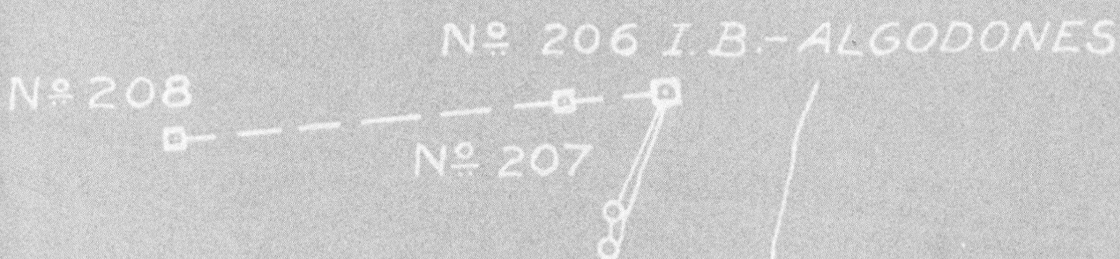
No. 206 I.B.-ALGODONES
No. 208
No. 207

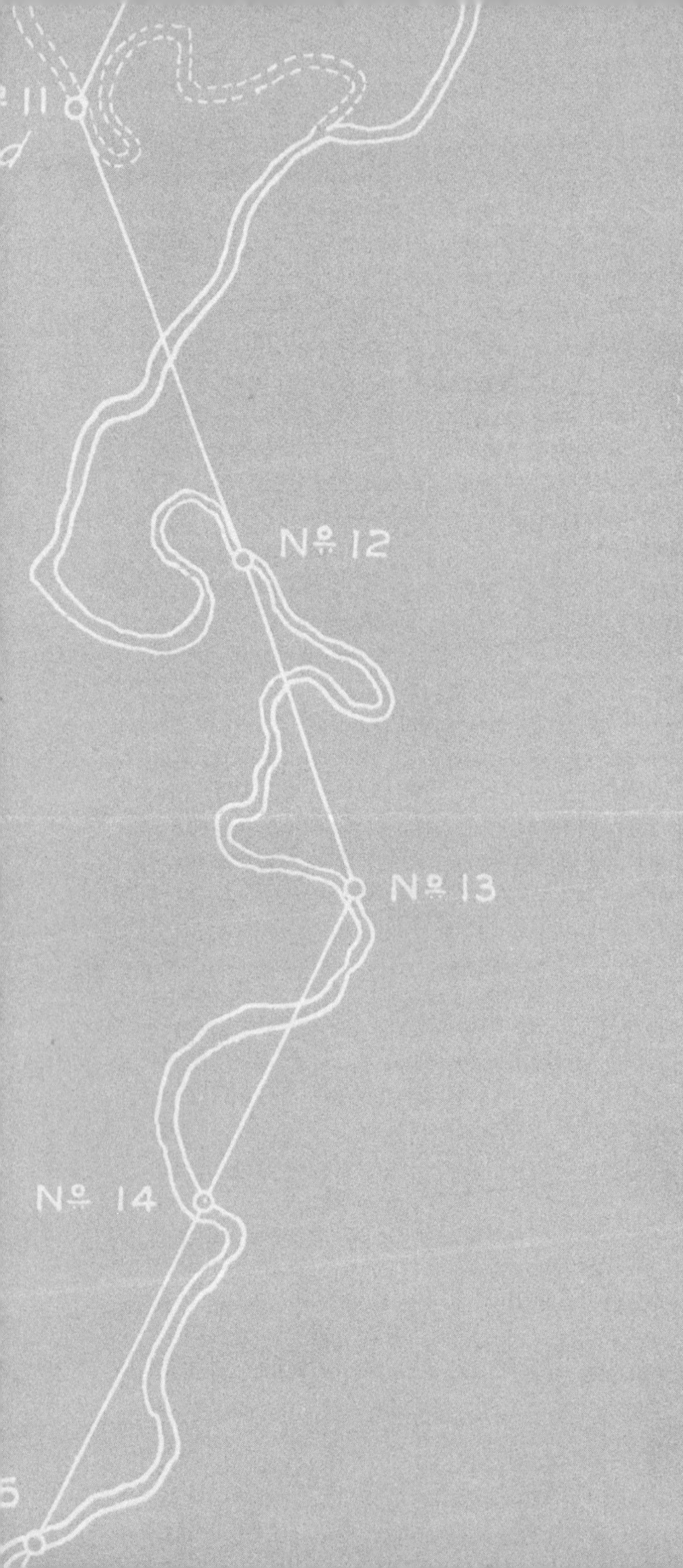
№ 12
№ 13
№ 14

IMPERIAL

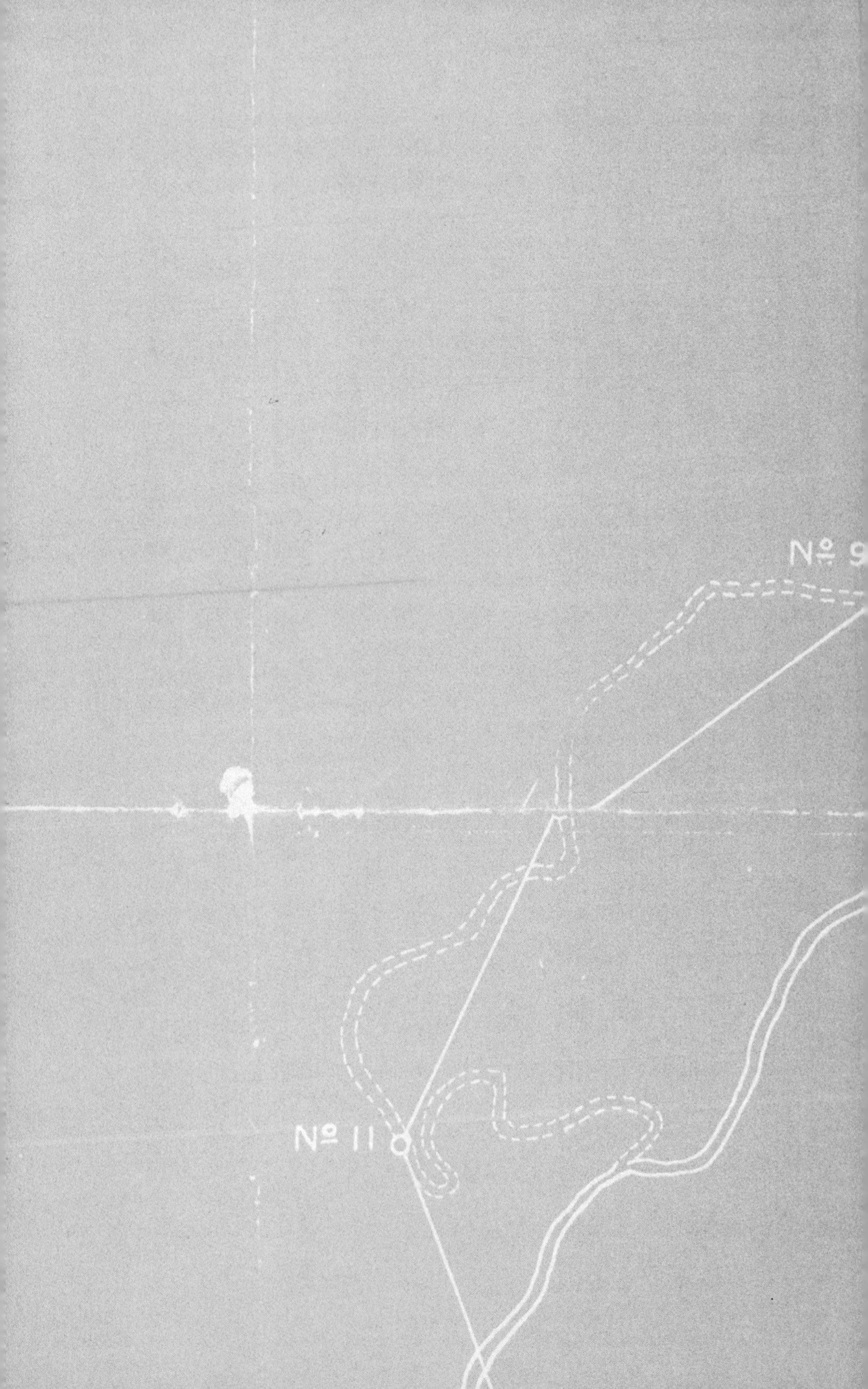
№ 9
№ 11

ALSO BY

WILLIAM T. VOLLMANN

You Bright and Risen Angels (1987)

The Rainbow Stories (1989)

The Ice-Shirt (1990)

Whores for Gloria (1991)

Thirteen Stories and Thirteen Epitaphs (1991)

An Afghanistan Picture Show (1992)

Fathers and Crows (1992)

Butterfly Stories (1993)

The Rifles (1994)

The Atlas (1996)

The Royal Family (2000)

Argall (2001)

Rising Up and Rising Down:
Some Thoughts on Violence, Freedom, and Urgent Means (2003)

Europe Central (2005)

Uncentering the Earth:
Copernicus and the Revolutions of the Heavenly Spheres (2006)

Poor People (2007)

Riding Toward Everywhere (2008)

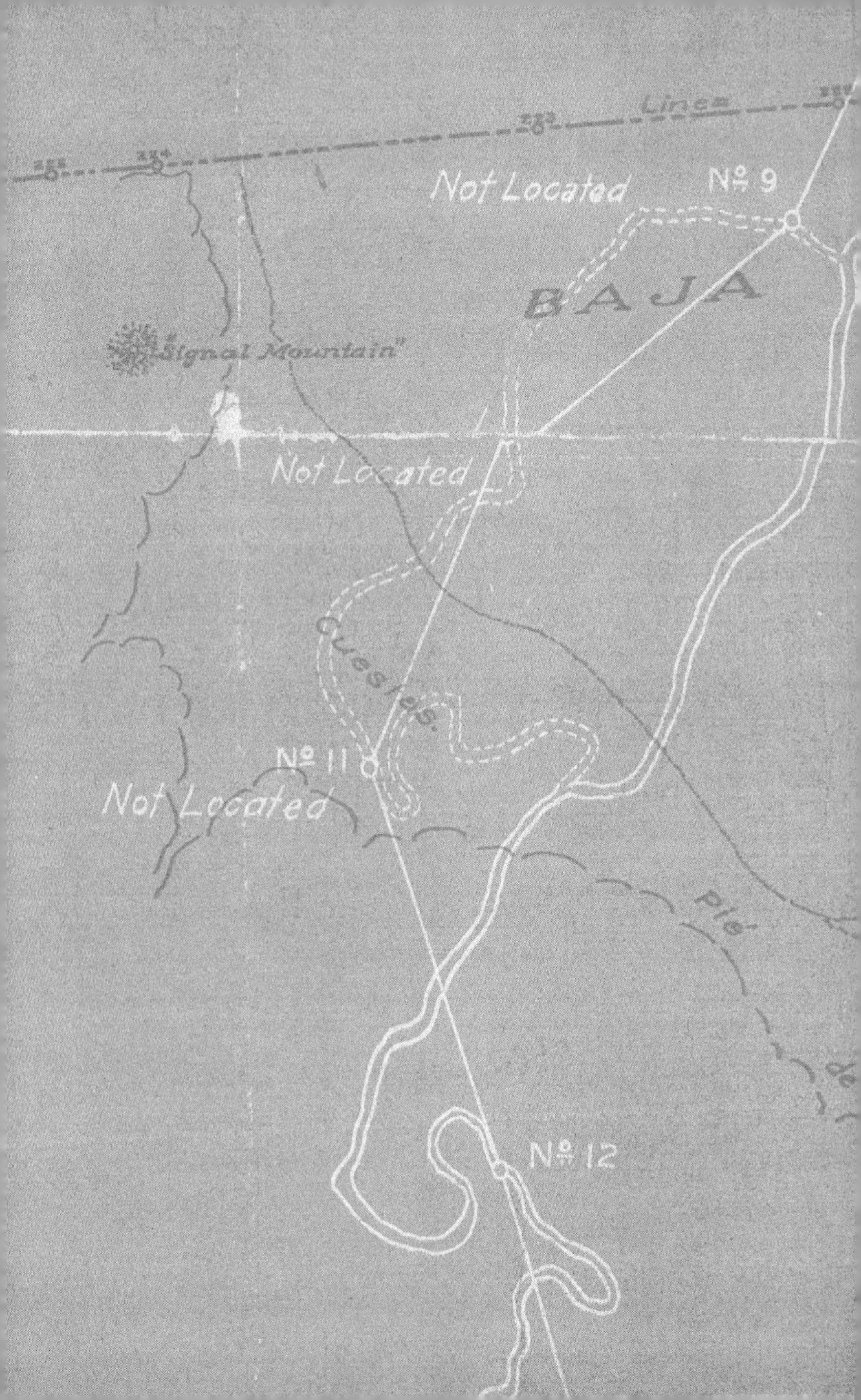

Lines

Not Located

№ 9

BAJA

"Signal Mountain"

Not Located

Guesias.

№ 11

Not Located

Pie

de

№ 12

WILLIAM T. VOLLMANN

IMPERIAL

VIKING

VIKING
Published by the Penguin Group
Penguin Group (USA) Inc., 375 Hudson Street, New York, New York 10014, U.S.A. • Penguin Group (Canada), 90 Eglinton Avenue East, Suite 700, Toronto, Ontario, Canada M4P 2Y3 (a division of Pearson Penguin Canada Inc.) • Penguin Books Ltd, 80 Strand, London WC2R 0RL, England • Penguin Ireland, 25 St. Stephen's Green, Dublin 2, Ireland (a division of Penguin Books Ltd) • Penguin Books Australia Ltd, 250 Camberwell Road, Camberwell, Victoria 3124, Australia (a division of Pearson Australia Group Pty Ltd) • Penguin Books India Pvt Ltd, 11 Community Centre, Panchsheel Park, New Delhi–110 017, India • Penguin Group (NZ), 67 Apollo Drive, Rosedale, North Shore 0632, New Zealand (a division of Pearson New Zealand Ltd) • Penguin Books (South Africa) (Pty) Ltd, 24 Sturdee Avenue, Rosebank, Johannesburg 2196, South Africa

Penguin Books Ltd, Registered Offices: 80 Strand, London WC2R 0RL, England

First published in 2009 by Viking Penguin, a member of Penguin Group (USA) Inc.

10 9 8 7 6 5 4 3 2 1

Grateful acknowledgment is made for permission to reprint excerpts from the following copyrighted works:

"Cartography" by Antonio Deltoro, translated by Christian Viveros-Faune, and "Arcana IV: The Emperor" by Veronica Volkow, translated by Margaret Sayers Peden, both from *Reversible Monuments: Contemporary Mexican Poetry*, edited by Monica de la Torre and Michael Weigers. Copyright © 2002 by Copper Canyon Press. Reprinted with permission of Copper Canyon Press. www.coppercanyonpress.org.

Poem by Nezahualcoyotl in *Native Mesoamerican Spirituality: Ancient Myths, Discourses, Stories, Doctrines, Hymns, Poems from the Aztecs, Yucatec, Quiche-Maya and Other Sacred Traditions*, edited by Miguel Leon-Portilla. Copyright © 1980 by Paulist Press, Inc. Reprinted by permission of Paulist Press, Inc., Mahwah, New Jersey. www.paulistpress.com.

"Portami il girasole" by Eugenio Montale, translated by Chris Glomski. Used by permission of Chris Glomski.

Acknowledgments for permission to reproduce copyrighted images appear in the credits section on pages 1301–1302.
Photographs and map illustrations are by the author unless otherwise cited.

LIBRARY OF CONGRESS CATALOGING-IN-PUBLICATION DATA
Vollmann, William T.
Imperial / by William T. Vollmann.
p. cm.
Includes bibliographical references.
ISBN 978-0-670-02061-4
1. Mexicans—California—Imperial County—History. 2. Mexicans—California—Imperial County—Social conditions. 3. Immigrants—California—Imperial County—History. 4. Immigrants—California—Imperial County—Social conditions. 5. Migrant agricultural laborers—California—Imperial County—History. 6. Migrant agricultural laborers—California—Imperial County—Social conditions. 7. Imperial County (Calif.)—Social conditions. I. Title.
F868.I2V65 2008
304.8'7949907208624—dc22 2008029532

Printed in the United States of America
Designed by Carla Bolte • Set in Scala with Scala Sans

As long as a farmer has an abundance of water, he almost
invariably yields to the temptation to use it freely,
even though he gets no increased
returns as a result.

—Yearbook of the United States Department of Agriculture, 1909

STATE OF CALIFORNIA
CERTIFICATION OF VITAL RECORD

COUNTY OF IMPERIAL

EL CENTRO, CALIFORNIA

California State Board of Health
BUREAU OF VITAL STATISTICS
STANDARD CERTIFICATE OF DEATH

1 PLACE OF DEATH 1,3,5,5
COUNTY OF Imperial
TOWN OF OR CITY OF Imperial (No. 1-mi ... S P track ST.; WARD)
State Index No.
Local Registered No. 28
[If death occurred in a hospital or institution, give its NAME instead of street and number, and fill out Nos. 18A and 18B.]

2 Full Name John Doe unknown Mexican

PERSONAL AND STATISTICAL PARTICULARS

3 SEX ...
4 COLOR OR RACE Mexican
5 SINGLE, MARRIED, WIDOWED, OR DIVORCED (Write the word) not known
5a HUSBAND OF
5b WIFE OF
6 DATE OF BIRTH (Month) (Day) 1 (Year)
7 AGE About 38 years months days If LESS than 1 day, hrs or min.?
8 OCCUPATION (a) Trade, profession or particular kind of work Apparently Labor
(b) General nature of industry, business, or establishment in which employed (or employer)
9 BIRTHPLACE (State or country) not known
PARENTS
10 NAME OF FATHER " "
11 BIRTHPLACE OF FATHER (State or country) " "
12 MAIDEN NAME OF MOTHER " "
13 BIRTHPLACE OF MOTHER (State or country) " "
18a LENGTH OF RESIDENCE
At Place of Death — years — months days
(Primary registration district)
In California — years — months days
14 THE ABOVE IS TRUE TO THE BEST OF MY KNOWLEDGE
(Informant) Mr Harris
(Address) Imperial
15 Filed 191 .
Subregistrar
Filed 7-31-1924 Lewis Foster
Registrar or Deputy.

MEDICAL CERTIFICATE OF DEATH

16 DATE OF DEATH July 29 1924 (Month) (Day) (Year)
17 I HEREBY CERTIFY, That I attended deceased from , 191 July 29 1924
that I last saw h alive on , 191 ;
and that death occurred on the date stated above at M.
The CAUSE OF DEATH* was as follows:
Heat Stroke found dead on S P track 1-mile no. Imperial
(Duration) years months days
Contributory
(Duration) years months days
State whether attributed to dangerous or insanitary conditions of employment
(Signed) B E Lemons Coroner
7-29-1924 (Address) El Centro
*State the DISEASE CAUSING DEATH, or, in deaths from VIOLENT CAUSES, state (1) MEANS OF INJURY; and (2) whether (probably) ACCIDENTAL, SUICIDAL, or HOMICIDAL.
18b SPECIAL INFORMATION FOR HOSPITALS, INSTITUTIONS, TRANSIENTS OR RECENT RESIDENTS
Where was disease contracted, if not at place of death?
Former or usual residence
19 PLACE OF BURIAL OR REMOVAL Mt View
DATE OF BURIAL 7-29-1924
20 UNDERTAKER B E Lemons El Centro
ADDRESS 641

13-72247

CERTIFIED COPY OF VITAL RECORDS
STATE OF CALIFORNIA, COUNTY OF IMPERIAL

This is a true and exact reproduction of the document officially registered and placed on file in the office of the IMPERIAL COUNTY CLERK-RECORDER.

Dolores Provencio
DOLORES PROVENCIO
CLERK-RECORDER
IMPERIAL COUNTY, CALIFORNIA

By M Maxine Hofer Deputy. DATE ISSUED OCT 22 2002

This copy not valid unless prepared on an engraved border displaying the seal, date of issuance and the original signature of the Deputy.

ANY ALTERATION OR ERASURE VOIDS THIS CERTIFICATE

In memory of

SERAFÍN RAMÍREZ HERNÁNDEZ

unknown, missing, illegal,

Mexican

CONTENTS

Part One

INTRODUCTIONS

Part Two

OUTLINES

Part Three

REVISIONS

Part Four

FOOTNOTES

Part Five

ELABORATIONS

Part Six

SUBPLOTS

Part Seven

CONTRADICTIONS

Part Eight

RESERVATIONS

Part Nine

CLIMAXES

Part Ten

DISSOLUTIONS

Part Eleven

POSTSCRIPTS

Part Twelve

DEFINITIONS

Part Thirteen

INSCRIPTIONS

MAPS

For explanations, excuses and derivations please see "Concerning the Maps" on page 1127.

For a map of my New River excursions, see page 84.

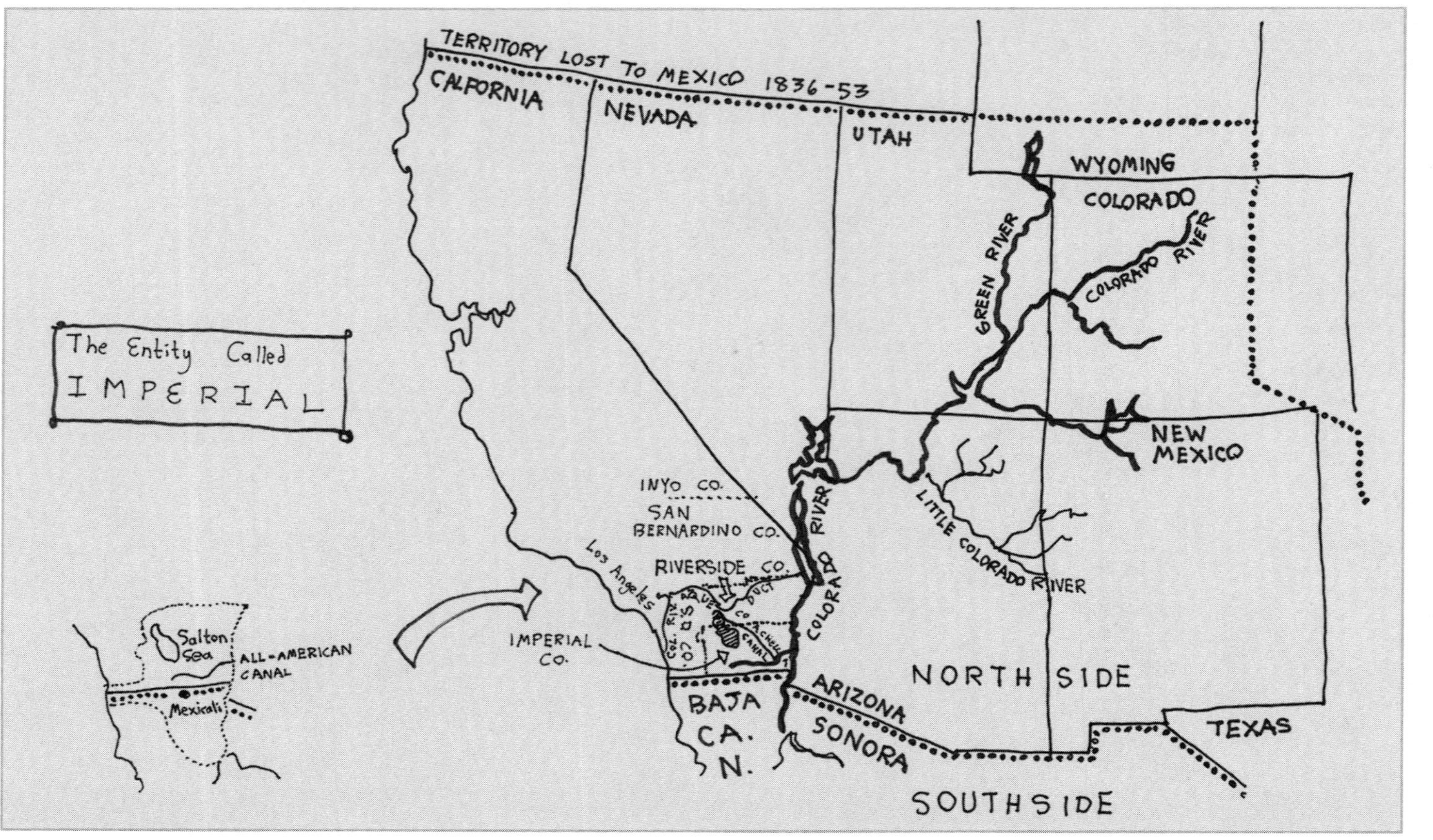

The Entity Called Imperial

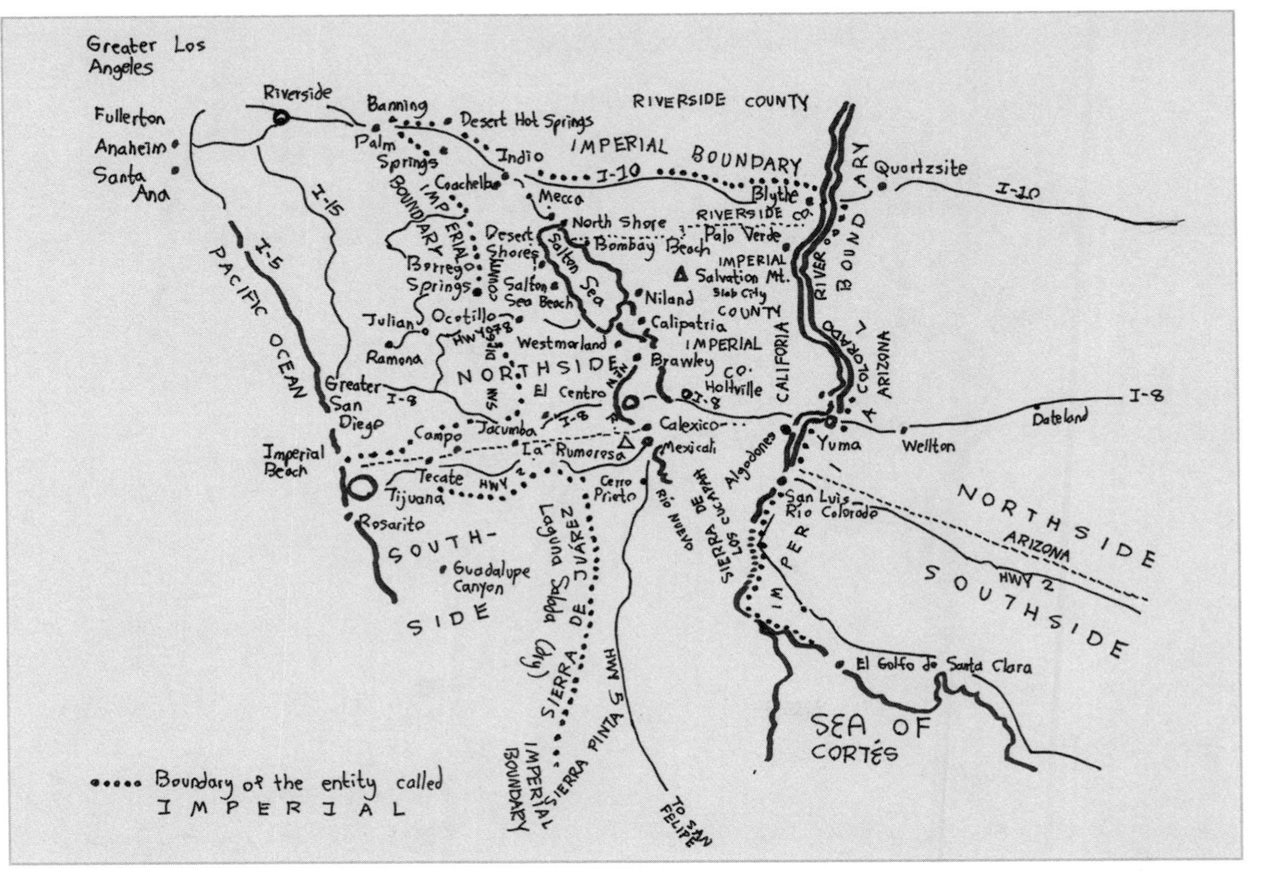

Closeup of Imperial

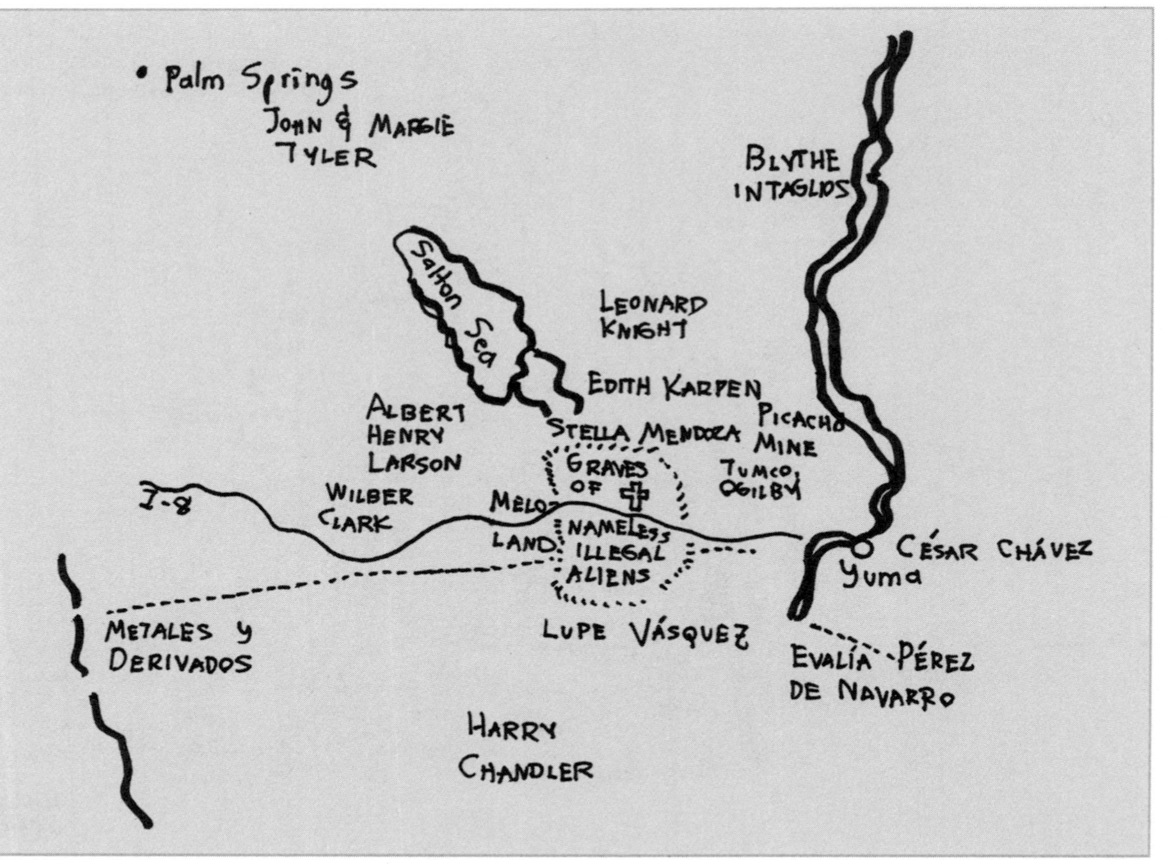

Persons and Places in Imperial

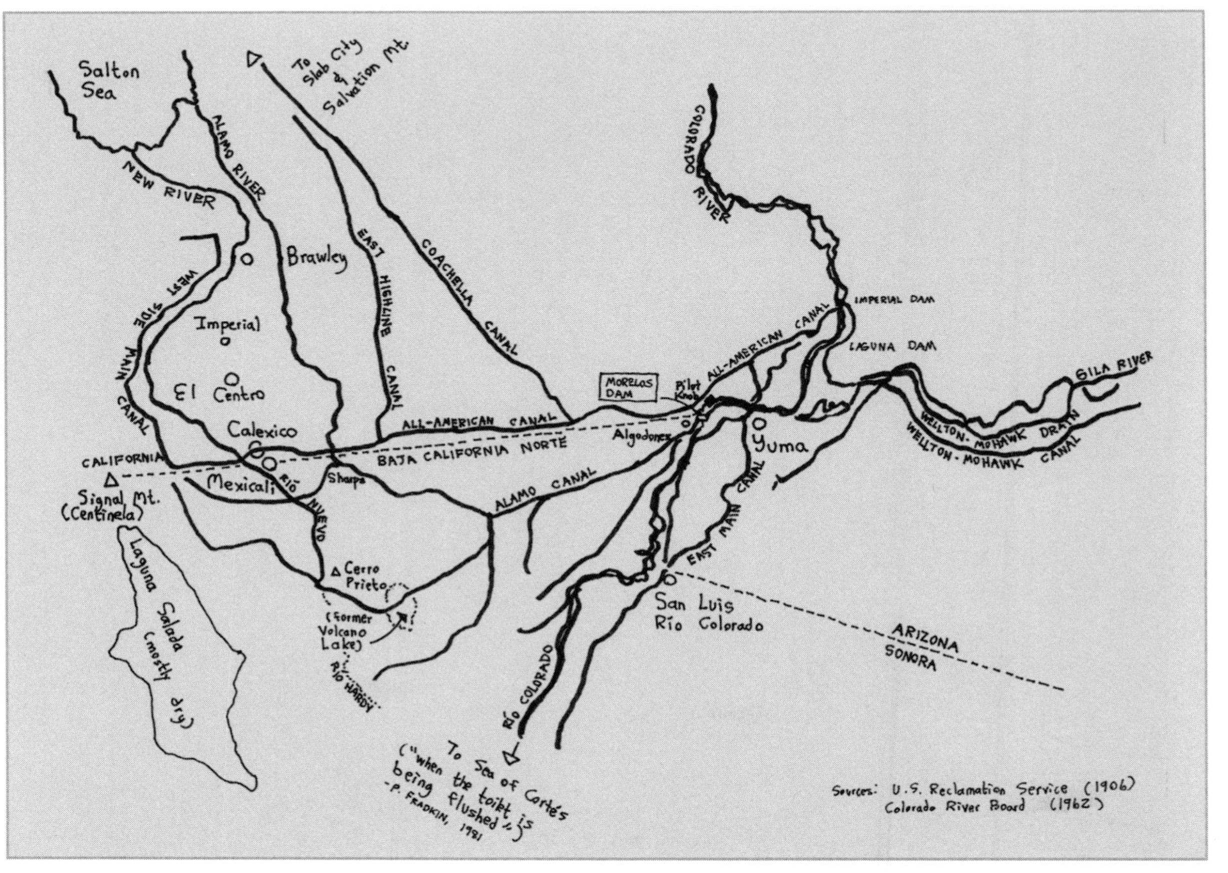

Rivers and Canals in Imperial

BRIEF GLOSSARY

The following terms are of considerable importance in what follows. Readers unfamiliar with Mexico or the Spanish language may not know them, as when beginning my research I certainly did not. Although they get defined in situ, they might as well be given all together here.

Acre-foot—The amount of water needed to cover an acre one foot deep. One acre-foot = 1,233.5 cubic meters = 326,000 gallons.

Campesino—Literally, "country person." Now a term used, with varying degrees of vagueness, to describe all tillers of the soil in Mexico. (Field workers employed in the United States are often excluded.) This encomium of commonality might have been first used by Catholic reformers shortly after the Mexican Revolution (1911). Before that, hacienda day laborers, indigenous inhabitants of pueblos, small-scale landowners, sharecroppers and former possessors of land reduced to vagabondage could well have seen one another simply as "other." The word quickly established a connotation of leftist militancy not much to the taste of the Catholic Church.

Colonia—Settlements of a less corporate character than ***ejidos.*** The residents can buy and own parcels, and sell them.

Coyote—See ***pollo.***

Ejido—Communal inalienable holdings, either from pre-Conquest times or else carved out of other lands by the Mexican Revolution.

Field worker—Somebody, in our context usually a Mexican, who labors in the fields of others, usually Americans. The words "campesinos" and "field workers" are often interchanged when speaking of the brownskinned people one sees stooping and sweating in the Imperial Valley. Acccording to the bargirl Emily at the Thirteen Negro dance hall in Mexicali, which is patronized by both groups, campesinos stay in Mexico, while field workers cross the line and do about fifty dollars a month* better.

*This estimate was from 2005.

Fracción—A newer ***colonia.***

Golondrina—Literally, a swallow (the bird, not what the throat does). Also, Southside slang for a fly-by-night ***maquiladora*** which shuts down without paying its workers.

Guía—A nice name for a **coyote.**

Hacienda—A plantation farm. Famous for gobbling up ***ejido*** lands. Very powerful under the Díaz regime. The Revolution of 1911 began to break up the haciendas.

Hectare—Generally employed in Southside in place of the acre. One hectare = 2.47 acres.

Maquiladora—A foreign-owned factory in Mexico, usually somewhere near the border. Pronounced with a single *l,* not a double, which would make it sound like something to do with makeup.

Northside—The United States.

Pollo—Someone who tries to cross the border illegally. Often guided by someone who is derogatorily referred to as a **coyote.** *(A.k.a. pollista* or *pollero.)*

Pueblo—A long-standing communal holding (often a village or town). Less formal a designation than ***ejido,*** and less tied to specifically agricultural land.

Rancho—A small private landholding. The owners were rancheros. Sometimes they allied themselves with the **campesinos**; occasionally, with the **hacienda** owners.

Solo—A person who attempts to cross the border illegally and alone.

Southside—Mexico. ("Northside" and "Southside" are employed mostly by the Border Patrol. I have appropriated them for my own purposes.)

IMPERIAL

PART ONE

INTRODUCTIONS

Chapter 1

THE GARDENS OF PARADISE

(1999)

I think we all feel sorry for 'em.

—Border Patrol Officer Gloria I. Chavez, on the subject of illegal aliens

BODY-SNATCHERS

The All-American Canal was now dark black with phosphorescent streaks where the border's eyes stained it with yellow tears.—These lights have been up for about two years, Officer Dan Murray said. Before that, it was generators. Before that, it was pitch black.

He was an older man, getting big in the waist, whose face had been hardened by knowledge into something legendary. For years he'd played his part in the work first begun by Eden's angel with the flaming sword, the methodical patrols and prowls to keep the have-not millions out of paradise—which in this case was Imperial County, California, whose fields of blondeness, of endless pallid asparagus, onion plants like great lollipops and honey-colored hay bales produced the lowest median tax income of any county in the state. Zone El Centro, named after the county seat, comprised Sectors 210 to 226, of which Sectors 217 to 223 happened to be Murray's responsibility. He kept the key to the armory, whose rows of M4 shotguns awaited a mass assault from Southside which never came. He knew how to deploy the stinger spikes, the rows of accordion-like grids like a row of caltrops: Pull a string and they opened up to puncture a tire. One car actually drove twelve desperate miles on four flat tires until it was wrecked beyond any conceivable utility to its confiscators.

They'll pop their heads up in a minute, he was always saying. He was always right.

An hour ago we might have been able to see through the bamboo and across the wrinkled brown water into Southside where Mexicans sat on the levee waiting to seize their chance, but at that time Murray and I had been over by the Port of Entry East bridge where two Mexicans waited, not aliens yet; while on our side, Northside, another agent sat calmly watching them in his car.

Hello, said Murray. Have those folks been there all day?

Yessir, the agent said.

Suddenly it was dusk, and the two men were already crossing. Now they were illegals.

Get out! an officer yelled at them. They turned and slowly, slowly walked back into Mexico across the humming throbbing bridge.

Then we drove west down the long horizon of border wall. Two Mexicans walked along the fence down in Southside, screaming obscenities at Murray.

Now, you see, this has got concrete, Murray explained. But it only goes down about four feet. They have their little spider holes. They pop up, throw a rock through the windshield, then go down again.

We drove west, down into the lights of Calexico and out again, passing the sandy waste whose incarnation as a golf course was memorialized by carcasses of palm trees.—See, another hole in the fence back there, Murray said. Usually you just hold back and wait. They'll pop up.—The golf course had gotten robbed once too often, and then somebody burned down the clubhouse after a fence-jumper from Southside was shot. So some townspeople told me. Their stories were weary and muddled, but in them as in this former golf course the border wall remained ever in the background, its long, rust-colored fence dwindling into lights. Then the dim red fence abruptly ended, and we met the All-American Canal, which comprises so much of this sector's border westward of the wall. Follow the All-American upstream on a map, and you'll see that it abruptly turns north, wraps around Calexico International Airport near that abandoned golf course (the hollow in this spot is a good place for *pollos* and *solos* to hide, and sometimes for bandits, too, who murdered somebody here half a year ago), and then it bends due east again just before Comacho Road, ducking under the railway and Imperial Avenue, streaming on eastward toward its source, until the last we see of it, it's overlined the streets named after southwestern riches: Turquoise Street, Sapphire Street, Garnet Street, Ruby Court, Emerald Way, Topaz Court—after which it runs off the map and out of Calexico. In the first four months of 1999 alone, eight people whom the authorities knew of had already drowned in the All-American's cool quick current, all of them presumably seekers of illegal self-improvement; and I imagine that other bodies were never found, being carried into jurisdictions where perhaps the nonhuman coyotes got them. In April 1999 the United States Navy began to wire the canal with a two-hundred-thousand-dollar noise-detection apparatus.—*The goal is to create a system that can alert authorities when someone is in trouble in the canal,* my home newspaper informed me blandly. Who am I to doubt the Navy's altruism?

You should see these guys pickin' watermelon, bent over all day, said Officer Murray. They do work most Americans wouldn't do.

We were close by the Wistaria Check, which lay opposite the place on the Mexican side where the taxi driver and Juan the cokehead had taken me the day before. The taxi driver had said: If you want, I'll jump into the canal and swim across, if you pay me.

Juan, whose scrawny back and shoulders most proudly bore a tattoo of the Virgin for which he'd paid two U.S. dollars back when he was twenty (he was now Christ's age), stopped the taxi to buy five hundred pesos' worth of powder in a twist of plastic. He was a true addict. Every day I had to advance him his wages. By late afternoon he needed a bonus. I had found him amidst the slow round of beggars and drunks on a street two blocks south of the United States where a poster announcing a **MILLION DOLLAR FINANCIAL SERVICE** depicted a giant identification card which among all its elysian proclamations faintly whispered NOT A GOVERNMENT DOCUMENT, then rushed on to proclaim **ORDER YOUR PERSONAL U.S. I.D. CARD HERE TODAY**. On that hot afternoon when we departed Mexicali's red and yellow storefronts and drove westward into the dirt, the houses shrinking into shacks, Juan and the taxi driver kept glancing at me and muttering together; but I told them that I would have even more cash when I came back tomorrow. Far away, deeper into Mexico, I could see the pale bluish-white mountains like concretions of dust. Now we came into Juan's hometown where several of the Mexicali street-whores lived, and although Juan wanted to stop to buy more coke, business, personified by me, demanded that we leave behind those long blocks of tiny houses of cracked dry mud whose yards were dirt instead of grass. So we turned onto a long dirt road in parallel to the All-American Canal, which we could not yet see. Here each of the many tiny cement or adobe houses was fenced away from the world. One fence derived from boxspring bedframes. Other fencepoles had been fashioned of twigs or columns of tires, and there were many hedges of thorns on that nameless road of prickly pears, bamboo, dust, beautiful palm trees, and turtles sleepily lurking in the stagnant ditchwater.

See all those cars in there? *Stolen,* my guide triumphantly explained. From America.

Well, I said, I'm glad they have a new home, Juan. How do you know they're stolen?

I don't think these people have enough money to buy a new car—or ten new cars.

He said that in Mexicali it cost two or three hundred dollars for a brand-new stolen American automobile, which I considered not a bad price. He said that another industry of the householders along this road was to hide emigrants on consignment until nightfall, then help them try to swim the canal. And just as he finished explaining these matters, we came upon a man in sunglasses who was driving a brand-new van with tinted windows. We had seen no other vehicles before, and we saw none afterward except for one water truck whose corroded white cylinder tank slowly bled water as it went. The man in sunglasses rolled down his night-dark window to study us, which was the only reason that we could see him at all. He was gripping a pair of binoculars against his face. When he had digested us, he drove slowly past, the window still down. He was watching the canal now through his binoculars.

Think he's a coyote? I asked.

What else?

Now we arrived at a little shrine to the Virgin and a cross. Someone had died, perhaps a *solo*. Juan read the inscription. Yes, he said, the man had drowned trying to cross into America, where everything was wider, cleaner, safer, more expensive, more controlled and more homogeneous. And by this shrine we parked the car and ascended the levee of crumbing mud-dust to gaze at the United States, where of the three of us only I could legally go. It was hot and thorny and dry on the Mexican side with all those American fields appearing so cruelly green like Paradise, *because the water belongs to America,* as Juan put it. Beside us, a skinny horse browsed in garbage.

Some chocolate-brown boys were swimming in the coffee-colored canal, and on Northside, very close to Wistaria Check as I said, a white truck was parked and two middle-aged white men were trying their luck at catfishing, ignoring the boys who ignored them. Juan pointed to the boys and said: See those poor people over there? They're gonna try for the night time, then they'll walk through all the fields . . .

Ask them where they're going.

They're gonna go to Canada, they say, unless Border Patrol catch them.

Ask them if they know where Canada is.

They say, they don't know, but somebody told them it's a real nice country where you don't get hassled like you do in America.

On our side, the dusty desert side, an obelisk marked American dominion, and later I learned from the Border Patrol that the canal actually lay slightly north of the true border, but those guardians found it needlessly troublesome to assert their authority over the few slender feet of United States sovereignty between the marker and the water. Officer Murray said to me: If I saw people on the Southside of the canal, I'd just wave to 'em. You see a raft, now, you just back off. Don't wanna spook anybody.

A day or two later the local papers carried a story about how Border Patrol agents had shot one of those rafts with a pellet gun. The raft capsized, and one or two aliens drowned. (There are Border Patrol officers in boats, and they're like *fishing,* a *solo* in Algodones told me. They cut open or shoot at the rafts and let 'em drift downriver.—Last night there were about seven shots, his comrade said, shrugging.) But the drownings, I hope, were an aberration.* I never at any time met a *solo* or *pollo* who expressed physical fear of the Border Patrol. Murray insisted that some agents bought fast food with their own money for the frightened Southside kids they'd captured.

But the Mexican consulate never hears that, Murray said bitterly.

They'll probably start rafting pretty soon, he muttered.

He stood listening to the canal, which was long, low, black with bamboo. His job was not to shape the destiny of those who sought America, but merely to postpone it. For what could he do to them, but lock them in a holding cell, then deport them back to Southside so that they could try again? And for a moment, as we stood there, each of us letting his private thoughts fall into the pit of the night, I almost pitied the futility of his occupation, as I suspect he did mine (the main purpose of my essays being to line birdcages), but then I fortunately persuaded myself that all vocations and callings are equally futile. He talked about how beautiful it was when he patrolled the shoulder of an onion field at dusk with the bees returning to their hives, and I started to like him. He told me about the fine catfishing he'd had in the canal, and we gazed at the sparse weak lights which shone from Mexico, until suddenly the radio said: There's already a rope across. Looks like it'll be near Martin Ranch.

Okay, said Murray, I'm up on the canal bank.

Okay, copy, replied the radio.

They could be running across the fields right now, he said to me. Okay, he's got sign.

We were in the car now, speeding toward the place. We stopped by a wall of hay, which we smelled more than saw in the dark humid night. Border Patrolmen were searching with their lights.

Right here you got the traffic, Murray said.

And he shone his flashlight on fresh footprints in the sand.

These kids should be easy to catch, he went on, half talking to himself. But I feel naked; I don't have a spotlight. I don't have any alleylights . . .

The long field appeared green through an agent's nightscope. The Border Patrolmen hunted and searched, as the crumbly earth devoured their feet up to the ankles. It was silt from the days of the ancient sea. They came through the field, stalking it with headlights which rendered the furrows cruelly bright.

*As a media spokeswoman at the Mexican consulate tactfully expressed it, "I assume there are some agents that are not very good, just like in a family, like if your brother is maybe not so good, but your father and your mother and your brothers make no problem. And some agents make some mistakes very bad, but it's not the whole Border Patrol. For instance, if they find a body now, they will phone us right away . . ."

Maybe we'll find the bodies, Murray said. Maybe not. It's just pure luck. But these kids tripped a sensor.

I can't see 'em anymore, another officer said, resting his hands on his Sam Browne belt.

I got an eye on your bodies, said the nightscope man, whose monitor made the word *bodies* seem chillingly appropriate, for in the green night the aliens glowed white like evil extraterrestial beings or zombies out of a science-fiction movie. The nightscope man could also reverse the contrast if he chose, so that the *bodies* became green silhouettes in a glowing white field of night-ness.—They're layin' up in the middle of the field, he went on, directing the hunters through a darkness which neither they nor the aliens, who surely thought themselves safe, could penetrate. How eerie it was! Only the nightscope man could see! The aliens lurked on faith that the darkness was their invincible friend. The Border Patrolmen could scarcely perceive where they set their own feet; they could have been approaching a precipice; but they approached the unseen *bodies* with equal and, as it proved, more justified faith.—Lookin' dead smack in the middle, said the nightscope man. Yeah, I got a fix on your bodies. Turn left. Three steps more. Another coupla steps. They should be right in front of you, right down there in those . . . Yeah, you got 'em.

Now came the wide circle of the spotlight. The hunters' cars circled the field. And the *bodies,* hopelessly silhouetted, resurrected themselves from the fresh earth, giving in to capture and deportation. They rose, becoming black on black. And the shadow of a man whose hands were on his head was replicated manifold. Two of them with their hands on their heads stood gazing down at the half-empty jugs of water they'd carried. Sad and submissive faces gazed into the darkness, half-blinded by the brightness as the Border Patrolmen frisked them. Yes, the *bodies* stood wide-eyed in the light, all in the line, with their hands obediently behind them. Coughing, shuffling, they began to cross the fields.

You know what? a Border Patrolman said to one of the *bodies.* You really need to brush your teeth. You've got wicked bad breath, guy.

The *body* was silent. In the nightscope it had been as white as one of the freshly dead fishes in the cool green poison (or should I say "reputed poison"?) of the Salton Sea. Now it began to reveal itself to be brown—Hispanic, sunburned and field-stained.

Let's go, *amigos.* Come on. Let's go; let's go.

None of the captives looked terrified. It was as Officer Murray had said: People realize they're not going to jail for the rest of their lives, so they calm down.

Now, that irrigator's car over there just happens to be in a convenient place, an agent was saying. We'll have to check him out . . .

The Mexicans walked more quickly now, carefully cradling their water jugs, attended by the bright, bright lights. Now they sat in a line on the roadside, a long line of them, with their jugs and bottles of water between their legs. Most of them wore baseball caps. They were young, wiry, strong to work. Their eyes shone alertly in the night. Already resigned, they quickly became philosophical, and in some cases even cheerful, slapping their knees and poking one another smilingly in the ribs. Soon they'd join the people staring out the panes of the holding cells. After eight hours or so, if they had no criminal history, they'd be sent back to Mexico.

(As I reread this chapter almost a decade later, in these days of "extraordinary rendition" and the Patriot Act, I suppose that a *body* fears capture more nowadays. But how can I be sure? Our Department of Homeland Security seems disinclined to let me watch any more hunts and chases.)

We got some that made the river, but we bagged the rest of 'em, an officer was saying, but already the Border Patrol had found other game.—Two made it up into the housing development, a woman's excited voice cried on the radio, but we're tryin' to inch up on 'em . . .

THE GARDENS OF PARADISE

What did the *bodies* come here for? We all know the answer. I remember how on one of my many bus rides south I was meditating on the heat and strangeness of this corner of California when the man beside me awoke, and turned toward the window like a plant toward the sun. Soon we would come to the sign which read IMPERIAL COUNTY LINE and a few minutes later we'd pass the Corvina Cafe, which would surely be as closed and dead as one of those corvina floating belly-up in the Salton Sea. The man sat gazing alertly eastward across the desert flats toward the long deep green stripe of date plantations and the dusty red and blue mountains beyond. I inferred that this landscape was his by birth or long residence. Perhaps he had been away from it for awhile. He'd told me that he was coming from a Fourth of July party at his sister's, but I'd seen the policeman standing in the loading area, watching to make sure that he boarded this bus whose disinfectant, pretending to be pine or lemon, stung the nose with its bad chemical smell. He'd slept with his chin in his hands all the way from Indio and past the tan silence of the Jewel Date Company's former factory parallel to the railroad tracks where rusty flatbed cars gave off heat. Now he sighed a little, and turned toward me as eagerly as he had strained toward the mountains. He offered me Mexican candy, praising it because it was cheap. Openhanded, gruff and husky, he longed to tell the tale of his life. He'd served twenty-four years in the Spanish army—or maybe he'd been an American soldier stationed in Spain, this fine point being occluded by his broken English and my ignorance of Spanish. At any rate, Spain had failed him, evidently by means of woman trouble. Now he was living in El Centro to be near his eighty-two-year-old father who had once been a mechanical genius but who lately did little more than putter around the air conditioner, trying to grow coolness like a vegetable and then inbreed and harvest it. When he spoke of his father, tenderness came into his voice in just the same way that the yellow flowers of the palo verde tree come briefly back even in July or August if there is rain. His father was too old to drive a car, so once our bus pulled into the El Centro station, my friend would be walking home in the hundred-and-ten-degree heat, which killed illegal aliens easily.

The ones who crossed alone were called *solos*. The ones who paid to be taken across were *pollos*—chickens. And who better to shepherd chickens through dangerous ways than a *coyote*? That's truly what they were called! Coyotes never eat chickens, do they? (Every day, many *pollos* die, a taxi driver told me with solemn exaggeration. The newspaper said that only two hundred and fifty-four illegals had died last year, to which the taxi driver replied: Liars—assassins! Two or three a day die right here! They hide the bodies under the sand so that the Border Patrol won't see.—They do die, a lifetime *pollo* later told me, but not that many.) Then there were the chicken-handlers, the *pollistas* or *polleros* whom the bigshot coyotes deputed to do the dirty work of canal-crossings and the like. Officer Murray called them "scouts."—They're pretty chicken, he said, not meaning the pun.—Like their bosses, they sometimes ran away when it was dangerous, leaving their passengers to die of thirst. For it was so very hot! When his father died, my seatmate might move away from Imperial County, on account of the heat. In his low, hoarse, not unpleasant voice, he remarked that he didn't mind sitting outside in a hundred and five degrees, but when it got up to a hundred and fifteen, then his cold beer turned into hot coffee, and it was time to go indoors. He uttered many a melancholy jest of this character. I'd already begun to think of him as *the old soldier*, and was almost appalled that he was my age, thirty-eight; he looked twenty years older. This working man, dark and wiry, had resisted many solar assaults, armored by no more than an upturned cap-brim, but each attack had shriveled him a little more, so that he'd eventually be desiccated to his very soul. The hot, dry sunlight instantly warms flesh to a state near burning, then cauterizes it and stains it brown. Born in Brawley, which our Greyhound soon would reach, he'd never been to the Salton Sea in his entire life. (How far was it? Half an hour's drive?) As a boy he'd been too busy in the fields, he said; after that he'd tried his luck in Spain. And now as we continued south on Highway 111 he began to explicate the crops to me, each time weighing himself down with a new story of dreary and dangerous drudgery.

Here came another date orchard to our left, with busy birds silhouetted in the palm-crests, uplifting their beaks, clicking and crying even in the heat of midday. I admired the shade and luxurious fruit of those trees, but the old soldier turned to me with a bitter smile and said that the most perilous labor of his life had been ascending toward the birds on a rickety ladder leaned against each tree in turn, with no one holding the bottom for him; his job was to tie bags around immature dates so that they'd not be lost. Little and lean, he'd scampered into the sun which burned him until he resembled the black fly with alert yellow eyes which one often finds crouching in the dusty crease of a palm's fan. Sometimes he got dizzy; sometimes the ladder slipped. His memories were stained with terror.

By the time he'd completed this relation, our Greyhound bus had drawn close to an onion field in glorious flower, and the old soldier croaked out that working in the onion fields had left him stinking of onion juice, his eyes watering day and night. After a week the onion juice was literally under his skin. (I thought of what Officer Murray had said: When you get people out of an onion field, you wanna roll your windows down.) No matter how long he bowed beneath the showerhead, scrubbing himself red, the onion smell kept oozing out of him so that he stank even to himself and coughed himself to sleep. Eventually he began to bring up blood from too much coughing.

No, I hung it up, the old soldier said. Don't wanna pick in the fields no more. I got me a ladyfriend, she about forty, forty-five years old. And every morning she drives from El Centro all the way to Yuma. There are four of them people; they share gas. Then she picks. Imagine that, a forty-five-year-old lady and still out there picking! What a tough gal! One time she brought me a cantaloupe from the field. Another time, it was a big watermelon . . .

And he smiled a smile of loving pride. But then his bitterness landed on him again, like flies on a sweaty face. We'd come to a place of white puffballs left behind in the dark fields. The old soldier said that they were cantaloupes—no plants, only the pale spheres sticking out. The migrant workers would turn them up later. He had been among the up-turners of cantaloupes and of so many other crops, following the harvesters on foot, gleaning up lost fruits under that hot, dusty, greyish-white sky. He began to tell me how it was, waving his withered hands as he angrily, dolefully whispered, describing the ache between the shoulderblades, the throbbing in the small of the back, the shooting pains in the arms, the hands that after gripping and lifting all day became dirt-stained baseball mitts which could no longer open or close, painfully throbbing in the bones. Beyond these agonies he remembered with all his hatred the Imperial summers, which had moved one woman on a hundred-degree Saturday evening in Indio to tell me how she had realized that this planet truly orbits a star of immense heat and brightness; whenever she stepped outside on an Imperial day, she could keep possession of only a slender slice of moments before being overpowered by stuporous confusion. Once she was safely back inside, everything on her person, every key or card, every square inch of her blouse, gave off heat. And yet the migrant workers had to spend all day outside, sometimes working for less than the legal minimum wage. The old soldier had finished with that. He could not bear it anymore.

The *Imperial Valley Press* stood on his side. In a section entitled "**OUR OPINION: TIME FOR A CHANGE**," that newspaper laid out the problem: **As important as agriculture is to the county, there are limits on a community with an economy so dependent on farming, because agricultural workers do not exactly get the highest salaries . . . Finally, agriculture is not as strong in the Imperial Valley as it has been in years past.** The *Press* slavered over the smoothly-named *Gateway to the Americas Project*, which would soon erect houses and industrial parks near the new Calexico East Port of Entry. It *could create thousands of jobs*. The hoped-for future of the Imperial Valley: strip malls, office parks, chain stores, Los Angelesization. Meanwhile the old soldier's ladyfriend went on fruit-picking, and in hopes of doing the same thing the *pollos* and *solos* slithered up and down the border fence.

THE FENCE

Yes, they slithered up and down the fence with ominous grace, like the floor-show girl in her summer dress who flew around the catpole at the Miau-Miau Club on the Mexican side, spreading her legs to show each sector of her audience in turn that she wore no underwear; she did pull-ups, flashing her bottom in the red rotisserie-light which translated her into meat; then she somersaulted naked up the pole and descended it upside down, her hands outstretched, gripping it between her thighs solely, until her long hair was sweeping the floor and the men shrieked in triumphant admiration. And the aspirants flowed palely up and down that metal fence in strange and elegant ways which should have elicited equal applause; but they were mere men who mopped their foreheads with bandannas and who stank of sweat, which is our humanity; maybe they'd earn a hundred dollars somewhere before the Border Patrol caught them. They became *bodies*. Another name for them was *EWIS*—entries without inspection. Bureaucrats subclassified them into *criminal aliens* and *administrative aliens*. The United States was their road mirage, a silver-blue illusion of refreshment far ahead upon their burning path. More than one *solo* told me that he'd rather do prison time in America than be free on the streets of Mexico, because in America he got better fed.—America! That was the dream in which they overwhelmed themselves. They'd glean cantaloupes, bag dates, or weed onions—anything. About the "average man" he arrested Officer Murray said: You never know if he just did fifteen years for shootin' a cop in Salt

Lake City or if he's just lookin' for work.—Yes, I occasionally meet such charmers as Hugo from San Salvador with his teardrop tattooed beside his left eye, and his ring which said 13; he kept saying he was good people; he'd been in prison a long stretch; and was I fuckin' INS? Hard and paranoid, he threatened me, and tried to rob me; in the end I had to punch him. Then there were the joy-riders, the Mexicans running across the night fields just to see what they could see, the businessmen in suits and slacks rushing over on a lark to steal American watermelons. But most of the people whom I interviewed, well, they were just looking for work. And they gathered and swarmed there against the literal edge of Southside, yearning, planning according to their resources: brute strength to leap, run, hide and suffer, or cunning to spy out an easy secret way, or wealth to pay a coyote. They waited literally in the wall's shadow, preparing to be brave, learning the weft of the forbidden country ahead. Near the post office, hot, filthy men settled down to sleep behind the bushes, laying out plastic bags of belongings. Yes, they told me; they aimed to cross into America. In Mexicali on that single night there were hundreds like them. (We get real busy in January, February and March, Murray said. Right now it'll be quiet. Last night we only caught eighty-five aliens. A week ago on midnight shift, we did five hundred and eighty.) They gathered, pooled, collected themselves into waves. How could one miss them? Merely approach the wall, the music of the strip clubs fading into faint strange shrillnesses as one walked north past hot alley lights. White white smoke arose from the sidewalk barbeque stands. A weary vendeuse, perhaps Mayan or Mixtec, walked by, her platter of stuffed animals strapped below her breasts. Now here came another alley, old style, cracked and dark, with shuttered luminescence reflected in its stygian puddles. A pool of urine, a brightly lit PEMEX station under construction, the gargantuan anthill of sand illuminated uselessly, a square area of dirt lit up like a nightmare grave . . . Then Cristóbal Colón the border fence stood silent. How apt was that street's name! For Cristóbal Colón was of course the discoverer of the New World *circa* 1492. And there indeed lay the United States of America, also known as Northside, hot and still beyond the fence through whose holes the eyes of a Border Patrol vehicle spied out Mexico unwinkingly. Closer to the legal crossing, at Morelos Street, ran a line of palms white-limed to head-height. Two rapid men in caps ghosted by. I saw them lunge at the fence and skitter partway up, hanging on it like those bees which cling with their forelegs to one of the many small yellow flowers of the palo verde tree; but then they leapt lightly back into Southside to free themselves from the alert green-clad men in white cars who'd instantly appeared—for to find a way across this subdelineation, and trade hunger for homesickness, was not so easy. The fence required that they be agile as well as desperate. It more than any other factor had inflated coyotes' prices from two hundred to twelve hundred dollars a head. The Border Patrol could be proud.

Well, at this time, said Duty Officer Michael Singh at Calexico Station, from inside of town it goes out approximately five miles, and about the same to the east. Right now we've got our crew putting up picket fence fifteen feet high . . .

That must have slowed the aliens down, I said.

Well, it has eliminated family groups. They're coming underneath, but we have to knock that out, too.

Officer Singh was right and wrong about the family groups. For at Madero and Ayuntamiento, in Niños Héroes Park, in sight of the big dullish grey water tower with the hidden camera, my friend Carlos, swarthy, big, tattooed, moustached, filthy, sweat-stinking, sat in the darkness of palms with a gang of other *solos* each of whom had come from a different Mexican state, one from Guatemala even, and all of whom planned to jump the fence either that night or the next, depending on how brave they felt and how many Border Patrol cars they saw. Most of those men had done prison time in both Mexico and in the United States—tattooed Mario, for instance, had passed fourteen months in Santa Nella. In Mexican prisons you got only one meal a day, a bowl of beans, so he liked Santa Nella better. Roberto said much the same. He was strong; he wanted to work in the American fields for three or four dollars an hour . . . They'd slept in the park that entire week. Whenever the police inquired their business, they replied: We're waiting for night to get across, at which the police shrugged and left them alone. And they literally called themselves a family. Whoever found food shared it with his brothers, they said.

Dan Murray, right as always, had said: See, we used to get a lot of groups, some female, some mixed. They go over, we chase 'em, they run back. This cat and mouse stuff, that's what this fence will stop.

Will the fence get any higher?

Well, what we've done, we've stopped the females and the heavier-set individuals.

For that reason Carlos was despondent, fearing that he'd grown too fat and old. He said: I am never goin' there, man. Here I am in the park, eatin' nothing. Where else can I go? Only people I know is these people. They gonna go tonight, but not me. I'm too heavy to get over.

And as he sat with his temporary brothers, lurking in the darkness beneath those white-painted palm trees, a policewoman pedaled her bicycle up to them and stopped, dropping her booted feet to the ground. A line of brass cartridges was strapped across her broad back. She told the family that she'd arrest them all if they were in the park half an hour from now. Her partner also cycled up and began writing down their names in his notebook.

Where else can I go? muttered Carlos, wringing his hands.

CANALS AND RIVERS

Well, there was always the All-American Canal. Carlos had swum it only two weeks ago, carrying thirty pounds' worth of supplies: bread and baloney, then water for two days. Once he'd crawled up into Northside, peeked through the bamboo, and crossed the levee road (Officer Murray's colleagues must have been hunting elsewhere), he'd begun to walk. He walked for two nights, all the way up to Niland, and then he got caught. He didn't mind so much. He'd been creeping into America ever since 1982, when coyotes charged only two hundred dollars from Tijuana, because there was no metal fence back then.* Now it cost twelve hundred dollars there—nearly the same as here. That corrugated steel wall of landing mat (some of it Air Force surplus from an easy little war of ours called Operation Desert Storm) presently extended three hundred and sixty-three feet into the ocean, then continued by fits and starts across all southern California. (We have so many gaps in this fence, lamented Gloria I. Chavez, the public affairs officer at Chula Vista. But these gaps are covered by agents.) Carlos saw no purpose in taking a bus all the way to Tijuana to gamble through one of those narrowing gaps. Sweating and stinking in the darkness, he told me that if his "family" went over without him, he might try the water route again. But his perils commenced even before he could drag his heavy, sodden body into Officer Murray's jurisdiction. Robbers preyed on the *solos*. So on occasion did uniformed agents of Mexican dominion.

In the clipped lingo of the Border Patrol, American sentinels were called Alpha, while their Mexican counterparts were Beta. Accurate as they undoubtedly were in their depiction of the power relation between the two nations, those designations scarcely overwhelmed me with their tact. Alpha pursued Beta's nationals whenever, like Carlos, they tried to breach Northside; Alpha's nationals swaggered around Southside like lords. And so Beta sometimes cooperated with Alpha in a less than enthusiastic spirit. In the grubby wilderness of freeways, warehouses and cut-rate stores between San Diego and Tijuana there is a municipality called Chula Vista, which like so many of its kind in California no longer exists as a distinct entity; its grid shades into those of National City to the North and Otay to the south; and here I met a handsome, pugnacious Border Patrolman named Brian Willett who told me about the bad old days when Beta had declined to cooperate with Alpha at all. Willett once witnessed a murder in No Man's Land, just beyond the gleaming corrugations of the wall. He radioed Beta on the special frequency set aside for such occasions (like many of his colleagues, he spoke fluent Spanish), but Beta would

*In 1982, according to a Mexican-American cab driver in Indio, a certain coyote had charged $1,500 to bring his chickens all the way from El Salvador through Mexico to Imperial County. By 2001 it cost $1,500 just to get across the border from Mexicali.

not come. All the while, the murderer kept staring into Willett's face. Finally he leisurely sawed off his victim's hand and flapped it at Willett in a mocking wave. Willett assured me that nowadays, whenever one side witnessed a crime in progress on the other, an officer employed the special frequency with excellent results. Beta sometimes even acted to interdict illegal border crossings! And on the Arizona line, in the Mexican border town of Algodones, one of Beta's representatives proudly informed me that Alpha had just given him a new white Bronco in which to chase criminals. The result—and a highly desirable one, to Alpha at least—was that Mexican cops had begun to squeeze the border-crossers harder—not so much the fence-jumpers, for they went over very quickly, but the canal- and river-swimmers such as Carlos who were slower and hesitated upon the Southside bank for hours or days, waiting for the perfect moment. Of these water-striders, the *solos* found themselves at greater risk of police interference than the *pollos,* because in one *solo*'s bitter words: Coyotes pay money for the police, so if the police ask you who you work for, and if your name is not on their list, you're fucked. You go to jail.

And Carlos said: The other day, I was by the All-American Canal, and I was with these seven guys, and then this Mexican cop showed up with that fuckin' automatic shotgun thing. Police started hitting us with their flashlights. They was gonna throw us in the canal. But really all they wanted was money. We said we don't got nothing. So they gave up and said just get out of here within half an hour. We don't want to see you here again. *Ay,* Mexican cops are a damn . . . They're a bunch of fuckin' . . .

Carlos might have been one of the waiting men I spied when I looked across from Northside. Perhaps Officer Murray would have recognized him. Sometimes when I was in Mexico I walked or took a taxi to that very hot and exposed spot where the steel wall ended by jutting forward at a right angle and down to the rippled brown water's edge; here there never failed to be homeless seekers bathing in the canal or washing their clothes or just sitting, awaiting dusk while on Northside an agent in a white vehicle watched them. They drank out of the All-American Canal, and carried its water with them. They huddled against the graffiti'd wall. They slept, paced, sat spraddle-legged in the litter of plastic and abandoned clothing, whose scraps reminded me of the bits of cloth worked into the earth of the killing-fields of Cambodia, for it was all sad cloth, lost or torn, the temporary skins of the desperate. In the hard and eroded earth, which at least smelled better than the ditch twenty feet farther into Southside, they sat, bowing, closing themselves up against the sun like human jackknives, and when the Border Patrol scanned eyes and binoculars in their direction, they sank their heads even lower into their chests. It was here that Carlos had been introduced to Beta's shotgun. When I was in Northside I never walked to the place opposite that place; I always took a taxi. The levee, hardpacked out of tan dust, carried on its lonely shoulder no one but myself, my taxi driver, and the inevitable Border Patrol agent, who waved and watched me. Over in Southside, Mexicans were sitting at dusk, their dark heads down, shadows in their faces. I went there on different nights at different months, and they were always there. I never saw Beta. (Beta frequently hit me up for fines and bribes closer to the legal crossing, in Niños Héroes Park and thereabouts.)

As Officer Murray now drove away from this spot, the Mexicans raised their heads and stood, gazing alertly into the United States. Once the last daylight had failed, the night vision van would be sure to show the rafters coming in, the All-American Canal milky-white on the scope with each raft a black dot, trees transformed into negatives of trees, lights solid black. Later the nightscope man would reverse the contrast to reveal the *bodies* as white as the egrets which prance on their long dark legs on the embankments of Imperial's irrigation ditches. On foggy nights he had trouble, but usually he could see aliens coming from over a mile away. They did not have much of a chance when he was around. His close-cropped head drank the light of the big screen he gazed into, his tattooed arm pulsing as he reached down at the control keypad, meanwhile keeping his left thumb hooked against the steering wheel out of some prudent habit or instinct; and on his shoulder shone the round patch where the words **U. S. BORDER PATROL** had been superimposed on an outline of continental Northside.

What do you see? Murray radioed him.

They're comin' across the check, sir, and I know they're still there.

All right, said Murray. I'm there.

An asparagus field was blowing in the warm wind, and near it a rope tautly and diagonally spanned the All-American Canal. A *pollista* had lashed it to a bamboo trunk. Rapidly, yet with an almost elegant meticulousness, Murray cut it with his knife. The rope lay in the sandy weedy night like a dead snake. Looking into my eyes, Murray suddenly said with almost ferocious bitterness: Now he'll write, *and then the heartless bastard cut the rope.*

I don't have anything against you, Dan, I said, but he grew silent.

Murray knew that what he was doing was not very nice. And Gloria Chavez in Chula Vista told me: I remember being on the bike unit and at five in the afternoon I hear *bing!* and they'd thrown a big steak knife at me. That was the kind of aggression I got. Another time we had what we call a *banzai*—thirty or more up there, a group there. Well, this woman started screaming. I said: What's wrong? She says: My leg, my leg! And when I went up to help her, I got pelted with rocks! I said: You stop throwing rocks or I'm gonna call Beta right now. Beta would've responded, although I don't know if they would have come around there right then. The lady had a broken ankle. I took care of her. The people who are gonna sometimes cause the problems are the smugglers and the guides, not the workers who follow them.

In 1996, a twenty-six-year-old Border Patrolman in Gloria's sector was blinded by a glass bottle hurled at him in darkness from the Ensenada Freeway. Now there were klieg lights to counter-blind Mexicans who came too near, while the agents lurked behind the lights in Northside's darkness, further protected by a secondary fence.

Here I had better tell you that in all the ten years it took me to write this book, I never met a single Mexican who could muster up good words for the United States Border Patrol.

See, on the west side you can't get this close to the fence or they'll bust your windshield, Murray said to me once, but I never had any such problems. And yet I was on his side. To be sure, I wished Carlos all the luck in the world—Carlos, Roberto, Mario and all the rest. But whether the laws which made them illegal from working on American soil were good or bad, and they were probably (so I suspected even then, and now I am sure) the latter, Murray's mandate was to prevent illegal entry, a necessary labor in and of itself, because any country unable to control its borders cannot adequately enforce nor even define itself. And the murderer whom Officer Willett got to meet, I do not want that fellow to saunter into California, kill me and saw off my hand.

If something catches your eye, there's a reason, Murray was saying. So I stopped right here and found a boat and a rope. I got thirty aliens . . .

He drove east to check the four tire-drags which lay in the sand near the Alamo River.—If anybody's walked, said Murray, it'll make a fresh wet depression.

I met a coyote who allowed that he sometimes brought his cargo over on the Alamo River, which crosses the border just east of Calexico's East Port of Entry, then ambles north by northwest past Holtville, Brawley and Calipatria; it goes on brown and secluded all the way to the Salton Sea. Where were the Alamo's *pollos* on this evening of crying birds which resembled all the other evenings? They might be on their way now; for to the west, the wall was going rustier and redder now against the orange sky; its lights came on, and the palm trees started to hide in the blackness that was the coyote's best friend.

Let's show 'im what's left of the old Ho Chi Minh Trail, another agent jocularly said.

Those Border Patrol agents in dark green with their Sam Browne belts loved to wargame everything, inflating their routines of searches and captures into a movie. They invoked the suicide-charges of our Japanese enemy half a century ago when they said: They'll *banzai* you with twenty or thirty people. You call a van over and you can hose that van out afterward . . .—And when they named the route up the east side of the Alamo River the *Ho Chi Minh Trail,* they got to fight the Vietnam War all over again. Leaning grasses tall and olive, tall bamboo groves and darkness smothered the place beneath an air of eerie exoticism. Not far away lay bright green fields which almost could have been Vietnamese ricefields.

They'll come over here and they'll even go over *here* on the west side or they'll have tunnels through the brush, an officer said.

They showed me windblown, rounded human tracks through the bamboo. They showed me tunnels. I was going to see many tunnels for the next few years.

We got three groups out of here in the last hour and a half, another agent said.

The cool convenience of the river water and the cover provided by the bamboo had served the *bodies* well for a long time, but now the Border Patrol had placed sensors in the bamboo pipes, so on the Mexicali streets I now met more adherents of the East Highline Canal, whose blue water was born from the rippled All-American approximately five miles east of the Ho Chi Minh Trail.

About the East Highline an agent told me: It runs north. It goes north forever.—And it did—all the way up to the county line, at least, where it met the Coachella Canal in the desert along the edge of the Chocolate Mountains. But the problem with the East Highline was that its long flatness left any fugitive enormously exposed. Therefore truly desperate and determined swimmers such as Carlos played their ghastly ace-in-the-hole: the New River.

It runs right through Mexicali, crossing into the United States just west of the West Port of Entry. Southside its cartographic name is the Río Nuevo, but the green canals feeding it are aptly called *shit water.*—I don't know why the American people want it, Juan the cokehead chuckled.—And at that time, water-illiterate, I still believed that naturally they didn't. The New River has been called the most polluted waterway in North America. (We will assess that accusation later on.) After sunset it runs black beneath the surveillance lights, with white scum on its surface. Near a million people's raw sewage thickens it; unregulated industrial runoff spices it. Through the corrugated gape in the steel wall it oozes, stinking, sometimes thick with evilly near-phosphorescent suds. Year by year the color changes, but the stink is always the same. To pick one's way through the weeds and black plastic bags of abandoned clothing, descending into the slimy ravine through which it flows, is sickening enough.—About ten diseases crawl right up your ass, an agent chuckled. And Dan Murray said: That's the worst river. If you wanna repaint your bicycle, dip the frame in for half an hour and it'll strip the old paint right off. Ten years ago, you might see the occasional two-headed fish. Now it's gotten so poisoned that the only life form you'll see is—*illegal aliens.*—He told the tale of how he'd dove into that literally feculent river one time to catch a *solo* and broke out with a giant sore that wouldn't heal for months. Two years later, when I myself took a cruise on the New River, I was granted a similar souvenir.

Carlos said that he'd never attempted the New River, but he was considering it. Maybe if he wrapped his bandanna tight over his nose and mouth, he could bear to give himself to that reeking brown cloaca. It would take an agent as dedicated as Murray to go in and get him. Others might let him pass rather than risking their own health and stinking up their patrol car . . .

Carlos, why do you want to go to Northside so bad?

I dunno. I . . . I been out of my house for about thirteen years. The best thing that ever happened to me was marriage to that white girl in America. Well, see, I took the train to go to Portland, Oregon. I hopped that freight. I got married. And . . . Well, after awhile I got drinking, and got stopped by the police. I didn't have no papers to the car I was drivin', or a green card or an ID, so they took me to jail, and then this Immigration officer questioned me, and they deported me to Juárez. I ain't never seen my wife again.

Do you want to try to find her?

Oh, I dunno, he said listlessly. I dunno if it would work out now . . .

THE WALK

River or wall, let's say they got across. Here is what happened next. If the Border Patrol did not catch them right away, they could lie low in the fields of Calexico, El Centro or another of those towns whose colors are muted silver and gold; the greys and whites all semiprecious with dust, the reds, yellows, greens, oranges bleached to a faint warm hue that might as well have been gold; but sooner or later they would need to cross a street or search for water. Shy, dark pedestrians where the streets were so wide and empty, a parked car almost an event, they could not evade the Border Patrol week in, week out. The Border Patrol was *everywhere*! Calexico Station, for instance, started as a seventy-man operation (that was what they told me, but we will go back in time and find sixty-nine men less); now two hundred agents operated there. The first time I set up my view camera in Calexico to photograph the international wallscape's tall narrow rusty bars, there appeared within less than a minute three white wagons, each with a Border Patrolman inside it. And how strangely quiet Calexico was at night, just cricket-songs, the asphalt still hot! Every footfall called attention to itself. The aliens had to go north fast. With luck, they might reach Indio. No matter that the *Indio Post* was filled with announcements such as: **NOTICE OF TRUSTEE'S SALE. File No.—9903005035 Servicer SOURCE ONE #505199724 Borrower—DEL CID YOU ARE IN DEFAULT UNDER A DEED OF TRUST, DATED 7/22/98. UNLESS YOU TAKE ACTION TO**

PROTECT YOUR PROPERTY, IT MAY BE SOLD AT A PUBLIC SALE. IF YOU NEED AN EXPLANATION OF THE NATURE OF THE PROCEEDINGS AGAINST YOU, YOU SHOULD CONTACT A LAWYER. These dark brown people lurking in the shade of white walls were not here to borrow. They needed no explanations. They would work hard and live quietly. (Any illegals? I asked at the Brown Jug liquor store.—Right across the street. They jump off the train all the time. But they're dangerous. If you see anybody in this here desert, don't ever give 'em money or they'll put the word out.) But the road to Indio was not easy. A few miles south of Salton City on Route 86, or somewhere on the hot and shimmering stretch of Highway 111 between Niland and Bombay Beach, the Greyhound would pull over at a surprise checkpoint. What happened next was not surprising at all. A man in Border Patrol green came aboard, with a pistol in his belt, and sunglasses perched upon his cap like fabled Argus's extra eyes. He commanded all passengers to ready their identification. The old lady across the aisle got out her green card. (Her generation used to call a green card "mica," because it came inside a shiny envelope like a sheet of that mineral.) The Mexican businessman beside me showed his visa, looking sad. Argus examined my passport with a quick, coldly searching look. (Aside from the driver and Argus, I was often the only Caucasian on that bus.) Now another Argus invited himself to this feast of identification and recognition.—Are you a United States citizen? I heard him say, and silence answered him.—The two Arguses took away a slender boy in a blue cap. His head hung low as he trudged forward between our seats. It was very hot outside, and flies came through the open door. The passengers craned their heads to watch him being led away. A moment later, the first Argus returned, and crooked his finger at someone behind me, as if he were slowly squeezing the trigger of a pistol. Another young man came sadly forward. Neither of them came back. The bus driver slammed the door closed, and off we went, north toward Indio. For a time the bus was silent, and then someone laughed too loudly.

That was why some *solos,* tough, brave, or merely stupid, chose to walk. Their ears burning in the sun, they found a place to hide until nightfall, then pushed on. When their water ran out, they sucked on the vague green sweetness of an unripe cotton ball. One cannot eat it, for even in its immature state the inside is full of white fibers. That is why younger is better. Younger is juicier. At least it gives one a little energy. But between the purple-hearted alfalfa fields along the border and the citrus orchards near Coachella one finds many utterly sun-exposed places—no fields or orchards, just green brush already going orange-brown in the heat. Yes, one can follow the East Highline or the Ho Chi Minh Trail, but now we know that that may not pan out. And the New River, well, that's hell. It might be wiser just to trudge the unremarked dust. But then, at a hundred fifteen degrees Fahrenheit, sucking on a cotton ball will carry a fugitive only so far. From Calexico north through El Centro and then Imperial to Brawley is not so bad, or might not be if the Border Patrol refrained from preying upon that route (here we might quote Officer Dan Murray again: If we see someone with mud on their shoes, we just say, c'mon, get in the car!), but then, as the Salton Sea begins to widen and devour the horizon, it comes time to choose: east side or west side. Either way one finds only nothingness tan and flat between sea and mountains, just going on and on, salt-baked sand and stinking dead birds, multicolored railroad cars speeding like cloud-blocks in a windy sky. Yes, the *bodies* walk by night, but from Calexico to Indio is nearly ninety miles if one stays on the road.* A well-trained soldier can walk this distance in a night and day; most people cannot. The sun will find them. It toasts the haystacks as brown as nuts. One *solo* whom I met in Mexicali told me how he had lain in a cave of honey-colored hay bales near the All-American Canal all day, then trudged the thirty miles from Calexico up to Niland between dusk and dawn. (Carlos had taken two days and nights to make the same trip, but Carlos was out of shape. Moreover, this other *solo* had crossed in the autumn, when the nights were longer and cooler.) Having the knowledge or good fortune to avoid the aerial gunnery range to the east, he followed the Ho Chi Minh Trail all the way up until it intersected Highway 111, then swung around Calipatria and headed through a long dry patch on the Slab City side. He was arrested in Niland in the middle of the following morning when, stained with dust and sweat, he sought to change sleeping places to better escape the sun. He was lucky. He didn't die.

THE RIDE

It was to escape such inconveniences that the *solos* who could afford it sometimes became *pollos*. The coyotes' recruiters, *polleros,*† were ubiquitous in Mexicali. Everybody who slept or worked on the street knew at least half a dozen.

What do they do? I asked Carlos.

They come up to you in the park and say: Hey, man, you goin' to L.A.?

How do you decide which to trust?

When you don't know nobody, you just go with the first one.

The coyotes promised a known route studded with safehouses, and motorized transportation where it was needed. Obviously, the faster a *body* could get out of the border area, the better became his odds of living underground in America. Consider the case of the elegantly dressed woman who sat sipping a drink in the

*Officer Gloria Chavez told of similar conditions in her sector: "They take advantage of darkness for sure and we know that. But they have three to four days' walking to the first freeway in the county."

†Or *las guías*, the guides.

lounge at Calexico International Airport. Officer Murray approached her. She happened to be an illegal from Peru. Usually it was easier to pick them out there at the airport, Murray said, because they were sweating and breathing heavily from their dash from the ravine, *puffing and puffing,* as he put it. The Peruvian woman looked plausible, but anybody with dark skin who sat that close to Southside was likely to get scrutinized. Farther north, in Mecca, Indio or Los Angeles, she might have gotten away with it. So that was her mistake, which she had full leisure to repent in the holding cell.*

And if a car could convey an immigrant across the hottest desert stretches of Imperial County, he had less reason to fear dying of thirst. In a surly testimony to the coyotes' effectiveness, Murray told me: You get hits out here, you gotta respond fast. You never know if they'll get pulled into a vehicle.

Why didn't they all arrange to get pulled into a vehicle, then?—Because in one man's words, *the farther you go, the more you pay.* When you can pay nothing, you go nowhere, unless you walk, swim or crawl, dragging your hunger along.

Coyotes offered the *pollos* one another's companionship. At least they wouldn't face the Northside all alone.—Officer Murray said to me: When you're out in a field, or east in the checks, you often get a group of thirty.—Those large groups, of course, were mainly coyote-run; *solos* by definition didn't travel in packs like that. Sometimes I saw heads popping up over the fence, waving arms all peculiar and inhuman in the dark, and the kids would run back out of a pool of light when the Border Patrol came. They were on their own, and I rarely saw more than half a dozen of them. Laughing and running, they gave one another courage to face the brightness of the wallscape. And if they'd had a guide, a wise coyote or his proxy, how much braver they would have been!

Then, too, some coyotes offered tricks and diversions, like the man I met in Mexicali who hired street youths at a hundred good American dollars per day to jump the fence and draw off the Border Patrol while he inserted his *pollos* into another section of wall. This coyote also knew the crops in the American fields very well, and the concealment they gave at various seasons. He knew how to introduce his clients to the pale heads of onion flowers at night. (You have groups here and all the onion juice comes out of 'em, Officer Murray repeatedly said. Sometimes it gets so powerful that I can't see.) He knew about those caves in the walls of hay bales, and tunnels in the tall corn. When I interviewed him, briefly and under uneasy circumstances, he said he'd never give away his best tricks. But he promoted

*The woman, so Murray's story continued, was well endowed. She pretended that she could not speak a word of English. Many of the agents peering into her holding cell made apppreciative remarks. When Murray learned that she could speak English quite well, she asked him not to tell anybody else, because she enjoyed listening to those men's compliments.

himself as if he were a circus ringmaster, promising thousands of bombastic marvels, experiences, colorful lures for the Border Patrol, whom he dismissed with exaggerated scorn. I did not much believe in him.

On occasion the coyotes could protect their *pollos* against American citizens who did not wear uniforms, such as the gaunt bald man in the Drops just east of Slab City who had pontificated to me for years about the manifold beauties of neighborliness; he gave anybody water who needed it; he loaned out his generator to a poor man with heat stroke; but when I asked him whether he'd ever seen illegal aliens come through, he laughed with vicious joy and told me that one night just last week a coyote and his passengers had stopped on this very back road. They needed help; their tire had blown and they had no spare.—'Cause I *know* what they was up to, he sneered. I was not about to let 'em do it for free. I charged 'em twenty-five dollars for my help. Yeah, they spoke a little English . . .—I wondered how much he would have assisted a Mexican who spoke no English and carried no cash.

Ah, sweet money! Money whispers that there are coyotes for every budget. I met a man in Sacramento whose friend's son, holder of an American passport, ran into some drug-related difficulties in Guadalajara. The United States consulate could do nothing. The man went to a friend of a friend in Sacramento. For five hundred dollars this coyote gave him a telephone number. For an additional fourteen thousand dollars (this happened in 1989, so I suppose it would have cost twenty-five grand in 1999, and after 2001 only Saint Juan Soldado knows), the Mexican guards were paid off, the prisoner loaded into an ambulance, ferried down a dirt road to an airstrip, and flown to Texas, where some bribed American official or employee (he did not tell; I did not ask) allowed them to continue on to Oakland without clearing customs. They landed on a private runway belonging to a certain large American corporation. The man who told me this story was along for the journey. I have been acquainted with him for years, and I trust him. How nice and friendly anyone's coyote would be, if one had fourteen thousand dollars . . .

A LIVING ADVERTISEMENT

Toward Yuma the state of California becomes even drier, burdened with sadly shifting sand dunes and grotesquely ancient crags; that's the Arizona look. Here the All-American Canal is wider and richer, almost a real river like the Colorado from which it flows, fringed with vegetation where the people hide. (It works both ways, a Mexican told me. The Border Patrol also has lots of places to hide.) And over at Southside, in the already mentioned town of Algodones, where two Mexican and two American states meet, the Morelos Dam supports a statue of the Virgin who looks out along the Colorado River. In the inevitable place upon which the Virgin's back was turned, I saw a hammock hanging upon girders like a weary pupa, shading a pair of sandals and a small daypack.

The man in the hammock stuck his head out at last. He felt sad now. His friend had tried the river crossing into Arizona just a day before. His plan, which was not very logical but better than no plan, was to wait here for three or four days, then, if his friend did not return, to make the attempt, hoping and believing that his friend must have made it, in which case he himself might succeed. Should his friend return, then they would try another place.—Not as easy as before, the man whispered, since many Border Patrol . . .

He was a timid man, leaving initiative up to others. The Border Patrol had caught him too many times now. Slender, richly bearded and moustachio'd, he said with a gentle smile that he wanted a restaurant job, maybe waiting tables or washing dishes. He wore a black cap emblazoned with the name of a famous American restaurant chain. He had attained Arizona not long before, but the freight train he tried to catch passed him by too quickly; then the Border Patrol arrested him. He was not angry with them, he interjected quickly; they did their job and he did his.

I gave him twenty pesos and he brightened, commending me to God. Now he would cross today, as soon as he had eaten. He would not wait for darkness, because he went alone. In the rich tangle of brush, robbers both Mexican and American would settle into their ambuscades by nightfall. They enforced their greed with knives and pistols. It had happened to him twice before. He'd be crawling low in the bristling darkness, and then suddenly he'd be caught; they'd stripped him naked, finding every coin.—They will shake you for pesos, *no importa* if you live or die, he said. I hope to God I get over there.

Sometimes the Mexican police had robbed him also. They did not come specifically for that, only to examine him for drugs, but if in the course of the examination any valuables were discovered, why then, they became the property of the discoverers.

His wife, like the wives of so many other *bodies,* awaited him in Los Angeles. It was now July, and he had not seen her since last May when they'd crossed the border successfully at Tijuana, the Border Patrol not yet having erected metal fence in the place that they had found. A month afterward, he'd learned that his mother was dying. So he went back to Morelos to say goodbye to her. His wife had remained in the United States. She was a chambermaid, a link in a hotel chain. She earned barely enough for rent and food. There was no possibility that he could pay any coyote. But if he only could . . .

If I didn't have my wife, he asked me, why would I be suffering and trying? She's the only thing I have in life. Without her I don't care if I die.

"YOU GOTTA CROSS"

The coyote came out with his shoulders down like a charging bull. I nodded and smiled, but he looked at me with a strangely flat, almost watery gaze which I have long since learned signifies a gazer who cares not what evil he does, someone utterly and inhumanly unreachable. I saw this gaze once in a Russian paramilitary policeman during the Yugoslav civil war; he soon held a bayonet to my throat to "test" me. I saw it in some teenagers in Harlem who seared my arm with a cigarette butt.

Ask him if it's okay to talk to him here in the street, I asked the cokehead.

Sure, the cokehead replied.

Ask him how he got started and why he—

The coyote stared into my face with his watery eyes and said in perfect English: I got started same as you, by asking questions. But I'm not gonna answer any of *your* fuckin' questions. Now get the hell out of here.

And turning to the cokehead, he told him in Spanish: If you don't cut this gringo loose right now, I'm gonna hurt you bad.

I'm just workin' for money, the cokehead protested, but the coyote roared at him like a bull and swung his big beefsteak arms.

He followed us for a good four blocks, threatening the cokehead, but not me.

The cokehead's name, as I said, was Juan. He had crossed the border illegally many times, sometimes as a *solo,* sometimes as a *pollo.* It depended on how much money he had.

What made you decide to go the first time? I asked him.

My sister lives there in America. I wanted to go and find out how it is.

How did she get there?

My parents went over by coyote and took my sister. My Dad came back alone. Then he died. I stayed here with my older sister.

So when you wanted to come to her, what happened?

Well, my sister find out about me over there, and they send a coyote to me. We started, but then the Border Patrol found us and the coyote ran. So the Border Patrol caught us. He just wrote my name and then we come back . . .

And then?

We got caught like three times until we finally made it.

Can you tell me the story of the successful time?

Coyote comes over here and talks to me, see. He tells me how they gonna do it. He got two or three workers, and they come with me and the other *pollos.* We go across the border at the night time. There's a field, and then another field, and then the coyote workers take us to a van. We all lay out in the second field. That day we were thirteen or fourteen people. We all had to keep quiet. We all had to lie down until after three hours, when Border Patrol weren't there no more.

Were you afraid?

You don't think that it's scary. All you think is, *you gotta cross*. The people that cross the border, sure they're riskin' somethin.' Like dyin' in the sun, you know . . .

Did you feel that?

No, because I was too young. I wasn't thinkin' at all.

And were you scared of the coyotes?

Naw. If you listen to them, they don't do nothin'.

You were boys and girls, men and women together?

That's right.

How were the girls treated?

Actually, like, they convince the girls that they're gonna cross the border for free, if they pay with their body.

But that's not true, is it?

The cokehead snickered.—Nope. The girls fuck the coyote, and then at the end they *still* gotta pay if they wanna get out of the hotel room where they keep 'em locked up . . .

All right. So you were in the second field until the Border Patrol left. What then?

From Mexicali to San Fernando it took us a day and a half. We had to sleep in the mountains. I forget the name of the place, but it was inside a ranch. The coyote took me over to my sister's house and she paid him the twelve hundred dollars.

So she didn't have to pay half up front?

Nope.

And then what?

I was in school over there. I was thirteen. That's the thing about America. You study for free. But then my Mom died, so I went back here. My Dad was already buried. When I got bored, I went back by coyote a second time. But now that I was big, I had a lot of problems with my brother-in-law. He told my sister that I didn't help him out with housework. They were really American people. And, just like most of them think, it actually *is* easy to make more money in America. But you *waste* more money over there, too. So I came back to Mexicali again. After that, I didn't need coyotes no more. I had my high school ID. So I came back a lot of times.

We stood together looking across a sealed parking lot which evilly shone with black puddles reflecting the border lights round and unreal like those not yet winnowed cantaloupes, and I asked him: You want to come over with me now? I'll buy you dinner in Calexico.

Oh, no! Can't do it now, man! That high school ID's twenty years old now . . .

So if you wanted to go to the U.S., you'd get a coyote?

Not if I can help it. They always talk *bastard and bitch, bastard and bitch* . . .

VARIOUS PUBLIC APPRECIATIONS

An old man in a Mexicali bar who kept buying me beers which were tinted bloodred with tomato juice and chili said: They are criminals. They traffic in human lives.—And he began to tell me a story about how when he was living in Arizona (illegally, as it happened; he'd been a *solo*) he'd found two human skeletons in the desert: relics, he was sure, of the coyotes. A coyote of his acquaintance claimed one skull, polished it and placed a red candle inside. The old man brooded over that for years.

And the Border Patrol? I asked him.

Also criminals.

We've had scores of people die in the last couple of years, a reporter in El Centro said. Probably four or five in Imperial County last month. (This was in May.) There would have been more, but it hasn't been so hot. They get stranded in the desert and the coyotes leave 'em. They'll do anything to move the people, like shuffling a hundred of 'em in back of a tractor-trailer rig. Last year one of them crashed and a lot of folks got hurt. And often they have to cross the All-American Canal. Ten to fifteen will drown there in the next several months. They're not highly thought of here. Most of the people who live here don't hold anything against illegal immigrants. They may call Border Patrol or they may not. But the coyotes . . .

Well, don't some of the coyotes perform a service?

The majority do not. They'll abandon 'em in a heartbeat. The really sad thing is when people try to cross the mountains and they freeze to death.

That was what the Americans tended to say, particularly when they were speaking officially. I remember when the *Calexico Chronicle* ran a front-page article entitled **Undocumented Migrants Speak of The Smugglers** [*sic*] **Total Disregard For Their Safety.** (Had the smugglers been considerate, would the *Calexico Chronicle* have said so?) Tom Wacker, chief of the El Centro sector, was quoted as saying: **We are trying to identify and prosecute the smuggler in every group that's apprehended. We need to get these criminals behind bars where they can't harm anyone.**

But one former *pollo* smiled when I quoted to him what Chief Wacker had said.

He replied: They choose one of their number to throw to the Border Patrol, the one they most dislike. In a chorus they denounce him as their coyote. And the judge doesn't have time to listen and figure it out.

And how often is the one they denounce the actual coyote?

Not very often. Because they might need to cross by coyote again next time.*

He was one of the members of another "family" in Algodones who on a very hot morning stood in their underwear, washing their clothes by hand against the rocks of the windy Colorado River, whose high clay banks were shagged with reeds. The white sand on the Arizona side told sad stories paragraphed with the naked, widely-spaced footprints of running men, and the tracks of Border Patrol vehicles curving and curling like immense wood shavings, whirling around the running men until they had caught them. The former *pollo* and his "family" were on the Mexican side, of course. After they finished washing their clothes, they'd go into the weeds to hide until nightfall.

We're gonna relax tonight, then try again tomorrow night, he said.

Why?

Well, we get used to it here. Not so different from our home.

An old coyote who'd led many chosen ones out of Algodones had told me how hard it could be to sleep there with the heat and the mosquitoes, but when I asked the former *pollo* about this, he said that after a week or two you got used to it. He'd already been there a month. In that month he and his "family" had tried six times, each time carrying four liters of water because it was not safe to drink from the Colorado.

I'm waiting to cross, he reiterated patiently.

But not by coyote?

No money.

He didn't blame the coyotes so much.—They don't wanna get caught by the Border Patrol, he explained. It's not that they're leaving 'em there.

In your experience, are they thieves or are they honorable men?

They sincerely do want to cross you over to win their money.

What chance do they give you?

Fifty-fifty. The coyote knows the road—but so does the Border Patrol . . .

His opinion was characteristic. The Americans called the coyotes villains. The Mexicans considered them useful—maybe a little cowardly sometimes, maybe mercenary; perhaps they did take advantage of their female passengers from time to time, but, still, where would most *pollos* be without them?

Yesterday when we crossed over on the east side, the Border Patrol let us walk

*"They don't like to be called coyote," Juan the cokehead reminded me. "Because the police are gonna take the coyote if they know who he is."

quite a distance, another *pollo* told me. I'm sure they'd already seen us. Then they caught us and verbally abused us. They like to let us get dehydrated and tired, so we can't run from them as fast.

How can you be sure they saw you?

He laughed.—They were watching from the freeway with binoculars.

And what happened to your coyote?

Well, he was safe in Mexicali, of course. As for the *pollista,* he ran.

You don't blame him?

No! I would have done the same!

THE PROCEDURE (1)

Well, there's all kinds of people who want to go to coyotes, remarked a man who smelled of stale sweat, dirt, prison, booze and tears. He was Roberto the Honduran, whose wife and children had all perished, every single one, in Hurricane Mitch. He wanted to cross over to Northside. But he could not afford the coyotes. He went on: One of them rounds up the others, and goes to the hotel room, where the coyotes pay him a commission. *They're* not looking for *pollos* on the street. Oh, no! They're in motel rooms, waiting for the people.

THE PROCEDURE (2)

From here to the crossing, it's the guide, one *pollo* explained. Then the coyote takes you across. Then your friend on the other side pays the coyote, who comes back and pays the guide.

CARLOS'S STORY

My friend Carlos, he who was too fat to clamber over the fence and too poor to hire a coyote, expressed a pseudo-American opinion one day when he said: The thing is, you know, they take you to the desert. No water. If someone's dying, they don't care. They leave you to die.

But when I said: You saw them leave somebody? he replied: Well, actually, I got across the border. I got to L.A. For me they weren't so bad.

I thought you didn't have money.

I ripped 'em off! he said, grinning.

You ripped off a coyote? That's pretty good. Tell me everything.

Well, they take me to a motel room and feed me. Beer and whatever you want.

They pay for everything. At three in the morning we go to the park. There's a hole under the ground, and we start running through the bushes and hide. They take me to Signal Mountain, one guide in the front, one at the end. There were seven people with me. So we started walking, walking, walkin' all night till we got to one town—I think it was, like, El Centro—and then another van was waiting for us.

You must have been tired, I said, for I had seen Signal Mountain from Northside, squat and blue on the horizon, veiled by blue-grey clouds. Crossing it at night must have been frightening and exhausting.

Yeah, he said. We hid near the Immigration checkpoint. After they searched the van, after we got the green light, then we got in the van. Then we ride our way to Santa Ana. There was an apartment out there and they take us. We don't pay till we get there. Your friend here pay money, and you're free to go.

Were there any women in your group?

Oh, they just rape 'em.

How many in your group?

Two.

And what happened to them?

They were fine. They fucked the guide, that's all.

And then what?

I just got off the truck and ran! You see, they told us there was some guys in the apartment with guns, and they would guard us until our relatives paid for us. Well, no relative was gonna come; I'd just lied to the coyotes, that's all. Before we get to the apartment, man, there was a stop sign, so I just jumped out and I ran. Because I had no money. They didn't follow me, because the others would have run out, too. I went to a house, you know, and there was this Mexican lady cleaning, and I asked if I could have some water. She told me to stay awhile, and then she gave me two dollars for the bus to L.A. Then I went straight to the mission,* man. Later I got a job passing out flyers on the street . . .

CASH ON DELIVERY

In his reference to that guarded apartment near Los Angeles, Carlos had touched on one of several necessary cruelties of the human-smuggling industry. Since the coyotes had little mind to bring people to Northside without compensation, and since most *pollos* could not afford to pay up front—indeed, the arrangement protected them, because the coyote had the best incentive to deliver them safely,

*Homeless shelter run by a religious charity.

instead of pocketing their money and murdering them—the merchandise, namely, the *pollo* himself, needed to be held until payment. Carlos had been gutsy, rash and lucky.

These holding areas could be found in almost any town in Imperial County. In Calexico, in that strip of border hotels on Fourth Street whose bathrooms stink of disinfectant like Greyhound bus terminals, whose weary curtains are often peep-holed with cigarette burns, whose televisions lean and leer, there was one owned by an old white man whose wife or companion was a beautiful, hard young Mexicana. When you asked this man how he was, he'd say: Well, I'm here.—He hated President Clinton and believed that America's problem was that it was being run by a bunch of goddamned intellectuals. He hated the Border Patrol, too. He called them flakes. He said that everybody accused the Mexicans of corruption, but it was worse over here. He had *goddamned* convincing proof that the Border Patrol sold entry cards to aliens for five *goddamned* grand a head, *goddammit*. The Border Patrol hated him, too; three officers told me so. This was the kind of hotel it was. In those days I always stayed there. It was not one of the rock-bottom haunts of street-whores and heroin addicts, the places whose filth lies beyond words. I never found one of those in Calexico. As the owner himself liked to say: It's not so bad.—Maybe because it was not so bad (it was not especially cheap, but it was private), I frequently heard darkskinned men say to the Mexicana: You have any rooms that face the street? Would it be okay if I see one?—Vans and panel trucks parked themselves in front of the tiny rooms. A former coyote who visited me there said quietly: What you have to imagine is twenty or thirty people all crammed into this room. And maybe somebody wants to sleep, but he can't sleep because there's no room on the floor. And maybe somebody wants to use the toilet, but he can't because the coyote's in the bathroom screwing all the girls one by one.

Officer Murray said that one time a woman in Calexico had telephoned an agent for help. It came out that she'd hired a coyote to get her son as far as Calexico, and then her money ran out, so the coyote's *pollistas* were holding the kid in a room in that hotel and would not let him go. The Border Patrol rescued and deported him. So the woman lost her money, and I don't know what the coyote did to her.

THE CARE AND FEEDING OF CHICKENS

One additional consequence of the cash-on-delivery system was that if the package got lost in transit, the shipper saw no reason to inform the recipient, who now would not be liable for payment. To my mind, this was the most evil aspect of the trade. A *pollo* trusted himself to a coyote, and either arrived in due course or else disappeared forever, in which case the ones who loved him never learned his doom.

If a people dies on a coyote, said Juan the cokehead, coyote's not gonna tell the other people that they died.

All right. But let's say your sister up in the San Fernando Valley paid the coyote half to bring you, and then you died. What would happen then?

Actually, the cokehead said, the people that come from south Mexico, at the beginning the coyote gets in touch with their family by phone. So then they never get the coyote's number and address. And if the *pollo* dies, the coyote just never call no more. So they never find out. The people that live here in Mexicali, they're more safe. Because they know who's the coyote in this town. But still it's not that safe. Sometimes, the *pollos* get out in that hot, hot desert where they never been before. And they'll be waitin' there for the ride that doesn't show up.

Border Patrol agents possessed any number of gruesome stories on this subject. Gloria Chavez, for instance, told of twenty-two people who were found in a boxcar in the heat of south Texas after sixteen hours. A sharp-eyed agent saw a feebly reaching hand. All of them were saved.

THE UNKNOWN END OF SERAFÍN RAMÍREZ HERNÁNDEZ

In the same palm-treed park where Carlos and his "family" prepared and hoped to cross the border, on a hot afternoon two young men were distributing flyers for a *pollo* who'd vanished twenty days ago, in company with twenty-one other hopeful chickens. The chicken-handlers had taken him across the desert to Northside in a 1979 Dodge van which overheated and finally caught fire south of Carrizo Wash. While the two men were telling me this nice story, a Mixteca street musician squeezed her accordion which butterflied so beautifully red and black, and the girl looked at me most mournfully and hopefully—in short, most professionally—while her younger sister held a beggar's cup in my face, wearing an even more plausible sad expression; and the smallest sister of all crawled in the dirt, drinking from the big water jug which she could barely lift. Who could blame those girls if they wanted to try their luck across the wall in Northside? The two leafleters waved them aside so that I could get the horror down reliably for this book. They feared that perhaps the missing man had been left to broil alive in the coyotes' van. The Border Patrol had found bodies inside the Dodge, they said—burned bodies.

As the *Calexico Chronicle*, which might or might not have been more accurate, told the same story, there were no corpses in the vehicle. A "concerned citizen," it said, had turned over an illegal to Border Patrol agents at the Highway 86 checkpoint.

The *pollo* led agents to the smoldering van. The agents then caught nine other people who'd straggled to scattered spots between two and five miles south of Highway 78 in that fearful heat. The remaining twelve were not found. Did one or two reach water somewhere? Was the missing man, Serafín Ramírez Hernández, whose blurred head stared out at me from the flyer most distantly, resolutely seeking something beyond and behind me, still alive?

What does he look like? I asked.

Same as me, but more thin, said one man.

He was a good man, said the other. He was the good friend of my brother. Looked same like me, but more tall. Married with three kids.

Why did he go?

To make money.

In the "Imperial Catechism" of 1903 one reads the following questions and answers about doing business there ("Water is King—Here is its Kingdom"):

What kind of labor can be had for ranch work?

The farm labor in the valley is principally foreign; some are Americans, but it is mostly Mexican.

They came to make money a century ago, and they were still coming now.

Do you know his coyote? I asked the two leafleters.

We don't. Maybe his brother knows him.

Which is more dangerous, to cross alone or with the coyotes?

It's the same, said one, but the other disagreed and said: If you know the way, it's more better if you cross by yourself. Because the *polleros* take advantage of you.

They wandered off to put up more flyers. Behind them, on the grass between the white-limed trees, two men squatted and one man lay, each of them guarding a small plastic bag of necessities as he waited for full dark to try America. The sleeping man was on his side, wearing the same plaid shirt and jeans I'd seen on many of the captured *bodies* in that Northside field. With or without coyotes the people would go.

INTERVIEW WITH A COYOTE

And the coyotes themselves, what do they say? Well, as you have heard, they are not so easy to talk to. I did talk to some, mostly on the fly.—Is it dangerous? I kept asking.—Yes, very dangerous, they always answered.

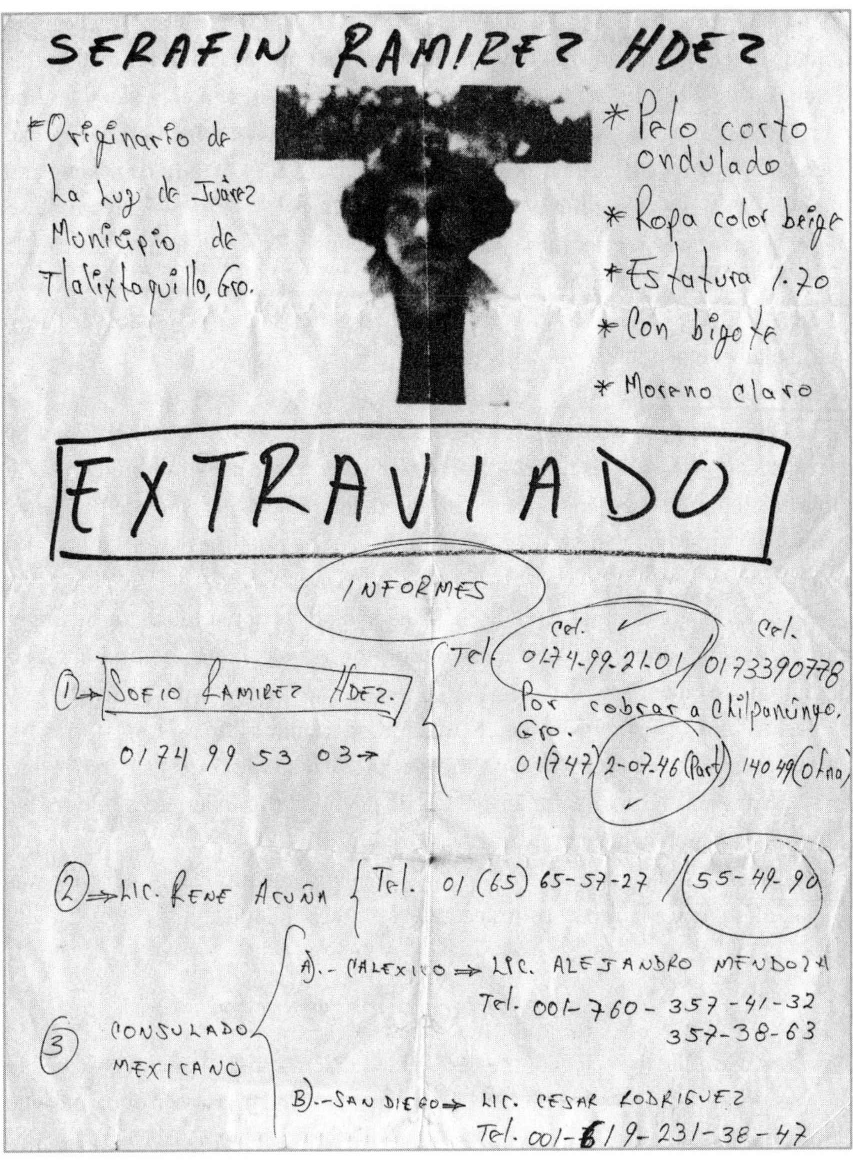

I met two men in Mexicali who confirmed what *pollos* and ex-*pollos* said about them. In a taciturn, colorless way, ever suspicious of exposure, they disclosed some details of their operations, and I have drawn on them here and there. But it was not until Los Angeles that I got to question a coyote for a good twenty minutes, a young one down on his luck; his many close calls with the Border Patrol had scared him into manual labor.

He said that in the days of his glory he had worked only by word of mouth.

Friends known to friends could hire him—no one else. He had always been careful (and he had always been small time). He swore that no *pollo* had ever died on his watch. But he did admit that there had been difficulties. For a considerable time he had led groups over Signal Mountain (this was the path on which Carlos had been taken). Once he came down into the Imperial Valley with his chickens and the *pollista*'s van was not there. It was very hot. They waited for two days and two nights without water. How they survived I don't know. The *pollista* never came. Finally he led them back into Mexico.

He also said that once he and his group had gotten lost, and the Border Patrol had actually helped them, showing them which way to go.

But mainly he feared the Border Patrol.

His answers were a series of lifeless banalities and feeble negations. Had he ever raped any hens in his flock?—No, he replied greyly (what else would he say?). How much had he charged?—Twelve hundred, the same as everybody else.—How many *pollistas* went with him?—Sometimes one, sometimes two, sometimes none.

He was less evasive than dull. Perhaps he had not suffered much; or he might have lacked the aspirations of his *pollos*. But now he was here, and must make a life for himself like them.

I asked him whether he wanted to make good money again.

The coyote looked upon me with the black gaze of an owl on a gate in full daylight, turning his head and blinking. He said he didn't think that he would try his old career again. Maybe he was only being politic.

Really he was like his chickens—shy, inarticulate, uneducated, hungry. He was no villain, merely a failure. He lurked and crept through life . . .

A BORDER PATROL SUCCESS STORY

Who was winning, the *bodies* or the body-snatchers? The rising price a *pollo* had to pay was one testament to the Border Patrol's success. And every *pollo* or coyote who ran scared was another.

In Mexicali I met a clean man of thirty-three years whose occupation was to pass out leaflets advertising dental implants. He usually slept in the street, but took a shower every day. He said: I tried to cross the border seven times, and I almost made it at Tecate. The coyotes took me out of Mexico with no money. But the Border Patrol catch me in Chula Vista. It was hard for me to come back. They kept me three days. They let me off in Juárez.

How did they treat you?

They feed you, but they verbally abuse you.

Do they beat you?

No, but sometimes they push you against the wall if you talk back to them.

Will you try again?

No, I don't wanna try. It's too hard.

And then there was Rubén, who'd lived in Las Vegas and Sacramento until he'd been caught. Now he was working in a taco stand in Mexicali trying to save up enough money to return to Nogales, where the coyotes charged only five hundred dollars instead of twelve hundred and he might not even need a coyote at all because the border crossings were so much easier; after all, he'd lucked out there before, saying to the officer: *Hey, I'm a citizen, man, but my papers were stolen.* He couldn't afford a Mexicali coyote now.

Before I started working here, said Dan Murray, I guess I thought our border was like the Berlin Wall. Well, when I saw all the holes and raggedy-ass places, I couldn't hardly believe it.

It was more like the Berlin Wall each year.

Nowadays, it's very clean out there, said Gloria Chavez in Chula Vista. Operation Gatekeeper began in 1994. At that time we had seven hundred agents in this sector. Now we have two thousand two hundred and fifty. We've established a nationwide database on each person we capture, along with fingerprints. This sector contains sixty-six miles of border, of which forty-four are fenced. There are twenty-four point two miles of secondary fencing. Fencewise, and it's very sad to say it, before Gatekeeper we had only eight miles. Before Gatekeeper, we were arresting half a million people a year. In 1998 there were only two hundred and forty-eight thousand in detention.

So you've cut the number in half, I said. Her statistics reminded me of the numbered sections of rusty landing-mat fence marching up and down the dry hills against which Tijuana pressed and strained.

That's right, she said. And we've cut the number of deaths also. In 1995, eighty-two aliens died in this sector. The main cause of death was homicide. The second cause was accident on the freeway. In 1998 we had only forty-two deaths, the leading cause of which was hypothermia. A hundred and forty-two were rescued. We're gonna do everything it takes to save those lives.

EPITAPHS IN A NEWSPAPER

I opened up my hometown newspaper and it said: **At least 168 people have died during the past 15 months trying to cross illegally into the United States from Mexico over treacherous mountain and desert terrain in eastern California and Arizona, a toll in large part the result of tighter U.S. patrols along the border in the San Diego**

area. Yet as tragic as these events are, the patrolling policy, known as Operation Gatekeeper, is the correct one.

I wonder what Serafín Ramírez Hernández would have made of that.

Six weeks after his disappearance, I telephoned the Mexican consulate in San Diego in hopes that he had been found.—His brother Sofio he has been in contact with us so many times, the woman sadly said. We also check with our contacts here. He's not in any hospital or detention center, or . . . The file is still open, and it will remain open until we find something.

How often does this sort of thing happen?

It's unfortunately very often, she said.*

Meanwhile, the front page of the *Calexico Chronicle* had proclaimed: **Border Patrol Unveils Public Service Announcements Featuring Widow of Smuggling Victim.** The figurehead of these announcements was to be the twenty-five-year-old spouse of a *pollo* who perished with ten other illegals near El Centro when their coyote or coyotes ran away. Sector Chief Wacker was quoted as saying: **I believe that Jackie's plea is very clear . . . We hope that the message will make everyone fully aware of the smugglers' priorities and of the dangers involved in entering illegally.** —My government had figured out that it could use deaths caused in part by its own policies to make propaganda.

MEMBERS OF OUR LABOR FORCE

Of course Operation Gatekeeper could foil some of those *bodies,* so that Serafín Ramírez Hernández became in truth a dead or missing body; and others were apprehended or discouraged. All the same, even if Murray's fantasy ever did come true, and the border became another Berlin Wall, it would never completely, much less permanently, contain the amazing boldness and determination of the *pollos* and *solos.* We were no match for them.

I think of Pedro, who employed no coyote, just swam the river to Texas, asked somebody what to do, figured out how to hop a train, and got all the way to Houston.

I remember Christofer, the slender, gentle, sad-eyed one with the cross around his neck and the New Testament in Spanish under his arm. His six-day deportation process from Los Angeles had concluded just yesterday, and already he was waiting at the fence on that cool fragrant dusk of flowers, considering whether to jump

*"When you find the dead body of a *pollo,* how often can it be identified?" I asked.—"Most of the time, after some work. But not all the time. There's a guy and he had an accident here. He's in a coma. He's been in a coma since he was detained. He fell in detention. It's very sad because the TV stations in Tijuana and everywhere have helped us show his photo, but nobody can identify him."

the fence in the place where I knew from Officer Murray that the video camera in the water tower was already watching us both, or else essay a ride on top of a railroad car—a more dangerous spot, to be sure, but he believed that the Border Patrol never checked it. Maybe he was correct there; I fear not. Fat Carlos had crossed six times on the train, but unfailingly found himself invited into a holding cell. (Last time I almost got by, he told me, but there was this big old rattlesnake on the road and it scared the shit out of me, man.) Christofer smiled quietly and told me that he had a feeling he would get through. His girlfriend, whose flesh was comprised of illegality equal to his, lived in Echo Park. He craved to return to her; he said that there was "no life" in Mexico (although it seemed to me that everything in Mexico was lower, dirtier, truer and above all more alive). We talked for perhaps half an hour, until it was dusk. I went back Northside, a journey accomplished in about ten minutes thanks to my United States passport, walked four blocks to my hotel, gathered up the tripod and eight by ten camera, and took a portrait of Christofer through the rusty bars where we had arranged a meeting. Day and night on the American side one can usually see somebody speaking softly and earnestly through these bars to another human being on the Mexican side. When it is very late, someone often wades through the humid night shadows to stand there looking across the border at the wide yellow lines of Mexicali. Here it was that I made my photograph. I offered to mail a copy to Christofer's girlfriend, but he knew her address only in a descriptive fashion; he could tell me which alleys to employ (none of them by name, only by topography); he related vividly every turn were I to walk from the Greyhound station all the way to his girlfriend's place in Echo Park; he could see the American streets swarming gloriously before him but could not name them because he was illiterate. That New Testament he carried upon his person thus proved to be no reference, but an icon. He could not read it, but believed in it. He trusted that the girl he loved would wait for him in Echo Park until he found his way back. He would cross the border again and again.

I think of the man who proudly boasted of having entered Northside illegally more than seventy-five times.*

Above all, I think of the brown people I saw picking lettuce outside Salinas on a foggy June day as a loudspeaker shouted at them in Spanish. They worked like devils. A melody began to shriek and blare on the loudspeaker, and they all sang along. Who would pick lettuce without them?

Across the three lines of shiny cars going to the U.S.A., a man stood among the

*"So, Gloria, what happens to an alien whom you keep catching over and over?"—"Well, the third time we arrest them, they get a notice to appear for formal deportation. The fourth time, it's up to the court system. They might be detained one day, then three days, then a week, and then . . ."—In these days of the Patriot Act, her answer now seems as quaint as the Geneva Conventions.

flowerbushes, still on the Mexican side, but pacing. He waited in the middle of the street, leaning against one of the yellow concrete barriers. He was longhaired, greasy, sunburned. He was rich with the fecal stink of the New River. He prowled and paced. He stared hungrily into America. He bore the immense burden of the heat.

Oh, he's waitin', Officer Dan Murray was most likely saying wisely, looking through the fence. He and his *amigos,* maybe they have plans. The way you're lookin' right now, if you look southwest, that's where you're gonna see him come through . . .

Chapter 2

DELINEATIONS

(2000)

> Our eyes scan only a small angle of view at any moment; as we move our direction of sight, our visual memory holds and builds impressions of larger and larger areas, while bringing each point concentrated upon into clarity and detail that only a very long-focus lens can approximate.
>
> —Ansel Adams, 1983

The fact that the perimeter of Imperial County resembles a distracted child's attempt to draw a square scarcely distinguishes it, since many other counties in America, especially in the Midwest and Great Plains states, were likewise enacted as defectively wearisome rectangles. Still, we need to start somewhere. It may well be that since this southeast corner of California is so peculiar, enigmatic, sad, beautiful and perfect as it stands, delineation of any sort should be forgone in favor of the recording of "pure" perceptions, for instance by means of a camera alone; or, failing that, by reliance upon word-pictures: a cityscape of withered palms, white tiles, glaring parking lots, and portico-shaded loungers who watch the boxcars groan by; a cropscape of a rich green basil field, whose fragrance rises up as massively resonant as an organ-chord. But I have seen so many old photographs in attics and archives, uncaptioned images of nameless California beauty queens, of lost canals and of obscure professional men in high white collars, all of them pinkening into specters even as the blank desert skies which frame them develop spots of "weather" (brown fixer stains), and maybe one of those professional men, whose hair was carefully sidecombed and whose moustachios tamed in order for him to best resemble the man he wanted to be by the time that photographer emerged from under the focusing cloth, withdrew the dark slide from the film and threw open the shutter on that long ago day before Imperial was a county and the Salton Sea was even born, maybe he, our professional man, deserves to be thanked or cursed for something important; maybe that pretty high school girl in the bathing suit who stands gripping a ship's wheel in her white, white fingers as she stands by the Salton Sea would mean more to me if I knew the extent to which her grandchildren mourned at her funeral and whether she ever once swam there, whether in her time it stank half as much as it does in mine with half-mummified birds and fishes crunching underfoot, which latter point would interest me extremely because some folks have told me that the Salton Sea is poisonous while others insist that there's nothing wrong except an extra pinch of salt perhaps. And what should we do about the Salton Sea, which is to say what should we think, and on what basis, not to mention how should we live? Without a past, no matter how controvertible, the present cannot be anything other than a tumble through darkness towards the darkness which neither past nor present can illuminate. Because I'd rather fall through patches of illuminated air, no documentary caption can possibly contain overmany facts to please me. Let the reader beware. At least the following attempts at delineation may entertain you by proving how badly I draw squares.

THE OFFICIAL LINE

Starting, then, at the county's southwest corner, where map-marks for Smugglers' Cave and Elliot Mine squat below the authoritative red downsnake of Interstate 8, we find the straight line of the Mexican border sloping slightly northeastward, prying apart those kissing cousins, Mexicali and Calexico, and from their severed embrace, memorialized by a sign which advises that ***WE PAY CASH FOR SCRAP METAL***, the line continues to shoot alongside rusty segments of American wall, with Mexico dim on our right, the music from the stripshows fading now, shrill and distorted. A century earlier, it had been like this: *A step over the ditch, and I was in Mexican territory. The contrast was noticeable. North of this imaginary line were modern structures, stores, shops and the commodious offices of the Imperial Water company, with vegetation on all sides, while on the south of it the eye rested upon a few Indian brush teepees scattered among the mesquite bushes that spread over a vast desert beyond.* And before that, of course, all this had been Mexico. The line hugs a dark road, then seals off a forest of lights along the edge of a richly sexually smelling kingdom of hay, reenters the desert and inscribes itself all the way to the Colorado River just north of Algodones. Here where California gives way to Arizona, the Colorado has bitten a ragged arc from Imperial County's southeast corner. It was within three miles of this spot that in 1904 a gambler's cut, made by American engineers without undue regard for Mexican sovereignty, gave the thirsty settlers of the Imperial Valley all the water they'd demanded, and more—and more, until flood-waves opened their fingers all the way from the Imperial Canal up to the New River, and an entire painfully shimmering whiteness of saline flats which had just begun to turn a profit for the New Liverpool Salt Company and then also for the Standard Salt Company was drowned by the county's new centerpiece, that Salton Sea. Well,

well, what could be more imperial than the purplish darkness of winter over water, the broken line of lights of some town along its far side (did I mention that either side is the far side?), some lonely town, decrepit town, ghost town whose beach adorns itself with salt-baked strata of carcasses? To close their breach, the saviors of what would soon be Imperial County had to throw in not only railroad cars full of gravel, rocks, boulders and clay, but the very railroad cars themselves. In 1907 that forfeit was paid and accepted. The farming could go on (hay brought in a decent ten dollars per ton in those days, and California's yields per acre exceeded the national average although Arizona's were twice as good), the sea subsided a trifle, and we pretended that our accident had been nature's. Appropriately enough, from this corner northward the county line is the Colorado River itself, which as it separates from Mexico slopes upstream widely southeast and then northeast around the Fort Yuma Indian Reservation to meet its next vampire, the All-American Canal; and then, looping and wriggling northeast to northwest against the Arizona counties of Yuma and La Paz, that aquatic boundary ropes in Imperial's mountains, railroad tracks and vandalized graves. Running past the Indian Pass National Wilderness, it nears, then veers from the Palo Verde Mountains, snaps northeastward one last time, and at the site of the old Taylor Ferry makes its third corner. Now at last we have an almost level line between Imperial and Riverside counties, as if the child-draftsman got sedated with a lollipop and settled down, allowing us to jog undeviatingly across Highway 78 and the live bombing area in the Chocolate Mountains. A dozen miles south of it as the crow flies, the gentle, wrinkled old prophet Leonard Knight lives alone at the base of a dry ridge whose terminus he has painted with an immense scarlet heart, a blue pond of Christian love, not to mention his slogans and multitudinous simple-styled birds and flowers. Soon it will be two decades that he'll have been laboring there. He only gets more excited. I remember one year when I happened to visit Salvation Mountain just after a rain, and Leonard's latest coat of oil paint was shiny and glowing like candy, brighter than ever before. Close up, the paint was still gooey, pleasantly reeking of newness. Leonard said: I believe someday you'll be able to stand here and see the whole mountain reflected in that shiny oil paint! I can see it comin'.—And if I could somehow reflect all Imperiality in this brief gloss job which you're now reading, I'd be much gratified. As it is, I'll have to be content with varnishing reality as reflectively as I can. From the top of the mountain, standing beside the hay-and-adobe pedestal from which Leonard's cross blooms, one looks down the great field of color-zones, lines and splotches (whose effect reminds me of a children's board game such as Candy Land) to find Leonard's mailbox, rows of paint buckets, then his two immensely decorated trailers, on both of whose roofs is spelled out (to me incongruously, since he's not stern or even monitory) **REPENT**, and then a flatness of tan scrubby desert where Leonard may sometimes be spied on his bicycle slowly pedaling around there way below; and beyond him, beyond that narrow dark straight road which leads from Salvation Mountain to Niland to the west and Slab City to the east, lies more desert, marked not randomly but mysteriously by dirt roads and a lone power pole, after which, far and far away, the low horizon, whose bright dry glory almost never gets impeded in this direction, halts both gaze and retrospection, being burdened by a dark ribbon: the Salton Sea. Leonard hasn't been there for years, he says. He just never seems to get the time, what with all he's got to do, embellishing and cherishing his mountain. The sea tapers northwest beyond our seeing until it gets sliced through by the Imperial County line just south of Bat Caves Buttes. Imagine that! People say it was miraculous that Christ walked across the water, and yet they don't think twice when the same is performed by this entity invisible everywhere except in its representations, whose substance is comprised of equal parts imagination, measurement, memory, authority and jurisdiction! Delineation is the merest, absurdest fiction, yet delineation engenders *control.* Crossing Highway 86, which hugs the southwest shore of the sea more than capriciously, the line runs a due and sober south, keeping the badlands of Anza Borrego State Park in San Diego County for no good reason, crossing Highway 78 again (somewhat south of the counterpart crossing on the east side), and then it lapses into squarish serrations around the perimeter of the ominously named Carrizo Impact Area. In the badlands by the Coyote Mountains, it resumes its straightness all the way back to Mexico.

ANNEXATIONS

Loyalty to literalism would have constrained me entirely within the perimeter of this desert polyhedron. But Imperial County's attributes overwash its borders on every side, as if they were squint-wrinkles extending like sun-rays from its inhabitants' eyes.* Spillovers are easy from a place where everything is long and low, even the mountains. From the levee in Bombay Beach one can see across rooftops, trailertops and treetops all the way to the arid mottlings of the Chocolate Range, which runs beyond the county line without indication of any official or approved transubstantiation. In Brawley and in Calipatria, lines of hay bales lead the eye to infinity. Let's therefore call Imperial County the center of the world, for so it is to

*"The presence of a boundary or measure necessarily implies the possibility of exceeding it . . . The consideration of this leads to a dialectical conception of the finite, according to which it may be understood only as the unity of its own being and its own nonbeing, as the mutual transition of one into the other."—*Great Soviet Encyclopedia* (entry on the finite).

anyone who pauses to stand within it, making it *here*. Having thus recognized its rightful place (meaning no disrespect to any other place), let's illuminate it with all the resources of eyesight, persuasion, bribery, book-study, the mystical "access" available for use and abuse by the holder of a press card, imagination again, second-hand experience, curiosity, romanticism, patience and chance, not to mention the pallid quadruple searchlights of the casino in Coachella where Jose the taxi driver sometimes parks at two in the morning, hoping for rich fares. When no rich fares come, he plays the keno machines. (He said to me: I like to play, but I never win.) This Imperial region about which I want to write and into which I've peeped for years without filling my understanding even halfway as much as wind-sand has lined the rusty cyanide vats of the Tumco Mine spreads itself into a number of overlapping, useless and sometimes superseded names: the Great Basin, the Open Basin, the Colorado Desert, the Desert Lower Sonoran Life Zone (which covers the lower righthand quadrant of the entire state), the Mojave-Sonoran ecotone, "the southwest," California incognita. Let's call it simply *Imperial.**

To my mind, the place extends westward along the border all the way to the Pacific Ocean,† on the shore of which a certain Officer Gloria I. Chavez of the Border Patrol gazed over the fence at Mexico and answered my question as follows: I think we all feel sorry for 'em.—More than just a line, but fluidly, variably so, this left arm of Imperial, thanks in part to Gloria, cannot ball up its muscle to any extent sufficient to breach San Diego, except maybe late at night, in evanescent, perishable globules of reconnaissance, immigration and trafficking; but it surges less deterred than redirected through all breaks in the ever failing border, its illegal hydra-heads popping over the wall south of Chula Vista where Officer Brian Willett remembers the murder he saw in No Man's Land; and it makes forays into the green grass and the red dirt, takes hold of the harsh eroded hills and the high mountains between San Diego and Calexico. Imperial rules all this. How then could we draw any borderline as sharp as a palm-crown against the desert sky?

*Practically every town in Imperial County seems to have its Imperial Avenue. Meanwhile, south of the line, Mexicali boasts Imperial Milk and the Imperial Hotel; on the edge of the Pacific stands Imperial Beach. Hence in the photograph now before me, whose caption reads, "Third Largest Department Store in San Diego County, Corner Imperial Avenue and Eighth Street," I can't even be sure which town I'm seeing—El Centro, probably. I see a parasol'd buggy reigning over much pale, crisscrossed dirt; I glimpse white-shirted humans in the awning's shade; I read two signs: BILLIARD HALL on the left; and on the right, **HICKORY WOOD**.

†Extract from the Treaty of Guadalupe Hidalgo (1848), Article V: *The Boundary line between the two Republics shall commence in the Gulf of Mexico* and continue all the way *across the Rio Colorado, following the division line between Upper and Lower California . . . And in order to preclude all difficulty in tracing upon the ground the limit separating Upper from Lower California, it is agreed that the said limit shall consist of a straight line, drawn from the middle of the Rio Gila, where it unites with the Colorado, to a point on the Coast of the Pacific Ocean, distant one marine league due south of the southernmost point of the Port of San Diego . . .*

(I keep marveling at the way I can walk across the line with legal ease when so many Mexicans can't. It may or may not be "necessary"; meanwhile, it makes me so sad.)

To the north, as I implied, Imperial certainly includes the topmost quarter of the Salton Sea, which where Highways 86 and 111 curve away from its stench becomes a narrowing stripe of multiply differentiated blueness riddled by a Mediterranean or Middle Eastern feeling. No matter that Riverside County has begun: in addition to four thousand one hundred and seventy-five square miles of an eponymous county, Imperial certainly contains within itself the ghost beach-towns of North Shore and Oasis Palms RV Park; past the Salton Sea where the date plantations rise and the perfect round yellow lemons and grapefuits are crowded like many breasts on the bushes of the Coachella Valley, it comprises Mecca, Thermal, Coachella and probably Indio, although the new city of La Quinta just west of Coachella must be excluded, for its clean wide streets and gated communities require us to lump it in with Palm Desert, Palm Springs and other stigmata of Los Angeles. Indio deserves at least qualified inclusion not only for the names of its streets (Sungold, Biskra, Arabia, Deglet Noor, Oasis and Grape), not only because long trains sigh across its eastward edge, with work-thirsty *pollos* jumping off and Border Patrol vehicles hunting them, but also because many of its hot wide streets are almost as lifeless as those of Brawley or Calexico. Within the next five or ten years, however, Indio will have seceded from Imperial. The second of its two casinos is slated for enlargement next spring. Angelenos drive the two or three hours from their behemoth to play in Indio, or, more telling still, to do business there. That business will enlarge Indio. As it speeds eastward, Highway 10 grazes the city, making it the last "important" watering hole on that road before Arizona. The other stops have become as alien to Imperial as is San Diego—no matter that some of them remain administration and transshipment points for Imperial produce which was nurtured by such instruments as, say, the bent backs of workers in a legume field, the big boss observing all as he squats beside his car, patient, distant and less than friendly. Yes, I'd have to say that Indio is Imperial's northwestern terminus.*

East of Mecca, the Orocopia Mountains and the Chocolate Range certainly deserve to be counted as Imperial territory, no matter which county they're in. After Brawley, you can ride east on Highway 178 past the East Highline Canal into the dune country around Glamis; and beyond the dune buggies, beyond the bearded

*If, however, we have it in ourselves to set aside the un-Imperial character of so much of Indio, we can follow Highway 10 westward to Banning, which is where the Colorado Desert visibly comes to an end, sand being succeeded by grass and smog beneath the gaze of Mount San Gorgonio. This is an equally plausible and less subjective frontier for Imperial.

hunters in camouflage shirts with guns and binoculars, beyond the stereotypical California blondes in tank tops who squealingly buggy-swerve between ocotillos, you'll find flat reddish-beige sand all the way southeast to the Cargo Muchacho Mountains. Here the twilight moon cannot ride over any sky of palm silhouettes. This is the place of beleaguered trading posts, of mine tailings and of ghost towns from whose marker-robbed graveyards fangs of bone peep out from the cracked earth. South of the dunes, along Highway 8, our zone declares itself in a pale green tendril-carpet of an asparagus field in the sand. No doubt it holds its own some distance east beyond the Arizona line, but I can't tell you how far, for I've never gone that way. Anyhow, the Colorado River would be as plausible a border as any. Imperial's towns owe their water to it, as we know; it's what the Book of Revelation calls *the river of the water of life, flowing from the throne of God and of the Lamb.* (By the way, it's dammed for the furtherance of expropriation and control. Nobody wants to waste stray droplets on any additional Salton Sea—Los Angeles and San Diego are too thirsty!) Even this far from its source, that parasitized watercourse, unlike Imperial's Salton Sea towns, remains rich in almost untainted water—never mind the taste of salt. Let's say, then, that the Colorado River's the eastern bound.

To the south, matters of definition become most problematic, since this region has been saddled with more administrative subdivisions than the others. Resurrect the confusing matter of names: North of the Riverside County line, the Imperial Valley gets called (doubtless as a concession to civic boosters) the Coachella Valley, while below the international border it's the Mexicali Valley, or formerly and binationally (in Spanish, of course) the Valley of Death. *Our Dutchman insisted that the plain over which we passed, should be named the devil's plain, for he insisted, that it was more hotter as hell, and that none but teyvils could live upon it.* Old newspapers call it "a section of Arid America." Certain memoirists and novelists know it as the Palm of the Hand of God. Geologists call it the Salton Trough, which is to say *a northwestern extension of the basin in which the Gulf of California lies.* To one-armed Major Powell, the Grand Canyon's most famous explorer, it was *Coahuila Valley, the most desolate region on the continent.* The technical label for the whole basin is the Colorado Valley, but since we've strongarmed so much of the Colorado from Mexico,* such an appellation seems as dryly, cruelly useless as the salt-infested lands for

*According to the 1976 *Britannica* (article on the Colorado River), the Colorado River Compact of 1922 between the seven concerned American states proceeded thus: "The total flow of the Colorado River was established at 17,000,000 acre-feet . . . of which 15,000,000 acre-feet were equally divided between the lower and the upper compact states. A water reserve was maintained for Mexico, which was agreed upon by treaty in 1944 . . . controversy continued between the United States and Mexico over the high salt content of the Colorado's water by the time it reaches Mexico." For bleak understatement this vies with Tacitus.

which our neighbors can thank the Americans. No, not for Mexicans the Imperial Valley's hypnotic sweeps of green, with water darkly sparkling in between them! If you travel the Mexican side from Algodones to Mexicali, the tawny dunes looming beyond the border, you'll find the cotton fields to be full of bald spots, and while it's always possible that the cause is bad farming, people will complain bitterly about salt from the United States. My floral guide to Baja California remarks in carefully neutral tones: *Vast agricultural areas of the Mexicali Valley that were formerly farmed now have been taken over by tamarisk. This is a result of agricultral salinization of the Colorado as it runs through Arizona.* And yet the border sometimes seems lusher on the American side, sometimes on the Mexican. Let's agree, therefore, that it's all one valley. Certainly Mexicali and Calexico are the same city, merely bifurcated, and distorted by that bifurcation as East and West Berlin used to be. How could Calexico be understood or even described without reference to Mexicali, which can be seen, heard and smelled between the steel pickets of border fence? I remember standing beside a certain Border Patrolman five feet north of the wall as he trained his binoculars curiously and almost wistfully upon a Mexican wedding, the veiled bride, her groom and her acolytes descending the church steps into the sunset-stained street. One member of the party intercepted his gaze and angrily lobbed it back into the United States of America as if it were an enemy grenade caught just in time; the others, reluctant I suppose to waste time on gringos on this day, refused to look. The Border Patrolman lowered his binoculars. He told me that he'd gone to Mexicali once on a day off, but only once. First of all, he'd been shocked at how little was in the stores. Secondly, it really wasn't healthy for him to go alone, even in civilian clothes. He knew that; he'd spent his professional nights staring southward, and yet the fascination of the line would not let him go. In that moment he seemed as lonely as the wan night-suns of hotel office lights. Embarrassed, he allowed that it looked to be kind of a nice wedding and that he "just liked to know what those folks in Southside are doing." So do I. And if Mexicali deserves to be included in this partly amorphous region which for want of an even less down to earth name I'm calling Imperial (no matter that a city of that title lies on Highway 86, between El Centro and Brawley), then perhaps some of the towns in the blinding white desert to the west and south of Mexicali on Highway 2 between Mexicali and Tijuana also deserve to be Imperialized.*—Not Tijuana, to be sure; Tijuana's not sleepy enough!—For Imperial is wide and slow and sunny like the streets of Mexicali with their long straight shadow-lines.

*For years I've made a hobby of asking people in Tijuana, Tecate, Mexicali and San Luis how far south they still "feel the border feeling"; the usual answer is: about a hundred and fifty kilometers. To the south of Mexicali, the town which best fits this bill is San Felipe; I accordingly decree that Imperial ends there.

DEFINITIONS OF IMPERIAL

Imperial is green, green fields, haystacks, and wide mountains. Imperial widens itself almost into boundlessness, like the Salton Sea as you go south. Imperial is bright fields, then desert wastes, stacks of hay bales almost Indian yellow. Imperial is a dark field glimmering white with irrigation sprays. *(There appears to be a widespread impression,* runs the 1909 Department of Agriculture Yearbook, *that the fertility of irrigated lands is inexhaustible . . . the experience of generations of farmers in humid regions is disregarded.)* Imperial is a loud lonely train whistling like darkness. Imperial dreams fragrant vegetable dreams. Imperial dreams resentfully of the wealth that it could have if the stink of death would only depart from the broken-windowed resorts on the Salton Sea. (THIS VALUABLE COMMERCIAL PROPERTY FOR SALE, says a hand-lettered sign in Bombay Beach. In Brawley, somebody who prefers to have it both ways has posted the following announcement on a ruined garage: **KEEP OUT! INQUIRE AT OFFICE.**) Imperial is the smell of a feedlot on a hot summer night. Imperial is the beautiful, smooth-skinned, reddish-brown fat girl with monumental breasts who replenishes the bowls of salsa and relish in a taco stand in Mexicali. Meat grease glistens upon her gigantic cleavage. Imperial is that nameless bygone California beauty queen in the uncaptioned photograph, and the nameless grave-inmates at Tumco. (Their names exist forever, like the Imperial County line, and if I hunted with sufficient exactitude I could discover them.) Imperial is Barbara Worth, the sentimental heroine of (and here I quote the commemorative edition's dust jacket) *A Saga of Love and Rivalries Set in the Pioneer Days of Imperial County*. Around the egg-shaped illustration, breathtakingly garish, of dark-haired, cherry-lipped Barbara Worth in her wide sombrero, staring dreamily past a cactus *(Often as Barbara sat looking over that great basin her heart cried out to know the secret it held)*, we're informed: *Movie Was Gary Cooper's Screen Debut* and (thank God for the quotation marks) *"A Clean and Wholesome Book"* and *"Strong People"* • *"High Ideals"* and finally: *Three Years on U.S. Top Ten Best Seller Lists,* those years being 1911, 1912 and 1922. *The pioneers in Barbara's Desert were, in fact, leaders in a far greater work that would add immeasurably to the nation's life.* In other words, **KEEP OUT! INQUIRE AT OFFICE.** Imperial is the slender, wrinkled inhabitants of Slab City, together with their trailers, weeds, and heaps of scrapwood. Imperial is the brown-skinned man who somehow missed every immigration amnesty and who now laments for the good old days of the 1950s when *all we needed back then was just a rancher to give a signature to back us up.* Imperial is solid white farmer-citizens, and the conglomerates who now own so many of them. Imperial is the grocery store clerk who begs every stranger to buy a plot of dust while he can, because the Salton

Sea's going to get entirely cleaned up within five years and then values will go through the roof! (You can hardly get away from the Salton Sea in Imperial.) Imperial is the grower who *changed our direction from dates to flowers, especially annual color for country clubs and hotels. They're quite lucrative.* (Annual color in this case meant poppies and petunias. Her corporation raised eighty thousand of each.) Imperial is Cahuilla Indians and East Indian liquor store clerks. But most of all, Imperial is "Mexicans" legal and illegal, and Imperial is also "Mexican-Americans."—They just dig in, a Border Patrolman once told me, as if he were speaking of a strange species of insect. They hide in the weirdest places.—Yes, they dig in, like us. Legally and illegally they establish themselves upon the land, and they try to stay; they want to live. (I can tell you that most of the people who come to the U.S.A. don't go back, said a taxi driver in Indio. Because I tell you, Mexico is beautiful but Mexico is tough.—He'd majored in electrical engineering, but then he fell in love and, as he put it, "went out of college." Now he was divorced, with alimony and child support to pay.) *Imperial is the continuum between Mexico and America.*

A CLARIFICATION ABOUT WHITENESS

The continuum between Mexico and America is, some people opine, the continuum between brown and white skin. Did you know that the California of the 1910 census, the very first in which Imperial County appears because before that it remained undissected from the flesh of San Diego County, was *ninety-five percent white?*—Well, in those days the census-takers seem to have called Hispanics white. Imperial County had a population density of between two and six persons per square mile then, and that population had increased by a hundred fourteen and a half percent in the previous decade, the decade when Imperial City and Holtville got incorporated and the Salton Sea flooded itself into being. (For every action there's an equal and opposite reaction, so of course the population of the Yuma Indian reservation had decreased in the same period, from eight hundred and seventeen to six hundred and sixty-nine souls.) What is whiteness? In 1824 a boy from Kentucky crosses the line into Mexican America and finds *much to my surprize and disappointment, not one white person among them.* A Latina in El Centro whose skin was lighter than mine said to me: A white boy gave me this tattoo. *Prominent among the wide-awake and progressive businessmen of Brawley is Walter P. Casey . . . He was married April 29, 1913 to Miss Irene La Fetra, native daughter and the first white girl born in Long Beach, California.*—Barbara Worth herself, who was white enough to be adopted by a banker and who possessed "the wholesome, challenging lure of an unmarred womanhood" (THIS VALUABLE COMMERCIAL PROPERTY FOR SALE), cantered out under the desert sun often enough to be "warmly browned." Where on our continuum did she ride? The submissively adoring Mexicans whom she saved called her *La Señorita*. Anyhow, if Hispanics are white then I imagine that Imperial is still ninety-five percent white at the very least . . .

UNDELINEATED MATTERS

What cautious hopes I possessed of becoming someday able to comprehend, however provisionally, "what made the people of Imperial who they are" had already begun to melt almost as quickly as a coolerful of old ice cubes dumped onto the sidewalk in El Centro. The Libyan-trained Thai terrorist leader and the Serbian intellectual had proved far easier to "understand," because, like me, they operated through the urban medium of *words*. Together we could construct, disassemble, inspect and blueprint thought-machines of remarkable and sometimes spurious complexity. With the finest-pinching calipers of definitions, explanations and synonyms, we could measure an idea or an expressible feeling with accuracy superior to what the competence of the translators generally permitted. Moreover, the city-dweller's psyche is often altered by its large collection of nouns and verbs. The ability to express something can engender the desire to express it. In short, city people tend to be less shy than country people. More often than I deserved, they've shared their spiritual, sexual, vulnerable and murderous moments with me. Country people can be more open, of course, less glib, but correspondingly more sparse or more undifferentiated in their tellings of tales. One reason that the gun owners of America are losing their Second Amendment rights is that they tend to be less articulate than their opponents, who may not be able to clean a pistol or gut a moose but who know quite well how to employ crime statistics, give press conferences and "network" with bureaucrats. Similarly, the lives of ranchers, farmers and their hired help tend to be lived in significant part through the verbally inexpressible labor of the body. You can ask a man how he is feeling and what he is thinking; and if he's been gripping his pair of hay-hooks into seventy-five-pound bales and raising them above his head for the next man to grab and raise to the next man, who aligns them with fervent care along the haystack's edge, knowing that he alone has the responsibility of keeping that tall, squarish green monster now much higher than a house from toppling onto them all, and if that man you're asking has been doing this until his shoulders ache and his arms begin to tremble and if he then keeps doing it and after that keeps doing it until the haystack is perfect, the hay secure, he might not answer you at all, or he might reply, smiling a little at the other workers: I'm not thinkin' much right now.—Unless you have stacked a few bales yourself, his experience remains alien to you. And while we are on the subject of unknowableness, Mexico is one of the most alien places on earth. No wonder that the *pollos* are called "illegal aliens"! Beneath that quick-smiling or watchful Catholicism lurks another far more elaborate hierarchicalism which in turn subdivides all supposed "Mexicans" into myriads of local spiritualities whose half-secret survival through all the long torments of the Spanish conquest promises their own continuance in bright-colored globules of coherence irrelevant to, hence safe from, the scrutiny of American capitalists. Shouldn't Imperial's pale tan soil therefore be subdivided to reflect its various Mexican cultures? (Perhaps the borders could be dark citrus hedges.) For consider: I've heard tell of a town where they believe in three Christs. I've met a man in a restaurant in Mexicali who called himself an Aztec and spoke of Cuauhtémoc and the other exterminated priest-kings as if they were his relatives. Maybe they were. What did he really think about those ancient days when on the pyramids people's hearts were cut out and their twitching carcasses hurled down steep, steep stairs? How long would it take me to learn what he thought? Once I visited a canyon high above Tijuana where smoothfaced oliveskinned Mixtec Indians of all ages were digging in a stone-piled hillside ditch. Behind them was a barrier of tires. They filled their wheelbarrow slowly with dirt and stones, while a transistor radio played; and down below them in their canyon were the dusty-plank-roofed houses, children and women and chickens in the shadows of trees, and clothes on the clotheslines in many bright colors as on the clotheslines above; and everything there was illegal; these people were squatters. Twenty-five years before, there had been only a few families. Now there were two thousand Indians in three adjoining canyons, and that was fifteen years ago, so I can hardly imagine what the place looks like now if I could even find it. I suppose I should incorporate it into Imperial because most of the money on which those people lived came from peddling chewing gum, puppets and toy animals on the streets, especially in the scarcely moving lines of cars waiting to cross back into American California; these vendors gave a certain color and content to the Mexican-American continuum. A wind rose up from the canyon, and the Mixtecs slowly chipped with picks and filled their wheelbarrow and stood around. We were guests, so they brought us sodas. They served themselves last. Their entire hillside was dirt of a parchment color resembling old map-flesh, and when the children scratched game-lines into it with dead sticks, that place became a map of itself, its delineation as real and eternal as any other even if it got scuffed out a minute later; and if you consider me frivolous, please tell me what and why a boundary is, or tell me how illegality is. Why must they live here, and not in your house? Those upper slopes were steep and hard and worn smooth, just baked hard dirt in the sun with litter and dirty paper and stinking decayed cloth; then they got steeper, at which point the Indians had cut tiny slippery steps into their substance and in still more difficult places affixed ladders down into their steep and narrow canyon where little girls in short dresses ran up and down the path. Piles of rocks and bones interrupted cement platforms. The canyon was terraced by means of tires, as neatly laid in as the boulders of New England farm walls. Upon these terraces, wooden house-boxes had been built and painted blue, yellow, green and firehouse red—all the hues of the clothes but far less bright than they, on account of Imperial's nearly unremitting sunlight. Looking down onto those house-islands, we saw lethargic women sweeping the concrete around themselves in motions much slower than those of their own chickens. Dogs barked. A little girl wearing only shorts moved a chair under a tree. We went through a muddy slippery yard past more little children; we passed by a fence, descended three tire-steps, paralleled another residential delineation comprised of old bedspring mattresses, and there in the doorway of the next house a woman said: I born in Mexcali. That's where I born. They have seven kids and I'm the youngest one. We were in Oaxaca. I remember that, but I don't remember why. My Dad died about sixteen years. After he died, my Mom took us all the way from San Felipe, then we came to Calican to work the fields, then to Mexicali. Then after that we came to Tijuana. I speak English, and my other little stepsister, and my stepbrother does. My Mom sent me to school. But now I forget. Now I don't know how to write my own name. My Mom, always she don't understand this. She's very mean to us. She thought my friend was my boyfriend. So she hate me. I was sixteen, and my husband was my boyfriend. She hit me. She was gonna take me to that place where you don't go no more. I woke up that morning, then before lunch I told my teacher I couldn't go to school no more. Then I went away with my husband, and we came back here. Now I was almost gonna be here three years now. I used to like to live here, but now, no more. I want to see green grass. Here it's just dirt. I want to go away . . .—Later this woman began to speak of magical practices, about how to pray to the Virgin by means of a bowl of water, and how often the spirits of dead relatives required food. Perhaps if I had lived in her house for a month or a year, I might have made some progress in apprehending the properties of that particular globule, after which I could have entered into an apprenticeship somewhere else, then if I were humble, patient, greedy, generous, respectful, unscrupulous, lucky and self-reliant enough, seek out other zones and lessons, appropriating rather than living all those lives, until at the end of my own life, I might have been able to utter a provisional delineation: *Imperial is . . .*—But that canyon was difficult to get to. Nor did I speak Spanish. Nor was I willing to give myself more than intermittently to Imperial. After three hours I departed that canyon forever. In brief, I couldn't quite expect to see into any of these Mexican lives as deeply as one can see into an open construction trench whose dark, raw, crumbly hole remains illuminated late at night by the glowing ferris wheels of the Imperial County Expo across the street . . .

MECCAN LIVES

If only these were the sole confusions and difficulties! But Imperial is not merely exotic to me, hence unknown; it's also the kingdom of secrets. Imperial is the crawling headlights and glowing road-dots on the two lanes of Highway 111. Where 111 becomes Grapefruit Boulevard, that's where you'll find the sign that crows: ***MECCA GOLD — CITRUS, FIGS, GRAPES***. And indeed it's not far from that advertisement where the pale bells of ripe grapefruits toll lusciously in a green darkness whose leaves layer it with depths as enigmatic as the lightless zones beneath the sea. For this we'd better thank the water we've sucked from the Colorado River, since in unirrigated places the sand stretches as blankly as the map of Imperial County itself, being occupied only by a cast-off bottle or boot, or in exceptional cases by a shaggy wild palm which has grown and grown in every direction, thickening itself with fronds, until it's lost much of its shape, hiding within itself. In Imperial, darkness is life; impenetrability is coolness. Hence those small and silent desert towns on whose streets every day is a shuttered Sunday, for the inhabitants harbor themselves at home, out of reach of the sun, or else they're *gone* to factories and fields. Why be exposed to that searing eye in the sky? Whatever doesn't hide gets half-bleached, half-effaced, like the lettering on the welcome-signs of those visionary cities around the Salton Sea. Is that convenience store open or closed? To find out, it's necessary to press one's nose against its dark-glazed windows. That's why the everydayness of Imperial is *mystery*. An Anglo man from El Centro said to me: This is a secret, secret place. In a way, it's like Nam. Just like the old guys don't make friends with the new guys, because most of 'em won't make it, here in the Imperial Valley you've got to ride out two summers before you're in.—Only the most determined voyeurism has any hope of reaching into the shade beneath a man's cap-brim, and then breaching the darkness of his sunglasses to read his eyes. Of course, it's not climate which can explain the divide between the wide-eyed, open faces of the *pollos* on their native border-side and the guarded smiles of legal and illegal farm workers in Imperial County. But the necessary secrecy of life itself throughout that sunstruck zone renders the guardedness less conspicuous. Even on the Mexican side, whose streets are not nearly so lifeless, vendors shelter beneath the awnings of their wheeled stands, beggar-children squat in shade, and prostitutes lurk in cool bars wherever they can, or in doorways of blessed sunlessness. If the Mexicans and Mexican-Americans of Imperial have any one thing in common, it's a resigned faith in the corruption of authority everywhere. For instance, one November a taxi driver from Indio claimed that the Border Patrol checkpoint at Salton City had been inactive "for six months." He thought that illegal entries would be condoned until the end of the grape harvest in December.—

If they don't make it easy, he reasoned, who's gonna pick the grapes? Don't you think the farmers are gonna give a nice present for Immigration?—And to the exponents of this majority doctrine, authority is not only greedy and unprincipled, but dangerously malicious. It certainly seems to be. From the **CLASSIFIEDS-LEGALS** of the *Calexico Chronicle:* **NOTICE IS HEREBY GIVEN that $903.00 (Nine Hundred, Three) U.S. currency was seized on May 29, 1999, from the person of Luis Alfred Garcia . . . by officers of the Brawley Police Department in connection with the violation of Health & Safety Code [sec] 11351.**—Moreover, dear reader, **NOTICE IS HEREBY GIVEN that a 1990 Honda Accord bearing California License No. ————, VIN ———— was seized on March 18, 1999 from the person of Paul Cesare de Jesus, on SR-86, . . . by officers of the Imperial County Narcotic Task Force in connection with the violation of Health & Safety Code sec. 11359, sec. 11360(a), sec. 12500(a) CVC (99–AF-007).**—Why should Luis Alfred García lose his cash, or Paul Cesare de Jesús his car, for having bought or sold drugs? More to the point, why should the cash and car of those two men accrue to G-men whose business lay in seizing people's property in order to finance the seizure of other people's property? At least in Mexico when you pay *la mordida,* the bite, to the policeman who arrests you, you may get your freedom in exchange. In the United States you'll get nothing. Punitive unto near-incorruptibility, the law of Northside executes statutes no more cruel and arbitrary than those of Southside, perhaps less, but unlike the law of Southside it does consistently execute them. I mentioned the vendors, beggar-children and prostitutes of Mexicali. In Sacramento, California, where I live, such people risk getting arrested. There used to be an excellent Mexican restaurant on wheels there; it had an Aztec name, and the burritos were as good as any in Mexicali. The sole proprietor couldn't afford a business permit, so he trolled his stand to and fro until omnipotence stepped on him. He could barely speak English; I wonder if he understood why they closed him down, fined him and arrested him for not being able to pay the fine. Enough. That didn't even happen in Imperial, so who am I to waste ink on his misfortune? The point is that to anxious semiliterate immigrants of any legal hue, authors, anthropologists, photographers and journalists—in short, record-taking outsiders—may well be authority's spies. Hence it is better to tell them nothing. (The man from El Centro again: So many people over here are either selling drugs or busting drugs. You learn who's who, and you shut your mouth.) On the Mexican side, people can afford to be more trusting, more confident, for it's unlikely that I with my mild deportment, ignorance of the Spanish language and foreign address could be in collusion with Mexican authority. And if I'm not asking questions related to drugs or illegal immigration, I probably don't work for the American government, either. But should my interlocutors and I happen to meet northwards of *la línea,* the line, who can say what I am? And so if we roll a trifle farther south on Highway 111, into Thermal, where the Jewel Date Co. building relieves us briefly from any eastern glare (the company itself, by the way, has moved), and if we then keep on past the Oasis Date Gardens and the subsequent desolaton of baked dust-flats, the traffic light with the sign which says MECCA, and if we in fact make the leftward turnoff into that aforementioned town, that small huddle of houses (to the east one quickly gets subsumed into fields; then the tan badlands of Painted Canyon with their smoke trees and soft sands run northeast all the way to Highway 10), the tightly closed enigma within it may not call any attention to itself. Just off the highway lies a small triangularish park of topheavy palms, a shade-haven where in summer Mexicans sleep on the grass, especially during the grape season, and where all year round certain shadowy souls sit in broken chairs. It could be a park in Mexicali, except that those shadowy men are much less friendly, and in place of, say, the brotherhood of sidewalk barbeque vendors perfuming the world with their savory white smoke; in place of the hulking, weary Indian peddler-woman strolling from shade to shade, with her shelf of stuffed animals strapped below her breasts, there's exactly no one, thanks I suppose to that American practice I've mentioned of extorting licensing fees from street vendors who are too poor to pay them, and thanks without a doubt to the Border Patrol, and thanks also to that same reclusiveness of Imperial life-forms, which would translate anybody who wandered through those sizzling open spaces in hopes of doing business with the public into a suspicious anomaly, especially since there's really no public to be found in Mecca, with the exception of those immensely private shadowy men. Just as from a distance, palm orchards seem to draw themselves up into compact armies of lushness, rich and dark between the desert and the Salton Sea, so these men appear to represent the same cause, compadres of idleness or perhaps illegality,* until one actually enters the park to see how in the afternoons, when their numbers are greatest, they subdivide into cliques. In their baseball caps or their white sombreros, they sit on chairs and sometimes even on kitchen stools in the park, watching the **DO NOT CROSS** yellow tape stirring in any breeze. In the stillness of their abiding, they resemble the lone dog who sleeps in the afternoon street. Hunching over cigarettes or kicking back their morning beers, they stare carefully at all the traffic going by, when there is any traffic, which is far from always.

Day after day I went there, hoping to invade their thoughts and steal their sto-

*An orchard keeper in Thermal told me that Mecca had the highest per capita violent crime in the U.S., the place being both somewhat violent and extremely unpopulated. Such numbers games amuse only in a shallow way. After Cain slew Abel, 33% of all humanity became murderers. At any rate, the couple whom I interviewed in Saint Anthony Trailer Park said that "everybody is friendly and peaceful; you can leave the garage door open," and Alice Solario, introduced below, likewise did not consider Mecca to be dangerous at all.

ries, but most refused to talk to me, eyeing me with a hatred as lushly soft as a smoke tree sweeping its hair against a sand dune. In July their watchfulness might perhaps have been diluted by the presence of all the migrant workers, the men sitting or squatting under trees, drinking out of bottles, the boys in sweaty white T-shirts sleeping in the grass whom I remembered from the previous summer, but it was not summer now. The shadowy men glared at me, their Spanish insults and obscenities also glaring like the glancing glints of sunlight on cars, which in Imperial are themselves as bright as suns; and then they looked away, far away at a long vertebral column of boxcars ghosting across the desert like a procession of hay bales. On the first afternoon one hard man strolled over, making a sexual proposition which involved himself, myself, his wife and the woman who had driven me to the park and who now sat in her car with the windows rolled up. I could see that my sweetheart was anxious, and I felt a trifle anxious about her, but my intention that day was to stay only for a quarter-hour and learn what if anything might be possible here, and since it was daylight and she was in the car, I decided not to worry. The man's face was as wrinkled as the cracked rows of earth in a sugarbeet field in high summer. Later, when I was photographing another man with the big camera, two others suddenly called that I'd better look out, and I saw him over there importuning her. (She'd rolled the window down; it was getting hot in the car.) The man was willing to tell me all about Mecca, but he required a thousand dollars, because it was "a deep story, the secret kind." By the end, he'd adjusted his demand to a dollar and twenty-five cents. He was ecstatic when I gave him five. In case I might keep my promise to send a copy of his photograph, he wrote down the number of a P.O. box in Mecca, but on subsequent days and nights, when I was hoping to find him, the other men all insisted that he lived in Palm Desert. I never saw him again.

In fact he'd been worth his five dollars, for when a tall, gentle-looking old cyclist came by to inspect me, the man of the sexual proposition had interpreted for the two of us. The cyclist allowed that he was a coyote. He was willing to tell me "everything," he said, and smilingly wrote down his address, which turned out to be right across from the railroad tracks. What location could be more strategic? An old lady laughingly told me that right there, where there'd formerly been bushes around the tracks, some clever Mecca boys had made a hole and hidden, waiting for the train to stop. Then they'd blowtorched their way through the train's underbelly and stolen microwaves, stereos and other appliances. After that, the train company had cut down all the bushes. This old lady had often seen *pollos* leap off the freight train from Algodones. That was how the tall cyclist had come. Now for a fee he helped others do the same. The old lady said that sometimes the train didn't slow, and then the *bodies* had to ride all the way to Palm Springs, which was considerably more dangerous. Whenever that happened, the tall cyclist lost his investment. All this, of course, was hearsay. The cyclist and I agreed that I'd come the following night at eight-o'-clock. But when the taxi pulled up on that dark dirt street at the appointed time, the cyclist refused to show, although the neighbors assured me that he was inside his fence watching me; and so it went the next day and the next night and the following day. The men in the park said that they hadn't seen him. I never saw him again, either. His property was studded with bottles of water on sticks as a protection against witchcraft.

Another Mexican-American taxi driver, the son of an illegal field worker who'd died amnestied, had once tried his hand as a salesman in Mecca. He explained to me: Sometimes they tell you come and they don't show. They hide. They're humble people. Once they open the door to you, they're very happy to make a friend, once they trust you.

I guess they don't trust me.

Mecca, Mecca, he sighed. Mostly farm people. People who work the fields. Sometimes they get to fighting. I heard somebody got killed . . .

He was a first-generation immigrant, still Mexican, and so he defined himself in relation to the Mexican-Americans, saying: We care about our families and the place where we come from. We don't forget what made us.* And we care about our religion. The Chicanos, the people who've been here more, they lose it. Some of them are *cholos,* you know, gangsters, low riders. They like to call us wetbacks . . .

The Mecca people of whom he had spoken were first generation like him. And yet a difference as sharp as the wicker-points of a fan-palm's skin had already arisen between himself and them, those "humble people," most of whom were living on unemployment right now, waiting for grape-pruning to begin the following month. He was not a humble person. He drove a cab. Perhaps he looked down on them a little. What then must they have thought about successes like him? A first-generation man in Calexico once remarked about three brothers whom we both knew: They're the kind of guys in Mexico you know we call strawberries, since they think they don't stink. Red on the outside, white on the inside. Fairskinned guys, not too dark . . .

Many of the Mecca people came from Michoacán, which of course lies far to the southeast of Imperial's lowest bound, the Sea of Cortés. In one palm orchard in Thermal, the other laborers pointed out to me a fullblooded Indian from there who

*First-generation immigrants rarely lost consciousness of their connections, which nourished and obligated them. This cab driver's brother schematized the matter thus: "Recently arrived immigrants that do not have relatives in the area or friends, these are the ones who work on the farm. The others, they are more likely to get a job in hotel, restaurant, construction, or as a gardener."

could not speak either Spanish or English; they said that he was a very good worker, but I don't know how they told him what tasks to do; nobody spoke his language except other Indians from Michoacán. There were also Spanish-tongued immigrants and *pollos* from that place who said that they were Mexicans, not Indians. Others came from Guanajuato, that arid "mummy capital" made famous by one cemetery's practice of digging up and exhibiting to admission-paying ghouls certain dead people whose relatives have defaulted in grave-rent. On the west side of Highway 111, in a dirt-paved Mecca cul-de-sac called Saint Anthony Trailer Park, where trailers and raised, graffiti'd houses lurked among the palm trees, some properties with fences around them and laundry on the fences, some fences made of metal and others of salvaged boards, I met an unmarried old couple from Guanajuato who agreed to speak with me only because my interpreter of that day also hailed from there. It was morning, the sandy ground just commencing to grow warm to the touch. I'd thought it better to try then than at the Mecca sunset, when Mexicans and Mexican-Americans leaned in the shade, and beside their small houses the people were sitting in their shaded yards; for sometimes a person might not wish to talk when the eyes of his neighbors are on him. I'm still not sure whether in this case it would have mattered. Openheartedly the couple gave me their names and even obligingly, pitifully presented their identity cards, I suppose in case I were some Immigration spy sent to entrap illegals. Both had come to Northside as *pollos* before they met. She came alone in 1980, "jumping onto a bus" as she casually told it, and eventually got amnestied. He paid a coyote two hundred and fifty dollars in Mexicali. That was back in 1972. He, too, was legal now. (Telling me this, he slowly interlocked his hands as if he were praying.) All the same, it seemed better not to write their names, for as I was speaking with them their Arab landlord, who told me with proud contempt that he couldn't speak Spanish, drove up and interrogated me while the two Guanajuato people smiled fixedly, waiting to get into trouble. To me it was extremely painful to see how anxious and helpless they immediately became. At last he was satisfied, having copied down my address in Indio, and off he went. The Guanajuato woman smiled in relief this time, wiping her forehead. The man said that I had been very lucky, since Saint Anthony Trailer Park was private property, and so the owner could have expelled me. The owner's concern, the man thought, was that I might be a building inspector, which may lead you to certain inferences about Saint Anthony Trailer Park.

How is the life here in Mecca? I asked.

Little work. Very sad. We work only on grapes. Waiting for the pruning. It would be good if assembly or other jobs came here.

Why can't you work on other crops such as watermelons?

The man said that the watermelons were the preserve of Central Americans, especially Salvadorans.—They push them very hard, he said. Salvador *pollos* working here, no legals, so they push them harder. Too hard, so they don't want us Mexicans. Discrimination.

These words now remind me of a sad man I met not long after, not a Mecca man but a city man, a pale yellow chunky man with curly hair and a faint moustache—he proudly showed me the map he'd drawn some weeks before so that he could find the Indio courthouse in sufficient time to be present for his arraignment on charges of driving while intoxicated—who seemed almost to be defending himself against the example of the inhabitants of Mecca, the ones from Michoacán and from Guanajuato (he himself was from Mexico City), the silent ones who were now harvesting far away near the horizon beneath the late afternoon moon which had already risen high above that cantaloupe field with its **NO TRESPASSING** signs (and yes, despite what the man from Guanajuato had said, a few of them were Mexicans) when the sad man explained: We U.S. born, new immigrants call us lazy, because we're not really willing to work our best for five dollars an hour. When I was a teenager, I didn't wanna work too hard for four dollars an hour . . .

How hard must somebody be willing to work to survive and prosper in Imperial? The couple from Guanajuato followed the harvest all the way to Bakersfield in their car. When the harvest came to Indio, ladies were allowed a little cart with an awning to shade them. The Guanajuato woman was grateful for that. Moreover, the family could work together. They *made a little group,* as they called it. He and his son did the picking, while she packed. In Bakersfield it was different.—That company is really racist, the man said. They want everything really strict. They can fire you just like that.—It was a vineyard with an Italian name, and this remark of his was the second reason I keep back his name. Both of them carried laminated identification cards bearing their photograph and the insignia of the winery. When they worked there, they had to stay in a camp where the field owner charged them seventy-six dollars per person per week for shelter, lunch included. The wage was six dollars and ten cents an hour, *but the small plants are piecework.* Perhaps the company could have everything its own way because in Bakersfield, only ten people that the Guanajuato couple knew of were legal. (Right here in Mecca, they said, the grape workers were *fifty-fifty legal and illegal.*)

After that, if they were lucky, they went on to Porterville. They worked from 25 May to 20 October, then they were laid off until December, when for a month and a half they could prune for piecework wages, thirty cents per plant. After that they were out of work again until the middle of March when the leaves came in, at which point it was culling time for another one and a half months.

We gotta stretch the money all our life, they said.

You want to stay here for good?

The woman, smiling and shaking her head, replied: When we retire, we plan to go back to Mexico, because here we can't survive on an income of four-sixty to five hundred a month.

They owned their mobile home. But the rent at Saint Anthony was a hundred and ninety dollars, and the utilities about two hundred thirty, so there went four hundred and twenty right there, and they needed food and gas. They had to pay rent whether they slept in Mecca or not.

In your hearts, do you consider yourselves to be Mexicans or Americans?

They say, they feel the same, returned the interpreter. They will give their lives for U.S.A. or for Mexico. Here, even though there's not always good pay, at least you can work. But when you get old, you can't get hired no more.

How soon would that day come? He was already sixty-five and still working because he couldn't afford to quit. She was forty-two. He looked much younger than his age, but she looked older.

If that Guanajuato couple were to emblematize Mecca, we'd have to call it a town of anxious, run-down lives—I don't know if the word "exploited" would be fair, since those people voluntarily came a long, long way north to work; let's consider this in another chapter, for I don't envy them. But across the highway where the big trucks exhaled a metal-sweating breeze, and behind another of those Mecca fences (orchard-jungle and barking dogs within, silent people behind those), there lived a round-faced, round-spectacled old woman named Señora Alice Solario, whom I met on one of those fruitless night visits to the cyclist-coyote who was never at home, and her joy in the town was as miraculous as dark citrus orchards springing out of chalky dirt. Born in the Philippines, lucky, she said, to get one bowl of rice a day, she'd married a Mexican and found herself here, living behind her tall fence with the moon above her and crickets all around her. She and her husband had dwelled in Mecca ever since 1986. For fourteen years she'd worked at the nearby factory manufacturing bomb-casings. Some of them had been used in Operation Desert Storm, she said proudly. I was a little saddened by the thought of Filipinos and Mexicans harming Iraqis whom they'd never seen for the sake of a bad cause, but at least one of poverty's graduates now possessed a stable job which was not as hard on her ageing body as picking grapes.

She said to me: This place, if you come here, for a family that's poor, there's always a place to get free food. There's watermelon and cantaloupe after the first picking. There's broccoli, tomatoes, bok choy, and over there is cilantro, cucumbers, lemons, zucchini . . .

She pointed into the darkness, showing where each field was. She knew where everything was. She said that the crops didn't much change in each field from year to year. The growers were kind to gleaners, she also said.

Over there, you have grapefruit, you have Chinese cabbage. We have a local mango grove, she added with a smile.

My taxi driver was amazed. Mangoes! he kept exclaiming in delight.

I asked Señora Solario whether Mecca was a community or merely a bivouac of mutually suspicious strangers, and she replied: My husband, people come here with no money, as long as he eats, they eat. It's 'cause he knows how it is to be hungry. And me, I remember how in the Philippines I was lucky to get one meal of rice a day. It's the Golden Rule.

GHOSTS AND OUTLINES

So that was Mecca, which was—what? I may have delineated Imperial, but as yet it resists my characterization. Imperial is pinched and infinite. Imperial is those tired old workers from Guanajuato. Imperial is Señora Solario. Imperial is the self-declared coyote who invites me home, then hides behind his fence and dogs, leaving me nothing but the gravel-scented breeze whipping across the railroad tracks, which begin to lead someplace special when the sharp bleak planes of the mountains behind them go slowly blue and fabulous. Imperial is Cortés the conqueror, as represented by a certain factotum, Francisco de Ulloa: Sailing as far as he could up into his master's eponymous sea, Ulloa very likely reached the mouth of the Colorado River, since we're told about "the bay at the end." *The sea there is vermilion in color; the tides rise and fall regularly. Along the coast are many little volcanoes; the hills are barren; it is a poor country.* That poor country is Imperial, the year 1539. And Imperial is a Border Patrolman calling into his radio: We just spotted eight El Sal juveniles and an obese Hondo female a mile east of the one-one-one check . . .—Fruitful and desperate, kingdom of recluses, shy folks and identity criminals, Imperial remains unknown. A Mexican-American inhabitant said to me: Near here, there's an Indian place full of ghosts and energy, and your hat, something takes it from you. I never been there but I heard about it. I wanna go there. I'm just kinda curious. I wanna see a ghost. People say they're just kinda clear, transparent . . .—I wished to see ghosts, too. And I wished to ask the Mexican illegals whether they were ridden (as was I whenever I wandered alone in Mexicali at night) by the feeling of being far from home. Now that I'd marked out, however approximately, some of the boundaries and difficulties of this mysterious place, it was time to begin work. Next time I'd traverse Imperial no more, but stand within the cool dark center of somewhere and try to *perceive.* Just as the humming and soughing of a fast long train reverberates more richly when it's heard from within a windy palm-orchard's dim, rustling aisles, so the qualities which make Imperial itself might well become more apparent to me should I write about a place in depth—perhaps Mecca, or one of the more sunstruck settlements to the south. Or maybe I ought to write about a given crop: dates, grapefruits, dense fields of corn with pale honey-colored tops, the tall grey fur of an onion field at night, or, if I felt "political" enough, grapes. Regardless, there seemed to be nothing for it but to return year after year, deepening friendships, exploring sandscapes and ruthlessly studying people's lives, until Imperial became as shockingly bright in my mind as the bands of sunny grass between the aisles of a palm-orchard.

For a more exact (and reasoned) delineation of the entity which I call Imperial, the reader is invited to study the comments on the maps at the end of this book (page 1127).

Chapter 3

THE WATER OF LIFE

(2001)

> And let him who is thirsty come; let him who desires take the water of life without any price.
>
> —Revelation 22:17

In the year 1997, the town of North Shore, shuttered, graffiti'd, ruined resort which, as you might have guessed, lies on the northern edge of the Salton Sea, was not very different from the way it would be in 2000, the beach literally comprised of barnacles, fish bones, fish scales, fish-corpses and bird-corpses whose symphonic accompaniment consisted of an almost unbearable ammoniac stench like rancid urine magnified. Fish carcasses in rows and rows, more sickening stenches, the underfoot-crunch of white cheek-plates like seashells—oh, rows and banks of whiteness, banks of vertebrae; feathers and vertebrae twitching in the water almost within reach of the occasional half-mummified bird, such were the basic elements of that district. Meanwhile, the dock was crowded with *live* birds—longnecked white pelicans, I think. Their coexistence with the dead ones jarred me, but then, so did the broken concrete, the **PRIVATE PROPERTY** sign (vestige of Americanism), the playground slide half-sunk in barnacle-sand. Could it be that everything in this world remains so fundamentally pure that nothing can ever be more than half ruined? This purity is particularly undeniable as expressed in the shimmer on the Salton Sea, which is sometimes dark blue, sometimes infinitely white, and always pitted with desert light.

In 1999 it had been worse—seven and a half million African perch died on a single August day—and in 2001 it happened to be better, on my two visits at least. Oh, death was still there, but matter had been ground down to sub-matter, just as on other beaches coarse sand gets gradually ground fine. The same dead scales, the barnacles licked at by waves of a raw sienna color richly evil in its algal depths, set the tone, let's say: crunch, crunch. Without great difficulty I spied the black mouth of a dead fish, then after an interval another black mouth, barnacles, a dead bird, and then of all things another black mouth; here lay wilted feathers in heaps of barnacles; here was a rotting fish covered with barnacles, but at least there *were* those intervals between them; the dead birds were fewer; there must not have been any newsworthy die-offs lately.* Scum and bubbles in the water's brownishness reminded me that it's not always wise to examine ideality up close. The far shore remained as beautiful as ever. When each shore is a far shore, when Imperial defines itself gradually through its long boxcars, hills, palm orchards, vineyards, and the blue pallor of the Salton Sea beyond, then the pseudo-Mediterranean look† of the west side as seen from the east side (rugged blue mountains, birds, a few boats) shimmers into full believability. Come closer, and a metallic taste sometimes alights upon your stinging lips. Stay awhile, and you might win a sore throat, an aching compression of the chest as if from smog, or honest nausea. I was feeling queasy on that April evening in 2001, but over the charnel a cool breeze played, and a Latino family approached the water's edge, the children running happily, sinking ankle-deep into scales and barnacles, nobody expressing any botheration about the stench or the relics underfoot. For them, perhaps, this was "normal." I stepped over another dead fish, proof that the Coachella Valley Historical Society's recent pamphlet was right on the mark: the Salton Sea, it informed me, was *one of the best and liveliest fishing areas on the West Coast. Stories of a polluted Salton Sea are greatly exaggerated . . . The real problem is too much salt . . .* In 1994 the author took a drive around the sea with her husband (she'd avoided it for thirty-five years, *believing the largely negative articles in newspapers and magazines depicting its sorry decline*), and experienced *a wonderful sense of what is right with the world.*

PRELUDE TO A RIVER CRUISE

How many Salton Seas on this planet already lay poisoned—if they *were* poisoned—for the long term? The Aral Sea? Love Canal? Lake Baikal? Would their new normality become normative for the rest of us? How badly off was the Salton Sea, really? One book published five years after that Coachella Valley Historical Society pamphlet described the Salton Sea as *a stinking reddish-brown sump rapidly growing too rancid for even the hardiest ocean fish. By 1996 the sea had become a deathtrap for birds . . . They died by the thousands. The coordinator of the [human] birth defect study admitted that her team was stumped by whatever was causing the deformities in the area.* But the authors of that book were not stumped at all. The Salton Sea has three

*According to Tom Kirk of the Salton Sea Authority, the birds were dying mostly from avian cholera, botulism and Newcastle's disease.—"We seem to have far too many of these," he said to me in 2001. "But keep this in mind. Twenty thousand birds died at the Salton Sea last year. That's less than one percent of the bird population."

†After writing this chapter, I had a chance to visit Yemen, and discovered that the Gulf of Aden, with its unfinished concrete structures, its garbage and its greasy gas stations was a near-perfect duplicate of the Salton Sea.

inflows: the Alamo River, in whose bamboo rushes Border Patrol agents play out their pretend-Vietnam cat-and-mouse exercises with illegal immigrants; the rather irrelevant Whitewater River, which flows in from the northwest not far from Valerie Jean's Date Shakes;* and our chief subject, the New River, which, we're told, *claims the distinction of being the filthiest stream in the nation. Picking up the untreated sewage, landfill leachate, and industrial wastes from the Mexican boomtown of Mexicali, the New River swings north to receive the salt, selenium, and pesticides running off the fields of the Imperial Valley . . . It dead-ends in the Salton Sea . . .* There you have it, but according to that confederation of counties and water districts called the Salton Sea Authority, what you have is no more than *Myth #5: "The Sea is a Toxic Dump Created by Agriculture." The Facts: Pesticides are not found at any significant level in the Sea.* Moreover, selenium levels are only one-fifth of the federal standard, and (if I may quote from the rebuttal to Myth #4), *water carried by the New River from Mexico is not a major contributor to the Sea's problems.* Reading this, I commenced to wonder, as this leaflet put it, *then what are the Sea's actual problems? The Facts,* and here come the facts: *Bird disease outbreaks* get freely confessed, and if that phrasing sounds euphemistic, well, who am I to say that the stinking bird corpses at North Shore are any "worse" than, say, the sweet-stenched feedlots, with mottled black and white cattle almost motionless under metal awnings? Those creatures likewise are destined for death. The next sad fact is *fluctuating surface levels,* which I take to be a reference to Bombay Beach's half-submerged houses getting sunk in salty sand, the considerably submerged Torres-Martinez Indian reservation, the drowned buildings of North Shore and Salton City. Finally come (and we may as well put them all in a row, since they amount to the same thing) *nutrient-rich water, algal blooms and fish kills.* To me, this phenomenon, which ecologists call eutrophication, seems symptomatic of *Myth #5: "The Sea is a Toxic Dump Created by Agriculture."* What else but fertilizer runoff could produce that "nutrient-rich water"? (Now that I think of it, Mexican sewage in the New River could.) The Salton Sea Authority mentions only a single cause for any of these problems, the one everybody agrees on: salinity—twenty-five percent higher than that of the ocean. Needless to say, salinity cannot explain algal blooms. But, to get right down to it, *we do not know all there is to know about the sea,* and I consider that statement definitive.

I decided to undertake a course of aquatic exploration. Specifically, I thought to ride the New River, which I'd never heard of anybody doing lately. An elderly lady at the Imperial County Historical Society Pioneers' Museum said that she used to swim in it all the time back in the 1940s. In 1901 a traveller found it studded with beautiful blue lakes, the most impressive of which, the eponymous Blue Lake, was

*The Audubon Society's spokesman Fred Cagle characterized the Alamo's fifty-two miles of water to me as "all irrigation runoff" and the Whitewater as "like the Alamo but less of it."

"bordered with mesquit trees, which hang gracefully over its banks," and "alive with fish of different varieties, sea gulls, ducks and other fowls"; all in all, he found it "very pleasant to the eye." Five years later Blue Lake would be gone forever. An album in the Archivo Histórico del Municipio de Mexicali bears a photo dated January 7, 1918: West Side Main Canal Flume Over New River, Mexico. There's the bridge across the tree-lined raw dirt gorge which the Río Nuevo made during the great floods of 1905–06. Through this wavery slit, destruction flows toward the border mountains; and everything remains open, uncrowded, the new water tower in the distance on its way to putting any and all "mesquit" trees in their places; Imperial is wild, empty and clean.—How navigable the river might now be, how dangerous or disgusting, not a soul could tell. My acquaintances in Imperial County said that yes, it did sound like a stupid thing to do, but probably not that unsafe; the worst that would likely befall me was disease. As for the Border Patrol, they advised against it, calling it "extremely dangerous" and incidentally promising me that should I cross from Southside to Northside by means of the New River, I'd infallibly be arrested.

MEMORY-HOLES

The New River curves and jitters in a backwards S sixty miles long from the Mexican border to an estuary (if I may call it that) of the Salton Sea equidistant from the towns of Calipatria and Westmorland. On a map of Imperial County, the towns and road-crossings of its progress are traced in blue, right down to the last demisemiquaver. We comprehend, or think we do, exactly what, or at least where, the New River is. We know how it got its name, for at the Irrigation Congress of 1900, Mr. L. M. Holt, who was one of the two eponymous heroes of Holtville, explained that some four decades back an engineer under contract to the state of California decided that the reclamation of Imperial's desert would be quite practical, thanks to *unmistakeable evidences of water having flowed* from the Colorado River *through innumerable channels, and finally concentrating into one of some magnitude, by which the water was conducted far up into the basin, or more properly speaking, far down into the basin. This stream was known as New River because of its comparative recent origin.* So really we do know everything. (In fact, we find the name in Bartlett's old narrative of 1850–53.) But immediately southward of Calexico's stubby fan palms, in bank parking lots, pawnshops and Spanish voices, runs a heavy line which demarcates the very end of California and the United States of America, which is to say the beginning of Mexico, and the state of Baja California. Here the New River becomes the Río Nuevo, and if we try to follow it upstream, it vanishes from all but one of the maps I've ever seen, each time in a different way.

Of course it comes from the Colorado River, said everyone I asked in Imperial County. *All* water here comes from the Colorado.*

Mexicans, on the other hand, assured me that the New River began somewhere near San Felipe, which lies a mere two hours south of the border by car. They said that the Río Nuevo had nothing to do with the Colorado River at all.

My plan was to cross into Mexicali, hire a taxi to take me to the source, wherever it was, find a boat, and ride the Río Nuevo downstream as far as I could. But now that I sought to zero in on the mysterious spot (excuse me, señor, but where exactly does it start?), people began to say that the river actually commenced in Mexicali itself, in one of the Parques Industriales, where a certain Xochimilco Lagoon, which in turn derived from Laguna Mexico, defined my Shangri-la. How could I take the cruise? Moreover, the municipal authorities of Mexicali were even now pressing on into the fifth year of a very fine project—namely, to entomb and forget the Río Nuevo, sealing it off underground beneath a cement wall in the median strip of the new highway, whose name happened to be Boulevard Río Nuevo and which was a hot white double ribbon of street adorned by dirt and tires, an upended car, broken things. Along this median they'd sunk segments of a long, long concrete tube which lay inconspicuous in the dirt; and between some of these segments were gratings, sometimes lifted, and beneath *them* lay square pits, with jet-black water flowing below, exuding a fierce sewer stench which could almost be some kind of cheese—yes, cheese and death, for actually it smelled like the bones in the catacombs of Paris.

What were some of the treasures which the Río Nuevo might be carrying to the United States today? The following chart encourages an inventory:

DISEASE RATES (per 100,000)

Disease	*U.S. average*	*California-Mexico border*	*Mexican average*
Amebiasis	1.34	1.38	798.8
Hepatitis A	12.6	37.1	50.1
Shigellosis	10.9	35.3	?
Typhoid[a]	0.2	0.4	36.1

[a]Dr. F. W. Peterson reported back in 1918: "Typhoid fever has been in evidence in the Valley since the first settlers arrived . . . The water is in most cases already polluted before it crosses the line into American territory." His solution: An all-American water supply.

Source: Environmental Protection Agency.

*In his memoirs, a certain "border mountain man" describes a journey to San Diego undertaken in 1845: "From Fort Yuma, we started again, going by way of New River and having to pass through a desert of sand sixty miles across, with water only at one place, and that a small pool hardly fit to drink . . . We travelled that day and night, and the next forenoon arrived at a small lake at the head of New River"—probably Blue Lake. Since Fort Yuma lies on the Colorado, his New River travelogue bears out the Imperial County residents.

A yellow truck sat roaring as its sewer hose, dangling deep down into the Río Nuevo, sucked up a measure of the effluvium of eight hundred thousand people. This liquid, called by the locals *aguas negras,* would be used in concrete mixing. Beside the truck were two wise shade-loungers in white-dusted boots, baseball caps and sunglasses. I asked what was the most interesting thing they could tell me about the Río Nuevo, and they thought for awhile and finally said that they'd seen a dead body in it last Saturday. The one who was the supervisor, Señor José Rigoberto Cruz Córdoba, explained that the purpose of this concrete shield was to end the old practice of spewing untreated sewage into the river, and maybe he even believed this; maybe it was even true. The assistant engineer whom I interviewed at the civic center a week later said that they'd already found hundreds of clandestine pipes which they were sealing off. He was very plausible, even though he, like so many others, sent me far wrong on my search for the headwaters of the New River. Well, why wouldn't the authorities seal off those pipes? My interpreter for that day, a man who like most Mexicans declined to pulse with idealism about civic life, interpreted the policy thus: See, they know who the big polluters are. They're all American companies or else Mexican millionaires. They'll just go to them and say, we've closed off your pipe. You can either pay us and we'll make you another opening right now, or else you're going to have to do it yourself with jackhammers and risk a much higher fine . . .—No doubt he was right. The clandestine pipes would soon be better hidden than ever, and subterranean spillways could vomit new poisons.*

The generator ran and the Río Nuevo stank. The yellow truck was almost full. Smiling pleasantly, Señor Córdoba remarked: I heard that people used to fish and swim and bathe here thirty years ago.

Perhaps even thirty years ago the river hadn't been quite so nice as he said, or perhaps people had fewer opportunities back then to be particular about where they bathed; for that night, in a taxi stand right in sight of the river, while a squat, very Indian-looking dispatcher lady in a sporty sweatshirt sat shouting into a box the size of a microwave, with the radio crackling like popcorn while the drivers sat at picnic tables under a sheetmetal awning, the old-timers told me how it had been twenty-five years ago. They'd always called it the Río Conca, which was short for the Río con Cagada, the River with Shit. Twenty-five years ago, the water level was lower because there'd been fewer irrigation canals to feed the watercourse, and the

*Here is a revealing excerpt from a California Environmental Protection Agency report. An EPA delegation crossed the border for a conference with Victor Hermosilio, the Mayor of Mexicali, specifically "to discuss New River issues." One of those issues was "monitoring of underground storm drains entering the New River concrete encasement project—prior verification of sewage spills into the New River from these storm drains was possible visually, *but can no longer be accomplished since the entire system is underground*" (my italics).

drivers used to play soccer here. When they saw turds floating by, they just laughed and jumped over them. The turds had floated like *tortugas,* they said, like turtles; and indeed they used to see real turtles here twenty-five years ago. Now they saw no animals at all.

Where does most of the sewage come from? I asked Señor Córdoba.

From the factories and from clandestine pollutants. It's a good thing that we're making this tube, so that now it'll just be natural sewage.

After the first hour on Boulevard Río Nuevo, I began to get a sore throat. The two sisters who were interpreting for me felt nauseous. After the second hour, so did I. (Maybe this wasn't entirely the Río Nuevo's fault; the temperature that day was a hundred and fourteen degrees.) Even now as I write this I can smell that stench. Well, in another year or two it would be out of mind—in Mexico, at least. I remember coming back near that place at twilight, and finding a sepulcher-shaped opening between highway lanes, a crypt attended by a single pale green weed, with the cheesey shit-smell rising from that greenish-black water which sucked like waves or tides. More concrete whale-ribs lay ready in the dust; soon this memory-hole also would be sealed. The assistant engineer at Centro Cívico said that his colleagues hoped to bury five point six kilometers more by the end of the year . . .

CALL IT GREEN

The taxi driver followed the Río Nuevo as well as he could. Sometimes the street was fenced off for construction, and sometimes the river ran mysteriously underground, but he always found it again. We could always smell it before we could see it. Now it disappeared again, beneath a wilderness of PEMEX gas stations. At Xochimilco Lagoon, liquid was coming out of pipes and foaming into the sickly greenness between tamarisk trees. The water didn't just stink; it reeked. Then it vanished into a culvert. Old men told me how clear it used to be twenty years ago. Thirty years past, people swam in it. Oh, yes, the Río Nuevo kept getting better and better in retrospect. At Mexico Lagoon the sight and the tale were much the same as at Xochimilco.

The end, said the taxi driver, smiling with pride in his English.

That, so I thought, was all of the Río Nuevo I could ever see except for the federal zone where in a gulley overlooked by low yellow houses, white houses and dirt-colored house-cubes (this gulley dated back a century ago, when the Colorado made the Salton Sea), the northernmost extremity of the river had been fenced off from the public and by the same logic allowed to run stinkingly free; the water was here very green.

A digression on greenness: A block or two up the western gulleyside, which is to say on the poor-hill which could be seen from the street by the Thirteen Negro dance hall, a legless man named Señor Ramón Flores was sitting in the porch-shade of his little yellow house on Michoacán Avenue. He used to be a taxi driver; another driver remarked that diabetes had done for his legs.—I've been here since 1937, he said. I've always lived in this house. I remember the Río Nuevo.—Raising his hands like a conductor, outstretching his fingers like rain, he sighed happily: It's *always* been green! There were *cachanillas* and tule plants. They were all over the Río Nuevo, but they're not there anymore. And I remember how in 1952 the river overflowed. People were camping around it then, in Colonia Pueblo Nuevo. The gringos threw water into the river on purpose so that people would get out of the area. So the government moved them from Colonia Pueblo Nuevo to Colonia Baja California . . .

So the *cachanillas* and the tule plants are gone, you said. How about the smell? Does it smell any worse than it used to?

Oh, it's always smelled that way, but in the summer it's worse. Have some more mescal. You know, down south there's another kind of mescal that's stronger. Three shots and you're in ecstasy; three shots will knock you out.

Thanks, Señor Flores, I will, and we enjoyed a long slow conversation on the subject of exactly why it was that Chinese food in Mexicali tasted different from Chinese food in Tijuana—it had to do with the *chiltepín* sauce—until the hot evening breeze sent another whiff of Río Nuevo my way, prompting me to inquire: Do you have any problems with the smell? Does it ever make you sick?

We're used to it, he said proudly.

Does it always smell like sewage, or is there sometimes a chemical smell?

No, it just smells like shit.

Do you think it's justice for the gringos that you send your sewage to America?

They asked for it, he laughed. They use it for fertilizer.

A Border Patrolman told me that the Río Nuevo will strip paint off metal. Do you think that's true or is it just propaganda?

Oh, that's true, he said contentedly.

Yes, the water was very green, no matter that an elegant woman in leopard-skin pants who'd lived beside the river for twenty years in the slum called Condominios Montealbán shook her long dark hair and said: Green? No green. No brown, no black. No color. Just dirty.—White foam-clots drifted down its surface as tranquilly as lamb's fleece clouds, but it was green, call it green, and green trees attended it right to the rusty border wall, where as I stood gazing at the river one of the two Hernández sisters pointed in the other direction; and between a painting of the

Trinity and a gilded tire from which other *pollos* began their illegal leap, half a dozen young men came running from a graffiti'd building to swarm up over the wall, forming that graceful human snake I had come to know so well, the first man being lifted over by the last, all of them linked, then the ones who were already over pulling the last ones over and down into the Northside, while Susana, the gentle sickly one, watched sadly from the taxi, and the other, Rebeca the dance choregrapher, crossed herself and said a prayer for them.

THE NATURAL SPRINGS

But *nobody* seemed to know where the New River came from. Mr. Jose Angel, Branch Chief of the Regional Water Control Board up in Palm Desert, seemed to think the source to be some sixteen miles *south* of Mexicali, he didn't exactly know the place.

Fitting his fingertips together, the assistant engineer at Centro Cívico mentioned "natural springs." He drew me a map which located these springs on the side of a squarish volcano called Cerro Prieto, which was located due *west* of Mexicali on the Tijuana road. A drain then carried the natural springs' contribution to civilization meanderingly southwest and then southeast to Laguna México, which as I've said drained into Laguna Xochimilco. My driver for that day accordingly sped me almost to Tecate before we found out that actually Cerro Prieto was due south of Mexicali, and not sixteen miles as Jose Angel had said but sixteen kilometers, so we careened back to take a southward turn on the San Felipe road, crossing the Río Nuevo once at five point two kilometers; and we kept faithfully on across the Colorado delta sands until from the direction of the broad purple volcano there came a faint but mucilaginous stink.

At the very beginning of the twentieth century, pioneer-farmers on the American side used to frequently see Cerro Prieto *thrown up by the mirage into the form of a battleship showing plainly the masts and turrets*. The woman who wrote down this recollection in 1931 added that such mirages were much rarer now, *because of the amount of land under present cultivation*. In 2001, Cerro Prieto sometimes grew quite indistinct, thanks to those clouds of commerce—well, well, Imperial's not about beauty after all; it's about money and need. Near the town of Nuevo León, trailers and gates marked out the restricted geothermal station; and in a certain air-conditioned office, an engineer looked up from the blueprints on his glass-topped table and said: As far as I know, it has no connection with the Colorado River.

It was true that no direct connection existed, not anymore.

In an undated map, hand done on grimy linen, which when unrolled takes an entire wide library table, we see all the California Development Company's canals in Mexico—the *former* California Development Company, I should say, for the map is entitled "Northern Part of the Colorado River Delta in Lower California, Compiled by California Development Company, W.H. Holabird, Receiver." (Receivership occurred in about 1910, once the California Development Company went bankrupt thanks to the Salton Sea accident.) The canals have been not only drawn, but tabulated with their lengths, the longest of these being the Alamo River (fifty-six miles), which evidently has been thoroughly tamed into a canal by or in the mind of the California Development Company. Then come fifty-two-odd miles of lesser arteries and drainages. The New River for its part swarms north by northwest from an immense blue Laguna de los Volcanes* in the neighborhood of Cerro Prieto. Accompanying the yellow-watercolored Volcano Lake Levee, it presently enters the New River Basin, which thanks to that accident has grown vaster than Calexico and Mexicali combined. And in this zone, which is not too far south of the border, we discover the largish colored square of the Packard Tract, which the West Side Main Canal diagonally bisects.

Well, so what? As we shall see, a few of these names bear passing relevance in the history of the Mexicali Valley. But the concern of this paragraph (and what if I never write another one?) is the source of the Río Nuevo. Near the righthand edge of Mr. Holabird's map, the Colorado River first flows south by southwest between the Southern Pacific Railroad's levee and a United States government levee, then splits, one branch wriggling almost due south from First Mesa to Second Mesa, then continuing off the map, all the way to the Sea of Cortés I presume, for these were the good old days, when the Colorado wasn't drained dry by farms and cities; while the other branch, the one of interest to us, flows through a rocky falls, passes the crevasse of September 1909, traces the falls of August 1909. Here the cartographer or his successor has pencilled in: *Present channel of the Colorado.* The river now goes west by southwest, nearly paralleling the Paredones River (dry as of 1911), until it fans out into a zone of pinkish watercolor wash labeled *Apex of Delta,* arrows like a school of minnows *(Swift Currents),* then almost touches the eastern extremity of this selfsame Laguna de los Volcanes upon whose dry bed this restricted geothermal station where the engineer looked up at me from the blueprints might even be standing. I imagine that back in the time of its freedom. the Colorado sometimes came here, sometimes didn't. But thanks to the All-American Canal, the *Present channel of the Colorado* bore no interest to the engineer, whose face I can no longer remember.

*According to a 1910 American history of the Imperial Valley, Cerro Prieto divides into two a certain Volcano Lake, one outflow of which is the New River, going north, and the other is the Río Hardy, or Hardy Colorado, which flows south to the Sea of Cortés.

On the last of his blueprints, the one I'd craved to see, the Río Nuevo evidently originated in a spiderweb of wriggling agricultural drains in Baja California's hot olive-drab and yellow-drab flatscape, some of them being named Dren Colector del Norte, Dren Xochimilco and Dren Ferrocarril, the last so called because it partly followed the course of the railroad tracks. My driver and I went to Ejido Hidalgo to discover, insofar as we could, the source of Dren Ferrocarril, and encountered more restricted areas which were scenic with white, sulphurous steam erupting on the horizon between latticeworks of pipes, everything guarded by shrugging sentries who had no authorization even to call anybody and who had never heard of the Río Nuevo. And now for the nearest of the assistant engineer at Centro Cívico's natural springs.—Oh, yes, here it was: a cement-walled canal in which liquid of an insanely phosphorescent bluish-white glowed in the sun.

MEDITATIONS OVER ANOTHER HOLE

In the United States, the New River is more or less denied and avoided; the Mexicans were doing what they could to achieve the same bliss; for now, though, the Río Nuevo remained a part of the human landscape. Begin, for instance, with the wildly spicy sour smell of a shop which sold dried chilis; then came a concrete ruin, scarcely even a foundation anymore, advertising itself for rent, after which, at the intersection of Calle Mariano Escobedo and Avenida Miguel Hidalgo, the street dipped down into a pale dry gulley of trees, houses, warehouses, taco stands, this view being centered by the following grime-stained red-on-yellow caption:

Hacienda S.A.

FABRICA DE TORTILLAS

and in this dip, which as I've said was made by the Colorado River during the floods of 1904–06, there ran two blue-grey dust-sugared ribbons of asphalt between which there seemed to be something resembling a segmented overturned bathtub of endless length; I could see darkness between the segments here and there; that was all. My legless acquaintance Señor Ramón Flores might have been watching me. (**Q.** Do you have any problems with the smell? Does it ever make you sick? **A.** We're used to it.) My nose could not detect dried chilis anymore; you can guess what it discovered. When I think about that arroyo now, I remember another album from the Archivo Histórico del Municipio de Mexicali; specifically, I remember a photograph entitled Puente sobre el Río Nuevo, the date being around 1920, probably; and the photograph depicts the airy trapezoid of a girder-bridge across our river, which was wide in those days and which glistened with the reflections of bushes and trees; it looked so cool and shining beneath the age-yellowed sky (a result of air pollution or improper fixing of the print)—so beautiful, in short; and on the bridge, a car of old-fashioned make preened itself, showing off huge, heavy-spoked tires and a perfectly flat roof; one didn't often come across such cars and rivers anymore. In 2001, pedestrians toiled across the dirt; garbage, especially plastic jugs, adorned it; and beside me, from a little trailer with a prison-barred window, a woman's hand every now and then flung out new garbage: a plastic plate with red rice stuck on it, a plastic bag of something, and finally—success!—a used condom.

Early one evening, the heat stinging my nose and forehead almost deliciously, I descended back into that gully, half-crossed the road which so many people hoped and believed would be the new straight shot to Calexico, found a square hole, and peered down into it, wondering whether I would stand a chance if anybody lowered me and a raft into it, and while I considered the matter, my latest taxi driver, who enjoyed flirting with my interpreter, stood on a mound of dirt and recited "El Ruego" by the Chilean poetess Gabriela Mistral. Thus Mexico, where the most obscene feculence cannot prevail over art.—The current appeared to be extremely strong, and there was no predicting where I would end up. At best I'd be washed out into the federal restricted area by the border, where I'd probably get arrested, since even after seeing my press credentials the Mexicans had denied me entry. Should there be any sort of underground barrier, my raft would smash against it. I'd probably capsize and eventually starve, choke or drown, for I didn't think I could swim against that speeding current whose stench was now making me gag, and even if I could, I didn't see how I could clamber up out of any hole. Just to be sure, I knocked on a few doors at Condominios Montealbán, whose grimy concrete apartments, home to poor people, *polleros,* prostitutes and car thieves, stood a few steps away. How bad did they think it would be if one had to take a swim?

Well, the kids have respiratory problems just from living here, said one lady who was standing in the broken courtyard. They have coughs, and on the skin some pimples and rashes. There used to be nothing but a fence here. *Pollos* would go in. We used to see them swimming. They used to die. Some of them made it to America, I don't know how many. Now in the Río Nuevo we see only dead people. They throw people in it like trash. Sometimes it's gays. Two months ago we found a body in there. He was naked. I saw the police and the ambulance, but I didn't go there because I don't wanna look at those things.

How about you? I asked a Chinese woman. Does the river ever make *you* sick?

A year ago, when they tubed this section, we stopped smelling it. I don't know anybody who's gotten sick.

(Some of the taxi drivers at that dispatch stand used to get sick from the Río Nuevo, they'd told me, but it was better now. None of them suffered from it anymore.)

I approached some knowing-looking, money-hungry, daredevil teenagers who sat in the shade of the old stone lion and asked whether any of them would be willing to ride underground in the Río Nuevo with me. They shook their heads sorrowfully and said: No oxygen.

That settled it. Since I couldn't spend my own death benefits, I decided to begin my little cruise in America.

FIRST RIVER CRUISE

Mr. Jose Lopez, who clerked at the motel where I was staying in Calexico, was an ex-Marine with a cheerful, steady, slightly impersonal can-do attitude. When I told him that nobody seemed willing to take me down the New River or even rent me a rowboat, he proposed that I go to one of those warehouse-style chain stores which now infested the United States and buy myself an inflatable dinghy. I asked whether he would keep me company, and he scarcely hesitated.—Anyway, he said, it will be something to tell our grandchildren about.

The store sold two-person, three-person and four-person rafts. I got the four-person variety for maximum buoyancy (since, as I've said, the idea of capsizing in the New River scarcely appealed to me), selected two medium-priced wooden oars, paid seventy dollars and felt good about the bargain. That evening at dusk, driving past the inky silhouettes of hay bales, I revisited the spot where the New River came through the gap in the border wall and, gazing back into that federal restricted area in Mexico, I thought more on what I was about to do, wondering whether I could prepare any better than I had. It was a hundred and fifteen degrees then, and sweat pattered down from my forehead onto the film holders of my view camera. Nobody had any idea how many of the New River's sixty American miles might be navigable; the Border Patrol (one of whose white vehicles now hunched just across the river, watching me) once again advised me not to attempt any such thing since it was "dangerous."

I'd prevailed upon Jose to bring his father from Mexicali. The old man would drive Jose's truck and wait for us at each crossing of the road that he could, proceeding always ahead rather than behind, so that if we had to walk in the heat, we could be sure in which direction to go. If we waved one arm at him, he'd know to drive to the next bridge. Two arms would mean that we were in trouble.

I worried about two possibilities. The first and more likely but less immediately detrimental one was that we might get poisoned by the New River. Should this happen, I supposed that our grace period would endure long enough for us to achieve our next rendezvous with Jose's father before ill effects overwhelmed us. The second peril, which seriously concerned me, was dehydration. Should we be forced to abandon the boat in an unlucky spot between widely spaced bridges, the heat might get us. Tomorrow's temperature was predicted not to significantly exceed a hundred and ten degrees, so that could have been worse. My daypack lay ready to hand, half filled with bottled water, juice and sugar-salted snacks. I'd told Jose to prepare his own supplies. He was behind his desk at the motel now, laboriously inflating the dinghy breath by breath whenever the customers gave him a chance, for he had no bicycle pump with him. This was the kind of fellow he was: determined, optimistic, ready to do his best with almost nothing.

His father had first come Northside as a teenaged *pollo* in the 1950s. A Japanese ranching family, recently unrelocated from some miserable American prison camp, proposed to pay him nothing except for food and clothing, but to teach him everything they knew. Just as Jose gladly accepted my offer to ride the New River with me in exchange for fifty dollars (I gave him a hundred plus the dinghy), so his father bore out Officer Murray's axiom: They do work most Americans wouldn't do.—Jose's father labored for two harvesting seasons. On each occasion, he'd walk along the border all the way to the terrible reddish barrenness of El Centinela, known on the American side as Signal Mountain. This journey required about twelve hours. He crossed at a certain place he told me about where there were no Border Patrolmen (they are there now). Then came thirty-eight miles in the heat. Sometimes there were taxi drivers who would take the illegals (who were not yet called *pollos* or *bodies*) that distance for ten dollars, and I hope I can imagine how much that would have been for a Mexican laborer in the 1950s, especially given Jose's father's wages. (In 2001, Jose got a twenty-dollar speeding ticket in Mexicali, and this fee infected him with anguish.) The first year Jose's father preferred to walk that thirty-eight miles. The second year he chose to spend the ten dollars, less to spare himself than to limit his risk of being arrested. As it happened, some other field workers were ahead of him. The taxi driver took their ten dollars, then turned them in to the Border Patrol. After this, Jose's father never trusted American taxi drivers; he went by foot. Each year when the last crop was harvested, he gave himself up to Immigration so that he'd get a free ride back to the border. At the beginning of his third year, the Japanese brothers began paying him twenty-five cents an hour. He was ecstatic. His grandfather, who'd been boarding him in Mexicali during the off season, was finally able to go back home to southern Mexico; Jose's father could fend for himself now . . .

Sheep-shaped clots of foam, white and wooly, floated down the New River. (That's domestic sewage foam, explained a scientist from the Environmental Protection Agency. Near Brawley there's lot of ag foam as well.) I stood on the trash-covered bank, inhaling the reek of excrement and of something bitter, too, which I guessed to be pesticides. Still and all, the water did not smell nearly as foul as in Mexicali. The cheesy stench had mellowed into something more tolerably sour and rancid, further diluted by sun and dust. The Border Patrolman on the other side of the river sat motionless in his wagon, watching me. After fifteen minutes my throat got sore and I went back to the motel. Another Border Patrol car followed me slowly through the white sand.

At seven-o'-clock the next morning, with Imperial already laying its hot hands on my thighs, my shoulders and the back of my neck, the three of us, Jose, his father and I, were in the parking lot across the river from the supermarket, squinting beneath our caps, squatting down to study Jose's father's stick-sketching in the dirt; he was mapping out the New River with the various road-crossings; and across the highway, on the dirt road where I'd stood the night before, another white Border Patrol vehicle idled. The first place that the old man would be able to wait for us was the bridge at Highway 98, about a mile due north, which equalled four miles' worth of river, thanks to a west-northwest north. After that, there might be a safe stopping place for the truck at either Kubler or Lyons Road, or perhaps the north-south overpass of S-30; but this depended on traffic, so the next spot which Jose's father could guarantee was Interstate 8, which looked to be a good ten miles from Highway 98 if one counted in river-bends and wriggles. Perhaps two miles after this began a longish stretch between crossings. If we got that far, I would be nervous then. But I hardly expected to; nobody knew if the river even remained navigable.

Now we dragged the dinghy out of the back of the truck, and Jose, who from somewhere had been able to borrow a tiny battery-powered pump, tautened his previous night's breath-work until every last wrinkle disappeared. From the weeds came another old man, evidently a *pollero,* for he, after laughing at the notion that Jose and I were about to be literally up Shit Creek, began very knowingly and solemnly to warn us of obstacles. We would not be able to reach even Highway 98 without a portage, he insisted; ahead lay a culvert through which the wiriest illegal field worker could not fit. He gazed at me with begging eyes, hoping, I think, to be hired as a guide. But our brave yellow craft, rated at four persons, appeared barely capable of keeping Jose and me afloat, so I could not encourage his aspirations. We dragged the boat down a steep path I'd found between the briars, and then the stench of the foaming green water was in our nostrils as we stood for one last glum instant on the bank, whose muck seemed to be at least halfway composed of rotting excrement. I could no longer see the palm-tree shadow, dark on grey, on the supermarket parking lot. Everyone waited for me to do something, so I slid the dinghy into the river. A fierce current snapped the bow downriver (the flow here has been measured at two hundred cubic feet per second). I held our conveyance parallel to the bank as Jose clambered in. Then, while Jose's father gripped it by the side-rope, I slid myself over the stern, while Jose's trapped breath jelly-quivered flaccidly beneath me. I had a bad feeling. The old man pushed us off, and we instantly rushed away, fending away snags as best we could. There was no time to glance back.

What a deep, deep green river it was! (It's *always* been green! Señor Ramón Flores had sighed.) Shaded on either side by mesquite trees, palo verdes, tamarisks (or "salt cedars" as they're sometimes called), bamboo and grass, it sped us down its canyon, whose banks were stratified with what appeared to be crusted salt. An occasional tire or scrap of clothing, a tin can or plastic cup wedged between branches, and once what I at first took to be the corpse of some small animal, then became a human fetus, and finally resolved into a lost doll floating face-downwards between black-smeared roots, these objects were our companions and guideposts as we whirled down toward the Salton Sea, end over end because Jose had never before been in a boat in his life. I tried to teach him how to paddle, but he, anxious behind his smiles, could not concentrate on what I was telling him, and kept dipping the oar as far underwater as he could reach, then pulling with all his might, like a panicked swimmer who needlessly exhausts his strength. Nor could I help him as much as I wanted to, on account of my self-appointed obligation to take notes and photographs. Every few moments I'd see us veering into the clutches of a bamboo thicket or some slimy slobbery tree branches, and I'd snatch up my oar, which was now caked with black matter (shall we be upbeat and call it mud?). Sometimes I'd be in time to stave off that shock. But frequently these woody fingers would seize us, raking muck and water across our shoulders as we poled ourselves away. Already we were sopping wet and patchily black-stained. The first few drops on my skin burned a little bit, but no doubt I imagined things. What might they have contained? In the Regional Water Quality Control Board's poetic words, *the pollutants of major concern are the pollutants identified by the Board in its 303(d) list. Namely, for the New River,* seventy percent of whose effluent comes from the United States, meaning that the contamination would presumably worsen as one approached the Salton Sea, *they are bacteria, silt, volatile organic constituents (VOCs), nutrients, and pesticides. The pollutants associated with agricultural runoff are salts, silt, pesticides, nutrients, and selenium.* Jose kept spraying me by accident. There was not much to do about that; certainly I couldn't imagine a gamer or more resolute companion. He was definitely getting tired now. Replacing my camera, which was speckled brownish-black from the New River, into its plastic bag, I laid down my notebook between my sodden ankles and began to paddle again. Here the stench was not much worse than that of marsh water. Had I simply grown accustomed to it (I remembered how my friend William had grimaced in disgust one night when we stood high on the bank), or was the New River really not so bad? The stink of a Florida mangrove swamp, or a Rhode Island cranberry bog, or a Cambodian riverbank on which the fishermen have thrown down many a wicker basket's worth of entrails, struck equivalency, in my memory at least. Although it was not much after eight in the morning, the water had already begun to approach blood temperature (the revised forecast for that day was a hundred and twelve, which turned out to be low). We rammed into another tamarisk thicket, and when the branches sprang up to catapault more river-droplets on our heads, it felt almost pleasant.

We were passing a secluded lagoon into which a fat pipe drained what appeared to be clear water. We sped around a bend, and for no reason I could fathom, the stench got much worse—sewage and carrion as in Mexicali. The greyish-black mud clung more stickily than ever to the paddle. I vaguely considered vomiting, but by then we were riding a deeper stretch which merely smelled like marsh again. The water's green hue gradually became brown, and that white foam, which occasionally imitated one of those faux-marble plastic tabletops in some Chinese restaurant in Mexicali, diluted itself into bubbles. Everything became very pretty again with the high bamboos around us, their reflections blocky and murky on the poisoned water. Occasionally we'd glimpse low warehouses off to the side; and wondering whether they might presage Highway 98 distracted me from the bitter taste in my mouth, which would continue to keep me company for days. Another inlet, another pipe (this one gushing coffee-colored liquid), and then we saw our first live creature, a duck which was swimming quite contentedly. Black-and-white birds, possibly phoebes, shrieked at us from the trees, fearing that we might pillage their nests. The heat was getting miserable. Narrowing, the river swerved under a bridge, and I got a beautiful view of more garbage snagged under dead trees . . .

I kept wondering when we would reach the pipe about which the old *pollero* had warned us; we never did. My end of the dinghy, having punched into one bamboo thicket too many, hissed sadly under me, sinking slowly. Since the price included several airtight compartments, I wasn't too worried, but I didn't really like it, either. Meanwhile the river had settled deeper into its canyon, and all we could see on either side were bamboos and salt cedars high above the bone-dry striated banks. A wild, lonely, beautiful feeling took possession of me. Not only had the New River become so unfrequented over the last few decades that it felt unexplored (no matter that every bend had been mapped and we couldn't get away from trash, poison, stench), but the isolating power of tree-walls, the knowledge that our adventure might in fact be a little dangerous if we extended it sufficiently, and the surprisingly dramatic loveliness of the scenery all made me feel as if Jose and I were nineteenth-century explorers of pre-American California. But it was so weird to experience this sensation *here,* where a half-mummified duck was hanging a foot above water in a dead tree! (What had slain it? Can we necessarily blame the New River? I recollected a certain old man on the shore of the Salton Sea who thought that nothing was really wrong there and said about the avian die-offs: How do those *scientists* know that all those birds weren't sick before they got here?) Lumps of excrement clung to the shore. Lumps of reeking black paste clung to my paddle. The river skittered from bend to bend in its sandy, crumbling canyon, and suddenly the sewage smell got sweeter and more horrid once again, I didn't know why. And now another splash from Jose's paddle flew between my lips, so that I could enter more deeply into my New River researches. (How did it taste? Well, as a child I was given to partake of the sickly-salty Salk polio vaccine—an ironic association, I suppose, for one of the thirty-odd diseases which lives in the New River is polio.) Not long afterward, fate awarded Jose the same privilege when a snagged tree sprang out of the water into his face.

At hot and smelly midmorning the river split into three channels, all of them impassable due to tires and garbage, and here again the water became the same rich lime as the neon border around the Mexicali sign for MUEBLES ECONOMICOS which as dusk arose gradually succeeded in staining its metal siding entirely green. Above us, Jose's father waited at the Highway 98 bridge. The Border Patrol had already paid him a visit. They prohibited him from coming to help us; and I remembered Officer Murray's colleague saying: Now, that irrigator's car over there just happens to be in a convenient place. We'll have to check him out . . .—Well, thank God I was white.—We hauled the sagging dinghy up the slope and through a fenced-in place where the earth was so pale that a brown jackrabbit, whose hue might in other jurisdictions match the color of dirt, seemed lushly alive. I didn't think we could count on enough buoyancy to make it all the way to Interstate 8, so I called it quits. Even after a shower, my hands kept burning, and the next day Jose and I still couldn't get the taste out of our mouths. We used up all his breath-mints lickety-split; then I went to Mexicali for tequilas and spicy tacos. The taste dug itself deeper. A week later, my arms were inflamed up to the elbow and my abdomen was red and burning. Well, who knows; maybe it was sunburn.

ANOTHER RIVER CRUISE

Ray Garnett, proprietor of Ray's Salton Sea Guide Service, was a duck hunter, but he preferred to take his birds in Nebraska. He knew quite a few men who hunted the wetlands around the Salton Sea, and he used to do that himself, but about their prizes he remarked: I don't like 'em, 'cause they taste like the water smells.

How about the fish, Ray?

I've been eatin' 'em since 1955, and I'm still here, so there's nothin' wrong with 'em.

As a matter of fact, he thought that the Salton Sea must have improved, because he used to get stinging rashes on his fingers when he cleaned too many fish, and that didn't happen anymore.

Ray went out on the sea pretty often. He'd been a fishing guide for decades. Now that he was retired, he still did it to break even. He called the Salton Sea *the most productive fishery in the world.*

About the New River, Ray possessed very little information. He'd never been on it in all his seventy-eight years, and neither had anybody else whom he knew.—Seems to me like a few years back I was down here duck hunting and then I heard a boat comin', he said. That was why he was willing to hazard this eight-hundred-dollar aluminum water-skimmer with its twelve-hundred-dollar outboard motor on the New River. He was even a little excited. He kept saying: This sure is different.

Ray preferred corvina to tilapia, and in fact he'd brought some home-smoked corvina in the cooler. It wasn't bad at all. Probably I was imagining the aftertaste. Thirty-four pounds was the record, he said. Fourteen to fifteen pounds was more average. He could gut one fish per minute.

In the sixties and seventies lots of people came down here, he told me. Then that bad publicity scared people away, but they're startin' to come back.

Today, as it turned out, Ray's boat was going to cover the river's final ten-odd miles. Poor Jose only got a hundred dollars. I had to give Ray five hundred before he'd consent to try the New River.

Stocky, red, hairy-handed, roundfaced, he did everything slowly and right, his old eyes seeing and sometimes not telling. We put the boat in near Lack Road by Westmorland, and the river curved us around the contours of a cantaloupe field, with whitish spheres in the bright greenness, then the brown of a fallow field, a dirt road, and at last the cocoa-brown of the very water which whirled us away from that sight.

The New River's stench was far milder here, the color less alarming; and I remembered how when I'd asked Tom Kirk of the Salton Sea Authority to what extent the Salton Sea's sickness derived from the New River, he promptly answered as his fact sheets did: None. People point their fingers at Mexico and at farmers. Neither of these are contributing factors to bird deaths or fish deaths in the Salton Sea.

Maybe he was right, God knows. Maybe something else was causing them.

You think there are any fish in this river, Ray?

Flathead catfish. I wouldn't eat 'em. One time we did core samples of the mud in these wetlands. It has just about everything in it.

Swallows flew down. The river was pleasant really, wide and coffee-colored, with olive-bleached tamarisk trees on either of its salt-banded banks—all in all, quite lovely, as Hemingway would have said. We can poison nature and go on poisoning it; yet something precious always remains. I thought about all the Indian tribes whom we'd forced off their hunting grounds—grazing ranges these days, or more likely industrial parks—and in exchange we'd awarded them "reservations" where we assumed the land to be most worthless. Coal and oil sometimes turned up there, or uranium . . . Our earth had gifts left to give, so we kept right on taking and taking. I wondered what Imperial must have been like in the old days—the very old days. Someday I should learn the history of this place. Lowering our heads, we passed beneath a fresh-painted girder bridge which framed a big pipe, probably for water, Ray believed. Rounding the bend, we met with a sudden faint whiff of sewage. But the river didn't stink a tenth as much as it had at the border, let alone in Mexico. Passing a long straight feeder canal with hardly any trash in it, we presently found ourselves running between tall green grass and flittering birds. Villager Peak in the Santa Rosa Mountains was a lovely blue ahead of us. Now the bamboo thickened on either side, rising much taller than our heads. When Ray duck-hunted, he refrained from shooting if his prey were to fall into a thicket like that, because it would be virtually irretrievable.

Have another piece of that corvina, he said.

Now the hills of bamboo and grass on either side resembled the Everglades. Four black-winged pelicans flew together over the grass. The sunken chocolate windings of the New River seemed to get richer and richer. But presently another odor began to thicken, the familiar stench of North Shore, Desert Shores and Salton City.—The sea's right on the side of these weeds here, my guide was saying.

What's that smell, Ray?

I think it's all the dying fish, and dead fish on the bottom. It forms some kind of a gas. It's just another die-off. It's natural.

Ducks flitted happily, and then we saw ever so many pelicans as we arrived at the mouth of the Salton Sea. Were the birds contented here or did they just have to take what they could get, since ninety-five percent of California's wetlands were

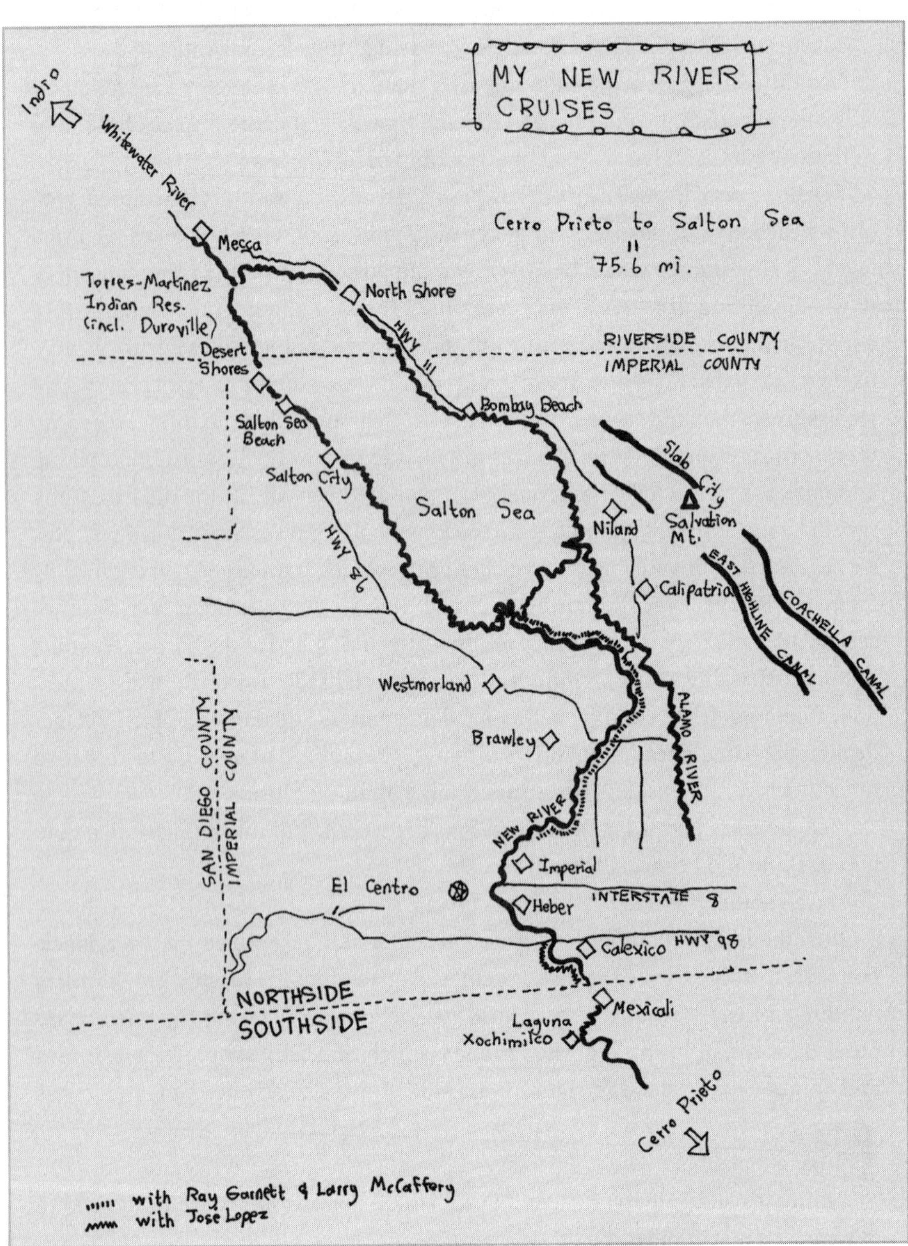
MY NEW RIVER CRUISES
Indio
Whitewater River
Mecca
Torres-Martinez Indian Res. (incl. Duroville)
North Shore
Cerro Prieto to Salton Sea
75.6 mi.
HWY 111
RIVERSIDE COUNTY
IMPERIAL COUNTY
Desert Shores
Bombay Beach
Salton Sea Beach
Salton City
Slab City
Salton Sea
Niland
Salvation Mt.
HWY 86
Calipatria
EAST HIGHLINE CANAL
COACHELLA CANAL
Westmorland
ALAMO RIVER
Brawley
SAN DIEGO COUNTY
IMPERIAL COUNTY
NEW RIVER
Imperial
El Centro
INTERSTATE 8
Heber
Calexico
HWY 98
NORTHSIDE
SOUTHSIDE
Mexicali
Laguna Xochimilco
Cerro Prieto
with Ray Garnett & Larry McCaffery
with Jose Lopez

Jose Lopez on the New River, 2001

Ray Garnett on the New River, 2001

already gone? I could see Obsidian Butte off to the right, and then the promontory of what must have been Red Hill Marina. How many dead fish did I spy around me on that day? I must be honest: Not one.

You get away from the smell when you get out here fishin', said Ray, and he was right, for far out on the greenish-brownish waves (that's algae bloom that made the water turn green, he explained. So there won't be any fish in here today. You don't fish in here), the only odor was ocean.

They've had studies and what have you ever since the late fifties, he sighed.

And did they conclude that water quality was getting worse?

That's what we thought in 1995 when we put four hundred and twenty hours in and didn't catch a fish. In '97 and '98 they started coming back. Whether the fish have gotten more tolerant or whether it's something else, I don't know.

It was pretty salty out here, all right. The Department of the Interior had announced that the sea's ecoystem was doomed unless nine million tons of salt could be removed every year. In the U.S. Department of Agriculture's yearbook for 1909, an article entitled "The Problems of an Irrigation Farmer" explains the necessity for adequate drainage to carry away the salt from cropland which like all the Imperial Valley once lay under some primeval sea; simply irrigating the soil is not enough, for as the evaporating water rises up through the topsoil, it draws dissolved salts with it, leaving the poor sad irrigation farmer ever more worse off. (Much of this book chronicles the continuing defiance of that principle.) What to do? Watch for creosote bushes if you can; they're a sign of low alkalinity. But if your homestead happens to lack those vegetable signals, you'll just have to flush out the soil, draining and draining, dispatching salt downward; and, as we know, the lowest point of the Imperial Valley just happens to be the Salton Sea.

Sabine Huynen of the University of Redlands Salton Sea Database Project had told me: The Salton Sea contains ninety-nine percent salt.

That sounds rather clean, I remarked.

There are very small traces of pesticides that are in the sea itself. The only places you find higher levels are in the bottom sediments. As of now there are no major issues in terms of pollutants. It used to be a lot worse. Due to pesticide regulations, the water quality has improved.

Would you feel comfortable drinking New River water near the sea's mouth?

She laughingly replied: Aside from the salt, yes.

Deep in a choppy orangish-green wave, Ray thought it best to turn around. As we approached the New River we grounded on a sandbar.

There were actually three of us in the boat: Ray, myself, and my friend Larry from Borrego Springs, who now in his autumnal years was becoming a natural history enthusiast. He'd come along for the adventure. Ray announced that somebody had to get out and help him push. I stared at the sores on my ankles which had arisen during the cruise with Jose, and while I stared, good old Larry leaped into the water; but my selfishness was all for nothing, because we were still grounded.

If you don't mind getting your feet wet, said Ray to me, it sure would make things easier.

We pushed. The water seemed to sting my feet, but that time I was most definitely imagining things.

Brown pelicans accompanied us overhead as we motored slowly upriver; then there were some bubbles, possibly from pollution or some geothermal source. A jackrabbit crouched on the bank. Now came again the lush, low banks of Westmorland, and up on either side the flat green fields to whose crop yields this river had in part been sacrificed (as the fellow from the Audubon Society told me: Nine million pounds of pesticides a year on Imperial Valley fields have got to go somewhere!), birds under concrete bridges, smoke trees, a fire pit, made perhaps by illegal aliens, beer cans, toilet paper, birds' nests, tamarisks, which choke out anything, and a dead palm trunk. The New River was turning chocolate-green again. Upstream of our starting point the water grew paler and creamier, greener and foamier than ever, with clots of detergent-like froth merging with the mysterious bubbles. Meanwhile, on the bank near a wall of seasoning hay bales, a man stood, getting ready to fish.

Must be something wrong with this water, said Ray, 'cause I don't see any bullfrogs. I been watchin' the bank. I seen a lot of 'em in the canals, but not a one here. No turtles, either. Bullfrogs and turtles can live in anything.

Now came a sickening sweet stench of rotting animals. That stench went away, but presently I got a sore throat and my eyes began to sting. I didn't ask Ray how he was doing. And presently we came to a burned, half-sunken bridge; it was too risky to try to get past it, so that was the end. My feet kept right on tingling. With a kind and gentle smile, Ray gave me an entire bag of smoked corvina.

"IT'S PROGRESSING ALONG REAL NICE" (PART ONE)

No face which we can give to a matter will stead us so well at last as the truth. That is what Thoreau wrote while he was measuring and meditating upon Walden Pond. He continues: *For the most part, we are not where we are, but in a false position. Through an infirmity of our natures, we suppose a case, and put ourselves into it, and hence are in two cases at the same time, and it is doubly difficult to get out.* Throughout my researches into the state of the New River and the Salton Sea, I found myself similarly in two cases at the same time, for once not so much thanks to my own fault as thanks to the errors and self-serving claims of others. But my fault did lie in this: I had drunk in a certain doctrine, whose sources are as obscurely ubiquitous and whose substance is as tainted as New River water, that only an "expert" has the right to judge the acceptability of the water of life. The Salton Sea is a dying sump or the Salton Sea is the most productive fishery in the world. (At Red Hill Marina a sign announced that as of A.D. 2000 all corvina taken must be at least eight inches long; there was no limit on sargo.) The New River is the most polluted watercourse in the United States, perhaps in North America, or the New River is—well, not virgin, but if its degree of purity became irrelevant, could we not then exhume ourselves from our double case, especially since ever more of its Mexican length is getting interred? And it bears merely ten percent of the Salton Sea's inflow, or thirteen percent, or whatever, so it must be nearly innocuous; moreover, the worst toxins are safely hidden in its sediments . . . The only way I could think of to decide the matter was to abrogate my own judgment, paying technicians to analyze one water sample from the river and another from the sea, in order to ascertain whether any pollutant happened to exceed standards which other technicians had decreed were acceptable. Then I'd know, because a printed report would tell me.

Can I say that Ray Garnett knew? His criterion for deciding that the New River must be in trouble was the absence of bullfrogs and turtles. He'd made up his mind; he was not straddling two opposing cases! But he'd also made up his mind about the Salton Sea, and I wasn't sure that I could agree with him there. Where lay my mind? *We suppose a case, and put ourselves into it.* It would be in my interest as a hack journalist to write something horrific about the Salton Sea or the New River. I'd supposed a case, the worst case, and on the basis of that supposition, a magazine had paid me to lower myself into the case and write this chapter of *Imperial;* wouldn't the magazine's readership be disappointed if the laboratory's numbers turned out to be ordinary? Well, the Salton Sea Authority would not feel disappointed at all.

Not having even collected my samples yet, I still knew the truth. The Salton Sea is ghastly. The New River is ghastly.

We might say that the sea, having been created by an engineering accident, was nobody's fault. Nor can anybody be held accountable for the fact that prior to the floods the Salton Sink had already glared and glistened with saltbeds.—Tom Kirk told me: Our salt levels are about twenty-five percent higher than the ocean and we support a marine environment that's pretty robust here. If the levels go up, we'll lose the fishery, then the shorebirds, then the benthic organisms.

The levels were going up, no question about that. The Alamo, Whitewater and

New rivers submissively accepted the runoff from ever so many salt-flushed fields.

Maybe the New River wasn't anybody's fault, either. People need to defecate, and if they are poor, they cannot afford to process their sewage. People need to eat, and so they work in the *maquiladoras*—factories owned by foreign polluters.* The polluters pollute to save money; then we buy their inexpensive and perhaps well-made tractor parts, fertilizers, pesticides. *It is doubly difficult to get out.* And it's all ghastly.

"IT'S PROGRESSING ALONG REAL NICE" (PART TWO)

The New River flows into what is not quite the southernmost extremity of the Salton Sea. Four miles due west, one strikes the other shore (where **SUNKEN TREES** adorn the map). Then it's a straight shot halfway up the sea to Salton City, followed by Salton Sea Beach where Ray lives, then the nearly defunct Sun Dial Beach, and finally Desert Shores, where beside the rickety dock, stinking white fishes gaped in the sun, some of them swirling with each greenish-brown wave (an algal bloom had struck), others washed farther up onto the boat ramp (*ANNUAL LAUNCH FEE $25. See Manager*), the rest squashed into the pavement. Halfway down the dock, which nearly broke under my weight, I gazed into the Salton Sea and saw a great fish split open like a sack; beneath the strips of its putrescent flesh, vermin were nuzzling like babies.

A couple backed their boat down the launching ramp, the man steering, the woman craning her head with extreme seriousness. Fish-corpses squished beneath their wheels.

See Manager, the sign had advised, so I went to see the manager, Mr. David Urbanoski, who'd lived in these parts for twenty years.

What's the state of the sea right now, Mr. Urbanoski?

It's progressing along real nice, he said. They've got desalting ponds goin' in, and there's another company that's putting desalting plants in . . .

Well, I'm happy to be back here, I told him. I don't come to Desert Shores so often, but every year I take pictures in Salton City, down by where the yacht club used to be.

(Salton City's attractions now included a broken motel with drawn-in palm fronds and shattered windows. Emblems of stereotypical cacti and flying fishes clung to the motel just as a fool clings to his dying love. They clung behind a **FOR**

* One derivation for this term: In old Spain, when a mill ground corn for someone, the miller kept part of the flour for his fee, his *maquila*. The *maquiladoras* get their own chapter further on in this book.

SALE fence, framed by boarded-up doors and windows. The motel's customers were heat, rubble, and cicada-songs. Meanwhile, out at the marina, a single fishing boat passed behind a rectangular pool of lavender or perhaps raspberry-colored water. Salton City offered me the sharp tang of decaying fish.)

Yeah, that was beautiful, Mr. Urbanoski said. It was a shame when they tore it down.

How was the life here twenty years ago?

Undescribable, really. Before they wiped out all the units down there, there was a place called Helen's Guest House with cabañas and all kinds of entertainment. Salton City was beautiful then. They had a real nice eighteen-hole golf course that was wiped out on account of the water. A lot of movie stars came there. It was a real neat place.

When did everything start to change?

Around '78 to '83. Right out there they used to have trailers. It was undermined by the Imperial Irrigation District. They bought everybody out. People were forced to sell.

How did the IID undermine them?

They were sued three years in a row. You'd walk outside and step in a hole. Water was coming in. It keeps coming in. We're at two hundred and twenty-seven feet below sea level right now. It keeps rising. IID got tired of being sued.

Mr. Urbanoski pointed out the window at a certain place half effaced by decrepitude and rising water. He said: The guy that owned this, he borrowed a hundred thousand dollars and was supposed to bring it up to code. He took the money and went to Tahiti with five women, had a heart attack and died. They said he died with a smile on his face.—And that building there, we lost that. I used to have a store . . .

What are all those dead fish out there?

The IID brought those tilapia in to clean out the canals, since they're algae-eating fish. The water temperature gets below fifty-eight degrees in the winter, and then they start dying off. Once in awhile you get to see a dead corvina, too, and that's standard.

It feels like at least a hundred and ten degrees today, I said. When did those tilapia die off?

Oh, those ones are pretty fresh. We just had an algae bloom a few days ago. That brownish look in the sea, that's plankton.

How about the birds?

We haven't had a die-off in a couple years.

So you'd say the Salton Sea is pretty clean?

San Bernardino County has tested the bottom for toxins. None. They got a little bit near the New River, of course . . .

Do a lot of people still fish around here?

I launch probably fifteen to twenty-five boats a week. (But what I'm gonna do, I'm gonna go down to Salton City and get some yellow police ribbon for that dock, seal it off. It's cheaper not to get sued.) They fish for corvina. If they get a big tilapia, three-four pounds, they'll keep that. It's very tasty. I would eat fish three times a week if my wife would cook it for me. I been eatin' it thirty years and I'm not dead, although my doctor said that's debatable.

We sat looking out the window at the Salton Sea, not that we could see all three hundred and fifty-two square miles of it, and he said: I'll tell you who ruined this: the *L.A. Times*. That bad PR: *Don't eat the fish in the sea because they're poison*. My buddies called me up and said: Hey, Dave, we can't come out here no more, because those fish are poisonous.

What's your favorite fish to eat?

Croaker. What I do is I fillet 'em and I brine 'em overnight in brown sugar, then I smoke 'em. You know how you peel an orange like *that*? That's how the skin comes off.

Smiling, he said then: It's so damn *tranquil* in here. I just seen a string of brown pelicans come in here an hour ago. It's real fun to watch the white ones, the way they herd the fish . . .

SAMPLING

Squatting over the stinking green water a few steps from the spot where Jose and I had launched our inflatable dinghy, I lowered the sterile sample bottles one by one in my latex-gloved hands. The air temperature that June afternoon was a warmish hundred and thirteen degrees. Up in the parking lot, my friend William sat in the rental car with the air-conditioning on while I did my business, standing partly on a fresh human turd to avoid falling into the water. The chemical odor seemed more dizzying than usual. What was it? Hopefully I'd find out, for, truth to tell, I'd cast my analytical nets rather wide. I was angling for your basic herbicide-pesticide sweep, including the chlorinateds (EPA method 8151), a CAM-17 for heavy metals at two hundred and twenty-five dollars, a full method 8260, needless to say, with MTBE and oxygenates, a TPH (that's total petroleum hydrocarbons to you, bud), a surfactant, and a diesel test while I was at it. Originally I'd craved a fecal coliform count so badly that I could taste it (and, come to think of it, right now I *could*), but Tom Kirk had said that the levels of fecal coliform, high at the border, dropped off steadily along the New River and then actually rose at the mouth of the Salton Sea, thanks to the worst polluters of all—birds. So to hell with it. Besides, then I would have had to keep the samples on ice, and it was boring to buy ice.

It really, really, really stank.

I'd told Mr. Kirk how happy I'd be if the water quality of the New River could be improved, at which he laughed sadly and said: Be careful what you wish for. Once the water's cleaned up, where do you think it will go, Bill? That will become very valuable water. The Mexicans won't drain it into the Salton Sea anymore. They'll use it for cooling power plants. Then the Salton Sea will get more saline than ever as the water level drops . . .

Should I have collected my sample where the river meets the sea? In that case, I would have been able to measure the total pollutant load—for, remember, seventy percent of those New River wastes do not originate in Mexico. But I was curious how lethal the Mexican outflow truly was. The United States Congressional General Accounting Office *finds that sewage from Mexico poses a health risk to public health.* What poet could have put it better? Anyhow, I wouldn't test for sewage itself. I'd test only for chemical poisons.

My hands felt wet. Lifting the last sample bottle out of the water and capping it, I discovered that the New River had more or less dissolved my gloves. My hands started stinging a few hours later. They stung for about a week.

(Actually, said the lab man, that probably wasn't the New River. That stuff at the bottom of the sampling bottles is nitric acid.)

William and I drove up to North Shore, where I took my other sample. North Shore seemed like a good place because it was far enough away from the New River to reflect the base level of filthiness, so to speak, and it was also good on account of all those fishbones and salt-stiffened feathers crunching beneath my feet. The sea was quite shallow here (the map shows a depth of two feet, and then the black silhouettes of a SUNKEN CITY), so I couldn't avoid getting sediment into the bottles, including bits of rotting fish and numerous cheerfully darting water-bugs which I felt guilty about inadvertently sentencing to doom (three days later, the laboratory reported that they were still alive), but I'd instruct the lab to shake up the bottle and homogenize it . . .

Every step I took made a splintering noise, like shards of glass. It was bone and barnacles, mainly, and scales, too. North Shore was a fairly grisly place.

Ray had found a swollen human corpse in the Salton Sea a few years back.—That's nothing new, he told me. They find 'em every week. That's just accidents. They're just tryin' to get across illegally.

And what about the finny remnants I saw all around me at North Shore? Tom Kirk explained: We don't take fish deaths as seriously as bird deaths from an ecological point of view.—(There was only one dead bird on the beach this time, a fluffy little baby.) And Jose Angel at the Regional Water Control Board had insisted: As long as there are fish in the Salton Sea, there will be fish kills. The prime cause is low oxygen. We have a warm body of salty water with major algal blooms, which when they decompose suck the air out of the water.

On the pier, a man was fishing, perhaps not impressed by the selenium health advisory (not more than four ounces of Salton Sea fish-meat per two weeks).

I took my two samples up to Sacramento and got them analyzed for a thousand dollars apiece. Sample one was the New River. Sample two was the Salton Sea.*

On the chlorinated acid herbicides, your 2–4 dichlorophenylacetic acid took a hit on sample one, said the lab man. On sample two, everything was non-detect. Let's see, now, your diesel in the very first sample took a very small hit; the second sample was non-detect. For metals your first sample showed beryllium and zinc,† and your second had barium and selenium. Both samples were well below the MCLs on all that.

What's an MCL?

Maximum contaminant level allowed by the Department of Health Services.

Silly me, I said.

Surfactants, surfactants, mumbled the lab man, and in my mind's eye I saw again the long white clouds of foam which drifted down the New River from Mexico—oh, here we go: a very small hit on sample one, and sample two was pretty close to sample one.

Are you sure about that? Sample one is supposed to be the most polluted river in North America.

Absolutely sure. Salinity: two point five grams per kilogram in sample one, forty-six grams per kilogram in sample two.

Here I gained confidence in the laboratory, because the Salton Sea Authority maintained that the sea's salinity was an almost identical forty-six grams per kilogram; and I had not disclosed the origin of my samples.

We ran the 8260 for volatiles plus oxygenates as you wanted. Both samples were clean.

And that was that. Unfortunately, they'd run out of water, or I'd run out of money, before they could get to the pesticides.

I sat there for awhile thinking. Then I inquired how my samples compared to other water they'd tested.

Relatively clean compared to other wastewater samples, the lab man said.

*In the reports reproduced here (I have omitted pages whose only result is "non-detect"), sample one corresponds to subsamples A, B, C and E; sample two includes subsamples E, F, G and H.

†Zinc is sometimes employed to reduce scaling in wastewater pipes.

They're certainly not nearly as nasty as some of our samples from Brazil, Singapore and China . . .

SELENIUM AND OTHER MYSTERIES

And so what do I actually know now about the dirtiness of the Salton Sea and the New River? (As to the constituents that you were listing, said Sabine Huynen of the University of Redlands Salton Sea Database Project, I can't give you my own opinions. I can't give you any information on whether these numbers are accurate. It would depend on how you sampled, what sort of personal equipment you had, and any number of factors.) It is too bad that I lacked the resources to test for other organic compounds; that the laboratory elected to test for herbicides instead of pesticides; that I couldn't have sampled the Río Nuevo at Xochimilco Lagoon and the New River at the mouth of the Salton Sea; I wish I could have repeated Ray Garnett's experience of testing Salton Sea sediments. But if I did learn anything, it was this: Neither the New River nor the Salton Sea was, on my sampling day, at least, as toxified as claimed—the relative absence of heavy metals appearing especially telling. Moreover, Mexico could not be the primary culprit for what little pollution of the Salton Sea my samples did detect. The New River's beryllium and zinc had nothing to do with the Salton Sea's barium and selenium.

I telephoned the Audubon Society man, Mr. Fred Cagle, who had always struck me as levelheaded and independent (no doubt it was these qualities which caused others to call him "jaded").

Do these results surprise you? I asked him.

Not at all.

Well, is the New River the most polluted body of water in North America, or one of the most polluted, or what? I can't figure it out.

It's been getting cleaner. But it still gets that reputation. It depends on who you talk to. They've found cholera, TB, all that kind of crap . . .

What about the metals and organics?

I don't know whether this is a low time or not in their pesticide application. You have to be careful. It varies tremendously. We've taken hundreds of samples, and they all come out different. And the stuff in the sediments may not be soluble; there are just so many variables. Of *course* you can't figure it out! Scientists can't figure it out.

And those nine million pounds of agricultural chemicals you mentioned, where do they go?

Some of them break down; some of them get oxidized by bacteria. But we don't know that. Scientists get confused, too.

Would you agree that the Salton Sea is the most productive fishery in the world?

It's the most productive fishery but it's the most limited fishery. All the fish are artificial. We're getting right close to the edge of the salinity window. And why spend a hundred million dollars to save a ten-million-dollar fishery? Tilapia are an amazing fish. You know, they're a freshwater fish, and in thirty generations they've modified themselves to live in the Salton Sea. But has anybody told you about the parasite levels on those fish? They're enormous. Parasites are in their lungs, everywhere. The people who eat those fish might not enjoy them as much if they knew that. But humans can't get those parasites, at least. Still, there *is* a selenium warning, as you know.

And that I can't figure out, since the selenium level of the water was so low.

What's in the water doesn't make too much difference. These fish feed on pileworms. Maybe these pileworms concentrate it. Nobody's completely researched how it gets concentrated in the food chain. But I know enough about selenium levels to tell you *I* wouldn't eat it.

I still have a little smoked corvina left. Maybe I won't send it to you.

Good idea.

Let's talk about selenium some more, I said, because I'd read that should the ever-thirsty municipalities of California succeed in diverting the inflows of the Salton Sea,* then, in one journalist's magnificent words, *a vast salt and selenium bed of dust of over 400 square miles would be driven throughout Southern California with any wind; tourism in Palm Springs, Palm Desert and the entire counties of Riverside, Imperial and Coachella would disappear . . . Certainly agriculture would disappear under the dust, and health problems would escalate to insurmountable proportions.* (As you know, the lab man had said to me, the concentrations of anything you find in there are going to increase as the water decreases.)

Again, said Cagle, we don't know how bad the selenium problem really is. But Imperial County already has one of highest asthma rates in the country on account of all the small particles in the air, which are present in concentrations double the federal ceiling. To me, that's the real problem. If this water transfer goes through and you lower the Salton Sea by fifteen feet, you have the potential for some Mono Lake–style clouds.

But the notion of a toxic selenium cloud is overblown, so to speak?

That would be my guess.

*In the words of Eugenia McNaughton, the EPA scientist, "California has to start reducing its take of Colorado River water. Agriculture's going to change in the valley. Either people will go out of business or they'll change their ways of husbanding their fields. It all points toward less water for the Salton Sea. It's not going to get a bucket unless some really powerful people sit on the heads of some other really powerful people."

(No air-quality models have been conducted, Sabine Huynen had said. It's very open as to what would happen. We only know that the scale is much larger than in the Owens Valley. People in the Imperial Valley don't realize how much declining water levels would affect them. Particulate matter would blow right onto their fields.)

All right, Mr. Cagle. Anything else I should know?

People have known about these problems for forty years. The farmers have had so much power that nothing's been done. Good chance nothing will get done.

What do you think we should do?

Dike off the two ends and let the rest become hypersaline. We'd still be saving an area eighteen times larger than Mission Bay. Our main concern at Audubon is keeping the bird habitat . . .

THE GOLDEN AGE

The article on California in the eleventh edition of the *Britannica* (published in 1911) states that *irrigation in the tropical area along the Colorado river, which is so arid that it naturally bears only desert vegetation, has made it a true humid-tropical region like Southern Florida, growing true tropical fruits.* Wasn't that the golden age? Actually, the golden age hasn't ended even now. I look around me at the Salton Sea's green margins of fields and palm orchards, and spy a lone palm tree far away at the convergence of tan furrows, then lavender mountains glazed with confectioners' sugar; this is the landscape, where all is beauty, the aloof desert mountains enriched despite themselves by the spectacle of the fields. Fertilization, irrigation, runoff, wastewater—the final admixtures of all these quantities flow into the Salton Sea. I couldn't condemn the state of the Salton Sea without rejecting the ring of emerald around it, which I refuse to do. About the continuing degradation of that sump, Jose Angel very reasonably said: It's a natural process because *the sea is a closed basin!* Pollutants cannot be flushed out. You could be discharging Colorado River water directly into the Salton Sea, or for that matter distilled water into the Salton Sea, and you would end up with a salinity problem, because the ground is full of salt! The regulations do not provide for a solution to this. You have to engineer a project. You have to build some sort of an outlet. Now when it comes to nutrients, I think there is a role for regulation to play. We can't blame Mexico for everything but they certainly play a role in the nutrients. They add to the problem but we have our hands full in the Imperial Valley, too. And what can we do? Because fertilizers have a legitimate agricultural use.

The stylized elegance of a palm grove's paragraph of tightly spaced green asterisks reified legitimate agricultural use, as did the ridge-striped fields south of Niland, where sheep and birds intermingled, the cottonballs on the khaki plants so white as to almost glitter. Suddenly came a brilliant green square of field on the righthand side of Highway 111, a red square of naked dirt on the left, a double row of palms in between, with their dangling clusters of reddish-yellow fruit . . . Legitimate use, to be sure, from which I benefited and from which the sea was getting more selenium-tainted and saltier and fouler with algae, creating carrion and carrion-stench, which kept sea-goers away, so that it was legitimate agricultural use which created that empty swimming pool in that motel in Salton City with cacti and flying fishes alternately painted on the two rows of broken-windowed rooms. The palm trees danced in a wind that stank of death. In its entry for Riverside County, the *California Blue Book* for 1950 offers a fine example of legitimate use: *The county is drained by the Whitewater River, which flows toward the Salton Sea*. Legitimate use made the half-scorched rubble of the Sundowner Motel, whose rusty lonely staircase comprised a vantage point to look out across the freeway to Superburger and then the sparse pale house-cubes of Salton City. On a clear day one could see right across the Salton Sea from those stairs, but if there was a little dust or haze, the cities on the far side faded into hidden aspects of the Chocolate Mountains' violet blur. Year by year, the Sundowner disappeared. By 2000, only the staircase was left, and in 2001 that had also been carried off by the myrmidons of desert time. Meanwhile the Alamo flowed stinking up from Holtville with its painted water tower (that river also commenced in Mexico somewhere), and the Whitewater flowed stinking, while the New River conveyed its stench of excrement and something bitter like pesticides. Imperial flowered and bore fruit; Imperial hid its excretions behind dark citrus hedges. Through that lush and luscious land whose hay bales are the color of honey and whose alfalfa fields are green skies, water flowed, ninety percent of it not from Mexico at all, carrying consequences out of sight to a sump three hundred and fifty-two square miles in area. *Pursuant to Section 303(d) of the U.S. Clean Water Act, the Regional Board approved its updated list of impaired surface waters in January 1998 (copy attached). Within the Salton Sea Watershed: the Salton Sea, the New River, the Alamo River, the Imperial Valley Agricultural Drains, and the Coachella Valley Stormwater Channel were all listed as impaired.* From a distance it looked lovely: first the handlettered sign of MAY'S OASIS, then the Salton Sea's Mediterranean blue seen through a distant line of palms, and the smell of ocean . . .

Chapter 4

SUBDELINEATIONS: LOVESCAPES

(2001)

> . . . an intelligent species might, for all we know, really be isolated emotionally from all surrounding species, might view them simply as moving objects and have no access to their moods. But this "theoretical" isolated possibility is actually very obscure and may perhaps not make much sense.
>
> —Mary Midgley, 1983

Imperial is—

A landscape remains itself without me, I think (I think, but cannot know. *There is nothing in all that I formerly believed to be true,* says Descartes, *of which I cannot in some measure doubt.*) Imperial does not need me to be itself, *I think.* The salinity of the Salton Sea will not alter its rate of increase on account of my absence, *I suppose.*

Nonetheless, just as the Salton Sea lies blue beneath a blue sky, grey under clouds, so any delineation of Imperial depends on the delineator, which means that whatever Imperial is must get expressed, no matter how scrupulously and intelligently, as a variety of shifting if hopefully overlapping entities even if we all confine ourselves to a single aspect of the place at a mutually agreed instant. My best hope (which doesn't seem awfully good) is that when we overlay those delineations, each plotted conscientiously upon its own translucent sheet of memory-vellum,* then a common core, however blurred in its boundaries, may appear. Why not lay a clean leaf of tracing paper upon the whole mess in order to construct an average shape? Well, we'd then be forced either to retain only the most conservative, hence tedious truisms ("Imperial is hot"), or else to extend the polygon outward, enclosing whichever debatable zones happened to conform to our own tastes. In other words, it would be going too far to claim, as in a previous delineation I nearly did, that Imperial remains unknowable, but yes, I did say that Imperial remains unknown.

*"Such simple 'sand maps' were frequently observed by early white travelers who were crossing territory unknown to them and who were asking Indians for directions. It is probably no accident that these records were made in the desert areas where Indians moved about a great deal . . . Among the more settled tribes of California, who traveled only within their own restricted territory, such maps would have been unnecessary."

In that chapter I tried to draw the best preliminary outline that I could, and now I can't help but make another. Overlay them if you will; I cannot.

Until a week ago this place had been hers and mine, *our place,* she said, and so it had been for years. In those days Imperial was as beautiful as a double rainbow over the desert, rain falling and evaporating as it fell when we came down Highway 78 into Ocotillo, with chollas on the reddish-grey knobby hills, pencil-smudged clouds of rain; and the noise of the windshield wipers was very mirthful; then came that stunning double rainbow with mountains shining through it like an overexposed color photograph. Imperial was a band of literally heavenly colors then, the most beautiful being the greenish-yellow arch in the middle of each rainbow like a celestial distillation of all the emerald fields, but then the rainbows faded into a fresh clean dust smell. The last time I ever spoke to her, she wept: And I don't even have a picture of us . . .—so here is the picture: Looking east, we came down into Imperial's magic afternoon light; soon we'd find the chalky glow of the Salton Sea. Grey ocotillos on the slopes were joyous to us, since lovers love the pathetic fallacy; and now we obtained our first faraway view of the Chocolate Mountains, and yes, the needle-narrow glint of the Salton Sea; somewhere in the deep purple mountains—I'm sure I've delineated the place—with white and grey cloud above, white sand below, came the sign IMPERIAL COUNTY LINE. It was our place. So many years later I read that sentence and almost smile; my ignorance of Imperial has filled a long book, so how could it have ever been my place? Who were she and I but travellers? No place was our place, and Imperial never belonged to me. Well, if it had been ours in any sense, now I must try to make it mine alone, and if she ever returned there, it must be hers alone. (And from many years later I almost smile again.) I had asked whether she wanted to accompany me just the same, but she'd replied that it would be too sad, *because it was our place,* and I thought her correct not only for that reason but because after that day anything would have been too sad. My life was mine alone now, not hers anymore, so I must try to carry the burden of my own dead or almost-dead Imperial, unless I simply chose never to go back there. It was not ours and could not be, not ever. But I didn't believe that yet. Well, well, so I was returning to Imperial just the same; but the Date Tree Motor Hotel in Indio, with its elegantly withered palms and the swimming pool she adored, the palm orchards of Mecca and Thermal, the sign below Leonard's mountain which said **LOVE**, those map-spots were so richly hers that I could not yet approach them without tears. Wait a bit, I tried to tell myself; Imperial's sun will fade her ghost. (But she was not dead.)

Imperial is not what I thought it was. It cannot exalt me anymore. But I've admitted already that Imperial does not need me to be itself. Imperial is whatever it is. Imperial is—

ONE MORE TIME

Had I implored, she might have done it. And because I hadn't, I longed for it, as at a funeral one wishes for just one more word and then one more word again from the dead; any addict thinks that the next fix will solve all his problems, and at that moment he is right. So I thought back on the last time when we actually *had* made love, an evening half-hour that felt tired and strained; now I understood that her body had already begun to grow away from mine; the decision was ripening in her in place of that child we could never have had, maybe she felt a little repulsed; well, for a long time she'd been asking me to brush my teeth before she allowed me to kiss her cunt; and then she'd stopped letting me do it at all. The morning after the last time we made love, it wasn't obvious to me, nor perhaps to her, that anything was different, because although we used to make love every morning we woke up together, over the last year she'd been getting more "delicate" as she put it, and so, that morning after our last time, when she made no move to touch me, nor any touching glance, I thought nothing of it. I believed that an enduring "is" had been calmly established between us long ago, so that if we did not make love at every opportunity, the rest of our lives remained; forgoing it therefore felt luxurious; we weren't starving. That was what I thought then. I was a fool, so Imperial could still be delineated by a twin rainbow.

And so what if we had made love one more time after she'd told me that it was over? First of all, I take back what I said at the beginning: Even if I'd implored, it never would have happened, and I wouldn't have, because the instant she told me, sobbing so hard that I grew terrified for her, I remembered how not long ago, on our very last trip to Imperial, in fact, she'd rushed into a teary rage of apprehension over nothing, and asserted that it was *over;* she could tell that I didn't get it but I would have to because it was *over, really over,* and I apologized and apologized as with her I had gained so much practice in doing, until she forgave me and we lay wearily in each other's arms. I now understood, and instantaneously, that on that night, she'd been begging me to let her go, but I'd been too blind and too selfish. Even now, when she sat bowed on the edge of the bed explaining that she just couldn't do this anymore, I retained the strongest conviction that if I were only to grovel, comfort and promise in the correct proportions I could lure her back for a little longer, but at the same time I recognized at last that I was truly harmful to her, so that any extension of our covenant would merely have poisoned her more deeply. Nonetheless, speaking purely selfishly (since I was as I've said selfish from the start), I very tentatively asked whether we could make love one more time, since I longed more than ever to be inside her right then, in part because she never ceased to manifest herself so divinely to me (and from years later I smile outright at this juncture, for "divinely" conveys none of the *unique* meaning which it once did for me) that I lusted after her beyond thirst no matter how many times we were together; and I now wanted her in part (impurest of all) as a desperate attempt to seduce her back to me by means of pleasure and pity; I knew her body very, very well by then, much better than I ever would Imperial; I knew precisely how to bring her to climax (now I forget); so how would *that* have been? Perhaps the Salton Sea's stinking radiance comprises a metaphor. Maybe it really could have been a pure goodbye, had I been good enough, but since I was not, it would have been a mixture of the love which cannot die, the love which dies, and was now looking over the edge of its oncoming dying, of terror, rage, grief, and pleading, of thinking that if I could only perform the act better than I ever had before, she'd be happily hypnotized out of the strength she'd so bravely discovered to leave me, just as when I rubbed her spine with just the right pressure, which is to say not too feathery, for she hated light touches, and not roughly, but firmly and steadily, as if I'd always be there with her. That is how it might have been for me; as for her, when I asked her (just once, in what I intended to be a gentle, hypothetical way) how it would be if we did that, she replied that she'd probably feel tortured by a terrible pressure to feel everything and make everything count forever, by which she communicated to my still astonished and unbelieving heart that the last time really *had* been the last time and she was trying not to change her mind, which meant that my having asked was all the more humiliating. She didn't want to touch me anymore. I had come to her today not knowing, and until she'd told me, we had still been together. First I knew nothing except that she was crying, so I kept asking who had been mean to her or what had gone wrong; and even after she told me that she just couldn't do this anymore, I continued to feel only that tenderest longing to comfort her which always came over me whenever she was suffering, and I held her tight, stroking her long hair; I said that of course I understood now and would do what she wished. But most of me, including the loving part, the comforting part, couldn't yet apprehend that what she wished was that I vanish from her life like water in Imperial sinking down into the sand. Very soon now the pain which turns like a worm in one's chest, the sharp, physically stabbing pain, the suffocating pain which awakens one gasping from a dream of winning her back or of losing her, the debilitating pain which takes up residence in the stomach, and the various kindred pains would enter into me. Right now they were swimming in the room like germs in New River water, but I couldn't yet perceive them. I was planning and fussing about how she was going to move all the heavy boxes out of her studio, because she had a bad back, and she said so gently, not weeping at all: Don't worry. *That's not your responsibility anymore.*—That was when the first pain, an eel-like one with very sharp teeth, began to eat my chest. The memory of her words would come back and back every day, and sometimes I nearly screamed. (Reading this over now, I feel a pain as sharp-spired as a smoke tree.) But even now, all I knew was that whenever she wept I always tried to be strong for her and help her, and I had done this again just now, freely and gladly, because I loved her and she loved me, although now we . . . Now we remained on the couch where we had so often lain together, and we were lying or sitting (I forget which) near each other, but not touching although we had been touching half an hour before when we came there and I had been holding her in my arms when she had told me, her face as white as the sands just east of Palm Springs. I felt weak and asked if we could lie down, and she said that she guessed that we could, as long as we didn't get too intimate, because that would make her confused. So I decided that it was better not to find out what too intimate was, better not to do anything. With shrill brightness she now began to treat me as though I were a friend. She proposed that we go for a drive or play a board game because she wanted us to always be friends; and because she had been so heartbroken when she was saying what she had to, I for her sake assured her that we always could, that in her words, *nothing will change except the stress and the sex,* and among the items which I can list to my credit concerning our relationship I am proud to mention that not only did I not implore or insist that we make love one last time, not only did I not beg her to take me back, but I even for an hour or two went through the motions of being just friends with this woman whom I longed to kiss on the mouth and name my sweetheart as I could have done just yesterday; until the slow, sharp fact that she was actually leaving me had twisted deep enough into the bright new wound to reach a certain depth, then a deeper depth, and then suddenly it approached unbearability, at which point I leaped up half-sobbing that she had better take me home now, although it was hours early, and she rose without protest, which she never would have done before. (She used to beg me for an extra five or ten minutes.) On the road she gave me a letter opener with a little business card window within which she'd inserted one of Leonard's Salvation Mountain postcards, cut to fit. Although she said she'd meant to give it to me before, it burned my hand, for it was a consolation prize. It was the first gift, and as I made sure, the last, which she had given me after she had left me. It was accursed. Sitting beside her (ordinarily we would have been holding hands), I decided to drop the thing into the Salton Sea as soon as I'd returned to Imperial, although in fact I failed to, proving too confused, weak and unsure of myself to reach the shore. It took several years to dispose of it. She remained silent and composed beside me. Then I got out of the car. This was the first time we failed to kiss goodbye, the first time that I went up the sidewalk without looking back at her and waving. Rushing inside my house, I stood and hid for a long time, dreading that she might still be there gazing at me. Finally I peeped out the window. She was gone. I began to choke with anguish.

She was not my darling anymore. If I ever saw her again, I would not be able to say *darling*. She would never make love with me again. I thought about this all the way to Imperial on that Greyhound bus which reeked so richly of unwashed human bodies that it was strange to think of the scent of her flesh, to sit there greedily imagining licking her private parts.

TERRITORIAL CONCESSIONS

And so, as always, the Greyhound went east on Highway 10, until even though the land was still grassy and tree-claimed, the long dry mountains of Imperial began snaking along off to the right; the grass got browner, shrubs shrank and darkened. At Beaumont an arguable western border of Imperial was reached, but as I have already told you, Banning looked more like it, it being here that mountain-chains approached on both sides. Now came Palm Springs, which used to be Cahuilla Indian territory (there's a Morongo reservation and casino now, and an Agua Caliente reservation also). I felt stone-cold, even when we passed within a few blocks of the restaurant where she always sweet-talked me into taking her. The Greyhound station there bore no associations except of previous Greyhound rides. Then we were approaching Indio (elevation: sea level), where I'd dreaded to see the Date Tree Hotel. I found myself feeling merely bored with Imperial, not to mention disgusted with myself for returning to collect more obscure details about a hot sad place when my life was draining away and everything felt stale.

Next the bus passed the sign for the Date Tree, and suddenly I *believed* that she wasn't with me and never would be again. My eyes sought through the colonies of low white houses between palm trees; and there it was, the Date Tree, empty. All of its palm trees were stunted. It was a dead grey place now. I wondered how she and I could ever have wanted to go there. Then it was quickly gone; I lacked the courage to look back.

When we halted for half an hour at the Greyhound station I went inside to get a drink of water and saw the vending machine for Mexican decals, one of which I'd bought her a couple of years back. And there was the corner where on another occasion she'd kissed me goodbye. I couldn't endure to approach it, so I went back out into the parking lot, where palm trees shook in the hot wind.

Well, she had taught me how to feel. Now that she was gone, I was struggling to unlearn the lesson for the sake of my own survival. As jilted lovers often will, I kept craving a death as cool and well-earned as Imperial's darkness. Imperial's mountains had gone away. It was freakishly cool (ninety-four degrees), and everything was dulled or else disappeared into haze. Here came the long line of palms she'd loved; it was dull and dusty, everything stained as if by smoke . . .

Suddenly I suffered a longing to telephone her and tell her that I was almost in sight of the palm-grove at Thermal where she had sketched and gouached so happily while I'd gone half a block away to photograph the sign for the Jewel Date Palm Co. (all the negatives from that trip appropriately disappeared in the mail, so that the catalogue entry for this image, number twenty-nine, reads: **IV-CS-THR-00–01. Wall of Jewel Date Co. Bldg, Thermal, mid morning, November, f/64 at 1/2 sec. Wall in shadow; camera in sun. Metered with incident dome flush against wall to stay in shadow. LOST.**); unable to leave her longer than a quarter of an hour, I'd rushed back into the cool darkness of the palm-grove to keep her company, and made other photographs there which also got lost. Her first gouache was almost done. She looked up and smiled at me. She'd loved that place so much that it was the heart of Imperial. How could I imagine not telling her that it continued to exist and that I was thinking of her? The way seemed so dreary, the whites greyish-tan with dust, the blues greyish with haze. There it was, and as the Greyhound went by, I saw the white shape of a person sitting in the darkness between palm trees, and wondered whether it could be her ghost, or the part of her which still loved me. No doubt it was just a legal worker, an illegal soul, a *body* who didn't count.

Now rolling on south from Mecca between armies of palms and citrus hedges, the Greyhound, untricked by varying greens, carried me in sight of the Salton Sea, which would ordinarily have uplifted my heart. That narrow tongue of blue which overlay the green grapevines widened and darkened like a concretion of my indifference. Thanks to the strange weather it turned grey, hazing itself away into nothing. As we approached Niland, following the "worked" tan flatness of the shore, I suddenly and thankfully was permitted to feel a stab of almost unbearable grief. Perhaps she was throwing out my toothbrush right now, the one on which she'd written my name and drawn a little heart; or perhaps she was disposing of the photographs of me she'd once kept upon her wall. It was the ninth day.

And now every time I saw something that reminded me of us in our once unbroken Imperial, my grief increased so sickeningly that I thought I would vomit.

Presently I was in Calexico with the knife-sharp evening shadows on the streets, and, a little weak after carrying my tripod, film holders and big camera through the streets after a day without much food or water, I entered the supermarket where she and I always shopped, went straight to the aisle of the foods which she liked best, and even started to pick up an avocado for her. I rushed back to my motel room and collapsed on the empty double bed for an hour.

I could not comprehend it. She loved me. Something was hurting me. Whenever something hurt me, I went to her. Now I could not go to her. Why couldn't I?

She'd wanted me to keep *in touch* with her, but I couldn't, I couldn't, I couldn't . . .

I thought about walking across the border as I had done so many times before, but even Mexico didn't interest me. I felt alone in the room, but outside would have been worse. I thought: I never should have come back to Imperial.

And of course Imperial never *has* been the same. I cannot escape all memories of the woman whose love for me, now lost through my own fault and hers, runs through many of these pages. That is why I so often longed to get rid of myself. Moment after moment it went on. I could pick up the telephone and dial her number, which I craved and which would be terrible,* or I could pick up my gun. Pistol or receiver, in either case right at the ear! If I get through this minute, there would be another minute to get through, and another day, maybe for the rest of what appeared to be my ruined life. And now, some years' worth of minutes since, I find myself grateful for my life and I've long since forgotten which corner of the Indio Greyhound station she kissed me in. This was but one subdelineation; now so many new ones have been overlaid upon it that if anyone asks me what is what, all I can hesitatingly reply is that Imperial is . . .

Searching the bedside drawer for a Bible, I found an Imperial County phone book on the front cover of which somebody named Piña had written: **I LOVE YOU Armando.** This comforted me slightly, to imagine that Piña and Armando might be happy. Then I opened the phone book and discovered on the inside cover:

*It might seem strange that I keep saying "she left me" when in fact I was the one who asked her please not to contact me in any way until (if there ever was an until) I felt ready to call her; but the reason was simple: After first trying to humor her when she proposed that we now become simply very, very good friends, I realized, and in our final conversation expressed to her, that I did not feel able to accept such a diminishment, for it would be agony for me not to be able to address her by our old endearments every minute, or to hold her tight. I see now that in telling her this I was already beginning to lay degrading hints: Maybe someday she might permit me to do those things again? Her gently definitive reply was that if she or I did slip up at first and call each other darling once in awhile, none of the people who'd known us from *before* would blame us.—She became, in fact, quite bitter about my change of heart. I had agreed to stay friends, and now I was reneging. She might now be compelled to "reassess" the value of the years we'd spent together. I replied that I needed to wait until a certain zone of my heart (which I did not delineate) died before I could endure to be her friend; in other words, I remained unable to see her until finding myself prepared to make her that promise which my never having made had caused her to leave me; or else until that place in my heart that was "our place" had died. This logic was absolutely correct, and I thought at the time that it bore no grovelling connotations of take-me-back, but I now see quite well through my photographer's loupe what I was hoping. Unfortunately, she carefully said, referring to the necessity for killing off that zone in my heart: Well, that makes psychological sense.—I told her that of course she could get in touch with me if it was an emergency. For weeks afterward, I couldn't understand why she never called me. Whenever the telephone rang, my heart vomited with crazy joy; but it was never the person I expected. Was she all right? I should really telephone her and see what the matter was, because it made no sense that she hadn't called me.

I love you
I love you
I love you 9-8-00 3.22 a.m.
good by my Love see you soon ????
We will be to gether?????
Armando E——— 1958 to 8-8-0000
I love you Armando
Armando y Piña
you to will always

I felt horrified. Then I thought: She loved him. She refused to cede her heart's Imperial. And so, if she'd had the guts, right now she slept with him for always.

I, of course, had only to pick up the telephone and make a certain promise which I could not make. Then I would have been with her. But the days of separation were widening; probably it was already too late; anyhow, I couldn't do it. I was damned.

Although ever since my mid-twenties I'd rarely remembered my dreams, I now dreamed of her every night with searing vividness. Upon the windows of Mexicali's seafood restaurants, painted representations of octopi and shrimp glow insistently, and the dreams were still more concentrated than that. I'd awake at once, gasping for air. At first the dreams offered dream-solutions: I paid off all her debts, and then we were able to be together; we agreed to change our names and hide from everyone who knew us, and so it was solved. But after a couple of weeks the dreams involved postmortem meetings with her: I fruitlessly begged her to take me back, and she replied with tears, anger, disgust. Knowing these scenarios to be accurate depictions of what would have happened had we actually spoken, I continued to squeeze out the strength to avoid dialling her telephone number for the next fifteen minutes,* and then for the hour after that; so it went day by day; that was the only thing to do, although I flattered myself that she, too, must be getting more miserable (and, knowing her, more angry) with each day of this silence which I'd imposed, not that that brought me any pleasure, for unkindness was never one of my faults. I knew very well that the instant I'd see her or hear her voice, I'd be my old self, relaxed, alert, capable, considerate and even joyous, because the undelineated portion of my heart (which we might as well call love) had not died at all. It was very strong yet. She was the love of my life. So I wanted to die.

At eight-o'-clock the smell of manure was in the air, and night had come to the asphalt of the streets, oozing upwards to dim the dun walls of hotels, freight trucks,

*At the end of the first month I began to dream that the phone would ring and then a female voice I didn't recognize would say her name. I knew it was she. That was all. I'd awake instantly in intense pain.

arcades, supermarkets; but the sky itself remained so luminous that it seemed the same as ever, imperishable as my image of her; the place within my heart could not, could not die, it seemed—now it is an old gulley nearly filled in with drift-sand—and yet this peculiar sky hovered in disconnection from the ground's darkness, where I weakly wandered, longing to disappear forever behind the silhouettes of palm trees.

A drunk, more drunks, drinkers not yet drunk, and drunks as yet unmentioned populated the so-called International Friendship Park. I paced there, more and more rapidly. Why wasn't she here? I could have been with her, but I couldn't have been with her. And then the guilt for failing her, as painful as myriad diagonal sunglares across a set of railroad tracks! I'd begged her forgiveness in the end, and thank God she'd forgiven me for everything, but I . . . A kind bullet, or . . .

I reached the border where a government sentinel's white vehicle watched the cars swimming like minnows through the narrow channels in that articulated reef of exclusion. Just out of my sight, they passed into Mexico.

A little girl in a pale skirt was dancing and swinging her pale purse, which resembled the crescent moon as it whirled about in the darkness. She was in Mexico; I gazed at her from between the metal bars of the border. Backlit by the red tail-eyes of the many cars waiting to cross into the country where I stood, she leaped joyously. Couples touched through the wall; pairs did drug deals on Southside; and the fence seemed to rock slightly; a man had jumped down illegally into the United States of America! I stood in Calexico, staring into the congested otherness of Mexicali, and felt that I would never comprehend the reason for differentiation of any sort, let alone separation. Yet what I watched brought me an instant of peace. It was possible to wait and to watch through walls. I would do this for the woman I loved, even though she no longer waited for me, so that the wait was hopeless. I refused to confess that. I would be very patient and good, and she would miss me enough to come back to me. Why not? The little girl had been waiting for her mother to return from Northside. Here she came; the child shrilled with delight, and they went off together, down the steps under the street and up again into Mexico.

So I did the same. I passed through the two clicking turnstiles, wound through that white pedestrian tunnel where the Mexican border guard sat with his head in his hands, and found myself gazing westward at the shacks whose high, pallid rows of lights on poles somehow resembled palm orchards. The streets were darker and meaner than I remembered. Well, I was unhappy, so of course I felt vulnerable, almost powerless.

My feet took me back to the red-lit Thirteen Negro dance hall where I'd come for half a dozen years now, sometimes with her, never once to dance. The beauty of the Mexican women, the way they swayed like underwater weeds, that fascinated me as much as ever, but this time they seemed so far above me, higher even than the sea-level mark on the squat white silo of the Holly Sugar Company, that when the waiter came to see whether I wanted a dance partner, I literally couldn't speak, so I shook my head. Sitting in the corner, I slowly drank my beer, watching the girls laughingly chattering to the men in white cowboy hats who were grinding their hips against them. I felt afraid and did not know why. I wanted to run back across the border and hide in my motel bed. I was afraid, but I pretended that she was beside me again, and that I was helping and protecting her from whatever I feared, because doing that had never failed to make me brave. Yes, she would always be with me, but only as my conscience, reminding me of the promise that I'd failed to make (and years later I insert the observation that "always" may not endure exceedingly long). It is no exaggeration that her presence tortured me; of course her utter absence would have been worse; I *had* to believe that she'd always be at the Date Tree Hotel, the palm grove in Mecca, Leonard's mountain and the cathedral in Mexicali.

Nowadays when I pass the Date Tree Hotel I sometimes feel a trifle sad, and sometimes the sight of the Jewel Date Co. creates a sensation not pleasant enough to be called "nostalgia." If I am with someone else, I hide my sadness, and my companion suspects nothing. Before I know it, the sorrow has gone. Frequently these places lack the power to hurt me. The cathedral has now presented itself to me in so many contexts that her ghost rarely attracts my attention. As for Salvation Mountain, who can visit Leonard and not like him? Who can resist his cheerfulness? There is a certain arch that Leonard built; it says **LOVE**. Never mind. And when I go to the Thirteen Negro year after year, I am happy. Well, that place always meant more to me than to her.

I took two sleeping pills and awoke after a full seven hours, filled with hope from a fairytale dream which resembled one of those paper animals which hang in the doorways of Mexican *dulcerías,* one of those giant garish animals furred with curling paper shavings: I'd paid off all her debts again, thereby solving the only problem. My heart was not yet in extremis. It tried to be resourceful. Just as when toward noon in Imperial one's patch of shade contracts and the head accordingly sinks down toward the chest, not only out of torpor but also to avoid squinting, so my heart drew in on itself a little, but disbelief still armored it against mortal injury; it could recover as soon as she telephoned or sent me the letter which I absolutely knew was coming. For a moment I lay there planning just how I would earn the money to accomplish this matter of her debts, and the grief crept back, staining my rising consciousness like some poison in the Salton Sea. I understood now how difficult it had always been for her to face the day, for she suffered from clinical depression. Often she could scarcely bear to get out of bed.

Early morning light in Imperial differs from evening light, the long shadows being softer, the light yellower, but in mornings as in evenings the zones of shadow remain so equally extensive that at, say, six-o'-clock A.M., old men can read their newspapers in comfort almost anywhere. Pigeons rise, transfigured into silhouettes like concretions of departing shade from the quiet streets. The mountains of Mexico stand beautifully clear behind the border fence. Certainly not on my next journey here, but perhaps on the one after that, if I could bear to make it, the Imperial mornings might soothe me with their beautiful proof of how unimportant I was, with all my buzzing little miseries; I wouldn't need oblivion as much by then, because in Imperial I was already invisible in comparison to the horizon. But at that moment all I could feel was the nearly unbearable vastness of this long hot day which I must now traverse, unless I could lose consciousness. If I took more sleeping pills now, I wouldn't be able to sleep tonight. As for that agony in my chest, it had resolved by now into a sort of sickness, punctuated by day-long fevers of crazy grief. (A month later, I would be more or less crazy, scrabbling to extract some sad or ominous meaning from every remark of anyone who knew both her and me. Because she hadn't replied to my letter on a Saturday, she must surely be spending the weekend preparing a perfect compromise which she would mail on Monday, so I would expect it on Tuesday. I lost myself in a forest of mirrors and symbols.) Hoping to grow too listless to care about my own sorrow, I was now so unsure of myself and so weak that I couldn't lift my big camera. I was supposed to be photographing the New River . . .

The alfalfa fields, fresh-shorn like a tropical girl's cunt-stubble, were golden-green and dense, textured with the row-lines which my love always used to remark on. She was an oil painter.

Earlier I'd understood (although by now, as I'd said, the pain had become so great, an acid, physical ache in my chest) that all I could try to do was to cherish my suffering, because it brought me closer to her, first of all because she too must be crying alone somewhere not so far away (when I closed my eyes I could almost see her, although half a decade later I could scarcely envision her at all, and preferred to suppose that instead of crying alone she had laughed in relief), and secondly because I had been hurting her year after year, so that at last I could feel what she had felt; this was what I had done to her; I kept whispering to myself, *it's my fault, my fault,* which comforted me, because then grief had a reason; I'd brought it on myself and needed to feel it so that I'd finally understand why she'd always sobbed and begged me to stay just another ten minutes; this desperate, inconsolable longing, which exploded from my eyes day after day, was also her longing for me, which she lost the capacity to bear. And all the time I'd kept soothing her: I'm so sorry. I understand.—But how could I have ever really understood until she went away, the love whom I loved more than my life (for I'd several times offered to kill myself for her), the one whose weeping presence had brought me guilty sadness and whose absence gave me agony? As the rift of days grew wider, I understood less, becoming stupider and baser every day; but I had to do my best to learn from this, and perhaps become a better person. I was one with her now, as long as I kept crying. (In our final conversation she'd angrily said: My recovery trajectory will be a lot slower than yours!—She had never been sweetnatured.) These feelings more than any childish pride saved me from lifting the telephone, dialling the number I knew by heart, and fruitlessly entreating: *Come back, come back, come back.*

A MEMORY-PHOTOGRAPH

Perhaps I have already betrayed her privacy a trifle, and certainly mine, in what's been written here. In this book, which attempts not only to delineate an arbitrary, semi-imaginary area called Imperial, but also to investigate how and why delineations are made, a revelation of the life we had, with its secret anguishes and now forever lost joys, would be disrespectful not only to the memory of that life but also to her. I will always cherish her so much that I must cherish her reclusive dignity, too. But precisely because I cherish her, my solace now, however inadequate, is to preserve my images of her. She was frequently annoyed at my poor memory, and already the stretch of days between our last day and this day has widened like the Salton Sea, and I am forgetting more. I don't think I will ever forget the way her mouth made a silent O when we made love, and the way she would suck her thumb when she came. But I never thought to really *look* at, for instance, her pretty little hands, and now it's too late; my memory-photograph of those has blurred. A week after my first visit to an Imperial now eternally withered and lost, I engraved her name into the sand near Ocotillo with a stylus of volcanic rock, and watched the hot wind very slowly begin to fill in the letter-grooves. Should I kill myself, all my pictures of her would be lost; if I lived to be old, her image would gradually blur away just like her name in the sand. What can I save here? (She's gone away. These words are all I can keep.) I lack the right to reveal who she was, the nature of my dirty secrets, or why I failed her. Let me say only that she was better than I. (Years later I add: And worse. And the same.) She was a woman, a human being; she had faults, perhaps the worst of which (the result of many bad experiences in earlier life) was an extreme mistrustfulness, which reacted with my own weaknesses to cause us misery. I might add that we were both sad and anxious people, sufficiently love-thirsty as to make nightmarish misdelineations of each other's fears, especially at first. But while I suffered unhappiness in the relationship, as she certainly did, to the harm of her health, there remained about it, and her, an almost indescribable quality, often masked by our own failures, which stood separate and perfect like that white figure I saw in the date palm grove, the being which seemed for a moment to be her spirit. Specifically, she had an almost boundlessly noble compassion for anything small, maimed or defenseless in this world. She possessed a rare capacity to love, even to her own destruction. One wellspring of this love was an immense sincerity. She could not be dishonest, nor mask her feelings; as a result, everything she said and did caught fire with its own spontaneous if volatile truth. She adored me. I will love her to the day I die.—So what? A friend saw her adoring someone else. I have had several sweethearts since.—She was never pretentious; much more intelligent than her insecurities permitted her to perceive, she expressed complex and interesting ideas in the most plainspoken way. Adorned with many talents and much artistic and technical knowledge, none of which unfortunately gave her joy in herself, she was more capable than most people of taking an interest in subjects new to her and discussing them without preconceptions. My own character, for better and worse, is rigid. I know what I know, and I follow my own muse; one of my university professors called me unteachable. Maimed, like her, by the cruelty of others in my younger years, I remain too often indifferent to the opinions and enthusiasms of others. Yet she was able to teach me. Above all she helped me to see the patterns of things, from the furrows in Imperial's fields to the architectonics of a Russian symphony to the nicely springloaded power dynamics implicit in all human relations. As much as the long hours when we lay in each other's arms I treasure the talks we had and the journeys we took, the books we gave each other, even the board games she taught me to enjoy. It was because she took such pleasure in Imperial that I began to write this book. In my mind's sad confusion after she was gone, I could not distinguish, much less define, any Imperial which did not include her. And so for the last time, as a way of saying goodbye to her, let me delineate her for you. Let me describe her.

She had a fair and freckled face, with thick eyebrows which I loved to stroke when we were making love; and, when she was not out of sorts, her brown eyes were extraordinary with some gentle painful truth shining out of them. (Again and again I cannot forbear the word "truth" when I speak of my darling.) She had long brown hair. On the rare occasions when she was happy enough with me to smile, that smile thrilled me with grateful joy. The very first time I saw her face, I was enthralled by her. She was the most beautiful woman in the world.

She was haunting, fascinating, dangerous, submissive, cautious, affectionate and affection-starved, intuitive sometimes to the point of telepathy but often paranoid, sensitive in both the good and bad sense, loyal, graceful, possessive and cruel, erotic, weak, indomitable, ethical, compulsive, generous, sweet-smelling, disorganized, sharp-tongued, anxious, and lavishly loving. She was my heart. She was my sorrowful angel.

AND ONE MORE TIME

Whenever I went to Imperial, my chief joy was to record through words and photographs the splendid colors, the fruits and stories of that world, to map it and as an act of worship to fix it in time.* And it was literally exciting to lay down on the light table my latest negative of the El Granero bar in Mexicali, or of Leonard the prophet and builder who was grinning and waving sweetly in paint-smeared overalls as he stood before his mountain.

I did not often photograph the woman I loved, because cameras made her shy; I had to coax her, and sometimes I thought that it was (to use one of her words) "invasive" to do that. Besides, I already knew that every time I saw the perfectly regular slanting evening shadows between orchard-rows I would think of her.

But, as it happened, on that very last trip of ours, about which, of course, as with the last time we made love, I had no suspicion that it was the last time, she requested that I photograph her, which she almost never did, and so when I think back on that April afternoon I have an eerie feeling, as if her heart already knew, and I suppose it did. (I kept asking her: When did you know? When did you finally arrive at this decision? Because the night before she left me, when we spoke on the telephone as usual, she seemed much less anxious than usual, cheerful even; she was going swimming with her friends. Next morning she said that she'd forced herself to be that way because it wasn't fair to tell me until we were face to face; in fact she'd gotten hysterical after hanging up the phone. She was correct, and I thank her for it, but it was so, so horrible.)

So I had my black plastic rectangles in a stack, and I laid them on the light table one by one as impatiently as I used to rip her clothes off. Yes, thank God, there she was. But I refrained from allowing my vision inside that special sheet of film just

*This must be related to the fact that I badly endure separation of any kind. It is almost impossible for me to leave anyone I've loved, for I never stop loving her. At great cost I did leave someone for the woman about whom I've been writing, and for months was half crazy with guilt. I could not talk about it with the one I loved best, for fear that she might interpret my expressions of pain as resentment against her. I left that one woman for her, and after that I was too weak or kindly-cowardly to do more. Separation is death. And after the one I loved so much left me, my friends and hers insisted it was necessary, which might have been fair and true; but I was being slowly executed by isolation, suffocation and darkness (say, by immersion in a drowning-chamber) while all witnesses and chaplains promised this to be the best medicine both for me and for my executioner. So I rejected them, raging against them like a little child; I hated the truth which, as the saying goes, had set me free, letting me fall into the drowning-chamber whose fluid was really a dark mixture of my needs, greeds and lies. God forgive me.

yet. I turned off the light table and let half the day pass, so grateful that I didn't crave suicide even once. Finally I went back upstairs to my study, locked the door, reached for the switch at the right side of the light table, and found my loupe. Now I was going to look at her face, her dear face, and by the miracle of photography I'd be able to see the way she'd been looking back at me when I was still hers and she still mine; and, most of important of all, that moment was the *true* last moment, which I'd not yet consumed; I was now about to live it, that is, experience it for the very first time, which is the only time one can live a moment, the reason being that when I take a photograph with a large-format camera, the cumbersome mechanics of preparation preclude more than the most superficial seeing of my own composition—the arrangement of it, mere geometry of upside-down shapes on the ground glass—whenever the subject is a human being, for should I take too long, she'll move on, just as she eventually did, and then life will pass me by! Moreover, after the focusing has been completed, the loupe lifted off the glass, it remains necessary to close the shutter, insert the big black film holder, set the f/stop, verify the speed, withdraw the dark slide and *then* click the shutter, feeling released by the spring-driven whirr. Of course I am locking eyes on my subject at this moment, but not to *see* her, for I lack the time; merely to persuade her to stand still just a trifle longer; and meanwhile any number of subtle positional shifts or alterations in her expression could have occurred. So it was that for the very last time I still had a future with her. Her few letters to me, my other photographs of her, all preserved a past in which she'd been my darling. If three weeks or ten years from now I did meet her, she'd be only my "friend." And beginning this night, my dreams of her no longer involved my solving everything, nor even my pleading; instead, they had to do with her arriving, wearing that gentle, distant smile, for she'd come to confiscate all the negatives, letters and memorabilia of our dead love, which she now must carry into oblivion.

To repeat, this negative yet existed in futurity. Because I had yet to learn how she was gazing at me in that photograph, it truly would be an unpredictable experience, a present moment stolen from within the boundaries of a lost past. This meant that I really *could* make love with her for the last time. I felt as happy and excited as when her face had swum toward mine to kiss me for the very first time. Already as I brought the negative toward the light table I could see the pure white arch of her negative-hair against black sand and black sky. I laid her down on the frosted glass. There she was, alive. Carefully I polished the convex glass surface of the loupe with the cleaning cloth. Then, sobbing in absolute anguish, I began to lower my head toward her, the loupe clenched against my right eye; any instant now I'd see the expression on her face.

Chapter 5

THE WIDEMOUTHED PIPE

(2002)

We attribute motives, agency, intention, and experiences to one another all the time. The investigation of who attributes what to whom, when, why and how is a science in itself.

—R. D. Laing, *Self and Others* (1969)

But Imperial is also a Mexican girl on flat white sand, her lovely legs silhouetted, her ankles together, who stands on her high heels, wearing a knee-length white flower-dress, and she is handing something to the first men in a rigid line, with the stadium behind her, her profiled face gentle and serious. In the Archivo Histórico del Municipio de Mexicali they could not tell me who she was. She might have been older than the Salton Sea! I'd swear she was rich. Imperial is a place I'll never know, a place of other souls than mine; and how can anyone know otherness?—Through study, perhaps; through history.—If I never came to know her, if I thought this landscape bereft of any feelings, which is to say just itself, beautiful and indifferent, then I would have failed. Always those wide, wide, empty streets! Upon Imperial's blankness, which might as well be a light table, it becomes all too easy to project myself, which is a way of discovering nothing. I sincerely wanted to do better and be better. In the brown fields between Mexicali and San Luis Río Colorado, pure water spews from a widemouthed pipe and falls three feet into a ditch. Imperial is water; it flows, and flows away. If I lack the strength to dig for it, I said to myself, may I nonetheless seek the water of life which comes glistening from the ground and then returns to earth! Let me seek something grander than myself, something that I have not known; because what I do know is nothing, which is to say myself. (Thoreau: *I should not talk so much about myself if there were any body else whom I knew as well.*) Who was she? Who was Imperial then and now? I closed their album and went outside, into the hot, wide, empty streets.

WARNING OF IMPENDING ARIDITY

This book represents my attempt to become a better-informed citizen of North America. Our "American dream" is founded on the notion of the self-sufficient homestead. The "Mexican dream" may be a trifle different, but requires its kindred material basis. Understanding how those two hopes played out over time required me to cultivate statistical parables about farm size, waterscapes, lettuce prices, et cetera. I have harvested them (doubtless bruising overripe numbers on the way), and now present them to you. Some may be too desiccated for your taste. If you skip the chapters devoted to them, you will finish the book sooner, and never suspect the existence of my arithmetical errors. As for you devotees of Dismal Science, I hope you will be awestruck by my sincerity about Mexicali Valley cotton prices.

Chapter 6

THEN AND NOW

(1844–2002)

Standing today by the grave of that infant civilization which blossomed, amidst such hardships, upon a desert, we would fain lift the veil and see the unthought-of transformation which fifty years will bring.

—Judge F. C. Farr, 1918

In January 1903, two months before Mexicali's official foundation date (by 1904 there were a dozen-odd adobe buildings in that city; they'd all get washed away two years hence), the *Imperial Press and Farmer* published a special holiday edition to celebrate the holy "ministry of capital" in prose as optimistic, if not quite as purple, as Harold Bell Wright's. The reclamation of Imperial is the largest irrigation enterprise in the nation! Imperial will be more fertile than the Nile Delta! *My experience this season,* writes Mr. V. Gant, *demonstrates the superiority of this land for producing feed crop, over any I have ever seen, either in California or Arizona.* How do such hopes and certainties stack up after a century? Imperial then and Imperial now cannot add up to Imperial, which is, we must never forget, infinite and hence unknowable, but to the extent that Imperial can stand in for something more limited (say, "America" and "Mexico"), the comparison might illuminate something. This land is stripes now, bands of white sand, road, then green-grown canal ditch, horizon and border wall, tree-line and power wire, furrow, everything harshly lit or shadowed, with the black silhouettes of hay bales reigning. Imperial is sheep, palm trees, flatness, then migrant workers clustered around their trucks in the leafy-lobed fields as if they were bees imparting sustenance to their hive. This is probably what Mr. Gant and his neighbors wanted, what they worked for. Their watchwords: own, use, delineate.

Imperial differs from their projections, to be sure. Where have the splendid duck-lakes of the New River gone? Where in particular is Blue Lake, and the brand-new township of Silsbee which abuts it?—Washed out by the flood which made the Salton Sea. Silsbee went to Seeley.—Whatever happened to Flowingwell? Where's Iris, where the Southern Pacific Railroad line reascends to sea level?—Vanished, just like those eight Mutual Water Companies whose stockholders were the owners of the irrigated farmlands.—For that matter, where did the perfect climate go? A. W. Patten, "a prominent citizen of Imperial," *reports that the weather is not uncomfortable in the New River section. The men, he said, work through the middle of the day without experiencing any discomfort. They have the opportunity of laying off during the warmest part of the day, but prefer to work right on through.* That might have been true, if they were paid by the hour.

I stand here on the Calexico side of the border, where Imperial is blonde and flat, emerald and flat, beautiful and fresh and eternally approaching harvest; all day a hot wind as if of molten gold pours down upon the yellowish-green sand, blowing north from Mexico, whose borderline of low buildings and trees runs on and on past the beginnings of the dark emerald fields, curving around the edge of the world under the squatness of Signal Mountain; that wind blasted Imperial yesterday as it will tomorow. Today's temperature is a mere one hundred and sixteen degrees, and A. W. Patten remains unrefuted; it is really not so bad; I can walk around for several hours with seventy pounds of photographic equipment on my shoulder, the sweat pattering down from my forehead onto the black film holders; it is, as the *Imperial Press and Farmer* continually reminds us, a dry heat; as long as I drink water I'm fine. But where are all my fellow climate-enthusiasts? (Thanks to air-conditioning, the Imperial Valley uses more electricity per capita than any other locality in the United States.)—Oh, here they are; see the lines of Mexican workers in the fields; as Officer Dan Murray remarked, they do the work Americans won't do. (*Another three Hondos just gave themselves up,* says the radio. The Border Patrolman points out Northside's latest wound: A section of picket fence only half a month old is already tunneled under, gapingly. *A group over the Alamitos on the west side,* warns the radio.) Aren't A. W. Patten's descendants working that land? If they're not, why not? Did the Ministry of Capital speak to them in tongues of fire, so that they learned that it was better, more profitable, to pay a minimum wage to the brownskinned ones while they pushed pencils and clickety-clacked at computer projections of harvest?

Going west, toward the the dusty-white pipes, rocket-shapes, funnels and boxcars of Plaster City, I find myself back in white, white sand, evidently unreclaimable by Mr. Gant and his colleagues despite its green tufts of vegetation, and closer to the greyish-blue translucent arrowpoints of mountains and the Lazy Lizard Saloon in Ocotillo, near which more thirst-killed illegal Mexicans will soon be found, including a couple of adolescent girls; Imperial asserts itself in bewildering dun-colored bluffs of crumbling earth, seasoned with lumps of gypsum (fragile shards of white mineral windowpane on tranlucent bone; it crumbles in the hands); a hot wind shakes the sparse golden weeds and nothing else moves because everything is rock and dirt. (Imperial County, by the way, is not as spectacular as the pastel-colored badlands of Anza-Borrego to the west with their mazes of washes and secret oases.) It was around here that back in 1903 they were finding fourteen-inch oyster shells *(some of the finest specimens will be presented to the Chamber of Commerce)*. But if he ever paced these yellowish humps of wrinkled crumbly dirt, Mr. Gant would have pronounced the verdict: Worthless, at least until we can get water here. And if we can't, then it's not Imperial.

Going east, the shines and shimmers of the East Highline Canal bid me farewell, after which Imperial gets sandier and scrubbier and more characterized by white salt stains; then it's all sand, sometimes yellowish, sometimes white, ornamented on the right by the All-American Canal's hydro plants; and thanks to that sand there are diamond-shaped hazard signs which reassure the lovelorn: SOFT SHOULDER. Yuma lies ahead. This zone also must be excluded from Mr. Gant's Imperial.

It is 1900. Blue Lake already boasts ten registered voters; the town of Imperial is inhabited; Silsbee, Heber, Calexico* and Brawley have just been staked out. J. B. Hoffman, Imperial's first justice of the peace, has just *invented the open air jail, consisting of a chain between two mesquite trees.* Imperial is a fallow virgin ready for the sowing. What makes her so? *Potash, lime, magnesia, sulphuric and a trifle of phosphoric acids.* I am quoting from the freshly expanded and vindicated edition of William E. Smythe's *The Conquest of Arid America.* In our eastern states, those "valuable elements" were dissolved in "the rains of centuries" and carried off to the sea. *On the other hand, these elements have been accumulating in the arid soil of the West during the same centuries. They lie there now like an inexhaustible bank account on which the plant-life of the future may draw at will without danger of protest.* Imperial equals profit to come, national assertion, universal improvement at a dollar and twenty-five cents per acre, plus a bit over eleven dollars more for water, supplied at bargain rates by the Imperial Land Company. And why the Imperial Land Company? Because *it took the Government a half century to wake up . . . The Government was too slow. It represented the people, and the people required too much time for educational purposes, and before the people got ready to act through their representatives, private enterprise . . . commenced the great work of illustrating the motto of the California Water and Forest Association, that "Moisture Means Millions."*—Or, as a grizzled pioneer puts it in his memoirs, *Throughout this history the almost pitiful dependence of the settlers on outside capital will be noted.*

Now let the canal be undertaken; let the story begin. (Before water there was no story; that is what Mr. Gant might say. So:)

Once upon a time, which is to say on Saturday, June 22, 1901, the *Imperial Press*

*A man who was there informs us that "Calexico, which derives its name from a combination of California and Mexico, simply happened." Mexicali's name comes from the same two sources.

and Farmer, in vast dark letters which march vertically down the front page, partially occluding the boxed and centered notice, **WATER IN THE TOWN OF IMPERIAL**: **Tuesday, May 15, 1901, the headgates of the Imperial canal were opened,** proclaims:

WATER IS HERE

Next week's headline reads: **THE DESERT DISAPPEARS**.

AN ESSAY ON THE INFINITE

The story of any life is the story of expectations fulfilled or disappointed, of "progress" from birth to death, projects accomplished or not (marry this person, farm this land, write this book), above all, of capital being drunk dry. Futurity spends itself; that's why Europe's long perished engravers so often depicted time as a hooded skeleton clutching an hourglass. Yes, the Colorado River can burst through the cut, sweep away Mexicali, and scour a deep gorge for the Río Nuevo to speed through, but someday that gorge will go dry; in fact it already has; the Río Nuevo's foul black spew is dead and buried. Someday the United States of America must come to an end. Someday the sun will be no more. Practically speaking, then, nothing we can touch is infinite, but that's only practically speaking; why not limit our awarenesses, as do meditators when they fill themselves with a single mystic syllable? Sooner or later, the woman I love will leave me, thanks to either her own choice or death. I know this, but it probably won't happen today. Today, therefore, remains infinite, so I shelter myself within it. And I submit to you that this faith in infinitude, which is simultaneously naive, noble and self-serving, remains the emblem of American character.

(What is Mexican character? I'll get to that, but it will take me several border crosssings.)

In an essay appropriately entitled "The Young American," Emerson writes (1844): *The bountiful continent is ours, state on state, and territory on territory, to the waves of the Pacific sea.* In other words, the days and lands of my life remain literally innumerable. These words which could have been coined by the Imperial Land Company.—"Imperial!" We patronize the monarchy against which we successfully rebelled; we patronize England as a busy man does his father gone senile; and yet, in the end, what word could be more American than "Imperial"? Half a century after Emerson's hymn to possession, a successful senatorial candidate advises us: *There are so many things to be done—canals to be dug, railways to be laid, forests to be felled, cities to be built, unviolated fields to be tilled, priceless markets to be won, ships to be launched, peoples to be saved, civilization to be proclaimed, and the flag of liberty flung to the eager air of every sea.* We peeled off half of Mexico; now we're off to Spanish Cuba! Our soon-to-be Senator elects *us* the chosen people; he dreams aloud of "commercial empire." In 1904 a mother in the town of Imperial names her newborn daughter Imperial Hazel Deed. In 1930 the author of an article entitled "Niland's Future" advises: *Give Salton Sea a new name. Call it Lake Imperial. The psychology of a name can often work wonders.* And in the first decade of the twenty-first century, the most self-confident American President ever proclaims civilization in Iraq and Afghanistan—mission accomplished! Meanwhile, Emerson envisions the arising on American soil of public gardens as lovely as the Villa Borghese in Rome. But he's a practical dreamer, a farmer; he will not object if those gardens are edible. *The vast majority of the people of this country live by the land,* he says, *and carry its quality in their manners and opinions.* How he would have loved Imperial's honey-colored hay bales, her alfalfa fields like green skies! Imperial is America; Imperial goes beyond all four horizons. Our holdings may not be quite infinite; indeed, Emerson mentions the railroad, which has already shrunk England by two-thirds; and steam power, whose magic has narrowed the Atlantic to a strait; still, *we have twenty degrees of latitude in which to choose a seat.* Someday, this book called *Imperial* will be completed, the last township-lot purchased, the last barrel of oil burned up in America or China or who knows where, my body stricken down into its grave; but that's a long way off, not this minute, and Emerson, who just as Koestler called Russia *the country of the revolution* calls Northside *the country of the Future,* sees futurity as an American will: *How much better when the whole land is a garden, and the people have grown up in the bowers of a paradise.*

Speaking of the gardens of Paradise, whose most memorable crop may well be Emersonians, dark-bearded, thinning-haired Mr. Smythe now stares out at us with melancholy tenderness from the frontispiece of his *Conquest of Arid America.* I've already quoted his simile of the desert as an inexhaustible bank account of nutrients. But this doesn't do the dreamy man justice. He's an opportunist only in the missionary sense; he too subscribes with touching literalness to the Ministry of Capital. His final chapter, fittingly entitled "Man's Partnership with God," informs us that *irrigation . . . is a religious rite. Such a prayer for rain is intelligent, scientific, worthy of man's divinity. And it is answered.* In the gloomy uneasiness of early-twenty-first-century America, these words seem questionable, to say the least. But Smythe has proved his case with enlightened practicality: The expense of such a Brobdingnagian apparatus of levees, sluices and dams as our new settlements require will defeat even a Stanford or a Huntington. *All this lay beyond the reach of the individual. Thus it was found that the association and organization of men were the price of life and prosperity in the arid West. The alternative was starvation.* So it is that Arid America, a huge domain which happens to include Imperial, will be settled not by speculators and their pawns but by ordinary farming families whose laborious canal-digging requires them to constitute themselves upon small allotments close together. The large farms of Massachusetts, the grand plantations of the South, with their attendant slaves and servitors, will never replicate themselves here! We'll all be equal and moderate neighbors here in Imperial, planting heterogeneous crops so that our mutual companies can weather anything. We'll be spared what one fellow (who unfortunately just happened to be Imperial's first engineer) describes as *the natural antagonism of any people living under a large water system toward the company controlling their source of supply.* No, we'll own that supply together! Living in common, we'll easily find opportunity to build our schools, libraries, electric grids and churches. *The essence of the industrial life which springs from irrigation is its democracy.*

To be honest with you, I find this assertion immensely touching. I want it to be true. How about you? Turning the page, I find a halftoned photograph of a man whose white hat enjoys distant cousinage with the pith helmet of an African explorer; in his sensibly light-colored suit he stands in profile on a grassy levee; he's put one foot before the other, as if we'd preserved him in the act of taking an immense step; his jaunty gaze directs us into shady grass while behind and above him I see an immense shade-tree whose radiating foliage should be considered an explosion of oxygenated coolness and blessedness; and I see more trees and more, blessed by a tranquil grassy-banked canal of mirror-brightness—abode, retreat, chapel to capital, Emersonian seat—and William E. Smythe writes the caption: **TWO YEARS AND FOUR MONTHS PRIOR TO THE TAKING OF THIS PHOTOGRAPH, NEITHER WATER, TREE, NOR MAN EXISTED IN THIS PLACE, IMPERIAL VALLEY, CALIFORNIA.**

The majority of the people of Northside no longer live by the land, so naturally they do not carry its quality in their manners and opinions. The rural population of California has decreased from seventy-nine percent in 1860 to five and a half percent in 2000.* Surely the few who feed the rest of us are ultra-rich? As it happens, although some millionaires and corporations now own empires of acres there, Imperial County, in incongruous defiance of Smythe's logic, is the poorest county in California; while Mexicali remains still wealthier in poverty. Imperial then, Imperial now—what has the Ministry of Capital accomplished? To be sure, we retain twenty degrees of latitude in which to choose a seat—which resembles an onion field less than a block of cheaply made houses in El Centro, a long low line of beige-roofed Sprawlsville with the sign: *VISIT ONE OF OUR NEW*

*Imperial County itself now encloses a rural population of only 14.8%.

HOME NEIGHBORHOODS. *The great cities of the western valleys will not be cities in the old sense, but a long series of beautiful villages, connected by lines of electric motors, which will move their products and people from place to place.* In so many ways Imperial is as forlorn as the face of a motorist who's just been pulled over by two Calexico policemen, one bending over either side of his car. **THE DESERT DISAPPEARS**, but Imperial is houses wide-spaced in sandy lots, some with palms around them, to be sure, but those palms are often dead; Imperial is two fan-palms struggling and dancing in the wind at Azure and North Marine, whose sign has been appropriately abbreviated NO MARINE, for we're at Salton City.

Imperial is the long trains which run through every evening, bearing freight less often from Brawley's cantaloupe fields (in 1905, wise townsmen are making a hundred dollars an acre from the fruit; in 1918 *nearly 3000 carloads of this delicious table dessert are annually shipped from this point;* in 1926 we find Southern Pacific fabricating twenty thousand refrigerator cars and deploying them all around the Imperial Valley for *the largest season in the history of the cantaloupe industry*) than from some syndicate in Asia. What went wrong? Oh, yes, in 2002 there will still be Imperial cantaloupes, but two hundred thousand metric tons of that fruit will originate in Mexico, where labor is cheaper than in Brawley. A certain time-chiseled resident of Heber who declined to be quoted by name glared at me when I mentioned free trade, then said: In Mexico you rent land for half as much, you don't have inspectors out in the fields, no bathrooms, no pesticide laws, and then they ship the stuff here and *all people look at is the price!*—(He himself was priceless, so in this book I'll quote him again and again.) To be sure, *this marvelous Valley where the land valuations have increased from nothing in 1900 to $14,000,000 in 1912, and $20,000,000 to $40,000,000 now,* which is to say in 1918, still meets Emerson's definition of an agricultural paradise; we know that it does for the *pollos* who make the snake over the border fence at night; I pick up today's *Imperial Valley Press* and read that the corpse of Rogelio Contreras-Navarette, who was one of ten-odd "undocumented immigrants," has been found near Signal Mountain, the cause of death being heat prostration; what could be a better testimony to Imperial's cantaloupe-wealth, of which Señor Contreras-Navarette must have hoped to drink dribs and drabs at an hourly rate?

But the urbanites who now operate the machines of our various grand and local governments take 1918 land valuation figures with a grain of that salt which is ruining the farms around Mexicali. What quality do these worthy legislators of ours carry in their manners and opinions? The quality of *commerce,* I would say; the judge who exulted over "this marvelous Valley" in 1918 might have liked it just as well if its treasures were gold mines or taxpayer-subsidized penitentiary industries;

perhaps even Emerson wasn't an agricultural enthusiast out of pure principle. The night-smell of Imperial's fields as rich as new tobacco, that's the smell of money, really. In 2002, the El Centro City Council and Planning Commission numbers its priorities from one to fifteen. *The city's No. 1 priority is that as growth occurs, public facilities and services must be in place to meet the needs of the community.* How reasonable! *Two principles at the bottom of the priority list—though still important, city officials said—are that the community's rural character be preserved and enhanced by new development and that the vitality of the region's agricultural base and prime agricultural lands are protected.* Well, at least one can still see palm trees reflected in the dark windows of City Hall.

Too bad, too bad; for some Emersonian entrants in Judge Farr's biographical directory of 1918 are not unattractive—for instance Wilber Clark, who worked in the raw new towns until he had enough money to buy his acres and improve them with water. Mr. Clark *is a book-worm, and possesses a library of several thousand volumes, containing some rare "Americana" and first editions, as well as books relating to the Southwest.* Meanwhile, he's already experimented with fifty different kinds of grapes. He reads, so possibly he wonders; perhaps at night he gazes at the stars. I hope he did, for in my day the sky is smog-stained and glary with the lights of El Centro. Year by year, my hair grows grey like the ribbons of salt in the dirt of Imperial. Imperial was dry before; someday Imperial will be dry again.

But for now, Imperial runs over with Colorado River nectar, infinitely. (The most lucrative crop as I write this book is winter lettuce.)* Water is life; Imperial is, among other things, water; we are Americans, so water must be infinite. If it isn't, what will happen to Brawley's cantaloupes? Brawley gets, on the average, two point three inches of rain per year. (The northwest corner of our state receives almost a hundred.) Let us now enter into the heaven of infinite water.

In no section of Arid America can there be found so large a tract of so fertile soil, capable of being furnished with a water supply so abundant at so low a price for the water right and with so cheap water for all time to come.

Being inclined to acknowledge Imperial's finitude, which cannot betray my own,

*Señor José López of Jalisco, who in his thirty-eight years has so far made sixteen successful illegal crossings of the international line, informs me: "The work I made the most money in was picking melons and the lettuce. They used to pay us piece rate. Back in the eighties and nineties, that's where the money was at, in the lettuce and in the cantaloupes. It used to be better when it was piece rate. The lettuce, Monday to Saturday you would get sometimes to take home four or five hundred dollars, sometimes three hundred. There's also been some bad times when it was only a hundred and fifty." Most of his cantaloupe-picking was done in the Central Valley near Fresno, in the towns of Mendota and Firebaugh. This surprised me in view of the Imperial Valley's reputation as "the winter garden of America," but José insisted that in the latter places the season went from July to October, whereas in Brawley and thereabouts the growing season was a mere six weeks.

I find myself nonetheless overruled by Mr. E. J. Swayne, who in a front page article entitled "E.J. Swayne Talks of the Imperial Country and Its Wonderful Possibilities"—and wonderful possibilities were all that they were in 1901—informs us: *It is simply needless to question the supply of water.*

Did we say needless? I mean blasphemous! In those days, our stockholders paid fifty cents per acre-foot for water, which is to say two cents per trickling inch per twenty-four hours, plus operational and maintenance expenses. Nowhere in California was cheaper. In Riverside, for instance, water cost fifteen cents per inch. A century later, it would still be cheap. Here's an article from 1902 entitled "Water Wasting," which invites us *to stand on the margin of the Colorado River and view the immense flow of water in that stream now passing to the sea, and then turn and scan the horizon east or westward.* We *will thus realize the fearful loss to humanity in allowing the waters to thus enter the fathomless sea.* Fortunately, Imperial is getting reclaimed at this very second; humanity can see profit coming, and quite soon the Colorado *will be utilized* so that *thousands of homes* will *dot the land where solitude now reigns supreme.**

Imperial is a dream and a lie; Imperial is a six-room suite in Providence, Rhode Island, back in 1894, where a certain promoter's display cases impress us with *oranges, lemons, bananas, figs, apricots, all products of the Colorado Desert, which, at that time, was producing nothing but a few horned toads and once in awhile a coyote.* And why not? This fortune-teller sees a green field-horizon with palm-silhouettes. A century later, I've found them and touched them. (Imperial is a truck for sale near Mexicali; $ $ has been fingerpainted most hopefully in its windshield-dust.) In 1915 the U.S. Customs Service will still be passing on rumors of a possible bridge at Algodones to connect with a hypothetical Colorado River Ferry. In 1918, Judge Farr slides his spectacles back up his nose and pronounces a verdict for the ages: *It is therefore apparent that the water supply in this vast area is inexhaustible.*

Contemplating the progress of Boulder and Parker dams, an Angeleno concludes: *The water problem seems to be solved for all time.* From 1931 on, the Colorado will be, in an engineer's appealing words, "smoothed out." And in 1934, construction of the All-American Canal begins, for the overt purpose of keeping Mexico's hydramouths out of our water. (President Herbert Hoover, on Mexicans' rights to the river: *We do not believe they ever had any rights.*) By 1942, ranchers in the Mexicali Valley are irrigating more than a quarter of a million acres. By 1975, the Mexicans and the Imperial Irrigation District will be irrigating half a million acres each.

*Once that happened, the headlines remained eerily similar: "Feds get involved in state water issues: $10 million worth of water to flow into ocean." But now the "fearful loss" was no longer the hypothetical one of unused potential; it had become the wastage of what Californians desperately needed.

An undated aerial photograph depicts an S-curve in the desert with a crane at the end of it, then sand and scrub all around. It will be eighty miles long. Every time I see it, I can't help but use the trite word *miraculous,* because it is so blue and cool as it speeds through the white hell of the desert. (Here come the blue-green rushings of the East Highline Canal through its locks.) Stripes of tan, stripes of emerald all the way to the haystack-horizon, they represent no mere infinity, but the conquest of infinity!

AN ESSAY ON URINE

Next issue: *With our magnificent water system (the pure fresh water coming from the mountains of Wyoming) and with our unparalleled drainage, which carries all undesirable matter toward the Salton sink, we need have no fear that our lands will not become better and better as the years go by.* These founders of American Imperial see "drainage," which is as necessary, hence as unobjectionable, and therefore as non-unpleasant, as the stream of urine which issues from each of us from time to time; I for my part see a stinking stream shaded by a freeway overpass and a railroad overpass, accompanied by grass, paper cups, plastic bags, litter and a drowned shopping cart as it flows toward the Salton Sea; and probably the founders are right and I am wrong, because the particular manner in which urine stinks remains irrelevant to its purpose. Cross the border, and ten minutes south by foot, just in front of the Playboy Club, there's a taco stand illuminated by bare bulbs, and around its bowls of watery green sauce, bloody angry red sauce, spicy beans and delicious pickled onions, the street-whores, tired vendors, excited children and passersby are gathered to eat while listening to the meat cleaver's rhythmic fall. A few steps to the westward, the aroma of fresh tortillas stales, then mingles with the smell of sewage, for we're overlooking the Río Nuevo, whose *aguas negras* wriggle horridly down there in that shantytowned gorge that the Colorado River made when it made the Salton Sea. (So it is in the year 2000. Next year they'll cover that cloaca over, in order to hide the stench; then it will vanish out of mind, becoming the merest "drainage" again.) Irrelevant! In the west, the sky's afire in the narrow strip between mountain and cloud, and that fire resembles the brown and black and gold of roasted Mexican corn; that's irrelevant, too, but don't think that the *Imperial Press and Farmer* will neglect it—oh, no, not these pages of smug boosterism whose repeated commonplaces (irrigation is cheaper than rain; grow alfalfa to increase the weight of your hogs; the businessman is known by his stationery; don't trust to luck when you are able to work; every crop on earth will grow in Imperial if you only buy it through the Imperial Farmers' Store) become as flat and dreary as the desert of those parts, for the *Press* is a company paper, the mouthpiece of the Imperial Land Company. Thank God some oases of jokes have been provided: the man who swears his love *by those lofty elms in yonder park* unnerves his sweetheart, *because those trees are slippery elms,* and whenever we get sick of him, we can laugh at the lethally incompetent doctor, the burglar who can't pull open the bedside drawer because humidity has warped it, the scolding woman, the effete woman, the spendthrift, the watermelon-stealing Negro,* the grasping proprietor of the "Jew store." Don't worry; I promise that these jokes will never get racy; you're on Northside, where we are or pretend to be as prudish as the characters in *The Winning of Barbara Worth,* since *no desert is a fit place for an idle or dissolute man.* Meanwhile, pure Colorado water, magnificent water, I mean, the Nile of America, enters Imperial's ditch-veins and percolates through the fields, nourishing cantaloupes, onions, date trees, grapefruits, alfalfa-heavens; it's a bit more turbid now, more saline with the wastes of those transactions; but other ditches playing kidneys' parts permit lucky Imperial to urinate endlessly, infinitely, I mean, right into the New River and the Whitewater and the Alamo, thence into the Salton Sea, whose salinity was three thousand three hundred fifty parts per million in 1905; in 1931 Mr. Otis B. Tout confided to his readers: *It is a surprise to many people today to find the waters of Salton Sea drinkable, although brackish;* in 1950 the salt content, now equalling that of ocean water, was almost ten times higher than the 1905 figure; in 1974, eleven and a half times greater; in 2001 it was nearly fourteen times more.

Excuse me, but you're not against pissing, are you? What the Regional Water Control Board's engineer, Jose Angel, said to me about the Salton Sea has already been accepted without reservation: *What can we do? Because fertilizers have a legitimate agricultural use.*—Moreover, I quote from the Executive Summary Report of the Colorado River Basin Salinity Control Forum (1984): *The Forum finds no reason to recommend changes in the numeric salinity criteria at the three lower main stem stations.*

Speaking of legitimate agriculture, the Colorado River may not be quite as mountain-pure as they say, but, as might be expected, the *Imperial Press and Farmer* offers reasons why that is actually advantageous: *The waters of the Colorado river carry a very large amount of commercial fertilizers . . . a tract of land irrigated during the season with water enough to cover the ground three feet deep would receive fertilizers to the value of over $10 per acre.*

If only those complainers down in Mexicali would see it that way! Salt's a fertilizer, too, isn't it?

*"The baseball craze has reached the negro population of the South to such an extent that it seriously interferes with their value as laborers during the season of picking cotton."

SALT CONTENT OF COLORADO RIVER WATER AT THE CALIFORNIA-MEXICO BORDER

Imperial Dam (constructed in 1938) is the last diversion site in the U.S.A. Morelos Dam (built in the middle of the century) is the first diversion site in Mexico. The greater salinity at Morelos results from what we euphemistically call "irrigation returns." The peculiar dip in salinity for 1963 may be the result of my placing it in the wrong column; I am guessing at Morelos Dam since the study is Mexican.

Years	*Imperial Dam*	*Morelos Dam*
1902	400 parts per million.[a]	
1932	600 ppm[b]	
1951–60	770 ppm	
1961–62	844 ppm	2110 ppm
1963		800 ppm[b]
1966	702 ppm	
1974	861 milligrams per liter	?? (4,000–5,000 mg/l "after the last Mexican diversion")
1984	879 mg/l	
1990	775 mg/l	910 mg/l
1995		1050 ppm[b]
2001	760 mg/l	921 mg/l

Note: 1 ppm approx. = 1 mg/l

[a]Imperial Dam was not built yet. Exact location not indicated in source text.
[b]Exact location not indicated in source text.

Sources: Colorado River Board of California (1951–62); Morton (1977; 1966 data); Philip L. Fradkin (1974); Colorado River Basin Salinity Control Forum (1984); Gerardo García Saillé et al (1990, 2001); Francisco Raul Venegas Cardoso (all other dates).

Again the word *irrelevant* blows across Imperial to me; my own time, the time they pretended they were doing it all for, could not have mattered to those pioneers as much as they pretended; the future they built for was their own; and in their now bygone time they, the Colorado River's self-adopted children, could never suckle their mother dry. Just as Salton City spreads out in the sand, each house, boarded up or not, comprising a single grain of cosmic dust in the universe, they themselves remained atoms in desert emptiness. What would they have made of Salton City? At Riviera Keys I tread on crusts of salt and dead fish; I observe an egret brooding on one leg, a garlicky stench of decomposition. This part of Salton City, like the others, is still and grey, the stench interrupted only occasionally by bird-cries.

What do you do for fun?

Ride around on my dirtbike, replies the fourteen-year-old.

Does the smell bother you?

We're used to it, he says, as proudly as anyone. Besides, I don't never go down there.

Irrelevant! Don't tanneries likewise stink? Reclamation justifies such inconveniences. *The green things growing are improving every shining hour, and making the farmer's heart glad . . .* writes Judge Farr. *The nights are always cool, affording restful sleep, while the sleeper dreams of his rapidly ripening fruit and their early arrival in the markets to catch the top prices ahead of other competitors in less favorable regions.*

THE COLORADO'S MOUTH (1775, 1796, 1827, 1845, 1895, 1903, 1910, 1925, 1950, 2002)

Passing the wrecking yard whose cars are the color of the desert earth, I leave Mexicali to the north of me. Stackyards, failed restaurants, propane trailers and tire fences decay infinitesimally upon this blank flat red desert land. A hand-painted sign announces that CARNE ASADA will be available in 100 Meters. But it isn't. Ten kilometers from San Luis Río Colorado, I see lush green fields of sugarbeets, water spewing silvery out of a pipe's throat, spilling luxuriously on the ground. The way that Mexican children play around open water emblematizes for me Imperial at its best: Water comes, and there is life, laughter. And I continue east. Here's a whole family bathing in an irrigation ditch beneath a pump of cold water. (Pests, said a Mexican rancher. Sometimes they leave broken bottles around. Then I fence it off.) Imperial grows dry again now. Here's the yellow bridge over the bush-lined Río Colorado, which seems to be paralleled by a canal. I cross the bridge and pass out of Imperial. Through the rearview mirror, I see that thin but fairly deep snake of a river turning south, toward the Golfo Santa Clara, for which I now find a sign. This way! Here's a cross, a concrete-lined irrigation ditch and then a roadside shrine for another accident victim, a silver-blue mirage in the black road, an ocher irrigation channel captioned by a beer bottle which glints by the side of the road as brightly as any flare. Here comes a field of something dark green-grey, then a tiny American-style field of alfalfa crowned by neatly staggered emerald bales. An unfinished (still roofless), turquoise-painted homestead secluded within a grove of carefully planted young palm trees makes me wonder what it would be like to live here; then the paved road becomes dirt, and the dirt gets too rough for the rental car. The Gulf may be this way, but all I can see is red dirt at fieldside, then a garbage dump, a green-choked ravine, a wide, white-sanded canyon.—Where's the Colorado?—Farther west, I suppose, past these old stoves and refrigerators and smoke trees, this toilet paper spotted yellow and brown, these paper plates. Everything has been too thoroughly sun-dried to stink very much. I turn around, re-encountering those black-burned palm trees with ornate fronds, that swaggering-looking scarecrow in a cowboy hat. Here stands a family in roadside shade, the children hooking up their shirts to expose their bellies to coolness, the wrinkled old mother staring fixedly across the road into nothingness. And the road goes on into San Luis Río Colorado, a hot town, an Imperial town, "a colorless town with a growing number of *maquiladoras,*" a town which feels wider and lower than Mexicali.

Here at the border the Colorado comes green-grey through a narrow gap in the wall, which must be as high as at Mexicali but seems less impressive; the boys in baseball caps and the tattooed boys make the snake and flow over it while the white Bronco idles on the Arizona side, its Border Patrolman waiting for them to come close enough for him to roll down his window, stick his hand out of the air-conditioning, and gesture them back into Mexican Imperial; and they obey; it was all in fun. That is on the north side of this uneven little bridge under which the Colorado flows. On the south side there's a narrow reed-grown dirt path alongside hanging laundry. And the Río Colorado runs by, narrow but deep, maybe even chest-deep; I don't believe I could jump over this river, not quite. What does my 1910 *Britannica* say about this spot? *From the Black Canyon to the sea the Colorado normally flows through a desert-like basin, to the west of which, in Mexico, is . . . Laguna Salada . . . which is frequently partially flooded . . . by the delta waters of the Colorado.* Every time I've seen Laguna Salada, it's been as dry as a bone. Well, let's be fair; even back at the end of the nineteenth century, water-holes might suddenly go dry . . . *Of the total length of the Colorado, about 2200 miles, 500 miles or more from the mouth are navigable by light steamers* . . . From here to the Colorado's mouth is about a hundred miles. A light steamer might still navigate this creek, a toy one pulled by a string.

FLOW OF THE COLORADO RIVER AT YUMA

Years	*Flow Volume (in million acre-feet)*
1909	26
1934	4

"The long-term average virgin flow of the river is approximately 15 million acre-feet per year."

Sources: Mary Montgomery (1943); The California Water Atlas (1979).

In 1775, the de Anza Expedition forded the Colorado near its confluence with the Gila and assessed its width *at some three or four hundred yards, and this at a time* *when the water is at its lowest, for when the river rises it is leagues wide.*[*] On their return in the following spring, they crossed at a different spot a few leagues away and estimated a width of about a hundred yards. In 1796, Governor Arrillaga found the Colorado unimpressive, *but this was undoubtedly due to its being the dry season . . . From the mouth until it enters full sea, it has considerable breadth.* In 1845, Colonel Cave Johnson Couts arrived in Yuma, where he discovered the river to be *about 200 yards wide but full of little sand islands & c.* In 1925 a traveller very appropriately named Frank Waters took the steamer from El Mayor, whose location I found marked by a trailer park, but whose steamers, landings, indeed whose *river* seemed just about bygone on the day in 2002 when I took the highway south from Mexicali, down past another lost town called La Bomba,[†] and into the Gulf. Frank Waters details the surprisingly swift current of the Río Colorado, the willows, lagoons and herons, the chocolate-colored water-windings which enter the Sea of Cortés, he claims at two hundred thousand feet per second. (A man who'd worked for the Bureau of Reclamation from 1948 to 1950 told me: It's all spread out at the Gulf, and it's kinda uninteresting. Swamp.)

Waters's memoir was reprinted in 1984, at which time he added a preface remarking (in exaggeration, but not by far) that ever since 1961, "not one drop" of the Colorado has reached the Gulf.

I stare from the little bridge in San Luis.—Is this really the Colorado?

Shrugging, a man assures me that it is.

And the retired Reclamation man said: There was more water once, yeah.

Here's another road to the Gulf. This one starts in the center of downtown and boasts a larger sign. Therefore the road will be better. My landmarks: goats, flatlands, tire-fences and unlined canals. An orchard of palm so thick and low it's really a thicket beguiles me; I've never seen any such thing on the American side. But this corroded schoolbus with the lean-to atached could be in Slab City. Someone has written **$ $** and **FOR SALE** on a wall next to the Bar Monalisa. Time to bisect another cement-lined canal. (James O. Pattie, 1827: *We continued to float slowly downwards, trapping beavers on our way almost as fast as we could wish . . . The river at this point is remarkably circuitous, and has a great number of islands . . .*) Finally I see a pencil-line, brighter and whiter than sky-blue, divorcing me from the west's blue mountains. *That* must be the Colorado. The green-pocked sand-plain, which in Frank Waters's time was a tule marsh screeching with birds, begins to tilt just slightly downward, and the mountains take on the hazy look of a coast observed

*In 1827, James O. Pattie found that that "Red river . . . is between two and three hundred yards wide, a deep bold stream, and the water at this point," where it meets the Gila, "entirely clear."

†In a guidebook from 1958, El Mayor still clings to life. From Mexicali to that hive is 42.2 miles; from Mexicali to La Bamba (alternate spelling) is 67.4 miles.

from the sea. A white plain bearing that widening web of water, well, it doesn't seem so bad; as far as I can tell, several drops of the Colorado are still reaching the sea. (John C. Van Dyke, 1903: *After the river crosses the border-line of Mexico it grows broader and flatter than ever. And still the color seems to deepen. For all its suggestion of blood it is not an unlovely color . . . And now at the full and the change of the moon, when the Gulf waters come in like a tidal wave, and the waters of the north meet the waters of the south, there is a mighty conflict of opposing forces . . . The red river rushes under, the blue tide rushes over.*) Oh, no, now I see; that's Santa Clara Slough, where Arizona's lethal brine comes to rest. (John Wesley Powell, 1895: *A million cascade brooks unite to form half a hundred rivers beset with cataracts; half a hundred roaring rivers unite to form the Colorado, which rolls, a mad, turbid stream, into the Gulf of California.* Philip L. Fradkin, 1981: *To follow the river from Morelos Dam to the gulf is a tricky business. First it is there, then it isn't, then it is, then it isn't. Its presence depends on when the toilet is being flushed.*) A woman and child sit silently by their overheated car, whose hood is open; steam comes out. Ahead I see a widening delta braided with ankle-deep streams, and then the Sea of Cortés itself, reddish-grey and thick; much of it is actually mud; the tide must be out.

The town of Golfo Santa Clara was literally built on sand. White-blossoming trees, palms and sea-coolness soften everything. It must be at least fifteen degrees colder here than San Luis Rey. Mexican and American families sit happily together on the beach, calling to their children who are splashing in the sea. As for the Colorado, it's lost in the mud, like the fish-heads and stingray skins, the rotting jellyfishes, the truckloads of teenagers speeding, splashing and exulting in the ooze. Water is infinite. Water is here.

"AND IN MATERIAL ADVANTAGES THEY ARE ALREADY VERY WELL SUPPLIED"

WATER IS HERE. THE DESERT DISAPPEARS. And now it's just like the tale of Jack and the Beanstalk! Plant the seed, and Imperial bursts out of the cracked desert, shoots upward with an audible whirr, and explodes into greenness! On the outskirts of Indio, *where two years ago not a living sprig could be found, ripe Thompson's seedless grapes are now being gathered and shipped to Los Angeles.* Everything and everyone comes to life in Imperial! Mrs. Leroy Holt is one of that zone's very first white women; she arrives by stagecoach to find a postal service already in operation; delivery means hanging up the mailbag at Fifteen Mile Tree. Sometimes dust storms blow so hard that no one can eat. *I had kept the children in bed fully dressed so if the tent-house should blow down they would be properly clothed . . . Why did we stay? We loved the days that were not windy and dusty; we loved the bigness of our surround-*

ings. In other words, her Imperial was infinite.—The lead story for Saturday, August 2, 1902, reports (with prudent belatedness, given the infant mortality rate of those days), that Miss Ruth Reed, the first child to be born in Imperial city, came into the world last September. *A half-tone portrait of Miss Reed,* who looks plump, adorable, etcetera, as she gazes out at us from a creased black lozenge, *is herewith presented to the readers of the Press. It shows a healthy child. In fact, it is well known that climates similar to that found in Imperial always develop very healthy children, who rarely need the services of the physician.* In 1904 they stake out Holtville, and water arrives in Brawley. El Centro will be founded next year. In 1905 there are close to ten thousand people in the Imperial Valley; by 1910 there will be twice that many. In 2000, Imperial County alone will contain more than a hundred and forty-two thousand souls.

"And in material advantages they are already well supplied. Here," said Mr. Atwood, as he pulled a crisp five-dollar note from his purse, "is a bill issued by the First National Bank of Imperial—a national bank away out in the center of the Colorado desert."

IRRELEVANT!

1902 was the year when Mr. Atwood pulled that crisp five-dollar note from his purse. The engineer who was bringing the water to Imperial later recalled: *We started out then, about the first of March 1902, with our bonds all gone, our mortgages depleted, not a dollar in the treasury, and individually so deeply in debt . . . that it was exceedingly doubtful whether we would ever be able to pull out.* Irrelevant! **WATER IS HERE**. By 1904 so were seven thousand people.

Then what? Imperial County tears itself out of San Diego's womb; tent cities become brick towns with churches and libraries; railroad tracks and electric lines come, then telephones; emerald alfalfa-squares (not to mention barley and corn) push back the desert; El Centro beats out Imperial to become the county seat. (What about our new Salton Sea? Irrelevant! An expert named Mr. Grunsky testifies to the Senate that it will be gone in twelve to fifteen years *if there were no resupply.*) **WATER IS HERE**. In 1910 parts of the Yuma Indian Reservation get opened up to white settlement.

Do you want to know how the American Imperial of those days portrayed itself? Those of you in so great a rush to get back to irrigating your fields that you have no time to read *The Winning of Barbara Worth* may now take heart: In this year of grace 1915, the grand Barbara Worth Hotel has just opened, with every important character painted in oils on the walls of the lobby. I now telegraph you the highlights, as abstracted from a newspaper article by Otis B. Tout: *Trade is leading Culture, a beautiful young woman . . . Miss Sawyer, a school teacher of Meloland, represents*

Culture . . . In the next "pendant" picture primitive life of the first inhabitants is described. The faithful Mexican Pablo and Jose, the Indian, are the chief characters in this sketch. To get the correct expression on their faces the artists made a trip of several days' duration into Mexico to see exactly how these same Mexicans and Indians live today . . . And how *do* they live today? Not like the folks in Barbara Worth's circle, it would seem. *The first picture on the south wall of the lobby will be that of the "Financial Genius," without which the Valley would have remained the land of nothing. Here W. F. Holt is shown as the Jefferson Worth of the story.* Oh, yes, and *merged into the green luxury of developed plenty there stands the maiden of the story, Barbara Worth. Miss Marjorie Paris, daughter of Mr. and Mrs. C. E. Paris of El Centro, posed for this scene. She is garbed in simple white. She rests against a bale of cotton.*

In 1911, the Imperial Irrigation District comes into being. In 1913, Mr. R. S. Smith of Silsbee wins first prize—a silver loving cup and forty dollars cash money—for his display of Hemskirk apricots. In 1918, Mr. John Baker advises us that *paved, well lighted streets will be the culmination of the Commercial Club's dream and efforts in the very near future.* A photograph's caption reads: "W. F. Holt Looks into the Future with the Direct Gaze of the Confident Man." It is W. F. Holt who said: *I can't help believing in people . . . I have never been cheated out of a dollar in my life . . . I've found that the way to get your money is to give a man a chance to pay you.*

ONE MORE ESSAY (A VERY SHORT ONE) ON THE INFINITE

Could it be that W. F. Holt is the American exemplar of this period? Ten years later, in the Soviet Union, our hero will be the Stakhanovite miner, farmer or factory worker who overfulfills his production quota by some superhuman multiple of your capacity and mine. Imperial smilingly murmurs that water and soil will do the same for us, and we can keep the gains for ourselves! *I have never been cheated out of a dollar in my life.* And I never will be, because Imperial's promise is infinite. **WATER IS HERE**. *One of the local men,* continues John Baker, *claims to have made a thousand dollars an acre from the growing of cucumbers* . . . If you're looked up to in Imperial, they'll say of you: *His farm has been highly improved.* They'll say: *He made a success through his own efforts.* They'll say: *He sold out at a fancy price.*

The entertainments of this epoch were in keeping with its aspirations. I read of Joseph Estudillo, who opened Calexico's first drugstore; he *often entertained crowds by shooting dimes tossed in the air.* Here's a caption in Otis B. Tout's history: **A Ten Dollar Bill on the End of a Greased Pole That Hung Over a Canal Furnished Much Amusement**. Herein dangles Imperial's ultimate metaphor.

Imperial is hot freeways and the snapped off stumps in the Salton Sea. Imperial is smoke trees between which stretch cradles of spiderwebs; Imperial's nothing but that algae'd ditch, the Colorado River. *We need have no fear that our lands will not become better and better as the years go by.* Toss another dime in the air! And now a train comes humming through! I count four yellow locomotives, then container cars loaded with immense crates commercially colored and marked. *And in material advantages they are already well supplied. He sold out at a fancy price.*

Chapter 7

THE OTHER SIDE OF THE DITCH

(1519–2005)

> No two people will agree on what makes a perfect vacation, but it's fun and helpful to know what others think.
>
> —*Fodor's Mexico, 1992*

The way that the man in the white, white dress shirt leads each stripper by the hand to gallantly escort her onto stage (the Chinese-pigtailed cocktail waitress, her white blouse glowing in the ultraviolet strobe, now sings happily along while the waiter catches our heroine's clothes one by one as she dances them off, both he and the waitress clapping for her not only encouragingly but exuberantly); the way that the powerless, in-and-out-of-prison drunk in a Mexicali park sincerely, sweetly invites me: You ever have any problem, you ask for me! and the grand way that the roadmender in the desert flags down my car; the way that when I promptly submit he's satisfied to wave me on with an ornately personal gesture; the old people who actually remember their muncipal history and are *proud* of it, the slogans of tire shops and restaurants painted in black or white letters on yellow- or blue-painted brick; the greater chaos and color of Southside, the multitudes on the sidewalks, the shoeshine boys and watermelon hawkers, the higher level of unevenness and humanness, the dirt, the formal Latin courtesy, the people peering out windows, the *life;* this is Mexico. *(The informal labor sector has grown nationwide,* writes Professor Ramón Eduardo Ruiz. *Child labor can be seen everywhere* . . . And in material advantages they are already well supplied. *Children of both sexes, no more than toddlers, drop out of school . . . and, when they reach adulthood, end up doing unskilled labor at low pay . . . American policy, as well as the exploding global economy, exacerbates these conditions.)* Far away across the twilit fields of San Luis Río Colorado there's a line of white lights, a night of whirling rattles, chants and honking horns, all from pickup trucks; everyone's so happy; their team's won. In Calexico late at night one might see a handful of Mexican men running, pursued by the screaming white vehicles of the Border Patrol. More often there will be blankness. Yes, Southside's where the life is; Northside's where the money is; I've never been cheated out of a dollar in my life.

Northsider born and bred, I actually do love my country, or at least the country that it wishes and occasionally even tries to be; besides, I've on occasion found, alone and at night in Southside, that I had no friends; I decline to claim that Mexico is "better." It was in Southside, after all, that hundreds of vigilantes, mistaking three undercover police agents for childnappers, beat them with pipes. Although they called for backup, their colleagues failed to arrive for three hours and thirty-five minutes, by which time two of them had been burned alive.—Again, on the very last night I spent in Mexicali for this book, I saw a pimp, stern and burly father that he was, staring down a desperate girl with a gruesome face who stood ten paces away; she pleaded with me to take her. Sorrowing for her with all my heart, I smiled at her, wished her goodnight and walked to the United States to use a pay phone. Forty minutes later, on my return to Mexico, there stood the pimp with another much younger girl, in fact a child. Across the street, two bored policewomen chatted; one kept scratching her buttocks. And the child looked me full in the face with fear in her eyes, trying to appear hardened and available; she did the same with the next man and the next, perfecting what Northside vice cops would have called her "prostitution stroll," while the pimp walked sometimes ahead and sometimes behind her. At the corner they were level, and the last I saw of them, he was angrily twisting her shoulder.

Steinbeck once wrote: *It is said so often in such ignorance that Mexicans are contented, happy people. "They don't want anything." This, of course, is not a description of the happiness of Mexicans, but of the unhappiness of the person who says it.*—He is right. And now let me quote to you the elegantly middle-aged woman at Condominios Montealbán whose son's life was going dangerously downhill, which might have been why she appeared no happier than one of Steinbeck's Americans as she stood in the doorway of her diabolically hot kitchen (it was nine-o'-clock at night, and the outside temperature had now ducked below a hundred); about the United States she said to me: You're not free there. It's terrible. You have to work all day, then sleep, then work again. Here we're free. Over there they live like robots.

She preferred to dwell in the stench of the Río Nuevo.

THE OTHER SIDE OF THE DITCH

Mexicali has always been the antithesis of Calexico. The parable runs that once upon a time, the city fathers of Calexico, namely George Chaffey and his son Andrew, prohibited alcohol, and thereby brought into being Mexicali, where *the very first place of business* (recalls Otis B. Tout) *was a plank set up under a mesquite tree, where mescal and tequila were dispensed at so much per drink.* To me there has always been something rather profound about this story. Here are Northside and Southside separated by a ten-foot-wide international ditch; in Northside we cannot drink, but on the other side of that ditch a Mexican, holding up his dipper there beneath the mesquite tree. What can poor George Chaffey do? Annex part of Mexico? But we already did that in 1846, and all that happened then and all that would happen now is that at the extremity of our reach, there the border will run, its far side offering what we forbid. By 1909 the first gaming-house has officially opened in Mexicali; no doubt there was already a plank beneath a tree to build on. In 2003, cocaine happens to be illegal in Calexico, so it's widely available in Mexicali. They frown on prostitution here, so come and get it there.

In 1915 California outlaws horseracing and prostitution. Come and get it down here. That very year, H. M. House informs the Chief Engineer: *The* Mexican *Collector states that a town is to be started at Algodones, the subdividing to be started tomorrow.* What sort of place will it be? I wonder. W. H. Holabird can imagine. He writes the United States Collector of Customs: *I greatly deplore this effort to start a town, because it has but one purpose and that is to sell liquor to the lawless element who can not obtain it in Yuma, nor in other California towns. I shall not build a bridge* to Algodones *across the canal, but I am powerless to prevent them if they wish to do it in Mexico.* And who might *they* be? W. J. Smith, Deputy Collector and Inspector of Andrade: *I understand a Mr. Ingraham of Yuma will start to build a saloon during next week.*

In 1917, California forbids pro boxing and dance halls. Where might we find those? In 1919, the Volstead Act prohibits liquor in the United States. *We need have no fear that our lands will not become better and better as the years go by.* "Sunny Jim" Cofforth now controls the racing in Tijuana. Carl Withington from Bakersfield operates the Mexicali Brewery. That Mexican under the mesquite tree works for *him.*

In 1920, the Imperial County Board of Supervisors publishes this incitement to make a home on our side of the ditch: *Calexico is one of the liveliest cities of its size in the southwest. It has four strong banks, large, well-stocked mercantile concerns, modern cotton gins, . . . and is a railroad center . . . Calexico has no saloons and the morality is high.* Meanwhile we learn that *Mexicali's cabarets and bars catered to farmers and ranchers of the Imperial Valley of California, the most notorious among them being the Southern Club, the Imperial Cabaret, the Black Cat, and the Tecolote Bar, a gambling casino and brothel where floor shows went on all night.*

One midnight in 1925 at the Tecate crossing, the Deputy Collector in Charge spies *two Mexicans in a tent on the Mexican side of the Line just west of the gate, selling liquor. I respectfully recommend that two Customs officers be stationed at Jacumba at the earliest date possible.*

Every now and then, Northsiders who take the other side of the ditch for granted get punished, as in the case of Dawn Marie Wilson, who buys innocuous prescription drugs from a Tijuana pharmacy without a Mexican doctor's prescription. The year is 2003. While easy sex and cheap cocaine continue to comprise much of Southside's allure, our forty-nine-year-old American protagonist's purpose has become ever more emblematic. In Mexicali, José López from Jalisco awaits his own customers beside the border fence: Some may be truckers in search of strip clubs, but many are elderly Northsiders who can't afford to buy their arthritis medication in their hometowns. Old men drive across the line to Algodones to buy Viagra at half the price; widows in Coachella form carpools to pick up Southside's generic drugs once a month. By the time Dawn Marie Wilson sets out to stock up on her anti-seizure medication, the price differential has become less advantageous than formerly. The way one elderly Coachella Valley resident described it to me, the other side of the ditch was less an *attraction* than a *secondary convenience.*—John used to go down to Yuma to a gun show, she said. Then we used to go to San Luis because it was so much cheaper. I take some kind of blood-pressure medicine but it isn't hardly worth it unless you know someone who's already going.—Indeed, one San Diego dweller I know who buys Tijuana pharmaceuticals for her friends reports that the counter cost per drug is virtually the same in Northside and Southside; the savings derive from the fact that in Southside nobody has to pay a doctor first.

And so the pharmacist happily sells Dawn Marie Wilson her pills, this being the other side of the ditch, after all, but in Ensenada the police stop her on the street, search her backpack, perhaps because she was involved in a small traffic accident the day before, and then she's awarded a five-year prison sentence at Ojos Negros. In the end, thanks to Representative Bob Filner, past whose slogans I sometimes wander in El Centro, she serves a mere seventeen months, followed by three months more in a Northside prison. American authorities, needless to say, employ the occasion to issue stern warnings about the dangers of flouting the law (our law) on the other side of the ditch.

In 1931, Otis B. Tout is constrained to write: *Thousands of automobiles cross the line every day,* and at one time it was just that, literally a line. I open another album in the Archivo Histórico and see the San Diego Cafe in Calexico with its eleven arches (the edifice remains, but now it's something else), then comes an octagonal kiosk in the middle of the street (also long gone), and under so many wires, like those within a piano, three squarish automobiles attend in a line, and behind them a dotted black line has been inked upon the photograph: the border. A queue of pedestrians waits to cross. The caption reads: Mexicali: Visto de Calexico. Hacia el Suroeste. (What is a border? Definitions vary. An old farmer told me that the C & M Ranch, now called the Bravo Ranch, used to straddle both sides of the border, but those days departed; we changed the definition.) *Thousands of automobiles cross the line every day,* writes Otis B. Tout, *and places of business in Mexicali enjoy an enormous patronage. The cafes, cantinas and palaces of chance offer a glamour of excitement.*

(Here's a grey old photo of a corner-building whose arched overhang shades its sidewalk: the sign reads **MEXICALI CABARET**.) One may encounter underworld types in Southside. *The strict control of undesirables by the Mexican authorities, however, is efficient,* and if you believe that last you'll believe anything.

What *does* poor George Chaffey do about it all? What can he do? (In his way this Canadian-born engineer is benevolent; he's an idealist, not to mention a busy real estate man; his passion is to improve the desert for the benefit of unborn me. He's the one who dreamed up the name "Imperial Valley.") I'd suppose he closes his eyes.

In Calexico there was a certain hotel on Fourth Street where I always stayed when I was writing about *pollos* and coyotes. Whenever I'd ask the proprietor how he was, he'd bitterly reply: I'm here.

We need some more toilet paper, I said.

Bang-bang paper, huh? I'll get you some. I don't want you thinkin' this place is bad. This place ain't so bad.

No, it's not bad.

He asked me where I'd go when I went across the border that night and I told him the Thirteen Negro (red and yellow lights flashing down on the metal dance floor, half-squeezed limes on the sticky table, tall men leaning against the dancers when they dance; in between dances, the women, most of whom are barelegged and some of whom are very bare, sit in dark-seeming clothes all in a row, many with lovely expressions on their faces simply because they are so young and beautiful that unloveliness would be an effort; they sport big buttocks and spread fat thighs; they're bored but docile, and the men gaze at them in longing as bright against that darkness as the fresh bluish-green cuttings in alfalfa fields), and the hotel proprietor said in amazement: What do you want to go to some nigger place for?

I didn't know whether to answer that I had nothing against nigger places or that the Thirteen Negro wasn't a nigger place; mainly I was astonished that this man did not know the Thirteen Negro at all, which meant that his world did not extend for even seven blocks, the last three of which lay south of the line. And he derived so much of his living from the other side of the ditch!

This place ain't so bad, he repeated almost apologetically. It's actually kinda funny really.—And I could see that he was proud of his hotel.

I got nothing against Mexicans, said an old lady outside the Brawley Market. It's just that there's nothing down there.

It had been ten or twenty years since she'd visited the other side of the ditch; she'd forgotten exactly how long.

There's nothing down there. What a revealing way of putting it! In my *National Geographic* optical disks containing California maps, Mexicali has been, doubtless for commercial reasons, so blanked out as to only half-exist. The same goes for Tijuana in my *Thomas Guide* to San Diego. Well, after all, is it so sinister that Y should fail to be wholeheartedly represented in a guide to X? And yet, San Diego would have been better defined, could we have appreciated its street-patterns in relation to those of the neighbor on the other side of the ditch. Indeed, what does this will to blank out Mexico say about us?

"NOW THEY GOT THE HUMVEES WITH THE GUNS MOUNTED ON THEM"

It was in June, when the desert ironwood's purple blooms were on the way to perishing, that through the recommendation of the Pioneers Museum I met that ancient man from Heber (his memory was the best of any in that cohort, they said), and I was hoping and halfway expecting many stories of Imperial then and now, not just the Imperial of *he sold out at a fancy price,* but the other side of the ditch, too. He said to me: In general, I think the border is too open. I don't know why our country is just doing lip service. Now I hear the people smugglers are getting so brazen, now they got the Humvees with the guns mounted on them. They got laws on the books and they're not being enforced.

He was a proud old patrician of Imperial, straight and narrow like George Chaffey. His profile was what a nineteenth-century capitalist-worshipper would have called Roman, chiseled; I forget whether he had the high forehead. So he thought that the border was too open, and at that moment our government was keeping seven or eight thousand agents across twenty-one sectors. Well, he had a point; Mexicans did get through. (An arrested *pollo* smiles at me with crooked-lipped pride; he may have gotten caught, but at least some gringo with a camera wants to take his picture; he's made the big time.)

That Heber man was born here, and he knew as much about Southside as the hotel proprietor. He disliked me more every minute, I suppose because he could smell my immorality. (I am actually not an entirely bad fellow in my way.) Soon he was instructing me neither to use his name nor quote him on anything, because this interview was not an interview, only background information; and he kept warning his contemporary, a cheery old farmer named Eugene Dahm, to be more careful in my hearing. I inquired of the Heber pioneer regarding the Chinese tunnels in Mexicali, about which every soul in Mexicali I ever questioned possessed some myth or rumor, and in annoyance he said he'd never heard any such nonsense. I asked about the coyote route over Signal Mountain and he informed me that he'd never wasted his time on that sort of business. Well, he had been busy with his Northside life.

Back after the war, though, we had a whole lot of wetbacks, said Eugene Dahm, trying to be helpful. Had a whole lot of guys, just give 'em a sack and let 'em pick cotton or sugar beets. Nowadays, if they come into the field and find a wet, they can fine you a thousand dollars. But they still hide out.

When he says "wet," I don't want you to write that down, warned the pioneer from Heber. "Wet" or "wetback" used to be a very common figure of speech. It's not racist. This is all just background.

I asked Eugene Dahm what he remembered about the other side of the ditch and he said: They had the best restaurants in the valley, both Mexican and Chinese. Alley Nineteen was a great one. Everybody had a filet mignon. They took about any part of the cow, wrapped it in bacon and called it filet mignon for two dollars. What's the name of the place down there where you can still bet on the horses? They had some real nice nightclubs until, oh, about 1955. They had good floor shows and then after 1955 they didn't seem to care if we came there.

But the old pioneer from Heber disgustedly interjected: The whole place was loose, shot through with *mordida*. Say you were eighteen, and you got served beer.

That does sound different, all right, I said.

Grimly he explained: When the King of Spain sent his conquistadors over here, every man expected to live like a king and skim off the top. Down there it's accepted. But this is just background information. Don't quote me on any of this.

Ignoring him, Eugene Dahm sighed dreamily: The night we graduated from Brawley High we went down to Mexicali . . .

"A TOTALLY NEEDLESS AND SENSELESS ACT"

A high-wheeled white carriage waits in front of a long house's white fence, suspended between white street and white sky. Every white spot, every place leached out by time and light, can be construed, if we want it to, as a zone of potential, not for the future, since that's come and gone, but for vision itself, without which the dead past has no value anyway. Crossing the line on a hundred-degree afternoon in June 2002, the pair of international turnstiles clinking musically overhead as they always do, I drain my lemonade, which is, like Mexico, so sweet, tart, dirty and vibrantly fresh. An old man waits patiently until I have finished; then he takes my paper cup from the trash. He goes to the lemonade vendor, negotiates a lower price, and the last I see of him he is drinking slowly and happily out of my cup. From here it's not far to the Archivo Histórico, where I find myself at ditch's edge again, gazing across the line at a faded photograph of a partially shadow-faced woman in white who is white-kneed, with dark-haired bangs above her white Mexican face;

beautiful, now eaten by time, she holds a parasol which blurs itself like a wheel-spoke, while two men in white suits and white hats stand beside her, the closest with his hand on his hip. Behind them looms their half-built house, and a peon bends over a wheelbarrow. If that lady is still alive, she must be a hundred. When she was twenty-five, that border between us was just a ditch. Now it has become a wall; and I'm separated from her not only by sunburned metal panels but also by time.

When anyone could jump across that ditch in either direction, was the estrangement between American and Mexican Imperial any less? In the beginning, of course, there was only the desert; then came human beings, and once they'd drawn that border between them, first administratively, subdividing that region of Mexico into Upper and Lower California, then violently, scoring Upper California away from Mexico to aggrandize the United States according to the desires of Texas slaveholders and their kin, each side became progressively more articulated into opposition toward the other. One sees that so evidently from Signal Mountain: It's green on the American side, greyish-tan on the Mexican. And yet the waves of transnational capital don't care about that; they only want to buy low and sell high, so like rivers they inevitably undercut their own sandy banks, buying low and then lower in Mexico, until their nourishing outwash of money stimulates local development, which gradually raises prices. That's the theory, anyhow.

From the very beginning, Northside has always pretended that it extends forever, to the very end of Imperial. In the seaside resorts of San Felipe and Santa Clara, many of the signs are in English, the prices in dollars. In a 1906 number of *Out West* magazine (**The Nation Back of Us, the World in Front**), I find an advertisement for *desirable tracts of from 100 to 100,000 acres* as far south as Sinaloa; their exclusive concessionaires operate out of not Mexico City, as a naive believer in national sovereignty might have expected, but Los Angeles.

Capitalist theory might be correct. Mexicali is cleaner and more prosperous than any Congolese or Malagasy city. Since I began going there it's won more parking lots now full of shiny cars. Let's all reserve million-dollar hopes for the Mexicans. Someday they'll be just as rich as us; they'll be us. Then we won't need the ditch.

Outside, right along Southside, says the radio. Yeah, we got a group that just ran across. Twelve bodies. We don't have 'em in sight . . .—And the white Bronco speeds down an alley of walls and fences, palms and streetlights. A man paces in his driveway, watching the officers.

We still don't have 'em in sight . . .

There was always a crossing, said the old pioneer from Heber, and there was free egress and entry for us, for U.S. citizens. We could just walk in and out of Mexico.

And Eugene Dahm added, with just the slightest wink (I liked him better and better): In the thirties, Mexico was open for gambling and you could play roulette and blackjack. But I remember during the war you had to use two-dollar bills because of counterfeits . . .

There was always a crossing; there was free egress and entry for *us* but there was always a crossing; there was a crossing when a van literally packed with *pollos,* people lying on people, twenty-seven of them, drove westward and without lights in the eastbound lane of Interstate 8 until it hit a Ford Explorer head-on, ending the life of that vehicle's driver, a legal U.S. citizen, while simultaneously killing its own driver and four of its passengers. *This was a totally needless and senseless act,* announces Border Patrol Agent Raleigh Leonard for the record. No doubt it would have been needless except for the fact that the Border Patrol had established a checkpoint on the westbound lane. There was always a crossing, but Agent Leonard knew that wasn't and shouldn't be lawful; he had no interest in the other side of the ditch.

"WAVES OF PEOPLE COMING ACROSS"

Near midnight and southeast of Mexicali, children are throwing a balloon back and forth until it finally ghosts over a whitewashed fence and ascends into the full moon beneath which a girl and her boyfriend are sitting on the trunk of a car, their fingers intertwined as they gaze together at the bright canopy of ***HAMBURGUESAS***. Around the corner, in a brightly lit courtyard, a mat imprinted with the likeness of the Virgin of Guadalupe hangs on the wall. And that moon, that orange moon ascends higher and higher into the purple sky; now it's white. Herewith, the other side of the ditch!* Here each store, house or bar feels different; one never knows what the building material will be. In a restaurant, not all tables are finished with the same type of veneer; indeed, not all are even the same shape. (Steinbeck repeats: *"They don't want anything." This is not a description of the happiness of Mexicans, but of the unhappiness of the person who says it.* So if I for my part opine that in Mexico each house "feels different," my God, what does that say about American houses?) The journey from Northside to Southside is a voyage from a grid to a place where streets do not announce their destination. What does that say about American streets? Northside fields are wide, low and emerald; they're vast, rectangular, uniformly colored; some are palm-avenues with mountains or Salton Sea blue between them. Southside fields are pale green with yellow-brown islands and

*The beginning of the other side, I should say. About most of Mexico, including the Mayan woman of clay who gnawed at her knuckles eternally, the idol from Veracruz with the cone-shaped lower lip, this book remains as silent as a mop swimming across marble floors in Mexico City.

sometimes with dikes in the middle. Mexicali's hay bales may be an almost garish yellow, like the signs in the new strip malls. A reddish-brown cornfield, a house walled round by dying plants in flowerpots, the merest dozen cows or so per feedlot, this is Southside agriculture. Sometimes Northside is long green ranches and Southside is sand-duned blankness; sometimes Northside's just a waste studded with boulders, sensors and lights (a white Bronco waits watchfully upon its private dirt road); then comes the wall, with Southside's houses crowding up against it all the way to the hill-horizon. In either case the wall comes slicing through everything, transforming continuum into opposition. Northside and Southside are antipodes; we all agree on that. But the line of workers in those fields, brightly clothed and stooping, oh yes, they could be anywhere in Imperial or out of it; I've seen them picking lettuce way up north in Salinas. People come from Southside to commit what Agent Leonard would call totally needless and senseless acts. They return to Southside to come home.

No habeas corpus in Mexico! cries the angry old pioneer from Heber. But, see, attitudes were different then. People were traditional. They were born in the village and they stayed in the village. They didn't have TVs. We didn't have those waves of people coming across.—Sitting opposite from him in that air-conditioned room of the Pioneers Museum, listening to him deplore the vanishing of traditional people, I remember from an album in the Archivo Histórico del Municipio de Mexicali, where he has never been and never will go, a certain photograph of blackhaired little girls in frilly white dresses and white tights and (in most cases) white shoes; there are seven or eight per row, nineteen girls in all, many with long black braids spilling down their chests, one with a necklace; I see black eyes in white faces, a white wall, a window and doorway behind them. Are they the ones he means when he speaks of traditional people? How many of them crossed the ditch in their nineteen lifetimes? I assume they're all dead now.

As for those *waves of people coming across,* they too have burned an image in the photo-emulsion of my memory: Carlos, Mario, Roberto and the other brothers in that "family" in Niños Héroes Park. Carlos crams his knuckles hard against the side of his chin, leaning forward a little, while beside him the brother in the skullcap gazes at me with his head up and back like a lord's, his eyes cool; when he smiles, raising a clenched fist with the two outermost fingers extended like insect antenna, a boyish joyousness rushes out of him like light, whereas Carlos's best smile is a grimly nervous show of teeth. Neither one of them smiles now. Tonight they're going to try for the other side of the ditch! Beside him, a brother nods out; his hairy arms don't show off their needletracks; in the back row stand Mario and Roberto, and between them a man in a sweat-stained striped shirt; his pallid face and glazed eyes resemble a corpse's. He looks so sad, so ghastly; what's his story?

And how will his story end? He cannot speak English, but through Carlos he tells me that he hopes to enter the service of some American fast food restaurant where his life will be air-conditioned and well-greased with fried sustenance. But he really doesn't look good. If he makes it over the wall tonight, perhaps tomorrow's sun will give him a passport to that stretch of sand in Holtville where forgotten *pollos* lie beneath crosses emblazoned **NOT FORGOTTEN.** Can't he see that? Or does he hate this side of the ditch more than he fears that side? (I have already quoted the migrant worker in Mecca who'd said: *I tell you, Mexico is beautiful but Mexico is tough.*) This restless coming and going of human beings, this hurrying of life into dry desert where it finally sinks without a sign, and this border walled off for the express purpose of denying the undeniable oneness of Imperial, there's many a parable in it all! Perhaps you've heard the tale of the man who got wind of the fact that Death was coming for him, so he set out for faraway Samarkand, where Death would never find him; and if you want to imagine Samarkand, just let yourself see Coachella's ranked lines of date palms with mountains beyond, the sign **SAY IT WITH DATES**, smoke trees squatting on the off-white sand. The journey was wretched and treacherous; the Border Patrol hunted him, but by sunup he was well beyond the wall and in due course he reached Samarkand, where with a clap of a skeleton-hand on his shoulder Death greeted him, saying: How kind of you to remember our appointment in Samarkand!—And here's another parable for you: An old man from Heber, so old that the skeleton must soon take *him* by the shoulder, fears getting drowned by a human wave! What does his inner eye see? Possibly he remembers the Pacific War, where the Japanese launched no-surrender "banzai attacks." He would have been old enough to fight in the Korean War, and maybe he did; maybe he encountered waves of Chinese suicide-volunteers. (Not long ago I visited the Korean War Museum in Dandong, China, just west of the North Korean border. It displayed a photograph of American GI's posing with decapitated Asian heads. I believe it. But that doesn't mean there weren't suicide-volunteers who played against them with equal mercilessness.) Human waves! Many's the time I've observed those encroachments upon my nation's sovereignty. First comes the desert dirt with its few cat-whiskers of grass, then the border wall, graffiti'd and almost too hot to touch, but someone is touching it; a teenaged boy's bare arms lie across the top of it (what's he standing on over there in Southside?) and his head peeps over; he's steady; the heat can hardly touch him; he'll wait and look and wait. As soon as that white Bronco drives away, if it ever does, he'll signal to his friends and then they'll make the snake; with luck they'll slither all the way to Samarkand. *Banzai, banzai!*

Now, do you want to hear about their weapons? At my request, one of the brothers in Carlos's "family" of *pollos* (he's a trifle embarrassed about this; he doesn't wish me to write which one of them he is) strips off his shirt. In the darkness, his muscular block of a body takes on the pallor of a tombstone. I can see the whiteness of his skull-skin beneath the hair he's cropped as close as a soldier's. Then comes neck and gleaming-beaded necklace, each bead as fat as a beetle, and his shoulders as wide as a billboard, the braces of that signboard being of course the arms, which are as hard and swollen with power as any champion's; let's consider the left arm first, for it bears a long shiny scar from the armpit halfway to the elbow; if it were smaller I'd say bullet, but I think I'll say knife; now for the right arm, on which a longhaired woman seductively nestles, and there's another tattoo as well, on the inside of the elbow, but I can see only the perimeter of it so I don't know what it is. Enough; what image does the signboard bear? Comfortably lodged upon that broad back, longhaired, bearded haloed Jesus looks lovingly at me. He wears a heart upon a necklace. His right hand is folded inward upon His breast, like a dead man's, and His closed fingers touch that heart. His left hand is also folded in, but at the wrist it upraises to form a gesture: the thumb vertical, the little finger and its fellow folded against the palm, the two fingers in the middle crossed and jutting high. Jesus wants me to pay attention to Him. Look at Me, he says; look at My heart. Look at My left hand. (Under this sign thou shalt conquer.) Don't you know what it means? Guess what, *amigo*? It's a secret. Maybe I'd be in on it, if I lived on his side of the ditch. (What do you want to go to some nigger place for?) The other side is by definition the secret side, the dark side of the moon. First there was only Imperial. But then we bifurcated it, so that it now contains mysteries without end. Here's another secret, another story whose end only Jesus knows: In the footprinted sand on the Mexican side of the All-American Canal, a thin-woven striped sweater lies trodden and half-buried; it reminds me of the scraps of clothing I once saw at the Choeung Ek killing fields in Cambodia, where by means of guns and iron bars and other convenient tools human beings were converted into flecks of bone and bits of cloth from which the threads grew like crazy grass; even had I never seen Choeung Ek, there would have been something sad to me about this garment, still serviceable, which some agency has flattened into the dirt. What became of its owner? Had he swum across the All-American, wouldn't he have taken it with him? Anyone who abides at this spot must be poor. It's a hot, glaring place, a hostile bit of No Man's Land. Perhaps he came here by day, knew he had to wait until nightfall to make his attempt, got hot and went for a dip, while from the other bank the white Bronco watched without comment. At this place I've so often seen would-be *pollos* in the blue-green water, wet and laughing *(those waves of people coming across)*, only their heads out; their shoes wait at the very edge of the shore, in case they need them quickly; their folded clothes crown the zone of flowering weeds where sand meets water. Then what? It's possible, but unlikely, that the owner of the sweater drowned; along this border only two people die per day. More likely the Mexican police came here by surprise, and either seized him or scared him off. Or—why not wish him the best?—maybe Jesus came along and whisked him right to America. Whatever the case, a poor man got parted from his clothes. *Now I hear the people smugglers are getting so brazen, now they got the Humvees with the guns mounted on them.*

BORDER GIRLS

And so I think I understand why the choreographer Rebeca Hernández once said to me: I'm not Mexican-American. I'm a border girl. A Mexican-American is someone who speaks English and Spanish at the same time. I can be a Mexican in Mexico, perfectly Mexican. I can be, not perfect American in America, but I can pass. I just connect better with Mexicans than with Mexican-Americans. The Virgin of Guadalupe is not European; she's syncretic. My face is syncretic. I'm Indian, African and European. But I'm not one or the other. Even my clothes. Let's see, today I'm wearing this bandage on my wrist, and that's from Mexicali, but the clasp is American. My sandals are Mexican; my shorts are American. My underwear is Mexican, so the size is *chica* instead of petite. My shirt, let's see, where the fuck did I buy this shirt? . . .

Is it true that the Virgin of Guadalupe is "not one or the other"? In 1904, the year of Mexicali's founding, Pope Pius conferred on her shrine the designation of basilica. She'd already been the official protector of New Spain since 1754. But back in 1531, when she first revealed herself to the Aztec (or Mexican as he would have called himself in the pre-Conquest sense of the word) Juan Diego Cuahtaloatzin, some Indians conflated her with their goddess Tonantzin. To them she was dark-skinned; for her they performed the outlawed pagan dances. A book called *The Wonder of Guadalupe,* which naturally never makes any such association, offers the following Northside view of Tonantzin: *A statue of this grim goddess . . . truly conveys the chilling nature of the Aztec mentality. Her head is a combination of loathsome snakes' heads and her garment a mass of writhing serpents . . .* Our Lady of Guadalupe, "She Who Tramples the Serpents," looks in no way serpentine. (And what about her supposed antithesis? One researcher reminds us that *another name for the Virgin Tonantzin is Coatlalopeuh, "she who crushes the serpent's head."*)

When she first appeared to him, Juan Diego thought that she might have been fourteen. Now her image shines forever upon his mantle of ayate fiber. Her eyes are almost closed; her gaze is far-off and sleepy; a gold-bordered, gold-starred mantle of celestial blue enwraps her dark hair and spills down to her ankles; she clasps her hands in prayer and wears the same black cross as the conquistadores. Good

Father Florencia of the Society of Jesus advises all women, rich or poor, to be guided by her in their own deportment, *how they must correct their dress, and what they must forego so that they may give no scandal.* As for Tonantzin, whose name not coincidentally means "Our Mother" and upon whose ruined temple the Virgin first appeared, some Northsiders seem quite sure that she *projects a visage of fathomless grief from her sightless eyes, as if in perpetual mourning over the self-slaughter of her children.*

Nine million Mexicans turned away from her—or, if you like, adored her new incarnation—and converted to Catholicism. So I read in *The Wonder of Guadalupe.* A migrant worker's child informs us that *Guadalupe predates Christianity. She was Tonantzin to the Aztecs. She is the compassionate mother of all Mexicans, but especially of the orphans and the disenfranchised.* A Northsider student of religion who visited her shrine more bluntly asserts: *The Virgin of Guadalupe is a figure through which the indigenous people fought back against their colonizers and the religion of their colonizers and continue to do so today, whether they are conscious of it or not. I would consider this technique to be "Cultural Guerrilla Warfare,"* and he goes on to quote Mao Zedong.

In 1545, the Virgin of Guadalupe halted a typhus epidemic. In 1737, upon being named Patroness of Mexico, she stopped another plague. In 1775 the de Anza Expedition sang a Mass to her and adopted her among their patron saints before setting out to traverse the sands of Imperial. In 1810 a priest raised up her likeness as an icon of independence from Spain. Over the Treaty of Guadalupe Hidalgo, by whose provisions Mexico lost half her territory to the United States, the Virgin of Guadalupe presided, gazing dreamily down into space. In 1921 she withstood a time bomb. In 1966, in his "Plan de Delano" speech, César Chávez announced that at the head of their penitential cavalcade from Delano to Sacramento, a good two hundred and fifty miles, *We carry LA VIRGEN DE LA GUADALUPE, because she is ours.* As I write, Mexicans on both sides of the border still rely on her to help them conceive children or cure a fright. A historian of stereotypes gives the following Northside interpretation of the Virgin Mary: *As a special pleader for sinners, the Virgin offered confidence in them that they could "beat the rap."*

In 2005 a dancer at the Thirteen Negro assured me that her youngest daughter had been truly and absolutely dying, so she named her María Guadalupe and promised to make an annual pilgrimage to the little hill above her hometown of Obregon, a sacred little hill because it was there that the Virgin of Guadalupe was once seen. Every year Emily fulfilled her vow; upon her dressing room mirror in Mexicali, the Virgin's image gazed down at her.

In 2004 the *Imperial Valley White Sheet* contained this advertisement: *GRACIAS VIRGEN de Guadalupe por escuchar oraciones M.P.* Thank you, Virgin of Guadalupe, for having heard our prayers—probably poor people's prayers. And why not? Juan Diego Cuahtaloatzin described himself to the Virgin as *a poor ordinary man. I carry burdens with the tumpline and carrying frame.*

In 2003 an old woman in Tecate who possessed three images of this syncretic goddess told me in a tone of quiet rapture: This is the religion I've been raised in. This is the Virgin I have the most feeling for. The Virgin of Guadalupe is for everyone, for the whole world . . . We're all under her blanket. When I was younger, especially around the time I had my first communion, I used to dream about her . . .

In 2002 a street-lounger and would-be *pollo* in Mexicali uncomfortably told me: Most of the people in this country, they do believe in that. Do I believe or not? I'm not sure about that. I believe in God and Jesus but I think I have to read more about that. But something's not right about that, because I hear a lot of old people, they don't believe in that.—Slowly his faith in her grew evident. I suspect that he wanted to be, or be considered, an ultra-orthodox Catholic; nonetheless he loved her; he was hers and she was his. He and his Virgin were syncretic.

In 2000, Vicente Fox ended seven decades of single party rule in Mexico. Just before he took the presidential oath, he went to pay his respects to the Virgin of Guadalupe.

Look! In the double line of waiting cars and trucks at Mexicali's western border crossing, darkskinned people in sports jackets are selling gigantic crucifixes; that's standard; that's Catholic; but over here an Indian girl is offering a white bas-relief of the Virgin of Guadalupe.

Syncretism goes back farther than that, at least to 1519, when Cortés came to Mexico and (after temporarily bestowing her on *a very grand gentleman* named Hernando Alonso Puertocarrero) took as his mistress the highborn woman, the "mistress of vassals" from Jalisco whom he christened Doña Marina, used as an interpreter and confidante throughout the Mexican Conquest, begat on her a son named Don Martín Cortés, and married her off to a certain Juan Jaramillo. Since then the denizens of what we might as well call Northside have looked across the ditch with race-mixing in their hearts. Why not? Doña Marina, who might have loved him, for she exerted herself to save him from being assassinated by the Cholulan Indians (then again, that might have simply been the wisest course for her career as she saw it; moreover, it has been asserted that there was no assassination plot), opined for the record that *God had been very gracious to her in freeing her from the worship of idols and making her a Christian, and giving her a son by her lord and master Cortes, also in marrying her to such a gentleman as her husband Juan Jaramillo.* What could be more syncretic than that? (She sold out at a fancy price.) She is better known now as Malinche, and Mexican politicians like to attack one another as *malinchistas,* meaning *that one is not truly Mexican. That one is susceptible to foreign influences. A traitor. Like Malinche.*

In the *Annals of Tlatelolco,* composed by the vanquished, Marina speaks to them like a haughty queen: *Do come here . . . Is Quauhtemoc still such a child?* One of Malinche's few biographers responds: *Mexico's problem with Malinche is, fundamentally, a question of how to honor a rape.* The Florentine Codex says: *. . . the Spaniards took things from people by force. They were looking for gold; they cared nothing for green-stone . . . They looked everywhere with the women, on their abdomens, under their skirts . . . And [they] took, picked out the beautiful women, with yellow bodies.* And in the same breath, the Codex describes the seizing and branding of men for slaves.

Perhaps she submitted willingly, relishing her important position. In the Florentine Codex *they placed a canopy of varicolored cloth over the Marqués,* which is to say Cortés; *then he sat down, and Marina sat beside him.* In the *Annals of Tlatelolco* the defeated ones bring to Cortés all the gold they can find, *but when the Captain and Marina saw it they became angry and said, "Is that what is being looked for?"* because they expected more; the writer seems to see them as equals. In a later Nahuatl folk tale, there is syncretic mention of *the White Woman, the great lady. She is known as the interpreter of Cortés.*

Perhaps she was a traitor to some phantasm of united indigenous Mexican-ness that did not yet exist; she was Mayan, and Cortés conquered the Aztecs. Who are we to say what she was? In the 1850s, some Los Angeles Rangers sent to arrest Mexicans at a fandango were instead *immediately taken into custody by an overwhelming array of black-eyed Señoritas.* And here's a Southside man in 2002, with eight brothers and four sisters, some of whom were born white, because his father had many girlfriends, some of whom have his dark skin and kinky hair. He gazes hungrily across the ditch and says: I'm gonna tell you the truth. I got a problem, 'cause all the girls to me are beautiful. But my speciality, I like one girl, maybe tomorrow I like another, maybe *morena* like that (you know *morena*? it means dark*), maybe tomorrow white, but to be married, I like a white girl. I don't know why.†

*A migrant child of the 1950s, born in south Texas, tells us that "the dark-skinned daughter in a Mexican family was always 'La Prieta.' The nickname of 'the black one' was given in love."

†In all of these respects he resembled Cortés, who had four children by his first Spanish wife, a son by Doña Marina, another son "by a Spanish woman," and three daughters by three other Indian women. Meanwhile he married another Spanish lady after the first one died. "He was much given to consorting with women," writes his personal secretary, "and always gave himself to them."

THE AZTECS ARE BACK

Here's another telling of Malinche's marriage-tale: If they won't swallow our Virgin, then mix her up with their goddess Tonantzin; that ought to make her stick! She's already preparing to engrave her image, supernaturally, of course, on that Indian blanket; call it one of the first Spanish flags to fly over Mexico. May they all believe in the Virgin of Guadalupe! But will we Northsiders ever believe in Tonantzin? What do you think? Her power springs from the other side of the ditch. In the last few years of writing *Imperial,* I began to notice that some Southsiders, particularly those who dwelled in Tijuana, referred to themselves as Aztecs. They did so with pride. Meanwhile, I read the following editorial in a national Northside newspaper: The Iraqi insurgents who carve off the heads of American hostages are not actually Muslims at all (thus opines Mr. Ralph Peters), but mere exemplars of *the elementary problem of our times: Frightened human beings and the longing for easy answers that lead to the most repugnant forms of faith. The Aztecs are back.*

And now it's midnight in Mexicali, with only the bars still open, whores flying or waddling brilliantly up the dark street, the churches glowing in their sleep; and at the border itself, under many yellow lights, with the sound of the turnstiles echoing in the cooling air, a mother sits on a bench, desperately kissing her child, a tramp sleeps on the next bench, a cockroach runs across the yellow-lit sidewalk, the Chinese *licuado* man laughingly plays snap-the-towel with his girlfriend, and up the railroad track the cars glow, waiting to clear the U.S. checkpoint on the other side of the ditch. A few steps away, it's darker than dark beside the Escuela Cuauhtémoc, Cuauhtémoc being the last Aztec prince, who surrendered to Cortés and whom Cortés, *who could not prevent their actions,* first allowed his lieutenants to torture by fire, in hopes of getting more gold, and later, this time on his own authority, hanged for conspiracy. That way, the Aztecs wouldn't be back. And now it's so dark, so quiet!—We didn't have those waves of people coming across, remarks the old pioneer from Heber.

And then slowly, like a juice vendor ladling his wares, keeping ice and liquid in their respective places, a *pollo* comes creeping toward the fence, with a friend who'll raise him up on his shoulders; he's getting ready to be syncretic; he's going to commit another totally needless and senseless act. He's a wiry little man in a soccer jersey and a baseball cap which spells out his wish: **CALIFORNIA**. He wears a cross around his neck. I nod to him, and he nods to me. Sucking in his cheeks, clenching an unlit cigarette between two fingers, he approaches the wall. His comrade murmurs in his ear, probably something along the lines of: *Go with God!* because he replies softly: *Gracias.* The Border Patrol won't drive to the detention center just for him; they'll wait until the whole van is full.

Chapter 8

SIGN OF SLOW GROWTH SENDS STOCKS LOWER

(2002)

Specialization is passing from the consideration of a given set of objects to that of a smaller set, or of just one object, contained in the smaller set. Specialization is often useful in the solution of problems.

—G. Polya, *How to Solve It* (1957)

I opened the newspaper and read: *The deaths are full of suffering. People have been suffocated in airless trucks* . . . Dateline: EL CENTRO, Calif. Operation Gatekeeper's harvest might well take the gold medal at the next county fair *in the more unguarded and desolate deserts of Arizona and eastern California,* a zone which naturally includes Imperial, because *June was the deadliest month ever there, with 67 migrants dying.* Fortunately, the majority of these perishings took place in Sector Tucson, which Officer Dan Murray had told me was "a hot spot for narcotics and immigration" and which lies outside this book's sphere of concern; let's say they never happened. In Sector El Centro, *which includes the vast Imperial Desert,* only fifty-two dead *pollos* had been found in the last ten months. *The sheriff's department believes the deaths could outpace last year's record of 95.*

Three ninety-nine, one seventy-seven, said the radio. Ninety-nine, you anywhere near the Highway 111 check?

Ninety-nine, that's me in the white Explorer.

We achieved two hundred and forty-eight thousand apprehensions last year, a Border Patrolman told me.

I congratulated him, and he proudly said to me: We're highly visible. We're on the border. We're in the hills, day in and day out, to try and deter them.

The dying season began early this year, with four bloated bodies found floating in the All-American Canal on March 14. Well, it wasn't the worst news on the front page: more air raids and suicide bombings in the Middle East, an attempt (fortunately foiled) to murder a hundred schoolchildren in a Christian school in Pakistan, and my government had snubbed Iraqi overtures; we were getting ready to bomb them again. I had been to Iraq; I had seen the sick and dying children in a medicine-embargoed hospital; so I had my mental picture; it's better not to have mental pictures. But why confess such a flinch? I'd rather clothe myself in principle: Communication for its own sake is not an interesting goal. (Does that sound plausible?) Unlimited access to information remains worthless without something to do with that information, or some way to verify its quality. What can I "do with" my image of that young mother whose hijab made a white crescent across her black hair as she held her baby's round head tight against her throat so that it was just their two heads filling my vision in that ward of Saddam Hussein Pediatric Hospital whose pharmacy was empty, while the baby, not knowing that anything was wrong with it, gazed sleepily upon the world and the mother stared into space, never at me, the corners of her mouth parenthesized by bitterness? I asked her if there was anything I could "do"—I'd already given the duffel bag of medicine to one of the doctors, and she probably wouldn't get any of it—and she replied, grinning with hate: End the sanctions.—Thank God her misery didn't take place in Sector El Centro! I won't need to write about her in this book.

Reading a newspaper, you see, is fundamentally a matter of delineation: Some people prefer the sports page; in the Sunday *Sacramento Bee,* I always go straight for the "Forum" section, which deals in opinions instead of information; in the *Sacramento News and Review* I seek out erotic classified ads. We irrigate our mental fields with the liquid of our choice. And the reclamation of "reality" is the largest irrigation enterprise in the nation! *The bountiful continent is ours, state on state, and territory on territory, to the waves of the Pacific sea.* Each morning a new continent awaits me on the glass table downstairs; because each newspaper's potentialities, like those of all entities blank or folded, are as vast as the wide silver-tan-ness of the concrete bay between El Centro's Greyhound station and its adjacent sheds and brickworks: "All the News That's Fit to Print." What rivers and mountains will get discovered next? I can remember the headline when that surgeon in South Africa performed the first human heart transplant; he did something. He died recently, making obituaries but not headlines. I can still see the heavy black headline about the Apollo lunar landing in 1969. When I grew up, I would be able to go to the moon. Pan American was selling tickets. Pan Am's bankrupt now. We'd colonize Mars, whose red craterscapes may not be conceptually distant from the tan sands of Imperial,* at least in the case of the County Refuse Disposal Area. Recently I reread Ray Bradbury's *Martian Chronicles* and realized that the Martians, at least at the end of that novel, when they're essentially ghosts (before that, when they're telepathic, magical, dangerous, tricky and treacherous, they resemble Puritans' nightmares about Indians), speak and behave in an eerily familiar ornate fashion—

* See "Subdelineations: Marsscapes," p. 1023, for a complete explication of this vital scientific issue.

why, of course! They're Mexicans! We conquered California from them, expelling their laws and ways; California, Imperial California, is our Mars, but *the Martians are coming back!* (Excuse me, but do you prefer more alien aliens? Note the three glowing eyes on a locomotive; I'll bet you can't find that face in your xenobiology guide! The steady mica-like gleam of some trailer, window or car across the Salton Sea could be the beacon of a rocket in distress. Do you want spacemen? The handsome Border Patrolman removes his sombrero, pinching the crown of it with the left three fingers of his right hand as he gazes down into the bamboo-shadows of the Ho Chi Minh Trail, his communicator comfortingly ready on his left shoulder; it looks a bit like the spare respirator which now comes standard in a scuba outfit. He's Neil Armstrong *and* Buck Rogers; he's looking for Martians. I want to find them, too, but where are they? I see old shell-fragments and mussels on the shore. I hear the bubbles from the brine shrimp sizzling like popcorn.) The Mars of Robert A. Heinlein's novels I remember, or think I do, from my childhood. Desert, difficult temperatures, colonists holding town meetings, fighting the wildlife and improving the sands into a democratic Eden, why does this strike a chord? *I can't help believing in people . . . I have never been cheated out of a dollar in my life . . . Ranchers in heavy boots stomped into luncheon conferences demanding water.* All this comes into my mind now, when I recollect that headline about the moon landing. All this is probably why I recollect it. I was nine years old. Several solar revolutions later there came a day in the Klong Toey slum when some skinny Thais sniggered into the window: *Big fire in your country! Buildings fall!* A blaze in California or Oregon must have nibbled at houses, maybe even a town; I thought of my friends in Borrego Springs; I'd once telephoned Larry to see how he was doing after his colostomy and he was busy watering down the roof and deck because flames might be coming; he explained, professorial to the last, that high temperatures and dry desert brush made for superheated conditions if a spark got lucky. When Imperial's heat comes, people's minds shut down; we don't want to think or try anything new; we don't want to know. (Ecclesiastes 1.18: *He who increases knowledge increases sorrow.*) And so it was only by accident (I wish I could have gone a week without knowing) that on the next day I happened to stroll past a sidewalk stand which displayed the *Bangkok Post* with its headline. For another minute I still couldn't believe it; my innermost Border Patrol was still fencing out feelings which once I felt them would be as sharp-edged as the shadows on a burning-hot sidewalk. That must have been on September 13 or 14, 2001. *The sheriff's department believes the deaths could outpace last year's record of 95.*

The sheriff's department believes the deaths could outpace last year's record of 95. Then came Palestine and Iraq on the same page. There was also a small boxed item which from my point of view was especially unfortunate: **Sign of Slow Growth**

Sends Stocks Lower. We mostly think of ourselves first. The bald shoeshine man on his throne, his hands crossed, gazing down at the world, how much time did he spend thinking of me? *I have never been cheated out of a dollar in my life.* I worried about my little girl's college fund. Since September 11 it had lost a third of its value. But I wouldn't want to imply that Imperial wasn't interesting, too. (A guidebook advises: *Mexicali's sights are few and far between, and most visitors are in Mexicali for business. A tourist-oriented strip of curio shops and sleazy bars is located along Avenida Francisco Madero, one block south of the border.* Another guidebook: *Mexicali lies at sea level . . . Be warned that it is unbearably hot here in the summer.*) Power plants and sugar beets, here and there a brief flash of onions, that was Imperial for you. Imperial was sticky sweets stacked up against a bakery window, each one hand-shaped, variable. That bakery closed, I think in 1998. No matter; I'd already photographed it.* Which sweet do you want? Give me Imperial; I'll skip Palestine. (An Algerian woman I know reads the latter article—something about retaliation and malnutrition—then starts wiping her red-rimmed eyes.) *Big fire in your country!* **Sign of Slow Growth Sends Stocks Lower.** *Bodies are being found in ever more remote areas . . . Here in the El Centro sector, five suspected illegal immigrants died of heat exposure in mid-July in an area of the Imperial Desert that resembles a moonscape.*

*Negative MX-SP-ELV-97-06, which will be sent to Ohio State University in due course. The woman in this picture, Elvira, disappeared in 2001. The other street prostitutes who recognized her in the picture claimed that she had been murdered.

Chapter 9

WATER IS HERE

(1849–2002)

Possibly there was more rainfall in those days than now . . .

—John C. Van Dyke, 1903

In about 1845 Captain James Hobbs set his face westwards and departed Fort Yuma, prudently keeping close to the New River, which at that particular moment *possessed water only at one place, and that a small pool hardly fit to drink. In passing through this desert we came upon the remains of an emigrant train, which a month previous had attempted to cross this desert in going from the United States to California.* From the United States to California! These words hint at how bleakly remote Imperial was in those days. A sandstorm had driven his predecessors off course, and Captain Hobbs spied their abandoned wagons almost in sight of that foul pool in the New River.* *We could see where they had lightened their loads by abandoning goods, but still their cattle had been obliged to yield to the terrible thirst. There were eight women and children, and nine men. The body of a child had been almost stripped of flesh by the buzzards and animals and its clothes were torn off; but most of the other bodies had their clothes on.* Different times, different mores; a Border Patrolman in Yuma once told me that *his* dead bodies were usually naked or nearly so, because in the final conscious stage of heat exhaustion one's flesh begins to swell; clothing becomes excruciatingly tight. Standing beside me as we faced the river, tall and neighborly with my passport in his hand (he'd just wanted to see what I was up to), that Border Patrolman said that whenever he came upon a T-shirt or a pair of pants in the sand beside the wavering spoor, he knew that the prize was near: another trophy for Op-

*The New River's course, by the way, was at this point in time a wide, shallow U dipping down into what is now left of Mexico and then back into California—well, well, in 1849 it was still Mexico; Imperial baked and basked in its last months of freedom from an international line. In 1850 we could coin the term "Arid America." Forgive these complications; in reference to the New River forgive reality as do several twenty-first-century maps, not even excluding a certain glossy double-page spread in the supposedly "scientific" *Salton Sea Atlas*, which I discovered in a bookstore in El Centro last week. No Dren Ferrocarril, no Cerro Prieto, no Laguna Xochimilco—all those human-poisoned springheads! Oh, no, we'll keep the New River simple; let's keep everything simple, subdividing creation into watercourses and arid wastelands. So pardon my interruption; the New River's an easily comprehensible twist of the Río Colorado; if you must enter the vicissitudes of Imperial, nourish yourself as best you can from that U-shaped umbilicus, and, God willing, you'll be saved.

eration Gatekeeper. *We could see where they had lightened their . . .* The sandy stretches around Yuma have always been particularly deadly for desert-crossers legal and illegal. Aside from that detail about indecent undress, and aside from the fact that they weren't Mexican, it was the same story as the Border Patrolman's, almost. What's the "almost"? Must I really tell it? All right then; here's a book for you; I found it in the same bookstore where I bought my pretty new *Salton Sea Atlas,* or maybe I wrote it; it's a book called *Imperial:*

CHAPTER I

In passing through this desert we came upon the remains of an emigrant train. There were eight women and children, and nine men. But someday these tragedies would be history, by which we Northsiders mean "obsolete"; we can forget them because Mars was going to be terraformed by Alistair MacLean at Ice Station Zebra, great clouds of oxygen becoming rain, Mars growing green; those ancient canals which an Italian astronomer first spied centuries ago (xenobiologists remain divided as to whether their builders were Cahuilla or Yuma Indians) beginning to shimmer with pure polar water, melted for us by Mexican bipeds whose spacesuit rental fees had been deducted from their wages in an easy payment plan: **WATER IS HERE**.

CHAPTER II

THE DESERT DISAPPEARS. *Call it Lake Imperial. The weather is not uncomfortable in the New River section.* Wilber Clark improves his ranch: Here comes water; jump out of the way, because his fruit trees are sprouting up! **TWO YEARS AND FOUR MONTHS PRIOR TO THE TAKING OF THIS PHOTOGRAPH, NEITHER WATER, TREE, NOR MAN EXISTED IN THIS PLACE, IMPERIAL VALLEY, CALIFORNIA.** Now for Boulder Dam and the All-American Canal! By 1945 Imperial County will possess 259,487 grapefruit trees and 627,467 orange trees, and I'll bet you the Coachella Valley's got a few, too. *We need have no fear that our lands will not become better and better as the years go by.* Imperial's heaven; water's in Brawley; we're safe from thirst forever.

CHAPTER III

The sheriff's department believes the deaths could outpace last year's record of 95.

Chapter 10

PREFACE

(2002–2003)

The concept of metadata—or data about data—which describes source, method, and appropriate uses . . . is a growing priority.

—*Salton Sea Atlas*, 2002

All these delineations and subdelineations had persuaded me that if I were going to write *Imperial,* that book should probably investigate what used to be called "the American dream," along with some border strips of its Mexican counterpart. Holt and Heber, George Chaffey and Judge Farr, Wilber Clark together with his wife and sister, they all must have sincerely believed, and in their own time proved, that upon the almost unregulated, practically infinite, fertile potentiality called "America," we may each of us delineate a principality, maybe even an Inland Empire, and then set about "improving" it with sweat, imagination, and, when appropriate, with commercial prayers asked of and answered by the Ministry of Capital whose Old Testament was (if one didn't care to go as far back as Emerson, Lincoln, Jefferson, Roger Williams) William E. Smythe's *The Conquest of Arid America* and whose New Testament was *The Winning of Barbara Worth* (imitated and in proportion to his literary capability extended by Otis B. Tout)—a realm whose county seal was and is—I'm doublechecking this on the death certificate of another unknown Mexican—a crown which hovers over irrigated fields, with Signal Mountain on the horizon. Who but the faithful would have named their baby Imperial Hazel Deed? And what if their faith actually justified itself by truth? For they succeeded, didn't they? They died richer and, in their own and their posterity's eyes, more blessed than they had begun. Imperial was going green on both sides of the line; **THE DESERT DISAPPEARS**. Do you remember what Smythe wrote? *The essence of the industrial life which springs from irrigation is its democracy.* No matter that nine out of every ten people in the democracy of Athens lived unenfranchised; American Imperial's democracy for its part sometimes proved less than democratic to Mexicans, Chinese, women; Mexican Imperial too often lacked rest from poverty's violence; nonetheless, within the strictures of its epoch, Imperial was giving and welcoming. Assemblyman Victor V. Vesey remembers that there was no higher education in Imperial County in 1949; the school districts refused to unify because *they opted for independence and local control.* I admire the principle if not its result.

He sold out at a fancy price. I don't glory in that sentiment at all; in fact, I suspect that it's the root of our American boorishness; nonetheless, in this world of peonage and poverty, it's nice to suppose, with how much justification it will be my task to determine, that those words could apply to almost anyone. *We need have no fear that our lands will not become better and better as the years go by.* "W. F. Holt Looks into the Future with the Direct Gaze of the Confident Man."

And now, as you know, Imperial County is the poorest county in California and its water is being robbed away by state threat and federal intimidation, not to mention private greed, and *the sheriff's department believes the deaths could outpace last year's record of 95.* So what went wrong? Or does Imperial in fact continue on course? Would Mr. Holt, were he alive today, feel pleased and proud about the housing subdivisions of El Centro? Is the county's high poverty rate simply an aspect of its transition from an agricultural to a commercial utopia? (Holt was, after all, a banker.) Would he and his fellow pioneers consider the deaths of illegal Mexicans to be no more consequential than the Athenians must have judged the deaths of a few slaves? In short, is the Imperial on the north side of the international line American or un-American, and what does the answer to that question say about what Americans profess?

Meanwhile, what Chinese tunnels or other secrets can I discover on the other side of the ditch? *Imperial is the continuum between Mexico and America.* What has the Ministry of Capital accomplished in Southside? I hope to investigate these questions in my book called *Imperial.*

Chapter 11

SUBDELINEATIONS: BOOKSCAPES

(1850–2003)

Perhaps you think I will tell you everything, so that you may be able to understand my story. I will begin to tell the story.

—Rabbi Nachman of Bratslav, eighteenth century

Imperial is whatever we want it to be, unless we're businessmen, in which case imagination requires capital. I have none; mirages satisfy me; I don't expect this book to achieve the fame of *Silt* by Otis B. Tout. Imperial has acres and acres of alluvium left; Imperial can find room even for me. I see a reddish-orange vastness below me, with Mexicali far, far away across the Laguna Salada, and Signal Mountain a broad half-oval like the sail of a dinosaur on this cool, cool evening, which has been graced with winds and clouds, everything fading into sandy dreams just as my youth did; this landscape reminds me of Afghanistan to the south of Jalalabad. I was young then and sure of what I could do; I was writing my own story. Soon it will be dark, and then to find a restaurant one must drive all the way to Tecate. Back to the car. Here come the first green trees at Arroyo de la Gloria; there stand more crosses and shrines for this road's dead; Imperial vanishes behind me as I ascend into this dimming coolness whose fruits are jigsaw rock-breasts with erect rock nipples. *The part of 1850 San Diego County that would later become Imperial County in 1907 was a mere thoroughfare for the adventurers, gold miners and settlers coming to California . . . There were no ranchos and no towns.* Thus runs the already-quoted encomium of a county-by-county guide to the California of a century and a half ago. Well-meaning sidebars and itineraries stud that book, like the tawny canvas bags which are hung in date trees to protect the fruit from birds and rain. But for Imperial there's only the following boldface marginal note, whose time-saving words have been as emphatically capitalized as those of an ancient washroom sign: *There are no 1850 Sites to Visit in Imperial County.* Imperial is (have you ever heard this before?) a blank page. What shall we inscribe on it?

THE PLEASURES OF BARBARA WORTH

Not long before 1911, when the Imperial Valley gave birth to one million, one hundred and twenty thousand pounds of cabbage and an almost equal quantity of grapeweight, Mr. Harold Bell Wright, who in his photographs looks nearly as gaunt as Abraham Lincoln, sat down in Holtville in an arrow-weed house he'd built with his own hands (how Imperial of him!), wrote out eight manuscript drafts whose internal organs he reshuffled through a system of hanging pockets, and reified Imperial into somebody he could adore: *To look at Barbara Worth was a pleasure; to be near her was a delight.* So what if to me his novel seems absurd? In the Flamingo Club in Mexicali* men drink their beers in rapture while a queenly, magnificently-buttocked woman unhooks her bra, undoes her hair, launches her panties in a slow slide to her ankles. Let an agronomist continue the story: *Sugar beets grew admirably. It was never my privilege to see finer cauliflower than was exhibited at Imperial. Eggplants and melons of mammoth proportions were shown.* The Flamingo Club is out of business now; a sports bar stands there now, but why not live in the past? Meanwhile, other ladies, ladies in fancy frilly clothes, ladies with long, long hair, invite themselves next to the men, whisperingly begging for four hundred pesos for six beers. Caressing all takers, they eschew underwear, as each man discovers when pretty fingers guide his hand into the darkness beneath a skirt; in short, they're fully prepared to illustrate the motto of the California Water and Forest Association: *"Moisture Means Millions"*; to look at them's a pleasure, to be near them a delight. *The dark-faced old plainsman . . . turned often to look at her now while his keen eyes, dark still under their grizzly brows, were soft with fond regard.* Yes, search into those men's eyes! Lust shines sweetly and sincerely there. For all we know, affection does, too. They sit in their Imperial; after six beers they will enter Paradise. *As she passed, the people turned to follow her with their eyes—the "old-timers" with smiles of recognition and picturesque words of admiring comment,* because Barbara Worth, who's so chaste that even come the happily-ever-after, she hasn't quite been kissed, was *so good to look at.*

I cannot think of this healthy, athletic horsewoman's sickly creator without wishing him well. He truly does love Barbara, so he's ahead of the game; isn't every Pygmalion's biography a success story? He also loves hard work, human better-

*No disrespect to our United States is intended by this reference to a Mexican business establishment. Can't we raise any crop that foreigners can? Indeed, as early as 1903 we find the various anti-liquor ordinances of American Imperial being disobeyed by "M. B. Davis, commonly known as Bob," who "bought a lot near the railroad and opened a regular saloon. He was very defiant for a few days, and at last two women came to town to make their headquarters at his place." Once the warrant had been issued, he fled across the border, and the prostitutes also apparently departed. And so vice ended in Imperial County forever.

ment and Imperial's desertscapes. So do I. May he dwell with her always, right there in Holtville. (In 1915 he had to depart for Tucson, on account of illness. He died in 1944.) *She passed into the hotel, followed by the eyes of every man in sight including the engineer, who had noted with surprise the purity and richness of her voice.* Why shouldn't we be able to form stories about and around ourselves? Or, as inclination invites us, why not follow in the wake of a story which writes itself? (Here's a story for you: *Over the years . . . the flow of the river gradually lessened and the salt content gradually increased.* Thus the story of every life except for Barbara Worth's.) In place of Harold Bell Wright's heroine I see (I don't need to imagine) that gorgeous reddish-brown fat girl at the taco stand in Mexicali; the grease from *carnitas* shines preciously between her vast breasts. Why not request permission to follow her for a day and write down everything she says and does, so that a thousand years from now we will still know her? Or why not mount a goal, any experiment or expedition, then go wherever it points us? In 1940, John Steinbeck and some comrades took a sail around most of the Baja Peninsula, which is to say (speaking approximately) a trip halfway around the perimeter of Imperial. He introduced his *Log from the* Sea of Cortez thus: *We have a book to write about the Gulf of California . . . We have decided to let it form itself: its boundaries a boat and a sea . . .*

This book also forms itself as it goes. Fields, hay-walls, towns and fences comprise my thoroughfare; I have no sites to visit in Imperial County or out of it; I'm free to chase after white birds in green alfalfa fields as long as the heat fails to discourage me; I don't care that I'll never finish anything; my delineations and subdelineations resemble those severed palm-fronds bleaching in the white sand at the border wall. Imperial will scour them away with its dry winds and the brooms of its five-dollars-an-hour Mexican laborers. Then what? Imperial will continue on, *silent and hot and fierce in its desolation, holding its treasures under the seal of death against the coming of the strong ones,* which is to say the ones whom Harold Bell Wright idealized, the ones whose epoch was *the age of the Seer and his companions, . . . the days of my story, the days of Barbara and her friends.* The alluvial soils of Imperial can grow anything, not least Harold Bell Wright's fields of purple-flowered prose. *To look at Barbara Worth was a pleasure; to be near her was a delight.* Why shouldn't I bloom a bit, too?

My original intent was to write a novel about Imperial, a story which followed the lives of *pollos* from Southside all the way across wall and desert to, say, Yuma, where they labored for low wages until they got caught and deported. Here is how it would have begun (I now reclaim the desert of this book's first chapter):

IMPERIAL

by

WILLIAM T. VOLLMANN

1

The man beside me now awoke, and turned toward the window like a plant toward the sun. Soon we would come to the sign which read IMPERIAL COUNTY LINE and a few minutes later we'd pass the Corvina Cafe, which would surely be as closed and dead as one of those corvina floating belly-up in the Salton Sea (to smell them was a pleasure; to eat them was a delight). The man sat gazing alertly eastward across the desert flats toward the long deep green stripe of date plantations and the dusty red and blue mountains beyond.

We all do it. We're all novelists. In the Imperial County Pioneers Museum I see a photograph of Westmorland's sixth-grade class in 1948. Bev Johnson, whom I presume to be the donor, has labeled only herself.

We all do it. Here's the title of a quarter-column novel which appeared complete with photograph in the *Fresno Morning Republican:* **Asked to Lead Evil Life, Girl Kills Sister.** That happened in 1920.

We all do it. We all want to win Barbara, be Barbara or stay in the Barbara Worth Hotel. A smoothskinned yet very, very Western glamour-girl in a soft white cowboy hat rests her chin on her fingers, clutching an elegant leather riding-glove. Is she alive or dead now? The photograph is yellow and undated. The caption reads: *Mrs. Bradshaw, contestant for lead, Barbara Worth film.*

NOVELS OF IMMIGRATION MEN

Oh, yes, we all do it; that's for sure. In the fall of 2002 I happened to be crossing the international line when the scraggly-bearded Immigration official, slowly, slowly turning the pages of my passport, discovered that my exit visa from Yemen was dated the day before yesterday. Yemen was where the USS *Cole* had been attacked in 2000; and this year, just two weeks earlier, which is to say while I had been in Yemen, several Yemenis were arrested in New York for possible links with the September 11 plot; my government announced that Special Forces operatives would be sent to Yemen to hunt down more terrorists; no doubt they succeeded for all time, like southern Californians with their aqueducts. And here I was.

Sometimes a Border Patrolman smiles white-toothed and friendly at me, with his arm on the windowsill of his white Bronco; he just wants to know what I am doing down here. I can't help but like him. He's so genuinely interested in me! But this wasn't quite like that; oh, no. The Immigration man, scratching his chin, asked me how long I had been in Mexico, and I said three hours. He stared at me for a long time. To me it was not so strange to go in and out of Mexico like that, especially if one is writing a book about the border, but evidently the Immigration man considered it quite aberrant. And so he began to fill out an orange slip, taking his time to look at me again and again; I hope that he derived as much satisfaction from his work as Harold Bell Wright once did. That dark-faced old plainsman turned often to look at me now while his keen eyes, dark still under their grizzly brows, were soft with I forget what. He had a shiny badge, too (an invented novelistic detail, for I could see him only from the chin up in his sad little window). Then it was time to pull into the special parking bay in order for a relentlessly smiling man in a white uniform to ask me if I had any bomb-making materials. Thanks to him, no doubt, *we need have no fear that our lands will not become better and better as the years go by.*

The woman I was with (the love of my life who had just replaced the love of my life) was getting very thirsty. Half an hour earlier, while our rental car idled at the tail of the queue, I'd promised her that the instant we reached Calexico I'd buy her a tall juice, a soda or whatever fruit of the gardens of Paradise she desired; she was tired; she'd done all the driving; and although she denied it, I suspect that she now began to be a little anxious. Meanwhile (the plot silts up), another official took my passport, studied my Yemeni visa for three utterly silent minutes (he'd never seen one before, I suppose, and the fact that it allowed multiple entries surely enhanced my aura of evil). He said: *Ai, yi, yi!*

Next came the bitter officer; perhaps Barbara Worth had jilted him. But please don't accuse him of slackness. He'd never been cheated out of a dollar in his life. And here I should tell you that they all wore what Otis B. Tout would have called "a grim smile"; everyone in *Silt* has a grim smile, and everyone talks like this: *Folks, no matter if the river eats up the entire towns of Alexico and Exical, we'll move back and let it eat. When it gets through, we'll build a bigger and better town.* It gives me pleasure to assume that had my bomb obliterated even more of Imperial than the Salton Sea flood, these protectors of Northside would have built bigger and better checkpoints in the end. As Border Officer Gloria I. Chavez once remarked, *I think we all feel sorry for 'em.*—But pardon me; my narrative flow's silting up; let the headgates open!

The officer who was bitter looked me up and down, said to the woman I was with: Does he ever change his expression?

That's just his expression, she said.

He smirked at me, grimly of course, and said: So how are you feeling now? Are you happy or sad?

I'm probably about as happy as you, officer, I replied.

They had all the luggage out of the car by now and their dog was sniffing under the seats. They were pretty sure that I'd sold out at a fancy price. The dog discovered nothing, so the officer who was bitter pushed the dog's head down and made him sniff again. **TREASON IS HERE**. Sad to report, the dog discovered nothing for the second time. So they sent us into a corridor to sit below a lady at a high desk. To look at that gal was a pleasure; to be near her was a delight. Actually, that was my novelization: I forgot what she looked like.

The woman I was with was too nice to complain, but I knew that she must be getting more thirsty now, so I asked the woman at the high desk if there might be a soda machine. Sipping at her soda, she replied that there wasn't, but there was hot water in the bathroom. The woman I was with then asked whether she could step outside and smoke, and the woman behind the desk told her that she could not.

To the right of the high desk there was an open door, through which I could see two brownskinned women sitting at a table while a female officer interrogated them. After awhile, one of the brownskinned women came out, silently weeping, with her wrists already cuffed behind her back. *As she passed, the people turned to follow her with their eyes—the "old-timers" with smiles of recognition and picturesque words of admiring comment.* The female officer followed her into the elevator, where she had to stand facing the wall, so that the last I saw of her was her crossed wrists locked together against her buttocks. The other woman, the one still in the interrogation room, was now also crying.

The officer behind the desk looked quite indifferent. She'd seen it all before. I can't help believing in people.

We all do it. The woman I was with (she was not the one who had been the love of my life, but the next one) became decidedly anxious; I decided that this must be the reason she was not holding my hand, but my interpretation might have been my novelization; she would soon stop holding my hand forever; anyhow, I let her be as we sat there, outwaiting the other detainees; sugar beets could have grown admirably in that eternity. I felt like novelizing just then, so I pretended that Yemen could have been Imperial, and Imperial could have been the Bedouin-haunted desert of northern Yemen, with the bittersweet smell of qat blowing in the wind, and two veiled women walking alone between mountains; then there was lovely desert nothingness all the way to honey-colored ovens in the earth. That was when I, sitting in the back seat of the Land Rover beside Mr. Ahmed, began to float higher and higher above this blankness, tasting the deliciousness of dreamy dissociation; I was daydreaming about Imperial and the blue beauty of the Salton Sea, pretending that I could get out of the Land Rover whenever I wanted, leave behind those two qat-chewing soldiers with machine guns who sat in the front seat. I'd wander wherever I chose; no one would kidnap me for being a foreigner, or hate me for being an American, which is to say a pawn of international Jewry; oh, I had tired of being hated! I could hardly wait to come home to Imperial. And now that I was in Imperial, awaiting my turn to be "processed" into American cheese, I daydreamed about the ancient mud skyscrapers of Yemen; in my visions I remained so free; I married both veiled women and disappeared with them behind the mountains forever.

Time went by and time went by, until finally the officer who'd said *ai, yi, yi!* came downstairs from some high and secret office whose filing system must have been still more intricate that Harold Bell Wright's, and he clutched a long printout of my international comings and goings, among which were doubtlessly included my visits to what they called "rogue nations": Iraq, Afghanistan, Serbia, and I don't know what all. He marched over to me and announced: We've found out quite a lot about you.

That's nice, officer, I said.

Perhaps I should have shown more gratitude for his efforts, for he looked sad and out of sorts then. I was cross with them all for not allowing the woman I was with to drink anything but hot bathroom water. Possibly the tears of those two brownskinned women had caused me to wonder how nice all this was. Otherwise I would have been more polite; I'm sure I would. Anyhow, the officer who'd said *ai, yi, yi!* strode to the woman at the high desk, showed her the printout, and said to her these magic words: *It reads just like a novel.*

That was when I truly did begin to feel sorry for him. He had written a novel in which I was a big fish, an al-Qaeda terrorist from Yemen, while he was Sherlock Holmes:

IMPERIAL

by

THE OFFICER OF THE UNITED STATES IMMIGRATION AND NATURALIZATION SERVICE WHO'D SAID *AI, YI, YI!*

1

We've found out quite a lot about you, I informed the suspect Vollmann, who turned pale and began to tremble. It was never my privilege to unmask finer subversion than was exhibited at Imperial on this day. It was quite a kick, if you know what I mean. Eggplants, bomblets and melons of mammoth proportions were shown. In short, the suspect Vollmann was everything you could ask for in a suspect. He thought that he could sneak an eggplant by me, but what scum like him will never understand is that we're highly visible. We're on the border. We're in the hills, day in and day out, to try and deter them. And I was the one! It was I who had foiled the conspiracy of the traitor Vollmann! *This was a totally needless and senseless act,* I informed him with a grim smile while Agent Marlowe was putting the handcuffs on.

This Vollmann had confederates, too. *Get out!* I yelled at them. They turned and slowly, slowly walked back into Mexico across the humming throbbing bridge.

Naturally there was a dame involved. In material advantages she was pretty damned well supplied, if you know what I mean. To look at her was a pleasure; to be near her was a delight. But I had the goods on Vollmann. I couldn't cut her any slack. I told her to listen up good. I told her to be a loyal American. If she didn't watch out, it was going to be hot bathroom water for her for the next twenty years!

You never should have gotten mixed up in this, I said to her with a grim smile.

She started bawling and wanting to know what she could do to help the suspect Vollmann. Now, dames have always been a mystery to me. But this was a pretty clear-cut case. I looked her right in the eye and said: That guy's no lily. Forget him.

She tried to plead one more time, but I said to her: You've already played your hole card. But I've trumped you. Agent Marlowe over there's going to take you upstairs. They're going to ask you a few questions.

Nothing changed; nothing even flickered in her greenish-brownish eyes. And I didn't like that.

You're holding out on me, angel, I said to her with a grim smile. What's the dope?

Just then I heard the ticking sound coming from her purse.

Get out, everyone! I shouted. Threat alert!

My colleagues evacuated the office, taking the dame with them. The last I saw of them, they were slowly, slowly walking back into Mexico across the humming throbbing bridge.

I went through her purse pretty fast and pretty careful, I can tell you. What I was thinking to myself was: *Ai, yi, yi!* I found a solid gold cigarette lighter, a rock of cocaine as big as Gibraltar, three illegal aliens, two of them with tentacles, and then (needless to say, it was in a secret compartment) I dug out the other bomb, the real one, a sweet little softnosed nuclear job set to go off within the hour. I whipped out my .45 and shot it to smithereens. Single-handed, I saved the entire towns of Alexico and Exical.

Now, you might think that's the end of the story, but it's not quite the end, because it's my story, if you see what I mean. It's a story about me.

My superior officer, the dark-faced old plainsman, turned often to look at me now, while his keen eyes, dark still under their grizzly brows, were soft with fond regard. In accordance with Führer Directive No. 27, Vollmann was handed over to a secret military tribunal. (We need to get these criminals behind bars where they can't harm anyone.) As for the dame, she's still doing time in Calipatria. I sort of steer clear of dames like that.

But nobody would ever read his novel now, because I turned out to be nothing but a dud bomb. Poor man!

As for the officer who was bitter, I never did feel sorry for him. I disliked his inquiry on the subject of my expression. When they finally let us go, he asked the woman I was with about the Russian tattoo on her arm, and the way he asked was ingratiating, which proved that he wanted to show amends, at least; he even waved when we drove away, but I wouldn't wave back; in fact I stared at him with the most expressionless face I possessed, because in my novel called *Imperial,* when brown-skinned women weep in handcuffs they must be victims even though I don't have a clue what they've done; and he was a part of "the system" which made those two women cry, so I didn't like him. Moreover, as it happened, he was black, and in my novel, when black men are rude to me, they must have it in for me because I'm white.

IMPERIAL

by

WILLIAM T. VOLLMANN

1

The officer with a chip on his shoulder looked me up and down and said to the woman I was with: Does he ever change his expression?

That's just his expression, she said.

He smirked at me and said: So how are you feeling now? Are you happy or sad?

I'm probably about as happy as you are, officer, I said.

I'm going to fuck you up, whitey! he said. Then he shot me in the face. After I was dead, he took out his truncheon and began to beat some women who were weeping in handcuffs. That was when I realized that I loved Big Brother. I sold out at a fancy price.

And so we all write stories to suit ourselves, and I wish happy endings, happy landings to all of us.

FLAUBERT'S HEROINE

There's a cleaning lady I know in Sacramento, a coarsely beautiful schoolteacher who now scrubs out other people's toilets; when her brother the accountant flies up from Mexico City to visit, he comes from house to house to help her; and if the homeowner's there, he'll rush to show his picture identification card, and his expression is pitiable beyond abject; it must be a reflex, the reflex of submission to this foreign power which took half his country but which repays the theft by oozing money from its bowels—what phrase could better locate his sister who cleans toilets?—She has encysted herself in Northside for many illegal years; unless somebody drops a dime on her, she'll probably die here. Wouldn't she be perfect to write a novel about? All I'd need to do to get inside her head is scrub toilets in Sweden for a few years, furtively and for cash. No, come to think of it, Sweden wouldn't be quite right; while it's true that it's cleaner than the United States and that I can't speak the language, Sweden hasn't taken anything from me; moreover it would be difficult for me to feel afraid there; finally, if they caught me scrubbing Swedish toilets and kicked me out, I'd get over it. So how could I learn enough about María's life to express the respect I have for her endurance, and the compassion I feel for her intellect which wastes itself on drudgery?—Parenthetically, I'm not saying that nobody should have to clean other people's toilets or that María simply because she's real to me is better than anybody else, only that it would be unfair to a janitor to make him teach high school, and it's unfair to María, who taught high school, to make her clean toilets—but *why* is it unfair? María chose to come here; it's not my fault, or my government's, or hers, so what am I saying?—How could I best pay tribute to María's life? I know how to invent character, upon which I suppose it would be possible to drizzle a few droplets of local fact, much as a Mexicali street vendor beset by July splashes water on his oranges and cherries. But life's sufficiently dishonest already; my oranges might taste like candy, but why? The truth is that I do not understand enough about border people to describe them without reference to specific individuals, which means that I remain too ill acquainted with them to fictionalize them. Only now do I feel capable of writing novels about American street prostitutes, with whom I have associated for two decades. The sun-wrinkled women who sell candy, when they sit chatting beneath their sidewalk parasols, what stories do they tell one another? I could learn Spanish and eavesdrop; then I'd know; but I wouldn't *really* know until I could invent their stories. Making up tales about María's life would not only be disrespectful to her, it would be bad art: *Suddenly, as a beast checked in its spring, they were still and motionless. By the side of the old frontiersman on the platform under the light stood Barbara.* The best compliment I can pay María is that I cannot imagine her life, especially the drudgery of it but also its various helplessnesses, humiliations and apprehensions. (What happened to those brownskinned women who were crying? What did the one in handcuffs see when the elevator doors opened?) Writing a novel about María would be like slapping her face. Someday, if I ever get out into the world and see more, suffer more, which might not be worth it, writing a novel about her might be an act of beauty and truth.

Have you ever read Flaubert's story "A Simple Heart"? It begins: *For half a century the women of Pont-l'Évêque envied Madame Aubain her maidservant Félicité,* and then we follow that half-century to its end, when Félicité leaves behind her a life of drudgery whose main enrichment was her capacity to love.* She keeps an old frock-coat of her mistress's long dead husband; she adores Madame Aubain's daughter Virginie at least as much as does the mother. The passion of her life is for her mistress's cast-off parrot. When it dies, she gets it stuffed, and gradually comes to associate it with the most perfect entity she knows: the Holy Ghost. *And as she breathed her last, she thought she could see, in the opening heavens, a giant parrot hovering above her head.* Félicité is, in a word, stupid. One of the reasons that "A Simple Heart" is a masterpiece is that Flaubert never hesitates to make her stupidity plain, meanwhile permitting us to realize that of all the characters in this story, she's by far the finest, a fact never noticed by any of the busy, self-absorbed human beings around her, who remain ordinary as she is. What "A Simple Heart" did for *my* heart when I first read it many years ago was to alert me to the probability that among the people whom I myself overlooked, there might be Félicités, whose hidden goodnesses would do *me* good to find. Later, when I began to write books, it occurred to me that discovering and describing those goodnesses might accomplish some external good as well, perhaps even to Félicité and María, who have less need of our pity than we might think (but more need of our cash). Suppose that Madame Aubain, after reading my version of "A Simple Heart," refrained just once from assaulting Félicité with harsh words. Or is that aspiration ridiculous?

Harriet Beecher Stowe tried to do something of the kind when she wrote *Uncle Tom's Cabin.* Our President is supposed to have said when he met her: So you're the little lady who started this great big war.—Nowadays an Uncle Tom is somebody who's servile, contemptible; yet his author meant him to be a martyr.† What made tastes change? What would Lenin say about Félicité? He would certainly call, as Flaubert never did, for the abolition of Madame Aubain. (He'd despise Uncle Tom.)

*Here is poor Harold Bell Wright's best shot at creating an equivalent character: *"The Mexican prepared the horses as Texas had instructed and then took up his position by the front gate, proud and happy that they had so honored him—that they had trusted him to guard his employer's daughter."*

†In a similar vein, Helen Hunt Jackson's *Ramona* offers a tale of nonwhite martyrdom on the boundary of Imperial itself. The heroine, half-Scottish, half-Indian, raised in a Mexican California hacienda as an unwanted niece, falls in love with a fullblooded Temecula Indian named Alessandro and runs away with him shortly after his home has been seized by white American settlers. Each time the young couple set up house, they prosper until the Americans take over their property again. Alessandro finally goes mad and gets murdered. Ramona is saved by her Mexican half-brother Felipe, whom she marries; they flee the Americans for Mexico just as she and Alessandro had fled the Americans for San Jacinto. Michael Dorris writes: "Ramona herself is lifeless, so uncomplex in her goodness, loyalty, piety and brave endurance that she exists more as a cipher than as flesh and blood."

Anyhow, might not María be far worse off than Félicité? That must be what I want: somebody who's badly off. And aren't the women who work in Mexicali's *maquiladoras* worse off than María? Their take-home pay is only one-fifth of hers. At the end of the twentieth century there were six hundred and thirty thousand of them, *primarily young women, who account for one-third of the republic's labor force . . . They are 10 to 15 percent more productive . . . than American workers . . . the* maquiladoras *have generated during the past years "a 47 percent increase in productivity coupled with a 29 percent decline in real wages"* . . . I have never been cheated out of a dollar in my life. *Few hire pregnant women, and some plants have compulsory pregnancy tests.* A maquiladora *in Ciudad Juárez, according to complaints by workers, requires new hires to "present bloody tampons for three consecutive months."* In other words, *in material advantages they are already well supplied.* This makes me so furious and sorrowful to read. (In another chapter of *Imperial* we'll find out whether it's true.) Even Napoleon before he hypnotized himself with domination's glittering honors is credited with having said: *Respect the burden, Madame.* He was referring to a workman who was carrying a heavy load.

IMPERIAL

by

GUSTAVE FLAUBERT

1

For five years the other foremen in the shoe factory envied Raúl Hernández his star worker, María. Only the bookkeeper knew her last name. María was absent for work only once, on the day her father died. She brought in a bloody tampon every month, and on demand she slept with Raúl Hernández, a service for which she asked no favor other than the continuation of her employment. Long after he had lost his sexual interest in her, Raúl Hernández continued to be fond of María because she could turn out more soles per shift than any other worker he ever had.

Once upon a time, I thought that I wanted to write a novel like that—what style! I understood *respect the burden*. That novel about María would have failed, because respect must encompass more than the heroine's victimhood. It needs also to embrace her various happinesses and her silliness about parrots.

In 1968, a doctor who works with poor people in the Deep South and Appalachia writes a book which breathes shame, guilt, compassion and indignation in a manner which I can only consider noble; the doctor is haunted by *Let Us Now Praise Famous Men*, whose passion may indeed have been one of the primary reasons he stands present in the land of goiters, stinking outhouses and seven-year-olds with degenerative joint disease—in which case James Agee and Walker Evans truly accomplished something; he looks at the photographs in their book and feels a sense of *déjà vu;* yet the people in his own book *seem different—perhaps more lonely, more confused by the ironies and paradoxes which this nation presents to them as much as to those of us who feel educated and sensitive.* It is very important to this doctor that his patients be different, because Agee has said over and over that no portrait of an individual family can stand in for everybody; there can be no types because human beings, so the doctor puts it, are *preciously unique and different even in the way they face starvation and die.*

Indeed our attitudes toward poverty are reflected in the two distinct stereotypes we apply to it. In order to earn . . . quickly forgotten sympathy, the lives of perfectly respectable and determined people are caricatured and distorted so that they emerge as useless, semi-retarded, pitiful creatures, in need of charity . . . Or else those lives are made so exclusively "different," so intractable, so proud, so "happy," so uncomplicated, natural, unaffected, stoic, beautifully patient and enduring—that awe or envy becomes the only suitable and justifiable response from "us."

What then does the doctor want? It may well be that the people with the leisure and inclination to read *Let Us Now Praise Famous Men* all the way through are not the go-getter people who have the ability to control resources, and thereby to direct them toward the poor. What does more good, a generation of indignant college students or several million dollars' worth of beans, flour and powdered milk sent to this nation's poorest counties? This is by no means a rhetorical question; I would be grateful to learn the answer.

The smell of fresh tortillas, the songs of birds, and the silences of the prostitutes young and old now standing in their doorway chrysalises, ready to fly into the cooling evening (the temperature has already fallen twenty degrees, down to ninety-four), these can go into a novel or an essay; it doesn't matter which; they could even be working notes for a poem. But once on a Greyhound bus from Calexico to Los Angeles I met a Mexican-American man whose best friend had lost three sisters, ages sixteen, fourteen and thirteen. It happened right on the eastern border of

Imperial, in Yuma, Arizona, and the reason that the man told me his friend's story was that fourteen more *pollos* had just died of thirst when their coyote abandoned them in the very same spot; so it must have been 2001 when I heard the story, which took place about fifteen years earlier; and you already know the ending. They'd paid their big money, then waited and waited, after which forensicists identified the decomposed bodies of those three young girls. They never found the coyote. The mother went crazy. And the man told this steadily and so softly that I thought that only I could hear, but when he had finished, everyone on the bus fell silent. How could it be right to make art out of this? And yet of course it *would* be right to make a poem or a song, a painting or a novel about it, if doing so would help anyone to *feel*. Steinbeck might have been able to do it. Maybe someday I will attempt to do it. At the moment, I cannot presume to do anything with this story except to show it to you, tiptoe around it, and walk away.

THE TIDE IS OUT

For now, all I can hope to do is learn as I go. I've kept returning to Imperial year after year, just as I promised; and I know the most important thing, which I know only because I'm getting old—namely, that I'll never do enough of that learning. As for the landscape, at least, I'm finally beginning to find my bearings in it; so many Imperial views are familiar now; when I come to them, I recognize them from my own photographs. (Sometimes the photographs trick me. I'd forgotten how yellow the Algodones Dunes are, since I mostly see them in black and white.)—It's night here, the tide out, the dark mud rivelled and wrinkled with water, studded with rocks and clamshells, consecrated by blue, pink, yellow and green stripes of reflected neon. Steinbeck almost got this far, but here at San Felipe the Sea of Cortés can be dangerously shallow; can you see these fishing boats sunk in the mud? In 1539, Cortés's lieutenant, Francisco de Ulloa, did get here, or near enough; after inspecting the whales, sheep, Indians and tortoises of Imperial he concluded that *the game was not worth the candle.*—The tide is out; the tide is out, and those white streaks of ocean have become long low flat subdued lines, scarcely worthy of being called breakers. The clean smell of Gulf proclaims finality; this is Imperial's frontier, and these long foamy lines whose whiteness seems phosphorescent in the night, they lie within another zone. My air-conditioning man in Sacramento sails out of here for his fishing vacations. Last time he caught a thirty-five-pound grouper and three squids ranging from eight to twenty-six pounds; they changed from reddish-brown to milky-luminescent while they died; but those successes occurred two hundred miles south of San Felipe, not in Imperial at all.

What is Imperial? A Mexican woman in a serape walks slowly along the beach, tilting back her head yet shading her eyes with a forearm. Suppose that I could "bring her alive," which means in part to appropriate her, in part to reimagine her, so that she (or the character, the alphabetical trick which pretended to be her) grew vivid, consistent, interesting, noble and flawed and serenely ordinary all at once—in short, "real." Moreover, suppose that her reality corresponded in some fashion, probably metonymically, to the reality of this imaginary "Imperial." Steinbeck's Okies in *The Grapes of Wrath* were well constructed puppets; one can actually grieve for them, and thereby be encouraged to ask important and maybe even practical questions about human rights, California agricultural policy, whatever; in other words, one can respect their burdens; whereas a purely statistical, objectively truer approach, by occluding the humanity of dispossession, and thereby obstructing our grieving, partakes of the worm-ball character of a fallen palm tree's inner flesh; we can touch its complex deadness, know it in a way that a living thing, for instance a woman in a serape, can never be known; the only way to approach knowing that woman in a serape, unless you live with her, is to invent her; but can knowing the dead palm tree profit us as much? I've written that Imperial widens itself almost into boundlessness, and so does my task.

Who should *my* heroine be?

Imperial is palm trees, tract houses, and the full moon. Imperial is the pale green lethal stars of chollas, whose spikes can go right through shoe leather. Imperial is a landscape like wrinkled mammoth-flesh; Imperial has broad breasts and innumerable pubic mounds, long reddish-grey tendons of crumblestone; Imperial's hair is comprised of snaky washes in the badlands. Imperial is mica; Imperial is gypsum: translucent pages of a rock's broken book. How many books might Imperial contain?—An infinite number, of course; but just as my eye has accustomed itself to retracing certain mapscapes (Highway 111, the Algodones Dunes, the border wall, the loop around the Salton Sea), my mind's eye, trying to see Imperial, overgazes a few very particular bookscapes: *Let Us Now Praise Famous Men,* and *The Winning of Barbara Worth,* of course; and *The Grapes of Wrath* . . . Oscar Lewis's great oral history *The Children of Sanchez* I meant to write about later in this book; I expected to reread the life of Cortés more closely . . .

STEINBECK, MOST AMERICAN OF US ALL

I feel protective toward this dead writer, who doesn't need my protection at all. A friend of mine has been teaching American literature for a long time in a certain California university. Year after year, she assigns *The Grapes of Wrath,* and they love it. Very likely on account of that selfsame popularity, the critics jeer that Steinbeck writes, if I remember correctly, *novels with training wheels.*

When a scientist embarks on a series of experiments to test a new hypothesis, it is likely that most of them will "fail," reality being more complicated than even the most torturous assertion. Science corrects, revises, goes on. In this respect writing is more like science than the other arts (except, of course, for musical composition), because we can replace one word by another as many times as we like, even resurrecting deleted choices; whereas I have only so many chances to paint over my bad oil painting before it turns into a sticky brick. Nonetheless, once a work of art gets sent out into the world, revision ends. (Writers such as James Branch Cabell, who corrected their novels after publication, are decidedly not the rule.) So what would prudence entail, should my *Grapes of Wrath* turn out imperfectly? We find one of Steinbeck's would-be mentors advising him to write the next *Grapes of Wrath,* set this time among the Puerto Rican population of New York City. Had Steinbeck accepted this counsel, he might have created something quite powerful. Who knows? Maybe he could have been another Zola, constructing an entire series of novels about dispossessed or underpossessing Americans. Instead, he chose to devote himself to loopy failures such as *The Winter of Our Discontent* and the never-to-be-finished translation from ancient English to archaic English of Malory's tale of King Arthur. I love him for it.

People simplify Steinbeck into a populist, a pseudo–common man who idealized the true common man, a socialist like Jack London. For an instant corrective to that notion, read his short story "The Vigilante," about a fellow who helps to lynch a "nigger fiend." *Somebody said he even confessed.* With genius's restraint, Steinbeck sets this tale in the hours *after* the murder, chronicling the changes in the vigilante's heart from emptiness to cocky pride. At the end he comes home to his bitter, shut-down wife, who gazes into his face in astonishment and decides that he must have been with another woman. *By God, she was right,* thinks the vigilante, admiring himself in the mirror. *That's just exactly how I do feel.* And the story ends. One quasi-socialist thread does spin itself through "The Vigilante" as it does through all of Steinbeck's work: the receptivity of human beings to one another, and specifically of the one to the many. It is the bloodthirstiness of the lynch mob, and later on the admiration of the bartender, and the look in his wife's eyes, which in turn tell the vigilante how to feel. Thus we are to one another, for good and for evil.

Steinbeck's astonishing novel *In Dubious Battle,* which narrates the course of a fruitpickers' strike in California's Central Valley, and which like all his best writing is unbelievably *real* down to the last detail (the mud between the tents, the look and smell of dinner-mush, the ugly dialogues between apple-pickers and the checkers who dock their pay, the practicalities of sanitation),* magnifies the vigilante's sus-

*I found myself remembering its images while researching Imperial's agricultural strikes of 1933–34.

ceptibility into something larger, less evil, if still problematic, and longer lasting: the way in which workers can be manipulated for political ends. Just as he did with the vigilante, Steinbeck dares to show the human nastiness of the strikers. *When we get down to business,* says one "sullen boy," *I'm gonna get me a nice big rock and I'm gonna sock that bastard.* But while he is helping us to see what is wrong about the rank and file strikers, Steinbeck does two more things: He makes it powerfully clear to us *why* they strike, putting much of himself into their cause; meanwhile, he savages the vanguardist puppeteers who so often infest political movements. Their motto: *The worse it is, the more effect it'll have.*

Were Steinbeck's writing to be simplified into anything at all, the motif would be *distrust of authority.* In 1947 he visited the Soviet Union, and in his account of that journey he reports that while Russians, or at least the Russian spokespeople whom he was allowed to meet, tend to support their government and believe that what it does is good, Americans prefer to begin with the profoundest suspicion of government and its coercive powers. Of course the latter is no longer true at all, if it ever was. Hence Steinbeck is one of the most un-American Americans of his time.

I want to be un-American like him, unaffiliated with anything but balance. I want to show Félicité's goodness and stupidity together. Maybe then, in the book called *Imperial* which I hope someday to write, I can achieve greater goodness while exposing my own stupidities.

Steinbeck desired all of us to be angry and sorry about the plight of the Okies, and his own outrage makes *The Grapes of Wrath* a great book. He wanted to tell us that the people in the Soviet Union were not the monsters that our Cold Warriors insisted they were; and because the apparatchiks distorted and limited what he could see, his *Russian Journal* is dated and slight, but true enough to annoy both Russians and Americans. (Let's call it a failure.) When he wrote *The Winter of Our Discontent,* he was worried about American materialism and hypocrisy. The defects of this novel remind me of those of socialist realism. Here lies a book with a message, and because that message is sometimes too stark, and other times camouflaged to the point of eccentric mysticism, it makes the story itself waver and warp. Well, fine; so he did have messages; he hoped to actually accomplish something in his own time, in which case I love him for that, too.

The book of his which I admire the most is *East of Eden.* For two decades now the character of Kate, whom some critics find unconvincing, has haunted my head; she's horrific, pathetic, steady, successful and lonely; she perfectly is what she is. The retelling of the Cain and Abel story is touchingly accomplished, the landscape descriptions lovely and lush, the plotting as careful and convincing as the best of George Eliot. And of course Steinbeck has written in a message, a flaw, personified by a Chinese servant who tells us, sometimes at great length, what to think. But Lee has never annoyed me. He speechifies intelligently, at times wittily, and sometimes compassionately. Do I care that nobody I've met talks like that? He is sincere because Steinbeck is sincere. And this is what I love about Steinbeck most of all, his sincerity.

He once wrote about his friend Ed Ricketts that the man loved what was true and hated what wasn't.* If Steinbeck occasionally mistook sentimentality for truth, well, there remain worse vices. Steinbeck worried and at times grew bitter, but he was never cynical. One aspect of his credo which too many of us misperceive as sentimental is his very Imperial glorification of individual choice. If I dislike, say, what America "stands for," and if I express that feeling in public, I may find that certain other Americans dislike *me*. That happened to Steinbeck. The many bannings of *The Grapes of Wrath* comprise its badge of honor. This book upset people. It actually had something to say. It was angry, unashamedly sexual and un-American. Being un-American, Steinbeck was the most American of us all.

IMPERIAL

by

John Steinbeck

1

María loved truth and hated untruth . . .

*Aside from its beautiful lament for the death of Ricketts, *The Log from the* Sea of Cortez is another "slight" book, in the *Russian Journal* category. Two things about it strike me. First of all, here is Steinbeck, living admirably, wanting to learn more about the world, to educate himself in a discipline which most people "have to" go to school to learn—marine biology—in hopes of applying what he has learned to the lives of human organisms; and he is throwing his own not-superabundant financial resources into the quest. I consider this noble. Secondly, on almost every page Steinbeck recounts or advises things which would now be considered unethical at the very least, and probably illegal—most often, the unsupervised gathering and pickling of sea creatures, many of whose corpses, thanks to the *Sea of Cortez*'s inadequate supply of storage vessels, ended up getting ruined in transit. His paean to the reproductive powers of Ed Ricketts falls in the same category. These frowned-upon activities may be victimless crimes, or worse. In any case, they are crimes of individualism and of individualism's experiments and discoveries.

Were I writing a *Grapes of Wrath* about Imperial, I would have to first attempt what Steinbeck did for the whole of agricultural California in "The Harvest Gypsies"; I'd construct a sociology of Imperial. *Let us see the fields that require the impact of their labor and the districts to which they must travel,* he writes, then inserts a true and pathetic detail, just as any novelist or journalist would do; afterwards, he gets down to delineating his data: *There are the vegetable crops of the Imperial Valley, the lettuce, cauliflower, tomatoes, cabbage to be picked and packed, to be hoed and irrigated. There are several crops a year to be harvested, but there is not time distribution sufficient to give the migrants permanent work.*

Maybe I don't get out as much as Steinbeck used to. In any event, before getting my shoes dirty in any Hoovervilles, I'll pick up the telephone to order up some piping-hot statistics. First I have to learn the female employment rate; then and only then may I go interview some Marías. The Department of Health Services has kindly ranked the fifty-eight counties of California in regard to various unpleasant things, a ranking of one being the best. And from these profiles I learned the following:

Imperial County comes in thirteenth for deaths due to all causes, fifty-second for fatal motor vehicle crashes, eighteenth for murder deaths, fourteenth for suicide deaths, seventh for cancer deaths, fiftieth for drug-related deaths, fifty-second for incidence of hepatitis C, fifty-seventh for incidence of tuberculosis (only San Francisco County is worse), nineteenth for infant mortality, forty-ninth for births among adolescent mothers, fifty-fifth for incidence of minors living in poverty. So what? We need a novelist to make sense of it.

What is the story of the Joad family? If you lack time to read *The Grapes of Wrath,* you can read the synopsis in "The Harvest Gypsies": *Families who had lived for many years on the little "cropper lands" were dispossessed because the land was in the hands of the banks and finance companies, and because these owners found that one man with a tractor could do the work of ten sharecropper families. Faced with the question of starving or moving, these dispossessed families came west.*

If I were going to write my *Grapes of Wrath* about Imperial, maybe I'd take my synopsis from Officer Dan Murray of the Border Patrol: *You should see these guys pickin' watermelon, bent over all day. They do work most Americans wouldn't do.*

The novel might open in a certain perfectly arrayed jungle on the border of Thermal, a humid, shady little kingdom across the street from the sign for the Jewel Date Palm Co. Each uprooted fan-palm made a royal progress, marching slowly down the road between the wheels of the white Bobcat, holding high its green-crowned head: The king was coming! With a proud white smile, José ground the vehicle down that rutted mud road, which could have been somewhere in Central

America, and then he emerged into the hot naked reality of Imperial where his colleague Marciano, who came from Michoacán and lived in Indio, was whacking each treetop into tight flat-topped bundles, then tying them off. José gripped the lever. The king's many fronds whirled; then he began to lurch, to dance, slowly bowing to the forces of severance, until José had laid him crosswise upon his fallen predecessor, expertly sliding the loop out from under his trunk. Mariano began binding and maiming the king. They shipped three hundred palms a month to the MGM Grand and other hotels in Las Vegas. And now José was grinding down the shady alleys, back to the place where a stinger-tailed chainsaw machine had already cut out a cube-shaped chunk of root from the earth. He said to me: To move the big one is very difficult because that's the most dangerous. If you no have strong machine, you can be killed.

His favorite kind of palm tree was the queen palm. That was what his people called a fan-palm. Just as I did, he saw them in terms of royal stateliness.

I could have come every day with my notebook to stand beneath the multitudinous, multipointed canopies of fan-palms, watching José and Marciano, writing down their stories and their slang, and after work I could have met their sweethearts and children. I could have described their homes. (As Officer Murray used to say, *if something catches your eye, there's a reason.*) Had they refused to invite me in, I could have gone to Michoacán to meet Marciano's mother. And if I failed to meet her, I could have appropriated that fat orangeskinned woman in Mexicali who stands in her flat square yard, which is bare earth, and she is hosing down the dust. This is how to write a novel: Gather details and plant them in the pale tan soil of narrative, which sometimes finds itself formed into levees and sometimes makes walls around orchards. My notebook is a fan-palm grove. I am José; I uproot the grandest trees which have grown there, and carry them out to Marciano, who is also me, to hack them up and pack them up, so that they can be potted in the lobby of my *Grapes of Wrath.* That is how one writes novels. Imperial County is fifty-seventh for incidence of tuberculosis, so we'd better give José tuberculosis. South of Mecca lies a watermelon field, then citrus groves, a fan-palm orchard. Once upon a time there was a man named José . . .

But in Mexicali there is a man named José López who has become my friend. And Lupe Vásquez is my friend. I would never consider changing a word of their stories. They are real and they have taught me many things that are true as I peer into the mystery called Mexico.

Chapter 12

THE GARDENS OF PARADISE

(2007)

Motivations, even if ideological, are not monolithic.

—Ross Hassig, 1988

As I said, this book forms itself as it goes. Fields, cemeteries, newspapers and death certificates beguile and delay me; I don't care that I'll never finish anything; Imperial will scour them away with its dry winds and the brooms of its five-dollar-an-hour laborers (and a very few Anglo farmers, too). It is they, the Mexicans and Mexican-Americans, the cabbage-pickers legal and illegal, whom it is slowly becoming my privilege to know. Imperial is what I want it to be, but they are ones who are what they are. The desert is real, as are they, but there is no such place as Imperial; and I, who don't belong there, was never anything but a word-haunted ghost. This is my life, and I love it. Books are whatever we want them to be. I am where I want to be, in Paradise.

Let me now commence the history of Paradise.

PART TWO

OUTLINES

Chapter 13

WHEN BREAD WAS LIGHT

(1768–1848)

> For years they had wandered alone in silence and solitude, where the sun burned white all day and the stars burned white all night, blindly following the whisper of a spirit.
>
> —Zane Grey, 1913

"CHIEFLY COVERED WITH FLOATING SAND"

Once upon a time, in that limbo of mostly dry centuries between Lake Cahuilla and the Salton Sea, Spanish delineators, knowing that assertion is necessary if not sufficient for possession, drew their northernmost boundary-line as far as (let me crib from Mr. Samuel T. Black) Nootka, while the English stretched their claim all the way down to San Domingo. Fortunately, my own system of grids and lines came along to save Imperial from this maddening doubleness—oh, the place is bifurcated now, to be sure, but that's a different thing from existing within two mutually exclusive zones of authority! Here is how Mr. Black tells the tale (he's writing a history of San Diego County, specifically, of San Diego County's *Settlement, Organization, Progress and Achievement*): *It was not until the Americans, by the seizure of Oregon, came in like a wedge and spread them apart, that their respective overlapping claims may be said to have come to an end.* Hurrah! Now it's us *versus* the Mexicans, with *our* overlapping claims comprising "California," "Arizona," "Texas," and other ill-defined entities. Well, where did Imperial end in the old days, before some fur trader's clerk invented Oregon? Any reasonable person can see that Imperial is contracting, imploding even, as Los Angeles, represented by Indio, comes in like a wedge, etcetera. Why not say that in those days before the first line it wandered indefinitely northward, all the way to where "California" begins to get cool, and deeply, vaguely southward down the Baja Peninsula where until 1768 the Jesuits had their fifteen missions?

Imperial is a dream without details. Imperial is a future of *Settlement, Organization, Progress and Achievement,* which its own pioneers, settlers and organizers might not like if they knew what was coming. *We need have no fear that our lands will not become better and better as the years go by.* Imperial is and unanswerably was:

Somewhere within its dust-clouds lay a white-ringed basin of indeterminate extent, within which the Mexicali Valley's nine hundred and eighty-eight thousand acres still cohered with (which is to say, remained equally unnamed as) the Imperial Valley's six hundred thousand; and these in turn, continuing to be themselves all the way down and up the gentle hollow of the Salton Sink, which in spite of its circles of stone (Indian fish-traps) had always been, so must always be, dry—who can foresee, much less believe in, the comings and goings of water?—had not yet been divorced from the Coachella Valley, whose palm forests, excepting an oasis or two, were as long gone as Lake Cahuilla—and I should probably tell you that the Coachella Valley would still have been the Cahuilla, after the Indians who lived there. In short, nobody had drawn either county or national line to trisect that long downsloping bed of a long-lost sea; the core of Imperial remained whole. (Only what's unknown is safe from dissection. Bow to the eternal vacuum!)

Somewhere, somewhere, potentiality slept. Somewhere the Sea of Cortés sent roaring tidal bores up the blood-red Río Colorado; east and west of it, unchristened Indians dug irrigation ditches. No one had gathered up Imperial's treasures, the concretions which resembled knurled unicorn horns; these lay on the north slopes of Signal Mountain, in the dry washes west of the Salton Sink, and around the travertine altars northwest of the latter, in a zone still blessedly unburdened by the Riverside County line. The artesian wells that would spurt a full thirty feet into the air still lay vaulted up beneath Imperial's maidenhead, which in the words of Lieutenant W. H. Emory (1846) *is chiefly covered with floating sand, the surface of which, in various places, is white with diminutive spinelas and everywhere over the whole surface is found the large and soft mussel-shell.* All over, you see, Imperial sported the spoor of bygone and future water. Half a century after him, the founders of El Centro would marvel at Imperial's petrified clam and oyster beds without wondering which dreams of theirs would fossilize into something for you and me to marvel over.

Imperial was an unprimed canvas which Mark Rothko would someday paint with glowing field-rectangles and name *Untitled;* Imperial drowsed more and then some, pillowing itself upon sandhills; Imperial sprawled inchoate within the more formless formlessness of California itself—California, island in a Spanish romance!* This island, as the concretions prove, is characterized by *treasure,* and its inhabitants are Negro Amazons about each of whom it may be fairly said: *To look at Barbara Worth was a pleasure; to be near her was a delight.* Or, if you'd rather, California is not actually an island, but a peninsula *somewhere on the way from Mexico to India* whose coordinates in space and history, so the founder of the Bancroft Li-

*Ordóñez de Montalvo's *Sergas of Espandian,* first printed in either 1510 or 1519.

brary concluded in the course of reading more than four thousand documents sixteen hundred of which predate the Gold Rush, were *vaguely fixed by such bounds as Asia, the north pole, Newfoundland and Florida.* Never again; vagueness has been illuminated away by the whiteness of American bread; we *know* California; we came in like a wedge and took it from the English.

And so: Between Asia and Florida lies California, which now lies wrapped in Mexico but will soon be partially stripped of Mexican-ness, with American and Russian bedclothes thrown haphazardly over her shoulders while she slumbers on, turning uneasily in her sleep so that one coverlet or another slips away; deep within her womb, Imperial gurgles with rivers and aquifers, but the cavity's sand-packed, so nobody hears anything; Imperial sleeps within her mother; not even the shining of bread can lure her out.

We know California. Now let's know her better than death. Let time begin: In 1804 the Spaniards draw a line bisecting this territory into Baja and Nueva California; twenty years later, Nueva California gets renamed Alta California; a quarter-century after that, this world will hold only one unqualified California, the American one; Mexican California we still call "Baja" to this day.

So much for context; now what about Imperial itself? (Or did I already ask that?) Well, let's talk about the portion lying in Lower California; the rest remains unknown. Imperial sprawls down far past Loreto in those days; she snores and fidgets, crossing her ankles; with one grimy toenail she scratches at a mosquito bite on her naked brown foot, never waking up; she opens her legs and spreads them across the Gulf of California; there, we have her now; let's say that Baja's her right leg and Sonora's her left. What about the rest of her? Surely Imperial's more than a pair of legs! With her right hip at Los Angeles and her right side running all the way to Nootka and her head in China and her—all right; I give up; she's nothing but a pair of legs. Lake Cahuilla's her womb, but Lake Cahuilla's dry now.

Do you feel as if you know Imperial yet? According to one of the Jesuits, the peripatetic Father Baegert, *it was altogether one of the most miserable countries in the world, fit only for three kinds of people: self-sacrificing priests; poor Spaniards, who could not make their living anywhere else; and native Indians, for whom anything was good enough.* (Baegert goes on to condemn the poverty of the Indians' language, which pressed metaphors into service to name those new things brought by the Fathers: A door was a mouth, bread was light, and wine was bad water.) Other visitors were equally enthusiastic. For instance, General Sherman called the Baja *a miserable, wretched, dried-up peninsula.* Well, but even then Imperial did have her points: the quicksilver monopoly, unauthorized pearl-fishing, the hope of one more El Dorado to rape.

So that was Imperial for you, amorphous, virgin and vast. On the west the Pacific Ocean did constrain her, no doubt, and to the east there was still the Río Colorado; oh, yes, there was that. A hundred years after we overthrew the Mexican regime in Imperial Norte, a scholar who was preening his talents for the *California Blue Book* laughingly recalled a map from 1564 in which *the Colorado, largest river in the world, rising in the mountains of Thibet and meandering through a course of 15,000 or 20,000 miles, pours its vast volume of waters into the Gulf of California.* Perhaps it was really almost like that, in those days when bread was light.

THE BODY-SNATCHERS

Beyond this streamlet, also known as the Buena Guila, lay the subdistrict of Pimería, which swept southeast through much of Sinaloa and which in those days was little more than an outline drawn in around unknown quantities. Strictly speaking (as we delineators do prefer to speak), the conquest of Pimería had commenced in 1687 with the erection of the latest palisaded mission, appropriately called Dolores; the tale of the two Yuman missions in Imperial territory would prove more dolorous by far, as you'll read. Speaking still more strictly, we should mention Hernando de Alarcón's voyage from embryonic Acapulco to unborn Yuma; that happened in 1540; the Río Colorado had begun to be mapped. Melchior Díaz also grazed Imperial that year, but we won't allow him into this book.

In 1697 Imperial got hemmed in from another direction when Loreto, first of the Baja California missions, cauterized itself off from the surrounding landscape of non-delineation: *la línea* was born! The Jesuits stood on one side of the ditch, with their mouths, lights and blood-colored bad water; on the other side were the people whose grandchildren would be Mexicans. And between Northside and Southside, I mean around the perimeters of those little Northside islands in the immense tan sea of Southside, stood soldiers; *their duties were to act as body guards for the missionaries, to stand watch at night, to keep an eye upon the Indians and inflict punishments.* The body-snatchers of my era wore uniforms and used night-vision technology to catch the half-Spanish-half-Indians of Southside; they enclosed them in a blare of police-light, lined them up on the silt of roadsides, standing over them, concentrating headlights on them, and then, when they'd accumulated enough to validate the trouble, expelled them back beyond the line. The body-snatchers of the old days cut the line, which was still infinite and had not yet been placed anywhere in particular, into manageable segments, then pulled each segment around themselves to make another loop of Northside, their dwelling place. Then they issued forth into Southside's surrounding blankness, hunted Indians, hauled them back to the new islands, and saved their souls by means of confinement and whiplashes,* not to mention the fresh-baked Host, which shone with magic light. (Acting Governor José Joaquín de Arrillaga, 1796: *I found about 150 Indians beside the women, who fled upon my arrival. The men remained passive. I took a Christian girl, 12 or 13 years old, who was running away and who belonged to Mission San Vicente.*) That is how it was in the missions, century after century. Perhaps it did get a little better toward the end, since it was worse in the beginning. (Petition of some of Cortés's allies against the Aztecs—the petitioners are pleading against a crushing new tax: . . . *when they gave us the holy gospel . . . with very good will and desire we received and grasped it . . .Not once was anyone of us . . . ever tortured or burned over this, as was done on every hand here in New Spain.*) My own hatred of the very idea of authoritarian compulsion, and the experiences of the century in which I was born—Hitler, Stalin, Mao, Pol Pot—incline me to see only the worst side of these establishments. But it might well have been that bread was, on occasion, light. There; now I've proven that I have an open mind; back to my axe-grinding: As late as 1826, a visitor to Alta California reported that *if any of the captured Indians show a repugnance to conversion, it is the practice to imprison them,* then once again offer them the sunny choice of Catholicism, sending them back to their dungeons should they still return the wrong answer.† Wait again, ask again, bring them back into the light! By that date there were fountains for the undecided to gaze upon, and tall trees shaded the body-snatchers' courtyards. Here is how a California county history tabulates the rewards of those who chose correctly: *The dress was, for the males, linen shirt, trousers, and a blanket. The women had each two undergarments a year, a gown and a blanket. What a dreamy secluded life it must have been . . .* But in those first Spanish centuries, delineation remained too feeble to ornament itself, at least in California. Bread was light, but it didn't shine very far. No fountains, and saplings or bare earth in place of trees! The Fathers did the best they could, but their rectilinear establishments were roofed with mud or tules. Only the very grandest, Mission San Diego, for instance, sported bronze cannons; and San Diego wouldn't be founded until 1769.

Nonetheless, mission after mission implanted itself on the far from fertile soil of the Baja. By 1730 some three hundred Spanish colonists lived in Pimería, and it

*In 1843 or 1844, James Hunter Bull, the first American to travel much of the Baja by foot, heard revolting tales, told by the Indians, of being lassoed to the missions and whipped for nine sunrises "to learn the delightful and mild doctrines of the Gospel of Christ," after which they were worked to death. One old Indian showed Bull how half of his thigh had been flogged away. Bull was no Catholic, and his story might be discounted, were it not for the fact that there are others.

†Ten years later, Richard Henry Dana, Jr., concurred that the mission priests were strict, but concluded: "Of the poor Indians very little care is taken," and cited the case of an Indian couple who had been married in church; the husband prostituted his wife to sailors and shared her earnings.

came time to push closer to Imperial herself, the "real" Imperial, the shrunken one, Imperial as I define her.* Spaniards had already sailed deep between Imperial's legs; who knew how far up the Colorado they'd go? Maybe to Thibet! Maybe, maybe; maybe luscious chocolate Amazons still awaited us somewhere; we hadn't explored every last sandhill. *Girls reached puberty at the age of twelve years; and they would often demand husbands before that age . . . Their word for husband had only a vulgar signification.* That is exactly what a conquistador likes to hear.

THE GARDENS OF PARADISE

The Franciscans now replaced the Jesuits. In 1771, the year that Mission San Gabriel was founded, Fray Francisco Gardés explored the Colorado Desert as far as Signal Mountain. Three years later we find Captain Juan Bautista de Anza setting out from Pimería all the way to Monterey, Alta California—an astonishing overland journey which could have easily ended as badly as those of the Forty-Niners and *pollos* whose desiccated corpses are shrouded in sand. But this de Anza knows exactly what he is about. For example, he establishes alliances. In that bygone wideness of water where the Gila met the Colorado (the terminus of Alarcón's voyage of 1540), there were, once upon a time, two islands, the larger of which was called Island de Trinidad, and here Captain de Anza and his soldiers are guested by the *Capitán and Chief of the Yuma Nation of savage Indians of the Colorado River drainage of Sonora in the Interior Provinces of this North America . . . known by the surname Palma,* whose real name is Olleyquotequiebe and whose baptismal name will be Salvador Carlos Antonio. The feast occurs in a lodge built especially for the occasion (and from de Anza's description I suspect that it scarcely differs except in size from the arrow-weed ramada in which Harold Bell Wright wrote *The Winning of Barbara Worth*). In those days the place remains "heavily timbered," hence surely cooler and less forbidding than it will appear to me. Palma's Yumans live lushly on river-irrigated watermelons, cantaloupes, Apache maize and diverse other crops. They go naked, and flatten the heads of their children by lashing boards tight against their skulls; they trade dried beans for scraps of red cloth. So an American trapper will report half a century later. In de Anza's time it may not have been much different. Palma, whom they promptly christen Salvador Palma, demeans himself as a reliable friend, and there is no good reason he should not have remained so. *After mass a proclamation was made prescribing rules tending to the better conduct of the people.* Then what? Guided by an Indian deserter from Mission San Gabriel, de

*Imperial was not yet Mexico by any means. In 1776 we find Fray Junípero Serra, founder of San Francisco, worrying about how to safely get some letters down to Mexico.

Anza fords the Colorado, thereby entering the area of interest to this book. Creosote bushes make his acquaintance. He descends into the Salton Sink. The New River in its then still modest canyon of clay might be wet or dry that year; either way, it doesn't detain him. If it's wet, it will have decorated itself with peppergrass and the occasional desert heliotrope. Regardless, there will be scant good water to drink in that channel. *It is a miserable place, without pasture and with very bad water,* which may be why they'll return home by a different route equally delectable to travel thanks to its sand dunes and dry plains. In the white sandhills over which unborn Imperial County will lay its road of oiled planks, and upon which Hollywood science fiction movies will be filmed, the expedition gets lost for ten days. Why should it be any different? Soldiers from Mission San Diego in search of runaway Indians had been defeated by Imperial's sand-mazes not two years since. Sebastián Tarabal, de Anza's guide, has already lost his wife in Imperial's deserts, and evidently (the sources conflict) his son as well. Eventually he succeeds in restoring the party to the Indians. They rest. Then once again de Anza marches down the "Devil's Road" in good and rapid order, sixty-one leagues southwest and northwest through Imperial, until they reach fair water at the Arroyo de Santa Catharina. *This place is in a canyon that runs on up, and through it passes the road that crosses the Sierra Madre de California.* We soon find him passing through the Cahuilla Valley, which I presume must have offered a palm oasis here and there; a century later there was one in what is now the southern sprawl of Indio. It takes about eight days to march from the west bank of the Colorado to Mission San Gabriel if one is unencumbered; with colonists it takes five or six weeks; de Anza shepherds none that time. He reaches Monterey without incident. Thanks to him, there's a proven line of supply to that outpost of adobe houses in the oak trees. His route *cannot be traced exactly,* says Bancroft, appropriately enough, for this is Imperial, where nothing's exact; if it's any help to you, Fonty's map of 1776 reveals, southeasterly of the intersection of the Gila and the Colorado, the territory of the Yumas, Cajuenches and Cucapahs, then westward of them the white emptiness of Imperial all the way to San Diego, which lies in Quemexa territory.

Home again. *We bade farewell to the Yumas with much tenderness on account of the fidelity and affection which they showed us.*

The following year, after stopping again at Palma's, he explores the Yuha Desert, which I imagine was almost the same then as now, the ocotillos tall and frail, the eponymous Anza-Borrego badlands beginning to swell, bluish-grey glass-shards of mountains to the west and southwest, the Imperial Valley sloping vastly and gently downwards toward what we now call Mexico, and I must not omit the pastel colors and waterless heat. Nobody ever bothers to garrison this spot. This time de Anza brings two hundred soldiers and colonists with him. Eight children are born on the way. While he's in the desert, Diegueño Indians promote Fray Luis Jayme into California's first martyr.

Once again de Anza arrives at San Gabriel in good order. Two years later will come the first public execution in Upper California, four insurgent Indian chiefs being shot by firing squad in San Diego for the greater glory of God.

In 1779, as I said, they baptize de Anza's host Palma (do they require him to remove the turquoise bead from his nose?) and establish two missions in his territory: Portezuela de la Concepción right where Yuma now is, Puerto de San Diablo about ten miles south of it. Imperial's commerce-inconvenient membrane will be deflowered at last. As a certain El Caballero de Croix explains in his instructions for the recruitment of soldiers and settlers for the upcoming expedition of 1781, *the two Provinces* of Lower and Upper California *should be united and have communication one with the other through the establishments on the Rivers Colorado and Gua.* In short, Portezuela de la Concepción and Puerto de San Diablo are "strategic." No doubt that's one reason the authorities trouble to save Palma's soul. But don't think they're not in earnest: The nudity of the Yumas has already been "discontinued," evidently by the Indians' own will, *seeing that all are covered with reasonable clothing acquired from the fabric of the Pima Nation.*

To be sure, the body-snatchers of 1980 may be distinguished from those of 1780, but only if we forget that the latter group aren't all priests! Some Northsiders catch natives and brainwash them; others catch them in order to drive them away. We've watched the map of Baja California become pimpled with religious islands of Northside; that's because the Fathers are celibate. When conquerors of both sexes congregate and procreate, then it won't be long before Southside itself gets surrounded. In 1566 the judge Alonso de Zorita completes his decade of helplessly compassionate witness in New Spain and sails home to the old. He advises the King: *To give a field or other land to a Spaniard is to cause great injury to the Indians. The Spaniards have taken their lands, pushed back their boundaries, and put them to an endless labor of guarding their fields against the Spaniards' cattle . . . some Indian towns are already so diminished and encircled by Spanish farms that the natives have no space in which to plant . . . They suffer need and hunger throughout the year.* In this book about Imperial we have no call to dwell upon the horrific *deliberate* cruelties of the Mexican Conquest: the workings to death, the hangings and burnings of children, the huntings-down of Indians by vicious dogs. Suffice it to say that as a direct result of the Conquest, disease, enslavement and spoliation killed four and a half million people in Mexico. The few lines which I have excerpted out of Zorita help us to understand the role which delineation plays in all this—or redelineation, I should say, for doubtless each Indian pueblo had its own shape before it gets enclosed, transected, shattered. How could the results of redelineation be any different?

And so, in 1780 the colonists arrived and began to treat Palma's people about as one would expect. Has bread lost its light, or is there no more bread for Indians? The friars are said to have seen the future, and try to prepare their flock for it by means of especially rigorous Loyolan meditations. In 1781 the inevitable Yuma Massacre, led by Palma himself, erases both missions, the men being put to death down to the very last priest, the women and children taken captive. After they manage to ransom them, the Spaniards proceed to the next phase: reprisals. Unfortunately for the delineators, these accomplish next to nothing. Hence the overlords of New Spain never again attempt to raise up missions in this area. Instead, they found Los Angeles.

And then? **THE DESERT DISAPPEARS.**

Chapter 14

LOS ANGELES

(1780)

Summer was counted from the time frogs were first heard to croak.

—Perfecto Hugo Reid, *ca.* 1800

What was Los Angeles like before there was a Los Angeles? What can we imagine of the quicksands and bears of Los Angeles, the California roses in the swamps of the Los Angeles River? To those of us who can read or write this book, it must have still been *once upon a time.*

Chapter 15

LOS ANGELES

(1781)

It is the destiny of every considerable stream in the west to become an irrigating ditch.

—Mary Austin, 1903

There were eleven families of settlers at first, all of them volunteers. It was sometime in June. A corporal and three soldiers,* whose red-collared blue uniforms were doubtlesss a bit grimy by now, led them to a place adjoining the Indian *ranchería* of Yabit, and there they founded Our Lady of the Angels of Porciúncula. **THE DESERT DISAPPEARS**. In August the Yuma Massacre would be discovered, and so the new Angelenos must have stayed on guard against their neighbors in Yabit, especially since Governor de Neve had recently noted that *the Pagans . . . anxiously ask especially for Sword blades, fragments of these, points of sharp Lances and every kind of cutting Instrument.* Fortunately, he was speaking generally; the pagans of Yabit were *docile and without malice but susceptible, like all Indians, to the first impressions of good or bad example.* Accordingly, the Governor had prudently *taken the necessary steps to prevent transmission of this news* of the massacre *to the natives* of other missions in Upper California. *I can't help believing in people.*

Although the destruction of the two Yuma missions had weakened their connection to Lower California, whose capital, Loreto, commanded them, the settlers were hardly alone in Upper California: San Diego with its three missions, San Carlos de Monterrey with its own three, San Francisco with its two and Mission San Gabriel itself already existed. Santa Barbara was just getting started. On the appended priestly establishments lived one thousand seven hundred and forty-nine Indians whose Christianity was undoubtedly at least as good as that of the Yumans. *We need have no fear that our lands will not become better and better as the years go by.*

Antonio Clemente Féliz Villavicencio of Chihuahua was the first to enlist. Who was he? *The Head or Father of each family must be a Man of the Soil, Healthy robust*

*The soldiers themselves, by the way, were married ten-year volunteers.

and without known vice or defect that would make him prejudicial to the Pueblos. We can be pretty sure that he, like the soldiers, wore a blue wool jacket, which, however, lacked insignia. He had probably put on his black campaign hat. He was a Spaniard. His wife, María de los Santos Serefina or Soberina, hailed from Durango. She was a fullblooded Indian. She would have worn one of her chemises of fine Brittany linen and a skirt of serge, blue baize or white cotton now probably gone dust-grey; if it were breezy that day, she might have worn the linen jacket she had made herself out of issued cloth. Very likely she wore one of her two shawls. He was thirty, and she twenty-six; their adopted daughter María Antonia Josefa, who was eight and a mestiza, would at the advanced age of thirteen marry a widower, at Mission San Gabriel. I see that this family purchased six *varas* of ribbons, and it pleases me to suppose that the little girl wore one or two of them in her black hair.

Not a single household consisted of Spaniards only. There were two Spanish-Indian couples; three Indian pairs, one wife of whom was *coyote Indian;* one mulatto couple, a mestizo married to a mulatta; a sixty-seven-year-old Indian with a forty-three-year-old mulatta wife; two Negroes married to mulattas; a mulatto whose wife's race was not specified; and a fifty-year-old widowed Chino accompanied by his eleven-year-old daughter—and, for your information, a Chino is the child of a salta-atrás with an Indian; a salta-atrás is *a child having negro characteristics but born of white parents.**

They dined sumptuously, no doubt. *Corn . . . is generally landed wormy,* the authorities advised. *Lard and cane sugar . . . the heat of the hold melts and ferments.* On the other hand, each settler and his family received, or at least were mandated to receive, two mares, two cows with one calf, two ewes and two she-goats, all four of the latter animals pregnant, a yoke of oxen, two horses, a cargo mule, and a multitude of tools including hoe, spade, musket and dagger . . . It may well be that some of these bestowals were subject to the equivalents of worminess, melt and fermentation; all the same, the intentions of this *reglamento* were admirable.

Still more remarkable to me are the instructions for land distribution. Each parcel was a square five hundred and fifty feet wide (two hundred *varas* in the measurement of the time), *this being the area ordinarily taken by one fanega of Corn in sowing.* Every settler was awarded two of these which could be irrigated and two more which could not. These land grants were not dissimilar to the *ejidos* which President Cárdenas would bring into being in Southside a century and a half later:

*My 1910 *Britannica* lists the following seven castes of New Spain: the Gachupines, or spurred ones, who were European-born and therefore at the apex, the creoles or native-born, then "mestizos (Indian and white), mulattoes (negro and white), Zambos (negro and Indian, who were regarded as specially vicious and dangerous), native Indians and negroes. But there were about a dozen intermediate 'named varieties . . .' "

They were *an inheritance in perpetuity . . . indivisible and inalienable forever,* immune to mortgage and subject to descent to whichever male descendant a family chose, *that the sons of the possessors of these grants may have the obedience and respect of their parents.* They could also go to landless daughters married to other settlers. All taxes were remitted for the first five years.

Sipping from their leather water bags, which they must have filled from the Los Angeles River *(it is simply needless to question the supply of water),* the settlers built their pueblo. In a decade, it had twenty-nine houses, containing a hundred and thirty-nine inhabitants. *And in material advantages they are already well supplied.*

Chapter 16

TÍA JUANA

(1825)

The dust rises, making swirls, with flowers of death.

—Aztec song

Next comes Tijuana, whose name's origin remains arguable. In 1825, Don José Dario Arguello obtains a grant of Rancho Tía Juana. The Inquisition has been abolished in Mexico five years since. Slavery was prohibited a year ago; to make up for that error, the new Constitution granted the presidency dictatorial powers in case of emergency, thereby guaranteeing that there would soon be an emergency.

In 1825, Tía Juana cannot even be said to boast the presence of Aunt Jane. The official founding date of the city will be 1889. On the other hand, Los Angeles has not yet gone too far ahead; in 1827 it will hold a mere eighty-two houses.

Tía Juana gets river water in dribs and drabs, but **WATER IS** not yet **HERE**. Accordingly, nor is the entity which will someday be called Tijuana.

Chapter 17

TECATE

(1830)

Before mapping can begin, control points must be defined.

—*The Compact NASA Atlas of the Solar System*, 2001

And doomed Juan Bandini somehow took title to sixteen hundred hectares of Cañada de Tecate, which needless to say did not stay in the family. In that time it was an unknown place with a name as obscure in meanining as Tía Juana's; it might have meant *the water in which a woman wets her hands while making tortillas* or it could have meant a gourd, or (least likely of all, given Tecate's proximity to Mexicali, which decidedly outdoes her in this respect), *where the sun shines* . . .

Chapter 18

LOS ANGELES

(1845)

And in spring the sweet goad of compelling desire and mating and mutual love are in season among all that move upon the fruitful earth . . .

—Oppian, *ca.* A.D. 194

For a certain grand ball in Los Angeles, in August 1845, the hosts incurred the following expenses: thirty dollars to prepare the dance floor,* fifteen dollars for spermaceti so that there would be an abundance of light, twenty-four dollars for four musicians, four dollars for servants and a hundred nineteen dollars for refreshments, in which *aguardiente* played a distinguished part. (Half a century afterward, one county history will define this beverage as *a sort of cognac, which was very agreeable to the palate and went like a flash to the brain.*) Now everything was ready. Soon the music would begin. Soon the gentlemen would doff their cord-tied, broad-brimmed hats and bow to the ladies. Amazons dwelled in California after all, and their names were Ramona, Josetta, Isadora, María Arcadia, Guadalupe and Juana.†

By now the stockaded redoubts of what Bancroft calls "pre-pastoral California" had been partially superseded. In 1834, Louis Vignes planted the first orange tree. Los Angeles rapidly became a kingdom of figs and oranges. *Every house had its inclosure of vineyard, which resembled a miniature orchard, the vines being very old, ranged in rows, trimmed very close, with irrigating ditches so arranged that a stream of water could be diverted between each row of vines.* That was how General Sherman remembered it; the Mexican War had called him here; the time was not come for him to scourge the American South. Nor would the Los Angeles River run dry for many years yet; accompanied by its cottonwoods and willows, it fed the pueblo's still modest thirst. Near the century's end it remained powerful enough to wash away

*I wonder if they paid in gold. A doubloon, or *Mexican ounce,* was sixteen dollars.

†James O. Pattie sends us this dispatch from the Mexican American village of Perdido, New Year's Eve, 1827: "When the ball broke up, it seemed to be expected of us, that we should each escort a lady home, in whose company we passed the night, and we none of us brought charges of severity against our fair companions."

bridges and drown people. People were killed by floods in 1825, 1861–62 and 1867. At the beginning of 1886, a huge flood inundated everything from Wilmington Street to the rise east of there.

Los Angeles was the destination of many runaway Mission Indians, for the missions had been secularized in 1834, and the Indians could no longer get food and clothing there. Indeed, the previous year, President Santa Anna had allowed the Liberals to end the Church's statutory tithe throughout Mexico. The missions crumbled; the padres grew poor and demoralized; Los Angeles swelled.

In 1845, per capita income in Mexico was fifty-six pesos; in 1800 it had been a hundred and sixteen pesos. What about California with her decrepit missions, fidgety converts, variegated *rancherías* and Indian serfs? Specifically, what about Los Angeles, surrounded by head-high fields of wild mustard? William Smythe: *The essence of the industrial life which springs from irrigation is its democracy.* We need have no fear that our lands will not become better and better as the years go by.

ANXIETIES OF AN ENCLAVE

The tiny equal plots of Los Angeles are long gone. *I can't help believing in people.* Her boggy, bear-infested thickets are getting drained bit by bit. There is now a ten-mile-long irrigation canal from the neighborhood of Redlands to San Gabriel. I wonder who did that work. For quite awhile now, the authorities have been renting out Indian field serfs to the original settlers. This policy justifies itself on the basis of its results: Since the beginning of the century, Los Angeles has grown more beans, corn, barley and wheat than it needs, and now it supplies Santa Barbara. In short, I have never been cheated out of a doubloon in my life. And why shouldn't this benevolent system be made perpetual? Since the 1820s, the Franciscan-owned vineyards of San Gabriel have been trodden by almost-naked Indians. A certain hundred-and-seventy-acre grapery produces several tons each day.

But how might the poor Fathers be managing now that their mission has been secularized? And how well do property owners sleep in Los Angeles? Mexican California is getting increasingly stung by Indian cattle raids; indeed, one commentator believes that by 1845 the Indians have actually succeeded in squeezing back the Spanish frontier. Will there be more Yuma massacres? Who lurks tonight in Los Angeles's tule swamps?

"OFTEN BEWITCHING TO MY SIGHT"

Los Angeles's fandango continues. An American clergyman's son who sees one in Baja California at about this time calls it *an exceedingly lascivious dance.* All the same, *I am not Platonist enough to deny that* the women *often appeared bewitching to my sight as they whirled through some of the intricate figures of the* Jota . . . And this old Los Angeles likewise bewitches my sight. I gaze upon it as upon the crowning of the Date Queen in Indio. How long can it last? For just as date royalty epitomizes that fading agricultural empire of smallholders, that American dream called Imperial, Los Angeles stands in for Alta California, where some trees were sixty feet high. (At midcentury, the railroads of our rival, the United States, reached no farther west than the Alleghenies. Carmel's mountains teemed with deer and bears as they now do with automobiles. And what did Los Angeles use for automobiles? Wooden-wheeled oxcarts.) In short, Los Angeles is the very capital of Imperial, not yet inimical to it.

The women wear short-sleeved gowns *after the European style.* They sport brilliant-hued belts or sashes, necklaces, earrings. (An American observer is interested to note that they go naked of corsets.) The men wear dark broad-brimmed hats whose bands are generally colored and sometimes even gilt. I suppose that they throw off their jackets of calico or silk when they dance, showing their open-necked shirts. Sometimes they wear short breeches and white stockings, sometimes gilt-laced pantaloons.

For an entertainment, bulls and grizzly bears get roped together in pairs, to maul and gore each other until one party perishes. James O. Pattie reports that on one occasion in San Carlos, fourteen bulls died to destroy five grizzlies. Meanwhile, at the fandango, the lady smashes on her chosen partner's head an eggshell filled with gilt and colored confetti.

An observer from the United States of America, a nation which at this juncture can merely be called Northeastside, looks upon this revelry and sees *the laxness and filth of a free brute, using freedom as a mere means of animal enjoyment . . . dancing and vomiting as occasion and inclination appear to require.*

Chapter 19

WEST OF THE RIVER

(1803)

God, there never was a bigger game! It couldn't flop—unless we spoiled it for ourselves. And that's what we've done. It was too big for us!

—Dashiell Hammett, 1924

Of course agricultural Los Angeles, like the Spanish Imperial it epitomizes, will endure forever. Spain's enemy, the United States, lacks interest in the region.

I grant that in 1803, Alexander Hamilton expresses relief over what he considers to be the fortuitous accident of the Louisiana Purchase; he's especially happy to gain the Mississippi River, which can someday be employed to recompense Spain for the Floridas, which are *obviously of far greater value to us than all the immense, undefined region west of the river.* May I be more specific? *On the whole, we think it may with candor be said, that whether the possession at this time of any territory west of the river Mississipi will be advantageous, is at best extremely problematical.*

Chapter 20

DRAWING THE LINE

(1803–1848)

We replied that the laws of our country did not require that honest, common citizens should carry passports . . .

—James O. Pattie, 1830

TÍPICO AMERICANO

Never, cries Jefferson to Bowdoin (1807), *did a nation act toward another with more perfidy and injustice than Spain has constantly practised against us; and if we have kept our hands off her till now, it has been purely out of respect to France, and from the value we set on the friendship of France. We expect, therefore, from the friendship of the Emperor that he will either compel Spain to do us justice or abandon her to us. We ask but one month to be in possession of the city of Mexico.*

In 1803 the Louisiana Purchase entitles the United States to an ill-defined stretch of property to the west, some of it extending into Mexico's equally unsurveyed claims. *I have never been cheated out of a dollar in my life.* Might Imperial be included in our new domains? No, but the Rio Grande surely is—never mind; forget the Rio Grande; we'll compromise on the Sabine River.

Just for once in this book, let's please think about Texas with its rivers and wild horses. As a Californian, I know that my state is bigger and better, but sometimes, simply to be fair, it's necessary to mention insignificant territories. Did you know that there's a town in Texas whose inhabitants dwell under the ground for fear of Indians? I just wanted to put that in. Corpus Christi, where the Americans traded tobacco and calico for Mexican silver, has nothing at all to do with Imperial. Neither do the Mexican massacres of Americans at Goliad and the Alamo, and the occasional American counter-murders. The point is this:

In 1827 the United States offers Mexico a million dollars for Texas. In 1828 the United States offers Mexico five million dollars for Texas. In 1831 the Treaty of Limits recognizes Mexican sovereignty over Texas. In 1836, year of the Alamo, Texas declares itself *sovereign and free*—that is, free of Mexico. The same year, so does California. By some coincidence, the majority of insurrectionists in both districts happen to bear Anglo-Saxon names. Or, as my 1976 *Britannica* tells it: *The Texan revolution was not simply a fight between Anglo-American settlers and Mexican troops; it was a revolution of all people living in Texas against what was regarded as tyrannical rule from a distant source,* Mexico City, I assume, not Washington. Now, how does my 1911 *Britannica* put it? *Three abortive Anglo-American invasions during the first few years of the century indicated the future trend of events.* Translation: *We need have no fear that our lands will not become better and better as the years go by.*

At first our insurgents vote dovishly against independence; they want a union with the Mexican Liberals against Santa Anna's dictatorship. But *the weakness of the Mexican Liberals and the necessity of securing aid in the States led the Austin party to abandon their opposition to independence.* In other words, they didn't mean to; they *had* to! And so in 1844, the year that the wagon route to California begins, the United States and Texas sign the Texas Annexation Treaty. The following year, Texas gets annexed; once more, we offer Mexico five million. Preposterously, Mexico refuses us. In 1846, the Mexican War accordingly begins. It is, like all wars, a just war. *We were sent to provoke a fight,* recalled Ulysses S. Grant, *but it was essential that Mexico should commence it.* The American flag goes up over San Diego, then the Battle of San Gabriel breaks Mexico's grip on Upper California. In General Sherman's summation, *California was yet a Mexican province,* although now *held by right of conquest.* Time to clarify that situation. Our numerically inferior but better drilled troops, generalled by Taylor and Scott, therefore set about overcoming Monterey's sandbagged parapets, the walls of Vera Cruz, the precipices of Cerro Gordo. Grant again: *My pity was aroused by the sight of the Mexican garrison of Monterey marching out of town as prisoners, and no doubt the same feeling was experienced by most of our army who witnessed it.* Escaping the yellow fever, winning Puebla, we enter the Valley of Mexico! If I weren't so parochial, I'd tell you about the battle of Churubusco. Creeping forward, sheltered by the aqueduct-arches of Mexico City, we recapitulate the feat of Cortés.

In 1848, our defeated enemy signs the Treaty of Guadelupe-Hidalgo. Instantly,* half of Mexico becomes American, for which we magnanimously pay fifteen million. The new international line runs right through the area which I call Imperial. **THE DESERT DISAPPEARS.**

*Which is to say by 1853, when the Gadsden Purchase gnawed away the final acres of New Mexico and Arizona.

Chapter 21

RANCH SIZE

(1800–1850)

Being of or from the Border can provide unique opportunities.

—James Bradley, *ca.* 1995

But before it does, let us peep like good realtors at the near-virgin territories around Imperial in their earliest subjection to European subdivision.

Horses are the cheapest thing in California; very fair ones not being worth more than ten dollars apiece . . . notes Richard Henry Dana, Jr., in 1836. *If you bring the saddle back safe, they care but little what becomes of the horse.*

Horses were cheap because properties were vast.

When Cortés's conquistadors, finding, as human nature inevitably will, less gold than cupidity expected, they compensated their disappointment with huge land grants. In the nineteeeth century, we find, for instance, Hacienda Sánchez-Navarro, which at one point possessed over fifteen million acres—ten times the areas of the Imperial and Mexicali valleys put together. The book from which I snatch this information does not claim that the Sánchez-Navarros owned the largest hacienda in Mexico, only that this is *the estate for which we have the most information.* Who knows what other leviathans darkened the murk of those times?

Meanwhile, out in the pueblos of Mexico, we continue to find the rural people, which is to say the *indios* and *mestizos,* clinging to family subsistence plots. I suspect that for them horses were not cheap. In California, however, any poor man could get his own horses. All he had to do was catch them and tame them.

The missions had been secularized by decree in 1833–34. The *mayordomos* who administered them devoured as many of their acres as possible. It was now, in the senility of Mexican California, that most of the land grants were made.

The mythos of Imperial on both sides of the line is this: *He made a success through his own efforts. His farm has been highly improved.* In the *ejidos* of the Mexicali Valley, and pioneer biographies of Imperial County, a parcel-holder's home is his castle. Subsistence farming was practiced in recent memory (in Southside, at least), even as I write. This ethos derives from the existence or pretense that most farms or ranchos are, like Los Angeles's original land grants, smallish and comparably equal.

Accordingly, this book will track the size of Imperial's farms and ranches. If water is the Marxist "substructure," then land is the "superstructure" whose history turned American Imperial into gardens of Paradise, on whose border Border Patrolman Dan Murray had been stationed; I can hear him saying: They'll pop their heads up in a minute.

An official of the district agrarian tribunal in Mexicali said to me: Before, the land parcels were huge. People would often say: *As far as you can see, that's mine.* There was a high proportion of large landowners. Since it was so sparsely populated, that was the bait.

By *before* he meant *before the Revolution.* As for the huge land parcels he referred to, to the extent that they existed in half-unsurveyed Mexican Imperial, they remained as inchoate as Tijuana, as old Spanish Imperial itself—at least until the Chandler Syndicate came from Northside. That story has not yet begun.

But not all Mexican California was the Valley of Death! Along the Pacific coast, livestock could graze without overmuch irrigation. And so that region, human nature being what it is, became a heaven of large land grants. I am informed that ranchos were legally required to be no more than eleven square leagues, which is to say forty-nine thousand acres; but some happened to be larger—as shown, for instance, by Rancho Cañón Santa Ana's thirteen thousand acres in present-day Chino, San Bernardino County. In 1850, most of what is now Orange County belonged to eleven families.

In what would soon be called the Inland Empire, the following grants displayed dizzily varying acreages:

MEXICAN RANCHOS IN RIVERSIDE COUNTY AREA

Jurupa (Rubidoux)	6,749.99 acres
Jurupa (Stearns)	25,509.17
El Rincon	4,431.47
San Jacinto Viejo	35,503.03
Near San Jacinto (Rubidoux)	4,439.57
La Laguna (Stearns)	13,338.80
Pauba	26,597.96
Temecula	26,608.94

Potrero de la Cienega	477.25
Potrero el Carizo	167.51
Little Temecula	2,233.42
San Jacinto Nuevo y Potrero	48,861.10
Santa Rosa (Moreno)	47,815.10
Sobrante de San Jacinto	48,847.28
La Sierra (Sepulveda)	17,774.19
La Sierra (Yorba)	17,786.89

As for Imperial itself, I repeat: Since irrigation had scarcely begun, most of it remained blank. (To a property owner, Indians are walking blanknesses.) *There are no 1850 Sites to Visit in Imperial County.*

Chapter 22

MEXICO

(1821–1911)

They did not recognize themselves as the only real hope for the future in a world caught in the grip of horrible ghosts of the past . . .

—Arkadi and Boris Strugatski, 1964

With his squat, dark features and a stature of not much more than five feet, Benito Juárez resembles, as well he should, the indigenous ones who people the images of Diego Rivera and José Clemente Orozco. This first Indian to become President of Mexico looks out at us from an engraving, stiff and straight, with his right hand on the open book on his desk (could it be a Bible?). Harsh, brave, enduring much, let him be our representative of poor Mexico herself, who, amputated at the waist by the Americans; invaded by the Spaniards in 1829 because they could not yet forgive the independence she had achieved in 1821; invaded again by France in 1838 in the so-called Pastry War; menaced in 1861 by England, Spain and France, so that she could be occupied in 1864 by that tall, pallid, bearded, gorgeously uniformed Hapsburg puppet of the French, Maximilian, a man who drew on an empty treasury in hopes of beautifying an ungrateful capital, and succeeded in syncretizing nothing but the music*—Juárez, once he finally won the guerrilla war, had him shot—meanwhile tormented herself with uprisings and civil wars. In his short black coat and his handmade white shirt (courtesy of his wife) he gazes at us with alert caution. His principal achievement, like Mexico's, is that he survived. *After the nation's humiliating defeat by the North Americans,* I read, *Juárez restored his nation's dignity and esteem.* But at midcentury the Caste War breaks out in Yucatán. Three years later a third of the Maya have been wiped out. Then here comes the Liberal uprising of Ayutla that kills four thousand; and, as Kurt Vonnegut would say, *so it goes.*

In 1856, the Ley Lerdo, second of the famous Reform Laws, required the Church to sell her remaining lands. Lumped into this same unprogressive category of corporate holdings were many of the shared fields of the pueblos. It is saddening,

*"And yet," writes Malcolm Lowry, "how they must have loved this land, those two lonely empurpled exiles . . . lovers out of their element—their Eden . . . beginning to turn under their noses into a prison . . ."

although not surprising, that Juárez, who came to power in 1867, thought facilitating centralism and capitalism to be more urgent than the preservation of communal autonomy.* In the short run he might have been correct: He intended to raise agricultural production, and haciendas could certainly do that. *In the long run,* writes Mark Wasserman, *the Reform served to concentrate landholding even more than previously.* One reason was that as the haciendas aimed at commercial crop production with modern methods, they needed more water. That water could be conveniently obtained by annexing pueblo lands.

Benito Juárez died in office in 1872. Five years later, the first presidential term of Porfirio Díaz began.

More gorgeously accoutered than Juárez in a uniform with epaulettes, medals and braids, he gazes out at us handsomely and remotely. His white moustache curves down. This proud old soldier-dictator made better luck for himself than his predecessor ever could have, for by now, thanks to his suppression of various internal instabilities, the foreigners who had bled away so much Mexican blood and pride had begun to appreciate their victim's investment possibilities. Under Díaz, the economy grew accordingly. He built railroads to get Mexico's silver ore, coffee beans and suchlike commodities to market in a cheap and timely fashion. Much of that market was in Northside, and the railroad lines were at first owned by Americans. So were ever so many other things, for Díaz's Mexico was a wonderland of foreign concessions.

Accordingly, here is an authorized Northsider version of the tale: *Then came the long, firm rule of Porfirio Diaz, who first broke up the organizations of bandits that infested the country, and then sought to raise Mexico from the state of discredit and disorganization into which it had fallen. Suspicion and jealousy of the foreigner is disappearing, and habits of industry are displacing the indolence and lawlessness that were once universally prevalent.* Thus my 1910 *Britannica.*

It was under the regime of Porfirio Díaz that Imperial finally announced: **WATER IS HERE**.

His Law of Colonization (1883) compensated the private sector for surveying vacant government lands. In Mexican Imperial, the new settlements this measure aimed to establish were facilitated by the higher wages of Northside, which forced

*Historians commonly believe that "villagers and small landholders held the balance of power" in much of Mexico during the middle six decades of the nineteenth century. During the second and third decades, Mexico's economic troubles destabilized many haciendas, and we read of villagers who pooled their pesos and succeeded in buying hacienda plots which they had previously rented. In the mid-1830s, it is true, centralists raised voting requirements, replaced local councils with officials answerable to the government, and took other such measures to exclude country people. But the officials were poorly trained and the central budget remained small; therefore, so did the government's powers of oppression. Arbitrary power was and is another matter.

Southside employers near the line to raise their own wages somewhat—a phenomenon that continues as I write. And so more Mexican migrant workers began coming to the United States. Other Mexicans passed through American Imperial in their eagerness to gamble in the California Gold Rush.

Seven thousand five hundred and eighty-three people lived in the entirety of Baja California Norte in 1900. Meanwhile a total of 13,607,259 people got counted in Mexico, *of which less than one-fifth (19%) were classed as whites* (the same proportion as in the census of 1810), *38% as Indians, and 43% as mixed bloods.* Out of less than fifty-eight thousand foreigners, there were *a few Chinese and Filipinos,* the Japanese exerting a more powerful presence.

And so Mexican Imperial remained "undeveloped." Elsewhere in Mexico, many government lands were vacant only of clear title; they belonged to the pueblos. No matter. The haciendas bought them up—and not from the pueblos, but from the government.

Díaz's method of crumbling up that impediment to Progress, indigenous communal property, approximated Northside's not only in its procedure but even in its timing. In 1877, the first year of Díaz's term, the United States set into motion the Dawes Act, which alienated Indian reservation land into individual parcels which could be, and by some unforeseen coincidence did get, sold away from their already impoverished owners. In 1915, our Marines would impose the same improvement upon the benighted communitarians of Dominica.

In Díaz's Mexico, land concentration continued. Luis Terrazas's ten million acres in Chihuahua, the million-acre Hearst ranch, these grew increasingly emblematic. Tied as it was to increased property values in the vicinity of the railroads, the expropriation of communal land grew especially marked during the construction of main railroad lines in the 1880s and then again when the secondary lines were built during the first decade of the twentieth century. *We need have no fear that our lands will not become better and better as the years go by.* Wasserman remarks: *Like so many other Latin American strongmen who preceded and succeeded him, Díaz failed in the end because his genius was only his own.* And another historian completes the point: *By 1910, most rural folk in Mexico . . . no longer possessed enough property to support their families.* That was when the Mexican Revolution began.

Like its French counterpart, it commenced among the elite, then spread unpredictably downward.

Chapter 23

THE LINE ITSELF

(1844–1911)

What are the colors of the map without a dream?

—Alberto Blanco, 1998

How did Northside and Southside distinguish each other in those days? After all, it took the Boundary Commission quite a spell even to set up markers, many of which remain today, if graffiti'd and even caged. At the close of the Mexican War, the line evidently resembled the metagalactic center in James Blish's mid-twentieth-century science-fiction tetralogy *Cities in Flight,* being the *neutral zone,* our side of which hopefully *coincides with* its analogue *in the anti-matter universe,* which is of course Mexico. As usual in Imperial, considerable delineation and subdelineation would be required, *for the metagalactic center was as featureless as the rest of intergalactic space, and only extreme care and the most complex instrumentation would tell the voyagers when they had arrived.* Hence the Boundary Commission.

But a certain American who trekked through much of the Baja four years before Mexican California fell must have trusted the complex instrumentation of his own sensibilities; for he insisted without the least equivocation that the Californians were less "servile" than their counterparts in what would soon be Southside. *The Californian boasts of California; he claims no kindred with Mexico. This strong disgust . . . is principally attributable to the fact that Mexico has been in the habit of sending to this province as soldiers of the Republic, the outcasts and criminals of other departments.*

As for the Mexican trekkers, as the nineteeenth century wound down, their vanguard continued to cross the not-quite-delineated blankness into Northside, going where the money was.

Chapter 24

LOS ANGELES

(1850)

> But I hope as soon as I set forth to reach lands more abundant in pasturage than those traversed up to this point . . .
>
> —de Anza to Bucareli, 1774

There were grand balls in Mexican Los Angeles; by definition there must be grander ones in American Los Angeles! On 26 October 1854, two years after the erection of the city's first brick house and two years before the first legal hanging, Juan Diego Valdez gets shot dead by John Chapman at a ball. My favorite Ranger remembers when *the streets were thronged throughout the entire day with splendidly mounted and richly dressed* caballeros, *most of whom wore suits of clothes that cost all the way from $500 to $1,000, with saddles and horse-trappings that cost even more* . . . One more detail: *All, however, had slung to their rear the never-failing pair of* Colt's, *generally with the accompaniment of the Bowie knife,* for spilled blood's as common as red *vicuña* hats used to be in Los Angeles!

In June 1852, an unknown Mexican prisoner winds up *shot by Mr. Lull while trying to escape.* Meanwhile, and this is all on the same page of these vital records, an unknown Indian is found murdered on Lalu Street, an unknown Indian dies on the street of head injuries, an unknown Indian is *found killed,* and for fairness I'd better mention an unknown *butcher shot by Mexicans,* balanced out by the unknown *Mexican shot by Dr. Osburn.* Another dead Indian in the street, another *Sonoran youth killed* and *two Americans found murdered, robbed,* reported the day after *two Mexicans found hung*—thus the 1850s in Los Angeles County, which is *then the greatest cow county in the state.* Our Ranger offers us more than one recollection of *Nigger Alley, which was the most perfect and full grown pandemonium that this writer, who had seen the* elephant *before . . . , has ever beheld . . . Every few minutes a rush would be made, and maybe a pistol shot would be heard . . . You would learn that it was only a knife fight between two Mexicans, or a gambler had caught somebody cheating and had perforated him with a bullet.*

On 4 August 1851, the Los Angeles County Recorder took note of the first marriage, in Spanish. He then closed the marriage register until October 1852.

Meanwhile, people fell in love, made love and even married without him. What was the result? An adventurer from the British Isles who came to the Mexican War remembers California as a mixture of *the portly Californian, under his ample-brimmed* sombrero *and gay* serapa, *the dark-skinned and half-clad Indian, and the Yankee, in his close European costume*. However, that mixture was not happy. *I have frequently seen a quiet and respectable party of natives,* meaning Mexican Californians, *intruded upon by drunken soldiers or sailors . . . It is not to be wondered at, that a people so isolated and so naturally courteous should have regarded the Americans and English somewhat in the light of savages.* The Americans and English certainly returned the favor.

In 1859 this pueblo boasted twenty thousand souls, *with brick sidewalks, and blocks of stone or brick houses.* Ever fewer of the inhabitants were Indians. *This general principle has been demonstrated repeatedly with the lower organisms in their parasite-host or predator-prey relationships . . . Since the quickest and easiest way to get rid of* the Indian's *troublesome presence was to kill him off, this procedure was adopted as standard for some years.*

(As for the Chinese, in 1850 only two were listed in the Los Angeles census. Their population would soon increase significantly.)

And the orchestra strikes up another number! Los Angeles calls out the next fandango. On 7 August 1852, a three-year-old child named María Antonio Albitre was *murdered while parents at dance; Dolores Higuera (male) suspected.* In 1855, Colonel W. Martin Keene was sent to his Maker by a grizzly bear at Fort Tejon. On 23 January 1857, Carlos K. Baker got killed in pursuit of outlaws of the Pancho Daniel band. Sheriff Santiago R. Barton, also known as James, Guillermo H. Little and another man likewise died on this excursion. Sheriff Barton's epitaph reads: *Murdered in line of duty.* (Pancho Daniel was duly lynched on 30 November 1858.) On 23 July 1858, Seth Lunt expired from wounds sustained in an Indian attack upon San Bernardino. Nicho Alepas and Dionisio (Lionisio) Alipaz both got shot by Governor Scholes on 9 January 1859. On 16 October 1859, a man whose last name was Alexis met the following fate: *Shot by Sonoran Manuel Ruiz.* In 1858, Hilliard P. Dorsey got shot by his father-in-law, although then again it might have been suicide. In 1859, Jean Debreuil was accidentally shot in front of a restaurant.

Knife fights, shootouts after arguments, executions, lynchings, murders by the Pancho Daniel band, killings with a hatchet, shootings during a ball, this was Los Angeles.* *I can't help believing in people.*

*It was also San Francisco, whose Vigilance Committee occupied a fortified office on Clay Street around 1855, conducting midnight trials and armed forays on the streets.

Chapter 25

LOST MINES

(1849–2005)

But a few miles from us on the east, the land falls off five thousand feet into the Colorado Desert, a sea of fiery sand broiling beneath an almost eternal sun . . . The desert is, of course, uninhabitable . . .

—*The City and County of San Diego,* 1888

Now that California's ours, what a convenient chance that James Marshall finds gold the very next year! I can't help believing in people.

Imperial is beehives on the edge of a lavender field, and the dark-blue wedge of the Salton Sea observed from the mouth of Painted Canyon. That is Imperial to me. But in 1849, a hundred thousand gold seekers cross the Imperial Valley, or was it ten thousand? What do they see? Desert milkweed, crucifixion thorn, sage, smoke trees, California fan-palms, desert century palms—if they're lucky. Mostly, Imperial lies ankle-deep in alkali. One of them, a man named Oliver Wozencraft, sees that *"Moisture Means Millions."* His prayers to the Ministry of Capital will go unanswered; he will die disappointed.

What is Imperial to you? What could Imperial ever be, but the ghastliest, most useless stretch of the Colorado Desert, which runs a hundred and fifty miles long by fifty miles wide? The Salton Trough now bears the scratch of an international line, but so what? Our snapshot of California at midcentury calls what we currently refer to as Imperial County *a mere thoroughfare for the adventurers, gold miners, and settlers coming to California . . . There were no ranchos and no towns.* South of the line, Mexicali remains a plain of clay.

Now it's already 1855! By telegraph from New Orleans, we learn that in that distant place called California, *business of every description is reported as being extremely dull.* But mining and crops are both anticipating better fortune, thanks to all the rain.

In 1864, news comes of *many miners going to work the mines at La Paz on Colorado River.* The hundred-and-seventy-five-mile stretch of San Diego County, spiced up with a little greasewood, will now serve up another chapter in the eternal tale of disappointment. Mexican miners dig for their dreams in American Imperial. They place small crosses throughout their mines, each subdivision of which is named after a saint. On one saint's day, they erect a large cross on a hill overlooking their mine and bedeck it with flowers. Not long afterward, special Yankee taxes, accompanied as needed by guns, run them out. The way is now clear for Peg-Leg Smith to search vainly all the rest of his life for that hilltop in Imperial's Cargo Muchacho Mountains where he'd once seen black-encrusted gold nuggets. In due course, "an old Yuma squaw" named Acoyhopuck will inform history that there were two Peg-Legs, one with a wooden left leg, the other with a wooden right leg; one in the Cargo Muchachos in 1830, the other in the Anza-Borrego Badlands in 1871. And so Peg-Leg's memory grows as blurred and ultimately as lost as his mines.

Imperial's Tumco Mine receives unimportant mention in 1870.—Do you remember what I saw there? A rusty cyanide vat.—In 1873 we read that the gold quartz mines seventy miles north of the city of San Diego (hence around the present day metropolis of Temecula, fifty miles due west of the northwest corner of the Salton Sea) are *the richest in the State of California*. Where are those mines now? Well, they were never quite within the entity called Imperial; why permit this history of successes and improvements to be marred by their demerits?

On 6 May 1886, E. W. and Harriet E. Alexander are the grantors, and the Ogilby Gold Mining Co. is the grantee. On 13 July 1894, the same couple are the grantors, and the California Picacho Gold Mines Co. is the grantee. Perhaps they had finally learned that Imperial would not be fated to provide overmuch nourishment from her rock-flesh, nor from her desert's blood-scabbed rock-nipples such as Pilot Knob. After that last sale they might have sold out and moved on. Or had they struck it rich in Picacho? The California Picacho Gold Mines Co. must have seen something there, to buy their claim.

Two hundred thousand ounces and more! Imperial's mines yielded that much, thanks to a hundred thousand gallons per day of Colorado River water, and oodles of cyanide, whose tailings remain at Tumco.—Then what?—Why, improvement, reclamation, Progress!

I remember Picacho, oh, yes. I remember Ogilby, where in the vandalized cemetery I found a fingernail-sized piece of human bone.

I remember Tumco on a hot July day, the mountains like bloody scabs upon the desert's skin, bleached ocotillos in the white gravel, a grand palo verde tree and then the black metal of the leaching vats on a bluff in the midst of the old Colorado floodplain. Thus the heartland of Arid America. I remember the American Girl mine: hot sand and steel, a little dead lizard in the sand. Although she must still be operating as late as 1914 (for the United Mines Company will telegraph the Governor on her behalf, asking for fifty soldiers to protect her from *excited Mexicans*), how much longer can she hope to persevere in her dreams of Imperial gold in the bright heat four miles north of Ogilby? Poor American girl! Her prospects are as pale as the ocotillos around Tumco.

Never mind. *Our* American girl will be Barbara Worth.

Chapter 26

WHITE EYELASHES

(1853–1926)

> The discourse of Cortés filled his companions with great hope . . . and now they felt such a keen desire to accompany him to a land that hardly anyone had even seen, that it seemed to them they were not going to war, but to certain victory and spoils.
>
> —Francisco López de Gómara, 1552

Other adventurers prospected more ruthlessly for Imperial's treasures. They called themselves the filibusters. Cormac McCarthy's horrific novel *Blood Meridian,* arguably his greatest, fictionalizes careers whose extremities scarcely called for embellishment. Meanwhile, in that multivolume history of California, Bancroft refers to *the cause of humanity bandied in filthy mouths to promote atrocious butcheries.* What was this cause? *It is generally admitted,* says my old *Britannica, that Mexico was provoked into aggression in order that additional territory might be available for the extension of slavery.*

A wonderful cause indeed! Let us accordingly pay reverence to the memory of a certain Watkins, convicted by a heartbroken judge who nonetheless proclaimed his admiration for *those spirited men who had gone forth to uphold the broken altars and rekindle the extinguished fires of liberty in Mexico and Lower California.*

Watkins and his colleague Emory were each assessed a fifteen-hundred-dollar fine, which they never had to pay.

Watkins was the Vice-President, and Emory the Secretary of State. Who then was President?

Bancroft marvels over his *seemingly pupilless, grey eyes, their large orbits, half concealed by white eyebrows and lashes, at once repelling and fascinating with their strong, steady penetration.* His physique resembled Napoleon's. Turning his grey eyes upon Southside, William Walker instantly spied out that it was a zone of race-mixing; hence inferior.

Ironically, he was a martyr to freedom of the press. Jailed in San Francisco for contempt of court because he condemned leniency toward criminals, he was eventually freed thanks to lobbying from his sympathizers. Then he opened his recruiting office. Denied the *Arrow* by the sole anti-slavery man in power, General Hitchcock (who, needless to say, would not rise high come the administration of Jefferson Davis), Walker sailed on the *Caroline* instead, with forty-one disciples. And so he entered La Paz, sporting a Mexican flag. Kidnapping the governor, our hero proclaimed Louisiana law! *The bountiful continent is ours, state on state, and territory on territory, to the waves of the Pacific sea.*

On he led them to Sonora, seeking to uphold the broken altars of slavery in this year 1853. But his knights of freedom abandoned him at the Río Colorado, so he marched back west through Mexican Imperial, all the way to Tijuana, and turned himself over to Americans, who treated him with compassionate comprehension. After all, why *not* bite off another piece of Southside?

Walker's career is an anomaly in the history of mankind, writes a historian who can't help believing in people. *Devoid of all the characteristics of a great leader . . . homely to the point of ugliness, in disposition cold, cruel, selfish, heartless, stolidly indifferent to the sufferings of others, living only to gratify the cravings of his inordinate ambition—it is strange that such a man could induce thousands to offer their lives for his aggrandizement . . .* I am sorry to say that I do not consider it strange at all.

His three expeditions against Nicaragua are outside the purview of this book. But you will be happy to know that on the first (1855), he did succeed in establishing the glorious institution of slavery, and declared himself head of state; his men then mutinied. Two years later, failing again, shipwrecked, rescued by the British and repatriated on the USS *Wabash,* he faced trial for piracy, a trial which conveniently never occurred. On his final attempt, the men rose up against him as before. The captain of a British warship handed him over to representatives of Honduras, who on 25 September 1860 perforated his nasty carcass.

Walker reminded Northside that the international line was the merest beginning. His spirit survived in Americans and Mexicans alike.

In 1916, the new Chairman of the Board of Supervisors of Imperial County instigated *a movement to secure the annexation of enough territory in Mexico to serve the purposes of the Irrigation District . . . It aroused international interest but the object was never realized.*

As late as 1926, General Enrique Estrada from Jalisco was captured not far from San Diego; he had plotted to overthrow the government of Baja California.

I am happy to report that none of the people I asked in Mexican Imperial remembered William Walker.

Chapter 27

COLONEL COUTS'S HOMESTEAD

(1839–*ca.* 1915)

I want and desire that I might enjoy their precious emerald, their fine turquoise, their bracelet that was forged and perforated at the throat and in the womb of the lady.

—Pro forma address of an Aztec ruler to the parents of a girl he would marry

Get an Indian wife. They're sweeter.

—Gilberto Sanders, 2003

The military conquest of Imperial now being complete, and attempts at further paramilitary annexations having failed for the present, the quest for desert gold being a dangerous game of chance, what was an American who wished to establish himself in California to do?—Why, marry a Mexican girl!

Syncretism is a slender Chinese girl at the restaurant counter, maybe with Mexican blood in her because her skin is darker and ruddier than that of the other Chinese; she speaks Spanish to her Mexican boyfriend. In 1877, on a ramble out of Pasadena, John Muir meets a Mexican-born mestizo who aims to *"make money and marry a Spanish woman."* Syncretism's banner gets complacently hoisted by a certain citizen of San Diego who's observed the last days of Alta California; in his opinion, the señoritas of San Diego, Santa Barbara and Los Angeles *preferred for husbands, not finely dressed, courtly, serenading cavaliers, but the colder blooded plainer dressed foreigners, who were more industrious, treated them better as wives, and took more care of their children.**

In 1835 a sea-captain in the sea-otter trade writes home to Maine: *I was Married on the 4th of November last at Santa Barbara to Miss Francisca Carillo of that place, her age is nineteen, have been attached to her for four years.* They will have six children who grow up speaking Spanish. In 1853 he writes his sister: *It is two years to-day*

*This San Diegan looks upon the Mexicans of his zone, or Californians as they were then quite accurately called, as follows: "Their chief faults they had brought with them in their blood from Mexico, but these faults have been more or less mellowed and softened by the equable sun and temperate breezes of the country"—not to mention that best cure for hereditary blood disorders, race-mixing.

since my Wife was burried, she was born the 28th day of Feby 1816, died the 26th day of Feby 1851, and was burried on her birthday: her Father Don Carlos Antonio Carrillo . . . was one of the handsomest Men in the State . . . He never remarries; I wish to believe that he truly loved her, although it might be that what Don Carlos had bestowed upon her sufficed him.

Syncretism is its own reward, and one can well imagine the longing and the real disappointment between the lines of that fable you already know of Spanish *conquistadors* who *heard that ten suns distant from there was an island of Amazons, a rich land; but these women were never found. In my opinion the error arose from the name of Cihuatlán, which means "place of women."* Or perhaps it arose from the name of California itself, which Cortés is said to have bestowed upon our peninsula in honor of a romance then the rage; the romancer's California was an island of jet-black Amazons. No matter; Imperial's Amazons suffice. Ladies' bare brown sweaty shoulders, women wearing loose white T-shirts pulled down over their bare brown thighs just far enough, so that it seems as if they were wearing nothing underneath; all this flesh calls to me when the evening gets cool and I stand on the northern side of that rust-red border fence, gazing through it as the Amazons of Southside gaze back at me; in search of syncretism I cross the line and meet a barefoot, reeking Indian girl in a gorgeous dress of white, red and purple. She's sweeping the sidewalk and lifting heavy boxes of garbage. She stops and smiles at me. She wants to syncretize. Did I tell you that she does her hair in two long black braids tied off in ribbons, just as the belles of Alta California used to do? They wore silk or calico bodices with embroidered sleeves, so I've read; their skirts were flounced and lace-trimmed; sometimes their shoes were satin, sometimes velvet; they wore dark *reboso* scarves over their shoulders; they wore rich necklaces, and sometimes headbands adorned with a cross or a star. When an American wanted to syncretize with one of them (where did he see her? why, from afar, riding a horse!), he addressed himself to her buckskin-shod father or her brother, presenting his case with courtesies and presents, until finally he was permitted to enter the family's house of whitewashed adobe and sup beneath their roof of burned-clay tiles. I imagine that if he thought it would help him or if he enjoyed entering into the spirit of the thing, he dandied up in a white shirt and a dark vest, with a serape over everything. Handsome or not, well-dressed one way or another, he sat at table, complimenting the mother's cooking, jesting with the cousins while shooting half-secret glances at his intended Ramona or Isadora to see if she also laughed, trying to impress the father with his life-dreams of cattle ranching, merchandising, or maybe even irrigation: *We need have no fear that our lands will not become better and better as the years go by.*

Syncretism is when you drink an orange juice and suddenly taste chili in the bottom of a glass. Syncretism is also one of control's most effective strategies. In 1521, Cortés sends a deputy into the as yet unbroken hinterlands to subdue Tuxtepec and Coatzacoalcos. Among them is a certain Gonzalo de Sandoval, who becomes an Amazon-hunter. *Sandoval had no desire to fight, but, having no choice* (we never have a choice), *he made a night attack on a village and there captured its lady, which made it possible for our men to reach the river without opposition, occupy its banks, and seize Coatzacoalcos.* We're never told the lady's name, much less her fate. Once she bears children, a Hispanicized dynasty may well endure.

The syncretic marriages and amours of Cortés's generation had been tied to two causes: a dearth of women from the homeland; and a calculated ambition to obtain, hold and legitimize both property and status by marriage into some high-ranking indigenous bloodline. For Cortés himself, who hoped to join the nobility through the blessing of that ultimate secular authority, the Spanish sovereign, a few thousand or million acres of Mexico made secure between the thighs of an indigenous "princess" would have been too insignificant a gain. To be sure, for some time after the Conquest he did enjoy his private harem of Aztec wards. Begin with Tecuichpotin, whom her father Moctezuma had married to Cuauhtémoc at twelve; long before the latter's execution Cortés removed her from that spouse and renamed her Doña Isabel; one Aztec lament runs: *But who is that at the side of the Captain-General? Ah, it is Doña Isabel, my little niece! Ah, it is true: the kings are prisoners now!* Her three sisters were also kept in that house in Coyoacán. Meanwhile, the famous-infamous Malinche and her daughter or niece Catalina provided their own diversions. Cortés's Spanish wife, who might not have approved, died peculiarly and rapidly after her arrival; but this deed, if such it was, was certainly not committed so that Cortés's five bedmates could supplant her. They shared Malinche's fate—abandonment—and in due course the conqueror obtained a new Spanish wife.

Captain Cornelius Jensen from Homburg sails to California in hopes of benefiting from the Gold Rush. In 1854 he arrives at the town of Agua Mansa, which happens to be five miles downriver from San Bernardino, and there marries Mercedes Alvarado, *the belle and beauty of Southern California, . . . a member of one of the then most aristocratic families in the country,* lives with her until they get flooded out, and in 1868 hires Chinese masons to built what is now the oldest brick building in Riverside County. Their syncretic marriage thus has its monument, which is officially known as the Jensen-Alvarado House.

The British sailor Michael White becomes Miguel Blanco and marries his Mexicana at Mission San Gabriel; in 1843, we find him already the patentee of Rancho Muscupiable! Meanwhile, California passes into Northside's control; and on 2 April 1858, Josefa Yorba marries a man whose name has been variously handed down to us as Juan Salmih, Juan Samith, and John S. Smythe.

The question of how many of these unions of white men with Mexicanas in these early days of Imperial might have been equivalent in spirit to Cortés's with Malinche is certainly a painful one. In the last decades of Mexican California, an American sailor catches sight of that scion of a once great family, Don Juan Bandini, and after variously condescending words about the man's ineffectuality continues: *I could not but feel a pity for him, especially when I saw him by the side of . . . a fat, coarse, vulgar, pretentious fellow of a Yankee trader, who had made money in San Diego, and was eating out the vitals of the Bandinis, fattening upon their extravagance, grinding them in their poverty; having mortgages on their lands,* which as you will remember included Tecate Canyon, site of the future Imperial city of that name, *forestalling their cattle, and already making an inroad upon their jewels, which were their last hope.* It is easy to imagine such a Yankee buying up that jewel of jewels and key to jewels, a daughter of the house.*

In Orozco's famous painting, the sinewy old snow-white patriarch's arm crosses Malinche's nakedness like a barrier, while she holds her naked lord's other hand, gazing at him in a kind of empty stolidity or perhaps grief. He sternly eyes the trampled faceless native below their feet. They sit in state, lord and temporary lady of Mexico, but he is holding her back, perhaps from weeping over the fallen one on whom he has set his right foot. Malinche is beautiful after a squatly crystalline fashion; nor has Orozco denied her master his own dignity. It is one of the saddest pictures I know.

So many choices! Ascension (or, if you like, Asunción), Juaquina, Eloisa, Soledad, Jacinta, María de la Luz (one of my favorite names), Catherine Magdalena! Cortés's generation could take their pick of such Aztec delicacies as Xicomoyahual. But in American California, she would have had too exotic a taste. Helen Hunt Jackson's novel *Ramona* does offer up a happily sentimentalized mating with an Indian woman, but the bridegroom is, after all, a mere Mexican Californian. A book on the California Indians notes that *the American civilization . . . viewed miscegenation with the greatest antipathy . . . No blood bond could ever become established which would mitigate the indifference and contempt with which the Indians were regarded,* and by the mid-nineteenth century, white males who defile themselves with Indians have earned a specific term of contempt: *squaw men.* Theodore H. Hittell, *History of California,* volume III (1897): *The marriage of Indian women by white men of course involved degradation of the latter.*

We do read of a certain Don Hugo Reid, who after getting naturalized in 1839

*When they themselves had been parvenus, the Aztecs followed the same syncretic prescription, but in their own kindly fashion. They requested that their host, Achitometl, King of Culhuacán, grant them his daughter to be queen among them, to which he acceded. That alliance proved especially intimate: When her father attended the wedding banquet, he found an Aztec priest dancing in her skin.

was married to Victoria, an Indian woman with a solid claim to the Rancho Santa Anita. But this ignoble ability to hold one's nose for the sake of commerce is un-American, no? Mr. Reid was British.

William Hartnell of Lancashire converts to Catholicism, visits a rich Don in Santa Barbara, and in the natural course of things espouses his daughter, Doña Teresa de la Guerra y Noriega. Perhaps there was love involved. Let us at least hope that Malinche, Mercedes, Josefa and Teresa all sang some version of the ancient song that the women of Chalco sang to their Aztec conquerors: *I have come to please my blooming vulva, my little mouth. I desire the lord . . .*—Why not hope so? A certain twentieth-century researcher has determined from studying rural California divorce records that the nineteenth century *is the decisive century in the development and realization of the companionate family.* Eighteenth-century divorce records mention children in relation to economic quantities; nineteenth-century records describe children as objections of affection. So let's extend our best wishes to these mixed marriages and their offspring. May our hopes be as lovely as the woman's name Cayetana.—Everyone has hope, a Mexicali barber once said to me, resting his hand upon my forehead in an almost loving gesture. I asked him what his hope was, and he replied: God. He said that God was his private hope, that all true hopes were private, and to explain himself he imagined an orange being passed about the barber shop; everyone could see it, but only he, the barber, had tasted it; no one could know whether that particular orange was sweet or sour. He asked me whether I had chosen the woman I was with or whether God had given her to me. I asked him his opinion of the matter and he said: God.—Surely the conquistadors felt so. So perhaps did the Yankees, if they believed with true faith in the Ministry of Capital.

SEEN AT THE CLUB ANAHUAC

San Diego County, which at this time stretched all the way from the Pacific to the Colorado, thereby encompassing the entire width of the entity I call Imperial, contained twenty-nine Mexican land grants, all of them in the west and center, and some, as we have seen, quite large. Colonel Cave Johnson Couts's twenty-two hundred nineteen and a half acres was one of the smallest.

Couts was born in Tennessee in 1821, the same year that Iturbide asserted Mexican independence from Spain. Now for his career: West Point (where he took his comrades' autographs), Indian Territory, Mexico, San Diego.

The Bandini family now comes back into the story. Couts marries Ysidora Bandini. In other words, he who trekked through Imperial and estimated the width of the Colorado River at Yuma now enters an Alta Californian house of whitewashed adobe, succeeds in his wooing, and settles with his new bride on *the Guajome Grant, a wedding gift.* Syncretism definitely has its advantages; and Mrs. Couts must have been ripe for it; for when she was still a maiden, she and her sister sewed the first American flag to fly over San Diego. Theodore Hittell again: *Much more suitable than the Indians as wives for the early comers were the Mexican women.*

Then what? The bridegroom carries on the tradition of Cortés's viceroys and deputies. *Having been appointed subagent for the San Luis Rey Indians, Colonel Couts was able to secure all the cheap labor needed for the improvement of his property.*

It was treeless; he caused orchards to rise. His orange grove was the first in San Diego County.

Rancho Guajome, by the way, was a wedding present not from the bride's father but from Abel Stearns, who had conveniently obtained it from *Andres, an Indian, and . . . his two sisters.* Speaking of this latter syncretizer, I might mention that his wife Arcadia, a rather plain woman who styles her hair in opposing diagonals across her face, is Ysidora's sister. Yes, Juan Bandini has mother and daughters enough for two Anglos! He will die, aged either fifty-nine or sixty, at the home of Abel and Arcadia Stearns.

(Speaking further of Mr. Stearns, in an 1873 booklet for southern California homesteaders, I see a map of the Abel Stearns Ranchos, *for sale in sections or fractions* by a San Francisco company, which announces **Farming Lands—Perfect Titles**, namely *Early Mexican Grants, confirmed by U. S. Courts.*)

One historian refers to Couts as *one of the worst abusers of Indian field hands.* A habitual drunk, Couts whipped two Indians to death, and also killed an anonymous Mexican, not to mention his children's tutor. But perhaps he was kind to his wife. A county history informs me that he was *the soul of honor . . . a genial companion . . . a perfect gentleman in society.*

He syncretized, prospered and died. His lineage survived awhile. Sometime around the end of the teens of the next century, we find a Señorita Couts at a dance at Los Angeles's exclusive Club Anahuac for Californios; one commentator insists that she is a descendant of this family.

It does indeed appear that the syncretic path was safer and more lucrative than the way of William Walker or the wearisome gamble of a Mexican miner at Picacho. The trouble was that in the eastern reaches of San Diego County, and even south of the line where Imperial's eponymous valley continued, there were no women to marry and no lush acres to acquire. Imperial continued to drowse beneath her sandy blanket.

Chapter 28

THE INDIANS DO ALL THE HARD WORK

(1769–1906)

> And as the concomitant differentiaton and specialization of occupation goes on, a still more unmitigated discipline falls upon ever-widening classes of the population . . .
>
> —Thorstein Veblen, 1904

Walker wanted slaves, as do we all. One definition of human contentment is *having somebody else do my chores.* Here is an outsider's description of Mexican California in the 1830s: *The Indians . . . do all the hard work, two or three being attached to the better house; and the poorest persons are able to keep one, at least, for they have only to feed them, and give them a small piece of coarse cloth and a belt for the men, and a coarse gown, without shoes or stockings, for the women.* O joy! O conveniency! I have never been cheated out of a peso in my life.

In 1769, Padre Crespi and Captain Rivera lead forty-two Cochimi campesinos from Loreto all the way north to San Diego. This must be the first use by Europeans of exploited labor within the entity that I call Imperial. By the time they arrive, thirty of these workers have run away or died.

Fifteen years later, the Ministry of Capital calculates the expense of shipping them from Baja, factors in the significant mortality rate, and decides to replace the Cochimis by Alta California natives. In 1828, a French sea-captain sees only one Cochimi field hand in Mission San Diego; all the others are Chumash. The Chumash will get used up in their turn; so will many others.

Indeed, the history of Imperial agriculture is the history of waves of farm labor, in this order: Native American, Chinese, Japanese, and then, with or without interludes of blacks and Filipinos, Mexicans.

This book has already alluded to the charms of the California missions. Since most of them lay outside Imperial,* I cannot devote many lines to them. All the same, it may be worth reflecting on an observation of the noted *Californio* Antonio

*The exceptions were the two Yuma missions, which as you remember were wiped out by the Indians in 1781, and Mission San Diego, which will get mentioned from time to time, as will Imperial's future archrival, Los Angeles.

María Osio: The mission registers display two-thirds more burials than baptisms. Let me give the final word to Richard Steven Street, whose massive *Beasts of the Field* relates the history of California farmworkers from the beginnings of the missions in 1769. This chapter and several others are heavily indebted to him. Although he grants that many Indians joined the missions voluntarily, they quickly learned that they could not leave. If they tried, they could expect the following: *rape, murder, execution, whippings and intimidation at the hands of the leather-jacketed mission soldiers.*

Another commentator believes that *the Ibero-Americans consistently followed the procedure of utilizing the natives and incorporating them in their social and economic structure,* while *the Anglo-American system . . . had no place for the Indian . . . All Indians were vermin, to be treated as such.* This oversimplifies the case; for California's Indians, who were indeed considered vermin, did get *utilized* on their way to extinction; and, as we say just now, a very few were even spared by syncretization; while Mexico's Indians, who got *incorporated,* to be sure, remained the lowest caste of all; so the divide between Southside's inescapable peonage and Northside's capricious enslavements and genocides might not have quite been as wide as one imagines. In the Yucatán, an American observer concluded that *the Indians worked . . . as if they had a lifetime for the job,* which they did, since their lives would hardly be spent doing anything but working. In Mexico City, a diplomat's wife noted *the innumerable Indians loaded like beasts of burden.* Meanwhile, Southside's Indian rebellions got punished with mass atrocities. They sometimes responded in kind. On one occasion in 1849, Comanches and Apaches murdered eighty-six Sonorans near the international line.

Back to Imperial's edge: In 1833, we find many secularized mission Indians doing unskilled vineyard labor in Los Angeles. By 1847, they have been placed firmly under the thumb of the United States government. In 1850 their word no longer means anything in court; "idle" Indians can be rounded up into serfdom. I will spare you the horrors of the roundups. A Ranger writes: *Indians did the labor and the white man spent the money in those happy days.* In 1860, California Indians are dying off rapidly; a still crueller law extends their indenture period; and the *Humboldt Times* enthuses: *What a pity the provisions of this law are not extended to Greasers, Kanakas and Asiatics. It would be so convenient to carry on a farm . . . when all the hard and dirty work is performed by apprentices.* The indenture law gets repealed in 1862; but the *utilizations* continue.

These Indians of California have large bodies, writes an 1870s Angeleno, *but small hands and feet . . . At one time long-lived, they are now becoming strongly addicted to brandy. The women drink as well as the men. This, together with the prevalence of syphilis, which has been brought in by the Europeans, is what has increased their death rate . . . When used—as they are throughout the county—as laborers they are harmless and industrious, although somewhat slow.*

He estimates that there were nearly a hundred and one thousand of them in 1823; now there are probably fewer than twenty thousand.

In 1906 we hear of five hundred workers, mostly Indian, gathering brush "mattresses" on which to found the dam of rocks and logs that will close Imperial's Colorado River break.

By then, Imperial has just begun to plough her gardens of Paradise. More labor, much more, will be needed.

Chapter 29

THE INLAND EMPIRE

(1860–1882)

> We wish to form a colony of intelligent, industrious and enterprising people, so that each one's industry will help to promote his neighbor's interest as well as his own.
>
> —Judge J. W. North, circular advertising the founding of Riverside, 1870

THE THREE STAGES OF DECOMPOSITION

True allegiance to the boundaries of the entity called Imperial would require me to exclude from this book the western marches of what is not yet Riverside County, whose settlements will be founded on vast *rancherías* such as Bernardo Yorba's. Talk about fairytale principalities! No wonder west Riverside's so far beyond the pale! The history of Imperial, like that of California and indeed our United States, may be summed up as follows:

(1) Exploration.
(2) Delineation.
(3) Subdivision.

Sixty miles east of San Diego, Warner's Ranch still embraces two Mexican land grants of San José del Valle and Valle de San José, 26,600 acres in toto. But just now as I write *Imperial,* in this forward-looking year of ours 1887 (by special permission of the Pope, our Virgin of Guadalupe's image has just been crowned in Mexico; meanwhile, the Wright Act has authorized the formation of local irrigation districts here in California), news comes to me that Warner has retired to Los Angeles. What will happen to Warner's Ranch? My prediction: Subdivision.

Truth to tell, we cannot all be Colonel Couts. How many Mexican land grants and rich Spanish wives are left? Nor does it seem profitable to follow William Walker's example. But that's not saying we can't center ourselves in petty empires of one kind or another. East of Los Angeles, where there were never multitudes of Indians, Chinese can do our laundry and waterworks will do the rest. So ring down the curtain on those vast *rancherías*! It's time for agrarian democracy!

Example of subdivision: The city of Jurupa, almost instantaneously renamed Riverside, sprouts upon the ranch of Luis Rubidoux and his Spanish wife. We may note that their sixty-seven hundred acres equal less than a quarter of Juan Bandini's original Jurupa Ranch; subdivision has already begun. And why do the Rubidouxes sell out? They're tired of paying property taxes on land they consider to be "utterly worthless," and indeed refuse to pay them. The great drought of 1862–64 renders cattle ranching unattractive. In 1869, the capitalists of the California Silk Center Association pay Mr. Rubidoux two and a half dollars per acre. In 1893, after several vicissitudes, that land will be worth between one and two thousand dollars an acre, and while the Riverside Directory assures us that *the Rubidoux family . . . were blessed with plenty and were then, as now, highly respected,* the five inhabitants of Riverside with that surname will be laborers, a hostler and a teamster, and the Rubidoux Cafe will belong to a fellow named Wentworth. That's life.

"A STRICTLY NEIGHBORHOOD AFFAIR"

Our epigraph, namely, Judge North's statement of intention, did not predate the actual foundation of Riverside by even so much as a year. The first house went up, and the first canal was gouged, in 1870. On the first of March in the following year, the first orange tree was planted in Riverside. And why not? Southern California had just succumbed to the condition called "orange fever." *Nothing contributes more to set off the appearance of a festive table than the orange.* I've read that for awhile the settlers employed orange seeds from Tahiti, but at some unremembered date, two navel orange seedlings were obtained from the Department of Agriculture in Washington by Mrs. L. C. Tibbetts, whose husband incidentally happened to be pathetically litigious. It's said that during dry spells she kept her seedlings alive on dishwater. Everyone adored the fruit she raised; navel oranges became the craze. Her first tree was replanted by Teddy Roosevelt and monumentalized behind a fence; you can see it on the label of Parent Tree Brand oranges, packed by G. R. Hand & Company; with two adobe edifices sharing a wide empty ivory-colored boulevard in the picture. (As of 1989 the tree was still alive.) In 1872, when some colonists experimented with planting pretty red opium poppies, came Riverside's first wedding; the bride was sweet sixteen; perhaps it took place in a shower of orange blossoms, for by the following year a promotional guide for home buyers in Los Angeles County and environs was already informing us that Riverside was irrigating itself nicely and that *here may be seen large nurseries of orange, lime, and lemon trees growing luxuriously.* Two years after that, the Evans-Sayward Syndicate bought the Southern California Colony Association's lands in Riverside and things really took off!—By the way, grapes fell behind oranges early in the course of Riverside's Darwinian profit-struggle. In the San Joaquin Valley they grew faster. Well, to hell with grapes; let's tell a tale of happy oranges.—Here came more canals, not to mention the first Citrus Fair. *We need have no fear that our lands will not become better and better as the years go by.* In 1883, Riverside incorporated.

Now, you might think that since Riverside was owned by a syndicate, it no longer conformed to the dictates of Judge North's prospectus: *Each one's industry will help to promote his neighbor's interest as well as his own.* I can't help believing in people. Indeed, I see Chinese workers before vast wooden islands and spillways of citrus in the Frank B. Devine Packing House, *circa* 1888. Their pale, wary, still faces, mostly in caps or hats, discourage me from watching the museum's **CITRUS FILM**, which anyhow is *OUT OF ORDER.*

In 1893 the Riverside Fruit Exchange, later to grow into the California Fruit Growers' Exchange, came into being, and you'll be reassured to know that *the foundation of the organization is the local association, a strictly neighborhood affair.*

THE GARDENS OF PARADISE

What is Riverside? This capital of the Inland Empire should be emblematized not only by its capitalists, but also by its homesteads—for instance, the mansion of Mrs. James Bettner, a "citrus pioneer's" widow. Her departed husband must have had better things to do than plant lemon seedlings, for he not only helped organize the Riverside exhibits at two New Orleans World's Fairs, but also became first President of the Southern California Lawn Tennis Association. I hope and suspect that the widow found herself well taken care of. In the 1893–94 city directory she appears as

Bettner, Mrs. Catherine, horticulturist, res Magnolia ave.

Sitting in the gazebo, whose shadow-outlined diamonds of sunlight are sometimes more or less glaring on the cloven hexagon of bench which runs around the inside perimeter, Mrs. Bettner centers herself in a universe of oranges. The gazebo floor is a sort of spiderweb; quadrilateral boards fixed in concentric parallels, painted grey.

Now that she is dead, and the orange groves almost gone, I, transit passenger through the Inland Empire, stop at her home, which is now called the Heritage House, and I note that her two storeys of indented porches are lovingly, ornately shaded. I see shutters on the windows, domes, seashell-like ledges under the windows, everything shuttered against heat and light because we are almost on the edge of Imperial.

Through the open crisscross around the arched doorway and through the doorway itself I see a gracious palm tree, widening as it ascends, ringed round with ferns on its island; and hoses sparkle silver on the lawns as the gardener rakes and trundles. Green, green trees cast the Heritage House in a spell of shade. It smells as fresh here as do Imperial's hayfields in the cool of a summer evening.

Did Mrs. Bettner plant this Japanese gingko? Surely she remains present in the smell of honey and of sun on old wood. The old white carriage house is almost blinding in the September afternoon sun.

I stand beneath a magnolialike tree which bears red petaled blossoms like labia wthin pine cones. I see, as she must have seen, palm trees reflected in her house's dark windows.

"SUCH A MAGNIFICENT SCENE"

Well, what happened next? Success, of course! I have never been cheated out of a dollar in my life. In 1895, Riverside was rated the richest city per capita in America. In 1904, an expert from the United States Department of Agriculture can't resist writing home about *the magnificent hills and valleys with their seas of orange groves . . . You look down the valley to Riverside six or eight miles away, and the groves are in one solid mass. . . . It is a miracle, the transformation of a desert country into such a magnificent scene, in about twenty years.* It's small-scale democracy at its finest: For instance, eight miles south of Riverside, I spy the Arlington Heights Trust Co. property: fifteen hundred acres of oranges, five hundred of lemons; it's *the largest orange and lemon ranch in California.*

In 1906, the Riverside Fire Department reports: *Riverside is essentially a city of homes.* Hence the air is clear. *And Riverside is clean morally as well as physically,* thank God.

In 1907, the California Fruit Growers' Exchange starts advertising, first in Iowa. (Nobody can see the day coming when our orange juice will come from Brazil.) And the Inland Empire keeps getting bigger and better, which must be why in 1930 I find an ad for the Inland Empire Gas Company in El Centro.

IMPERIAL PRELUDE

Forty-eight miles east of Los Angeles, Etiwanda subdelineates itself in blocks from A to T, each block containing sixteen lots. This colony lies at a sufficient remove from the coast for her embryonic orange groves to remain untouched by the common scale and the black fungus. Land goes for a hundred dollars an acre. In 1882, the year of her incorporation, Etiwanda installs the first electric lights in southern

California. No one can call George Chaffey anything but progessive. Besides, he's partnered up with that arch-boomer L. M. Holt! (George's brother William also signs on, but keeps himself largely irrelevant to the entity I call Imperial.) Holt now owns the *Riverside Press and Horticulturist.* He publishes advertisements and editorials about Etiwanda. (A sample headline: **Promises Fulfilled**.) By the second year, there's already a Congregational church. Next comes Ontario, subdelineated out of Rancho Cucamonga. A mutual company of water shares (one parcel of land, one share) keeps irritgation democratic. Before we know it, rows of orange trees already stretch all the way to their convergence point in the dust beneath the mountains—hurrah for Euclid Avenue! In 1904, our USDA man will visit this city, which is now called Ontario, and name it *one of the great orange centres.* By then, the Chaffeys' name will already be associated with Imperial. Praise the Inland Empire!

REALITY IS IN THE EYE OF THE REALTOR

By the way, what is the Inland Empire? The pictorial on my lap opines that it must have been *a term . . . conjured up by real estate developers probably during the first decade of the 20th century,* in which case it would have been an attempt to copycat Imperial herself. Once upon a time, the Inland Empire was Riverside County. By 1920 the *San Bernardino Sun* had counted in its own readers and advertisers. At the beginning of the twenty-first century, most of Riverside and San Bernardino counties and some of eastern Lost Angeles County (for instance, Claremont and Pomona) have enrolled. Call it twenty-eight thousand square miles, and confess (as is the case with the entity that I call Imperial) that nobody knows precisely where it ends.

THE VALE OF DEATH

And the Inland Empire keeps annexing whatever it can, but whatever it can goes only so far, to San Gorgonio Pass, which is the gateway to the entity which I call Imperial. A county history gives the lie of that land: *On the other side,* which of course is the Imperial side, the dark side of the moon, *is a low range of sandhills. Beyond is a sandy waste devoid of vegetation . . . called Whitewater Valley.*

Chapter 30

SUBDELINEATIONS: WATERSCAPES

(1850–1900)

Nearly all of California that slopes toward the Colorado, and drains into it . . . is an absolute desert, within whose limits is included nearly three fourths of the entire area of San Diego county.

—William Hall, State Engineer, 1888

Down here, behind the Coast Mountains, is a vast, strange, hot land that used to have no water . . . This Desert Region we shall mark now with the red chalk. Later on you will hear a wonderful story about this land . . .

—Irmagarde Richards, 1933

SUMMER FAILURES

On the other side lies a low range of sandhills, but so what? Who needs Imperial? On our side, in our Inland Empire, the earth literally swells with water. Do you want any? Drill a hole, and water will spurt out! In San Bernardino Valley, artesian wells ejaculate sixteen million gallons of pure water into the sky *every day!* Judge Willis over in Old San Bernardino has a well four hundred and ten feet deep which vomits up small sucker-fish. (How many artesian wells in San Bernardino in 2007? I telephoned a bureaucrat and she didn't know.)

In Imperial, the intermittently existing New River, *formed by the surplus waters of the Colorado,* is accompanied by an honor guard of giant sunflowers on its descent to Dry Lake. A geologist named William Blake trekked through here in 1853. Spotting the ancient shoreline of Lake Cahuilla, Blake understood Imperial's possibilities, and won the visionary's customary reward: nothing.

But more practical men, which is to say men with their eyes on today's dollar instead of tomorrow's, poise armies of shovelers upon neighboring waterscapes.—*In the southwest,* explains *Scribner's* magazine, *this labor must be largely Mexican, now that public opinion prevents the employment of Chinese. If not Mexican, then it must be the scarce, highly paid, independent white labor of the West.* Therefore, reservoirs are expensive. We need our real estate boomers to lure homesteaders out here; then they'll invest in waterworks, because I can't help believing in people. Once they buy ranches and put down their taproots, how much should I charge them per miner's inch? Evidence that *"Moisture Means Millions"* is provided by the fact that between 1880 and 1902, no fewer than fifty-seven irrigation companies see fit to gamble in the foothills east of Los Angeles alone.

In short, to pay for our reservoirs we'll increase our population, who will then need more water. Never mind that; **WATER IS HERE**. An inventory follows:

Now, in the forty-two hundred square miles of western San Diego, which will be all that remains of that county once Imperial and Riverside counties break away, we find seven main rivers, flowing more or less in parallel southwest into the Pacific. Proceeding northwards from the border, we first encounter the Tia Juana, which loops in and out of Mexico and whose main American extension, Cottonwood Creek, *to a limited extent . . . may be advantageously utilized for winter irrigation on bottom lands near the coast.* Small springs in the Tia Juana's upper watershed could be tapped in the future. Next comes the Otay, *comparatively insignificant as a source of irrigation supply,* but it might be good for two reservoirs. The Sweetwater gets dammed in 1886–87, as a result of which twenty or twenty-five thousand irrigable acres come into being. Then comes the San Diego, whose flow only a realtor would dare call perennial; the San Dieguito, which on the contrary is eminently tappable, has been tapped, but can be quite a bit more; the San Luis Rey, which comprises *the largest and most reliable water-supply in the county;* we pass over the Temecula, which requires damming due to the scantness of its summer trickle; and the San Jacinto* with its various branches *(local testimony on the relative permanence and volume of these tributaries is conflicting).*

All of these rivers fail in summer. Moreover, the amount of annual rainfall in their waterscapes can vary by more than a factor of seven. Good Boy Scouts had better plan for the worst case! Throughout the early years of the approaching century, our water frequently falls short. (In 1904 the citrus groves of National City and Chula Vista will die of thirst.) But have faith; since **WATER IS HERE**, all the engineers need to do is convey it to **THERE**, where we'll bank it in dams and withdraw it through wells and ditches. The Mount Tecarte Land and Water Company has already picked out eight reservoir sites on the Tia Juana River. *A subsidy of one fourth of certain large bodies on these lands is being negotiated by the company with land owners, as a consideration for water-rights for the remainder.* Meanwhile, the Riverside Water Company builds three main canals and diversions. Orange groves, arise!

*These last two rivers will later be called the San Luis Rey and the Santa Margarita, respectively.

HOME ROCKET SCIENCE

This era reminds me of the science-fiction novels I used to read. Two boys build their own spaceship and blast off to Mars! An inventor and an entrepreneur construct a sphere of Cavourite, and they shoot straight up to the moon! Who could have imagined a government space agency, whose salaried astronauts follow the orders of Mission Control? *The bountiful continent is ours, state on state, and territory on territory, to the waves of the Pacific sea;* and by *ours* I mean not the government's but *mine,* should I only get enough money to take it. In short, private enterprise builds its own reservoirs. For instance, here is a fine extra-Imperial fable of success and reconciliation which the *California Cultivator* entitles **Up-to-date Cattle Raising.** Henry Miller is *the greatest cattle-raiser in California, a man whose ranches extend from the Tehachapi to Oregon . . .* He and his partner Lux *with their barbed wire fences, and branding chutes, did their part to change the rope-swinging cowboy into a hired man.* (In other words, no more roping, boys; that makes the stock lose weight.) What gave Miller and Lux their leg up? It might have been that 1886 State Supreme Court decision that awarded them the entire Kern River: **THE DESERT DISAPPEARS.** Upon protest of the lawsuit's losers, who will presently become the Kern County Land Company, our two neighborly cattle barons give back two-thirds of the river, in exchange for which the rival company builds them a reservoir in which to bank their one-third. And in material advantages they are well supplied.

Private enterprise, I said, builds its own reservoirs. And so it will continue to do until 1928, when the spectacular collapse of William Mulholland's Saint Francis Dam, killing half a thousand Angelenos, compels the coroner's jury to conclude: *The construction of a municipal dam should never be left to the sole judgment of one man, no matter how eminent.*

WATER RIGHTS, *or*, A DEFENSE OF R. R. SUTHERLAND

A 1933 children's primer on *Our California Home* explains that *at first, you see, each farmer tried to get a farm that was beside a stream. Then he built his own dam, dug his own ditch . . . That worked well enough for awhile. But soon another man would take land on the same stream, higher up . . . The trouble was, each man tried to work alone, for himself.*

The doctrine of unhindered sovereignty over the watercourse adjoining one's landholdings is an ancient one, known as riparian rights. It happens to be well suited to bullies. As late as 1920, a power company begins to lower the water level of Lake Tahoe for its own purposes; in the end, the public has to go all the way to Washington to stop it.

In Los Angeles I hear gunfire between the men of the Azusa and Corvina neighborhoods! They're fighting over the water that runs down San Gabriel Cañón. Thus Los Angeles in the 1880s. On the other hand, what with all the barroom gunfights, Mexican bandits, woman-knappings in Nigger Alley, what else is new? I can't help believing in people.

Since **WATER IS** not only **HERE** but infinite, California still hopes that riparianists can continue to enjoy unrestricted use of the streams within their domains, returning the water when they are finished with it (never mind that much or most of it will sink into their fields); meanwhile, the rest of us can get what we need from reservoirs. And so *The City and County of San Diego,* published in 1882, enthuses about various "large schemes" to catch the riverine outflows of that huge zone, and then store them. The Hemmet Valley Reservoir Company, the San Marcos Water Company along the coast and in Encinitas; the San Luis Rey Flume Company, the Otay Valley Water Company, the Fallbrook Water and Power Company, all busy themselves on the Temecula River. I've already intimated that the Sweetwater Valley Water Company is digging for our good at Jacumba, *and whenever it will be safe to trust a flume outside of the American line, the Tia Juana may be brought in from Mexico to reclaim some twenty thousand* acres *more.* After all, there are hardly any Mexicans at Tia Juana; they won't need that water!* Besides, President Díaz is a friend of Northside; he'll write us a concession anytime . . .

Unfortunately, even if we take it all for Northside, not enough **WATER IS HERE**; and so, in a series of court cases, riparian doctrine gets superseded by the doctrine of *first appropriation for beneficial use.*

The methods of beneficial use have been defined as *those that produce the* best results *from the most* economical *use.*

H.R. 13846, the genesis of the 1902 Reclamation Act, contains this language: *The right to the use of water shall be perpetually appurtenant to the land irrigated and beneficial use shall be the basis, the measure, and the limit of the right.*

The builders of private dams learn to roll the phrase *beneficial use* out of their mouths,† and the game goes on. Here's news from 1904: *R. R. Sutherland filed*

*I am informed that only about 15% of Mexico is arable *even with man-made improvements.*

†The riparian doctrine endured, at least in name, for many more decades. The year 1928 marked the collapse not only of the Saint Francis Dam but also, according to *The California Water Atlas,* which favors appropriative rights, of "an era which depended on individualism, local control, and private enterprise for the development of California's water resources. The new era, characterized by cooperation, centralized supervision, and the use of public funds and authority, was already well advanced by this time . . . thanks in part to the pressing needs of California's cities, which by 1900 had become critical." The crucial legislative event of that year was *Herminghaus v. Southern California Edison.* Against the utility's determination to store water for hydroelectricity, Herminghaus clung to his riparian right to natural irrigation, which occurred only during the spring snow melt. In 1928, a constitutional amendment was passed which undid a prior California Supreme Court decision in Herminghaus's favor. To be sure, as late as 1950, an editorial in the 1950 *California Farmer* crowed that vested water rights still existed in California, because when the Bureau of Reclamation sought to "grab" some streams in the San Joaquin Valley on the grounds that they

notice at Riverside Monday, of his appropriation of 1500 inches of water in the east fork of Snow creek, 1500 inches in the west fork of Snow creek and 2500 inches in White water, all for power purposes.

We now pause to discuss the ostensible setting of this book. A rival volume on Imperial accuses the valley's irrigators, Chaffey and Rockwood, of criminal hubris: *They sought economic gain by means of appropriating as their private property the waters of a free-flowing river . . . Equally, their shared objective required that they deliberately and systemically undermine the land laws of the United States . . .* But what did they do that R. R. Sutherland didn't do?

BLYTHE'S OASIS

Onward to the Salton Sink: In 1877, evidently with the assistance of our Riverside boomer friend L. M. Holt, California passes the Wright Act, which explicitly undoes riparian law and thereby facilitates the creation of local water districts. In that same year, Congress passes the Desert Land Act of 1877, which in the accurately leftist view of one historian is *founded upon a false assumption: that the desert could be watered simply by giving 320 acres to anyone who would agree to irrigate it.* The result, he insists: monopoly. Will that be so? This book hopes to learn the answer.

Once again in 1877, the boomer Thomas Blythe begins to underwrite the irrigation of his eponymous acres, which enjoy the rare advantage of lying both adjacent to and below the Colorado. (The long valley from Coachella through Mexicali is similar in this respect, but it will be five years yet before George Chaffey even gets to Etiwanda, let alone the Salton Sink.)

If you go north from Pilot Knob, where the irrigation of the Imperial Valley will begin not quite a quarter-century hence, you can crawl for many miles across the desert's dry breast; then presently there will be a bit of yellow grass and purple mountain ahead. Steer past the orange maze to the west, over which purple rocks crookedly jut; dip down into the small green world of Palo Verde, a world which Thomas Blythe began. The native American intaglios near Blythe roll westward on a gravel road. Then comes a mons veneris of earth, whose pubic hair consists of rays of white and black. Here where the land rises away from the Colorado, the red rocks often have scorched-looking edges; in summer they're nearly too hot to touch. I remember a rock like a burned horse's hoof, with two bonelike yellow cylinders embedded in it. Rocks tinkle underfoot in the searing breeze. Now you are high enough to gaze downward and get a comprehensive glimpse of one of the giant intaglio figures. Is that a rounded letter **W** on its side, or veins in an insect's wing?

---

were navigable; the Supreme Court ruled in favor of local irrigators. The *Farmer*'s stance was, of course, wishful thinking.

And then you can lift up your eyes a trifle to gaze across the Colorado and down into the blue-green squares of field on the Arizona side. The entity that I call Imperial begins here.

Blythe's gamble deserves to be called shrewd; for not only does the Colorado never fail, but in this epoch it still reaches the sea! In 1880 another boomer stands on Blythe Townsite and praises the *water communication from the center of the tract with all the harbors of the world.*

THE SONG OF NANAYA

We now prepare and improve ourselves for irrigation. The California Convention of 1878–79 inserts a three-hundred-and-twenty-acre limitation on state grants into the constitution. Thank God we've saved ourselves from monopolists! *(Henry Miller is the greatest cattle-raiser in California, a man whose ranches extend from the Tehachapi to Oregon . . .)*

Then what?

At the Irrigation Congress of 1891 (this body will assemble almost yearly in various Western cities throughout the decade), Francis G. Newlands of Nevada warns that *irrigation has reached almost a stationary period . . . The field of individual effort has been almost exhausted . . .*

Why exhausted? Our leftwing historian, Paul S. Taylor (once the husband of Dorothea Lange, whose heartrending photograph of a migrant mother and child will achieve more fame than any project of his), sums up the tale of California's waterscape improvements thus far as follows: Cooperative development by farmers has failed due to cost; development by capital will produce monopoly; development by government is the only alternative. That will begin with the Reclamation Act, a year after George Chaffey's headgates open in Imperial.—And so the Irrigation Congress, following just this logic, calls upon the United States to cede public lands to individual states and territories for irrigation. For Imperial, the eventual result will be great dams on the Colorado, not to mention the All-American Canal.

Meanwhile, Chaffey irrigates Etiwanda; Rockwood seeks partners; and at last the day comes when Imperial opens her eyes, spreads her legs and sings a song as ancient as Sumer—the Song of Nanaya:

Dig no canal; I'll be your canal.
Plough no field; I'll be your field.
Farmer, seek no wet place;
My precious sweet, I'll be your wet place.

Chapter 31

THEIR NEEDS ARE EASILY SATISFIED

(1871–1906)

You look at a man's eyes, you see that he expects pidgin and a shuffle, so you speak pidgin and shuffle.

—Lee, character in Steinbeck's *East of Eden,* 1952

I have never been cheated out of a dollar in my life. *The Indians,* as I said before, *do all the hard work,* but unfortunately we're running out of Indians!

Here come the Chinese, about whom an Angeleno explains: *In fact, now that they are here, their presence has become essential to most inhabitants of California . . . They make especially capable laundrymen. Chinamen are hard workers and do not drink excessively. Since their needs are easily satisfied they are contented to work for much lower wages than white workers.* He adds: *All in all, they are not popular and in Los Angeles the anti-Chinese feeling is highly developed.*

By 1871, Chinese laborers have set to work in Riverside ranches. A decade later they are in the citrus groves, taking over from Indians. I see two pigtailed Celestials in snow-white clothes and hats (their garments would actually have been blue) planting a white narcissus, one of them standing with his hand on his hip, leaning on the shovel, while the other kneels on the near-blank flat foregrounds of this 1870s-era engraving, smoothing the bright dirt around the plant with his hand, and an orange tree ripe with moon-white fruit frames them as a young orange grove organizes itself military-wise behind them, and then on the white horizon stands a vast white house of many gables and chimneys and a shaded porch all around.

In the homes and ranches of the whites, Chinese cooks and servants stand ready to work for sixteen to twenty-five dollars a month. Chinese citrus packers make a dollar a day, working from six in the morning until seven at night, with an hour off for the lunch they must bring themselves. You see, *since their needs are easily satisfied they are contented to work for much lower wages than white workers.**

*How much less was this than the prevailing wage for white labor? A man with the not very Chinese name of Leo Klotz remembers working in the packinghouse of the Cucamonga Lemon Association in 1910–14; among many other jobs, most of which sound miserable, he made wooden lemon-packing boxes by hand

(One Riverside historian has noticed that photographs of fruit packers at the beginning of the twentieth century tend to show mainly Anglo women. He wonders whether Chinese and Japanese were deliberately excluded from these images in deference to *popular antagonism.*)

In 1876, a saloonkeeper named Al Rodgers starts the first Anti-Chinese Society in San Bernardino. I wonder what set him off; did the Chinese refuse to patronize his bar? Anyhow, he enjoys good timing; for that year Chinese are the victims of violence all over the state. In 1878 the San Bernardino Town Board expels Chinese prostitutes but not prostitutes of other nationalities. In 1880, the Glenwood City Hack prohibits Chinese passengers between Riverside and Colton.

In 1881, the *Pacific Rural Press* worries: *It is difficult to see how the present fruit crop, which is bringing such fine prices, or the immense grape crop now ripening, could be handled at all without Celestial aid.* In 1885 the Chinese are growing and delivering nearly the entirety of Riverside's produce.

All the same, their future prospects are as slender as the circular Chinese bone-chess pieces, each inscribed with the character for horse, which resemble many windblown grassblades. From his headquarters at Eighth and Orange, L. M. Holt, that boomer of Coachella and Imperial, editorializes against them in the *Riverside Press and Horticulturist,* which he has owned since 1880; in its pages he calls for a race war. That fall, rents to some Chinese go up astronomically; the others are simply evicted. An arsonist solves the Chinatown problem. The new Chinatown will be tolerated at the center of town. Then comes 1893, year of the Great Chinatown Fire in Riverside.

In 1897, regarding the possibility of delegating a Riverside policeman to protect Chinese laborers, Holt pitilesssly opines: . . . *if packers persisted in hiring Chinamen they should protect them.*

Call him a man in touch with the popular pulse. He's a true American Californian, all right. In the glorious year 1882, the First Chinese Exclusion Act is signed by President Arthur. In 1889 we begin to hear of illegal Chinese laborers crossing the border from Mexico, and I can almost hear Border Patrolman Dan Murray say: *They'll pop their heads up in a minute.*—By 1891, Chinese are already coming from Los Angeles to help with Etiwanda's grape harvest; so in 1892 the Geary Act prohibits Chinese immigration for ten years. Accordingly, Colis Huntington the railroad magnate begins soliciting Mexican labor in 1893. (Judge Farr, 1918: *Cotton has been especially valuable on the Mexican side of the line on account of the favorable labor conditions where Chinese could be imported and where Mexican labor was available . . .*) Fresno fruit packers threaten to sue the county if their Chinese workers

at two dollars a day; sometimes he packed lemons at eight cents per box; on a very good day he could pack sixty-five boxes in a nine hour day, making close to five dollars.

are deported, but they're swimming against the good old American tide. That year, Deputy U.S. Marshals take five Chinese into custody in Cahuenga and deport them. Later they arrest ten Chinese in Riverside. And there are many other raids; I might as well be reading today's newspaper, except that there is no Border Patrol yet, which is why good citizens must get proactive for the sake of their beloved country. Hence the patriots of Burbank expel their Chinese residents, all eight of them; they were merely railroad workers; we don't need them anymore. Here comes a similar occurrence in Norwalk.

In 1906, a Chinese is discovered to be dying of leprosy in Santa Ana's Chinatown. They put him in a wire stockade for a week or two until he dies. The City Council condemns Chinatown, and burns it down. Once upon a time, two hundred people lived there.

BROKEN TREASURES

When the burnt, buried remains of Riverside's Chinatown got dug up at the end of the twentieth century, archaeologists found more opium-related artifacts there than at any other single site in America. The inventory includes a man's jade bracelet, hairpicks of carved bone, opium pipes of orange or grey paste earthenware. The marks on opium pipe bowls included *chiu,* the number nine; *meng,* the budding of plants; and *tung,* meaning east. They uncovered wooden Chinese dominoes with circular holes bored shallowly into them for the numbers.

I myself would soon descend into the half-mythical Chinese tunnels of Mexicali, discovering my own rat-gnawed treasures; and when we get to that part of Imperial's history I will tell you all about it. But for now we ought to return to the nineteenth century, because we are closing in on Imperial's birth-by-irrigation; meanwhile, in the highest interests of democratic Americanism, the Chinese have been legally excluded, and to replace them, in come the Japanese, who are expected to work harder and for less . . .

Chapter 32

LOS ANGELES

(1875)

> The constant ripening of fruits and the maturing of vegetables in this county . . . astonish persons unfamiliar with the peculiar nature of the soil and climate.
>
> —*An Illustrated History of Los Angeles County*, 1889

Once upon a time was still once upon a time, when Imperial contained Los Angeles. To be sure, Los Angeles's almost bygone acorns, deer and shell-beads wouldn't hold on much longer. Nobody cared that Yang-Na had been the Indian name for Ranchería Los Angeles. Sonag-na was now known as Mr. White's place. In 1851 and 1852, federal commissioners met with tribes all over California to extinguish title to most of their lands, granting them reservations in exchange. The editor of the *Los Angeles Star* warned that if these treaties were ratified, *the most degraded race of aborigines upon the North American Continent* would receive dangerously unwarranted respect. *We can see no solution of the difficulties which will grow up around us . . . except a general and exterminating war* . . . Fortunately, the treaties remained unratified. More fortunately still, in 1863 most of the Indians in Los Angeles died of smallpox. We need have no fear that our lands will not become better and better as the years go by. For the rest of the century, Los Angeles would be periodically distinguished by smallpox, flower festivals and Chinese festivals, fires, floods, murders and improvements.

The telegraph line to San Jose had been in existence ever since 1860. In 1868 Los Angeles began to expand rapidly, getting its first three-storey building. Two years later it possessed a hundred and ten liquor establishments. *Drunkenness and pistol shooting rampant for months, especially among the Indians of the town . . . "Nigger Alley" described as the vilest of resorts.* In 1872 Los Angeles had a day of three bullfights, one bull being ridden bareback while crowned with firecrackers; two years after that the population was eleven thousand. By 1882, electricity arrived.

Best of all, two years after that, Los Angeles gained title to all water rights of the Los Angeles River. Moreover, artesian wells could be *had at pleasure, at depths of 40 to 200 feet.* A boomer accordingly assured us that the water supply is *ample for a very large city.*

Indeed, Los Angeles was now a city of sorts. In 1887, five hundred devotees of the latest land boom waited in line all night to buy lots in Paradise; men sold their places in line for up to a hundred and fifty dollars. All the same, Los Angeles remained nearly as much of an enclave as a seventeenth-century mission in the Baja; for in the midst of the land boom, two brothers killed a seven-hundred-pound grizzly in Tejunga Cañón, and coyotes were still preying on Angelenos' chickens, lambs and piglets. Compared to the Los Angeles of my own time, the place might as well have been what it was to a young American wanderer in 1829: a *small town,* remarkable only for the *bituminous pitch* with which its houses were roofed.

In 1856 the Los Angeles assessor had found no more than a hundred and fifty-one bearing orange trees to record. In a promotional guide to *Homes in Los Angeles City and County,* published in 1873, we read of Miss Francisca Wolfskill's inheritance of eighteen hundred orange trees on the west side of Alameda Street. Fifteen hundred oranges per tree! *Broad carriage-ways lead through and around the grove, and almost every day may be seen tourists on horseback and handsome coupes and barouches . . . visiting this golden Hesperides. Here and there rippling streams (called* zanjas) *reflect the shadows of the scene above . . .*

Meanwhile, in the San Fernando Mountains lies the largest beehive in the world, in a rocky cleft containing at least eight to ten tons of honey!

Chapter 33

THE SECOND LINE

(1893)

A map of the real world is no less imaginary than the map of an imaginary world.

—Alberto Blanco, 1998

BUT WHAT ABOUT MASSACHUSETTS?

Exactly forty years after William Walker's attempt to liberate Sonora for the greater good of slavery, we Californians score another wound upon the wide silt-flesh of Imperial: Riverside County breaks the brainpan of Lake Cahuilla, now marked on maps as Dry Lake, in two.

Were I a more accurate old gentleman, which is to say a "historian," I should have dated this chapter 1853, the year of Walker's foray, because it was then that San Diego County, which once reached all the way to Death Valley, got robbed of San Bernardino County, which is presently the largest in the United States; call that theft the second line. But then again, perhaps I should have set my sights on 1851, the precise year when Los Angeles County nibbled a prior bite out of San Diego; or for that matter on 1866, when Inyo County cost San Diego its northern triangular knife-edge. No, I'll stand my ground; the following two sentences will vindicate me to posterity: *Most of present-day Riverside County* (to be precise, six thousand and forty-four square miles of it) *was within 1850 San Diego County until 1893*. As a matter of fact, there was no Riverside County at all until 1893. *A small northwestern portion* (which we'll neglect in this decidedly unpedantic book) *was part of Los Angeles County until 1853 and a northern strip* (five hundred and ninety square miles) *was in San Bernardino County between 1853 and 1893*.

If you wish, I can make this chapter even more tedious than the polygon of Riverside County itself, which is immensely complex in shape, requiring the spelling out of many ranchos, townships and sections for its accurate delineation. (In 1907, defining the limits of Imperial County will not take nearly so many words.) Computing the area of this geometric form is no mere schoolchild's exercise, as proved by the fact that on page 133 of the book I'm cribbing from, Riverside County is the size of Massachusetts; on page 168 it's twice the size of Masachusetts. I wish I had a hundred pages to devote to the subject of Riverside's elasticity;* unfortunately, the northwestern part of Riverside County avoids coming anywhere near the entity which I call Imperial; nor does that irrelevant strip of San Bernardino. Conclusion: Until 1893, Imperial was not galled by any delineation excepting the international frontier.

THE CUT

On W. E. Elliott's map of California in 1883, San Diego County still forms an immense triangle whose base is the international line and whose hypotenuse wanders down from Los Angeles to Yuma, encompassing the famed Imperial landmarks of New River Station, Dry Lake (that will be Salton Sea to us), Coyote Village, Indian Wells (which looks awfully like Indio), Soda Spring (gone without a hint), Agua Calienta, or Caliente (which is to say Palm Springs), another Palm Springs now dried up and gone to hell, a Green Palms, a White Water.

But on all maps after 1893, the line comes crashing through the Santa Rosa Mountains, which are of absolutely no interest to you and me, then sunders the ancient sea valley at Imperial's heart, already once sundered by the international line, into those imaginary constructs, the Imperial and Cahuilla valleys. I grant you that the gentle green star-spiders of palms are more populous in Cahuilla; maybe that means something. Still and all, the absurdity of the separation will be proved after the Salton Sea accident, when a county division runs foolishly through water. Well, so what? It's only a line; and since 1893 happens to mark the worst economic depression thus far in United States history, it may well be that people in Ohio or New York or Virginia fail to give this latest subdelineation their best attention. But now the destinies of "Imperial" and "Cahuilla" (soon to be "Coachella") will begin to draw away from each other ever more visibly.

THE BUCK STOPS HERE

The line of 1848 was a tragedy for Mexico, of course; and a century after that, with the completion of the All-American Canal, the ecological, economic and moral effects of the line will become ever more hurtful to the portion of Imperial which remains on Southside; that is why Border Patrol Officer Gloria I. Chavez looked

*Specifically, if I could only be sufficiently impartial to admit that the rival entities which ring Imperial round have their own justification for life, I'd devote this chapter to the doings of that now very energetic and self-willed young child, the Inland Empire, instead of to the second line's effects on Imperial.—Statement of Mr. Warren, missionary, *circa* 1883: "When I first came to Riverside, it had only a ditch and a future, and the future was in the ditch." But I've no time for Mr. Warren. Imperial's own ditch and future are on their way.

across the fence near Chula Vista on that day in 1999 and said to me: *I think we all feel sorry for 'em.* Nonetheless, *la línea* does enrich Imperial much as the Salton Sea does: By subdividing so strikingly, it creates mysteries and stories.

What about the line of 1893?

A certain philosopher asserts that *a space is something that has been made room for, something that is cleared and free, namely within a boundary,* and I'll leave out his Greek derivation. *A boundary is not that at which something stops, but, as the Greeks recognized, the boundary is that from which something* begins its presencing. End of citation. Is the glass half full or half empty? When we gaze into a prison, do we see a place where freedom stops or a place at which confinement with all its horrors begins its presencing?

"AS THIS IS NEARLY ALL DESERT WE HAVE NOT INCLUDED IT"

These semi-gruesome speculations remain academic to Imperial in 1893, when the business directory's map of Riverside County ends not far beyond Beaumont and Banning, with this legend on the rightward edge: *The County extends Easterly to Colorado River, 125 miles.* Why should Riverside Imperial be deleted? *Our handsome map shows clearly every part of the county except the eastern, and as this is nearly all desert we have not included it, as it would make the map a bad shape for handling.*

We do at least find mention of Indio in the directory. *The peculiar situation makes it extremely warm, it being about 200 feet below sea level . . . Fruit ripens here very early.* The place is recommended to consumptives. Two station agents reside there; likewise two section foremen, a coal heaver, two pumpers, a viticulturist, a lady hotel proprietor . . .—in short, less than a page's worth of inhabitants, in comparison to Riverside City's eighty. As for Palm Springs, that's *a small settlement on the Southern Pacific railroad.* Its population is comparable to Indio's, but they're mostly farmers and laborers.

Am I making myself clear? Ten years before the cut, a county history advises: *Though large parts of this may certainly be reclaimed by the waters of the Colorado, we are not at present recommending our desert.*

Chapter 34

THE DIRECT GAZE OF THE CONFIDENT MAN

(1900)

"We have only one standard in the West, Mr. Holmes."
"And that?"
"What can you do?" came the words as if spoken by cold iron.

—Harold Bell Wright, 1911

And then, right at the turn of the next century, I see W. F. Holt standing in a brimmed bullet-shaped hat, blurrily grinning and clenching his fists beside a railroad track. "W. F. Holt Looks Into the Future with the Direct Gaze of the Confident Man." *I can't help believing in people . . . I have never been cheated out of a dollar in my life . . . I've found that the way to get your money is to give a man a chance to pay you.* Thanks to men like him, **THE DESERT DISAPPEARS**.

Chapter 35

ADVERTISEMENT OF SALE

(2002)

Prof. David B. Chaplin, formerly principal of the B-street school, . . . resigned a month ago because he saw an opportunity to make a fortune at Imperial . . . The professor wanted to get away several weeks before he did, and declares that thrice the amount of his salary . . . was slipping through his fingers every day he remained after the opportunity opened for him at Imperial. He says that there is a veritable boom on the desert . . .

—*Imperial Valley Press and Farmer* (1903)

PUBLIC NOTICE:

ADVERTISEMENT OF SALE

NOTICE HEREBY GIVEN that the undersigned intends to sell the personal property described below to enforce a lien imposed on said property under the California Self-Service Storage Facility Act . . .

SPACE	NAME	DESCRIPTION
E33	MARTHA G. VERDUGO LUQUE	. . . BOXES UNKNOWN . . .
H58	ESFRAIN CASTELLANOS	. . . EYEGLASSES . . .
D141	REYNALDO MIRANDA CHACON	HOUSEHOLD GOODS . . .
D43	PRISCILLA ANN SANDOVAL	. . . BOXES—CONTENTS UNKNOWN

And in material advantages they are already well supplied. He sold out at a fancy price.

Chapter 36

IMPERIAL TOWNS

(1877–1910)

He saw the country already dotted with the white tent-houses of the settlers . . . He drew a deep breath, and, taking off his sombrero, drank in the scene.

—Harold Bell Wright, 1911

Holt didn't do it alone; he was preceded by missionaries of capital. Do you remember how the Jesuit and Franciscan missions crept up Baja California and northwestward through Sonora, then commenced to stipple Alta California itself? I've claimed that each of these was a thread of borderline cut to length and wrapped around itself to keep Southside out. The Imperial of W. F. Holt lay mostly within the bounds of Northside; now the islands no longer had to be walled and soldiered; for they housed not authority, which already controlled the paper blankness of the maps, but *money*, or, to be more specific, property development. What else could live in Imperial? *During our passage across it,* writes Pattie in 1830, *we saw not a single bird, nor the track of any quadruped, or in fact any thing that had life, not even a sprig, weed or grass blade, except a single shrubby tree.* Tortured by prickly pear thorns, compelled to moisten their lips with their own urine, Pattie's expedition staggered across *this very extensive plain, the Sahara of California,* and were saved at the last hour by a stream of snow-water.

In the 1880s, the appropriately named locality of Cactus first appears upon Imperial's blankness;* a decade later, Glamis and Hedges will keep her company there. Next comes Picacho, on which Mexican prospectors have actually been feasting since 1862. Meanwhile, in southwestern parts of Imperial, cattlemen begin to send their stock to gorge on wild grass during the cooler months. In 1893 the engineer Charles Robinson Rockwood, who will bear much responsibility for the disaster that causes the Salton Sea, surveys much of Imperial. In comes our friend George Chaffey, "the father of the Imperial Valley." In 1900 he and Rockwood sign a contract. **WATER IS HERE**. Rockwood will force him out in 1902; I

*A photograph of Amos Cemetery in 1878 already shows a few wooden crosses. And where was Amos Cemetery? Somewhere in the Imperial Valley.

can't help believing in people. Between 1900 and 1910 come Ogilby, also known as Ogilvy (twenty-one residents listed in the San Diego County directory for 1901); Andrade, which unlike Ogilby is not quite long, long gone, even though it's sufficiently out of the way to be more than fifty percent of the time on the wrong side of the All-American Canal; Calexico; Heber; Blue Lake (I mean Silsbee); Mobile; Meloland (the former Gleason Switch); Imperial; Braley, which is now Brawley because Mr. Braley refused to have any town in that godforsaken place named after him; Holtville, which would have stayed Holton except that the Postal Service objected to the similarity to Colton; Cabarker, which, showing marked ingratitude to Holt's partner C. A. Barker, we refer to nowadays as El Centro; Imperial Junction, which has gone blank but was not entirely unrelated to Niland (date of birth: 1914); and we shouldn't neglect dear Westmorland with and without its *e*. In 1963, the Ball Advertising Co. will proclaim Westmorland *one of the state's top cotton-producing areas*. What might it look like on its incorporation in 1910? Well, well, it was an Imperial town.

The rattler was the most dreaded thing & there was little else living here, writes an old Imperialite lady in 1956. *As to humans, a prospector now and then came thro in his way to the hills.*

A mid-twentieth-century author who is sour about his own era and correspondingly sentimental about the past assures us that the years 1890 to 1915 constituted *a halfway Utopia of civilized development* in southern California. To be specific, *blacksmiths' shops were community centers for men. While the men baled hay together they sang together. In summer when the apricots were ripe the young people worked cheerfully and flirted in the orchards* . . . If this vision ever possessed any more reality than its analogue in the brightly exhortatory posters of Maoists, I cannot believe that it survived the scorching emptiness of, for instance, Cameron Lake in 1896, which was a longish tract of milk with green-fogged dirt around it, on the far side a low and indistinct coast of shrubs or trees, no scale anywhere, everything lost—the result of improper fixing by the dead photographer, but nonetheless poetically true, for Cameron Lake, like so many Imperial towns, has become itself quite well and sufficiently lost. In those days the dichotomy between Imperial and its antithesis in greater southern California was not only less marked, everything being less "developed," but it also had less to do with what we now define as rural *versus* urban than with the ancient delineation of aridity *versus* lushness, which meant, from a homesteader's point of view, near-impossibility *versus* some kind of guarantee, for which one paid accordingly to the land development office.

Ever since the middle of that century, railroads had been crawling out of Los Angeles, northwest and west, south and southeast, with a long eastward arm jiggling through El Monte, Pomona, Cucamonga, Colton, Riverside. Soon the Bee-Line

Railroad would connect San Diego Bay right over the Colorado River and across Sonora, Mexico, all the way to Calabazas in the Arizona Territory. In 1887, fifteen hundred Chinese were working on the railroad from Oceanside to Santa Ana. When we finished kicking the Chinese in the teeth, it would be time for Colis P. Huntington to solicit more Mexican workers; one way or another, the railroads grew every which way; and I imagine that from the point of view of Capital, as reified by the direct gaze of the confident man, all this was already meant to be one entity, so that Cameron Lake could look forward to matrimony with San Diego County's two-storey houses with their second-storey porches looking out over picket-fences at mountains, mineral springs, orchards and wild deer. But who wants to kiss a bride whose lips are dry and whose mouth is a travertine cave packed with sand? *"Moisture Means Millions."*

Emblematic, therefore, was Blythe, whose eponymous millionaire founder, you will remember, had been irrigating his acres there ever since 1877. The irrigators of the Imperial Valley would take note of Blythe.

WIDE-AWAKE WHITE MEN

Across the county line, Indian Wells and Woodspur already stake their claim to the Cahuilla Valley; they'll become Indio and Coachella. (In 1877, twelve hundred Chinese, five hundred Indians and a hundred-odd individuals described as "white trash" were working on the railroad thereabouts; we need have no fear that our lands will not become better and better as the years go by.) The first homesteader files on his hundred and sixty acres there in 1885. In 1887, on the very edge of the entity known as Imperial, lands of old Spanish settlements on what was then called San Gorgonio get bought up by a syndicate which changes the name to Beaumont. And not far east of Beaumont we find a Big Palm Spring, which has been here since 1871. It now changes its name to Agua Caliente, a far from unique appellation; the de Anza Expedition had applied it to a Cucapah town just east of Imperial. In the new Agua Caliente, which in my time (1887) will go on the real estate market as Palm Springs,* *you rent your adobe house from an Indian family, who move into a brush shantey near by, on short notice—charging you, for their vacant domicile, in a ratio which is truly "childlike and bland."* How tragic, this guidebook continues, that some "wide-awake white man" can't get ahold of Agua Caliente! Well, well; that just may happen.

In 1894 somebody strikes an artesian flow at Mecca. Farming begins. Thermal has been there for an unspecified number of years, hiding beneath the unpromis-

*Platted in October, opened for sale in November. A hundred and thirty-seven lots were sold on the first day.

ing name of Kokell. Kenworthy has appeared by 1900. We next find, in this order, Marshall Cove and Arabia. Out of order, we get Salton and Dry Camp.

A TOUR OF MEXICAN IMPERIAL

We introduced Tecate in 1830, when its sixteen hundred hectares were granted to poor Juan Bandini, metonym of the Mexican Californians; Tecate comes into civic being in 1885, the same year that white people begin to stake their claims at Agua Caliente, the future Palm Springs; or in 1876, when it becomes Colonia Agrícola Tecate; or in 1917, when heroic-villainous Governor Cantú enacts it into a municipality. Meanwhile, Chula Vista's townsite has just been laid out in Northside.

In 1898, we find settlers at La Laguna del Alamo, the future site of Mexicali. It seems that there might have been a Cocopah Indian village in the neighborhood, but the Cocopahs have moved south. Mexicali snuggles sleepily closer to the commencement of her irrigated history. Guillermo Andrade has owned most of the Mexicali Valley for a good ten years now. Ever since 1874 his syndicate has been irrigating a settlement called Colonia Lerdo, forty-five miles south of Yuma. Shall I forewarn you of his next great plan? He's going to sell out to Los Angeles.

Tía Juana's sulphur springs are already growing famous; they're as good as anything in Arkansas; lands down there now go for fifty to a hundred dollars an acre. Who knows what prices an oncoming century will bring? In the boom of the late 1880s, Tía Juana is called *the El Paso of California*. In 1901 the San Diego directory will obligingly extend its purview across the line to "Tia Juana,"* listing twenty-three residents, including a fireman; several ranchers; Miss Alice G. Stearns, P.M.; two deputy U.S. Customs collectors and their Mexican counterpart; not to mention T. Arguelo, actual proprietor of the Tia Juana Hot Springs. In the guides and histories of this period there is no real difference between California and Mexico, no firm delineation; Mexico may be considered an attraction of San Diego. One book from 1887 advises "for recreation and health seekers": *On the southeast, at Tia Juana, there is a well-kept hotel, and only half an hour's drive farther on the well-known hot sulphur springs in Lower California, Mexico, are reached.* All the same, Imperial's first and most consequential cut has already begun to bite. On 21 March 1895, Mr. Fred W. Wadham, who is Deputy Collector, etc., at Tia Juana, Cal., receives his instructions from San Diego: *I advise that you carefully search every person that crosses the line, making a careful examination by passing your hands over their clothing.*

*Tía Juana means Aunt Jane. I have also read that "Tijuan" is an Indian word signifying "by the sea."

Chapter 37

THE BOOMERS

(1880–1912)

They sold hundred-dollar property at $300 to $500 per acre, promising that it would yield $1,000 in orange profits . . .

—Glenn S. Dumke, 1944

Holt didn't do it alone, I repeat, but it isn't for nothing that Holt (by whom I naturally mean W. F. Holt) was known as the Empire Builder. *He stood staunch as Mount Signal,* says the very first historian of the Pioneers Society, a certain Mrs. John Kavanaugh, who then goes on to list a few of his good works in the Imperial Valley: the first telephone line, printing press, church, power plant, gas plant, cotton gin! *He founded Holtville and El Centro, giving each a park and school grounds. He built the Alamo Hotel in Holtville and the Barbara Worth Hotel in El Centro; also the Holt Theatre and 30 brick business buildings in El Centro.*

The County Recorder's Index is a more appropriate monument. Here are a very few of Mr. Holt's real estate transactions in the years 1902 to 1905:

On December 23, 1902, A. F. and Nell K. Cornell are the grantors; W. F. Holt is the grantee. On August 20, 1903, the California Development Company is the grantor; W. F. Holt is the grantee. On October 14, 1903, W. F. Holt and his wife Fannie sell real estate to Elliott B. Mabel, Marinus O. Klitten, the Imperial Valley Bank of Brawley, and the Holton Power Company, whose name (as Mrs. John Kavanaugh hinted in her tribute) bears more than a coincidental resemblance to Mr. Holt's.

On April 16, 1904, Mr. and Mrs. Holt sell lots to N. A. Ross and Delphia E. Redman. On June 20, 1904, Grace Chaplin is the grantor; the Holton Power Company is the grantee. On July 6, 1904, the Brawley Town Company is one grantor and the Heber Town Company is another; W. F. Holt is the grantee. On October 1, 1904, the Calexico Town Company is the grantor; W. F. Holt is the grantee.

I omit several pages whose every item records the Holton Town Company as grantor; but this one's circularity pleases me: On March 15, 1905, the Holtville Town Company sells land to the Holton Power Company.

He is said to have owned nearly eighteen thousand acres of the Imperial Valley. A historian bluntly concludes: *By 1910, when Wright was writing* The Winning of Barbara Worth, *the Imperial Valley was Holt country . . .*

Born in Merced City, Missouri, when Maximilian was still Emperor of Mexico, he had at age nineteen married his childhood sweetheart, the former Fannie Jones, who never stopped trusting in him no matter how many business failures he suffered *(I can't help believing in people)*. The children were named Catharine, who sometimes appears in census records as Catherine, and Esther Chloe, who occasionally becomes Estel Chloe. They would never marry.

One of Mr. Holt's first moves in the Imperial Valley *was to acquire for himself and his wife six hundred and forty acres of desert land.* Another was to acquire the *Imperial Valley Press and Farmer.*

He built Canal No. 7's entire fifty or so miles, and sold the water stock without down payments. *I have never been cheated out of a dollar in my life . . . I've found that the way to get your money is to give a man a chance to pay you.*

(On June 3, 1903, we find a letter from W. F. Holt on his personalized stationery, with an address on West Olive Avenue in Redlands. He writes with the spelling of a self-made man: *Dear sir: Herewith find Cirtifficate for 320 shares of water Stock all paid up . . .* He is also a frugal man. The address on the stationery has been changed by hand from 406 to 113.)

Ignoring nay-saying engineers, Mr. Holt's four-hundred-horsepower Holton Power Company established itself in the drop at the Alamo, generating enough power for the entire valley!

He built the first telephone line in those parts, and the first church, of course; he began the first railroad. He financed the first gas company, and donated Holt Park, complete with twelve hundred pepper trees and twelve hundred palm trees. (In my day, not all of those have been kept up.) Appropriately, and I am sure without considerations of vanity, he *built or financed the Barbara Worth Hotel.* By 1905 he'd already finished electrifying the valley! In 1906 he founded the Valley State Bank at El Centro and the Citizens Bank at Holtville.

"The Little Giant" is a modern Moses who led people not out of, but into a desert, which he has transformed into an electric-lighted, power run, fertile garden, and the warm little twenty thousand dollars he took into the valley ten years ago has been converted into a cool million.

How Imperial! He enriched himself by doing good! *Mr. Holt's wife and daughters live in Redlands in a fine home . . .* Better yet, he has *associates, Redlands capitalists.*

Three-quarters of a century after Imperial's first announcement that **WATER IS HERE**, a new generation of boomers will be busy selling Salton City. (Every time I go there, the stench stings my nose.) About these knights of commerce it has been written: *The fog of this particular kind of war is the fog of believing that you can prey upon suckers and do them a favor at the same time.*

Did Holt think of the people to whom he sold land and loaned money as suckers? I suspect not. In 1907 he is Chairman of the Board of a certain church in Redlands. One member of the flock is Harold Bell Wright, whom he induces to visit the Imperial Valley. Wright stays awhile, writes *The Winning of Barbara Worth,* and dedicates the book to Holt, who thus became Jefferson Worth, Minister of Capital. Frances A. Groff, reporter for the *Redlands Federal Standard,* sees in Holt *a look of quiet power combined with the naiveté and sweetness of a child.* Were I Jefferson Worth, how could I not wish to believe in my own goodness?

He works too hard to have time to sit around the corner store stove and whittle with the rest of the fellows, so when they get out to work they find the Holt fields are all plowed . . . Lots of people don't like Holt; lots do.

Reader, what about you? Are you on board? Are you ready to work as hard as Mr. Holt, or are you a mere stoveside whittler? Don't you believe in Progress?

My next door neighbor moved to Sacramento in about 1960. He sold his house for more than he paid for it, and bought another. Housing prices kept going up. Year after year, he'd say: The market has to level off sometime.—It kept going up.—Finally in 2006 there was a *correction,* but all my realtor friends, even the ones who can't pay their own mortgages, know that Progress will return to save us all, just as surely as diamond cholla marks dry ground. They worship at California's number one church, the Ministry of Capital.

By his business sagacity, remarkable resourcefulness, and exalted Christian principles, he became a builder of banks and railroads, a founder of cities . . .

In line with his genius for development and expansion, rhapsodizes *American Biography and Genealogy, he has even spread his enterprises over the international boundary into Mexico. For one man to be virtually the source of supply for the power and light, and the means of transportation and communication, enjoyed by the people of a truly Imperial Valley, is honor enough—but Mr. Holt is even a greater source of benefits . . .*

On 14 April 1912, a certain W. F. Holt was listed among the *Titanic*'s perished. But from the census of 1920 we learn that he had actually done what ever so many Imperialites do when it is time to go to heaven: He had moved the family to Los Angeles.

In 1923, Mr. Holt invested nearly three hundred thousand dollars in the Utah "dry farming" settlement of Widtsoe, named after a Mormon Apostle. It was going to have irrigation, phone lines and lettuce just like Imperial. The *Salt Lake Tribune* reports: *Drought, erosion and rodents doomed the project, and Widtsoe was soon infamous as the most destitute area in the state . . .*

BELIEVERS IN THE FUTURE

Reader, may I introduce you to another boomer or two? They're very jolly fellows to be around, because they're always optimistic.

Capsule sketch of a boomer in Redlands, 1904: *I took lunch at the University Club yesterday noon with a Mr. Morrison, President of the First National Bank. He is a hustling young man, an orange grower of the finest type, as well as a good financier.*

George Chaffey was a boomer, too, of course; in Etiwanda he had a fountain that gushed only whenever a train of land-seekers came in.

And do you remember L. M. Holt, whose editorials helped run the Chinese out of central Riverside? This cripple, popularly known as "Limpy" (his Christian name was Luther), is said to have named Mexicali and Calexico, if you don't believe that George Chaffey did it; and if you don't ask Mexicans, who will tell you that Colonel Augustín Sangínez accomplished that acrostic feat. Holt had a soft pale schoolteacher's face, with round glasses and a firm but rather meager-lipped mouth, and fine hair parted on one side. We can thank him above others for bringing about the statewide Irrigation Convention of 1885. Just as George Chaffey would rename the Valley of Death *the Imperial Valley,* so Southern California got christened "Semi-Tropic California" thanks to our hero, L. M. Holt. Why not set a tone? *Mr. Holt was a boomer by temperament and training. He believed in the future of horticulture in Southern California . . .*

Chapter 38

CONTINUED FROM PAGE A1

(2003)

> To them, the Romantic Hero was no longer the knight . . . but the great sales-manager . . . whose title of nobility was "Go-getter," and who had devoted himself and all his young nobility to the cosmic purpose of Selling . . .
>
> —Sinclair Lewis, 1922

IMPERIAL

CONTINUED FROM PAGE A1

Boosters see opportunity with each new mall

Chapter 39

LOS ANGELES

(1900)

As you grow bolder you explore your world outward from the firepit (which is the center of each universe) . . .

—Gary Snyder, 1990

TÍPICO AMERICANO

In 1900 the population of the United States is already forty percent urban. Los Angeles waxes. To be sure, it's not quite the Los Angeles of 2000. *Every house had its inclosure of vineyard, which resembled a miniature orchard.* The Los Angeles of 1900 still resembles the Los Angeles of 1845 in this respect. On the other hand, we don't pay in Mexican ounces anymore.

A visitor from the East thinks Los Angeles to be one of the prettiest metropolises he has ever encountered, thanks to the large lawns and yards around every house, these being planted with eucalyptus, orange, pepper, and English walnut trees. At the same time, Los Angeles is busy, progressive, with all the amenities! The visitor writes: *I have not seen a city so honeycombed by trolleycar lines as this.* We need have no fear that our lands will not become better and better as the years go by.

And they *are* getting better, oh, yes! Look out; here comes another boom! Los Angeles County, which was the merest blankness back in 1850, now teems with little towns and settlements whose names are not yet mockeries: Olive is here now, and Artesia, Clearwater, Santa Fe, Charter Oak, Vineland (which as I write roars with cars and stinks of smog), Lemon, which in my day has long vanished from the map . . . In 1900, Los Angeles already holds nearly one-third as many residents as her big sister, San Francisco. Los Angeles intends to keep right on growing.

Subdivide the old Garvey Ranch near Allhambra, change the name to Garvalia, and you're ready for business. Here comes Mr. C. H. Newcombe from Minnesota; he's tired of the cold winters. Buying twenty acres, he plants seventeen of them in lemons. *The water comes from an artesian well on the tract and the thirty shares that Mr. Newcombe owns give him the right to thirty inches of water five days a month at a cost of only $2.50 per day. This is ample to thoroughly irrigate the ranch* by means of underground pipes. Last year he got four thousand sixty-pound boxes of lemons, which he sold to the packing house at San Gabriel for a dollar twenty-five per hundred pounds, cash, of course. Oh, he's happy he moved to southern California, and I'll bet that his wife is happy, too.

The Los Angeles River was the greatest attraction. It was a beautiful, limpid little stream, with willows on its banks . . . That recollection is furnished by none other than Willliam Mulholland, soon to be Riverine Emperor of Southern California.

And the label of Old Mission Brand oranges (office: Los Angeles, Cal.) assures me that fruit packed under this brand, namely, the Pacific Fruit Company, is grown in the finest orange section of California, so Los Angeles must look just like this! Three jolly old monks admire an orange-clustered branch on a desk, with the archway of the picturesquely dilapidated mission behind them, and the sky softly blue and yellow overhead. A cactus-stockinged palmetto spreads its fronds in the foreground, beside two oranges which must each be five feet in diameter. Darling, will you marry me? We'll move west and live forever. *Ten thousand people from the east have been brought to California during the past two weeks by the railroads, on colonist tickets . . . It is predicted by the railroad companies, that this influx will continue.*

The railroad companies, God bless them, are correct. (Good thing Los Angeles *has secured options on the Owens river water, amounting to about 25,000 inches.*) During the first decade of the new century, San Diego and Imperial counties will each grow by a hundred fourteen and one-half percent; Los Angeles County will grow by *a hundred and ninety-six percent.* By that time, although Los Angeles still possesses Orange Slope, Orange Heights, Orange, Orange Grove Place and Orange Crest, these places have begun to alter away from their names. Across Orange Slope Tract alone, the Los Angeles Brick Company, the Huntington Land & Improvement Company, and Marengo Street now stamp themselves, each one a different pastel shade of blankness in Baist's Real Estate Atlas, with here and there an orange-colored building-rectangle.

Do you know why business smells so sweet in Los Angeles? Because *Los Angeles, Ventura and Santa Barbara Counties are leaders in the honey industry.*

And now it's time to describe the locus of Imperial's ever-optimistic lust: the Los Angeles Market on Third and Central, where so many horses and wagons cluster in the dirt street that the impression is of a stockyard. The people who harvest the hilly, wide-open tomatoscapes of West Hollywood surely bring their wooden crates down here. Parking there costs fifty cents per morning, but it's worth it, for to take just one case, in Los Angeles *onions are still as good as gold mines. Some Australians have come in the past week which have sold at 6 cents a pound.* That's why I now see farmers and commission men carrying in boxes of produce to their divinely (I mean commercially) ordained places in the market's hundred and fifty stalls, *every one of which is filled, with now and then a man standing looking on wishing he could get in.* Outside, on the market-grounds, wait the *smaller sheds, in which stalls of Chinese and other market men are located.* Sometimes I hear arguments between farmers and commission men; sometimes the farmers don't sort their stock, or else they try to sell it themselves until it wilts; then they blame the commission men—who do every now and then, of course, cheat them. (As for me, I, like Imperial, have never been cheated out of a dollar in my life.)

But let's abandon the vulgarly individual perspective, which Marxists have entirely disproven. Let's consider this scene from the vantage point of economic superorganisms:—Is Los Angeles aware of Imperial, I mean *really* aware, commercially aware? Absolutely! In 1908 a vast row of men in suits and hats will stand in the flour-white potentiality of El Centro; they stretch three boxcars long; they're the Los Angeles Chamber of Commerce; they stand with their fists at their sides, or jauntily, with their hands on their pockets, or with folded arms; some are fat, some are thin; one bold spirit in the front row even crouches in the sand! They're an army!

And in 1913, a circular put out by the California Land and Water Company, which offers FREE LECTURES DAILY in its Imperial Valley Exhibit and Lecture Room, oh, yes, a very nice company, coincidentally headquartered in Los Angeles, will offer this incitement to buy the newest batch of irrigation-ready land: *Brawley, more than other towns, is possessed of the "Los Angeles Idea," which means she is united on the one idea of assuming and maintaining her present ascendancy.*

Chapter 40

THE IMPERIAL IDEA

(1901–2004)

I am not against packing holidays, per se, but I insist on my individual prerogative of choosing those days myself, without the help of some all-knowing Committee.

—Harry Carian, Jr., grape grower in Coachella, 1967

And was there an Imperial Idea to oppose the Los Angeles idea? I think so. The boomers certainly opined that there was. Among their number we find the commercial photographer Leo Hetzel, who, like Otis P. Tout, could always be counted on to portray Imperial County as an exemplar of agrarian wholesomeness and success. *We need have no fear that our lands will not become better and better as the years go by.* A Hetzel image from 1920 introduces us to a farmer with a pipe in his mouth; he's resting his hands on the top of his quadrilateral pig corral, where a dozen piglets with dust-matted fur are gobbling, heads down; while on the running board of the Model T, remaining in place by gripping the canopy above her head, stands a cross-legged Lolita of a girl who leans in toward the steering wheel, gazing coyly at us from around her arm; behind her are fields and behind *them* are trees. Isn't this the Imperial Idea? The difference between this eternal picture and the equally eternal days of my friend Mr. Lupe Vásquez,* who gets up at three-thirty to pick crops in and for another nation, is the difference between the right to happiness, which none of us can be guaranteed, and the right to happiness's pursuit, which I do find written into a certain early document of my United States. So what really *is* the Imperial Idea? What makes me, no thanks to my increasingly un-American government, proud to be an American?

Imperial is the farmer with his pipe and Lolita; it is also the farmer Albert Henry Larson, who killed himself gruesomely six years after Hetzel clicked the shutter. The Imperial Idea is that we have the right to go to hell in our own way. To be sure, one of America's most prized illusions† is, or at least used to be, that self-reliant

*See below, "The Days of Lupe Vásquez," p. 358.

†Or hypocrisies, if you will. From the Chinese Exclusion Act to the exploitation of Mexican field labor, the observances-in-the-breach of the American idea are so ubiquitous as to find their way even into this very

individuals could achieve some kind of free fulfillment in associations of their own choosing; and Imperial has certainly been memorialized in an ancient photograph of a Holtville banquet under the palms, the gentlemen in hats, everything self-serve, laid out on long tables with stacks of plates awaiting all of us, some of the ladies wearing aprons, and every last one of them in ankle-length skirts. (A century later, when I pass through Holtville, I see no one under the palms.) The public meetings of the Imperial Irrigation District begin with the Pledge of Allegiance, and it touches my heart to see everybody in the room rise and place his hand on his heart.

I want to believe than an American is free to belong or to remain aloof, to prosper or to destroy himself, to govern himself well or badly. Among the exponents of this very Imperial Idea I find Leonard Knight, the gentle old painter-builder of Salvation Mountain. Somewhere around 1995 he was heard to say: *I love people,* and I actually believe that Leonard does. He went on: *But when I get too close to people, they always want me to do it their way. And then it looks like I want to do it my way. And most of the times, their way is right. But I still like to do it my way.*

---

pro-American book. In 1923 a Los Angeles booster proudly informs us that "the several neighborhood schools in our city are exactly what their name implies. Each school is a social center, a community house, and a place from which the American idea must radiate." Then again: "Our schools are carrying the burden of Americanization of the country." Here Americanization might simply mean de-Mexicanization. But why not give him the benefit of the doubt? Why not assume a well-meaning earnestness and desire to improve us all?

Chapter 41

WILBER CLARK'S HOMESTEAD

(1901–2005)

For an hour or more Barbara, at the piano, sang for them the simple songs they loved, while many a tired horseman, riding past on his way to his lonely desert shack . . . paused to listen to the sweet voice and to dream perhaps of the time to come when such sounds would no longer seem strange on the Desert.

—Harold Bell Wright, 1911

Wilber Clark arrives in Imperial in 1901, possibly by means of that newfangled miracle of self-sufficiency, the automobile. Why has he come, if not to improve the land? Mr. Frank B. Moson, President of the Green Cattle Company, will soon be citing *the wonderful advantage of the Imperial Valley as a fattening center.* Who says we can't fatten our own fortunes? Imperial, reifying herself in an eponymous town at her valley's geographical center, has already begun rising grey and grimy from her own creased silt. Next will come the municipal water tank, creamery, warehouse, barley crusher, ice factory—and not least the jail! *We need have no fear that our lands will not become better and better as the years go by.*

Along the county's eastern edge (it's still San Diego County, of course), miners scratch out gold at Tumco and Picacho. Picacho will run out first; Tumco remains in operation until the First World War. I've heard that everything happens at Picacho, even bullfights. Many miners there speak Spanish, you see; they come from the other side of the ditch.—And what other human novelties mark Imperial? Well, there's been a railroad depot in the sand and boulders of Old Beach for twenty-four years now. (Someday Old Beach will turn into Niland.) Meanwhile, the Cahuilla Valley finally changes its name to Coachella, a combination of "Cahuilla" and the little seashells called *conchas.** As for Imperial Valley, thanks to George Chaffey it has worn that title for a full year now; it used to be the Valley of Death.

Almost in sight of that adobe ruin where the Butterfield Stage depot used to be, Blue Lake holds no fewer than ten registered voters, who will be allotted another

*Another version: A printer's error for "Conchella," or place of shells.

five years of groundbreaking before the great flood cleans them out. In a caption to a picture of that locality's single white tent and awning, with Signal Mountain in the background just as it will be in the Imperial County seal, while a flag flies over flat grey nothingness, Otis B. Tout informs me that *before Imperial was laid out Blue Lake was Headquarters for Surveyors and Visitors.* And what a well stocked headquarters it had been! The *Imperial Press and Farmer* finds in it *more ducks and other water fowl on the lakes than an army could slaughter. Standing room only for new birds.* On the other hand, nobody has briefed us about mosquitoes. So forget about Blue Lake. After all, Imperial has now indeed been laid out. It boasts the Hotel Imperial (on Imperial Avenue, naturally); this establishment offers *tent house accommodations.*

But such amenities are nascent when Wilber Clark is packing up in Los Angeles. Imperial townsite comprises *less than a dozen souls in* March of 1901—in other words, about the same as Blue Lake. Almost all of them are male. I presume that George W. Donley belongs to this first wave, for he *came to Imperial when the town consisted of only three tent houses.* L. E. Cooley *entered the town as pioneer, driving a pair of mules and followed by a spotted dog;* he too is probably improving his quarter-section of land by the time Wilber Clark pulls the starter cord of his automobile.

Again, this automobile is hypothetical. His biography in Judge Farr's tome simply has him *driving down from Los Angeles;* he could have done so by stagecoach; on the other hand, other pioneers generally *removed to* Imperial or simply got there; ignorance gives us leave, as to any science-fiction writer, to entertain ourselves speculatively; so I'll suppose him to be one of that brave new breed, a motorist.

On Tuesday, the fifteenth of May, 1901, the headgates of the Imperial Canal resemble a giant loom upon whose top lean many men in hats, accompanied by a seated lady or two. They're here to see our century begin: **WATER IS HERE**. Water descends from Pilot Knob, which is a rolling purplish-dark hunk of something volcanic sprawling quite far away from Imperial with one white streak wriggling down it. And water deigns to return twice a week, swirling right down the Imperial town ditch! By year's end, so they say, five settlers are pulling in each day.

So a newcomer such as Wilber Clark would have found a handful of homesteaders at work inscribing visible alterations within the invisible property-squares they've bought. He's in on the ground floor; banking on the fact that **WATER IS HERE**, he'll work hard and take chances to win his stack of silver dimes, but I'm sure he's a careful gambler, for, after all, in this Arid America of ours, first is not best. Don't you remember what Captain Hobbs found here? *There were eight women and children, and nine men. The body of a child had been almost stripped of flesh . . .* And Wilber Clark has his family with him in that automobile: his father

John, who's a former Superior Court judge of Tulare County, and his sister Margaret S., who will in due course become Mrs. W. H. Dickinson of Yuma. These details are courtesy of Judge Farr's biographical directory. Lacking their marriage certificate (for in the county nuptial index, the only groom of even the vaguest relevance was a Frank Oscar Clark), I believe that Wilber Clark has not at this juncture espoused the mysterious Elizabeth F.; Farr would scarcely have neglected her if she were in that car, which must have been crowded, noisy, buttock-bruising and precarious on that journey down from Los Angeles.

What does it mean to enter into Imperial by automobile in 1901? They certainly didn't have to come that way. There was a stagecoach from Old Beach right to Imperial, pulled by three pairs of horses. There was a train to Old Beach.

I suppose that they must have proceeded by way of Indio, since the way along Imperial's western tail remained the rockiest of roads. Four years later, the newspaper reports that two married couples *tried to drive to the mountains by way of Calexico, got lost on the desert and almost died. They made their way back to the Valley just in time.* That is why I am willing to call Wilber Clark a gambler.

In Campo, California, which lies a few miles northeast of Tecate, Mexico, there is a Motor Transport Museum, one of whose ancient mechanic-restorers advised me on this question.

If it was 1901 he would have had to go through Palm Springs and Banning, said Mr. Calvert. Are you sure it was 1901? Maybe it would have been closer to 1905.

No, I'm pretty sure it was 1901.

There was very, very few cars in Los Angeles in that year. Maybe ten cars then. Anybody that had a car, there was notoriety about that. Only the wealthy could afford it. You were looking at a thousand dollars, or maybe seven hundred and fifty . . . Do you know what kind of car he had?

No, Judge Farr only says an automobile, or implies it. Would he have had a license plate I could track down?

Before 1910 they issued you a number, and you made it yourself, out of leather or wood. Starting in 1914, they started issuing porcelain plates every year; actually it was porcelain on steel . . .

I called the California Department of Motor Vehicles, whose robotized switchboard connected me to a lady who referred me to a woman at Information Services who passed me on to Customer Relations where the phone rang and rang eternally. So we will have to imagine the Clarks' journey.

We know from Judge Farr that the Paradise he will eventually build holds experiments with *some fifty varieties of grapes . . . A profitable express business has been worked out on the same.* Undoubtedly he has inspected the vineyards of Los Angeles. And as he motors east of Ontario, he spies Secondo Guasti's new young realm of grapevines, the first of which was planted just last year; in due time they will take up thousands of acres. The Inland Empire's orchards tempt him all around.

It pleases me to imagine that he rested here, perhaps even in Riverside, whose citrusscapes would have been glowing along quite nicely by now, for it had already been thirty years since the planting of Mrs. Tibbetts's first orange seedling. From his earliness and civic-mindedness (proofs of which will appear), I believe Wilber Clark to have been a well informed man. Resolved to homestead in Semi-Tropic California, he knew that Riverside navel oranges usually took first prize in the Citrus Fair—all the more reason to imagine him taking his family for a cool stroll along Magnolia Avenue! Besides, the townsite of Imperial was so far and lonely a distance away from Riverside (it now takes about two and half hours in light traffic) that they might never be back there. Although 1901 was not a great year for oranges and lemons in Riverside, the heart of the Inland Empire must have been pretty nonetheless. Mrs. Bettner's mansion had been in place for a decade now; and I like to imagine Wilber imagining being married to someone like Elizabeth F. and dwelling happily and forever with her in a home like this, hidden away from the sun and illuminated by oranges. His father and sister dream equally glorious dreams, because they're Imperial bound!

Then they get back into their car and smoke and shudder down the road toward Indio. It's getting hotter with every mile. Horses shy out of their way.

One photograph in the Imperial County Historical Society Pioneers Museum is captioned *Mr. [and] Mrs. Virgil Patterson Dec. 2, 1907 Holding 13th marriage liscense [sic] of Imperial County in one of first three cars in the Valley.* Wilber Clark's auto must have been quite a conversation piece.

VESEY'S MAXIM

In my mind I have this idea about Imperialites: They're sparsely settled agriculturalists, which implies that throughout much of the twentieth century they resemble pioneers, which in turn means that they can make something out of nothing. Assemblyman Victor V. Vesey, lifelong Republican in a Democratic county, which says something for him right there, arrived in Brawley in 1949 (he would have been about thirty-four) to take over his dead father's ranch: six hundred and forty acres of cattle, which he, a neophyte, decided to transform into sugar beets, cotton, grain, alfalfa! Here is what a neighbor advised him to do: Drive around the road until you find a crop that looks good. Go and see that farmer and talk to him about it. Find out what he did and didn't do.—Victor Vesey made that maxim his own. And he succeeded. I respect his success.

Wilber Clark is Victor Vesey; he's quite Imperial. He motors cautiously toward the unknown, determined to buy a piece of desert and flourish on it. He'll build his Wilfrieda Ranch amidst the creosote bushes of Imperial.

A TRAVELLER IN TROPICAL CALIFORNIA

So that is who he is. But who *was* he, really, this person whose voice we will never hear?

The *California 1890 Great Register of Voters Index* lists a Wilber Clark, aged twenty-nine, of 128 North Johnston Street, Los Angeles. He is the only person of that name in all the entries for Los Angeles. In that year, Hollywood has grown into a handful of houses in empty grey desert.

Out of the many John Clarks in the 1870 census, there's exactly one in Tulare County, a John L., aged thirty-one years, who hails from Ohio. The Mormon genealogists I hired in Utah assured me that in fact this John Clark was born in Tennessee in about 1827. As for his son Wilber, they believed that his birthplace was Iowa and that his life began in about 1861. In 1880 he left traces in Kaweah and Mineral King, Tulare, where the census taker recorded his occupation as farmhand.

In September of 1874, we find a John Clark elected county judge in Tulare County; I also spy a Mrs. Mary A. Clark, *née* Graves, who happens to be a survivor of the Donner Party. One of the cannibals, George Foster, had proposed her for eating, she being neither wife nor mother; another man had defended her. Could Wilber Clark be her son? Mary Ann Graves, who was twenty years old, got married in 1847, only one month after her rescue; for (so another survivor giggled): *Tell the girls that this is the best place for marrying they ever saw.*

Since Wilber Clark was twenty-nine in 1890, then, just as the genealogists claimed, he would have been born in about 1861, fourteen years after the marriage of this Mary Ann Graves, who would have reached the age of thirty-four. Why not? In the novel that I plotted, a historical fiction entitled *Imperial,* Wilber Clark's childhood was a trifle dark-tinted by his mother's ordeal. When rats are experimentally starved, they can learn to hoard food, a behavior which persists even after plenitude has been restored by their laboratory god. A likely result of Mary Ann Clark's maiden days might have been prudent stewardship, if not outright acquisitiveness. Wouldn't her son, especially given that he also knew quite well enough the exhaustion of farm labor, have become a careful, cautious man?

Why then would he have trusted himself to the desert? Perhaps he possessed what a certain Indian Commissioner assures that the red man lacks, namely, a sense of *the divine angel of discontent . . . The desire for property of his own may become an intense educating force.*

Well, my geneaologists bestowed on him a mother named Laura or Matilda Robinson.—So much for Mary Ann Graves!

Our subsequent Mrs. Clark was born in Ohio in around 1820, a date with which my hired private detective concurred. She would therefore have been forty-one at Wilber's birth, hence quite elderly had she lingered on to 1901; since we do not see her riding to Imperial in that hypothetical automobile, she must have been in her grave.

What about her son? How long did *he* remain on this planet? My friend Paul Foster, pitying me because I had learned scarcely anything concerning another of this book's subjects, a young girl named Imperial Hazel Deed, grazed various electronic fields on my behalf and rapidly plucked up the death date of a certain Wilber Clark: Pasadena, August 1967. But I had already established that *our* Wilber Clark's spouse Elizabeth F. would enter widowhood in the 1920s. Moreover, Paul's Wilber Clark was eighty-five when he passed on, his birth date being 1 March 1882, or approximately two decades later than his namesake's. Wishing this unknown ghost well, I then disqualifed him.

Having circumvented my hero's double, and his mother's, I scarcely knew what to suppose about him. Well, what did he have in the way of what is now called *occupational experience*? When he arrived in Imperial, he commenced a hardware business. So perhaps he owned a hardware store in Los Angeles.

Why had he removed from Tulare in the first place? Much of the southern California land boom of the 1880s took place in Los Angeles. In 1887, a price war between the Southern Pacific and the Santa Fe railroads reduced the price of a ticket from Kansas City to the City of the Angels from a hundred and twenty-five dollars to one dollar. Although fares soon rose to twenty-five dollars, the boom was on. Between 1886 and 1888, seventeen hundred and seventy subdivisions, replats and tract maps got filed in Los Angeles County. *We need have no fear that our lands will not become better and better as the years go by.*

But in 1890 the Census Department made it official: The American frontier was now closed. What was a pioneer to do next?

That railroad price war occurred exactly when the Wright Act permitted the formation of irrigation districts. By 1890, nine percent of Los Angeles County and one percent of San Diego County possessed irrigated farmland. Possibilities for future irrigation smelled delicious. *The bountiful continent is ours, state on state, and territory on territory, to the waves of the Pacific sea.*

Wilber Clark might well have heard of the failure of Barrett's Boring Outfit to find oil in the Imperial Valley. Surely he read of the birth and almost immediate bankruptcy of the California Irrigation Company, whose aim was to do intentionally what the great Colorado flood would soon do by accident. For Wilber Clark was scarcely the only California gambler!

Perhaps he attended that year's Irrigation Congress, which assembled in Los Angeles. If so, he surely heard the following: (1) *I can't help believing in people.* (2) *The essence of the industrial life which springs from irrigation is its democracy.*

John Wesley Powell's voyage down the Colorado made the newspapers in 1895. That river contained an infinite amount of water, didn't it? Meanwhile, L. M. Holt kept us all abreast of "Semi-Tropical California," now also known as **TROPICAL CALIFORNIA**, in this case Palm Springs, which is to say ***The Land of Early Fruits and Vegetables.*** (Thirty-eight years later, in the same book that features a glowing biography of Wilber Clark, Judge Farr will make identical claims about the Imperial Valley.) *There is no known valley in the State that can compare with Palm Valley for its early fruits and vegetables.*

And here came the cantaloupe price boom of 1898–99! These exotic melons originated in Mecca, a space colony in the soon-to-be-named Coachella Valley. The first Imperial Valley cantaloupes of 1919 would retail in Los Angeles for no less than fifteen dollars apiece.

The Chaffey brothers kept selling lots in Etiwanda. In 1900, George Chaffey became President of the California Development Company and coined the name "Imperial Valley."

Why did Wilber Clark decline to become a citizen of the Inland Empire? I'd imagine because *there is plenty of good land to be had but all Government land worth taking is about gone,* which means that land prices in that dominion now began at the extortionate figure of ten dollars an acre.

But If I were Wilber Clark and possessed an automobile, I would certainly pay a visit to Etiwanda. (Why did that place fail to suit? Perhaps he arrived between trains, which meant that George Chaffey's civic fountain was off.) I would also send away to George Chaffey's new entity, the Imperial Land Company, for a map, and study the layout of the Imperial townsite, which for your information lies in the district of Imperial Water Company No. 1, whose area is in turn bounded by the sweet-smelling New River, the Mexican border, the Alamo River, and the edge of Imperial Water Company No. 4. I would wait until the headgates of the Imperial Canal were opened. Then, after filling my water jugs and my spare petrol can, I would join the next wave.

"THE WONDERFULLY FERTILE VALLEY OF THE NEW RIVER IS NOW BEING OPENED UP"

Hence, I imagine that his dreams fly toward San Diego County, which according to its own directory for that year is *larger than the State of Masachusetts . . . For one hundred and fifty miles it borders on the Mexican boundary; the Colorado River separating the eastern part of the county from the territory of Arizona . . . The wonderfully fertile valley of the New River in the eastern part of the county is now being opened up . . . The richest and most fertile section of the state . . . will soon teem with life, furnishing homes for thousands of families.*

In spite of this praise, in spite of the twenty-one residents accounted for in Ogilby or Ogilvy, the directory has no listing whatsoever for the town of Imperial—another indication that Wilber Clark must be a gambler.

THE ARRIVAL

So what do the Clarks see upon their emergence from L.A.? Maybe something like what Raymond Chandler will decades later: *This is the ultimate end of the fog belt, and the beginning of that semi-desert region where the sun is as light and dry as sherry in the morning, as hot as a blast furnace at noon, and drops like an angry brick at nightfall.* That sums up Pomona, which was laid out by a company managed by Mr. Holt's late father. After Pomona the semi-desert region becomes the desert region in which Riverside remains a modest oasis; then it's definitely blast furnace, all right.

How long would it have taken him to get to Imperial? I asked Carl Calvert.

I'd say two days. It was difficult, because it was sandy. Dry sand. People would carry with 'em burlap bags and like that, to avoid getting stuck.

(In 1909 an auto touring club will motor from Oakland to Maine. They'll report that the very worst stretch of road is from Palm Springs to Indio.)

I see a view of the road through Brawley in 1908, running wide, sandy and rutted; the caption says that *clouds of dust and sand pursued each automobile,* except when rain turned it to muck. I imagine our voyagers choking on dust, Miss Clark with a scarf over her mouth. *A 1921 Studebaker, manned by four stalwart and begoggled adventurers, skids through the sandy ruts on the road near Blythe, typical of early desert roads.*

I suppose that our explorers stop again amidst the tent-houses of Indio, some of which are now a good decade and a half old. But the town is scarcely a green spot. Northwest of the Salton Sink, the Coachella Valley remains almost dry, the only exception being the Apostle Palm Oasis, which will later burn, then be superseded by the junction of Indio's Madison Street and Avenue 38. In 1903, darkhaired Howard Gard stands with his hands in his pockets; the photo does not allow me to distinguish whether he is wearing vest or coveralls; slender palm-trunks rise behind him, and then there is his dark-windowed grocery store, which is also the post office; perhaps he waited on the Clarks in 1901: Steam comes out of the car. Chickens run away. The travellers alight. They buy water, and perhaps fresh fruit. Horse manure desiccates in the streets.

They continue south to Coachella, some of whose native trees persist. (I see a faded photograph of men doing something around an open boxcar. The caption reads: *Fred, Paul and I loading 65,860 pounds of mesquite which we hauled from my farm and sold for firewood to an LA firm.*) The town is getting platted out; a convocation of seventeen men has lately abolished the old appellation of Woodspur. I presume that Wilber Clark sees the wooden water tank over Jack Holliday's well; surely he must drive past the miraculous white spurts of artesian wells. Could there be any of those where he's going? No doubt; for George Chaffey has promised us: **WATER IS HERE**. Imagine a ranch—for instance, the Wilfrieda Ranch—built around such a pillar of delight! Imagine a home of comfort and cool green abundance.

He drives on. Arabia is not yet a ghost town. Mecca is still hard-pressed from the total loss of last year's melon crop, thanks to a hundred-and-thirty-five-degree spell in June.

Ahead of them glares the Salton Sink. The two rival salt companies have just reconciled and are mining *this wonderful saline deposit* in mercantile concord at the Southern Pacific spur line called Salton. *It is common to find the mercury here as high as 105 degrees Fahrenheit in the shade . . . and in the full sun's rays 130,* so, needless to say, the companies employ Indians to plough the salt. I would not suppose that Wilber Clark's party stops here, but they likely motor past it, for the wagon road to Old Beach, nowadays known as Niland, to which Leonard Knight bicycles from Salvation Mountain to get his water; his is the railroad disembarkation for many Imperial immigrants. *In a short time that point will be the base of supplies for the Imperial country.* So the Clarks might pause in Old Beach, for the same purpose as Leonard.

In 1901, most of Imperial townsite's immigrants arrive in October. Wilber Clark is a trifle more cautious—or perhaps he simply takes longer to make up his mind. An item in the *Los Angeles Times,* dated 28 November 1901,* informs us that *the Imperial country continues to fill up, more than fifty people having come in the last week.*

*It is not insignificant that (so the dateline reveals) the *Times* saw fit to list a "resident correspondent" as the author. Imperial was not yet large enough to require a bureau, but it was already newsworthy, since I have never been cheated out of a dollar in my life.

Among the recent arrivals in the valley are Wilbur [sic] Clark and sister, and their father, from Los Angeles. Clark is building a residence in Imperial, and will at once put in a hardware store.

In November, Imperial is almost cool. They stop. They gaze at the saltbush-blotched desert around Imperial City. In a month, Margaret Clark will already be postmistress.

THE ASTRONAUTS

As Judge Farr implied, the love and labor of Wilber Clark's life will be the Wilfrieda Ranch, also known as the Wilfreds Ranch. At this point in time it remains "unimproved," which is to say waterless. What might be its appearance in that condition? Here's the residence of Joseph Becker on Eighth Street, one mile west of Imperial Avenue: A squat cone roofs it, almost like a miniature Signal Mountain; it has a shaded porch all the way round, with three steps between it and the flat dirt which goes on forever; near the leftward edge of this old photo a gentleman stands on the topmost step, while a lady, beautifully proportioned but unknown, since her hatted face entirely has been shadowed by the awning, sits in a coach behind two splendid white horses. Oh, but Imperial is flat and grey all around them! Their house crouches like a newly landed flying saucer; how can this extraterrestrial couple (could they likewise hail from the planet of Los Angeles?) hope even to breathe the air of Imperial, which feels nearly as hot as the air of Venus (seven hundred degrees Fahrenheit)? Imperial's a science-fiction story. For that matter, how can they find anything to drink?

But then what happens? George Chaffey opens the gates of the Imperial Canal, and the Colorado rushes down the riverbed of the Alamo! **WATER IS HERE**.

Can you imagine it? It must have been as fantastic as the scene in H. G. Wells's *The First Men in the Moon* (published that same year): Sunrise's unbearable light strikes a crater drifted high with frozen oxygen, and promptly slushifies and liquefies the snow into air,* then seedcases burst and grow into spiky olive-green plants, at which point the insectoid Selenites open the shafts beneath, and out come the pale white mooncalves to graze. **THE DESERT DISAPPEARS**.

But for now the moon continues to partake of a decidedly lunar character; and Wilber Clark has not yet even purchased the site of the Wilfrieda Ranch. His home in Imperial City is provisional, like irrigation itself.

*Indeed, by 1904 a Coachella company "proposes to furnish the people of that valley with liquid air, ice, etc. It will also carry on a cold storage plant, handle milk and eggs, manufacture butter, and furnish electric power"—how luxurious and convenient!

So for the time being he plies the retail trade in town; that's his contribution to Empire. More specifically, as we've just been informed, he opens Imperial's first hardware store (which Judge Farr, always good for such details, informs us will soon be bought by A. L. Hill), while his busy sister starts a stationery business which in due course she sells to H. E. Allat. One day in the Pioneers Museum, turning over photograph after photograph, I came across an oval portrait of *Miss Clark—Imperial Valley's first postmistress. Later became the wife of Mr. Archie Priest,* who presumably precedes or succeeds W. H. Dickinson of Yuma. Since pioneers had to do many, many things, *she was also a school teacher.* Curlyhaired, fairskinned and ovalfaced, she wears a lace scarf tied tight around her collar and a light-colored quilted dress of many vertical stripes. She gazes far away. Her jaw is slightly clenched, perhaps due to the stress of being photographed; but her face is so very smooth and young that the impression escapes unpleasantness. She's a beautiful, serious lady of thirty-six years—ripe for marrying.

What might her brother's hardware store have looked like? Here's another photograph from the Pioneers Museum: A man in a Western hat leans his wrist on a post; he has a moustache and the half-sad, half-insouciant expression of a French-Canadian *voyageur;* beside him stands a prim-looking, plain woman in a pale ankle-length dress; she wears no hat; from them radiates Imperial emptiness with a stake in it; behind them is a building, slightly grander than a shed, of vertical planks, with surprisingly large square compound window-panes in its facade; the caption reads: *First Post Office and Hardware Store, Mr. and Mrs. J. Stanley Brown.* First hardware store where? Consulting both Judge Farr and Otis P. Tout, I discover no answer.

W. W. Master is working sixty horses on our lateral canal, which will be fourteen feet wide! A drugstore is to be *put in immediately,* not to mention a harness store. Los Angeles must be proud. Mostly, I suppose, Imperial is Tent City, as Indio was and Salton City will be in 1958. I quote from an envisoner of that third epoch: *There were enough tents to house a circus now, flying pennants from their masts as if for a coronation or a festival.* Or, if you would rather repeat the sermon of William Smythe: *The essence of the industrial life which springs from irrigation is its democracy.*

In the spring of 1902 we hear that the first four brick buildings of Imperial will be erected soon; one is Wilber Clark's hardware store. Oh, Imperial's dreams are all coming true! As two of her citizens will later recall, *water was in the ditches, seeds were in the ground, green was becoming abundant, and the whole area was dotted with the homes of hopeful, industrious, devoted persons.*

He runs an advertisement, not the largest, not the smallest:

Refrigerators,
Ice Cream Freezers,

Everything in Hardware

If we havent got what you
want we will get it for you.

WILBUR CLARK

Postoffice Store, Imperial, Cal.

On 20 September 1902, Wilber Clark registers a purchase of land from the Imperial Town Company. Is this a belated formality connected with his hardware store, or has he become a petty W. F. Holt, a speculator like so many others?

The following month, the Farmers' Institute calls the roll in *the new brick block of the Imperial Land Company.* Signing the roster, widely separated by other names, are W. F. Holt and Leroy Holt, Margaret S. Clark—so she remains yet unmarried—and old John Clark. Wilber Clark's name is absent. The newspaper reports that he has gone with some friends to Carriso Creek for a week's hunting. *We have the temerity to suggest that they were possibly hunting oil land but were informed that such was not the case.*

Nor does he appear in the self-congratulatory *Valley Imperial* published by the county historical society half a century later. We're informed that the Edgar Brothers, as had the Clarks, rolled into the town of Imperial in 1901; *they soon founded a farm implement and heavy hardware business in Imperial . . . Early in the firm's history a policy of offering only first class merchandise with guarantees . . . was decided and adopted.* I have never been cheated out of a dollar in my life. By 1903, the Edgar Brothers own a store in Calexico; soon they have branches in Brawley and Holtville, too. What about Wilber Clark? He's straining his reddish-brown drinking water out of the ditches with the rest of them.

In 1903 his hardware store receives brief mention in the newspaper. I see that he owns a hundred and seventy-five acres of Imperial Water Company No. 1. And the crop acreage of the Imperial Valley quadruples, from twenty-five thousand to a hundred thousand acres!

His advertisement is larger now. I see that he is offering ellwood and kokomo steel wite fences, barbed wire, hogs, sheep, cattle, poultry. Sometimes it changes borders. He soon has a harness department, a paint department offering white lead, oils, glass, asbestos, cold water paint.

At the end of that year, after a tenure of twelve months, Margaret Clark resigns as postmistress, perhaps because she will soon become Mrs. Archie Priest. The marriage will take place next April; in the write-up, the bride's brother will be referred to as *our popular businessman, Wilber Clark.*

Meanwhile, on 11 September 1903, canny Wilber Clark sells land to the county of San Diego.

On 12 April 1904, an auction of lots is held in Imperial. Under a tent-awning men in hats and overalls sit on long benches. Other people stand, including one lady in a white blouse and a long, long dress; they must be purchasers, for we see them approaching the table where three men sit facing us and one black-clad lady in a remarkable hat sits in profile; perhaps she's the stenographer, although it's early in the century to count on that. A man in black and white stands, resting his white sleeve on the table; he's the auctioneer. Behind him an enlarged map of PART OF TOWNSITE OF IMPERIAL tempts us all. So we approach him one by one, to buy our American dream. The seller: George Chaffey's California Development Company, which controls water rights to these public domain lands. The water supply this year as last year remains irregular enough to cost us many a tight-clenched dime, but next year Rockwood and Chaffey will surely unkink the Imperial Canal. One of the citizens in that line may be Wilber Clark—unless, of course, he's bought his lot long since. This is the year we find him proving to be by the standards of Imperial an almost fanatical participant in the political process: He signs a petition to incorporate Imperial as a city of the sixth class. (In those days, cities were ranked by population size.) *Thirty-seven votes were cast,* reports Otis B. Tout, *although the town had 800 inhabitants.* San Diego accordingly disqualifies the result. A second attempt succeeds three months later. Otis B. Tout doesn't tell us, but I'd wager my hammer and nails that Wilber Clark has signed that petition, too.

We can count on his sister to accompany him on civic and mercantile adventures; the very next month she'll buy land from the Imperial Town Company—twice. Beloved of the Ministry of Capital, she's not only a true believer but a woman of means.

IRRIGATION'S POWER

Two months later, the Dutch botanist Hugo de Vries happens by Imperial. Since in 1904 there is only one game in town, we know where he sleeps: the Hotel Imperial, which beginning this year is no longer a conglomeration of tents but an *edifice* whose colonnade supports a graceful skirt of wood above the balcony, which runs around all four sides, and beneath which three ladies in long white bell-skirts recline in rocking chairs while a farmer-type gentleman in a hat and overalls stands behind them at the double door, with his hand in his pocket; meanwhile, a second gentleman in a suit, who for all I know could be Hugo de Vries himself, seeing that the dates of his visit and this photograph match, rocks in his own world somewhat leftward of the ladies; this scene, like everything else in Imperial, has been divinely framed by glaring whiteness above, around and below. Presently Hugo de Vries arises from his rocking chair and takes a stroll past Wilber Clark's hardware store. Noting the wide, wide streets, which make the teeming thoroughfares of Chicago seem like alleyways, he concludes, I know not whether with ingenuous admiration or Old World irony: *Like all cities in the west, Imperial has been designed on the chance that it will one day be the largest city of America.*

In 1905, when the first aircraft, a skeletal, blocky biplane, lands at Imperial town, *freight receipts at Imperial, $70,000 for the month of May, placed that station third in size on the S.P. western lines. Los Angeles is first and San Pedro is second.* Imperial has awakened now! In a darkening, vignetted, badly mounted old photograph datelined simply "Imperial" we see a horse and buggy, a hitching post, an arcade of sorts roofed with wavy metal siding; within its shade stands a line of men and ladies in their light-colored best, the latters' dresses ankle length; I see a boy, too, in a little cowboy hat; the dark door behind them is open; the store window reads VARNEY BROTHERS DRY GOODS. Perhaps Wilber Clark's little store looked pretty shabby compared to that. *We need have no fear that our lands will not become better and better as the years go by.* Next year our neighbor Mr. McKim will already possess twenty-five hundred hogs on his ranch east of Imperial. **THE DESERT DISAPPEARS.** To be sure, *Sharp's Heading is a cheap wooden structure and has been for some time in imminent danger of washing out,* but never mind that; we trust our engineers here in Imperial! When the Salton Sea accident occurs, I'd be surprised if Wilber Clark did not appear among the active citizens who dig and dynamite the New River in efforts to save Calexico, Seeley, Imperial, El Centro.

By now we've already raised several homes in Heber. Brawley shows off fifty houses, a hotel and of course a church; Mecca boasts its first school and an experimental date station; the population of the Imperial Valley has increased from two to seven thousand; fifty thousand acres now lie under cultivation! In the Coachella Valley the first Japanese arrive. William E. Smythe is on the verge of publishing his triumphalist revision of *The Conquest of Arid America.* To quote de Vries again: *I was particularly surprised at the speed with which all kinds of weeds and European plants spread under the influence of irrigation . . . Soon the endemic flora will have been displaced largely by these foreigners.*

THE SUBMARINERS

Again, who was Wilber Clark?

An old man in Campo once told me of the turn-of-the-century Imperial sanctum called the *submarine:* One erected a tent inside one's house and hung soaking wet sheets on it. The water ran down the tent and condensed on the inner walls of the house. Not everyone could afford to do that, the old man said.*

*In 1998 I was interviewing a mother and son in Slab City, about which they said: "Once you get here, it's hard to get back out. It's like a hole." The son then said: I hope we get out of here before it gets too hot. I'm afraid this heat will kill me. Put a wet towel on me; it's the only thing that keeps me cool. And then this happened, he said, telling me a sad story of violence and the law.—My plan was to be out of here before the summer hit, he said. But his plan did not work, and *the submarine* was still alive and well among some of the poor of Imperial.

To me, these conditions sound ghastly. Who was Wilber Clark, to give up the orange groves of Los Angeles for *that*? What were his motivations? Did he long so much for Emersonian self-sufficiency that discomfort was no object? Or did he simply aspire to be said of: *He sold out at a fancy price?* He certainly could aspire to making any number of silver dimes. *Cattle and hogs are going forward to market now on nearly every train, says the* Imperial Press.

This judge's son, buyer and seller of land, retail capitalist and possible automobile owner, could not have been desperate. He must have been something else.

VISION OF A HARDWARE STORE

Raymond Chandler, whose hatred for the hypocrisy and corruption of America is symbolized in and localized by Los Angeles, puts these words in the mouth of a millionaire: *There's a peculiar thing about money . . . In large quantities it tends to have a life of its own, even a conscience of its own.* Chandler musters no admiration for that conscience. He hates the magnates; despising the cheap grifters and the cops who beat suspects, he sneers at the blondes who laugh too loudly; he smells out dishonesty everywhere, so it's not surprising that the small-town ideals espoused in American Imperial under-impress him. Here is how he imagines himself into Wilber Clark's life: *I would have stayed in the town where I was born,* which my hero declined to do, *and worked in the hardware store,* which he certainly did, *and married the boss's daughter and had five kids and read them the funny paper on Sunday morning and smacked their heads when they got out of line . . . I might have even got rich—small-town rich, an eight-room house, . . . chicken every Sunday, . . . a wife with a cast iron permanent and me with a brain like a sack of Portland cement.* For Chandler, the hardware store symbolized inability to escape one's narrow origins. For Clark, it was the frontier itself.

What is Imperial to you? I have never been cheated out of a dollar in my life.

THE AMERICAN DREAM

In 1907, a man whose name the County Recorder spells Wilbur Clark buys land from Harry Cross; and in the same month, he buys a new lot from the Imperial Land (not Town) Company.

We presently find him in Calexico, in the company of Elizabeth F., whom he must have married out of the county, since the marriage isn't recorded in its books; and in that city the couple establish a new hardware store. (The first permanent structure in Calexico was an adobe; the rest being tents or else ramadas such as Harold Bell Wright wrote *The Winning of Barbara Worth* in.) I wish him joy in his

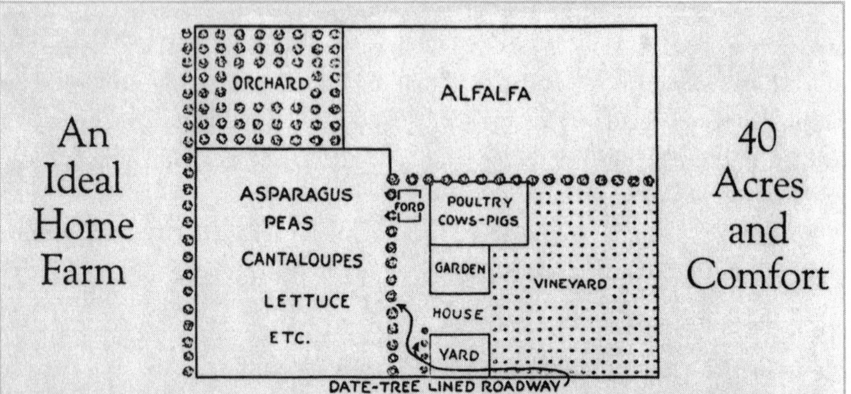

AN ideal home farm in Imperial valley is a 40-acre tract. Rich soil, abundance of water and the possibilities of whole-year culture and a wide variety of products combine to make the small farm the best for practical results.

The foregoing diagram shows in a graphic way how such a farm may be divided. It provides a central location for the home, and the things immediately pertaining to it. Not only is diversification of crops suggested but the possibility of their rotation is provided. The alfalfa field and the vegetable acreage can be rotated as desired. The only permanent plantings are the orchard and vineyard.

Alfalfa grows in such abundance that dairying is a profitable venture on the small farm. Through it cream checks are kept coming to the farmer with monthly regularity throughout the whole year. Poultry and hogs go with the combination to make it one of an appealing character. The vegetable plots offer a wide latitude of choice.

A factor not to be overlooked favoring the 40-acre farm is the problem of labor. Planned as suggested in the foregoing, the average farmer and his family can care for crops without help. This gives a degree of independence not otherwise possible.

marriage, and I hope that he takes his bride to Mexicali at least once. Why shouldn't they feel at home there? It's not as if they've left the Salton Trough.

I don't suppose there's much to buy in Mexicali in 1907; but once the Colorado is finally diverted back into its old bed, entrepreneurs begin to rebuild Southside. Do the Clarks ever find time, as so many of the Mexican field workers I have interviewed in Imperial County never did, to visit the new Salton Sea? I can almost see them trying on a holiday mood as soon as they've set foot on the other side of the ditch; the weariness of their labor and their money worries briefly depart them when a Mexican beckons them through a tall palisade and into an adobe house which is the same grey as the dirt in this old photo I'm now dreaming over in the Archivo Histórico del Municipio de Mexicali; the house stands steep-roofed beside the steep-roofed skeleton of a corral's framework; I see a horse and buggy off to the right, the horse's silhouette shockingly skinny. Soon they come out with his arm around her; he has bought her a pretty Mexican blanket.

Who was she? I perceive little in common between her and Barbara Worth, whom a historian describes as *the "Imperial Daughter" of the Imperial Valley: a tall, outdoorsy Girl of the Golden West who speaks fluent Spanish and spends much of her time riding the desert on horseback.* On the subject of Imperial Daughters, Judge Farr writes: *Most of these are country born and bred, with an ancestry of sturdy farmers of which they have been proud to boast . . . plain women with big, noble souls, ready for any honorable and worthy task that was set before them.*

Elizabeth F.'s maiden name was Schultz. Census data indicate her to be a German immigrant, born in about 1874, who had entered the United States aged eleven, in the year when Tecate was founded, the first store sprang up in Indio, and the first Chinatown was torched in Riverside. I therefore suppose that all her life she will speak English with a slight German accent. Perhaps this charms her husband, who may himself retain a midwestern drawl. In 1907 he is forty-six and she is thirty-three. Lucky Wilber Clark!

On March 15 of the previous year, Wilber Clark sold unspecified real estate to G. W. McCollum, a rival hardware store man. I am guessing, therefore, that what Clark conveyed to him was the business in Calexico. Perhaps it is this very sale which affords sufficient capital to build a dream at last.

Indeed, the Clarks eventually settle on the *now greatly improved* Wilfrieda Ranch, or Wilfreds Ranch, a hundred and seventy-one acres in area. The year of their land patent is 1911. They pay in full and in cash.

THE GARDENS OF PARADISE

And where might this haven be? By now I longed to see it. I hoped and imagined to find a small family business, ideally a Clark Date Farm or the like, employing Wilber and Elizabeth's descendants of the fourth and fifth generation.

Well, there's a Clark ranch, said Edith Karpen, who was ninety-one. He lived out there, he was still alive; he lived on the road from El Centro to Mount Signal. I know this Clark was one of the early pioneers there. There was Imperial Hardware and there was that independent one; Alice, do you remember that one that brought you to us when you wandered away from us on that Saturday night? That man who had the hardware store left his business and brought her along; and then Alice came along so happily with her hand in his.

So I set hopefully out on another expedition across the foxed paper Imperial that lives only in libraries.

In the *Imperial Valley Business and Resident Directory 1912–1913*, we are apprised before anything else that *IMPERIAL COUNTY SHOWS RAPID INCREASE: Is*

Growing Rapidly Richer, Accepting the Tax Man's Appraisement as Evidence. Next come the listings, bordered by multiply replicated advertisements; and on page 77 there dwells a

Clark, Wilber, dairy and vineyard, Mobile, P O El Centro.

Dairy and vineyard! What a busy place, this Wilfrieda Ranch! I wonder if the Clarks ordered an Empire milking machine from Los Angeles or a De Laval junior milking outfit for small herds from San Francisco? On page 309, we find him listed among the two hundred and fifty–odd dairies of Imperial County.—Imperial is a Swiss dairyman in his white hat, holding his gleaming pails of milk, walled in by his cows' rumps. I saw that photo at the Pioneers Museum.

Oh, my, dairying is the newest new thing! It might prove more enriching than grapes, dates and hogs together! As early as 1905, Chase Creamery at Imperial was making seven hundred and fifty pounds of butter per day, and shipping his daily five hundred pounds of cream to Riverside. That same year the first meeting of the Imperial Valley Dairymen's Association took place at Heber; the Cardiff Creamery of San Bernardino was already preparing to relocate to Silsbee. **MILK IS HERE**.

By 1916 the County Development Agent can safely inform me that

> **IMPERIAL COUNTY** is second among the 58 counties of California in butter production.
>
> **IMPERIAL COUNTY** makes one-tenth of the butter made in the state.
>
> . . .
>
> **IMPERIAL COUNTY** increased its butter 235% and rose from seventh to second place during the last six years.
>
> . . .
>
> "Opportunities for profit in dairying are greater in **IMPERIAL VALLEY** than in any district that I know of in the United States." —E. W. Webster, former chief of the Dairy division, United States Department of Agriculture . . .

In short, we need have no fear that our lands will not become better and better as the years go by.

A Hetzel photograph shows a long line of white-clad soldiers of both sexes beneath the banner of their cause: **IMPERIAL VALLEY MILK PRODUCERS ASSOCIATION--CHALLENGE OF BUTTER**. My fellow Americans, how could they not meet their challenge?

Two hundred and fifty dairies in 1912! Eight years later there will be only three.

Six years after that there will be eleven. In 1930 there will be six. Dairying is no sinecure, it would seem.* The yellow pages for 2001 list no dairies at all in Imperial County, although Nudairy One does sell the equipment and supplies of that profession.

Indeed, Wilber and Elizabeth Clark must have experienced the instability of the profession, for the 1914 directory and its successors decline to mention any dairy business at **Mobile, P O El Centro.**

Now, where is this Mobile? It seems to be near El Centro. Otis P. Tout advises me to *USE THE INDICES* of his *First Thirty Years,* but these, alas, contain no Mobile. Judge Farr omits any indication of the ranch's location; however, on the back endpapers of the 1912 directory, an offering for the Seeley Townsite Company announces that *a strong syndicate has been organized, with W. F. Holt as president, to help develop the resources of the great west side of the valley.* I have never been cheated out of a dollar in my life. *Associated with Mr. Holt are G. G. Chapman, leading orange grower and capitalist of Fullerton; W. T. Bill, president of the El Centro Townsite Co; N. A. Ross, well-known capitalist of Los Angeles; A. R. Ferguson of Seeley; R. R. Crabtree, and others.* I gather that San Diego men are likewise involved. It would seem that Mr. Holt has allied himself with a mixture of locals and outside speculators—ah, the direct gaze of the confident man! The advertisement continues: *This company has purchased the townsites of Seeley and Mobile. The fertile lands around Mobile station, comprising about 240 acres, will all be set to alfalfa in the fall and subdivided into small tracts . . .* And facing these words, well glued down against the coverboards, a crude engraving from a bird's-eye perspective depicts agrarian checkerboard all the way to the horizon, with the Salton Sea a series of parallel lines above which the tops of Iowa-style cumulus clouds play peekaboo. The legend reads: **DIXIELAND . . . IMPERIAL VALLEY**. In the foreground, a triangle

*My dear friend Mr. Paul Foster, who grew up on a farm in the great dairying state of Minnesota, and who is equally adept at running spreadsheets and peafield combines, concludes that "the growth, peak, and total collapse of the Imperial Valley dairy industry follows closely the national experience for dairy farming . . . In particular, the decline from over 3000 dairies in 1920 to 2 dairies today" in Imperial County. . . "can be traced to the transition to the sanitary 'Grade A' dairy system . . . which required a substantial investment in milking parlors, hot water for cleaning, and cold storage stainless steel tanks. This wiped out lots of small dairy farmers who had previously eked out a supplemental income by keeping a few cows and moving them from one leased pasture to another. It also wiped out milk as the source of a variety of unpleasant diseases . . . The resulting move by small farmers into marginal dairy production led to the glut which resulted in price controls and the rise of the single most powerful agricultural lobby in America . . . Interestingly enough, the Imperial website has a promotion inviting dairy farmers to check out Imperial as a place to set up operations, thanks to the new 'misting barns' which keep cows cool during the summer . . . Since Imperial has always suffered a dramatic fall-off in summer milk production due to the heat . . . it's hard to believe that the increased cost of air-conditioned cows is offset by the supply of large amounts of relatively cheap water. Even if true, it seems like a near-criminal misdirection of resources. Whether I like it or not, they seem to have succeeded in at least one case: there are now 3 dairies in Imperial County, including the only Swiss cheese maker in California."

of trees and cross-hatched field-squares has been labeled FRUIT LANDS. What would it be like to live there? I remember as a child reading a certain strangely alluring potboiler of a desert valley reclaimed by irrigation, of good Western men, aided by a noble Indian, winning out over the corrupt Easterners who've dynamited a spring.* (Somehow the Holt Syndicate does not fit in with this tale—unless one believes fervently in the Ministry of Capital.) If only I could have been a good Western man, dreaming my life away in FRUIT LANDS! As it happens, however, this region was enacted only to help frame a heavy square grid of blank plots demarcated by a family of roads whose east-west members have been deliciously lined with shade trees parallel to which the San Diego and Arizona Railroad (they actually won't be completed for six years more) comes straight through; while south to north, Dixieland gets bisected again by the West Side Main Canal, which then curves northeast into the checkerboard dreams around the Salton Sea. I look due east, and find the New River's arc swinging up from Calexico to the dots of Silsbee and Seeley, the former known for its cornscapes, the latter, freshly inscribed in 1911, right on the San Diego and Arizona tracks, which continue eastward, first crossing the Southern Pacific Railroad's perpendicular axis (Imperial–El Centro–Calexico), then soldiering on toward Holtville at the very edge of the world. Right on this line, about one-third of the way from Seeley to El Centro, hence very near to where the Mormon Battalion camped one January night in 1847, roasting confiscated Mexican beef for the furtherance of Northside's noble war, I discover the dot called Mobile.

So Wilber and Elizabeth Clark live here. (A twenty-first-century backcountry gazetteer calls it *a siding on the San Diego & Arizona Railway.*) Are they pleased that Mr. Holt's syndicate has purchased the lands around them? Since they have done their own buying and selling, they may well hope to benefit from oncoming assessed valuations. As for me, I can't help believing in people. Do you want to know why? Well, I'll tell you! In 1917, Imperial County holds the largest ostrich herd in America!

I hope that he and Elizabeth find joy in each other to the end, that until the boom ends they sell their milk for high prices in Los Angeles, and that they find occasional leisure to take a spin to El Centro, a city now so teeming with automobiles that Wilber Clark's own machine must be lost: *During trading hours the streets are lined with rows of automobiles . . . at times so numerous as to render traffic difficult.* (Those words date from 1918.) He puts on his best suit, and she her best dress.

*This novel, Zane Grey's *Desert Gold,* actually looks into Imperial, when the fleeing cowboys with the aristocratic Mexican bride they seek to save from rape gaze westwards from the Sonoran lava-fields and see "a seemingly endless arm of the blue sea. This was the Gulf of California. Beyond the Gulf rose dim, bold mountains, and above them hung the setting sun, dusky red, flooding all that barren empire with a sinister light."

They don their motoring goggles. Brushing the dust off each other, they pay a call on D. G. Whiting, who brought the first Jersey herd into the Imperial Valley, which is why I imagine a kinship between him and that other dairyman and innovator, Wilber Clark. Do their wives like each other? All that I know of Elizabeth F. is her name.

I like to imagine that the Clarks have just experienced one of several good seasons. *He made a success through his own efforts.* They deposit their cotton earnings in the bank. Then he takes her for dinner at the Barbara Worth Hotel, which has been open for three years now. Surely he is proud of his young wife. Her mother is with them; she adores him. They finish their steaks and ice creams. His sunburned hand touches her knee under the table. Then, knowing that they'll be up before dawn to milk the cows, she helps her mother back inside the dusty car and sits down beside her husband just before he pulls the starter.

Between El Centro and Mobile one encounters *"the Poole Place," which is noted for its high state of cultivation, with many fine shade trees and a prosperous looking home.* Poole and his family own two thousand two hundred and twenty acres—a bit more than the statutory hundred and sixty—and they lease three hundred and twenty more. Their fancy house has stood there since 1910. Although Otis P. Tout neglects to mention the Clarks at all, why not suppose the Wilfrieda Ranch to be nearly as nice as this? I quote again from Judge Farr's account:

Mr. Clark is a book-worm, and possesses a library of several thousand volumes, containing some rare "Americana" and first editions, as well as books relating to the Southwest.

How often does he have moments to read? And does she enjoy reading? I would not expect so, English being her second language and her days so hot and flat, but who am I to guess? Perhaps he reads to her, or at night as she combs out her hair before bed he tells her what he imagines de Anza saw at Yuma; or he shows her an old bullet he's found; he dates it from the Mormon Battalion. Whenever her mother cleans the house, she tenderly brushes the dust off his first editions. They chat about taking a motoring trip back to Los Angeles, perhaps even next year. He subscribes in advance to Judge Farr's *History,* I would imagine; and when it arrives, he opens it up and shows her how *he and his wife, Elizabeth F., settled on the now greatly improved Wilfrieda Ranch.* His mother-in-law smiles, puts on her spectacles, holds the book close to assure herself that Elizabeth's name is truly there. Someday they will visit Los Angeles, to be sure; he will buy more books and some new tools, and she wants a brand new dress; she thinks that the Varney Brothers charge too much for sundries, so it will be a pleasure to bring a lot of things back home at a reasonable price. Her mother is curious to see those new oil wells in Los Angeles. How many millionaires there must be! And now to bed, and now to rise. The labor will be hot today because *some fifty varieties of grapes have been tried out and a profitable express business has been worked out on the same. Of great interest to Mr. Clark is the six-acre date orchard; many of the trees are in full bearing, producing fine tasting dates* in this utopian spot somewhere near Mobile.

Having now found Mobile, I have grown worthy to reread Otis P. Tout! In Chapter XXX, "Unincorporated Towns and Trade Centers," Seeley receives a page and a half. *A new business is the Valley Cream Company, which handles over 12,000 pounds of milk daily, converting it into ice cream, buttermilk and cheese.* That description was written in 1930. Too bad that Wilber Clark's dairy fell out of business long before! From Seeley to Mobile can't be more than three miles. A creamery that huge would certainly have been convenient for him. I wonder where he lives in 1930, or *does* he still live? He must be about sixty-nine now. Elizabeth needs to work a trifle more than her share now, no doubt.—In the Imperial County Assessor's map books, number 16–112–1 (TR 65) depicts the townsite of Seeley, with U.S. 80 sloping diagonally upwards, licking Fudge Co.'s one and a half acres; and it pleases me to imagine Wilber and Elizabeth Clark treating themselves to store-bought fudge, because I want them to be happy. In the photographs of Hetzel, the ditches are wide, practically canals—well, of course they are!—and there are heads of dark horses on white sand, dark cows on salt-and-silver fields, men bucking bales in horse-drawn wagons. Hugo de Vries remarks on the red purslane flowers along the edges of the canals, but I have never seen them. I see only hot wide wastes. But the Wilfrieda Ranch, walled coolly in by dates and other fruit, must shade the two lovebirds nearly as nicely as does Mrs. Bettner's stately house in Riverside. Can they fall asleep without employing *submarines*?

And they dwell near the amenities! Seeley was a concatenation of sand dunes in 1912. Five years later, three hundred and fifty pioneers live there, patronizing its meat market, doctor, hardware store and billiard parlor.* My word, I can't help believing in people!

As for their actual residence, *Dixieland was planned when an effort was made in 1909 to bring a high line canal west of the present canal on the western boundary of the irrigated area.* In other words, that West Side Main Canal is as fictitious as the railroad line from San Diego to Yuma, not to mention those FRUIT LANDS. Otis P. Tout continues by naming two promoters, neither of whom appeared in the Seeley Townsite Company's advertisement; they must be modest. *A brick building or two bear mute witness to the fact that Dixieland still awaits the coming of water on a higher level. With the construction of the All-American Canal the old plans for a town at this point will no doubt be revived;* oh, no doubt.

*The population was 150 in 1910, and 1,228 in 1990.

Opening the map I bought in Calexico last year, I learn from its margins that the Imperial Valley Dental Group is committed to my health, that the Calipatria Inn and Suites has wisely placed in quotation marks its self-assigned encomium, *"The Beautiful,"* and that the Evan Hewes Highway, more realistically known as S80, proceeds due west out of El Centro, reaches an indeterminate portion of the Salton Sea–to–Mexicali street grid, meets the label **Seeley** and swerves southwest right at the **y** to underline the town at a respectful distance, resumes its westward trajectory, crosses the New River, which in the map is a laughably pristine blue—by the way, Seeley seems to have moved across the river since 1911—and reaches **Dixieland**, which in obedience to the syndicate's vision does now indeed straddle the Westside Main Canal! Moreover, this road parallels the Southern Pacific Railroad all the way. I'm ashamed now, that I saw duplicity in the direct gaze of the confident man!

By now, everyone who's anyone has heard of Dixieland. In 1914, Customs Service headquarters in Los Angeles informs the Deputy Collector in Charge, Calexico, Cal.: *The latest shipment of opium by this crowd which we now have under arrest is supposed to have come through Jacumba and gone to Dixieland.* In 1916, D. Steffano, proprietor of the San Diego Bar in Mexicali, gets denounced by his confederate as an opium smuggler. *For some time Steffano has been suspected and officers from this office have, on two separate occasions, inspected his auto at Dixieland.** Unfortunately, Wilber Clark remains less renowned than these heroes. He is not the director of the Chamber of Commerce for Seeley or Dixieland in 1913. His name appears on no more resolutions or petitions. Did he drown himself happily in domestic obscurity with Elizabeth F., or has he become a struggling nobody?

I went to Seeley and asked around, but not even the most grizzled Imperialites had heard of Mobile. The clerk at the County Assessor's office lived near Seeley, despised me for an outsider, played with her hair and denied that Mobile ever existed.

Fortunately, the 1914 directory gave me a new clue to the Clarks' location:

Clark, Wilber R (Elizabeth F) o 175–a, 40 cotton, 120 alfalfa, dairy **Elder Ditch** 6 mi w El Centro, P O Seeley

Their date orchard failed, it would seem. Much of the alfalfa goes to feed their cows; and cotton has become their speculative cash crop. Well, why should it be otherwise? Mr. Holt's syndicate likewise went in for cotton; by 1917 Seeley is so cotton-rich that it boasts two gins already and a third will be built in 1918 to process the even hundred acres of *Egyptian varieties.*

*The next letter in the file reveals that the confederate who accused Steffano has shot him dead in Mexicali.

In 1920, their adddress is **2 mi e Seeley** at the same post office. Wilber Clark is now fifty-eight—better than sixty-nine. Elizabeth is forty-six. According to the census, Elizabeth's mother Maria still lives with them. It is no surprise to learn of the pioneer automobilist that he and his wife may now be reached by telephone.

TRACT 281

The records in the County Assessor's office went back only to 1960. However, the nice lady at the desk brought out one of the immense leather-covered books I'd read about in the California Board of Equalization county report of 1949, whose author complained about having to carry them into the field; indeed, the Imperial County Assessor had yearned for sufficient money to do away with those books, and it seemed as if that wish had been granted. The lady at the desk said to me: Please be very careful with this. I think it's even older than I am.

That was in 2002. When I returned in 2005 I was told there were not and never had been any such books. However, by then I had hired a private detective, and so I learned the parcel number.

In County Assessor's Mapbook 51, page 51–13, there's a tract along Elder Canal in the townsite of Seeley; it's euphoniously named 182A, and the parcel number,

Tract 281 in 2005 (Signal Mountain in background)

indicated by a circle, is seven.—Oh, excuse me; it's actually in Book 52–48; and it's Tract 281, lying not quite on Elder Canal as I thought, but two east-west horizontals northward of there.—To be more specific, the former property of Wilber and Elizabeth Clark consists of a rectangle bordered on the north by the Evan Hewes Highway, on the west by Elder Lateral Ten, on the south by Elm Lateral Two just up from Ross Road, and on the east by Low Road.

On a hundred-and-four-degree day, I meet brown stagnant water in the lateral and I find various smells of mud. The Clarks' field remains green, but it is just blind greenness now, lacking spoor of a house, although it does offer a fine view of Mount Signal to the southwest. The few haywalls warped against the sun could not have been stacked by Wilber Clark. The Wilfrieda Ranch has vanished like Imperial's grapescapes near Holtville.

On Evan Hewes Highway, I gaze into a pale, cracked dry lateral on the edge of the property. I look northwest across it at the mountains of Anza-Borrego, then east to a low and broken line of blue-grey trees, and west where in the distance an open-framed train sleeps. Hay bales are baking in the sun like cookies. From there it is walking distance to the brown-green New River, which is clotted, foamy and stinking, with bush-lined wriggles deep in its desert ditch. As the crow flies I am less than nineteen miles from where Ray Garnett first eased his motorboat into this river at Lack Road; our farthest upstream, where the wrecked bridge defeated us, can be no more than fifteen or sixteen miles.

A huge peeling eucalyptus shades the northwest corner, a tree whose many white trunks rise up and spread in the sky.

About this property, the eloquent farmer across the street informs me through the almost-closed door: Don't know. Haven't been here that long.

"JOYOUS AWAKENING"

Did the ranch fail before the dairy did? Did they live out their years here or did they sell out? What befell Wilber Clark's books, grapes and dates?

Wilber and Elizabeth Clark must not have done as well as expected, since the pioneer hagiographies cease mentioning them. One tribute to a rancher near Imperial townsite enthuses: *A home, good friends, a fair day's labor, a pipe and a night's sleep are luxuries to him.* Do the Clarks likewise live simply but well? Shouldn't they now own nearly as many refined objects as the Pooles and the Wilsies? In 1925, when almost every American housewife still possesses both a sewing machine and a washtub, a Maytag washer advertisement lets us in on *The Secret of Happy Wives,* namely: *Joyous awakening . . . unhurried breakfast . . . wash day . . . movie or club or Farm Bureau . . . perhaps Reading or Study . . . refreshed and rested for Friend Husband's*

Home Coming at night. Could this ever have been true? Would it be pleasing if the Clarks had had such a relationship? I can't help believing in people.

THE GARDENS OF PARADISE REVISITED

What happened next is what always happens. To discover when it happened, I opened the heavy death indexes in the Imperial County office. They were big volumes on tarnished brass rollers instead of shelves, the rollers' colors variously changing with time. **Nathan W. Clark Jan 28 52 66/1** was not my man, but should that make him less worthwhile to me? Judge Farr, which is to say **Finis Calvert Farr Apr. 8 1918**, now resided in certificate 30, book 6A; out of gratitude to him for introducing me to Wilber Clark, I purchased a copy of his death certificate.

In the California State Library in Sacramento, on page 1964 of volume 2 of the *California Death Index* for 1905–29, I found a W. Clarke and a Wilbur Clarke, both of whom I provisionally parted from due to spelling mismatches, especially since on page 1957 there proved to be

NAME OF DECEDENT

Last	First	Initial	Initials of Spouse	Age Units	No. of Units	Sex	Race
CLARK	WILBER		E F	1	67		

PLACE OF DEATH		DATE OF DEATH			DATE REGISTERED		LOCAL FILE NUMBER	
County	City	Month	Day	Year	Month	Year	District	Number
70		10	11	28		28		

STATE FILE NUMBER

51520

This would seem to be our man, since both the name and the wife's initials match up. The age is also correct (the unit code of one means that at death his age was sixty-seven years, not sixty-seven days, minutes or hours). What unnerves me is that although this Wilber Clark died in 1928, the Wilber Clark whose biography I am now trying to write disappeared from the *Imperial Valley Directory* prior to 1924.

Could anyone else be our Wilber Clark? Two other dead candidates offer themselves on this page: Wilbur Clark, middle initial G., and Wilbar Clark, middle initial L., the latter lacking a spouse. Wilbar died in 1916, which is much too early; Wilbur, whose wife's initial was H., died in 1923 in County No. 60, which is Alameda. By far the best match is the one whose name is actually Wilber Clark.

Presumably either Wilber or Elizabeth Clark, or both of them, got worn out—I would guess Wilber, since he was the elder—and so they moved to County No. 70, which is Imperial's enemy, Los Angeles County, and died.

The 1930 census shows us a fifty-six-year-old head of household named Elizabeth Clark, widow. She owns her domicile, which happens to be a farm in Pasadena Township. She has not attended school in the previous year. She can read and write. She belongs to the white race. She was born in Homburg, Germany, and both her parents were also born in Germany. Her native tongue was German, but she can speak English. Her occupation is *poultryman*. She worked the day before the census taker came to her door.

Wilber Clark's sister Margaret, now definitely Mrs. W. H. Dickinson, lived until 1942 and died in San Diego at about age seventy-seven.

One wonders whether when they sold out and departed the Imperial Valley it was with the emotions expressed in the song of that period:

> Oh, Harvest Land—Sweet Burning Sand!
> —As on the sun-kissed field I stand
> I look away across the plain
> And wonder if it's going to rain—
> I vow, by all the Brands of Cain,
> That I will not be here again.

Chapter 42

MEXICALI

(1904–1905)

Mexican lands are entitled to half the water that enters the Imperial Valley . . . They have never taken it and probably never will take it.

—The *Los Angeles Times,* 1925

A horse and buggy far away, and a shaded profiled horse hitched to a wriggly palisade; a man standing in a doorway beneath a sign which, although bold, remains too small for me to make out despite my brand-new reading glasses—why didn't I bring a photographic loupe to the archives?—a few edifices intermediate in character between huts and houses, facing off in two rows, with a wide wet street of dirt between them (wet because **WATER IS HERE**; Baja California has just now entered a forty-seven-year rainy spell, meaning that precipitation will be slightly above zero), a street which keeps coming toward me until it fills up the world; this is Mexicali in 1905, and the caption reads, of course, "Main Street." The foreground of the street is in sharpest focus. The street displays its naked wagon-ruts which waver like a stripper's hips; the street presents its sand, its silt and its little heaps of Imperial dirt. That's all. Well, I forgot that one house is adorned by a dead tree whose top was snapped off by unknown agents.

As usual, a map increases reality's impressiveness. By 1904, Mexicali boasts five named streets: Calle Luis E Torres and Calle Celso Vega running north-south; and Avenida Porfirio Díaz, Avenida Ramón Corral and Avenida Juárez running east-west. Of all these, only the last will retain its name. The border appears to run slightly northeast (it's actually dead level), so that between it and Avenida Porfirio Díaz, which parallels it, the one unlabeled and the two labeled plazas form parallelograms and trapezoids; next comes Avenida Ramón Corral, which does in fact run east-west; so that the blocks of lots between it and Porfirio Díaz are trapezoids subdivided into smaller trapezoids on the north and rectangles on the south. After that, Mexicali's all rectangles—or it would be if a certain wide and unnamed boulevard didn't come arcing through it.

Could this ever be mistaken for any Northside town? The city where Wilber Clark lived for a time possesses—here's that list again—its own water tank, creamery and the rest; it boasts Wilber Clark's hardware store. But, after all, it's *Headquarters for Surveyors and Visitors.* And it was established four years ago. That's a long time for such doers of deeds as Wilber Clark, L. M. Holt, George Chaffey. Mexicali remains officially only two years old—never mind those settlers from 1898.

Do we blame the Treaty of Guadalupe Hidalgo, now fifty-seven years old, for Mexicali's failure to be an irrigated Imperial boomtown in 1905? Arid America is young and well capitalized. Arid Mexico is simply poor.

—Oh, but I forgot. Without the line, why would Mexicali come into being at all?

But what would Imperial be to me without its two manmade accidents of the Salton Sea and the international line? Here's a cyanotype of Mrs. Ethel Wellcome's social at the boundary marking-stone in 1906. Some ladies are holding their hats, in order for me to admire their faces all the better. It's certainly nice to see an image of Imperial which is blue and white instead of grey and white; it makes the place look almost cool.—On either side of the marker there's nothing but flatness. Absent that imaginary line, why would Mrs. Wellcome have brought her guests here?

Still, delineation has begun to spawn consequences. Mexico established a customs house here last year. (Meanwhile, near Mexico City, the Virgin of Guadalupe's shrine was upgraded to a basilica.)

What next? Well, Chinese laborers are arriving; and a secretive entity called the Lower California Development Company is now preparing to irrigate two hundred thousand acres *below the international boundary line . . . as has been done at Imperial.*

Chapter 43

THE SWEET YOUNG NIGHT

(2002)

But there was always Mexicali, a half hour south down Mexico way. *Mexicali Rose, I'm dreaming* . . . As long as I shall remember, the great blazing signs of the "Southern Club" and the "Owl" will loom aloft in the velvety night as portals of a world that will never exist again.

—Frank Waters, 1946

Time spends itself in Imperial as carefully and silently as the long old American automobiles. Past days and their future reenactments preserve themselves in the semblances of specific bars, currency exchange windows, Chinese restaurants. Mexicali's wide-arched, white-lit arcades comprise a calendar as cyclical as the Aztec variety. One returns, for instance, to the Thirteen Negro dance hall, which never ceases to be itself even if the queen-sized mammaries and the moustache-underlined cowboy hats might wax and wane around a Platonic core, if the price of the drinks goes up a trifle and the streetfront gets decorated by variant assemblages of long, ancient, shining, angle-parked cars. By day, everything is still and bright, by night still and dark, warmish-cool. The leaden, pitted night sidewalks under those archways of light allow anybody to stroll about in time, scarcely impeded by fellow time travellers (for one characteristic of Imperial is low population density).* The day of my birth will always be here, reified in the border crossing. I can wander over to it and even "document" it with my big camera if I choose, at seven dollars per click of the shutter, and God only knows how much per print, depending on the gold chloride I waste. The day of my death awaits my inspection also, except that I have not determined which edifice, nightscape or streetscape represents it, and which is a huckster-shuck. It's probably some border feature—maybe even the same station I passed so easily and legally through when I entered this world of Imperial: I've told you that in 1900 the border was nothing but a ditch ten feet wide; in 1925 it sported "great wire gates" which closed at nine-o'-clock sharp, which is why *at five minutes to nine began the exodus back to the United States;*

*According to one mayoral candidate whom I met in the spring of 2001, the population of Mexicali is 800,000, of which 40% have crossed the border at some point and 30% possess green cards.

in 1942 only telephone poles marked it, but it remained *serious* all the same: a nightclub singer who'd larkishly intended to enter Southside on the shoulders of her date, a British airman, received instructions to cross on her own feet *because of the "White Slave Law,"* which had been written, they told her, to prevent prostitutes from being taken to Mexico against their will. Coming Northside in 2000 we entered an air-conditioned station and queued to show our picture identification cards, thereby delaying ourselves by an additional five or ten minutes; in 2002, thanks to terrorism in New York the previous autumn, three soldiers with machine-guns had been added for the purpose of teasing me about my big camera and teaching me erotic Spanish phrases.—But should my death be of the sordid, furtive or desperate variety, then I'll need to "document" another alley, an old style one, cracked and dark, with shuttered luminescence reflected in its stygian puddles. No fear; we're still alive, at least on the Mexican side (your eyes are border lights reflected in a pool of urine), but we're going to scale the fence of crossing before we know it, in a state of grim and dirty panic, and on Northside death will be waiting in a silent Bronco: WELCOME TO CALIFORNIA. Therefore, please visit a different concretion of time—Good Friday evening, the church door swinging open and shut, briefly baring light as people enter one by one (some carrying flowers), or, much more rarely, exit; while a dirty man whose baseball cap has gotten censored by the night into the same warm grey pallor as the street itself (Avenida Reforma) sits on the steps, his elbows on his grimy knees. An amplified cousin of a Gregorian chant comes up the flat warm street-cobbles; the truck's headlights blink slowly, followed by the Procession of Silence. Next year we might happen on a Corpus Christi Procession; the previous year there was a funeral. The crowd, not immense but a crowd nonetheless, collects itself in front of the church; and its first member, a middle-aged woman, glides forward, passing into sanctuary as she upholds her candle within a shade of paper so light-rich as to seem a glowing bell of glass. She ascends to the arched door. The lefthand member of that pair of wooden church portals, each punched with cookie-cutter holes delineating bells and crosses, now parts for her. She vanishes into the inner light where somebody else is sitting out of my sight—the woman who soon will leave me because she loves me too much; this will be our last evening together in Mexicali, and it will be short and sad since she is disappointed in me and I am afraid of her. Now a year has passed; a year has drained into the Salton Sea. She sits forever in the church as long as I do not attempt to look inside, just as whenever I happen to pass the Date Tree Hotel in Indio I am pleased to understand that she is there and will always be, subject to the same gentleman's agreement. Here's that palm-grove by the sign for the Jewel Date Co. She loves it there; I wouldn't dream of disturbing her. As the *Imperial Press and Farmer* explained back in 1903: *The collection of pictures is unlimited, for they come from nature's storehouse, and none will be used more than once . . . The pictures are the result of an Imperial mirage. The sun, as it rises, starts the images in motion . . . The setting sun is not far behind.* The pictures are as variously piquant as the red sauces on the table of a Mexican restaurant: the hot vinegar kind, the hot sweet kind, the gentle kind, the kind that is fire-essence. I want to taste them all, so I am making her wait while I complete another longish exposure—sixteen minutes at f/45—while she sits in the church thinking I now know what. (Eventually I made her wait too long.) Meanwhile, the flatbed truck approaches. I begin to spy the immense crucifix which it bears. Will it enter my lens's omnivorous or should I say catholic consciousness? Around it, the first woman's followers, imitators, siblings and descendants pool together ever more tightly, streaming up the church steps with their candles in the paper bells and paper cones. Oh, yes, past days preserve themselves: Here comes Judas, betrayer of Christ; he'll betray Him next year as he did last year; in 1835, when Alta California still belonged to Mexico, a spy from Northside sailed across the ditch and witnessed the hanging and burning of Judas's effigy in Santa Barbara. In Imperial, nothing is lost. The loudspeaker moans: *María, la Madre de Jesús.* And on the truckbed, María herself weeps over the wooden Jesus, her kerchiefed head bowed in a fashion whose stylized character does not at all reduce sorrow to a formula, but indeed focuses it just as each paper cone does its flame. Do her eyes truly utter tears? How can her sorrow be real when she knows as well as I that the one she mourns will return to life the day after tomorrow? Yet although I'm among the most nominal of Christians, I begin to feel it myself, perhaps by analogy with the death of my much loved little sister, on the anniversary of whose drowning each year I cannot escape the grief and horror again, again, again. The rest of the year she is dead, and on that late summer's day (a day for swimming, hence for drowning), she dies simply deeper, at each reenactment sinking farther into the slime at the bottom of the pond where the decomposition of her memory-image leaves nothing but gruesomeness—or almost nothing; somewhere within the mucky skeleton there lives, in an inversion of quotidian anatomy, a shy, pretty six-year-old girl with brown bangs and brown eyes, who may still love me and has possibly even forgiven my part in the accident. For now, that's as much resurrection as I can accept, which is why (does this mean I'm damned?) Easter frequently strikes me as the merest and most meretricious mockery even as I unfailingly feel Good Friday, Bad Friday my mother used to call it . . .

It was on this night, at this church not far from the border wall, that I first met the sisters Susana and Rebeca Hernández. Rebeca, who was always less shy (she was the "border girl" I've already told you about, the syncretic one, the one who'd made love but never had sex), said to me: In every Mexican city there's a small group of rich people. Most of them don't mix with the others. I used to go to church in my grandmother's parish. The governor's house was two blocks away, and if you ever dressed badly they would look at you really bad. So I started coming here. Here everybody is welcome. Did you see that dirty beggar who went all the way up to the altar on his knees?

Yes—

In that long misery ahead of me, I often returned to that church on Avenida Reforma, because Rebeca had said that everybody was welcome—therefore, even me, who had and was nobody, being no longer part of the woman I still loved; and one hot Tuesday toward the end of the following month, which was to say about two weeks after she had left me, I entered that church, and sat in the rearmost bench of one of the four rows, while people came in around me, sighed, fanned themselves, knelt on the *prie-dieux,* and began to pray. There were perhaps a dozen souls in all. Some entered just for a moment, praying briefly and in silence, then rose to cross themselves. Boys with doffed baseball caps, a broken old woman, three anxious dirty men who might have been about to try their luck at the border fence, they came and prayed while birds spoke faintly from somewhere outside the tall white stained-glass-inset coolness. It was a very ordinary church, consecrated in 1955, neither particularly clean nor well built; it had rickety benches. An old grey man knelt on the floor; a taper flickered near the altar. Everything was humdrum, and all the more sincere for that; there was nothing here except faith.

Presently the priest came in. His Mass seemed to me perfunctory, echoing and void; maybe that was the good of it; and maybe thanks to heartsickness my perceptions were as sharp yet distorted as the shadow of a moving bus on a Mexicali street. I prayed: God, I don't ask for Your help. I can't even ask You to help the woman who loved me. All I can do is apologize for my failures, and try to believe that You will do whatever is best.

I refrained from asking for comfort, and got none, but it seemed somehow befitting to watch the other prayers flow past me as steadily and unspectacularly as the brownish water in the drainage ditches, which crawled away, sinking into the dry earth. Around not so very many corners, another heavyset whore stood leaning in the doorway of the Hotel 16 de Septiembre.

Sometimes I walked past the Restaurante Nuevo Oriente, which was the last place I ever sat in Mexicali with her whom I'd loved; after visiting the cathedral we quarreled on a sidewalk bench and then entered the restaurant to keep a hungry friend company; the two of us didn't eat anything, but he did (chow mein; I myself would have ordered *carnitas coloradas:* a heap of scarlet pork garnished with emerald cilantro, another mound of rice on a separate plate, the breasts of life and death); as soon as his plate was bare, we all three returned across the border, and I can't even remember what she and I did then for the remainder of our last night together in Imperial; I do recall that on the following night, coming to rest a few miles outside of Imperial, we also quarreled . . .

But there was more in Barbara's Desert now than pictures woven magically in the air. There were beautiful scenes of farms with houses and barns and fences and stacks, with cattle and horses in the pastures, and fields of growing grain . . . —not to mention that swanlike girl in a white slit gown, showing leg and showing more leg and showing hip and showing buttock and flicking her long dark hair as the disco ball's lights rushed over everybody like foam on the Río Nuevo. A flash of green light on her breast, her panties very white in the cool darkness; off with those, and she slid down the catpole to please the young men who kissed her and tipped her, not to mention the old men who stared. Back in 1925, before there was a church, when Avenida Reforma was still flat dirt crisscrossed with trenches, furrows and the scaffolds of emerging houses, there had been elegant gaming rooms where *not a vulgar greenback, not a piece of silver was allowed to cross the felt. Only gold. Heavy, yellow gold.* Now silver was permitted; surely it must be the constituting element of those cracked grey streets (paved in 1947) whose bumps seemed all the more interesting because thanks to the heat one tended to wander across them so slowly. In the 1830s, back when San Diego still belonged to the entity which I call Imperial, men threw silver dollars at ladies who danced "El Son." Had one of them danced beautifully enough, or if they were relatives or lovers, the man might place his hat on the woman's head at the end; that promised a present. Oh, yes; past days hoard themselves like silver and gold in the vaults of Imperial; nothing is lost. In 1925 the lights of Mexicali's gaming-houses went out promptly at nine, and the whores stood in the courtyards, illuminating their offerings by torchlight. In 1997 they stood in the hotel doorways in the streets, mutely presenting themselves to a world they seemed not to acknowledge, a world of men who would use them, as they used the channels of prayer, like drainage ditches; and these women for their part would use the men for their sustenance. The sky was cool now. Dreams stopped sweating and began to rise into the sky. I dreamed of the woman who'd left me; I yearned; I could have been one of these men who came slowly striding with backthrust shoulders and upraised heads, majestically reaching toward the sweet young night. Moment by moment, more people came out. Mexicali became inhabited. But I wasn't there anymore. I felt hollowed out, ready to cross the border from life to death, from the urgent color and filth of Mexicali to the museum called Calexico, whose regular sidewalks empty long before dusk.

Chapter 44

IMPERIAL'S CENTER

(1904–1907)

It was with a singular feeling that I saw the slowly oncoming waters drive back the tokens of an advancing civilization.

—George Wharton James, 1906

Next, in photograph number P85.13.1, we see a cypress-shaped plume of muck burst out of dark water. The caption: *Calexico, California: Dynamiting in an Attempt to Change Channel of New River July 1906*. In Mexicali, men in sombreros stand at the edge of a street of steep-roofed white houses, watching the waters eat and eat. Now they are almost at the edge of the end house. Far away, a family poses, very still. The President of the United States calls matters *serious and urgent*.

Once upon a time, less than four years into Wilber Clark's Imperial sojourn, the too shallow intake of the Imperial Canal clogged up. In the immortal words of Otis B. Tout, *silt—that's the devil we've got to fight!* Otis B. Tout was right on the money. The Colorado's silt content exceeded the Nile's tenfold.—In 1928 alone the residents of Imperial County will spend one and a half million dollars getting rid of silt.

Since our dollar-conscious California Development Company declines to supply sufficiently powerful dredges, there's nothing for it but to puncture the Colorado again—temporarily, I promise—down in Mexican territory where the Alamo River grade will make up for lost time. *We hesitated about making this cut, not so much because we believed we were incurring danger of the river's breaking through, as from the fact that we had been unable to obtain the consent of the Government of Mexico to make it.* Well, he who hesitates is lost. Our attorney in Mexico City will get that consent, a year or so after the fact.

The Imperial Canal now runs through Mexico for sixty miles (some say fifty-two). *Out West* magazine reproduces a dim photo made more melancholy by its lack of focus: "Mexican Dwellers Along the Canal"—namely, women and girls in long skirts, holding sombreros in their laps; we also see an arrow-weed ramada and a dog's hindquarters.

High water comes early. Unfortunately, the California Development Company is so engrossed in quarreling with the Southern Pacific Railroad about Imperial's future treasures that the neglected cut widens. An engineer now describes the levee as *sandy soil that eats away like so much sugar.* The Southern Pacific wins the dispute. Flood follows flood; the gap's half a thousand feet wide now.

On Thanksgiving 1905, a flood greater than its predecessors wrecks the Company's miserly attempts at diversion. In 1906 it will be worse. (Imperial is a sermon of capital, to be sure—an object parable of short-sighted greed.) *J. C. Thompson has rigged a double cable across New River . . . When one wishes to cross he gets in the box and pulls himself across by the other wire.*

A blurred little photograph in *Out West* magazine depicts a man in a wide hat who stands up to his calves in the Salton Sea; he seems to be the chemist of the salt works; *it was he who discovered the source of the water; searching by boat and wading till the muddy waters from New River were encountered. He then traced the water to Calexico and finally to the source of the trouble, . . . the canal below Yuma,* which in companion photographs looks mirror-wide. Even he, I suspect, can hardly imagine that the Salton Sea's current rate of rise—half an inch per day—will soon increase dramatically enough to drown his salt works for a century and counting.

The New River continues to rush, no matter what channel it might gush in. *The great cataract, which resembles Niagara Falls and is 1,500 to 1,800 yards wide and has a fall of 90 to 100 feet, is working backward at the rate of one-third of a mile a day. If not checked it will . . . ultimately deprive of water every farm along the Colorado River up to the Grand Canyon . . .* Another still more ominous headline: **THE SAFETY OF $100,000,000 IN THE BALANCE.**

(An American doctor remembers Mexicali: *Here was the gay, careless life of the land of mañana . . . A town it was, more distinctively Mexican than it has ever been since. The Colorado washed it away, with only a touch of the corruption which later has become the whole life of the community.*)

Now the Southern Pacific sets out in earnest to close the gap, and on the third attempt, in February 1907, eleven thousand flatcar loads of gravel save the world! Then Northside returns to business, with the Southern Pacific now in full control of the California Development Company. Oh, Harvest Land—Sweet Burning Sand! *Characteristically American,* a settler recalls, *they forgot the river in a week, and in a month few of them could remember the day of closure.*

But the Salton Sea is born. Imperial has a center.

Chapter 45

THE THIRD LINE

(1907)

Because no single version of a map can serve all purposes, maps are commonly produced in several versions to emphasize landforms, surface markings, albedo, or other planetary characteristics.

—*The Compact NASA Atlas of the Solar System,* 2001

Now comes Imperial's third and to date final cut, each boundary not so much enacted as compelled, and with a great deal of bad feeling.

First the line of 1848 divided Imperial into Northside and Southside; then came the line of 1893, which tore off Imperial's topmost pseudopod, bearing it away in Riverside County's jaws. Now in 1907 Imperial County creates itself and breaks away from San Diego, which no longer reaches east of the Anza-Borrego badlands.

(In spite of an old photo I've seen of a wistful crowd beneath the legend BRAWLEY FOR THE COUNTY SEAT, El Centro takes the prize.)

The entity I call Imperial accordingly sprawls through all or part of four bureaucratic divisions: Imperial County, Riverside County, San Diego County, and Baja California, Mexico. In the ancient Norse *Eddas* we read how the lovely Svanhild was executed by being torn apart by four horses; Imperial, just as lovely, is fortunately not quite so killable, but she'll certainly be pulled in four different directions from now on. Her severed parts live on as parts of other bodies, forgetting where they came from; only you and I, reader, will be able to see her entire . . .

Chapter 46

SUBDELINEATIONS: PAINTSCAPES

(1903–1970)

The magnitude, on every level of experience and meaning, of the task in which you have involved me, exceeds all my preconceptions. And it is teaching me to extend myself beyond what I thought was possible for me.

—Mark Rothko, 1966

The first time I came to the Imperial Valley, it unimpressed me as hot, flat, muted and dull. The badlands and mountains in San Diego County appealed to me more; in the most objective sense, they offered entities to look at. Because I'm driven to "understand" things, my own prints and drawings tend to be representational. And mountains are representational, no? From a distance, a mountain may well present itself as something "abstract"—for instance, as a long, wavering zone of blue-grey glazed down by the dusty atmosphere of southern California to a matte acrylic finish; in place of canyons I can discover only a few randomly underpainted brushstrokes. These aren't mountains at all; so what can they be, but background?—And the freeways of Los Angeles, what are *they,* if not grey-washed zones within which spilled beads of traffic display themselves?—So by "representation" I must mean in part "definition." A human face, a sun-cracked old woman's face at Slab City, they're representational. So I respect the myriad figures in a seventeenth-century French monumentalist canvas more than the colored rectangles of, say, Mark Rothko, no matter that the French painter's allegories might be stale if not drolly absurd! I've enlisted with the Artistic Border Patrol. A painter who proves his ability to render the human form competently has flashed me a valid passport. I'll permit his entry into Northside. Should the face be proportioned properly, then I can trust him to make blotches and squiggles of his own proportioning. On the other hand, if he "can't draw," then how can I judge his proficiency when he paints in an unknown language? I could learn this language, but how bitter I'd feel if his grammar turned out to be fraudulent! Some of us speak English only, we citizens of Northside.

Kandinsky I trust, because his early work identifies him as a competent purveyor of images whose "accuracy" is intuitively measurable. Klee and Picasso may be "abstractionists," but their pictures remain pictorial enough in the old sense for me to appreciate the figures. Imperial's petroglyphs and pictographs for their part offer me simple yet deliberate geometric organizations. In about 1600, the Elizabethan miniaturist Hilliard writes: *Now knowe that all* Paintinge *imitateth nature, or the life in euery thinge, it resembleth so fare forth as the* Painters *memory or skill can serue him to expresse . . . but of all things the perfection is to imitate the face of man kind, or the hardest part of it, and which carieth most prayesse and comendations.* More specifically, *the goodnes of a picture after the liffe* (life) consists of *life, favor and likeness.* What comprises likeness? When I see a nude by Gauguin, I can judge it. I have loved women; so has Gauguin; I trust and believe in him. But when I see the rectangular zones of a color within the fieldscape of a Rothko image, how can I determine its degree of perfection?

Of course this diffculty, which I so stiffly resist acknowledging, arises even with that most representational of all arts, photography. Perhaps you know the famous "Clearing Winter Storm" by Ansel Adams. In this view of New Inspiration Point (December 1940), the artist's eight-by-ten-inch camera has framed a sort of bowl: On the left, a slope stubbled with snow and trees curves ever more gently toward the tree-choked center, which then meets a craggier upcurve to the right. It's a lovely, peaceful composition, stamped with life, favor and likeness. One could draw a horizontal line from the point where the lefthand curve ascends beyond the image frame to a certain crag about two-thirds of the way to the righthand edge; from this mostly snowy tooth begins a dropoff to a waterfall, after which the bowl curves up again, this time rising considerably above its lefthand counterpart before departing the frame. Is this photograph balanced or not? The vale between rocks is nicely centered; on the other hand, Adams could have panned his tripod head more to the left, so that both of Yosemite's walls would depart the borders of the picture at precisely the same coordinate along the vertical axis. But then that narrow, sunken, shadowed place of snowy trees to which our eye is drawn would have been off center. What was the artist's thinking? *I first related the trees to the background mountains as well as the possible camera positions allowed, and I waited for the clouds to form within the top areas of the image.* There seems to be a hint of expediency here; and indeed we are informed that the camera could not have been moved more than a hundred feet to the left without reaching *the nearly perpendicular cliffs above the Merced River,* nor to the right without encountering *a screen of trees* or *an impractical position on the road;* nor forward, which *would invite disaster on a very steep slope falling to the east,* nor backward, for that must *bring the esplanade and the protective rock wall into the field of focus. Hence the camera position was determined . . .* It still seems to me that Adams could have panned an inch left, as opposed to moving the camera a much greater distance in the same direction, and that had he done so, the slightly altered angle of view would not have distorted his distant subject appreciably. But who am I to say that the distortion would not have been appreciable to *him*? Nor can I claim that the composition as I've hypothetically reenvisioned it would be any more *favored,* more beautiful; presumably its *life and likeness* would remain as unimproved as Imperial before irrigation.

What is *life*? At the end of his commentary on this photograph, Adams, whose pictures do not emote to me at all—they're beautiful meditations in which I can refresh myself (as I also can when in "real life" I spy dewdrops on a fern); but they never cause me to *feel* as, say, a Napoleonic battle-scene might—insists that a photographer's subject ought to be what moves him. *Intellectual and critical preevaluation of work,* concludes this extraordinarily meticulous preevaluator, *is not helpful to creativity; regimenting perception into functional requirements is likewise restrictive.*

I go down Imperial's hot wide street (the shady boardwalks, being more private, usually stink of urine); standing in the barrenness and narrowness of No Man's Land, I try to see why I would ever desire a non-representationalist to paint me a sunset in a date orchard. (Well, why should a sunset be painted at all? And why not? Ansel Adams's image of dewdrops on a fern is no more or less valuable than dewdrops on a fern.) Why would I ever want to open the aperture of my view camera's lens wider than f/64? As it is, I'm obtaining my maximum depth of field; I want canyons on my mountains, not brushwork. I don't care to exclude any detail; everything is precious to me.

All the same, Imperial is flatness; Imperial is background. Shall we approach its abstractness by degrees; just as Rothko approached his final commission?

It commenced as early as 1948, although back then the colors were too bright and puddled to be Imperial; they actually seemed *interesting* at first glance, which would never do. But gradually the inset daubs become more rectilinear; he was still in his red period then, with globs of blue or yellow on those fiery fields. The "Mauve Intersection" of 1949 encloses more yellow and white than red within itself, and its blue is as dark as the Salton Sea; it's rectangular, like all the rest; it could be a reservoir or a flooded field. Just as on the way from the Anza-Borrego Desert to Imperial the country's washes, arroyos and canyons keep thinning out (it's actually surprising that God allowed anything but flatness into Imperial County, but He did, here and there), so in the career of Rothko concretions of representation keep thinning away. He tells Stanley Kunitz that he wants to erase the Old Masters and *start new* in *a new land.* He's coming into his Imperial. So many people I know prefer Borrego's mountains! And I can see their point; I'm that way myself; I prefer *life, favor and likeness.* What do Rothko's paintings bear the likeness of? Until I know that, I can't "understand" them.

Here's one from that same year—called, as are so many, "Untitled"; while it's a far cry from the famous Blackform Paintings of 1960–64, it's already conspicuously dark within its glowing edges; the sun has almost set over a glinting-wet field; other colors lie hidden in it, under the dark water; we will never get to the bottom of them. When morning comes . . .—but of course morning will never come to the Blackform District of Imperial. In self-defense I turn to another bright painting; its luminescence partakes of what used to be called "false color" in infrared renditions of Mercury or Venus; perhaps somewhere on earth there are fields like this, of mustard and rapeseed sown in with patches of wildflowers here and there, but they're too strange; they're too inhuman. Bright, bright! His biographer Breslin feels that these so-called multiforms (namely, *his classic simplified format of two or three stacked rectangles which seem to locate a viewer at a "doorway" between the physical and transcendent worlds*) rarely appear to have *emerged from a torturous creative process. Their warm, intense colors, their fertile variety of shape and hue, their ebullient sense of freedom and creative search* express *infatuation with his medium*. We can look at Imperial that way, too. We can admire the field-colors and field-rectangles of it, noting that the Mexican sweat which waters Imperial cannot affect its beauty one way or another. How intense those colors are! And warm, very certainly, and fertile—where did that fertility come from? What is Imperial? Simply because its patterns are large and strange, does that make them inhuman? If not, then Rothko's canvases aren't inhuman, either. They rarely appear to have emerged from a torturous creative process. Not many successes do. The blankness of a late Rothko canvas gets first touched by glue infused with hand-ground pigment, then painted in oil, then glazed, the glazes often containing more pulverized pigments and even whole eggs. His associates remember him as pondering over these unsown fields, sometimes for days. And of all that, nothing's left except the result. Borrego's mountains lie unseen behind us now, not to mention the so-called automatist works of the 1940s, which are almost Klee-like. Even the ovals and circles are gone. Inhuman, did I say? The golden rectangle of painting Number 10 (1950) has been called a "humanized sun" because it will not burn the eyes. In 1951 Rothko paints a field of two red lips with wheatgrass growing around them and between their parting; maybe this is Alberta somewhere, not Imperial; but he's getting closer, I can feel it. I'm getting closer; the airplane lands; the paintings feel bigger and bigger. *To paint a small picture is to place yourself outside your experience* . . . he once said. *However you paint the large picture, you are in it. It isn't something you command.* Then come the paintings of yellows and blues: sky-fields and wheat-fields bordering one another on the same page of the County Assessor's property book, but which county? What if it were Imperial already? What can I learn from these softly blended rectangles of color within their canvas plots? Is this what life is? Is it what Imperial is? Why and how can it make me feel anything? *What were they made of, after all?* marvels one collector. *A monochrome flat ground and a few blobs of color. Larger and smaller rectangular canvases.* And more and more of less and less. The often expressed idea that "Rothko painted a vacuum" holds truth; so does the painter's own assertion that an artist steadily works toward increasing clarity. But isn't representation, by being definition, clarity? How can a vacuum stand in for that? And if it can, wouldn't it follow that everything is the same as nothing? How could Rothko do it? How could he somehow replicate *the emotions present in the orchestral music he so loved?* But he did. *Rothko's paintings grow beautiful, reaching out to a viewer with their sensuous color* . . . These boundaries between color-sectors in each field, I can't quite "understand" them, although when I think about a vacant lot in sight of the international fence, something hot and living but fallow in human terms, something altered most peculiarly by delineation, I can almost put my finger on what Rothko is trying to "say." (He knows the secret of Imperial.) But now, just as I think I might be onto something, his colors begin to become earthier and more muted, the orange descending to tan, the red closer to poppy or even chocolate than it used to be to lipstick; Rothko is going agricultural! We vegetate forever. Do you remember what Judge Farr wrote in 1918? *The sleeper dreams of his rapidly ripening fruit and their early arrival in the markets to catch the top prices ahead of other competitors in less favorable regions.* This is the kind of dream we dream, but without commerce; there's only fruit, growing imperceptibly within those subplots of color in the Rothko Tract. (Breslin again: *Rothko's empty canvases are filled with ceaseless movement, a perceptual abundance.*) It's scarcely a steady progression; here in 1954 I find more blue-and-yellow, more bloody red and urine-yellow, but over time the colors do mute and darken; in the "Saffron" of 1957 I once again see Canadian wheat-plains; in the "Black Stripe" of 1958 I find a reservoir of real darkness; it's night on the Salton Sea, and this pool perhaps contains the *aguas negras* of the New River. That same year, Rothko paints "Four Darks in Red." Sunset bleeds upon the irrigated zones of a dark wet field. It's so mysterious; it is saying something to me, maybe something about Rothko's suicide; I want to "understand" it but cannot. If I write a book about Imperial, will I comprehend it? If not, what did I do wrong? About the boundaries between his sub-zones of color I wrote *softly blended.* Imperial as seen from the air remains a chessboard of almost shockingly distinct agricultural squares. But wait until you've seen a hundred-and-nineteen-degree day at Bombay Beach, where sky and sea ooze together, the horizon erased by haze. You've fallen into a Rothko canvas then. Or when you descend west to east, coming from the high desert near Tecate into a hazier softer brownish-greenness of Mexicali's fields, you sink into heat and haze. Call it Rothko. "White and Black on Wine" (1959) is another field in another sunset; soon it will be dark and then too late forever; the sky is white like a new white car between the date palms at sunset—but here in Rothko County, local ordinances prohibit the beards and wickerwork skins of the palm trees; there's a law against the Mexicali I love, whose walls are painted with fishes, shrimps, and *femme fatale* octopi on the facades of seafood restaurants. Are these losses a loss?* Certainly, but no matter how much I want to see and "understand" all within Imperial, I can't help the fact that details drain away in that sweet summer darkness when Judge Farr lies down to sleep; he thinks that he'll get up tomorrow but it's already 1918, the date of his apoplexy; last week in El Centro I purchased a copy of his death certificate. And we're all going down there, deep into the rich silt soil of past seas; our ocean must run dry; the sun fails; we thought we hated the sun because it sweltered us but it helped us rush our fruit to market. Softening sunlight makes the desert green; the western edge of Imperial glows pale with Plaster City's sparse white structures in the distance; Rothko paints squares of paleness; I believe he owns *likeness* because east of Ocotillo a zone of flat white sand runs all the way to Westmorland. *The sleeper dreams of his rapidly ripening fruit.* He dreams and dreams forever. By the time of the Harvard Murals of 1961–62 we find Rothko planting a lot of grey and maroon in his homestead; *we need have no fear that our lands will not become better and better as the years go by.* In either 1961 or 1964 he paints "Untitled (Light Plum and Black)"; to me it seems to be bursting with darkness and grief, but maybe he was happy and I am imagining all this. Here's "Untitled (Plum and Dark Brown)." Imperial's silt is sown but not yet harvested; the dark water feeds it. And then that fuzzy-edged bloody rectangle in an indigo-greyness (number 207, painted in 1961), what does that remind me of? I used to think that red was too "unrealistic," but that was before I saw the Salton Sea in those flooded lots beyond the levee at Bombay Beach. I *know* that the Salton Sea can be red like that; it can also be reddish-green; tea-green; greenish-brown; and as for Rothko's strange blue, I remember what I saw at that restricted geothermal plant near Cerro Prieto south of Mexicali; that canal or drain or whatever it was, a source of the New River, was an impossibly glowing blue! In Imperial anything's possible. You think that only dullish tans and beiges flourish in that place, but what about the yellow-green spray of palo verde bushes west of Brawley? More blue in this next painting—well, here comes a line of blue beyond the orchards: the Salton Sea. (The sign says ***FIRE DEPARTMENT VOLUNTEERS WANTED.***) I give in; Rothko can paint Imperial any color he likes. What then *is* Imperial? It may be something richer, literally more fruitful than I can ever devour. Can two or three rectangles of oil paint likewise add up to Imperial? And if so, is that the result of Rothko's genius, or of the obvious fact (not that it used to be obvious to me) that

*It could be that I exaggerate them. In Rothko County you can still find, for instance, the waist-high counter of orange tiles in the chicken-and-beans restaurant in Mexicali. If Rothko paints it, you may not know that there are tiles in that smeary band of orange, but that gives one's imagination something to do.

everything is inconceivably grand? What is Imperial? (What is New Inspiration Point? Did Ansel Adams "understand" it?) Imperial is "Untitled." Back in the days when the conquistadors claimed it without knowing it, and in the centuries when bread was light, Imperial was untitled; now what is it? Sector El Centro. I give in. I study a Rothko canvas, and its deliberate labor helps me see beauty; as a result, I see more beauty in Imperial, too. Rothko can paint Imperial any way he likes (except the last way, the way of the Houston Chapel, which achieves his stated goal of being *something you don't want to look at.*) Oh, but Rothko's giving in, too; he paints red on red and black on black, shutting down his tonal scale; for instance, "Number 8," painted in 1964, could be a representationalist painter's primed and black-gessoed board without any image. Rothko calls it finished. The representationalist for his part will paint subtractively, just as time does. (Do you want to know what's left when a painter takes blackness away? Imperial! Imperial's subsectors of earth are nearly as white as salt.) Rothko's mother dies in 1948, when the colored multiforms commence. In 1957 he begins to take away everything but blackness. His name for this project of reduction: "the dark pictures." Staring into a Rothko image, I discern a darker black rectangle within the other black rectangle, and within the darkest black may dwell prior hints and rustlings of night. "Untitled," "Untitled" and "Untitled." Black and grey, grey and white, slate-blue (I remember driving westward on Highway 8, with the pale blue mountains beyond Imperial floating above a snowy haze); nothing is or can be distinct; we've almost come to that chapel in Houston where, in one admirer's words, *all that remains of Rothko's once rich colors is a deep darkness from which everything . . . slowly emerges.*

Chapter 47

IMPERIAL REPRISE

(1781–1920)

> They had all kinds of picturesque names for highways [in southern California] . . . Also, there were Spanish names, reverently cherished by the pious realtors of the country.
>
> —Upton Sinclair, 1927

1

The Head or Father of each family must be a Man of the Soil. . . *He stood staunch as Mount Signal.* The women had each two undergarments a year, a gown and a blanket. *Tell the girls that this is the best place for marrying they ever saw.* I think we all feel sorry for 'em.

It was altogether one of the most miserable countries in the world. *It is a miserable place, without pasture and with very bad water.* WELCOME TO CALIFORNIA. **WATER IS HERE**. *And in material advantages they are already well supplied.*

I can't help believing in people . . . The Indians do all the hard work. *I found about 150 Indians beside the women, who fled upon my arrival.* Soon the endemic flora will have been displaced largely by these foreigners. *It is predicted by the railroad companies, that this influx will continue.* **THE DESERT DISAPPEARS**.

2

There is plenty of good land to be had but all Government land worth taking is about gone. *As this is nearly all desert we have not included it.*

The wonderfully fertile valley of the New River in the eastern part of the county is now being opened up . . . *Rothko's empty canvases are filled with ceaseless movement, a perceptual abundance.* Green was becoming abundant, and the whole area was dotted with the homes of hopeful, industrious, devoted persons. *We need have no fear that our lands will not become better and better as the years go by.* He has even spread his enterprises over the international boundary into Mexico.

3

I have never been cheated out of a dollar in my life. It would be so convenient to carry on a farm . . . when all the hard and dirty work is performed by apprentices. **WATER IS HERE**. *Every house had its inclosure of vineyard, which resembled a miniature orchard.* A brick building or two bear mute witness to the fact that Dixieland still awaits the coming of water on a higher level. **WATER IS HERE**.

PART THREE

REVISIONS

Chapter 48

FUTURES

(1883–2007)

> In compiling the present report, we have found the area to be characterized by little systematic knowledge of either its prehistory or its archaeological inventory.
>
> —Bureau of Land Management, 1974

In 1883, Wallace W. Elliott announces in his county history that *the future of San Bernardino Valley is fruit culture.* How might that future look? Helen Hunt Jackson's famous tearjerker *Ramona,* published in 1884, describes *one of those midsummer days of which Southern California has so many in spring. The almonds had bloomed and the blossoms fallen; the apricots also, and the peaches and pears; on all the orchards of these fruits had come a filmy tint of green, and the orange groves dark and glossy like laurel.*

Of course the future of San Bernardino Valley, and of Ramonaland, too, not to mention Los Angeles and suchlike fruitpatches, is actually subdivisions.

"NO PARTICULAR COMPARATIVE ADVANTAGE"

But why couldn't the future of southern California have been, for instance, barley?

In 1884, wheat production in California begins to recede; in 1880 it was fifty-four million bushels; in 1906, it will be twenty-seven thousand. *There has been a general parallelism between the amount of rain and the amount of wheat produced; but as yet irrigation is little used for this crop.* In any event, wheat declines (in the Imperial Valley, a rust infection kills much of it off); barley goes up.

Mr. Paul Foster, who analyzed Imperial County agriculture statistics for me and is himself a grainland farmboy, describes wheat as *a classic swing commodity, with farmers moving in and out of wheat (see acreages planted) based on commodity prices. The same holds true to a lesser extent for barley and milo. Imperial has no particular comparative advantage in wheat production over other regions, so production of wheat and other grains shifted generally with beef prices (another opportunistic commodity) and away from commodities that might produce more stable profits over the long run. Isn't everyone tempted to double down at blackjack when the opportunity arises?*

NEW YORK'S BARLEY YEARS

But why wasn't southern California's future barley?

In *Appletons' Annual Cyclopaedia*, 1892, the entry for California informs us: *Two States in the Union produce half of the entire barley crop of the country, and of those two California takes the lead, New York being second . . . The bay counties and those adjacent to the ocean are the largest barley producers.*

Judge Farr writes that the history of Imperial County began with grain and alfalfa. *Barley and wheat were the winter crops and grain sorghums were the summer crops. Alfalfa was usually planted as soon as the land was properly leveled.* Both wheat and barley acreages were already dwindling in the pioneer years.

APRICOT HOPES

What would replace them? Fruit trees would come once the pioneers could pay for them. Someday Imperial's orange groves would be laurel-glossy and her future might also contain wide acres of pearscapes *(one orchard consists of sixty acres and is reported as successful)*; and since *it is almost unbelievable how fast apricot trees grow in this Valley*, why shouldn't the future of Imperial be fruit culture? Unfortunately, in 2005 the gross value of Imperial County's fruits and tree nuts was $37,061,000 out of $1,236,066,000 for all commodities, or less than three percent of the total.

What then were the top five crops of 2005? Number one was cattle, as in the old days of Mexican California; Judge Farr knew of Imperial cattle ranches both north and south of the international line; and by the time his history was published in 1918, livestock was *an important part of the Valley's industries;* in 2005, cattle made up almost twenty-three percent of gross revenues! Number two was alfalfa, another constant from Judge Farr's time. Then came leaf lettuce, carrots and just plain lettuce.

To an agronomist, what is Imperial? Imperial is cantaloupes and watermelons; Imperial is lettuce, asparagus and, sporadically, cotton.

In 2005, cantaloupes did respectably, being ranked number ten (watermelons were number thirty); asparagus was a mediocre number thirty-one; cotton lint was number twenty-five. Poor sad citrus was number forty. Perhaps even in Judge Farr's time that outcome was suspected, as I infer by reading between the lines of faint praise: *During the past years nearly every kind of fruit and nuts grown have been planted here, and it is possible to raise at least enough of them for family use, with the exception of the cherry and the walnut.*

THE CRYSTAL BALL

What might California's wheat blackjack players have been thinking at the beginning of their American game? How many moves ahead did they scheme? Did they expect to move in and out of it as commodity prices dictated, or were they set for life? Did they possess what we pompously call a "vision"? And was that vision subverted or fulfilled when wheatscapes became first citrusscapes, then houses, factories, freeways?

As for Imperial's fruit gamblers, can they be said to have gone wrong? Citrus continues to thrive in the Bard Subdistrict; I always buy a sack of blood oranges when I pass through there.

Setting citrus aside, and a few other flashes in the pan such as dairy, Imperial County's agricultural productions have remained remarkably constant over her century of autonomous life (she remains officially a hundred years old as I write this, in 2007). As for southern California, she has changed into a thirsty city lady. And Imperial owns the water. That is why she and Imperial are enemies.

But Imperial is also at cross purposes with herself.

There is in America a nomadic race of beings, always pressing toward the frontier and carving empires to endure for the ages. Call them blackjack players. Some of them played for homesteads, like Wilber Clark. After all, there was a hundred-and-sixty-acre limitation on the books. Taxpayers' money, spent by the millions on reclamation dams, was meant to keep the frontier open a trifle longer for the sake of pioneering families. On the other hand, what is any limitation to a true empire seeker, but a challenge? I can't help believing in people.

It is but a few pages since we buried Wilber Clark, and said goodbye to his widow. Before he sinks out of our memories, let us now make the acquaintance of his antithesis, the Chandler Syndicate.

Another still more striking opposition must be laid out in this section, in order for us to appreciate the strange nuances of Imperial's history north and south: Mexican and American Imperial dream very different agrarian dreams. Now that settlement has begun in earnest in both of those zones, it is high time to introduce you to those two reifications of happiness, the self-sufficient American homestead and the Mexican *ejido*.

Chapter 49

HARRY CHANDLER'S HOMESTEAD

(1898–1938)

> The model ranch of the Valley, owned by a stock company of Los Angeles businessmen, comprises 1,100 acres of highly developed ranch land in California and 876,000 acres just across the line in Mexican territory.
>
> —Edgar F. Howe and Wilbur Jay Hall, 1910

When I think of him, I remember the old sunken lobby of the Biltmore Hotel in Los Angeles, with its echoing fountain, whose sound is surprisingly loud given the slenderness of the white streams; I see the vaulted ceiling's gilded ribs and Moorish stars. Some of the chandeliers resemble immense yellow-glowing quartz crystals, and others are more like glass beetles.

I think of his cotton sampling room in Mexicali, *with a north exposure, the entire length of the room from floor to ceiling being of glass. The soft, subdued tint, light blue, on walls and ceiling,* not to mention the various window shades, *combine to make it possible to have at any time of day an ideal light.* Outside, a fountain plays, and there is a garden of appropriately giant cacti.

In a blurry old photograph we see him standing beside and slightly behind the President of Mexico, who gazes away. Mr. Chandler wears a black stovepipe hat which shadows his eyes. A benign fringe of white beard (or is it simply Mexicali sunlight?) clings like moss below his mouth, and he seems to be smiling in his black and white suit. The year is about 1925. If so, the President, who seems out of focus, must have been Calles. Chandler's wife and daughter sat beside him at the inauguration.

Here is Harry Chandler in 1922, receiving a previous President of Mexico's invitation to raise with him personally all issues of the development of Baja California. In return, Chandler promises that the *Los Angeles Times* will publish nothing but nice things about Mexico and her President. In practically the same breath, the President signs decrees undoing the titles on which Chandler's property rights were based, and nationalizing one of Chandler's holdings: Volcano Lake, the source of the Río Nuevo. But since this is Mexico, the President can cancel the undoing at any time, should the Chandler Syndicate give satisfaction. The so-called Volcano

Lake Compromise rings like a deal between statesmen, and indeed it is: Who could be more literally Imperial than Harry Chandler himself, eighty-five-percent owner of the Colorado Land River Company, Emperor of Mexicali, San Fernando, Hollywoodland, Tejon and God knows how many other domains?

But who is more *typically and fundamentally* Imperial—Wilber Clark or Harry Chandler? Whose career says most about the American dream?

ALL HAIL NORTHSIDE

The following portion of Mr. Chandler's American dream (for of course he possessed many, many other portions) took place on the other side of the line, where everything was blanker, and all means and ends lay readier to hand. Why not invoke the American dream just the same? After all, in its service, we'd taken half of Mexico and drawn Imperial's first line. Moreover, his obituary assures us that he *took a prominent part in the organization of the company which built the irrigation canals which transfomed Imperial Valley from a desert into the most productive farming region on the continent.*

POSTERITY'S OPTIONS

In the Imperial Valley, Wilber Clark has been forgotten. In the Mexicali Valley, Harry Chandler is remembered and hated. They blame him for locking up the land for decades, for creating their "Chinese problem," for making them his peons, for being the rich gringo whose shadow they could not escape. Even the Salton Sea accident is sometimes called *Chandler's mistake.*

CAPITAL OR LAND?

Up in Northside, we (supposedly) encounter what has been described as "the agrarian mind," one of whose preeminent qualities is *a longing for independence—that is, for an appropriate degree of personal and local self-sufficiency. Agrarians wish to earn and deserve what they have.* I would call that a fair if faintly sentimentalized description of Wilber Clark as I imagine him.

How might we characterize the divide between Wilber Clark and his opposite? I continue to quote the same source, the literary eco-farmer Wendell Berry: *The fundamental difference between agrarianism and industrialism* is this: whereas indus-*

*Berry approvingly quotes, and seemingly derives his dichotomy from, a 1930 compilation entitled *I'll Take My Stand: The South and the Agrarian Tradition.* One history of the Great Depression refers to this volume as "a nativistic reaction to a changing world"; in the historian's opinion, its essays uniformly ignore

trialism is a way of thought based on monetary capital and technology, agrarianism is a way of thought based on land. Agrarianism, furthermore, is a culture at the same time that it is an economy. Industrialism is an economy before it is a culture.

In sum, the difference between Clark and Chandler was as the difference between the low earth-hills at the beginning of Painted Canyon and the high blue-grey mountains on the west side of the Salton Sea, which is to say, the difference between mere sweat and capital itself.

A MAP OF THE MEXICALI VALLEY

Wilber Clark was born in about 1861; Harry Chandler in about 1864. Harry Chandler lived longer and was richer—definitely richer.

In spite of his thousands of volumes of Americana and first editions, Wilber Clark has, as I have intimated, left fewer fossil traces in the shale of history than Judge Farr's biographical entry caused me to expect. Perhaps that is because he was a typical member of his class.

Harry Chandler was most certainly typical of his. After all, E. T. Earl, who owned the *Los Angeles Express,* possessed three million corporate acres in Sinaloa; and William Randolph Hearst, who expressed himself through the *Los Angeles Examiner,* had his private Mexican concessions. Chandler's homestead was comparable to theirs, and I will detail it as follows:

On an undated map of the Mexicali Valley, faded and stained, made probably before 1940 since in the margin a different hand has pencilled within Mesa de Sonora: *Inundated since 1940,* we see Mexicali in the form of a faint pencil grid the length and half the width of the first joint of my forefinger; it rests near the westward apex of an inverted triangle stretching from my shoulder just past my fully outstretched hand, and I am a tall man; this figure comprises the Mexicali Valley itself, suitably subdivided into the following properties: **A**, just below Mexicali, is the property of a certain C.R.L. Co. S.A., and consists of 906 steaming hectares (2,238 hot acres, or if you please 474,456 square feet of heaven) running all the way down to Canal Packard, which is a tiny, tiny piece of the valley; as it chances, **B**'s 203 hectares slightly north of the east-west-running Canal Corona belong to this same C.R.L. Co. S.A.; **C**, separated from **B** by *colonias* numbers one through ten, is the merest 36 hectares, and happens to belong to the C.R.L. Co. S.A. **D**, which the map informs us is the legal possession of the C.R.L. Co. S.A., consists of 4,603 hectares. **E**, which coincidentally belongs to the C.R.L. Co. S.A., is a 184-

"the failures of an economic system that had created a culture of dependency and subjection": the exploitation of sharecroppers and tenant farmers, the rape of the soil for the sake of King Cotton—in short, the evils which Berry lays at the door of industrialism.

hectare triangle near the east vertex of the great triangle, next to three deep wells. **F** is 862 hectares; **G** is 604 hectares; both are in keeping of the same entity. **H** is 5,607 hectares; **I**, 12,384 hectares; **J**, 4,806 hectares; **K**, 7,985 hectares; **L** is 7,616 hectares; and at first I thought that nobody owned them, until I saw, printed leisurely-wise across their areas and subdelineations, **COLORADO RIVER LAND COMPANY, S.A.** Strange to say, **M**, 1,437 hectares in extent, really does remain unlabeled. Just west of that lie the substantial two *colonias* Nuevo León and Coahuilla, 6,321.1301 hectares in total; the Colorado River Land Company lacks those. But **N**, 210 hectares, belongs to the C.R.L. Co. S.A. **O**, at 12,161 hectares, a bit northwest of El Mayor, is included in the same super-zone (walled in by the Sierra El Mayor on the left; the Colorado River runs down the middle; on the right I see the Mesa de Andrade, the Rancho Caterpillar, and other makers) as **P** at 9,275 hectares, **Q** at 12,765 hectares, **R** at 10,172 hectares, **S** at 4,145 hectares, **T** at 4,868 hectares, **U West** at 7,883 hectares, and **U East** at 8,305 hectares; the Colorado River Land Company controls them all. On the top left of the great triangle and eating into it from the side, is an unowned blankness of about twenty percent . . . and there goes most of the Colorado River delta.

ANOTHER PRAYER TO THE MINISTRY OF CAPITAL

Harry Chandler *versus* Wilber Clark, subsistence homesteader *versus* landed capitalist, that is certainly one divide which the history of Imperial leads us to meditate on. Another dichotomy remains to be considered: Harry Chandler *versus* Jefferson Worth.

Did the latter ever exist? We remember that he was modeled on W. F. Holt. *He works too hard to have time to sit around the corner store stove and whittle with the rest of the fellows, so when they get out to work they find the Holt fields are all plowed . . . Lots of people don't like Holt; lots do.*

If we consider *The Winning of Barbara Worth* not as "literature," from which standpoint it obviously falls as far short as some Imperial drainage ditch gasping out its last trickle into the sand, but as the capitalist equivalent of socialist realism, which was never "realistic" at all but in fact deployed stereotypes and happy endings to show everybody how life ought to be, then this novel becomes as revealing as any manifesto. I have always believed that in spite of the dreariness, inefficiency, menace and sheer murderousness with which it has been most often practiced, socialism *as an idea* remains superior to capitalism, which is really a philosphy of selfishness. Marx wrote: *From each according to his ability, to each according to his needs.* To me this is as sublime as anything in the Gospels; and to envision a system under which we actually live for each other and a better world is wonderful for me.

Hence I cannot help but sympathize with *ejiditarios.* By contrast, the social order in which American Imperial and I now happen to find ourselves consists of freedom, selfish aloofness and disinterest in our neighbors, greed, corporate in place of "proletarian" ugliness, hierarchy, jingoistic commercialism. Who could justify all that better than a writer of "capitalist realism"? The works of Ayn Rand come to mind, exemplified by her *Virtue of Selfishness.* As for Harold Bell Wright, he professed, as had William Smythe in his *Conquest of Arid America,* that the irrigation of Imperial was actually undertaken for some higher good:

The methods of The King's Basin Land and Irrigation Company . . . were the methods of capital, impersonal, inhuman, the methods of a force governed by laws as fixed as the laws of nature, neither cruel nor kind . . . The methods of Jefferson Worth were the methods of a man laboring with his brother men, sharing their hardships, sharing their returns; a man using money as a workman uses his tools . . . It was inevitable that the Company and Jefferson Worth should war.

James Greenfield served Capital; Jefferson Worth sought to make Capital serve the race.

As you might have guessed, I am skeptical that the methods of Jefferson Worth ever existed. We find Mr. Holt hiring a special train to bring Angeleno investors to the Imperial Valley; the Southern Pacific Railroad commissioned him to reconnoiter Mexican Imperial for precisely the sort of irrigation projects soon to be undertaken by Harry Chandler—who for his own part would argue in due course that his methods were good for Mexico. His justifications were as milk-white as the Salton Sea sometimes appears to be at twilight. To *agraristas* of the 1930s, his enterprise would be the *horrible company that hoarded the land.*

FRIENDS OF JEFFERSON WORTH

And now to our tale, whose plot might be summed up as follows: **THE DESERT DISAPPEARS.**

You may remember that Wilber Clark's arrival in Imperial was early enough, and hence newsworthy enough, to be reported by a *Los Angeles Times* correspondent. The year before that, a *Times* editor named J. W. Jeffrey sent back such glowing accounts of Imperial's prospects that Harry Chandler and four colleagues paid a visit and filed land claims. Indeed, such was his eagerness that Chandler apparently became the third person to file a claim on Imperial Valley Lands.

I now list some of the members of his syndicate.

General Harrison Gray Otis, who then owned the *Los Angeles Times,* was Chandler's father-in-law. (After he died, the syndicate would propose to rename its still hypothetical railroad terminus at Port Isabel, Sonora, Port Otis. For isn't to name

Imperial to possess her?) At the time of their purchase from Andrade, Chandler was the *Times'* business manager. He would inherit the entire enterprise. As for C. E. Richardson, Albert McFarland and Frank X. Pfaffinger; they all worked for the *Times* in more middling capacities. The Title Insurance and Trust Company got represented by Messieurs Allen, Clark and Brant; the Los Angeles and Salt Lake Railroad Company, a subsidiary of the Southern Pacific, found occasion to send in its own tentacle; First National Bank and Merchants Bank both had their men in, and although I'll end here, the truth is that I'm not done. For instance, I never mentioned that builder of interurban railways, Moses H. Sherman. Why then should I personalize the Colorado River Land Company as Harry Chandler? Because for most of its long tenure in the Mexicali Valley, he owned eighty-five percent of the stock.

Here is an epitaph for all those boomers, empire-builders and union-haters: *There is no doubt that they sought wealth and power, but they also viewed themselves as performing a civic duty* by helping to build the support facilities of an expanding Los Angeles* . . . In other words, *Jefferson Worth sought to make Capital serve the race.*

HIGH FINANCE AND A LOW CANAL

In his hypocritically threadbare fictionalization (he's such a pious Imperialist that he never would have blasphemed against the Ministry of Capital, so why not name names and be done with it?), Otis B. Tout informs us that *Henry Auster, head of a syndicate of wealthy men, had been farsighted enough* (would a Marxist put it quite this way?) *to lend quite a sizable sum of money to the careless scion of an ancient Castilian family some years before. The family held a grant of land of more than half a million acres in Mexico.* This Henry Auster expressed the Los Angeles Idea very well and called in his debt when the time was right. In Mr. Tout's novel, the Mexican voluptuary is happy enough to shrug off his half-million arid acres in exchange for forgiveness of the debt and enough money to keep him in cigarettes and gambling-chips; money is here; money will always be here. Later he reads in the newspaper that the Auster Syndicate is irrigating half a million acres of Mexican Imperial. How does he feel then? That's not in the story.

But in his official history of the Imperial Valley, Mr. Tout is content with the more accurate observation that the land *was purchased outright from the Mexican government.*

The Mexican government originally consisted of two millionaires: Guillermo An-

*Some historians have implied that the Chandler Syndicate was the William Walker of capital. Harry Chandler was actually indicted for attempting a revolution against Mexico to seize Baja California, but got acquitted, and probably rightfully so.

drade, on whose eponymous mesa (they now call it simply *la mesa*) I generally find campesinos harvesting green onions; and Thomas Blythe, the founder of Blythe. What had happened was that when Andrade's first attempt at a syndicate failed, Blythe stepped in. Thanks to Blythe's money, Andrade's connections, and of course the eternal beneficence of that upstanding Minister of Capital, President Díaz, the partners *now held title to virtually the entire Mexican portion of the delta . . .*

When Blythe died in 1883, and thirty court cases eventually decided against both the estranged mistress and the current mistress who'd passed as his niece, the illegitimate daughter won what remained. Through maneuvers of his own, Andrade eventually got most of his Mexican land back, but by so doing he overextended himself. He sold some of his lands to a Petaluma syndicate in 1887–88. Clever Harry Chandler would eventually gain possession of these, too, once the rival syndicate defaulted.

In 1898, the year before the California Development Company suckered George Chaffey into taking on the Imperial Valley's reclamation-through-irrigation, an entity named the California-Mexico Land and Cattle Company bought from Andrade 832,337 more acres of the Mexicali Valley, which is to say nearly ninety percent of it—an area larger than the future Imperial Irrigation District. In due course, this landowner became known as the Colorado River Land Company.*

But first, and we are still in 1898, the California Development Company created a puppet called the Sociedad de Irrigación y Terrenos de la Baja California, S.A., one of whose stockholders happened to be a certain Guillermo Andrade.

Since topographic considerations obliged George Chaffey to dig his Imperial Canal through Mexican territory, Andrade sold the required hundred thousand acres to the Sociedad de Irrigación y Terrenos de la Baja California, S.A.—with the canny proviso that half the water in the canal was his. It was this particular perk (transferable to any subsequent owner of Andrade's lands) that made the Mexicali Valley particularly attractive to the Chandler Syndicate.

ACCOUNTINGS

In 1901, George Chaffey raised his headgates in Northside. **WATER IS HERE**.

In 1902, two giants were born: the United States Reclamation Service and the

*It would be an overstatement to say that the Colorado River Land Company owned the entirety of the Mexicali Valley. Mexicali, for instance, remained a small autonomous island; so do a few *colonias*. In 1910, Mr. Jefferson Worth himself, which is to say W. F. Holt, "announced the improvement of 32,000 acres in Mexico" by an entity called the Inter-California Land Company. This Inter-California Land Company had bought thirty thousand acres from the California-Mexico Land and Cattle Company, "with Cocopah as the point of entry, and the plan is to colonize this land, which is particularly fine soil."

Colorado River Land Company. Both of them spent extravagantly for irrigation, and neither one ever turned a profit. About the latter, which was first called the California-Mexico Land and Cattle Company, the *Imperial Valley Press and Farmer* shouts on page one: **LARGEST IRRIGATED RANCH IN THE WORLD**.

Almost anytime I like in 1903, I can open my *Imperial Valley Press and Farmer* and discover an advertisement from the Sociedad de Irrigación y Terrenos de la Baja California, S.A., G. Andrade, Vice-President. In that year, a certain W. H. Holabird, whose name I will often discover in connection with various water matters of Mexican Imperial, takes a ten-day hunting trip across the line with an unnamed party of good fellows, successful Los Angeles businessmen who "do things," sees deer, meets a Mexican cowboy, shoots ducks, visits Volcano Lake, and concludes that the delta of the Río Colorado is unsurpassably rich! I wonder who those businessmen could have been?

On 23 May 1904, Guillermo Andrade is the grantor and the Colorado River Land Company the grantee in a transaction recorded in the Imperial County property records. On 13 June 1904, the Colorado River Land Company is the grantee, receiving property from the Sociedad de Irrigación y Terrenos de la Baja California, which happens to be a subsidiary of the Southern Pacific Railroad. Meanwhile, on one side or the other of that irrelevant international line, that Chandler subsidiary the California-Mexico Land and Cattle Company is already accepting delivery of another herd of Texas cattle for fattening.

As a much later book tells the tale, *their plan was simple: to grow cotton with free water and cheap labor and sell it in the United States for top dollar.* The water was not free, although the charge that the Chandler Syndicate did not pay for it has been often repeated. Otis P. Tout's assertion is far more credible, and just as disconcerting to believers in small scale agrarian democracy: *It may be said that the Chandler interests are the largest cash customer the Imperial Irrigation District has.** As for the cheap labor and the hoped-for top dollar, that part was accurate enough.

And so by the end of 1904, the Colorado River Land Company has already begun to operate a goodly amount of Mexican acres *from the Colorado River to the Cocopah Mountains, and from the international line to the Gulf of California.* In the Imperial Valley, angry settlers berate the California Development Company for shortchanging them on water they need to irrigate their acres. But here in Mexico, it's more difficult to make trouble for corporate interests. After all, Porfirio Díaz is still President, and surely will be until doomsday!

By 1907, we hear a sober citizen remarking to a Congressional subcommittee

*Rather than calling them a customer, one Mexican source prefers to call the syndicate "the partners of IID. It cannot be denied that the Colorado River Land Company organized and rationalized, in some way, the exploitation of farmland in the Mexicali Valley."

that *the most valuable portion of the valley is on the Mexican side of the line, owned by the Otis-Chandler syndicate.* To what extent that value has been tapped remains in dispute; one historian asserts that in 1908 a hundred and fifty thousand American Imperial acres have already been irrigated as green as dollar bills, while south of the line fewer than seven thousand acres are in cultivation. But the Chandler Syndicate, after all, must simultaneously pursue many other titanic projects; Mexicali wasn't built in a day.

In 1910 the California-Mexico Land and Cattle Company, which we might as well call the Colorado River Land Company, will comprise *1,100 acres of highly developed ranch land in California and 876,000 acres just across the line in Mexican territory.* In 1918, Judge Farr praises *this model ranch owned by a Los Angeles stock syndicate . . . More stock is produced there than on any other ranch in Southern California . . . Walter Bowker is the manager of this vast tract.*

By 1929, the Colorado River Land Company keeps busy four thousand to eight thousand workers per year.

Well, then why did Harry Chandler and his partners fail to achieve what they had dreamed? They certainly turned a profit here and there. In the course of 1904, the Colorado River Land Company made five purchases, thereby ending up with eight hundred and fifty thousand acres of the Mexicali Valley. The land cost them $533,959. In 1910 they sold a thirty-thousand-acre piece of it for eight hundred thousand dollars. More impressive than this, because for several years it was repeated, is that between the end of World War I and the Depression, Harry Chandler's homestead grew eighteen million dollars' worth of cotton per annum.

But the Colorado River Land Company remained eternally undercapitalized. Chandler had hoped to borrow sufficient capital to build railways, cotton gins and suchlike refiners and carriers of agricultural wealth. Then his tenants could make money, the shareholders would do the same, the capital loans might finally be repaid, more capital could be borrowed; and presently the lands would be subdivided and sold—a *model community,* Chandler called it, a new southern California! But in 1920, he and his associates had to bail out two Calexico banks owned by one of their dependent syndicates. The Colorado River Land Company never paid any dividends at all, although in 1923 and 1924 it did send some modest disbursements to reimburse stockholders what they had originally laid out, without interest. In 1928, thirst for finance capital required it to give up majority control of the Mexicali Valley's fledgling cottonseed industry. In 1930, the Colorado River Land Company was obliged to rescue the Bank of Mexicali . . .

Meanwhile, various Mexican administrations expected Chandler to develop the valley at his own expense; when the time came, they would wrest it from him.

Throughout the 1920s, they played cat-and-mouse, intermittently threatening to undo his titles unless he built more railroads, canals, etcetera.

Squeezed on two fronts, Harry Chandler, like Wilber Clark, failed to strike it rich in his Imperial gamble. Poor man!

In 1935 one of Los Angeles's glorifiers gives Chandler this epitaph: *It was his inspiration that turned the Imperial Valley from a desert into the truck garden of America.*

Another epitaph, from 1988: *The syndicate's members viewed the entire Colorado River delta—both Imperial Valley and Mexicali Valley—as part of the greater Los Angeles commercial nexus . . .*

The best tribute of all dates from 1936, when the Secretary-General of the Union of Peasant Day Laborers of Alamo Mocho cries out that in Mexicali *there is no law nor revolutionary principles . . . There is nothing more than Mr. Chandler, and he is the owner of everything.*

Chapter 50

PRACTICALLY SELF-SUPPORTING IN THREE YEARS

(1865–2004)

"But this is tremendous!" I cried. "This is Imperial! I haven't been dreaming of this sort of thing!"

—H. G. Wells, 1901

The individual holdings of American Imperial, I've said, enlarged themselves beyond the statutory limits of the 1902 Reclamation Act. How much and when? Oh, our dream of the self-sufficient little homestead! Isn't that the American dream? I have a book called *Remembering the Family Farm: 150 Years of American Prints*. Confessing the sentimentality of some images, the preface remarks: *There is no escaping the stereotype of an ideal agrarian world,* which is to say a realm *where there is harmony and balance between humankind and nature . . . and labor leads to simple but ample rewards, and where the family is central to social fabric.* I look down into John Steuart Curry's "Valley of the Wisconsin," which was lithographed almost at midcentury, when Mexican and American Imperial had both come into their glory; and I see Eden on a meadow that slopes ever so gently toward a horizon of fields and trees, the clean little two-storey farmhouse beside its gambrel-roofed barn reminding me of my boyhood years in New Hampshire nearly half a century ago; I remember snowy farmhouses that were warm inside, and a little girl who took me home from school with her; because I never grew up in such a place, I remember her family's home on its hill of snow as being better than it probably was; *there is no escaping the stereotype of an ideal agrarian world.* What were her chores like? That I never had to learn.

In the middle of the nineteeth century, John Muir was put to work by his father, building up a family farm in Wisconsin. *Many of our old neighbors toiled and sweated and grubbed themselves into their graves years before their natural dying days . . . I was put to the plough at the age of twelve, when my head reached but little above the handles . . . We were all made slaves through the vice of over-industry.* No wonder that he spent the rest of his life wandering through and proselytizing for wilderness!

Meanwhile, in an undated stock photo which strangely resembles Nazi homeland propaganda, two little white boys, one of them blond, the other merely fairhaired, facing each other, the one we can see smiling; they're each holding a shock of flax; and in this lush grassy California field the pale shocks go marching in wide rows back to the row of trees. And down in Imperial, Wilber Clark and *his wife, Elizabeth F.,* have *settled* happily ever after *on the now greatly improved Wilfrieda Ranch.*

"WHAT THE HELL CAN I DO WITH TEN ACRES?"

Once upon a time, Imperial, also known as the **BEST FARMING LANDS in the WORLD**, stretched all the way to Illinois, whose eponymous Central Railroad Company offered nine hundred thousand acres for sale. *The rapid development of Illinois, its steady increase in population, and its capacity to produce cheap food, are matters for wonder and admiration.* In 1864, this state yields *more than one-fourth of the corn*—Indian corn, that is—*more than one-fifth of the wheat, and almost one-seventh of the oats produced in all the United States.* So buy your forty- or eighty-acre parcels, *or in larger tracts, as may be required by the capitalist or stock raiser,* at nine to fifteen dollars per acre! *The attention of persons, whose limited means forbid the purchase of a homestead in the older States, is particularly invited to these lands.*

Turning to Schedule Two of the 1880 California census, namely to "Productions of Agriculture in Los Angeles, in the County of Los Angeles, State of California," I find mostly under fifty, and often fewer than ten acres per farm. To be sure, Andrew Smith owns forty-five improved acres and Andrew Briswalter two hundred; over in Supervisor's District Four, Enumeration District Twenty-seven N, a certain Patrick Kooch possesses five hundred acres! But he's far from average.

In 1901 the first President Roosevelt turned his attention to Arid America and said: *The object of the Government is to dispose of this land to settlers who will build homes on it.* Hence the Reclamation Act of 1902, which allowed a single homesteader up to a hundred and sixty acres—three hundred and twenty for a married couple. What pioneer would need more than that?

In 1917, a glowing tract entitled *Reclaiming the Arid West* explained why it was that American Imperial's parades, once commenced, would never die away: *The Reclamation Act forbade the delivery of water on any government project to privately owned lands to a greater extent than 160 acres. Thus an effort was made to take it out of the power of capitalists and speculators in land to take selfish advantage of the beneficent work of a government of democracy . . .*

That very same year, an Imperialite advises that *experienced men with small means* might be able to get by subsistence farming on ten or fifteen acres, although he doesn't make it sound easy. Judge Farr (who by the way owns a hundred sixty acres in Mesquite Lake, a hundred seventy-five more near Imperial and eighty near Calexico) insists that *Imperial County was settled in a large part by those who did not have a large amount of capital.* You remember his praise of Wilber Clark's agricultural experiments: *Some fifty varieties of grapes have been tried out and a profitable express business has been worked up on the same.* How many acres might have been involved? A mere hundred and seventy-one. *Of great interest to Mr. Clark is the six-acre date orchard . . .*

But half a century after the publication of Farr's history, we overhear local grape growers testifying at a hearing in Coachella. The industry is getting "consolidated"; small-timers disappear left and right. In light of these progressive developments, somebody proposes an amendment to define a grower *as anyone who grows or leases ten acres or more,* to which a certain Mr. Reider replies: What the hell can I do with ten acres?

"A PICTURE FROM THE MIDWEST"

In 2004, portly old Richard Brogan, whose paid reminiscences will figure from time to time in this book because his ongoing career as an informant to private investigators gave him interesting knowledge (as he beautifully put it: *That's what I do for a living, is personalities. Without threatening, without exposing my motives*), sipped at his Coke in the Burgers and Beer Restaurant in Calexico and said: I've worked wheat, alfalfa, sudan, barley, cotton, lettuce. I've worked as a laborer, as a tractor operator; I've worked insecticide; I've worked for fertilizer companies; I've bought and sold commodities. I have farmed my own ground and I have had my custom harvesting equipment, both cotton and alfalfa. And as a deputy sheriff here and in Yuma County, I had a quasi-official capacity to represent enforcement issues in that capacity. It's my life. I know enough to know that without money you can't do anything. This is a complex financial thing. If I had a couple million dollars I don't know why you'd put it in here in Imperial. Because the returns are small and the potential loss is great every day. I myself dreamed that I could farm, and I tried, and I failed.

I said nothing, waiting, and Richard Brogan said: I kinda think that the family farm is a picture from the Midwest. We work in the corporate farming here. The water costs are the first thing, the land costs are the second. We have an ideal growing climate, and we have an ideal growing climate for bugs, for weeds. That means more money you've got to put in. So if your land starts out high, and your water is expensive, well. The date trees are the only crop that looks like you could win with, but even they, you can't grow anything without water. And that means money. We have two seasons for melons. We have a summer melon and a fall melon. Not watermelons but cantaloupes. There are times when I know we've been the world supplier of melons. And that means money. That means acreage. The family farm picture is just a few hundred acres and a family on the premises. That's not realistic.

Was it ever?

I believe it probably was.

When did it change?

When lettuce became big here. When Bud Antle started making a million dollars off lettuce in a hundred days.* The only people equivalent to that are the oil people. If you can make a million dollars off eighty acres in between thirty and ninety days, the potential is unbelievable. But the flip side of it, the threat, is you can lose a million pretty fast.

Well, Richard, what's the minimum one needs now?

I don't think that a small operator can farm less than seven hundred or a thousand acres.† A diversification of crops is also needed.

Why did the Roosevelt administration insist on that hundred-and-sixty-acre limitation?

I think they picked a figure and they had to have a start. Communication wasn't what it was. You look at our subsidized agriculture system since Roosevelt, our college system. We got intelligent people teaching this stuff now. It is a science. So whatever applied then, my quick response is, they didn't have a fax machine. You have to have a practical approach to that, and a hundred and sixty acres probably isn't enough to justify buying a hundred-thousand-dollar tractor. You have to understand: A lot of people are farming on leased ground! Our sprinkler systems, we've devised a way to sprinkle an even inch and we can control that. That's a natural remedy to alkali. If you just run water through canals, that deposits alkali. If you sprinkle 'em, that draws down the alkali. A guy with a hundred acres of ground couldn't afford one of these elaborate sprinkler systems. We need to rewrite the limitation law.

PAUL TAYLOR'S COMPLAINT

In 1967, Paul S. Taylor, consulting economist to the Social Security Board, Interior Department, etcetera, formerly the husband of the great documentary photographer Dorothea Lange (with whom he travelled through the Imperial Valley during

*In 1971, César Chávez speaks at Riverside Church. Dow Chemical has obtained an anti-strike injunction against the United Farm Workers. Chávez says: *The fact is that Dow Chemical owns about 17,000 acres that are farmed by Bud Antle.*

†When he uttered those words, the average size of a California farm was 320 to 330 acres.

the Depression years), and now an ancient professor emeritus, steps forward at a public hearing to say: *The Reclamation Law provides for tremendous subsidies for water development, which . . . now runs perhaps at a thousand dollars per acre. In that law is a provision known as the 160-acre law. The purpose of that law is to insure that water does not go to the pre-existing property owner for a tract of larger than 160 acres. It's to control speculation. It's to control monopoly. It's to diffuse benefits widely, to see that they reach all elements of the population.*

Taylor then raises the uncomfortable subject of nine hundred thousand California acres either irrigated or about to be irrigated—larger, he remarks, than the state of Rhode Island—which violate the hundred-and-sixty-acre limitation. He urges that the limitation be modernized and continued.

Is there any other public comment? inquires the chairman—for we have a democracy, ladies and gentlemen; even Paul S. Taylor can say what he wants! Well, *is* there any other comment? There is none. America agrees with Richard Brogan.

"WE HAD EVERYTHING"

And does Mexico agree?

In 2004, in Colonia Sieto de Cierro Prieto, not far past the glass factory a few kilometers south of Mexicali, there lived a lady named Teresa García.

Originally we were eleven brothers and sisters, she said, but four have sold their parcels to people from other states. We were given ten hectares each.* And the family of my brother's wife has bought some land . . .

How many hectares does a person need to survive without working outside one's own fields? I asked.

If you don't have the implements to work, you can't do it, said her son. It's very expensive.—And he said again: You can't do it.

The proprietress of a small restaurant not far away from Rancho García was more optimistic than he. I asked her: In your opinion, how many hectares would you need to support yourself, if you lived only off the land? And how many to support yourself, your spouse and children?

Here in the valley, she replied, people who work really hard can live on eight or nine hectares. If you were going to plant wheat or cotton, yes, you would need more land. For orchards, ten hectares, a family would live well. Now they rotate planting, of course. With this restaurant I know many farmers . . .

I quoted Richard Brogan's assessment: *I don't think that a small operator can farm less than seven hundred or a thousand acres,* in other words, two hundred eighty or

*Slightly less than twenty-five acres.

four hundred hectares. And I told her: That's what many Americans say to me in this same valley, on their side of the line.

The woman replied: Well, here the concept of living well is different, and also the Americans are addicted to machinery.

My father's sister had six hectares* and seven children, she remarked, and they lived perfectly well. They harvested cotton, melons and tomatoes. And all the kids studied; they had a house in Mexicali; they had a farm. There were many of them; they did nothing else; they lived well. They dressed well; they ate well; they travelled a lot, to Mexico City and Guadalajara.

How long ago did this happen?

This was thirty years ago.

Could they live in a similar way now?

Not really, because people want more. What happens now is that people are more demanding, especially due to technology. Back then, if people had good food and cattle, especially beef and pork, and good clothes, they could be happy. We picked cotton, but when there wasn't cotton to pick, my father worked construction. We had the first television and the first washing machine in the area; we had everything.

THE POINT OF IT

So in Mexican as in American Imperial the expectations of the farmers have increased. But whereas in Northside *I don't think that a small operator can farm less than seven hundred or a thousand acres,* when I ask the homesteaders of the Mexicali Valley how much land they hold, they usually say: Twenty hectares.—That works out to less than fifty acres.

ANOTHER ESSAY ON THE INFINITE

I wish well to Wilber and Elizabeth Clark. However representative or unrepresentative they may be,† I desire for them good harvests, a comfortable life, success, which in America means expansion of income and capital. If they lived in Imperial today, drawing their water from the All-American Canal, which the taxes of other citizens had paid for, would I wish on them the power to gain property in excess of

*Slightly less than fifteen acres.

†In a draft from 1981, Taylor insists that, being a child of the Ministry of Capital, the Imperial Valley never even commenced as "a community of farmers with their families working their own land, in the tradition of the Homestead and Reclamation Acts. On the contrary, it was a divided, polarized society. One-third of the Valley population was of Mexican origin, largely of Mexican birth, and field wage laborers by occupation."

the limitation law? Would I wish them to extend their holdings until they could contemptuously say: What the hell can I do with ten acres?

By 1918, Paul Taylor's description of limitation law was already behind the times; for the brains in the Agriculture Department had come up with the notion of an *enlarged homestead* which *may contain 320 acres, provided the land is nonmineral, nontimbered, and nonirrigable.* Then there were *stock raising lands,* six hundred and forty acres each, no watering holes allowed. Most conveniently of all, *a regulation has recently been issued increasing the area of a homestead from 160 to 320 acres on land having no water supply, in Los Angeles, Imperial, San Diego and Riverside counties.* In 1958, the United States Supreme Court will uphold the original hundred-and-sixty-acre limitation in its famous *Ivanhoe* decision; but don't worry; Imperial will get around that in a decade or two.

Imperial is family farms. Imperial is corporate farms. Imperial is Wilber Clark, and also the Chandler Syndicate. *Imperial County,* we have read, *was settled in a large part by those who did not have a large amount of capital,* but what if the souls with small capital weren't all farmers, but—small capitalists?

You
Calipatria
Fortune

Get the meaning of this heading?

* * *

Get busy now and buy a lot or two.
Calipatria had to be — it was a necessity.
Calipatria will grow, and grow fast.
Let this growth mean money in your pocket.

That was a newspaper advertisement from 1914. The real estate company's main office was in Calipatria, but it just happened to have a Los Angeles branch office. One of the men to whom the Calipatria townsite lands belonged was Harry Chandler.

In 1925, Mark M. Rose, one of the Imperial Irrigation District's five directors, introduces himself to a Senate committee by remarking that he owns four hundred acres in the Imperial Valley. His colleague Ira Aten possesses more than nine hundred acres together with his family. (Richard Brogan: *And that means money. That means acreage.*)

Consider *these Lyons boys,* who in 1907 *baled more hay and threshed more grain than any other combination in the district. They operated on a large scale* . . . Emulating the Chandler Syndicate, *they bought 565 acres in Mexico, near Calexico, which they proposed to use as a model stock farm or a cotton plantation.* Meanwhile, *Dave Williams has five hundred and sixty acres near Holtville.* Harry Van den Heuvel arrives from Riverside in 1903 with twenty-five borrowed dollars, files on a quarter-section, and by the time Judge Farr's history comes out in 1918 he owns six hundred acres!

Then there is W. F. Holt, of course. Only God and the Redlands syndicate know how much *he* owns.

The purpose of that law is to insure that water does not go to the pre-existing property owner for a tract of larger than 160 acres. Or, if you prefer, *I don't think that a small operator can farm less than seven hundred or a thousand acres.* (Alice Woodside, an ex-Imperialite whose recollections figure in the middle sections of this book, opined: *I think that first of all, a hundred and sixty acres you're not going to survive. I would think in the neighborhood of two thousand acres is what you need now.*)

When does self-sufficiency become evil? Here's an encomium in the November 1954 issue of *Quick Frozen Foods.* (Is there anything wrong about it? Ask a Marxist. For an opposing reply, ask Alice Woodside.) *FROM A RURAL MAIL BOX TO A FARM SO BIG IT HAS A POST OFFICE OF ITS OWN. Few American success stories are so dramatic as those of Charles F. Seabrook and the giant farming enterprise he built. The story begins half a century ago when a boy began farming his family's 57-acre homestead . . . When young Charlie Seabrook could walk from the north field to the south pasture in a few minutes, today he can drive for 45 minutes and still be on land that belongs to his Farms,* with that corporate or maybe merely worshipful capital *F.*

The fable of Charlie Seabrook is set in New Jersey, which lacks a limitation law. Does this put him in a separate category from Mr. Reider, who spits on his ten acres in the entity which I call Imperial? Anyhow, can't every American aspire to be a millionaire?

More fundamentally, why did the pioneers settle in Imperial? *As has already been learned by the reader of this volume,* writes Judge Farr, *the financial end of the great project in this Valley has overshadowed every other feature from its inception.* In that case, is my reconstruction of Wilber Clark's life the merest sentimental fantasy?

These questions cannot be answered with any degree of consensus. But this book will stick uselessly to its duty, and keep asking them.

THE ROMANCE OF GARDEN TRACT SITES

Setting aside unknowable dreams of others, and considering only results, what progressions can we discover in Imperial's story?

Two doctors who have studied American rural poverty assure me that *between 1910 and 1920 there began for the first time a trend toward an absolute as well as a relative decrease in the farm population.* That ideal agrarian world was cashing out, bit by bit. The ability of the formerly Imperial state of Illinois *to produce cheap food* might remain a *matter for wonder and admiration;* but the cheap food producers were not only farmtowns anymore; they were the stockyards of Chicago. And speaking of Chicago, that city long since transformed its corn-acres into a Los Angeles–like concatenation. In short, *we need have no fear that our lands will not become better and better as the years go by.* But the allure of the family farm only increased as it became more utopian.

In 1920, while a certain fifteen-year-old girl, daughter of Imperial homesteaders and subject of another chapter, lies freshly cold in her hospital bed in Fresno, California, *Garden Tract Sites* are being advertised in that same city: Get in on the ground floor and in three years your investment will be *Practically self-supporting!*

As late as 1933, we find the President of the United States, no less, expressing his desire to settle twenty-five thousand more poor families on small farms (*Garden Tract Sites,* if you will) at a cost to the government of a thousand dollars each; and so the Subsistence Homestead Program begins.

Sometimes we read about *the myth of the family farm.* But it was not yet a myth even then, not to our noble, compassionate and practical President.

No boy should be deprived of the experience of harvesting, wrote an old man in the last quarter of the twentieth century; he used to do it himself. The implication: Harvesting is fulfilling, defining, American, valuable beyond cash. And advertisements (which of course are eternally to be trusted) make the same point. I see a little orange-roofed farmhouse wreathed with leaves; a small boy waves to me from the doorway; the mother in mauve ankle-length skirts holds the youngest girl by the hand; her elder sister gazes at me by the edge of the front lawn; there's the father in his khaki coat and the old grandfather leaning on a barrel-hoop; the rest is all lovely orange groves widening back to the mountains, because this is the label for Home Brand oranges from High Grove, California.

Chapter 51

THE *EJIDOS*

(1903–2005)

> A calpulli or chinacalli is a barrio of known people or of an ancient lineage which holds its lands and boundaries from a time of great antiquity. These lands belong to the said kindred, barrio, or lineage . . .
>
> —Alonso de Zorita, 1585

Let us now center ourselves in a certain bleached necropolis which endures infinity apart on one edge of a tan mound of cracked dirt whose particles are even finer than a child's hair; and beyond the last row of faded crosses and white angels, bottles and fallen crosses lead the eye down to more dirt marked here and there by alkali; then a canal bisects the world, with emerald fieldscapes immediately beyond, bearing their furrows, ranchos and palm-groves westward through an atmosphere of bird-songs, so that it seems as if from that canal all the way to the horizon, which comprises Cerro Prieto and the Sierra Cucapá range—the western extremity of the Mexicali Valley, in short—it's all green! And so this cemetery-mound on which we stand seems to be the only island of desert in this place, which ironically happens to be called Islas Agrarias, the Agrarian Islands. To the east, more green and more reddish fields obligingly continue the illusion.

Come to think of it, it's no illusion at all, but the central human reality of Mexican Imperial, not to mention Mexico herself: the *ejidos.*

An *ejido* is a territory with limits, owned by the federal government of Mexio but intended for the perpetual use and benefit of its inhabitants, *ejidatarios,* each of whom has been granted a specific amount of land (typically, twenty or forty hectares)* to work and bequeath.

A *colonia* is an area of houses, and it possesses a name and a limit.

In 2004, there were two hundred and twenty-eight *ejidos* in Baja California. Around Tijuana there were five hundred and four *colonias* but seven hundred and sixty "named areas" which were not formally colonias. There were many, many

*In Mexican Imperial it is more commonly twenty. In other parts of the republic it is sometimes much less.

ejidos around Mexicali—over a hundred—and perhaps a dozen in the vicinity of Tijuana, thanks to urban sprawl, *maquiladora* voraciousness and water scarcity.

The history of Mexican Imperial over the first half of the twentieth century is in large part the tale of the Colorado Land Company and its expropriation by the *ejidos*. The history of American Imperial is a mirror image of that: Wilber Clark's homestead gives way to Bud Antle's endless empire of lettuce.

In the second half of the century we will find the water farmers, the Interior Department, and God knows who else beginning to transform American Imperial farmscape back into desert for the greater good of housing developments in San Diego.

In Mexican Imperial, the *ejidos*, although they are weakening, have not entirely failed to hold their own.

A DEFINITION

We read that *ejido* is *a colonial-era term that had been used to describe indigenous communities' common lands ever since the colonial period*. In conception it is surely more ancient than that, as this chapter's mid-sixteenth-century epigraph reminds us. The epigraph's author, Alonso de Zorita, travelled sadly, honestly and laboriously through post-Conquest Mexico, recording practicalities of interest to the Spanish Crown while raising his unavailing voice against the dispossession and enslavement of Indians. His data have been variously interpreted ever since. Some say that the *ejidos* were merely administrative divisions of land belonging to, for instance, Moctezuma; others see them as true communal holdings. Indeed, one would be shocked had the forms of land ownership *not* varied across Mexico! In recognition of the fact that some villagers he knew held their *ejido* lands in common, while others subdivided them into individual plots, the revolutionary Emiliano Zapata left it up to each locality to decide the details of land allocation. But the essential characteristics of *ejidos* remained: autonomy, preexisting right, inalienability.

DREAMS

The Mexican Revolution begins in 1911. Zapata fights for the right of his neighbors to keep their village land against the *haciendero* equivalents of Harry Chandler. (Thank God, Chandler couldn't reach quite that far.) By 1912, the eloquent ex-lawyer Luis Cabrera calls for the new Chamber of Deputies to honor *rights established in the epoch of the Aztecs*. And so a bill is introduced for *the reconstitution of the* ejidos. Article Twenty-seven of the new constitution of 1917 gives villages the right to hold property as such. And in his beloved Plan de Ayala, Zapata announces that fields, woodlands and water taken from the people will immediately revert to them, they *maintaining at any cost with arms in hand the mentioned possession.* Furthermore—and here ancient rights get reduced from justification to inspiration—large landholders may now be expropriated of one-third of their holdings so that new *ejidos* can be formed. Although we find *ejidos* getting parcelled out in dribs and drabs, for instance, during the administration of President Calles in the mid-1920s (he seems to have considered them merely a *Realpolitik* measure of temporary subsistence and tried to privatize them), not until the presidency of Lázaro Cárdenas in the mid-1930s will this notion be carried out on a large scale. Never mind. The Revolution has begun. At a stroke the conception of *ejidos* has become dynamic, militant.

Almost from the start, runs one Northside account, *the* ejidos *bore the taste of salty tears,* being undercapitalized, created from tiny pieces of arid lands, squeezed by rigid state-controlled prices and hindered by bad bureaucracy. Accordingly, the campesinos gained little if anything from the *ejidos.* This may or may not be true for Mexico generally; regarding Mexican Imperial I completely disagree.

José López from Jalisco said:

In the *ejidos,* like I'm telling you, there's *rules,* there's *laws* that are applied, and yes, the land is divided equally, whereas in the Imperial Valley a few powerful ranchers work the land because they have the money. Some of them, like M—— S——, whom I worked for, he's even Hindu, he's a foreigner. But they have the money, the land. Over here the land is divided equally. Then it depends on how your harvest goes. That is the truth here in Mexico. If a rain destroys your harvest, you're not going to get a big insurance refund like you would in the States, so that's gonna put you in the hole. If you have the money and use all the hectares you got, it's almost guaranteed you will come out doing good at the end of the season. Sometimes you don't have the capital, Bill, to work all the land you have. Then the *ejidos* don't help you out there. If you spend all the season drinking and partying out, you're not gonna be helped. You have to look after yourself.

In Jalisco, he continued, there are big haciendas, but I guess it started out being *ejidos* here in Mexicali. (José never mentioned the Chandler Syndicate.) People saw the *ejidos* were a good way of living, he said, a more or less equal way of living. So if a big *haciendero* were to come over here and buy a big chunk of land, no *ejido* guy would go and work for him. A hacienda would probably go broke.

So basically what you're saying is that this land was settled later.

That's true. After the revolution, people with money became *hacienderos.* Most of them, as time progressed and we came into the seventies, the eighties, some of them went broke, and the laws were changing in Mexico, and there wasn't so much repression as before. Haciendas I've heard in Chiapas, they call 'em *casicas,* where they just exploit the people, you know, Bill, you just work the skin off 'em . . .

Why is Jalisco more exploitative?

Because it's a very old province, Bill. Baja is a baby province.

And I thought of the expression *as old as sin.*

Once upon a time, the *ejidos* had also been old. But the Revolution renewed them, particularly in Mexican Imperial, which despite the Colorado River Land Company preserved a certain virginal blankness. As early as 1915, the councilmen of Mexicali began to propose the creation of *ejidos* expropriated from the lands owned by Harry Chandler's syndicate. For weren't those still largely blank lands?

Indeed, when I invited myself into the Sunday afternoon of the middle-aged rancher Don Carlos Cayetano Sanders-Collins, who sat in the yard with his family in a built-up *ejido* called Ciudad Morelos, his unnamed wife, who did much of the answering, at first described the *ejidos* not as legal reversions or revolutionary seizures, but as simple pioneering in the desert nothingness, so that for a moment we seemed to have returned to the Imperial of Wilber Clark, where *water was in the ditches, seeds were in the ground, green was becoming abundant, and the whole area was dotted with the homes of hopeful, industrious, devoted persons.* But in place of, say, L. E. Cooley, who *entered the town as pioneer, driving a pair of mules and followed by a spotted dog,* a first *ejidatario,* at least as the lady told it, seemed to have settled with and among his old neighbors; for she said:

Mexicali was started by people from many different countries who came at the time of the railroads. They were contracted from the interior to work on the railroads. Many went back home afterwards, but those who stayed spread out to begin the *ejidos.* The *ejidos* were started by different indigenous groups, for instance the Cucapahs. So their thinking is based not on where they live but on who started their *ejidos.*

So which group of people formed this *ejido*?

She had to ask Don Carlos, who replied: Cucapah.

Do you have Cucapah relatives?

No.

She said then: In each *ejido,* people often speak a dialect that is different from in other places. But as time has gone by, they have lost their differences. A lot of people born here have gone to work in the United States, so the *ejidos* are losing many people.

Don Carlos was born in Ejido Indo. He said: This *ejido* is Ciudad Morelos. Before, this was Estación Cuervos, Crows Station.

Don Carlos, why do you live in a house and your two brothers live on a ranch?

He shrugged and said: They like it better.

To what extent this answer was intended simply to shut up a nosy outsider I cannot say, but in any event it was a very Mexican reply, expressing that sense of volition which is much more commonly heard on the south side of the ditch than here where I write in the Land of the Free; my neighbors would have provided me with such explanations as: *To be nearer to my job,* or *Because my mortgage requires it.* Among the few farmers whom I have actually been able to interview in American Imperial (they being more closed than their Southside counterparts), I am more likely to hear answers of this non-mechanistic caliber than in urban California. Come to think of it, Alice Woodside, for instance, whom you met a few pages ago in Sacramento, loves and values her Imperial Valley childhood more and more as the years go by. (We will hear her recollections in their place, along with those of her mother.) Her friend Kay Brockman Bishop, also Valley born, expressed the contentment that I felt as I sat on her back patio watching the sunset over the fields while her husband took the dog for a walk, then went to putter in his garage and machine shop, which was also Kay's studio; between the two of them, they could build almost anything.

As for Don Carlos, he was also a farmer, raising cotton, corn, maize, onions, radishes and chilis. He owned *between twenty and thirty hectares.* Pretty much everybody has the same, he said. I'm the owner. There's an agricultural law. The person who has the responsibility for taking care of the parents has the right to all the land.

The *ejido* families had crossed the line often enough, or knew enough others who had, to express satisfied incuriosity about Northside. They sipped coconut juice in cafés of concrete or fiberboard, or, far more often, they stayed home. When I asked Don Carlos how often he went into the United States, he replied: All the time.

How is the life here different from there?

He shrugged, waved his heavy hand, and said: Oh, very different.

The wife said: The United States acts very paternalistically to all its citizens. In Mexico, everybody has to fight for his own life. But if you have a good education, you can figure out how to get what you want.

She was polite, but I got the point: She was quite happy in her *ejido,* thank you.

Being Imperialites, the *ejidatarios* existed at the center of their dreamy cosmos; green tranquillity went on forever all around them, as far as they cared to lift up their eyes, and that was not very far. Don Carlos's wife did eventually tell me how the Cardenistas violently expropriated the two *factories where they took care of the wheat and the cotton,* and so this family ended up with a ranch; but that was long ago and might never have happened, for in the *ejidos* there is nothing but peace.

And so a certain restaurant proprietress, the same one who in the previous chapter had insisted that six hectares used to be enough and that *we had everything,* did not refer, as Zapata might have done, to ancient indigenous titles, but to creation *ex nihilo,* saying: An *ejido* is founded by agricultural people who own parcels. And a *colonia* is started by people who work for the *ejidos.* So here's a parcel with twenty hectares; here's another; each parcel has its house. In a *colonia,* it's just houses: journalists, workers, teachers.

If they want to start an *ejido,* they must buy land from the government. Really now you can only start an *ejido* in a place with a very small population. Because to buy parcels it can take years.

To start more *colonias,* it's easier. They are always close to a city or an *ejido.* Now they call them *fraccionamientos.* If a man buys a parcel of land, he can subdivide and sell the parcels to others as *fraccionamientos.*

Reader, never mind the *colonias* or *fraccionamientos,* at least not for now. What are the *ejidos?* Like all other places, they are worlds within worlds. Beyond the frond-roofed cages of Señor Hector's fighting cocks in Ejido Monterey begins his world of ruined cars, rows of them in the desert, then the broken engines and electronic parts. He is the ruler of his empire.

Lupe Vásquez's aunt had a dream; she thought her *ejido*stead was safe forever, but another nephew, Rubén, the one with the sweet distinguished face, sold it out from under her. Be that as it may, in the course of my travels in Imperial I never met as many happy people, at least by their own definition, as in the *ejidos.**

Wilber Clark's homestead was a dream; and perhaps the reality was as harsh as the shadows of birds scuttering across a flat baked field on the way to Algodones. But who are we to say that the illusion didn't hold good all the way to the property line?

What did they used to say in American Imperial? *His farm has been highly improved. He made a success through his own efforts. He sold out at a fancy price.*

In the *ejidos* somebody's farm might or might not get improved, and nobody else will give a damn. He might or might not make a success; he might spend the harvest season getting drunk with his mistress, and that is literally his affair. He has no intention of selling out, not ever; he is home.

AROUND THE WORLD

May I lay out for you the *ejidos* of the Mexicali Valley?

Due east of Mexicali, some *ejidos* are very green, thanks to seepage from the All-American Canal. (Well, as you'll read later in this book, that will soon be over. I've never been cheated out of a dollar in my life.) This is the mesa where they grow green onions. There are also many fields of squash and watermelons.

*Reader, do you think I sentimentalize Southside, Wilber Clark, the reclamation laws, the self-sufficient American dream? If you do, please tell me whether this book would be better if I were more cynical.

Irrigation ditch, Mexicali Valley, 2004

East-southeast of Mexicali, Plácido's Cucapah, vendor of herbicides and insecticides, is surrounded by *ejidos,* with factory smokestacks across the street; and in the mud yards and the dust yards of the *colonias* people sometimes vend their old clothes by hanging them on a fence; and in the *ejidos,* some people sit all day beneath their shade trees, and some work the fields. In one of these *colonias* I once sought out the mother of the street prostitute Karla, Karla whose singing voice bore all the cracked brilliancies of salt on the southeastern end of Laguna Salada and whose skin was a reddish-brown overlay in the salt. The mother was not kind. So I passed on to the *ejidos,* where no one turned me away; I could knock on any door I liked and someone would spend an hour or an afternoon with me, offering me water, telling me stories, inviting me to his daughter's *quinceañera* or her family's Christmas. They'd been everywhere, even past Mexicali. I'd ask them how life was here and they'd slowly fan a child's sweaty face and say: I like it, because things are tranquil.

Keep going that way, all the way to San Luis Río Colorado, and *ejidos* will accompany you.* It will get hotter and humider and there will be many small cemeteries but there will also be green *ejidos* just off the road.

*There are ranchos in Mexicali also—private, family-owned farms. One treatise on the valley claims that there is a division, perhaps even antagonism, between the ranchers and the *ejidatarios.* Over the decades, however, the *ejidos* bear a fainter stamp of cooperative socialism than they did under Cárdenas. The differences between the two forms of farm property have lessened. If antagonism remains, I have not heard it expressed.

West of Mexicali, after the half-hearted green fields, there comes a dip, and we are practically out of the *ejidos,* passing through low plains, greenish shrubs, tan sand, then the dry greenish ovoid of Laguna Salada, meaning "salty lagoon," and a whitewashed roadside restaurant with an immense painted Christ on a crucifix, peacocks in a cage, proud fat chickens strutting on the sand. There is also a café with hubcaps strung like trophies on barbed wire, many painted boasts of ***COCOS HELADOS***, a truckload of greenish-yellow hay bales parked in front. Weeds like upturned golden candelabra drink light instead of giving it. As we begin to ascend beyond the Colorado's bygone reach, we see the desert as it always must have been, and Imperial becomes once again the old Valley of Death.

South of Mexicali, near the volcano called Cerro Prieto, grey-green little smoke trees survive in the pale wastes, and there are scattered tires, the occasional dead dog at roadside, the Sierra Cucapá mountains ahead. Even here there are *ejidos,* the fields not so green as Northside's, of course, and always smaller, less regular, bordered with mesquite and smoke trees, the Sierra Cucapá over everything, everything shaggier. Here I have seen fields of corn and alfalfa and sometimes specialty crops such as garlic.

Southeast of Mexicali, even in the reddish foothills of the Sierra el Mayor you may find a homestead. I asked one leathery old couple why they had built their shack away from other human beings, and the woman glared at me in hatred of my presence while the man replied with a proud uplifting of the corners of his mouth: We prefer to be free.

The junked cars in the sand along Mexican Route 2, the haystack pyramid under palm trees in somebody's front yard in the *ejidos,* it's all of a piece with that clothing of grey-green on the desert beneath the dry mountains; humanity's artifacts line the dry land thinly and unevenly; call it paltry and trashy and you will be, as we say in Northside, on the money. But in the *ejidos* they're off the money.

I never would have believed it if I had merely read about it in a book like this. It took me years of seeing and asking before I finally believed. *They harvested cotton, melons and tomatoes. There were many of them; they did nothing else; they lived well.*

This book investigates many secrets, from the Chinese tunnels to the *maquiladoras* to the New River. But the deepest of them all, and the best, is the secret that in the *ejidos* they live well. I do not want that life and could not live it happily. They might get dangerously drunk and their daughters sometimes run away to be prostitutes and they read very little and lose their teeth early. Many of them work very hard beneath Imperial's sun. *I like it, because things are tranquil.*

Chapter 52

IMPERIAL REPRISE

(1901—2006)

1

It is almost unbelievable how fast apricot trees grow in this Valley. Calipatria will grow, and grow fast.

It is almost unbelievable how fast apricot trees grow in this Valley. The date trees are the only crop that looks like you could win with, but even they, you can't grow anything without water.

2

James Greenfield served Capital; Jefferson Worth sought to make Capital serve the race. Isn't everyone tempted to double down at blackjack when the opportunity arises? But even they, you can't grow anything without water.

WATER IS HERE.

3

I like it, because things are tranquil. There is no escaping the stereotype of an ideal agrarian world. For orchards, ten hectares, a family would live well. *Of great interest to Mr. Clark is the six-acre date orchard . . .* What the hell can I do with ten acres?

My father's sister had six hectares and seven children, and they lived perfectly well. *I don't think that a small operator can farm less than seven hundred or a thousand acres.*

4

Over here the land is divided equally. Then it depends on how your harvest goes. *So when they get out to work they find the Holt fields are all plowed . . .* WELCOME TO CALIFORNIA.

He stood staunch as Mount Signal. I can't help believing in people. *It was his inspiration that turned the Imperial Valley from a desert into the truck garden of America.* It may be said that the Chandler interests are the largest cash customer the Imperial

Irrigation District has. *The most valuable portion of the valley is on the Mexican side of the line, owned by the Otis-Chandler syndicate.* There is nothing more than Mr. Chandler, and he is the owner of everything.

5

It is almost unbelievable how fast apricot trees grow in this Valley. *Thus an effort was made to take it out of the power of capitalists and speculators in land to take selfish advantage of the beneficent work of a government of democracy* . . . I know enough to know that without money you can't do anything.

PART FOUR

FOOTNOTES

Chapter 53

WHAT I WISH I KNEW ABOUT MELOLAND

(1907—1998)

Half way between El Centro and Holtville Meloland is an important shipping center. Plans were made there in an early day for a town of considerable size.

—Otis B. Tout, 1931

This important shipping center did not quite live up to those plans.

Meloland's efflorescence, such as it was, seems emblematic of Imperial itself. It was here, six miles east of El Centro, four and a half miles west of Holtville, that Harold Bell Wright wrote *The Winning of Barbara Worth* in that arrow-weed ramada of his. He also named the place, exclaiming: What a mellow land!

I am reliably informed that *the well-known Rancho Meloland of 280 acres* was begun in October 1907, so W. F. Holt must have introduced Mr. Wright to the place about then. His classic of world literature would be published four years later. Fifty thousand sour stock orange seeds were planted, among other varieties. The first child was born there in April 1909: the daughter of Mr. and Mrs. Joseph Loftus. A month later, the boomers were already unloading fifty-by-a-hundred-and-forty-foot lots of Meloland Townsite at a hundred dollars each, ten dollars down and five dollars per month.

I know from the *Imperial Valley Business and Resident Directory* that in 1912 Walter E. Packard, whose name figures occasionally and forgettably in this book, on both sides of the international line, was in charge of the agricultural experimental station there. From the *Imperial Valley Press* ("Covers the Valley Like the Sunshine") I've kept abreast of all **MELOLAND SOCIAL EVENTS OF THE WEEK**—for example, the May festival of 1926, a great success, which took place in the playground, adorned by *long strings of electric lights.*

By then the Barbara Worth Hotel had opened. I've already quoted to you Otis B. Tout's description of the mural: *Trade is leading Culture, a beautiful young woman . . . Miss Sawyer, a school teacher of Meloland, represents Culture . . .*

Meloland remains on the 1916 California state road map; so does Hazelwood in the whiteness of the eastern desert of Imperial's southeast corner; I never heard of Hazelwood until I saw it there. May I read off to you some of the other important shipping centers?

South of *la línea,* a railroad runs through Mexicali, continuing southeast to Packard, which may well be named after Walter; then to Pascuality, continuing to Seabania or Sesbania, not to mention Cocopah, after which it flattens out, and presently angles northeast up to Yuma. Well, Mexicali and Yuma remain, at least. In Coachella, Salton clings absurdly to the map; you'll find it on the northeast shore of the Salton Sea. Mortmere, Dos Palmas and Caleb are all there, more or less in an east-west line below Mecca. Rest in peace, you mummified ghost towns and salted railroad sidings!

Now for the stunning alteration of Meloland into a metropolis: In 1910 the population was ten. By 1920 it had doubled; in 1930 it had achieved perfect stability (which means that it remained the same as in 1920); in 1940 it was only five persons less (several of them being schoolchildren brown, yellow, white and freckled); in 1950 it stayed proudly unaltered.

Meloland, so we're informed, is *listed as rural from 1960,* which may be why we have no population figure for that year. At any rate, in 1965, the very next listing, Meloland reported a hectic population of fifty. The compilation I cite was published in 1998; nonetheless, after 1965 there is only Imperial blankness in the row of the chart devoted to Meloland. In other words, Meloland appears to be *actively developed, highly improved, and is becoming thickly settled.*

I asked a veteran Imperialite about Harold Bell Wright's ramada and she replied: There's nothing there. I know where it was. It was there when I was younger. It was just to the west of the Barbara Worth Country Club. I think it fell down in the fifties, sixties, something like that.

Geologists have named a Meloland soil, not to mention an Imperial, a Superstition, a Holtville and a Gila. The County Recorder once believed in the existence of a Meloland Orange Tract, on which a breach of obligation of a certain Deed of Trust took place in 1924; another pioneer or speculator had defaulted on his mortgage. Lots eleven, twelve, twenty-three and twenty-four in Meloland, together with others on another page, would be sold in three months. So don't tell me that Meloland did not exist, no matter that if I buttonhole somebody in El Centro and ask him how to get there, he'll say he never heard of it. The canals and green fields of Meloland are jewel-like in the evening light. The hay bales like green bullion on the pool tables of alfalfa fields now turn golden-orange. They are *highly improved.*

Chapter 54

SAN DIEGO

(1769–1925)

San Diego is wedded to her lethergy [*sic*] and will do nothing. Let the sleeper sleep. In the meantime, Imperial will continue to do business with Los Angeles.

—The *Calexico Chronicle, ca.* 1907

Imperially speaking, San Diego, first occupied by the Spaniards in 1769, remains an irrelevance. Captain Gaspar de Portolá won't even get a footnote in my book. The feeling's mutual: San Diego couldn't care less about Imperial until Imperial breaks away. Out of San Diego County's eight million five hundred thousand acres, two million two hundred thousand are *adapted to grazing and farm culture.* As for the rest, namely *the area covered by the Colorado River Desert, and mountains and canyons,* who esteems it in 1873?

Helen Hunt Jackson's melodramatic novel *Ramona* is likewise of small use to us, for it scarcely looks east of San Jacinto Mountain. All the same, it does describe the Pacific coast just north of San Diego, with many oak-clad canyons, or *cañons* as Mrs. Jackson obligingly orthographizes them. They have long since been urbanized.

As for the urbanizers themselves, in 1777, Governor de Neve found the troops of that pueblo *deplorable, . . . first because they were seen not to conform to uniformity . . .* [*the clothes of*] *many have so greatly deteriorated that they are almost indecent.* In 1796, Acting Governor Arrillaga had nothing to say about the Presidio itself, where he rested for four days after a grueling expedition through the area which I call Imperial; but he noted *small houses of gentiles,* meaning unchristened Indians, *as one enters the arroyo. This arroyo is lush, with lots of poplar, alder, and willow trees. It has water for some distance.* **WATER IS HERE**. And so early in the following century, the Franciscan Fathers build the first reservoir, no doubt with the help of Indian labor.

In 1833 a certain Yankee merchant visits San Diego and advises his colleague: *Hides are plenty in the Pueblo, and no goods in the market, if you get there before any vessel, you can sell your cargo off immediately. Calicoes and cottons will bring any price asked.*

(Richard Henry Dana, Jr., the author of the famous *Two Years Before the Mast,* passed a significant proportion of those two years in flensing hides at various California ports; then he got to carry them on his head, going barefoot through rocks and surf. In San Diego he counted *about forty dark brown looking huts, or houses, and three or four larger ones, whitewashed, which belonged to the "gente de razon."*)

In 1839, William Hartnell, who's followed the requisite path to success in Mexican California—marriage to a wealthy Don's daughter and conversion to the True Faith—sets out to fulfill the thankless duty of Visitador General of the Missions of Alta California. Never mind his vicissitudes; I grant him entry into our kingdom only for the purposes of quantifying San Diego's attributes, which he does as follows: *There is a vineyard in San Diego with 5000 stocks, and 350 olive trees and another with 3600 stocks and 167 olive trees,* not to mention pomegranates, a cornfield and a beanfield. *There are also about three or four barrels of spoiled white wine and other than that, nothing worth the trouble to note.* Most of the Mission's Indians have fled to Los Angeles in search of food and clothing.

In 1851 a British adventurer describes San Diego as *a number of small* adobè *houses . . . situated at the north side of the bay.* Two decades later, the population is estimated at three thousand. *It has a large park containing several hundred acres, which, when improved, will not only prove an ornament but a source of comfort.*

Eight years after that, the aforesaid Richard Henry Dana, Jr., now an ageing celebrity, visits San Diego as a passenger and finds *no change whatever that I can see. It has certainly not grown. It is still . . . a Mexican town.*

Here's an old ranch near Mission San Diego. By the standards of my century it's not much more than a pale cottage half lost in palm trees. The corrals are nearly as empty as the semidesert horizon behind them, part of which is shrub-dotted mountains, everything grey on grey in this photograph from about 1880.

The first transcontinental train pulls into San Diego in 1885. The Sweetwater Dam goes up in 1888. A realtor enthuses: *We may say that San Diego has a population of 150,000, only they are not all here yet.*

Here come half a dozen large dams in 1887–97; between 1918 and 1924 five more dams appear, so that San Diego's thirst is solved for all time. **THE DESERT DISAPPEARS.** In 1925, county reservoirs stand ready to hold nearly half a million acre-feet!

By the way, rest assured that Los Angeles suffers no apprehensions on the score of San Diego. *Where do the fine fruits come from that are now piled on the fruit stands of San Diego? . . . from the great groves of Los Angeles City.* May poor San Diego grow and prosper! There's not water enough for true commercial accomplishment down there. Therefore, *as it could offer little by way of barter or exchange, our products would necessarily sell for gold.* Imperial County feels the same.

Chapter 55

IN MEMORIAM, IMPERIAL HAZEL DEED

(1905–2002)

> . . . we realize that California at its worst would be beyond the aspirations of people anywhere, and that California at its best, as we see it now, is beyond even their dreams.
>
> —The *Fresno Morning Republican*, 1920

Ruth Reed, daughter of the *Imperial Valley Press and Farmer*'s first editor, was actually the first child born in Imperial. Her life might have made a sweet footnote to the triumphalist saga of the Ministry of Capital which you are now reading. But what eponym could be superior to *Imperial Hazel Deed*?

She was born on 14 August 1905, to Mrs. Mary Deed. Wilber Clark had been in Imperial for four years. Who knew when Mrs. Deed got there? Imperial's green fields were a small huddle in those days, and the baby girl named Imperial might well have opened her eyes in some hot tent buzzing with flies; soon she must have obtained a view of greyish-black mountains in rows upon yellow sand so far away. Her mother must have stood holding her, looking down the swells and bulges of gravel mountains to the blue and yellow horizon, past a salt lake as smooth and hazy as a dream.

Otis P. Tout, who customarily names both parents in these announcements *(the birth of a daughter to Mr. and Mrs. A. H. Rehkopf . . .)* omits any mention of her father. Indeed, his two-sentence account specifically singles out the mother, who must therefore have been alone: *She named the child Imperial Hazel Deed.*

Any one of three motives could explain such a name: pride, hope or calculation. If I had to guess, I would choose the first, given that almost everybody in the Imperial Valley in those days must have been either a boomer or a believer. **WATER IS HERE**. *We need have no fear that our lands will not become better and better as the years go by.* Don't you think the neighbors loved that name?

Had she been less conspicuously named, I never would have tried to learn about her life. Then I devoted years and dollars to find out almost nothing.

The absence of the father, Oren Deed (all I know of him is that he was born in Kansas of Danish parents and that he wedded Mary in about 1903) is a trifle ominous, but didn't Barbara Worth herself, happiest and most accomplished of girls, begin life as an orphan? I looked up Imperial Hazel Deed in the death index volumes for Imperial County all the way up to 1980 and missed her, which meant she had married and therefore yielded up her maiden name, or sold out and moved like Wilber and Elizabeth Clark, or was still alive; I could almost imagine meeting some happy, sun-weathered crone sitting in a porch swing near Meloland, lovingly cared for by a clan of children and grandchildren. That was what I wanted.

But in that case, why did the Deeds not appear in the newspapers, the histories?

My hired genealogists believed Mary Deed to be identical with Mary Kunkel, who was a dressmaker in 1910 and a clerk in 1915. She might or might not have married Albert Benjamin Webster in 1915.

This lady was born in 1880 in Bell Creek, Craig, Nebraska, which I suppose from acquaintance with that state to be another hot, dry place. (Nebraska, you will be happy to know, possesses a town called Imperial.) Her mother was from Virginia, her father from Pennsylvania. They seem to have been farmers, and therefore the perfect ancestors of an Imperial pioneer. On the census for that year, she was listed as *baby daughter,* and her mother's profession was *keeping house.* Her sister Birdie was a year older than she. Her brothers George and Luther became chicken farmers. In 1900, they shared a home with Birdie.* Mary, who would have been twenty, must have already gone ahead to California by then, for she is not listed on their page of the census schedule. The Chocolate Mountains would have been dusty blue, although there would not yet have been any Salvation Mountain ahead like a bunch of melted candles. Surely Mary would not have been in the Imperial Valley. George Chaffey had not opened his headgates.

Who came to Imperial first, Mary or her younger brother George? The latter owned a farm in El Centro in 1910, but like Mary he was invisible; neither Judge Farr nor Otis P. Tout mentions him. At that time he was twenty-seven and single. The genealogists determined him to have possessed *black hair, brown eyes, short build.* By 1920 he had married and removed to Tulare County with his wife Virginia; they were sufficiently well off to board a hired maid.

Here are Mary Deed's children: the one we care about, whom my genealogists could find listed only as Hazel G. Deed, *in California in about 1906,* an error of only a few months, but all the same a reminder not to trust overmuch in apodictic fact; Mildred M. Deed, born in Nebraska in about 1908, so evidently Mary Deed had returned to her birthplace by then; and Clarence Deed, born in Sacramento in 1911. The family's continued absence from the territory of this book is further implied

*By 1910, Luther and his wife Alice were in Santa Barbara, living with their brother- and sister-in-law and two nephews. Their parents would also be living there in 1920. Luther had "blue eyes, full build, brown hair." What else should the census taker have asked him? Now it is too late.

by the fact that no one named Deed is listed in the *Imperial Valley Business and Resident Directory 1912–1913*. There are no Deeds in the county indices of grantors and grantees up to 1919, no Deeds in the marriage index, either. The closest I could find was the registered marriage in Holtville of a certain Samuel Deed, or more probably (the handwriting is difficult) Dees, who was twenty-three and a scion of Arkansas, to an Uloa Harlan of Texas, aged eighteen, on 9 October 1911, six years after Imperial Hazel Deed was born. So now you know that I have exercised due diligence.

The fact that Imperial was now known as Hazel I take to be evidence of her mother's disillusionment with the subject area of this book. They had left Imperial County, and did not want to remember it.

Who was she? What sort of person was she? What did she look like? Perhaps she had *black hair, brown eyes, short build.*

In the archives of Mexicali there is a photograph of a bleached and bygone señorita in a short skirt as blindingly white as her thighs; she holds a grey parasol, smiling with awkward grace.—This is not enough, but it is something. As for Imperial Hazel Deed, all I know of her is her name.

Mary was thirty in 1910, and may well have kept enough of her youth to allure Albert Benjamin Webster five years later. In the federal census record she was listed as head of household.

In 1920, Imperial Hazel Deed was fourteen, according to the census. Once again, her estimated birth year was *about 1906*. She could read and write. She was living in Selma, Fresno, California. What do we know about her? *White, female, single, daughter, able to read, able to write.* Her mother, now on the verge of forty, was a widow, and therefore still head of household. She could not have been in dire circumstances, for she owned her own home. Like her daughter, she was literate. Her former father-in-law, Frank Deed, was living in that home, which makes me think that Imperial Hazel's father must have died instead of abandoning the family. If Mary had indeed married Albert Benjamin Webster in 1915, then she was twice widowed in short order. Frank Deed was sixty-three by then. The young girl's brother Clarence would have been about nine years old. In 1942 he was going to join the Navy. He died in 1984 and is buried in the Inland Empire—in Riverside National Cemetery, to be exact. What about Mildred? *White, female, single, daughter.*

What was the story of Imperial Hazel Deed? I tried birth and death certificates for San Diego County. There were no matches. The county clerk was nice enough not to charge me. Another county clerk named Alejandra found a girl named Bernstein Deed, born in 1992.—It's the only one that pops up, she said. The father was born in California in 1965.

Then in the State Library I finally tried the *California Death Index 1905–1929,* where I found: DEED HAZEL. AGE 14. COUNTY 10 (which was Fresno). MONTH 3, DAY 20, YEAR 20, DATE REGISTERED 20, STATE FILE #11526.

So I went to the Office of Vital Statistics for a death certificate and it was certainly hers.

She died at nine-thirty in the morning on Saturday, the twentieth of March, 1920, of peritonitis brought on by a ruptured appendix. An operation had been attempted the previous day. She died in the hospital. There was no autopsy.

I searched the *Fresno Morning Republican* for her obituary. Well, probably the paper had already gone to press by the time she died. On Sunday, the "Commercial News" section reported this datum from the San Francisco market: *Eggplant, Imperial Valley, nominal.* On Monday, Imperial Hazel Deed was buried. (The undertaker was J. L. Robinson of Selma, embalmer's license number #312.) On Tuesday, the state of Washington ratified female suffrage. Every day there was more commercial news, but the child who had already been shucked of her grandiose name continued to be ignored in death. For instance, on Saturday the twenty-seventh, the citrus column announced that in Boston, oranges were up but the lemon market was unchanged. In Cleveland six cars of oranges were sold. In New York the market was steady on lemons and tangerines. Then an advertisement advised us to **PHONE 3700 FOR THESE SPECIALS TODAY**, LETTUCE, namely **Fine Fancy Imperial Valley** lettuce, was on sale for fifteen cents per two heads. April thirtieth was going to be Raisin Day in Fresno . . .

STATE OF CALIFORNIA
CERTIFICATION OF VITAL RECORD

STATE OF CALIFORNIA
DEPARTMENT OF HEALTH SERVICES

PLACE OF DEATH. DIST. No. 1054 (To be inserted by Registrar) — California State Board of Health 20-011526 1036
BUREAU OF VITAL STATISTICS — State Index No. 145
STANDARD CERTIFICATE OF DEATH — Local Registered No. 145

County of Fresno
City or Town of
Rural Registration District Fresno
(No. County Hospital St.; G P.R. Ward) [If death occurred in a hospital or institution, give its NAME instead of street and number and fill out Nos. 18a and 18b.]

FULL NAME Hazel Deed

PERSONAL AND STATISTICAL PARTICULARS

SEX Female — COLOR OR RACE White — SINGLE, MARRIED, WIDOWED, OR DIVORCED (Write the word) single

If married, widowed, or divorced HUSBAND of (or) WIFE of

DATE OF BIRTH Aug. 14, 1905 (Month) (Day) (Year)

AGE 14 years 7 months 6 days — If LESS than 1 day, ...hrs. or ...min.

OCCUPATION (a) Trade, profession, or particular kind of work none
(b) General nature of industry, business, or establishment in which employed (or employer)
(c) Name of employer

BIRTHPLACE (State or country) (city or town) California

PARENTS
NAME OF FATHER Oren Deed
BIRTHPLACE OF FATHER (city or town) (State or country) Kansas
MAIDEN NAME OF MOTHER Mary Kunkel
BIRTHPLACE OF MOTHER (city or town) (State or country) Nebraska

LENGTH OF RESIDENCE
At Place of Death ...years ...months 1 days
(Primary registration district)
(If nonresident, give city or town and state)
In California life ...years ...months ...days
How long in U.S., if of foreign birth? ...years ...months ...days

THE ABOVE IS TRUE TO THE BEST OF MY KNOWLEDGE
(Informant) Fresno County Hospital
(Address) Fresno Cal.

Filed ...19...
Filed Mar 21, 19 20 R N Carlson — Subregistrar / Registrar or Deputy

MEDICAL CERTIFICATE OF DEATH

DATE OF DEATH March 20 1920 (Month) (Day) (Year)

I HEREBY CERTIFY, That I attended deceased from March 19 1920, to March 20 1920
that I last saw her alive on March 20 1920
and that death occurred on the date stated above at 9:30A m.
The CAUSE OF DEATH* was as follows:

1st Peritonitis-- General

Ruptured Appendix

(Duration) ...years ...months ...days

Contributory

(Duration) ...years ...months ...days

Where was disease contracted if not at place of death?
Did an operation precede death? yes Date of March 19, 1920
Was there an autopsy? no
What test confirmed diagnosis?

(Signed) C. M. Vanderburg M.D.
Mar. 20 1920 (Address) County Hospital

*State the DISEASE CAUSING DEATH, or, in deaths from VIOLENT CAUSES, state (1) MEANS OF INJURY; and (2) whether (probably) ACCIDENTAL, SUICIDAL, or HOMICIDAL. (See reverse side for additional space.)

PLACE OF BURIAL OR REMOVAL Odd Fellows Cem — DATE OF BURIAL Mar 22 1920

UNDERTAKER J. L. ROBINSON — EMBALMER'S LICENSE No. 312
ADDRESS SELMA CAL.

This is to certify that this document is a true copy of the official record filed with the Office of Vital Records.

02 NOV 25 AM 10: 04

MICHAEL L. RODRIAN
STATE REGISTRAR OF VITAL RECORDS — DATE ISSUED

001540520

This copy not valid unless prepared on engraved border displaying seal and signature of Registrar.

ANY ALTERATION OR ERASURE VOIDS THIS CERTIFICATE

Chapter 56

STOLID OF FACE AND LANGUID

(1901–2003)

> Mexican women turned their tortillas on improvised griddles; Indian women, stolid of face and languid, did their share, fed the bucks on the levee and took care of their naked youngsters who huddled like frightened rabbits under the mesquites.
>
> —Otis B. Tout, 1928

If Imperial County "went wrong" somewhere, transforming "potentially . . . the most valuable land in the United States" into the poorest county in California, *how* did it go wrong? I asked an official of the Employment Development Department in El Centro this question, and he said that he hadn't been working there very long, so he didn't know. A plausible Marxist-Leninist answer might be that many homesteaders became rich enough (or that the Ministry of Capital started rich enough) to hire poor people to work their land. Holdings enlarged themselves beyond the statutory limits of the 1902 Reclamation Act, therefore requiring ever more legal and illegal laborers for the harvest, so that the county's per capita income went down once those laborers began to get counted. They are certainly *undercounted*. One study begins by asserting that migrant farmworkers are *by any reckoning . . . the poorest, the least represented and the most abused class of working people in the United States.* As for Hispanic workers in particular, after Mexico lost the war of 1846–47, *throughout much of the area, Mexican Americans were reduced to the status of menial laborers serving white masters. This is a fair description of the state of affairs that exists in the border region today.*

In 2003, Mr. Philip Ricker of Holtville writes this letter to the editor: *The great percentage of farm workers are green carders from Mexico who are seasonal . . .* They *cause the Valley to have the highest unemployment and poverty rating in the state. They contribute little to the economy of the Valley, even though the farmers hype that they do . . .*

Indeed, if you read *The Conquest of Arid America,* or *The Winning of Barbara Worth,* you may believe that white farmers did everything on their democratically small homesteads. When the Barbara Worth Hotel opened in El Centro on 8 May

1915, everyone got to see the Imperial Valley's beginnings depicted in oils, one or two of *which will stand for the ages, no doubt,* never mind that the Barbara Worth burned to ashes in 1962. Anyhow, here is "Labor": *Picture a man in desert garb, his throat open to the sun and wind, his arms bare to the elbows—yes, just such a man you will see, a hundred times every day in Imperial Valley—the laborer. Well knit muscles, strong in body, sturdy in character, the laborer bears the load of work faithfully.* In *The Winning of Barbara Worth,* his name is Pat.

In Mexican Imperial, his name is José or Manuel; and in the *ejidos,* he has truly built and labored for himself. In American Imperial, his name is Pat, or Wilber Clark, if you like, but he has many helpers even though *The Winning of Barbara Worth* would have us believe that *he made a success through his own efforts.* It is bemusing, and ultimately chilling, to watch how American Imperial uses up one race after another for her ends, and then they're *gone,* because *I have never been cheated out of a dollar in my life.* Mexican labor has lasted the longest, a good century now; and as I write this sentence on a muggy spring day in 2006 I remember the title of a movie that came out recently: "A Day Without a Mexican." What if all the gardeners, babysitters and waitresses refused to appear? In 1886, the *Rural Californian* inquires: *Suppose, for instance, that every Chinaman is driven out of the Santa Ana Valley next week, who is to take his place in the field, in the laundry, and in the kitchen?*

In 2004 I asked Alice Woodside (born in Imperial County in the early 1940s) whether she recollected any whites who worked their own farms. She replied:

You know, maybe when I was a kid maybe there were a few leftovers, people who lived in very dilapidated homes, very poor, where there was still white labor. I was unaware if they had money or if they didn't, because nobody did. There was such a population of people who were pretty impoverished, I would say, but I didn't even look at it that way . . .

Chapter 57

THE DAYS OF LUPE VÁSQUEZ

(2003)

The Imperial Valley's fertile soil and mild climate allow farmers to enjoy year-round planting, cultivation and harvest.

—Imperial Irrigation District, fact sheet on agriculture, 2001

When I wake up in the morning I don't feel like getting up. It's too cold and I'm tired from the day before and the first thing that comes into my head is it's gonna be a long day. If there's ice, I'm not gonna get paid for that time. It sucks. At least I'll get paid something. Most of these places pay every day.

When you take a sandwich, they say, *Don't get up, honey, I'll buy a torta.* They make fun of you. They say, *Don't get up, honey,* when you break out a sandwich. They know damn well your wife's not gonna get up. Why should she get up at three-thirty in the morning?

And the sex, there's no sex. They make fun of it. They say, turn your back on your wife. Eat, shower, *nada.* I don't worry about it, 'cause Sancho does it. She's in Sancho's hands. That's what they say. You might as well laugh and make fun. Day goes easier.

At three-thirty I get up, drink coffee, get dressed, sometimes eat breakfast. I'll drink a beer in the morning, one or two. There's always this guy selling beer at Donut Avenue, at a dollar a beer. He has slanted eyes, but he's Mexican. They call him Chino. He's been caught but he just sells his beer and goes on home. He's a smart old man.

From my *colonia* it's a twenty-minute walk to where I catch the taxi and another ten-minute walk when I get here in Calexico at four-thirty. The first thing I try to do is get myself in a good crew where they're gonna pay me. I decide on what kinda work I wanna do. I pick the easiest, and for me the easiest is broccoli, because I don't wanna crouch.* Some people say that lettuce is easier, but you crouch and

*On 23 September 2004, the state of California finally banned most hand-weeding, "declaring the practice an immediate danger to the health of thousands of workers." But there is little that lettuce-pickers can do about the fact that heads of lettuce lie on the ground. I suppose that humanitarians will soothe aching backs by inventing an automatic lettuce-picker which will throw people out of work.

get wet. With broccoli you get wet, you get cold, but once the sun is out, you warm up. On Donut Avenue some guy's yelling, *Broccoli, broccoli! I'll pay you every day!* This guy is hustling for the foreman. I watch for that guy.

In June, there's cantaloupes and watermelons. There's tomatoes. In July, August, September, there's no work, hardly none, 'cause it's too hot. In October they start thinning out the broccoli fields, start planting.

If you work for a crew for ten straight days, most of the guys will be the same. Well, maybe not most, but some, I'll know their faces. Lot of times the word will be passed: Don't work for that asshole; he yells too much.

Sometimes there'll be a bus that'll take you over there, and sometimes there'll be vehicles that'll charge you two dollars or three dollars for a ride. So I prefer the bus.

You never see the Border Patrol.

When you get to the field and the ice hasn't melted, you can wait inside, but a lot of people make bonfires. You can play cards, joke around. Some might smoke their joint, shoot their heroin. A lot of the girls are used to dick-tease the guys, but most guys never get some. The guys really think they're gonna get some! It used to be, years ago, that the foreman used to get pussy: If you don't gimme some, you won't get no work tomorrow. But even now, some of them just get to take it easy, just write down the employees' names and jobs in exchange for giving pussy. For the guys, what they do doesn't matter. For the other women, some of them get jealous. I never even try. I mean, women, it doesn't matter what race and what creed, they all have the same spirit of vengeance against you.

Most of the time, the ice will disappear by about nine-thirty. But sometimes there's that black ice and you wait till noon. You don't get paid for that time. That's just another way they rob us. We work till dark. I've worked places where they shine lights on the field so we can keep working at night. That's in December, January, February. But when I've been working all the days of one of those months, usually there's ice only for about a week.

When there's no ice, you start working as soon as you can see.

The foreman says, *Muchachitos,* little kids, let's go! Or, come on, ladies! Just like the way they talk to us in the military. Then everybody gets their tool, a hoe or knife or whatever. And then I'm feeling terrible, horrible, like you don't wanna start.

It's worst when you're on your last couple of hours. The last hour is always the worst. The foreman understands that everyone's tired. Most of the time he won't say nothin', 'cause by then the job's almost done. A few will grab a hoe and help you out for a little while.

For an eight-hour job, it's forty-five bucks. When I first started, in the early seventies, I used to make about seventeen dollars a day. Two-fifty an hour times eight hours is what?* With taxes you'd take home about seventeen, eighteen bucks. I'd say the work's the same now; it's the same.† Maybe the foremen don't hurry you up and treat you as bad as they used to. We were scared, you know. We had to hurry up. For the foremen, money is more important to them than their own people. They gotta kiss ass, and the way they do that is by making us work harder.

They usually let us off where the railroad is, right back by that seafood place on Imperial Avenue, I think on Second Street.

A lot of times, after work you drink a beer with two or three work buddies. Not friends, not buddies, just work buddies. I'm in the mood to go home right away. Once in awhile I'll do it, but when I was younger and single I used to party all night, screw whores all night and come to work broke.

In January it's broccoli, lettuce, asparagus, and caulifower. In February it's the same, and then also carrots in February, March, April. I never done carrots. In March it's all lettuce, just lettuce left and a few broccoli. It'll end by the end of this month.

In April there's hardly anything. It's kinda like a break. A lot of people have no work. All that's been done in this month is the weeding of the cantaloupes, of the watermelons, and they're weeding it, they're cleaning it, they're uncovering it from the plastic for the freezing season.

May's onions, lots of onions. Everyone's talking onions. They pay you piecework, sixty, seventy cents a sack. It takes me about five minutes, three minutes a sack. And they pay on how fast you top. At the beginning of the topping season, the ground is still muddy and sticky, so it takes a long time to shake the mud out of it. Later on, when the land is dry, it's faster. When the land is sandy, it's loose.

In May and June there's also cauliflower and tomatoes. In June you have cantaloupes, watermelons, tomatoes, bell peppers. Bell peppers, you just pick 'em off the plant, fill the basket, carry it to the end of the row. Now they say it's different; I don't know. They say they have a machine. I don't know if they pour it in a truck or boxes, I don't know.

There's hardly anything in July.‡ They're still the last of the cantaloupes, maybe the last of the watermelons. People collect unemployment. A lot of people go up north to the Salinas Valley to do lettuce, or to the Coachella Valley to do grapes.

In August it's dead, Bill. Totally dead. There ain't nothin'. You don't hardly see no soul. I just stay inside, kick back, drink a lot of beer.

And in September there's no crops, Bill. It's dead. They start planting the lettuce

*It would have been twenty dollars.

†I wish you could have heard the weariness in his voice as he said this.

‡Indeed, Imperial County's unemployment rate tended to increase during the summer months.

and broccoli and stuff on the ranches, but the farming is asleep that month. In October there's no harvesting. In November they start harvesting some broccoli, some lettuce.

December, that's when all the work starts. Lettuce, cauliflower, asparagus, some spinach, some cabbage. Corn . . .

God, so that's my life.

Chapter 58

"LUPE IS LUCKIER"

The Days of José López from Jalisco

(2003)

> The spectacular incidents connected with the reclamation of the desert and with the subduing of the turbulent Colorado have given Imperial Valley a charm of romance that is hard to equal. A history of agriculture under such conditions must be a story of human interest as well as a statistical record of development . . .
>
> —Judge F. C. Farr, 1918

I usually wake up between five and six. I just don't get up real quickly, because those abandoned buildings, a lot of 'em are used by addicts to go smoke and do whatever they do, so I wait until they're done doing their thing, but all the same I got to get up early. Myself, been a few months since I smoked any coke. In Mexicali it's hard to get rock. What you have to do is buy the concentrated stuff and make your own rock. Well, anyways, that's one of the reasons I get up early, before the police come.

There are usually other people there. Sometimes I go to sleep alone and wake up with other people. We're almost all men.

When I go to sleep, I take with me a gallon of tap water. You gotta go ask somebody you see watering their garden. Some people don't even wanna give you water, man. Some people are just mean. So I bring it to the abandoned house at night, so I can wash up in the morning, so I don't have to go out and then come back again and maybe get caught by the police. I go to the public showers once or twice a week: thirty-three pesos. The other days I just shower from a jug in an abandoned house. So I get up, take a shower, take a leak, whatever. In restaurants I get napkins, whatever, to wipe myself. Sometimes I have to use a paper bag.

So I walk toward the border, stop over at a stand over there by the taxis, and if I have the funds, I get a coffee, a pastry maybe. Then I sit down right here by the wall. I try to be here around seven, seven-thirty. Sometimes I walk and sit over at that bench over there if this gate is closed. They open this gate at eight in the morning. Then I watch for tourists, people who might need some help, and try to hit 'em up. I say: Good morning. Can I help you? Do you need a taxicab? If they say no, I still insist: Are you looking for a good pharmacy even if you lost your prescription? I'm friends with the head pharmacist. Or do you want to eat good, or shop good? Do you want to know where there's a shopping mall just like in your country? I just try to convince 'em! I have about two minutes before their voice changes and the way they say no changes; then it's hopeless.

For taking 'em to a taxi, opening the door for 'em, and telling the driver where they want to go, I might get more; I might get less. They might gimme a dollar, two dollars . . . My biggest tip for escorting a couple to a cab was twenty dollars. They were middle-aged people, really nice.

That's what I do from seven A.M. to eight P.M. The most I've made during one day is close to two hundred dollars. That happens rarely, maybe five times a year. And the least, some days I haven't even made a single peso. On an average day, I make, say, twenty dollars.

I try to stick to a fare, a price, so as soon as I start workin' for 'em, I tell 'em I'm expecting twenty dollars, and I usually get it. But sometimes they don't pay. Then, since I done my work, my part of the deal, for them to say, I'm payin' you nothing, that gets me mad. But that's pretty rare.

Most of the people I get are like truck drivers who gotta stay overnight in Calexico and they wanna go to a strip bar and get a girl and like that. Part of my job is to see those waitresses don't rip 'em off. I take pride in my job, man. I care. Sometimes they want me to drink with 'em but I say, no, no, just one beer, two beers or a soda, so I can watch out for 'em. Sometimes it makes me feel lousy, like *wanting;* I wish I had the money for a girl. But on the occasions when they offer to buy me a girl, I always say: Thank you very much, but I got expenses; I'd rather have the money.

The girls, some of 'em are nice; some of 'em have stuck-up ways. Some tell me: Jack up the price so I can give you something. With the price as it is, I can't give you anything.—But I say: Don't worry about it. I'm already getting paid.

If I have only a little bit of money I'll probably wait until two or three in the afternoon to eat lunch, because sometimes I can't afford to eat three meals. At eight I might have something for my dinner, a little piece of bread, some milk, whatever.

Where to sleep depends on the situation. When a building's abandoned, you can tell right away, here in Mexico. All of us homeless, we know 'em all by sight. You gotta do what you gotta do. Scariest thing was waking up and this guy was dead. He had OD'd.* I called the ambulance, and the police took me in for investigation for forty-eight hours. When we found the guy, I was the last one to leave that building, man. The others were rushing out. I just thought it wasn't right.

Sometimes, you know, I get bored, especially if I'm getting turned down, so I might start a conversation with some guys or one of the girls. There are disappointments every day. Lupe is luckier than me, just by the simple fact that he can be on *that side.*

(And José pointed across the border wall.)

Why don't you work in a *maquiladora*? I asked him.

Oh, wages are miserable.†

I know who to go to, he said then, and I understood that he was referring to a border guide.—You know, you get to knowing stories and meeting people. You try to find out who's the best. The one I have in mind, I see him three or four days out of the week.

How often do you go to jail?

I would say, once a month at least. It's twenty-four or thirty-six hours. It's just when they're making raids and I'm not having permanent ID when I'm here. Now it's changed. Say, you might even find your money when you get out! *La mordida*‡ not to get arrested, is maybe twenty dollars. I've done it a few times. Then they won't mess with you all day.

In prison, show respect but don't be a coward. If you fight, win it or lose it, you're all right, because you stood up for yourself.

How often do you go with a girl?

Once a month. Sometimes it's that girl María. Sometimes I get lucky and find another. If I have a lot of money I might do it every two weeks, maybe in the Nuevo Pacífico. Usually I tell the girls, you know what, you'd better take good care of me. I say the same for my customers, and they give them, not the royal treatment, but it's okay.

How often do you keep in touch with your family?

I try to phone or wire them every week or every two weeks. I gotta call this little

*Overdosed.

†On another occasion he remarked: "The jobs around here, they don't pay good. I don't wanna bring my family over here and be struggling. The wage here, it's fifty dollars a week. Over there"—and he pointed across the line, into America—"it's fifty dollars a day."—This reminded me that at the beginning of the twentieth century, the cost of labor on the Riverside citrus plantations had been a dollar to a dollar-fifty per day. In south China, where so many of Riverside's citrus workers originated, it was ten or fifteen cents. Do some gradients remain unalterable, or is it only the shorthand for expressing them that remains the same?

‡*The bite.* A bribe.

pharmacy store right in town. I send a messenger to go call 'em, since they don't have a phone or nothing.

Who misses you the most?

I would say none of 'em.

That was the personal information of my friend José López, for which I paid him ten dollars. Why was it that that one thing made me the saddest? *Who misses you the most? I would say none of 'em.* That made me sad, all right. The fact that he had to pay the police just to be left alone to beg all day, that was rough. The fear he suffered when he slept in those abandoned buildings, that I read more in his face than in his words, but it made me pity him. Still, the worst of all was this: *Lupe is luckier.* And at once I could hear Lupe with his head between his hands, groaning: *God, so that's my life.*

Chapter 59

IMPERIAL REPRISE

(1905–2003)

1

WATER IS HERE. *Some people don't even wanna give you water, man. Some people are just mean.* I can't help believing in people . . .

2

Yes, just such a man you will see, a hundred times every day in Imperial Valley—the laborer. I think we all feel sorry for 'em. You know, maybe when I was a kid maybe there were a few leftovers, people who lived in very dilapidated homes, very poor, where there was still white labor. *Trade is leading Culture, a beautiful young woman.* She named the child Imperial Hazel Deed. **White, female, single, daughter, able to read, able to write.** It's just another die-off. It's natural.

3

Yes, just such a man you will see, a hundred times every day in Imperial Valley—the laborer. They contribute little to the economy of the Valley, even though the farmers hype that they do. *But sometimes there's that black ice and you wait till noon. I've worked places where they shine lights on the field so we can keep working at night.* God, so that's my life.

4

He sold out at a fancy price. I think we all feel sorry for 'em. God, so that's my life.

PART FIVE

ELABORATIONS

Chapter 60

THE LINE ITSELF

(1895–1926)

Every now and then a word
crosses the border,
. . . marrying another . . .
little by little words turn mestiza . . .
The dark-hued family of words
produces a blond daughter . . .

—Antonio Deltoro, 1999

In 1895, San Diego dispatches an alert to lonely Mr. Wadham, the Customs Collector at Tia Juana, California: *I have reason to believe that Mexicans or others who are carrying wood across the line into this country, are engaged in smuggling Cigars and Opium* . . . But what can Mr. Wadham do about it? The line remains little more than an idea.

In 1907, one year after Northside begins to require competency in English as a precondition of naturalization and two years before the first Immigration officials arrive at Calexico, the Asiatic Exclusion League sounds its own call: *Of 2,182 Japs arriving at Mazatlan, advices from mexico informed us that they had nearly all made a bee-line for the border* . . . How terrible! Fortunately, I read in the newspaper ninety-nine years later that the President will take care of everything. *"It makes sense to use fencing along the border in key locations in order to do our job," Mr. Bush said in a speech at the headquarters of the Yuma Sector Border Patrol. "We're in the process of making our border the most technologically advanced border in the world."*

Alas, we remain near the beginning of that novel! In 1914, the year after a bridge finally spans the Colorado at Yuma, our Collector at Calexico seizes six cans (three pounds) of smoking opium, but it is only the opium that he gets: *I halted two mexicans on 2nd Street, three blocks east of the Custom House at 6 P.M. Jan. 3rd. One was carrying a sack which I demanded they allow me to search and when I took hold of it, he released his hold and ran for the boundary line which was a block distant. I was unable to overtake or halt him and the other made his escape in the opposite direction.*

Such failures to enforce Northside's authority must have been the rule . . . *Said W. M. Tiller crossed over from Mexico at 11 A.M. April 9, 1914, when hailed by me he started to run. I ran after him and when I had nearly overtaken him he threw himself into an irrigation ditch at the same time throwing the opium into the water.*

On the other hand, delineation's tenuousness facilitated that selfsame authority's incursions into Southside. In 1906, Colonel William Greene, proprietor of the Sonoran company town of Cananea, suffers inconvenience when his copper miners, whose wages he will not raise to match those of their American coworkers, go on strike. Both sides rack up fatalities. What to do? Colonel Greene calls Governor Izabal, who obligingly accedes to a visit from two hundred and seventy-five Arizona Rangers. There being a line of sorts between Arizona and Mexico, Rangers cross it in dribs and drabs, quite unofficially. Then they commence the job of killing and being killed by Mexicans. Reinforced by the *rurales,* they break the strike.

Returning to territory more directly relevant to this book, I report that in 1915 *the Collector cites our amicable relations here, that we have been allowed to pass into Mexico with motor car along our levee track without inspection, or even bothering to give notice . . . as near as I could gather from his Spanish without interrogating him about the matter particularly, he cited the fact that our Imperial* [Canal?] *was allowed to get partly over the line without comment or trouble, and that our shore pipe line is partly in Mexico.*

Indeed, ease proffers advantages for civilians, too. The Imperial Valley directory for 1920 informs us that *Imperial Irrigation District comprises 603,841 acres of which 412,000 are under cultivation in the United States and 360,000 are in Imperial Valley, Mexico.** Harry Chandler's entity, the Colorado River Land Company, wins easy permission from the government of Northside for its livestock to range between Mexican and American Imperial, so long as they have no diseases and stay six months or less. More than a quarter of the way into the century, the *Los Angeles Times* can still headline the latest factory in Mexicali as **A New Kind of Pioneering in Imperial**. And why not conceptualize Imperial in our way? Didn't we win the war? I accordingly encomiumize the grandeur of *CALEXICO*, shown on Imperial County Assessor's Map number 17–15, as a big rectangle with a square eaten from its upper righthand corner, the property owner's name pencilled in and then erased from it. South of the border is *Mexicali*, not in capital letters; the word indicates merely a railroad.

(On this map, signed *Th* and dated 1911, we do see a yellowing blankness named *MEXICO*, into which the Encino Canal speeds south by southwest from Sharp's Heading on the Main Canal . . .)

*This acreage fluctuated from year to year. For instance, in 1918, when the total crop area of the Imperial Irrigation District comprised 410,201 acres, "in addition to the above," continued the Imperial County Development Agent, "it might be interesting to note that in the territory in Lower California immediately adjacent to Imperial County, there is an acreage of about 90,000, mostly planted to cotton and grain, grown by American farmers and marketed in Imperial County."

But the authorities deeper in Northside deem these to be perilous conveniencies. And so they make their policies and send out their orders. At the beginning of 1915, the Customs Collector at Andrade, which lies on the line almost at Imperial County's southeast extremity, reports that he *would strongly recommend, as a preventive measure against smuggling, that the Geological Survey (or whatever department erects International fencing) and the Mexican government, be interested in building a good substantial fence from the Colorado River west along the boundary for about five miles.*

By the beginning of Prohibition, the line has begun to enforce itself more stringently. To be sure, some indications of mutability remain. Senator Henry Ashurst proposes to cut the Gordian knot and buy Lower California outright; our dear friend Harry Chandler has already been indicted for and acquitted of seeking to alter the government of Baja California. But no one undoes our ditch. Therefore, we'd better dig it deeper!

After a shootout between two Mexican smugglers and Customs officers *(Inspector Norman G. Ross was killed by an apprehended alien . . . Inspector Frank G. Goddell was shot and wounded by an autoist)*, Los Angeles sends out the following directive to Calexico, Tia Juana, and other Imperial border stations: *You are directed to instruct all officers under your jurisdiction to shoot to kill any known smugglers of this character who are detected in the act of smuggling and who are armed and evidently intending to resist United States officers.* But those officers remain more or less in Mr. Wadham's situation. In 1923 the Deputy Collector in Charge at Tecate recommends *that authority be secured from the State . . . to place cement blocks on each side of the road at various places, where we inspect traffic,* in order for the officers to *perform our duties in a manner that will not leave us at the mercy of outlaws . . .*—for two years earlier, an Immigration officer in Campo had been run over and killed by whiskey smugglers. Once cement blocks have been stationed, Northside's guardians hope to close off the entryway with a chain. This notion of the Deputy Collector's conveys some sense of how open the remainder of the line must be. Compared to Homeland Security officers of my own day, these isolated sentinels appear hapless.

Chapter 61

THE FIRST COYOTE

(1895–1926)

On the 28th of last February I informed Your Excellency of the decision that I had made to try to reach Northern California.

—de Anza to Bucareli, 1774

From the standpoint of Operation Gatekeeper, the very first Entry Without Inspection must have taken place within moments of when the Treaty of Guadalupe Hidalgo was ratified. If that sounds absurd, it is only because Gatekeeper is absurd. No matter. For decades, people of Mexican, American and various tribal nationalities made their way across the line without deference. Where did it exist, as I said, but on maps and other documents, and in a few white steles convenient to overlook? Even Northside offficialdom overlooked them, at first. When San Diego advised Mr. Wadham, *I have reason to believe that Mexicans or others who are carrying wood across the line into this country, are engaged in smuggling Cigars and Opium . . . ,* it was not the wood-carrying that was problematic. In the era of Gatekeeper, of course, any untracked movement across the border is forbidden. As de Sade remarks, it's a multitude of laws that creates a multitude of crimes. Once the flow of goods over the line became subject to control, smugglers appeared. Once this control applied to people, the body-smugglers—*polleros,* guides, coyotes—began to flourish. In 2006, the price of a coyote in San Luis Río Colorado was approximately two thousand dollars. A century earlier, it was still easy to be a *solo,* as long as one showed no evidence of Asian descent.

But who was Imperial's first coyote? He must have appeared quite soon after Chaffey's headgates opened and maybe even before; since the very first official warning I can find (14 February 1915), duly telegraphed to us from the Mounted Inspector Jacumba, expresses no surprise about the existence of PARTIES WILLIAM WALKER AND JAMES CHILLISON OF CALEXICO, WHO ARE ALLEDGED [*sic*] TO BE IN THE BUSINESS of smuggling opium and Chinese. Los Angeles has just telegraphed to Calexico: Proceed immediately to Thermal; thence Martinez Indian Agency. Gather evidence smuggling Chinese by Seddles and Chillison who escaped. Goldie Evans and H. Bugkley and six Chinese arrested by Stanley. Two automobiles still there . . . If opium in automobiles machines may be confiscated.

In 1924, Border Patrol subdistrict headquarters was founded at El Centro; and that same year, coincident with the Johnson-Reed Immigration Act, which aimed to be a new Chinese Exclusion Act just for Mexicans, the first patrol went out. *They'll pop their heads up in a minute. They do work most Americans wouldn't do. We're in the hills, day in and day out, to try and deter them. I think we all feel sorry for 'em.*

Chapter 62

THE FIRST HOBO

(1901)

> Two men, declared to be the first hoboes to visit the Valley, wandered into Imperial in December, 1901. They missed fame by failing to leave their names with the editor of the Press.
>
> —The *Imperial Valley Press*, 1901

And who was the first hobo? Who was the first have-not to wander through Imperial? Who was the first to die? On page eighty-seven of Book Two at the Imperial County Recorder's office we find a date of burial of 17 June 1909 for a sixty-year-old male of unknown race, unknown date of birth, unknown date of death; cause of death: *from heat while crossing the desert. Brought in from about 35 miles out in the desert.* Was he a hobo or a *pollo*? He missed fame by failing to leave his name with the editor of the *Press*.

Chapter 63

TWENTY THOUSAND IN 1920

(1906–1922)

Bigger crops mean bigger money.

—Advertisement in the *California Cultivator,* 1920

What is Imperial to you? Imperial is **TWELVE BANKS; DEPOSITS MORE THAN TWO MILLIONS**. Imperial is **10 TONS OF BUTTER SHIPPED DAILY (Largest Output of Any County in Cal.)**. Imperial is above all

NO WINTER--NO SNOW

NO CROP FAILURES

All these incantations reach you courtesy of the California Land and Water Company, which in its altruistic zeal to continue improving Arid America even maintains a special Imperial Valley exhibition room in its office in Los Angeles, and which has coined the capitalist prayer for Brawley: **20,000 IN 1920**.

El Centro, less ambitious by half, boasts the Women's 10,000 Club, which calls upon the females of that city to take all necessary measures to increase the population to ten thousand and which soon absorbs the Woman's Club of Imperial. On Thursday, 7 May 1914, our good ladies unanimously vote to purchase the Gary Corner on Seventh and Olive. The house they built still stands.* *The club colors are green and white. The club motto is, "The aim if reached or not, makes great the life."*†—*Browning*. El Centro, you see, dreams her Imperial dreams. Why not? Between 1910

*Depicted in 8" x 10" negative IV-CS-ELC-03–03. It was late afternoon and coolish when I took this picture, and I still remember the long shadows and the green foliage around the house, so green that I decided to use the green filter; I was sure that this picture would be spectacular although the woman I was with couldn't see the point; she was right and I was wrong, but "the aim if reached or not, makes great the life."

†An old lady who took up residence in the valley in 1933 told me: "We used to have bridge parties at the Women's 10,000 Club. We had our own Calexico women's club by the time I left. In Calipat I think the Methodist church was the social center. When I was in Calexico, I belonged to the Daughters of the American Revolution. My aunt was very active in the Mayflower Association. The interesting thing was how

and 1920, Imperial will be the third-fastest-growing county in the U.S.A.! The *Imperial Valley Business and Resident Directory* for 1912–13 crows: *YOU MAY FIGURE THAT . . . the Population Is Increasing at the rate of 40 per cent Every 24 Months.* In the same publication we find a proud and complete seventeen-page list of every book in the El Centro Public Library. Two years later there's even a library at the Colored School!

20,000 IN 1920! Why not? **THE DESERT DISAPPEARS**. Why not? In 1911, when Harold Bell Wright publishes *The Winning of Barbara Worth,* a ditch rank with trees runs toward Signal Mountain, from which the god of delineation has set Mexicali just a trifle back, within a No Man's Land of white flatness belonging largely to the Chandler Syndicate; and Calexico's first line of houses and yards stand flush against Southside, fronting a white sand street nearly as wide as the properties; then comes a second row, smaller, unlawned, reminiscent to me of those Slab City trailers parked in the sand. By 1920 that ditch is gone; instead, huge letters spell out UNITED STATES against the sky, and the archway's buildings of the Calexico I know are in place. *Long before the present generation was born it was ordained that Calexico should exist, and that Calexico should become the capital of a great inland empire.*

Reader, don't you believe in great beginnings? *The Imperial valley now leads in the production of early grapes,* whose Sweetwater variety were picked in Brawley on 9 June 1905. At the same time, more than a hundred and fifty loads of grain and melons pour into Brawley every day.

Great beginnings! In the years 1904, 1905, 1906, the Brawley Town Company, like the Calexico Town Company, looms large in county records, selling land to individuals with such surnames as McClermont, Mead, Blinn, Johnson, Bennett, Rupert, and to such fine organizations as the *Southern California Mission Society of Chris. Church* and the *Imperial Investment Co.* There don't seem to be too many Hispanic or Chinese names; I guess those people are busy digging ditches. Well, the McClermonts and Johnsons come through! Brawley's main street in 1910 is all dirt and low brick buildings, men and ladies crossing the photo frame side by side in their horse-and-buggy progesses, and Brawley in 1912 is brighter still. Since that 1912 directory is in front of me, let 1912 be the once-upon-a-time seed of magnificent fruit to come. Imperial is *x*. Imperial is *y*. Imperial is this book of heroes and heroines whose greatness will live down the ages (for instance: McClermont, Mead, Blinn, Johnson). White-faded ladies and white-bleached gentlemen at a never-ending party, they're a happy, weatherbeaten crew in cowboy hats.

many people belonged. I think we had thirty members. Somehow those kinds of people just congregated in a place like the Imperial Valley. Out here in Sacramento we couldn't get thirty."

In El Centro we find a line item for the law firm of Eshleman & Swing, whose second member sometimes doubles as Imperial County's District Attorney; he's the man who will truly make good by bringing home the All-American Canal! Imperial Junction, as the whole valley from Coachella down to *la línea* is still sometimes called in those days, already anticipates a high line canal, *so that there will be room for more towns and settlers as soon as water can be provided.*

In the city of Imperial, Judge Farr also lists himself as an attorney. His mammoth *History of Imperial County, California,* to which my book so often refers, will be published in 1918—posthumously, alas, and not quite finished. For awhile I kept a copy of his death certificate to remind myself that any castle I can ever build will be founded on sand. (You don't think so? You're correct, of course. I'd forgotten that ever efficacious magic charm, **THE DESERT DISAPPEARS**.) And Mrs. Robert Vaile is president of the Women's 10,000 Club, which will after all achieve its aim (not in 1920, alas, but in 1940); Mrs. Laura Waters runs the Hotel Imperial in Imperial, at the corner of Ninth and Imperial; that establishment has come along nicely since Wilber Clark's time and will undoubtedly improve forever; unfortunately, in 2003 I can't locate it. Other businesses send down their own taproots. For instance, *the Special Agent's Office at this place advises that Charles Hayward and Burt Hall, now located at Imperial, Cal., are engaged in the opium business . . . watch their movements carefully . . .*

In Holtville, Mr. Franklin Hardison advertises himself as an artesian well driller,* which is a sweet and kindly occupation: sink a hole, and water will gush paradisiacally into the air forever, gracing the family homestead with another of God's miracles. In my California, water is metered and chlorinated. I cannot believe in Franklin Hardison. He's a ghost from a better past.

Sometime between 1906 and 1910 (these dates being posterity's approximation, pencilled on the back of the fading photo), El Centro dispatches King Cotton to pose at the Imperial County Fair, accompanied by the giant simulacrum of a twenty-dollar goldpiece hanging in an arch of cheap wooden beams.

In 1913 men and horses begin to excavate the site of the new Barbara Worth Hotel. In 1915 that establishment opens. *Trade is leading Culture, a beautiful young woman . . .*

Imperial is Brawley's volunteer fire department, whose members look proud as they pose eternally beneath the smoke trees. Imperial is California herself, that feckless growing girl who would rather run than walk. So would I. *Buy Hercules Dynamite and* blast *the holes for that new orchard. Your trees will soon show you that*

*Under "Holtville City Government," the 1914 Imperial Valley directory lists L. Kendle as Water King.

they like to be planted in blasted holes. They'll grow better, bear sooner and give better grade fruit than any trees you've ever planted in the old-fashioned way. So, sign the coupon and send it in today. *Your copy of "Progressive Cultivation" is waiting for you.*

By 1920, at which time the population of Brawley is actually 5,392, and of El Centro, 5,462, the El Centro National Bank is ready to show off. First and foremost one sees the safe, suitably labeled, and in raised letters EL CENTRO BANK; it is high and mighty and shiny like an immense ingot, with a murky picture on its double doors. After taking in that marvel, the eye begins to notice the line of female tellers behind their opened ledgers, all pretty and dark-haired, all serious except for the one who is smiling as if she knows the photographer; the adding machine glitters like an Imperial town seen from the air; the tellers' cages achieve a wonderful darkness in mastery of Imperial's shining glare; then on the right are Mr. Weber and Mr. Adams, whose gender reduces their interest to me.

A history book from this era calls *the winning of the desert wastes of Imperial Valley . . . one of the most striking chapters in the wonderful romance of California history.* That's patently true, for in 1922, Imperial County becomes America's number one lettuce producer.

Chapter 64

COACHELLA WAITS

(1912–1917)

The citrus belt is largely along the foothills from Los Angeles to Redlands and across the upper part of the valley at Redlands and Riverside. All the rest of the country from this valley east . . . is made of the most broken type of foothills . . .

—G. Harold Powell, 1904

Here, in what was once deemed a hopeless desert, around the towns of Coachella, Indio, Mecca and Thermal, the people are demonstrating the peculiar fitness of the soil and climate . . .

So runs a history of Riverside County, published in 1912. Next year, thanks to an army of mules and men,* first water will enter the East Highline Canal down in Imperial; meanwhile, first water will travel those two hundred and thirty-three famous miles from the Owens Valley all the way down to San Fernando through Los Angeles's spanking new aqueduct. (You will be proud to know that Harry Chandler, owner of the *Los Angeles Times* and of most of the Mexicali Valley, *aided the promotion of the Los Angeles Aqueduct to tap the water from Owens Valley.*) Los Angeles can grow and grow. So can Imperial County.

As for Coachella . . .

What if that second line had never been drawn back in 1893? The "Coachella Valley" and the "Imperial Valley" are one, I keep saying, just as much as are the "Imperial Valley" and the "Mexicali Valley." Geographers disagree; they insist that the Imperial Valley's soil derives from mixed sedimentary deposits from the Colorado River, whereas Coachella dirt would never be what it is without the particles of granitic rock borne by the Whitewater River. But I know what I know.

The city of Riverside has kept up in the race. During the first decade of the twentieth century, Los Angeles's population tripled; San Diego's and Riverside's

*I see a glaring white road through volunteer alfalfa as short as the stubble on a pubis that was shaved two weeks ago; then, just below the sharp edge of the field itself, there is a line all the way across the photo of brim-hatted ploughmen standing tall between the wheels just behind their animals.

each slightly more than doubled. The Southern Pacific Railroad advises us that Magnolia Avenue's seven lovely miles may now be *traversed by luxurious electric cars . . . The city itself is an orange grove . . .* And the pomologist G. Harold Powell writes his wife: *I don't expect to have such a time anywhere else in California, as I have had in Riverside. There I met the cream of the orange growers and business men.* What kind of time was that exactly? *There is a grand ball here tonight, a masquerade affair. A lot of the young folks are around with their powder and puffs and big wigs . . . The orchestra is making things lively as it does every night.*

But in the southeastern reaches of the county, where the entity called Imperial holds sway, the ballroom is a patch of sand.

Brawley hopes to be **20,000 IN 1920**; while Palm Springs, once taken notice of for its ability to ripen grapes early for the Chicago market, is still described as a "little settlement." The grapes are gone now. *At present the town is known widely as a health resort.* It possesses a store and four hotels. Consumptives live in tents near the *agua caliente* which they pray will cure them. *In a moment the warm liquid sand closes around the body and it feels as if* the *bather were being sucked in and down by the clinging tentacles of some living creature that had the power to hold the body in a most soothing and satisfactory embrace.* Dr. Murray's hotel has enlarged itself over the years; palm trees and rose-bushes crown it *(he made a success through his own efforts; he'll sell out at a fancy price);* across the street, the Indian reservation's figs achieve the Los Angeles market; but isn't this as good as life will ever get? Once upon a time, we dug irrigation channels from the Whitewater River, but the milk-white sand which gave that watercourse its name kept clogging our intakes; finally, irrigation proved too expensive.* Palm Springs seems doomed to remain, now and forever, a *little settlement.* Indeed, what if littleness itself cannot be maintained? Not far away from Palm Springs lie the dead orange groves of Palmdale, which became a ghost town because *water complications arose.*

Meanwhile, Imperial, within her eponymous county, at least, drinks in the *agua caliente* of perpetual water and intoxicates herself with visions of moneyplums! Imperial paves herself, improves her arterial system with new canals, rushes new crops to market! **THE DESERT DISAPPEARS**.

But in the town of Coachella, which belongs much more to Imperial than to Palm Springs, **WATER IS** not quite **HERE**, not entirely. To be sure, ever since 1906 Coachella has overcome the necessity of importing beets, carrots, rad-

*An old-timer in Indio hinted at water-wars which all sides lost; I don't know that this outcome wasn't preferable to another, as demonstrated by what happened to the neighboring Indian village of Rincon: "A wealthy white man of Riverside" piped all the water away for the sake of a speculative venture entitled the Garden of Eden. "In a sheltered spot hidden by rocks and shrubs we found a stone mortar and three pottery ollas, placed there doubtless by some broken-hearted woman who hoped one day to return for them."

ishes, lettuce and other vegetables. Local water suffices for that. So Coachella picks up heart. But how could she ever hope to stand beside Queen Riverside or even Duchess Calexico without hanging her head?

Margaret Tyler, born in 1916, grew up on a ranch southwest of Coachella. In 2004 she said to me: I can remember back when we didn't have an automobile; we just had a horse and wagon. I don't know; I guess there were roads, sort of. People just drove their wagons across the desert to get to town. I can remember, it must have been in 1920 or so, when they paved the highway, and that seemed pretty upscale! Sometimes I couldn't get to school because there used to be flooded fields. I don't think they have rain like that now . . .

We sat around the coffee table in the Tylers' air-conditioned home in Palm Desert, and the morning promised to be hot.—Coachella was the big town early on, the old lady said.

The big town! I thought. Where paved roads were upscale, and even the Date Festival couldn't be counted on!—In 1911 there was one in Coachella, another old-timer had told me. They made efforts for volunteers, and the next year you wouldn't have volunteers.

To be sure, Coachella grows cantaloupes just as does her antagonist. But Brawley's cantaloupe-packing sheds, not Indio's and certainly not Palm Springs's, remain the largest in the world! In 1907, while Imperial County tears herself out of San Diego's womb, Coachella manages to plant seven or eight hundred acres of cantaloupes. But her artesian wells are already running dry near Indio. *Where three years ago wells flowed several inches over the casing they now have to be pumped . . . This has been the history of all artesian districts . . .*

Coachella's anxious. *A farmer from near Coachella and Mecca last week told us of many wells in that section flowing hundreds of inches, much of the time going to absolute waste. Such action is unfortunate—worse, it is criminal, morally if not legally. It should be made legally criminal . . .*

Indio was a railroad center, Mrs. Tyler was saying. By the time I came along there was some green, but there was a lot of desert in between. The town was just about one block. There were some office buildings facing the railroads. The main street was Highway 111, which used to be Cantaloupe Avenue. Oh, yes, there used to be cantaloupes there, probably before my time. When they first started they had an artesian well that would flow at night.

Her husband John interjected: They'd take tractors and build a dike around the area, or a horse and a fresno,* probably, and anyway they'd make this dike and then at night they'd let the artesian well flow.

*The fresno scraper was a commonly used type of plough.

By the time I came along they had pumps, said Mrs. Tyler.—Reader, we know why they needed pumps. Poor thirsty Coachella!

In 1917, Coachella gets wind of what one of her historians describes as *a plan proposed at an El Centro meeting to build a canal from Palm Springs to the Imperial Valley. It would carry water from the Whitewater River . . . for domestic use in the towns of the Imperal Valley.* The Whitewater is practically all that Coachella has. Coachella cries: *All the north end of the Salton Sea Valley . . . objects to El Centro and the Imperial Valley taking this water . . .*

In Imperial County, **WATER IS HERE**. In Riverside County, Coachella waits.

And that is why the county history, blandly smoothing out its hope, envy and terrible need, lets us know that Riverside Imperial now licks her lips, *waiting only for the application of the water which the great river,* meaning of course the Colorado, *can supply, to duplicate the experience of the Imperial Valley and make of the country tributary to Blythe another rich country for California.*

Chapter 65

CITY OF IMPERIAL

(1925)

Pavements in time hid the dust of the main thoroughfares, and Imperial, changed in outward form and much in the spirit of the people, had become a modern municipality.

—Edgar F. Howe, 1918

As the Valley's first and oldest settlement Imperial continues to forge ahead without the aid of booms or other artificial impulse.

—Otis P. Tout, 1931

Imperial is still an important town in the Valley . . . Imperial is still important in Valley affairs.

—Elizabeth Harris, *ca.* 1958

Meanwhile, El Centro's failed competitor, the loser in the war for county seat, remained a few buildings surrounded by fields. At least some trees were starting to come . . .

Imperial is an up-to-date little city, furnished with good telephone and railroad service, electric light and power, and all the modern requirements of an intelligent and progressive community. These words were published in around 1912. God bless the city of Imperial with her cottonwood-shaded streets!

The Imperial Hotel was still listed in the county directory in 1914. By 1920 it was gone.

According to the Federal census of 1920 Imperial County exceeded in its agricultural production that of eleven states of the Union. But Imperial City's population remains only two thousand in 1926.

(Imperial reminds us that she's *the metropolis of the Imperial Valley.* She's wide and pretty, with horses and citizens on her white dirt streets.)

In 1926 Imperial City's ten *business buildings, halls, etc.,* still overshadowed El Centro's seven; moreover, I am proud to report that the former metropolis possessed both a Methodist Episcopal church and a Methodist Episcopal (colored).

As the decades went on, while Calexico grew in importance thanks to Mexican trade, El Centro continued its growth slowly, inertially, and thanks in part to bureaucratic centralism; while Holtville became, if such a noun is appropriate for a Paradise of irrigation, a backwater, and Imperial simply withered. In my day it is easy to pass through Imperial County without ever noticing, let alone stopping in, those two latter towns. Holtville by virtue of its stagnant isolation just off the freeway does at least remain a shell of itself; whereas Imperial is nothing but a junction of roads in northeastern El Centro, a flatness of whiteness and tanness, an unpainted Rothkoscape upon which was once painted, decades into the empire of the infinite past, fifteen young men in gorgeous-squiggled uniforms, brandishing their brass instruments, gazing straight at us from beneath their caps which said **IMPERIAL**; their drum said **QUEEN CITY INDEPENDENT BAND**; in the center, upon a rich dark heart, the same darkness as their uniforms, was superimposed the word IMPERIAL. Then decade after decade went by with the newspapers saying **BROCCOLI: MARKET ABOUT STEADY.**

In 1950, Imperial actually comprised fewer people than in 1920. Over the course of the twentieth century, Tijuana, which began with slightly fewer residents than Imperial, increased her population by a factor of four thousand seven hundred and forty-seven, while Imperial increased hers by a factor of eight.

Did the busy boomers of El Centro, Brawley, Calexico and Holtville ever ask themselves: Could this happen here? After all, it was occurring in Meloland; Salton, Mortmere, Dos Palmas and Caleb had already grown equivalent to Coachella's Palmdale—but of course all of those latter failures had taken place north of the Imperial Valley; and who could say that Meloland wouldn't pull through?

ABSOLUTELY NO EXCUSE

To me, Imperial City is a metonym for the greater entity I call Imperial; one decline mirrors the other. But when the city went down, who cared for socioeconomic prophecy when a more straightforward narrative conveniently anchored in present and past stood ready to hand, a narrative, moreover, peopled with humans rather than forces? All the losers needed to do was blame their arch-boomer, hero of *The Winning of Barbara Worth,* compassionate banker, developer-savior of the valley, who although a town was named for him there actually lived in Redlands with his two maiden daughters?

The narrative runs: W. F. Holt and his partner C. A. Barker form one of their accustomed syndicates, buy land cheap from A. R. Robinson and establish the railroad junction which will become El Centro. Our "Little Giant" owns the *Imperial Valley Press,* so it is a simple matter to get that publication to write: *There will be absolutely no excuse for Imperial when El Centro gets the county seat.*

The engineer Rockwood, to whom we telegraph some of our thanks for the Salton Sea accident, never liked the location of Imperial in the first place, because *the rough and salt lands between Imperial and Brawley* would give prospective settlers a terrible impression, and because flowers and shrubs w*hich residents of the Valley would naturally desire to put about their homes* did not do well in Imperial's soil. Had it been up to him, he would have established Imperial a mile and a half north of El Centro; then there would never have been an El Centro.

Imperial City had absolutely no excuse. That's why she died. As for the rest of us, who find plenty of excuses for ourselves, why shouldn't our cantaloupe and asparagus empires endure forever? After all, **WATER IS HERE**.

Chapter 66

THEIR NEEDS ARE EVEN MORE EASILY SATISFIED

(1893–1927)

> It is an interesting commentary on the effective development of public opinion throughout the rest of the United States concerning the Japanese "problem" in California, that the Japanese constitute but 1.7 per cent of the total population of that state, while Mexicans constitute 6.5 per cent.
>
> —Paul S. Taylor, 1934

My fellow Californians, do you remember the Chinese? Not me! They were never here; they're gone.

In 1893 the Chinese population of Redlands was over two hundred; by 1896, patriotic advocates of American labor have reduced it to twenty-four. Masked men with shotguns evict seven Chinese from Casablanca. Meanwhile, Japanese laborers have begun to arrive in California. By 1897 we already find a Japanese Christian Mission in Riverside. The annotated chronology from which I have been taking many of these dates flags 1899 as the year when *Japanese workers rapidly replace white section hands of the Santa Fe Railroad in the desert areas of southern California.* (Accordingly, in 1900 the U.S. Deputy Collector of Customs in San Diego warns that *large numbers of Chinese laborers are crossing the border.* They'll pop their heads up in a minute.) In 1900 a Japanese orange picker attacks his Chinese rival with a knife while on the job in Riverside. In 1904, masked Caucasians menace Japanese fruit packers in Cucamonga; Japanese get attacked in Highlands and Corona. All the same, the Japanese are working out so nicely that the *California Cultivator* sees fit to advise: *Lemons which made the size known as 300s, only, should be picked. There is a difference of $1 a box between 300s and 360s. A man who picks 360s ought to be put off the ranch. If you cannot get a white man to pick 300s, then get Japs, and if they cannot do it properly, then get a woman . . .*

That same year, Japanese commence harvesting cotton and melons in the Imperial Valley, more than satisfying their labor-hungry employers. For the year 1906 we read that *Japanese citrus workers* are *gradually replacing the Chinese* in Riverside.

We need have no fear that our lands will not become better and better as the years go by.

In 1900, ninety-seven Japanese dwell in the city of Riverside. Ten years later there are seven hundred and sixty-five; during the citrus harvest there might be three thousand. In 1907, the six hundred citrus workers of greater Riverside comprise forty or fifty Spanish speakers, fifty or sixty Caucasians, and Japanese.

Our lands may be getting better and better; but by 1907 the Asiatic Exclusion League has grown extremely alarmed. *The general persistency with which the Japanese are breaking into many industries, their frugality, their ambition, and their lack of business morality render them more formidable than the Chinese.* For instance, in Japanese restaurants in San Francisco, employees often work twelve-hour days; workers in white-owned restaurants work two hours less. Talk about crimes against nature!

In the summer of 1908, unemployed whites attack Japanese melon pickers in the Imperial Valley; the Japanese Consul General telegraphs to express his concern. No doubt we listened to him; for by 1909, Japanese make up forty-two percent of all California's farmworkers.—How well off does that make them? In 1912, Japanese own only three hundred and thirty-one farms in California. No Japanese farmers own any acreage in Imperial County that year, although I do see seven Japanese leases totalling eight hundred and forty-eight acres.

(In an undated Imperial County photograph captioned *Masako, Eiko and Marie Yukawa at Date School across Date Canal from Ranch,* I see three little girls, the tallest with her arms around the others, dressed mainly in white, standing on a white dirt street in front of a white house.)

The collective bargaining procedures of the Japanese being more effective than those of Chinese, growers are already seeking to replace them, with Sikhs, Mexicans, midwestern farmboys, anybody. Their part in the Oxnard beet workers' strike of 1903 was particularly shocking. In 1906 the *California Cultivator,* perhaps regretting its advice of 1904, sends out the alarm: *The Jap laborers in the fields around Watsonville struck, on Saturday night, for a raise of 2 ½ cents an hour.*

Here are two letters to us from the year 1910: *I consider the Japanese immigration a thousand-fold more harmful and threatening than Chinese immigration ever was, or ever could have been,* advises Edwin A. Meserve, candidate for the United States Senate. *They are doing our laundry work with our machinery, following our own methods—which they have adopted.* Meanwhile, William Kent writes in from the Second Congressional District: *I have made it a large part of my campaign on the Asiatic exclusion idea, comparing it with the racial troubles brought on by the heedless importation of negroes.*

Is the World Going to Starve? wonders the *California Cultivator* in 1920.

Out of the bigness of her domain and bigness of her heart America has said—and still is saying: "Come, we have enough for you all, help us reclaim our rich valleys, our hillsides, our deserts." That was mighty white of us, and guess what happened? *Take, for instance, the rich valleys around the city of Los Angeles. But a few years since they were filled with attractive homes of American gardeners and truck farmers. Today 85 per cent of Los Angeles' vegetables are grown by Japanese. The change has been gradual . . . excepting to the American farmer who has been forced off the farm . . .The birthrate on California farms is being increased with wonderful swiftness by the shipping to this country of women who are sent purely for breeding purposes . . .* I wish I could have met one of those.

What shall we do? Why, make a Gentlemen's Agreement—which goes into effect in 1909. Japanese immigrant labor arrives in ever smaller numbers; Northside has been saved.

NO REST FOR THE GUARDIANS OF AGRICULTURE

But that scarcely means that she can relax her vigilance; for certain other laborers with easily satisfied needs—laborers whom the Japanese had supplanted—wait just beyond the international line, plotting to force the American farmer off the farm!

In 1910, the *Riverside Daily Press* warns that thirty thousand *contraband Chinese* have come into Canada and are waiting their chance to infiltrate our pure United States.

In 1915, a lady named Goldie Evans leads a gang of Chinese-smugglers from Mexico up through the Coachella Valley and into the orchards of California. A posse of Apaches track them; we report a gun battle in Thermal; Cahuilla Indians track the escapees; they do work Americans wouldn't do.

In 1922, America's heroes capture thirteen Chinese concealed in packing boxes in Oceanside. We'll solve that problem once and for all! In 1924, the Second Exclusion Act establishes a rigid immigration maximum. Unfortunately, by 1927 Chinese are getting smuggled in airplanes!

STILL NO REST

And if this was the result of Chinese exclusion, how would the Japanese react? A historian from that enlightened epoch picks up his pen in the year 1926 and darkly alerts us all: *But whereas the Chinese were good losers, the more aggressive Japanese have by no means proved so meek and docile.*

Chapter 67

NEGROES AND MEXICANS FOR COTTON

(1901–1930)

. . . the Latin-American does not propose that anyone shall know him, he is ever on the defensive, he will not "Let you in." This is the result of the treatment he has received from the so called superior people.

—Reverend A. B. DeRoos, 1920

The question of competent labor has become a most serious proposition to the fruit-growers of California . . . runs an item in (you guessed it) the *Western Fruit-Grower.* The year is 1903. Wilber Clark is now established in the Imperial Valley if not yet at his Wilfrieda Ranch; one of his lives will be lived amidst fruit trees. And there's a school in Mecca; oh, yes, the Coachella Valley's orchards are coming along, coming along. *We need have no fear that our lands will not become better and better as the years go by.* Back to the labor question: *The Chinese and Japanese labor in California is not equal to the work, it seems, and a writer in the* California Fruit-Grower *suggests that an effort be made to locate colored families on fruit farms, claiming that they will in time learn the work as thoroughly as the Japanese or Chinese. Any plan which will remove some of the colored families from the cities of the country, where they are subjected to every form of temptation, will be a good move. It is a fact that the colored people of the city are not as good citizens as they would be in the country, nor is their health so good . . . But when one gets a darky on the farm, how is he to be kept there? It's a hard proposition, anyway.**

And so, once *the basic strata of the population* have been established, the Swiss, *a frugal, industrious people,* begin to build dairies in Imperial County; *the next class to come in considerable numbers were colored people from the cotton States of the South . . . Schools and churches are affording the people of this race an opportunity and encouragement to attain higher development.* Meanwhile, Muslims and Hindus also start to arrive in Imperial.

Fifteen years after that item in the *Western Fruit-Grower,* Judge Farr posthumously

*Meanwhile, a rival periodical depicts *A Rare and Handsome "Nigger-Head" Cactus from Central Mexico.* (Echinocactus Trollietti.)

explains that *cotton has been especially valuable on the Mexican side of the line on account of the favorable labor conditions where Chinese could be imported and where Mexican labor was available . . .*

Those Chinese have certainly become an anachronism in Northside! Allow me to quote from a magisterial history of California, published in 1926: *While the history of Chinese immigration is not a record in which the American can take much pride, and admitting that political ambition, bigotry, and race prejudice have had a prominent part in the agitation, nevertheless, few thoughtful students of the exclusion will now deny the contention that exclusion has been of distinct benefit to the United States.*

It must surely be coincidental that on Northside *some difficulty has been experienced in securing labor.* Never mind; *but this difficulty has not proved so serious . . . Cotton is well adapted to the small farm, and it is probable that the labor difficulty will be finally overcome by planting Egyptian cotton on small farms, where the labor of the family can be utilized in the harvest season.*

Small farms, oh, yes! I'd forgotten that Imperial is self-sufficient Emersonian homesteads. Meanwhile, a history of the Coachella Valley explains that even at the beginning of the twentieth century, *labor was supplied by the Indians already living in the area and by Mexican families drawn to the developing ranches.*

Between 1914 and 1919, the number of Mexican laborers in Inland Empire citrus increases from twenty-three hundred to just over seven thousand. By 1973, two-thirds of those citrus workers will be Mexican.

In the southerly reaches of American Imperial, *reliable and efficient men* set one back about forty-five dollars a month plus board; day laborers a dollar seventy-five or more, up to two-fifty, for a nine-hour Imperial Valley stretch. *The majority of the farm labor is American,* thank God for that, boomers and boosters! Now to the exceptions: Negroes for cotton, of course, but not elsewhere to any great degree; Hindus for contract labor such as picking milo, *Mexicans to some extent on the larger ranches and to do contract work, but not by the month on the smaller farms. Japanese are important factors in the production of fruit and garden truck, especially cantaloupes,* and Southern Europeans can be handily employed for dairy and hog.

Migrant workers will certainly prove a great convenience to those who value a speedy picking schedule. One reason is that their employers need not spend too much on them. The State Commission of Immigration and Housing reports: *Camp conditions in 1914 were unspeakably bad throughout the state . . . men sleeping in little filthy hovels, eight or ten in a room designed for two . . . men and women compelled to labor in the field on hot summer days without a drop of water to drink for whole afternoons.* By 2005 conditions have so vastly improved that *the emergency rules will allow farm workers to seek at least five minutes of shade (even if it's only under an umbrella) if they are experiencing symptoms of heatstroke.* Of course it goes without saying that *farm workers will be reluctant to ask for a water break under the umbrella . . . if they think they might not get hired the next day.* Do you remember what Border Patrolman Dan Murray said? *You should see these guys pickin' watermelon, bent over all day.*

Chapter 68

MEXICANS GETTING UGLY

(1911–1926)

> Say, old boy, there's something doing in Mexico . . . Across that line there are crazy revolutionists, ill-paid soldiers, guerrilla leaders, raiders, robbers, outlaws, bandits galore, starving peons by the thousands, girls and women in terror.
>
> —Zane Grey, 1913

In 1911, the year that Mrs. M. A. Ritter of El Centro sits down in the far left seat in the back row, blurred, with only a weird hat to identify her sex, to become, so the caption explains, the *first woman JUROR in State of California*; the year also that Harold Bell Wright walks out of his arklike studio and back into his home, which is encircled by young palm trees—he has just completed *The Winning of Barbara Worth* (here he comes now, tall and lean in a suit, inclining his head toward his darkhaired, chubby-faced wife; he has lines in his face and his hair is receding)—Porfirio Díaz abdicates. Bad business for Northside!—Good business, too, because exactly now a certain wealthy rancher from Nuevo León leads his three sons across the line to save them from being conscripted into Pancho Villa's army of bandits and left-wing altruists; they'll become migrant workers for life, as will many of the grandchildren. Thousands do the same. Work awaits them, not only because the need for farmhands in the Imperial Valley's mushrooming acres approaches desperation, but also because the merest year later, Imperial's Anglo labor force has soured with the socialist virus, and *the Valley was uneasy on account of depredations and fires caused, it was said, by I. W. W. gangsters.*—The Industrial Workers of the World! Although Russia remains half a decade away yet from going Bolshevik, the Wobblies embody radical threat well enough on their own. Here's one of their songs:

> The boss will be leery, the "stiffs" will be cheery
> When we hit Farmer John hard,
> They'll all be affrighted, when we stand united
> And carry that Red, Red Card.

Who could Farmer John represent? He's surely not Wilber Clark. Since migrant workers carry the red card, Farmer John must be their employer, which is to say the owner of a grand expanse of irrigated acres. In this era they begin to call him, or the corporation that will supplant him, a *grower.* They'll put the squeeze on him, and he will do the same to them. Thus class struggle.

In Upton Sinclair's 1924 play "Singing Jailbirds," which as late as 1983 the American Civil Liberties Union declines to stage because it remains after all these decades *too angry, too bitter,* the hero, an imprisoned workingman whose name just happens to be Red Adams, warns the District Attorney: *Ever hear of Joe Hill? . . . Out in Utah the master-class stood him up against the wall and shot him with a firing-squad . . . But now Joe Hill's songs are all over the land.* To the extent that this is actually true, it must be a nightmare for Farmer John, not to mention the District Attorney. The nightmare deepens, for Red continues: *We sing 'em in Dago and Mex, in Hunkie and Wop, we even sing 'em in Jap and Chink!*

Just imagine, if Mexican farmworkers started believing in Joe Hill . . . ! And advance detachments of the Mexican Revolution have already infiltrated the Wobblies . . .

"THE MOST PITILESS EGOTISM"

Speaking of Southside, Joe Hill is already there, if only on the horizon.

In 1906, as you may remember, the miners strike at Cananea; in 1907 the Río Blanco textile workers appeal against the miseries of their twelve-hour workdays to President Díaz, who inevitably finds against them; so they strike and they riot; the forces of law and order shoot down a hundred of them. As that taxi driver in Indio remarked: *Because I tell you, Mexico is beautiful but Mexico is tough.*

In 1910 the opposition candidate, Madero, gets arrested and jailed for running against the President. Eventually Madero wins; that is when Díaz flees. But Madero will not be Joe Hill.

Article Twenty-seven of the new Constitution (1916) calls for the expropriation of the haciendas and the creation of *ejidos.* These enactions fail to realize themselves just yet, thanks to the cautious nondescriptness of the landowner Madero, who for all his pains gets assassinated and replaced by Huerta, possibly with Northside's connivance. In comes Carranza, another landowner, who fights over Mexico's carcass against Zapata and the famous-infamous Pancho Villa. In my time, Zapata is remembered almost as a saint, probably thanks to his own martydom; all the same, his side committed its portion of atrocities. *When the men of Zapata entered the town, they came to kill . . . They also carried off girls. People said that they took them to the woods and raped them there . . . No one knows whether they were devoured by wild animals or whether the Zapatistas murdered and buried them there.* Against Carranza, who again signs a bill to expropriate the haciendas but never meant it, and Villa, who is less ideological than mercurial, must be set their greater crimes. Zapata and Villa do talk a bit like Joe Hill. They share some few of his qualities. Meanwhile, the Revolution leads itself, or, as I should say, gnaws at itself and its original enemies with equal desperation. A Michoacán woman remarks that the violence concludes only when the swine flu epidemic of 1918 paralyzes everyone. By 1919, a million people have become elevated into corpses or refugees. The great muralist and printmaker José Clemente Orozco remembers: *People grew used to killing, to the most pitiless egotism. . . Farce, drama, barbarity. Buffoons and dwarfs trailing after the gentlemen of noose and dagger, in conference with smiling procuresses.* Worst of all, if true, is a certain Northsider historian's summation: *a triumph for capitalism.*

Thus Harry Chandler's vast homestead in American Imperial continues to flourish. Confluence of interest with successive administrations, and occasional bribery, safeguards the Colorado River Land Company.

But by the mid-1920s, despite incentives to sideline local incarnations of the struggle into issues of religion or water rights, the Revolution's concatenation of Indians, Catholics, good citizens, small landholders, mestizos, day laborers, sharecroppers, and other partially overlapping subcategories have begun to call themselves campesinos—an angry political term and also a comfortingly inclusive one.

Who are campesinos? What do they look like? Go to the Thirteen Negro in late afternoon, when the foremen have let them off until tomorrow, and you will see them drinking beer in the red-winking darkness, stinking of sweat. Sometimes you will see one who resembles Orozco's "Head of a Mexican Peasant," the face wide and blocky, the narrowed eyes resembling double-bladed knives, long moustachios sweeping down like another two crescent knives: He is wary, suspicious, cunning, ferocious. You will certainly find smoothfaced young men who are still strong enough, as Lupe Vásquez used to be, to work all day in the hot sun, then drink and whore all night, returning to the fields before dawn, sleepless, broke and cheerful. You will always see hard old men and sad old men. You might buy them a beer and they might buy you one, but does that mean they trust you?

In 1928, Cárdenas becomes Governor of Michoacán. His manifesto proclaims: *The only way for campesinos to protect their lives and their material interests is if they are given adequate armament.* His Revolutionary Labor Confederation of Michoacán (CRMDT) drowns the province in ominous red and black flags, each bearing the Bolshevik-like emblem of a scythe and sickle upon a book. Sometimes his activists wreck churches. They do expropriate haciendas and create *ejidos,* although most of those actions cannot be ratified until he becomes President of Mexico in 1934. Meanwhile, murders and home-burnings continue on all sides, so that too many campesinos and activists came to feel, as one historian puts it, that *social harmony was a dangerous fantasy.* What if they are correct?

Northside has long since taken notice. Her Southside concessions are endangered or lost. In 1920, a California newspaper explains it all to us in this headline: **MEXICO CENTER FOR BOLSHEVISM**.

"MEXICANS PUZZLED BY U.S. TROOPS"

What should Northside *do* about this Revolution? That we truehearted Americans eschew the cowardliness of lukewarmness is indicated by the following: On 14 February 1914, the Collector of Customs informs the Deputy Collector in Calexico that the President (Wilson) has rescinded the prohibition on exportation to Mexico of weapons of war. *In view of this fact, such articles may now be exported to Mexico without restriction.* I can't help believing in people.

Wilson, it seems, has determined Huerta to be the wrong leader for Mexico. Well, it's true that the man murdered his predecessor. What ought Northside to do?—Why, send in the Marines! *The bountiful continent is ours, state on state, and territory on territory, to the waves of the Pacific sea.*

And so, in May, the *Imperial Valley Press* regales us with various front-page items: **American Troops Save Life of Dr. Urrutia in Vera Cruz**; ***Battle of Saltillo Believed On Today***. Speaking of unhappy Vera Cruz, which has been overrun by foreigners more than once,* the *Press* informs us, in the midst of conveying to us the spectacles of a **Great Battle** there: ***MEXICANS PUZZLED BY U.S. TROOPS***, because we've made the city of Vera Cruz safer and nicer than ever before, instead of pillaging it. Meanwhile, here's a Mexican headline: **WHILE MEXICANS CUT GRINGO PIGS' THROATS, IN THE CHURCHES LA GLORIA RINGS OUT.**—I'm reminded of the nice old lady in El Centro who remarked to me during the second or third year of our occupation of Iraq: We went in there to liberate them. We helped those Iraqis. But they don't appreciate it. They're *mean.*

*Certainly not only by Americans. In 1683, French-led pirates raped almost every female in the place and tortured some people for dessert. But we did our share. During the Mexican-American War, thirteen thousand shells landed in the city, killing mostly women and children.

"VIRTUALLY LANDLESS"

Fortunately for the inhabitants of Calexico, San Diego and suchlike Northside border towns, the Revolution weighs lightly on Mexican Imperial, although Madero does enter Sonora, to be sure, and Pancho Villa operates on both sides of the international line; his infamous foray into Northside will kill a few of us. But up here in American Imperial, we're mostly too busy making sure we'll never get cheated out of a dollar in our lives to worry about foreign events.* (I cite again the stern old pioneer from Heber: This is just background information. Don't quote me on any of this.)

Chandler frets, no doubt. So do his stockholders. But the Colorado River Land Company continues to drive livestock almost unmolested; the first cotton plantings go in, and still the revolutionaries are too busy attacking one another to trouble Baja California.

In 1912, A. F. Andrade, receiver of the Mexican company that controls the canal from the Colorado River into the Imperial Valley, demands *absolute control of all the canals in Mexico.* The American receiver of the now defunct California Development Company, Colonel Holabird, responds that *the Mexican company is simply a creature of the California Development Company erected to comply with the laws of Mexico,* and it may well be that these laws are not held in the strictest regard by Colonel Holabird. Well, why should they be? Who can say that next week they won't all change?

The Revolution continues; so does Imperial's canal. Moreover, the following item in the *California Cultivator,* datelined southern California, 1925, gives Northside's cotton and melon magnates all the more reason to bear with their misguided Mexican brethren, tolerating their errors in pious obedience to the Ministry of Capital: There continues to be *a marked labor shortage in Imperial, Coachella and Palo Verde Valleys.*

So thank God for those hungrily industrious young men from Nuevo León and other parts south and east of Mexican Imperial; we need have no fear that our lands will not become better and better as the years go by.

Who are the new refugees to us? We decline to think of them any longer as noble Californios; a 1912 history of Riverside County falls more on the mark when it describes them as *the miserable half-breed race* which steals white people's cattle and horses; at least they're not Chinese; our Exclusion Acts will keep the Celestials

*Back in 1836, Richard Henry Dana, Jr., had concluded that "revolutions are matters of frequent occurrence in California . . . The only object, of course, is the loaves and fishes; and instead of caucusing, paragraphing, libelling, feasting, promising, and lying, they take muskets and bayonets, and, seizing upon the presidio and custom-house, divide the spoils and declare a new dynasty."

in Southside, picking cotton for the Colorado River Land Company.—In 1919, only five percent of the arrestees in Imperial County will be Americans, *the rest being Mexicans, Hindus and other foreigners.*

Now let's put those foreigners to work!—I wonder what the result might be?—Irrigation democracy at its best, no doubt.

Santiago Gonzales from Las Barrancas sets off for Northside. He gets a job in the California gold mines. When he returns, he's so well off that while preparing to throw a party he washes down the patio with expensive tequila. *Well, from then on many of the men from Las Barrancas went.*

Near the end of a long career studying California's underclasses and water politics, with frequent reference to American Imperial, Paul S. Taylor compiles a list of numbered points in his "Imperial Valley, Notes, Drafts," dated 1979. Here are two of them:

> 13. The applicability of acreage limitation to Imperial Valley . . . is the essence of national policy on how land should be used. Without the law, Imperial Valley is a polarized society. Virtually 9 out of every 10 persons engaged in its agriculture are part of a "lower class" "mass of laborers."

(Who might they be? *Well, from then on many of the men from Las Barrancas went.*)

> 14. . . . These people, overwhelmingly of Mexican origin, are virtually landless. The purpose of applying acreage limitation law as defined by the U.S. Supreme Court, is "to benefit people, not land."

Well, they did it to themselves; nobody forced them to come. And until 1913 there's not a single labor union in Imperial County.

A PAGEANT FOR SCHOOL TEACHERS

And so Northside watches Southside, apprehensive of trouble but hoping still to get while the getting's good. Comforting herself with her superiority *(the entire equipment of the United States regulars at Calexico is considered far in advance of that of the Mexicans across the border)*, American Imperial enjoys Mexican Imperial as exotic theater—trusting, I should suppose, that the performance will stay literally within bounds.

We see ladies in long dresses and big hats, adorned by purses, all smiling or half-smiling upon the dirt. The caption reads: **TWENTY-FIVE IMPERIAL VALLEY SCHOOL TEACHERS VIEWING THE ACTIONS OF THE REVOLUTIONISTS IN MEXICALI, BC, FEBRUARY 11, 1911.** The border post will be razed by arson that night.

In 1914, the following page-one news arrives from Southside: **Embargo Is Established On Huerta's Orders** . . . *No mention is made of the rebels' claim yesterday that Mazatlan had fallen* . . . On the same page, we read Northside's counter-preparation: ***Platoon of Machine Guns Arrives; Militia to Depart*** . . . *With the arrival of a platoon of machine guns of the First cavalry, Calexico's military garrison was greatly strengthened.* Seventh California Infantry has also been dispatched to Calexico. And finally, again on page one, we find the most important news of all: **Cotton Industry Reaching Giant Proportions Here.** We have two weeks yet before the opening of the cantaloupe season; the Holton Power Company is supplying us with mountains of ice . . .

THE PAGEANT THREATENS THE AUDIENCE

But there come moments when ice cannot keep the Imperial Valley cool.

At the end of 1910, which is to say of the grand year that Westmorland incorporates, Huey Stanley leads the Wobblies across the line, establishing socialism in Mexicali's wide white streets! The following February, his army defeats the troops of Kelso Vega, Governor of Baja California. But in April he falls in battle, leaving Mexicali as he found it, namely, sandy and mostly bereft of buildings, the few in existence being scaffolded and low, while blurred people in antique dress walk past a now antique car.

Then come those American revolutionists of 1911, who incarnate William Walker all over again. But after all, who *isn't* trying to put his face on the Revolution? In the Imperial County Historical Society Pioneers Museum there is a Hetzel photograph captioned *Horses stolen by insurgents, Mexicali, Mexicali, Jan. 29, 1911.* I see a blur; I see four men and four horses. I see *Lieutenant Berthold inspecting insurgent troops, Mexicali, 1911.* They are a blurry line of hatless men standing on a grey blur; possibly they are the same people who belong to the *detachment of Revolutionists patrolling the railroad in Mexicali, 1911.*

The events of 1911 remain not only convoluted almost beyond belief, but obscure in their details. On 28 January, Ricardo Flores Magón, revolutionary anarchosocialist and therefore natural enemy of Porfirio Díaz, sends his Magonistas to Mexicali. Or do they go by themselves? What can be the true role of this unbending dreamer, who passes so much of his life in various Mexican and American jails? Perhaps in his honor, the Magonistas kill the jailer in Mexicali and release all prisoners; the government runs; two bridges get destroyed. In answer, certain altruistic Northsiders (call them friends of the Colorado River Land Company, some of whose stockholders have now utterly lost heart and long to get rid of their Southside properties) form a private army. On 7 March, thirty thousand American soldiers stand along the border, ready to come in. Who stationed them there? Did Harry Chandler send somebody a telegram? On 12 March, the Wobblies take Tecate. Meanwhile the mercenary Caryl Ap Rhys Pryce attacks Tijuana, which falls on the ninth of May. Upholding the highest principles of international liberation, Pryce's men pillage the city. They charge tourists a quarter per visit. Then they get ready to seize Ensenada. It is actually now that Madero becomes President and calls for the factionalists to make peace. Pryce refuses, embezzles funds and leaves. In Northside, Magón likewise keeps the faith. Now Dick Ferris from Los Angeles, who once tried to blackmail Díaz into selling the entire Baja Peninsula, tries to pull a William Walker in Tijuana. Magón's replacement general, Jack Mosby, accordingly denounces Ferris; the Federales retake Tijuana; Mosby flees to Northside but gets arrested, as does Magón, who, sentenced to twenty-three months, dies in jail after years and years. South of Tijuana there's an Ejido Flores Magón; that's all that's left of him.

Just to thicken the plot, other altruistic Northsiders, who evidently bear less connection to the Colorado River Land Company than to the dreams of some new William Walker—or who knows? maybe they're even Magonistas—send a night letter to the Governor of California:

We, the people of Los Angeles, in mass meeting assembled have adopted a resolution in sympathy with the Mexican Insurrectionists and have asked our government at Washington to declare the revolutionists to be belligerents, so that they may receive all the rights of soldiers under international law.

Perhaps on their account, or on account of people like them, in 1914 the *Imperial Valley Press* complains of a certain hardening of the line: *It is not possible any longer to make a dash across the Mexican border into Mexicali, as the Mexican customs officials have inaugurated a policy of minutely searching all who enter the city.* In the same breath, one speaks of Apricot Day. **Fruit and Vegetable Day Reflects Wealth of Valley.**

In that same year we hear and pass on rumors that Mexicans might cut the part of the American Irrigation Canal which lies on their side. We form home guard volunteers. In 1916, the Adjutant General of California receives a panicked communication from none other than Charles Rockwood, whose imprudent engineering gave us the Salton Sea. The telegram deserves to be shown in full, since every word of it is classic, right down to the determined refusal to capitalize the word "Mexican":*

CHARGES
CHARGE TO

TELEGRAPH COMPANY

Hiram W. Johnson Papers
Bancroft Library

STATE OF CALIFORNIA
THE ADJUTANT GENERAL'S OFFICE

TELEGRAM

SACRAMENTO, CAL.

COPY.

868F JO 100 Blue

Herber Cal 1222P June 25, 1916.

Thomas Adj. Gen.

Sacramento, Calif.

Mexicans getting ugly I doubt Cantus ability to control situation their force nearly three times ours and better equipped with field guns our present force inadequate to prevent destruction of Calexico and Canals system believe one thousand more men if sent today will prevent bloodshed and disaster I have eight hundred men mostly mexicans and seventeen hundred mules working in Mexico on river protection and emergency works river at flood height now destruction of levees spells ruin rapid movement of mexican laborers from valley to Mexicali yesterday for obvious reasons my name should not be connected publicly with this information.

. C. R. Rockwood.

Calexico mysteriously survives.

And it goes on and on like this in the border cities of Southside, while Northside watches from as far away, perhaps, as the Tinken Ranch in Calexico with its twin silos one of which reads PERFECTION. Surely there must be other times when the pageant threatens this audience. Did you know that in 1919, one out of every five American laborers went on strike? That was the year of the Red Summer Race Riots. The Ministry of Capital doesn't care for that. Moreover, some of the shouts we hear from the other side of the ditch sound pretty damned Red.

*This may have been the doing not of Rockwood but of the telegraph operator or the person who made the official copy.

HOLDING THE LINE

And so, come 1925, when Phil Swing demands an All-American Canal, he deplores for the edification of the appropriate Senate Committee *the uneconomic method of that great irrigation district,* namely Imperial County's, *which has to spend between two and three million dollars annually in operation and trying to do business under two flags, and one of those flags a nation which has not maintained for some eighteen years any very stable form of government, whose people have not in recent decades shown any particular friendship for our people.*

(I wonder why they don't like us? In 1920 an American crosses the line at Calexico, asks to be taken to Cantú, the current Governor of Baja California Norte, and offers to smuggle weapons and ammunition to the good people of Southside. What credentials might he possess? Well, he has already transacted this same business with *Carrancistas and revolutionists in Mexico.* Cantú questions him in detail, then turns him over to the Americans.—In 1926 the *Imperial Valley Press* warns us of a certain M. Y. Mejía or Mejís, *believed to be the leader of bands which were partially organized in this section for an intended attack on Mexicali at the time of General Estrada's ill-fated expedition . . . Mejis is known to have been in Seeley Sunday.*)

Phil Swing calls for more ruthless and complete delineation.

The canal in Mexico is for a great many miles above ground, he warns, *and open to attack and destruction—when I was there as a county officer we were in great fear during the fight between the contending factions, when one faction held the capital, Mexicali, another army of another faction was camped upon the Colorado River and planning to . . . with a few sticks of dynamite cut off the water supply of the city of Mexicali.* Worse yet (for who cares about Mexicali?), they could have forced *us* out, all sixty thousand of us; because in the Imperial Valley we have stockpiled no more than three or four days' worth of water.

Chapter 69

THE NEXT STEP

(*ca.* 1925)

By *the mid-twenties,* writes Paul S. Taylor, *they succeeded in obtaining legislation assigning quotas to immigration from nations of Europe, Asia and Africa . . . The next step . . . was to try to close the western doors also, and especially to limit the recently emerging flow of immigrants from Mexico.*

Chapter 70

EL CENTRO

(1925)

The husbandman here does not think of his fields being moistened by the falling rain. He digs ditches around them, in which water is conveyed from a stream . . . whenever moisture is required.

—James O. Pattie, 1830

Roth and Marshall's Feed Store, El Centro: Two men, one in a hat, stand duty behind the long counter one pan of whose scales rests upon a box of bag balm; from the ceiling hangs an immense proclamation of American realism: **OUR TERMS ARE CASH. NO NEW ACCOUNTS OPENED.** *I have never been cheated out of a dollar in my life.* How could I be? For in 1925, the El Centro Chamber of Commerce announces what we all knew would happen: Imperial County, California, is *THE THIRD RICHEST GROWING COUNTY IN THE UNITED STATES AND THE RICHEST PRODUCING AREA IN THE WORLD.* A hundred and sixty thousand acres of alfalfa now, ha! And thirty-four hundred acres of tomatoes, twenty-three thousand acres of lettuce, forty-six thousand acres of barley, seven point nine million pounds of butter, all in 1925; don't you dare think I couldn't go on. And El Centro must therefore be—just think of it!—the county seat of the richest-producing area in the world! No wonder that here we find the chosen residence of Cary K. Cooper, Assistant Secretary and Manager of the Pioneer Title Insurance Company. *Mr. Cooper richly deserves whatever success has come to him, for he now holds a prominent place in the business world.* He sold out at a fancy price. Not far from Mr. Cooper (for one can easily stroll from one end to the other of this young city), at 513 Brighton Avenue, dwells Imperial County's own Herodotus, Otis P. Tout. About him and the ones he chronicled it could well be said: *He had enormous and poetic admiration, though very little understanding, of all mechanical devices. These were his symbols of truth and beauty.* The above words were published in 1922, in Sinclair Lewis's now classic *Babbitt,* whose vulgar, greedy, jingoistic protagonist is oddly sympathetic in his feeble and indeed mostly unconscious rebellion against the world of multiply replicated emptiness which he inhabits and busily sustains. *I have never been cheated out of a dollar in my life.* Isn't that the most

Babbittish thing you ever heard? *He now holds a prominent place in the business world.* Is that so bad? Not necessarily; nor is Babbitt, whose home is *a high-colored, banging, exciting region* of new factories and old; the author means it to be any small American city, so could it be El Centro, too? **OUR TERMS ARE CASH.** *You can't hate them properly,* says one of Lewis's characters, *and yet their standardized minds are the enemy.*

At the beginning of this century only four out of every ten Americans live in cities. By 1925, more than half of them may be found there. Roth and Marshall's Feed Store isn't yet an anachronism, but new sorts of businesses are definitely in evidence: Peering down Main Street in 1918, I find automobile supplies in the Davis Building; then comes the opera house (on the other side of the empty dirt street, the Hotel El Centro bestrides the archway'd establishment of John E. Davis, druggist; and other arches beyond counting recede on both sides of the street). In 1926 we find the Imperial Valley Motor Agency selling Studebakers in El Centro. I can almost see Babbitt smoking an exultant cigarette behind the wheel of one of those ultra-modern machines. By 1930 El Centro will possess two of the county's four *automobile laundries* and eight of its twenty-four automobile dealerships.

El Centro has not acquired a large Japanese population, many more East Indians, Mohammedans and Hindus being seen on the streets. These people are not residents of the town, however, being wholly rural in their habits.

The Hotel Barbara Worth remains bright and white in 1928, with its American flag and its white, white pavement; and Miss El Centro 1928, Wanda Johnson (Garret Johnson's sister), poses with a chipmunk smile beside a Dodge whose headlights resemble breasts; my grandfather, who was born not long after Imperial County broke away from San Diego, always called women's breasts headlights, and now I know why. Wanda wears a fringy shawl of a thing wrapped around her shoulders and tickling her white shoes; her stretchy one-piece garment is like a swimsuit, her legs shockingly naked from the lower hips down.

Chapter 71

MEXICALI

(1925)

Impressed with the success of numerous small commercial farmers in the Imperial Valley, they recommended following a similar development pattern on the Mexican side.

—Dorothy Pierson Kerig, 1988

"PUBLIC OPINION WOULD NOT SUPPORT IT"

Puente Blanco, also known as the Colorado Bridge and the New Town Bridge, now ran fresh and quadruple-railed across the Río Nuevo gorge so that the city of Mexicali could be joined to her first *colonia,* Pueblo Nuevo, which the photograph shows to have still been surprisingly tree-lined in that year 1925, the year that the Teatro Municipal (which resembles a Hopi pueblo) and the Biblioteca Municipal were constructed, the year that Don Federico Palacios was Presidente del Concejo Municipal. Next year the Masonic Temple would go up. The Southern Pacific Railroad had promised to lay track all the way to the Río Hardy and maybe even to San Felipe, so that the cotton crop could ship straight to Europe or Japan! And so Mexicali possessed due justification for sporting boomers and boosters. As a certain Hector González explained, *due perhaps to the rosy prospects which the cultivation of cotton offers capital, enterprise and enthusiasm have gathered with more vigor around Mexicali than around any other place.* No doubt that's it. We'll leave out the other vigorous enterprises made possible by Northside's Prohibition-disease.

Mexicali was still a long flat swath of dirt, textured with ruts, furrows and the odd house. Avenida Reforma was dirt and houses—not to mention (as Mexican boosters often didn't) the Chinesca's two Chinese theaters, three teahouses and twenty-eight associations, not all of which survived the fire of 1923. An album in the Archivo Histórico del Municipio de Mexicali shows us blurred flat fields of silver-grained dirt, corduroy'd plough-stripes, low houses far away. The date is 1920. We see a picket-fenced house at the intersection of Avenida Madero and Calle Oriente, and in the photograph the unpaved street resembles white beach sand, everything emptily immaculate. Shacks display their laundry above the dirt. In

March 1924 they are laying drinking-water pipes on Avenida Lerdo de Tejado. Why not? Mexicali's cotton fields are already drinking deep.

When I imagine those days I smell again the dust and manure from the feedlot, the smell that enters my nose as I come northwards toward Mexicali in the golden sunlight; and of course the feedlot would not have existed had there not been cattle and dust; and then as now there would certainly have been white birds, fluttering in the brown grass. Going west alongside the border toward the mountains, there would have been the same beautiful palm trees and many more rabbits. And I am quite sure that then as now, somewhere on one of Mexicali's wide dirt *avenidas* a little girl with an immense spade-shaped stick of roasted corn clutched her father's hand.

I've read a book which assures me that starting in 1907, once the Salton Sea had been stabilized, Mexicali began to boom, especially since *the concession policies of the Porfirio Díaz Administration . . . promoted U.S. investment in the Mexicali Valley, which led to the establishment of the Colorado River Land Company.* And that company needed workers. Workers came, many of them, then as now, from the interior. Indeed, by 1910 Mexicali's population was more than half of Tijuana's; in 1930, close to *fifteen thousand* residents were counted in Mexicali, fewer than eighty-four hundred in Tijuana. Be that as it may, here are the memories of one who was born into the serene stasis of those days:

In all of my childhood, insisted an old man named Hermenegildo Pérez Cervantes, Mexicali did not grow. I was living in Calle B. From the edge of Mexicali, the northern edge, to where the social security office is now, on F Street, there was a drain, a *canalito,* and that was the southern border of Mexicali. It ran right alongside Avenida de Larroque. The canal is covered up but the street is still there. But the western edge was Calle Eleven. The *colonia* was called Pueblo Nuevo. There was a wooden bridge at the end of Reforma that was called the White Bridge. The bridge took you right to the corner of Avenida Baja California and Fourth Street. That was in Pueblo Nuevo. Before the flood, there was nothing there, but when the flood came it made a big wide canal. So the houses that were on that side disappeared; in 1906 there were houses. In my childhood it was a canal about as wide as this room. But I remember that the water, it wasn't dirty. It was slightly muddy. There were no fish; that's true. Just in front of F Street, which would take you down to that canal called Drain One Hundred Thirty-four, that was the southern edge. The Río Nuevo divided Mexicali into two parts, Old Mexicali and Pueblo Nuevo. Between F and G Street would have been your eastern border.

(One reason why Mexicali had not grown might have been that the Colorado River Land Company's holdings enclosed it. In 1920–21, the municipality was allowed two hundred and forty acres from Chandler's syndicate *to enlarge its urban area.* Kindly Chandler threw in a free thirty-one acres for a park.)

The first thing I remember, continued Hermenegildo Pérez Cervantes, is the musical group formed by the owner of the Industrial Soap Company of the Pacific. It was a military marching band. But they also played old Mexican music, like *corridos.* That would have been in 1929. I was born in 1924.

Now, the Industrial Soap Company of the Pacific was owned by—and he jerked his hand at the border fence, which was just outside the window; and his meaning passed so magically and freely right through it into Northside. (*The entire plant is of steel and concrete,* enthused the *Los Angeles Times, and the machinery bears the labels of manufacturing firms at Chicago, Pittsburgh, East Bridgewater and Piqua. It all came from the United States.* So did the investors. The Industrial Soap Company was of course a partner of the Colorado River Land Company.)—They wore sailor uniforms, Hermenegildo Pérez Cervantes said, very handsome. Black shoes, white pants, a sea-blue stripe all the way down, *muy bonito!* A closed vest with golden buttons. And they had epaulettes. The vest was navy blue, a cropped jacket with long sleeves, with a golden ball and stripes. And a white cap with a black brim.

Do you remember some of the songs they played?

He smiled.—The "Zacateca March"! Some North American marches, but I don't remember. They played a lot in the parades. There were about eighteen of them. They were there for three years: 1929, 1930 and 1931 . . .

He did not know how old the Thirteen Negro was. He had never been there. Well, after all the Thirteen Negro had a bad reputation . . .

What did people say about Chandler and the Colorado River Land Company? I asked that ancient man, who responded: They were from San Francisco, right? Everybody talked about the fact that these North Americans were basically the owners of the whole valley. The Colorado River Land Company bought the land from Señor Guillermo Andrade. He was the first owner. I think the Mexican government sold Andrade the land for ten cents per hectare. But it was all desert. And anyway, that was before they closed the canal.* I never saw them. They must have come, but not very often.

In the flatness outside Mexicali's flatness lay the first few rural schools (established in 1915); beyond them, bales of cotton, squared up on flatbed wagons, awaited their turn between the sheds, towers and railroad tracks of the Colorado River Ginning Company. Through this fertile blankness, the Colorado River Land Company had begun to build the Mexicali and Gulf Railroad, so that cotton bales

*Meaning before the completion of the All-American Canal in 1942 caused the old Imperial Main Canal in Mexico to go dry.

could be shipped to San Felipe without the *complications* of crossing the border. The company had already cleared many of the mesquites and willows in the Colorado Delta, and carted them to Los Angeles for firewood. Then it had raised livestock. Next, bit by bit, as it could borrow more capital, it sought to irrigate and therefore to expand its cultivated holdings. It wanted to turn Mexican Imperial into a perfect mirror of the American side. No Southsider could stop it.

In 1923, it undid Marcelino Magaña's expropriation of thirteen thousand eight hundred acres. By 1927, it had sold off three large parcels, totalling thirty-two thousand acres; it still had about eight hundred thousand acres left. As a rule, it preferred not to sell, but to lease.

Speaking of leasing, the company has always been accused of putting Mexicans last among its parcelees.

Since 1916, Chinese had been subletting parcels from the Colorado River Land Company. Indeed, there were now fifty Chinese ranches in the Mexicali Valley, the largest being the Kam Lin Yuen, whose wages fed and sheltered four hundred souls. In 1926 the Colorado River Company rented out forty acres to the China Leasing Company to grow *potatoes on a large scale for local and Southern California markets.*—There have always been Chinese people since 1903! laughed Hermenegildo Pérez Cervantes, wagging a finger. As for the Chinese tunnels, I never knew about them exactly, but all the people *knew* there were tunnels. The first thing I really heard about it was the fire in 1924. All the people who heard about it said the people just came up out of the ground! The ones who came up still had the long queue, all men! They all slept there. But they worked in the grocery stores, *lavanderías,* restaurants.

Did Mexicali hold eleven thousand Chinese and fifteen hundred Mexicans or fifteen hundred Mexicans and a hundred and fifty Chinese? It depends on which book you read. From the standpoint of a certain Phil Swing, whom I have already introduced to you as one of American Imperial's most ambitious lawyer-orators, the trend was ominous no matter what. He cautioned the United States Senate: *There have been 8,000 Chinese imported into Mexico, and while no more Chinese can be imported because of the exclusion act, there is no exclusion act against Japanese, and Japanese have been looking for years toward Lower California as a possible colony.*

So what? Why would Mr. Swing care about Southside?

Well, by 1920 fifty thousand hectares had already submitted to the plough in the Mexicali Valley. (That's a hundred and twenty-three thousand, five hundred acres to you, my fellow Americans.) Eighty percent of that was cotton, grown for the greater good of the Colorado River Land Company. In 1925, one of the Imperial Irrigation District's five directors insisted that Southside now contained over two hundred and nineteen thousand moist acres! Perhaps not all these figures were precise; who am I to say? Anyhow, prescient Mr. Swing spelled out the potential consequences to the American Imperial: *If Mexico should succeed in putting 600,000 or 800,000 or 1,000,000 acres under cultivation, I challenge any one of us here to make the assertion . . . that we could . . . subsequently withdraw that water from that land. Public opinion of the world would not support it.*

ENSLAVED BY MANUELITA PERALTA

No matter. We Northsiders *love* Mexicali.

In 1930 the Climax, "Mexicali's Fashionable and Leading Cafe" (Jimmy Alvarez, proprietor) was still advertising its American and Chinese dishes, its *private booths for families,* in the Imperial Valley directory. I would have enjoyed a meal at the Climax. Still more I would have liked to attend the Carnival of 1929, when Manuelita Peralta was Queen . . .

Chapter 72

VOLSTEAD

(1919–1933)

The Mexican side of the border is a place where free-spending Americans go to do things they're not allowed to do at home. Loose money always attracts persons of questionable character, and the border cities have plenty of those.

—Mexican teacher, 1962

Why did the Climax advertise in Northside? What made Mexicali grow? Both questions can be answered with a name: Volstead.

ENCOMIUMS TO A WHITE REPUBLIC

In 1903, as soon as Imperial County is born, the Valley Woman's Christian Temperance Union *took on the dignified name of Imperial County W.C.T.U. Through continued effort the county was born white,* meaning dry, *and the first legal act of the first supervisors was a strong prohibition ordinance* . . . Next, our good ladies establish *a detective fund* and prepare *an apparatus for ascertaining the per cent of alcohol in liquids.* In 1914 they hold a barbeque in Calipatria and perform the cantata "The White Republic."

Imperial is the only wet city in Imperial; and soon the white-ribboners claim victory there, too.* And why shouldn't they? They've long since succeeded in shutting down all saloons in the city of Riverside. Meanwhile, *Calexico W.C.T.U. is located on the Mexican border, and has strong, staunch workers who are doing a grand work* on the near side of the ditch. *This local . . . has flourished and won every battle toward keeping Calexico dry.*

Setting aside Victorian prudery (or attempting to contextualize it), why had the

*In 1912, the first legal liquor establishment opened in Imperial County (in Imperial, as a matter of fact). Meanwhile, in the Imperial Valley directory for 1912–13, under the heading **BILLIARDS AND POOL**, we find an astonishing eleven establishments distributed throughout Calexico, Brawley, El Centro, Seeley, Holtville, Imperial. Two years later a wholesale liquor dealer took up residence in the Zimmer Building, Imperial, California. By then there were six listed bars in Imperial (although none in any other city in the county, I admit). In 2001 there were eleven, widely distributed throughout the county.

city fathers of the majority of American Imperial been so quick to enact vice away? Perhaps they feared all the murders and such which other people resign themselves to as "usual to all new countries." To them, the violence of Los Angeles must have offered a terrible example. As soon as California fell under American control, if not before, Los Angeles had its "lewd women." The following statistic comes from 1854: *Average number of violent deaths in the city not less than one a day!—mostly of Mexicans and Indians—but not unfrequently persons in the higher walks of life.* Two years later a vigilance committee was formed; lynchings were already commonplace. The first legal hanging in Los Angeles was considered worthy of remark. Arguably, given the comparative ineffectiveness of statutory authority in that epoch, drinking, whoring and other acts which many of us consider "victimless crimes" were not at all victimless then. Men went armed in the streets as a matter of course; if lust inflamed them, or alcohol weakened their judgment, who would cool them down? The Chinese Massacre of 1871 was said to have started when rivals for a woman's favors exchanged gunfire in Nigger Alley.

Another way of putting this is that from the perspective of the micromonitored California in which I find myself in this year 2003, a place where I can be fined for riding my bicycle without a helmet or holding an unauthorized barbeque, the rapes and woman-nappings of the Moreno Gang were the result of inadequate police control. From the point of view of an American Imperial pioneer, they would have been the result of bad character, or of susceptibility to evil influences and poisons. Logic calls upon the true believer to ban those influences and poisons. Hence Prohibition and the so-called "war on drugs."

A TOAST TO MY HERO

In 1916 Imperial County votes in favor of Prohibition by the widest margin in California. Hurrah for the Volstead Act! Ten years later, the county will be against Prohibition by the same wide margin. We need have no fear that our lands will not become better and better as the years go by. Meanwhile, in Mexican Imperial, Ensenada runs out of gold, and so Colonel Esteban Cantú determines that the capital of the Northern District of Lower California shall be Mexicali. Before we know it, there's a cavalry barracks, an infantry barracks, that famous bridge over the Río Nuevo! (I find on a page of another album in the Archivo Histórico del Municipio de Mexicali a photograph of a water tower surrounded by squares of trees, white field-squares, a grid of empty white streets, here and there an inconspicuous house.) Best of all, bars and whorehouses bloom. In a certain Professor Ruiz's account, this military governor is one of those who *sold their souls to the devil . . . Having no other source of revenue, he opened his door to vice*—namely, American vice, created by Prohibition in 1919. In 1922, Cantú gets succeeded by General Abelardo Rodríguez, who enriches himself by exactly the same means.

Accordingly, the Tia Juana Warm Springs, known for their iodine, lime and magnesia, adorned by cottonwood trees, start getting known for other things, too. Call it a trend. Back in 1915, even as that wholesome exemplar of the Ministry of Capital W. F. Holt made the newspapers by *coming by special motor car* to meet the actors of the new play "The Winning of Barbara Worth" *(Mr. Holt, who figures in the book and play as Jefferson Worth, is having the actors here to look at the exact* spot where Barbara was found *so that they may be able to feel as nearly as possible the real thrill of the* imaginary *incident)*, a Customs Collector in Andrade had warned us all of our decidedly unwholesome future: *It is very well known that the town of Algodones will be based on drink and gambling. Also, I am well satisfied that prostitution will soon run them hard as one of the basic money-makers, and with such a combination smuggling is a natural consequence.* Should we blame the Mexicans as usual? Our good officer continues: . . . *I understand a Mr. Ingraham of Yuma will start to build a saloon during next week.*

(Where might Southside's developers have picked up their ideas? I seem to see Aleck Gibson's gambling house, where the bar clamored and roared while a half-dozen monte banks operated in honest accordance with the laws of suckerdom, each green-baized table heaped with fifty-dollar gold ingots. That could have been Mexicali in 1930. It was really Los Angeles in 1852.—And in June of 1904, Imperial County's *"red light" district was raided by Constable Taggart. Five women and three men were fined.* In 1920, a Volstead year, the District Attorney, Sheriff and thirty deputies *raided thirty gambling joints and houses of ill fame in Calexico, Imperial and El Centro, arresting* 150. Perhaps some of the arrestees went to work for Mr. Ingraham of Yuma.)

The *Imperial Valley Press* runs a recipe for "Russian punch," whose strongest ingredient is carbonated water. On the other side of the ditch, the *Press*'s readers can drink themselves into the ditch.

From what I remember, said Hermenegildo Pérez Cervantes, there were a lot of North Americans who came here to drink in a big cantina called the Owl. But it wasn't just a cantina; it was a cabaret. They had an orchestra and a dance floor, and a big bar. Every kind of drink! There were dancers; there was poker, baccarat, roulette, all kind of games! There was *everything.*—And here the old man smiled so tenderly that for a moment I would have exchanged my middle age for his decrepitude just to have seen *everything* at the Owl.

It would be full of North Americans, he said. The dancers wore these dresses; I can't really describe them, and here again he smiled very gently, lovingly and sadly. They wore those little short, *short* shorts and these shirts; I don't remember whether they were long-sleeved or short, and they danced together, seven or eight of them. You could not dance with them. You would be sitting at a table, and if you wanted to dance, you would dance with people in your family. Usually people came in couples. I was seven years old the first time I saw this. I just looked. I was like a vagabond as a child; I went in wherever I wanted and looked around; I was a shoeshine boy. I just took a look because the door was open, and then I left. I took stock of what was there.

An informant, whose identity the Agent in Charge declines to reveal, reports that *Charles Hoy and James Coffroth, the latter being connected with the Tiajuana race track, were smuggling opium into the United States from Tiajuana, in automobile tanks.* "Sunny Jim" Coffroth gets mentioned in connection with Mexicali, too; but Hermenegildo Pérez Cervantes could not place him.—The name I remember was Jimmy Álvarez, he said. He was the owner of a very, very good bar where the dishes were served on fine china. It was named the Golden Lion. The lion is still there.

Meanwhile, *petitions, resolutions, articles for the papers and other modes of protest swept the Valley against the evils of gambling, drinking and debauchery in Mexicali.* Thus reports Otis P. Tout in 1923. Señor Pérez informs us of the outcome of those protests: Mostly through the late twenties I remember Mexicali getting bigger. The thing that made Mexicali grow was Prohibition. The North Americans came and spent all their money here and the money circulated throughout Mexicali.

To be sure, the money that Americans actually invest in Mexicali's casinos, racetracks and saloons is only about a thirteenth of what the Colorado River Land Company's owners have sent south; but every little bit helps the locals, especially the local talent. And the local talent is industrious and has been ever since a ditch separated Northside from Southside! As early as 1909, the *jefe político* of Mexicali had allegedly received a take of thirty-four saloons, each with its attached whorehouse or gambling hell.

And so Volstead stimulates Imperial's entire international line. In 1925, the Deputy Collector in Charge at Tecate urgently advises Los Angeles that a beer garden will soon be opening at Jacumba Hot Springs, Mexico. The proprietor *intends running a stage to and from the Gate at the International Line. With the limited number of Inspectors at this Fort I will be unable to properly manage the situation at Jacumba.* We may confidently congratulate that beer garden on its success, for by 1926 Navy men in uniform are driving illegally to Tecate to get drunk! Moreover, *at the present time no immigration officer is stationed at the border at the Tecate gate . . .*

In 1924, Dashiell Hammett interrupts the action of one of his crime stories to sum it all up: *This Tijuana happened to be in Mexico—by about a mile—but it's an American town, run by Americans, who sell American artificial booze at American prices.* Meanwhile, in a Hetzel photograph from 1927, we spy on a WCTU luncheon in El Centro: they are mostly elderly or middle-aged ladies in shapeless dresses and tragic hats, and above them spiral the pillars of the Hotel Barbara Worth. They deserve the gratitude of every one of us for keeping American Imperial clean.

But how terribly the Devil's minions fight back! A woman gets caught in Boston with a gallon jug of brandy beneath the dress of the doll she was cradling. The *Imperial Valley Press* reports from Fresno: **Beautiful Girl Pays Big Fine for Bootlegging.** And now a huge whiskey still, doubtlesss built by Satan himself, has just been discovered in Madera!

I suppose that our heroines of temperance are able to soldier on in good heart just the same, until that ghastly year 1926, when even Volstead gets quoted as saying that three point seven five percent beer is *innocuous*. Lift up mine eyes, O Lord! And in 1933, Prohibition is undone. Poor ladies!*

What remains? Why, Mexicali, of course, not to mention San Luis Río Colorado, Tecate, Tijuana.

From my time and place, Hermenegildo Pérez Cervantes's description of the Owl sounds positively innocent, compared with, for instance, the Miau-Miau in 2003, where long, long legs in shining fish-scales, high heels and sinuous leanness enchant my vicious eyes; and behind the triple nickel catty-poles, the waiter in the blue-glowing white shirt leads another stripper by the hand, while on the table a girl in panties permits one man to sniff her ass just as another man slides the panties off her ankle, and the girl of the long, long fish-scale suit has let that suit slip down to her waist; it's down to her ankles now, so that she can all the more freely chase the happiness of the disco ball's spots; the girl on the table is naked and laughing along with everyone. When the dazzlingly naked girl who was formerly in the long fish-scale suit comes offstage, the man in the blue-white shirt leads her by the hand into the flowery light of the dressing room. I sit with Lupe Vásquez, and we both clink our tequila-glasses in memory of the great Volstead.

BATTERIES AND CORN PRICES

In Volstead's spirit, Northside's enforcement agents seek through sternness to transform enacted hypocrisy into literal truth. In my era, the Border Patrol and the Drug Enforcement Administration will throw their police powers into equally impossible tasks.

At first opium is Enemy Number One. They catch *a negro, by name Casino S. Glenn,* in Los Angeles, when he attempts to smuggle opium and morphine from

*Some of the sincerest mourners were Mexicans. I have read that Prohibition's end, followed by Cárdenas's ban on gambling, compelled thirty-five thousand people to leave Baja in two years.

Tia Juana to San Diego by foot. And they achieve many more such successes. Dutifully reporting rumors *that opium in large quantities is being transported from Ensenada to San Diego in lard cans,* they open lard cans, I suppose. But just when they've told one another what to watch for, the forces of evil invent an opium container disguised as a flashlight battery! And then, quite suddenly (surely it must be a coincidence that this occurs the year after Volstead goes into effect), much of the opium mutates into whiskey, concealed in false-bottomed cars or whatever, as attested in letters signed by Federal Prohibition Agents. Our harried guardians of Northside must now keep their eyes peeled not only for suspicious batteries but also for the odd quart of sherry wine concealed in a compartment of a Cadillac roadster.

In keeping with their sometimes discreetly packaged products, the smugglers can show a prudent guardedness in their writings. Witness the following intercepted letter from Jesús Guaderama of San Diego, to David Ochoa of Jerome, Arizona. The writer pretends to be discussing the price of corn: *Well in Mexicali three or four months ago it went as high as $150.00 each load but when I came here in May it went down to $120.00 . . . I will tell you to be very careful when you buy it because there is so much fake.* Señor Guaderama has some possessions in pawn, and accordingly needs to borrow money. *I will pay you back as soon as I can go to Mexicali because I can make money over there.*

Like the product, the smugglers themselves alter characteristics. They become more likely to be Mexican.

In 1916 a druggist and a veterinarian, both of Holtville, are anonymously accused of smuggling opium and egret feathers from Southside; the veterinarian is *in conjunction with an unknown woman.* In that same year, the Special Agent in Charge at Los Angeles advises us that two musicians in Hoy's dance hall in Mexicali, one named Emil Block and the other simply called Wolf, are in the opium business. Meanwhile, Los Angeles warns Calexico that Max Singer, Oscar Kirshon and Jack Norton, alias Big Jack, probable members of the Alexander Gladstone opium smuggling gang, *may be operating in this district.*

Now for some Mexicans: The convicted opium smugglers V. Zurbano and T. de la Fuente come briefly to life in the old Customs documents because the Special Deputy Collector took the trouble to describe them for us. Zurbano had blue eyes and black hair. He weighed a hundred and forty-seven pounds and was twenty-seven years old. Since he pled guilty, he received four months in the San Diego County Jail. (What would he get now? Twenty-five years?) Tibicia de la Fuente might have been his sweetheart, since her time and date of arrest were the same as his and her criminal number was 1765 when his was 1766; those two must at least have been travelling together. After pleading guilty to smuggling five cans of opium, she got six months. She was thirty-six years old, five and a half feet, a hundred and fifty pounds, with brown eyes and *Ch. hair.*

In the same year, agents of Northside spy on a certain Francisco Gonzales in Calexico, who may be implicated in pearl-smuggling from Lower California. *Gonzales is a small Spanish appearing person, having some resemblance to a Hebrew.*

In 1918 we learn that *Miguel Gonzalez is a Mexican and resides at San Diego, Calif. He is well known as one of the leading merchants and importers of Lower California . . . I must say that his business has always been more or less under surveillance by this office on account of his great opportunity to engage in illegal operations, but nothing definite has ever been found against him.*

Mexicans may pass for Anglos on occasion. A certain Mark Yeates, sometimes seen *in a mixed gray suit, soft round crown hat,* turns out to be Juan Mata, alias Mark Yeater. His is of *dark complexion, height about 5 feet 5 inches, dresses like a working man.* The eyes of Northside detect him setting out for El Centro and Mexicali in company of someone named J. L. Whitton. That fall they arrest him in San Diego for opium possession.

Sometimes Anglos and Hispanics are in it together: In 1919, Ben Hodges, a bartender for "a Spaniard" named Mr. Barrera, seems to be his partner in the opium smuggling trade. In 1921, A. Leyra and two unknown Americans get arrested by Mexican officials in Southside *for transporting, without a permit, 5 three-gallon copper canteens of whiskey.*

Oh, yes, it takes all kinds to smuggle, even Asiatics! The following alert has just come in over the wire from 1922: *N. Sakiyama now in Mexicali, Mexico, believed to be from San Diego, Calif., is in smuggling booze game in large scale.*

"EITHER WHISKEY, DOPE, OR CHINESE"

Speaking of Asiatics, it is now time to remind ourselves that Volstead's ancestor, the Chinese Exclusion Act, remains in force, and with equivalent aims and methods. And so Chinese may be found in the ranks of the smugglers, among the contraband commodities themselves, or both. The following letter from Inspector H. G. Dunlap is typical. This officer has heard on the train to Yuma that a man named Cecil Dennis *was engaged in smuggling, either whiskey, dope, or Chinese, or perhaps all three; that Dennis was good for nothing. . . that Dennis made frequent trips to the Mexican border . . . that Dennis always left the house after dark, and would always get back before daylight . . . that when he returned . . . he was always well supplied with money . . .*

Thus Chinese as items. Now for Chinese as agents: Watch out for *Leon Maddox,*

Los Angeles police number 13762, who it is alleged on or about the 1st instant traded a stolen Ford automobile to a Chinaman in Mexicali named Louie Yee or You, in return for eight cans of prepared smoking opium, and that Maddox smuggled the opium at Calexico and brought same to Los Angeles.

Given their magical fungibility, it is no wonder that Chinese need merely to be on the scene for Northside's spies to take suspicion. Do you remember the Owl, about which Hermenegildo Pérez Cervantes dreamily assured me that there had been *everything?* Even prior to Volstead, Northside keeps an eye on the Owl. In 1916 the following alert goes out on Dan Hayes of Calexico: *He is 5' 8", dark complexion, smooth shaven, wears blue trousers with fine white stripe, black shoes and black hat; and while he is reported to be a Cherokee Indian he would invariable* [sic] *be called a Spaniard in this section. . . Hays has lived in Imperial Valley at least two years . . . He was recently employed by Edwards Brothers cotton growers in Mexico who have a house directly on the boundary three miles west of Calexico. The place has long been under suspicion . . . The city marshall* [sic] *reports that Hays always seems to have plenty of money without doing much for it, also that he is supposed to have had some sort of criminal record or trouble in the East. He is now stopping in Calexico and spends a great deal of time in Mexicali. Inspector Stott reports that hays* [sic] *was seen conversing with several chinese* [sic] *in the Owl Saloon in Mexicali yesterday evening.*

What were the Chinese up to in Mexicali? I promise that it will take me less than a hundred pages to tell you.

Chapter 73

THE CHINESE TUNNELS

(1849–2003)

Stay home and lose opportunities;
A hundred considerations led me to Mexico.
Political parties are like wolves and tigers
exterminating each other;
Hatred and prejudice against foreigners take
our property and many lives.
Unable to stay on,
I creep across the border to the America,
But collide with an immigration officer . . .

—"Gold Mountain Song," 1911–15

I've already told you that it was on Good Friday night, at the threshold of that church on Avenida Reforma, with the Virgin of Guadalupe's image invisible overhead and the border wall faintly discernable, like a phosphorescent log in a dark forest, that I first met the sisters Hernández. When the loudspeaker sighed *María, la Madre de Jesús,* I thought that they looked sincerely distressed, Susana in particular: the Crucifixion had just occurred again. When they mentioned Jesús, María and Judas, they were speaking of people they knew. Later our talk turned to Mexicali, and they began to tell me about the time of the great fire when all the Chinese who lived secretly and illegally under the ground came out "like ants," to escape the burning; and everybody was shocked at how many of them there were. Susana and Rebeca had not yet been born when that happened, but it remained as real to them as the betrayal of Christ. I couldn't decide whether to believe them. When was this great fire? They weren't sure. (In fact there were at least three great fires.) But they knew that Chinese, *many, many* Chinese as they kept saying, used to hide in tunnels beneath Mexicali.

Well, why shouldn't there be tunnels? I'd seen the Valley of the Queens in Egypt (dirt and gravel hills, sharp-edged rockshards, then caves); I'd convinced myself of the existence of Pompeii's Anfiteatro, which is mainly a collar of grass now, with a few concentric ribs of stone beneath—oh, there are so many parts of the earth comprised of dirt, tunnels and sunlight; sometimes there's even a Catholic church's tower among the four cypress trees above it all! Havre, Montana, maintains its underground quarter as a source of tourist revenue: Here's the bordello; there's the purple-glassed skylight, originally clear, now stained by the decades of sunlight reacting with magnesium in the glass. Don't forget to see the old black leather dentist drill—a foot-drill, actually, which was operated by the patient! So why shouldn't there be more than sand beneath Mexicali?

Jose Lopez, my fine and cheerful co-navigator of the New River, told me that a year or two ago a friend of his (Mexican, not Chinese; Jose didn't have so many Chinese friends; come to think of it, he didn't have any) delivered a truckload of fresh fish from San Felipe up to a certain Chinese produce market in Mexicali. What was the address of this market? Jose couldn't say. It was surely somewhere in the Chinesca, which you or I would call Chinatown. At any rate, the merchant opened a door, and Jose's friend glimpsed a long dark tunnel walled with earth.—What's that? he asked.—You don't need to know, came the answer.—Jose's understanding was that even now the Chinese didn't trust banks. They kept their money under the ground.

The owner of the Golden Dragon Restaurant believed that there were four or five thousand Chinese in Mexicali. A certain Mr. Auyón, who will figure significantly in this report and whose statistics always took first prize for magnitude, informed me that there were currently eight thousand Chinese, thirty-two thousand half-Chinese and a hundred Chinese restaurants.

Most were legal now, but in the old days they'd come illegally from San Felipe, and then their relatives or Tong associates had concealed them in those tunnels, which, it was widely believed, still extended under "all downtown"; and there was even supposed to be a passageway to Calexico, as why wouldn't there be, although none of the storytellers had seen it, and some allowed that it might have been discovered and sealed off decades ago by the Border Patrol. I've read that during Prohibition *in the Chinese district of Mexicali, tunnels led to opium dens and brothels, and for the convenience of bootleggers, some of them burrowed under the international line to Calexico,* which might have been that tunnel or a precursor. In the cantina around the corner from the Hotel Malibu, Mexicans bought me drinks and insisted that the tunnel was still there. As Jose Lopez liked to say about every conceivable legend, why not believe it? A tunnel under the Hotel Del Norte got discovered and closed in the 1980s; the Chinese didn't have anything to do with that one, I'm told. In the autumn of 2003, when I was concluding this investigation, people with guns and uniforms found another tunnel which began in a mechanic's shop east of the Chinesca and came up in Calexico, someone told me in a fireplace, but it wasn't a Chinese tunnel so I paid no attention. A whore in the Hotel Altamirano knew for a fact that the Chinese had been behind it because *they always work in secret.* It made her happy to believe that; it made life more mysterious. And who was I to say that she didn't know what she knew? Frank Waters recalls in his memoir of the days when the Colorado River still flowed to the sea that in 1925, Chinese were smuggled across the border *in crates of melons, disguised as old Mexican señoras, and even carried by plane from Laguna Salada.* Why not suppose they went by tunnel, too? They went from Mexicali's Chinatown to Los Angeles's Chintatown, both of which have since burned. *They came out like ants!*

My own mental image of the tunnels grew strangely similar to those long aboveground arcades on both sides of the border; on certain very hot summer nights when I have been under a fever's sway, with sweat bursting out on the back of my neck and running down my sides, the archways have seemed endless; their sidewalks pulse red like some science-fiction nightmare about plunging into the sun, and as I walk home out of Mexico, the drunken woman and the empty throne of the shoeshine man are but artifacts, lonely and sparse, within those immense corridors of night. I wander down below the street and up again for the border formalities, which pass like a dream, and suddenly I find myself in the continuation of those same arcades, which are quieter and cooler than their Mexican equivalents. Bereft of the sulphur-sweet stink of the New River, which loops northwest as soon as it enters the United States, they still go block after block in the same late-night dream.

Why not in Mexicali indeed? It seemed that everybody knew about these tunnels—everybody on Southside, that is; for when I crossed the line to inquire at the Pioneers Museum, two old white men who'd lived in Imperial County all their lives stared at me, not amused at all, and replied they'd never heard anything about any tunnels. Up in Brawley, Stella Mendoza, wife, mother, ex-President and continuing representative of her Imperial Irrigation District, passionate defender and lifelong resident of Mexican America, who spoke Spanish, traced back her ancestry to Sonora, and went to Mexicali "all the time," said that the tunnels were likewise new to her. Well, but why should *we* know? Mexico lay on the other side of the ditch.

VAMPIRES AND CIGARETTES

The clandestine nature of the tunnels lent itself to supernatural evocations. About thirty years ago a rumor had settled on Mexicali that the Chinese were harboring a vampire down there. Later it came out that the being was human, but a "mutant," very hairy, two of whose lower teeth had grown like fangs right through the skin above his upper lip. He "escaped," said the woman who'd seen him, but the

Chinese recaptured him and that was the end of the story.—I asked Jose Lopez whether he credited this, and he replied: Look. You have to keep an open mind. In the 1960s the Devil himself came to Mexicali. He actually killed a woman! Everybody knew it was the Devil. If you keep a closed mind, you can't believe it. But why not believe it?

They live like cigarettes, said a Mexican journalist on a Sunday, cramming all his upright fingers together as if he'd shoved them into a box. He advised me to search for people who looked *like this* (pulling his eye-corners upwards), because only they could tell me everything. Although he'd never seen one, his sources inclined him to believe that there might be a tunnel under Condominios Montealbán, those ill-famed grimy concrete apartments beside the Río Nuevo, where tired women, some Chinese-looking, some not, complained about the illnesses of their children, and teenagers sat day after day in the shade of the old stone lion. It had been at Condominios Montealbán that that Mexican mother had compared her country and my country thus: Here we're free. Over there they live like robots.—So we lived like robots; Chinese lived like cigarettes. To repeat: They lived like cigarettes, they protected a vampire, they came out like ants; might it be that not all Mexicans invited them into their hearts?

Granted, many of the local informants and interpreters I employed were poor. Why else would they work for me? Extrapolating from their opinions as a means of determining how Mexicans felt about Chinese was junk science, equivalent to interviewing a few railroad bums to learn how Americans of all classes felt about the war against Iraq. The people who were most ready and available to inform me about the Chinese tunnels could be well represented by the Mexican boy who had worked at a certain Chinese restaurant for five years now (it was the one we'll call the Nuevo Peiping, which, conveniently located near to two floor shows, offered bronze bas-reliefs of Chinese ideograms, an octagonally recessed ceiling, thick plastic on all the tables, mariachi musicians whose patrons took life as it came because for them it came easy; when a waiter such as this Mexican boy rushed over, shouldering a heavy platter of Chinese dishes, they regarded his service without surprise), and the Mexican boy explained: They come from far away from here, so their character is different from ours, and it's bad. They don't share.

The boy's salary was seven hundred pesos per week. His labor ran five days a week, from one-o'-clock to ten-o'-clock. That was a dollar-fifty an hour, not so far from what he might have made working in a *maquiladora*.

He got a mother, he got three sisters, the interpreter bitterly informed me. He says, the Chinese always get angry over nothing. And if somebody comes hungry or thirsty, they never help; they never share.

Has he ever heard anything about tunnels?

Never, because these kinda people, they don't wanna talk to no one about their life.

A whitehaired, pleasant, roundfaced lady named Lupita, who had once worked in the office of a semi company, had graduated to being a security guard in a prostitute discotheque, and now held afternoon duty as the moneytaker for a parking lot beside a shut-down supermarket, allowed that her favorite aspect of Mexicali was her friends, and her second favorite was the Chinese food. Would she consider marrying a Chinese? I inquired, and she replied: No! I'm not a racist, but no Chinese, no nigger!

So the people I met on the street didn't like the Chinese; unfortunately, I have to tell you that many of the intelligentsia, the journalists and archivists, didn't seem to like them, either.

"THEM DAMNED NAGURS"

Imperial is a boarded-up billiard arcade, white and tan; Imperial is Calexico's rows of palms, flat tan sand, oleanders and squarish buildings, namely the Golden Dragon restaurant, Yum Yum Chinese Food, McDonald's, Mexican insurance; Imperial contains a photograph of a charred building and a heap of dirt: *Planta Despepitadora de Algodón "Chino-Mexicana,"* an establishment which has vanished like the Climax Grill. Imperial is a map of the way to wealth; the map has sun-bleached back to blankness. Leave an opened newspaper outside for a month and step on it; the way it crumbles, that's Imperial. Imperial is a Mexicali wall at twilight: tan, crudely smoothed, and hot to the touch. Imperial is a siltscape so featureless that every little dip made by last century's flood gets a christening, even if the name is only X Wash. In spite of its wide, flat streets and buildings, Imperial is actually a mountain, Gold Mountain to be precise.

In 1849 the California gold rush begins. Mr. Chung Ming gets rich right away. Hearing the news, his friend Cheong Yum rushes to California and achieves equal success. By 1852, twenty thousand Chinese a year, mostly Cantonese,* are trying their luck. A decade later, we find twelve thousand of them digging, blasting, mortaring and shoveling on the transcontinental railroad. *Wherever we put them we found them good,* reports a white magnate who happily paid them less than he did his Irishmen. The Irishmen take notice. One of them laments: *Begad if it wasn't for them damned nagurs we would get $50 and not do half the work.*

*According to the owner of the Golden Dragon Restaurant, in 2003 this was still the case although a number of Mexicali's Chinese also came from Shanghai.

"Chinamen" and Indians get preference for employment in the vineyards around Los Angeles, I assume because *we found them good,* and in 1860 a contingent of white laborers gives up and departs for Texas. In 1876 a chronicle of Los Angeles reports this news: *City still rapidly improving. During June anti-Chinese meetings were the order of the day.* Those words depress me all the more because they were written a mere five years after the infamous Chinese Massacre.* In spite of the anti-Asian movement's best efforts, *An Illustrated History of Los Angeles County,* published in 1889, estimates that between two and three thousand Chinese walk the streets: *The Chinese are a prominent factor in the population of Los Angeles . . . The Chinaman, as a rule, with occasional exceptions, is not desirable help in the household. On the ranch . . . he can be tolerated, when white men are not obtainable.*

Meanwhile, in 1898, the Britannica Company contracts with Mr. Ma You Yong to bring a thousand Chinese to Mexico for railroad work. A tunnel cave-in kills seventy-seven. And they keep right on, from Oaxaca all the way to Salinas Cruz and Jesús Carranza. No doubt, onlookers remark that they live together like cigarettes. In the sixth year of their labors, Jack London publishes a bitterly logical little essay entitled "The Scab." *When a striker kills with a brick the man who has taken his place, he has no sense of wrong-doing . . . Behind every brick thrown by the striker is the selfish will "to live" of himself, and the slightly altruistic will "to live" of his family.*

Under capitalism, continues London, we are all scabs, and we all hate scabs. But not everyone takes his reasoning that far. The Chinese coolie, whom London mentions in the same breath as the Caucasian professor who scabs by being meeker than his predecessor, is to haters of *damned nagurs* a dangerously particular case. You see, in California the Chinese do more than we, in exchange for less. Moreover, they keep what they get. (An eyewitness judgment: *They sent up to the mines for their use supplies of Chinese provisions and clothing, and thus all the gold taken out by them remained in Chinese hands and benefited the rest of the community but little . . . In fact, the Chinese formed a distinct class which enriched itself at the expense of the country.*) In that case, we'd better make it hot for the Chinese. Hence anti-Chinese riots; hence the Chinese Exclusion Act of 1882 and its many descendants.

"The Scab" saw print on the official date of Mexicali's founding. The Chinese were already there.

*The way one county history tells it, two rival Chinese mobs fighting over a woman "on either side of Negro alley" began shooting at each other on 23 October 1871. On the following day, a policeman and two citizens who were doing what they could to bring peace got wounded in the crossfire; one citizen died. "The news of his death spread like wild-fire, and brought together a large crowd, composed principally of the lower class of Mexicans and the scum of the foreigners." The predictable result: lynchings, shootings, arson, pillaging. Eighteen Chinese were murdered. (Another source gives the casualty figure of a probably inflated seventy-two.) The United States later paid reparations to China.

"THEY CAME FOR THE WORK"

My Chinese interpreter Clare Ng (about whom more later) interviewed an old couple at Condominios Montealbán and reported: Those two people tell me, the Chinese people start the whole city, but I don't know.

In 1890 two Chinese named Mariano Ma and Chang Peio arrived in Ensenada, from where I don't know (after all, this is a creation myth). Thirteen years later they made the twenty-six-day journey to Mexicali. They might or might not have been the first. They were not the last.

A softspoken old Chinese shoe-store owner at Altamirano and Juárez (who became less open with me once I started badgering him about tunnels) said from behind the glass counter: Before me, my grandfather was here. When the city was founded, my grandfather came in 1906. He had heard from people who were here before that there wasn't a city, nothing but land; they came for the work. There were no buildings. My grandfather came to pick cotton.

Was he in business for himself?

He worked for someone else, an American company. I didn't remember the name.

I suspect that the name was the Colorado River Land Company, which had already hired Mariano Ma. In later years he'd be seen at the racetrack with the Governor of Baja California, but in 1903 he spent his days with Chang Peio and the other braceros, leveling roads, digging canals, all for a wage of fifty centavos (twenty-five additional for food); whether this was paid daily or weekly is not recorded. Señor Ma remarks: *In that place there were a lot of mosquitoes. Many people died on account of the various sicknesses caused by insect bites, rattlesnakes and the intense heat. Some people were buried underground by quicksand and whirlwinds.*

The old Chinese-Mexican mestiza Carmen Jaham told it this way: *Mexicali began with about a hundred or a hundred and fifty Chinese.* And between 1902 and 1921, forty or fifty thousand Chinese came to Mexico, some of them sent for by the Colorado River Land Company. In 1913 there were a thousand in Mexicali alone. And they kept coming.

On Calle Altamirano there stands a photo shop whose glass cases contain as fine a selection of merchandise as anything this side of Palm Springs; the owner was a middle-aged third-generation Chinese named Steve Leung, and here is how he told it:

When American people brought in Chinese to build the railroad, there was a big buildup in the Chinese population. After the project finished, there started being a concentration in San Francisco. Chinese culture, even though we can recognize them by a lot of invention like gunpowder, paper, etcetera, they do a lot of agriculture. So the first thing they saw was the wasteland here in the desert. There was nobody here, especially here in the Mexican side. Same thing happened here like in Las Vegas. So they started moving in and they started growing cotton. This was eighteen something; in the whole Mexicali Valley it was about ninety percent Chinese. There was no official power or authority that was Mexican, so the Chinese could do what they wanted. So downtown was a replica of what used to be San Francisco at this time. They were doing cotton and they were doing fine.

Then Mexican government started coming in. As Mexican people came in, Chinese people started putting in grocery stores and other services that will provide to the Mexican sector—laundries, etcetera. But of course they have some success and some failures. What they were able to keep were the grocery stores.

Then Mexican people started taking over the grocery stores, so they pulled back to the restaurants. Mexican people have not been able to take that over, since Chinese work longer hours. They don't fight with the local people; they let them come in, they just pull back.

And in my mind's eye, as Mr. Leung said this, I could see them pulling back into the tunnels.

Whether or not his version of events correctly explains the facts, it certainly fits in with them, for the photo albums in the Archivo Histórico del Municipio de Mexicali do show an awful lot of Chinese grocery stores. By about 1915 the Chinese must have pulled considerable commercial weight in Mexicali, for in a photograph from that year we find a storefront for C. B. Williams & Sons, Cotton Selling Agents, Hardware Implements and Wagons; the same legend appears in both Spanish and Chinese. One Northsider claims they might have made up forty-two percent of Mexicali's population then. By 1923 the Chinese have a Masonic lodge on Avenida Juárez at the intersection with Calle Altamirano. (According to Mr. Auyón, it was here that the Associación China de Mexicali began the confederation of Tongs in 1919.) The facade of this edifice boasts four pillars, and between the engraved dates 1916 and 1923 I see the words CHEE KUNG TONG. The Logia Masónica proudly shows off its own pillared portico, its roof facade of grandly spaced pillars which widen like doublebladed axeheads.

On the same block, at about the same time (this photo is dated 1923) we discover the long rectangular cube of the Chong Kee general store right next to the business of Harry E. Bowman. On the corner of Altamirano and Guerrero, Juan Chong Mercantile Cía. S.A. offers the world Mexicali Beer and a high trio of ideograms, gazing out on the blank white street.

And so they kept coming, but not everybody liked them. The ultraleftist Mexican Labor Party, which called for the exploited masses to rise up against President Díaz, could not resist reviling the exploited Chinese. In 1911, the locals down in Torreón,

Coahuila, had a party and murdered three hundred and three of them, not to mention five Japanese; but Coahuila's not in Imperial; it's not in this story, so never mind.—Many times I've heard the tale of how when the Chinese illegals arrived in San Felipe, many of them paid money to a certain captain who advised them to walk in the direction of a certain hill; they'd see Mexicali within half an hour. From San Felipe to Mexicali is two hours by car. These luckless people walked into the desert and died. I've been told that the ghosts of the Chinese victims continue to haunt the now long dead captain's spirit, and sometimes the flitting specter of his ship is seen.* All the same, they kept coming. They spread out through the Mexicali Valley and across the Colorado River into Sonora and Sinaloa, where they were persecuted especially violently. At the beginning of the twenty-first century I found an almost inconceivable number of Chinese restaurants one after the other in San Luis Río Colorado, all of them wearing the same sign: an upturned-boat affair which was sometimes red, sometimes green. A fighting-cock breeder from near there, not the older man whom I usually interviewed but one of his competitors, said to me during a match in Islas Agrarias that *of course the Chinese are all into slavery*. That was why one never saw any Chinese beggars. He got even more animated in the course of telling me that seven years ago, the authorities had rounded up many illegal Chinese in Mexicali and sequestered them in a stadium under heavy guard, but some had mysteriously escaped, an occurrence which he considered both uncanny and hateful; he turned bitter when he mentioned it. He supposed that they had disappeared into one of their tunnels . . .

It's always the same story. *Begad if it wasn't for them damned nagurs* . . . And it never matters what color the niggers are. In 1962 a Texan farmhand who'd moved to the Imperial Valley *'cause they told us it was the land of plenty* ended up standing in soup lines.—I have nothing against the Mexican nationals, he told a journalist. All I'm saying is how can domestics compete with guys who will work harder and for less?

*Thus the most common Mexican version of the tale which I have heard over the years. In *El Dragón en el Desierto*, whose half-Chinese author will come up from time to time in this chapter, the story is slightly different but no less sad: A certain band of Chinese from Sonora were ferried by a Japanese to San Felipe. Perhaps it was this Japanese who became the Mexican sea-captain in the local variant. At any rate, *El Dragón en el Desierto* claims that the Chinese were shown the proper road to Mexicali, but that they got lost and "began to wander directionless; starving and thirsty with temperatures of 125 degrees F., they began to die one by one as their bodies fell upon the sand . . . The Cucapa Sierra is where the Chinese braceros died and is actually known as 'Sierra of the Chinese' or 'the Chinero.' "

"THE CLASS WE USE IN OUR CAMPS"

Employers, of course, love scabs. In the very same year that Mariano Ma and Chang Peio first raise shovels in Mexicali, the "Imperial Catechism" advises settlers to the new American towns of eastern San Diego County how to harvest the richest crop of nickels from their fields. For your ranch hands *you can get Chinese or Japanese cooks, which is the class we use in our camps. There is no female help to be had in that valley. Chinese or Japanese make good house-servants as well as cooks.*

In his biographical directory of 1918, Judge Farr writes a few words about Mrs. Julia Lyon, wife of a postmaster-baker-dairyman-hardwareman: *When Mr. Lyon had his large ranch holdings in Lower California,* which means Mexico, *Mrs. Lyon . . . rode horseback and looked after seventy-five Chinese, thus saving the expense of a foreman.* I suspect that her seventy-five Chinese saved her other expenses as well. Let's assume that what she paid was what the Colorado River Land Company paid. Fifty centavos daily or weekly still sounds awfully cheap.

"TRULY IN EVERY SENSE ALIENS"

One never knows to what extent economic competition exacerbates racism, as opposed to being exacerbated by it. In any event, both were present. The historian Bancroft, whose many-volumed work on California comprises a monument nearly as eminent as the border wall, expresses his epoch when he tells us: *These people were truly in every sense aliens. The color of their skins, the repulsiveness of their features, their under-size of figure, their incomprehensible language, strange customs and heathen religion . . . conspired to set them apart.* This thinking continues to thrive in Mexicali today.—Goddamned gooks! cried my interpreter, Lupe Vásquez. I know you don't like that word, Bill. But look at that old gook there! See how he won't even look at us? Goddamned old gook!

In Condominios Montealbán, on one of whose four-storey cubes was graffiti'd **BROTHER FOREFER**, a middle-aged man was working with jumper cables on a rusty car; he had all the time and kindness in the world for me; yes, he agreed, he had more liberty than any American; on the other hand, he couldn't own as many things. Well, that was all right with him. His pretty young wife, whom I first took for his daughter, came to get a cigarette, and they smoked lovingly together. He had lived here for twenty-seven years. Yes, Chinese lived here, too, and they said hello to him, but *they keep to themselves and we keep to ourselves.*

We're not like friends, the man went on. It's like the whites and Negroes in your country.

That was the day that my poor interpreter, José López from Jalisco, not to be confused with the Jose Lopez with whom I rode the New River, kept getting kicked out of one Chinese restaurant after another when I sent him to inquire about tunnels; since I paid him by the hour, it is fortunate that Mexicali had somewhere between a hundred and a hundred and fifty Chinese restaurants* for him to get kicked out of; he came to me redfaced with angry humiliation. (Those gooks *yelled* at him? cried Lupe in amazement. I wouldn't have let no gook raise his voice to me. Those gooks need to get hit upside the head!) At first I wondered whether José's incomplete success had anything to do with the fact that he smelled rank; that day he kept disappearing behind a bush or a garbage heap to have diarrhea (fortunately, Condominios Montealbán was rich in garbage heaps); then there was the fact that he didn't project a dynamic attitude, having fallen asleep on one of the border benches at three in the morning; the sun woke him much too early, and so he kept nodding off today. In short, how much responsibility did he bear for his failure to gain high-quality intelligence on Chinese tunnels? Well, I proved for myself that whenever I greeted a Mexican at Condominios Montealbán, my greeting was invariably returned; when I greeted a Chinese, it usually wasn't. Here came another young Chinese man; José and I called out a greeting, but he didn't even turn. A pretty Chinese girl returned my *buenos días* in a low voice and kept walking. I politely requested her help, and she kept walking.

Next I met Alicia and her fifteen-year-old daughter Luisa. They came from Sonora. Condominios Montealbán had been their home for twelve years, ever since Alicia's divorce. They had no Chinese friends. The reason, said the mother, was this: *Chinese aren't happy the way we Mexicans are. When I have some problem, I go to a neighbor. The Chinese keep it all to themselves.*

On Saturday night there was a *quinceañera* for Luisa, right there where I'd first met Alicia when she was sweeping, in the plaza beneath the freeway overpass. It was the night before the year's heat settled back upon Imperial. Twin disco balls which strangely resembled police car lights sped their spatters of luminescence across the Aztec-style reliefs. Behind the tables, a sun-colored banner had been taped to the graffiti'd wall to frame the three-layer white cake on the red-colored table. Lupe Vásquez was with me, and he had a fine time, although he was so used to getting up early for his field work that by eleven he felt exhausted. Still, it brought his youth back. He used to know where all the *quinceañeras* in Calexico, Heber, El Centro and Mexicali would be held; he and his friends would crash these parties almost every weekend, for the free drinks and the dancing. His memories rushed like searchlight beams across the cracked plaza. Oh, he remembered the good old

*This figure was quoted to me by Mr. Leung, who ought to know. He claimed that Chinese restaurants accounted for 70 or 80% of the total business.

days in San Luis Río Colorado when they had a nice *zona rosa* with back rooms in the bars so that it wasn't necessary to rent a hotel room just for fifteen minutes; unfortunately, San Luis Río Colorado had grown too much, and the *zona rosa* got torn down. That was how he and I passed the time at Luisa's *quinceañera*. My friend Larry from Borrego Springs was there, too; he had such a fine time that on the next day his cheeks were sore from smiling. Here came the "waltz of the last doll," the song whose words were *I bought my daughter her last doll today, then noticed she had grown up; now the bud has become a rose;* Luisa and her stepfather were dancing slowly to this like lovers. Now she was dancing with her brother and her mother. A huge tree, I think a eucalyptus, towered over the first two apartment blocks, which it had grown between, and meanwhile there was a certain dancer, a dancer in red. Lupe loved to look at her. He said that he wanted some white meat. It had been a long time since he'd tasted any of that, if I knew what he meant. He'd repeatedly expressed this wish to his brother-in-law, who advised him to go buy a can of tuna. Every now and then the Río Nuevo, which was maybe thirty paces away, sent us a whiff or two to remind us that it might be interred but it refused to be forgotten; and there was Luisa, dressed like a bride, nestling her head on her stepfather's shoulder; there she was dancing with all her girlfriends, smiling and clapping her delicate arms. A little boy also danced dartingly among them; and high up on a narrow ledge between the Aztec reliefs, little children danced in the night, with the disco ball raking across them. Only half the tables were occupied, but nobody seemed to mind. Alicia brought every two or three guests a big bottle of beer, and when Lupe was so tired that we had to go, she offered to make a dinner for us. Her daughter danced on, her white dress distinguishing her from the others, who were all dark almost beyond visibility in that warm grey night against the spinning lights. All the young girls were dancing to a happy song about a cuckold: *It's only rumors, rumors, that he's around the corner,* Lupe chuckling goodnaturedly; now came another song of sexual innuendo: *I want to eat a banana with whipped cream on top,* the guests smiling, the fifteen-year-old dancing happily while her mother clapped. I loved this Mexican expression of the sunniness and funniness of sexuality; I loved the fact that these materially poor people could find joy right in the midst of the Río Nuevo's stench; up on the overpass, a man leaned over the railing to watch and listen; he stood there smiling for an hour. And Luisa danced with her girlfriends to a song about getting so wasted that I have forgotten my name and I don't give a damn.

By the way, said Lupe, how many Chinese do you see? Alicia's been here for how long did you say, and she's a nice lady, a real nice lady to welcome us like this, and these Chinese are her neighbors, and there's not a single goddamned Chinese. They won't even give her that much respect. Goddamned gooks.

THE ANSWER TO EVERYTHING

A few months after this *quinceañera* I met a very friendly, pretty, educated Chinese waitress who lived in Condominios Montealbán. I asked her why she had refrained from coming to Luisa's party, and she replied, not without contempt, *I don't care for that sort of event.*

"UNTIL THE LAST ALIEN SERF IS RETURNED TO THE ORIENT"

It is particularly painful, not to mention significant, to find that even the utopias of turn-of-the-century irrigation dreamers fail the test: Democracy will be built on small plots of equal size, none of which ought to belong to Chinese.* I quote from the second edition of *The Conquest of Arid America* (1905): California *has distinctly failed as a land of big things, and achieved its best successes in the opposite direction. Its true and final greatness will consist of the aggregate of small things . . . Progress toward this end is already well begun. It must go on until the last great estate is dismembered and the last alien serf is returned to the Orient.* Let's count it irrelevant to the serf's alienness that life in China at this period bears a strange resemblance to the Imperial goal. According to my 1910 *Britannica,* most Chinese *are cultivators of the soil. The holdings are in general very small, and the methods of farming primitive. Water is abundant, and irrigation common over large areas.* Well, who cares? Goddamned gooks!

"WHERE THEIR HABITS WOULD BE LESS OFFENSIVE"

As it happened, many Chinese do not get "returned to the Orient," so their employers in and around Imperial do the next best thing. A 1912 history of Riverside County remarks about its eponymous city: *The older citizens will remember when the back portion of the block, where the Reynolds Department Store now stands, was largely occupied by Chinese, mostly used as grape pickers in those days, and how rough and filthy a quarter this shanty section was in consequence.* Fortunately, a solution lay at hand: Remove that Chinatown and reestablish it *in the Arroyo, where their habits would be less offensive.* In the fullness of time comes a still better result: *The Chinese are no longer employed in Riverside,* because grapes and apricots, in whose tending they were employed, have been replaced by oranges and lemons.

*Mr. Clark of Missouri to his fellow Congressmen, 1902: "The Chinese problem is to the Pacific coast what the negro problem is to the Southern States, except that the race question of the South is entirely a domestic question . . . Upon these race questions I unhesitatingly take my position with the white people of the South and the white people of the Pacific coast."

"A HIGH-PITCHED VOICE WAS SCREAMING CHINESE ORDERS"

What if the alien serfs didn't want to be returned to the Orient?

In around 1905 we find Mr. Hutchins, the Chinese inspector, carrying out his task at Jacumba, *which is to allow no unentitled Mongolian to cross from Mexico into the United States.* When he catches them, they're jailed and tried. But something tells me that my government wouldn't keep paying Mr. Hutchins if the Chinese didn't keep crossing.

In one of Zane Grey's novels, published in 1913, a rancher on the Arizona side of Sonora explains to a cowboy that *of course, my job is to keep tabs on Chinese and Japs trying to get into the U.S. from Magdalena Bay.* (That same year, the Colorado River Land Company imports another five hundred Chinese into Mexico from Hong Kong.)

So why on earth wouldn't there be tunnels?

In 2003 the man in the *casa de cambio* on First Street assured me in a gleeful murmur that of course there were tunnels *everywhere* in Calexico because if they started over *there* in Mexico then it stood to reason that they'd come up over *here.* He was Chinese. His building had three tunnel entrances, he said, but unfortunately he couldn't show them to me because they were closed. But he knew for a fact that the old building which now housed the Sam Ellis store had a tunnel. The kindly old proprietor of the latter establishment showed me photographs of the way the border used to be; he advised me to go to the Chamber of Commerce for an interpreter; as for the tunnels, every time I asked if I could just take a peek in his basement he didn't seem to hear me, but he did say: You're never gonna find any of those tunnels. Anyhow, it's all passé. It's all hearsay . . .

It's all *secret,* he might as well have said.

Hence the supernaturalization of the Chinese in the minds of others. Do you remember that old pioneer from Heber who had his mind made up about *pollos,* coyotes, and their *modus operandi*? It was all I could do not to burst out laughing when he'd assured me: *Now I hear the people smugglers are getting so brazen, now they got the Humvees with the guns mounted on them.* I remembered the shy boys in the dark, the hopeful and hopeless trying to make the snake or swimming amidst the suds and turds of the New River, and I thought: This old man was born here. He has lived next to Mexico and with Mexicans all his life. And still he believes this. Is it any wonder that far stranger things might be believed about people who *live together like cigarettes*?

In 1925, Dashiell Hammett's crime story "Dead Yellow Women" envisions Chinese tunnels in San Francisco, all the while keeping faithful to the expectations of his public:* *The passageway was solid and alive with stinking bodies. Hands and teeth began to take my clothes away from me . . . A high-pitched voice was screaming Chinese orders . . .* That was one passageway to alienness. In another, which the protagonist reached through a trapdoor, *the queen of something stood there! . . . A butterfly-shaped headdress decked with the loot of a dozen jewelry stores exaggerated her height.*

When Fu Manchu movies went out of fashion, new authentications of menacing alienness became available. Zulema Rashid, born in Calexico in 1945, remembers being scared every time she had to buy something in the Chinese store on Imperial Avenue *because the Chinese were Communists who tortured people.*

Of course they continued to be everywhere, wanted or not. The reliably unreliable *El Dragón en el Desierto* assures me that in 1919 Mexicali held more than eleven thousand Chinese as compared to only fifteen hundred Mexicans. An equally suspect book claims that by 1930, Mexicali's population was one-third Chinese.† (Thirty percent sounds high to me, said the third-generation immigrant Steve Leung. Below ten percent I would say.) Opening another album in the Archivo Histórico del Municipio de Mexicali, I see a photograph of a Chinese procession, the photograph greyer and a little vaguer than the long perished reality must have looked on the other side of the lens; I see a car with round headlights like eyes, a Chinese banner like some giantess's half-undone sash, a palanquin which bears two uniformed Chinese boys; and in this picture there's also something resembling both an altar and a sail, tall and huge; it looms over us in the street like another of Imperial's dreams.

A FLASHLIGHT ON BLACK WATER

Almost all my life I've lived in the Chinesca, said Carmen Jaham, whose mother was Mexican, whose father was Chinese, and whose last name other Chinese fam-

*The famous burglar, robber and addict Jack Black disappointed those expectations in his memoir, first published in 1926: "The hypos I spent the night with in the city prison had aroused my curiosity about Chinatown. I put in many nights prowling through the alleys watching these mysterious people gambling, smoking opium, and trafficking in their women slaves. There were rumors of strange, mysterious underground passages below the streets and under the buildings, but I never saw them and I have since come to doubt whether they ever existed."

†This is far, far higher than it ever got immediately across the line. In 2000, the population of Imperial County was 142,361, its proportions being as follows: forty-nine and a half percent white, four percent black, slightly under two percent American Indian, two percent Asian, a tenth of a percent Hawaiian, and thirty-nine percent "other." What were they, I wonder? Seventy-two percent of all whites were "persons of Hispanic origin." Perhaps the others might have been persons of Hispanic origin, too.

In 1910, Imperial County officially held 13,591 human beings, including 682 Indians, 217 Japanese and 32 Chinese. What were the other ninety-five percent, do you think? A hint: California was ninety-five percent white. (How many Hispanics were white, how many were "Mexican" we don't know.)

ilies usually choose to spell either *Hom* or *Tam*. (Her maiden name was Yee.) The shoe store in which she talked to me had belonged to her husband since 1932. He died very young; she was widowed at twenty-four and never remarried. She'd outlived one of her two children; the other one was in Los Angeles. In 2003 her empire consisted of four stores, some for shoes, others for clothes, and she quite naturally opined that *we now have more power, since there are more than three hundred restaurants and shoe stores in Mexicali.*—It's changed a lot, she said, and of course that's what she would say; that's what every old person says. But then she said something which revealed the extent of that vanished universe for me, revealed it in the same eerie, half-illusory sense as a flashlight-gleam upon black water in a Chinese tunnel shows something; what has been shown? It's opaque; its feculence hinders us; we know neither its depth nor its extent, but the yellow play of light on that black water brings us into the recognition of a previously unknown realm—about which we still know nothing. Señora Jaham's utterance was of this character. She said to me: *Back then, there was nothing but the Chinesca.*

NOTHING BUT WALLETS AND MEDICINES

By the time I began my search for the tunnels, Chinese made up a much smaller proportion of Mexicali's inhabitants than before. Steve Leung's figure was *maybe two percent or less in 1950, and now maybe one percent.*—The new Mexican owner of Restaurant Nineteen proposed that *between halfbreeds and fullbreeds there's fifty thousand in Mexicali,* thus translated by José López from Jalisco, who went on to say: But that's ridiculous; there's more than that!

In any event, it wasn't hard to find them; it was only difficult to get them to say anything.

It was dusk when I closed the door of my hotel room in Calexico and walked across the line, the white taxis and goldfish-gleaming pickup trucks sighing across the wide grey streets beneath the full moon, while in the lefthandmost of four archways a man leaned thoughtfully within the glass window of his *casa de cambio,* whose revolving light seemed policecarlike and whose other light, the electric-blue one, was also vaguely official; beyond him, where the street bent away from the Hotel Imperial, lay the Chinesca with its alleys, hotels, restaurants, its roofed *callejones* with their barbershops and boutiques offering cheap medicines and wallets for sale: an old place, grimy and inconspicuous, the Chinese themselves scarcely noticeable on its streets . . .

"A *RAW* SMELL"

They came out of the ground like ants. So why shouldn't there be tunnels?—They exist, asserted Beatriz Limón, who was a reporter for *La Crónica.* She, however, had never seen one. One of her colleagues had entered a tunnel with Chinese guides, but the smell had been too terrible for her—a *raw* smell, said Beatriz with distaste, a smell like a sewage—and Lupe, who'd been my interpreter for this interview, later told me that the way he imagined that it had gone down was that the Chinese took the woman's money and then said: All right, bitch! You wanna see a tunnel? We'll show you a tunnel!—and took her to some disgusting place in order to cheat her, scare her away, and amuse themselves; Lupe supposed that those Chinese were still laughing.

Oscar Sánchez from the Archivo Histórico looked up at me from behind his desk and said: They are there. But I can tell you nothing concrete. Originally they were there for shelter from the heat, but then they started to install the casinos. Oh, but it is difficult. These people are very closed!

Men said that there once had been tunnels beneath the dance hall Thirteen Negro, which was whitewashed over its ancientness and cracked through its whitewash, doing business on and on at the center of the brick-fringed archways of arcades, lord of not quite closed sidewalk gratings, with blackness beneath; why wouldn't there be tunnels under the Thirteen Negro? (José López: *Why not believe it?*) And if they were there, why wouldn't they still be there? But the waiter denied it. What did his denial mean? I asked him how often he got Chinese customers and he said every night. I asked him if he could introduce me to a Chinese regular; maybe I could buy the man a drink and . . . But the waiter said he didn't want any trouble.

They live together like cigarettes. And so I can't pretend that I was shocked when old Mr. Wong, who'd lived in Calexico for decades and read a Chinese-language newspaper, didn't know anybody who could help me; his own explanation was that *the Chinese always go back to Mexicali at night.*

Once upon a time, in 2002 I think it was, I hired a tour guide named Carlos. He had a very nice car and liked money. We went to a certain restaurant in the Chinesca where Señor Armando, friend of the Chinese owner, sat tranquilly in the cool dimness. He assured me that he had been gambling in a Chinese tunnel on several occasions. I bought him a beer and wondered aloud whether I could make it worth his while to bring me there, and he was happy and sure that he could. Then I paid Carlos a full day's rate for the half day's work and waited. After a month he dolefully reported that Armando was afraid; Armando never wanted to see me again. Maybe Armando never knew anything about Chinese tunnels at all. Or maybe *these people are very closed.*

THE TALE OF THE AIR DUCTS

My next tactic was to bang on Mexicali's nearest prominently ideogrammed metal gate, and that is how, ushered down a tree-shaded walkway and into a courtyard, Lupe Vásquez and I had the inestimable pleasure of meeting Professor Eduardo Auyón Gerardo of the Chinese Association "Chung Shan."

This *world-renowned painter, known especially for his paintings of horses and nude women,* had a Chinese mother and a Mexican father. In 1960, when he was thirteen years old, his father brought him to Mexicali to join his grandmother.

Mr. Auyón was not especially pleased to see me. He told me that I really should have made an appointment. In fact I'd banged on the gate two days ago, and made an appointment through his nephew. This did not mollify the *world-renowned painter,* who sat unsmiling amidst his sumi paintings and brass lions. Well, to business: First he tried to sell me a gold-plated commemorative medallion which he had designed. It was pretty, but expensive. Then he offered me a dusty copy of *El Dragón en el Desierto: Los Pioneros Chinos en Mexicali* for the special price of thirty dollars. On a future occasion he would sell another copy to my new interpreter Terrie for twenty. (I quote from her summary: *The last twenty to twenty-five years in the book only mention cultural activities, visits from dignitaries and beauty queens, and some of the exploits of Mr. Auyón.*) Comprehending that if I didn't buy something from him my interview would be terminated, I paid for *El Dragón en el Desierto,* after which he brightened slightly and began to relate snippets of Chinese-Mexican history. Wide-eyed with worshipful amazement, I scribbled down everything which Lupe could be bothered to translate. As the younger member of my mother-and-daughter team of Chinese interpreters would later report: *Further cooperation in the future: likely (but must make an appointment first). I also do not know if this guy is telling the absolute truth. He seemed a bit tricky to me, and I got a very strange vibe from him, as did my mother . . .*

To Mr. Auyón, 1919 was the magic date when the twenty-eight-odd Chinese organizations (other people sometimes told me twenty-six) amalgamated into the Asociación China de Mexicali. A countryman named Wong Gok Kia donated two lots at Juárez and Altamirano to make it happen. It was this event which his gold-plated commemorative medallion immortalized, he explained, frowningly offering me one more chance to buy. His own Chung Shan organization was one of the original twenty-eight; it was a district organization named after *a hero in China who founded a dynasty.*

I asked him if I could please meet a Chinese family.

It's very difficult, he explained, because my countrymen are not very communicative. But *El Dragón en el Desierto* does have ten chapters. You can read all about Chinese in there.

That was perfect, of course. My research was now at an end. We agreed that if and only if I read his book thoroughly and maybe memorized it, then came back in a month, it was possible that he might have found a Chinese family to tell me something innocuous.

That point having been settled, I asked him about the Chinese tunnels.

They don't exist, the world-renowned painter of horses assured me. The people couldn't survive in them if they did. They could not sleep. It would be too hot down there.

He gave me a brief tour of his martial arts school, where a dragon lay on the floor in pieces. I would have rather seen some of his world-renowned paintings of nude women. The paintings of horses weren't bad. My thirty dollars' worth of him seemed to have been used up. On a per-minute basis, he was somewhat more expensive than the prostitutes of the Hotel Nuevo Pacífico; he was certainly less good-natured.

Just in case there were tunnels after all, Mr. Auyón, where do you think they might be?

That heat, the body cannot resist it, he replied. In the night time one has to sleep. One has to live down there; that's why the snakes live underground; but in the summer it's too hot.

So there are no tunnels?

Every locality has tunnels like a house has a cellar. There are businesses which have two or three branches. They have cellars and connections. On Juárez at Reforma, one man has seven businesses. Underneath, it looks like another city.

Could I see one of those cellars?

He didn't think that that was possible. He did want most anxiously and insistently to make sure that I would give him credit in my book, which I hereby do. I feel a little sorry for Mr. Auyón.

Then, looking into my face, and this was the one moment when I felt that he was actually being genuine with me, he said: Do you want to know the history of Mexicali? *Every ten acres, one Chinese died.*

I'm sorry, I said.

He looked at his watch. The world-renowned medallionist had an important appointment.

I asked him if it was really, really true that there were no tunnels, and he said that it was. I asked him if he could show me one of the cellars that he'd mentioned. He took me into the Hotel Chinesca next door and past the fancy lobby into the open-air courtyard giving onto tiny doublebedded rooms; and from a chambermaid he got the key to the cellar, which smelled like a cellar; there he pointed to a "communication" passage in the corner of the wall; it was small and square and had a screen over it; it was, he said, an air duct. Inside it I could see light and stoneworked walls. A small child could have hidden there. Triumphantly, Mr. Auyón said: This is what they call a tunnel. The tunnels don't exist.

What about the tunnel you mentioned on Juárez at Reforma?

The tunnels don't exist.

MY INTERPRETER READS BETWEEN THE LINES

As for Lupe, he thought that Mr. Auyón was a liar, a crook, a goddamned gook. Lupe's own opinion* ran as follows: The Chinese used those tunnels to transport illegal immigrants and heroin to the United States. He might have been right. Why not? Here's a telegram from Northside's guardians, dateline 1915:

COLLECTOR CUSTOMS
TIAJUANA [*sic*] CALIF.

ALEXANDER REPORTS ATTEMPT WILL BE MADE TONIGHT TO PICK UP FOUR CHINESE NEAR COYOTE WELLS AND TAKE THEM TO SAN DIEGO IN AUTOMOBILE WEBB AND CLARKE LEAVING NOW IN AUTOMOBILE TO TRY TO INTERCEPT THEM

MACUMBER

Did that say anything about tunnels? Never mind. Now back to Lupe's theories: And another strange thing I've seen, Bill: There's a lot of Chinese restaurants in Mexicali, but I have never seen an old Chinese! I mean, Chinese live to be a hundred! I think they hide 'em and don't want the Mexicans to make fun of 'em or laugh at 'em. In the streets you never see old Chinese. I've heard they have another city down there in the tunnels, for the old people.

"IF I KNEW, I WOULD INVITE YOU!"

Mr. Auyón's niece was standing in the courtyard as we departed the world-renowned author of *El Dragón en el Desierto*. She was very innocent and beautiful. Her name was Jasmine Brambilla Auyón. I requested an appointment. The next day, Lupe and I were in an old taxi which groaned down into the Río Nuevo gorge and across the freeway which pressed down the stinking waters, then up into the *colonias,* turning south now past broken walls, concrete houses, a fire station, a tiny

*Interview in Calexico, 2002.

truck with a red shrimp painted on the back; next came the church, at which point the young driver crossed himself; after the Internet Club and **SUPER CARNES**, we entered a zone of fancier houses behind white walls; this was Colonia Vía Fontana. The rows of white-limed palm trees reminded me of what the center of Mexicali used to look like in the 1920s.

I rang the bell. Like the fashionable young lady that she was, Jasmine proved to be almost on time.

The interview was conducted in the immaculate living room, with Coca-Colas brought us on a tray, and the mother listening behind the railing, sometimes calling out the right answers. Everything was white-tiled, and the phone continually rang for the mother, who wore heavy eyeliner and a leopard-skin-patterned chemise which didn't quite reach down to her pretty belly button.

Jasmine was third-generation part-Chinese, she said. Her great-great-grandmother could speak a few words of Chinese. Smiling, she sat perfectly still. She'd once been chosen as Queen of the Chinese Association. Everything about her expressed the same elegance as the gilded fan upon the mantelpiece.

I asked her what was unique about Mexicali and she replied: The people here in Mexicali are more simple, more kind, more loving.

Do Mexicanos and Chinos have good relations here?

My friends are Mexican and my relatives are Chinese.

Lupe gazed uncomfortably down at his shabby boots on the white-tiled floor. He sat beside me, worried, so he later told me, that he might be getting the sofa dirty.

Jasmine thought that there might be a tunnel under the Nuevo Mandarin restaurant.—I don't know, she remarked, but I have heard rumors also.

The mother was silent. I could see her in the gilt-edged mirror which hung over the fireplace—a fireplace in Mexicali! Why not air-conditioning in the Arctic? I almost felt that I was back in Northside.

What else have you heard about the tunnels, Jasmine?

Since the Chinese came here first, they made the tunnels to protect themselves. I've also heard about casino tunnels, but I don't know. If I knew, I would invite you! she cried out with a sweet smile in which I believed.

I proposed to take her out for lunch at one of the oldest Chinese restaurants in *centro,* paying her for her time; perhaps she could sweet-talk the owner into letting us see the underworld. The girl excitedly asked her mother for permission, which was granted. They both thought that the restaurant Jing Tung near the Hotel Cecil might be a good candidate. (I remember a photograph of the Hotel Cecil from the Archivo Histórico; the caption said 1948. It dominated all businesses on its left and right, thanks to its third storey; it was not only the Hotel Cecil, it was the Edificio Fernando J. Chee; its neighbors were the Cantina Los Angeles Bar and the restaurant Mexicali on the right, the Tienda Mexico and the Casa something-or-other-blurry on the left; one's gaze went right to the Cecil.) Then the girl and her mother went into the other room to confer some more, while Lupe stared at his boots and I inspected the white-necked, brass-winged swan which was built into the white sofa. The arrangement was confirmed. The girl was to meet us tomorrow at twelve-thirty. We stood up to thank her.

It would be very beautiful if we could find out that the tunnels are still there, the mother remarked. I don't think that they are there. We in the third generation have always had that doubt, and that curiosity.

She was a widow who had taken on her husband's used car business. Both of her grandfathers had been Chinese.—Chinese blood is strong, she said to us. It tends to disappear, but sometimes my kids come out looking Chinese.* I have a brother whose daughter is a Chinese original.

Do you feel Chinese when Mexicans look at you?

When people look at me, they know that I'm a mestiza. People are very observant. They know that we are Auyóns and that we have lived in the United States, in Los Angeles, in San Diego! she said proudly. My father, all his life he worked for the government here and also for the FBI. My Dad was dealing cars, so I learned from him. My grandfather was treated badly by the Communist government, so we came here. His house was confiscated. They made it a military base. Now it's a museum. It's European style.

Can you speak Chinese?

I can speak words that my parents taught me: the colors, the numbers, minimum.

Do you feel at home here?

Mexicali is my home forever. It's very tranquil here, so you can do anything.

Lupe gazed at her in admiration.† Later that night he kept saying: A rich lady like that, to take us into her house and be so nice! And such a beautiful lady . . .

We said goodbye. The Chinese girl offered her cheek to be kissed.

At twelve-fifteen the next day we arrived at the Chinese restaurant. Then we waited and waited. Lupe grew sullen. I sent him to the telephone. When he came back, he was more bitter than ever, and he said: The señora says her daughter has no time to meet with us today. The señora suggests that if we want more information there's a guy who knows everything and he's our friend, in other words that goddamned Auyón. They're all a bunch of goddamned gooks.

*It should be remembered that Lupe was interpreting, and that her words might have actually been more mellifluous than this.

†Lupe Vásquez, 2002: "A lot of Chinese have Mexican concubines. My compadre is one-half Chinese and one-half Mexican."

YOLANDA SÁNCHEZ OGÁS

So it went. I could tell you about my interview with the taxi driver who knew for a fact that a tunnel had once led from the Chinesca right across the border, but they closed it; I shouldn't detain you with the tale of Leonardo, the "tour guide" from Tijuana who was down on his luck, so he followed me from the street at midnight, trying to interest me in young girls. Did I want fifteen-year-olds? But I didn't, not just then. Well, so, he could get me twelve-year-olds. He could deliver 'em right to me if I went to the Hotel México. He had a hatchet-shaped, smooth little face and he was little and vicious. Since he could do anything (he'd already told me the story of how he'd obtained excellent false papers for *pollos* in TJ), I told him to take me into the Chinese tunnels, about which he'd never heard. So he did research. It took him a day. He found me an underground casino which would be possible to visit before opening time, but I had to promise not to talk to anyone and he couldn't guarantee that I could take photographs. When he saw that I really wanted to take photographs he said that he could work it out. Leonardo was the man, all right. Why shouldn't it be true? There'd been gaming-houses in Mexicali since 1909. He described so well how it would be that I could almost see it. Soon a note was waiting for me at the Hotel Chinesca: **Bill Hey it's me Leo the guy you met yesterday I have your ticket for to day at 7.30 p.m. I will be back at 7.00 p.m. Your friend, Leonardo**. The tour would cost me fifty dollars, and I had to pay in advance. I paid; oh, yes, I did; I have never been cheated out of a dollar in my life. Leonardo went first to give the password; he'd be back in two minutes. At least Terrie the Mormon girl got a thrill out of it as we stood in the pitch dark alley on the edge of the Río Nuevo; the moon resembled an orange darkly pitted by cyanide fumigation injury, and we waited and waited for admission to that splendid underground world which Leonardo had promised us.

What else should I relate? I definitely ought to assure you that zealous José López from Jalisco continued to troll the streets for me; his latest progress report (twenty dollars cash) went like this:

Finally I see this half-breed; I mean his color was not so yellow; and he was just standing there same as I, so I said to him, excuse me, I don't mean to offend you, but you don't look a hundred percent Chinese, and he told me he was third-generation Chinese. So I said, hey, you know what? I read about some opium dens and some tunnels have been busted by police, and was it true? He said, yeah, it was true; there were special places where you went and smoked opium. There were several here in the Chinesca, he said, from his grandfather. But it was mainly Chinese who went there. It was the time of Prohibition. Some Mexicans went to the opium den, but Mexicans were more into drinking.

There was a fee, he said, but I don't think it was that much and it was an old tradition. And I said to him, I said. . .

To my rescue now came Professor Yolanda Sánchez Ogás, lifelong resident of Mexicali (born in 1940), historian, anthropologist, and author of *Bajo el Sol de Mexicali* and *A La Orilla del Río Colorado: Los Cucapá,* both of which she sold me out of the closet of her house. Yolanda is my Mexican wife, and I adore her; I am faithful and loyal to her, thereby rendering amends for my gringo blood; in other words, I pay for dinner. She in turn is endlessly patient with me, considering me a somewhat ill-mannered but by no means hopeless young puppy. The first time I asked about Chinese tunnels, she said that she didn't know anything about them but would find out. The next time I saw her she calmly said: I went into the tunnels. That entire area under La Chinesca has a subterranean level. As for the casino, I know there *was* one, but right now I don't think so. But under the volleyball court many Chinos live.

Have you seen them living there?

No, but I have heard. And someone told me that under the Restaurante ———* there is a tunnel where they get together. I met an old man who lived all his life under Restaurante Ocho.

Will you take me into the tunnels?

Why not?

When do you have time?

Tomorrow.

Yolanda, you are the little heart of my little heart!

I will tell you that tomorrow where we're going it's very ugly and it smells very bad.

WHERE THEY TAKE OUT THE TRASH

Next morning in Callejón Chinesca the proprietors of the watch stores and clothing stores were already rolling up their gratings. I had with me my brave, discreet and intelligent interpreter, Terrie, who has already been introduced to you and who spoke excellent Spanish thanks to her missionary year in Spain. She was better liked by Yolanda than poor Lupe had been, and, moreover, less likely to yell out: *Goddamned gook!* as we walked down Reforma Street; that was where we were going. It was right around here that the Restaurant Jing Tung was supposed to be; that was the one that Mr. Auyón's niece and her mother had thought so promising.

*Name removed on request.

Nobody in the street had ever heard of it. But that didn't mean it wasn't there. As the other José López would have said, why not believe in it?

Yolanda led us to the Hotel Cecil, which I'm told was the labor of love of a Chinese named Cecil Chin. We went upstairs. Yolanda said that there had once been a tunnel with bars, casinos and a restaurant.

This is all new, said the manager, gesturing around him. When they constructed this hotel in 1947, the tunnel was already there. There used to be an entrance on the first floor.

Can we go into the tunnel? I asked.

The manager wearily spread his hands.—It's closed, he said. He didn't care to nourish any myths.

Across the street from the Cecil, in another roofed passageway called Pasajes Prendes, there was an ancient barber shop whose owner's white hair resembled his ribbed and whitewashed concrete ceiling, and he said: No, you walked in from the street and the restaurant was on the left by the bar and it had really big chairs and a piano, and there was a man who played the piano. They took the piano away many years ago. In the tunnel there was a store and right here in front there was a butcher shop aboveground. The hotel was finished in April of '47 and there was nothing here before, he said, beaming through his round glasses. Oh, he was happy, smiling, talking about the past.

So what are in the tunnels now? I asked.

Pure trash.

His single customer, who was tub-shaped, chimed in: And rats!

Yolanda said nothing. I knew that she hated rats.

I went down there, said the customer, and it's all trash. Rats, cockroaches, because of the humidity . . .

Yolanda said: But the other day we went down and there weren't any rats.

A woman over here had a store, said the barber. There is still an entrance over there and it's full of water. There was a cantina below. Cecil Chin owned the cantina. The whole building, there's tunnels all over the place. Anyone could go in. It was public property.

Where were the casinos below?

No, there were never any casinos.

I thought there was a casino under the Callejo.

There could have been, said the barber happily. There was a barber shop, a shoe store, a bowling alley, pool tables . . .

I think there are some places where people get together to play cards, said Yolanda.

The tubby man, who was a foreman, shrugged and said: There are tunnels all through here, and also on Juárez and Reforma. It's like a labyrinth.

As the fan slowly rotated along the edge of the mirror, they talked happily about the old days of *the big problem when they were all killing each other.* It sounds as if they missed the excitement of the Tong wars.

Around '46 a lot of this was burned, said the barber.—Slowly he reached up to turn on the auxilliary ceiling fan.—The first of these buildings caught on fire, in '45 and '46, a lot of Chinese died. The second fire, nobody was inside. That was in '91. That second fire was so big that they came from Calexico and El Centro to put it out. And by the way, it seems to me that there used to be a tunnel under the Hotel Imperial. There used to be a cantina . . .

There still is, but not underneath, said the fat man.

Were there ever any opium dens? I asked.

The barber said: I worked in the Hotel Cecil for six years. I started in '49 as a waiter. Then I became a manager of the laundry department. When I was up there washing clothes, I saw the Chinese people smoking opium. There was a basketball court—

Oh, the same, said Yolanda.

And under there were six or seven Chinese men with a big pipe, passing it around. The pipe was as long as my arm!

Another old man had come in to get his hair cut, and he said: Yeah, I was there then, too. They were up all night smoking and gambling. They were playing *baraja* for a lot of money. That happened in the tunnels. I am seventy-six and I was born here.

Were there prostitutes in the tunnels?

No, that was above.

Did anyone live in the tunnels?

Over in this part, in the Chinesca, sure.

Can we see the place where the water is? I asked.

A woman named Inocencia had the key. I never had the key.

Who would have it now?

It's probably closed. It's very dirty. The smell would make you sick.

That sounds perfect, I said. I think I'd really like to go there.

Why?

It would be interesting. As far as how it might smell, I took a boat ride down the Río Nuevo, so I don't think I'd mind.

The Río Nuevo? That's pretty much how it smells.

We thanked the barber and wished him good business. As he was saying good-bye to us, he remarked: In all the *callejones* you see a lot of vents.

For the tunnels?

Yes.

He also said, very sadly: There really aren't any businesses here anymore. It's all boutiques. All the Americans come here to buy medicines.

And I knew that he himself, like me, would have loved to go back in time, even just for a day, to wander in the tunnels when they were crammed with life, glamour, commerce and vice.

As we were walking down the next alley I said to Yolanda: If I were the owner of one of these properties, I would fix up my tunnels, make them exotic, and charge the gringos a lot of money to come down inside them and drink.

But people like to walk in the streets with music! replied Yolanda. Here in the *callejones,* it's where they take out the trash.

MY FIRST TUNNEL

Near the Hotel Capri there was a certain clothing business owned by an elderly Mexican who knew Yolanda quite well since, after all, he had already taken her into his Chinese tunnel, not that the Chinese tunnels existed, and behind the counter, next to the water closet, there was a metal door which the man unlocked, inviting us into a concrete room where clothes hung on a line. The man lifted up a trapdoor, and I wish I could tell you how thrilled I felt. I saw stairs. Yolanda had her flashlight, and Terrie was carrying the other flashlight, which we had bought an hour earlier for just this occasion. Smiling, the man stood aside, and there were the stairs.

Yolanda wanted me to go first, because as I said she was afraid of rats, so I did, and she came after me into that sweltering darkness, gamely half-smiling with her pale, sweat-drenched shirt unbuttoned almost to the breast and her head high and sweat shining on her cheekbones and sparkling in her short grey hair and her kind, proud eyes alertly seeking just as the straight white beam of her flashlight did, cutting through the darkness like a knife. Terrie's flashlight was very steady. Where were we? The humidity was almost incredible. Dirt and darkness, flaring pillars comprised my immediate impression. Lumber-heaps leaped up as pale as bone-piles under those twin beams of battery-powered light. I saw no rats. How stifling it was! Graffiti'd beams (a sample of their announcements being EL MEMO 13 Sinaloa 19/01/92) ran overhead, higher than I would have expected but still in arm's reach; and wire hangers with flaring underparts hung like the skeletal outlines of headless women. I glimpsed the folding X-frames of something, a table, and a metal wheel of protruding spokes. Beneath the heavy rectangular archways, the tunnel went on and on. Quite evidently it was much vaster than the store above it, even allowing for the fact that everything is always larger in darkness. Somewhere ahead of us, skeletal perspective-lines approached one another palely within the ceiling-darkness; the place where they lost themselves seemed to be a hundred feet away and was probably ten. I thought I could see a squarish passage. The floor was littered with trash, and broken chairs and empty cardboard boxes. Here gaped an open safe. I picked my way as carefully as I could; for all I knew, ahead of me there might be an uncovered well that would lead straight to death in cheesy black currents of the Río Nuevo, which, thank God, I couldn't smell at the moment. Yolanda and Terrie were out of sight; they were in other worlds; I could see only one or the other of their flashlight beams. I felt almost alone. Chamber after chamber went on, connected by squarish archways. How many rooms were there, actually? I can't say now, but probably no more than half a dozen. A palish blotch on the black wall gazed at me; my mind was beginning its usual game of dreaming up faces. Drumming and music came down to me from somewhere above. The old Mexican who owned the place had said that he thought there had been a casino down here, and when I heard that music I could almost imagine it.

It might well be that the quality of the tunnels which haunted so many of us was quite simply their *goneness*. When I imagine them, my ignorance allows them to be what they will. Before we knew how hot the surface of Venus is, we used to be able to write beautiful science-fiction stories of swamps and greenskinned Venusians. I could almost see myself descending the stairs into this place in the years when the electric lights still worked. What if it hadn't been a casino after all? I refused to believe that. Sometime between the first and second fires it might have been perfect down here. (That so-called Great Fire which the sisters Hernández had told me of, the one which in their telling strangely resembled the Biblical tale of the Deluge, that must have been the second fire, because the tunnels were almost uninhabited by the time of the third fire, and before the first the Chinesca was still very, very small.) Having smoked opium in Thailand, I could imagine that one of these chambers might have had mats on the floor where I could have lain, watching the opium smoke rise sweetly from my pipe between inhalations. And from Thailand I also remembered Chinese men in black trousers, shiny black shoes and white dress shirts; at an open-to-the-street restaurant in Chinatown, with stainless steel tables and white tile walls, we were all drinking delicious sweet chrysanthemum juice the color of urine, and the handsomest man of all leaned on his elbow and gazed dreamily over his crossed fingers. Was this how the Chinese would have dressed when they went underground to drink, gamble and womanize in Mexicali? Or would they have possessed nothing but the rough cotton clothes of the braceros? (Since Mariano Ma had been seen at the horseraces with the Governor of Baja California, very likely he at least possessed shiny black shoes.) There might have been a piano player here as there had been at Cecil Chin's, and when he paused to take a drink of Mexicali Beer, I would have heard all around me the lovely bone-clicks of mah-jongg. One hot summer day in the Chinese city of Nan Ning I wandered through a park of lotus leaves and exotic flowers to a pagoda where ancient women sat, drowsily, happily playing mah-jongg amidst the scent of flowers, and that excellent sound of clicking tiles enchanted me; I was far from home, but that long slow summer afternoon with the mah-jongg sounds brought me back to my own continent, and specifically to Mexicali, whose summer tranquillity never ends. (How I love Mexicali! Everyone tells every story slightly differently; every secret is delightfully inconsequential. Ultimately, what's the difference whether this tunnel was a casino or not?)

I remember a lady who smiled when she was dancing naked, a sweet smile of black eyes and glowing white teeth; she seemed so hopeful, so enthusiastic, so "sincere," if that word makes any sense between two strangers, and she was smiling right at me! She held my hand; that's right, she held my hand all the way to the hotel; I kissed her plump red lips and sucked on them as much as I wanted; she kissed me back. *Caliente!* the men in the street said approvingly. She rode me as a bull rides a cow; delicious hot drops of sweat flew off her face, breasts and shoulders, landing on my mouth; and although she faked nearly every moan, she did it with such enthusiasm, I say again, with such *sincerity;* and when it was my turn to be on top, she slapped my buttocks so happily with every thrust, that I felt her to be inexhaustibly perfect. Afterwards we walked hand in hand back to the dance hall, and all the men applauded.* She was Mexican, not Chinese, and the place where she'd rented me her illusion of love lay several blocks beyond the edge of the Chinesca; all the same, it was she whom I now thought of in that tunnel whose revelry had turned to lumber and broken chairs; those clickclacking mah-jongg tiles in Nan Ning, the laughter and preposterously exaggerated moans of that prostitute, the sensations of opium intoxication in Thailand, these were the buried treasures which my flashlight beam sought in the Chinese tunnels of Mexicali, my memories, my happy dissipations, let's say my youth. No wonder I'd wanted to

*Two years later, this same lovely, chubby brunette was still working at the Olé-Olé; she was bending over a table, whispering into the ear of a man whose hand reclined so joyously on her breast. She recognized me at once. Her first look was wary; what if I was jealous? When she saw that I wasn't, never had been and never would be, all of which I am positive that she did see—moreover, I was with another woman—she smilingly returned to her business, which must have been unsuccessful, since when the woman and I left, my fine brunette was still on the scene. I waved to her then, and she to me, each of us gazing at the other in a happy sad moment of renewed friendship: she liked me, and I her. I perhaps was still more happy than she, happy to know that she was still alive and here; she'd given me so much pleasure, and I'd paid her so well; but even if that was the only reason she liked me, and perhaps it was not, wouldn't that have been good enough? When I remember our first encounter, I feel gratitude. When I think about the second, my heart goes out to her; why not say I feel love? Her name was and is Michel.

believe Leonardo the "tour guide"! Waiting for nothing in the hot thick night, with the ducklike quacking of a radio coming from one of the tin walls of that alley, that rather evil sand-paved alley overlooking Condominios Montealbán, I was already a citizen of this darkness; I was a spider luxuriously centered in the silk web of my own fantasies.

Don't we all do it? Can't you see the smile on that barber's face as he descends into his past? *The Chinesca was the center of Mexicali; there was nothing else,* said Carmen Jaham.

THE TUNNEL LETTERS

Next came the Restaurante Victoria, a tranquil paradise of coolness and reliably bland food (the Dong Cheng was better) where the waitresses were the only ones who hurried; the customers, who were mostly Mexican, lived out the hours with their sombreros or baseball caps on, lingering over their rice; here I had tried and failed on several prior occasions to find out if there might be any tunnels in the neighborhood; come to think of it, the all-enduring José López from Jalisco had been twice honorably expelled from the Victoria in the cause of duty, for which suffering he charged me five dollars, plus two dollars for two sodas. I don't have the receipt. But it was just as my father always said, *It's not what you know; it's who you know,* and I knew Yolanda, who happened to be here, and who knew Miguel, the Chinese owner, a slender youngish man with jet-black hair who'd come here from Canton two decades since. He led us through the restaurant—white ceiling, white incandescent lights, white tables, at one of which a fat old lady and a young girl, both Chinese, sat slowly eating while the television uttered music which was sad and dramatic and patriotically Mexican; I had once spent a very happy day at that very table, interviewing an old Communist journalist about Mexicali in 1950; now the white walls gave way to pinkish bathroomlike tiles as we passed beneath the rapidly whirling white fans and admired from afar the Chinese-captioned painting of the red sun floating on a turquoise sea—and through the swinging doors he led us, straight into the kitchen, where the Mexican cook and the Chinese dishwasher goggled at us; turning right, we came into a long narrow courtyard and entered a detached two-storey building with what appeared to be an ancestral shrine just within the entrance. To the right, next to a shopping cart full of stale burned bread and a hand mill to grind the bread to flour for gravy, wide stairs descended.

This tunnel was less dark, uncluttered, and more self-contained. Indeed, it disappointed me at first; it appeared to be little more than a concrete cellar. Then I noticed that a five-socketed chandelier crouched on the ceiling like a potbellied spider, four of its sockets encased in ornate floral doughnuts, the fifth a bare metal bell. The ceiling itself was comprised of fancy-edged blocks like parquet flooring. But some blocks were stained or charred and some were moldy and some were entirely missing, leaving rectangles of darkness peering down from behind the rafters. It was a wide chamber which could have held many people, especially if they'd lived together like cigarettes. What had they done here? Had they gambled or simply banqueted? Had this place been an opium den? Thanks to F. E. Johnson, Special Agent, U.S. Customs, I knew what to look for (dateline Los Angeles, 1915): *Round one-pound tins coated with crimson lacquer, with gilt letters on red side label bearing the following Chinese and Japanese inscriptions: "Number one smoking opium . . . The Monopoly Bureau, Government of Formosa. Anyone found imitating this mark or label will be imprisoned. The smoker of this opium must have a license to smoke opium."*

And what did I find? A tub held old Chinese porcelain bowls with floral designs. Then there were several dark and empty side-chambers.

The Victoria was in Miguel's estimation sixty years old, maybe eighty. (Upstairs, according to the Victoria's posted autobiography, one was informed that it had been **FUNDADO EN** . . . but here the red letters ended; the refrigerator case prevented me from learning when it had been founded.) Since we were in the heart of the Chinesca, this tunnel would possibly already have been here, but so what and how could I possibly speculate anyhow? On my second visit to this tunnel I saw a few more traces of fire and I also found what might or might not have been a trapdoor in the concrete floor of the first chamber; it would not budge. In the dark room beneath the beds was a stack of bedframes.—*Muchas prostitutas!* opined José López from Jalisco.

At the extreme end of the farthest room, another passageway had been bricked up. I asked Miguel how much it would cost me to have that obstruction broken down and then sealed up again when I had seen whatever there was to see. Smiling, he replied that there was no need for that; all I had to do was ask the pastor of the Sinai Christian Center down the street to let me into *his* tunnel. This I later did, with the ever helpful José López from Jalisco. To José, who slept every night in places whose decrepitude resembled that of the tunnels, it was going to be a busman's holiday. But as a woman once told me when I requested her to perform certain sexual acts, we can't always get what we want. I helped the pastor, whose whitewashed church (denomination: Pentecostal) had held these premises for only three years, to drag the wooden cover aside—I can't really name it a trapdoor because it wasn't attached to anything—and there lay a grubby plank running end to end across a square shaft down which went other grubby planks called stairs, these being filthy with dust, dirt, ashes, scraps of newspaper, rags, used plastic utensils and other garbage; the farther down I looked, the more garbage there was. It wasn't sickening, merely dirty. Down I went; down went José. Yolanda and Beatriz Limón, that *Crónica* reporter, were both with me that day; they peered into the hole and refrained from descending. I can't say they missed much. To be sure, there were also many doors, each one of them sealed; once upon a time this so-called cellar must have led to many other branches of the underworld. The tunnel ran at right angles to the Victoria's. In the glory days its primary axes must have gone westward under all the businesses in Avenida Juárez, maybe even to Condominios Montealbán, although I was now quite sure that if there were in fact any tunnels in or around Condominios Montealbán, I was never going to see them. Another toilet without a tank, more chairs; that was what I found; this was like the first tunnel but smaller. The pastor, who stood above with the two ladies, would have liked to turn these subterranean quarters into a place of study or recreation but hadn't the money; his rent was far too high, he complained; his landlord was the Chinese Association. And here was the other side of the Victoria's brick wall.

José had already gone back up into the light. I remember gazing up through the rectangular floor-hole at the boy in the church; he might have been the pastor's son; nobody ever introduced him; he was crouching down up there in the sky with his hand on his knee, gripping the plank which ran across the hole; he was foreshortened and far away, framed by pale ceiling-blocks which were mildewed and also charred by this or that great fire.

Meanwhile, on that earlier June day in that tunnel under the Victoria, I had seen that brick wall and turned back to the middle chamber where beside another tall narrow doorway which led into more blind-walled darkness, we saw a desk, and approached it without any great expectations since it was not so many steps away from the entrance to this place; all we had to do was turn around and we could see the supernaturally bright daylight of Mexicali burning down into the stairwell. I remember that a spiderweb as wide as a hammock hung on the wall; I remember how dismally humid it was in that place; I could almost believe Mr. Auyón, who'd claimed that of course the Chinese never lived underground because that would have been too uncomfortable. In other words, I couldn't help but assume this desk to be a counterpart of the first tunnel's safe, more specifically speaking the first tunnel's Sentry model 1230, which sat upon the skeleton of a table which might once have had a glass top, lording it over broken beams and pipe-lengths. Dust and filth speckled the top of the safe; behind rose a partly charred concrete wall. The door gaped open. Inside was nothing but dirt.

But as it turned out, under the Restaurante Victoria, in that rolltop desk whose writing surface was wood slats now beginning to warp away from one another just enough to let the darkness in between them, lay treasures far more valuable to me than any Chinese gold: a hoard of letters, some of them rat-gnawed, all of them smelly, moldy and spiderwebbed; when Yolanda Ogás saw them she caught her breath, standing rigid with excitement against the wall whose pale sea-waves of stains were as fanciful as the serpent-plumes of painted Chinese dragons; they warped and curved, white-edged and sometimes dark-patched upon that wall where Yolanda stood rigid and rapt, watching Miguel bend over the desk, fingering the old letters which had been crammed into blackened drawers for who knows how long. The darkness was hot, wet and slightly rotten. For a long time the Chinese bent over a book of blank forms;* then he rose and turned away indifferently.

Yolanda was the one to ask whether any of the tunnel letters could be borrowed. Miguel, who was a nice man, assented at once. One of my Chinese translators would later remark that he *didn't seem to care in the least about* the tunnels *or what [they] might have been used for in the past.* When I chatted with him upstairs, in the richly glowing shade of the Restaurante Victoria itself, looking out through the lingerie-translucent curtains and the double glass doors with the red ideograms on them, the white rectangles of the streetwalls, and dried-blood-colored gratings of other Chinese businesses, the world one-third occluded by angle-parked cars and trucks, I found that he didn't want to talk, because he'd only been here for twenty years, which, so he reminded me, *wasn't long enough to voice an opinion.* He referred us to the Chinese Association. There were actually either twenty-six or twenty-eight of those, but he meant the Chinese Association whose head was a certain Mr. Auyón.

I photocopied Yolanda's originals and took the copies back Northside to translate them. Later I sent my interpreters back to gather in the rest of the letters. You will find a few of them quoted here. For me they bring alive the time when there was light in the partly stripped chandelier, when that ceiling whose fanciness has long since been gutted into occasional waffle-pits of darkness was still whole, when the stacked tables were still laid out for reading, drinking, arguing and gambling, a time before the walls were stained and the ceiling-squares dangled down like laundry on the line. I am not saying that it was necessarily a better time for the Chinese; I wouldn't presume to know that, and many of the tunnel letters are very sad, for instance this one, an undated message from a wife in China to her husband here in Mexico; perhaps he brought it downstairs to ask his Tong brothers what he could possibly do:

Everything goes well at home, except that my father-in-law cannot understand why there is no letter from you. Father-in-law questioned money sent via Hong Kong via Rong-Shi, and Rong-Shi denied receiving money. We borrowed money from neighbors. Father-

*About one of these sheets my translators would inform me: "The paper is symmetrically split in half and divided by perforations. Both halves are the same in terms of content. The right side is meant for the person who paid the money. The left side is for the person who received the money and recorded the transaction (treasurer at Wong Kong Ja Tong). After the transaction is made, the paper is then folded in half, and each half is given to the person it is meant for. In between the two halves, a large 'Number 180' is partly handwritten, partly pre-printed. That way, when the halves are once again brought together and placed side by side, the perfect match in calligraphy will prove its validity. Not having a perfect match up will prove that one of the people forged the receipt. This was to prevent stealing both inside and outside of the tong."

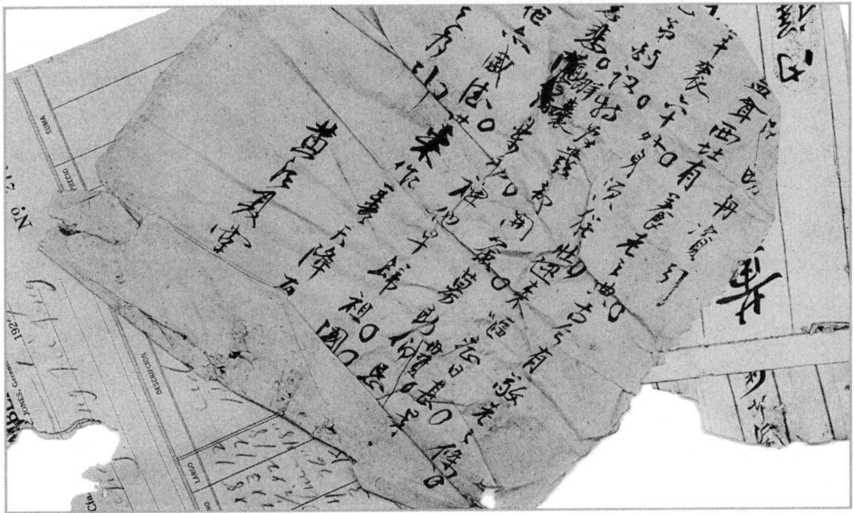

in-law is not in good health. Please send money home. Also, when you send money home, do not send money via Rong-Shi, but addressed to . . .

Thinking of you. The way I miss you is heavy and long; however, the paper is too short to carry the feelings.

When my Chinese proxies Clare and Rosalyn Ng, about whom more shortly, saw this tunnel a month later, this is how Rosalyn saw it: *The red sign above the stairs with the Chinese writing says luck/celebration/happiness. It is a very common character/word/phrase still used today, especially at weddings,* and the Chinese waitress from the Dong Cheng Restaurant down the street said the same when I brought her here.

But I highly doubt it was written/hung there for that specific purpose, even though the place would have been ideal for a wedding with its exquisite interior decorations and loads of round tables and chairs . . . You thought the place might've been used for gambling. My mom and I . . . find that greatly possible . . . It might also have been a place where people gathered, just like a community club or tong, and business matters were taken care of in back rooms. Also, the numerous tables and chairs would be available for anyone who wished to sit down, read the newspaper, or just have a conversation with a friend or neighbor. The tables also would have been great for playing mah-jongg, gambling or not. Either way, I believe the place was for public use and for entertainment purposes, especially since the sign at the entrance embodies that sentiment of fun and celebration . . .

Then suddenly I could almost see it; I imagined that I almost knew it; I know so well that much of the life in this hot harsh bright place which I call Imperial is lived indoors, in the lush nourishment of secrecy; cross the line to Northside, head for the Salton Sea, and when you get to Niland you'll find the I. V. Restaurant (Chinese Food to Go; **BURGERS**; *Sandwiches*) crouched beside the empty road. From the outside you might think that it was closed; the curtains are drawn; but when you come in, it's cool and dark and loud with the lively roaring of the air conditioner; the Chinese waitress scoops relish out of a huge plastic bucket; old men with bent backs sit in plastic chairs, eating at the counter; a Hispanic couple gaze at each other from across a small table; his massive arms are folded; she reaches for the salt, then wipes herself with a napkin. It's a hundred and fifteen degrees outside, so people stay and stay and stay. Another root beer float, please, with lots of ice cream! Another medium-sized soda as big as a house! Drink it down to appease the need. Now order another one and make it last! How cool and wonderful it is in here; if only we could hide from the sun all day . . .

Now imagine Mexicali back in, say, 1920, with no air-conditioning, the unpaved *avenida* blank and empty except for a single old woman in a white shawl limping across the blinding dirt (now the *avenida*'s asphalted, to be sure, and even late at night in Mexicali one feels the heat coming up from the pavement); imagine being Chinese and knowing that the nearest Chinese consulate was all the way in Ensenada; imagine longing for shelter not only from the hellish brightness of each day, but also from the people and institutions of Mexico herself whom one did not understand and by whom one was not understood.* *They live together like cigarettes. They came out like ants. Goddamned gooks!*

*In reference to loneliness, I can't quote you equivalent figures for the Mexicali Valley, but in 1910, the overall sex ratio in the Imperial Valley was 125.5 males per one hundred females. ("There is no female help to be had in that valley.") For Indians this figure was 104 to one, for Japanese, 562, and for Chinese, an astounding 1,017 to one. For this they could thank the Chinese Exclusion Act. No wonder that so many of the Gold Mountain Songs dwell on the following happy phantasm: "I turn around, and I'm no longer a part of that miserable lot! . . . Right now I can open a bank . . . I will buy land, build a house and get myself a concubine."

Ever since 1915, Chinese had been fleeing their murderers in Sinaloa and Sonora. Other Chinese kept coming all the way from Canton and Hong Kong to work for the Colorado River Land Company. The braceros of 1902 who'd saved up enough money to do so were sending for their relatives. Mr. Auyón insists that by 1919 *the Chinese called the city of Mexicali "Little Can-Choo" (the capital of Canton), because there were more Chinese than Mexicans.* If this were in fact the case, one can imagine what the Mexicans were saying about the Chinese. In 1921, Mexico passed its own version of Northside's various Exclusion Acts, and banned further importation of coolie labor.

I was beginning to see that the tale of the tunnels was not only the tale of myths and dreams, but it was also the story of how and why one world, which was dominant, hot and bright, forced the creation of another, which was subterranean and secret. Just why did they live together like cigarettes? Was it simply because they liked to?

Here is how that photo-studio owner, Mr. Steve Leung, who as I've said was a third-generation Chinese immigrant and whose birth certificate read Esteban León, described the differences between Chinese, Mexicans and Americans, and you should remember that his words were spoken in 2003, exactly a hundred years after Mexicali was founded; and please understand that Mr. Leung was sufficiently Mexicanized to keep an image of the Virgin of Guadalupe on the wall of his small triangular darkroom. In 1920, differences and perceptions of differences would have been even greater.—Mr. Leung said:

The Mexicans like to drink alcohol and as well to fool around with women, same as the Chinese would like to gamble a lot and they're workaholic. As for Americans, they like to enjoy their life, but they want to work, but they're not willing to sacrifice too much of their own time. Culturally thinking, Mexicans don't have the precise discipline that the Americans have, and yet the Chinese people is still not yet a developed country, because they overlook their own needs; they're always thinking of the next generation. Whatever your generation was passed to you materially, you can add one dollar or one percent, and pass it on to the next generation, and you succeed in the goal that was expected of you. Now, the American says, you got to build your own wealth; you don't receive anything from the parents' generation. And the Mexicans, they normally pass on debts, more than adding on anything. Businesswise, I think I can describe the culture like this: Always an American is thinking this year, *What is the projection of profits?* When he asks this of my Chinese friend, this Chinese owner, he says, *Forget about profit;* he says, *we're going for sales right now, penetration in the market; we're going for a hundred years.** The Mexican

*When I was in China, my interpreter said to me: "Every Chinese always believes that every store has a life, but a life longer than people. Never die."

right away will put as many relatives and friends into the payroll, see how much he can spend without putting any in.

The Mexicans said: *They live together like cigarettes.* The Chinese replied: *They normally pass on debts, more than adding on anything.*

Rosalyn Ng reported to me that *for a long time,* Mr. Auyón *went on and on about how Chinese need to come together and stand strong as one all over the world, especially when they immigrate to other nations. Thankfully, the Chinese already had this concept of unity . . . From this tight knit sense of closeness, tongs* began to develop based on the common bond of having the last name,* a case in point being the Wong Kong Ja Tong, whose letters rotted beneath the Victoria.†

Or, as a Mexican might put it, *they live together like cigarettes.*

Members of a Tong who had never met personally seemed to have been capable of instant mutual trust, as this letter from 1924 implies:

Dear Ging Gei (and perhaps this was the same Ging Gei who'd written in the tunnel letter already quoted: *Ten to thirty people were caught here . . .). There is still no sign of their being released in the future. In response to your letter, we understand your situation. I asked Bak Gei to go to Wong Gei for the money Bak Gei had asked for to lend his friend for medical bills since Wong Gei owes your brother Bak Sei money. If you do not know who Wong Gei is, please go to Chung Wei for further clarification.*

Another letter tells us that in 1928, thanks to the assistance of twenty-seven different communities, whose donations ranged between ten and ninety-nine dollars each, an elder by the name of Ting Zen *was able to go back to [the] home country and reunite with his family members . . . This announcement, in the name of Huan-Jiang-Xia General Association, was made to thank all the brother and sister donors.*

The Mexican perception, fostered by such well-intentioned spokesmen as Mr. Auyón, that the Chinese always acted *en bloc* bears scant examination. In 1911, or perhaps a year or two before, a Chinese named Shi-Ping gets murdered by a "westerner" in Mexico. The Mexican government forecloses his property, whose eventual release two Chinese associations co-guarantee. The representative of one of the organizations, a man named Yu, begins to occupy the property. Huan-Jiang-Xia Association, which I presume is the other group, appoints someone to look into the case. *I went to the venue where brother Shi-Ping was murdered,* he reports. *I found everything was true, and there was [a] goods list with prices. The total value should be*

*It is unclear to me as to whether or not the word "Tong" is now considered perjorative. The Ngs used it without discomfort; Clare Ng assured me that it was a "good" word. Carmen Jaham tried to define it for me and couldn't. Steve Leung said: "Used to be, society, or some sort of a club, a different kind of thing; maybe it's Mandarin, I'm not really sure, since I just speak Cantonese. I guess they are really more underground society. I guess they are Mafia, actually." Yet Wong Kong Ja Tong was not considered a Mafia.

†The second most popular point of commonality was work (in other words, a Tong could be equivalent to a guild); thirdly, a Tong might support people from the same city or district of origin.

4,414.90 rubies (currency denomination). He meets with the consular officer, who rejects his determination, informing him that only eleven hundred rubies will be requested from the Mexican court.

Twelve years later, in 1923, a report from the Huan-Jiang-Xia Association concludes that the consular officer is "not capable," *so if necessary, Huan-Jiang-Xia Association would take over the issue*. In other words, Huan-Jiang-Xia remains quite willing to lock horns with Yu and his Group Sub-Association. *Anyway*, the report goes on, *it is really unfair that brother Shi-Ping was murdered and his property was occupied illegally. We are of the same ancestor; we should help each other.**

And so one went downstairs to slowly read the *Chinese Republic Journal* with one's brothers from Wong Kong Ja Tong, the association of Wongs, whose name appears on the letterheads and envelopes of many of these tunnel letters. (They're still active, said Steve Leung in 2003. They still participate. They still send their members to the General Association. They still invite all of us to the New Year.) Maybe there'd be a game of mah-jongg. Maybe one stepped into the back room to negotiate a loan, building equity for the next generation. Perhaps one discussed with other brothers how to most appropriately benefit a destitute wife back in China. And probably one shared the fear, the grief when the Mexican government began to arrest Chinese, some of whom were one's Tong brothers. How many people hid down here, and not merely against the sun itself, waiting at the bottom of the sea of light not simply until it was pleasant to surface in one of Mexicali's twilight park-islands of screeching birds, but for weeks or maybe years? On one of my later visits to this tunnel, the Mexican cook, who was now forty-seven and had begun working at the Victoria when he was fifteen, came downstairs smiling and remembering, and he said to me: It was full of people—that room, too! There were seventeen apartments. Down here there were ten, and upstairs there were seven. It used to be really pretty down here . . .

What else do the Chinese tunnel letters say about these times? In 1925, we find Wong Kong Ja Tong in Sonora writing to Wong Kong Ja Tong in the Chinese city of Bukelesy, trying to track money its members have contributed to the Anti-Chinese Discrimination Organization. I discovered two letters on this topic. The reason Tongs subscribed to newspapers was that their members could not afford their own copies. *They overlook their own needs; they're always thinking of the next generation*. That being the case, one can well imagine that these men of Wong Kong Ja Tong wouldn't have donated money to the Anti-Chinese Discrimination Organization without cause.

Steve Leung said: In all the time I have been here, no Chinese has gotten

*When I read him these two letters, Steve Leung remarked that he considered this "a common case."

murdered in Mexicali. But at the beginning of the twentieth century it was different. In that time, you can see a high concentration of Chinese people only here in Baja California. They started expanding into Sonora and Sinaloa, and the Mexicans didn't like it, so they started killing the Chinese. So many were getting murdered. The government was kind of allowing it. You could shoot them and nothing would happen; the police would not prosecute the cases; a Mexican would take over the properties. There were some killed in Mexicali, a few dozen I would conservatively say; but the majority who were killed were in Sonora and Sinaloa; that was a few hundred Chinese who got murdered.

I find a letter on the letterhead of Wong Kong Ja Tong, with two witness signatures. It is written, so the translator notes, in excellent Chinese. *In response to your letter, I would like to inform you that ten to thirty people* (Chinese people, my translator clarifies) *were caught here. There is still no sign of their being released in the future. If I hear of any further news pertaining to this matter, I will let you know . . . 1924, October 29. From your brother, Ging Gei Chung Hi.*

It was in 1919 that Prohibition began over in Northside. Guess which vices moved to Mexico? I read in the ever unreliable pages of Ramón Eduardo Ruiz that in this epoch, Mexicali's Chinese casinos paid the police twenty-eight thousand pesos a month to stay open. In 1920, Chinese are said by one source to have owned ninety-two percent of the businesses in the city. (Do you want to know which source? Old Carmen Jaham referred me to him; he was *a certain painter; he knows what's going on;* his name was Mr. Auyón.) If that were even half true, then what happened next would be predictable: In 1921, the Migratory Legislation prohibited Chinese immigration to Mexico. (The Chinese solution to that was equally predictable: Hide in tunnels.)

In 1924, the year after the first great fire which destroyed most of the Chinesca, the Governor of Baja California Norte signed a measure compelling the hiring of Mexicans at gambling establishments. At first this was enforced only against Mexicali Chinese. In Tijuana it took no effect against Americans until 1927, following a grassroots boycott. In his *Memoria administrativa del gobierno del Distrito Norte de la Baja California 1924–1927,* the Governor offers us the following account of the "Expulsion of Pernicious Individuals of the Chinese Nationality": *A large quantity of individuals of the Chinese nationality who live in the municipality of Mexicali have created a problem which interrupts domestic tranquility . . . There are many secret Mafias amongst the Chinese, and they have the tendency to excite hatred and death between them. There have been horrendous homicides, many crimes. When the police tried to investigate these crimes it was almost impossible to accomplish anything due to bribery and obstructionism. In May of 1924 Señor Francisco Chiyoc, a prominent member of the Chinese colony, was murdered. Two months later the authorities and the police could not find any leads because the Chinese refused to help them.* (It was in that same year 1924 that Dashiell Hammett remarked in his latest San Francisco detective story: *Once more Tai ran true to racial form. When a Chinese shoots, he keeps on shooting until his gun is empty.*)

Governor Rodríguez continues his account: *The secretary of the Chinese Mafia was killed. Our Mexican constitution allows one to legally expel those who shed the blood of other people. So four citizens were deported.* (And in 2003 at the Archivo Histórico del Municipio de Mexicali, the ever kindly Señor Oscar Sánchez is searching through a book, trying to help me. He says: I'm trying to find where they threw out the Chinese because they were killing each other, one Tong against another.) On 2 October 1924 the Secretariat of Mexico sent a telegram to Mexicali stating there was in fact a Chinese Mafia, whose members were political enemies of the Republic. The authorities in Mexicali were authorized to expel the directors of said Mafia. Accordingly, forty-three more Chinese got deported.

Then came a respite from Chinese gang warfare until August 1927, when police discovered that forty pistols and two thousand cartridges were being delivered to local Mafias. *The inactivity of the past three years was just a big trick,* wrote the Governor. *What they were doing was making plans to kill each other.* So once again the authorities of Mexicali wrote the President of the Republic for permission to use Article Thirty-three of the Constitution. They expelled seven people. *It should be highlighted that the circumstances behind these cases involved serious previous investigation to arrive at the government's being apprised of the imperious necessity to nip in the bud the cause of these bad happenings.*

Although its references remain partially enigmatic, a certain tunnel letter from this year hints at some great weakness, suffering or disaster in the Chinese community when it says: *Thanks very much for flattering me and naming me to the position. However, I really can't run for senator. The social-moral standard is going down day by day, and political situation[s] change easily. I am reflecting Yuan-Ji's failure. Please select another capable candidate to rebuild our morale.*

More heartbreaking is a letter dated November of 1934, which is to say a year after Prohibition was repealed and two years after the Anti-Chinese Campaign drove more families out of Sinaloa. (Here I transcribe a *New York Times* headline from 1931: **5 MEXICAN STATES CLEARED OF CHINESE.** ***Nearly All of 10,000 Orientals Who Lived There Are Gone . . .*** **MANY REDUCED TO POVERTY.** The states were Sonora, Jalisco, Chihuahua, Sinaloa and Nayarit, but not Baja California Norte. Here also I quote the old Chinese shoe-store owner in Mexicali who said: I came in 1957. From 1950 to '60 there were no problems between Chinese and Mexicans at all. But my grandfather said from 1930 to 1935 there were anti-Chinese activities.—I asked him what kind of activities these might have been, and he was silent, so I asked him again, and he looked away from my Mexican interpreter and said that he had never really heard and couldn't answer much in detail.) The writer of this document is a certain Wu Ma Pho, whereabouts unknown. The recipient is Wong Kong Ja Tong in Mexicali:

The government has arrested a total of more than two hundred people. In Mexicali, of the twelve [Mexicali residents] of the two hundred arrested, four are our brothers (Huang brothers, adds the translator). *They are being jailed for thirty days and will be released on the twelfth and thirteenth of this month. Please do not worry, but we still do not know what may happen in the future. According to the newspaper, seventeen of the merchants from your city will be deported and are currently waiting at the Golden Gate Bridge at San Francisco. The newspaper has no proof so we cannot attain confirmation. So we asked one of our connections but he was not there. We do not know where he is. Another source informed us that on the twenty-sixth of last month, the seventeen hostages were shipped off in* (and here the translator uses the words "cow cages" and "trucks," with the note: "typically used for transporting criminals"), *to an unknown destination. Yet another source said that these seventeen merchants were killed on the thirty-first in San Francisco at the Golden Gate Bridge. And another informant said that they are in Honolulu waiting for deportation. This is a sad, desperate and terrifying moment. There are innumerable rumors. We do not know the real truth. But do you know if any of these seventeen people are Huang brothers? If so, we will have the Chinese Ambassador Yun* (in China) *contact the Mexican government so that they will be spared. If you have any further news, please promptly let us know.*

What finally happened to those seventeen merchants? How will we ever know? I find it hard to believe that they were killed at the Golden Gate Bridge, but the fact that such a possibility could have been considered at all shows how fearful and isolated these Chinese must have felt. Can you imagine them, sitting quietly in the hot humid darkness under Mexicali, playing mah-jongg and wondering whether the police would find them?

From what I heard, there was some Mafias, Steve Leung readily agreed. But the Mexicans were being unfair. As you see, Mexican society is very conservative, actually. They don't want to let anybody in. So there is always some discrimination. At that time the Chinese when they got in here, they didn't want to mingle. So that kept them a little apart from the Mexican society. In 1920–25, the Chinese society got so strong, so they started killing the Chinese people, taking their properties. My father had a boat ready with all the family, so they could go to the United States if those killers came into Ensenada.

I'm very sorry that your family had to suffer in that way.

Well, at the current moment, we're still spending about ten or fifteen thousand dollars to bring a Chinese over here, which makes no economic sense, and we still don't want to hire a Mexican person. So we also have our faults.

I found the chandelier, ornate wall-paper, nice molding and windows to be very fascinating, Rosalyn continued, *especially since they were all Western styled as opposed to traditional Asian. We also found some portraits in the right back corner of the large room, which are probably of the past owners of the place. Mom did not recognize the people painted and so that rules out them being famous historical characters. She usually knows her Chinese history quite well . . . Terrie,* my Spanish-speaking interpreter, *took one of the ceramic bowls/plates, but I taught her how to pray forgiveness from the dead the Buddhist way so no spirits haunt her. My mom said it wasn't good to be down there too long due to her superstitions and respecting the dead and their possessions. Her suspicions were confirmed when, on our way out, climbing up the stairs, we spotted a swarm of cockroaches in the nearest corner to us. Being girly girls, we sprinted out of that place as fast as our fat legs could carry us.*

"WE'RE VERY NICE TO THEM!"

Next to the Victoria was a passageway whose lefthand wall was comprised of double-padlocked doors. I knocked on a door, which was finally opened by a scared young Chinese girl who denied being able to speak Spanish. I knocked on another door. Through the bars of the inner door, another girl said *no* and *no* and *no*. At the very end of the passageway, a young man said through bars that yes, they all came from Canton, and no, the Mexicans were not nice to them. At this, Yolanda bristled and cried out: *We're very nice to them!*

The young Chinese man and the old Mexican woman stood hating each other.

No, the man then said, I could not interview him. He didn't want my money. All the Chinese were in a panic now; they were all hiding, locking their doors. As we departed, we passed a grating through which our flashlight revealed winding steps and rubbish. A Chinese woman said that she didn't know what was down there or what it was for. I looked over my shoulder, and saw her anxiously polishing the grating.

"I'VE NEVER REALLY HEARD ABOUT THE TUNNELS"

After that, I was more than willing to admit that I needed at least two sorts of people if I were to investigate these tunnels. On the one hand, I needed somebody like Yolanda, whose local knowledge and connections had made it possible to find the tunnels at all. On the other hand, I needed somebody Chinese, and not just any

Chinese but an adventuresome individual who *wasn't* from Mexicali, who couldn't be controlled by Señor Auyón, and who had nothing to lose by discovering secrets and sharing them with me. Originally I had hoped that Calexico would be far away enough, but my experience with old Mr. Wong was typical; I'd had several others; after my first peek beneath the Victoria, when I actually had a sheaf of letters from a Chinese tunnel, and wanted only to translate them, I went to the Yum Yum Restaurant on Imperial Avenue, an old-timey sort of place whose owner had been recommended to me; he wasn't there, but members of his family skimmed several of the letters as I stood before them, cast hard gazes upon me, and insinuated that I was a bad man to have stolen these dead people's letters. I assured them that I had only borrowed the letters, and with full permission of that tunnel's current owner, but the restaurateurs only became more and more unfriendly. So ended my attempts to hire a Chinese Calexican.

Sacramento, my home town, seemed far enough away. My little girl's piano teacher is Chinese, so I asked her whether she knew anybody who could help me, and she did; I hired the mother-daughter team of Clare and Rosalyn Ng on the spot. A couple of weeks later, while I lay in bed, I mean at Headquarters, those two ladies were flying off to San Diego, where in a well-coordinated espionage operation of almost inconceivable scope, they would rendezvous with Terrie, who now knew where to take them. As a sample of what they got out of Mexicali Chinese *versus* what I so often did, here is an interview I conducted with a fourteen-year-old boy named Tim, with insertions from their own interview.

On that hot October night, across the street from the red-skirted whores in the doorway of the Nuevo Pacífico, the alley where the boy lived, the night-roofed passageway as I should really call it since it was so narrow and high-walled, ran like a deep slit into the night. This was the place where Yolanda had shouted: *We're very nice to them!* An old man stood just within the mouth of that slit, gazing out. When the interpreter and I entered, he began to follow us. The interpreter told him the name of the boy we were seeking, and he nodded and kept following. At the second flight of steep wooden stairs we began to ascend, and he stopped following. Then what? On our right and below us stretched the nightscape of a torn flat roof. Below us a pigtailed Chinese girl five or six years old darted back and forth in the brighter part of the passageway we had entered. The interpreter tapped on a screen door, and the brother of the boy we were looking for came; he remembered Terrie but could scarcely communicate in Spanish; all that we established was that the boy was not there; perhaps he was working at the restaurant. The next morning I got him out of bed, and the interview went like this:

Why did your parents want to come to Mexico?

My father thought that here would be easier to find work.

From what province did you come?

He thought a long time, digging his thumbnail into the cleft of his chin.—Kuong Tong, he said, and helped me spell it. It's a very big city. Tai San is the province.

(Rosalyn Ng's note: *Canton/Guangdong*. As it happened, the owner of the Golden Dragon Restaurant, where Tim worked as a busboy, came from Tai San.)

What do you remember about that province?

Prettier than here, he said after a long hesitation.

What did it look like?

Lots of really big houses and buildings.

And were the people more friendly or less friendly?

Of course they are friendlier there.

How do the people treat you here?

Like an immigrant.

So when they treat you like an immigrant, how do they treat you?

I'm not sure how to say it. They think that I don't know.

How does that make you feel?

It makes me feel that I don't know how to speak so well, to communicate so well.

Do you want to go back?

I don't know.

(Rosalyn's note: *The kids hate it here and don't have many friends. Kids think parents do not particularly like it in Mexicali either. However, it is very hard to just pick up and move back to Canton because plane tickets to go back home are extremely expensive and they've yet to pay off the tickets they bought to get to Mexicali . . . Kids don't really keep in touch with old friends. Not only is talking on the phone expensive and writing letters time-consuming, everyone back home thinks they are living a [more] wonderful and better life than they had in China. They are too embarrassed to reveal the truth to their friends. By not keeping in touch, they neither have to lie [n]or tell the truth, but their friends will continue to imagine them living "the" life.*)

How long have you lived here?

A year.

Are you in school with Mexicans?

Mexicans and Chinese.

What do you study in the school?

Spanish. Everything is in Spanish. We study math, history, science . . .

What is your father's job now?

Restaurant.

What is your job and what is your father's job?

He is a cook and I am a busboy.

Why did your father decide to come to Mexico and not to another place?

He wanted to come here.

(Rosalyn's note: *Dad first came from China ten years ago for work. It was hard to find a job in China and the pay was bad. The mother, Tim and his younger brother came here a year ago.*)

Who told him about Mexico?

He has family here.

For how long?

Oh, for a lot of years.

Do they live here in the Chinesca?

No, in San Luis Río Colorado.

Why do you live here and not with them?

Because my father likes it here. You can buy a lot of things here in Mexicali.

(Rosalyn's note: *Whole family was basically tricked into coming. They were told that Mexicali would be a huge, beautiful, and cosmopolitan city booming with possibilities and jobs to make money. However, especially compared to Canton, the city turned out to be an absolute disappointment. Not only is Canton better than Mexicali, it is actually harder to find a job and make a living in Mexicali than in Canton. The language barrier also proves to be a drawback.*)

How often do you go to San Luis?

A few times.

What is your mother's work?

Same as me.

What does your brother do?

Works in a shoe store.

Is that better money as you or the same?

The same.

What do your parents say about Mexico?

They think it's really bad.

Why?

Because this area is very old and very poor.

In San Luis is it also old and poor?

Yes.

Which is worse?

Here.

When your father came here alone, how did he know where to go in Mexicali?

When he got to Mexico City there were friends here who told him where to go.

Is your father a member of a Tong?

No.

So how did your father meet those friends who helped him?

They're friends of my uncle.

Your relatives in San Luis, have they done enough for you, or are you disappointed?

They've done plenty. They come and they visit.

(Rosalyn's note: *The family has relatives in Mexicali, but don't see much of them.* No mention of the San Luis relatives.)

How much is the rent?

Ninety dollars a month.

(Rosalyn's note: *The family lives in a one-room apartment and pays twelve hundred pesos,* nearly a hundred and twenty dollars, *for rent. The room is divided in two by a curtain, so there is a bedroom for all four family members to sleep in and a living room. The bedroom consists of one queen-sized bed and a bunch of sleeping bags on the floor. When the dad lived here alone, the space proved to be sufficient. But now that the whole family is here, the parents are looking for a larger place to move to . . .*)

In one month, how much do you make at the restaurant?

Three thousand pesos.

Must you give all the money to your family, or can you keep some for yourself?

A little bit for myself, and the rest I give to my mother.

Do you know what *pollos* are?

He shook his head quickly. So I told him what *pollos* were.—Yeah, he said, I've heard of that.

And what Chinese word do you use for that?

I don't know.

Do you ever wish to go to the United States yourself?

Of course.

If you could cross like a *pollo,* would you do it?

He shook his head very quickly, laughed nervously and said: Very dangerous.

(Rosalyn's note: *Gaining legal status . . . is very easy to attain and keep, as long as you don't try to escape to the United States. Takes ten years to get a Mexican passport.*)

He wanted to bring me back to Mr. Auyón's office, so I asked him: Are you friends with Mr. Auyón?

No, he replied dully.

Now that I've showed you photos of the tunnels, do you believe that the tunnels exist?

He shook his head.

I don't know, because I've never really heard about the tunnels.

But now that I've showed you pictures of the tunnels, do you believe in the tunnels?

Today is the first day I've heard about them.

If you told your father or mother or brother about the tunnels, would they be interested or wouldn't they care?

I don't know how to answer. My Dad wouldn't want to go down in one.

Why?

Because it's better here. He wouldn't be interested even to see one. And I wouldn't be interested even to see one.

Why are the Chinese losing their power in the Chinesca and more and more Mexicans coming in?

The Mexicans are coming here because they need work.

But why can the Mexicans take over the Chinesca?

The Mexicans are taking work from the Chinese because they can and they like to.

Does it make you angry?

No.

Why doesn't it make you angry?

I like to talk with the Mexicans.

When you see the girls standing across the street in the doorway of the Nuevo Pacífico, what is their work?

Their work is to stay at home and take care of the children.

So are they doing their work?

No, they're just talking.

Tell me a story about something interesting that has happened to you.

When I first got here, I felt very unhappy, very bad. I felt as if I were in the middle of nowhere. But then as I got to know Chinese people here and Mexicans, I started to like it more, and now I can speak Spanish, and it's good to know another country, another language.

So you have a lot of Chinese friends now?

Yes.

Can we meet one who has been here a long time?

I have one friend who lives very near here but he doesn't speak Spanish at all.

Then you can translate.

I don't know where he lives.

If he lives so near, then how come you don't know where he lives?

Tim declined to answer.

DAYS OF IVORY

I've never really heard about the tunnels. The tunnels don't exist. Meanwhile, I kept going into tunnels, sometimes with José López from Jalisco, who remained alert but unimpressed, sometimes with Terrie the Mormon girl, for whom it was as much of an adventure as it was for me even though her friends usually got disappointed when she showed them the photographs. Half a dozen times I had the experience of descending below a Mexican-owned boutique or pharmacy, asking the owner where another tunnel might be, getting referred to this or that shop a door or three away, going to this or that shop's proprietor, and being told: There are no tunnels here. Sometimes they'd say: There is a tunnel but I don't have a key. The boss has the key. How long are you here until? Tuesday? Well, the boss will be in San Diego until Tuesday.—One lady assured me that the tunnels were a myth; another said that her establishment's tunnel was being rented out as a storage space and she didn't have the key; a third, who'd operated her business in the Chinesca for twenty-two years, assured me that there had never been any tunnels in the Chinesca. For some reason, of all the people in the Chinesca it was most often the female Mexican shopkeepers who lied and denied.

Of course, with every passing year the tunnels did come that much closer to a state of nonexistence. Restaurant Nineteen, one of the oldest in Mexicali, was abandoned half a decade ago and in the early summer of 2003 had already been for three months now reincarnated as a poolhall with blue-felted billiard tables imported from Belgium. The Mexican owner, who wore blue to match his tables, was actually less interested in billiards than in carambola, which employs only three balls. He'd bought the building outright from the Chinese. He'd remodeled extensively, and knew that there had never been any tunnels. I asked if I could visit his basement but he didn't hear me. I asked again but he still didn't hear me. Yolanda Ogás, Beatriz Limón and José López from Jalisco were there; we each ordered a Clamato juice with real clams in it, and when he brought me the bill (I was the gringo; I always paid) it came to thirty-five dollars. He had one young Chinese customer who came to play; perhaps through him I could reach his father. The big fire? Yes, everyone still talked about that. He believed that it had happened in 1985; that had been when *those Chinese came running everywhere;* he didn't know where they'd run from. He couldn't care less about the past, except in one respect: He sighed for the days when cue balls were still made out of real ivory.

THE RED HANDPRINTS

Smiling a little grimly or more probably just anxiously, the Mexican girl held the candle-jar out before her. From an oval decal on the side of this light, the Virgin of Guadalupe protected her. Although her family had owned the boutique overhead for several years, she had never dared to go down here, thanks to her fear of ghosts. Behind her, the other girl struck a match; a whitish-yellow glob of light suddenly hurt my eyes. I looked up, and glimpsed a faraway ceiling's parallel beams which might have been wood or concrete. Then the match went out. I went down and down. Suddenly the flashlight picked out something shiny-black: water. I thought then that it might be impossible to explore that tunnel, that it might be ten feet deep or more in feculence. When I was in high school in Indiana I'd once gone spelunking with some friends in a cave which required several hundred feet of belly-crawl with our noses almost in the mud and the backs of our heads grazing against rock; sometimes when it rained, fools like us were trapped and drowned. As I peered down into that Chinese tunnel, the feelings that I had had in that cave came back to me. And yet when I'd reached the bottom step and the flashlight split the darkness a trifle deeper, I could already see pale islands of dryness. Moreover, the floor appeared to be flat. So I stepped down into the wetness, and it came nowhere near the top of my shoe. Another step and another; that black water could have been a hundred miles deep the way it looked, but so far it wasn't. As always, my concern was that there might be a deep pit I couldn't see. I remembered helping a man from the Hudson's Bay Company drag a boat across weak sea-ice, which broke under me without warning; that was how I took my first swim in the Arctic Ocean. This memory proved as inapplicable as the first. With pettish, trifling steps I made my way, and presently so did the others. In time the flashlight picked out the end of the pool; aside from a snake of darkness which narrowed and dwindled like the Colorado River, the rest of that tunnel was dry.

We were under Avenida Reforma. The two darkhaired Mexicanas said that they believed that in this wide, high-ceilinged chamber Chinese had lived. Always that pair stayed close together, often forming a right angle as they gazed or tried to gaze at something, usually close to the wall, whose blocks rewarded their candle's nourishment with paleness.

Behind the stairs were three more huge rooms. At the end of the farthest, diagonal bars blocked us from the darkness's continuation.

The question of how vast the tunnels had been and still were preoccupied me. Old photographs seem to tell us how far they could have extended at any given moment: In 1925, for instance, when Mexicali finally got its Chinese consulate, Avenida Reforma resembled a long, wide, well-ploughed field of dirt, with little square wooden houses going up behind a rail fence; Avenida Madero was much the same. How or why could there have been any subterranean passages here? But evidently these views must have been taken far from the heart of things, perhaps even as far as the future cathedral on Reforma; for here's a vista of the *edificio ubicado* on Reforma at Azueta *en zona "la chinesca," circa* 1920: a sign for the Mexicali Cabaret, pricked out in lightbulbs or wires, rises into the dirty-white sky above a two-storey corner block of solid brick, fronted by squarish-arched arcades. Why *wouldn't* there have been Chinese tunnels there? Here's Chinese New Year, 1921: Two young boys, uniformed like soldiers or policemen, clasp hands atop a great float upon whose faded legend I can just barely make out the word CHINA; flowers, perhaps made of paper, bestrew the scene; behind them comes another float like a tall rectangular sail; an automobile's round blank eyes shine beneath it; a crowd of Chinese men and boys, their faces washed out by sun and time, gaze at us; everything is frozen, grainy, blurry, lost. Where are they? I don't know. I tried to shine my feeble light as deep down into the past as I could, but I couldn't even see the bottom step of the tunnel's entrance. (The tunnels don't exist.) And however many tunnels I ultimately got to enter, of course I'd never have any idea how many more remained unknown.

The two Mexicanas said that they thought this tunnel went all the way to the Restaurante Victoria, which would have been several city blocks from here. Shuffling with my careful old man's steps, I came across a mysterious square well of black water which might have been one foot deep or a hundred. Had I been a drainage engineer I might have known what it was. Instead, I thought of Edgar Allan Poe.

The older girl, whose name was Karina, shyly said she'd heard that at one time people tried to kill the Chinese, so they came down here and hid. The other girl had already begun to feel nervous, and declined to tell me her name.

Each concrete pillar in every niche had many shelves of dark spiderwebs. (The tunnels don't exist.) Receding rectangular arches of paleness made me feel as if I were inside some monster's ribcage. Perhaps everything was reinforced so well on account of earthquakes.

In the large chamber immediately under the stairs we discovered an odd cabinet which was really a thick hollow wooden beam subdivided into shelves and compartments, with empty darkness above and below its dust—no, it actually had three sides which went from floor to ceiling; it was simply that some of the back's slats had been pried off; on the back, in a niche whose ceiling was pegboard, someone had taped three picures of space shuttles beside an image of the Virgin of Guadalupe, who presided with clasped hands and almost-closed eyes over the two plastic flowers which her admirer had also taped to that wall; and then below the cabinet the Chinese tunnel went on to its barren bricked-up end. I found no evidence of anyone Chinese. On the front of the cabinet, in one of the compartments, lay an envelope containing the X-rays of Señor Herman La Roche; in the next niche, beneath several old telephones, a Mexican newspaper from 1982 announced the foundation of the Urban Female Soccer League, while *La Voz de la Frontera* (Mexicali, Friday, 11 May 1984), appropriately brittle and dusty, informed us all of **Frankness, friendship and respect between Reagan and Madrid**. In still another pigeonhole lay a hoard of pillbottles whose pills and whose whiteness were both long gone. The labels all said methotrexate. Not knowing my drugs very well, I wondered whether the *meth* prefix meant that somebody had been operating a methamphetamine lab in here. A doctor laughed: Somebody had a lot of arthritis!

The nameless woman had already gone almost to the top of the stairs, and my flashlight caught the impossibly white cylinders of her ankles almost out of sight, while Karina, holding the candle, stood sideways on two steps, gazing at me with her dark eyes. Her wet sandal-prints on the stairs were almost as dark as her eyes. I remember her standing there and looking at me, looking at the darkness I remained in, and I will always wonder what she was thinking. Then she ascended the stairs and was gone.

I returned to that framework of bars from floor to ceiling; the tunnel kept going, but only rats and water could get through. Then I searched the niche behind the stairs.

On one whitewashed wall the flashlight suddenly picked out human handprints made in red; at first I thought that this might be blood, but an experiment made with the rusty water on the floor proved that these handprints comprised a far less sinister game. Dashiell Hammett never wrote this.

Upstairs, the old woman who might have been Karina's mother said that the pharmacy next door also had a tunnel. The pharmacist said that he was renting out his tunnel for storage, he didn't know to whom; even the doorway wasn't in his property. The tunnels don't exist.

CREATION MYTHS

Do you want to know how they started? Clare Ng told me how she and her daughter Ros went down to Condominios Montealbán as I had asked them to do, trying to find tunnels or at least ask about tunnels, and she told it like this: Night time, it was that big apartment down there, and we saw some Chinese woman who was give the water for the vegetable down there, and in the beginning she was scared to talk. The husband has been there for ten years and she has been there only for three years. I asked how do you like it, and she said just since my husband is here

I like it; that is the only reason.* The daughter is not speak Spanish yet. The husband told me actually ninety-five percent of the Mexican people were really nice to them. (Actually I feel Mexican people were very friendly and as long as you don't kinda overdo it they don't care. Their thinking is, why you American people and you Chinese people wanna work so hard? They are not very aggressive.) So we were there, and they opened their heart. They told us it's many many years ago, and it's too hot. These Chinese people cannot take the heat, so they decide to live under in the tunnel. There's a big fire, and everything was burned. They don't live there anymore, but they still keep some things there anymore. They say there's still a casino down there. Maybe it is kind of secret, or . . .

According to a certain *world-renowned painter, known especially for his paintings of horses and nude women,* as noted in the top-secret Ng Report on Nonexistent Tunnels, *Mexicali started off being 90% Asian; the other 10% was made up of Mexicans, white people and a few Japanese. [He] proudly said that the city Mexicali was originally started by and built up by the Chinese people due to the fact that only the Chinese were strong enough to tolerate the extreme heat.*† *He went on and on about how Mexicans and Americans can't bear the heat and only the great Chinese could. Clearly, this man has a lot of Asian/Chinese pride even though he is only half.*

Mr. Auyón then ventured a few meters deeper than he had with Lupe and me, relating to the ladies that *as a result of numerous people dying above ground due to the heat (especially sleeping on the sand), people would dig holes in the ground and sleep in them like frogs because it was cooler underground . . . Eventually, these developed into the tunnels and became a huge city network underground. At first, there were tunnels that connected only the people that were in that specific community. Soon after, tunnels that connected communities to each other evolved . . . Initially, there were surfacing holes from the tunnels about every ten acres, but then people began digging their own and they began to pop up everywhere.*

(One Mexican I met in a cantina authoritatively located the very first tunnel *at Calle 18 down the walls at where the advertisements start.* Why not? His word was at least as good as Mr. Auyón's.)

Mr. Auyón then added that *there are about 26 tunnels left now. They also happen to all be linked to each other.*

*"I think the husband come because those people they are from small village and over there they don't have the chance to make a big living. They say in the beginning they need to pay for the people taking care of the visa and apply for them. He said in 1990, after they came, first they come on a tourist visa or something, but in 1992 the new Mexican president was really nice to the Chinese, so he said everybody can get a green card over there."

†Jasmine Brambilla Auyón believed that "the Chinese suffered more" than anyone, "because they were the first ones to come to Mexicali. It was uninhabited. They started building, litle by litle, and started establishing the business commerce."

"MAINLY THEY WAS MADE BY THE MEXICANS, ACTUALLY"

That was one version. But since Chinese tunnels are involved, no version is definitive. When I asked Steve Leung where the tunnels had come from, he first advised me to meet a certain Professor Auyón, then, when I continued to question him, proposed this explanation:

Mainly they was made by the Mexicans, actually. Way before, there were Chinese tunnels, to smuggle Chinese across the border, actually; but then they were taken over for the drugs by the Mexicans; they copied our idea, but that was taken over ten years ago. Of course there were some casinos, three or two that only served exclusively Chinese people, and they are all closed now, due to Mexican pressure. It is still a corrupt government, definitely, but it is more elegant now; it used to be you didn't need much connection as long as you got the money. Now you need the connection, too.

Were these casinos in tunnels?

They were in a room that was closed. Of course there's a lot of individual gambling going on every night, but not a casino the way it used to be. It looked just like a room, a few tables for pai gow and mah-jongg. And there was a Chinese poker that has thirteen cards and you make a hand with it.

Are there any Chinese without papers who are still living under the ground?

Yes, he said. Some of them.

We were both silent for a moment, and then Steve Leung said: It used to be, a lot of Chinese people liked to live under the ground because there was no air-conditioning at that time. It was sort of a little bit cooler. But with air-conditioning nowadays, I don't know anybody who would live in a tunnel all the time.

Nobody at all? I asked.

I know a block from here there is a Chinese restaurant and there is a room under the ground to play mah-jongg, but not because it is illegal, just because the space is there. And I heard at the time that there were some tunnels that were crossing the United States. Whether they're still operating, I don't know and I don't want to know.

But why would the Chinese have wanted these tunnels to go everywhere in the old days? I could see having a storage space or sleeping space under your business on Juárez, but why would all the businesses in the Chinesca want to be linked by a tunnel network?

Well, you got me on that one. Maybe the purpose in that time was you could sleep in it and you could use it as a warehouse.

That very day I'd just heard another Mexican mention of the big fire, my informant this time being Lupita the ageing parking lot attendant. She had come to Mexicali in 1973 from points south. I asked her why so many of the Chinesca's businesses had fallen into Mexican hands, and she said: The Chinesca burned. Two times. That was the end.

Did you see it?

Yes. It was all burned. Chinese were coming out of the ground and running like cockroaches!

Where did they come out from?

They used to live under the ground. Maybe they still do.

Why would they do that?

She shrugged.—Maybe no papers.

No, I never heard that, Mr. Leung insisted. Even though it's true that locally, Mexicali has about ten to fifteen diferent clubs, for the New Yorker, for the East, for Baja; they have rooms for their members, to shelter them, so there were plenty of those spaces at the time. And it was some sort of reunion location for those people, to cook a meal or play mah-jongg or something. Each of them had their own incomes. Each of these Chinese clubs had their own President, and they would send their President to the main Chinese Association that would represent them to the Mexican government. I belong to one of these associations, and it's called Sam Yap,* and it has about ten or twenty rooms, and I'm the Treasurer of that association, and for the people who belong to that association, they can have shelter and rice; we expect them as soon as they got their job to move on and let other people use it. No business at all; it's a shelter.

(The Chinese tunnel letters show that these organizations did help the destitute, and, as mentioned, subscribed to newspapers for the benefit of their members, who could not afford individual copies; furthermore they contributed to the Anti-Chinese Discrimination Organization, and investigated frauds, foreclosures and even murders.)

I looked at Mr. Leung and asked: Where do you think illegal Chinese might live now?

Well, in that alley you will see an apartment there and there's old Chinese who live there; there's about ten, twelve apartments; people without papers could be there, I guess. Anyhow, there's plenty of spaces; they don't have to live in a tunnel!

*"That one, its members come from a certain geographic association in China. Others often come from the last name."

WOMEN ON BLACK VELVET

I remember tunnels which pretended to be cellars, and real cellars, and other tunnels of various sorts. I remember a plywood door partially ajar with two blood-dark ideograms painted on it, a hasp, a slender padlock. I remember cylindrical holes in the floor with locking hatchcovers; these were the old Chinese safes. I remember how the palings of one tunnel wall resembled bamboo poles packed together, and around the top of them ran a stained metal collar. Then over a gap hung a torn ceiling, with strings and wires dangling down. The floor was a forest of paint buckets, toilets without tanks, cardboard and upended chairs. To me it never stopped being thrilling. Well, well, it's all in how we tell our stories, isn't it? I could tell you, *I just went into another Chinese tunnel!* or I could tell you, *I went into a butcher's basement.*

Señor Daniel Ávila was that butcher. Late in the evening the sun caught the orangeness on the backwards Restaurante Victoria lettering on the white window-curtains, and the pleats of the curtains began sweating yellow and gold. A man on a crutch slowly hobbled out, and a boy held the door for him. For a long time I could see him creeping along outside, with backwards Chinese lettering superimposed across his journey. The girls were already working across the street in the doorway of the Hotel Nuevo Pacífico; I counted six of them; Señor Ávila, who'd worked at a certain supermarket for forty years and now owned a butcher shop, said that his son had once clerked at the Pacífico and that he had found tunnels but was never allowed to go inside them.

In your opinion, what is down there? I asked him.

He laughed and said: Secrets.*

He took me down into his snow-white cellar-tunnels, which had once been Chinese tunnels, and assured me that in a tunnel which had once connected with the tunnels under the supermarket and perhaps still did, there had been a cantina with paintings of naked women on black velvet; he knew for a fact that the paintings were still there, although he wasn't sure what condition they might be in. He was positive that the Chinese still lived underground just across the street. He couldn't

*José López from Jalisco sometimes stayed at the Nuevo Pacífico when he was flush, which was rarely; he never rented any of the girls; he liked the safe, clean rooms and the showers. He'd never seen the tunnels which Daniel Ávila mentioned. I had visited the Nuevo Pacífico myself on various nights, and when my companion of the hour led me past the reception desk and far down that U-shaped concrete hall with its stairwells and its closed doors (the ones which were closed for business purposes were so indicated by clots of toilet paper jammed into the doorframe), I also used to watch for darkly mysterious descents, but, as Lupe Vásquez, another habitué of the place remarked, the Nuevo Pacífico was not the kind of place where you'd be allowed to wander around.

say exactly where their tunnel was, because they entered at night *like rats*. I remember him standing far away at the end of his farthest tunnel, an end installed at the termination of Chinese prehistory; he owned the place now, and didn't want thieves to get in. His whitewashed empire was a combination of a church and a nuclear submarine, being not only clean and grand, but also subdivided into compartments. In that wonderfully Mexican way he had, he made everything seem possible; anytime now I was going to descend through the floor of a pharmacy or watch-repair store and hear piano music; I'd smell opium; I'd hear laughter and the click of mah-jongg tiles.

He knew a woman who trusted him and who could help me, but the next time I saw him he was more doubtful that she could help me, and the time after that, he was in a hurry to go to the cemetery for the Day of the Dead.

"A CHINESE LIVED AND DIED HERE"

To the supermarket which he had mentioned there sometimes came a Mexican caretaker who requested that I not use his name. He had worked long and faithfully for the Chinese owner, who had recently died and whose memory he adored. The children did not care to operate it anymore, and goods sat decaying on the shelves. Really it was no supermarket anymore, but the shell of a supermarket. His job was to air the place out. He proudly said: This is one of the first stores that the Chinese opened in Mexicali, in about 1920.

(Scaffolding and shacks defining the curves of a wide dirt thoroughfare with two boxy automobiles on it, and several men, mostly hatted against the sun, striding across the blankness; that's the corner of Reforma and Altamirano during the construction of the "Teatro China" in 1920. The supermarket was a few steps from there.)

After persuasion which did not entirely lack a financial character (twenty dollars), the Mexican took me inside and through the double red curtains to the back, past an elevator cage (one of the first elevators in Mexicali, he loyally announced), and then we went downstairs into a white corridor. He said to me: This passageway originally went all the way to the cathedral on Reforma.

That gave me an eerie feeling. Aboveground it would have been a good fifteen-minute walk to that cathedral.

With his hand on his hip, thinking for awhile amidst the humming electric whine of the lights, he finally said that the last time any Chinese had lived down here was in 1975.

Why did they stay in the tunnels?

They didn't have their papers, so they hid here. Around 1970 was the big fire. A lot of them came out, *with long beards!* I saw them. All old people! Many went back to China.

He pointed down into a cylindrical hole like many which I had seen in other tunnels, and he said: The Chinese didn't keep their money in the bank, but in the wall. Here you would have had a safe, but it is full of water.

The tunnel went on and on, wide and humid, with salt-white stains on the walls. Huge beams spanned the ceiling. It was very well made.

Pointing to a square tunnel which went upward into darkness, he said: An emergency exit. This is how they came out during the fire.

In a vast whitewashed chamber which was nearly filled with wooden pallets, I assume for produce, we came to another safe-hole, and he said admiringly: The old Chinese, if they earned ten pesos, they saved five. When they made a meal, they made it for a big group. Chinese are a suffering people. You Americans, you're not as economical as you are commercial. With Chinese, it's the opposite.

He laughingly told the tale of how one day the big boss approached a boy at the checkout counter and asked him what size shoes he wore; the boy, certain that he was about to receive a gift, replied that he was a size eleven.—And if I gave you size thirteen shoes, would they fit? inquired the boss.—Oh, no, sir!—In that case, when people buy something small, don't put it in a large bag!

That was the kind of person the boss had been. But the Mexican had another story to tell: A Mexican woman had once been caught shoplifting food. They detained her until the boss arrived. He asked: Why did you steal? She replied that she was hungry. Instead of turning her over to the police, he allowed her to return to her children, and after that gave her free food once a month.

The large room had once been a Chinese restaurant called Super Cocina, and ideograms still remained on the walls, in various stages of obliteration. In the corner, a flight of stairs led up to the ceiling. Once they had gone to the street. The place had been very famous, sighed the Mexican; the food had been very good. And I could see that he, too, was happy to live for a few moments in the past.

Why don't robbers and gangsters live down here? I asked.

Mexicans are kind of timid. They think there are ghosts here. I have been working with the Chinese since I was twenty-seven. Now I am sixty. I myself believe in ghosts.

How do the ghosts reveal themselves?

The doors will open and close; the lights go on and off.

I asked him what it had been like for him to work for the Chinese all those years, and he said: Chinese don't trust people. They don't want to lose their culture. But when a Chinese gives you his confidence, he's the most faithful of all your friends.

When I began to work at the supermarket, there was an assembly of the Chinese and they decided to accept me. El Jefe, the owner, had given me his approval. But before that, for five or six months, no one talked to me. It was very difficult. I don't know why I put up with it. I could have just left. But when they saw that I was trustworthy and hardworking, they offered me their friendship.—By the way, since we're below sea level now, water comes out of the walls.

We had left the restaurant and reentered one of the middle chambers. The floor was stained white. The Mexican said: They slept in rows on small wooden beds.

Could I see one of the tunnels where they slept?

All that's disappeared. It was over where the Chinese Association is.

You mean Mr. Auyón?

That's right. Twenty meters from there. They slept there and smoked opium.

He took me back upstairs, then up more stairs to the boss's office. Sometimes he called the boss El Jefe and sometimes he called him Señor Chino. A rattle of keys, and we were inside the stifling room, with a chalkboard whose Spanish plans and phrases remained unerased, a dead adding machine on the table, and a photograph on the wall: An old Chinese was sitting palely, sadly at a desk.—This is my boss, said the Mexican with a strange formality. He's dead. He came here with one hand behind his back and the other hand in China.

I said nothing, and the Mexican went on: In my eyes, he was like a godfather. And all came to him; the young people bowed to him.

Did you ever want to marry a Chinese?

No, he laughed, spreading his hands.

We left the office, returning to a sort of catwalk from which we could see down into the dark, half-empty market with its canned goods filthy and spiderwebbed on the shelves; then we ascended to the third floor, which was an atticlike space with brick partitions which resembled those of a stable; it would have been a hotel had El Jefe lived. At the far end lay a great chamber with many tiny windows; the Mexican said that this had been a place where the Chinese came to dance. A private staircase went to the street.

More stairs brought us to another unfinished hotel floor; finally came the flat roof, with a three-room suite running partway along one side; within these apartments, which reeked of feathers and bird droppings, many pigeons lived, and some had died and decayed upon the floors; they flew violently in and out when we peered in.

The roof was open and bright, the reverse of the tunnels, and yet it felt the same; it felt like death.

The Mexican was saying: My Chinese friends used to only need two changes of clothing, one to put on and one to take off. Chinese love gambling and women . . .

I was hardly listening. I could see the pinkish-orange cupola of the cathedral on Reforma, so far away across the roofs and palms; it was hard to believe that the tunnels went all the way there.

The fire started with a man who sold tamales, the Mexican was saying. It burned right down to here, and he pointed off the edge of the roof. This whole street was cantinas back in 1955. There was a lot of conflict, delinquency, prostitution. It was like an old cowboy town, he said longingly.

And you're sure you can't show me the cantina where the velvet paintings are? I asked, slipping a ten-dollar bill into his hand.

And so now we were in the street behind the supermarket—in an alley, I should say, a narrow dark place which smelled of the Río Nuevo and of birds, and on the far side of this there was a wall in which was set a white grating; when the Mexican unlocked this, the recess within was square, and within that stood another door. He had to go back to the supermarket to find the right keyring for that one. Laughingly he said: The Chinese have a lot of doors and a lot of keys.

This was all a cantina, he added with a sudden sadness. Pedro Infante sang here. Like Frank Sinatra.

He unlocked the inner door and pulled it open, a task which took most of his strength. Here at street level ran a very dark high-ceilinged space which seemed to have been gutted or perhaps was never finished; there were many wooden pallets, and he explained that illegal things had been stored here.—What kinds of illegal things? I wanted to know.—Oh, butter and rice, he hastily said.

Dark stairs led down into black water; that was the cantina where the black velvet paintings were. He said that it would take three weeks to pump it out and he wasn't sure about the price. Three weeks later I was back and he said that the pump had broken; he stood frowning with folded arms and said that the old Chino who would have shown me more had refused; I could tell that he wanted me to go away and never come back. But that was three weeks later; right now we still had an everlasting friendship ahead of us, and so after the flashlight finished glimmering on the stinking black tunnel in the cantina of the velvet paintings he took me up a crazy flight of wooden steps through the darkness to a concrete cell with three windows which looked down into that chamber of illegal butter and rice.

A Chinese lived and died here, he said.

There had been a stove, he told me, but the stove was gone. The dresser was still there. The bed was gone. It was a ghastly, lonely place.

It was a long time ago that he died, but I was already working at the supermarket, he said. I remember him.

He was silent for awhile. The place was so hot and humid that it was difficult to breathe. The Mexican said slowly: Our race is like Italians. We like to party. But they are very strange. Look down, and you can see that tunnel; it's full of water . . .

Where does it go?

They say that that one also goes to the cathedral, but I don't know.

We descended the stairs, happy to get out of that eerie place, and we went back out to the street, and he locked the inner door and the outer door. In the doorway of the abandoned supermarket he said: When I got here, fifteen or twenty people lived below.

You mean, where you first took me?

Yes. They never left.

He pointed to another building and said: When the fire came, this is where the Chinese came out, the old ones with the beards . . .

ONCE UPON A TIME IN THE CHINESCA

Now what? I had established that the tunnels really existed and had seen them with my own eyes. Thanks to the letters, I could imagine, however incompletely and incorrectly, a little of what life must have been like for Chinese in Mexicali during the golden age of tunnels. (The Methodist church has a *subterráneo*, said Carmen Jaham. That's where my school was; I went down there from when I was seven or eight until I was seventeen. I don't know what they've done with it. It looked like a tunnel down there; when we had recess we'd come up and play basketball on the patio. We had desks. There were two teachers and about fifty or sixty students, organized by last name. We had an electric light and a big chalkboard; that was it. That's where we had English, Chinese and Spanish classes. We were all brothers and sisters. At that time, we didn't care if you had money or not. What was important was whether people were kind to us.)* But I still didn't know whether any tunnels were still active, and, if so, who or what might be down there. There might well be tunnels leading under the wall into Northside, but finding those, and seeing people smuggled through them, did not seem worth the expenditure of risk or treasure. I would be satisfied to find an illegal casino, which might or might not exist, or a few pallets where impoverished or illegal Chinese slept in the hot darkness.

Yolanda Ogás had claimed to have met an old man who'd lived in the tunnels for much of his life, and even to have seen the stove he used down there; unfortunately, when I asked her to introduce me to him, she neglected to return my telephone calls.

*She got married in that Methodist church, although she later became a Catholic. About the tunnels she simply remarked: "It was hot, so they slept there."

Lupe Vásquez proposed a procedure which probably would have borne fruit, but wasn't quite my style: Go to a Mexican cop (he recommended his cousin), give the cop a hundred dollars, and tell the cop to put his pistol against the head of the nearest old gook. Then they'd goddamned sure as hell show me their fucking tunnels!

Clare Ng telephoned her Chinese friend in Los Angeles who was in the trading business; he went to Mexicali often, and assured her that in this year of grace 2003 there remained at least one locale where Chinese played mah-jongg secretly; she tried, and he tried, but they didn't care to invite me. At least they didn't refer me to a world-famous painter of horses named Mr. Auyón.

Once upon a time in the Chinesca I peered in through the closed cracked window of the store that sold sombreros; there was supposed to be a tunnel underneath but the owner had assured Yolanda and me that he'd never heard of anything like that. I looked in and everything was dim; how had I advanced my knowledge of tunnels? Now it was already six-thirty, and a few steps from me the fat lady was locking the white-painted, dirt-tinted gates of a roofed alley for the night. Sweet dreams to the store that sold Communion dresses! A pleasant rest to the barbershop! There went the white Number 99 bus, crowded with standees; a man wheeled a dollyload of boxes down the grey sidewalk; a female radio voice was babbling cheerily from a store, and beneath that Mexican *carnicería,* which was very old, there presumably lay secrets dormant or active.

There was the old, low Restaurant Dong Cheng (COMIDA CHINA MEXICANA), where from time to time for half a dozen years now I've dropped in to get a beer or a half-order of fried rice, which was always as comfortingly large as a fat lady's breast. No matter how hungry I was, it was inexhaustible. Then a white fence stretched across a vacant lot, a palm tree behind; there was a parking lot, more Chinese restaurants, the Hotel Nuevo Pacífico, which as I might have told you three or four times already is famed for its beautiful whores, many of whom are Chinese or half-Chinese; this was the Chinesca.

Once upon a time, in a certain street whose name I have already mentioned, not far from the sign where it said **BILLARES** and *JAGUAR* and unsurprisingly near to the ironwork letters which spelled out **CHEE HOW OAK TIN**, there was a gate, and a Mexican woman pointed to it and said to me: All the Chinese go there.

Do you think I can go inside?

They won't let you.

Why?

She shrugged. Who knows? A lot of Chinese come out of there to work. At night they come back here. Everybody says they live underground.

We were nearly at the volleyball court, which was also the basketball court and which Yolanda had told me was the place beneath which the Chinese supposedly lived. (The tunnels don't exist.)

Every day that I passed by, I glanced at the **CHEE HOW OAK TIN** gate, but it was always closed until one morning in November when it wasn't; nakedly interpreterless, I went in, and there was a Mexican standing in the courtyard. I gave him twenty dollars and said to him: *Por favor, señor, dónde está una subterráneo?* He laughed at me. He could speak English perfectly well. He told me not to tell anyone his name or where the tunnel was, but I can let you know that it was less than three doors from there. And it wasn't even a real *subterráneo,* only a *sotano,* a cellar, on whose floor a man in a blanket was sleeping; he was old and Chinese and might have been drunk; he did have a beard, although not as long as in the Mexicans' stories; a bag of clothes lay beside him, so let's say he lived there; perhaps I should have photographed him but it didn't seem very nice to steal a picture of a sleeping man; I have done that sometimes if I hope to obtain a moving picture of the wretchedness of homelessness, but this man seemed neither wretched nor homeless, so I left him in peace; it all happened in a moment. And so now I had achieved my objective; I could say that people still slept in the tunnels; the myths were true; there remained secrets and subterraneans, just as there used to be once upon a time in the Chinesca. I came back into the sunlight, passing **BILLARES** and *JAGUAR*; and for some reason I felt very, very sad.

MISS XU'S FIRST TUNNEL

Once upon a time in the Chinesca I asked the waitress in the Dong Cheng if I could talk to her, and she said yes. (I don't know why I bother to tell you this. This story has already achieved its climax; I've assured you that the tunnels are inhabited; it's all over.) She was a tiny, pretty Chinese girl, aged twenty-six. Her parents had brought her to Mexicali when she was nine years old.

What do you remember from Kwang Tung?*

To tell the truth, very little. It's hotter here, and there were more people there.

Now that you are grown up, would you prefer to stay here or go back to China?

Here.

Would you marry a Mexican?

It doesn't matter to me, but my parents would want me to marry a Chinese.

Have Mexicans been nice to you, or do you feel like a foreigner?

Smiling, spreading her hands, she replied: My friends and the people I study

* Guangdong.

with are very nice, but every now and then the people yell something at me in the street . . .

What are the personality differences between Chinese, Mexicans and Americans?

Chinese are more conservative, she said at once. Then she thought for a very long time, first smiling, then pursing her lips.—I don't know exactly what Americans are like, but they're more liberal. Mexicans are friendly and nice . . .

Do you have any knowledge of the tunnels?

The truth is, she said, I've never been in a *subterráneo.*

So I took her down Avenida Juárez (every Mexican city offers us its avenue or boulevard named Benito Juárez) and through the red-lettered double glass doors of the Victoria; then with permission, *con permiso,* we passed through the kitchen and went down into the tunnel. Now we were home; now we were sheltered from the pure yellow loneliness of the Mexicali streetlights.

Have you ever seen a ceiling like that before? I asked her.

No, said Miss Xu.

Is it as you expected here?

I did not think it would look like this. I thought it would be more like a cave. This seems like a house.

(By the way, she never, ever let me see the inside of her own house. She lived in Condominios Montealbán. She was the one who'd said about Luisa's *quinceañera: I don't care for that sort of event.* Her dream for her life was to finish her studies in business administration and then work, maybe as a factory manager.)

The cook came down into the tunnel to visit me again; now that the boss had said that I was okay, he loved to use me as an excuse to descend into his memories. He was a jolly, pleasant man. He said: I used to eat and sleep down here with the Chinese. It was like a hotel down here! Mostly they have retired now; some have died; the rest went away. It's been more than ten years since they've stopped living here.

I asked him if he could say more about what had changed,* and Miss Xu gazed at him without any expression that I could see, and he said: After they rented out

*Before his thirty-two-year tenure there must have been many other changes of all kinds. Sad to say, it was right here that the May 1923 fire did its worst. Unlucky Mexicali! First the Colorado River flood of 1905, then this; in 1940 an earthquake would start another fire; there'd be a fire after that. (According to Mr. Auyón, the fire of 1940 was the big fire.) One of the Chinese tunnel letters from 1923 reads: "I recently heard that Huan-Jiang-Xia General Association was burned to ashes; however there was no casualty. What is the insurance?" The writer is worried about his loans, whether paying them back or getting repaid is unclear. Another letter informs us that "Huan-Jiang-Xia General Association is holding its grand opening in the Third City," which may or may not be Mexicali. Unfortunately, it is undated, so we don't know whether this was the first opening or a reopening after it arose from its ashes.

this space, water began to drip down from above. So I didn't want to sleep down here anymore. It used to be like a new house. Now it's like a haunted house . . .

He hesitated and said: I do mean haunted. You know, when one died, the rest leave . . .

That was all he would say. The Chinese waitress continued to be silent. In the darkness I could see her face surprisingly well, because it was so pale that it almost glowed; and now I watched the girl's tiny pale hands gripping the loop of her belt; when the Mexican said *haunted,* her hands tightened, and that was all.

DARKNESS AND BROKEN CHAIRS

Those old, old letters, partially rat-eaten, and the memories of old men, the myths of farmworkers and drunks, the lies of Mr. Auyón and the evasions of Chinese and Mexican business owners alike, the photographs in the Archivo Histórico del Municipio de Mexicali and the passages in old books, they all added up to something beautiful, stinking, empty and infinitely rich, like Imperial itself. On the threshold of the tunnel under the Victoria where the letters were found, Rosalyn Ng had tried as I had to imagine herself back into that world, and decided however tentatively that *I believe the place was for public use and for entertainment purposes, especially since the sign at the entrance embodies that sentiment of fun and celebration* . . . What was she talking about, but a warped and mildewed wooden door with the rectangular wirework over the top of it and the Chinese ideogram affixed to it, an ideogram which to me resembled two figures dancing together with outstretched arms upon a bridge supported by the shoulders of two kneeling figures? Behind and around the door was darkness; to the right of it was a high wirework window giving on darkness; below the doorknob and the padlock which passed through the crude-bored hole was a Chinese notice, nailed to the wood. What was in the darkness now? Not much but broken chairs.

What really happened to turn the tunnels from restaurants and hideouts into cloacas constipated by their own trash? Was it all the fires? As had several Mexican boutique owners, the owner of the Golden Dragon Restaurant said that the tunnels used to be populous "fifty plus years ago," but then came the great conflagration, which ruined and killed. *After that, everyone moved to above town or ran off to somewhere else.* For more information, he referred me to a certain artist and professor by name of Eduardo Auyón.

Yolanda Ogás for her part said to me: This used to be the commercial center of Mexicali, but when they built the Plaza Cachanilla with a lot of stores, the Chinese started going to buy those stores . . .

Señorita Xu's uncle, that exceedingly smoothfaced old man with very narrow-lensed spectacles, stood in his shoe store and said that in 1992, when *all the Chinesca burned down and firefighters from the other side had to come; that's the fire I've seen,* there were no people in the basements anymore. His own uncle had told him stories about *one fire when all this section burned down and a lot of people were living down there and a lot of people died.*

When you came to Mexicali in 1957, were people still living in the tunnels?

Yes.

Why did they stop?

Back then, there was no air-conditioning, so people had to live like rabbits. I never slept underground but I sometimes used to go there just to take a break from the heat. As time progressed and Mexicali progressed, they left those places. It was in the seventies that they started leaving.

I've heard there were a few old men who still live there.

Not anymore, he said softly, folding his arms. Most of that generation are retired. They may have their rooms under the stairs; there are rooms where they go and relax in the summertime.

Could you introduce me to one of those people?

Hardly any of them are left. Either they're dead or they've gone back to China to die.

He might have said more; after I'd entreated him three or four times he even took me down into his cellar, which once had been much more than a cellar although the bricked-up door was almost hidden behind boxes of shoes; he remarked that once this cellar had been connected to the cellar of the store across the street but that was long ago when they had been one business, he said; he urged me to proceed to the other business since its cellar was larger. Had he ever been down in that cellar? No; he didn't know anything about it. He refused to let me photograph him in his cellar, which he angrily insisted was indeed a cellar, a *sotano,* by no means a *subterráneo;* and he declined to give me his name for my book because his wife, who stood beside him behind the counter, kept angrily reading a Chinese newspaper and making deadly-sounding Chinese remarks in a very low voice; I think that by the time I left him he was in trouble with his spouse. The tunnels don't exist.*

*When asked, Señorita Xu reassured me that I had not behaved incorrectly, which was a relief; I'd never been welcome; after the first quarter-hour I'd finally invited myself to sit down. José López from Jalisco had been translating, and he later told me that the old Chinese had refused to answer many questions, a difficulty which José had tried to solve by raising his voice and stepping closer and closer to the poor old man, who probably noticed that José didn't smell so good; José had slept last night in some abandoned buildings by Condominios Montealbán, slept poorly, in fact, because there had been a shootout between district police and federal police after the federal police had gotten drunk in a nightclub; José had worried about getting shot by a stray bullet, and frankly admitted to me that on account of his sleeplessness, his loyal best with Señorita Xu's uncle might not have been good enough; all the same, the old man might

Meanwhile, at the Chinese Association, Mr. Auyón was thankfully absent, so a sort of deputy showed me around; when I asked him about tunnels he said that the tunnel under the Hotel Chinesca was going to be turned into a museum! Which tunnel? I wanted to know. It turned out to be the cellar that Mr. Auyón had taken me to in order to prove that there were no tunnels. The Mexican girl at the reception desk of the Chinesca had heard about the museum, but she didn't think it would be a museum, actually, because they were Chinese, so they would use it for drinking and gambling . . .

She kindly took me back down there. I looked around and saw not much more than darkness. There was the square opening which Mr. Auyón had named an air duct; the girl said that it was a tunnel; it went all the way under the Chinesca, she said . . .

I asked her why Chinese didn't live underground anymore, and she said that they still did. Then she thought twice and advised me to discuss the matter with Mr. Auyón.*

The elderly clerk of a store who didn't possess the key to that particular tunnel (the owner did, but he just happened to be in Los Angeles for an indefinite period) said that her brother had gone down into the darkness in the 1940s to do something with the water; he was an engineer. He'd seen so much depravity down there: wine, opium, prostitutes . . .

Why did it all stop? I asked her.

Nobody talks about it, she said. Nobody knows.

I asked Steve Leung what happened to his own family in the big fire, and he replied: At that time we owned a complete block in the Chinesca that we had rented. It was affected. It was in the 1950s that that fire happened. We had to make a big loan.

Did the fire drive any Chinese businesses away?

Some, yes.

How would you describe the Chinese influence in Mexicali now as compared to when you first arrived?

Chinese power and presence in the Chinesca is less. Before, Mexican Immigration was very touchy issuing Chinese people to come in; since Cedillo, which is five or six years ago, they opened up quite a bit. Now I would say that seventy percent of the Chinese people here has their own family and have brought them in from China even though we have a special rate from the Mexican Immigration. Cur-

---

have been more cooperative if only his wife hadn't been there; it was all her fault. I told him it was all right and invited him into my room at the Hotel Chinesca to take a shower. When I closed my eyes, the old man's almost wrinkleless face swam before me. I closed my eyes more tightly, and saw blackness.

*She knew me and liked me, but refused to let me photograph her down there.

rently they charge about eight thousand dollars per person for the Chinese, just to make them come in legally. Japanese and Koreans don't pay anything.

That's not nice.

Well, that's the way it is.

And why did the Chinese presence in Chinesca decrease?

The Immigration was getting tougher with the Chinese, and normally when the old Chinese get old, they take their money back to China. No replenishment was coming in.

Mr. Auyón had asserted that all twenty-six (or twenty-eight) Chinese associations remained in business; Steve Leung for his part said calmly: Should be around ten or twelve that are still active. In 1969 there were more. Lot of people died and went back to China, and the new guys don't care about those things.

Which one has the most power?

The biggest association is the general one. They still have an income of about ten thousand a month.

And what about your association?

Sam Yap, our income is about five hundred dollars a month. Our members is about five, ten. Well, technically around twelve, actually.

How much are your dues?

Twenty dollars a month. Most of the Chinese associations, we charge twenty, thirty, forty dollars a month.—He then remarked: There is another association in the United States with my last name and the President was getting tired and wanted me to step in but I said forget it.

Does it make you sad to think that the organizations are fading away?

Well, the purpose of these association was since the guys came in and left behind all the families in China and didn't know what to do here, they were spending time with their friends and other Chinese. So they were kinda lonely here. But nowadays, the young generation, they are not in the same situation. For instance, in Sam Yap, we have about fourteen rooms. The purpose of those rooms is if you have a problem, you can have those rooms but just for a short time. But right now our members don't have any problems, so I think there's just one person. So if the associations disappear now, the purpose is served.

Why did you choose Sam Yap? Was it for family reasons?

Of course. My father used to be the oldest member there . . .

On my next visit he took me there. Behind the iron gate was what so often appeared in Imperial: a surprising vastness. The unroofed corridor, walled with white doors, went on and on, although its concrete might have contained a little sand, since it was crumbly and in one spot I could see down into darkness. Mr. Leung's Mexican assistant busily wrenched the nails out of doors so that I could see what was inside: two storehouses of dead men's belongings (what I remember most is a cheap little frame with a cheaper print inside it, brochure quality, of an Asian beauty who was captioned **MADE IN HONG KONG**. Then came the *sótano,* which Mr. Leung called simply a place to play mah-jongg. There was no light, but my friend Larry, who was along for this tour, clicked his cigarette lighter a few times so that we could see how small and square the place was; a table leaned against the wall; I assumed that like the chairs in the main office or the tables in the rental living quarters it was stencilled with the Chinese characters for Sam Yap Association. In one corner, light came down through a pinhole.

Aboveground, at the very end of the shut up rooms, a man's laundry was hanging. It belonged to Sam Yap's last remaining tenant, a very old man whom Mr. Leung implied was not all there. I couldn't help but think of that hideous dark cell by the old supermarket where the unknown Chinese had lived and died.

I should probably also describe the main office, with its old group photographs leaning against the wall, its stacks of folded chairs, a few of which might have been broken, and its long table. The last time the association had met here was New Year's. Mr. Leung said that as usual they had impressed upon one another the necessity not to be "high key," not to display their successes, because the Mexicans needed to feel that this was still their country. Hearing this made me feel very sad, but I said nothing. Mr. Leung shut up the office and locked it, leaving darkness and broken chairs within.

"WHAT KIND OF LIFE IT IS?"

This decent, honest man who shared his life with me when he hardly knew me seemed dissatisfied, I won't say disappointed, for he had succeeded according to his stated cultural lights; certainly he would leave his extra one percent or more for the next family generation; his clean, cool establishment with the glass cases of cameras and tripods and graduated cylinders and darkroom chemicals was far superior to anything of its kind in the whole Imperial Valley; all the same; that flat *that's the way it is,* which he said in a calm and almost cheerful tone of voice, I suppose because he was proud and he was strong, made me melancholy, although not to the same degree as when Mr. Auyón had told me: *Every ten acres, one Chinese died.*

It is hardly surprising that a person who'd lived out most of his years in a place whose inhabitants said about his race: *They live like cigarettes. They're very closed. They came out like ants. They came out like cockroaches!* would have suffered from a bit of animus, all the more so because his behavioral code required him to believe or pretend that there was better harmony between Chinese Mexicans and Mexican

Mexicans than there actually was.*—You know, he said at one point, there's a mix of a culture here; you got Chinese, Japanese, everything; they think different from the Mexicans; that's one reason that I think Mexicans can't hang on to the *maquiladora* businesses.

This was the style in which he usually expressed his feelings. Sometimes he got more direct.

I asked Mr. Leung to tell me about his life, and he wanted me to ask him a more specific question, so I said: What kind of house did you grow up in?

An old house. I was eight; that was forty years ago; I was there in Ensenada until 1961. I was born in 1950. My grandfather, when he came here to Mexico, he started doing jewel repairing. Then afterwards he was married already. So after they built up a little capital, he put up a grocery store, and he brought my grandmother from China, to Ensenada, and she stayed in Ensenada for ten or twelve years; she had two boys and one girl; by the time they were about ten or twelve years old she went back to China and stayed there another ten or twelve years; one of the two boys was my father.

(Unless he were specifically asked to do so, it is unlikely that an American would have begun his autobiography with anybody but himself—a fact founded not only on my culture's egotism, but also on its own definition of consideration for the other: cut to the chase; don't bore the other with context; avoid riding on your ancestors' coattails. For his own part, a Mexican heeded his lineage. Lupe Vásquez took great pride in his wife's Indian blood, his outlaw-murderer grandfather from Sonora who wouldn't be pushed around. He derived himself from adventures and legends; his people were storybook people, larger than others. A Chinese knew more about his forebears and romanticized them less. They *were* his context, necessary and ordinary. Moreover, Lupe might enjoy imagining his ancestors on the same plane as himself—he was the equal of gunslinging heroes—whereas Chinese Confucianism exalts the ancestor. I feel uncomfortable in going too far with this; it would be easy for me to fall into a tunnel of ignorance. But I remember all the New Year's Days in Los Angeles when I have seen Chinese, the men in suits, the ladies often in their traditional pastel-gauzy dresses, praying at Forest Lawn, singing hymns, occasionally bowing outright. And I quote you this undated letter from the Chinese tunnels: *I received your letter yesterday. We're all very happy to learn that our family temple has been rebuilt. Your passion and love for the clan is highly appreciated. We will arrange your son's trip to Sheng City through our place.* Was Sheng City

*I was happy to learn that the Chinese whom Clare and Rosalyn Ng interviewed for me usually said that most Mexicans were decent to them. For instance, "Tim said that at school, the Spanish and the non-Spanish keep to themselves. Fluent Spanish-speaking Chinese stay with the Mexicans. There is no animosity between them, though. Most of the Mexicans even know all the Cantonese bad words, but do [not] use them with an insulting intention, only jokingly."

the same as Third City? Was Third City Mexicali? I don't know. But I see Steve Leung here.)

And when I was eleven years old, he said, they sent me to Hong Kong to study Chinese; then they sent me to United States. I stayed for two or three years; and then they sent me back to Ensenada, to my home town. I stayed there for one year and did some high school; then I came here to Mexicali because we didn't have university at that time in Ensenada; so I came all by myself. I was studying for my business degree, and staying in a boardinghouse. From 1969 up to today I've been in Mexicali.

How did you learn photography?

These two brothers, my father and my uncle, they started by repairing things; then they went into the grocery store business for twenty or thirty years; then they split up and my father started a photography business in Ensenada. He didn't quite learn; he just hired somebody from the competition. Then later on he set up another branch in Tijuana and put my uncle up there. Afterward, when I came up to Mexicali, this store had a financial problem, so my father bought the Mexican owner out and gave it to me. In high school I was already a businessman; I already had my own checking account and my car. And now this building has now been about fifty, sixty years doing business in photography.

Did you feel any particular distance between yourself and the Mexican majority?

Even for myself, I studied four years in China and three years in the United States, but I grew up here in Mexico, so I don't have too much problem thinking like them. I felt myself as part of the Mexican society. Actually I was expecting to get married to a Mexican girl, at which my father was very angry, but I was going to break that rule; I think race doesn't have anything to do with it. But I knew that was one way that my parents were raised: race discrimination. So I respect that in a way. As you see, I married a Chinese girl. I didn't have much problem to be accepted in the Mexican society, nor in the Chinese society, since our roots were pretty strong in Baja California.

What did Mexicali look like in 1969?

Small town, very hot, very seldom a place that has air-conditioning, so that makes it hotter yet, roads not much paved, people were poor. You could hardly see much of high end, class people.* It was pretty much of a structure of a triangle:

*Mr. Leung's class outlook was multidimensional. On the one hand, he was a successful scion of a small business dynasty. And "in China even though I was in an elementary school, two years I was staying in a boarding religion school, so I didn't have any hardship, let's put it that way. I was living with my aunt, in a high medium class society." On the other hand, he frankly believed that "the Maoist revolution I think was very helpful for Chinese. That first time I went was in 1965. At that time Mexico and China didn't have any relations. So they took our Mexican passport, my father and I, in Hong Kong, and gave us some sort of credential that we were citizens of Hong Kong, and when we came out of Hong Kong, they give us

eighty percent poor and maybe ten percent rich, and not much medium classes.

So what was it like for you when you first arrived in Mexicali?

Oh, boy, I was nineteen years old; I was happy with my new toy, my power, my checking account, definitely! I thought it was a good opportunity for my goals. It was a poor city but could give me a lot of opportunity if I took my chances. It was not a nice place to live in, but it would give me an opportunity.

Is it a nice place now?

No.

Why?

When I was young I always had a lot of faith in Mexican society, but after twenty years or thirty years, I've been living with Mexicans, the lack of discipline in the family, in the behavior of the society, in the way they plan things, is a disappointment to me. They don't have much conscience; they expect in everything help from the government; they're not willing to sacrifice. After twenty or thirty years you still have the same problems that were here before and they're still not able to solve them, and educational-wise, the Mexican is losing his effectiveness more and more. You don't see much improvement, let's put it that way. You do see people that have improved their life in Calexico.

The Mexicali Chinese often seemed to speak in this strain, from the Chinese Couple at Condominios Montealbán, who'd remarked to Clare and Rosalyn Ng that *it is not too hard to make a living and just get by in Mexicali, but if you are not satisfied with merely getting by, then it is a lot harder to make a good living for yourself and your family,* to Mr. Auyón, who told the Ngs that economic success in Mexicali was farther out of reach of new Chinese immigrants than it had been for previous generations. Mr. Auyón's niece and her mother said that they were happy in Mexicali. They were the only people of Chinese extraction who said that. The Chinese tunnels would seem to be a good metaphor for the racial antipathies so frequently denied and so near at hand beneath the surface of the city.

Clare Ng came to see me in my house once, with some Chinese food which she had made herself. We were chatting about this and that when all of a sudden she said to me: I have kinda mixed feelings about looking at Mexicali, after I was there. Why did those innocent people come there? To have a better life. But actually they didn't have a better life. Must be some people cheat them, to tell them they must have a better life. And it was their own people! Think about those people, eighty

---

Chinese citizenship, and then Mexican. We were very closely supervised at that time by somebody. At that time we had a lot of relative in China from my mother's side; at that time I was in business administration; I had a way to peek into the way they were thinking; they were not too much in agreement with the government, although the older generation was too much happy with the government for giving them a job. But the younger generation, they didn't know what was an automatic transmission even. So they kind of released some tension with the Cultural Revolution."

years ago! In the tunnel, living underground! And so hot! I don't know. I tried to tell myself, it was their choice. But actually they didn't have a choice. Eighty years ago, they couldn't have a choice. Eighty years ago, the Chinese government was very poor. And the men who come here, they cannot bring the wife. Go every four years, make the baby, then go back. What kind of life it is?

Tim? What kind of life it is? He is fifteen, my daughter is seventeen, and when he see us he is so happy. He never open the door to the stranger. He doesn't have life over there. I think the father came first. As long as you have money it's not difficult to get the paper. All the same, Tim said when he got here he was so surprised. Life was completely different from the way the people told him. He was really disappointed. He just stay at home watching the Chinese nonsense television. He say he go to school but I don't believe he improve his Spanish much. He's working part-time at the Chinese restaurant.

It's really nice, that new restaurant. The owner has been here thirty-five years, so he can make money. It's very nice decoration inside, more nice than here in Sacramento. He said, even though China is more open now, the kids they don't want to go back there. Some of them even marry with the Mexican. They just stay there, making money, go to China maybe once a year. He say he go to California maybe once a week, come to enjoy the life in San Diego Chinatown. He can afford it, but the other people, I hear they can live there for five years, they can come to America; they live there in Mexico for ten years, they can become an American citizen, but that's a long hard time. I talk with one waitress in a different Chinese restaurant, and she was only there for six months. She think she can go to Mexico but can change the visa and go to America pretty soon. After that, she find out it take her five years. She is young, she is unmarried; what kind of people gonna marry her? Those Mexicans, all the woman working like crazy, and some store they don't even have air-conditioning, and the men just fooling around. When we start going away, she look like she gonna cry . . .

Chapter 74

INDIO

(1925)

Indio will soon have a seventy-two-room hotel, at a cost of seventy thousand dollars. We need have no fear that our lands will not become better and better as the years go by.

Chapter 75

THE INLAND EMPIRE

(1925)

The citrus industry remained unchallenged as the major source of income and the identifying badge of the community.

—Tom Patterson, 1971

Riverside, city and county—how are those two entities holding their own in the great race? Tetley's Nurseries on Main Street in Riverside advertises itself as "Largest Citrus Nursery in California," which sounds awfully unbeatable. From the streets of Upland we continue to admire the snow on Mounts Cucamonga and Ontario; no cars are parked in front of the Ontario-Cucamonga Fruit Exchange today (**ORANGES—LEMONS**), but three Fords prepare to ***Serve the Surface with*** **BRADLEY'S PAINT**. Meanwhile, in Pomona, we can motor down Second Street from Locust, and receive Imperial inspiration from the sign which says: **PIGGLY WIGGLY** *All Over the World.*

Riverside County performs "Ramona" thrice, with a cast of a hundred. Pity the heroine and her troupe of doomed Indians; we'll applaud at the end when she moves to Old Mexico. And now Hollywood comes to Ontario and shoots films right here on Euclid Avenue!

In 1905 I gave you a photoportrait of *The World Famous Magnolia Avenue, Riverside,* with its towering dark trees lining an empty dirt road, and bushes on either side. Can you imagine how grand Magnolia Avenue has become now? Since 1913, Pacific Electric has been running trolleys there, fondly hoping that we will soon be able to travel by electric car all the way to Long Beach. Look upon my works, ye mighty, and despair.

In 1906, Riverside had controlled an irrigated area of a mere thirteen thousand acres. By 1921 she is prepared to introduce herself as *A city of American homes, institutions and ideals. A city of opportunity, especially for those seeking ideal farms and fruit lands.*

Here are some of her inhabitants in 1921:

Alta Cresta Groves Mrs. Mary E Rumsey prop S end of Maude
Altona Chas H auto trimmer
Ames Geo T (Blanche) fruit buyer . . .
Ammerman Moses A (Hannah) rancher h 13 McKenzie
Hungate Zack (May) rancher h 295 Kansas Ave
Hunter Wm J (Eleanor) orange grower h Ruston R D 2 Riverside

(We also find the

Imperial Valley Investment Co 771 W 8th.)

In 1924 the first motel opens on Magnolia Avenue; in 1925, the Ku Klux Klan commences operations in our city of American ideals. Chinatown is already fading anyhow; and Chinese of both sexes have begun wearing Occidental clothing. In the thirties the Klan will threaten a certain George Wong, and he will chase them off with a shotgun. *He made a success through his own efforts.*

In 1929, Riverside holds sixteen thousand orange-grove acres within her city limits! Palm Springs possesses trees, too—palm trees. Forty-seven Agua Caliente Indians still live there. In between dry spells, clear water flows amidst the pale slanting rock shelves of Palm Canyon.

Chapter 76

LOS ANGELES

(1925)

> It is a clean city—a good town. Its skirts have always been kept clean. The grafter and the looter have never been able to exploit it.
>
> —John Steven McGroarty, 1923

CAPITAL'S ALTAR

Between 1900 and 1920, the population of Los Angeles grows fivefold. Her thirst enlarges comparably. As late as 1921, some of the city's drinking water derives from the Crystal Springs wells, which lie either one or three miles downstream, depending on whom we ask, from the new Burbank Sewer Farm. Don't worry; that funny taste is temporary. *The Los Angeles aqueduct will carry ten times as much water as all the famous aqueducts of Rome combined.* And in 1913, William Mulholland, who recently received a grateful acknowledgment in *The Winning of Barbara Worth,* pulls the lanyard that unfurls the flag that gives the signal that turns the wheel that opens the sluice gates of that aqueduct. I can't help believing in people. *Only water was needed to make this region a rich and productive empire, and now we have it. This rude platform is an altar, and on it we are consecrating this water supply . . .* Hurrah! San Fernando explodes into citrusscapes!

By the way, do you remember the Chandler Syndicate? The Mexicali Valley is but one of their zones of interest. In 1924, we find Harry Chandler planning to superimpose a grid of automotive thoroughfares upon Los Angeles. He had prudently optioned fifty thousand acres of San Fernando before less wide awake citizens realized that Mulholland's aqueduct would raise property values up there. I've never been cheated out of a dollar in my life.

Between 1923 and 1925, more than a hundred thousand acres of Los Angeles get subdelineated into *city and suburban lots.* We need have no fear that our lands will not become better and better as the years go by. In 1927 Upton Sinclair praises such *subdivisions with no "restrictions"—that is, you might build any kind of house you pleased, and rent it to people of any race or color; which meant an ugly slum, spreading like a great sore, with shanties of tin and tar-paper and unpainted boards.* But for home-hungry migrants born too late to be pioneer homesteaders, these new tracts look

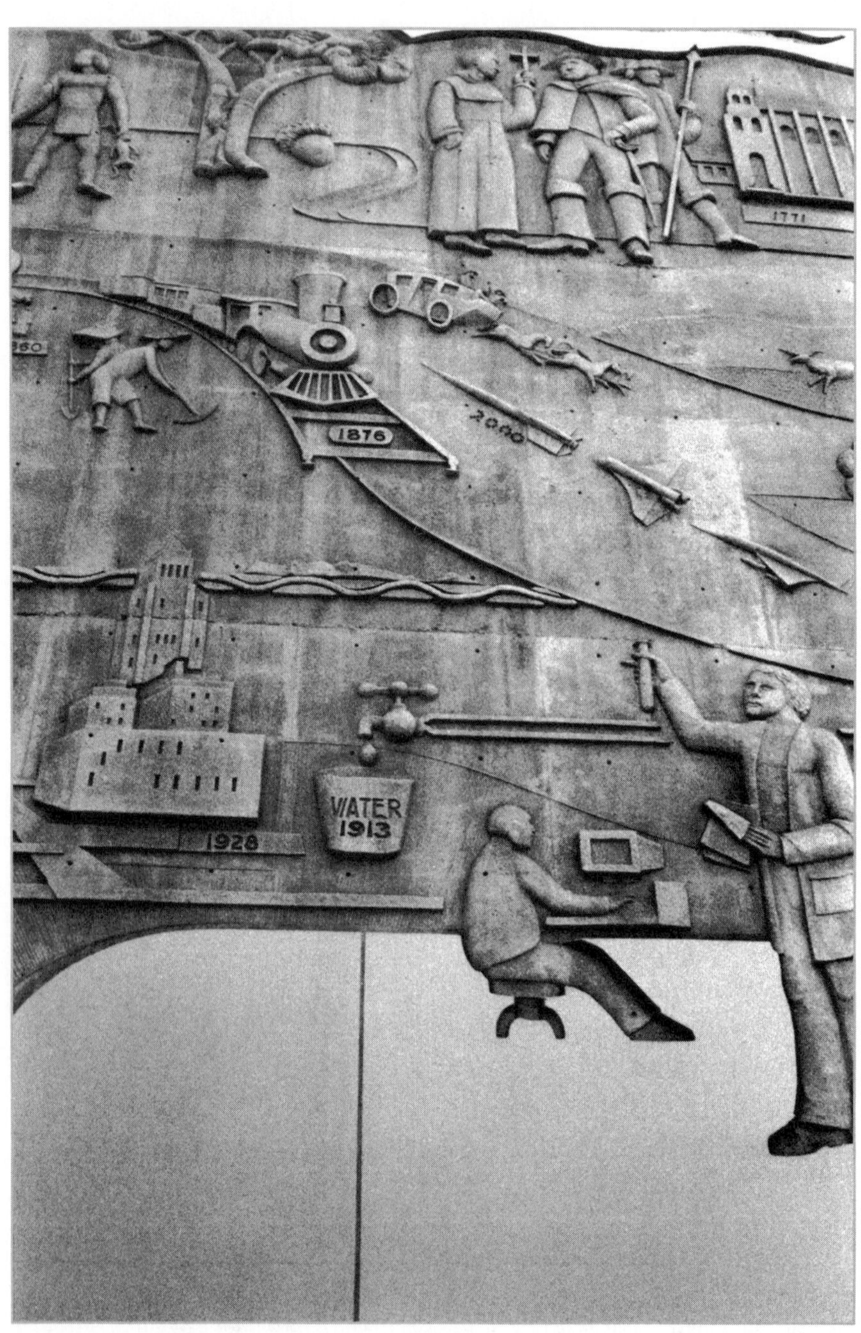

Los Angeles celebrates Mulholland's aqueduct in a bas-relief.

prettier. Of course, even now irrigated or waterless acres remain for sale in Imperial (flavors: irrigated or waterless). But not everybody likes the heat. Besides, the Ministry of Capital is now drilling in Los Angeles, and I'll make more money leasing out the gusher of "black gold" in my backyard than I ever could growing cantaloupes! Gardena and Lomita, Huntington Park and Torrance, even Signal Hill, all sprout oilscapes! White clots of smoke soften the bases of tapering black skeleton-towers. Cylindrical tanks shine and shimmer. In 1923, Los Angeles becomes the biggest oil exporter on the globe.

The city hovers disheveled between farms and factories, between manure and concrete. On one single map from the real estate atlas of 1910 we see the Barber Asphalt Paving Company, L.A. Pressed Brick, the Puente Oil Company, and Southern Refining Companies A and B, all sprawling across the Sepulveda Vinyard [*sic*] Th., bisected by the Southern Pacific tracks shooting down Alhambra Ave. And so Los Angeles's potentialities have grown as elongated as those Art Deco figures in the Biltmore Hotel: nymphs with breasts and crests, angel-devils as stretched out as the future's limousines. In the Los Angeles of 1925, blue-collar surburbanites keep chicken-hutches in their front yards while oil derricks tower behind them; higher up the ladder of moneyed worth, a professional man can still be both an osteopath and a citrus grower.

RABBITS IN CHEAP JEWELRY

Speaking of giganticism, a California history from this period proudly explains that Los Angeles *is sometimes referred to as "earth's biggest city"; and some men of vision* predict that in the future this might even mean something. Now for the dark side: Swiveling its considered judgments upon the barrios of East Los Angeles, the *Saturday Evening Post* concludes that their brownskinned inhabitants have brought *countless numbers of American citizens into the world with the reckless prodigality of rabbits.*

This admiration of Southsiders and their descendants may not be confined solely to the *Post*. One-third of Los Angeles employers regard Mexican women as poor workers: unreliable, slow, unintelligent. By some peculiar coincidence, they earn less than females of other ethnic groups,* evidently since most *were from the lower class*—which is to say *predominantly Indian*. Our researcher finds them concentrated in the canneries, laundries and clothing trades; in the citrus industry they tend to be packers, not sorters, since the latter work is more skilled. Three-fourths are between ages sixteen and twenty-three; nine-tenths are unmarried. (Nowadays

*In Los Angeles in 1930, both genders of *unskilled labor, American*, will earn fifty to sixty cents per hour, while *unskilled labor, Mexican*, will make forty-five to fifty cents per hour.

the *maquiladoras* in Tijuana and Mexicali also like to use young unmarried women, and doubtless for the same reasons.) Their homes tend to be cleaner than those of Mexicanas who have not entered the workforce: The windows sport curtains; sometimes they even own a radio. But their luxury knows limits: Although Southern California Edison has recently commenced advertising *refrigeration without ice,* I see no indication that they own the new gadgets called *refrigerators.*

In words which describe him no less than them, our sociologist (who is, once again, Paul S. Taylor)* builds an exemplar: *Distinguishable on the streets: generally fairly well dressed, perhaps too loudly; she tended to use cosmetics excessively and wore a good deal of cheap jewelry . . . She preferred to be with her "boyfriends" unchaperoned,* causing *a great deal of distress in these Mexican homes* since *a young girl was frequently found to be an expectant mother, though unmarried.*

NO BOASTING, PLEASE

Well, forget about them—everybody else does! Los Angeles has everything from meatpacking to moviemaking. *These industries, fostered by genial climate and contented population, have the further advantages of cheap and abundant water supply, & c.* In 1928, the Lockheed Aircraft Company will move into the abandoned Mission Glass Works in the orchards of Burbank, and build its first two wooden hangars. A decade later, the Vega Aircraft Company will take over the adjacent pottery works of the Empire China Company. But in 1925, Los Angeles is still horses in the streets, with and without buggies and automobiles; a two-dimensional horse prances atop a two-storeyed, balconied brickfront, labeled **HARNESS**. Los Angeles has sidewalks, wide streets, baths. (In Anaheim, which is not yet Los Angeles, the Tanaka Citrus Nursery advertises forty-three thousand trees.) Los Angeles is Henry Kruse of Germany, who came to California in 1903 with fifty cents, *and is now one of the well-to-do citizens of the El Monte community.* Los Angeles is not only *"earth's biggest city";* better yet, it's the largest city on the west coast, the tenth-largest in America! *It is difficult to speak of what the Los Angeles of today is without "boasting."* Over Imperial's flat blankness, Los Angeles towers like the immense right-angled castle of the Pacific Mutual Life Insurance Company Building.

*The reader surely remembers that this man is a fiercely compassionate advocate of Imperial Valley field workers. Therefore, the following description of working Latinas should be construed not as an ethnic slur but an artifact of his generation's (and class's) interpretation of gender roles. What strikes Taylor as loudness of taste would have been captivatingly vibrant to many men who met the belles of Alta California. As for the cheap jewelry, well, *predominantly Indian* women had not yet ceased being poor.

KISSING COUSINS

How did Los Angeles regard Imperial in those days? Were they water-rivals yet? If so, their emnity bubbled under the surface, in an aquifer. At the end of May 1914, a hundred and forty *ardent boosters* from the Los Angeles Chamber of Commerce arrived in El Centro and were greeted by the mayor himself! Their button-down shirts were white and waxy, like male date flowers (the female is yellow and resembles a pussy willow). Scottish bagpipers marked the world-historic moment. **Los Angeles Boosters Delighted With City**, reported the newspaper. And I imagine that Imperial continued to be delighted with Los Angeles, whose growth necessarily decreased local farm acreage while increasing the number of hungry mouths (Judge Farr again: *The sleeper dreams of his rapidly ripening fruit and their early arrival in the markets to catch the top prices ahead of other competitors in less favorable regions.*) Why shouldn't Imperial and Los Angeles have stayed happily married forever? In 1924, Los Angeles begins to transform Tenth Street into Olympic Boulevard in order to reach the Pacific Ocean to the west, and to the east, *by way of Telegraph Road and Whittier Boulevard, . . . San Diego and the Imperial Valley.*

TÍPICO AMERICANO

Well, you see the grapes? inquired a very knowing lover of Los Angeles named Marjorie Sa'adah. We were in the old lobby of the Biltmore Hotel, first looking down into a fountain, then standing on the verge of a two-dimensional world which might for all its stylizations have been derived from some Imperial dream.—You see so much detail that you almost can't tell, Marjorie said. But you see so much detail around *produce*. And these are all fake coats of arms, fake grandeur . . .

She took me to One Bunker Hill and gestured at the muted frescoes, murmuring: This was a different time.

Looking out at us from old Los Angeles, a painted girl leans over the gear of Progress.

Deco is so incredibly post–Industrial Revolution, Marjorie told me. Deco is saying: Machines won't kill us; we'll celebrate them.

I asked her to describe the *feeling* of Art Deco, and she replied: Deco takes the columns and flattens them against the windows. They recess the windows. Your eye keeps going up, going up.

She led me into the Cathedral of Saint Vibiana (1876), from which Angelenos of 1925 could look down into a white courtyard of spider-leaved trees whose fountain echoed in that secret sunny water preserve amidst the trees and towers. When

I went there with Marjorie in 2004, the cathedral had already been deconsecrated, its marble now marked with workmen's footprints, and the old round sun-window streaked with amber as if smog were a honey or other colloid which could run down the panes and bake; but even then I felt as if I had entered one of the labels of Old Mission Brand oranges (headquarters: Los Angeles, Cal.).—Well, why not make believe? Angelenos do.—In 1927, the Mayan Theater opens with a Gershwin musical; and Lupe Velez, "the Wild Cat of Mexico," flirts with the camera, playing the jealous sweetheart of Douglas Fairbanks. In 1928, Dolores Del Rio, *our greatest screen star,* accepts adoring worship at the Fiesta Mexicana. (She proudly refuses to become an American citizen.)

In time the orange groves of Los Angeles will remain only in the decorations of the Biltmore Hotel and a few street signs; but not yet in 1925. An old-timer recalls his much-loved city: *Looking north from downtown you could see the mountains probably 340 days a year . . . they didn't appear any farther away than Elysian Park. When the orange trees were in blossom, and out of the east came a gentle breeze, all downtown filled with sweet fragrance . . .* His memoir tells of farms and stingrays. In his honor I pore over the label of California Eve Brand oranges, packed expressly for United Fruit Distributors (J. H. Grande, your broker): Darkhaired Eve in her darkbanded straw hat sits blackstockinged atop a white mission wall, plucking one perfect orange from the tree not of knowledge but of pleasure; she smiles at me as sunset gilds the mission tower behind her. Please don't tell me Los Angeles was unlike this! Like Eve's, her skirts have always remained clean.

Chapter 77

TAMERLANE'S WARRIORS GALLOP INTO THE SQUARE

(1924–2003)

> The city of Los Angeles is asking for a very modest supply, to wit, 1,500 second-feet. That is about the supply of the city of Chicago for domestic use. About 600,000,000 gallons a day. If we get that much in addition to the water we have already here, . . . why, we will be all right here for a population . . . I would say, of eight to ten millions of people.
>
> —William Mulholland, 1925

In the novel which I originally meant to write about Imperial, I'd respect the burden; that was certainly my intention. I had before me the death certificate of Owens Valley, which obligated me to write about how wicked Los Angeles was. In 1919, six years after Mulholland completed the first aqueduct *(his sole interest,* explains a biographer, *was in advancing the good and fulfilling his vision—to make desert-locked Los Angeles into a thriving metropolis),* it came time to slurp a little harder; surface water failed to fill the glass, oh, dear; so groundwater pumping commenced. That was when Owens Valley began to desertify. Almost a century later, in the museum in Lone Pine, not far off a sad dirt road called Citrus Street, I saw an old photo of a wide silver lake, silver trees and silver mountains, tall crops of this and that, with a gleam of water behind cowboys on horses: That's how Owens Lake used to be. And south of Lone Pine, which is to say considerably south of Citrus Street, I gazed down upon a vast line of white light: Owens Lake, now known as Owens Dry Lake. It did not stink a trifle as much as the Salton Sea. Nor can I call it as desolate as the Mexicali Valley's Laguna Salada. For one thing, balls of sagebrush encircled it. Moreover, tiny sprinklers sprayed driblets of dark blue water onto its dead white flats, thereby accomplishing what was gloriously known as *mitigation* of the phenomenon described by the part-time cowgirl who sold me a soda in Independence: *Everyone who works on it* (the lake) *gets sick. The first year or two, you have trouble breathing. And when that dust blows, if you hold out your hand you can hardly see it . . .*—The wind-ripples in the blue-green pools, the crust of salt, which was sometimes white, sometimes grey like epoxy curing, and whose deadness crossed the valley floor to touch the mountains; the greyish channels of dampness into the cracked white crust, it was the shadow of a lake, the lake of shadows. Shadows on the tiny white pebbles and the miniature ridges in sand and salt reminded me of nothing so much as hard-frozen Arctic snow.

Anything on the valley floor is DWP,* said the museum woman in Lone Pine—not entirely accurately, for the federal government holds quite a bit of land, too.—The towns are landlocked, she said. Every now and then, L.A. does a land release and then they compete . . .

By 1923, agents of Los Angeles were breaking open privately owned dams, and Mulholland was prowling the Colorado River in preparation for the All-American Canal. That was the year that Upton Sinclair got jailed for eighteen hours for reading aloud from the Bill of Rights, on private property, with written permission, because his purpose was to support a Wobbly strike in San Pedro Harbor. Los Angeles couldn't have that; Los Angeles was wicked; everybody knew it.

In 1924, ruined Owens Valley ranchers blew up the aqueduct by Alabama Gate. Los Angeles repaired the damage in two days. Three years later the ranchers tried again, but cunning Los Angeles had instigated a state audit of their savings banks. Meanwhile, Owens Valley dynamiters faced Water Department shotguns. *On August 4, 1927,* writes a Valley resident, *I observed a little cluster of excited men reading a small sign on the front door of the First National bank of Bishop . . . All the banks in the Valley were closed and assigned to receivers. The resistance in the struggle against the Great City came to an end. Soon the desolation . . . was all around us.* Los Angeles was the enemy, and I had every right to say so because I was born there.

Los Angeles is in fact the Bullocks Wilshire department store, whose facade, one guidebook remarks, is *at a scale that makes window-shopping possible for drivers.* The cool dark windowpanes will someday be fabulous reflection-treasuries of concrete honeycombs; but in their first year, 1929, they merely reflect beanfields. Los Angeles's boomers and boosters remain Imperial's even now. The approaching Depression will drag Imperial irretrievably behind Los Angeles, but at the beginning of 1929 it's not entirely grotesque to compare John Bullock with W. F. Holt. *He made a success through his own efforts.* The Los Angeles emblematized by Bullocks Wilshire is an empire of opulence, optimism, even beauty. The architects, John and Donald Parkinson, could fairly be called artists. That turquoise-veined spire, those distorted rectangles of glossy black stone at the base of the edifice, aren't those products of something which could without irony be called Civilization? Los Angeles is that cylindrical lamp like an ancient seal superimposed on the reflections swimming within its windows. Celtic-like swirls and spirals occupy

* Department of Water and Power.

other plaques of bronze, brass or copper at Bullocks Wilshire; they could almost represent an agricultural cornucopia: shapes of corn still in the husk, sprouting beans and grapevines, all heaped together in rectangular market-crates whose walls mark the edges of the plaques themselves. Los Angeles is this wonderful ten-storey tower of tan stone with its double vein of turquoise-verdigrised copper latticework shooting up into the clouds, complete with balconies, angular Art Deco figures, and Mr. Bullock's chiseled prayer: Almighty Dollar, help me TO BVILD A BVSINESS THAT WILL NEVER KNOW COMPLETION. Isn't Los Angeles just such a business?

I shamefacedly admit that over the years I came to love Los Angeles nearly as much as Imperial. But Bullocks Wilshire won't do for my novel. Here's a more befitting Los Angeles metaphor for you: Between Algodones and Mexicali one sees palm trees, brownish fields, smoke trees, men sheltering themselves in concrete cantinas, while on the horizon, across the border, shine beautifully threatening dunes, almost honey-colored, accompanied by white sand and shrubs; one wonders whether they might someday slide over everything like the old Colorado flood, obliterating Mexicali's blocks of flatroofed little houses, each of which has its own fence. What can we do but build sand walls against sand, sand walls with tires on top of them? What can we do against Los Angeles?

TO BVILD A BVSINESS THAT WILL NEVER KNOW COMPLETION, that's what Los Angeles aims to do, and of course it's what Imperial desires—likewise the Inland Empire and San Diego. Should Los Angeles succeed, what will happen to Imperial North and South?

In a certain Hetzel photo, three men float down the wide, curving canal, whose banks are idyllically grassy; they're operating a suction dredge which resembles a series of gallowses on a barge, with engines packed on; a curvy hose or pipe rests on the bank, spewing unwanted dark sludge onto the tan flatnesss of Imperial. Everything's slow and wide open. There's the Imperial Idea for you! A canal can be not only a means, but an end. *There is no escaping the stereotype of an ideal agrarian world.* The Los Angeles idea, not least in respect to canals, will be different. So my novel-in-progress pretended, ignoring the existence of Bullocks Wilshire.

In 2003, the Imperial Irrigation District voted three to two in favor of transferring water to Los Angeles and San Diego. As my novel tells the tale, the evil megalopolis had won.

A SEQUENCE FROM "FERGHANA CANAL" (1939)

Oh, yes, it was the end of stasis; moving pictures had come into favor now. I quote from this unproduced shooting script by the great Soviet director Eisenstein:

SHOT 102

. . . The imprisoned wives of the Emir are dying in their harem, like quail in festive cages . . .

SHOT 104

. . . At the edge of a dried sunken basin, a young wife of the Emir is dying of thirst. At the bottom of the basin are some dead fish. Over all these pictures of death expands the music of roaring and crashing sound.

SHOT 105

. . . Two of the Emir's wives have died in each other's arms . . .

SHOT 107

. . . The Emir stares before him, whispering:

"He who controls water--is the victor . . ."

He dies.

SHOT 108

. . . Tamerlane's warriors gallop into the square . . .

Chapter 78

SUBDELINEATIONS: WATERSCAPES

(1901–1925)

. . . why, Granddaddy, there couldn't *be* any town without all that water, just rivers of it, everywhere. My goodness, Granddaddy, where in the world does it all come from?

—Irmagarde Richards, 1933

The California Experiment Station's record for 1920 contains a troubling parable. Two agronomists researched hither and thither in the southern reaches of our Golden State, then concluded: *Severe alkali injury was observed in a number of citrus groves in several districts, and a large percentage of this injury was due to irrigation water.* Sometimes the water contained chlorides, which yellowed citrus leaves around the edges; in more serious cases the leaves turned brown and fell off. Sulphate and bicarbonate poisoning, on the other hand, prevented the trees from growing. *The irrigation supplies rarely contained enough alkali to harm citrus trees directly, but the injury was due to the concentration of salts after a variable period of years . . .*

What to do? *When saline water is the only source of irrigation, the use of basin or flooding systems instead of the furrow system of irrigation may afford temporary relief . . . By increasing the alkaline content of the drainage water, however, the ground water may ultimately become heavily charged with salts.*

Temporary relief is only temporary relief. *The most effective treatment for injured groves consists of thorough tillage, plowing down manure, and the application of irrigation water free from alkali.* When that's not possible, we Americans fall back on Plan B: Use it up, run it down, move on.

In 1904, a mere twenty years after Riverside became the citrus capital of the Inland Empire, we find the USDA pomologist G. Harold Powell writing home to his wife that *the first settled part of Riverside . . . has now gone out of orange growing, with many a tale of woe hanging thereby; the land is now used for alfalfa.* What happened to this land? It *has been ruined by the accumulation of alkali from the seepage water from higher lands.* **THE DESERT DISAPPEARS**. No matter. The Inland Empire can easily cede a few square miles to property developers. In 1917 a paean to the United States Reclamation Service can still sing out: *It is in this regard—the pure democratization of the great irrigation systems—that the methods of the United States differ from those of all other nations, ancient and modern.*

"DRAINAGE IS THE MOST SATISFACTORY WAY"

In American Imperial, these exigencies and conceptions continue to act upon the waterscape. By 1909, a thousand miles and more of main and lateral canals bring Colorado River water to the brave new farmlands of Wilber and Elizabeth Clark, the speculative tracts of W. F. Holt, the date and citrus orchards of steely experimenters, the canteen (if he has one) of the Customs Collector at Calexico, the barrel, scoop and cup—again, this is my supposition—of the Imperial Investment Company (*YOU MAY FIGURE THAT . . . The Population Is Increasing at the rate of 40 per cent Every 24 Months*), and, of course, the embryonic Mexicali cottonscapes of Harry Chandler. On Imperial County Assessor's Map number 17–15 (dated 1911), the Central Main Canal droops into Southside like a phone wire, offers itself to the Chandler Syndicate, and finally makes it back west-northwest into the United States, feeding Briar Canal, which runs across Birch Street, where in my day the Border Patrol office will hunch, and irrigating the farms of Visbreek, United Farms et al., Lavigne, Farley Fruit Company, etcetera. Ash Canal flows north-northwest of all that before striking Northside. These branches derive from the Alamo River, which comes from our Main Canal. The Río Nuevo opens its sweet blue vein to Harry Chandler's Mexican cotton, crosses the line and becomes the New River; American farms line up to drink it.

As yet there is no one entity to control and coordinate all these waterways, but the Imperial Irrigation District strengthens year by year. That model of journalistic impartiality, the *Los Angeles Times,* explains that *landowners were from the first opposed to the organization of the Imperial Irrigation District. They did not want the important business of handling the water mixed with Imperial Valley politics.* The *Times* then quotes a certain disinterested entity, the Colorado River Land Company, which accuses IID of high rates and highhandedness. *The land company has grown tired of these outrages.* Unfortunately for the Chandler Syndicate, American Imperial's water companies continue to get folded in; and by 1922, IID's hegemony will be perfect, at which point this will be the largest irrigation district in the Western Hemisphere. Dig me another canal, please! *We need have no fear that our lands will not become better and better as the years go by.* I'll drink to that! How about you? I've read that *by 1919 about a quarter of the irrigated land in Imperial Valley had been spoiled by a high water table loaded with Colorado River salts.* **THE DESERT**

DISAPPEARS. But no one in the Imperial Valley has ever told me any such thing; maybe no irrigated land there ever got spoiled at all.

Drainage is the most satisfactory way of reclaiming alkali land, advises a circular from 1917. *When good drainage outlets, such as the Alamo or New River channels, are available, drains can be constructed to carry off the surplus water with much of the alkali . . .* And so the Salton Sea's salinity increases, and the Alamo and New Rivers, drains for more than alkali, begin to stink.

"THAT WHICH HAD NEVER HAPPENED BEFORE"

On the subject of those delicious ureters and sinks of Imperial, it may be of interest to learn how well the people who used them foresaw their future.

The flood had subsided, and to-day, July 10, 1906, as I write, instead of a turbulent torrent of water rushing on its way to the Salton Sea, a stream about seven hundred feet wide and from ten to twenty feet deep flows past the towns, confined within banks thirty feet high and with a current of not more than six miles an hour.

As soon as the Colorado is returned to its original channel the flow in New River will become normal—that is, it will be a small stream depending for its main supply of water from Volcano Lake and the surplusage from the main canal of the Imperial system.

Well, that reads accurately enough. In 1914 the Volcano Lake levee will break, and the New River will once again snatch away highway bridges, but in the long run the river does get *normal,* so that in days to come we will all feel inclined to hold our noses.

And what about the sea itself?

The area of the present Salton Sea is about 400 square miles, and its depth about 90 feet. If the river discharges no water into the sea, it will probably dry up in about 10 or 12 years. Those words were written in 1906. The sea is two hundred and twenty-seven feet deep now.

By 1922, when *The Winning of Barbara Worth* makes its third appearance on the best seller list, Imperial has grown proud of its center, which some booster or other has dubbed *the Dead Sea of America.* (In 1932 the mudpots will be magnificently dubbed *California's "Little Yellowstone."*) Salton Sea mullet, caught in nets baited with fresh alfalfa, sell in San Francisco restaurants. (Salton Sea tilapia sells in restaurants now; I make a point of not ordering it.) *The flesh is so oily that a ten-pound fish will yield nearly a quarter of clear white oil.* Salton Sea Beach gets platted; tourists plunk down their dollars and become speculators. One of the sea's many exotic attractions is Mullet Island, where a photo shows a pipe-smoking hatted man standing before a lightbulb-strung structure called **HELL'S KITCHEN**. I hope he makes a million.

By the end of the twentieth century, no Imperial County farmer I can find expresses any sentiment about the Salton Sea but indifference or disdain. Moreover, Mullet Island has been a peninsula since at least 1932.

Well, who could have guessed? The engineer Rockwood, who bears much of the blame for the Salton Sea accident, exculpates himself thus: *We have since been accused of gross negligence and criminal carelessness in making this cut, but I doubt as to whether anyone should be accused of negligence or carelessness in failing to foresee that which had never happened before.*

"SOUTHERN CALIFORNIA HAS MUCH WATER"

Speaking of unforeseen events, at the beginning of the twentieth century, the artesian wells of Artesia, California, begin to fail. Who would have thought it? In 1903, a certain Clarence Dougherty solves the problem for all time, installing *the first centrifugal pump, driven by a gas engine,* an innovation *soon followed by many others. These pumps . . . furnished a plentiful supply of water for several years.*

In 1904 a professor in Claremont, California, having chatted with *thoughtful men,* detects some *misgiving* on their part, because with all the pumping going on, the water table has begun to drop. Fortunately, *if we note the records of the past we discover that we have had ever and anon years that gave a great down pour. We may safely expect another of these very soon, I feel sure. Thus the men that plow in hope and faith, I believe will not reckon without their host.*

In 1915, the ever-trustworthy Mr. Rockwood reassures us all that *there is ample water for the irrigation of every acre of available land, including Mexico. If this is the case, you are greatly benefited, not injured, by any increase in the irrigated area across the line. The insinuation that the "Otis-Chandler" syndicate influenced the adoption of this plan, if true,* should therefore be cause for gratitude. So let the water flow!

In 1917, twenty-three years after a fellow in Indio pierced the ground and made the region's first artesian well, a circular for settlers assures us that *practically twice the present area can be irrigated from wells if the water is rightly handled and conserved.* One had better hope so, for *all* Coachella water is artesian in that period, the wells being from a hundred to more than half a thousand feet deep, and giving nine to fifty inches of sweet water. (Down in Imperial County, only Holtville possesses decent wells.) In 1918, the Coachella Valley Water District frets about certain artesian wells *being exhausted.* In 1922, the Water District reports *an overdraft on the artesian basin of 15,000 acre-feet.* Indeed, Coachella's water table has fallen seven feet in the last five years.

Between 1922 and 1925 alone, the State Engineer reports a drastic sinking of groundwater in Southern California. In some places this decline is as much as fifteen feet. Hence the fate of Clarence Dougherty's innovation: *As the water levels receded, this type of pump became obsolete, larger wells were drilled, and today [1932] water is drawn from greater depths by electrically operated deep well pumps.*

In 1925 the Honorable John I. Bacon, Mayor of San Diego, warns the United States Senate that *we have, to-day, about four years' supply of water ahead, and we are praying for rain this winter, because if we do not get it I do not know where we will be.*

And what about Los Angeles? The famous and infamous William Mulholland genially informs the same gathering that *in the last two years we have been close to the edge two or three times.*

> THE CHAIRMAN. Has the city exhausted all the water supply in the Owens Lake country?
>
> MR. MULHOLLAND. Yes, sir.

All the same, I read in the latest issue of my *California Cultivator* (1925) that here in the Golden State all is golden: *We have about 30,000,000 acres in farms, 4,250,000 under water, other millions to be brought under the ditch. We produce from $500,000,000 to $1,000,000,000 of agricultural wealth each twelvemonth.* (Meanwhile, on the next page, I read that the water table in the Fillmore section of Ventura County is falling; we'll have to deepen our wells.) In 1926 I find the following headline in the *Imperial Valley Press,* which as it turns out is simply making the point that Southern California possesses more water reserves now than a year ago; the phrasing, however, is emblematic: **SOUTHERN CALIFORNIA HAS MUCH WATER.**

Chapter 79

THE MEXICAN USER IS A CUSTOMER, NOT AN OWNER

(1904–1918)

Anything can be removed from water except salt and politics.

—Leon B. Reynolds, Professor of Sanitary Engineering, 1930

Fortunately, **WATER IS HERE**. In 1904, the Secretary of the Interior authorizes the Reclamation Service to commence Laguna Dam. It will be forty-seven hundred and eighty feet long and two hundred and fifty feet wide. *Now that modern irrigation methods are conducted on a large scale, the dam of Assouan is matched by that of Laguna.*

You're saying that Laguna isn't good enough? In 1918 Judge Farr's history of Imperial County assures us that *the construction of a series of huge reservoirs* sucked from the Colorado *is now under contemplation*, a deed which *would be sufficient to irrigate all the irrigable land below the Grand Canyon in Colorado, Wyoming, Utah, Nevada, Arizona, California and New Mexico, leaving a vast surplus for Mexico.**

In 1925, the Imperial Irrigation District's Calexico director repeats: *I believe that if the river is controlled and conserved, that there will be sufficient water for both sides,* meaning Northside and Southside. But regarding Southside, a member of the Colorado River Control Club elaborates: *The Mexican user is a customer; he is not an owner.*

*The Colorado has been bridged at Yuma for only five years. Catarino Mesina still finds it profitable to run a stage line from Mexicali to the river's mouth; I suppose that Laguna Dam and Imperial's thirst have not yet narrowed the Colorado into finitude.

Chapter 80

MARKET PRICES

(1925)

My country is abundant in wheat, maize, beans, cotton, tobacco, watermelons, calabashes, and cantaloupes . . .

—Palma, Chief of the Yumas, to Bucareli, 1776

Coachella green beans were going for twelve to fourteen cents a pound, while Kentucky wonder beans were going from eighteen to twenty cents. *Local Imp[erial] cucumbers 2.25 to 2.50 per lug.* Tamerlane's warriors come galloping into the square, but who says they're the enemy? We're going to sell them lettuce! *Lettuce: Local: Best, 79@90; poorer, 60 per field crate. Imperial Valley: all sizes. 2.00@2.25; few, 2.50 crate.* I have never been cheated out of a dollar in my life. You could buy tomatoes from Mexico, and Mexican peppers, too, of course, especially chili peppers. Now for cattle. *Steer prices advanced generally 25@40 over a week ago. The week's top on steers was 9.50, for five cars of good 1,181 pound Imperial Valley fed bullocks, establishing a new high mark for the current year. The price spread of 8.50@9.25 took in the bulk of steer offerings, mostly 885 to 1,250 pound Imperial Valley, Utah and Texas fed, although a few lots of more desirable kinds cleared from 9.34@9.40.*

These price quotations on the Los Angeles market, what do they say about Imperial? Well, we certainly need have no fear that our lands will not become better and better as the years go by.

These are the actual prices obtained between 7 and 8 o'clock, March 30, 1925 . . . Terms: Cash on the walk.

Chapter 81

SAN DIEGO

(1925)

. . . and then I shall return to the solitary church in that enchanted world . . .

—J. G. Ballard, 1966

We hurled off her yoke back in 1907 and became our own county. All the same, throughout the first quarter of the twentieth century San Diego still shares with Imperial a single agricultural empire. In 1910, Los Angeles and San Diego are among the top six counties for corn production, while Imperial has achieved that same exalted rank for both kaffir corn and milo maize. (Meanwhile, Los Angeles and Riverside are up there for hay and forage; Los Angeles alone, for potatoes and sweet potatoes.)

How could this not continue forever? What could San Diego's progress ever entail but richer fields? In 1925 Escondido has already shipped out two hundred and fifty tons of tomatoes by April. A new fifty-thousand-dollar citrus packing house announces itself; a twenty-acre apricot orchard goes on sale in Oceanside. In 1936, *San Diego supports extensive ranches and groves of oranges, lemons and various agricultural products.* San Diego is nearly Imperial. *I doubt as to whether anyone should be accused of negligence or carelessness in failing to foresee that which had never happened before.*

Chapter 82

THE LONG DEATH OF ALBERT HENRY LARSON

(1903–1926)

> This is the spirit of the Imperial Valley. There is ability coupled with willingness, abounding health, mental, moral and physical, faith in the district leading inevitably to faith in oneself, and a cheerful optimism that makes life worth something.
>
> —Edgar F. Howe and Wilbur Jay Hall, 1910

WHY MY DATES ARE UNIMPEACHABLE

The death certificate of Albert Henry Larson, filed in the city and county of Imperial, tells us that he was a sixty-year-old farmer whose date of birth even the listed informant, his wife Elizabeth, didn't exactly know (or perhaps the coroner desired not to trouble her at this bad time; he had not learned her date of birth, either), that like the majority of the county's farmers he was white, that the names and birthplaces of his parents were also, as you might have guessed, unknown, that the address of the home he and Elizabeth had shared was *7 Miles No. West,* that he died on the thirtieth of March, 1926, and that the cause of death was as follows: *Jury Verdict: Suicide by shooting and slashing wrist with a razor.*

He had lived on that farm, or near it, for twenty-three years, and in California for twenty-six. Accordingly I will suppose that he arrived in Imperial in 1903, some two years after Wilber Clark. Miss Margaret Clark would then have been completing her tenure as postmistress, so I'd imagine she would have been acquainted with him just as functionaries of communication know everybody in little pioneer towns—unless, of course, the Larsons lived gloomily alone. Was Albert Henry Larson even married in 1903? Did a man whose parents remained *unknown* ever receive mail? Unlike, for instance, W. F. Holt, he is not listed in the Imperial County Recorder's index of grantors, 1851–1907, nor in the corresponding index of grantees. If he bought or sold land before Imperial became its own county, that transaction must not have been legally registered. And so I begin to wonder whether Paul S. Taylor's contention that from the very beginning Imperial County was meant to be an exploitative empire of vast acreages tended by migrant workers—call it a factory farm, or Chandlerscape—was a touch propagandistic. How many Mexicans, Japanese or Filipinos worked for Wilber Clark? We have no idea; very possibly none; the last we saw of her, his widow was a laborer. And what about Albert Henry Larson? Could he have become a capitalist bigshot without buying and selling land?

(On 13 August 1904, a Gustav Larson appears as the grantee in a real estate transaction with Charles W. Fernald; on 15 April 1907, a Gus Larson, who may or may not be Gustav, buys land from Nathan D. Nichols. What does this have to do with Albert Henry Larson? I wish I could take out my ouijah board and ask Judge Farr. Larson does not even show up in Farr's biographical index of 1918. Perhaps he failed to represent *the spirit of the Imperial Valley* in its most boosterish light.)

My hired genealogists hesitantly disinterred an Albert Henry Larson who was naturalized in Anoka County, Minnesota, between 1917 and 1918. Should we believe them? The birthplace is a three-letter masterpiece of illegibility on the death certificate.—Turning to Otis P. Tout, I discover only an Olaf Larson, who seems to have been a clerk. Howe and Hall inform me that a certain John Larson, *four and one-half miles northwest of Imperial, is the most contented man I ever met. He came to the Valley in 1902 with his friend Joseph Hanson . . .* The date is almost the same; likewise the address; it would seem that he threshes his barley crop within two and a half miles of Albert Henry Larson. Does this Larson have a wife named Elizabeth? (As I implied, Albert Henry Larson remains obstinately absent from the county index of marriages from 1903 to 1923.) *A bachelor, with the passion for neatness of a man-of-warsman*—this is John Larson—*he has a home place scrupulously clean; so that one instinctively looks about for the woman who keeps it so.* It hardly sounds like our man. Certainly I wouldn't suppose Albert Henry Larson to have been the most contented pioneer in all Imperial.

Imperial is a hot flat diorama of this world, most of whose inhabitants live and die without a name. Imperial Hazel Deed, we'll never learn who she was. Wilber and Elizabeth Clark, did they consider themselves deserving of the Imperial encomium *he made a success through his own efforts*? And Albert Henry Larson, about him I can tell you scarcely more than I could about an illegal Chinese laborer who lived and died in a tunnel under Mexicali. What is *the spirit of the Imperial Valley*? What is the spirit of this world?

In the photographs of Hetzel, who arrived in the Valley a decade after Larson, the canals are wide and there are herds of dark horses on white sand, not to mention dark cows on salt-and-silver fields. Men in brimmed hats buck hay bales on the beds of horsedrawn wagons, and one horseman, who for all I know could be

Larson himself, clasps his hands together with the reins between them, the gesture strangely combining utility with worshipfulness. Faded cowboys lead their fading herds across bleached desert prints. It would be too easy to say that they are all gone; even now Imperial County beef brings in the silver dimes of American success.

A man in boots and waders stands in muck. He reflects himself in irrigation rivulets. Oh, yes, Imperial's all parallel lines; Imperial is water-furrowed all the way to the horizon. What if this uncaptioned old photograph were of Albert Henry Larson? Since what made his story begin for me was his end (I was flicking randomly through ancient death certificates in El Centro, and caught him), I imagine him as the antithesis of Judge Farr's Wilber Clark; a failure, a tired man without books or a date orchard, a man whose life must have for whatever reason become a long death. And I want to know why.

Bearded men stand raptly admiring their own huge sugar beets. (There is something masturbatory about this image.) A satisfied pioneer stands stalwart between stalks of his own sugarcane-forest. Did Larson experience seasons like this, when he could have believed in unlimited improvements?

The *Imperial Valley Business and Resident Directory 1912–1913* does inform us of the existence of a

Larson, Albert H, rancher, R F D No 2 bx 77, Imperial, r 6 mi NW.

Six miles or seven miles, who cares? The death certificate shows signs of haste. Or did Larson change farms? In that case, why can I not find him in the list of grantees?

Two years later, the directory has consolidated and improved Wilber Clark's address from a vague place in Mobile to Elder Ditch in Seeley; but Albert Larson's address remains unchanged; it's "northwest of" but not anywhere in its own right. Perhaps land speculators have scarcened in that vicinity now that El Centro won the contest for county seat. I have been out there, staring down into a stock farm from Larsen Road, vainly guessing at the suicide's former whereabouts (for on that day the County Recorder's office was closed), and the land seems fertile enough, thanks in part to proximity to the New River flood, whose gorge is even wider and deeper here than in Mexicali. **Rancher, R F D No 2**, and *suicide by shooting and slashing wrist with a razor;* what else is sure? I've found a Larson's Road in County Assessor's Mapbook 43; but which Larson was that named for?

Come 1920, Larson's address finally gains the spurious exactitude of Wilber Clark's:

Larson, Albt H r Wideawake Sch Dist nr New River P O bx 635 Imperial

Wideawake appears on Thurston's map (page xv), west of and equidistant between Imperial and El Centro. Larson would have almost been Wilber Clark's neighbor. Perhaps the two men met at Roth and Marshall's Feed Store in El Centro; perhaps their Elizabeths once sat side by side at a Fourth of July barbeque in Holtville. P. C. Johnson, who bought up much of Larson's land after his death, is described by the County Recorder as a dairyman; *he* certainly knew the dairyman Wilber Clark; that zone of American Imperial was a small flat world.

Elizabeth Larson, formerly and later known as Elizabeth Black, must have lived in the neighborhood for years, since on 26 November 1923 we find the County Recorder announcing an action in California Superior Court filed by Eleanor Clark, plaintiff, against seventeen defendants, four of whom are John Does, two of which are banks (there is also a mill and lumber company) and one of whom is Elizabeth Larson. Their mortgage—two adjacent lots in Imperial Townsite—had gone into foreclosure back in December 1917. Perhaps these entities and individuals had speculated together on the commercial prosperity of Imperial. Elizabeth Larson must have gambled in a very small way, which implies no grand capital on her part; and as we've just read, she lost the gamble. In any event, a year before Eleanor Clark sued her, she had already made her mark on the other side of a bad mortgage, in a noticeably peculiar transaction: Albert Henry Larson somehow received the appointment of California Superior Court Commissioner, for the purpose of selling to his own wife, for $3,121.85, lawful money, sixty foreclosed acres regarding which Elizabeth had been plaintiff against three Donleys.

On the eighteenth of April, 1924, an Albert H Larson pays cash for a parcel in Imperial township. See the direct gaze of the confident man! In June of that year, T. A. Brumbelow and Albert H. Larson, *by occupation Ranchers,* appear in a sad document whereby *the said mortgagers mortgages* [*sic*] to Farmers and Merchants Bank for ten percent per year *all that certain personal property situate and described as follows, to-wit:*

`One (1) roan horse, 4 yrs. old, weight 1400 lbs. branded (AL) on left shoulder`

and a black horse, a black mare, a bay horse, two sets of double harnesses, a cow and a calf, a wagon, three ploughs, *the entire crop of corn, consisting of about twenty acres and the entire crop of cotton consisting of about forty acres,* etcetera, etcetera, all of which *shall be kept and cared for on Larson Ranch,* since they no longer belong to Larson and Brumbelow, at least until they have been redeemed for three hundred dollars in gold coin, which is to say less than half the going rate of a Buick touring car, the collateral on the very next chattel mortgage in the County Recorder's book. Three hundred dollars, yes—oh, and that ten percent. If Larson and Brumbelow default, why, the Farmers and Merchants Bank *may take possession of said property, using all necessary force to do so.* I have never been cheated out of a dollar in my life.

This time Larson squeaks by; he must have even succeeded in paying off Brumbelow (who like the other people in this chapter fails to appear in Otis P. Tout's celestial index); for in 1925, a Deed of Trust on essentially these same mortgaged acres is conveyed to Albert and Elizabeth Larson, who will manage to avoid taking out any new chattel mortgages. Mindful of the impending suicide, I wonder whether the formalization of this transaction implies anything about the closeness of man and wife: They appeared on different days before different notaries.

In the same year, 1925, the Senate Committee on the Colorado River Basin issues its report, into the second of whose two hardbound volumes the Colorado River Control Club, which opposes digging any All American Canal but could live with a dam, submits a memorandum. Among its members we find two names:

Larson, Albert H, 76.62 acres valued at $3,740.00
Larson, Elizabeth, 90 acres valued at $2,000.00*

(Wilber Clark's name is absent.)

Perhaps the Larsons believed their irrigation assessment to be already high enough. But how could they trust that Colorado or New River floods had finally been taken care of? On Imperial County Assessor's Map 12-12, where Westmorland Union meets Westmorland, the New River squiggles toward the Salton Sea, then suddenly and finally makes two inhumanly straight bends labeled **NEW RIVER CUT 1924**. Perhaps that was good enough for Albert Henry Larson. In 1926, however, another levee would break, flooding bits and pieces of Mexicali once more, and—one would think—endangering any property in **Imperial, r 6 mi NW**. So life would and must go, until the Colorado got utterly *smoothed out.*

Had Larson invested in the Chandler Syndicate's Mexican lands? *That* contingent did not support the All American Canal, which would render their water rights worthless. I have not succeeded in finding any roster of Harry Chandler's stockholders, so I cannot tell you. Larson's motivation in opposing the canal, like his other thoughts and drives, will never be revealed to me.

I keep wondering whether his suicide had anything to do with *the spirit of the*

*Presumably Elizabeth's acres, which she will sell off in late 1926, are the Donley lands which her husband had conveyed to her as Superior Court Commissioner. They lie in Township 15 S, Range 16 E, Section 35, and the Larson Ranch consists of either four or five lots over in Range 13 E, Sections 4 and 5.

Imperial Valley. In this period the U.S. Department of Agriculture expresses worry about the way the development and agriculture land, which used to result from individual will, now takes place *under the guidance of private agencies engaged in promoting the settlement and sale of land for profit.* Mr. Holt's various syndicates, and the California Land and Water Company in Los Angeles (which shows such kind care for Brawley's future), not to mention the Colorado River Land Company, do any of these fit the bill of accusation? *I have never been cheated out of a dollar in my life.* The USDA continues: . . . *numerous agencies, whose volume of business is very great, are preying on the impulse to buy farm land* . . . The USDA laments *the results in misdirected investment of capital, futile labor through years of unavailing struggle against hopeless odds, and consequent discouragement* . . . What wore Larson down? Was Elizabeth about to leave him, or was it business that destroyed him, or was he ill?

On the day of Larson's autopsy, Jack Armstrong is selling forty acres for three hundred dollars, half of which is *under ditch and easy to level.* **WATER IS HERE**. *We need to have no fear that our lands will not become better and better as the years go by.* Meanwhile, Armand Jessup has two addresses, one in San Diego, the other in Seeley; he has a hundred acres of ditched and leveled land for sale, rent or trade; evidently any arrangement would be better than the one he has. Is he an Imperial sellout or a San Diego speculator? On the thirtieth of April, a notice informs us that H. L. Boone is holding a closing out sale on all his horses, his twenty cows, his mules, his trucks and even his slop cans, with six tons of head corn thrown in. *NOTE—Mr. Boone has leased his ranch and everything goes.* It's just another die-off. It's natural. I guess we all feel sorry for 'em.

(That last sentence, expressed, as you may remember, by Border Patrolwoman Gloria I. Chavez, referred to illegal aliens. Officer Dan Murray on a related subject: *They do work Americans wouldn't do.* And on this hot California day, as I meditate on the long death of Albert Henry Larson, I wonder whether Mexican ranchers and *ejidatarios,* given the land and crops that Larson possessed, would have failed as he did. Who was he? Again I ask, and again, why did he kill himself? Had he reached *the results in misdirected investment of capital,* in other words unlucky speculation, or did he take up gun and razor after *futile labor through years of unavailing struggle against hopeless odds, and consequent discouragement?* In either case, what might the defeats of all these Anglo farmers say about the Imperial idea?—Probably nothing. Most Imperialites don't kill themselves.—And never mind the *unavailing struggle against hopeless odds, and consequent discouragement* that a Mexican field worker may or may not face in the Imperial Valley while he sells his youth and strength for piecework; after all, *they do work Americans wouldn't do.* Why did this become the rule? Can field workers perform any tasks that Wilber Clark and Albert Henry Larson would have declined? When are homesteaders succeeded by growers?)

Now Larson's listed domicile has become Rural Route 1, Box 37, Calexico, but the address on the death certificate, *7 Miles No. West* of Imperial city, renders his sojourn in Calexico all the more provisional. Was he trying one last business venture, perhaps something to do with Southside, before finally returning to stare down death at Wideawake? Meanwhile he buys another lot near the Larson Ranch.

Less than two weeks before his suicide, Larson proceeds to the County Recorder's office and makes an official declaration of homestead. The listed acres are, as usual, *7 Miles No. West* of Imperial.

THE BACKBONE OF THE NATION

Larson would have been born at the end of the Civil War—out of California, I presume. (Seventeen Larsons are listed in the 1870 California census, from Andrew to Peter S., all white males, one from Los Angeles, one from Copperopolis. There are also nineteen Larsens. None is our man.) When he came into Imperial he would have been thirty-seven or thereabouts. He had slightly more than a third of his life left to live.

Life, and especially Imperial life, is a narrow, precarious thoroughfare in the midst of arid death, like the dark double tier of the old plank road, winding across the sand dunes, with Signal Mountain on the horizon; that used to be Route 80.

He got no obituary in the *Imperial Valley Press,* but shortly before Larson's suicide, a French economist wrote: *The industrial wealth of the United States must not deceive us. Agriculture is still the greatest American industry. That is why the farmer is the prime element, one might say the backbone of the nation.* So now we know what he was.

No, he lacked an obituary, although I did come across an ad for Rin Tin Tin, starring in "The Night Cry," and on Thursday, May 6, the following was reported: **MRS. LEROY HOLT HOSTESS AT TWO PRETTY AFFAIRS.** Life goes on, doesn't it? Fred Nebel Than has already set off *for eastern points to boost the sales of cantaloupes throughout the country;* last year he did the same for lettuce. On the day that Mrs. Holt's pretty affairs astonish the world, the first trainlot of cantaloupes rolls out of El Centro; and Southern Pacific brings twenty thousand refrigerator cars to bear for the biggest cantaloupe season in history.

Reader, do you want to know what a real Imperial image looks like? Here we go: A year after Larson took up gun and razor, we find five girls in knee-length skirts posing amidst the produce crates of Jack Brothers and McBurney Co., known for their GOLDEN QUALITY brand. The photograph is captioned Brawley, California. The two young ladies in front are holding bristling fans of many gleaming carrots; the rightmost and leftmost in the back hold melons, and the middle one, the straightest, properest girl, whose black bangs have been cropped perfectly even and whose stockinged legs are welded politely together beneath the dark skirt, cradles on her lap a monstrous ball of kale or spinach. This must be *the spirit of the Imperial Valley*. And I somehow still believe that if I were to prowl round and round this epoch as I did the Chinesca, I would finally discover some tunnel into the Imperial's underside where Larson's death has left us messages in a rat-gnawed desk.

LAVENDER

Larson is gone. We need have no fear that our lands will not become better and better as the years go by. In the old cemetery on the outskirts of Imperial I see Greenleaf, Ingram, Wood. I cannot find any Larsons. Albert Henry Larson, as it happened, was autopsied and buried in El Centro. In keeping with the apodictic certainty of those days that Imperial would soon be a citrus paradise, the name of his undertaker, who doubled as coroner, was B. E. Lemons. They interred him on April Fool's Day. What about Elizabeth? Where might she reside nowadays? Well, there are many almost obliterated inscriptions on the flat reddish earth. By 1929 she had sold all her acres and his. Greenleaf, Ingram, Wood . . . Markers are missing. It is very flat and empty, hot and dreary. A nearby lavender field is singing out perfume at a hundred and sixteen degrees.

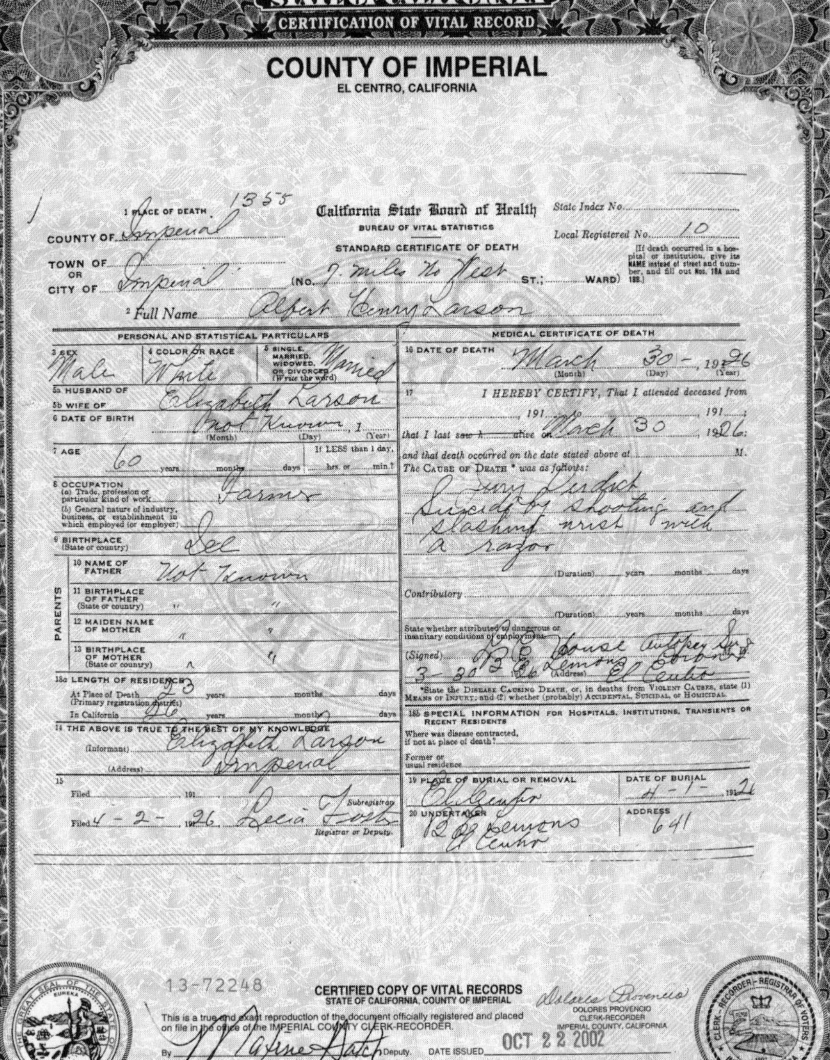

STATE OF CALIFORNIA
CERTIFICATION OF VITAL RECORD

COUNTY OF IMPERIAL
EL CENTRO, CALIFORNIA

1355

California State Board of Health
BUREAU OF VITAL STATISTICS
STANDARD CERTIFICATE OF DEATH

State Index No.
Local Registered No. 10

1 PLACE OF DEATH
COUNTY OF Imperial
TOWN OF OR CITY OF Imperial (No. 7 miles No West ST.; WARD)
[If death occurred in a hospital or institution, give its NAME instead of street and number, and fill out Nos. 18A and 18B.]

2 Full Name Albert Henry Larson

PERSONAL AND STATISTICAL PARTICULARS

3 SEX Male
4 COLOR OR RACE White
5 SINGLE, MARRIED, WIDOWED, OR DIVORCED (Write the word) Married
5a HUSBAND OF
5b WIFE OF Elizabeth Larson
6 DATE OF BIRTH Not Known
7 AGE 60 years
8 OCCUPATION (a) Trade, profession or particular kind of work Farmer
9 BIRTHPLACE (State or country) Swe
10 NAME OF FATHER Not Known
11 BIRTHPLACE OF FATHER (State or country) "
12 MAIDEN NAME OF MOTHER "
13 BIRTHPLACE OF MOTHER (State or country) "
18a LENGTH OF RESIDENCE At Place of Death 23 years; In California 26 years
14 THE ABOVE IS TRUE TO THE BEST OF MY KNOWLEDGE
(Informant) Elizabeth Larson
(Address) Imperial
15 Filed 4-2-1926 Lecia Foster, Registrar or Deputy.

MEDICAL CERTIFICATE OF DEATH

16 DATE OF DEATH March 30, 1926
17 I HEREBY CERTIFY, That I attended deceased from 191 to 191; that I last saw h alive on March 30 1926; and that death occurred on the date stated above at M.
The CAUSE OF DEATH* was as follows:
Jury Verdict
Suicide by shooting and slashing wrist with a razor
(Duration) years months days
Contributory
(Signed) D.C. House Autopsy Surg.
3-30 1926 B. Lemons Coroner El Centro
*State the DISEASE CAUSING DEATH, or, in deaths from VIOLENT CAUSES, state (1) MEANS OF INJURY; and (2) whether (probably) ACCIDENTAL, SUICIDAL, or HOMICIDAL.
18b SPECIAL INFORMATION FOR HOSPITALS, INSTITUTIONS, TRANSIENTS OR RECENT RESIDENTS
19 PLACE OF BURIAL OR REMOVAL El Centro — DATE OF BURIAL 4-1-1926
20 UNDERTAKER B. Lemons, El Centro — ADDRESS 641

13-72248
CERTIFIED COPY OF VITAL RECORDS
STATE OF CALIFORNIA, COUNTY OF IMPERIAL
This is a true and exact reproduction of the document officially registered and placed on file in the office of the IMPERIAL COUNTY CLERK-RECORDER.
DOLORES PROVENCIO
CLERK-RECORDER
IMPERIAL COUNTY, CALIFORNIA
By Deputy. DATE ISSUED OCT 22 2002
This copy not valid unless prepared on an engraved border displaying the seal, date of issuance and the original signature of the Deputy.
ANY ALTERATION OR ERASURE VOIDS THIS CERTIFICATE

Chapter 83

SUBDELINEATIONS: SCROLLSCAPES

(1611–2004)

Imperial is ink on decorated paper. Imperial is the poetry anthology *Waka Roei Shu,* inscribed by Asuka Mosaki (1611–79). Imperial is, in short, a scroll of a fabulous landscape, gold on white: gold palmlike trees, gold rice dikes which might as well be lettuce fields, gold clouds. Imperial's wide landscape unrolls in either direction, potentially forever, dusty and hazy and sunny.

The *Waka Roei Shu* is but one of many treasures at the Tokyo National Museum. It is but one of Imperial's myriad scrollscapes.

Once upon a time at twilight, a dusty wind began to rise in Mexicali. It soon became a rainless storm whose cold flurries of dust attacked our eyeballs, ears, nostrils, teeth and throats; our hats blew off; we had to squint almost to blindness. People ducked their heads; awnings were shaking; and that taste of Imperial dust saturated our mouths, not unpleasantly. With stinging eyes we watched signboards blow over. By eight the dust had mostly fallen wherever it was going to fall on that occasion, and there remained merely a cold wind, depositing the occasional mote in our eyes to remind us of ourselves. That wind smelled of Imperial, which smells of dust. The prostitutes in the Hotel Nuevo Pacífico sheltered behind their glass doors; the prostitutes at the Hotel 16 de Septiembre withdrew far up their steep warm stairway, some of them reading as they sat on the stairs because who was going to visit them on a night like this? Besides, if anyone did come, they'd know it when he poked his head in. At the Hotel Altamirano I saw only one whore, who stood in the doorway a single step back from the sidewalk just as usual; she must have been tougher or more desperate than the others. She blew a half-smile my way, and my penis became as stiff as laundry which has been washed in Mexicali tapwater. At the taco stand outside the Playboy Club, the various bowls of guacamole, salsa, beans and chopped cabbage had been covered with plastic wrap, with a plastic spoon wiggling around in each dedicated hole. A customer's used plate blew off into the sky, and the taco man cursed.

It's progressing along real nice, the marina manager at Desert Shores had said in reference to the Salton Sea. And Imperial's night was progressing as nicely as a white plastic bag puffing and whirling down Avenida Juárez, white against black in meaningless semblance of a struggle; the stars shone patiently above it all once more, reminding me, no matter how cold I might have accidentally felt, of holes in Imperial's black roof, holes discovered and invaded by the glaring sun. After all, aren't stars suns? And the wind blew, and a cat hid beneath an angle-parked car in front of the Hotel Chinesca. An old lady made a special detour across the street in order to request money from me. I gave her two pesos.—*Magnífico,* she said calmly. Then two girls with long naked legs and big bottoms went giggling by, their hair lashing each other's faces, and the sidewalk fell silent; the archways dwindled down beneath their occasional incandescent tubes and reached their finish line, the barber pole, against which a bundled-up figure crouched, silhouetted almost hellishly; that was the whore who'd threatened to wait outside for me; she also wished to become a serial killer. In fact I'd looked for her a half-hour earlier—too bad she'd been off on business. Later I brought consolation money, arriving just in time to see her pinching her fifteen-year-old daughter, whom she was trying to sell; I couldn't be certain that the selling was wrong, but I disliked the pinching, so I walked quietly on around the corner to watch another awning blow over. A cowboy wandered across the street, swaying in the wind, and came to haven at the Restaurante No. 8 (Comida China). And so many more things happened that night that it would take a hundred nights to tell you; and next morning, going south on the highway toward San Felipe, I came to the grand ballroom and café El 13 Viejo, where I found the manager on a scaffold refastening the tarps which comprised its walls; the wind had come this far and farther; it had been infinite.

All these vastly important doings and happenings take up the tiniest bit of Imperial's fifteenth-century scrollscapes, which Nature painted with tautologically inhuman delicacy.

Indeed, there really *are* scrolls, almost: the Imperial County Assessor's maps! Many are credited to Geo. H. Derby 1854, R. C. Matthenson 1855, H. S. Washburn 1856, then elaborated on decade after decade.

In Niland 11–14, my consciousness flows through the East High Line Canal, then down the Southern Pacific Railroad to Yuma, after which, south of Niland, I reach the green-bordered tracts of Fidelity Citrus Growers No. 1, 2 and 3; Imperial Grapefruit Growers, Inc., and various other laterals named after letters of the alphabet; finally I come home to a minuscule point with the grand name Date City . . . Of these entities, the canal and the two towns remain.

In Map 13-17, where Sunset Spring meets Pine Union below the Third Standard Parallel South, I adventure into a blank grid whose legend reads *Drifting Sand Hills;* on Map 14-18 I encounter *Rolling Sand Hills.*

Please never forget Holly Sugar on Tract 178 No. 3—six hundred and forty acres on Map 14–14. That's still there. A migrant farmhand once told me that he had worked at Holly Sugar for a day, but whatever it was they used to make their product white made him feel sick.

In Map 15–15 I see Holtville in lower right, then Pear, and the corner of the page has broken off, but here is Meloland 42A Orange Tract as the Alamo River flows through Rosita Dam; then I let my dreams carry me up through squares, rectangles and occasionally rectangles with strange bites taken out of them; I dream myself through bygone Imperial, serenaded by the smell of old paper.

Chapter 84

IMPERIAL REPRISE

(1901–1929)

The sword created the shape of empire;
the chisel, the dead, the statues we inhabit.

—Veronica Volkow, 1996

1

The wonderfully fertile valley of the New River in the eastern part of the county is now being opened up . . . **WATER IS HERE**. *We are praying for rain this winter, because if we do not get it I do not know where we will be.* **WATER IS HERE**. **Water was in the ditches, seeds were in the ground, green was becoming abundant, and the whole area was dotted with the homes of hopeful, industrious, devoted persons.** *Soon the endemic flora will have been displaced largely by these foreigners.* "Opportunities for profit in dairying are greater in **IMPERIAL VALLEY** than in any district that I know of in the United States." *The essence of the industrial life which springs from irrigation is its democracy.* **Enterprise and enthusiasm have gathered with more vigor around Mexicali than around any other place.** *IMPERIAL COUNTY SHOWS RAPID INCREASE: Is Growing Rapidly Richer. Accepting the Tax Man's Appraisement as Evidence.* **A strong syndicate has been organized, with W. F. Holt as president.** *The club motto is, "The aim if reached or not, makes great the life."* So, sign the coupon and send it in *today.*

2

I can't help believing in people . . . I can't help believing in people . . . I have never been cheated out of a dollar in my life. There is no escaping the stereotype of an ideal agrarian world.

3

OUR TERMS ARE CASH. *It is in this regard—the pure democratization of the great irrigation systems—that the methods of the United States differ from those of all other nations, ancient and modern.*

4

The orchestra is making things lively as it does every night. *This has been the history of all artesian districts . . .*

5

The wonderfully fertile valley of the New River in the eastern part of the county is now being opened up . . . **Larson, Albt H** r Wideawake Sch Dist nr New River. **Jury Verdict: Suicide by shooting and slashing wrist with a razor.**

PART SIX

SUBPLOT

Chapter 85

ALMOST AS EFFICIENTLY AS WASHING MACHINES

(1891–1936)

So, then, to every man his chance . . . to every man the right to live, to work, to be himself, and to become whatever thing his manhood and his vision can combine to make him—this, seeker, is the promise of America.

—Thomas Wolfe, before 1938

What thing does our vision make us? Judge J. S. Emory, Kansas delegate to the Irrigation Conference of 1891, still held out for a democratic conquest of Arid America: *Four weeks ago I rode across a farm in Texas twenty-eight miles long, and I was sick . . . Why, I would be sick to my stomach if I rode down that valley in California, over those long miles owned by one man.* But the *California Cultivator,* whose articles and essays are ostensibly geared to agrarian democrats, keeps its stomach despite any one man's success. In a series called "The Call of the Hen: A Visit to the World's Largest Poultry Farms," we learn that Ed J. Callon up in Marin County owns twenty-five hundred laying hens and four or five thousand growing chicks. Well, who am I to begrudge Mr. Callon his kingdom? The promise of America, isn't that the promise of wealth? Haven't the excesses of the French Revolution shown that too much equality is bad for liberty? (This long parable of Imperial, and indeed much of the American story, proves for its part that unbridled liberty kills equality, but never mind.) Two years later, in 1906, the *Cultivator* makes more emblematic use of chickens, this time in an advertisement. *You have chickens,* runs the copy. *Did you ever consider them as machines—machines that make eggs? Did you see in a recent Sunday paper where hens were made to lay SEVEN TIMES THEIR OWN WEIGHT in eggs in a year?*

That sentiment quickly becomes the official line. In 1925, in an essay entitled "Where Are We Going?," the *Cultivator* extols *the great ranches of South America, where beef cattle are turned out almost as efficiently as washing machines from an Iowa factory.*

"EXACTLY OPPOSITE TO THE INDUSTRIAL REVOLUTION"

When I began to study the history of the period, my mind remained unbiased by knowledge. All I knew was that somehow Imperial County had altered from being one of the richest bits of farmland in the United States to the poorest county in California, and I couldn't fathom how.

John Steinbeck's *The Pearl,* set in Baja not far south of Imperial, is a parable about how lives can be ruined by wealth. When a poor man finds the pearl, everyone wants to get it from him; he becomes endangered and dangerous.

The great wealth of Imperial, the pearl whose discovery revived her parched silt, was the water to which one accident of geography, a second of relative seniority, and a third of American water law's generosity (left over from an epoch which believed, as had Judge Emory, in agricultural democracy) entitled her. And, like most of us, Imperial saw her water as a means, not an end. (Judge Farr: *The sleeper dreams of his rapidly ripening fruit and their early arrival in the markets to catch the top prices ahead of other competitors in less favorable regions.*) When exactly it was that Los Angeles and San Diego decided that buying Imperial's produce was the merest side game, that what really needed to be done was to take Imperial's water, remains a secret locked in the vaults of the respective water agencies. But when beef cows were just starting to be considered as somehow equivalent to washing machines, Imperial was neither endangered by nor dangerous to her neighbors, with the possible exceptions of various produce consortiums which could not hope to compete against her twelve-month growing season.

That was a once upon a lettuce time, when citrus still lived happily ever after. *He sold out at a fancy price.* But there now sprouted up two mutually exclusive problems for Imperial, and indeed for all American agriculture:

1. How can we maximize production?
2. How can we sell the resulting surplus?

We twenty-first-century consumers of genetically engineered soybean milk which comes in vacuum-sealed little plastic-or-paper boxes can see how those problems solved themselves: through the creation of imperial agribusinesses. *I would be sick to my stomach if I rode down that valley in California, over those long miles owned by one man,* but suppose a corporation owned them?

Well, let's not go gently into that good night! Let's close our eyes right up to the end! *The history of agriculture,* continues that 1925 explication of where we are presumably going, *is that the large holdings come first . . . As the population grows these* *large holdings are cut into smaller farms.* These in turn are cut still more . . . into city and suburban lots. This fact is particularly noticeable in California . . .*

And what might subdivision prove? Something quite reassuring to readers of the *Cultivator: The individual spinners, weavers, shoemakers and such industrial workers have long ceased to be and large scale operation is doing their work. But large scale farming operation is giving way to the agricultural producers. The agricultural revolution is working exactly opposite to the industrial revolution.* Thank God for that! *I would be sick to my stomach if I rode down that valley in California, over those long miles owned by one man.*

ECSTASIES OF A SAFEWAY FARM REPORTER

In 1936 that most unprejudiced source, the Safeway Farm Reporter, pays a call upon Mr. Charles Anderson, who owns an eleven-hundred-acre walnut farm near Stockton. Mr. Anderson takes time out of his busy, successful life to explain to us that *I don't believe it would pay nowadays to operate a big walnut holding like ours if marketing conditions were as they were some 15 or 20 years ago . . .* In other words, I have never been cheated out of a dollar in my life. *I am willing to give a good deal of credit to the new methods of retail food stores. Modern merchants like the Safeway grocers increase the demand for farm products . . . Compare the inviting, well-arranged stores of the Safeway type with the kind we can all remember.*

Well, bully for him and his big walnut holding! The agricultural revolution seems to be following the Industrial Revolution in his case, for which *I am willing to give a good deal of credit to the new methods of retail food stores.*

As for those *machines that make eggs,* well, what can we say about them but that progress continues? In 1953, their productive life lasts for three hundred and twenty-five days and a hundred and ninety-eight eggs. By 1973, their care and feeding and perhaps even their composition have been upgraded for a productive life of five hundred and twenty-two days and three hundred and thirty-four eggs. In consequence, I am proud to say that the average California chicken flock has increased from three thousand in 1950 to fifty-two thousand in 1970. In 1975 an "egg farm" in San Diego County will proudly describe itself thus: *Petitioner's operation is more akin to a light industry than to a farm, and Petitioner employs the latest engineering and computer techniques in an effort to maintain rigorous quality control over its product.* Petitioner's holdings: Two million chickens. Take that, Ed J. Callon! We need have no fear that our lands will not become better and better as the years go by.

*This was true in part. As we saw, California's Mexican land grants did get subdivided.

AN ENDNOTE ABOUT WATER

Had the Safeway Farm Reporter gone back in time to 1925 and dropped in upon a Coachella Valley rancher, physician and landowner named Doctor Jennings, he would have heard the same tune. When we look in on him, the good doctor is on the warpath against certain small-minded citizens who complain of an overproduction of farm goods, which they then point to as evidence that there is no earthly need for a Highline Canal to Coachella. *Most of the inability to dispose of farm products,* he aphorizes, *is perhaps not due to an overproduction, but rather to an improper distribution and improper marketing of such products.* This is what the orange-juice people will also say in time, and the broccoli associations, lettuce cabals, watermelon magnates, and finally (I suspect, although I cannot prove it) the water farmers. Doctor Jennings concludes, and I am sure that all Coachella stands with him (by the way, he happens to be a member of the Board of Directors of the Coachella Valley Water District): *We accept in theory and fact the principles of the Colorado River compact and expect to receive our benefits subject to its terms.*

Chapter 86

SUBDELINEATIONS: LETTUCESCAPES

(1922–1975)

> The main reason we cannot read these early texts is the fact that writing initially was nothing more than a means, more comprehensive than those employed before, of recording the details of economic transactions.
>
> —Joan Aruz, 2003

What might Imperial's signature crop be? Doubtless the confident men of 1912, who coined the slogan *IMPERIAL VALLEY: Cotton Is King,* would have proposed cotton, and we will give it a short chapter later—but cotton proved to be one of Imperial's many intermittent disappointments. Then what about sugar beets? According to Paul S. Taylor, it was the mechanized monoculture embodied by both cotton and sugar beets which brought Mexican migrant labor into being; but the history of the latter commodity in the Imperial Valley, delightfully soporific as our research might be, would need to account for the tragic fact that on occasion San Luis Obispo County, not Imperial, has grown the nation's earliest sugar beets. Dates, oranges and grapefruits, my three personal favorites, are all frivolous choices and must be confined to subdelineations at best.

I therefore propose either lettuce or cantaloupes. The first of these is a safely ubiquitous staple; the second, as you may recall, originates early enough to be found in most pioneer histories of American Imperial. Moreover, both of these bring Imperial particular lucre in the winter months, being among the so-called early crops which make her *The Winter Garden of America.* For cantaloupes that archive tiger Mr. Paul Foster furnishes the chart and commentary on page 532.

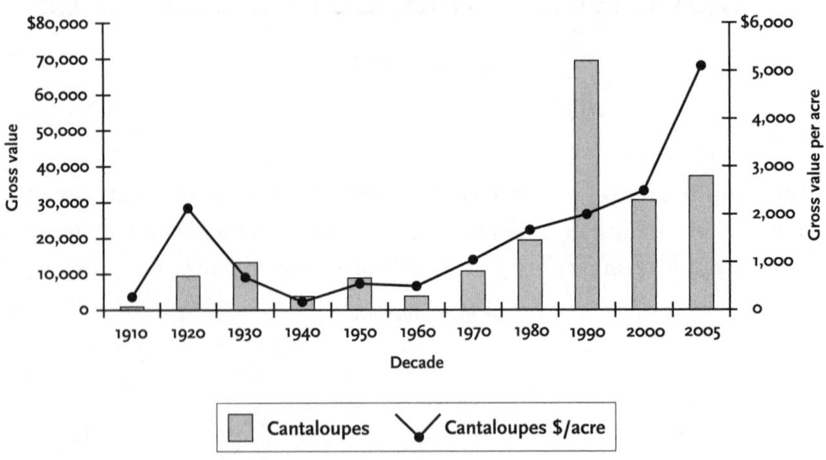

A startling contrast to dairy, Paul concludes. *This crop is the most obvious and consistent beneficiary of Imperial's two clear advantages: a long growing season and a consistent and plentiful water supply . . . With only a couple of exceptions (most likely due to crop problems or worldwide depression), cantaloupes and honeydews have been a remarkably stable and profitable contributor to valley agriculture. As with several other crops, Imperial is typically the first US growing region to bring these melons to market in the late fall and early winter, and improvements in per acre productivity have helped keep this niche crop remarkably profitable. This crop is also aided by the fact that almost all of it is picked during the cooler seasons, with the result that it's easier to find labor for the harvest.*

Cantaloupes are utterly Imperial, all right. And I do wish to take this after-dinner occasion to celebrate the fortitude of men in the Brawley Cantaloupe Growers' Association, who wear suits, ties and jackets for their group portrait in the heat of 1910. However, to quote from the historical record: *This is a lettuce hearing and we object to anything that relates to cantaloupes.* Hence the remainder of this chapter:

In 1922, the Horticultural Commissioner gleefully reports that *there were 12,000 acres planted to lettuce. The frost cut down the production but raised the price to unheard of profits.*

In 1924, Imperial County ships out nine thousand four hundred and eighty-nine carloads, more than half of California's total production. In 1925, *growers in the Imperial Valley are alarmed at the estimate of 30,000 acres of lettuce in the fall plant-*

ing, fearing overproduction. (Undeterred, Ed Miller ships out the first carload of lettuce ever from Blythe that year.)

Because of market conditions in 1934, the equivalent of 300,000 crates of lettuce *were unharvested in the Imperial Valley.* Therefore,* in 1935, the Valley cuts its lettuce acreage to less than half.

Suddenly Arizona has become Imperial's rival for winter lettuce! A quarter-century later, an Imperial lettuce man named Mr. Bunn will say: . . . *in the last few years Arizona has been stepping on our toes.* The two contestants grapple eternally.

The first trainload of Imperial Valley lettuce of the 1936 season departed on the third of December, 1935, and brought the impressive price of two dollars and twenty-five cents per crate. It arrived in New York city on the day after Christmas, there winning a wholesale price of three to three and a half dollars! But light demand, combined with heavy shipments from the arch-enemy Arizona, had already begun to press revenues downward. Almost a hundred traincars' worth of our dollar-colored crop ended up unharvested in the Valley. By the third of January, the cash price was merely eighty to eighty-five cents a crate for Phoenix lettuce-heads; the Imperial crop did slightly better at ninety cents to a dollar. The California Board of Agriculture consoled us: *Distribution of the 1936 crop in Imperial Valley extended to 263 cities in 45 states, the District of Columbia, and Canada.*†

Two years later it was worse, not just in Imperial but all over California, and the Board of Agriculture had to admit that *in most branches the returns realized were most discouraging.* The Director went on to complain about the *lack of harmony and lack of support for a marketing order on canning cling peaches. Producers were able to realize only the cost of harvesting their crops, whereas under a marketing order in 1937 they received one of the highest prices paid peach growers in almost a decade.*

What do you think caused those discouraging returns? After all, Imperial Valley enjoyed the vastest carrot crop ever, forty-three percent greater than the previous record, which had been set last year, and thanks to low competition, the growers did slightly better than break even. Cantaloupes likewise fulfilled the dreams of Imperial's pioneers, and so it was an acrimonious cantaloupe season, marked by arguments over whether or not to plough under a third of the acreage to reduce supply. Lettuce prices remained steady in Los Angeles, but that did Imperial no good. *The 1938 lettuce season was probably the most disastrous in the history of the*

*An anomalous shortage of irrigation water may also have affected this decision.

†Moreover, 1936 was the most lucrative year for cantaloupes since 1929—no matter that carrots lost money or barely broke even. Imperial's lettuce-gamblers had lost, but they would have been consoled if an economist explained to them that the booming rewards of our free market must sometimes be paid for by "corrections."

Imperial Valley. The quality was excellent, you'll be happy to know, but the soil was just too damned good! *The constant threat of heavy shipments . . . seemed to be the depressing factor.* (Jean-Jacques Rousseau, 1754: *I have seen men wicked enough to weep for sorrow at the prospect of a plentiful season; and the great and fatal fire of London, which cost so many unhappy persons their lives or their fortunes, made the fortunes of perhaps ten thousand others.*) After a lukewarm start at a dollar five to a dollar twenty-five, prices wilted to eighty-five cents to a dollar ten.* Almost all of the lettuce sold below cost.

In 1949, some of Imperial's gamblers must leave the casino table, for thanks to a freeze and a general price decline the total cash valuation of the county's crops decreases from the previous year's, but *the lettuce deal, due to seasonal conditions, was the exception,* the County Agriculture Commissioner consoles us. *Markets were steady and F.O.B. prices were a near high record from January to April when the season closed.* Imperial is truly America's winter garden. Lettuce revenues increase sixty percent from 1951 to 1952.

And in 1958, when market price is *a dollar and a quarter for the best,* at ten-o'-clock in the morning and not much more than a week before Christmas, a hearing on a proposed marketing order for winter lettuce comes to order in the Barbara Worth Hotel in El Centro.

WHO IS WHO

To set the scene, let us cast a quick eye all around the lettucescape.

This year Imperial Valley has shipped more than ninety percent of all American lettuce, and there is no reason not to refer glowingly, as does a certain Mr. Dannenberg, to *that particular period of time when Imperial Valley shipped three thousand two hundred and fifty-nine cars and the great state of Texas shipped six cars*—but the Valley's victory endured only from 6 to 20 February. Since winter lettuce is harvested between 15 November and 31 March, the Valley, unfortunately for its boosters, cannot be said to control the winter lettuce market at all.

Blythe holds perhaps twenty percent of Imperial County's lettuce acreage. The shipping season there runs from mid-November to mid-January, and then from late February until mid-April. So Blythe scarcely overlaps with the Valley.

The Valley wars with Blythe. Meanwhile, Yuma is the common enemy. Riverside and Los Angeles continue to be players.

*In 4-5-doz. crates, F.O.B., 6-doz. crates being priced lower.

THANKING GOD THAT WE ALL LIVE IN AMERICA

Among others, the above-mentioned Danny Dannenberg from El Centro is present; so is John Norton from Blythe (he owns land both at home and in Phoenix); Earl Nielsen of El Centro will rivet us all with his gnomic remarks, such as: *You may have too much lettuce which is not enough and not enough lettuce which is too much.*

The legendary Lester (Bud) V. Antle of Phoenix has also put in an appearance.—Do you remember what Richard Brogan said about him? I was asking when the family farm stopped being, in Brogan's words, *unrealistic* in Imperial, and he replied: *When lettuce became big here. When Bud Antle started making a million dollars off lettuce in a hundred days. The only people equivalent to that are the oil people.*—We are apprised that in 1956–57, Antle *owned and had interest in* four thousand six hundred and ninety-four acres in the Imperial Valley. In the following season his acreage had dipped by half (did he sell out at a fancy price?); now in 1958–59 it is rebounding slightly.

He says: Opponents have used in one of their arguments to smaller growers and smaller handlers of lettuce that some of us are trying to control the market.

Dannenberg asks him if *he* is trying to take control, which he denies.

Joe Martori of Phoenix, who admits that *well, I have an interest in lettuce, if that is what you mean, yes,* in California, in Phoenix but not in Yuma, and who also allows that *surely we right now are competitive with Imperial Valley and so is Yuma and so is the Gila,* feels that lettuce production dangerously exceeds demand. *Now, that is the situation as many of us see it in Arizona.* The Yuma Vegetable Shippers Association agrees with him.

Martori reiterates: Not only the production but the acreages are increasing all the time.

S. C. Arena from Phoenix says: If it keeps going like this I am going to go broke. He estimates the cost of cutting and marketing to be *up close to a dollar a carton just for packing lettuce.*

The oracular Earl Nielsen, who lives two and a half miles south of El Centro, wants a marketing order for a production ceiling. He has made the Valley his home since 1937 and grown lettuce since 1942. This year he left his lettuce field unharvested. He speaks like a stock market trader: *Blythe and Imperial Valley can control the market today on a downward trend, but they cannot control the market today on an upward trend.*

Mike Schultz of El Centro, acknowledging that over the last four years the Imperial Valley has shipped nearly three-fourths of America's lettuce, explains that 1954–55 was Imperial's last successful season. The following year was *disastrous,* thanks to the acreage increase; acreage increased again last year. This year he's kept about five hundred acres in lettuce. It eventually comes out that Mr. Schultz has done quite well on this commodity, at which point he coyly remarks: *I think it is common knowledge that I shipped a portion of my acreage to a gentleman in this room, and I made a slight—I saw a glut in the market, or thought I did—I sold my crop at a slight profit, or a good portion of it—up to that point I had a loss.*

The hearing officer then helpfully says: I must instruct the witness, however, that he isn't required to reveal any confidential data.

Reginald Knox, an attorney who represents *a number of growers and producers,* asks Mr. Schultz: Now, do you contend that the figures that you gave us for the period February 6th to February 20th 1958 are representative of the entire season of 1957–58?

I don't contend that at all, replies Mr. Schultz. I am just showing the period for which I am testifying.

Mr. Knox: You just wanted to show that during that particular period that the market was low.

Mr. Schultz: No audible answer.

Who are these gentlemen? Somehow they don't strike me as family smallholders. What is going on here? Why would Mr. Schultz wish to hide his profits?

Perhaps the testimony of Richard Campbell, who's been for fourteen years the manager for William B. Hubbard in El Centro *(and they have some operations in Arizona)* will supply a hint: *I think the record will show over the past ten or twenty years that there has been a steady increase both in the number of acres available in this area for lettuce and also the number of producers . . . And I think that the real problem in this thing has not been the fact that we have lost so darn much money, but it is the fact that we are making so much.*

Mr. Campbell is, in one adversary's words, *testifying against the Blythe group, and they constitute a group of seventeen shippers over there, nine of which ship in Imperial Valley.*

He wants lettuce to continue to be speculative because *when you reduce your risk you invite more competition,* and what canny agribusinessman craves that? He worries further that a prorate *will allow men with bad lettuce to put it out and men with good lettuce to lose some of it.*

At this, Mr. Kurht, the hearing officer, jumps in again: I think this testimony here that you have some sort of a voluntary prorate in effect is mighty dangerous for all of you, and I suggest that you just quit talking about it because you know that it is illegal . . .

What might be the difference between a prorate and a marketing order? In the latter course, the Department of Agriculture sets acreage limits. In the former case, which must be more in tune with the Imperial Idea, the growers do it themselves, without interference. That is also called *monopoly.**

Never mind all that! Mr. John Norton, Jr., believes that *this marketing order is necessary to preserve a reasonable correlation between supply and demand for winter lettuce,* a sentiment seconded by that exemplar of Imperial, Mr. Dannenberg, whose unctuous words, so appropriately spoken in the Barbara Worth Hotel, reinvoke the sacred Ministry of Capital: Profit is not only sacred, it's patriotic! To wit: *Collection* [*sic*] *action by farmers is as American as apple pie . . . We are finally going to vote on this in a democratic secret ballot . . . and I can't help but feel that we are still all lucky regardless of which way this comes out, because you came here in a democratic fashion, as Americans, and I think we can all thank God that we still live in America.*

Needless to say, the record reports applause.

*This distinction remains unclear to many of the attendees—for instance, Don Deol, who must be a small local grower, since none of these titans seem to know him and since he was born here in the Valley. He says straightforwardly and sincerely: "There are a lot of us that only grow forty acres of lettuce—thirty acres of lettuce—fifteen acres of lettuce. Now, if the market is eighty-five cents, or eighty cents or seventy cents, why, we stand a chance to lose, and there are a lot of them small little growers. But if we can have a program where it can be prorated then we'd at least have a chance to say to the companies 'well, take over my field and pack it and ship it for me.' "

Chapter 87

THE NIGHTS OF LUPE VÁSQUEZ

(2003)

. . . the highest honours within human reach may, even yet, be those gained by an unfolding of extraordinary predatory efficiency . . .

—Thorstein Veblen, 1899

You see that one with the big ass? God, she is beautiful! I want to dance with her and check her out. Usually it takes two dances or one drink to check them out, because not all of these girls are *putas,* you know. Some of them only want you to buy dances and drinks all night, spending your money for nothing. So I just say: Do you want to fuck? If no, that's it. She's fired. They appreciate that, because it saves their time. Where's that one with the big ass? I can't see her. Can you see her? Where is she? *Hola,* there she is! She's dancing with someone else, the bitch!

Chapter 88

IMPERIAL REPRISE

(1891–2003)

I can't help believing in people. *Did you ever consider them as machines—machines that make eggs?* And in material advantages they are already well supplied.

Why, I would be sick to my stomach if I rode down that valley in California, over those long miles owned by one man. He sold out at a fancy price. *IMPERIAL COUNTY SHOWS RAPID INCREASE. The constant threat of heavy shipments . . . seemed to be the depressing factor.* I am willing to give a good deal of credit to the new methods of retail food stores.

Because of market conditions in 1934, the equivalent of 300,000 crates of lettuce *were unharvested in the Imperial Valley.* She's dancing with someone else, the bitch!

PART SEVEN

CONTRADICTIONS

Chapter 89

CREDIT WILL BE RESTORED

(1929–1939)

"Credit will be restored and business will hum again—"

"When?"

"When Empire Valley wins a clear victory for the Boulder dam and the all-American canal. Then the bugaboos will disappear and prosperity will ride rampant."

—Otis B. Tout, 1928

In 1929, many, many dark, squarish automobiles lie angle-parked alongside the multiple archways of Brawley's main street, which is an almost textureless white in the sunstruck, timestruck photograph; I myself, coming to Brawley almost seven decades later, will never see so many cars parked there. *We need have no fear that our lands will not become better and better as the years go by.* American Imperial approaches her cusp. Mexican migration to the United States achieves a peak. More than fifty thousand railroad cars of produce pass clitterclattering out of the Imperial Valley every year! *He sold out at a fancy price.* Between 1919 and 1929, Imperial County moves up from forty-first to eleventh *in value of its agricultural production among all counties in the United States. In the past ten years, this county has made the greatest gain in value of its agricultural production of any county in the nation.* Imperial County is number one for lettuce, cantaloupes, melons, fresh vegetables! (Thank you, El Centro Chamber of Commerce.) In 1932, nearly three million unsold watermelons, a million and a half tons of unsold cantaloupes, and mountains of unsold tomatoes will be converted to waste, because if we once began to give our produce away to the hungry, wouldn't every sly rascal pretend to be famished? *I have never been cheated out of a dollar in my life.* But in 1929 the future's the merest black Rothkoscape whose darkness has no bearing on our emerald alfalfa-zones, our yellow-polka-dotted grapefruitscapes. Mr. Robert Hays announces: *The First Thirty Years of Imperial Valley's existence far exceeded in accomplishment anything which the most hopeful of its valient [sic] pioneers ever dreamed of . . . My vision beholds the greater Imperial Valley of thirty years hence, then as now conceded the most productive agricultural area in the world.*

Here comes Black Thursday and Black Tuesday; the stock market shrivels just as will cake-dough when you slam the oven door, but we don't care; out here in Arid America we have better things to do than read about another Wall Street panic.* In 1930 the monetary value of Imperial County's tangible property, at least as measured by the assessor's office, reaches a summit of $6,257,231. Out go fifty-seven thousand, seven hundred and one carloads of Imperial Valley products!

SEARCHES MADE FOR DEFENDANTS IN ALL DIRECTORIES

Imperial is men with hats, men with beards, sitting half a dozen at once in a horse buggy whose huge wheels are half sunk in the dirt; Imperial is a photograph captioned *Calipatria 1927:* the American flag waves over the dirt.—But now the bad years are upon California. Here's a photo from an album: hats on the table, bowed heads, men grim on courtroom benches, and a woman looking down as she writes. Men bend over paperwork. The title: *Sheriff's sale of foreclosed farm.*

The Imperial Valley directory for 1930 offers this advertisement as a sign of the times:

Attorneys, Attention!

Searches Made for Defendants in All Directories
Throughout the United States.

AFFIDAVITS FURNISHED.

Meanwhile, we're also advised of the following:

Confidence in the continued growth of Imperial Valley's wealth, industry and population . . . will be created as sections of this directory are consulted.

If only other Americans had consulted sections of this directory! Maybe then the year 1931 wouldn't have been worse than 1930. Next up: 1932 and 1933. *Because of market conditions in 1934, the equivalent of 300,000 crates* of lettuce *were unhar-*

*The great printmaker-muralist José Clemente Orozco was in New York when it happened, his already bitter sensibility sharpened by the Mexican Revolution, his feelings about Northside enhanced by the loss of a number of his drawings—officials of the United States had seized and destroyed them in order to protect citizens from their moral pollution—and so he reported on the crash with the same mordant coolness as he had done describing the disasters of his own country: "Office boys no longer bet on whether the boss would commit suicide but on whether he would do it before or after lunch." A Northsider—John Steinbeck, for instance—would have told the tale with more compassion. To a Southsider, it was simply what it was, and what Orozco kept seeing—queues of hungry bankrupts in the snow, "red-faced, hard, desperate, angry men, with opaque eyes and clenched fists"—did perhaps excite his compassion, but also, I should suppose, his cautious realism; he recognized class hatred when he saw it.

vested in the Imperial Valley. In 1935 the national unemployment rate will remain steady at almost twenty-two percent.

As for farmworkers, Paul S. Taylor concludes: . . . *the Depression . . . altered the political terrain, by reversing the actual flow of Mexicans from an incoming tide to an outgoing tide of unemployed.*

I'VE NEVER BEEN CHEATED OUT OF A DOLLAR IN MY LIFE

In a filing cabinet in the archives of the Imperial County Historical Society Pioneers Museum, a five-page typescript entitled "How It Feels to Be Broke at Sixty, or, High Finance in Imperial Valley" looks back upon its author's career with a resentment aggrandized by typically Imperial rhetoric into a eulogy for a historical mission betrayed:

I could see our little family as we had come on to [the] desert, years before. Wife and I in the prime of life, willing to work and sacrifice, that the forces of nature might be controlled; the desert reclaimed; our children educated and a little accumulated, for our old age, and perhaps something to give our children a start . . .

I could see the desert boundless . . . a vast sea of rolling sand . . . while the sun's rays danced and in the mirages [came] . . . buildings and ships and castles and mountains, creating scenes as awful as they were attractive.

I could see the sun as it appeared in the eastern horizon in the early morn, a big red ball of fire, the size or redness of which was never seen after vegetation began to grow . . . I could see the farm as it began to take shape and was being covered with cattle and hogs and barley and corn.

The farm must have been attractive; for Otis P. Tout informs us that *W. E. Wilsie's new home two miles west of El Centro was the finest in the Valley.* The Wilsies were close neighbors to Wilber and Elizabeth Clark.

I could see my wife in her kitchen about her daily work, Mr. Wilsie continues, *and the children as they became old enough, each taking their place, boys and girls on horseback, herding, in the milk yard, and in every way doing their share toward accomplishing the task that we had set out to do . . .*

I could see the development of . . . the greatest enterprise of the kind the world has ever known . . .

In short, **THE DESERT DISAPPEARS**. *"Moisture Means Millions."* **WATER IS HERE**. Then what?

I saw our fine ranch divided and sold through a system of profiteering and high financing, as shameful as it was unjust. I saw our three boys volunteer and set off for the war without a tear, but with a hearty Godspeed from their loyal, heroic mother.

But the profiteers, he bitterly notes, didn't send *their* boys.

I saw our fine ranch divided and sold. But isn't subdivision the name of the California game? In our introduction to the Inland Empire, the point was already made, and out of laziness I quote myself verbatim, that the history of Imperial, like that of California and the United States itself, may be summed up as follows:

(1) Exploration.
(2) Delineation.
(3) Subdivision.

By all means subdivide desert emptiness. For that matter, subdivide the Mexican land grants; those grand old delineations were made in the name of an obsolete alienness; Northside has taken over now! But when the Wilsie Ranch gets subdivided, please don't expect W. E. Wilsie himself to call that procedure *the greatest enterprise of the kind the world has ever known.*

Two points ought to be made about this sad document. The first is that it was written *long before* the Great Depression began. In fact, Mr. Wilsie lost his ranch during the war boom year 1916.

The second has to do with how the ranch was lost. Do you remember the direct gaze of that confident man, Barbara Worth's father? Mr. Holt is said to have loaned Wilsie a few mule teams; when he tried to return them, Holt said he didn't need them at the time. Later on, he presented his victim with a huge bill. *I have never been cheated out of a dollar in my life.*—But another story simply runs that Holt had nothing to do with it: Wilsie had planted too much cotton.—Reader, are you a leftist or a rightist? Take your pick of causes.

We often tend to think of the Depression as a shockingly unique event. But the Wilsie Ranch's epitaph for itself suggests otherwise. What are we to make of the characterization of Mr. Holt? After 1929's Black Thursday, the Ministry of Capital temporarily lost its good name. *Since 1930, the most despised and detested group of men in the Union is the bankers . . .*

In 1930, Henry L. Loud still hopefully advertises his real estate and insurance business from the Barbara Worth Hotel. Imperial County's hundred and one fruit-packing and loading sheds, her nine icemaking plants, her two hundred and forty miles of paved highway and above all her twenty-five hundred miles of irrigation and drainage canals still pulse and struggle; she is young yet; her organism can still fight. *I have never been cheated out of a dollar in my life.*

Chapter 90

MARKET PRICES

(1919–1931)

Sometimes it seems that Fortune deliberately plays with us.

—Montaigne, before 1588

Cotton almost reached forty-four cents a pound on the New York Exchange in 1919. In 1931 the low was five cents.

This two-sentence tale goes far to explain the class warfare that exploded in all sectors of Imperial in the 1930s.

Chapter 91

IN A STILL MORE ADVANTAGEOUS POSITION

(1928–1942)

> Of all the western myths, it is the myth of the family farmer, for whom the dams were claimed to be built, that has taken the longest to vanish.
>
> —Sandra S. Phillips, 1996

The Imperial Main Canal of 1901 was a hundred feet wide, which sounds awfully wide to me, but pretty soon it wasn't wide enough.

The novel which this book struggles to write, called *Once Upon a Time in Imperial*, takes place back when Imperial's canals were wider so that Imperial herself was lusher, bushier and more beautiful; as I persist in informing you, those days of the old photos were coming to an end. The good news is that everyone wanted them to, except for the Mexicans and the Colorado River Land Company.

In 1922 the Swing-Johnson bill was introduced. It passed in 1928.

You have already met Phil Swing. I should also introduce you to Mark Rose, "father of the All-American Canal," also director of Holtville's Imperial Irrigation District: youngish, a tight necktie and buttoned down collar, a tight-clenched mouth, baby cheeks; I would have picked him for a small-town reverend. Among its complaints against IID, the *Los Angeles Times* (in other words, the Colorado River Land Company) singles out *schemers or impractical dreamers of the Mark Rose type.*— But back to our hero: *Swing is energetic, popular and efficient; his ability being recognized by his fellow citizens who have made him secretary of his Masonic lodge.* That is a distinctly Imperial point of view. For entirely unknown reasons, the *Los Angeles Times* is less enthusiastic about him.

In 1920, the Imperial Irrigation District crosses the ditch to pay a call upon individuals ingenuously referred to as *the Mexican interests.* Their members, it seems, have been paying less for irrigation than Northside's ranchers. Mr. Allison of the Colorado River Land Company expresses willingness to let Southside's rents go up, which will lower American Imperial's acre taxes; unfortunately, Señor Luis Romero, deputy of the Mexican government, will not concur. Still, Mr. Allison (who hails, by the way, from San Diego and the Imperial Valley) holds out hope that the

Mexicans, if handled gently, can be brought around. He is well aware of the danger if they do not: They might be punished with *the All-American Canal and the denial of all Mexican rights,* meaning the very probable drying up of the Colorado River Land Company's cottonscapes.* The canal's proponents have, he well knows, *their own schemes, under the camouflage of looking after the valley's interests.*

Oh, Imperial and those wicked, wicked schemes of hers! In the drought year 1924, Phil Swing accuses the Colorado River Land Company of intending to irrigate its Mexican acres just as much as ever, while the good ranchers of Northside go thirsty. Immediately, the company dispatches a public letter to the Imperial Irrigation District, stating its happy acceptance of a fair pro rate cut in water deliveries. Indeed, such is the Chandler Syndicate's civic-mindedness that it has declined to order a single drop for its alfalfa until everybody has enough. Don't say they're not good Americans down in Mexican Imperial!

Cut to 1925, when the Senate Committee on the Colorado River Basin meets in the Biltmore Hotel in Los Angeles—a place which you and I have already visited, reader; we know it's even swankier than the Barbara Worth. The Honorable John I. Bacon, Mayor of San Diego, takes the floor to warn that the Colorado is silting up so much that in seventeen years it may back up and flood the Imperial Valley, which I suppose he worries about for sentimental reasons. We need an All-American Canal, no two ways about it!

E. F. Scattergood, Manager of the Bureau of Power and Light of the City of Los Angeles, sees the amount of electric power generated by the proposed Boulder Dam as comparable to that of Niagara Falls. He's for it, no doubt.

Now for the statement of William Mulholland: *Unless there is a dam, and unless there is a high and capacious dam that will regulate the flow of the Colorado River, this city will not be justified in having a thing to do with it.*

But the *Los Angeles Times* predicts that an All-American Canal will bankrupt seventy percent of the landowners in the Imperial Valley. I would predict that at this moment Mulholland and Harry Chandler are not friends.

On Mayday 1926, in a magnificent display of self-interest rightly understood, the Democrats of Imperial Valley join the Republicans in urging the President not to permit politics to further delay Swing-Johnson. The Associated Chambers of Commerce of Imperial Valley pass their own kindred resolution. Meanwhile, A. Giraudo sends the Hon. George E. Cryer the first crate of cantaloupes from his ranch in thanks for the latter's labors on behalf of Swing-Johnson, *which when con-*

*Another Northsider puts this more kindly: "Because it had a vested interest in the crucial resource that made its own lands economically useful" . . . the company became "the staunchest defender of Mexico's rights to an equitable share of Colorado River water at a moderate price—rights that some people north of the border contested . . ."

summated will undoubtedly be the greatest feat in human history. Well, isn't he right? A quarter-century later, Shields Date Gardens in Indio will describe its charms to tourists as follows: *The All-American Canal on the eastern shoreline is the old-timer's dream come true . . . A comfortable day's outing. Again carry grapefruit.*

Tuesday, May 4, 1926, page one: **ACTION IS ASKED ON BOULDER. Imperial County Supervisors Go On Record for Quick Action.**

Friday, May 7, 1926, page one: **BOULDER DAM BILL AGAIN DELAYED BY MEXICO QUESTION**, that is, Mexican rights to Colorado River water. *The need for money is desperate. Your dollars are the only way we can continue the fight . . .*

In October, the new movie version of "The Winning of Barbara Worth" premiers in Los Angeles, of all places, at a conference *to discuss the allocation of funds and distribution of water for reclamation projects.* Perhaps because of that, probably thanks to Los Angeles's *exhibit boosting the Boulder Dam* at Brawley's Imperial Valley Midwinter Fair, very likely on account of *your dollars,* and certainly in spite of Arizona's infamous filibuster of 1928, Swing-Johnson passes!

The Western Union telegram has been pinned to the flower-heaped table; a man in a necktie grins wide-mouthed, holding up one finger. Another man, plumper, who wears a tie and a white shirt, beams in front of an American flag. Lights have been strung across the scene, from a smoke tree to a pole. And in the foreground, the crowd gazes up at the grinners; most of them are men and they are holding their hats in their hands; **WATER IS HERE**.

That grizzled Imperial County farmer named Eugene Dahm told me with a shrug: I remember in 1934 there was a drought in the Southwest. There was so little water you could hardly get any in. The canal went fifty miles into Mexico but *they* were using water like there was no tomorrow; they didn't care about the gringos!

(*They* must mostly have been the Colorado River Land Company.)

In 1937 we moved to the ranch, said a lady named Edith Karpen, who figures in several chapters of this book. It was out at Mount Signal, eight miles out from Calexico, right by what is now right by the Woodbine Drop of the All-American Canal. One of the first events I went to, Jack took me out to Holtville, and they had a big celebration there, and it was celebrating the passage of the Swing-Johnson thing. See, before that, the water left the Colorado and went through Mexico, and of course when *they* got through stealing it, *we* got some back. So this was to have it on the American side. So the whole valley celebrated. You have no idea of the *spontaneity*! Someone would mention Swing-Johnson and everybody would get happy!

So they took the south end of our ranch for the All-American Canal, and you know, I remember watching them. And they had mules that pulled these scrapers!

That was the area in our section that was done by mule teams. A fella named Lee Little had the contract for that area. He lived out from Mexicali but he was an American citizen. It was a full section we had—six hundred and forty acres—before they started scooping away at it. Then it was about four hundred acres.

How did you feel about that?

We were happy.

She was happy, as were Swing, Johnson, America, Imperial & Co.! Early in the next century I find a social anthropologist looking back on this epoch and concluding that the All-American Canal was *from the very beginning* perfect, which is to say *an inappropriate answer to a misconceived problem*. Well, so what? We need have no fear that our lands will not become better and better as the years go by.

By 1931 El Centro's official map already gloats: *When new lands are added through construction of the All-American Canal, under the Boulder Dam Project, there will be one million acres of the most fertile land in the world, with El Centro as its center.** The Mexicali Valley might become a trifle *less* fertile as a result, but that's hardly Northside's business. In 1939 the Chamber elaborates: Our million acres, now revised to eight hundred and fifty thousand, will comprise *about one-fifth of all the land in California under the plow.*

On Christmas Eve of 1932 the first workmen begin to build a camp in Fargo Canyon, *signaling the beginning of work on the Metropolitan Water District aqueduct through the Coachella Valley.* And in the old map books from the Imperial County Assessor's office, I've seen a page from that very year, a hand-drawn bird's-eye snapshot of moneyscapes which sports a blackish fissure labeled in pencil *All American Canal—Coachella Branch.*

In 1934 Indio calls an "Aqueduct Miners' Day." That's the year I see Evan T. Hewes, President of the Imperial Irrigation District, at his desk, smiling, pretending to be about to write something, his fat pen poised above a document . . .

In 1940, first water comes through the All-American Canal. By 1942, the old Imperial Main Canal is dry.

PHOTOGRAPHS OF HEAVEN

I see still water on the very edge of the sky, reflecting blocky concrete towers with concrete arches between them, and a massive cylindrical assemblage boring through everything. The desert hills are low and distinct behind them, like the edge of the world. All is still; all is clean. These are the dam gates of the All-American Canal, and they double themselves upside down in the pool of liquid capital in

*Imperial County now holds six hundred thousand fertile acres.

IMPERIAL IR

WATER TR

HOOVER D

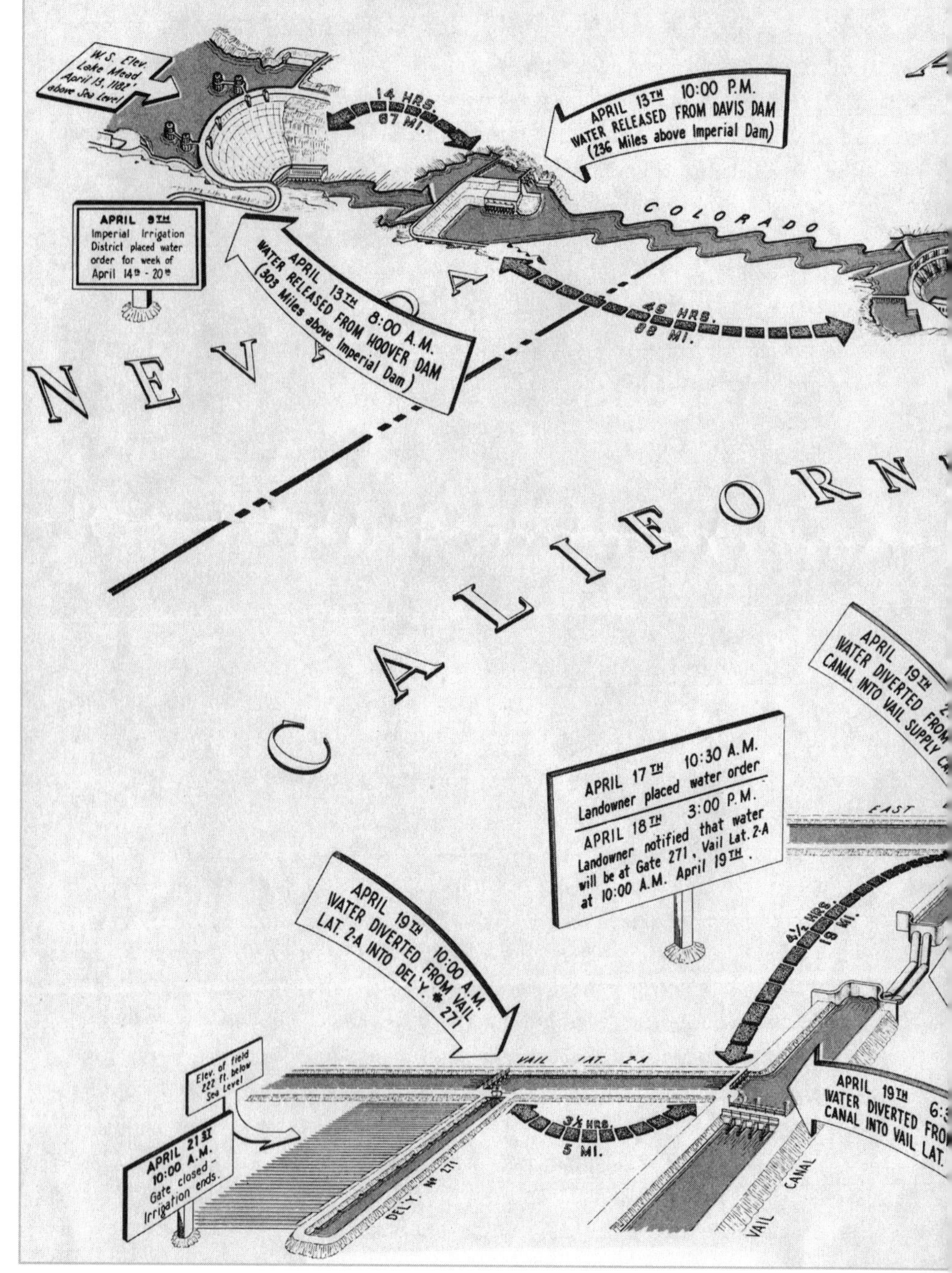

ON DISTRICT

SPORTATION

TO USER

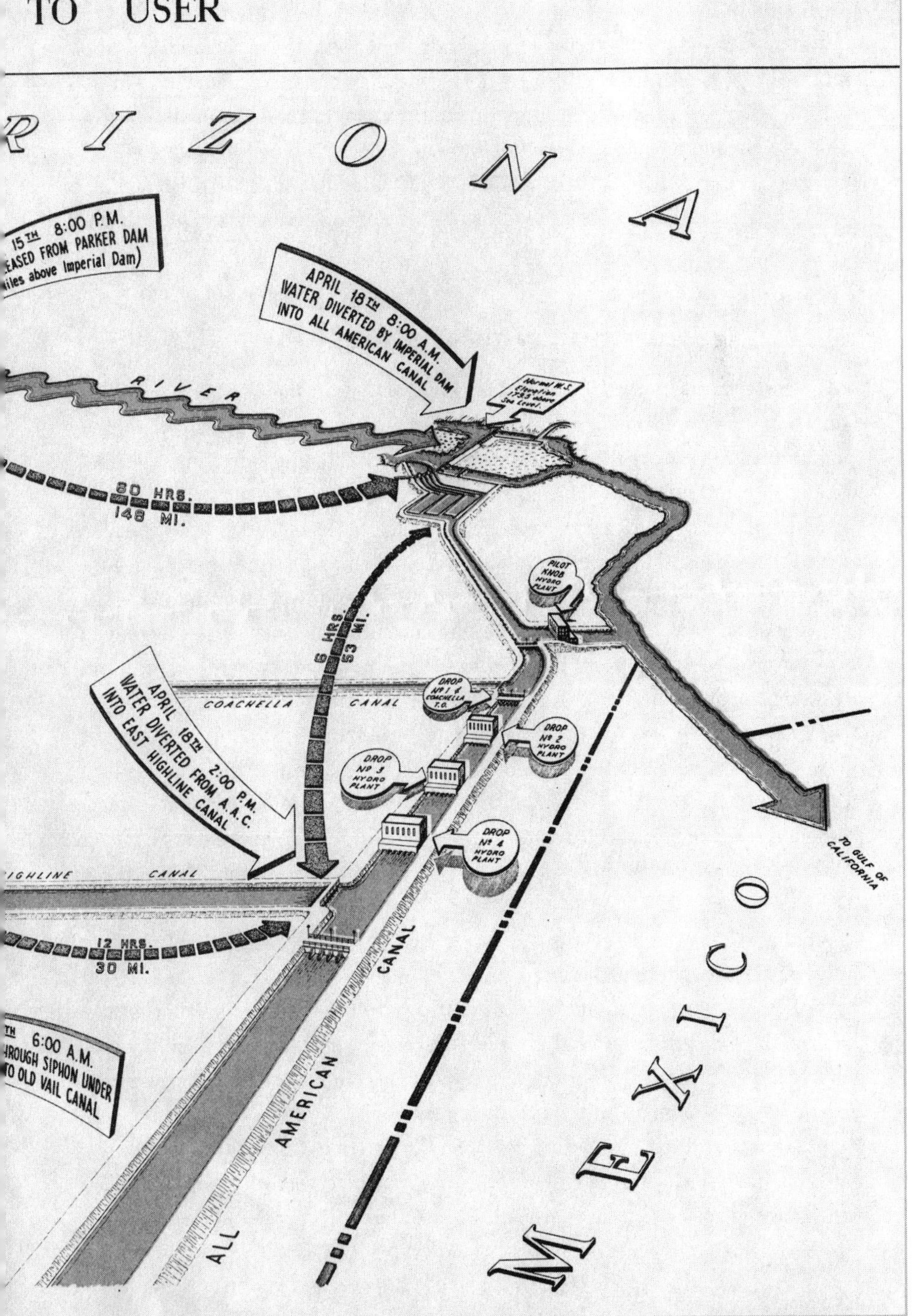

Horace Bristol's photograph of 1941. An aqueduct S-curves through the mountains for eighty miles, two hundred and thirty-two feet wide, filled high and clean with water that foams and ripples through the scrubby desertscape. We've conquered Nature.

Workmen stand mostly facing outwards on the upper level of a cylindrical concrete tower whose flat floor of timbers holds workbenches galore and whose inner wall is spiderwebbed with dark rods or cables which remind me of the jointed metal legs behind typewriter keys; this Bureau of Reclamation photo, dated October 1951, is stamped **BOULDER CANYON PROJECT** and **BOULDER CITY, NEVADA.** *We need have no fear that our lands will not become better and better as the years go by.*

"BOLDER THAN BRITISH DREAMS OF EGYPT"

With the practically limitless Boulder Canyon power now available, the city has been placed in a still more advantageous position. These words, of course, issue from the mouth not of El Centro or Coachella, much less Mexicali, but from Imperial's foe, lover, or threatening friend, Los Angeles.

No doubt there was trickery involved against the yokels of Owens Valley, maybe even a little rough stuff (Tamerlane's warriors gallop into the square); but I'm sure that the following words from *Babbitt* apply to every man involved, from the lowest-paid construction worker right up to Mulholland himself: *Then he goes happily to bed, his conscience clear, having contributed his mite to the prosperity of the city, and to his own bank-account.* Besides, the yokels weren't compliant. They kept on with dynamite. In return, Los Angeles was forgiving, merciful. In 1934, the city bought out the ranchers whom it had ruined. So that was the year of the last apple crop. *Today the trees that bore that crop are again white with blossoms, but the petals of these blossoms will fall on parched ground. The boughs will never more bend under their load of fruit. The water is gone. It flows southward to the Great City. Be it so. The sin is not ours.*

What next? Another aqueduct.

Imperial County, tranquil and removed, continues to dream her dreams of lucre. *The boughs will never more bend under their load of fruit* in the Owens Valley; but to the Imperial Valley, more water than ever will come. And so Imperial County prepares to draw up her yearly agricultural report. *These statistics were compiled by the Imperial County Board of Trade under the supervision of the Board of Supervisors,* explains a sheet entitled "1928 Statistics." So far, so good; this is how the county wants others to see it. *Anyone wishing further information concerning Imperial Valley farm lands and lands affected by Boulder Dam project may write Imperial County Board of Trade, Court House, El Centro,* again, so far, so good, but here's the peculiar part, *or may obtain it at Imperial Valley desk located in Chamber of Commerce Building, Los Angeles, 12th and Hill Streets.*

THE DESERT DISAPPEARS

Was that last hint too obscure? All right, then: In 1923, while the Chinesca burned and Imperial County readjusted its borders one last time, William Mulholland and company boated down the Colorado.—And Mulholland said: Well, here's where we get our water.

Sixteen more survey parties went out under his authority, investigating the respective merits of Boulder Canyon, Bull's Head, Shaver's Summit, Picacho through the Imperial and Coachella valleys; please don't think that Los Angeles wasn't interested in the Colorado . . .

THE NEXT TWIST

Meanwhile, *with what amounted to secrecy, . . . my deputy and I went by auto over the then-unpaved mountain and desert highway and onto the plank road through the sand dunes to Yuma.* So we are informed by Shelly J. Higgins, attorney for the city of San Diego. It was summer, he complained—but when wasn't it summer in Imperial? Imperial is this: When you come out of the July sun, your shoulders slowly relax. *Early one morning—the sun was working itself into a white-hot rage . . .—we went for a distance up river and piled rocks into a cairn and in the middle we placed our legal notice of filing for water and power, stuffed into a tin can.*

San Diego thereby claimed a hundred and twelve thousand acre-feet per year of Boulder Dam water.

Chapter 92

THERE IS EVEN EVIDENCE OF A SMALL FRUIT ORCHARD

(1931–2005)

It is well known that civilization demands water, and that it shifts in pursuit of it, because the former is dependent on the latter.

—Al-Biruni, A.D. 1025

Gale Robbins, slender, sleek and cold silver, perhaps a redhead in "real" life, smiles in an oval of perfect teeth and dark lipstick, her eyes expressionless beneath arched brows, the orchestra playing behind her. Four handsome, smiling men in dark suits groom her as would ants their queen, the two seated ones in the foreground kissing one wrist apiece, the other two, standing, touching their goblets to the air around her naked shoulders—ah, invocation; oh, hieratic pleasure! And it is all happening in Los Angeles. Just think how much water it all takes!

In November 1935, consumption of water is two hundred and two second-feet for domestic use, forty second-feet for irrigation. In November 1936, Los Angeles is up to two hundred twenty second-feet and sixty-five second-feet, respectively. *Of the total consumption for the month* of November 1936 *(284.9 second feet), 221.3 second feet was drawn from the* Owens Valley *aqueduct supply and 63.6 second feet from the Los Angeles River supply and local wells.* Thank God for Mulholland and the Owens River! Daily flow from that watercourse and various Owens Valley wells through the Los Angeles Aqueduct varies from three hundred and fifty second-feet in November 1935 to two hundred and forty-three second-feet a year later. Los Angeles keeps pumping. Owens Lake has long since become a dustbowl. By 1941, four of Mono Lake's tributary creeks have also been sucked dry.

Principal products of Los Angeles, 1942: aircraft, petroleum, motion pictures, women's clothing. Don't those require water, too?

In 2005 an Owens Valley tourist pamphlet which bears self-congratulations from the Los Angeles Department of Water and Power on the inside front cover *(We're proud to be a major recreation provider in the Eastern Sierra!)* passes on the following must-see hiking vista: *Higher up the road notice the mine site and ranch on the left; there is even evidence of a small fruit orchard here.*

Los Angeles enthusiastically obeys legal mandate to environmentally mitigate Owens Lake, 2005.

Chapter 93

COACHELLA'S SHARE

(1918–1948)

The Coachella Valley County Water District board spent years negotiating for its own allotment of Colorado River water. Had they become a part of the Imperial Irrigation District they would have had to assume a share of its large indebtedness. I have never been cheated out of a dollar in my life.

And so in 1918, hearing of Imperial County's attempts to fund an All-American Canal, Coachella forms her own water district. The Highline branch is due her, and she will get it.

In 1920, the Coachella Valley County Water District may be found in the Masonic Temple at Sixth and Cantaloupe. Is it then a secret society of fecundity? I never entered the Holy of Holies. But surely the water district's high priests advanced the First Commandment: *"Moisture Means Millions."*

In 1921, Coachella files suit against Los Angeles in hopes of preventing her from appropriating electric power from Coachella's preserve, Boulder Dam.

In 1922, Coachella wires Phil Swing in Imperial County: **WE CANNOT AND WILL NOT BE SET ASIDE WITHOUT RECEIVING JUST CONSIDERATION AND COMPENSATION FOR OUR EFFORTS . . .**

In 1938, workmen start digging the Highline Canal. In 1949, first water arrives in Coachella.

Chapter 94

SUBDELINEATIONS: WATERSCAPES

(1925–1950)

Only in our own day has California reached virile maturity full-armed for many a worthy conquest . . .

—Rockwell D. Hunt, A.M., Ph.D., *California and Californians, Issued in Five Volumes* (1926)

In 1936, one year after San Diego finishes her El Capitan Dam, a certain Major Wyman draws up his project report regarding control of the Los Angeles River. The great flood of 1938, which kills forty-nine people, makes his proposals all the more attractive. *The ineffective and dangerous practices of building mountain reservoirs and small, inexpensive check dams were also brought out,* notes the U.S. Army Corps of Engineers in another attack on irrigation democracy.

At that point, the Los Angeles River has been about halfway altered. *Prior to 1935 the three basic stream patterns—Los Angeles River, San Gabriel River and Rio Honda, and Ballona Creek—draining the Los Angeles area followed meandering natural water courses.* By 1921 the lower Los Angeles River had already been, in a fine neologism, *realined.* Next, the channel between southern Los Angeles and the San Fernando Valley got *improved.* So did Ballona Creek. Then it came time to build dams.

The Colorado River now gets similarly improved,* and not only for safety reasons. In 1927 the State Engineer calculates that *four-fifths of the local supplies on the Pacific slope of southern California, excluding Owens Valley, are now in use . . . In order that growth and expansion may continue, . . . the Pacific slope . . . will require three times the volume of water that can be obtained from nature's allotment . . .* We'll need *a continuous supply of fifteen hundred second feet* for greater Los Angeles alone. Thank God for the Colorado!

But a memorandum of 1929 caps California's take of that watercourse at four million, four hundred thousand acre-feet per year. Poor San Diego gets lower priority than Imperial County, Palo Verde and Yuma, *where rights have been established by long usage.* Alas! But Phil Swing himself offers reassurance: *These technical priorities, however, are of little importance, since the total of all California contracts is ad-*

*According to the Bureau of Reclamation, "the river's flow can be manipulated in the same fashion as the garden hose on the tap outside your home, and is."

mittedly well within our legal limit. In short, it is simply needless to question the supply of water, at least up here in Northside.

In 1942, Imperial's first and most fundamental line, the one between the two nations, receives visual ratification at last upon completion of the All-American Canal. The inevitable treaty of 1944 awards Southside the munificent allowance of one and a half million acre-feet per year. For an arithmetical understanding of this little adjustment, consider the following: During the month of April 1926, the Colorado's total discharge at Yuma was 1,404,000 acre-feet, shared equally by Northside and Southside through the Alamo Canal. Before George Chaffey opened the headgate of the Imperial Canal in 1901, Mexico would have received all of that water. She then by the Andrade patent remained entitled to half of it (no matter that Harry Chandler's enterprises drank most of that half). She will now be permitted to receive one-twelfth of it.

Well, isn't even that too much to waste on foreigners? Los Angeles complains that each acre-foot gained by Mexico will lose us five Angelenos.

Here's a long concrete facade of many tall narrow niches through which the whitewater spews; its concrete pillars and its tall narrow louvered slits remind me of Nazi architecture, particularly of the Reichsbank, but appearances can be deceiving; I'll never say that I'm against it. Shall I tell you what it actually is? *Exterior view of Nevada wing of Hoover Dam power plant which supplies city with 65 percent of all power requirements.* Which city? Do you have to ask? *Giant transformers raise generated voltage to 287,500 for power transmission to Los Angeles, 266 miles distant, over three transmission lines of Department of Water and Power.*

Not many years after the completion of Hoover Dam,* pearl oysters, shrimps and several species of fish have nearly disappeared from a number of their accustomed dwelling-places in the Gulf of Mexico. (No one has informed me just when the last Delta jaguar died out; perhaps that was long ago, before irrigation.) In 1940 an adventurer sails up the Colorado's mouth and determines that *there is something back of the rumors that the Colorado is a changed stream since it has been paralyzed by the building of Boulder Dam.* To wit, he *sees an immense and apparently ever-widening desolation* of dead cottonwoods, osage oranges, willows, grasses. *The region had formerly been a marshland, saturated with fresh water.* To be sure, subdelineation's bite can be temporarily undone, and in 1949 another observer of the Delta enjoys an experience right out of Mexican California: *Often we seemed to be going silently down long, lavender aisles where tens of thousands of the salt cedar trees in full bloom trailed their blossoms in the water.* But Progress—bless her!—pulls Mexican Imperial in a drier, saltier direction. And so we find the farmers of the Mexicali Valley drilling

*Formerly called Boulder Dam; hence formerly referred to as such in this book.

into their aquifer, which gets some replenishment thanks to seepage from the as yet unlined All-American Canal; by the century's end, six hundred and fifty-eight wells will pump out eight or nine hundred thousand acre-feet of water each year, gaining them half again as much as what Northside had allowed her.

But seepage can repair only so much, and Imperial's bifurcation remains visible: While the irrigated zone of American Imperial most often equals immense emerald rectangles both flat and dense, the counterpart area of the Mexicali Valley is, for instance, sagging honeycolored hay bales, ***METALES PROGRESO***, the smell of refried beans and then the smell of boiling sewage, a young couple walking along the grey wall, an empty plastic garbage bag rising in the wind and hovering high over the street, laundry hanging out of windows on littered hillsides. Could these two different landscapes have anything to do with underlying waterscapes?

The rest of Mexican Imperial is in very good shape, thank you. Tijuana finishes the Abelardo L. Rodríguez Dam in the middle of the thirties. Now she is taken care of forever; it is simply needless to question the supply of water. Tecate's five hundred and sixty-six residents cannot drink much.

Our newsflash now takes you back across the line to report other good news: In 1930 we find an advertisement for **IMPERIAL VALLEY "TRIPLE A" ARTESIAN WATER**, with company branches in El Centro, Brawley, Thermal, Mexicali* and Yuma—twenty-five cents a bottle.

More than a decade later, Riverside can also draw on artesian wells here and there; they just need to be drilled deeper. Some say Riverside water is sweeter than the Colorado River's, which may be one reason why in 1931, Riversiders vote four to one against joining the Los Angeles–centered octopus known as the Metropolitan Water District. Speaking of sweetness, it may be a sign of the times that in 1937 a U.S. Salinity laboratory is established at Riverside.

By 1941, sinking water tables have begun to alarm a few superbrains in Los Angeles who note *the imminent danger of infiltration of immense quantities of sea water into an area 475 miles square,* including the Santa Ana and Los Angeles rivers.

But why couldn't Imperial, and Riverside if necessary, and Los Angeles and all southern California, go on fixing the problem indefinitely by flooding the fields with Colorado River water?

*The Colorado River Land Company discovered the vast Mexicali aquifer in 1923, and promptly began to tap into it, since no water concessions were needed.

Chapter 95

THE LINE ITSELF

(1927–1950)

> This drift toward a warlike fatality has been facilitated by subsidiary consequences . . .
>
> —Thorstein Veblen, 1915

Although Imperial County Assessor's Map 17-10 depicts the International Border Line *(public reserve 60 feet wide)*, as yet the blank white maps on which the Salton Sea is sadly, foolishly subdelineated into numbered squares seem to remain almost of a piece with the international line.—Back in those days, said Hermenegildo Pérez Cervantes of Mexicali, referring to the 1920s, the American Immigration had a passport with the mother and all her kids. That was on one passport. So from very young I went to Calexico. I went with my mother. She took me often. It was very, very small over there, ooh, very little! Just on the other side of the border was a store owned by an American Japanese man named Kawakita. My mother bought jars of lard, canned goods, beans, sugar, salt, rice, sausages, clothes, all in thick paper bags with handles. You could buy most everything there . . .

And a rancher woman in Calexico once told me, speaking of a neighbor: Before they had a border there, his family farmed on the Mexican side without knowing it!

But the years bite deeper into Imperial's former coherence, as revealed by the line at Tijuana in 1932: *Down its yellow slopes drops a gangling fence, a tall network of wires supported on spindles, quickly to disappear in the thickets of a willow-bottom . . .*

And consider the instructive business failure of a Riversider named Bing Wong. In 1933, the year after Hetzel took that classic photograph of snow on Signal Mountain, Bing Wong opens his first restaurant. Some of his best customers come over from Mexicali. But then authority decrees that the border must close at midnight! In nine months he goes out of business.

In the 1940s, subdelineation gashes deeper still. I've already told you about the All-American Canal. Meanwhile, Southsiders' prospects of venturing Northside decrease. A woman born near the beginning of that decade and raised close by

Signal Mountain remembers: We were three hundred yards from the All-American Canal. I remember at two in the morning waking up from all the activity, all the Mexicans singing; or sometimes here came the Border Patrol, chasing those people with flashlights . . .

THE RAPIST-SAINT

Those people who get chased with flashlights, between then and now they come to define the border with ever increasing persistence. For Northsiders, the other side of the ditch continues to be a place of *yes*. As for inhabitants of Mexican Imperial, for them the line is an ever more bitterly reified exclusion. Hence the tale of Juan Soldado.

It happens in Tijuana. In 1938, an eight-year-old named Olga Comacho fails to come home. The little corpse shows evidence of rape. Juan Castillo Morales, aged twenty-four, possibly from Jalisco, is arrested; his clothes are bloodstained. His continued existence incites a riot. Accordingly, three days after the discovery of Olga's body, the army, having tried him without undue ceremoniousness, conducts him to the cemetery, in some versions makes him dig his grave, then shoots him. On the following day, an unknown old lady lays a stone on the earth that covers him and invites us all to pray, whether to him or for him is unrecorded.

Those who pray *to* him claim that John the Soldier was framed by the real rapist, his commanding officer. Accordingly, he is said to help those who suffer persecution by such authority figures as the Border Patrol. To be sure, numerous ex-votos praise him for this successful medical operation and that fertile conception, although the following seems more à propos: *I give you infinite thanks, Juan Soldado, for having granted me the miracle of saving me from the big prison that awaited me.* Passport-sized photos of men adorn the chapel which now frames the site of his execution. People thank him for assistance with their immigration documents. He is especially beloved of *pollos, solos, bodies*. Why not? There must be kinship between the rapist-murderer and the unwanted Mexican who risks death for the privilege of picking Imperial Valley lettuce: the powers that be disdain them both . . .

In the one image purporting to be of him, he resembles a little boy in his private's uniform, simultaneously jaunty, martial and wide-eyed as he stands facing us, with his pale hand on a round, draped little table which bears a statuette of Jesus on the Cross. He has crossed the line. We can never hope to know who he is.

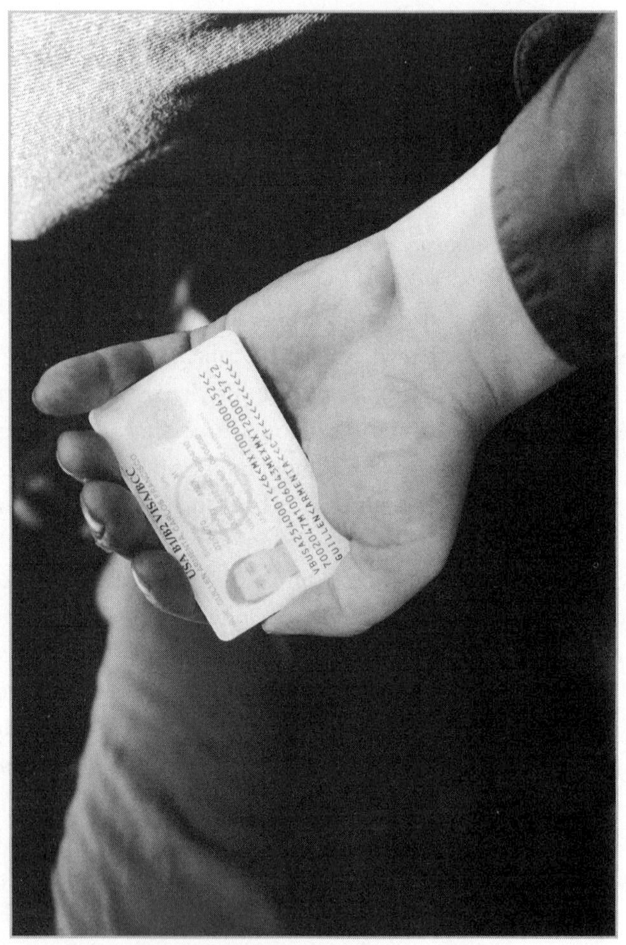

A limited-use visa for a Mexican national to visit the Northside, 2004

Chapter 96

DIFFERENT FROM ANYTHING I'D EVER KNOWN

(1933–1950)

. . . they entered a world where the normal laws of the physical universe were suspended.

—J. G. Ballard, 1966

Edith Karpen, born in Los Angeles, came of age just in time for the Depression.—And then I looked for a job, she said. And you know what teaching jobs were like then.

In 1933 I got a job offer in Calipatria. At that time, it was very, let's say, I don't want to say primitive, but a frontier-type town. It had two hotels, and if you went a block in one direction, you were out in the country. The other direction, you were out in a very small residential area. I lived at the hotel. It was the Hotel del Lingo. It was run by a widow, and periodically her sister would come to visit her, and she was the sister-in-law of Byrd the explorer. I don't think she knew too much about his accomplishments, but it was interesting. I do remember at that time, I signed a contract for the school year for eight hundred and eighty-nine dollars, and I was thrilled to get that job, because in Los Angeles I had been working at the first Bullock accessory shop at twenty-five cents an hour. Anyhow, the school district found some extra money and I ended up with twelve hundred dollars. I was thrilled to death.

If you want to know my first impression, I was so lonesome when my parents brought me down there! I decided to go for a walk. I walked in the direction where the wilderness was, about two blocks, and there I heard this Mexican music, and they had a campfire and they had these workers around it, singing. I just stood out of sight and listened.

I was a curiosity, because the teachers there were mostly the wives of farmers, and it was during the Depression, so they weren't about to give up their jobs. I always overheard them say, *There's the new teacher!* Across from where I lived there was a drugstore with a soda fountain, and whenever I went in there, I was a celebrity.

To me it had a feeling as though it wasn't part of California, because it was different from everything that I had ever known. For instance, they'd bring in a busload of kids, and then stop at the Fremont School to let off the American children and the Chinese children; I think they had only one Chinese then. Then they went to the Benita school, where I was teaching, and they let off the blacks and the Mexicans. Completely segregated. We had only a few blacks, I think about two families.

We had four rooms, and when the crops were in—we were largely a pea-picking area then—I'd have as many as sixty students, and then when they had a freeze or when the crops were in, I'd be down to about thirty or thirty-five, just overnight. They'd gone up to Salinas.

So these were the children of migrant workers?

That's right. I had what would be called preschool. Pre-kindergarten, starting about five.

And were they American citizens, Mexican citizens, or all of the above?

I don't think anybody ever cared.

Were there Mexican field workers who crossed the line routinely?

At that time, the growers would bring workers from the New River gorge.

How was the smell there in the thirties?

When I first got there, it wasn't too bad. It got worse all the time. I had a friend who was very outspoken, and when I was there, he was lobbying, I would say, to build a dam, so that the water couldn't come from Mexico!

How was your Spanish?

I was hired because I didn't speak Spanish. Complete immersion! They called it Americanization.

So what would you do if a child had to go to the bathroom and couldn't tell you?

They were pretty good with body language. I'll tell you one story. I don't know what they would think about this today, but shortly after I got there, we had gnats, and my kids were all getting pinkeye; they had this dirty muddy hair, and so when they came in from recess, I gave 'em all a Dutch haircut! They never talked back to me. You see, when I started at age twenty, I had to kind of lay down the law. The first Spanish words I learned were *amarillo* and *azul,* 'cause I was blonde and blue-eyed. Sometimes they used to touch my hair.

What was your impression the first time you crossed the border?

My first impression was complete awe. Mexicali was really booming back then. They had cabarets. The Gambrinas . . . The big one, it was the Owl. We never, ever called it the Teclote; we called it the Owl! You would walk in, and here were all these gambling tables. I had led a very, very sheltered life, and you would go back and there was the gambling and the bar, and you would go back to the dining area, and it was real plush.

And how would you describe the El Centro of 1933?

El Centro on Saturday night was bustling, but the rest of the time was kind of sleepy. In El Centro they had the famous Barbara Worth Hotel. I stayed there once right after we were married.* It was very nice; it was always nice. Then the buyers for the grapefruit and peas and all, they would congregate, and a lot of business was done. There was a nice dining room. Jack used to take me there most Sundays. It was really top drawer.

Did you dress up for those Sunday dinners?

Oh, yes.

What did you wear?

I never went in for long dresses, just nice street dresses. In the summer I wore skirts and blouses . . .

And what was the rest of the valley like?

The north end of the valley and Niland was a hobo center, 'cause that's where the trains switched. Then between Niland and the sea was the mud pots. There were different colors of mud, and it would go up and then go plop. They plopped up carbon dioxide, and a company came in and that was the origin of the Birds Eye frozen peas.† Where Slab City is now, that was good area for growing tomatoes. They like the sandy soil. But the desert was just desert. Ocotillos.

When I first came to the valley, she said, you'd still go part of the distance to Yuma on the plank road,‡ going out from Calexico, since the sand dunes were always shifting. Maybe seven miles of plank road were still left. It didn't take very long; you'd just go slowly. Of course *everything* was slow then.

*In Edith's obituary, her daughter describes the marriage: "Happily, the love of her life . . . Jack Donlevy, was then living in Mexicali where he owned Donlevy Bourbon . . . In her later years she loved to tell of going to Mexicali with him . . . It was a town brimming of [*sic*] celebrities and movie stars who would come for legal alcohol, Donlevy Bourbon, gambling and hunting."

†Here's that glorious year, 1944, when Imperial became the state's number one county in carbon dioxide production! The gas was used to make dry ice.

‡In 1916 the first plank road, comprised of pine boards, marches across the Imperial Sand Dunes. In 1924 it will need replacement, and the authorities try two thousand feet of redwood boards, but conclude: "No permanent solution of the problem has yet been found."

Chapter 97

FARM SIZE

(1910–1944)

Our economy is based on the exchange of goods and services through the medium of money . . . Thus farming for the market gradually became the predominant pattern for successful agriculture.

—Frederick D. Mott, M.D., and Milton I. Roemer, M.D., M.P.H., 1948

Of course everything was slow then; but everything was also enlarging. The property rectangles on the early Imperial County Assessor's maps respect at least the spirit of the Reclamation Act: The large parcels outweigh the small to no obscene degree; and many farmsteads remain identical in size. *There is no escaping the stereotype of an ideal agrarian world.* But Emersonian dreams, no matter how passionately syndicates and realtors invoked them, rapidly grew more phantasmal in an America where between 1910 and 1940, the proportion of farms five hundred acres and larger rose from twenty-eight to forty-five percent! In 1939, a utilitarian calculated that the gross income which a farmer needed to survive was fifteen hundred dollars; only one farm in five achieved this minimum. Although poor crop yields, low prices, etcetera, might well impoverish large farms more than small, on balance the former had a better chance . . .

But never mind the rest of America. *My vision beholds the greater Imperial Valley of thirty years hence, then as now conceded the most productive agricultural area in the world.* Why shouldn't the Wilfrieda Ranch prosper forever?

In 1940, Ernest Hemingway's *For Whom the Bell Tolls* introduces us to the fascinatingly date-specific concatenation of a good American from Montana who has placed himself under Communist discipline in order to fight in the Spanish Civil War. The guerrillas ask him whether in his country land is owned by the peasants. He replies: *Most land is owned by those who farm it. Originally the land was owned by the state and by living on it and declaring the intention of improving it, a man could obtain title to a hundred and fifty hectares.*

Tell me how this is done, says one of his interlocutors. *This is an agrarian reform which means something.*

Robert Jordan, bemused by the notion that this is an agrarian reform, explains that this is simply *done under the Republic*. In other words, it is American, plain and simple.

They ask him about large proprietors and he expresses the guarded hope that *taxes will break them up*. They inquire whether there are many Fascists in his country and he replies: *There are many who do not know they are fascists but will find out when the time comes.*

Poor Robert Jordan! No wonder that his creator makes him die with noble uselessness for a doomed cause! Here in the agrarian paradise called Northside, farms keep right on getting larger and fewer.

MIDAS'S HELL

Wilber and Elizabeth Clark had been among the last generation of homesteaders in the continental United States. Between 1900 and 1918, California's vacant public lands shrank from forty-two and a half million to twenty and a half million acres. In 1920, when Imperial still boomed north and south of the line, the United States Department of Agriculture Yearbook bravely confessed the inevitable: *We have always been able to look beyond the frontier of cultivation to new and untouched fields ready to supply the landless farmer with a homestead . . . That untouched reserve has about disappeared.* Never mind, my fellow optimists; we need have no fear that our lands will not become better and better as the years go by; because we possess a new reserve: the potential yield of science and efficiency! In fact, we have just now achieved nearly the largest harvest in American history; our corn crop alone equals more than eighty percent of world production!

To a family farm ensnared in the money economy, this accomplishment is catastrophic. If we produced only for ourselves, doing our own work,* and could be satisfied with that, we might have been happy. Unfortunately, people have a way of wanting washing machines, movies and store-bought dresses. And even if everybody on the farm could somehow resist the lure of a commodity produced by someone else, by now we've found ourselves assessed for various social services unknown to Wilber Clark. One source from the mid-1940s lists road districts, reclamation districts, drainage districts, pest-control districts, all presenting their obligatory invoices on top of the irrigation district charges without which Imperial would return to salty silt. This financial burden on farmers is significant, increasing and non-negotiable.—Never mind; we live in the greatest democracy on earth;

*By the way, merely subdividing large farms into family-sized units could not achieve Emersonian self-reliance: They'd need to be *diversified* family farms in order to utilize the labor of their inhabitants throughout the entire year. Granted, this requirement becomes less onerous in the almost-perpetual growing season of Imperial.

that means we pay those bills because we *want* to; roads and pest control benefit us, so how could we not love to do our part?—In any event, these "wants" invite us to produce as much as possible in order to maximize our power to fulfill them. Therefore we become vulnerable to the conditions of our time: shocking price jumps for the fertilizers and machines to which we've addicted ourselves, and shrinking reservoirs of willing farmhands. This latter scarcity not only (as Marx would say) commodifies labor but also makes it more expensive. (Thank God for Mexicans!) *Altogether, in the spring of 1920 the American farmers were confronted with the most difficult situation they had ever experienced.* Our only hope of paying these new costs is to produce even *more*. Since our neighbors follow the same logic, and supply lowers demand, we drown in our own golden harvest!* The crop of 1920 is accordingly *worth, at current prices,* three million dollars less than the previous year's, even though the latter was smaller, and a million less than the year before's, which was smaller still.

Call this foreseeable. Back around the time of the Mexican War, Thoreau had cast his Olympian pity upon any farmer who strove for more than subsistence. *To get his shoestrings he speculates in herds of cattle. With consummate skill he has set his trap with a hair spring to catch comfort and independence, and then, as he turned away, got his own leg into it.* And so Thoreau escaped poverty by doing without the supposed necessities of the poor—for instance, their coffee. His sojourn at Walden Pond is instructive—not least because he declined to remain there. And so, although the crisis of family farms was indeed foreseeable, it was also inevitable. Even one of Southside's greatest (because stubbornest) agrarian revolutionaries, Emiliano Zapata, who rose up against the encroachments upon village land of the sugarcane haciendas, and fought year after year to safeguard the *ejidos* of Morelos, counseled his neighbors to exceed mere subsistence, because it sometimes wasn't even that: *If you keep on growing chile peppers, onions, and tomatoes, you'll never get out of the state of poverty you've always lived in. That's why, as I advise you, you have to grow cane . . .* Rich or poor, we human beings continue most faithfully to set our traps to catch more comfort and independence. We'll sell out at a fancy price.

All is relative, to be sure; the difficulties of American farmers in 1920 compare paradisiacally to those of their counterparts in the Revolution-razed Mexico of 1915,

*As usual, Paul S. Taylor tells the story very well: "The farmer buys a tractor. He thinks it will make work easier and hours shorter . . . Also his wife will not have to feed and do the washing for the hired man." At first he's happy with the time he's saved. But "after a while the farmer realizes that after all the tractor in the shed is "eating up" something while it sits . . .—interest and depreciation . . . These hours and days begin to look to him like idle time . . . He sees that he could handle more land than he does . . . If the farmer is slow to realize these possibilities, there are articles in the farm journals to help him. . . . Most of them won't see—or heed it if they saw it—the little 1936 pamphlet of the Federal Department of Agriculture which asks the farmer in black-faced type, "If you bought machinery to get increased returns, what would happen if your neighbors did likewise?"

when Zapata uttered the words just quoted, but that gives us no right to trivialize Northside's desperation. What should the farmers do? They can go to market in cooperatives and associations, as the citrus ranchers did.—In 1905, D. D. Gage, *a prominent citizen in Riverside,* came home from the East and advised his fellow orange growers that *the salvation of the industry lies with the big department stores of the great cities.* (The Safeway Farm Reporter knew all that.)—Unfortunately, the big department stores won't stock Imperial's alfalfa, but maybe some middleman could peddle it away. And wouldn't it be fine if that middleman were somehow accountable or beholden to the growers? Perhaps, in other words, American farmers can survive being assimilated into an economic superorganism through the expedient of superorganizing themselves. Who knows? This is about all that the Department of Agriculture can advise.

In time, the farmers will accept this logic. That 1958 hearing on the proposed marketing order for winter lettuce is evidence of that. Rival entrepreneurs that they have become, they remain nonetheless united in their bafflement before the common problem. Norman Ward, sales manager for Farley Fruit in El Centro, remarks that both lettuce and cantaloupes remain in eternal oversupply. He refers to *a terrible glut from which we can never dig out.*

"THE DIVORCE OF OWNERSHIP FROM MANAGEMENT"

California held a hundred and fifty thousand farms in 1940—only two point two percent of all farms in the United States, but thirty-six point seven percent of all large-scale farms.* The Department of Agriculture concluded: *The tendency toward larger farms is likely to throw an almost insurmountable barrier in the way of a man who wishes to progress up the so-called agricultural ladder . . . The divorce of ownership from management tends to eliminate the small-scale producer, and hastens the development of a group of rural people who have no property and must sell their labor in order to live.*

In this respect, the California of 1940 was moving in the direction of the Mexico of 1540. Again, it goes without saying that even in the worst Depression years, California's homesteaders never got dispossessed as indigenous Mexicans had been by the conquistadors (or indigenous and Mexican Californians by the Anglo-Americans); but the process, however attenuated in American California, and however different in its cause—capitalist concentration, not foreign expropriation—was similar. Cortés had made a habit of bestowing captured Aztec towns on his conquistadors; this scheme was called the *encomienda.* The town's owner got Indian

*At that time the USDA defined a large-scale farm as one whose produce was valued at $30,000 or more.

tribute and labor. We read of a colonist *of the northern frontier,* a zone approximating Imperial, who assembled a Chandleresque domain of 11,626,850 acres. Three and a half centuries later, while the haciendas enlarged themselves under the benign eye of President Díaz, the *encomienda* reinvented itself, complete with a company store. In twentieth-century American Imperial, the longterm trend toward average acreage increase, combined with population growth, logically reduced the ratio of owners to tenants. Is tenancy necessarily a state of exploitation? That is not for me to say. But it is evidently a less secure state than ownership.

Steinbeck's *Grapes of Wrath* was about Okies. California had her own Okies. So did Arizona. In 1927, just a few miles east of the entity I call Imperial, in the neighborhood of Yuma, a child was born to a Mexican-American family who soon lost their statutory hundred and sixty acres. That child was the future farmworker organizer César Chávez. Meanwhile, in Imperial County itself, by 1930 almost three thousand of the forty-seven hundred farms in existence were operated by their tenants, not their owners. In other words, a shocking three-fifths of the county's farms were no longer, if they ever had been, self-sufficient family homesteads.

(In a Dorothea Lange photograph from the Imperial Valley, a former tenant farmer now on relief leans slightly toward us, his eyes narrowed in what is probably a habitual squint although the shiny pupils and the clenched grimace bestow on him the distinction of anguish. The year is 1936.)

In 1910 there had been only thirteen hundred and twenty-two farms in Imperial County. Fifty-one of them comprised less than three acres, ten were owned by petty Harry Chandler types, being a thousand acres and over;* four hundred were in the bailiwick of the old limitation law: a hundred to a hundred and seventy-five acres. By 1913, certain large-scale Imperial Valley cotton growers had already leased cotton hectares from the Colorado River Land Company. A year later, the Chandler Syndicate, in cahoots with *a number of Los Angeles business and professional men,* was preparing to grow citrus on Imperial Valley parcels of forty to six hundred and forty acres apiece.

The numbers I possess simplify this complex situation. They seem to show that between 1928 and 1950, average acreage increased from a hundred and ten to a hundred and eighty-five acres per farm—no more than average California acreage, and probably less. But the unreliability of the data must be emphasized; for example, note that the 1950 entry in the following table is not exactly a hundred and eighty-five acres. All we can say for certain is that the general tendency of average acreage is *increase.*

*Here is one of them, admiringly introduced to us by Judge Farr in 1918: Willis F. Beal, who filed on his hundred and sixty acres in Water Company No. 8 (Brawley) in 1903, "still owns the original homestead and has added to his holdings until he now has, all told, one thousand acres in Imperial County."

AVERAGE ACREAGES OF FARMS IN IMPERIAL COUNTY

The Reclamation Act of 1902 fixed a 160-acre homestead limit, 320 acres for a married couple. By 1918 the homestead limitation had been adjusted to 320 acres for an arid homestead and 640 acres for cattle lands without a watering hole.

Year	*Number of Farms*	*Total Acreage*	*Average Acreage per Farm*
1909	3,947	181,545[a]	50
1910	1,322		?
1920	2,843		?
1930	4,769	525,797[b]	110
1939	2,696	418,029	155 (CBE figure)
			80 (IVD 1939)
1944	2,932	489,260	167
1945	2,696	489,260	181
1949			"about 105"
1950	4,500	432,000	96
1954	1,633	550,075	337

[a]The County Assessor's records for 1909 (at least as quoted by Otis B. Tout, p. 191) fail to give the total farm acreage. There is an "acres assessed" figure of 731,520. Since even in 2000 only half a million acres had been irrigated, much of this land must have been held by speculators or city fathers. Under "total acreage" for this year I have used the figure for acres irrigated.

[b]The actual figure given (p. 12) is for "irrigable area," so irrigated area was probably less. On p. 14, the Secretary of the El Centro Chamber of Commerce informs us that more than 60,000 acres have been irrigated and cultivated and that the average farm "is about one hundred acres in size."

Sources: California Board of Agriculture (1918) for 1910; Imperial County Agricultural Commissioner's papers (1920); Imperial Valley Directory (1930); Otis B. Tout (1931); Imperial Valley Directory (1939); Imperial Valley Directory (1949); California Board of Equalization (1949); California Blue Book (1950).

At the beginning of this period, total acreage in the county approximately doubled. The number of farms stayed constant at less than forty-eight hundred, which I interpret as good news for local farmers: It would seem that they did not sell out and were able to increase their holdings. Of course their expansion would have increased their dependence on hired field labor; in other words, it would have facilitated *the divorce of ownership from management.*

In 1934, the Dean of Agriculture at University of California, Berkeley, visits the Imperial Valley and writes in his personal notes: *Sharp Reduction in acreage 67% of valley absentee land owners.* In 1942, the first year of All-American Canal water, the Bureau of Agricultural Economics concludes: *About 40 percent of the total number of farm owners do not live in the valley but collectively control almost one-half (48 percent) of the total acreage in farms . . .*

Here's another statistic which bodes poorly for the family farm: By 1940, only forty-five percent of Imperial County's workforce engages in agriculture.

The extreme fluctuations in the number of farms shown in the table disturb the imagination. The change between 1944 and 1945 is especially distressing, implying defaults, foreclosures and abandonments—unless, of course, one or both of the figures for those two years was bogus. In any case, most commentators draw sharp conclusions. An essay on the All-American Canal opines that the lure of Colorado River water brought speculators and agribusiness managers to the Imperial Valley, causing it to be *populated by a small handful of owners and operators at the top of the social pyramid and a great lower class of workers, mostly of Mexican origin . . .* In other words, there are many who do not know they are fascists but will find out when the time comes. Another historian writes: *It did not take long for the Imperial Valley, eventually subsidized by the reclamation-built All American Canal . . . to become dominated by the same landowner class already present in 1900 when Harrison Gray Otis and his partner Moses H. Sherman purchased a 700,000-acre ranch adjacent to the Imperial Valley, and extending into Mexico.* Here is one last opinion: *From the first years of settlement to the present,* runs a book called *Salt Dreams, the average size of Imperial Valley holdings steadily increased.* What its authors make of that statement we shall see when we look in on farm size once more, during the latter half of the twentieth century. For now, let us stay in the Depression years.

In those days,* I asked Edith Karpen, who owned the farms in the Imperial Valley?

Mostly, Americans owned the farms. At that time you could hardly make a living because they had field crops. Most of them had a section—six hundred and forty acres.

So a hundred and sixty acres wouldn't have been enough? I've read about that hundred-and-sixty-acre limitation.

Oh, no. You couldn't have made ends meet.

*She had just been telling me about the pea pickers' strike, so "those days" would have been the middle 1930s.

"THEY PUT UP THE RED FLAGS"

In Mexican Imperial, the case was rather different. Harry Chandler was about to lose his empire of acres!

We have seen that even the Zapatistas, who were among the most radical elements of the early Mexican Revolution, considered the *ejidos* less as utopian vehicles of redistribution than as the restoration of hoarded land titles dating from the Conquest. In Zapata's zone, progressive young land surveyors consulted elders in order to mark the traditional borders of village holdings. Zapata did eventually seek to dispossess haciendas of certain lands to which no village had ever asserted a claim, but it was with the caution of a de Anza in hostile desert that he proceeded beyond his premise of restoring prior legal rights.

Much of the Mexicali Valley had not been irrigated or cultivated before the Colorado River Land Company got there. No matter; Mr. Chandler's prior rights did not count. Nor should they have; his company disdainfully disregarded Mexicanness. In 1927, for example, even as the Peasant Union of two Mexicali *colonias* ominously petitioned to expropriate thirty-five thousand of its acres the company had proposed *to bring hundreds of thrifty ranchers from Germany and Central Europe* into the place that it liked to call *Mexican Imperial Valley.* Two hundred thousand acres would be subdivided into parcels of thirty, forty and more acres for these Europeans. Thus, the Colorado River Land Company was ironically promoting small, relatively egalitarian landholdings, perhaps because it saw the revolutionary handwriting on the wall. Meanwhile, by an odd coincidence, the company's manager, H. H. Clark, *has the distinction of being the world's largest cotton rancher.*

The table on page 576 gives some indication of Mr. Clark's supremacy.

An additional cause of the hatred so many Mexicans felt toward the Colorado River Land Company had to do with the local grantees of its leases. In 1924, for example, its ninety-five *protocolized leases* consisted of the following: fifty-six to Chinese, twenty-two to Japanese, nine to Mexicans and eight to Americans. One report to stockholders opined that Chinese worked harder to improve their parcels than did any white man. Whether or not that was so, Mexicans felt not merely oppressed by the situation, but insulted.

Chandler repeatedly expressed his intention of subdividing Mexicali Valley lands and selling them to colonists. Why then did he continue to lease them out, thereby inflaming campesinos against him ever more year after year? In part, I am sure, his congenital opposition to organized labor would have left him cold to peasant demands. A second reason was that if he could ever finish his cotton railroad to the sea, and irrigate the valley more grandly, he could fetch a higher price for his

LAND OWNERSHIP IN THE COLORADO RIVER DELTA, *ca.* 1930

Acres	*Percent of Total*	*Entity*
800,000	80	Colorado River Land Company
50,000	5	Andrade estate
35,500	3.6	Mexican government
29,000	2.9	Sold by Southern Pacific Railroad
28,500	2.8	Kept by Southern Pacific Railroad
16,000	1.6	Imperial Development Co.
12,000	1.2	Globe Mills Co.
10,000	1	Mt. Signal Land & Cattle Co.
8,000	0.8	Shintani Ranch
999,000	**98.9** (due to rounding)	

Note: The lands sold by the Southern Pacific Railroad went to four ranches and development companies, three of whose owners had Anglo names. The remaining 16,634 acres of those lands were "miscellaneous (including roads and canals and some doubtful areas)."

Source: Otis P. Tout (1931), citing a Congressional report.

properties—hurrah for the Ministry of Capital! Finally (and here I almost feel sympathy for him), since the Revolution prohibited most foreign ownership of Mexican land, particularly in those politically sensitive areas near the border, Chandler and his partners worried that if they did sell, only Mexicans would be legally allowed to buy, not those *thrifty ranchers from Germany and Central Europe;* and should the unthrifty Mexicans default on their mortgage payments, the company, whose title survived only through an increasingly precarious grandfather clause, might not be able to repossess the land.

This was why Chandler fantasized about selling to Italian immigrants, or English, or even the hated Chinese and Japanese. The Pueblo Brant subdivision of 1926, which he magnanimously planned to offer to Mexicans who had gained their farming experience on the northern side of the ditch, was too little and definitely too late, because by then the land invasions of hungry campesinos had already begun.

In 1924, the Colorado River Land Company was pressured into developing infrastructure in the Mexicali Valley in exchange for retaining most of its land titles. The pressure continued. By 1930, although the company *remained the dominant economic force in Mexicali Valley,* it was four million dollars in debt and still had not yielded any dividends. In 1936, a convenient new American syndicate called the Chandler-Sherman Corporation sued that Mexican entity, the Colorado River Land Corporation, for recovery of moneys lost by such stockholders as Harry Chandler, winning a four-million-dollar judgment. I have never been cheated out of a dollar in my life. That was just as well for Chandler, because expropriation was coming ever closer.

By 1937, the All-American Canal had nearly been completed. The Imperial Canal would soon go dry, and with it much of Harry Chandler's utility to Mexico, for the rights to half the water in the old canal—which is to say almost all of the water in the Mexicali Valley—would now be the rights to nothing. For years, Chandler and his *Los Angeles Times* lobbied Northside not to set aside those rights. They had lost that battle. Now Mexico must soon find other water from other ditches. Hoping to establish a case for herself under the Northsider legalism of prior and beneficial water use,* Mexico now wished to finish settling and irrigating the valley immediately, before the All-American Canal was finished.

And where were her settlers? They kept coming. They could not afford to rent parcels from the Colorado River Land Company, let alone buy land. In 1930, some campesinos whose attempted legal expropriation of Chandler's fields for *ejidos* had failed remained as squatters. They were jailed. Among them we find the charismatic devotee of agitprop Felipa Velázquez, then forty-eight years old. Her watchword: *We are going to fight, no matter what happens.* When they arrested her and her children, the *agraristas* were performing an anti-capitalist play by Ricardo Flores Magón, who you may remember had been a leader in the movement that briefly seized Mexicali in 1911. The detentions caused such a stink that after five months the land-invaders were released. Meanwhile, Baja's territorial representative in Mexico City demanded the revocation of the Colorado River Land Company's legal title. A manifesto of the Bar and Restaurant Employees Union in Mexicali cried out *from our very soul that Mexico is for the Mexicans . . .*but *the heart of the city is owned especially by chines, japanese and jews* [*sic*]—in other words, Chandler's preferred tenants. Seeing where the winds blew, Chandler tried to sell off his lands before they were simply seized. In 1936, he signed a colonization agreement with the Cárdenas government. The Colorado River Land Company promised to finish surveying its holdings and sell them off over twenty years.

Almost immediately afterward, Cárdenas intimated that these transfers ought to occur in five or six years, not twenty. Chandler must have been furious. As it

*For definitions, see above, p. 237.

turned out, Cárdenas was a moderate, for the field workers of the Mexicali Valley now took over. Among their leaders were many of the campesinos who had been arrested with Felipa Velázquez.

As 1937 began, a committee of campesinos petitioned once again to carve their own *ejidos* out of the company's parcels. They demanded arms. While the authorities hesitated, four hundred of them occupied Chandler's fields and expelled the paying tenants—most of whom were Chinese, of course, so to the *agraristas* they did not count.

One very hot afternoon, Yolanda Sánchez Ogás, to whom this book is so indebted in regard to Chinese tunnels and Cucapá Indians, was in a car with me, en route to a filthy barracks in Ejido Tabasco where some campesinos had recently been living, as she said, like slaves, and when I asked her to tell me the tale of the *ejidos,* she said:

We kicked out Díaz in 1910,* but there were still plantations until 1937. We tried many times to get rid of the Colorado River Land Company, but in '36 here and in Nayarit, our agrarian groups finally got together. They made different ranches. There were five different agrarian committees that formed a federation. They took the land they worked. They didn't use weapons, but they put red flags around ranches and said: *This land is ours,* because they knew that President Cárdenas would support them. On 27 January 1937 they put up the red flags in our valley. The Colorado River Company had White Guards;† their job was to prevent campesinos from organizing. The company had arrived in the valley in 1904. They preferred to rent land only to Chinese, Japanese and Americans, not to Mexicans, since Mexicans possessed real rights to the land.

So the White Guards and soldiers came, she continued. They put many campesinos in prison. The prisoners sent a telegram to Cárdenas. The Secretary of Agriculture came fifteen days later. And they formed the first *ejidos.*

Were all the fields the same size?

Here in Baja California, on account of the desert climate, the *ejido* land parcels had to be twenty hectares. (At first, they were much smaller, some as little as four hectares.)‡ There might be forty people in one *ejido,* a hundred in another. But each had a parcel. The government did this to get settlers up here. Even Americans came, but—Yolanda smiled—they *left.*

How could Americans settle here?

*He actually left the country a year later.

†This was of course the term that the Bolsheviks used for their reactionary opponents in the Russian Civil War. Whether the CRLC called its security detachments by this name I cannot say. If not, it would be indicative of Yolanda's politics that she used it.

‡Indeed, in Oaxaca, the average parcel size was one to three hectares.

They had parcels from the Colorado River Land Company. But of course no foreigners had rights here, only Mexicans. Cárdenas bought out the company at eighty pesos per hectare and also started the *colonias* at that time.

What was life like on the *ejidos* then?

The first *ejidos* were like kibbutzes. They all worked together. In 1939 they told Cárdenas that they didn't want to work collectively anymore, since there had been many fights. So private property was introduced. One hectare got donated for a park.

"THERE WERE NO GUNFIGHTS"

The scope, effectiveness and good faith of Mexico's agrarian revolution has been debated since the 1960s. Without exception, the *ejidatarios* whom I interviewed in Mexican Imperial considered themselves the beneficiaries of Cárdenas; and almost without exception, they expressed satisfaction with their lives, which they tended to characterize with the word *tranquilo*. They personalized that President and told anecdotes about him, such as the following, which I heard from the proprietress of a small highway restaurant south of Mexicali: *Cárdenas came here* and saw a house falling down and a new car in front of it. He got upset.* She adored him.†

By one account, Cárdenas granted fourteen million hectares to almost a million campesinos. About a hundred and sixty-eight thousand of those hectares had been Harry Chandler's.

Not all the grants stood. Down south in Morelos, the heartland of the Zapatista revolution, Cárdenas passed out many acres, and yet, thanks to disputes between villages, rising land values and growing populations, *ejidos* there frequently shrank, both in total extent and in plot size. One historian concludes that by 1943, Zapata's hometown *was in desperate straits.* Another source writes that because many Mexicali campesinos lacked the means even to purchase water, much less seed and other supplies, by 1943, not even eighteen percent of the valley's *ejido* fields were being worked. Meanwhile, another scholar explains that *Cárdenas's agrarian reform paid off because both output and productivity rose.*

I cannot speak on the current fortunes of Zapata's hometown. But Mexicali's *ejidos* continue even today to dream their rich green Imperial dreams.

When Cárdenas was President, explained a rancher's wife in the *ejidos* west of

*Cárdenas visited Mexicali from 3 to 6 July 1939.

†Predictably, this adoration lessened in the urban centers: San Luis, Mexicali, Tecate, Tijuana. The *maquiladora* workers in the dirt hills overlooking Tijuana did not strike me as excessively happy; they never mentioned Cárdenas of their own accord, and many had no idea who he was. Those who remembered him sometimes blamed him (with justice) for closing the border's gambling dens. Among city dwellers, it was mostly the citizens of Mexicali who paid Cárdenas lip service.

CIA. MEXICANA DE TERRENOS DEL RIO COLORADO, S. A.

Se hace del Conocimiento de los ocupantes legales de terrenos en proceso de colonización en el Valle de Mexicali, que por acuerdo de esta compañía y de la Comisión Nacional de Colonización SE AMPLIO EL PLAZO HASTA EL DIA 31 DE JULIO DE 1949.

Para que regularicen su situación en relación con su Admisión como colonos y con la celebración de sus contratos de compra venta, conforme al contrato de colonización de 23 de Abril de 1948 y sus Reformas de 9 de Septiembre del mismo año.

ATENTAMENTE

Mexicali, B. Cfa., Abril de 1949.

Ing. Alberto Celaya V.- Gerente

Circular regarding the sale of Colorado River Land Company plots

Algodones, he divided up the land and gave it to the families who were already living here. When the first father died, it went down to the family. Our rancho was in the family since the time of Cárdenas. On the twenty-seventh of January, that's when they got the ranch. That was when that group of men took over all the factories. There were two factories there where they took care of the wheat and the cotton. They stormed the factories here and that's when Cárdenas started this system.

I asked how her life was, and she smilingly replied: *Tranquilo.*

Cárdenas was rapid and determined. Between March and August 1937, nearly a hundred thousand Colorado River Land Company hectares had already been confiscated and converted into about forty *ejidos.* The confiscations continued. In 1938 the company's irrigation canals were nationalized. Chandler and his partners received compensation in annual payments which finally ended in 1956. After an investment of four decades, they gained nothing and lost nothing. In 1972 the company's Mexican receiver finally dissolved.

As I write this, there remain more than two hundred *ejidos* in the valley.

Yolanda would have been born shortly after these events. In 1937, Hermenegildo Pérez Cervantes would have been thirteen. His account of what happened was both more local and less enthusiastic. He said to me:

In 1937, that's when they divided up the land. So basically Cárdenas expropriated the land. That's when people started arriving from Michoacán, Guanajuato, etcetera. That's when you started to see campesinos. That's why you see the *ejidos* with the names like Zacatecas, Guanajuato, because the people came from there. There were no gunfights when it happened. There were some farmers who were renting land from the Colorado River Land Company. The expropriators took the land from them, too. Well, there was a sit-in by these people with their families in front of the Governor's Palace. They had a kiosk where they were giving speeches to the public. They were there a month and a half at least. They sent a delegation to Mexico City to talk to the government. I was really little; I really didn't know what opinion to have about them. But what I heard was that somebody had taken their land. So people were sympathetic toward them. The business owners sent them food. And the women, they had a little wood fire and they made their dinners right there. And finally they were given other land. The few who had bought land from the Colorado River Land Company were not expropriated.

I asked him if he believed Cárdenas to have been a great man, and he assented, but not emphatically; he did not even say *claro,* meaning *of course.* This old survivor who so happily remembered the marching band created by that Chandler ally or entity, the Industrial Soap Company of the Pacific, told me about 1937 without Yolanda's smiles. But, after all, he was a city dweller, no *ejidatario.*

In his great novel *Under the Volcano,* which is set in 1938, Malcolm Lowry describes Mexico with cynical sadness. For him, the era of Porfirio Díaz continues in the Cárdenas years: *Yet was it a country with free speech, and the guarantee of life, liberty and the pursuit of happiness? A country of brilliantly muralled schools . . . where . . . the land was owned by its people free to express their native genius? A country of model farms: of hope? It was a country of slavery, where human beings were sold like cattle, and its native peoples . . . exterminated through deportation, or reduced to worse than peonage . . .*

In Mexicali there was an official of the Tribunal Unitario Agrario named Carlos E. Tinoco. With his nearly shaved head, his moustache and goatee, he had a somewhat Leninist appearance. He said to me: So it's important to understand first that Cárdenas came out of the Revolution. One of the things that gave rise to the Revolution was land inequality—a lot of land and few owners. So there were social revolutionaries like Madero and Zapata, and they were interested in turning that around. And that's when they started to have Presidents who came from the ideals of the Revolution. Zapata was not a campesino. He was a big landowner. His land was divided up among the campesinos. He took up arms. His motto was: **FREE LAND; LAND OF LIBERTY.** It kind of just happened that when Cárdenas was President, they had the opportunity to divide up the land. Cárdenas basically left the large landowners without any recourse. I think that was a little heavyhanded. A person could get four hectares to eight hectares, and the landowner would have to give it up.

Cárdenas helped the whole country, Señor Tinoco continued, but especially people living in Baja California. In the United States and in most of the states of Mexico, the division is not equal. Baja California is just one of the places where a parcel is almost always twenty hectares, perhaps because there are so many plains and a lot of water, so you can irrigate more places. But the actual motives for why the parcels are twenty hectares, no one knows exactly.

When you go into the *campo* now, he said, what is the average farm size? Still twenty hectares. And, at least before 1992, you were not allowed to divide up your parcel. It's called the indivisibility principle. You go with your group of friends to form this *ejido* and then if you get married you put your spouse's name as the inheritor. If you divorce, that's a different problem. If your name is on the paper, you don't have to leave it to your wife but to whomever you want to. So if you got divorced the wife might have no right to the land,* or if you had several children, they could not break up the property. The order usually goes: You leave it to your wife, your concubine, or your children, or your parents. But you still can't subdivide it.

"ALTHOUGH ACCURATE DATA ARE LACKING"

After Cárdenas, Camacho performed a tightrope dance between *ejidatarios* and landowners, and for better and worse the pace of redistribution slowed. Landowners and *ejido* families were encouraged to reconcile.

Southside was and perhaps in part remains (likewise Northside) *a country of slavery;* and yet I tentatively believe that in these years the borderlands of Mexican Imperial did indeed offer *a country of model farms: of hope.* Astonishingly, even the American Ambassador thought so.

On Northside, *although accurate data are lacking, the belief is rather widespread that concentration of ownership and control is increasing.* On Southside accurate data are equally lacking, but the perception, thanks to the Revolution and especially to Cárdenas, is the opposite.

*In 2004, the Rural Development Institute favored privatizing the *ejidos* on several grounds, one of which was the fact that most women who live on them are not full *ejidatarios*.

Should we grow food as efficiently as possible, which will benefit consumers with uniform quality and low prices; or should we support the family farm? Posing the dilemma in this way creates the illusion that somebody in power has actually made a choice, when of course it's all (let's pretend) *market preferences,* hence nobody's fault when the Okies get tractored out. *There are many who do not know they are fascists but will find out when the time comes.*

But in Mexico someone *has* made a choice.

Imperial's delineation grows unbearably real: Northside has gone in one direction, Southside another.

Chapter 98

THE LINE ITSELF: JAPANESE ADDENDUM

(1941–1945)

"Well, that's the way the world goes," the shadow told him, "and that's the way it will keep on going."

—Hans Christian Andersen, 1847

We rotated crops, Edith Karpen said. Part of the time there were melons. Between that there'd be alfalfa to rebuild the land. Milo maize, that was a summer crop. Kawakita was one of them that leased our land periodically to raise melons. Jack didn't raise them; he leased the land to people who raised them. Kawakita was very pro-Japanese when the war broke out. His son Meatball went back to Japan, and he had these radio broadcasts against the United States, and he was held responsible. After the war, they held a trial for him. At least one daughter went back to Japan because he didn't want her to marry an American Japanese.

Were most people in favor of locking up the Japanese?

They were all in favor of it. My friend Harold Brockman had a friend who was Japanese who was interned, and he stored all his things in Harold's garage. They thought there was a real threat to the Valley, because they thought the Japanese might come up through the Baja. So they took training so they could recognize the silhouettes of Japanese planes, and they used to patrol the All-American Canal. Jack used to take a gun and go. I remember sitting eating breakfast in my kitchen and the rain was pouring down; we had harvested alfalfa and they had put up temporary fences around the alfalfa to keep out the sheep, and suddenly I heard all this racket when Jack was out on patrol, and the sheep were milling all around the house and I had the radio on and they had sunk one of our big ships, the British ship, too, and it just looked so threatening to our forces, I just sat there and cried. I had a brother who was taken prisoner.

Chapter 99

BROAD AND SINISTER MOTIVES

(1928–1946)

> Finally, the Committee recommends that a group of representatives of the agricultural interests of California wait upon the Governor . . . to advise him of the broad and sinister motives and objectives of the recent labor disturbances and their serious threat to California's greatest industry and to urge upon him the necessity of using every means for the protection of the State.
>
> —Report of the Special Investigating Committee, 1934

"CALLING WORKERS FROM THE FIELDS"

A dusty old truck, squarish with round headlights like spectacles, poses at the edge of an empty dirt road. A small army of slender young men, all but one of them wearing pale, close-fitting mushroom-shaped hats, stands on the truckbed, leaning up around the cab to envelop this sign: **DISARM THE RICH FARMER OR ARM THE WORKER FOR SELF-DEFENSE**. The capless one has sleek black hair; he looks boyish, Hispanic. The others are harder to see, their faces gone to shadow beneath their caps in that harsh white California light. On the back of the photo someone has handwritten: *These Mexican men* are out to canvas* [*sic*] *the country side* [*sic*] *for people working in the cotton fields.*

Fortunately, those Mexicans aren't relevant to my book; why worry about their demands? They're way up north in Corcoran. The year is 1933. Edith Karpen had just begun teaching school in Imperial. I asked whether society had been stratified in those days and she replied: It was very stratified, oh, yes. The ranch owners and people like that were one stratum, and then there were the salespeople and that stratum, and then the Mexicans that were not . . . They lived, well, you can't imagine the squalor that they lived in. They lived on the ditch banks, with just a tarp for . . . Throughout the valley that was how they lived, but I think we were the most primitive. There was a department store in San Diego, Marston's, that was kind of the top store for that area, and they had a daughter, I've forgotten her name,

*That year there were fifteen thousand pickers in the area, three-quarters of them Mexican.

but I think it was Adele, and Adele Marston became incensed with the living conditions down there, and she came down there and held meetings. They had the pea pickers' strike and the Highway Patrol came in to maintain order. I remember looking out the window of my hotel and seeing the Highway Patrol on either side. The buildup lasted maybe a week, but the worst part was over quickly. They say it was put down with force; I never saw any force. I just stayed away. That was probably in '34. Of course in the classroom my kids didn't talk about it.

A tubby, ageing man in a white shirt, dark overalls and a dark hat raises a bugle to his lips and blows! A younger man, clutching his straw hat behind him, leans forward to yell. One of the men in the truck behind him has raised his right arm in what resembles a Fascist salute. In the crowd of men, a man sits on a canted motorcycle. They're on duty now, and they're staring across the road, into a place which the photographer has not shown us. The caption reads: *Pickets on the highway calling workers from the fields.* Well, that's still far away in Corcoran. We'd better hope that our Mexicans don't hear that bugle. *Of course in the classroom my kids didn't talk about it.*

In 1934, Upton Sinclair runs for Governor of the Golden State on the ticket of EPIC—End Poverty in California. Part of his platform reads: *The people of our State find themselves in a permanent crisis . . . We have too many steel mills, oil wells, coal mines, automobile factories . . . What causes overproduction? The fact that the wealth of our country has become concentrated in a few hands.*

EPIC owns the answers. What about the lot of Mexican field workers down in American Imperial? What about the days of Lupe Vásquez? *In a State system conducted by the workers for their own benefit, such work will be in the nature of a holiday excursion . . . There will be comfort and recreation for all . . .*

What if that could have been made true? *The farmers of America have not been told about what is going on in Russia,* Sinclair continues, *and few . . . realize that under the new system of collective farming, the Soviet Union produced last year a crop more than ten per cent larger than any in its history.* As a matter of fact, between 1929 and 1933, fifteen or sixteen million people were murdered for the sake of collectivization; moreover, Soviet grain and cattle production figures did not surpass their prerevolutionary analogues until 1954. But what if idealists had forged a better way?

Down in Southside, Cárdenas, fresh from his labors in Michoacán, runs for President on the platform of hope, comes into power, then does the unthinkable: He begins to carry out his promises!

In Northside, Sinclair loses—of course!—while the Depression worsens, and the unemployed, the newly farmless, the beaten down, listen desperately for the far-off trumpet of any rescuing angel. What do they hear? *Pickets on the highway calling workers from the fields.*

A Wobbly organizer announces that in the fight between labor and capital, *there is no compromise or arbitration . . . that can solve or settle it; either labor has to come into its own or go down . . .* In other words, **DISARM THE RICH FARMER OR ARM THE WORKER FOR SELF-DEFENSE**.

In 1935, Paul S. Taylor's wife, the great photographer Dorothea Lange, records the faces and backgrounds of migrant laborers in the Imperial Valley. In 1937, now employed by the Resettlement Administration, she returns there in order to produce the ninety-seven images now in Lot 345 of the Administration's files. She writes her boss: . . . *what goes on in the Imperial is beyond belief. The Imperial Valley has a social structure all its own and partly because of its isolation in the state those in control get away with it. But this year's freeze practically wiped out the crop . . . The region is swamped with homeless moving families.* I just stayed away. Of course in the classroom my kids didn't talk about it.

A man in a banded hat, brilliant white cigarette in his mouth, hunches above the wheel of a truck, peering over his shoulder at us through the open door. In the truck bed, which is barred with planks like a cage, no doubt to prevent agricultural wealth from spilling onto the road, ten women and girls stand, leaning against or gripping the planks; they look anxious, distressed. Their sign reads: **THE GOVERNOR SENDS AID TO PIXLEY: 24 DEPUTY SHERIFFS, 11 HIGHWAY PATROLMEN. WE WANT FOOD!** Shall I tell you who they are? *A crowd of young Mexican women at the picket lines. They are fighters when they get mad. Some are educated.*

And now grinning men in pale hats, white shirts and dark trousers are standing against the wooden wall between truck bed and cab; their sign reads: **JOIN THE PICKET LINES. DON'T SCAB.** Behind them are two more trucks and more men walking; it's a procession on this still grey road. On the back is written: *Out to picket again . . . The officers, however, kept them on the move. In some fields the farmers stood with guns and held them off, in others they swarmed over the fields and beat the men and women who were working there with clubs until they had all the people who were willing to work scared . . .* Fortunately, this is Pixley, not Imperial, where a brown girl, perhaps ten years old, bends as if to curtsey at the end of that narrow wooden pier, and dips her drinking water out of a cloudy canal near El Centro. Behind her is a field, with distant trees on the horizon.

"SCHOOL CHIEF IN DENIAL OF COMMUNISM HERE"

It would be false to suggest that white Californians emoted toward their brown brothers and sisters with anywhere near the same degree of obsessiveness that white Southerners did to the people then called Negroes. If the newspapers of those decades are any indication, Californians were more frightened of Reds and gypsy burglars than of Mexicans. To be sure, the *Fresno Morning Republican* informs us that three men with Hispanic names have been arrested in the murder of a Japanese peddler in Coalinga; two days later the same publication advises us that the Department of the Interior has sent out *circulars urging measures to prevent the entry of Mexican workers into the United States . . . It is pointed out that many Mexicans are in a miserable plight in southern [American] states, where they can find no work. It is also said that unrestricted emigration endangers Mexican agriculture and industry.* But in the first place, the three murderers with Hispanic-sounding names are explicitly pointed out as murderers; in the second, as you see, the Interior Department's circular genteelly pretends to be helping Mexicans, not defending whites from them. This is not at all the case with gypsies, who are eternally sinister in some sordid, unknown way; nor is it so with Reds.

As long as Mexicans refrain from going Red, we can use them. But shall I tell you what we don't like? *A crowd of young Mexican women at the picket lines. They are fighters when they get mad. Some are educated.*

And now these Red Mexicans are beating the good Mexicans who accept *our* wage to harvest our crops in season. (In 1909, we paid a dollar per hundredweight of cotton picked in the Imperial Valley. In 1938 we pay seventy-five cents.) Talk about broad and sinister motives!

Here's California's position: *We farmers want to be fair, and we think we are, but we won't deal with any alien Reds.*

These business practices may be informed by memories of lurid headlines about the Mexican Revolution, which once seemed to have subsided but which may be rearing up again, thanks to that dangerous, crazy fellow, Cárdenas. How could at least the cannier growers forget atrocities committed (as a historian of the Zapatistas acutely puts it) *by men who wore white pajamas and sandals to work, carried machetes, and presented swarthy complexions, in this last betraying themselves unmistakably as members of an "inferior race"?** For the Revolution was no mere brown-skinned irrelevance. The expropriation of the haciendas affected the economy of Northside itself. What if alien Reds tried to repeat the procedure in Imperial? That would be unfair, positively un-American.

Not all employers of farm labor dig in their heels. We are informed, almost unbelievably, that a certain powerful grape grower gets *forced to that belief against my own prejudices . . . As an employer of labor, I would welcome the unionization of the common laborer, if it can be done. I don't know if it can be done.*

It can't be done, I suppose. Let's hide our heads in the sand. *Imperial Valley Press*, Tuesday, April 1, 1926, front page: **SCHOOL CHIEF IN DENIAL OF COM-**

*In every respect but the swarthiness, this description anticipates 1960s images of Viet Cong.

MUNISM HERE: Says There Is No Cancer of Anarchy Among the California Students.

Unfortunately for the school chief, Reds will soon make themselves known right here at the center of the world where the Pacific Land and Cattle Co., Inc., offers **IMPERIAL QUALITY** lard; and in due course, a history of the Great Depression will describe *the huge irrigated farms of California's Imperial Valley, San Joaquin Valley and Sacramento Valley, the three most important agricultural regions in the second most important agricultural state in the nation,* as *the principal arenas* of class conflict.

"THE WORST PART WAS OVER QUICKLY" (CONTINUED)

As early as 1925, the authorities in the Mexicali Valley began to find it necessary to send home seasonally unemployed campesinos, encouraging them to believe, with or without grounds, that *ejido* grants might await them.—You see, there were months when the Chandler Syndicate's acres required no tending.—Accordingly, those who could crossed the ditch into Northside, radicalized and desperate.

In 1927 there were already thirty-seven thousand migrant children in California.

In 1928 the Imperial Valley Workers Union, eventually renamed the Asociación Mutual del Valle Imperial (AMVI), commences business in the Benito Juárez Mutual Benefit Society Hall. The Mexican consulate gives cautious advice and direction. I cannot tell you what that kindhearted grape grower says about it all. Meanwhile, cantaloupe pickers demand higher wages, not to mention payment of wages already owed. These insolent attempts at extortion being manfully resisted, the pickers initiate a series of wildcat strikes. Imperial County Sheriff C. L. Gillett musters forty deputies, arrests sixty alien Reds, closes down poolhalls and holds the line.

In January 1930, Imperial County growers, drowning in overproduction, lower vegetable and fruit wages, so new strikes naturally arise, the AMVI receiving assistance from three Communist organizers from Los Angeles. The fellowship between the latter and the former achieves such success that the AMVI actually joins with the Chamber of Commerce to denounce them. Undaunted, the Communists prepare a grand conference, to be held on 14 April in El Centro. The name of their organization, the Agricultural Workers' Industrial League (AWIL), implies, at least to me, a proto-Maoist attempt to conflate migrant workers with that urban proletariat which by orthodox Marxist theory comprises the truly revolutionary class. It might be their hesitation to be enrolled into this brotherhood which explains the leeriness of the field workers; then again, it might be their menacing situation in American Imperial: expendable, replaceable, deportable, lacking representation and many legal rights, and quite aware that their situation in the Mexican pueblos where they originated might be worse. (Juan Rulfo, 1953: *What land have they given us, Melitón? There isn't even enough here for the wind to blow up a dust cloud.*) In any event, the AWIL finds itself not exactly alone, but certainly isolated. As for the ruling class of Imperial County, no doubt they still *want to be fair, and we think we are, but we won't deal with any alien Reds.* Moreover, as a government book will later explain, *the demands . . . came at a time when the farm owners were least able to meet them.* And so the worst is over quickly, the lettuce and cantaloupe strikes both defeated, and more than a hundred workers and organizers arrested. Eight leaders receive long prison sentences, although they will be paroled by 1933.

Early in 1931, strong rains make fields impossible to work in the Mexicali Valley. Three thousand hungry campesinos promise to loot Mexicali unless they get jobs within twenty-four hours. Grocers distribute free food in hopes of saving themselves from complete expropriation. Governor Trejo y Lordo calls out the army and expels *all Americans employed in Mexicali,* particularly—here the reference must be to the Colorado River Land Company—*several veteran American cotton ranch foremen, employed below the line.* The effect of these events on labor relations in American Imperial can be imagined. What next? *We need have no fear that our lands will not become better and better as the years go by.* Indeed, a history of California farmworkers has this to say about Imperial County: *Working and living conditions, which had long been recognized as the worst in the state, had become unspeakable by 1933.*

But don't worry! Wasn't Chinese exclusion a patriotic success? Didn't we save ourselves from insolent Japanese labor contractors? Why not similarly clean up our Mexican problem? And so, three hundred thousand Mexican workers in American border states, half of them in California, conveniently return home. You will be pleased to know, courtesy of the *Los Angeles Times,* that *those who have already gone did so of their own volition. No "pressure" whatsoever was applied . . .* And a retired minister, who evidently knows how to do well by doing good, explains: *By helping Mexicans return to their own country, we relieve conditions in this country.* Nine hundred of the repatriates will take part in *a vast co-operative farming scheme* in the Colorado River Delta. The crop is, of course, cotton. *Co-operating were the Colorado River Land Company, the Pacific Oil Mills and the Globe Mills.* Shall I give you a morale report? *A peso a day is paid the colonists in provisions and clothing, and many went through the season without so much as a centavo in their pockets, yet were comfortable and happy.*

What if they weren't? **DISARM THE RICH FARMER OR ARM THE WORKER FOR SELF-DEFENSE.**

Meanwhile, even more hungry would-laborers have arrived in American Imperial. They are squatting along the banks of our canals and ditches. Fortunately, few of them could be labeled alien Reds, for they hail from the heartland.

Once upon a time, twelve years before George Chaffey opened his headgates, the Oklahoma Territory was Imperial. Almost two million acres got staked out in a single day. A novel about this epoch rings with rhetoric which would have coaxed Barbara Worth's cherry-red lips into their sweetest smile: *There's never been a chance like it in the world. We can make a model empire out of this Oklahoma country . . .*

But just as the Owens Valley in the mid-1920s began to dry up, her farms and stores abandoned, so ten years later the Okies saw their model empire blow away. They did not even have Mulholland to blame.

I see a pale farmhouse whose windmill is as white as a skeleton against the immense oncoming black spheres of dust-cloud. The door to an outbuilding hangs blackly open. Perhaps the family has already gone. The woodcut artist who carved this in 1938 remarks: *A typical scene of the "Dirty Thirties" of the Dust Bowl Days . . . Windows and doors failed to keep out the fine dust.* In another woodcut by the same man, a farmhouse sits half buried in white dust, its trees dead silhouettes, its wagon wheels sunk into the new desert which eerily resembles Imperial, the slatted windmill standing above everything like a clock of doom. A lithograph by a different artist five years earlier portrays the sand as rippling with dune-stripes; and before the black-cavitied hulk of a farmhouse stands a shovel, stuck slantwise into the sand as if someone had begun to dig a grave and fled.

In Padua, Oklahoma, Wallace Case stays safely out of debt so that the banks can't get him. One day his grandson sees him weeping for the first time. Following the mandate of the Agricultural Adjustment Act, G-men have shot his cattle. Doing everything right was not good enough, it would seem.

Oklahoma lost ever more fields to the dust devils; meanwhile, Imperial had too much produce for her own good! Reader, can you connect the dots?

A hobo who wandered the country through those years remembers *Yuma and the Imperial Valley where you could usually pick up a few days work on a ranch or farm . . .*

But in *The Grapes of Wrath,* Steinbeck details the plight of desperate Okies* who went all the way to California, only to find that there was no work for them. There was food, of course—but the growers were destroying surpluses, to keep the price down.

A boy named H. T. Roach is riding the rails in 1935. Los Angeles had just formed

*One of Steinbeck's many fans kindly explains the derivation of the term "Okie": "This word was born in the mind of a novelist whose current book portrayed the tenant farmers and sharecroppers of the state of Oklahoma as a slovenly, hopeless, dirty-thinking, vile-talking class of people."

a Committee on Indigent Alien Transients, and will refuse entry to people without jobs or money until overruled by the California Attorney General. *Los Angeles declared war on us,* he says. *I was on a freight train that was stopped at the Arizona-California border. A small army of railroad agents swept the train and kicked off upwards of six hundred of us. They left us standing in the silent desert.* Did he get work in Imperial? He does not say.

Philip Bonosky remembers: *We saw the ruling class on the defensive. We saw breadlines and thousands of workers rioting to get a dozen jobs. We saw cops raising fountains of blood on the heads of ex-servicemen and workers in steel towns and coal towns.*

As for the campesinos whose hunger had impelled them across the line into the fields of American Imperial, they must have been aware that their own blood could be invited out of their skulls should they fail to mind their manners.

So thank goodness for politeness: Mr. E. B. Goodman of El Centro *(lived here off & on since 1889)* assures us: *No Red lives here. Desert doesn't breed reds. They are trying to come in however.* His next remark, alas, sounds like something that a Red would say: *Brokers-shippers others interested in vegetable business exploiting this Country—thinking only of profit. Don't own land.*

But let's all of us think only of profit! Isn't that how Arid America's supposed to reclaim herself? Barbara Worth's verdant Ministry of Capital harks back to Adam Smith and his invisible hand! W. F. Holt builds up his Redland Syndicate by means of the Three Sacred Axioms: *I can't help believing in people . . . I have never been cheated out of a dollar in my life . . . I've found that the way to get your money is to give a man a chance to pay you.* So why can't the growers and the field workers all get rich? In Mexican Imperial they pay three pesos a day—less than the cost of living. Here on the Northside the wage is three times higher. What do we need Reds for? *The first picture on the south wall of the lobby will be that of the "Financial Genius," without which the Valley would have remained the land of nothing. He made a success through his own efforts. He sold out at a fancy price.*

In 1933 and 1934, Imperial County's years of worst violence, we find Communists still pitted against the Mexican consulate, whose labor organization therefore becomes almost palatable to growers. The first strike (lettuce again) ends to the growers' satisfaction, and the Consul is their hero. An outside investigator reports: *Consul last year made a survey of whole valley of living conditions—absolutely no complaint.* By the way, the Consul is said to collect or extort bribes from his countrymen upon their arrival in Northside, so I wonder whether the Chamber of Commerce might also take up occasional collections for him? *Consul: Mexicans recognize they & the growers have a common problem with the agitators.* In any event, his exhortations together with the police's own exertions rescue the growers again during the following strike, of pea pickers; it was concerning this success that Edith Karpen said to me: *The worst part was over quickly.*

But now the Communists are in force, and the trick harder to pull off. A Communist cell operates in Brawley. The Party-run Cannery and Agricultural Workers Industrial Union also sets up shop. The union's two organizers, however, possess little experience. Stanley Hancock, twenty-five, has been called *a functionary, and* Dorothy Ray, age nineteen, has not yet graduated from the Communist Youth League. Their bravery must have been immense. Like their predecessors, they will end by doing hard prison time. As the Party will be informed in a disapproving report: ...THEY AGITATED THE WORKERS FOR A STRIKE INSTEAD OF EMPHASIZING ORGANIZATION SO AS TO PREPARE FOR A STRIKE...

Perhaps even fullfledged apparatchiks could not have better directed the workers, given the ugly confluence then squeezing Imperial—that unsold produce withheld from hungry hordes, whose newest members were Dustbowl refugees competing economically and racially with Mexican labor; the failure of previous strikes, which must have inflamed all parties; the increasing militancy in Mexicali, the impending rupture between Cárdenas and the Chandler Syndicate. One must grant that Hancock and Ray chose their battleground well. Have you forgotten that Imperial County remains America's number-one provider of early lettuce? As a matter of fact, the lettuce growers are already over a barrel. The pro rate system of idling production so as to keep crop prices up will soon become an American institution. In fact, it has recently commenced right here, with lettuce, in self-reliant, Republican Imperial County. What does that indicate, but soft demand? Now is the time. Accordingly, at the beginning of 1934, the Communists call a general lettuce strike. Their primary demand: thirty-five cents an hour.

Growers respond by raising wages from fifteen to twenty-two and a half cents per hour, with a five-hour minimum; they immediately default. Well, even a kept promise might not have kept the peace. Twenty-two and a half cents is not thirty-five.

I see pale tents crammed all the way to the field-horizon, women and children in a line on the pale dirt, a banner for the CIRCO AZTECA; groups of people under almost every awning; in this tiny print it takes awhile for the eye to realize how teeming this camp really is. On the back is written: *The camp site at Corcoran, Calif.* Mexican labor camps in Imperial must have looked similar. *There were about 2000 here. The Circo Azteca, at the left, was for some show that was in camp—probably to excite the workers.*

Analogues to that Mexican labor camp may certainly be found in the entity called Imperial. The Colorado River Land Company does not seem to be hiring

Okies. In 1934, the United States Special Commission on Agricultural Labor Disturbances in Imperial Valley reports on squatters' camps: . . . *we found filth, squalor, an entire absence of sanitation, and a crowding of human beings into totally inadequate tents or crude structures built of boards . . . During the warm weather, when the temperature rises considerably above 100 degrees, the flies and insects become a pest, the children are fretful, the attitude of the parents can be imagined . . . In this environment there is bred a social sullenness which is to be deplored, but which can be understood by those who have viewed the scenes that violate all the recognized standards of living . . .*

That year we see people with milk-jugs and bottles lining up to get their free water from a railroad car, FOR FAMILY USE ONLY.

Men in work clothes are sitting on long wooden benches in the California Employment Relief Station Camp, whose corrugated metal walls make everything slightly greyer. It is meal time beneath the bare bulbs. The great Hetzel himself has signed this photograph, which is as nondescript as most of his other productions. We get the gist of it: In Imperial in 1934, many, many people have gone on relief. How many would decline to scab? Perhaps this will not be the most propitious time for the Communists' lettuce strike.

In the Bancroft Library at Berkeley, in a carton labeled *Farm labor situation 1933–34*, I have seen, among many other faded souvenirs of angry drama, two sheets of stationery bearing the image of Imperial's heroine, Barbara Worth. Some of the handwriting—evidently Dean Hutchinson's from Berkeley; he must have been preparing one of his reports on broad and sinister motives—is difficult to make out; most of its references are enigmatic. And yet even an abbreviated version conveys that time's ugliness, the secretive preparations for worse:

Tried to get the opposing factions together here. Was arrested. Not jailed. Contacted all groups. Even going to & from Azteca hall, looked suspicious. Did Kris under orders of MacCullough arr.? leave of absence from girl's office at time.

The lettuce strike begins. Five thousand field workers take part. By now the Consul and his union are utterly discredited, so that the growers feel compelled to meet the picketers with naked violence. Fortunately, many Imperial sheriffs, police, and kindred deputies of legal force happen to be growers, so they can be counted on to enforce the law in the most impartial spirit. Our oracle, the *Imperial Valley Press*, reveals all with kindred objectivity:

On Monday, 8 January 1934, we read with relief that the strikers abstain from violence, so there is *no trouble in the sheds*. A certain woman has convened a radical meeting near State and Second; Filipinos are driving in with strike banners. Meanwhile, the Cannery and Agricultural Workers Industrial Union calls for, among other insolences, equal pay for women and free clean drinking water on the job. On the following morning almost a thousand lettuce strikers (not five thousand as we read a paragraph ago; perhaps both sides deploy figures with a light hand) refuse to disperse, compelling the police to charge and tear gas them, an action which, I am happy to say, *broke up the meeting without violence of any sort.* Eight people have already been arrested for *investigation relative to picketing activities.*

As for the Communist agitators, Dean Hutchinson's notes indicate that the police already know who they are: *Jan 9th crowd formed* in Brawley . . . *& blocaded* [*sic*] *traffic. Milling about excited—Chief* [*of Police*] *asked what going to do. Said hold a parade. Told them they could not do so. Some yelled let's go pay no attention to Police—no leaders. Went around in front of group in his car. Americans Filipinos negroes gathered out of curiosity but apparently not in group. Streets blocked two blocks. Threatened to shoot tear gas. They did shoot tear gas—riot gun short range projectile, hit one man—then a hand grenade of gas—maybe another one thrown. Mob dispersed. Woman—Dorothy Ray does a lot of talking, agitation. Chief filed complaint about John Do Hancock, Pat Chambers & Dorothy Ray and told his men to pick them up.*

On the tenth, the *Press* reassures us that life continues in the same tranquil spirit, I suppose because another hundred-odd strikers are just now marching to jail in order to be investigated for picketing activities. What might these crimes be—intimidation of scabs, or merely holding up signs? Well, after all, if we want our fields to be almost as efficient as washing machines, can we let any demands whatsoever interrupt the spin cycle? The authorities now arrest more people with Mexican-sounding names, and on the next day the *Press* reports that the strike is *believed to have weakened,* thank goodness. Accordingly, on the day after that (we have now reached the twelfth), a front-page headline promises: **Legionnaires Assist Officers Who Declare Militia Will Not Be Required**. The character of the Legion's assistance may be imagined. Meanwhile, Sheriff Campbell sends a telegram to the Governor's office giving notice that he may need the National Guard.

When officers threw bombs into the meeting room they closed the doors. Within a few seconds a gasping crowd composed entirely of Mexicans began breaking the glass. Meanwhile, eight women and twelve men get arrested on the fields. *The American Legion has answered the emergency call* . . . Other sources verify that the Legion does indeed perform its patriotic part, employing clubs as necessary. I can't help believing in people. If Dean Hutchinson's notes are to be believed, the picketers do not exactly adhere to Gandhi, either:

. . . Brawley Meeting Azteca Hall 12th January. Police had 3 warrants for arrest for holding illegal meetings. Mexicans gathered around & prevented ar-

rest. Amer. Legion has at Brawley emergency committee. Patroled and garded [sic] streets in case of Earthquake. Commander refused 2–3 times before calling out his committee. 60 members responded. All sworn in as deputies. Tried to get in building. Chief of Police hit over head with bar. Tear gas bomb thrown in, Came out fighting. Found under platform bunch of 4–600 clubs. Many had spikes thru end. Claimed to be used for firewood.

By the thirteenth the *Press* hears the music of quietude in the lettuce fields! . . . **THE DESERT DISAPPEARS**. Seventy people now sit in prison. It is Saturday, and I hope that on this very night, Edith Karpen, who must have been strongwilled, self-reliant and effective, will dine with her sweetheart at the Owl in Mexicali. *You would go back and there was the gambling and the bar, and you would go back to the dining area, and it was real plush.* At the Owl, beer remains five cents a glass for Bock, and the management is advertising a new floor show—new faces in the chorus, exotic dancers, beautiful girls! On Sunday, Imperial's finest raid two locations, arresting six Filipinos and two whites, one of whom, you will be sad to read, is female. In addition, officers seize and confiscate alleged Red literature from two people whom they accuse of *roaming about from place to place without any lawful business.* Where do these types originate, anyway?

I rejoice to see the following news from Tuesday: **ALL QUIET ON STRIKE FRONT**. On Wednesday, **OFFICIALS BELIEVE BACKBONE OF LETTUCE STRIKE BROKEN**, although *alleged attorneys* do annoy the peacemakers by asking for writs of habeas corpus. A Constitution is one of those magic exemplars of crockeryware whose beauty remains untouched for those who break them. On Friday, Imperial issues a bench warrant for the arrest of a misguided attorney. By the way, I have it on the reliable authority of the *Press* that the valley's troubles are not at all homegrown; Reds from outside are the villains; and so in obedience to agitators, not by locals. And so Dorothy Ray, Stanley Hancock and a third Communist, Frank Nieto, now view events through prison bars. The latter two enroll in a chain gang, and vigilantes allegedly greet them with death threats. As for Ray, *the tank in which she is held reaches a summer temperature of 122 degrees.* That same day, the California state police chief denies that his officers have used any violence against strikers. How could I have doubted it?

A week later, on Wednesday the twenty-fourth, A. L. Wirin, an American Civil Liberties Union lawyer who has expressed concern about the treatment of strikers, answers a knock on the door of his hotel room (unlike Dean Hutchinson, he is staying at the Planters' Inn in Brawley). His guests throw a sheet over his head, drag him off, and reward him with *a cut lip and other bruises alleged to have been received during the scuffle.* After rolling his Ford roadster down into the dump, then robbing him and threatening to burn him, they leave him in the desert north of Calipatria. He walks eleven barefoot miles before finding help. In my own time it will not be uncommon for illegal *pollos* and *solos* to walk such distances and more (in the opposite direction); but presumably, being agricultural laborers, they are habituated to the outdoors, and they surely have shoes or tough feet.* Mr. Wirin was lucky to have survived. But why dwell on such pranks? *Calm and quiet ruled in Imperial Valley today.* And on page five, the *Press* sets our souls at rest regarding the methods by which calm and quiet was achieved: *Contrary to rumors spread about the streets, it was learned this morning from authoritative American Legion sources that the Legion had little or nothing to do with the abduction of Wirin . . .* Well, nothing like going to the source!

Wirin files suit against the Governor, the head of the Los Angeles police "Red squad," the police chief of Brawley, the chief of the state Highway Patrol and one of his officers, and twenty-five John Does. But when he is summoned before the El Centro District Court, he declines to appear, expressing fear for his life.

Perhaps he was wise, for I read that another lawyer for the strikers is attacked in Niland, still another arrested within three hours of his arrival and imprisoned for thirty-five days; a third is *assaulted on the very steps of the Court House by a band which included county officials.*

Or perhaps, as Dean Hutchinson's investigating committee concludes, the accounts of Mr. Wirin's "kidnapping" (quotation marks supplied by the Committee) have been embellished.

And now it is the end of January, and the strike has finally been foiled. I suppose that fewer brown faces and more white ones now appear in the lettuce fields. (The following exclamation of pleasure comes from the San Joaquin Valley Agriculture Labor Bureau, and hence bears no relevance to Imperial: *The labor that came voluntarily from the drought area,* in other words Oklahoma, *came at the opportune time.*) Not everything is heavenly; Brawley's anti-strike ordinance has been found unconstitutional in district court; and lettuce prices continue so low that the growers declare a three-day holiday. But at least the Imperial Valley remains unsullied by any farmworkers' union.

The strikes resume in February. The Imperial County Board of Supervisors addresses them with a new ordinance: Strikes will now be illegal near public thoroughfares! Just in case that measure fails to achieve expectations, a number of Imperial Valley growers join together with like-minded souls to form the Associated Farmers of America. After all, the injunction against Brawley's ordinance implies that the authorities can no longer protect us from alien Reds. That eerily real

*Some of the forty-two Chinese who set out from San Felipe for Mexicali in 1902 lacked shoes and hats. Thirty-five died.

IMPERIAL VALLEY PRODUCTS!

The Growers and Shippers of Imperial Valley have organized murderous gangs into so-called Vigilantes and in the past week have kidnapped four persons, viciously slugged five, and driven out of Imperial Valley fifteen persons, some of them workers who have lived in the Valley over fifteen years and are torn from their families and relatives.

THIS TERRORIZATION CAMPAIGN IS ORGANIZED BY THE GROWERS AND SHIPPERS TO PREVENT THE ORGANIZATION OF WORKERS FOR STRUGGLE AGAINST STARVATION WAGES AND INTOLERABLE CONDITIONS.

ANSWER THIS TERROR BY REFUSING TO BUY IMPERIAL VALLEY GOODS

Issued by the: Cannery & Agricultural Workers Industrial Union, 852 Eight Ave., San Diego, Calif.

novel *Babbitt,* published more than a decade before these happenings, invented a nationwide organization called the Good Citizens' League, which found its greatest strength in *commercial cities of a few hundred thousand inhabitants, most of which . . . lay inland, against a background of cornfields and mines and of small towns which depended upon them for mortgage-loans, table-manners, art, social philosophy and millinery . . .* It was our Good Citizens' credo that *the working-classes must be kept in their place; and all of them perceived that American Democracy did not imply any equality of wealth, but did demand a wholesome sameness of thought . . .* The creed of the Good Citizens strangely resembled that of the new Associated Farmers, whose weapons include axe handles and whose helpers include a Colonel of the U.S. Army Reserve and that same chief of the California Highway Patrol whom Wirin named in his lawsuit. In June, one of their kind will deliver a speech to the Commonwealth Club of San Francisco on the subject of "California's Embattled Farmer." Here is a sample: *We object most strenuously to inferences that those workers were required either to live in those camps or to consume muddy water. What they get out of that ditch water is up to them, just as it is up to their employers.*

Despite the forces and resources on their side, the growers must have found it unprofitable or otherwise impractical to hold the line absolutely; for at the end of March, the growers agree to wages of a quarter per hour for field labor and thirteen cents per hour for cantaloupe picking (the strikers had wanted thirty-five and sixteen). The Communists accordingly prepare to attack the May cantaloupe harvest.

Did you know who Imperial County's truest friend is?—Why, Los Angeles.—On March 28, this disinterestedly altruistic neighbor, as represented by a certain G.P.C., Secretary and General Manager of her Chamber of Commerce, dictates a letter to Congressman Dockweiler in Washington, D.C. Los Angeles informs her representative that she opposes the dispatch of any federal labor conciliator to the Imperial Valley in this matter of the cantaloupe strike, because *the temper of the Californian or any other American under such stress* will lead to bloodshed. Los Angeles may not think that such a bad thing. *Instead of a kid glove, we need an iron hand . . . These communistic leaders must be deported and the soviet propaganda stamped out.*

Their strike will be defeated, of course; and in 1935 we see a Mexican field worker in a white straw hat and a bandanna about his throat on the verge of leaving for the melon fields, his left hand hooked in his heavy belt, whose buckle is square, his right arm hanging loose, his trouser legs tied tight over his shoes at the ankle. Grim and wary, sweaty and tough, this young man clenches his mouth, gazing past us. Here comes his competition: Between June 1935 and August 1936, more than eighty-six thousand Dustbowl refugees arrive in California. (Now for the important news! By mid-July 1936, the Imperial Valley has shipped seven thousand nine hundred and ninety-three carloads of melons in seventy-two days!) By March 1938 there will be a hundred and twenty thousand new refugees.

Date: March 15, 1935.

To: Harry E. Drobish, Director of Rural Rehabilitation.

From: Paul S. Taylor, Regional Director.

Subject: Establishment of Rural Rehabilitation Camps for Migrants in California. Item VIIIC.

Among suitable locations for initial camps, the following are recommended:...Riverside County: Indio, Oasis; Imperial County: Westmoreland, Mt. Signal, Calipatria...

A white man from 1935, stubbled, in bib overalls, stares not quite toward us from the Imperial Valley. His eyes are pits of shadow. His neck is bent and there are wrinkles in the bridge of his nose. The shadows catch his cheekbones. There is nothing behind him but solid tan, like some ancient badly fixed photograph of an Imperial landscape.

His day may be coming; the growers surely prefer him to alien Reds! For by the autumn of that year, broad and sinister motives have infected even the hinterlands of Los Angeles: Citrus pickers, *most of whom were Mexicans,* dare to make demands—rejected since winter citrus is small business anyway. *That Orange county should be chosen for this purpose showed very definitely some deeply laid plot. The pickers have been well paid . . .* at five and a half cents per box. They dare to ask forty cents an hour for a nine-hour day, a day's work being thirty boxes; after that, they want seven cents a box. The confrontation builds until July of 1936, when strikers with clubs, knives and chains attack picking crews and packing-house workers. Both sides suffer injuries; hundreds arrested. *Interrogation of the arrested rioters showed that only four per cent of them are American citizens.*

From 1936 a man in work boots and corduroy pants sits in the driver's seat of his square, grimy vehicle, his face blasted white by the Coachella sun. The silhouette of his wife (only the lenses of her spectacles can be seen) lurks in the passenger side, hunching toward him, or perhaps just toward the center of the cab, which is farthest from that hot light. They are hoping to be taken on picking carrots. I suspect they have already found, as had the author of the 1936 *Motor Tales and Travels In and Out of California,* that *disappointment was in store in the Imperial Valley, for El Centro was reached during a period of intense heat.* If they do get jobs, I hope they remember to demean themselves submissively; for by September the Associated Farmers will be beating and gassing white strikers up in Salinas. *The essence of the industrial life which springs from irrigation is its democracy.*

In 1937, when they complete Barbara Worth Junior High School in Brawley, a Mexican pea field worker stands in front of his shack, whose cardboard is peeling from the outer walls; in the darkness, a small girl peeks from the doorway, clinging to it; and the man stands mournfully with one foot on the tailgate of his vehicle, holding a swaddled baby. It is March and the peas have frozen, and he does not know what will happen. Who cares? There's only a four percent chance that he's an American citizen.

"When a person's able to work, what's the use of beggin'? We ain't that kind of people," said elderly pea pickers near Calipatria.

Is that so, Okies? Your wish is our command! Caption to a Dorothea Lange photograph (#LC USF34-16338-DC): *March 1937. Drought and depression refugee from Oklahoma now working in the pea fields of California. She has picked cotton since the age of four. Imperial Valley, California.*

Of course not everyone will be as lucky as she. In another Dorothea Lange photograph, a skinny man in a beaten-up broadbrimmed hat sits with drawn-up knees on a ridge of dirt, with planted furrows receding to the horizon, whose righthand edge is marked by the commencement of a single upslope which may well be Signal Mountain. Clasping his hands, he looks away from us. His cheeks are wrinkled and his neck is corded. The caption: *Jobless on Edge of Pea Field, Imperial Valley, California, 1937.*

(Dean Hutchinson's notes, sheet 4: *Doc. W. F. Fox County Courthouse El Centro County Health Officer Thursday A.M. Apr. 5th 1934. Camp sanitation pea fields hasn't changed in last 4 years—no improvement. Industry itself has developed very rapidly same time. Tremendous influx of migratory labor from district to district in Calif & Arizona . . .*)

And they trek into California, Paul S. Taylor told the Commonwealth Club of California, *these California whites, at the end of a long immigrant line of Chinese, Japanese, Koreans, Negroes, Hindustanis, Mexicans, Filipinos, to serve the crops and farmers of our state.* Taylor calls them *a rural proletariat.*

Imperial embraces them, and in 1937 we find this paean of welcome in the *Brawley Daily News:*

> Jonathon Garst, Regional Director of the Resettlement Administration has declared that the migratory camp for Brawley is to be built despite all the objections that have been raised.
>
> Mayor Carey and others wanted to know why they were not consulted. Garst asserted that he was more interested in the people on the "ditch banks" than the people of Brawley.
>
> The growers declared that experience had demonstrated that the class of persons found on the "ditch bank" camps are not suitable for field work, such as thinning and cultivating lettuce. They might be used as pea pickers in some instances—but the season for this class of labor is short.

In other words, **Water was in the ditches, seeds were in the ground, green was becoming abundant, and the whole area was dotted with the homes of hopeful, industrious, devoted persons.** *The club motto is, "The aim if reached or not, makes great the life."*

In 1946, the College of Agriculture at UC Berkeley will conclude that *the seasonal farm workers . . . continue to present a major social problem.*

Fortunately, this story does not end unhappily for all parties: A historian of the period concludes that *the Imperial Valley authorities enjoyed an unlimited range of power.*

And now; and *now . . . IMPERIAL COUNTY SHOWS RAPID INCREASE . . . We need have no fear that our lands will not become better and better as the years go by.* In 1940, Imperial County's gross cash income from agriculture achieves twenty-one million dollars (three point one two percent of California's total). Out of California's fifty-eight counties, Imperial is number seven for cash farm lucre! *Why, I would be sick to my stomach if I rode down that valley in California, over those long miles owned by one man.*

And here comes a second happy ending: Japan bombs Pearl Harbor, and the Okies' problems explode into bits! They can join the army or work in a factory . . .

What about the Mexicans? I think we all feel sorry for 'em.

Chapter 100

BUTTER CREAM BREAD

(*ca.* 1936)

Once upon a time it was indisputably true that *Butter Cream Bread enriches every recipe in which bread is used . . . Baked in the Imperial Valley by Cramer's Bakery.* And in that fairytale time, if a good Imperial Valley housewife were to prepare a dinner with proportions for fifty guests, she'd lay in twenty-five cantaloupes, six quarter-pounds of butter, twenty-five pounds of roast pork, four average-sized cakes or nine average-sized pies, and seven quarts of ice cream. What does this tell us about the conviviality of the epoch, not to mention its prosperity for those who did not have to camp out along the sides of ditches, its ideas about nutrition, its level of physical activity (for we are fatter than they were)?

If I could only eat a slice of fresh-baked butter cream bread, then I would *know* the American Imperial of that time, because I could taste it. But just as Baja's fossil oysters, some of them two feet long and twenty pounds heavy, were expended in making brickmakers' lime, so American Imperial's butter cream bread got eaten up; nobody fossilized any of it for my private museum; Imperial hurtled along toward me, not imagining that it existed only in the past. *And in material advantages they are already well supplied.*

Chapter 101

COACHELLA

(1936–1950)

Dr. John Tyler came to the Coachella Valley in June of 1936. The following month, a Riverside County woman trapped two mountain lions.

I met Margie in the dental office, he told me. I came down and I worked on a percentage basis and a small salary for Frank Purcell, the established dentist. We got married in 1938. Practically the only time that I considered moving away from the area was a very short period of time in 1936 when the dental association were trying to locate dentists. And they had places like Fallbrook that had no dentists. When I came here, Frank Purcell and Rufus Choate, we had four, there were five dentists operating in the valley but when I married Margie I decided to stay put. With the aqueduct in here and all the workers, we had lots of work. The valley was growing, like mad.

It would hardly surprise me to learn that Dr. Tyler *decided to stay put* not only for the sake of his career, but also on his wife's account; for she was born on a ranch in Coachella in 1916. At any rate, when I asked him what made the area special, his reply expressed an elderly person's concerns: I think it's the climate. I think it's the heat. I think that air-conditioning has made it practical so that people can live here all through the summer, and people who have afflictions of the arthritic nature feel better than they ever have in their lives.

The main event in the first year or two that I was here, he said, was the arrival of the workers who were building the Metropolitan aqueduct going to Los Angeles, and the town was flooded with the wives of the aqueduct workers and so on, and for awhile getting a place to stay was a big thing. They came in literally by the hundreds to work on the aqueduct.

Where does it begin? I asked, wondering whether he would answer, *The Colorado* or *Imperial County,* but he simply replied: The aqueduct brings water from Parker.

And how did you feel about it?

Well, the local people, most of them, accepted the workers pretty well. At that time we still depended on wells, so we didn't mind too much one way or the other. But there was a lot of contention about the All-American Canal. They had planned that canal to go up to Coachella and they wanted the farms up here to be paying to furnish water for Imperial Valley for some time.

Did the Imperial Valley seem close or far away?

No, in those days distances seemed much further, said Mrs. Tyler.

Was Imperial poorer than Coachella?

Everybody was poor, said Mrs. Tyler, and Imperial wanted us to help pay for the canal when we weren't yet getting the water ourselves.

When did you feel that Coachella really started to boom?

There was kind of a boom in the twenties, before the Depression, said Mrs. Tyler. People building nice homes for tourists. Then that stopped. The farming industry burgeoned after the war. But the real boom, I think it was in the early thirties, and it had to do with air-conditioning. We had swamp coolers and people could live here without living too uncomfortable. When air-conditioning came in, it really burgeoned. The swamp coolers were a great help. As long as it's dry and not humid, they work beautifully.

Her husband put in: By the time we got married, well, the development was going so rapidly that building could hardly keep up.

Was the Date Festival pretty well established by then?

Well, it didn't start until the thirties. The first festivals were held in the Indio Park. And I don't remember exactly when it started at the fairground, said the old woman, wearily shaking her head.

I think the Indio Civic Club sponsored some of the early events that were in the park there, said her husband, trying to be helpful.

And how was Coachella in the forties?

I thought the war years here were kind of interesting when Patton's troops descended, he replied. All of a sudden we were inundated by Army people and Army wives. Poor things, they were trying to find even a room to rent. So people were renting their bedrooms. It was kind of a wild time. Most of us stayed off the streets. Lots of saloons. They had special buses on weekends when the soldiers had leave. Shall we tell 'em about the time the .45 was shot? We lived in the back of a bungalow court. We had the rear apartment. Between the rear apartment and the neighbor's garage was a place about four-and-a-half to five feet wide. One night there was all this commotion and yelling and gunshots. Some soldier from Patton's camp had stolen a car and he stopped outside. He was AWOL and wanted to leave and the military police didn't see it that way. The .45 bullet hit our house . . .

When did you start to hear about Slab City?

Well, not way back. I don't know whether Slab City was formed by the military police. I think it was a military police training camp. They had nothing but the cement slabs and the tents. And of course they moved off everything afterward. People took up on the slabs because it was a nice place to camp.

The Tylers were unacquainted with Salvation Mountain. When I mentioned Leonard Knight, they said: Oh, there were always hermits here.

And how was the Salton Sea in the forties?

It was nice, said Mrs. Tyler. It didn't have dead fish floating around in it. When I was going to high school we had school picnics and it was nice.

I went fishing down there many times in the forties, said Dr. Tyler. Well, it was nice.* There were boat landings and a group would get together and they would either charter a boat or get their own and the fishing was quite good. They just backed up to the sea along the Mecca shores, close to the town of Mecca. We'd usually just go down in the early morning and come back when the sun set. Usually we'd bring back all the fish we wanted.

Would you eat corvina from the sea now?

No. Apparently it's pretty bad.

I've heard that the Indians built fish traps around Coolidge Springs.

Oh, I know where the fish traps are, he said. I used to go there a lot. It's all private property now. I think you can still see them.

And what's your opinion on the situation in Coachella now?

I think we're getting overbuilt but how would I know? said Mrs. Tyler. It makes me sad but in another way it's kind of exciting. The only thing that would stop it is lack of water.

*A photograph from this period shows a floating grandstand with a great clock on it, and a shore lined with people; it's the Salton Sea Regatta.

Chapter 102

HAVE YOU EVER SEEN A FLAX FIELD IN BLOOM?

(1940s)

Here the land is green, and words are its fruits.

—Gabriel Trujillo Muñoz, 1993

Edith Karpen's daughter Alice Woodside, now aged sixty-two, had predominantly happy memories of her girlhood on the ranch at Mount Signal.* She said: The whole valley went to flax during the first part of the World War,† because they needed the linseed oil for planes. Have you ever seen a flax field in bloom? It's the most beautiful blue! They were growing it when I was really small, but I haven't forgotten the blue butterflies. There isn't anything I have ever seen with the intensity of a flax field.

They tried raising saffron, said her mother, but it didn't take.

Well, you know, said Alice, I was an only child. I really had no trouble just wandering around. My father's father acquired the ranch. That probably would have been, let's see, maybe in 1915, 1920. The people who worked on it, I always kind of liked to hang out and talk to. Most of them were quite frankly illegal, and quite frankly those were my favorites. Very gentle. Francisco, Jesús. I would just follow them around when they were irrigating. I don't think my parents worried about my safety. You know, I was completely comfortable about these guys. My father had a couple of tractor drivers, middle-aged men, who'd never been married, and I used to hang out with them. There was one old guy who lived in a shack, and my mother never thought about him but my Dad warned her to kind of keep an eye on me when I was around him. I guess I mused a lot. You know, my Dad would take me around with him. He taught me how to drive a pickup when I was six years old. One of the Caterpillar tractors, I could drive one of those when I was eight. He'd take me out, and I was shooting a .22 at cans; I remember it used to kick a lot. He

*About the mountain she wrote that her mother "loved its electric blue in the morning and she couldn't resist stopping to watch the everchanging mauves and purples at dusk."

†In 1949 flax continued to be Imperial County's number one crop at 130,779 acres out of more than 600,000. (Flax had also been the largest single crop in 1948.) Alfalfa was second at 127,790 acres.

had a .45, and I could never shoot that very well. I remember the blistering echo. I keep saying to my husband what my Dad always said to me: (a) *you don't force things;* (b) *you just stand back and look at it and think.* I was just today shrieking at him. He had just gotten some tool of ours that didn't work and he was just tearing it apart.

We had a lock on the front door, which is kind of silly when you consider the back door which had just a hook. My mother always used to have ladies who'd come in to do the washing and the cleaning and they never spoke English. I was left alone with them. I remember an Anglo guy who came up on a motorbike, and he banged and he banged and he banged. The Mexican lady just hid in the closet! I was just petrified! As a kid, how wonderful it was to have those ladies around if you were sick or if you were crying, because they could make you feel good. That's what I remember, is these quiet people coming in, fixing you tea; that's the way you get well. It's just that wonderful warm feeling.

Harold and Dorothy Brockman adored me because they thought they could never have children and their house was seven miles from ours. Their house was built I believe around 1910, and the main portion was interior and they had the screened-in porches all around. They made the house very picturesque. There was this very big walkway area where you'd step out from the glass doors. And all those years, it never had a lock on the door.

Harold was a man of very, very few words. I learned to get along with people of few words.* You'd see him under a truck taking care of his own pickup. He was a wealthy man but you wouldn't know it, she said proudly.

He had a lot of Mexicans working for him, Mexican families on a compound on his land. He treated them very well. But there was always a line. They were not included in any social activities.† There were maybe fifteen or twenty of them. I played with some of them. They had one man and one woman who were the elders of the family: Margarita, she was a lovely, lovely Mexican lady who spoke no English, and Francisco also spoke no English. Juan was the one I used to play with. Many years later, when Harold died, it was an Elks funeral, and the pallbearers were all the Mexicans dressed in white, plus my father. He always cared for their feelings. And yet they kept a line. There were two get-togethers at his funeral, one for Mexicans, one for whites. Actually, it embarrasses me to say so.

My main playmates were black, and twins, and they lived in that little house up

*In a letter written to me after her mother's death, Alice likewise described her father as "a man of very few words . . . so typically Imperial Valley. He was an old time rancher."

†Her mother mentioned still another distinction: "The Mexican women had their own society, and the Spanish Mexicans had theirs."

the way. I was an only child and the ranch was ten miles out of town. I played with whatever living thing I could find.

My school was called Mount Signal School; it would have been north of where we lived; there were three classes; first and second. It was just a country school. I can assure you that there was no other Anglo child there. All the kids I grew up with, they all yelled out, *Viva Villa!* My Mom had already taught me in kindergarten level to read. I remember being a problem for the teacher, because I was bored to death! I think during my school years my really good friends were Mexican, and they came from kind of another cut of class you haven't heard about. I could understand what they said, but I felt a little shy; my Mexican friend who was the leader always liked me to know who was boss; he liked to laugh at my Spanish.

Here Alice's mother smilingly interjected: I always knew when she was talking to Nicky or to his cousin Conchita, because she would put on a certain lilt, even in her English. One reason for her not acquiring Spanish earlier was that this was a period of total immersion and you weren't supposed to speak Spanish on the schoolground. When I was teaching, we enforced it.

Well, Mom, said Alice, on our playground we spoke Spanish all the way along.

When Alice and I were alone, I asked her how on balance she would characterize growing up in the Imperial Valley.

I think as I get older, so much about it I value more and more and more. But there's not enough to do. I think that really, unless you're a real self-starter, there's not a lot of room for real personal growth. I think that operating in that heat slows you down. It's just too bloody hot. I remember just sitting in those classrooms in June just sweltering, watching that clock just inch along until I could go outside and get a breath of fresh air. That bus ride home was an hour!

Here in the big city, kids don't have to learn to adjust as much. I used to think it was kind of hard, but . . . I guess it forced me to read. We didn't have television out on the ranch, and there was hardly anything on the radio. And, as I told you, I could drive a tractor when I was six years old . . .

Chapter 103

THE DAYS OF CARMEN CARILLO AND SUSANA CAUDILLO*

(2003)

They do work most Americans wouldn't do.

—Border Patrol Officer Dan Murray

When I go to the grapes at Coachella,† I get up at one in the morning. I wash my face and make lunch and let's go! No perfume! I feel tired, not wanting to go. And then with the heat, it's worse. At two-o'-clock I leave the house. I pay nine dollars for a ride. Sometimes it's the same person; sometimes it's not. The ride goes from Holtville where I live to Calexico and then to Coachella. Sometimes in Calexico we wait half an hour at Donut Avenue‡ for the people to cross the border.

We arrive at four A.M. Sometimes we go to Mecca; sometimes we go past Mecca toward Indio. When it's Mecca, we can sleep two more hours. The reason we have to get there so early is that if they change us from one field to another field they don't want to lose time. At four A.M the foreman is already there. We sleep in the vehicle with our heads on each other's shoulders. If it's a station wagon, there are six or seven people inside. If it's a van, there are nine or ten people. We don't sleep outside, because there are snakes! We've seen big ones. And there are snakes with horns, short ones. They're meaner than the rattlesnakes, those *chiquitas.* Right there on Highway 86 where you have the Alamo, there's an Indian reservation; that's where I've seen the small snakes. They're this color, the color of dirt, so you can't see them. And sometimes they're in the grapevines. If they bite you, if you don't get medical attention soon enough, you die. That's why we sleep in the car. We sleep with one eye open and one eye asleep.

At six-o'-clock we get up. They give us a briefing on how to pack the grapes and

*Most of these words are Susana's, with interjections and corrections from her friend.

†In contradistinction to the *Desert Sun,* which informs me that the season in the Coachella Valley runs from late April to early July, Carmen Carillo said: "The grape season starts in March. There's green ones; there's purple ones; there's black ones. They're all the same."

‡A bakery-restaurant.

how they want them cut. That takes ten minutes. The foreman does that. A lot of us workers are there, about a hundred. Often the same people go two or three seasons and you know them, and then all of a sudden it changes. Basically it's the same people. And it's mainly women. We are better workers, because mostly the men are *borrachos*.* The men respect us and the foreman respects us, too. Everything's fine. Everyone respects each other. Depends on the person, too. If you get people giving you unwanted attention, you gotta stop it.

At the briefing is when they start counting the hours and paying us.

They give you scissors. They are a special kind because they've got a little curved hook on them to take out the rotten parts. If we work eight hours, after five hours we start getting tired. You feel it all over. The whole body aches. At ten A.M. we get a fifteen-minute break. At twelve, we eat lunch under the vines, watching for snakes. We get half an hour then. At two-o'-clock we get another fifteen minutes. We finish at three.

They pay us weekly. It's minimum wage, but sometimes they pay a bonus. So we get about three hundred dollars, three-fifty, three-sixty, sometimes two-fifty, depending on the hours. If you have a lot of boxes, you gotta hurry up and pack. There's two cutters and a packer in each group. If the packer is behind, you gotta help the packer at three-o'-clock. We don't get paid for that. It's fifteen or twenty minutes extra. At three-fifteen, three-thirty, we get in the car. At five-thirty we get home, straight home to Holtville.

I stop in the store for a soda. Then I take off all the dirt, take a shower. I start cooking and turn on the washing machine. I cook something for my family, something fast. I don't even eat dinner. I go to sleep at seven P.M.

It's a sad life because it's cold; it's freezing and you cannot go home; you have to work. In the summer it's also sad with the dirt and the sweat. Sometimes you even feel like crying. It's hard when it's cold and you're wet. And not enough sleep. It's miserable. But once we get paid, it changes!

You pay the ride, the food and the bills, and there's only a little bit left. But we're happy not to have husbands. God freed us from husbands. With them, it would really be miserable.

*Drunks.

Chapter 104

IMPERIAL REPRISE

(1754–1940)

WATER IS HERE. **Sign of Slow Growth Sends Stocks Lower.** *IMPERIAL COUNTY SHOWS RAPID INCREASE.* In the past ten years, this county has made the greatest gain in value of its agricultural production of any county in the nation. *The 1938 lettuce season was probably the most disastrous in the history of the Imperial Valley. The constant threat of heavy shipments seemed to be the depressing factor.* I have seen men wicked enough to weep for sorrow at the prospect of a plentiful season.

I can't help believing in people. There are many who do not know they are fascists but will find out when the time comes. Amer. Legion has at Brawley emergency committee. On 27 January 1937 they put up the red flags. I have never been cheated out of a dollar in my life.

I can't help believing in people. The growers declared that experience had demonstrated that the class of persons found on the "ditch bank" camps are not suitable for field work.

I can't help believing in people. I never saw any force. I just stayed away. Of course in the classroom my kids didn't talk about it.

PART EIGHT

RESERVATIONS

Chapter 105

A DEFINITIVE INTERPRETATION OF THE BLYTHE INTAGLIOS

(*ca.* 13,000 B.C.–2006)

> . . . there is something unsatisfying about characterizing whole groups of people simply as those who used Clovis-like points . . .
>
> —Robert F. Heizer and Albert B. Elasser, 1980

We find in the treaty of Guadalupe Hidalgo a promise on the part of the United States to restrain and punish *with equal diligence and energy, as if the same incursions were meditated or committed within it's* [*sic*] *own territory against it's* [*sic*] *own citizens,* all raids into Mexico by "savage tribes." This article continues: *It shall not be lawful, under any pretext whatever, for any inhabitant of the United States,* where slavery was of course still legal, *to purchase or acquire any Mexican or any foreigner residing in Mexico, who may have been captured by Indians inhabiting the territory of either of the two Republics; nor to purchase or acquire horses, mules, cattle or property of any kind, stolen within Mexican territory by such Indians.* That this is relevant to Imperial will be proved the very next year, which is to say 1849: Colonel Cave Johnson Couts (we met him long ago in the chapter on syncretic marriages), having just crossed the two-hundred-yard vastness of the Colorado River, confides the following to his journal respecting the Yuma, or "Juma" as he calls them: *They sold Capt. Kane a small girl (prisoner of war) about 10 years of age and whom they had* scalped, accepting in payment a dead horse. (Captain Kane broke the treaty of Guadalupe Hidalgo, it would seem. I wonder what he did with the child? Probably he meant well.) *There is no doubt of their* Cannibalism. *They are by far the most filthy, miserable, wretched beings that we have ever met or known of. No happiness or pleasure can exist with them unless in the simple absence of* pain.*

*Couts on "Jumas" west of the Colorado: "They use blood generally for painting and are so filthy that their presence is nauseating. They watch the slaughter ground, and whenever a beef is butchered secure the entrails, the whole of them, and when the blood has cooled and begins thickening, clogging up, they scoop it up with both hands, as we do water in washing, and rub it over their entire face and neck, then with their fingernails make waving lines over their cheeks and forehead. Blood is frequently made to stick until quite an inch thick. The women although they use the same for painting ordinarily do not clot it upon their faces as the men, except during the time of their *courses* when they invariably do it, and it is probably required of them by their men."

Southside subscribes to some of Northside's views on the Indian question. *There are educated people in Mexico,* explains a member of that class, *who consider themselves polluted by the mere fact of having to think of the Indian.**

Who are Indians? As the good citizens of Mexicali say about their Chinese neighbors, *they're very closed.* No matter: In the perfect treatise I once meant to write, a book entitled *Imperial,* I was going to go at least as deeply into the story of each tribe as I went into the Chinese tunnels. Perhaps I might have even made friends with someone on a reservation or two. Now my money is gone. I have spent more than fifty thousand dollars of my own and other people's cash on *Imperial.* This section will not and cannot do justice to its subjects. I am sorry.

Who are Indians? They are those whose lands so often fail to be recorded as theirs, and whose names so often fail to be recorded at all. On 7 May 1853, Helena marries Vicente at San Juan Capistrano. Neither one has a surname; the note reads: *Indians.* The same is true of Trinidad and Sylvestre in 1858, of Maria de Jesus in 1856 (her groom, Santiago Gales, was luckier), of Maria Antonia and Pedro in 1857, Catalina and Jose Alejandro de Jesus in 1853 . . .

The 1901 San Diego city and county directory offers us eighteen entries for the locality of Warner, each one an individual's name except for the first: *Agua Caliente Indians, about 350.* A century later there will be about the same number of Agua Caliente on an eponymous reservation in Riverside County near Palm Springs.

Indians die nameless, in page after page.

A GRASS-GROWN SPIRAL

The Yuma is quiet and docile now, observed a settler in 1910, *but he does not seem to absorb American civilization rapidly, even when young, and there has been found a most discouraging tendency among the tribesmen to return to their heathenish ways when once the heavy hand of the school-mistress is removed.* A decade later, an educator reports that although it had been *difficult for the Indians to see the advantage of the school training,* which from a between-the-lines reading seems to have been forced upon them, and although *the Yuma are clannish, cling to their own language, and progress*

*About the Indians of Mexico my 1910 *Britannica* informs me: "Neglect of their children, unsanitary habits and surroundings, tribal intermarriage and peonage are the principal causes of the decreasing Indian population . . . The death rate among their children is estimated at an average of not less than 50%, which in families of five and six children, on the average, permits only a very small natural increase." But we are mainly talking about southern Mexico, it would seem, where "the native population on the plateau of Mexico, mainly Aztecs, may still be seen by the thousands . . . The face is oval, with low forehead, high cheek-bones, long eyes sloping outward toward the temples, fleshy lips, nose wide and in some cases flattish but in others aquiline, coarsely molded features, with a stolid and gloomy expression . . . The complexion varies from yellow-brown to chocolate (about 40 to 43 in the anthropological scale) . . ."

is slow, nonetheless *the Yuma Indian is considered the best laborer among the Indians and he is on the road to prosperity.*

Ninety-two years later, I saw an *Indio* selling newspapers and all-yellow balloons. He was Quechan,* he said, meaning Yuman; he must have been on the road to prosperity.

Just north of the line and in sight of the Colorado River, the Quecha Reservation, which occupies 33,613 Imperial County acres, shows off its prosperity of mesas, dunes, scant fields, broken glass, rusted cans, the tank painted with the message **PLEASE REMOVE THIS TANK**, the tan rocks; it is a world made of dried dirt. A long train is breathing and clanking through a cut in the dirt. Prosperity is a bedspring beneath a palo verde tree, a field of green lettuce with red lettuce darkening on one corner of it, abandoned couches, the shell of an adobe building with two walls standing.

In the Yuman creation myth, Wallapais, Mohaves, whites and Mexicans are latecomers. *Some of these held themselves aloof from the other people,* so the Creator, Kwikumat, stamped until fire came, at which the Mexican and the white ran away. Kwikumat's son and successor *told the whites that if they would enter the darkhouse he would instruct them. But they distrusted him. They were rich and stingy.* I have never been cheated out of a dollar in my life.

I am confident there is a great future for this place, writes "a Kern citizen who has recently visited Imperial." *Since being here I have been over lots of country and everywhere I have been are signs of a former vast population of Indians; the country is covered with old pottery and remains of Indian villages,* which proves to him once again that the Colorado River will be as productive as the Nile Delta.

In another issue of this same newspaper we find an illustration of structures which seem to be a cross between giant mushrooms and the grass huts of Africa, with the caption: **INDIAN DWELLINGS ON THE PLAINS NEAR THE IMPERIAL CANAL SYSTEM IN LOWER CALIFORNIA**, meaning Mexico, **WHERE PROVISIONS ARE KEPT TO BE ON TOP OF THE HOUSE INSTEAD OF UNDER IT.**

Skeletal debris of human beings have been found in the Yuha Desert near El Centro; they are more than fifteen thousand years old. Who were they? If we entertain no expectations of getting them right, then there is no reason not to imagine them, for our own sake, certainly not for theirs; I myself have experienced the way that the Blythe intaglios, those snaky paths of paleness in the dark brown desert varnish, resolve into figures, some of which are human, at least one of which bears a phallus; I remember an A-shaped figure, not immediately noticeable as human

*Pronounced *Kwatzan.*

or even artificial except for the straight line of the arm at perpendiculars to the head. The animal and the spiral are much less noticeable, particularly the latter, which has begun to disappear beneath tufts of olive grass. On the first figure are grasses growing at left hand and crotch. They are all fenced in to protect them from a certain subgroup of the victors. Because they may be seen with better understanding from above, I've gazed at them from a high mound, where they foreground the glint of a wide bend in the Colorado—yes, nowadays one discovers water instead of water's tree-lined intimations—then to the southeast, there's a dark green agricultural checkerboard of considerable size forcing its pale white roads toward convergence; this is the Imperial version of a geoglyph. In the south there goes a pallid grey riverslit, seemingly bottomless, around the gaze to the outlying fields and ranches of Blythe. Beyond those, Imperial offers worn-toothed and fluid-humped swellings of her desert hills.

The Blythe intaglios now constitute a tourist attraction, like Coachella's Dead Indian Rock near the Palms to Pines Highway, and the Indian fish-weirs west of the Salton Sea, right on the county line. We crush the Indians, then turn them into pixies, hobgoblins, magicians, supernatural figures, so that they are magic or magical expression of the dirt.

South and almost into Blythe, there's a wide dirt-lined canal, then another. I see a white ranch under huge trees, a row of campers, of palms, then a tawny wall of hay, and more ranches under cool tree-huddles, a third canal.

A bit farther south, the desert preserves kindred inscriptions: for instance, the depictions at Mule Tank. One gets there by means of a winding narrow arroyo whose hot basalt is nearly painful to the touch, and past a ring of dark stones in the sand, in the center of a vast view of vastness, one comes into a great flat-bottomed arroyo, golden and ocher, seeing far away the mountains to the north, and the mountains of Imperial, very blue and cool to the south. In a swirling rocky hole amidst the open golden shadows on the rock are pale red loops, nested circles, waves, infinity signs, insectoid and humanoid figures scratched into the dark shiny rock, and perhaps it would be worth the effort of a lifetime to understand the female figure with golden vegetation lunging below her, sun gilding the top of her shadowed rock; from her, one clambers down past spirals and leaves, sun and white-pebbled pavement.

Anthropologists of American Imperial inform us that the Indians here partake of the Hokan language family,* whose mainly extinct representatives existed in several territorial globs upon the California map; for American Imperial we have a long backwards L-shape extending across the bottom of the state and then run-

*A linguist now informs me: "Hokan hypothesis never substantiated, seems very unlikely."

ning up the eastern edge almost all the way to the beginning of the long diagonal in which Nevada is nested. What do I know of Hokan? To me in my ignorance it's but another grass-grown spiral.

In the spirit of failure, I accordingly catalogue some of the people of Imperial.

THEY MAKE DOLLS OF DEAD CHILDREN

In the Coachella Valley we find the Cahuillas, and if I were to do them justice I'd at least retell their tale of the Topa Chisera, or Devil Gopher. In the old records of Los Angeles we find some of them among the members of the *Caguillas tribe,* or *Caquillas Indians,* or *mother Indian,* or *parents gentiles of Palluchis tribe,* or *Luiseños.* The word *gentiles* means, of course, *unbaptized.* On 12 January 1853, Maria Encarnacion Esperiaza, born at San Gabriel, receives baptism; she could easily be a few days old, or she could be, as is Maria del Refugio Ysidora, *adult Indian of Caguillas tribe, widow,* sixty years old; as it happens, Maria Encarnacion Esperiaza gets baptized on the first anniversary of her birth. Her mother and her father remain unknown to us, an omission to which the fact that they were *gentiles* is surely relevant. In their stead, the child's godparents are listed: Jose Gabriel Corillos and Maria Josefa Miranda.

Did I tell you that the Cahuillas fear eclipses, that for them the bear is taboo, that once a year, parents make dolls of their dead children, weep, and then burn them? Shall I insert into the record that both the Cahuilla and the Kamia are renowned for pottery in brown, red and grey? They fashion bladder-shaped vessels decorated with diamonds, spirals and double lines.

The Cahuillas have not had a head-chief since the death of the one they called "Razon," meaning, so I read, white man.* They have intermarried with the Serrano. Many have become homeless, thanks no doubt to Progress. *They nearly all live upon the large ranches now, doing the roughest and most disagreeable work for small pay. The new era of fruit farming has thrown many of them out of employment . . . The women have no virtue, and many of the males live from the proceeds of a life of shame followed by the females.*

In 1999, the Cabazon Band of Cahuilla Mission Indians, population twenty-five, subsisted on a gross acreage of thirteen hundred and eighty-two near Indio; while the Cahuilla Band of Mission Indians, population two hundred and sixty, could be visited on their gross acreage of not quite nineteen thousand near Anza.

I have never to my knowledge spoken with one.

*My copy editor writes, "That's interesting—it means 'reason' in Spanish."

WATER IS HERE

Next group: In 1911, the population of the Martinez tribe is three hundred and twenty men, *generally well employed*. They hold their land in common. You'll be relieved to know that the agent restricts each allotment to ten acres per Indian. That way the rest of us can get our hundred and sixty. Meanwhile, the Torres reservation boasts more than nineteen thousand acres and a population of two hundred and thirteen. In my time there will be a joint Torres-Martinez Indian reservation, of which Imperial County's portion makes up eight thousand acres. Thanks to the Salton Sea, much of it is underwater.

TOUCHED UP WITH RED PAINT

East of the Colorado lived the Yuma, Halchichoma and Mohave tribes, all of them warlike; from San Diego up along the line to Jacumba and just into Imperial County, much evidence remains of the Diegueño, now called by their own name, the Kumeyaay.

In the Imperial Valley itself, settlers found the Kamia, who were not identical with the Kumeyaay, and also the Cocopah or Cucapah, whom Judge Farr benevolently describes as *closely related to the Yumas, though more industrious than the latter.* One or both of those two latter tribes quarried obsidian in the valley. (South of Laguna Salada, there was a hill where one could pick up Apache tears.)

Here I must tell you that Diegueños are actually Ipai. Kamia are Tipai. In the *Handbook of North American Indians,* the protohistorical Ipai and Tipai territories are depicted as an undifferentiated shaded zone on which **Ipai** has been inscribed northwards of **Tipai**. This area begins northwestward at the Pacific coast, at Agua Hedionda, not far south of the San Luis Rey River, which it first parallels, then follows; continuing eastwards along and slightly north of San Felipe Creek, then goes due east across the lower fifth of the Salton Sea, continues east about halfway across Imperial County, then slants southeast along a boundary marked *Sand Hills*. At the same latitude as Cuyapaipe, it suddenly slants southwest. So far it has been bordered by the Cahuilla on the north and the Quechan on the east. Now on the east it is bordered by the Cocopah. It goes down to the Río Hardy, makes an arc northwest to southwest through the Cocopah Mountains almost to La Rumerosa, then goes due south to La Huerta de los Indios, continues evenly southwest to the Pacific coast some twenty-five miles south of Todos Santos Bay.* The essayist calls these boundaries *fluid*.

*A different source ascribes to the Kumeyaay, identified as "southern Diegueño," the land from the San Diego River to beyond Ensenada to the sandhills east of the Imperial Valley. What did that culture come up against? Still another source, a mid-twentieth-century anthropologist who specializes in the Four Cor-

What are those people now? Well, here's the Campo Band of Diegueño Mission Indians in 1999, two hundred and ninety souls on fifteen and a half thousand gross acres . . .

If you wish to see more, then when entering Imperial County, feel free to stop at the Desert View Tower's green chollas in spring amidst the sunny granite boulders of a certain Ratcliffe's creature-garden; and here you may wish to admire the *yohnee stone,* which somebody in the vicinity who does not want his name used admits to have touched up with red paint, just to make it more decorative.

Speaking of vulviforms, *of the five yoni formations at W-1133, three are vertical and closely resemble vulvas. The other two are horizontal and also resemble eyes.* Were I to do these people justice, I would seek to understand the roasting ceremony after which Diegueño girls were introduced to a vulva stone. One anthropologist believes that the numerous yoni rocks in this zone *represent vaginal openings into the uterus of mother earth.*

How does she know? How would I ever know?

INSCRIPTION ILLEGIBLE

Although the Diegueño, as we just now read, used to maintain a presence into part of the Mexicali Valley, the only Indians I myself have met who speak of that part of Imperial as their homeland are the Cucapah, there orthographized to Cucapá.—I once met the man who'd worked for the Bureau of Reclamation from 1948 to 1950, surveying the area from the international line south to the Gulf of California. I asked him what he remembered from his experiences, and he said: Well, we found a cave with Indian corn in it. I only got down there once, but what I vividly recall is that they had a grapefruit-packing plant in Yuma and their culls, they would throw them into the river and we would pull 'em out and eat 'em up. And south of the border there were some Indians with long poles, and they were pullin' 'em in. Very unfriendly Indians.—I asked him which Indians they were, and he said that they were so difficult to approach that he never found out.

The Yuma, Maricopa and Cucapah all sold captives to Mexicans; the Mohave did not. The Yuma were allied with the Mohaves. The Kamia traded foods with the Diegueño. The Yuma and Cucapah were long-term enemies. Does any of this help you? These facts remind me of the Hetzel photograph of *mud volcanoes six miles from the village of Cucapaugh Indians in L. . . .*—inscription illegible—the print faded

---

ners region (Arizona, New Mexico, Colorado, Utah) refers to "the long arm of the Corn God's northerly conquests," which stretched almost to the frost of the Great Lakes. "A shorter arm reached into the arid Colorado River basin to halt finally in the latitude of Great Salt Lake, with the harsh desert zone of the western Colorado River drainage," namely Imperial, "barring it from the Pacific."

to milky-green, the squat mush-heaps and the wide oval mush-craters steaming into the fog of the ruined photographic paper, like Escher's famous print of the hand which draws itself.

"WE SAY ONE THING AND THEY SAY ANOTHER"

In 1776, it seems that the Cajuenches, Valliacuamais and Cucupash are all in a state of "contentment" to meet the Spaniards, and *I praise God for such a good disposition in which they receive the fathers and the Spaniards in their lands, to be taught the doctrine, to which I am dedicated.*

In 1796, Governor Arrillaga meets some Cucapah along the as yet unnamed Río Hardy, which in my epoch is famous for being the conveyance for six to eleven thousand acre-feet per year of *agricultural drainage water;* and the Cucapah act friendly at first—cigarettes for watermelons! *I spotted several little huts, some people, and their farms of melons, watermelons, and pumpkin.* It is drier than that now. In a twinkling, the Cucapah have begun to menace the party, and Arrillaga feels obliged to warn his boy guide that should they be led into danger, he will kill him at lance-point. *I continued my journey in good order,* firing when attacked. The end of these skirmishes reflected the usual technological disparities: five Indians killed, one of Arrillaga's soldiers and eight of his horses wounded, and one mule killed with a sharpened stick. *I must frankly confess,* he concludes, *that, although the previous afternoon they gave me ample reason to punish them, I had pity on their wretched state . . . I could have destroyed their rancherías and families . . .*

Writing in from the early twentieth century, Otis P. Tout reports that *Cocopah Indians could get all the liquor they wanted in Mexicali. The men would bring their women to* Calexico *town Saturday nights, get them drunk, tie them to mesquite bushes in bunches and then 'enjoy' their own drunken carousals. But woe to him, white, Mexican or Indian, who touched a drunken Cocopah woman!*

(We fought over women, since we couldn't marry in the family.—That was what a Cucapah man told me, down in Southside.)

A Cucapah man from 1900 stares at the camera, his black hair falling in two streams, many white necklaces about his throat, his forehead furrowed as he gazes at us with alert suspicion. I saw his portrait once, in a museum in Mexicali.

Twice I visited Cucapah El Mayor: blue barrels for water and for trash, gravel shaded by mesquites, cinderblock houses and metal latrines, like the ones on construction sites, whitish grime. The community El Mayor Indigenes Cucupá was the only primarily Cucapah settlement in the Mexicali Valley, but they also lived in other *ejidos* such as Oviedo Mota; they had another settlement in San Luis, called

Posa Derviso.* In 1932 a certain Mexicali Delegation promised the future that *the aforementioned territory, consisting of 54,381.00 hectares, shall hereby be known as Territory "Los Cucapás,"* and there you have it.

In 2002, Lupe Vásquez took me to visit Pascuala on the Hill of the Metates. She was the oldest Cucapah alive, Lupe said, hearing which, being a gringo, I eagerly asked for exact numbers. First she was a hundred and twenty. Then she was a hundred. Then we compromised on eighty or ninety.

In 2003 there were thirty-eight families in El Mayor—four hundred throughout Mexico, and some in Somerton, Arizona.

Yolanda Sánchez Ogás, who had written a book about the Cucapah and was a friend of several of them, said: Mestizos came here in the nineteenth century, and gringos starting at the building of canals. Cucapahs worked building the canals. This is *la patria de los Cucapahs;* the region of the Colorado Delta was all theirs, on both sides of the border in that whole area. Guillermo Andrade made a pueblo; he was the first owner of the Delta. He made Ciudad Lerdo. There are documents where they give the names of Cucapah Indian chiefs who worked in Ciudad Lerdo cutting hemp.

Article Twenty-seven of the Mexican Constitution is about land, Yolanda continued. There are three kinds of property: first, small property, either in an *ejido* or in a communal property. The Cucapah have the second. They possess title to one hundred and forty-three thousand hectares. It belongs to all who live in El Mayor.— When Díaz was here, she said, her tone becoming angry and bitter, all this land was one plantation belonging to Otis Chandler.

That day Yolanda introduced me to darkhaired Juana Torres Glez Cucapá, to Antonia Torres Cucapá and to Jaziel Soto Torres Cucapá. Two of them were sisters.

Maybe ten people out of thirty families in this community can speak Cucapah, they said.

What makes the Cucapah unique? I asked them as we sat at a round table under a mesquite tree, chewing sour-sweet mesquite seeds.

The necklaces that we make, they replied, and the skirts. We make them out of the bark of the willow. The beaded headbands, we wear them while we dance and then we sell them. The black one is two hundred pesos. It took me three days. It's bad for my eyes, all the sewing. I just made it for the dance. It's made out of glass beads. We used to make them out of shells.

They said that *mai* meant sky. Sky plus earth made *mot,* universe.

*Spelled by a local informant. "Both words seem unlikely to be spelled correctly," writes a linguist.

Everything was still—weak rivers and palms. From a neighboring white cubehouse came Cucapah music on a cassette player, a droning chant like that of the Inuit.

Is there different thinking between Cucapah and Mexicans?

Yes. We say one thing and they say another . . .

"WE DON'T HAVE A GOOD DRUNK ANYMORE"

Now back to the people whom the Spaniards first met when they crossed the Colorado into Imperial.

In 1775 Font called the Yuma *shameless and excessive* in their promiscuity; he must not have enjoyed the rattling of the women's treebark skirts. The men painted themselves with red hematite, black earth and white colors; the women usually only with red. Perhaps the blood-painting that Couts observed had something to do with this. *They usually kill some woman,* said Font, *or someone who has been careless, and try to capture a few children . . . to sell in the lands of the Spaniards.* His summation: *These people are as a rule gentle, gay, and happy.*

In 1918 the California Board of Agriculture explained: *The Yuma reservation contains an area of 71-3/4 square miles, the Indians living in this section being the most primitive of the California tribes in manners and customs.*

Richard Brogan and I were talking about the Bard Subdistrict, and he said: They have interesting water issues in the Bard. The river changed course. There was a No Man's Land of supposed Indian territory then. In the fifties and sixties the Quechan Indians were destitute.

Ever see them out here?

A lot of them, in jail. As soon as they're sober they're good people. Wild people then. Jekyll and Hyde transformation. They were beloved by the sheriff's office. We would leave their cell doors open. If one of the deputies was in trouble we would call them and four three-hundred-pound Indians would be on top of somebody.

(In other words, *the Yuma is quiet and docile now.*)

We don't have a good drunk anymore, Mr. Brogan continued. Now it's gluesniffing and methamphetamine . . .

A MORONGAN INSPIRATION

Crossing the river into California, gazing down on the reservation's wide green and yellow bottomlands, I received this greeting: **WELCOME TO PARADISE CASINO.**

I don't know if you'll find anybody who wants to talk, said the girl at the convenience store.

How about you?

Nope.

Well then, I said, I guess I don't want to talk to you, either.

At the first house where I knocked, the people invited me in. Their names were Cameron and Diana Chino. He was Quechan; she was white. There was green leafy iceberg right across the dirt road, on Indian land leased out to agribusinesses which hired brownskinned men to tend and harvest it.

Mr. Chino was born and raised here. In 1991, when he was twenty, he had gone away. He had returned this June with some graphic-design ability and an interest in collecting samurai swords. He was a blocky, shaveheaded man; two days later I met the proprietor of a coffee shop in Mexicali who looked much like him.

I see a big change for the better, he said. Twelve years ago it was a little bit bad, propertywise. My family was the landowner here.

He estimated the population on the reservation at about five thousand. Most of them leased out their land, or worked at the casino or the tribal offices, such as the diabetes institute. Mr. Chino: said: The boundary of the res is pretty much up on Baseline Road, all the way up Ross Road, and then it veers off to another section and then up to the town of Bard. Anything not used by dates is reservation land. And the houses we have, they're all the same throughout the whole area.

And the wife added: The ordinary concrete reservation houses.

Broccoli, over here, he said. Dates and palms, that's Bard.

He was happy to get money twice a year from the casino. Their last distribution from the casino was almost four thousand dollars, and the check from the previous six months had been almost five thousand.

About the Cucapah he said: We're not related. They're just our neighbors.

I asked him what he had done for fun as a kid, and he laughed. His wife, who was extremely beautiful, with long red hair, said: It's a bunch of bored kids with a whole bunch of back road.—And he said: Being a teenager, those were the days!

Yeah, said his wife. Your mother came by her grey hairs honestly, dear. She did.

There's been a comeback with the language, he said. And fun nowadays involved basketball, movie night . . . He proudly named the names of various tribal organizations.

About herself, Diana Chino said: We were going to spend a winter in Idaho. But Mother didn't like the cold. I was a white kid dropped into an Indian school. But now it's better. Our son is as blond and blue as they come, and he has had no trouble.

Did the heat take any getting used to?

She said: We've got the fields around the house, so once the sun goes down it starts to dissipate.

I asked Mr. Chino whether he considered himself to be part of Imperial County in his mind.

Pretty much, we're just Yuma people, he replied. We've been here a long time. Technically our tribe is considered an Arizona tribe. Farming has always been Yuma as well. Yuma thrives on lettuce. They use the land here sometimes. It's all iceberg across the street. It's darker green because it's fresh.

He spoke of Imperial as if it were another country, saying things like: *Imperial has hayfields and so forth over there . . .*

If you go through like Brawley, he said, it looks like time has stood still. Old-time El Centro is something out of the fifties. When I was in the Midwest, I would see houses and buildings like that

Do you ever go to Mexico?

We usually go to Algodones, she said. Sometimes we go to San Luis. I like to go get my vanilla for cooking. It's real vanilla. You can get a screamin' deal on Kahlúa.

How often do the *pollos* come through here?

She said: One of my friends on the west side, she says there are quite a few who come through. That's why we have a lot of dogs. So of course the Border Patrol comes through. A lot of helicopters.

I asked about their water situation, and he said: We had the water-rights issue twenty-odd years ago. The tribe was given the water rights in federal court. Each member was distributed about three thousand dollars. We went to San Diego; we went to Mexico; we went to Disneyland! We had to sign over the land where the All-American Canal runs through.

He showed me his drawings and one of his swords. She gave me some of her home-baked pastries. They were kind, patient people, and I was sorry to leave them.

I asked him whether he had any vision for the future of the reservation. He wanted the Quechan to emulate the Morongo tribes up near Palm Springs.—They have a really high end outlet, he said.

Regarding Palm Springs, by the way, one of our favorite boomers, L. M. Holt, possessed an equally enticing sense of the future encompassing these *eight thousand acres of choice land . . . About 3000 acres belongs to the Government, and is being reserved temporarily for the use of Indians, of which there are five or six families in the valley, who are peaceful and valuable laborers for the white men who are now developing these hitherto unknown lands.*

Chapter 106

THE ISLAND

(2003–2006)

On the Quechan Reservation I had asked Cameron Chino about a section called the Island, and he'd answered: That's always been where the black people live. So I've not really gone into the Island. There's this levee road all through here, through the subdivision, and then it would turn easterly into another levee round into Bard. From that road to down *here,* that's the Island. It's pretty big.

It used to be all bushes here, said a black man named James Wilson. The All-American Canal busted a few things. Killed some woman on horseback, a real white girl.

(The Island really had been an island, once upon a time. Someday, perhaps, it would be again.)

Mr. Wilson was forty-five years old. I asked him to please tell me some of his memories, and he said:

Used to go swimmin' in the water for fun. Had old pump irrigation. My first job was choppin' cotton. Went away about fifteen or twenty years ago. We used to plant often, too. Had a twenty allotment. I must have been about ten years old. Used horses to plough. Then my Dad worked on the Southern Pacific Railroad. When I got a little bigger I went to work on a date farm. Still doin' it thirty-five years later. They used to hire on wetbacks, but then Immigration got on them. Didn't really affect me.

I own about seventy-nine acres. I grow a few date trees; I must have about eighty. Some people have a hundred fifty or a hundred sixty. Trees might be bigger over there in Coachella. Started putting in trees here about 1945.

Lemons came on pretty strong, and some grapefruits, too, here in Bard. Dates is pretty good right now. Look like a lot of date growing to move to Yuma.

What's the best thing about living here?

Got a house and everything I need.

And what's the biggest change?

Biggest change is all the big companies coming over.

He got electricity and water from the Bard Subdistrict, but paid the land lease to Arizona, because before the Colorado shifted, this part of Imperial County had actually been in Yuma.

THREE COMMENTARIES ON MR. WILSON'S DWELLING PLACE

Yuma has a split season, remarked Richard Brogan. Yuma very much grows in smaller plots than we do. Mostly Yuma is Colorado riverbed. They've got better soil. That's completely corporate farming. They never shut down the cotton farming there like we did. The Winterhaven area, the Bard Subdistrict, that's a separate area, and they voted to keep cotton in and they did. Bard relies on Yuma as their provider. It's funny; they rely on Arizona time. There's a lot of people that don't even know a lot about Bard. They're *different*.

Kay Brockman Bishop, who had lived in Imperial County off and on since her birth there in 1947, and had even climbed Signal Mountain, had this to say about Bard: I don't know a soul up there.

In October the flower-fields near the Cloud Museum were all chocolate-brown, furrowed and empty. But everything was lusher than elsewhere in the Imperial Valley, thanks to the proximity of the Colorado's tree-packed gorge. The crystalline beauty of the palm trees in their staggered rows reminded me of Coachella. Cooling myself in a rectangle of evening shadow elongating out of Imperial Date Gardens, I discovered that it was already that moment before dusk when every furrow is sharp and clear. At the side of the road, in flatbeds, bunches of handpipe were stacked like bundles of asparagus. Driving straight into the evening sun, I found Bard full of wild palms, grasses and shrubs. Now I was almost at the Salamander Mobile Home park with its attached bar. And Imperial Date Gardens had fallen entirely into shadow.

By the Cloud Museum I looked west, and between two palm-rows the sun basked like some strange squash or maybe a fallen grapefruit. It had melted into a pink stain between mountains by the time I'd reached **RANCHERO DE LUX DATES**. The Island lay already under the rules of darkness.

How many people on this earth truly know Imperial County? And of those, who knows Bard? And even to a good portion of Bard's inhabitants, the Island remains unknown, secret, like so many other subzones in the entity which I call Imperial. When I left James Wilson's homestead, the night was as thick as cloth, and his aged father sat dreaming under a tree. This was Imperial, center of all secrets and therefore center of the world.

PART NINE

CLIMAXES

Chapter 107

THE LARGEST IRRIGATED DISTRICT IN THE WORLD

(1950)

The extent of Alta California in ancient times was altogether indefinite.

—Samuel T. Black, 1913

In those days Imperial County's stationery proclaimed itself *The Largest Irrigated District in the World.* Imperial County, and much of the rest of Imperial itself, had also become *The Winter Garden of America.* By twenty-first-century standards it remained curiously undifferentiated. Exactly a century after the Treaty of Guadalupe Hidalgo there was still no border wall, of course, and in that same year, 1948, the population of the county seat, El Centro, was only five hundred more than that of Brawley, whose thirteen thousand souls comprised a respectable enough crop. But please don't think El Centro wasn't on the map; in one of his bitterest detective novels, published in 1949, Raymond Chandler generously gave one of his characters, who got murdered with an icepick, seven business cards, each bearing a false address and telephone number from that city.

The county as a whole held more than sixty-two thousand people, which is to say that it was still, by the urban standards of my own time, empty. Coyotes remained *a serious menace to sheep during the lambing period.* Although it was the ninth-largest county in the state, only one-half of one percent of all Californians lived there. But fly high enough and not even Los Angeles will show any people! Los Angeles's muted blue-grey coolness, where skies and concrete are often the same, must have been blue-grey even before the foundation of that city in 1781. Ladies and gentlemen, hold onto your hats! The airplane (a chubby little plane which wears our American flag and the twin legends **TRANS WORLD AIRWAYS** and **LOS ANGELES AIRWAYS**) rises into a grey cloud through whose weave I can see with great distinctness the breakers of the Pacific Ocean; they're as white as the sclerae of your eyes. Here we are, coming in from above a long white wave; we're suspended directly above and perpendicular to the not quite infinite boulevard of trees and tree-shadows like ranks of rockets shoulder to shoulder. Around us and below us lie more trees, grassy rectangles, bungalows; this is the sea-edge of Los

Angeles at midcentury. Ascending into the fog until these details are quite lost, we spiral into brighter and whiter air. We break through, proceeding southeast over a cold white desert of clouds. After awhile we pass a many-fingered blue handprint which admits our vision all the way down to earth. Here's another hole. The clouds are riddled now; they won't hold up much longer. Below me, the darker blueness of the San Gabriel Mountains parts the sky. The coast, brown and blue with white roads on it, is long gone, left to its own fog-dressed aridity. The hills below are fuzzed with blue-green trees, and sandy valleys of greenish-ocher lie between them. In effect, we're in the Rothko paintings of 1948, whose shapes frequently remain circular and oval; we haven't reached the field-rectangles yet. But the sand-patches are already getting bigger; and the vegetation's taking on a worn look. And now, beyond the sharp-edged mountains, I see deeper vermilion than I've ever met with. If only I knew how to tell you how beautiful it is! The valleys go grey; the blue-greenness of the high hills is quite gone. This really could be Mars. Farther ahead the land is lower, paler, brighter and flatter: Imperial.

Yes, even after a century of irrigation, settlement and road-building it's still almost otherworldly, with here and there a small simple grid of streets, houses laid between the squares like clusters of glass-shards—how they sparkle! Here's a complex of field-rectangles blown white and grey with dust. More field-grids lie ahead, still greyish but a bit grey-green, too: **WATER IS HERE**. The Salton Sea is an inviting toy pond in the middle of them. According to the Ball Advertising Co., this place, *235 feet below sea level, is rapidly becoming one of America's most popular water sport and fishing areas.* Shields Date Gardens explains that its salt content is presently *about the same as the ocean.* Never mind that trend; there will soon be launching facilities for power boats! The latest issue of *National Motorist* is thrilled to report that *low barometric pressure and greater water density make the Salton Sea the fastest body of water in the world for speedboat racing.* No wonder that by 1960 the number of visitors to the Salton Sea's state beach park will surpass those to Yosemite. A booster from 1962 assures me: *At our little desert hideaway near Mecca, on the North Shore close to the Salton Sea, we have a beautiful artesian well which flows copiously all the time, much to the delight of the nearby palms, tamarisks and mesquites.* From my post-Imperial vantage point, this tale is equivalent in dreamy fantasy to the following: *They had a house of crystal pillars on the planet Mars by the edge of an empty sea . . . Afterwards, when the fossil sea was warm and motionless, and the wine trees stood stiff in the yard, and the little distant Martian bone town was all enclosed,* the Martian Mr. K liked to read from his metal book with the Braille-like hieroglyphs, stroking it so that it sang to him; and sometimes he would compose his own chants, such as—imagine! Water, on Mars! Imagine a Salton Sea around which tourists actually wished to play! Fly over it, and its blueness darkens eerily. Everything I see is so greyed up or down by dust that it might as well be a black-and-white photograph; in fact, let's say that it is, because then it will never change. To the extent that Imperial is actually a Rothkoscape it surpasses my colorblind comprehension with its infinity of half-hidden tonal changes beneath a field of seemingly solid color; precisely this makes the Salton Sea so alive; but I'm not capable enough to render this phenomenon for you at all, much less in perpetuity (nor was Rothko himself; his black, black panels in the stiflingly ominous Houston Chapel have already begun to fade), so let's keep this snapshot of Imperial simple; just the facts, ma'am. A waggling line of whiteness like a single breaker extends far out into the sea from a turbid zone near shore: subaqueous mudpots, I presume. In 1950 more of them would have been above water, not unlike *Salton City, a bustling young community of modern homes.* And Imperial radiates around me in every direction. What is Imperial? Whatever it is, it is all one. (Rothko, 1943: *A picture is not its color, its form, or its anecdote, but an intent entity idea whose implications transcend any of its parts.*) To my left I can see into Riverside County, a part of which, no matter what the state of California asserts, belongs to my Imperial; here is how a civic booster tells that story: *One of the great sagas of the Old West took place in the twentieth century. It was the transformation of the Salton Basin into the rich winter gardens, date groves, and fabulous resort and vacation centers of the Coachella Valley.* How strange! It's as if the Coachella Valley had nothing to do with the Imperial Valley! As you know, I subscribe to all the opinions of Edgar F. Howe, who therefore might as well be looking out the window beside me; here is what he wrote in 1910: *We can see today more clearly the possibility of building a new Egypt. We can see the possible unification of Imperial and Coachella Valleys in a continuous garden from the Mexican line to the mountains which cleave Southern California in two parts.* A continuous garden indeed—the Winter Garden of America! But in midcentury that still hadn't happened, not quite. *From the air,* two geographers will report in 1957, *the Coachella Valley looks much like the Imperial, except that the Imperial has solid blocks or irrigated greenery between its eastern and western canals, whereas the Coachella has only smaller and scattered irrigated patches.* Never mind. We won't go to Coachella for a few paragraphs more. Instead, we begin to descend toward the field-squares to the south, which take on more greenness the closer we get; we're coming into Brawley and Imperial. (Brawley's slogan: *Where it's Sun-Day every day!* Why doesn't this apply everywhere else in Imperial? Take it up with the Ball Advertising Co.) Along the perimeter of these emerald and chocolate squares, a thin silver glint of water catches the light like tooling on a leather book. And over there's the New River, looking strangely tropical in its green-frizzed gorge; it's the only uneven thing in sight. How badly do you suppose it stank in 1950? (Worse than in 1940; better than in 1960.) There's Signal Mountain far away, squat and blindingly mysterious over the green, green fields. Off to the left I see Calexico, which *is rightly called the "city of air-conditioning,"* and which offers us *the annual Dove-Hunters' Fiesta, the Wine Tasting Fiesta, the Cotton Carnival and other Mexican and American holidays. One would think that every day is a fiesta on the exciting Mexican-American border!*

We touch down in the city of Imperial, with the dust dulling down the grey-roofed houses and the lawns peeling off the lots like old pool-felt. That is how it was in 2002, and that is more or less how it would have been in 1950. Come to think of it, maybe it wasn't as dusty then; for the President of the Imperial Valley Pioneers noted that *Imperial Valley is more than a highly-developed farming area—it is a wonderland of factories running 24 hours a day, 365 days a year. Its products are moved to every point in the nation and some few of them all over the world.*

In *The Largest Irrigated District in the World,* retail sales and income for civilian residents had both more than tripled between 1939 and 1947, and it kept rising. "W. F. Holt Looks into the Future with the Direct Gaze of the Confident Man." In Brawley, some of them were well-off and leisured enough to hold their 1950 annual picnic in the coolness of Long Beach. I know it; I've seen the photo in the Imperial County Historical Society Pioneers Museum.

Agriculture remained the primary source of income, of course: Twenty-nine and a half percent of all the county's wages and salaries came from fruits, vegetables, fodder and beef. A pound of beef, by the way, needs twenty-five hundred gallons of water to raise the alfalfa, keep the cow from dying of thirst, and hose down the barn. Good thing we're in *The Largest Irrigated District in the World!*

"THEY REALLY HAD THEIR EYE ON THE DOLLAR"

Unfortunately, Imperial County's percentage of California's locally assessed tangible property values remained one-third lower than it had been before the Depression. Relative to other California counties, Imperial had by some measures fallen into near insignificance. In 1950, California collected more than twenty million dollars in county inheritance taxes. Nearly half of this derived from Los Angeles, which overshadowed San Diego by a factor of almost ten. San Diego in turn approached being six times richer than Riverside, which came close to a sevenfold victory over poor Imperial. In short, if Los Angeles counted for half, Imperial counted for less than an eight-hundredth. Well, after all, we're only talking dollars and cents, not more meaningful things—but wasn't it dollars and cents that Imperial (American Imperial at least) was built on?

A man who'd worked for the Bureau of Reclamation from 1948 to 1950, surveying the Colorado and taking samples of the bottom *to see what was shifting,* told me the following about this *wonderland of factories:* The fields were working, sure, but all you ever had were little shabby motels and cabins to stay in! The pickers were white and Filipino in those days. Not as many Mexicans as now. The whites were hardworking and aggressive. The whole families would work; they really had their eye on the dollar. They looked like they were from Oklahoma. One group of Filipinos, pickers, they had one Cadillac convertible and they had one blonde livin' with 'em. They probably had only one suit between 'em!

Well, so what? The cash value of Imperial County farm products had risen even faster than income! In 1940, that all-important number was a bit under fourteen million dollars. In 1953 it would be more than a hundred and thirty million. (Simone de Beauvoir, 1948: *It is because of the abstract climate in which they live that the importance of money is so disproportionate.* Please don't take it personally, dear Imperial; her observations were formulated in Chicago. *It is because they cannot frame or declare real values that Americans are satisfied with this symbol.*)

"AN IMMENSE GREEN-GOLD GARDEN"

Lettuce was the most lucrative crop at twenty-five million dollars. Herbert Marcuse, 1955: *The sacrifice of libido for culture has paid off well: in the technically advanced areas of civilization, the conquest of nature is practically complete, and more needs of a greater number of people are fulfilled than ever before.* In other words, we're a wonderland of factories running twenty-four hours a day, three hundred and sixty-five days a year!

And what makes a wonderland even more wonderful is that improvements can always be made. For instance, the Imperial Valley's production norm of six-tie carrots under the travel-packs system (you know what I mean) has been raised from thirty crates per packer per hour to forty-five crates per hour. Don't worry; this is no recapitulation of the Soviet Gulag; it's a celebration of our helpful machines! I'm sure the Mexicans won't complain. Another revolutionary scientific advance: If we use pallets, lift trucks and low-bed trailers in our orchards, we can *cut this phase of the labor by a third.* Hopefully that can translate into fewer laborers (the excess can just go back to Southside); in any case it will mean higher profits. You see, I've never been cheated out of a dollar in my life.

But what if Progress cheated me?

One might imagine from the foregoing that the agribusiness magnates of Imperial were selfish, callous individuals who sought to squeeze more out of their laborers simply in order to raise their own profits. In fact, they, too, were getting squeezed. In his Agricultural Crop Report of 1950, B. A. Harrigan writes: *I wish to emphasize that these values are Gross Values, F. O. B. Shipping Point . . . The net income to farmers was not increased in proportion to the gross sales due to lower farm prices and increased costs of labor and all materials used in harvesting and handling the crops.* What then can the farmers do?

All the same, they and their laborers are unlikely to become better friends as a result.

In a distinctly half-hearted vein of reassurance, Marcuse continues: *Neither the mechanization and standardization of life, nor the mental impoverishment, nor the growing destructiveness of present-day progress provides sufficient grounds for questioning the "principle" which has governed the progress of Western civilization.* Should we question it now?

The 1950 high school commencement program at Wilson School in El Centro consists of a processional, an invocation by the perfectly named Reverend Hypes, the Pledge of Allegiance, of course, and no less naturally "The Star-Spangled Banner," played by the Wilson School Band, and so forth and so on, up to the presentation of the American Legion Award to not the most outstanding but the *Most Representative Girl,* Prudy Lydecker, and the *Most Representative Boy,* Russell Kirk. American Imperial is America indeed, which deifies the average. What was average in 1950 is no longer so in my era; I sometimes worry that that is the main reason I love American Imperial.

But even then, Imperial was never average!

At first I thought we'd come to the end of the world, said Mrs. Claude Finnell, the retired Agriculture Commissioner's wife. See, we lived in Bakersfield first, so I was used to the heat. But the streets were just covered with these crickets and the cockroaches. And we just had one air conditioner in the bedroom, so we just lived in that bedroom.

Her husband showed me a photograph of their house on Barbara Worth Road, *a three or four room house with three or four kids,* he called it.

I asked her whether the towns and cities of Imperial had shown much growth during the fifties, and she said: The biggest problem was the heat, of course, so as we got more air-conditioning, the farmers began to move to town, and the mothers and the wives got next to the other wives. It's interesting to be in the country and see one of those old farmhouses. You wonder why they wanted to be there at all!

From that answer, it sounds as if Imperial had become a trifle less isolated, but when I asked Alice Woodside to tell me what her future husband had made of the place when he first visited, in around 1962, she replied: He had *no idea*! At that time Calexico was maybe ten thousand. And there had not been a whole lot of development. The old part of Calexico was about all there was. He was out there looking around and it was about a hundred and eighty outside! He was just wondering what on earth he had gotten into. We took him to Comacho's. And he had never had one scintilla of Mexican food in his mouth. Mexicali, now, I don't think he had ever in his life been exposed to so much poverty, so much filth . . .

Her family had moved into town in about 1956, when she was fourteen.

And how was your life then? I asked her.

Let's just say that I hated it here in Sacramento at first. I was used to Calexico where everybody knew me. The brewmaster of the Mexicali Brewery lived right down the street from us in Calexico. He was German. Mexicali beer, now, that beer, my parents used to have it on hot afternoons, and they poured it into pitchers and it would get that big head on it! Just wonderful! They had a pretty bottle. I think there was a sun on it and a lot of gold printing. The beer had a very golden color . . .

Back to business: After lettuce came in descending order carrots (whose high commodity status was a postwar phenomenon), sugar beets, melons, tomatoes and of course alfalfa, at over a million dollars apiece!—Next year, alfalfa would be the premier crop, occupying a hundred and seventy thousand acres. (It comes and goes, said Kate Brockman Bishop in 2006. It sort of depends on the number of cows in L.A.)—I'm sorry to say that by midcentury, grapefruit profits were down to under half a million a year, but these moon-jewels still shone most lucratively of any in the Imperial Valley's citrus treasury. (Try not to worry about Coachella, Yuma, Borrego, Florida.)—We had citrus here, an oldtimer would tell me in 2004. It was proven to be a difficult crop and probably not a dollarwise crop.—Meanwhile, cotton was coming back: forty thousand acres in 1951 (that's the year that Barbara Worth's "Empire Builder," W. F. Holt, passed on in Los Angeles),* eighty-five thousand in 1952 (in which connection please allow me to introduce you to the smiling, sturdy blonde in what must be a two-piece bathing suit—it resembles a pale bra with mid-grey shorts—who curves her hips, swings her right knee, and flaps her polka-dotted cape beside the FIRST BALE 1952 PLANTED I.V. COTTON), nearly a hundred thirteen thousand in 1953. At midcentury, Jack Kerouac, en route from Yuma to San Diego, looked out his bus window and in his journal noted only the following three specific commodities: *Orange groves, cotton—new houses . . .*

As for farm pests, Mr. Finnell, the former County Agriculture Commissioner, assured me: We worked together in those days with the Mexicans on the capra beetles. We've always worked very good with them. Never had any trouble.—*We need have no fear that our lands will not become better and better as the years go by.* Oh,

*He died on 21 November 1951, almost forgotten; the only notice I could find was a small picture-obituary in the *San Rafael Independent Journal* labeling him "the man most responsible for changing southern California's Imperial Valley into rich farm land." Harry Chandler had died in 1944; his obituary said much the same.

yes; oh, yes! Even the Imperial County Assessor's office couldn't help pausing in the midst of cash tallies to rhapsodize about *the flourishing fields and the mile-long trains that carry Imperial County products to the market places of the Nation.* In other words, *his farm has been highly improved. He made a success through his own efforts. He sold out at a fancy price.* As for that commercial Bible, the *California Blue Book* (Harold Bell Wright's heroes might as well have consulted it), it doesn't in the least mind interrupting its tabulations to opine that *Imperial's warm, sunny winters and many strange desert attractions make it a pleasant playland.* In fact, it's *an immense green-gold garden.*

"EVERYTHING WAS OPEN"

Zulema Rashid, who grew up in that garden, was born in Calexico in 1945. About her native city she said to me: I think it is so beautiful, the skies, the houses. It seems like James Dean will appear, in a movie from the fifties. Those tall palm streets. I think it's just great! But I didn't see that then. All I saw was Mexicali.

She was an elegant redhaired woman, divorced not terribly long since, who'd come back home *for the summer,* which proves her to be a real Imperialite. And in her origins, in the success story of her family, she was utterly Imperial, too.

My mother is Mexican, from Sonora, she said. Most of the people in Mexicali are from the states of Sinaloa or Sonora. My Dad came from Lebanon. He established himself here in Calexico and brought himself over. My mother is extremely Mexican, and she brought us up and said: You are Mexicans, and I don't want you to be confused with ugly Mexicans, and you speak Spanish at home and you speak English outside the home.

Now I feel American in mind in many ways and I feel Mexican at heart. I feel very proud and very grateful for an education in the United States, and I am very grateful to be brought up in the different culture, a culture which is more sensitive and has more family values and is more open to other values.

My grandfather went to Argentina at the end of the nineteenth century for land and then he sent for his wife, who was only a fourteen-year-old girl, and my father was born in Argentina. But my grandfather had a quarrel with one of his brothers and shot him and thought he had killed him,* so he ran away to San Francisco and he stayed there for I don't know how many years, and he came here to the valley as a merchant in about 1910. Once he had enough money, he sent for his family. My grandmother had had to wait for eighteen years. So my father came here at the age of twenty-five. He was an illiterate; he only spoke Arabic.

*About this deed, Zulema later remarked: "We Middle Eastern people, we're very passionate and very subjective."

This must have been in 1925 or '26. He helped out in the store and then he inherited it, he and his brother. My father and my uncle, they both became landowners, merchants. They had their stores right here in the center of town. They became landowners, for commercial use, right here between First and Second streets.

I retired two years ago. I just live off the rents off what our father made, coming in here. A total illiterate! It took him time to become a resident, a citizen. But he did it.

My grandfather must have passed away in about 1935. My Dad, he missed of course his tradition, and what was more similar than the American culture was the Mexican culture, so he would cross the culture and come to Mexicali, just for those social events, and that was how he met my Mom. He was going to marry his first cousin, but instead his brother fell into the trap!

My Dad believed that he was supposed to be the support of the family—he never took a vacation in his life—but the mother was the heart. Whatever she wanted, he thought that she was right. They had six kids, one of whom is now deceased. I was the one before last.

What makes the greatest impression on you when you remember your childhood?

I guess being free, being safe all the time. This was a safe little town. Everything was open. Something that I remember was crossing the border, which was like crossing the street. We lived just in one town. I hate the border wall now. When I lived in Mexico City, I hated the high walls. Here I was so happy all the time. Never thought about the heat. I guess I had a very protected time.

What did you do for fun?

We would go around on our bikes; we would go to the YMCA to take swimming lessons. Sometimes there were special events in the De Anza Hotel. The Fox Theater was the only theater in Calexico. And they had these matinees: "Tom and Jerry" for a double feature, cartoons of course . . . First of all, it was *safe*. Just like any little town, I guess you could say. I guess everybody knew each other. It was fun. You know, I could never say to you, God, it was intolerably hot! Because I didn't know any better! It was just a regular life. Going to school Monday through Friday, partying in Mexicali on Saturdays and Sundays, that's what I remember. Going up and down on Reforma flirting. All the life was going on in Mexicali. Most balls and theme parties were organized in the Casino de Mexicali. That's gone now, long gone. It's the mothers that will organize the theme parties now, not the girls. Halloween and like that.

So Mexicali wasn't Sin City at that time?

Mexicali was the whorehouse of the Imperial Valley, I did read, but it was only here in the borderline that they had these nightclubs, and they were very low-class ones, the Cage and the Green Cat especially. And there were other terrible places, those women of the night and whatever! But no, I never saw Mexicali as a Sin City, because we only went for family affairs. There is always this morbid thing about finding out what is behind these dark places. Right after my wedding, which ended at three in the morning, my friends took us to the Cage, and I said, so this is it! You have seen across the way all those abandoned buildings parallel to the international line, right by the Hotel del Norte? That was El Gato Verde. And there was a restaurant, too, El León del Oro, and it was also a betting place, but it was a family place, and also an intellectual place where the men would like to get together and have their beers and whatever. We were only interested in the family fun. First we had to have our Mass, and then we'd go out flirting, and then we'd go out to a Chinese restaurant, either the Shangri-La or else the Restaurante 19 . . .

It says something about Zulema Rashid's social class that although she flirted on Avenida Reforma every Sunday after Mass, she almost never attended Mass in that church on Reforma, the church which Rebeca Hernández had praised to me because *everybody is welcome. Did you see that dirty beggar who went all the way up to the altar on his knees?*—Here is how Zulema described it: It's like a little postcard. It's a very simple, provincial cathedral, a very plain church. And Zulema went on to say: Most of the people from the social elite, they would go to church in the Colonia Nueva, which has very nice residential houses, very well furnished. I would go often there, yes, because my grandmother lived very close by. Because of the heat, they wore pastel clothes. I never missed a Mass on Sunday, never. But maybe that was because I was afraid of committing a capital sin and dying and going to hell.—Laughingly, she added: I'm not scared of that now!

Did you ever go to church on the American side?

Oh, yes, to Our Lady of Guadalupe Church here in Calexico, on Fifth and Rockwood. By the way, there was also an Episcopalian church there, and it was a big mystery, a *big* mystery, and sometimes we would kind of sneak on in, like into a haunted house . . .

And where did you go to school?

There were two schools at the time. One was the public school; one was private. The private school belonged to the nuns from Jalisco. You will find my father's name on the plaque, because he helped bring in the nuns. In that private school, ninety-five percent of the students were from Mexicali. But there was a little problem there. The nuns were from Guadalajara, so we got black points if we spoke Spanish during recess! We were all Mexicans, so it was very hard to make us speak English. All my friends were from Mexicali. I had no friends in Calexico. When I got married, we came to the courthouse to get married, but the ceremony was in Mexicali.

What was your goal in life at that time?

All I wanted to do ever since I was sixteen was to get married to Prince Charming and have twelve children! I just wanted to be a Mom the rest of my life. When I turned twenty, I went to this black-and-white ball which is very important traditionally in Mexico. It was in Hermosillo, Sonora. I was sent as an ambassador. I got the crown. But I wanted to study. I wanted to go to Mexico City, but my Mom said that was too far.

Did you have a *quinceañera*?

Oh, yes, I had one! Because I was very romantic at the time, so I wanted one! My sisters never did. My Dad didn't believe in luxury. I wanted my fourteen maids and all the rest of it . . .

(Here I couldn't help but remember the *quinceañera* of the child Luisa in that graffiti'd freeway plaza of Condominios Montealbán, with the Río Nuevo stinking up the spring night.* But why shouldn't Zulema have had her fourteen maids? And why shouldn't Luisa?)

And did you find Prince Charming?

I thought so at the time. Anyhow, I was very happy. I worked in the bank here and it was so dry and so strict and so boring. But in Mexicali as an accountant it was like partying all the time!

"A FORTHRIGHT, INQUISITIVE MIND"

In 1940, a woman who had toured Okie camps in hopes of uncovering *The Real Causes of Our Migrant Problem* shared this eternal truth with us: *If there's one thing I'm certain of, it's the big-heartedness of the men who head this country's oil industry.* But when it came to agriculture, she still defined bigheartedness in nonindustrial terms: *It's a sad change that has come over our farm owners . . . To them a farm is just a business that uses soil, water, sunlight, seed . . . in order to turn out food products.*

Oh, but that was once upon a time. Now Imperial was *a wonderland of factories running 24 hours a day, 365 days a year,* even if Zulema Rashid retained no definite impression of which miracle crop her father's factory grew; Imperial was *The Largest Irrigated District in the World.*

In 2004, stout old Richard Brogan made me a reasonably attractive case for the bigheartedness of Imperial-as-factory-wonderland. He said: The nature of the American farmer is that it's a forthright, inquisitive mind. It's like, *I'm gonna try and I'm gonna win and I hope you do, too. You might!* A very industrial, a very free-

*Described on p. 428.

wheeling free spirit. That's not corporate agriculture; it's large family agriculture. It's very emotional. A family farm still cares. I do grant that the larger associations, whether they be corporate or large family, seem to be the successful controlling people in the produce business. When you turn that around, is it because produce makes money? I honestly believe that a lot of these people started with a hundred and sixty acres and went to ten thousands. That economic feature is certainly a controlling thing in a lot of ways.

He belonged to the Imperial Valley almost as much as Zulema Rashid. Indeed, he must have been a schoolboy there when she was a schoolgirl, for he said simply: My mother had TB when I was born and by the time that was corrected it was decided medically that the desert climate would be beneficial. I was born in La Jolla in 1944, but I grew up here.

What did it look like?

Well, I don't know. Looked like big farmland. I didn't understand what I was seeing the way I can now. I was driving a tractor at seventeen, eighteen years of age. When I was twenty-one, I finally became a deputy sheriff in this county. I still drove a tractor part-time . . .

THE ALGERIAN WONDERLAND

It is a wonderland of factories running 24 hours a day, 365 days a year.

And what else was it?

Well, Calexico was a lot quieter, a lot whiter, said Kay Brockman Bishop. I ran into a friend the other day and *her* friend described her as the last white girl in Calexico. There's still a lot of community here, but there was more back then. People went to dance class but there was not so much of that as 4-H and so forth. You went and helped your neighbors. If you saw smoke, you went and saw if they were in trouble.

We were sitting in sight of her childhood home. She pointed at it and said: It was originally a Sears Roebuck kit house. Has a screen porch that went all the way around it. It originally was two bedrooms and it had a great big kitchen.

My grandfather built it in 1904. When my grandfather moved down here, he had the idea of raising teams of buggy horses. Then the car was invented and that took care of that! So he started raising workhorses. Daddy used to say the worst place to be was in a pen of yearlings because they all wanted attention and they all wanted to fight.

My Dad was born in 1906 in L.A. and they brought him down here. He lived his whole life in that house. My Dad used to drive a schoolbus across the plank road to Yuma if they had a football game. That would have been in about 1922. Daddy shot this mountain lion right down the corner where you turned off 98 . . .—She showed me a newspaper clipping from 1947.

What did you do for fun?

Rode my horse. I had a girlfriend that lived about a mile and half from me and I rode to her house a lot. And when I was growing up—I was an only child—I got to do an awful lot of stuff. If Daddy had to haul grain to town, he would take me. I worked weekends moving cattle and I had to ride to work before daylight. Things are a little different down here when you have your own ranch. My son George was driving tractor when he was in first grade; he was raking hay. We had to refit the tractor for him.

Meanwhile, all through the middle of the next decade, which is to say after Alice Woodside's husband had first seen Calexico and Mexicali, *Imperial Valley, the big, sunny, windy Algeria of the "Southland,"* was still annexing further and higher mesas for purposes of irrigation, populating her new territories with flax, alfalfa (six cuttings a year), sugar beets . . .

FRUIT, FLOWERS AND SUNSHINE

Why did they come here? Why did they stay? . . . asks a woman who herself arrived in the Imperial Valley back in 1918. *Now one sees the answers, written in the fields, the homes and the towns; one hears the answers in the sound of working tractors on summer nights and the hum of air conditioners, in the winter concert series and in the train whistles as produce starts to the market place; one feels the answers in the winter sun and the summer evenings and in the certain knowledge that "home" is held fast in the "Hollow of God's Hand."*

Imperial is fossils and vacation fun; Imperial is a picnic in painted canyon; Imperial is a shopping trip in Mexicali; Imperial is bird-hunting in the tules along the south shore of the Salton Sea.

Imperial is in God's hand, all right. *No other area in the U.S. can produce any more crops per acre than those grown in Imperial Valley because of the year-round growing season, B. A. Harrigan, county agricultural commissioner, told the El Centro Kiwanis Club.* Imperial is sweet—so sweet! To be exact, Imperial yields one million eight hundred thousand pounds of honey in 1950. Speak of sweet! *At Calexico it was Christmas shopping time on Main Street with incredible perfect astonished Mexican beauties* . . . Speak of still more sweetness: In 1958, Richard Campbell remembers once upon a time in his fourteen years in Imperial Valley when December lettuce went to seven dollars a carton at a time that two or three would have been high. Why shouldn't our lettuce go up to eight dollars in 1959?

Thanks to the Salton Sea's mud volcanoes, Imperial at midcentury is number one among California counties for carbon dioxide production; Imperial is another "Cavalcade Parade," God knows precisely when or why; the archivist didn't, although in the background I see the old Allhambra Motel in Calexico, which is long gone now; three little girls in lacy white dresses advance, bearing round placards for FRUIT, FLOWERS, and SUNSHINE.

Chapter 108

THERE WAS ALWAYS FOOD ON THE TABLE

(1950s)

In 2003, Stella Mendoza, who not long before had completed her term as President of the Imperial Irrigation District, had just baked cookies in her kitchen in Brawley, and she offered me all I wanted.

I was born in Brawley, she said. My Dad came across in the 1920s, when they were about eleven years old. They came by horse. They hired a Yaqui scout to bring them into Nogales. They came into the Imperial Valley where there was cotton. My mother met my Dad here. It used to be that families in groups of four or five would travel at the same time. Her father worked for the railroad in Arizona. The family lived there for two or three years, to save money to go to California. She lived there up to fifth grade, I believe. Then they ended up in the Imperial Valley. My Dad was ten years older than my Mom, and my mother's parents didn't like my Dad, because they said he was too old and he drank too much and he was a womanizer. So they went away to Sonora. Then they had nothing to eat. So he came back and got them and he was the best son-in-law.

We used to go from Brawley to Los Banos for the labor season, for the cantaloupes.

Well, going back to my childhood, well, growing up, with an extended family, it was a very small house but it was always full of friends and relatives, who were there for something to eat; and I grew up in that kind of an atmosphere. There were twelve of us and nine of us survived. My Dad provided for us. He was never a farmer but he worked for the farmers. In fact, my brother, when he was ten years old, he was run over by a melon truck in Los Banos. Eduardo. My mother was pregnant. He died two years before I was born. He just went to hang around, and he saw the truck pull away, and he jumped, and he slipped and fell, and by the time they took him to the hospital he was dead.

In Sonora, they're famous for making those big tortillas. In the back of the house, my Mom had that fifty-five-gallon drum on which to make the tortillas. They would fold them in a triangle. I grew up eating tortillas for everything. None of us learned to do that. We depended on our Mom to make those.

I would dry the meat from Safeway in a little cage and I would pound it; I would pound the dried meat in a *metate* made out of petrified wood. Then I would make the *machaca* for a stew, and my Dad loved it.

You know, when I was growing up in Brawley, we had the east side and the west side, divided by the railroad tracks. My mother would tell me, back in the 1930s the east side was a real thriving community. It had restaurants and pharmacies. I think there was more economic development back then than now. Why it changed—I don't know. I remember on the east side of Brawley, we would leave in the summer, to go to Los Banos, we would always come back around Halloween, and especially—you have to understand that the valley—the politics have always been controlled by the landowner. And that has been one of the reasons why development has taken so long. I'll tell you when the big change came, was when the prisons came into the valley, and they started giving their opinion. I was on the Brawley City Council at that time, and we lobbied for it. I felt it was good, because it would provide good jobs for people here. The biggest employers are the county, the IID and the prisons, the schools. So it's mainly service related. The county, they have the courts, human resources, roads, welfare department, sheriff's department.

All I know is that my Dad, and our extended family, they always worked the fields, and they always had work. There was always food on the table.

Growing up, my mother's sisters lived in Mexicali, and I was maybe eight years old, and we could go on a Sunday morning and spend the whole day and come back. My Mom gave me money to go to the corner store, and they said of me: Who is she? My friend said: She's from the other side.

What I remember was that life in Mexicali was a lot harder. They have more freedom, but maybe they have less to lose.

My Mom would always help her sisters. She would always take them food and money. My mother lived in Kilometer Fifty-seven. My mother died before my aunt. When she died, she told me, you need to take care of her; so we, her daughters, we continued to take care of my aunt. She liked canned roast beef . . .

Chapter 109

COACHELLA

(1950)

. . . the road was anisotropic—just as history is. There is no way back. And he went right ahead anyway. And met up with a chained skeleton.

—Arkadi and Boris Strugatski, 1964

In 1947, when Coachella green corn drinks sunbeams for two thousand five hundred and seventy-five acres, a certain Mr. and Mrs. La Londe, who before then had been living in Riverside with the bride's parents, complete their first year of residence in the entity which I call Imperial. In that part of Riverside County with which we are concerned—namely, Indio, Coachella and "surrounding desert areas"—population has more than doubled between 1940 and 1950. Indio's growth has been especially spectacular: a hundred and thirty percent! *I have never been cheated out of a dollar in my life.* That was for sure. Banning and Palm Springs had experienced an increase somewhere between seventy and eighty percent. And it was only going to get better and better, because, well, because **WATER IS** finally **HERE!***

The La Londes arrived in Thermal during a cool spell. Coachella incorporated just the previous year; Thermal remains unincorporated as I write. As Art La Londe put it: It was October and it rained. October twentieth was the date I got hired, and also my discharge date from World War II. We thought it was great. Weather was great. We had an outhouse which was about a hundred feet from the back.

His wife Helen sat in her wheelchair and said: We had to go to Riverside to my parents to take a bath. We had to go to Indio to use the wringer.

I was hired to be the seventh-grade teacher, said Mr. La Londe, who had once, so I was told, been a hale, large-presenced man but who was now skeletal.—I had two grades, sixth and seventh. I had two rows of one and three or four rows of the others. I'd just say there were around thirty students at this point. I do remember that the next year I had around fifty, including two sixteen- or seventeen-year-olds. We had the little green schoolhouses where the Mexicans went. See, when we got

*In the middle 1950s, the irrigated areas in Coachella, Borrego, Palo Verde and Bard will add up to 563,000 acres.

here, the World War had ended. Anyway, they had eliminated any kind of segregation.

Mexican families were very well thought of, Helen put in, and we keep in touch with them to this day.

Thermal had about three hundred students in '46, her husband continued. And then they combined with a school district called Ensign. We got three teachers from that school. Thermal, it's way up there now. Close to five thousand. Now, in '56 the superintendent died and I got the job. I ran the district for seventeen years.

We like it when you go on Saturday afternoon, go to Indio and see all your friends. It took fifteen minutes in '46. Thermal to Coachella is still two lanes, one each way. Then when you get to Coachella, well, they have a road that goes around it now, an expressway. That's where they made a mistake. Freeway means you can drive straight through and can never worry about intersections. Expressway means you can have access to it. They have had some very bad accidents.

How often have you gone to Mexico over the years?

The only trip we took to Mexico was a rail trip, from Mexicali. This was a one-day trip. I don't even think we stayed over.

Do you see any difference between Tijuana and Mexicali?

Mexicali and TJ, they're about the same. Third World. Oh, the poverty! On the other hand, Mexicali had a hospital, and one of my teachers had a gallbladder problem and went down for surgery. We didn't have such a thing as health insurance. That didn't come along until the middle sixties.

How would you differentiate Coachella from Imperial?

Well, geologically they are one big area* with the Salton Sea in between, but actually the Coachella Valley and the Imperial Valley are two separate entities economically and in all ways I'd say.

The La Londes were very proud of their sector of the long binational valley; they were certainly not the only ones. A booster called it "America's Garden of Allah." Carolyn Cooke, who arrived in Coachella in 1957, expressed much the same feelings; and when I asked her whether Imperial was different from Coachella she replied:

Yeah, well, they are different. For one thing, they are based solely on agriculture. We used to go back and forth a lot into Imperial, and it was strictly agricultural, and they would be growing alfalfa or corn or sugar beets, where up here there were the citrus ranches and grape ranches and there was a lot of sophistication here that there wasn't down there. We started from Palm Springs and their little core of

*I am assured that Coachella is perfect for dates, whereas the Imperial Valley is so only in "some sections" (El Centro and Bard), since its soil contains so much clay.

movie stars and it spread from there and became the golf capital of the world and went from there, and enormous wealth came into Indian Wells and Rancho Mirage and set the tone totally differently than in Imperial Valley. There's a lot of roving population down there, a lot of vacant houses.

On another occasion, the old lady put matters slightly differently: I have lived briefly in the Imperial Valley, in El Centro. Imperial Valley is agricultural pure and simple. There is very little tourism. There is definitely no glamour. It's just a farming valley and I envy them. I love farming valleys and ours is rapidly losing that. Now I haven't been down there for years. We used to go back and forth all the time. I don't know where the line is even. I don't know what it's like anymore, but it used to be there'd be like reduction of civilization as it were, for many miles, and then you'd get to Brawley and you'd start to see the ranches and the farms and so on.

The headgates of the Imperial Canal first opened, as you'll recall, back in 1901, which was Wilber Clark's time; whereas the first water didn't make it down the Coachella Branch of the All-American Canal until 1948, just two years before this chapter opens. Reader, you can be sure that that waterway would be treated as a jewel! I remember all the people at Slab City who liked to cool off in it at the turn of the following century, all of them hoping that the *irrigation goons* wouldn't come and give them a ticket. (That's what we call *by the people and for the people.*)—Now here's an idyllic midcentury photograph of two men in a broad flatboat, one piloting it, facing forward into the future, the other standing facing us, spraying many overlapping chevrons of aerated liquid at the shrubs on the white and sandy bank of the Coachella Canal, which goes on straight and flat, bisecting Imperial's grander flatness. The caption explains that this is a weed-control boat. Weeds drink water, you see, and we don't want to waste a drop. (I remember a scene from the Preston Ranch near Calexico in 1904: A man sits contentedly fishing at the Imperial Canal's edge, with verdure all about. We don't do that anymore. We're all business.)

Like Imperial County, Riverside County was enjoying an income boom. How could she not, with all those new people coming in? In 1950 Riverside County produced more than ninety percent of California's dates, and most of the date plantations were in the Coachella Valley, which accordingly looked forward to even greater things, because *about 20,000 acres are now under cultivation and 75,000 more can be put into crops when the All-American Canal is completed in the near future.* (De Beauvoir: *Their own existence is a thing of chance to which they attach no importance. That is why they are interested in net results, and not in the spirit which engenders them.*)

Speaking of net results, Coachella will outperform Palo Verde in income by twenty-one to fifteen in 1952, by twenty-three to seventeen in 1953.—My beloved brethen, shall we speak next of the spirit? Anytime you want to experience that, we kindly invite you to attend our next Date Festival.*—Now for the procedure: *The scientifically clean dates then move down an endless belt, over the grading tables, where medically approved girls, dressed in immaculate white, remove the culls and separate the fruit into lots of uniform ripeness, consistency, size and general appearance.* Peering down through a square metal framework studded with lamps, we spy the medically approved girls, who wear striped party hairbands and white uniforms, their white arms out on the work surface before them as they studiously sort dates into boxes. They appear to be lost in ecstasies of concentration. Within the square perimeter of date-boxes frozen in mid-conveyance, parallel belts run beyond the photographic horizon. The mild exoticism of the dates and the pleasing spectacle of youthful femininity save this industrial spectacle from the usual factory dreariness, although I wonder whether it is any more fun or at least more profitable for the girls than it would have been for me.

Now, what about Coachella green corn?

In 1947, the opinion of C. H. Hollis, corn grower and shipper in Thermal, is this: *Well, one man and a Ford tractor or two horses can easily plant ten acres a day, four dollars and a half to five dollars.* That does not sound too bad. But that is hardly the total cost to grow corn. In 1954, one farmer calculates the total cost at a hundred and fifty-one dollars per acre. Both field and tractor labor at ninety cents an hour. Gifford Price, who farms in Mecca, says to us: *Most of us have to go out and borrow our money . . .*

A rancher in Thermal named Douglass Nance now utters that dreaded phrase, *crisis of overproduction.* A thousand new Coachella acres this year are going into corn due to cotton going out! This is a marketing order hearing, of course; and Mr. Nance's expressions are all to a purpose: We want *to try to bring the Imperial Valley and Borrego Valley in with us so we would all be operating on the same basis.* This strategy may well prove essential to the salvation of Western civilization; for Paul Sandoval of Indio worries that *if we stabilize and have a good market up here in the Coachella Valley and they see we are doing fairly well, they can put in some big acreages* in Calipatria.

It's not only the Imperial Valley that Coachella must watch out of the side of her eye. This area of early corn competes with Alabama and Florida. And thank God Texas doesn't ship good corn! J. L. Mapes in Indio, who grows, packs and ships all the way to Detroit, Boston, even Indianapolis,† expresses his worries about that

*This book would not be complete without mention of R.M.C. Fullenwider, who became Date Festival Manager in 1943 and "replaced the Western theme with an Arabian theme to coincide with the names of some Coachella communities . . . and streets . . ."

†Los Angeles is not all bad, either, since he can send his inferior corn to that hive of honest commerce, there being "always someone that wants to—different stores that use a cheaper grade of corn."

giant tract of formerly Mexican real estate: *I think this year they have taken about all of the eastern play on the carrot market, which they could very easily do on corn if they ever grew the quality of corn down there.*

Even as Coachella's farmers worry about competition and overproduction, they stand on the verge of decline. One of their own dearest wishes, a branch of the All-American Canal, will gradually, if so far partially, undo them. For a long while yet, Mexican-Americans and a few others will continue to get their living in Coachella by hand-sorting lemons into one of four classes on a rubberized canvas belt. As early as the mid-fifties, however, a regional geography perceives all too well that *agriculture was long the chief source of income in the Coachella, but now a booming urban development along the Valley's western edges and below San Jacinto Peak is beginning to encroach upon the farming land.*

The La Londes were part of that urban development. As you remember, Coachella had hired on Mr. La Londe as a teacher. (Carolyn Cooke became a grape grower's bookkeeper, so we can call her agricultural.) I myself would have enrolled in the residential legions; why not confide to you that one of my greatest, sleepiest pleasures in entering the entity known as Imperial is to imagine myself living young and newly married to the woman I love in a little American homestead in about 1950? To be sure, ever so many Imperial homes have caught my fancy on both sides of the line: high desert ranches around Tecate and La Rumorosa, tree-shaded, pastel-colored concrete houses in Mexicali, farms in Campo, Seeley's residences set apart from the world by being centered in furrowed fields, semi-secret eucalyptus-shaded dreamhouses in Brawley, Heber or even El Centro—but where I so often crave to be is in Coachella, in sight of a date palm grove and the Salton Sea with its mountains either east or west; I'd want to be on the porch beneath the grapefruit tree, in late afternoon in the love swing with my pregnant wife beside me and date shakes in cold glasses in our hands; yes, in 1950, when the All American Canal brings me all the water I'll ever lust for and we all still believe in progress and my own real life (commenced in 1959) has not scorched me with any problems; *it is simply needless to question the supply of water.* Never mind the Cold War, black segregation and Mexican peonage; particularly don't worry about DDT. Exclude the self-congratulatory parochialism which has defined America from Babbitt to President George W. Bush and which might have reached its zenith in 1950; the Imperial Idea likewise seemed to be an eternal desert star; I can make my own life and to hell with the rest of the world!

Maybe I could have been a reporter for the newspaper in Indio. In my student days I dabbled at unskilled ranch labor; I never could have supported a family doing it. But my Imperial dream is luxurious precisely because it will never see the sun of truth.

Would I plant grapefruits in my back yard? Why not? *How fortunate we are in planting our grove at this late date, as formerly we would have been required to have drilled a deep well, . . . but with the coming of the canal from the Colorado River, we are definitely assured of adequate water at a cost considerably less than were we to depend on pump irrigation.* By the middle of the decade, many farmers already need tile drains due to salinity caused by over-irrigation.

Chapter 110

RIVERSIDE

(1950)

Confidence in the continued growth of Riverside's wealth, industry and population, and in the advancement of its municipal and social activities will be created as this directory is consulted; for the directory is a mirror reflecting Riverside to the world.

—Riverside City Directory (1951)

It took exactly the entire twenty-five miles to get out of the smog of Los Angeles; the sun was clear in Riverside.* Jack Kerouac wrote the words of that novel in about 1956. It is nice to think that Riverside was still pretty then. Her smog visitations had begun during World War II.

Riverside City's slogan was: *Birthplace of the Navel Orange.* One of the two original navel orange trees planted by Mrs. Tibbetts in 1873 was still alive in 1951; I never did find out when it died.

Riverside is an ideal residential community . . . From Mt. Rubidoux, towering over the city, it resembles an immense wooded estate. It is known for its beautiful boulevards, lined with palms, eucalypti and roses, and lighted with distinctive "Indian Rain Cross" electroliers.

The Ramona Freeway, known in my epoch as Interstate 10, will commence operation in 1954. I've seen it from the air just before it opened: a canal-like artery of white that forever bisects the dark yarn-puffs of orange-rows. One history of the Inland Empire perceives this new artery of Progress as *opening the door of suburbia and ending the era of agriculture.* In fact, the city of Riverside had been subdividing and building crazily ever since 1950.

Therefore, why don't you move into the subdivision of your choice? Why not dwell amidst the palms, eucalypti and roses before our smog makes them obsolete? The J. H. Jeter Co. (REALTORS: CITRUS GROVES — HOMES) will gladly bestow on you a homey house surrounded by sunny and shady trees. As for me, I could take you for the prettiest little home-viewing drive down a street

*According to the county directory, the city of Riverside was actually fifty-three miles east of Los Angeles.

THE J. H. JETER CO.
REALTORS
CITRUS GROVES — HOMES

"Complete Real Estate Service for Riverside and Vicinity"

APPRAISALS
CITRUS GROVE AND FARM LOANS
4½% — 20 YEARS
Farm Loan Correspondent for The Equitable Life Assurance Society
3662 Market St. Telephone 0111

called **LEMON**, which runs *South from PE Ry tracks bet Orange and Lime* until *Hewitt ends,* then continues across non-citrus roads.

No, don't look at me that way; let's get down to business. How can I sell you a homestead in Riverside? Twenty-two thousand telephones, fifty-five churches, thirty-nine point two square miles of city, orange trees galore (under **Citrus Groves**, the county directory gives two entries, both for realtors), more than forty-six thousand citizens, and—most important to those who chant invocations to the Ministry of Capital—assessed valuation: $59,761,360! I have never been cheated out of a dollar in my life. (Will you be needing a mortgage? By golly, I'll bet that if I motored you down to the Citrus Belt Building and Loan Association, Mr. Alger J. Fast, our Secretary-Manager, could fix you up!) While we are on the subject of Capital's ministers, I hasten to inform you that there were a hundred and thirteen Holts in Riverside, not counting spouses, and of this clan the most powerful-sounding was the *dist mgr State Controller.*

EVERYTHING IS HERE

Predominating nationalities in the city are American and Mexican. Shall we browse through the county directory and see which of these tend to be employed at what?

As people say, there's a lot in a name.

Meet the Angel family:

Angel Antonia fruit pkr r 9343 Canal av
" **Enedina Mrs.** orange pkr h9343 Canal av . . .
" **Jas R (Josephine R)** tab opr CEPCo h 4581 Arlington av
California Electric Power Co.
tab? operator
" **Mercedes** fruit pkr r 9343 Canal av
" **Pentelion** (Josefa) lab h7458 Emerald
laborer

Randomly, and still in the **A**'s, we meet

Acosta Lupe fruitwkr r7642 Fern av

and

Aguilar Isabel L fruit pkr L V W Brown Est r Colton

Now for some Anglos:

Hoover Alva (Nellie) aircrftgwkr
Hopkins Pansy M Mrs with U S Salinity Lbty
Hopper Frank J (Ernestina) aircrftwrkr
SMITH F NORMAN (Lolita K) "All Lines of Insurance" on Seventh

And here are a couple of foreign names, just to show you that we Americans assimilate all kinds:

Ahlswede Karl P (Harriet R) fertilizer 9758 Magnolia av . . .
Zymkie Alex A (Gertrude M) rancher h1245 Ruby Highgrove

From the occupations of the Angel family alone I can nearly believe the directory's assertion that . . . *today Riverside is the center of the Citrus Empire. Riverside County has 26,958 acres devoted to citrus fruit . . .*

Of course, the Ontario city directory, whose front cover sports an advertisement for Ford Citrus Motors, 115 South Palm Ave., Ontario, counter-assures us that *Ontario is ideally situated in the heart of the citrus belt, thirty-eight miles east of Los Angeles . . .*

Reader, would you rather live in Riverside or Ontario? *One of Ontario's most prized assets is the incomparable Euclid Avenue, a majestic tree-shaded thoroughfare, 200 feet wide, with roadways on each side of a central parkway of velvety lawn and pepper trees . . . Euclid Avenue is considered one of the seven most beautiful avenues in North*

America . . . Something tells me that none of the other six run through the entity that I call Imperial.

Do you remember *The Largest Irrigated District in the World?* Well, who cares about those rubes down there? Here in the Inland Empire, *citrus fruits provide the largest parts of the agricultural revenue but directly east of Ontario stretch vineyards including the largest vineyard in the world.*

In short, don't you just love the Inland Empire? For manufacturing we can offer you General Electric, Barbara Jane's Sportswear, Fluffee Novelty Co. and Hollywood Junior. Meanwhile, George Chaffey's proto-Imperial lives on as Etiwanda the Beautiful: *Nestling among its orange and lemon groves and its expanse of vineyards, abounding in every kind of grapes, its people are among the most comfortable, enterprising and happy in all the state.*

Orange groves and freeways, Euclid Avenue and General Electric, ranches and subdivisions, why can't we keep the whole lot? As Border Patrolwoman Gloria Chavez said: I think we all feel sorry for 'em.

Chapter 111

MARKET PRICES

(1950)

But it is presumably all for the best or at least it is expedient for business-as-usual, that the farmer should continue to nurse his illusions and go about his work, that he should go on his way to complete that destiny to which it has pleased an all-seeing and merciful Providence to call him.

—Thorstein Veblen, 1923

Coachella green Valentine beans were going for twenty-eight to thirty cents a pound in Los Angeles, while Kentucky wonder beans, replaced by another variety, for the wonder eventually drains out of everything, were going from sixty to sixty-five cents. Where were the local Imperial cucumbers of 1925? By year's end, Imperial County would send a hundred and seven carloads of those down the hot black ribbon of track, chattering past palo verdes and smoke trees, swinging along on the sides of the white crumbly berm all the way to Indio, then to the markets of this wider world!

In 1925 the only cabbage listed on the Los Angeles exchange had been local ($1.25 to $1.35 for good quality). We now find: *Cabbage: White, local, $2.00–2.50; lidded Yuma $3.00–3.25; Imp. Vly $2.00–2.50; Red, local, $4.00–4.50.* In other words, Imperial cabbage, like Imperial's status in American agriculture, was high ticket, not top ticket.

Nor had the Valley supplied carrots to the City of Angels in 1925 (back then they were listed under "bunched vegetables" at thirty-five to forty cents per dozen bunches; imagine that!). But Imperial had achieved a success through her own efforts. She was selling orange jewels at a fancy price: *Carrots: Iced 6-doz. Imp. Vly, $3.25–3.50; small $2.85–3.00; local unlidded 3-doz $1.00–1.15.* This year, Imperial County would ship nineteen thousand and twenty-nine carloads of those, making more than three million dollars.

Now for our signature commodity: *Lettuce: Dry pckd. Imp. Vly 4s $2.00–2.25; Yuma $3.00–3.25; Imp. Vly $2.00–2.50; Red, local unlidded 3-doz. 50–75c.* More than fifteen thousand carloads will go to market this year, which works out to more than fifteen million dollars—don't tell me we don't know how to play lettuce roulette here in Imperial!

In 1925, neither Imperial nor Coachella squashes had been listed on the market; but in this department also, the entity which I call Imperial had accomplished cash magic: *Squash: Italian, Imp. Vly Crts., flts., $3.50–4.00, ord. $1.25–1.50; Coach Vly flts $3.75–4.00.* We'll forget about the white summers, yellow crooknecks, and locals of both the banana and Hubbard variety, since they're not prefaced by "Imp. Vly." In the fullness of the year, Imperial Valley ordinary and banana squash will rack up a respectable two hundred and sixty-two carloads.

Why does Imperial continue to thrive in this cutthroat market? Because we've held the line against unions, thank God. As Richard Johnson, Jr., explains it for all time: *A minimum wage to marginal workers would force the farmer's costs above the break-even point.* Meanwhile, Jack T. Pickett is outraged that the unions want growers to pay a minimum wage of no less than a dollar per hour.

Chapter 112

CROP REPORTS

(1946–1957)

If a year's crop were good, Juan's happiness was assured for the next six months.

—Helen Hunt Jackson, 1884

And how well *were* the owners of Imperial's fields thriving?

1946: *I wish to emphasize that these values are Gross Values . . . The net income to farmers was not increased in proportion to the gross sales due to lower efficiency from inexperienced agricultural labor, worn out equipment, and increased costs of all materials used in harvesting and handling the crops.*

Inexperienced agricultural labor! If the brown hands of field workers and tenant farmers failed to reach the efficiency that, say, Wilber Clark might have demanded of himself, why did the growers invite them into the carrot fields of Holtville; the date plantations of Indio, Coachella and Bard; the lettuce empires of El Centro; not to mention Coachella's citrus orchards, beyond which the Salton Sea appeared so wide and cool and gentle, too far away from the future to stink? I can think of only one answer, the answer of Border Patrolman Dan Murray: *They do work most Americans wouldn't do.*

1947: *I wish to emphasize that these values are Gross Values . . . The net income to farmers was not increased in proportion to the gross sales . . .*

The farmer remains caught in the same economic coils that the Department of Agriculture detected in 1920. The family farm grows ever more expensive and "needs" to produce more. Failure causes bankruptcy; success imperils all producers of a given crop. Overproduction and overindebtedness, these are Imperial's Scylla and Charybdis. The Department of Agriculture concluded: *The tendency toward larger farms is likely to throw an almost insurmountable barrier in the way of a man who wishes to progress up the so-called agricultural ladder . . .* But we need have no fear that our lands will not become better and better as the years go by.

1949: *I wish to emphasize that these values are Gross Values . . . The net income to farmers was not increased in proportion to the gross sales due to lower farm prices and increased costs of labor and all materials used in harvesting and handling the crops.*

Evidently some field workers have negotiated a higher wage.

1954: *I wish to emphasize that these values are* *Gross* *Values . . . The net income to farmers was not increased in proportion to the gross sales . . .*

1955: *This report is a compilation of the gross value of all the commodities produced in Imperial County and represents the gross F.O.B. Shipping Point values. It is not intended to show the net income to farmers, which due to lower farm prices, increased cost of labor and other materials purchased by farmers, was in most cases lower than in 1954.*

1956: *This report is a compilation of the gross value of all the commodities produced . . . It is not intended to show the net income to farmers, which due to lower farm prices, increased incidence of pests and diseases, primarily curly top virus, reduced values of some crops drastically. This was offset in some measure by increased production for some commodities.*

But don't get me wrong. We've never been cheated out of a dollar in our lives. *The 1957 crop values are the second highest ever reported from Imperial County.*

Chapter 113

CANTALOUPE ANXIETIES

(1958)

So, concludes Mr. Frank R. Coit, if some research could be made as to how they look on the fruit stand, I think it would be a good thing—compared to oranges or peaches or something else. At the time we are shipping we have to compete with other fruits and vegetables.

He is a grower and shipper of cantaloupes, of course, and we are eavesdropping on him in this marketing order hearing in Fresno.

He complains: I have seen letters given to Paul Smith from ladies that couldn't find a good melon—why couldn't she find a good melon?

Replies a Dr. Braun: There is a long ways from the field to the housewife.

But Mr. Coit, fearless investigator, wants to *follow it and research it and control it from the field to the housewife.*

Mr. F. J. Harkness, Jr., now gives utterance to the American dread: *overproduction.* (My parents used to tell me to finish all the frozen succotash on my plate because other little children were starving in China.) Mr. Harkness says: Most of us here on this board were talking back somewhere on the twentieth to the twenty-fifth of July there would be a lot of cantaloupes—perhaps way too many.

What can we do with them? Well, there is *cantaloupe a la mode; they can be frozen; they can be pickled; they can be worked in with salads* . . . And perhaps if we growers and shippers assess ourselves two cents per crate to finance promotion, we can sweet-talk Americans into buying more cantaloupes.

Where are all these cantaloupes coming from? Turning the page in high excitement, I expected to read: *The Imperial Valley,* which encompasses a royal seventy-five percent of the state's spring melon acreage! But in fact our glut must be credited to the southern San Joaquin Valley. And then I remember that Imperial has suffered from mosaic disease lately; moreover, acreage has shrunk. That must mean that my favorite zone of California is afflicted by a crisis of over- or under-production . . .

Chapter 114

THE BRACEROS

(1942–1965)

. . . Imperial would not be the Magic Land it is today without help from across the border. Many of the vegetable and other crops of Imperial Valley, are "row crops" and require a huge lot of what is generally known as "stoop labor." It is doubtful if anything like enough labor could be secured in the United States for this type of work.

—Elizabeth Harris, 1956

Well, good, said Javier Lupercio, getting ready to talk about the past. In 1958 and '59, all around the railroad tracks here in Mexicali, there used to be a lot of people in tents just resting and living; those were the contractors, the braceros. Bosses from the United States would come and hire; they would call them by name or number, and as many people as that boss needed, he would hire.

Were there about the same number as we see now on the other side, in front of Donut Avenue?

Oh, no—more! Back in that bracero program, all the states of Mexico wanted to take advantage of that program. In one city block there would be maybe two hundred persons, since the train and bus station were there. There were a lot of cantinas. The Owl (Tecolote) was still around, and so was the Nopal, the White Hat, the Molino Rojo. They all closed down around 1975.

And Señor Lupercio nodded and smiled a trifle, remembering the Owl and the White Hat. It was hot and bright there in the park of the Child Heroes, and he licked his lips; soon he and José López from Jalisco and I would go to drink beer and praise women. But how could anything be as good as everything was in the old days, before we'd strayed closer to death?

Back then, he said, most of the people who went to work on the other side were contractors under the bracero program. The patrolling wasn't as strict but there was constant checking and they went to the fields. If you didn't have your permit you would get loaded into a van and taken back to the border.

And his face changed, and the good days became no longer quite so good.

HARRY SINGH & SONS
P.O. Box 1850 Oceanside, CA 92051

0118363

HOURS REGULAR	HOURS OVERTIME	RATE	REGULAR EARNINGS	OVERTIME EARNINGS	OTHER PAY UNITS	OTHER PAY RATE	OTHER PAY AMOUNT	GROSS	PERIOD ENDING
31.50		8.00 12.00				0.20 0.30			10/5/03

TOTAL GROSS: 252.00

DEDUCTIONS

F.I.C.A.	FED. W/H	STATE W/H	SDI	Food	Beverages	LUNCH
19.28			2.27	25.10	2.60	18.71
				Food Tax	Advance	Transportation
				2.15	11.23	12.00

CONTROL NUMBER: 8785

TOTAL DEDUCTIONS: 93.34

EMPLOYEE'S NAME AND SOC. SEC. NO.: JAVIER LUPERCIO

FINAL CHECK

NET PAY $ 158.66

Pay stub of Javier Lupercio, purchased by WTV in 2003

But they were not all bad, either. In 1947, Don Ezekiel Pérez from Las Barrancas works as a bracero on a Montana ranch. *They treated us like family, and we sat and ate with them.* Isaías Ignacio Vázquez Pimentel remembers his bracero father in 1957. *After five months his contract ended and my dad came lighter-skinned, with his suitcase and red boots.* He brings home a dress and gives his wife his earnings.

How did it all begin? You know that—with the Chinese, and then the Japanese, then others.

Claude Finnell, the retired Imperial County Agricultural Commissioner, explained to me across his kitchen table: When people came in here to homestead, they were farming with horses. They couldn't farm great numbers of acres because they didn't have the power. Some of the farmers were using people from Mexico. But there weren't many people from Mexico in the time. Mexicali was a very small town. Then they needed more and more workers. So as Mexicali filled up and ran over, so to speak, it made it easier to get those people for work. So it started during World War II. When I came here in '54, the Mexicans were pretty well here. As I mentioned, they had houses for 'em. We were really booming in those days in terms of farming: Hay and wheat and vegetables.

So were the crickets! laughed Mrs. Finnell. Big black crickets in the street and they were singing!

Four point six million braceros stooped and sweated in Northside between 1942 and 1962. (A poster from a 2002 demonstration in Mexico City reads: *They made us strip, then fumigated us.*) Mexicali swelled with braceros and their families, waiting for the call from Northside.

We see a man in a white paper mask spraying a naked bracero with DDT. Behind them wait many other naked men in a double line. The chemical mist is white like cigarette smoke. The man who is getting sprayed (right in the face) closes his eyes and submits calmly. His penis is very conspicuous in this photo, and so is the sombrero of the man behind him.

That's the beginning. Now for the happy ending: A Mexican leans out the window of his train, which has been chalked: BRACEROS MEXICANOS—VIVA MEXICO! He wears a long rectangular ribbon at his left lapel. It says: **BIENVENIDOS A LOS TRABAJADORES MEXICANOS**. His hair is uncombed (after all, he has been in transit for five days), and the creases at the corners of his eyes curve down, although he is young; and his lips are parted as he grips his right hand with his left hand, as if in bewilderment.

There were fifty-two thousand braceros in 1943. Four hundred and sixty-seven thousand worked the fields in the peak year 1957. After that, the numbers began to go down.

In her little restaurant south of Mexicali, Señora Socorro Rámirez said to me: When my father left here, he worked as a bracero in the U.S.—She bitterly added: He left a great ranch, with water.

And I wondered what it was that hurt so. Was it the abandonment of *her*, or the humiliation implicit in his abandonment of Mexico? Was the ranch lost forever? Did he return to his family? I flicked a glance at her smoldering eyes, and chose not to pry.

By the 1950s, braceros made up a quarter of all California farm laborers. We find, for instance, fifteen hundred of them crammed into the former San Bernardino jail, in quarters meant for a thousand, tending citrus. When forest fires broke out, they could be commandeered to fight them without extra pay.

Up in Coachella, Ray Heckman grows green corn on rented land. In 1947, he gets a hundred and twenty-five crates of corn per acre. Do you think he's working that corn all by himself? Labor for applying water costs him seven dollars an acre (less than half the cost of the water itself, and the rent is fifty). He pays two dollars and twenty-four cents a crate for picking and packing. His total costs work out to two hundred and eighteen dollars an acre. Thank God labor is such a small proportion of these expenses! Does he employ bracero labor? At this marketing-order hearing (held in the Coachella Valley Water District Building), Mr. Heckman does not say. I guess there is a three-out-of-four chance that he doesn't. But I'll bet you my bandanna he's got Mexicans working for him. *So as Mexicali filled up and ran over, so to speak, it made it easier to get those people for work.*

See, in those days there was a bracero program, said Kay Brockman Bishop in Calexico. A lot of those guys came and stayed in labor camps. But you know, it was the same out here. You didn't go to town every day.

My father had a bracero camp around eleven miles from here in the desert, said

Zulema Rashid. I remember my father going over there. There were about four barracks, and they had beds, and there was the main barrack, the large one, and my Dad, he would get up at three in the morning to prepare breakfast for the braceros, and take the big pans into the fields to feed them. What did he grow? Maybe it was cotton, Bill. I don't know. I wouldn't remember. I saw parents of my friends losing everything they had from a bad year in cotton, and also gaining everything. Those gains and losses were mainly in Mexicali. I think I can also remember some on the U.S. side. The barracks were still there a few years back. They housed maybe three hundred braceros, all men.

(Three hundred braceros! Something tells me that Mr. Rashid owned more than the statutory hundred and sixty acres!)

C. H. Hollis, corn grower in Thermal, 1947: *I have one man that irrigates a hundred and sixty acres of grapes, corn, and alfalfa, and he does a pretty good job all by himself* . . . I wonder where that irrigator comes from?

In that same year, when Jack Kerouac went weaving through the San Joaquin Valley with his short-time Mexican girl whose *breasts stuck out straight and true,* farmers were paying three dollars for every hundred pounds of picked cotton. Kerouac went to work with a will, but could make only a dollar-fifty a day. (Border Patrolman Dan Murray: *They do work most Americans wouldn't do.*) And Kerouac decided not to do it, either. He leaves us no descriptions of barracked braceros. Instead, he gives us *the wild streets of Fresno Mextown. Strange Chinese hung out of windows, digging the Sunday night streets; groups of Mex chicks swaggered around in slacks; mambo blasted from jukeboxes; the lights were festooned around like Halloween.*

Thus the San Joaquin in 1947. In 1950 the cotton crop will be seven hundred thousand bales. But only forty-seven thousand pickers will be needed, as opposed to the hundred and twenty thousand of the boom year of 1949. Hence the Producers Cotton Oil Company advises the Farm Placement Service *to do everything possible to discourage farm workers from migrating into the San Joaquin Valley.* The Producers Cotton Oil Company seems quite altruistic! It wants only to avoid *the tragic situation where at the peak of harvest there were more unemployed cotton pickers than pickers who were working.*

Wouldn't it be just super if a grower could pick up the telephone and order forty-seven thousand cotton pickers, no more, no less? Braceros would come in handy for that. We could just count them off like other commodities.

As it just so happens, bracero agriculture is the epitome of contract labor. In this connection let me now quote our familiar companion Paul S. Taylor, writing in that bracero year 1943:

This system of labor contractors in the west began with the Chinese and continues to the present. By relieving employers of many responsibilities it has strong appeal to them;

it offers some advantages to employees, finding employment and sometimes housing for them.

Happily for growers, this arrangement has nothing to do with any union, since *a contractor is an intermediary whose interest is sometimes to exploit the employer for his own advantage and possibly that of its workers and sometimes to exploit his workers for his own advantage and possibly that of the employer.*

How does a contractor work? He might troll a poolhall in Sonora, or a bar he knows in Mexicali; he can avoid or even replace local labor if it's acting uppity.*

So we can understand who might like the bracero system. Who do you think dislikes it?—Some braceros, undoubtedly; for it's not unheard of to pay Mexican officials a bribe of six hundred or even a thousand pesos to get on the approved list. But, after all, braceros are only foreign laborers; since when did their opinion count? The following is more germane:

In 1950, we find certain angels in a familiar Paradise of family farms busily fluttering their wings, trying to pass Senate Bill 272 in order to reinstate *the old "crossing card" permit system for Mexican National stoop labor* so that *some of the labor difficulties of the Imperial Valley will be solved.* Which difficulties, I wonder? *Led by the Imperial Valley Farmers Association, the growers have argued that they are being forced to pay a premium for Mexican Nationals imported under the contract which was developed a couple years ago by the State Department . . . Instead of recruiting in Mexicali, where it would cost the farmers practically nothing, the USES† goes deep into Mexico for the workers.*

Imperial will triumph as usual. Here's Border Patrolman Dan Murray again, 1999: *Now, everything's quiet here, but this street will be packed at three or four in the morning. That's when the field workers come across with their work authorization cards.*

In 1951, when Northside saves herself by arresting a hundred and twenty-seven thousand wetbacks, we see a jail cell in Calexico in which half a dozen men sit against the wall, one sleeping with his head in his arms, another, whose face is utter shadow, cupping his chin in his hands; another glares up into Imperial's white light, and one, who is young and graceful, stands with his hands in his pockets; and a grid of shadows from the cell bars superimposes itself upon all of them in homage to the subdelineation which has caused their fate.

In 1962, in addition to the two hundred thousand braceros for that year, we find sixty thousand commuter field workers across the entire U.S.-Mexican border. Perhaps Kerouac saw some of these in Fresno; perhaps many of the laborers in "Mex-

*These are real cases I have read in Agricultural Labor Relations Board restricted files from the seventies; it was surely like this in the forties and fifties.

†United States Employment Service.

town" were naturalized Mexican-Americans. Others must have followed the example of Don Maclovio Medina, 1946: *Well, those who had good luck went with contracts from Mexicali, the* braceros. *The only thing was, we weren't picked, but we were there, too.* He scales Signal Mountain and comes into American Imperial. A Japanese rancher named Jimmy takes him on. Every field worker there is illegal, because *they wouldn't give the Japanese contract labor.* Don Maclovio would not seem to be in competition with any bracero. But there must be instances when commuter workers, braceros and illegals all vie for the same jobs. As for the few native-born Anglo-Americans still stooping in the fields of others, how could they bear affection for any of these Southsiders?

In 1961 President Kennedy had unwillingly extended the bracero program, worried about the pressure it puts on native-borns. Senator Aaron Quick of Calexico (Democrat) stands firm against it. So does a Mexican-American leader in Los Angeles named Dionicio Morales. Braceros and commuter workers are taking away the farm jobs of Mexican-American laborers, he says. Dr. Ben Yeller down in Brawley hates the bracero system but blames the cheapskate growers who put native-born Imperial Valley farmhands out of business: *They do not want to pay American wages.* They want the cheap labor from Mexico.*

Mike Miranda is one those farmhands, and he cries: *Mexicali is swallowing us.* Robert Louis Kramer is another. He says: *You can't keep up with those Mexican nationals. They work harder and for less than anyone else.*

In El Centro, two unions come out with cardboard signs: **ON STRIKE FOR FAIR WAGE $1.25** and **MERCHANTS: LOCAL WORKERS NEED YOUR HELP**. They stare straight ahead at us. They need *our* help.—My fellow Americans, wouldn't you say it's time for a new Exclusion Act?

On the first of January, 1965, the bracero program ends.

*Braceros are guaranteed a dollar an hour; domestic workers have no contract minimum.

Chapter 115

OPERATION WETBACK

(1954–1955)

> Why is it estimated that at certain times of the year there are at least 80,000 wetbacks working in California? Because employers are willing to hire them.
>
> —Ruben Salazar, 1970

And wherever Exclusion establishes itself, up springs its opposite from the other side of the ditch.

By 1959, Jack T. Pickett knows it all. Let him explain: *In addition to the Mexican Nationals, there are a few Mexicans called "wetbacks" who want to work in this country so badly that they sneak in across the border. Some will work for less money, but what we consider "less" money in this country is to them a veritable gold-mine . . .*

Before you know it, Northside is up in arms about *the wetback problem.*

Ruben Salazar, 1970: *A wetback lives in constant fear. Fear that he will be discovered. Fear of what might happen to him once* la migra *finds him. Fear that he will not be paid before being deported.*

And what do Northside's nativists have to fear? Those wetbacks who for sometimes uncollected wages seek out the musty-geranium odor of brown rot in lemons in Coachella, or who enjoy the supreme pleasures of stooping in Imperial Valley watermelon fields, might be stealing American jobs!

Why does Northside have anything left to complain about? Back in 1954, you see, General Joseph Swing had launched Operation Wetback, and at first Northside averaged seventeen hundred and twenty-seven wetbacks caught per day! Victor Orozco Ochoa: *I was seven years old, American, and didn't speak any Spanish at all . . . They had long trench coats and big-brimmed hats. They came in the nighttime.* General Swing soon announced: *The border has been secured.*

Meanwhile, here comes another parade! The Rotary International float represents Mexicali and Calexico together, our bulging-breasted young ladies dressed in flowing neoclassical style; and there's a little girl on top, and one man just to round things out; he's darkhaired and serious.

Chapter 116

MEXICALI

(1950)

During the 1940s and 1950s the valley's economy consolidated around cotton.

—José Luis Castro Ruiz, 2006

In 1955 a pale-dressed man in a white-and-tan hat stands chest deep in corn, with the Sierra Cucapah behind him and a dirt road in front of him. Around him, Mexican Imperial's pyramids of hay bales like miniature Aztec temples overlook seas of cotton and corn; small houses swim in leafy productions of the soil. Although Baja California's forty-seven years of plentiful rain have ended, open canals still flow from deep wells, the water placid and clean with grasses on either side; this could be Northside's Imperial Canal in 1901; and indeed it seems to be the rule that whenever history visits Imperial, it stops off at Northside first. Unfortunately, my attempts to coin rules of Imperial history achieve no more success than Lupe Vásquez's attempts to translate Mexican political cartoons for me: He holds the newspaper at arm's length and strains to read, muttering: In the sun I can see . . .—for Southside has certainly overtaken Northside in at least one department: population. In 1950, between sixty-four and sixty-five thousand people lived in Mexicali alone—more than in all Imperial County. If we count all the *ejidos* and *colonias* of the Valle de Mexicali, the number more than doubles. I see a dairy ranch in Colonia Rodríguez. Meanwhile, the city grows and grows! Five years later, Mexicali holds eighty thousand souls.

You see, **WATER IS HERE**. Northside has the All-American Canal; Southside now boasts the Canal Todo Mexicano. Moreover, ever since decree number 1276 began the Sonora-Baja Railroad in 1936, Mexicali has been easier to get to. The valley swells with braceros, ranchers, shopkeepers and *ejidatarios*. Even gringos drop in from time to time. A hit song by the Coasters assures Northsiders that a night spent "Down in Mexico," and specifically in Mexicali, will reward the adventurer with chili-hot drinks and equally spicy señoritas. *And in material advantages they are already well supplied.*

In short, these are the grand old days when Mexicali was, according to a famous journalist from Mexico City whose words were remembered by an ancient leftist ex-journalist in Mexicali and translated for me one long hot morning in the Restaurante Victoria by the masterful Lupe Vásquez, *four paved streets, sixteen alleyways, two rivers full of shit and a whole lot of assholes!*

Many times people come to Mexicali hoping to cross to the other side, a woman said. But they stay here. And you rarely see people from Mexicali going elsewhere. They stay here because there's opportunity here.

Look—here comes Señor Francisco Arellano Olvera! On 17 September 1951, he pays thirty-nine hundred forty-six pesos fifty-six centavos for six hundred and fifty-seven point seven-six square meters in the Packard Tract, lot 6885. (In other words, he pays exactly six pesos per square meter.)

Look—here comes Mr. Claude Finnell, the Imperial County Agricultural Commissioner, ready to enjoy a dinner with his wife.—We used to go there a lot, she told me, to take friends to eat. We used to go about once a week. In El Centro, the Barbara Worth, oh, they were special on steaks. A really good steakhouse. The produce people all lived there. Except for the Barbara Worth, there wasn't anything else here. They had nice places and singers in Mexicali. I think we ate mostly at the Mission. Chinese food. Mexcali was . . . they had a lot of wealthy people there. We had a lot of people in the movies and so forth who used to play there in those days.

And Kay Brockman Bishop is running past them!—Here is how she remembered it: We always went to Alley Nineteen and Shangri-la for Chinese food and the Golden Lion for steaks. God, they were good! We always went to the country club in Calexico for Sunday night, but I bet you once a week we went to Mexicali.

I got stuck down there one time when I was very little, she went on. I was with Margarita, who came to the ranch the day I was born. Margarita, now, I basically thought I was—if the Immigration guys came, *they* hid under the bed, *I* hid under the bed. I didn't know I was different. One time I got to the border coming back and I didn't have papers and I was talking Mexican like a little Mexican kid and Margarita kept telling them I was white, and they took me into the office. My Dad said: Daughter, what daughter? He had a sense of humor.

Look—here comes Jack Kerouac! The narrator of his best novel, *The Dharma Bums,* visits Mexicali in about 1956, crossing into Southside and then perhaps gazing back over his shoulder across the line, as I have done when I let myself sink into period photographs, to the little pyramidal-roofed kiosk and the arched scaffold bearing the following words, one letter to each suspended signboard square: **U N I T E D S T A T E S**, after which he reports that he *turned sharp right at the gate to avoid the hawker street.* This seems to imply that there was only one hawker street—Cristóbal Colón, perhaps, for that is the first *avenida* in Mexicali. Our narrator's westward turn brings him to construction dirt and a muddy road. At this point he must be standing on the rim of the Río Nuevo gorge, for *I came to a hill and saw the great mudflat riverbottoms with stinks and tarns and awful paths with women and burros ambling in the dusk . . . I crossed the flats and narrow board bridge over the yellow water and over to the poor adobe district of Mexicali,* in other words Pueblo Nuevo. Then what? Do the croonings of the Coasters incite him into a chili-hot hour amidst the stinks and tarns? On this subject Kerouac is sadly silent. But it is clear that the Mexicali of 1956 resembles the Tijuana of 1924: *Still the same six or seven hundred feet of dusty and dingy streets running between two almost solid rows of saloons . . . with dirtier side streets taking care of the dives that couldn't find room on the main street* (thank you, Dashiell Hammett), which in turn must have equated more or less to Los Angeles in 1867, courtesy of Major Ben C. Truman: *Crooked, ungraded, unpaved streets, . . . adobe houses, with flat asphaltum roofs; with here and there an indolent native hugging himself inside a blanket or burying his head in the inside of a watermelon.*

THE WHITE GOLD

Thanks to cotton, said Lupe Vásquez, that's what helped us out. After World War II, my grandfather had two big trucks; he had horses. He was a lot better off than the *ejidos* are now. I'll never forget cotton, no sir! They used to call it the white gold. Then the United States stopped buying.

In an unnumbered photo album in the Archivo Histórico del Municipio de Mexicali I find a grey-on-grey image of two horses dragging something through what at first seems to be lacy grey mud-clods; the face of the rider has gone featureless grey beneath his white hat; the sky is speckled with dirty grey; everything is hot, flat and dismal; the legend reads *Pulverizadora de tracción animal, para combatir la plaga de la hoja del algodón.* Other photographs show more of this *algodón,* white-constellated fields of it growing on to the horizon. Ever since 1912, the valley's yield had dragged along one and a quarter bales per hectare or even less; suddenly, right now at midcentury, productivity doubled. Production goes up! 1912: fifteen bales. 1925: more than eighty thousand. 1950: two hundred and forty-four thousand, six hundred and thirty-eight. Five years later, the yield will be more than four hundred and twenty thousand. And so a closeup shows great white puffs in clusters of three or four; they look softer than anything can possibly be. In still another view, two men stand amidst a sea of bales. The caption reads: *Patio of the cotton mill of Mr. West.*

And now I begin to understand why in one hot bright flat spot in the northeastern Mexicali Valley there's a place called Algodones, "The Cottons."*

Oh, cotton perfected everything; why worry about how much those cottonlands cost? Receipt number 6669, dated 7 December 1954, bears witness that the Cía. Mexicana de Terrenos del Río Colorado, S.A., based in Mexicali, received the sum of 14,252.70 pesos, of which 1,965.99 went for *intereses vencidos sobre* [accrued interest for] *el valor del Lote #13-Porción Sur de la Colonia "Uno", División Dos*. The other 12,286.82 was for the lot itself, which according to a notarized map from 1936 consisted of 118.5 hectares and adjoined the west side of the Canal Largo del Sur, which flowed into the Río Nuevo. That's a hundred and four pesos an acre! An attached letter announces that the debtor, Señor Eusebio Meléndrez, was rescued by a Señor Cota Arballo. Is this a sad or happy story? We lack the information to know.

Most of the names on these land documents belong to Mexican men, although amidst the nine names pertaining to Colonia El Triángulo those of two women stand out: Isabel M. de Cervantes enjoys the use of forty one point six hectares, which is nearly twice the average per capita farm size in the Triangle; while Carmen Castro comes in slightly under average at a respectable twenty point six.

So the second gender is present. What about people of foreign extraction? Colonia Hindu contains everyone from Dionisio Castro Flores to Man Singh, Bir Singh, Josefina Castro de Singh and Mala Singh; indeed, out of the twenty-one names, seven are Singhs, my favorite being that of Eva Vega de Singh, who lives and farms on fifty hectares exactly. As for the Chinese, by and large they appear in these documents all too rarely, considering their numbers and considering also the fact that they were the first farmers in the Mexicali Valley. Chong Suey and Juan Wong own fifty hectares together in Colonia Independencia Número Uno. Over in Colonia El Mayor, Delmiro González has two of the nine lots, one at twenty and the other at forty hectares, while Samuel Yee Fong and his señora hold three hundred and eighty-one hectares. Of course we know from the very name Chinesca that they have impressed themselves upon the center of Mexicali, where just before midcentury we find a hundred and thirty-four Chinese businesses, fifty-three of those being grocery stores—and let's not forget the four Chinese cabarets and three poolhalls. But the expropriation of the Colorado River Land Company in 1937 dispossessed many tentacks of which one Mexicali labor union called *the everlasting yellow octopus, which continues sucking the mexican* [*sic*] *workers' blood*. And so in

*South of Mexicali a woman said to me: "The wheat you plant in December and harvest in August. Your second planting can be cotton. Right here you're going to see a lot of vegetables planted, and cardamom. But if you go further east," meaning toward Algodones, "that's where they plant the cotton. All of this here is wheat . . ."

1930, there were more than twenty-nine hundred Chinese in Baja California. In 1940 there were slightly more than six hundred.

In 2002, when the television was clashing with a mariachi band, Señor Armando sat in the Café Canton beneath a ceramic cosmos of birds, lotuses, classical Asian beauties whose looks were not superior to those of the Chinese-Mexican girls in semipermanent residence at the tables; and Señor Armando, who was narrow-eyed and looked both Chinese and Mexican, said: There were more Chinese people than Mexicans. They lived in the Mexicali Valley. Then came the two world wars. The Chinese cannot go to USA. Then came more Chinese.* Then they opened restaurants because that always worked for them. All the old restaurants here had a basement, and then a tunnel to other basements. The government find them now because they dig up the street. And the Chinese keep a casino in the basement. That was in around 1950. As for now, they don't say nothing. But Chinese people love the casino! And some Chinese go to play near the border and see the race . . . The tunnels, I have never seen them. Often the Chinese people can go down. You can see tables, cards, but not roulette or Chinese dominoes . . .

Señorita Xu, the pretty Chinese waitress at the Dong Cheng Restaurant, had an uncle down the street whom I interviewed in his *zapatería,* and he stood behind the counter in the year 2003 with shoes on the walls all around him and his wife reading the Chinese newspaper as he said: I came in 1957, when I was twenty-two. I came with my grandfather's brother. We flew from Hong Kong to Los Angeles, then drove in one of Uncle's cars from Los Angeles to Mexicali with a stop in Tijuana.

What was your impression of Mexicali?

There wasn't so much land anymore. The city had been founded. There was still land where they had cotton, and still cotton, a lot of it. My uncle already had businesses here. This business was Uncle's.

And what were your feelings about the place?

I had lots of feelings about the climate and the people, he said, folding his arms and looking my Mexican interpreter in the face. I spoke no Spanish at all. I had studied no Spanish . . .

And what are your feelings now?

He was silent.

He didn't want to turn the Chinese tunnels into a myth for me; oh, not at all; he did the opposite. After I entreated him to take me down into his cellar, he did, but, as I have already told you in the chapter about the tunnels, things took a bad

*In fact the Chinese population declined throughout Baja, not only thanks to the expulsion of non-Mexican tenants of the Colorado River Land Company, but also thanks to market economics: The Depression lowered cotton prices.

turn then. Something in his eyes told me that for him the lost universe was not secret casinos but cotton; perhaps he would rather have cultivated his own hectares of "white gold" in the *ejidos* than sold shoes; anyhow, his life was done, and the Chinese legacy of cotton not much more now than an old photo in an unnumbered album in the Archivo Histórico del Municipio de Mexicali: PLANTA DESPEPITADORA DE ALGODON "Chino-Mexicana." Soft white mountains of what only the caption informs us must be cotton (for otherwise they could be dirt, sawdust, powdered gypsum or saffron) command the middle ground of a hot white flatness interrupted by the sharp-edged black shadows of the sheds.

WHEN MONEY HAD POWER

Javier Lupercio was born in Mexicali in 1945.—Well, good, he said in 2004, pointing into the air. In those days, Mexicali was a small town. One of the first *colonias* was Colonia Baja California. There's a big store, straight through this street right here. Where that big store is located, that's where the train station used to be located. Right next to it was a bus station also; the buses would go south in Mexico. You know where that mall, Plaza Cachanilla, is located at? There used to be a soap factory there in about 1958, 1960. Back then there was more poverty than now, but back then they used to plant a lot of cotton in the Mexicali Valley.

When did it stop and why?

The thing started going bad when the government wouldn't give out no more loans to the small farmers to help with their planting and like that. When the season's over and you make your money, give it over. Like that. The people who would pick the cotton would be people from the south of Mexico like Oaxaca and like that. When those people saw that there wasn't enough work, they started going to Ensenada for the pulp tomato season in September, just running after the work. There was like a lot of vegetables grown in that area; they used to plant bell pepper. A lot of people that were migrant workers from that state are now natives of Ensenada.

What was your childhood like?

I was kinda lucky because my grandparents had some land and they were one of the farmers who planted the cotton. We were a middle-class family. What I remember, it was a nice childhood. The city wasn't as big as it is now. You could see plantations where there are *colonias* now. That was around 1978. Up until then they still planted up into the city. Colonia Wisteria, Palaco, Aurora, those were the places. Colonia Santo Niño and all those are basically new colonies.

Where did you live with your family?

Toward Algodones, there's a community called Cuervos, *crows*. Ten hectares of cotton was what we had. They sold it. My grandparents, who used to work the land, died, and we started going to the United States and looked to better opportunities. We got our green card so we decided to sell. We sold it in 1970. I was just a grandson. My grandparents were on my mother's side.

(José López, who was interpreting, said out of the side of his mouth: Maybe a little family fight, I'm figuring. That can get dirty, you know, so the other side divided the land.)

They sold it for around fifteen or eighteen thousand pesos, so I've heard. The dollar was at twelve-fifty around that time, but there's a big difference now. Back then the money had power. With two thousand pesos you could buy a good new car. For all the night,* fifty pesos, and for just in-and-out, ten pesos. At the Thirteen Negro, it was twenty centavos to hold a woman and dance with her. With one peso you could dance five songs.

AURORAS AND ALFALFA TOWERS

Those were the days, all right, when a new car cost the equivalent of two hundred acts of intercourse and the Thirteen Negro was in its glory. But many of the farmers, ranchers and *ejidatarios* had no use for the pleasures of the metropolis, and, as I learned from year after year of knocking on people's doors in the *ejidos*, they still don't.

I remember driving westward down a rutted dirt road which smelled like cattle, with ear-numbered cows in the barbed-wired field of Bermuda grass, and after the road crossed a levee of heaped powdery earth in great clods, there came palms and cottonwoods and a shallow ditch of greenish-brownish water, with the Sierra Cucapah Mountains ahead. This was the view from Rancho García, which in 2004 was slightly decrepit and secluded by palms. Looking northeast from the front door, one could see the four ribbons of dirty smoke twisting up from the glass factory where they would not let us in because we did not have an appointment.

Señora Teresa García said: My parents came here in 1936 or '37. They bought some land little by little from the Colorado River Land Company. In 1937 it was finalized. My father died in 1951 and we were still paying the Colorado River Land Company. The company helped us out; they even gave us the seed, for cotton and alfalfa. We grew cotton through the seventies. Now it's all wheat in this area.

Why did you stop growing cotton?

Because the land started to lose its strength, because the water was really

*With a whore. But you don't need to believe him, because a guidebook from this period assures us that "about the only reminder of Mexicali's unsavory past is the relatively large number of bars and night clubs."

salty. The United States was sending water down here that was supposed to go straight to the ocean, but the Mexican government manipulated that and used it for irrigation.

How salty is the land now?

She smiled and touched her cheek.—Not that much.

But the land gets tired, said her son.

So what grows now is rye grass and Bermuda grass and Sudan grass, because they don't mind the salt, said Señora García. Rye grass they just use to feed the cattle, and Bermuda the same. We bale the Sudan grass. What you feed the cattle earns more than other crops we can grow.

How much can you make?

The ranch just up the road did pretty well since they planted it, harvested, watered, and got two harvests.

So you have lived here all your life?

I was born here in Rancho García. Both of my parents were Garcías. I was born in 1940. The first thing I remember, my father used to bale the alfalfa, and he would stack it up, very high, and the children would climb up. When you grow up on a ranch you're not afraid of anything. It was very high! she laughed. You could see all the ranches. Back then they also harvested a lot of corn, many pumpkins and watermelons and vegetables. And the cotton would be so high! And the alfalfa was also that high! Very high and very high! You could hide in it!

When I went to school it was all the way in Palaco. You get on the highway to San Felipe, ten kilometers. We went by bus. It was the only school, so there were many students. I was five. There were forty students in every room. The name of this whole area is Colonia Sieto de Cierro Prieto.

When you were a child, did you always know you wanted to stay here?

We talked about buying a house in the city, but that's when my father passed away. I got married and would have stayed. Even if my father hadn't died I would have ended up back here. Here you're alone and it's very quiet and you don't open the door and see a neighbor. Very tranquil!

Right now, the ranch down the road, they're bringing about four hundred head of cattle from Sonora. On that other road down there, we see many rabbits. When I was little, there were many coyotes and snakes. I don't know where they went; they disappeared.

What is the most beautiful thing you have seen out here?

One of the most beautiful things is that at night you can see the stars and they look very clean. When I was little I would see comets go by and the aurora borealis. But now because the air is so dirty you don't see it anymore.

EIGHTEEN PESOS FOR A HUNDRED KILOS

On the highway's edge a few kilometers south of Mexicali there is a little restaurant called Yocojihua. The proprietress was a woman in late middle age named Señora Socorro Ramírez. She said to me:

The difference between Mexicali and other places is the diversity of the people here. People from other states came looking for work. I came here in 1952, and the people are not your classic lazy people who don't want to look for work. The people here are *looking*. There was nothing here in '52. It was desert. Some people came because they were given land. Others came just to work the land. President Cárdenas would even pay the travel expenses for those who wanted to come, in order to populate the new state. My parents decided to come here to work, because they had a big family; at that time there were six children. So in Jalisco my father had the ranch which had belonged to his parents, but it was divided up among the heirs, which made it not large enough to support everyone. So my parents decided to move here. My parents came here to pick cotton, working for different people who had been given the land by President Cárdenas. At that time they were all working for the Colorado River Land Company.* I remember picking cotton when I was little. Around 1958 other companies started showing up. I would pick for the individual landowners, and they would sell their cotton to the Colorado River Land Company. I was paid between sixteen and eighteen centavos per kilo, so you had to pick a hundred kilos to earn eighteen pesos. An adult in one day, which was from five in the morning until the sun went down, could pick between a hundred and a hundred fifty kilos a day. It was nice. Of course you enjoy things more when you were a kid. We would go out together as a family, and the people we worked for would always take good care of us. They gave us hot lunch and cold water. At six I could pick only twenty kilos. I did more running around! I went to school, but only from January to June, because everyone was picking cotton. Sometimes the teachers would give classes in the cotton fields.

What did you do for fun?

We played with the animals, rode our bicycles, fished; at school we played volleyball, football. In the afternoons we played Cops and Robbers. I fished a lot. I liked to catch carp and shrimp and other fish.

Did your parents get rich? After all, people called cotton the white gold.

No. The white gold, yes, some got rich, but the workers, no. And it was only for

*I asked her whether on the whole the Colorado River Land Company had been good or bad, and she replied: "It was good because it was the first company to arrive here and because the things they did brought people here. But it was bad because they did not have any competition."

a very short time that it was good. I'll tell you why it didn't last very long. What happened with the white gold was that people started getting really rich really fast, so they bought a new car or something for their wife so when the good times ended they had to go to the bank and get a loan. At first the parcel owners got loans from the Colorado River Land Company. They paid it back. Then the banks came, and people started borrowing from the banks, and it just caved in, because the banks were charging a lot of interest. Also, when the government got involved, people borrowed from the government, saying, If I don't pay it back this year, I'll pay it back next year, because it's only the government, so what can they do to me?

So here's the difference between the people here, she resumed. In other places they wait for it to rain. They wait for the government to come to help them. Here, no. When people first arrived, there was no water, so they built the canals, she said proudly. And now they take the canals all the way to Tijuana and other places! Here, the people know they have to protect the plants from the heat and in other places they just throw water on the ground . . .

The ways of farming my parents knew worked in the south of Mexico, but here it is different. In Jalisco they were used to farming but they were also used to going to the cantina with their friends. But here you had to work much harder.

I had just begun to perceive the sorrow and bitterness beneath her pride when she said: This is something that I will never understand, that people will sell everything and come here, get a new life, a new wife. So many doctors and lawyers end up here washing dishes. Where they come from there's work. But here there's *hard* work . . .

END OF THE GOLDEN AGE

In spite of that *hard* work, some people enveloped their recollections in a nostalgic luminescence of white gold; and for the ending of the White Gold Epoch, most of the rememberers I had the privilege of listening to did not, like Señora Ramírez, blame the banks; they followed habit and blamed the gringos. It seemed that there was a Northsider plot to get the good people of the Mexicali Valley to plant as many cotton acres as possible, on the promise of high prices; then the prices dropped.

Strangely enough, Northsiders did not remember it quite that way. Richard Brogan for his part said: In the 1950s in Mexicali the boll weevil was probably as problematic as anywhere else in the world. They don't have ploughdown times. There can be stalks and debris on the ground. We ran the weevil out of here and they probably all went to Mexicali and thrived! That hurt their cotton. And then cotton is a world-driven commodity. We're not growing cotton on our Cotton Belt like we used to. Imperial's not producing hardly any. We were able to grow three bales–plus here per acre, even with salinity and boll weevil problems. I don't know if at one time we weren't realizing at least a gross of a thousand dollars an acre. But we've lost everything. The cotton gins are gone. The structures are gone. The pickers have been sold off. I believe Finnell* and his farm connection did it for some reason. I don't know why. People who were in the cotton business will sit back and remember the cost. They didn't realize that there could be somebody gaining in that process. I always thought that Claude was of such stature that no one would question. And here he is, a major key player in this water thing. The Kuhn family, they were big cotton growers but it doesn't matter to them . . .

*Claude Finnell's long reign as Imperial County Agriculture Commissioner lasted from 1954 to 1986. Mr. Finnell's own recollections appear here and there throughout this book, and especially on pp. 983–986.

Chapter 117

SUBDELINEATIONS: COTTONSCAPES

(1796–2007)

Cotton would grow very well if it were sown.

—José Joaquín Arrillaga, exploring the Mexicali Valley near the Río Hardy, 1796

A man stands quizzical in cotton which has already grown up to his elbows. This must be the tale of Jack and the Beanstalk!

A tan-colored man in a tan-colored suit grips an immense tan-colored blossom with boyish pride; the stalks rise above his head to lose themselves in a tan-colored fog; the tan ground cracks at his feet.

At Pomona, *no definite conclusion as to the value of Egyptian cotton culture in that region has been reached.* That was in 1903–04, exactly forty years after Sacramento offered the first-ever cotton exhibit at the State Fair. In Imperial, of course, where we're wide awake, the first experimental planting took place in 1902. In strict obedience to that hundred-and-sixty-acre limitation, Joe Macdonald announces that he plans to raise six hundred acres of cotton in the Imperial Valley come 1905. Whatever happened to him? Judge Farr swears to me that the first commercial planting of three hundred acres did not occur until 1909; moreover, it might have failed to please the Ministry of Capital; for in 1910, a mere fourteen acres get consecrated unto cotton. But in 1911, that statistic enlarges to fourteen *thousand* acres! Next year, Imperial Valley cotton will take first prize at the New York fair. Gaze with me at this old photo of the white loveliness of the cottonballs in a field's variegated darkness: The caption reads *Meloland, one of Imperial's first cotton fields!* Harold Bell Wright surely admires those cottonscapes likewise; he emerges from his ramada from time to time, blinking in the sun, trying to invent another plot twist for cherry-lipped Barbara Worth. Within an oval in the 1912–13 Imperial Valley directory I read: *IMPERIAL VALLEY: Cotton Is King.* There's a Hotel King Cotton in Imperial. The Imperial Valley Oil & Cotton Co. has built five cotton gins, one in each major town. In 1914, the *Imperial Valley Press* advises: **Cotton Industry Reaching Giant Proportions Here**. ("The valley" being still only weakly delineated, the paper refers to an estimated *40,000 acres of the crop on each side of the international line.*) Meanwhile, the 1914 Imperial Valley directory informs us that *this year* cotton covers *over*

28,000 acres, and some say as high as 80,000 (the reader may accept either of the figures). The beanstalk shoots up! *The outlook for the crop is so good that it is believed the yield will average a bale to the acre.* In 1917, seventy thousand Imperial acres produce thirty-five thousand bales!

In 1910, a certain foreman of the Colorado River Land Company leases six hundred Mexicali hectacres, plants some of them in cotton, and becomes ecstatic. In 1912 the company plants twelve hectares;* in 1920, fifty thousand. The peak year is 1927 at sixty-four thousand hectares. A historian will define the *white gold* as follows: *cotton—the key to Baja's economic growth and independence.* On the other side of the line, the California Board of Agriculture utters its own invocation of praise: *The yield per acre in the Imperial Valley is much larger than in any other state in the Union.* Indeed, the average production of 1916 was four hundred pounds an acre, Virginia, whose name one can't help but associate with cotton, coming in a very distant second at three hundred and ten.

The pickers walk beneath the rows, writes Paul S. Taylor, *or crawl if the stalks are short, and pick with both hands into a sack suspended from the shoulders or waist, and dragged either at the side or between the legs.* In Kern County there will be ten to fifteen thousand pickers in 1933. More than ninety percent of that year's production will be shipped to Japan. A crop and chattel mortgage will be taken, as the farmers say, on *everything except the farmer's wife.* But what do we care about Kern County down here in the Paradise of self-sufficient homelands, I mean *the wonderland of factories?*—Well, you see, Imperial has competition; everybody in California wants to get in on the white money! (For the California crop, a new grade has been created: *extra white.* Poor old Virginia!) By 1929 nearly one-third of all large cotton farms in the United States may be found in California, *where the pattern of cotton culture approximated industrial rather than family farm production.* Here in Imperial, we'd better watch them.

Palo Verde and Coachella have already begun to emulate us. The San Joaquin enters the game during World War I. Production grows and sprouts and buds until the depression of 1921. May we hover, please, in the peak year 1920?† That was when eighty-six percent of all California cotton came from the Imperial Valley, Palo Verde and Coachella, and only fourteen percent from the San Joaquin.

Since 1920, however, the advantages of the northern valley in yield per acre have been so marked, and the effects in Imperial Valley of the encroachments of alkali, and

*Mr. Auyón, the renowned painter of horses and nude women, claims that in 1913 there were a thousand Chinese in Mexicali, who grew thirteen and a half thousand hectares of cotton.

†In 1920, the California Cultivator profiles **America's Champion Cotton Grower**, a Mr. John Walthall, who has achieved $365 worth of cotton per acre. Alas, he dwells across the great river, in Scottsdale, Arizona.

competing vegetable crops so great, that by 1932 the percentage of California cotton grown there had risen to 96 per cent . . .

In 1929 we find H. H. Clark, General Manager of the Colorado River Land Company, addressing the California–Arizona–New Mexico Cotton Association in a congratulatory mood: This year's crop is worth a hundred billion dollars! *He believes the time is ripe* for *a selling agency.* We need have no fear that our monopolies will not become better and better as the years go by.

In 1930–31, cotton acreage is down to twenty-seven thousand six hundred hectares in the Mexicali Valley.

In 1932, the Imperial Valley produces less than one percent of California's cotton.

The national crop limitation of 1933 destroys only thirteeen thousand acres, or six percent of Northside's cotton. The Colorado River Land Company considers increasing cotton production, since it is not bound by Northside's laws, but finally decides that this would not be in the economic interest of the Chandler Syndicate.

SWINGS OF A GRAPH

What is cotton, but swings of a graph? In 1953, Imperial County acreage peaks at nearly a hundred and thirteen thousand; in 1957 fewer than forty-four thousand will be planted, due to *acreage controls.*

The *California Cultivator* told the parable in 1925. The protagonist could have been practically any crop over almost any longish period: *Many fell into it. Cotton fell in price. Growers were ruined. Their only asset was gone. Cotton was abandoned as a crop. Cotton rose in price. Many land owners rushed again into cotton, to sow every acre thereto.*

In 1917, Imperial's average cotton yield was a bale per acre. In 1953, it achieves over a bale and a half; in 1954, nearly two bales.

In 1958, a lettuce grower complains from El Centro: *The cotton deal, we have lost—the United States has lost their world outlet for cotton because of your controlled marketing.*

A Minnesota farmboy has a rather different take on it: *Here is a cautionary tale on failure to diversify. Buoyed by the peak in agricultural markets in 1920 (lots of reasons, most related to the aftermath of WWI), Imperial farmers began a spectacular climb in the 1920s followed by an even more spectacular crash (Column D, lines 2–16, and Rows 22 & 39, Ag Census). It's primarily for the sake of cotton that I include the acreages for the even-numbered years between 1910 and 1920, and the dollar production number for 1920 is not a typo. Unfortunately, cotton was devastated by declining prices in the 1920s combined with the eventual arrival of all the pests that devastated cotton in the south.*

This was the simple result of short-sightedness, as the use of cheap cotton batting from boll-weevil states for packing vegetable and fruit crops was common at the time. Despite optimistic reports in the 1920s and 30s on the number of bales coming into the county that were burned by inspectors due to pests, cotton virtually disappeared from Imperial in the 1930s and 40s as low prices and unreliable yields drove farmers to other crops. Comparative advantage eventually won out (along with improvements in pest control), and Imperial is a leading (and profitable) US producer in the niche market of high quality long-staple cotton, thanks mainly to its long growing season and stable water supply.

Meanwhile, Lupe Vásquez blames coldblooded manipulation by the gringos for the cotton recision in Mexican Imperial, and Señora García accuses salinity; while Señora Ramírez shakes her head and sighs: It was only for a very short time that it was good . . .

Yet what is any of it, but the merest, craziest swings of a graph?

In 1965, California is second only to Texas for cotton. How much of that do you think is Imperial County cotton? I assure you that that year cotton comes in a glorious number two for profitability; I have never been cheated out of a bale in my life!

The 1974 edition of the *Great Soviet Encyclopedia* informs us that *some of the land between the Colorado River and the Salton Sea is irrigated; the principal crop is cotton.* Imperial County grows more than seventy-three thousand cotton acres that year;* the yield is over two and a half bales per acre. Mexican Imperial contains a disproportionate number of cornscapes, but in 2000 we find seventy-one thousand, three hundred and twenty acres of cotton in the northeast corner of the Mexicali Valley alone.

We don't grow cotton here anymore, lamented Richard Brogan in 2004.† I think the government just expired the program. The money that went out, I used to marvel at it. I wanted to get it myself.

The following year, cotton came in a respectable twenty-fifth out of the county's forty top-earning crops . . .

*Riverside grows 20,087 acres; Los Angeles's acreage is zero.

†That year the world yield of cotton was 22.43 million tons, of which 86% was grown by the ten primary cotton producing countries. Of these, China was number one at almost 5.5 million tons, followed by the United States at 4.39 million tons. Mexico did not make the top ten.

Chapter 118

SAN LUIS RÍO DE COLORADO

(*ca.* 1968)

> And when the carpenters had hurried on, the women came in with flowerpots and chintz and pans and set up a kitchen clamor to cover the silence that Mars made waiting outside the door and the shaded window.
>
> —Ray Bradbury, 1950

San Luis lies on the far side of the Colorado—in Sonora, actually, where in 1777 the explorer de Anza found some petrified wood to send to His Excellency down in Mexico. Two hundred and twenty-six years later, in my hotel room, ants ran across my belly with remarkable speed.

The next day I asked a hairdresser what the city had contained when she first arrived thirty-five years previous, which is to say in about 1968, and she replied: *Nada*. Just a train station. Then markets, shoe stores came, because the people from the ranches would come. I started my business after three years. I studied cosmetology in Nayarit and married a lawyer here. More than twenty years ago, the bars arrived. On account of the climate, the people drink a lot of beer.

It's a nice place if you like to dance, she said. Me, I don't like to dance.

Chapter 119

CERTIFIED SEED

(1959)

Nor can I sing in lyric strains
Of private, little woes,
When Greed is reaping golden gains
From bloody seeds it sows.

—IWW Song, before 1923

In the year of my birth, 1959, Imperial's crop reports introduce two new categories. The first, **MILLION DOLLAR CROPS** (carrots, lettuce, cantaloupes, watermelons, cotton, alfalfa, and other fine commodities, in whose company we unfortunately fail to find grapefruits), all of us should have seen coming, because what could be more Imperial? I have never been cheated out of a dollar in my life. But the second category shows a more novel species of genius. Seed crops are now divided into ***NON CERTIFIED*** and ***CERTIFIED SEED***, in the latter of whose ranks stand such grandees as New River Flax (sixty acres), Imperial Flax, Star Millet, Brawley Sorghum, DD 38 Milo and D Imperial Kafir.

Won't agriculture be better off, when its manifold productions have been *certified,* when an agency, a laboratory or at least a brand name stands behind each and every one? We're on the way to never-ripe tomatoes that will not squish in transit, to genetically engineered alfalfa, to crops with consistent characteristics, so that everything can be more predictably grown, moved and marketed. Speaking of marketing, in 1958 we find a lettuce producer fretting at a marketing order meeting in El Centro that chain stores are controlling the buying more. What if they decide to buy only lettuce derived from a specific certified seed? What if the company that sells that seed gives the supermarkets a kickback? Well, then the lettuce growers will know their marching orders. *We need have no fear that our lands will not become better and better as the years go by.*

Chapter 120

SUBDELINEATIONS: OCEAN PARKSCAPES

(1966–1993)

. . . the tension of "something about to happen" . . . recurs years later in some of Diebenkorn's . . . *Ocean Park* paintings . . .

—Jane Livingston, 1997

Imperial is Rothko's flat bright multiforms and then his earthy canvases going gradually toward black.—What then defines Imperial's antitheses, Los Angeles and San Diego?

I nominate the Ocean Park paintings of Richard Diebenkorn.

In 1966, he moves into a new studio in Ocean Park, Venice. Jane Livingston writes of him: *Rarely has an artist been more finely attuned to nuances of changing light, temperature, landscape, and streetscape.* What then might we expect the coast of Los Angeles to do to him? Diebenkorn writes that his paintings flattened out.

The place called Ocean Park ends at the ultramarine-blue Pacific itself, the flat horizon sharp as a brush-line across masking tape; I also remember the ocean sky, pale and vague just above the horizon, gradually darkening into a lovely blue which is still much less than half as dark as the ocean itself; the tan rectangle of beach—an assumed rectangle, that is, for its ends project beyond my eye-canvas on either side—the palm trees, the cocky seagulls whose crops pulse in their throats; they stand webfooted on the sidewalks and dip their beaks in the puddles.* On the lawn, an Anglo couple sit at a rectangular concrete picnic table with their baby in its pram; another man, Hispanic, sits on a table making silent love to his guitar.

In "Ocean Park No. 107" (1978) we see a coastline of Rothko-like colored zones: green for a park, yellow for sunshine;† the red is your guess—a sporty car, let's say;

*In place of Imperial's old Plank Road, Ocean Park has invented a boardwalk of dark planks, possibly creosoted like train tracks, in the tan sand, its destination not the sea, which lies a few paces farther on, but a beach umbrella striped blue and white in imitation of that ocean.

†In downtown Los Angeles, early sunlight often warms the west side of the tall white canyon called Flower Street. Beneath a lush awning of tree-leaves against the scaffolded coast of the University Club, a bus blinks its red lights. The shadow of one skyscraper upon another seems as ancient as any survivor of geologic or

and all this clings across the topmost quarter of the canvas; the rest consists of ocean squares of various milkinesses, bleached indigos and blueprint etherealities.

That was "Ocean Park No. 107." What about Nos. 41 and 94? *Each one creates its own, self-contained chromatic universe,* continues Jane Livingston; and in complexity, *Mark Rothko takes a distant second place to Richard Diebenkorn.* Imperial-lover that I am, I take proud exception to this, as I do to her assertion that seeing the Ocean Park series as landscapes or cityscapes is *well off the mark.*

What is Los Angeles to me, but *abundance of water?*—In 1881, that ex-Ranger named Horace Bell looked back on his early days in southern California and remembered his journey from San Pedro Harbor to the new American metropolis: *Finally, when all hands were seated, a portly looking young man . . . offered to each of the passengers an ominous looking black bottle, remarking, "Gentlemen, there is no* water *between here and Los Angeles . . ."* But through an assertion of will far more effective than Imperial's, because Imperial's Ministry of Capital was only occasionally visited by the Chandler Syndicate, whereas Los Angeles was developed through the undivided attention of the big boys, Los Angeles has achieved water everywhere!

The water that Diebenkorn paints is indeed ocean, therefore saline, nonpotable. His Los Angeles thus becomes not only an antipode to Imperial, but also a twin. Someday, when civilization ends, the sea may kiss the remains of Los Angeles; but Imperial will lose her green fields, and her canals will fill with dust.

What then is Ocean Park, and Los Angeles itself, but an ironic waterscape which defies physical and other laws?

Two characteristics of the Ocean Park series, so a monograph informs us, are *the hesitant-yet-defining diagonal cutaway* and *the half-erased boundary.* Indeed, Diebenkorn writes, probably from this period, that *what I enjoyed almost exclusively, was altering . . .* Thus as his series progresses, doing the same thing over and over again, sometimes more boldly, sometimes more discreetly, subdelineation asserts itself more steadfastly in him than in its object. He enjoys the altering; he's the William Mulholland of painting in that respect; he works and reworks his images; but his goal, unlike Mulholland's, remains beyond expression. So, of course, does the "real" universe that we live in and feel. In a pretty essay, John Elderfield describes a typically altered Ocean Park canvas as *a visibly imperfect surface that shows signs of its repair.* I disagree. For me, Diebenkorn's surface takes on an ever more "worked" texture until it approaches the infinitude of earth itself.

In "Ocean Park No. 32" (1970), a gorgeous rectangle which is not quite Mars yellow has been subdivided by a white strip, like a highway; in the lefthand lane, a dipper-shaped zone of dark blue has been set; this immediately transforms itself

---

even celestial time. But bit by bit, the shadow shrinks and thins; the yellow-tan glow takes over, brightening all the while; and Flower Street becomes busy with people and cars. This is Diebenkorn light.

into a hole, because it is the same blue as the ocean at the upper righthand corner, which the almost–Mars yellow sector protects itself from through a scuffed-white cap, like a beach or parking lot that follows the coast; inset in this is a wide triangle of green, like one of Los Angeles's traffic islands. All this occupies the righthand two-thirds of the canvas. The lefthand third consists of a rectangle not quite bisected by a warm white triangle and a milky-blue quadrilateral. To me the almost–Mars yellow area, together with the white and green that caps it, resembles the entrance and exit roads to a marina; and the dark blue dipper might be a puddle of rain or seawater; this entire assemblage cleaves the rest of the painting, like the deck of an aircraft carrier moving through the sea on a mission.

Several of the other Ocean Park paintings, such as Nos. 14½ and 24 (1968), convey more of a feel of pavement. Going away from Ocean Park's blocky buildings, palm trees, and dandelions in the median strip, going eastward, there comes a dip on the dark road with its white and yellow lines and inscriptions, then almost immediately the ocean feeling begins to be lost. And I think of how quickly the plants beyond the edge of Palo Verde or Calexico go olive, then yellow, then grey. Heat rises from parking lots even at Ocean Park. Yet in these canvases as in the utramarine ones, Diebenkorn keeps his colors crisper than in many Rothkoscapes, as if they have been sharpened by the sea air; and even the grey polygons of asphalt have been blued. Although in 1970 and 1971 the series does approach the bright field yellows of a Rothkoscape, by 1972, certainly by 1973, the ocean blues come back; then for a time everything gets increasingly vivid, like Ocean Park itself after a drizzly night. Sometimes they dull down or go yellow again, but always the water comes back—spectacularly so in "Ocean Park No. 116" (1979), which is a softer version of the same aerial view as No. 108. What John Elderfield calls *an architecture . . . increasingly . . . eroded of complexity* may be seen in, for instance, the hundred and twentieth member of the series (1980), whose tonal values have sharpened considerably; meanwhile the water has shrunk down to a dullish rectangle in the upper lefthand corner. In 1986, Diebenkorn accomplishes "Untitled (Ocean Park)" in ink and charcoal. The effect is not unlike that of a Plains Indian ledger drawing. And always the ultramarine waxes and wanes, taking up most of the canvas in "Ocean Park No. 128" (1984), eating by means of a rectangular bay into the topmost coast of warm white, yellow and green. More yellow forms a solid lower coast, and an extremely thin coastal strip along the lefthand edge of the painting. In "Ocean Park No. 133," which may be the most beautiful of all, the sea has nearly triumphed, swallowing most of the painting in blueprint-hued zones incised with white and flushed with purple; its subdelineations are utterly true to life; for doesn't Los Angeles sunshine sometimes gild my downtown hotel's window-blinds in threes, with glassy shadows and right angles, cubes and squares and lines, white sliced towers?—And then the white and yellow coast hugs the top of Diebenkorn's canvas as usual.

Omitted, at least overtly, are the longhaired darkhaired women in their sundresses and miniskirts, who walk slowly along the boundary between beach and grass, their legs almost the same pale tan as the sand; undepicted are the slow cyclists and joggers, whose hair rises and falls more slowly than the sea-waves. In the Imperial Valley, who could survive in a sundress except for a Mexicana? Whose legs can stay pale, but a Northsider's who bunkers himself in long sleeves, long pants and a hat when besieged by the sun?

Not omitted at all is the sea air, the deliciously cool breeze, the sea-waves so refreshing to the eye after Imperial's sandy glare. Los Angeles can be paradise!

I remember palm tree shadows on the well-kept grass, the smell of salt; all is clean, cool and moist.

In Ocean Park there is a reddish-vermilion irregular pentagon isolated in white; to the left of it, a triangular blue pond is surrounded by sidewalk, and a street separates a green field, a turquoise field and a grey field from a series of pale yellow Imperial-like fields which have been pierced but not entirely severed by a grey aqueduct ending in a beak. All this is coastline; for on the righthand edge of California is a sea-stripe of the same blue as the pond. This 1970 painting ("Ocean Park No. 27") is more arid than my memories—but, after all, Ocean Park is over so quickly; and then one comes into greater Los Angeles, which sprouts water here and there, for instance in the fountain by the library, and hums with secret aquatic arteries, but remains nonetheless an almost-desert, fragile and therefore pitiable, worthy of compassion.

A girl rapidly rollerskates down the smooth grey street of Ocean Park, leaning forward, her hands clasped behind her buttocks. What is she but a liquid vessel of beautiful mortality, approaching the desiccation that Imperial seeks nobly, crazily, selfishly and impossibly to overcome. Everything around her has been tamed and perfected, excepting only the still low crash of waves.

Beyond her, the sea is an almost solid blue, with only the unruly white shinings of a single breaker-concretion marking the boundary with land, which, like one of Diebenkorn's canvases, is perfectly flat in its sandy zone, then worked and wiggly-squiggly where there is grass.

Elderfield believes that the artist had nearly abandoned the Ocean Park series when he died in 1993. *Still, he always seemed to be in the process of leaving for a destination that was unknown.* What could that be, but the antithesis of Ocean Park, which is to say Imperial?

As a matter of fact, in 1970, a year of several Ocean Park works on paper, we find Diebenkorn accompanying the Bureau of Reclamation to one of Imperial's other rival zones, this one in Arid America itself: namely, Salt River Canyon, Arizona. The two specimens I have in my book of reproductions ("Lower Colorado," Nos. 2 and 6) each portray a zone of confined darkness like water, enclosed in other mostly rectangular sectors of varying desiccation.

TOWARD IMPERIAL AND BACK AGAIN

I have left Ocean Park with the mountains ahead, and as I cross Lincoln with its many, many yellow painted lines and come up to Tenth, the mountains continue to disappear. I go up a hill lined with trees and small square houses, up past the small white blocky apartments of Euclid where it flattens out like a Diebenkorn canvas so that again I can see past the dark green trees and pale green palms (which are paler green past the Sunset Grill). In this smooth-rolling California automobile I have now achieved a perspective convergence of Ocean Park with the mountains ahead, which become paler and greyer block by block; at first, thanks to the sea air, they were almost as ultramarine as the sea.

At Twenty-fifth I turn around at Clover Park. It is here that Ocean Park readies itself to become a Diebenkornscape on my windshield's gallery wall. From here, we first see the colored signals in black vertical dominoes. A giant plantain or banana tree here and there reminds me that Los Angeles never was nor could be desert; other trees have been landscaped into balls on branches; some hedges have been manicured into cylinders.

At Seventeenth I receive the first intimation that Ocean Park will drop into greyness; indeed, it will end abruptly. At Fourteenth I begin to discover a growing line of sea above the low horizon. Tree shadows on the sidewalk, then the dark gentle drop of pavement on either side of Ocean Park, past well-treed side streets, prepare me for the drive down the dip at Euclid; and the ocean flattens and widens before me and it is also now above me, because Ocean Park will ascend again, so that the ocean is above the next horizon; this is very strange water over me. I ride down another dip, bottoming out at Lincoln, at which point the ocean has once again been lost; but once I get to Highland and Beverly, I see the ocean there again, flat ultramarine zone above a concrete road-bridge and the first intimation of tan beach; all water lies over the bridge.

The bridge was at Fourth, and I pass beneath that overpass and come out onto one more dip, a very gentle one which is marked by white crosswalk lines and double yellow lines that curve. Ahead I see three walls of trees, the center one of which is palm trees, and then I have reached the final edge of Los Angeles.

Chapter 121

LOS ANGELES

(1950)

The Indians sternly beckoned us to be up and onward, now for the first time explaining to us, that there was no water until we had reached the mountains in view.

—James O. Pattie, 1830

TÍPICO AMERICANO

Do you remember the orange groves of Los Angeles and the Inland Empire? Oh, I'm not saying they've dried up and gone, not quite yet. As late as 1960, we overhear Mr. R. J. Smith of Sunnyland Citrus informing his colleagues in the Mirror Building of Los Angeles: *Well, I think that there are a number of people, Harry, in the orange juice business that we run across occasionally. I believe there is a processor in Long Beach. I'm not too sure. I have heard of him. I know that there is a small one in Anaheim.* But Los Angles sternly beckons us up and onward; there will be no oranges anymore, not until we've reached the mountains of commercial prosperity. I've never been cheated out of a dollar in my life.

In 1931, Otis P. Tout crowed that *Imperial County since the war has been the beneficiary of the great "era of concrete"* which renders highways numerous, fast and convenient. And now at midcentury, lucky Los Angeles has derived even more benefits from concrete!

In 1947 Jack Kerouac finds Hollywood Boulevard *a great, screaming frenzy of cars.*

In about 1950 they first started complaining about parking downtown, said Marjorie Sa'adah. Currently there are seven storeys of parking under Pershing Square . . .

A historian helpfully explains that *the city's transportation system resulted not from conspiracy and not from consensus but from temporary convergences of diverse and sometimes impractical agendas.*

That must be why it is that in 1956 Kerouac updates his report to mention the eye-watering smog: *A regular hell is L.A.*

And the improvements continue! By 1955 the Los Angeles River will boast channel-inert paving with continuous reinforcing steel, not to mention the double-gated pipes which empty into manholes on five-hundred-foot centers—a triumphal advance over the previous era of four-inch weep holes on ten-foot centers. *We need have no fear that our lands will not become better and better as the years go by.*

New residents come to California, and come and come, . . . reports an angry observer. *Old maids change addresses almost as often as call girls do . . . The question "Where d'you live now?" is as common and as necessary as "What's your present job?" or "Still married to the same one?"*

Among those new arrivals were my parents. This is how they remember their half a dozen–odd years in that zone at the end of the 1950s:

At first we lived in Santa Monica—it was a sleepy town, with charming Spanish style houses, not very large . . . We lived 2 blocks from the Brentwood Country Mart and sometimes we glimpsed a movie star shopping there.

Downtown L.A. hardly existed—it was mostly warehouses and freeway interchanges. Once we took Grandma Louise and Grandpa Archie there for a delicious Mexican dinner in the Mexican neighborhood of Alvira (sp) Street, but it was pretty much terra incognita to us at the time. There were no skyscrapers in West L.A. or Santa Monica, but they were just beginning to build some in Westwood (very sophisticated, everyone thought, like New York City) . . .

In West L.A., there was a Japanese community with several (very cheap) little restaurants and shops. We took you and Julie to eat there sometimes—it was about all we could afford! These people were left over from the concentration camps and usually worked as gardeners.

The yards were smaller than we were accustomed to, but still there was a great deal of open space. Driving from Santa Monica to Long Beach or on to Irvine, one passed along empty beaches and through many orange groves . . .

We loved to go to the desert—partly because it was cheap, but also because we could see the stars there so well at night . . . We used to stop and buy date shakes and tangerines . . . We also went to the high desert near Palmdale, usually with some friends. We usually had guns and shot at tin cans.

So for my parents it was not quite *a great, screaming frenzy of cars* in Los Angeles. Their experience encourages me to browse through the 1951 Orange County directory with less cynicism. ***From Swim Suit to Ski Lift in Less Than Two Hours***, it proclaims. If it was ever true, could it still be so even now? In 2007 I telephoned my friend Jake in Long Beach; he burst out laughing, then began to consider it as a literal proposition, and finally said: Do we have to assume that one end of that trip is in Orange County? You could probably take the 605. So the thing you'd want to do is start at the northernmost point, say, Seal Beach . . . I think it would be a near thing but you do it now. Hell, it might be easier now, thanks to the freeways . . .

In short, not everybody believes that *a regular hell is L.A.* Not even Kerouac consistently believes it. He grants South Main Street to be *a fantastic carnival of lights and wildness.* (He goes on to say: *Booted cops frisked people on practically every corner.*) He pays due tribute to the Angeleno incarnation of the feminine: *The most beautiful little gone girls in the world cut by in slacks; they came to be starlets; they ended up in drive-ins.* If Los Angeles is to him, as it was to Nathanael West in *The Day of the Locust,* a sickbed of desperate and perishing illusions, those illusions can sometimes be lovely indeed, and the California Dream need not remain entirely bereft of reality. *One passed along empty beaches and through many orange groves . . .*

Moreover, the Colorado River Aqueduct (length: four hundred and fifty-seven miles) will soon be able to deliver one million, two hundred and twelve thousand acre-feet per year; and by 1966 the Lockheed Aircraft Company considers it safe to report that water is one of the commodities still available *in abundant supply at fair costs.*

Chapter 122

SAN DIEGO

(1920–1960)

So, you see, we have to add to Barbara's list of the uses of water the curious thing it did for the Indians. Streams of water decided where they should live, who should be their friends, who should be their enemies, and what languages they should speak!

—Irmagarde Richards, 1933

TÍPICO AMERICANO

The San Diego city directory of 1950, which is about four times as thick as the San Diego city and county directory of 1901, announces that the city's population is now three hundred and sixty thousand, and the county's is five hundred and fifty thousand. No, wait! Our figures have fallen out of date; five hundred thousand people now live in the city *alone.*

And there's no cost to agriculture, because San Diego is perfect! For 1950 I proudly report a new high for San Diego crop returns: $62,391,353.00. Wowie, zowie; I sure can't help believing in people!

Needless to say, there's no more glowing talk about the fertile New River Valley, which along with the rest of Imperial County was robbed away back in 1907. But San Diego is big in every sense; San Diego has gotten over the slight. There remains a great deal to boost and boast about. For instance, the capacity of San Diego's water reservoirs is 133,700,600,000 gallons. The average daily water usage in the county is 44,360,000 gallons. The latter figure goes into the former three thousand and fourteen times; that's more than eight years' worth of water we have stored up! Another interesting exercise in division yields that the average per capita water usage in San Diego County is not quite eighty-one gallons per day. In 2000, that figure will have increased to a hundred and twenty-five gallons per day. Well, why not? **WATER IS HERE**.

Shall I say how and why? It didn't look promising at first. Between 1941 and 1943, water usage doubled. *Luckily the rainy years before the war left the reservoirs brimming. Still, it was clear that the city—and the Navy—would soon need the water from the Colorado River.* What to do? In 1944, the San Diego County Water Authority commences operations. In 1946, the San Diego County Water Authority joins the Metropolitan Water Authority (which you will remember equals Los Angeles) in order that, in the Authority's own words, *it could receive deliveries when the pipeline from the Colorado River Aqueduct was complete.* In 1947, when only three weeks' worth of water remain available to the county, the first drop of water from the Colorado reaches the San Vicente Reservoir of San Diego.

Thank God for the Colorado! But Pipeline Number One isn't enough. Better add Pipeline Number Two! That happens in 1954. And so capacity is doubled.

Chapter 123

TIJUANA

(1966–2065)

> Tijuana multiplies film's capacity for spectacle . . . Film can further exploit the spectacular character of the city as an astonishing and scandalous space by reproducing its strong stereotypes and the intensity, strangenesses and pain of its social dynamics.
>
> —Norman V. Iglesias Prieto, 2006

A LEER OF CHROMIUM TEETH

In 1966 the great science-fiction writer Philip K. Dick publishes *Now Wait for Last Year,* one of his most resonant parables about addiction, futility, disorientation and painful choices. The setting is, at times, Tijuana. His prominent narrative device being time travel, our dates may now vary more dramatically than is customarily the case in this book called *Imperial.*

The Tijuana of 2055 is a place where one can check into a hotel room with an insectoid enemy alien. *It had always been like this here, and even now, in wartime, Tijuana remained unchanged. You could obtain anything, do anything, you wanted. As long as it was not done blatantly on the public street. Especially if it had been consummated at night . . . Once,* presumably in 1966, *it had been abortions, narcotics, women, and gambling. Now it was concourse with the enemy.*

Let us ingest a capsule of JJ-180 to find out what happens next: In 2065, Dr. Eric Sweetscent, anguished by guilt over his failed marriage, his wife's addiction to a toxic drug, and his own inadvertent complicity in precipitating the occupation of Earth by the empire of Lilistar, enters a pharmacy in Tijuana. *A different pharmacist, this one a black-haired elderly female, greeted him.* Sí? *she leered, showing cheap chromium teeth.* Dr. Sweetscent has come to purchase a poison of West German manufacture, perfectly named g-Totex blau. *As he signed she wrapped the black carton. "You are going to kill yourself, señor?" she asked acutely. "Yes, I can tell. This will not hurt with this product; I have seen it. No pain; just no heart all of a sudden."* And Sweetscent thinks to himself: Tijuana is as it always was.

The Tijuana that always was did not exist prior to the Volstead Act, of course. The sprawling, slum-riddled, increasingly water-impoverished entity of my time was emphatically present in the midcentury years when Dick's typewriter excreted pulp manuscripts like bullets; but we ought to remember that as late as 1960, Mexicali continued to dominate Southside Imperial, with more than a hundred and seventy-nine thousand inhabitants to Tijuana's hundred and fifty-two thousand.

In 1932, just before the end of Volstead, an American crossed the line and after *several blocks where there is no make-believe,* in other words shanties and shacks, arrived at his rendezvous with Tijuana officialdom: *We pass through the portal, the postoffice to one side and the bureau for prostitutes on the other.* He picked up his permit to sail and collect specimens. *Work over, . . . we dropped in Caesar's, brass rail and all, and ordered a couple of silver fizzes.* For him, the setup was much the same as for other Volstead tourists: *From the new West Gate to the far end of the track* the management, customers and choice of merchandise were all American. Tijuana was still a precursor of the Las Vegas of my time. But Volstead died, immigrants from southern Mexico began to squat in the dry hills, Caesar's brass rail grew tarnished, and while many customers remained American, Tijuana grew out from under American management and became *Tijuana as it always was.*

My parents got married in the late fifties, when Tijuana was, they said, *a dirty, sleepy but wide-open town. The standard joke was, "Do you want to get married? Divorced? My sister is available."* My parents' memories, like mine a half-century later, play a pageant of excitingly unpredictable and therefore potentially menacing exoticism on the other side of the ditch:

. . . For our honeymoon, incredible as it now seems, we drove down to Tijuana one morning with 3 friends to see the jai alai games. (We were taking a 4-day honeymoon in Pasadena!) As the games didn't start until evening, we went on to Rosarita Beach . . . and the guys gambled in the casino of a hotel. This was advertised in the L.A. papers and we (22 years old) assumed all was on the up and up. We actually won enough money to buy dinner at the hotel! But—exactly one week later, the Federales swooped down and arrested all the Americans who were gambling there . . .

In 1966, Mexicali and Tijuana were nearly equal in population. By 1970, Tijuana had pressed ahead, but by a margin of less than fifteen thousand. The *maquiladoras* began to arrive. By the century's end Tijuana would have passed the million mark while Mexicali barely exceeded half a million souls.

She might have been fully grown in 1966, but Tijuana, like a fifteen-year-old hooker on Avenida Insurgentes, was already herself. In 2055 she will be vaster and more wrinkled, but no less herself.

Imperial is bifurcation. The Salton Trough is a worm almost cut through by steel fence, the two halves writhing and leaping. The fence shoots westward, its Northside keepers steadily overcoming its intermittence, and arrives at the Pacific, where

Tijuana presses longingly against San Diego, like a prisoner kissing his wife through the glass window of the visiting cell. Imperial is constraint indeed. Therefore, Imperial is possibility, and within Imperial it is Tijuana where possibility gets reified above all. *You could obtain anything, do anything, you wanted.* And in material advantages they are already well supplied.

MIRAGES OF A TIME TRAVELLER

Dick's contention that *nothing changes in Tijuana and yet nothing lives out its normal span* derives in part from his observation of Mexican street prostitutes, who, like their sisters in Northside, do flower and age more quickly than other women. In this respect, his maxim is not especially true. But there is a cheapness to much of Tijuana, and therefore an expendability. The shantytown *colonias* which now begin to found themselves in the dry hills, the *maquilas* which desperately seek employees and then move to China, the infamously evanescent dental work, the warping, mildewed hotel rooms, these legitimately impress themselves upon time-travelling Northsiders whose muteness and deafness in Spanish and whose inability to stay put for more than a night or two cuts them off from the vibrancy of the place, which is far more than the nightmare luxuriance of the red-light district.—I want to marry Tijuana, but look! She was fifteen when I met her, and now she's a skeleton!—But was her ageing innate to her, or did it happen because the JJ-180 was wearing off and I had to come down to my day job in Northside? Tijuana pretends to want to marry me, but she knows that I'll soon be gone, back behind the wall where she cannot follow, so she'd better hustle me while she can, all the while cocking a smile at her next ten husbands. *Time moves too fast here and also not at all,* because I never stay long, and I always come for the same thing: free trade. A trumpeter from Northside, enraptured by the rhythms of bullfights, which are prohibited on his side of the ditch, establishes a musical ensemble called Herb Alpert and the Tijuana Brass. Then he carries his new rhythms home. So do I. Border Patrolman Dan Murray remarks that illegals do the work Americans won't do; and whenever he time-trips into Tijuana, Dr. Eric Sweetscent will tempt himself with the possibilities that Americans won't provide. *You are going to kill yourself, señor?* I can't help believing in people.

Chapter 124

TECATE

(1950)

Meanwhile, Tecate drowses on.

In 1900, Mexicali's non-indigenous population was perhaps one or two *Chinos* growing cotton along the banks of the Río Nuevo. Let's generously allow her a population of one. Tecate then boasted a hundred and twenty-seven residents—half the number of Tijuana's hordes.

By 1950, three thousand, six hundred and seventy-nine people dwell in Tecate. But Tijuana's population exceeds hers by more than a factor of sixteen; Mexicali's, by eighteen. At the end of the century, thanks to the tourist trade, the brewery, her cooler climate and her eventual conveniency for *pollos* and *coyotes,* Tecate will be more vibrant than many a failed Northsider agricultural town, but she will remain overlooked, another Imperial placeholder.*

(How could it be otherwise? In Northside one often gets a sense of a person's accidentalness in a place, or at least of the person's feeling that this place is neither better nor worse than any other; whereas on Southside people frequently privilege their own over any other place, even the place next door. I remember the old man on the park bench in Tecate who informed me: Mexicali is very big—*too* big! A lot of farming and agriculture! And it's very hot, *mucho, mucho!* Here it's nice and cool. The only problem is that here in winter it gets cold and rains a lot. Winter is very long.—That was the view from Tecate, center of the universe. But in a single city to the west, which is to say down in Tijuana, a newspaper reporter explained the following: Nobody cares about Tecate! They only go there to get to the United States. You can follow the cans of tuna across the line to the United States . . .—And in Mexicali, of course, the trueblood *cachanillas* shone with civic pride; they would never want to live anywhere else, including Tecate.)

Tecate drowses on; throughout the century she will drowse on. Tecate is a slow street, a fat palm tree, a man in white chopping meat for tacos, mariachi music canned and on low, a single honking horn, two blackhaired girls wearing white hair-ribbons and navy-and-white gold-buttoned school uniforms in the back of a white Chevrolet on Benito Juárez.

*See comparative population table, p. 1222.

Chapter 125

HOLTVILLE

(1905–1964)

The "Carrot Capital of the World" is a homey community of 3,000 with every resident excited over the city's present progress . . .

—Holtville Chamber of Commerce, 1952

Once upon a time in 1905, we find Mr. C. C. Bowles roasting a million bricks for the new brick plant in Holtville, and I would not be surprised if "the Little Giant," by whom I mean W. F. Holt himself, wagons or motors regularly down from Redlands to boost this and that in his eponymous city.

Holtville, what can we say about Holtville? Just a little bit east we can find barrel cacti; there are also some of those on Imperial County's southwest corner.

Here is Holtville advice from 1964: *When you stop at Fifth and Holt, entrance to the park, drop in at the Chamber of Commerce office and say "Howdy." The Chamber Manager will bid you a hearty welcome. (He'll give you a free booklet containing more than 100 carrot recipes too!)*

In an undated photograph, a doll in a wide white bell skirt like a *quinceañera* dress squats a trifle precariously upon a pyramid of vegetables entitled **CALIFORNIA'S WINTER WONDERLAND** and ***HOLTVILLE: CARROT CAPITAL OF THE WORLD***. More produce and then labeled open dishes of minced edibles lie before her like offerings. Three flags rise from behind her head, one of them being the American. And, resting one manicured, nail-painted hand on what might be a giant cabbage just behind the toy pig (this picture has faded considerably), and wearing a Vikingesque helm with fringe on top like the brush of a vacuum cleaner attachment, a lady grips another flag, which resembles the Tricouleur of France, and life goes on forever . . .

Do You Want a Home IN Southern California

At the Government Price of $1.25 per Acre?

With the best water right in the world at the lowest price ever offered?

These can be had nowhere but in the

IMPERIAL SETTLEMENT

In the Eastern part of San Diego County, California

The Colorado Delta, located in Riverside and San Diego counties in Southern California and extending down into Lower California, comprises about 1,000,000 acres of level, irrigable land that has been made during the past ages by alluvial deposits carried down by the waters of the Colorado River.

The Imperial Setttlement is located on this delta, and comprises about five hundred thousand acres of level, fertile land, free from alkali, with sufficient slope to be easily irrigated. It is all Government land and can be taken up under the desert land law or the homestead law. 320 acres can be taken up by each person under the desert land law, and residence on the land is not required. This liberal law is liable to early repeal or unfavorable modification.

This country is suited to the production of alfalfa and the fattening of cattle, (a line of business that can never be overdone) and to other agricultural and horticultural productions usual to Southern California.

The climate is the finest in the world for eight months in the year, and the summers are not one-half as hot as you have been told. Any healthy man can stay and work with comfort all the year round.

The Colorado River furnishes the most abundant supply of water for irrigation purposes to be found west of the Rocky Mountains. Its greatest flood is during the month of June, when it is needed the most, and the least supply during December, when it is needed the least—being about nine feet higher in June than in December.

The river carries enough water to irrigate 8,000,000 acres of land, hence the supply can never be cut short by dry seasons.

An extensive irrigation system is now being constructed to reclaim this large tract of country. The main canal will be enlarged and the branch canals extended to meet the demand for water as the irrigated area is enlarged.

Water is now flowing in the main canal, and will be ready for use for fall and winter crops.

The waters of this river carry more fertilizers than is carried by the waters of any other river in world, not excepting even the Nile.

The soil of this Delta is as fertile as soil can be, and when cultivated and irrigated with this water it must continue to remain fertile, as each season's irrigation will deposit on each acre irrigated more than $10 worth of commercial fertilizers without extra expense.

The land will be irrigated by mutual water companies, designated as Imperial Water Company No. 1, No. 2, No. 3, etc., formed to distribute water to stockholders only, at cost.

The Imperial Land Company sells this water stock to the landowners—one share to each acre. The price is now only $11.25 per share.

A railroad through the Imperial Settlement, connecting with Yuma on the east and San Diego on the west, and with the Southern Pacific on the north, is on the program.

A large area of land under this irrigation system has already been taken up, principally by residents of Southern California, who have had experience and understand soil and irrigation.

Read in the Imperial Press what the editors of Southern California say about this country and this enter prise.

Visit Imperial and receive the object lesson of a lifetime on irrigation on a large scale.

For circular matter and full information, address

IMPERIAL LAND CO.

S. W. FERGUSSON, General Manager. IMPERIAL, SAN DIEGO CO., CAL.

Chapter 126

WHAT A COLD STARRY NIGHT USED TO BE LIKE

(1949–1989)

And giants lived in this Sun.

—Codex Cuauhtitlán (Aztec)

It was just such a wonderful thing that happened to me, said Alice Woodside. Our little house was out in the middle of the fields, and my eye was accustomed to distant horizons. One morning, very early, my father came and woke me up. I think I was maybe five years old. He took me to the north end of the field, where you can see west forever. For miles, I could see wooden towns, old towns, old houses, in a kind of a pinkish peach atmosphere. I said: Those houses have never been there before! Where have they come from? And then as the sun came up they began to dissipate very slowly. And then my father explained to me it was the mirage to end all mirages. It could have come in all the way from some Colorado mining town.

He had a bad heart. I think he was pretty much aware that he was going to die. I called him on a Saturday, I think it was in 1989. I said, Dad, I keep forgetting to ask you: Did I really see that? He said yes. He also said, you know, Alice, once I had to go out at night and flood the fields because there was going to be frost. And I saw a rainbow around the moon. That was what he said. And he died that night. I never can talk about it without getting choked up.

You just can never believe what a cold starry night used to be like. They used to be blazing, those stars. Even up at Lake Tahoe, you don't see that blaze. Everything's filmed over.

Chapter 127

IMPERIAL REPRISE

(*ca.* 1950–2066)

1

I 'll never forget cotton, no sir! They used to call it the white gold. Then the United States stopped buying.

When I was little I would see comets go by and the aurora borealis. But now because the air is so dirty you don't see it anymore.

Back then the money had power. For all the night, fifty pesos, and for just in-and-out, ten pesos. *I wish to emphasize that these values are Gross Values, F. O. B. Shipping Point . . .*

You could obtain anything, do anything, you wanted. As long as it was not done blatantly on the public street.

Everything was open. Something that I remember was crossing the border, which was like crossing the street.

2

It took him time to become a resident, a citizen. But he did it.

The whole families would work; they really had their eye on the dollar. *One would think that every day is a fiesta on the exciting Mexican-American border!* The seasonal farmworkers . . . continue to present a major social problem. The net income to farmers was not increased in proportion to the gross sales.

3

We have a beautiful artesian well which flows copiously all the time. Still, it was clear that the city—and the Navy—would soon need the water from the Colorado River. **THE DESERT DISAPPEARS**. The city wasn't as big as it is now. *IMPERIAL COUNTY SHOWS RAPID INCREASE . . . We can see the possible unification of Imperial and Coachella Valleys in a continuous garden from the Mexican line.* Why, I would be sick to my stomach if I rode down that valley in California, over those long miles owned by one man. *The bountiful continent is ours, state on state, and territory on territory, to the waves of the Pacific sea.*

4

Imperial Valley is more than a highly-developed farming area—it is a wonderland of factories running 24 hours a day, 365 days a year. Today Riverside is the center of the Citrus Empire. *A regular hell is L.A.* And in material advantages they are already well supplied: *four paved streets, sixteen alleyways, two rivers full of shit and a whole lot of assholes!* I can't help believing in people. *You are going to kill yourself, señor?*

PART TEN

DISSOLUTIONS

Chapter 128

PROBABLY THE WEATHER

(2002–2003)

There is no ill which lasts a hundred years, nor anybody who can resist it.

—Mexican proverb

ICE COLD (2003)

Probably the weather, replied Mr. Larry Grogan, freshly elevated from Mayor of El Centro to former Mayor as he sat lean-faced and long-limbed over a desk full of papers in the back office of his pawnshop, beyond the guitars on the walls, the bicycle locks for sale, the boom boxes, the hordes of wrenches both rusty and perfectly nickeled; I saw a grinding wheel; the vending machine proclaimed its contents **ICE COLD**; a DeWalt drill could have been mine for half price, a saxophone for $599.95; on the outer wall of Mr. Grogan's office hung a *CASH EXPRESS PAYDAY ADVANCE* chart which explained that to receive, for instance, a hundred dollars, the fee would be seventeen dollars and fifty cents, which was why one needed to make out one's check to Valley Pawn for one hundred and seventeen dollars and fifty cents; *I have never been cheated out of a dollar in my life.* I also discovered an appreciation plaque from the Centinela State Prison Citizens' Advisory Committee, another from the Lions International, one from the El Centro Police Activities League, and one from the Volunteers of America Imperial Alcohol and Drug Service Center.

Probably the weather was his answer when I asked him why Imperial County had not lived up to dreams of her boomers and boosters forever and ever, Amen. And it might even have been the perfect answer;* for in this empire, even beehives need awnings.

"SAY KA-CHEEPO"

Probably it was the weather, to be sure, but by now the ninety-one-degree autumn afternoon had entirely departed, the sky dark violet at seven P.M. like the Martian

*For other answers of a more quantitative sort, see the source notes to this chapter (excerpt from Paul Foster's Imperial color commentary).

atmosphere. When the air got as cool as this, I for one wouldn't pawn El Centro away! A man in a wheelchair sat in front of the nightclub on Main Street; his gaze was a sentry's; nothing got past him on that long wide flat street, because there was nothing. Probably it was the weather. At least he'd never have to worry that in his grave he'd turn **ICE COLD**. A coolish breeze began to breathe from the wide tan alleyways. I read the sign which said **SEXY LINGERIE** – WE HAVE TOYS AND THING'S FOR WOMEN! But for which women? I'd lost my belief in the slender cowgirl with long soft bangs who stands with her hands on her buckskin-fringed hips, grinning like the perfect stewardess; she's on the cover of Ball Advertising's pamphlet: "Visitors' Recreation Guide Book to Imperial County California: 36 Pages of Information." I think she's supposed to be Barbara Worth. What prevented her from existing? Probably the weather. Having reached this conclusion, I then passed very slowly through one of the alleys, wondering as always what had gone wrong and fallen silent here, or was this how Imperial was supposed to be? Before the Valley of Death got settled, its sands were silent, but the silence of an uninhabited place or of potentiality differs from the silence of a corpse. I remembered an old photograph of Main Street, with the El Centro Hotel proudly front and center (where was it now?); the arches of its arcade had spelled out STATIONERY and **CONFECTIONERY** and CIGARS and **DRUGS** and **CAMERAS** and CACHIPO Say Ka-Cheepo for your Stomach Liver etc. I remembered the days when Imperial was the third-fastest-growing county in America. If only the Virgin of Guadalupe would help us all!

Or do some happy homesteads endure? Consider this: NOTICE: PARKING RESERVED FOR FARM AMERICA.

THE COURTHOUSE (2002)

Generally speaking, when one walks eastward in this part of El Centro, the businesses become bail bonds offices and pawnshops; while going westward, they tend to become title companies. So I went a block south. On State Street, the bright phony yellow welcome of the Roberta Hotel's doorway blasted into a jet-black silhouette of the black man who was riding his bicycle round and round the parking lot. *He made a success through his own efforts.* There were several other yellow-lit parking lots whose blackness had been delimited and verified by tan buildings; there was block after block of multilayered square arches from whose ceilings more yellow lights hung down like pig-teats. The insurance company had closed for the night, but the Fraternal Order of Eagles (founded in 1907) offered a glowingly open doorway with a garbage can just inside. (The Eagles used to meet in Holtville, I recall, back when the world knew that *IMPERIAL COUNTY SHOWS RAPID INCREASE: Is Growing Rapidly Richer.*)

I heard crickets. Old people said that half a century ago they were "everywhere" in Mexicali. I never heard them in that city anymore, at least not downtown. Well, but El Centro wasn't as busy as Mexicali nowadays. (TAKE NOTICE. **"PALMBREAD" *Made in El Centro Sold All Over the Valley*.** That message comes to you from 1912.) Sooner or later business would pick up, once Imperial County had finished building those industrial parks. *His farm has been highly improved.*

Dawn was enacted by the liquid chucklings of pigeons, taking State Street by surprise, for it had not yet fully organized its shadows into razor-edged tightness as it certainly would by eight-o'-clock. Soon each pillar in each archway possessed a downward-diagonal shadow of itself. I wandered back to Main Street, turned west, and reached the courthouse* just as it opened.

This graceful white edifice, its staircase flanked by hedges, exemplifies bifurcation as much as anything in Imperial. On the left stand a trash can and a graciously deciduous tree; on the right, a regal palm, a mailbox, and our American flag. Straight up the middle of the stairs runs a railing, almost all the way to the place between the central pair of pillars where the double doors meet. There are, in fact, six pillars, each outermost pair clumped together, so that the portico is divided into thirds, each third adorned by a molding and a rectangular window divided in two both horizontally and vertically, the smaller pair of topmost panels then subdivided in a star-boned square of six triangles. To the left of those grand copper doors, and also to the right, there is a wide glass-paned bulletin board, and within the rightmost of these misery-windows there hang from rows of clips, sometimes with their sides curling inwards, like the wings of sleeping bats, NOTICES OF TRUSTEE'S SALE from this or that foreclosure department of Anyzone's title or "service" company; while the leftmost pane presents corresponding notices of sale and probate. The probate doesn't bother me; we all have to die. But what about those presumably still-living wretches who have lost their homes?

That lovely white courthouse, eternally quiet behind its hedges! Open the door, and you'll find it filled with brownskinned people who murmur in low sad rapid voices.

*Depicted in my 8 x 10" negative IV-CS-ELC-01-02. This is El Centro's second courthouse. The first, now not very far from **SEXY LINGERIE** – WE HAVE TOYS AND THING'S FOR WOMEN!, has since become an Elks Lodge. From across the street the courthouse appears almost inexpressibly inviting. That cool white portico, the copper doors, the thirteen white steps are perfect embellishments to that old Imperial adage "He sold out at a fancy price."

EVEN MORE ICE COLD (2003)

After looking through a loupe at the ring which a lady sought to pawn, Mr. Grogan said tenderly: You see, girl, it's very . . .—and then he took her fat wrist. Then, turning to the biggest of his clerks, he said in a firm, all-business voice: *Seventy-five dollars.*

Is seventy-five dollars too much? Do you want to save? I'll tell you how, courtesy of the following advertisement from the Pure Ice Company, one of whose three plants was in El Centro: *SAVE WITH ICE*.

Here's another helpful hint for all you scrimpers: In El Centro, California, our Furniture Palace proclaims **1 YEAR SAME AS CASH**.

A SECOND OPINION (1936)

What caused Imperial to go wrong? Probably the weather. And here's another explanation, courtesy of a book on citrus diseases: *A large list of special fruit rots and spots occurs . . . The last one,* dry rot, *has been found only in the Imperial Valley.*

Chapter 129

FROM TEN GALS DOWN TO THREE

(1914–2004)

All Riverside County "shows off" during this one week period. Horses, cattle, dramatics and pretty girls galore in Arabian costumes.

—Shields Date Gardens, 1952

Well, I worked there fifty years, said Mr. Ray House, rotund and grey. Well, the first year we called it Tent City. Through the years it's been upgraded. I worked there in the Junior Department, 4-H and so forth. And then I served nine years on the Board of Trustees of the fair, you know, the Fair Board. Then I served the rest of the time just working on the fairs. I had a Date Queen exhibit at the Fair for pretty much fifty years.

It started out, looks was very important. You got a bathing suit, and things like that. Well, that's started to phase out. But they still use skimpy costumes and you see. It's been Arabian costumes since 1947. Bob was the manager. Guess his daughter suggested it. They were looking for a theme to follow. They chose the Arabian theme because of the desert. Looks was very important at first, and then it phased into knowledge of the date industry being an important part. And then the communications skills come in there.

We used to take a week off from school for the Fair, but that phased out.

It was all volunteer work at first. We didn't have sponsors before. Used to have the Christian church with all the foods. Now we have a hundred and fifteen kinds of foods, and all not local. One reason is that the kids don't want to work as hard as their parents. They got tired. They got other interests. They got surfboards.

We did go from ten gals down to three, you know, one Date Queen and nine Princesses down to a Queen and two Princesses; and the reason for that was financial. It was countywide at first, and then it got littler and littler as far as it covered. We had a Queen of California, a Queen of the County, all that. But we always had the publicity based on the Queens. When we had ten of 'em, a Queen and nine Princesses, we could go to L.A. and get anything on TV we wanted. And locally here, when we brought the Queens down, they got a free meal every day they were here, for the ten days, to, to, go before the Lions Club.

He smiled into the past very sweetly, as if he could see all the way back to the day Miss Helen Shaw got elected Imperial County Queen *and held court on the fair grounds, awarding prize winners their trophies.* She'd commanded ten Maids of Honor. That was in 1914, at the Seventh County Fair.

They'd always wear their costumes, he said. One thing you notice, the costumes weren't as fancy in the beginning. They weren't as colorful; they weren't as skimpy. Then that changed. Toward the end, they'd make communications about the date industry the centerpiece. (It was really dates and citrus and all that, but mainly dates.) I guess the last five years or maybe ten, I made a book for every Queen or Princess and gave it to 'em. And the Fair gave me no money for my book, but they paid for the expense of printing the pictures.

In 1947 there were ten gals. We had ten for years. I started with the Fair in '51, and then it went to five, and then to three. I can't tell you when, exactly.

But there's some people who will never give up on the Queen.

You gotta have a Queen, agreed his friend Art La Londe.

There's been a lot of pressure to change the emphasis from Queens to Ambassadors. They think it should not be so much emphasis on beauty, Mr. House continued, and I could tell that this made him sad.

From ten gals down to three! Isn't that life? Across the line in Mexicali, the bank of flesh-red lights began winking at the Thirteen Negro, and I ordered a beer from Mario the waiter, after which I bought a beer for Mario, who was by no means as old as Mr. House but had known the Thirteen Negro for many eternities just the same. On the subject of royalty, he remarked that there were very few dancing-girls nowadays; even on Fridays, Saturdays and Sundays you saw no more than thirty; eight or nine years ago there had been seventy-six; and when he remembered that, he got happy even in his sadness that seventy-six had gone to thirty and the Río Colorado no longer reached the sea, that he was no longer the lover of the bargirl Emily and that someday the Thirteen Negro itself would come to an end.

When I asked how I could meet a Date Queen from long ago, Mr. House replied: There's only one that I know that's dead. One of 'em passed away. Passed away at an early age. I know where a beautiful one is in Redlands.

It was a very hot still July morning in Coachella, and Mr. House sat unmoving for a time with the sunlight harshly shadowing his face. Finally he said: I would tell you that the one from 1947, when I saw her in 1997, she was just as beautiful as she was then. Trim and petite. You couldn't believe how elegant she was.

Chapter 130

YOU CAN'T PRODUCE THINGS THE WAY YOU USED TO

(2003–2004)

Migratory working man, I'm on my way—
I am done with sun and sand and new-mown hay;
I have worked from sun to sun,
Nothing have I ever won
And now, thank God, my harvesting is done.

—IWW song, before 1923

CRYING IN YOUR BEER (2003)

What caused Imperial to go wrong?—Why, what on earth are you talking about? Nothing's wrong.

Way over in Carol, Illinois, which has been detached from Imperial for some years now, the President of a corporation with the Imperial name of Prince Industries *dismisses gloomy industry talk of the disappearance of U.S. manufacturing as "a big lie."*

"There's a lot of crying-in-your-beer stuff going on" because of China, lost jobs and other pressures, he said.

Prince Industries makes *precision metal products.* What would have taken the company *dozens of humans* to accomplish, it learned to do with three machines, which then got replaced by one machine.

Manufacturing is hitting another level of evolution, explains the President of Prince Industries. *You can't produce things the way you used to.*

Once farming changes from a way of life to a means to an end, once crops become equivalent to precision metal products, why, then you can't produce things the way you used to. It's as simple as that.

South of Mexicali, where *maquiladoras* have begun to gobble up ranchos and *ejidos,* a woman said to me: There's still much cotton in the valley, and right now it goes for a good price. It used to be that from August to January there was a large movement of people all over Mexico to harvest the cotton. It's just like Mexicans now in the United States. But what happened is that machinery came in, so they didn't need the workers so much.

What will happen to those workers? *There's a lot of crying-in-your-beer stuff going on.*

Maybe the President of Prince Industries is right. Ten years ago, Winzeler Gear in Chicago needed fifty-five people to make two million gears a month. Now, with thirty-five people, it makes sixteen million gears a month. I'll bet gears are cheaper. I won't cry in my beer about that!

In California, annual crop production has increased by two and a half times in the short interval from 1939 to 1959. Just imagine the magnitude of the increase over the lifetime of Imperial County! Shall we pat ourselves on our backs? On the contrary, let's start weeping into our alcoholic beverage of choice, in deference to Mr. S. M. Beard of Salinas, 1958: *The widespread use of Great Lakes seed increased production in all districts; and this has had a detrimental effect on the western lettuce industry.* (Rousseau: *I have seen men wicked enough to weep for sorrow at the prospect of a plentiful season.*) Well, since lettuce overproduction drives down the price of lettuce, I'll simply have to produce more lettuce in order to make the income as I used to. But how to manage that? I can't afford the lettuce-harvesting machine which will make my previous lettuce-harvesting machine obsolete. Nor can I harvest lettuce as cheaply as the big boys do. What will happen to me? *There's a lot of crying-in-your-beer stuff going on.*

In the 1940s there were at least fifteen citrus packers in the city of Riverside. In 1996 there were only six—processing more fruit than before.

In 1950, California contained a hundred and forty-four thousand farms of about two hundred and sixty acres each. In 2000, there were only eighty-seven thousand five hundred farms; average acreage had risen to three hundred and eighteen; but the total acreage farmed in the state had fallen from thirty-seven and a half million to twenty-seven point eight million. *Manufacturing is hitting another level of evolution.*

What *is* a farm, anyhow?

It's a great feeling, when winter bears down or a drouth comes along, to go down cellar and look over hams and bacon, barrels of sauer kraut and pickles, sacks of dried beans, and plenty of turnips and potatoes and pumpkins. Say, boys and girls, that's when you realize that the good earth is your best chance for security in your old age. An old farmwife wrote those words in 1940. Read between the lines, and her definition is evident enough. But my *California Agricultural Directory* informs me that *starting in 1975, the new definition of farm[s] is "places with annual sales of agricultural products of $1,000 or more."*

In short, insists Victor Davis Hanson, *democracy—once created through bloodshed by those who owned land for the salvation of a few million others who owned land, in a society that was mostly independent, physical, poor, and rural—was now to be the unconscious entitlement of hundreds of millions who were mostly dependent, leisured, secure, and suburban. Land that was once understood to grow citizens as well as food was now to grow only food for those without land.*

(Paul S. Taylor, 1981: *U.S. agriculture is the most productive in the world . . . Yet only four percent of all Americans work on the land.*)

Does Victor Davis Hanson deserve to cry in his beer? Are farmers the victims of the leisure class? But perhaps some of them (for instance, the members of the Chandler Syndicate) have belonged to that class.—One afternoon in Calexico, Richard Brogan was explaining to me some of the doings of the Agricultural Stabilization Board, and he said: They have a complete grid mapping of every county. Those subsidies are based on a past history of production. They will then have the current allotment or what have you for each acreage. If you have a thousand acres of ground and forty acres has a cotton base, I think you can move it around on the ground you control. Well, there's people who really don't understand it or are jealous. There's enforcement, monitoring. But people who know how to lease land are just good, savvy, crafty people.

Let's say that the times we live in, when every field gets subdelineated down to the last cent, have transformed farmers from stockpilers of their own cellars to savvy, crafty lessors and lessees of the soil. *Manufacturing is hitting another level of evolution.* Let's thank science, without which we wouldn't possess that brand-new dehydrating method which allows Imperial County to sell asparagus to Europe.

In 1982, Imperial remains in fact the fourth most agriculturally productive county in the state—first for cattle and calves, alfalfa hay, wheat, sugar beets and lettuce! *We need have no fear that our lands will not become better and better as the years go by.*

A private investigator from San Diego whose business had taken him into Imperial County for years told me that he used to see *sweaty guys in farm clothes* in the bars there; he saw fewer and fewer of them now. He said: The really rich ones own or control eighty-five percent of all agribusiness. Fifteen percent are controlled by the blue-collar guys.

Will the small farms go under? I asked.

Sure, just like in the Central Valley. The Mom and Pop farms are being swallowed up by the housing tracts. The whole thing's being crunched. That way of life is going now.

Reader, do you want to watch it go?

Imperial County Agricultural Commissioner's report, 1970: *As you will note, there was an increase in the gross income of 4%, which on the surface appears to be substantial; however, the cost of farming continued to increase at an even greater rate. The result of the continued price squeeze is being felt throughout the community . . .*

Imperial County Agricultural Commissioner's report, 1980: *The disastrous marketing season for the 1979–80 lettuce crop, as well as a declining market in livestock, were the major factors in lowering the gross income for this year.*

But wait a minute! Imperial County Agricultural Commissioner's report, 1990: *. . . the total County Agricultural production values have surpassed the one billion dollar mark for the first time.* Manufacturing must be hitting another level of evolution.

Sometime between 1971, when he hand-lettered the beautiful title page of *I Remember America,* and 1985, when he died, the writer-painter Eric Sloane wrote: *The extraordinary family spirit and agrarian economy that originally sparked America are gone; only the old stone barns are left to remind us of it.* I myself wouldn't cry in my beer about that. I never saw a stone barn in Imperial anyhow.

CRYING IN YOUR BEER (2004)

My *New York Times* informs me that *American agriculture is at a dangerous crossroads* because *the United States could soon become a net importer of food for the first time in about 50 years. In part because of Nafta and globalization, consumers often find it cheaper to eat tomatoes from Mexico . . . than what is grown a few miles away. Meanwhile, especially in the fast-growing states of the South and West, medium-sized farmers find that selling their land is more profitable than cultivating it.*

I personally feel that this country can't depend on the Mexican industrial sector, Richard Brogan told me bitterly. Just because it's cheap labor today and everybody wants to outsource, they accept less quality. There's the issue of the graft, the greed, the corruption. It's not a level field.

Manufacturing is hitting another level of evolution. We need have no fear that our lands will not become better and better as the years go by.

Chapter 131

THE AZTECS ARE BACK

(2004)

> He was beginning to yearn for Mexico,—for Mexico, which he had never seen, yet yearned for like an exile.
>
> —Helen Hunt Jackson, 1884

What caused Imperial to go wrong?—Nothing's wrong, at least not on Southside.

A huge blonde sails by, her double chins bearded with sweat-pearls, and a man in a white sombrero chats without hurry or limit to a man in a baseball cap as they lean against the IMPORTMEX window behind the line of angle-parked cars; there is more traffic than there used to be, and it goes faster: more once-yellow buses and men drinking alertly from water bottles, more men raising their sunglasses to their foreheads to study each suspicious situation, more young boys in baseball caps, more pale white cars and even more gringos, who occasionally muse, as did I just this morning, over the shop window of immense silver belt buckles incised with golden bulls' heads; in the end, I contented myself with a narrow belt with horse-shaped appliqué, and the first red shoelaces of my life; oh, I felt free then; I was a dandy; and I could see the same awareness of becoming free in my fellow gringo's eyes—he could wear a belt buckle of greater immensity than he had ever imagined! He could walk down the street and everybody would look at him and think about his penis. In the end I didn't buy the belt buckle, for I feared that my penis might not live up to it. Back to the eternal present: It is hot, I feel dreamy and happy; and two pretty whores from the Hotel 16 Septiembre will soon remind me that if I wish I have permission to deploy the organ just mentioned. Right now they are leaning against a restaurant window, correcting their eyebrows with the aid of a tiny pink-framed mirror. One is much taller and prettier than the other. Her white-toothed smile rivals the river of sunlight on the street. The other, the blonde, keeps going over and over her hair with one hand. They lean; they chat, then sleepily call out to men, all the while correcting their eyebrows. The tall one, whose dark hair resembles a shroud, smiles again sideways, and by now her teeth are even brighter than the pavement; they glow and glow, but nobody cares. **Sign of Slow Growth Sends Stocks Lower.**

Compared to American Imperial, Southside's stocks have always been low; and that's why a Northsider sees dirty poverty on the other side of the ditch. But Northside's boomers turned much of American Imperial from a desert to a crazy-growing wonderland of money and agriculture, and this wonderland failed to keep its edge. Meanwhile, Southside augments itself. Its day is finally coming. Oh, yes, **THE AZTECS ARE BACK**. In the *ejidos* west of Algodones I remember meeting in a field of watermelon-pickers a young woman as squat, stone-hard, wide, huge and sinister as an ancient statue of the Aztec goddess Coatlicue, whose skirts are serpents, whose bifurcated face sports insect mandibles and whose hands show a skull to the world. Sweat bloomed on her round face and on her meaty arms as she stooped and straightened, cradling between cannonball-breasts this or that immense green fruit; she worked laughing; it seemed that nothing could ever kill her; she could have trampled the entire world.

In the northern zone of sunroasted Imperial, some hide in defeat, some sell out, and some do deals with everyone's water; some command field-worker armies upon their flat crop-empires. On Southside the campesinos sweat no less; sometimes they complain; but the heat somehow becomes them; they own it and are even proud of it. They work in the squash fields when it is a hundred and fifteen degrees, drinking jugs of water, and in later years sodas; the time will soon be here when they will slowly, patiently assemble products for foreigners in hot industrial parks. Why is Mexicali busier than El Centro? Why has Southside narrowed the gap between Northside and themselves?—Probably the weather, replies Mr. Larry Grogan.

Manufacturing is hitting another level of evolution, explains the President of Prince Industries. So outsource to the Aztecs! It's only in American Imperial that *you can't produce things the way you used to.*

Chapter 132

THE LINE ITSELF

(1950–2006)

. . . in the new landscape around them humanitarian considerations were becoming irrelevant.

—J. G. Ballard, 1964

Back then, said Javier Lupercio, meaning *back in the 1950s*, there were wooden benches at the crossing for people to rest, and the buildings were real small wooden buildings, and for the pedestrians there was only one customs officer. Up until 1980 and 1981, they had a patio-like thing that was the old one. They tore it down in about 1981. When that Port of Entry was built in Calexico, there weren't all those businesses that are like in the tunnel when you come into Mexicali. There were a lot of robberies and muggings going on.

(The *Imperial Valley Press* reminds us that the Port of Entry was a triumph of human civilization. Dateline 1974: **POE opens new door to Mexico in era of friendship**.)

How old were you the first time you went to the United States?

Around seven or eight years.* At that young age, my mother had already put my papers in. She'd applied for green cards for the whole family.

What seemed different about the other side?

I noticed right away there were more job opportunities. The people were also different. Their way of being was different. I noticed all those small things that are also big things . . .—and he concluded with a yawn, because we were in the Park of the Child Heroes in midafternoon when it was very hot, so that the peculiar existence of Northside now and then remained of small importance.

It was afternoon; it was hot; indeed, in those long past days before the wall went up, Imperial's binational delineation could still be overlooked on occasion. It had certainly not infected Greater Northside to any significant extent. That was the reason that by the time Operation Gatekeeper began, the Native American writer Leslie Marmon Silko would find herself looking back, with that special sort of angry

*Since he was born in 1945, this would have been *circa* 1952. Perhaps this was the first time he stayed in Northside for a significant period, since he later dated his "first time across" as 1949 or 1950.

cynicism that implies nostalgia, upon the 1950s, when they taught her in school that Americans could travel without restriction from state to state; for she had just learned what it was like to be stopped in the small hours in New Mexico by the Border Patrol. *I will never forget that night beside the highway. There was an awful feeling of menace and violence straining to break loose.*

I myself never experienced that sensation, even when they detained me. The Border Patrolmen were often courteous; the Border Patrolwomen smilingly accepted my compliments. They could be kind. Sometimes they bought their prisoners soap with their own money, or they might share their dinner with a scared and hungry child. Once when a busload of captured illegals rolled past Salvation Mountain, the Border Patrol granted Leonard permission to board the bus so that he could pass out postcards for them to take home to Mexico.

On 28 August 1970, the day before he was shot dead by Los Angeles County sheriffs, Ruben Salazar published his last column, which stated in part: *The Mexican-American has the lowest education level, below either black or Anglo; the highest dropout rate; and the highest illiteracy rate.* Money trickles down like water; Mexican-Americans occupy lower dips of the moneyscape than Anglo-Americans, but there are lower places still. Four months earlier, this same journalist had written that *anyone who has seen the fetid shacks in which potential wetbacks live on the Mexican side of the border can better understand why those people become wetbacks.*

Not wishing them to become wetbacks, Northside reacted accordingly. First there was no wall, then there were wall sections here and there, and immediately there were holes in them. (Even in 1999 I remember huge window-gaps in Calexico itself, huge spaces. You could reach through; you could step through. The next time I was there, those gaps were gone. Fresh stacks of fence lay in the setting sun, ready to be deployed elsewhere along the line. In 2005 there were still many easy gaps near Jacumba, in sight of the dirt road. My friend Larry and I stopped to admire one of those, and unsmiling Border Patrolmen drove up to us right away.)

In 1964, Northside caught forty-four thousand Mexican illegals—a decade later, seven hundred and ten thousand. Not content with the latter figure, a certain César Chávez informs us: *The worst invasion of illegal aliens in our history is taking a shameful toll of human misery . . . All of this stems from the unwillingness of the Border Patrol to do its job when that job might threaten the profits of the growers . . .*

Poor Border Patrol! Couldn't they please anyone?—They went on holding the line.

And what was the line itself but the red-reflectored white posts, staggered in height, the fresh-dragged tracks, the Border Patrol trucks everywhere? What is it now? Life continues to ignore and resist it. Very early on a Sunday morning in Calexico, a cool, cool manure-scented wind transforms palmtops into pennants, blowing away from the missing half of the high white moon, while the sun blazes dazzlingly but harmlessly at the end of the alley between Third and Second, gilding the crowns of the old square buildings and of the signs. The street remains unpeopled save by one darkskinned man with his jacket under his arm, slowly striding toward the border; the consciousness of Calexico is still plastered over with Chinese newspapers like the windows of the Aguila Super Market. As I transect another alley which last year was filled with water, I remember, an old citizen walks northward, toward me, with a newspaper tucked beneath his arm; an elderly Chinese lady in shorts briskly crosses Second Street, passing the triple-arched facade for Crystal Dream Travel; on the corner stands a security officer in white. I greet him and he replies with reserved courtesy, so I leave him.—Here in the windows of Christina's Lingerie, a blonde mannequin in a loose blue camisole and matching blue panties whose translucence proves that she lacks a vulva gazes steadily outward, pushing at the window with her eternally outstretched hands, and beside her, another face has been newspapered over; a note reads: WE'VE MOVED TO THE NEW PARADISE, and then follows the name of an automobile. More female mannequins, these in summery outfits, and a plump golden dog trots toward a golden dumpster. Crossing First Street (Yoing Ju Ginseng Tea), I enter the bay between buildings which leads to the wall itself, where two white buses with people in them now begin to pull away, going north. And so I stand at the wall and gaze into Mexico. There's the green sign for SAN LUIS RIO C, for SAN FELIPE and TIJUANA. It's not yet seven, and traffic already waits to enter my country. A man named Señor Juan Pérez, tattooed and thirtyish, comes to shake my hand through the fence (Operation Gatekeeper has since made those handshakes impossible); he tells me about the old days of General Cantú, while a few feet deeper into Mexico, a girl in orange with a delightful sweatband is flirting with a newspaper vendor.

Chapter 133

FARM SIZE

(1950–2006)

As the number of farmers decrease [*sic*], each farmer's responsibility for feeding more people and animals increases. A gallon of gasoline or diesel produces more power in an hour than 300,000 pounds of horseflesh.

—The *California Farmer*, 1959

Why am I so struck with the *bygoneness* of the hay-heaps in the field of Mrs. Josephine Runge of Brawley, who got almost ten tons to the acre—the Imperial Valley record for 1927? First of all, because the competition of human beings for prizes and maximums is much less evident than it used to be. Secondly, more fields than ever are corporate Rothkoscapes: One resembles another. And if Company A produces a higher yield than Company B, I will never know it; in fact, when I go to the supermarket I lack any clue as to whose crops I am buying.

How did that bygoneness manifest itself? In American Imperial, it diminished the number of farms—and farmers—over time, correspondingly increasing each farm's average acreage. In Mexican Imperial, it made the farmers more desperate for land. How could it not? At the beginning of the twenty-first century, twenty-five percent of working Mexicans were still farmers, while fewer than two percent of working Americans remained in that life.

In the Archivo Histórico del Municipio de Mexicali there is a twenty-nine-page list of *colonias* and their inhabitants drawn up in 1947. (Most of the *colonias*, by the way, contained just ten or twenty plots, although Colonia Mariana was not far beyond the pale with thirty-six.) This list is the only information the archive possesses regarding property holdings in the entire Mexicali Valley at this time, so it is as representative as we are going to get; and it proves that in spite of President Cárdenas's best efforts to subdivide the Chandler Syndicate's estates into equitable parcels, in spite of the protestations of an official of the Tribunal Unitario Agrario that in Baja California the *ejidos* were drawn up even more equitably than in other provinces—twenty hectares apiece, no more, no less—the few land documents from this period which survive show much the same sorts of small-scale inequality in acreages as prevailed in Los Angeles a century before! Well, but after all, these were *colonias,* not *ejidos.* The official was inclined to credit human error, remarking to me: *Not all the land was divided at once. So what you're dealing with is land in the process of being divided up. So somebody probably thought he had twenty hectares, but it was really only seventeen.*

Two examples:* In 1947, Colonia Villarreal divides eight hundred hectares among eighteen persons, families or partnerships. There seem to be twenty-five lots in all.† So each lot averages thirty-two hectares; the per capita acreage for those eighteen landholders works out to forty-four and a half. Meanwhile, Colonia Zacatecas in its two divisions has assigned nearly twenty-seven thousand hectares to three hundred and fifty-two landholders, who use four hundred and seventeen lots in all. The average acreage per lot is nearly sixty-four hectares (not quite Roosevelt's hundred and sixty acres); per capita acreage is seventy-five and a half hectares.

What can be said? Yes, these inequalities may be locally significant; but compared to those within American Imperial, that hymn-singer of agrarian democracy, they are trifling.

In 1949, a young Congressman named Richard M. Nixon—who must have possessed extensive agricultural connections, for hadn't he proved to the world that Alger Hiss hid Communist secrets inside a pumpkin?—visits Imperial County, a place where, according to a regional geography from that period, *farming is characterized by highly commercialized large scale operations . . .* (Where did Wilber Clark's homestead go? I guess he couldn't produce things the way he used to.) *Two statements made by Nixon should prove popular with the people of Imperial Valley. Nixon declared he is against the 160-acre limitation of ownership of lands demanded by the bureau of reclamation,* one of several institutions which the *Brawley News* resolutely relegates to lowercase, *and that he is against the department of interior's grab for power.*

Imperial remains victorious in both respects, for now. Although the United States Supreme Court will uphold the limitation, eight to zero, in its famous *Ivanhoe* decision of 1958, the Court then immediately permits the federal government to exempt certain water projects; and Chairman Clinton P. Anderson of the Subcommittee on Irrigation and Reclamation to the Committee on Interior and Insular Affairs reminds us all: *It should be made clear to every Member of the Senate that, in many areas, 160 acres will not produce enough to support a family under today's costs for machinery, transportation, and labor,* while Mr. Barrett (the Senator from

*More data may be found in the citation to this information.

†At this time most of the rural *colonias* sport only a handful of landholders, some of whom rent and some of whom own outright: Colonia Astorago has five families, Colonia Bravo ten; among the most populous of these islets are Colonia Chapultepeo at fifty-nine households, Colonia Silva at seventy-eight (on the average, they work around fifty hectares each) and, grandest of all, the below-mentioned Colonia Zacatecas at three hundred and fifty-two. Colonia Moctezuma is already substantial at forty-nine lots.

ZACATECAS (Continúa)

Núm.	Nombre:	Contrato.	Lote	Sup.	Cobrables	Inc.
328	Fco. Villavicencio	Aparc.	246-A	40.0		Ver Lote 237
329	Ramona Tánuri	"	246-B y 247	100.0	2100 –	
330	Julio Espinosa	"	251	110.0	2310 –	
331	David Gibson	"	253, 254 y 255	300.0	6300 –	
	ZACATECAS # 2.-					
332	Basilio y Elodio Angulo	"	1	100.0	10000 –	350270
333	Melitón Fuentes	"	2	31.0	2081 30	
334	Fco. Necochea	"	3	25.0	1171 79	
335	Juan Fuentes, Agustín Merín y Humberto Mayoral	"	4	160.0	Ver Lote 193 Zacatec	
336	Cristóbal Angulo	"	5	72.3	1512 75	
337	Salvador Farah	"	6	130.0	Ver Lotes 10 y 11	
338	Genaro Palacios	"	6-A	65.0		
339	Victoriano Angulo	"	7	25.0		
340	Pedro J. Aguirre y R. Hashem.	"	8 y 9	198.876	12316.79	
341	Raul Zenteno y S. Farah	"	10 y 11	222.345	40900 – ?	240400 05 ?
342	Ramón y Manuel Rubio	"	12	106.7373	10,700.–	169196 53
343	Arturo P. Noriega	"	13	130.4031		Ver Lotes 178
344	Carmen Z. de Farah	"	14	57.26		Ver Lotes 10 y 11
345	Fco. Villavicencio	"	15	159.173		Ver Lote 237
346	Leopoldo Verdugo	"	16	28.593		Ver Lote 237-B
347	Leopoldo Verdugo y Ss.	"	17,18 y 19	330.4063		
348	Lee Ying Kee y Ss.	"	21,22,23,24 y 25	494.535	18085.26	
349	Adalberto Walter Meade	"	26 y 27	200.0		
350	Federico Sánchez y J. Aviña	"	30,31,32,33 y 34	451.146	3481.47	
351	Lee Kee	"	28,28-A,29,35,36, 37 y 38.-	650.0		
352	Cesáreo Hernández	"	39 y 40	200.0	4200 –	

Page from a list of landholders and renters in Colonia Zacatecas, 1947

Wyoming) adds his mite: *I say to the Senator from New Mexico now, as I have said to him privately, that I am hopeful his subcommittee will report the bill which will authorize a limitation higher than 160 acres for the Seedskadee project in my State.* So Imperial remains in step with her times; who could be more American than Imperial?

In fact, how huge *are* Imperial County's parcels? The regional geography just quoted from this period sees five thousand farms of a mere hundred acres each, tended by their *Mexicans, Orientals, Negroes, and migrant Caucasians under the direction of Caucasian foremen.* The place also had room for Harold Hunt's eight-hundred-acre ranch near Holtville. Brahman blood survives hot climates, so a three-eighths Brahman X five-eighths Charollais was his choice cow. He had factory production so well worked out that his pastures carried two thousand pounds of beef per acre!

(By the way, if a pound of beef needs twenty-five hundred gallons of water, then each of Mr. Hunt's acres will require five million gallons of water to achieve its quota; his ranch therefore must drink four trillion gallons.)

In 1962, the Coachella Valley was apparently complying with the hundred-and-sixty-acre limit, but not the Imperial Valley. Steven H. Elmore of Brawley owned thousands of acres.

Far from fulfilling William Smythe's breathless promise that irrigation agriculture would build a bulwark of middle-class democracy, the Imperial Valley became instead one of the most feudal landscapes in North America. These words appear in a book called *Salt Dreams,* which asserts that average farm size in this area continually increased from the very beginning—this we have seen to be the case—and that in 1990 one in four Imperial County residents was officially classified as poor, which, alas, is also all too true. *If one includes in such a calculation the circumstances of approximately eight hundred thousand farmworkers who live in greater Mexicali but work seasonally in Imperial Valley, the gap between rich and poor grows even broader.*

Such emphatic precision raises my suspicions—for who can even agree what constitutes a farm, let alone how to measure its size? For instance, in 1974, the number of farms in California was sixty-seven thousand, six hundred seventy-four by the 1974 definition, seventy-three thousand, nine hundred fifty-five by the 1959 definition.

Between 1969 and 1974, California's total farm acreage decreased by four point six percent, while the average farm size increased from four hundred fifty-four to four hundred ninety-three acres. Since two-thirds of all California farms remained under a hundred acres in 1974, there must have been a few farms of nearly Chandleresque magnitude. This shows how useless, even treacherous, an average can be—a point which I will soon be compelled to make again. Nonetheless, since mathematical fanciness will only increase my conclusion's self-doubt, let us proceed cautiously ahead, swiping at all obstacles with the Census Bureau's 1974 definition of a farm.

Between 1940, when Hemingway's hero Robert Jordan promised us that *most land is owned by those who farm it,* and 1974, the number of farms in California decreased by nearly half, and the average acreage almost doubled.

Now, what about American Imperial, or at least Imperial County?

When last we looked in upon the place from this perspective, in 1940–50, the numbers indicated that average farm size was growing less than California's generally. In 1940 it was a hundred-odd acres.* In 1974 that was no longer the case; by the end of the century, hundred-acre Imperial farms would be positively quaint.

FARMS IN CALIFORNIA AND VARIOUS COUNTIES, 1969–74

	Number of Farms				
Year	*Imperial*	*Riverside*	*San Diego*	*Los Angeles*	*CALIFORNIA*
1969	831	2,170	2,609	11,916	62,148
1974	771	2,333	3,829	797	67,674

Sources: Census Bureau (1974), for both 1969 and 1974.

By 1974, the average farm acreages of those counties were: Imperial, six hundred sixty-six (down thirteen from 1969); Riverside, two hundred forty; San Diego, a hundred and seventy-nine; Los Angeles, two hundred and twenty-three.

Imperial County reported eight hundred and ninety-six *farm operators* in 1969 (do you think Wilber Clark would have been considered one of those?); in 1974 there were seven hundred and seventy-one. (You may remember that there were forty-five hundred separate farms in 1950.) Total land in farms decreased during that short interval from six hundred and eight thousand to five hundred and thirteen thousand acres,† although the acreage of actual harvested cropland remained about the same.

In 1974, Imperial County's farm operators were burdened with a much higher average debt than their counterparts in the other counties. I wonder what the solution might be? Expand acreage, I suppose.

(Meanwhile, in 1976, hungry peasants from Sonora seized thousands of acres from eight hundred rich families. President Echeverría backed them up, then bestowed on them a quarter of a million acres more. Who was appeased? Landowners and capitalists were appalled; leftists sneered that it was only theater. People from this area, and from Jalisco and many other places south of Mexican Imperial, migrated in increasing multitudes to the border, forming *colonias* where they could and squatting otherwise.)

*Above, "Farm Size (1910–1944)," p. 568.

†In 1969, 22½% of Imperial County was farmland; by 1974, it was 18.9%.

In 1979, Paul S. Taylor took out a sheet of yellow paper and once more propounded his ancient question:

*Is it "unfair" to require residents of Imperial Valley to observe reclamation law?**

1. *Large landowners using the slogan "Call for Fairness" are appealing to Congress "to continue to exclude Imperial Valley from any acreage limitation on the land we own. We are asking this country to keep its promises to its citizens."*

In 1980, the Supreme Court answered Taylor at last, and overturned the hundred-and-sixty-acre limitation.

In 1982, only a hundred and fifty of Imperial County's eight hundred and thirty-three farms occupied a thousand acres or more; but in 1993, the Bass brothers began to buy land in the county. Three years later they owned forty-two thousand acres—almost ten percent of the Imperial Valley.

In 2002, the United States Department of Agriculture prepared a county summary. The average size of a farm in Imperial County was now nine hundred and fifty-seven acres. The median size was four hundred and two acres. A hundred and fifty-eight of the county's five hundred and thirty-seven farms were a thousand acres or more. Three hundred and seventy-one farms grossed a hundred thousand dollars or more.

One morning in Calexico when I asked the farmworker and occasional foreman Celestino Rivas, aged sixty-two, whether he thought Imperial County was rich or poor, he laughed contemptuously and said: It's too rich! They call the ranchers here *the millionaires*! Right here, the farmers, when they sell their crops, they sell at a high price. When the season jumps to Bakersfield, *the millionaires* have sold to Bakersfield already . . .

He named a grower in El Centro with whom he had had dealings, and said: He's like all the Americans: *I'm out of money!* A person who plants twenty-five hundred acres of broccoli . . .

*On 24 February 1933, Interior Secretary Ray Lyman Wilbur had informed the Imperial Irrigation District that the limitation would not apply to Imperial and Coachella. In 1945, Interior Solicitor Fowler Harper repudiated that good news, at least for Coachella. A subsequent Interior Secretary, J. A. Krug, in Taylor's description "left the situation as he found it. He stood by the Ickes decision to apply the law to Coachella Valley" but not Imperial although the latter "action might now be subject to valid question." In 1957, Solicitor General J. Lee Rankin arrived at Harper's opinion and said: "The limitations of the reclamation law upon the quantity of privately owned lands which might receive irrigation water under the All-American Canal are applicable in the Imperial Valley . . ." In 1964, Solicitor Frank J. Barry invalidated the old Wilbur ruling, noting that "long practice, especially long practice of neglect, cannot make legal that which was initially illegal."

FARM SIZE IN SELECTED CALIFORNIA COUNTIES, 2002

For purposes of comparison, the Reclamation Act of 1902 fixed a 160-acre homestead limit, and allowed 320 acres for a married couple. By 1918 the homestead limit had been adjusted to 320 acres for an arid homestead, and to 640 acres for cattle lands without a watering hole.

		Acreage	
	Number of Farms	*Average Acreage*	*Median Acreage*
California	**79,631**	**346**	**35**
Counties in the entity which I call Imperial, and their rivals			
Imperial	537 (41)[a]	957 (7)	402 (1)
Riverside	3,186 (5)	180 (40)	10 (53)
San Diego	5,255 (3)	78 (54)	5 (tied for 54)
Los Angeles	1,543 (15)	72 (55)	5 (tied for 54)
Highest-ranking other counties in chosen categories			
Fresno	6,281 (1)		
Inyo	2,668 (1)		
Modoc	400 (2)		

[a]The number in parentheses after each entry indicates the county's rank for that datum. For instance, the "(1)" following Imperial County's median acreage value shows that it has the highest median acreage of any of the state's 58 counties.

Source: USDA, National Agricultural Statistics Service: 2002 Census of Agriculture, County Data (accessed online, 4/4/07).

And Lupe Vásquez nodded, his eyes glittering with rage.

In 2002, Imperial County's total farm acreage was 514,101—a less than seven percent decrease since 1954. But the county retained only a third as many farms.

As for Mexican Imperial, how much of that was being leased by Northsiders? God knows. I remember for instance Ejido Morelos, where they told me: *All of this is rented, mostly by Americans.* (José López from Jalisco, Mexico, 2003: *They grow a lot of crops here. I've heard there's a lot of American companies that come here to pay cheaper wages.*)

In 2006 I asked Kay Brockman Bishop whether to her knowledge any family farms still existed in the valley, and she replied: But they're still around!—She and her husband named several names, most of which I omit here.—Some of the farms have gotten huge, she continued, but the boys all farm with Dad. The Priest boys, some still work just like Dad did. Cute little kids. Then there's Joe Wilson, who is probably sixty-seven, sixty-eight, something like that. He rents most of the ground on our ranch. His son who is forty-two or forty-three did most of the farming for him. Now he's working another farm and so his Dad now has to hire everything. But he definitely learned from his Dad; I know so many people who farmed under their Dad . . .

Was it ever a hundred and sixty acres here?

It was always bigger farming here than that. It was harder to grow everything you need all year round. It was always a business, you'd say. I think it has to be.

Then she said: If you think Las Vegas has gamblers, try those vegetable guys.—She named a man and said: He went up and down just as far as you could go . . .

Chapter 134

WE NOW WORRY ABOUT THE SALE OF THE FRUIT COCKTAIL IN EUROPE

(1948–2003)

The concept of progress acts as a protective mechanism to shield us from the terrors of the future.

—Frank Herbert, 1965

And so American agriculture had truly won the victory. As for California (not to mention Imperial), she had beaten many competitors. Do you remember what Judge Farr, dead now these eighty-five years, wrote in his history? *The nights are always cool, affording restful sleep, while the sleeper dreams of his rapidly ripening fruit and their early arrival in the markets to catch the top prices ahead of other competitors in less favorable regions.* His dream came to pass. And Imperial's fruit went on ripening, summer and winter. Imperial seized the day and perfumed the night with grapefruit blossoms.

Moreover, once that rapidly ripening fruit had entered the narrow zone between green hardness and bruisable softness, picking it had never been easier! In that midpoint year of the twentieth century, a U.S. Department of Agriculture article entitled "Science in the Agriculture of Tomorrow" boasted that in 1945 one *farm worker* (I guess the word *farmer* was no longer in fashion) *produced twice as much as did one farm worker 50 years ago.* That was on page one. Page two admitted: *Surpluses and how to dispose of them with a minimum of loss will always constitute a problem.* But please! Let the sleeper dream!

At the beginning of 1975, the California Freestone Peach Association reported that it had just had *the kind of year farmers pray for, with a good crop and a realistic price.* In 2003 an editorial in *The Sacramento Bee* explained that canned California peaches were falling out of favor, because Americans now preferred fresh Chilean grapes and other goodies. That was why *California peach farmers are intentionally shaking their trees with giant machines so that 14.5 million tons—yes, tons—of the fruit intended for canneries will instead fall to the ground and simply rot . . .* But it was not all bad news for the entity called Imperial, because *on the demand side, consumers in the winter increasingly are opting for fresh fruit available from the Imperial Valley, Mexico, Chile and other countries.*

Imperial County's growing season lasted just about three hundred and sixty-five days a year, to be sure, but why should big grocery stores care about that? If it wasn't summer in Oregon, it might be summer in Peru. You can't produce things the way you used to.

In 1948, California pears took in a hundred and twenty dollars a ton. A year later, they earned only thirty dollars a ton. The *California Farmer* advised: *It behooves every grower to produce a* moderate *quantity of top quality fruit in 1975.* A few pages later came this item: *We now worry about the sale of the fruit cocktail in Europe.*

Chapter 135

THE WATER FARMERS

(1951–2003)

> In the first place, we might look into the American's greed for gold. A German observes immediately that the American does not prize his possessions much unless he has worked for them himself; of this there are innumerable proofs, in spite of opposite appearances on the surface.
>
> —Hugo Münsterberg, 1904

And if *you can't produce things the way you used to,* can we blame a farmer for getting out of the farming game? If he buys water cheap at government rates and sells his lettuce to Los Angeles for whatever the market will bear, we fondly say: *He made a success through his own efforts.* We say: *He sold out at a fancy price.* If he buys water cheap and sells to Los Angeles for whatever the market will bear nothing but that water itself, shouldn't we say the same? Some people don't like it. *There's a lot of crying-in-your-beer stuff going on.*

I don't have a lot of trouble with it, said Alice Woodside. I do think it's a shame that farmers can structure the sale of the water rights. But a big farmer that buys something and works it, I don't have any problem with it. Brockman, now, he never did anything that was not honest and aboveboard.

The American does not prize his possessions much unless he has worked for them himself. Do the water farmers truly work for their possessions themselves, or should we regard these people as would a Marxist—namely, as parasites, who do nothing but buy water cheap and sell it at a higher price, adding no actual value to it? A water farmer would argue that what he adds is the service of moving it from here to there. Khun Sa, the "Opium King" of Burma, once reminded me with a bitter smile that he wasn't putting a pistol to anybody's head; people bought his heroin because they chose to. For their part, the water farmers never told the good citizens of San Diego: Buy our water, or else!—Quite the contrary; San Diego *needed* the water.

In 1959, eight point three percent of American farms happen to be irrigated. In California, that figure becomes seventy-four point seven percent. In Imperial County, unless we count hypothetical range-cattle operations on the edge of a river, it's got to be a hundred percent. Won't Imperial's farms always need that water?

But in 1960–61, San Diego receives the lowest rainfall on record: three and a half inches. (The high occurred in 1883–84: twenty-six inches.) Water farmers, take note! "Moisture Means Millions." Meanwhile, crop prices ride up and down as usual. Thus the old story: The more successfully farmers master their lands, which is to say the more they produce, the worse they accordingly devalue their produce. Rousseau thought it *easy to see, from the very nature of agriculture, that it must be the least lucrative of the arts; for, its produce being the most universally necessary, the price must be proportionate to the abilities of the very poorest of mankind.* The farmers had thought to control the prices they got by limiting production; but agriculture resists Sovietization; therefore, whatever we do over here in Imperial they can undo over there in Florida.

Water, however, is different.

Do you remember what was supposed to happen? I invoke the prophecy of Mr. Robert Hays, *circa* 1930: *As the increasing population of the seacoast cities in California encroaches annually upon the adjacent lands, Imperial Valley, with its assured supply of Colorado River water, its perpetual sunshine, its twelve months' growing season, its perennially green fields, will be called upon more insistently to feed hungry mouths. She will respond. In so doing, wealth will come to her.*

The cities are encroaching, all right. In 1967, Paul S. Taylor, who we've encountered before in these pages, reminds the National Commission on Urban Projects that *what is agricultural land today is urban land tomorrow. It's becoming urbanized at about the rate of three to four hundred acres per day.* Well, doesn't scarcity translate into value? As the decades pass, won't Imperial be sitting prettier and prettier? *We need have no fear that our lands will not become better and better as the years go by.*

And haven't they? According to that most unbiased of sources, the El Centro Chamber of Commerce, in 1970, Imperial County ranks fifth in agricultural production among all American counties, and first for the number of pen-fed cattle.

But wasn't Imperial County supposed to sew up the early lettuce market? In 1974, a good mid-range year of our "dissolutions" epoch, we find that Imperial comprises a respectable eighteen percent of California's three hundred and thirty-three head lettuce farms, and nearly twenty-nine percent of the state's acreage for that crop—but against Imperial's not quite forty thousand acres, one must set Monterey's more than sixty thousand. For romaine and other lettuce, Imperial makes a still duller showing—better than San Diego and Riverside, to be sure, while Los Angeles cannot muster up any recorded lettucescapes at all; but didn't the boomers of 1922 insist that Imperial County had become America's number-one lettuce producer?

What about her other signature crop, cantaloupes?—About the same.

Remembering my friend Lupe Vásquez, who has passed so much of his life in harvesting Imperial County broccoli, I am shocked to find that in that department also Imperial's way behind Monterey—nine hundred nineteen *versus* eighteen thousand six hundred acres.

Imperial's showing amongst the great champions of California asparagus is likewise poor in 1974.

In 1971, the Irvine Company, based in Santa Ana, owns five hundred and twenty-five acres of asparagus in the Imperial Valley and another thousand and fifty acres of the same crop in Orange County (four hundred and twenty-five acres *direct farmed* and the rest leased). The Irvine Company complains about a weed problem everywhere. If they could sell their water allotment for more than they sell their asparagus, why wouldn't they become water farmers?

In 2003, a resident of Holtville writes in to the newspaper: *The crops in the Valley are only 1/27 of the total farm output in the state. I have heard the Valley feeds the world. What a joke—maybe if you eat Sudan grass or alfalfa.**

In that case, why shouldn't Imperial County feed thirsty mouths instead of hungry mouths? Especially since **WATER IS HERE**?

In 1947, a farmer in Coachella named Ray Heckman† wants a marketing order *to provide for an even flow of corn into the Los Angeles market.* In 1958, Norman Ward, sales manager for Farley Fruit in El Centro, informs a meeting at the Barbara Worth Hotel that he is proud to have achieved *a more orderly flow of melons to the consuming public.* In 1967, a grape farmer who identifies himself only as King *(I'm . . . a small grower—real small)* stands up at a public hearing in Coachella to express a pretty metaphor: Grapes are water! He speaks of *a pipeline of grapes that can go to market . . . It's a good deal like a district water supply which has to be flowed out in advance.*

So why not flow out everything else, too? Why not flow out the water itself? (So many times in Imperial I have seen a field whose sole production seems to be the white waterspouts elongating and crisscrossing at a great height, bowing toward one another like grass-heads in changing winds; they issue from silver pipes in the raw brown soil; they grow up and up, eternally, bearing rainbows. Isn't this a water farm?) I've never been cheated out of a dollar in my life, and if I can get more for my water than for my grapes, why should I grow grapes at all? "Moisture Means

*Kay Brockman Bishop explained: "Sudan, we grow a lot of it, because the Orient needs a backhaul for all their computers that come this way. And Texas is becoming a great big market for our Bermuda grass because they just can't grow it down there. Horses like it and it's good for them. The truck driver says: I can't get enough of it to haul."

†We met him briefly in "The Braceros," p. 664.

Millions." Of course, if I sell every last acre-foot of water that belongs to me, then my piece of Imperial will just have to dry up. **THE DESERT REAPPEARS**.

THE DESERT DISAPPEARS. In celebration of that fact, here come two grinning girls past *FRESH MEATS*; in their matching skirts they march down the center of the street and support the banner of our Imperial Tigers. In material advantages they are very well supplied. (This photograph, which seems to have been taken in the early 1960s, must depict the town of Imperial.) Yes, it's a parade! At the head of a marching band's quintuple uniformed columns, a confident, pretty girl in white shorts raises her right arm up so high that her outspread hand almost occludes the sign **LIQUORS** which lurks between the two American flags. Citizens watch, some of them shaded by the arch of the snack shop (***Drink Coca Cola***). If **THE DESERT REAPPEARS**, all the way, I mean, then the Imperial Tigers will perish of thirst; the water farmers will stay in Los Angeles or San Diego, getting rich; meanwhile, only dust devils will march in our small-town parades.

EXCERPT FROM A REPORT

1. Imperial is TOO HOT. In the summer, it's too hot for people, too hot for dairy cows to produce milk, and too hot for feeder cattle to gain weight. With average soil temperatures peaking near 106 degrees, it's too hot for a wide variety of temperate-climate plants (obviously, desert and oasis plants will do just fine). Even in those cases where Imperial's climate gives it a comparative advantage (winter melons, numerous vegetable crops, alfalfa thanks to irrigation), being too hot for people is a big problem: labor productivity is lower, available labor pool is smaller, the list goes on and on. Despite endless promotion of itself from the 1900s forward, ultimately Imperial's growth will be limited by its high heat and its high humidity (a nasty side effect of being below sea level). Absent climate change, it's hard to see how Imperial will suddenly "take off", especially compared to the rest of Southern California.
2. Imperial was over-promoted by its boosters. This is true for many agricultural communities, but seldom have the promoters been more enamored of their own PR. When a region is virtually uninhabitable for 3 months of the year and everyone who can afford to flees, it's hard to see how you maintain your stable base for economic growth. Imperial is that rare California county that suffered a population *decline* in the 1930s and virtually

no growth in the 1940s. This is more like counties in Texas, Oklahoma, and Kansas, than California, and this is despite the fact that Imperial had a stable agricultural water supply. Of course, part of this was undoubtedly simple in-migration to coastal urban areas, but it's a stunning fact nonetheless: people who moved there based on the press releases actually *left*.

3. The sturdy, independent, agriculturist of Rousseau never really existed in Imperial. A startlingly high proportion of farmers even in the 1920s were tenants, and water rights established a caste system that exists to this day. To the extent that tenant farmers gave up and moved to LA, this is probably a good thing.
4. The remaining sturdy, landowning farmers were too conservative (small-c) in their adoption of new farming practices and crops. Dairy farming died a slow, agonizing death in Imperial, and livestock farming is likely to remain a marginal contributor to profitability (most likely via boom and bust cycles) even as it maintains its position as a significant (though no longer major) contributor to the ag economy. It may also be that the bankers were too slow to lend to these farmers (this is a common failing of rural banking) to allow them to invest in new crops and growing methods, so it might be more fair to say that the region suffered (suffers?) from the lack of a clear vision of Imperial's comparative advantages and how best to exploit them for permanent, sustainable, agricultural advantage.
5. This leads to a fairly direct materialist explanation for water farming. Simply put, if I can't make money anymore (or can't afford to continue slowly losing money) raising dairy cows or feeder cattle, or wheat, or barley, or milo (only feeder cattle look viable from recent statistics), and I have to learn to raise a new crop and borrow lots of money for the equipment to raise it, why shouldn't I just take money for my water allocation? All these other things are risky and expensive, while with no investment whatsoever, I can earn an assured return on something I own (water rights). Lots of farmers would resist this, since it defies the values they were raised with and contradicts their general experience of the world, but enough years of barely scraping by farming the same things, combined

with a lack of capital to learn how to do something new and risky, and water farming looks like a way to keep from losing what you've got, at least financially.

6. Sustainable agriculture with irrigation is a very tricky thing to accomplish, and very few civilizations have succeeded in doing so (one could argue that none have, given Egypt's experience with the Aswan dam). Soil salination, erosion, invasive pests, and a variety of environmental ills are likely consequences of industrial-scale irrigation methods. I feel bad for the people faced with these choices, but we shouldn't rule out the possibility that in the long run decreased reliance on flood irrigation methods might be better for the Imperial Valley environment.

So why not be a water farmer?

I remember one old man in El Centro saying to another as he prepared to pay for coffee with a roll of dimes: One time when I was still working at the bank, I got two rolls of *silver* dimes; every dime in every roll was a genuine *silver* dime! And the way he expressed his reverence for rarity and purity, perhaps even for silveriness, was sweet to me, because back in the old days, when all dimes were silver, the value of a dime was exactly ten cents, but now a silver dime was a concretion of the good old days; far more precious than a silver ingot of equivalent weight, it epitomized Imperial's tarnished glamour.

And closing my eyes I can almost see, instead of silver drops of water springing out of those rainbirds over the brown fields, silver dimes jetting up to heaven.

Chapter 136

COACHELLA

(1975)

Welcome to the Coachella Valley. Desert scrub is the dominant habitat here, but the influences of nearby agriculture, urbanization and natural and ornamental oases add to the richness of the avifauna.

—Coachella Valley Audubon Society, 1983

What caused Imperial to go wrong?—Well, nothing's wrong in Coachella! *The wildest dreams of men in the first 40 years of this century have been exceeded. The advent of Colorado River water reduced the demand on the underground basin making possible the development of the area above Point Happy into what has become America's "Golf Capital."* Those words were published in 1968.

At the beginning of the 1940s, Coachella was irrigating sixteen thousand acres. By the end of the sixties, over sixty-six thousand acres had come into production. **WATER IS HERE**, and so it is only natural that as we peer down upon this whirling world in the year 1975, Coachella Valley leads Riverside County in agricultural income, ringing in $74,657,000! *This 1973 aerial view, looking south from Bermuda Dunes Airport toward La Quinta, shows vividly how much open desert has disappeared in the past 27 years.* We need have no fear that our lands will not become better and better as the years go by.

Chapter 137

THE IMPERIAL IDEA

(1950–2000)

He was fast becoming that most tragic yet often sublime sight, a man who had survived, not only his own time, but the ideas and ideals of it.

—Helen Hunt Jackson, 1884

"AND NOT SEE A NEIGHBOR'S LIGHT"

I happened to be down in Calexico for my thirtieth class reunion, said Alice Woodside, and I was really saddened and horrified. They've led hard lives. The signs of wear and tear were really there. You know, bad diets . . .

By 1975, in spite of her nine-passenger Imperial Airlines Queenaires and her yellow Air West F-27s, the Imperial Idea was similarly evincing a few wrinkles. By 1985, although a gazetteer could still say of the Imperial Valley: *Principal economic base: market gardens, cotton, sugar beets, alfalfa, gypsum quarries,* the Imperial Idea was going to hell.

Do you remember the Imperial Idea? My homestead is my castle, which I have greatly improved through my own efforts. I have never been cheated out of a dollar in my life. Anytime I'm ready, not before, not after, I'll sell out at a fancy price.

The Imperial Idea was going to hell, but I'll go to hell in my own way. I'll call that dirt-ridge over there Salvation Mountain, and I'll paint it whatever color I want to. If you don't like it, go paint your own dirt-ridge; just don't run me off of mine. I pledge allegiance to the flag, because America is the land of the free, and I'm free.

But they're starting to close in on me a trifle. I don't like the fact that the Agricultural Commissioner can tell me to destroy my bees. I distrust his power to issue a **STOP SALE** order against me for whatever reason, and even to prosecute me if I try to get around him.

I'm not saying he has no reason to do as he does. The Oriental fruit fly is coming. The citrus black fly and the citrus white fly are on the way. The Mexican fruit fly's out to get me. Peach mosaic and olive scale are already in the state. But don't I have my own reasons to do what I do?

I especially dislike being told what I can and cannot grow on my own farm.

At a meeting in El Centro, Richard Campbell, who's been for fourteen years the manager for William B. Hubbard in El Centro ("and they have some operations in Arizona") complains about the fundamental concept of a marketing order that *to put it in after the man has planted and grown his crop, then you are taking something away from him.* He elaborates: *And when they can specify that, and the State of California has the authority to do that* [and] *they can enforce this by legal machinery which can put a man in jail if he doesn't do it, then I say that you are jeopardizing his rights.* In utter Imperial style he declaims, and my heart sincerely goes out to him: *I believe that even if one single individual handler, grower, farmer, or what have you here in this business be saddled at this time with this marketing order that he would have a perfect right to ignore the provisions of it in this particular season and following.*

What else defines Richard Campbell? *I was opposed to FDR when I was a kid and I am still opposed to him, even though he is not here any more.*

This confession is significant, because FDR was America's Cárdenas. He was a friend to the poor and an enemy to monopolists, whose hatred he explicitly welcomed. Were William B. Hubbard a sufficiently powerful company, Roosevelt would have been against them, and therefore against Richard Campbell. (Paul S. Taylor bitterly defines the Imperial Idea, beginning with the valley's rescue from the Salton Sea accident and continuing with the All-American Canal: *Public assistance came to be highly valued, provided that it came free of public control.*) It may well be (which I possess no evidence to believe) that Richard Campbell pushes his Mexican field workers a trifle. In the 1960s and '70s, two U.S. Supreme Court decisions would ensure that an employer's right to control property could no longer keep agents of employee collective bargaining off the property. That laudable outcome certainly goes against the Imperial Idea, and in this context it is all too easy to imagine Richard Campbell uttering thunderations about his outraged rights. But what if (which I also possess no evidence to believe) Richard Campbell had been simply a struggling loner who refused to believe in handouts? *He made a success through his own efforts.*

There is a moment in John Gardner's elegiac *Nickel Mountain* (published 1973, set two decades earlier) when state troopers begin to question a fanatical Jehovah's Witness who is suspected of having burned down his own home. The interrogation, like the novel itself, takes place in the diner owned by fat, slobbery, Christlike Henry Soames, because it is Henry who shelters the man; and here I should mention that the Nickel Mountain, which looms somewhere in the forests of the Catskills, is nearly as isolated as Imperial itself. What now happens engages us with two peculiarities. The first is that the questioning goes on right at Henry's counter. Whenever I myself get detained by Homeland Security—even in Imperial County, I'm sad to say—they keep me in one of their nasty little rooms. The second odd thing is that when the troopers first show up, *Henry wouldn't hear of their talking to Simon until the following day, after he'd rested a little and pulled himself together.* Now, Simon is not a pleasant man. He's used violence against his children whenever they've "sinned." But Henry intercedes for him with his usual charity, and when the officers try to resume the questioning, Henry's friend George tells them to cut it out, and they do. Something tells me that life doesn't play out like that anymore.

Another novel from the same period, *Vandenberg,* follows its eponymous protagonist through a fatal collision with authority. In those years, thrillers and science-fiction tales about Soviet-occupied America were as ubiquitous as cantaloupes in Imperial, not only because we feared the unknown Slavic other, and the possibility of nuclear extinction which our politics and theirs mutually symbolized, but also because the hive mentality which we projected, with some justification, onto Communism had much to do with what was happening in our own cities and towns. The frontier officially closed back in Wilber Clark's day; and the Agricultural Commissioner had arrived. In theory he was one of us, appointed for us, and it is the genius of *Vandenberg* to keep Northside's Soviet puppetmasters mostly between the lines. American functionaries do their work for them; ordinary citizens adjust. Unfortunately for Vandenberg, he exemplifies the Imperial Idea, which he describes as follows: *Heavy-handedly I went after one of the last options around: the privilege to make mistakes, to foul up one's life-style beyond repair.* This is something that Leonard might have said (no doubt with sly humility) about Salvation Mountain. Henry Soames for his part chose to gorge himself to death, knowing quite well what he was doing. In his day, one's friends, not to mention the state troopers, respected a man's choices; and Vandenberg recalls: *As long as I made even a token show of following society's rules, I was left alone . . .* Well, well; Henry dropped dead, and Richard Campbell lost the battle. *I think, very shortly, that somebody like me will be so out of tune, so out of place and out of grace, that death will be welcome.* When the inevitable occurs, and he gets sent to a reeducation camp, I glory in Vandenberg's secret psychiatric report, which could have been written about me: *Superficially, he shows some indication of cooperation, though making little effort to conceal deep-rooted distrust and resentment.*

The interrogator, a good American of the new type, hints that Vandenberg has failed to meet his social obligations. *With the ranch, we turned our backs on all that,* Vandenberg explains, and a host of Imperial characters come rushing into my mind. *People thought we were crazy for buying ninety acres of unimproved grazing land, a wrecked house, no water, no well, no electricity.* I remember sitting beside Kay Brockman Bishop on her back patio on the edge of Calexico, gazing across her ranch at the sunset as she told me: This girlfriend of mine that lives down on the Donlevy ranch now, she took off, her husband had to work until Wednesday night, so she took the kids and they camped in the desert. I never did much of that with my Dad. We usually went fishing for marlin. Anything in the ocean. My Dad used to take us down into the Gulf . . .—Vandenberg again: *My house is on a hill, and at night I could look for miles in any direction and not see a neighbor's light.*

A gaunt, bearded man stands in a pumpkin field. The pumpkins are as immense as boulders. They go on and on, pale against the turmoil of the field; then the eye starts to make out other human figures, first the old man in the white shirt and dark vest who stands with his arms at his sides, holding his hat; he's between pumpkins; then the little boy in the grubby jacket who rests his tiny white hand on top of a pumpkin which comes up to his nose; I see two strapping men supporting a pumpkin in midair between them; from the look of it, it's as heavy as a bag of cement; then there are the two pretty, darkhaired ladies, one in an apron, the other in bloomers; each one sits on a big pumpkin, with a little pumpkin in her lap; each one stares off into some diagonal distance; far behind all these people (who without exception are Caucasian-looking) is a fence, then a shed and a tiny farmhouse.—Where are we? The land's too dark and moist for this reification of the Imperial Idea to have taken place in Imperial; the print bears no caption; the series (seven boxes at the California State Archives) is described simply thus: *Stock photographs, c. 1930–1970*. Once upon a time, the Imperial Idea was the California Idea; so, too, the American Dream; once upon a time, Emerson was right.

And then—what?

Nietzsche: *Nihilism . . . is the recognition of the long* waste *of strength, the agony of the "in vain" . . . being ashamed in front of oneself, as if one had* deceived *oneself all too long. This meaning could have been . . . the gradual approximation of a state of human happiness; or even the development toward a state of universal annihilation—any goal at least constitutes some meaning,* In other words, we need have no fear that our lands will not become better and better as the years go by. But it used to be up to me to make it better, and now it's up to the string-pullers who write market orders.

Once upon a time, which is to say from the late 1950s until some indefinite year or decade, Richard Brogan lived an Imperial life without undue annoyance from any neighbor's light.

I was bulletproof, he told me, and I wanted to go out and fight the world of crime. Yuma was forty years back in time. The Cucapah were still living in mud huts. Yuma hadn't divided; now it's two counties. My beat, there wasn't a soul out there, from the Mexican border to a stone cabin. We were granted a lot of authority, a lot of leeway to just work a case to fruition. By the time I was twenty-eight years old, I had worked homicide, sex crimes, child abuse, and I'd worked alone, very limited supervision, with the District Attorney's office to bring them to trial. The quickest and the saddest thing I ever had to deal with in law enforcement was a traffic accident in Yuma. A drunk driver hit a family. The parents got out and the kids burned up. The next day I was asked to come to deal with the autopsy room and I can remember seeing a couple of tiny burned hands and then I went home to my children. I was involved in a shooting here when two highway patrolmen were shot. I was the dispatcher. One was shot dead and the other kept wrestling the shooter for about two hours. He had a bullet in one lung. Shortly after that I was assaulted in jail and woke up in the hospital . . .

He told me these stories with what I took to be a deadpan pride in himself and his self-reliance in those times when *there wasn't a soul out there* and a cop might have to wrestle the man who'd shot him in the lung for two hours. He had lived the Imperial idea, and survived, so it is no wonder that he did not like interference. His views on César Chávez, when we get to them, will be quite consistent with this ethos. FDR and Cárdenas both would have sympathized with Chávez. Richard Brogan and Richard Campbell took the other side, because *when they can specify that,* and by *that* I mean anything whatsoever that outside authority can specify, including a minimum wage, *and they can enforce this by legal machinery which can put a man in jail if he doesn't do it, then I say that you are jeopardizing his rights.*

Perhaps *they* are not quite as evil as Vandenberg's would-be brainwashers. In 1965, the Imperial Valley receives $7,221,448 in federal agricultural subsidies, the number of recipients being two hundred and thirty-one. That's more than thirty-one grand apiece. But after we make due deductions for natural human greed and hypocrisy, there may remain some grounds for empathy with exponents of the weakening Imperial Idea.

"I JUST LIKE TO BE HERE"

Meanwhile, in Mexican Imperial, Cárdenas's undoing of the Chandler Syndicate—as attested by the document from 1949 in which Conrad C. Caldwell, representing the Colorado River Land Company, conveys to the señores Chi Chun Chan, Chiu Chon Yee, Yee Sue Chan and Alfredo Chang Fong a single parcel: lot number twenty in Villarreal, extent twenty hectares—has strengthened the Imperial Idea. Yes, those with smaller means or different agendas may buy their Imperial dream jointly; but does that make them any less enterprising than Wilber Clark? No doubt the bifurcation between competitive individualism and *ejidatarianismo* strains the Idea a trifle, but Southsiders are less burdened by grandiose expectations. They certainly say less about their rights.

(On the subject of rights, here is José López's codicil to the Imperial Idea: *What you have is what you are worth.* If he, too, could have owned a ranch, perhaps José could have been as proud as Vandenberg. But he did not, so he said: It's like this thing with the police. If I have a backpack and my clothes are dirty, and I haven't got an address to show, I've been taken in to jail for thirty-six hours, just for being poor. There's no food, no blanket, no heating, no air-conditioning, and it's filthy. Especially here in Mexico, you have to fight to survive. I've seen fights break out just for a piece of bread or a taco somebody got sent from outside. Then they want to kill each other. And then you have to defend yourself or they'll take you for a pussy. Me, I've always been left alone, 'cause I respect people and I won't let anybody just walk over me.)

In 2004, in Colonia Santo Niño, I met an employee of the State Commission of Public Services in Mexicali, a kind and hospitable man of late middle age who in true Imperial fashion declined to have his name printed in my book. When I asked him why he had chosen to live in this particular patch of sand, he replied: I don't really like the city, so I came out here. Too many people out there! I was the first person in the place.

Did it look the same as it does now but without houses?

Pointing to dirt, flatness, tires and rubbish, he said: That vacant lot out there, that's how it was.

And why did you choose this particular *colonia*?

Because I got tired of the noise, he said. I like solitude.

(Translation: *My house is on a hill, and at night I could look for miles in any direction and not see a neighbor's light.* So what if there was no hill?)

Who named the *colonia*?

The state government. They named it because of the Rancho Santo Niño, which has been there I don't know how long. I was transferred from Tijuana and the ranch was already here. I have been here for eighteen years. The people who were paying rent in Centro began to come here. And because of that it got big.

And did that disappoint you? Because there's not so much solitude now.

No. Because I'm right here on the edge it doesn't matter.

So the *colonia* began to grow. Then what happened?

Services. Water, light, electricity, telephone . . .

Did you build your house yourself?

Yes. *Sólo*. I learned how to do it when I was working in Costa Mesa, San Diego County. I did it in one month. I have been married here for four years. I met my wife right here, when I was four blocks away from where I am now. My wife lived two blocks away.

It's very calm here, he added. You can leave the door open.

What's your favorite thing to do here?

I like to be here alone, or with my wife, just the two of us. I just like to be here.

What's the future of this *colonia*? Skyscrapers?

I think so. It's happening little by little.

That makes you sad?

No, the opposite. Because in Centro I rented, and here this is mine.

Chapter 138

IT SEEMS LIKE THE MONEY IS BEING TAKEN BY SOMEBODY

(2003)

Lupe Vásquez was born in Newman, California, a Central Valley town whose exit sign I pass when riding Highway 5 between Los Angeles and Sacramento. I have never been to Newman, which is, of course, a hot, flat agricultural town. When Lupe came into the world (sometime in the 1950s, I believe), his father was picking melons.

He was raised in the Imperial Valley, in Heber. He met his wife while picking broccoli.

When I was about six years old, he said, up in the summer, we used to pick prunes, grapes, so we could make some money for clothes, shoes. My father taught us how to make our money for ourselves. It wasn't hard, it was *fun*! he cried, glaring at me.—We stayed in this camp without electricity. We had oil lamps. I hear there are still some places like that in San Diego, north county: Oceanside, Fallbrook, Escondido. The people stay in shacks in the bushes, and they pick strawberries, lemons . . .

Which crop is your favorite?

Well, none! They're all a bitch to pick. But the easiest I've done is corn, 'cause you don't have to cut it with a knife; you just break it off. The women pack it off in the machine. The broccoli is a bitch because you get wet. You have to wear rain equipment, and cloth gloves on the inside and rubber gloves on the outside. Plus, a lot of times you have *la perdida,* what they want from you: A lot of time. They want three loads. They don't care how long we work. I don't know how long, because I just work on the ground, cutting. We use a thin shredding blade, thin blade knife, the same you use to cut lettuce. It's dangerous because it's very sharp. There's incidents where people get drunk and they fight with the knife. When you come into Mexicali, don't carry it with you after work, because the cops will say it's a deadly weapon. I put it in my backpack where they can't see it. Anyway, it's only an *arma blanca,* a white weapon. It's not as dangerous as an explosive or a gun.

I've picked bell peppers and grapes up in Coachella. I'd say the conditions are better up there. They don't work you as hard. Over here it's hurry up, hurry up. The cooler wants two loads . . .

Cantaloupes, you just pick 'em up and off. There's a packing machine. The ones that come off the stem easy are ripe, and you see the color: The ones that are a little bit yellow are the ones that are ripe. But sometimes they want the ones that are not ripe, too, although that's not too common.

I think the Mexican labor started in 1910, 1915, he said then. That's when they built the All-American Canal. That's when they were selling the acres, ten cents an acre. I don't know why Mexicans didn't buy.

Why are Mexicans often so poor?

Because there's exploitation. Those contractors, the farmers pay them fourteen dollars and they pay the workers six dollars and seventy-five cents. That money, where does it go? It seems to me like somebody's taking the money. This valley produces *everything.* I've even heard of *mangoes.* It seems like the money is being taken by somebody.

Chapter 139

CHÁVEZ'S GRAPES

(1962–2006)

So we went and stood tall outside the vineyards where we had stooped for years.

—Proclamation of the Delano Grape Workers, 1969

Once upon a time, Jim Holcomb still lived at Dead Man's Hole, right on the edge of the Great Warner Ranch where Highway 79 crossed the cattleguard. He used to prove his mettle by shooting at the merchandise at "Bob" Gun's saloon and store, after which he'd pay the bill. He arrested a Mexican fugitive at gunpoint and turned him over to the sheriff. Who knows exactly when these feats of Imperial valor took place? *Old-Timers of Southeastern California*, published in 1967, replies: *No doubt those were the good old days before we had Civil Rights Marches, riots, and the many other situations of which we find ourselves complaining so much of the time today.*

But you and I remember that even in those good old days, the Wobblies were singing:

They'll all be affrighted, when we stand united
And carry that Red, Red Card.*

Never mind those freaks—the good old days remain! In 1975, I read in my *California Farmer* that **INDEPENDENT GROWERS KEEP WORKERS HAPPY** in Salinas.

"I WILL *NOT* FOLLOW IN MY MOTHER'S FOOTSTEPS"

How happy might workers feel within the entity I call Imperial?—Ecstatic, no doubt. In proof, I invite you to read the *California Farmer*, which reassures our pub-

*This may be considered proof of their proletarian internationalism. But the Wobblies had another song: "And Scissor Bill, he says, 'This country must be freed / From Niggers, Japs and Dutchmen and the gol durn Swede.'"

lic that the United Farm Workers' lemon strike in Yuma drags on *without any notable success.* Moreover, the UFW has fallen out with the Confederation of Mexican Laborers! I can't help believing in people.

All over California, growers, shippers and authorities stand resolutely affrighted and united against the United Farm Workers!

In Delano, home of the dangerous militant César Chávez, there's now a reactivated South Central Farmers Committee and I pause to quote Mark Zainovich, Market Information Chairman of that organization: *We don't have time to propagandize as the United Farm Workers of America are doing. All we have to do is tell the truth . . .* In other words, **INDEPENDENT GROWERS KEEP WORKERS HAPPY**. Why wouldn't they be?

In Imperial County, a man is irrigating onions on Good Friday. He begins at six in the morning and his shift is supposed to last twenty-four hours. That night, winds eat away the levee, and, as the Agricultural Labor Relations Board hearing understates it, the man *had a very difficult night.* At six on Saturday morning, the foreman tells him to stay on the job a bit longer. At ten in the morning the foreman visits him again, still without anybody to replace him. The irrigator says that he is very tired, to which the foreman replies that if he sleeps he'll be fired. The irrigator repeats that he is tired. In that case, says the foreman, he can come back on Monday for his final paycheck.

Paul S. Taylor, 1973: *Among the results of delay by Mexican-Americans in deciding to accept and affirm American citizenship, has been prolonged civic inaction to protect their own self-interest. A dramatic example has been the survival—under very dubious legality—of concentrated ownership in Imperial Valley, California.*

In 2004, Edith Karpen looks back upon that time from her own point of view: *The farmers were the ones that got the Mercedeses and the ones like that. There was an emerging middle class. As the peon type became more educated and sophisticated, then the bilingual storekeepers and all came in. So starting in the sixties they started more bilingual speakers. Then, from being just very grateful for being included, they became very demanding.*

How demanding, exactly? Sometime in the late 1950s or early 1960s, a migrant child named Delmira Treviño promised herself: I will *not* follow in my mother's footsteps. I swear that I will *not* marry a man who has dirt under his fingernails, and who drags me from field to field.

César Chávez stood on the horizon.

HINT

Years later, people would still be scarred by the memories.

On this subject Richard Brogan advised me: You need to talk to people who are extremely intelligent, because all you get is emotion. Hell, they don't have a clue what hard work is all about. They don't work the fields.

APRICOTS

He was right. In a museum folder labeled "Apricots," which contains images of many things other than apricots, the first photograph depicts a space between many parallel beams to which a single line of lightbulbs is perpendicularly oriented. Beyond all this lie two railroad cars, one of which says **CENTRAL PACIFIC** and **EXPRESS**, while the other says **FRUIT**, for this zone has been consecrated to fruit! These ovoid globes of it as pale as onions, what are they? The folder says "Apricots," but . . .

Mexican-looking men in caps and brimmed hats stand along the long sorting troughs, which are rollered like the filing shelves of the County Recorder's office in El Centro (this allows the heavy death index ledgers to be more easily slid out); the men reach for the pale fruits with their dark hands; they seem as if they are concentrating each and every one on choosing the single apricot or whatever it is which will ensure their happiness; they look bemused and relaxed, yet grave; are they going slowly at the orders of *Hetzel the Photographer*, so that they won't be degraded into blurs; or does Imperial's heat require of them the dreamy care and slowness licensed to the inhabitants of other tropical regions? In Thailand I knew a woman who hated Caucasians; she particularly liked to tell the story of the German lady who sneered at how sluggishly southeast Asians worked; after a few days in Thailand this foreigner, trying to do as she would have done in Germany, overexerted herself and nearly died; after that, she learned to move slowly. In Imperial, where every shadow in every footprint is bordered by glaring light, campesinos and field workers must work with analogous caution. So they work longer to make their quota. (Lupe Vásquez: *They don't care how long we work.*)

Because I was studying this Hetzel photograph in an air-conditioned archive (anyhow, it wasn't hot outside that day, only ninety-two or -three), I remained free to imagine that its subjects were also cool, in which case their pondering and musing over perfect fruits might have been as pleasant as a woman's browsing through her jeweler's emeralds and rubies, each of which could be bought at a fancy price.

The pretty young Mexican-American intern, who from the look of her hands and long painted fingernails had passed few of her days in agricultural work, knew that those white fruits had to be apricots because they were in a folder labeled "Apricots."—Oh, those are definitely onions, said the archivist, who actually knew something.

I knew that I needed never to forget how little *we* know about *them* (and that in the *we* I include the Mexican-American intern, and in the *them* I include Lupe Vásquez and also José López from Jalisco), and I knew that *they* knew almost as little about us, since they saw us mainly in our weakness, luxury and arrogance, judging us accordingly; moreover, to varying degrees their powers of observation must have been damaged by the narrowness, ignorance and fatigue of a consciousness constrained to work in the fields or sleep in the street; as opposed to our shallow broadness, our undertired ennui, and, above all, the ignorance on our part of specifics, especially of that most specific thing of all, *pain*.

On that subject, here is one Imperial field worker's fate: *Until his termination, he missed only six months of work due to a work-related injury suffered when he fell into an irrigation ditch filled with toxic pesticides.* He had made the mistake of telling his foreman that he supported the United Farm Workers. They canned him the day before the election.

THOUGHTS ABOUT RUFINO CONTRERAS

The war between the United Farm Workers and the growers of Imperial deserves its own book, which I am not equipped to write. Thanks to my friendships with Lupe, José and others, I understand that this was in fact a three-cornered war, the third faction consisting, naturally, of the group to which Lupe belonged and José López longed to rejoin: the commuter field workers from Mexicali, who to Mexican-American Chavistas were fundamentally scabs. (César Chávez had called the end of the bracero program *the birth of serious hope for a farm union.*) During the great march from Coachella to Calexico in 1969, the marchers, singing, shouting and trudging, many of them carrying the Virgin of Guadalupe, tried to get commuter workers to unionize so that they would no longer be strikebreakers. I imagine that pressure was applied.

The suffering of the growers remains mostly untold, Imperial County's farming dynasties being in some respects as closemouthed as the Chinese of Mexicali. Richard Brogan, to whom I paid a thousand dollars for telling me the various things that he did, was much nearer to these events than I can tell you, and in the end he would not let some of his experiences go on the record.

What the militants experienced is slightly less unknown. But they, too, have kept many secrets.

We read that the organizer Rufino Contreras got murdered during a strike in 1979, probably by a strikebreaker. (In Calexico, César Chávez cries out: *On this day greed and injustice struck down our brother Rufino Contreras . . . the company sent hired guns to quiet Rufino Contreras.*) No charges were filed. Whether his killing was premeditated and organized, and, if so, how high up in which organization the decision went, we cannot know.

I am fortunate enough to have received access to certain restricted files of the California Agricultural Labor Relations Board, these being kept at the California State Archives in Sacramento. I promised to change the names of individuals and organizations, and whenever possible to dilute direct quotations into paraphrases, to further disguise the speakers.

These documents permit me to make a beginning. That is all.

HORACE CALDWELL'S VICTORY

In 1905 a nurseryman from Fresno visits Brawley and gets *especially enthusiastic over the possibilities for orchards and vineyards.* In 1906 the *Imperial Standard* surveys those vineyards and reports: *In five years' time, Imperial valley will be recognized as the greatest grape land in the world.* Malaga and Black Hamburg grapes do better in Imperial than Muscat and Tokay, which sunburn since they grow less foliage. Somebody offers a Coachella grape grower six hundred dollars for a single acre's worth of his Málagas; such is the buyer's eagerness that he'll even do his own picking. In 1917, the *Manual for Settlers* assures us that table grapes will be *one of the most profitable industries in this section,* which from context I infer to include Coachella.

Coachella gradually takes over. Why not? Her soils must be better for this fruit. Imperial County hangs on, but mainly in the Calipatria and Mount Signal districts.

And so it's no wonder that the appellant in the following California Supreme Court case happens to be a table grape grower in the Coachella Valley. Call him "Horace Caldwell." He employs four hundred harvesters once or twice a year, for a week each.* Caldwell owns three labor camps. In the spring of 1977, the United Farm Workers of America serve Caldwell notice of intention to organize his workers. The law requires that within five days of being served, he must send the Agricultural Labor Relations Board a complete list of his employees, with their addresses. After eight days, he does provide a list, with omissions. Half of his labor force lives in one of his three labor camps, but only seven employees from there appear in the list. Of these seven, several are associated with post office boxes. The United Farm Workers and the ALRB inform him that this will not do. So helpful Horace Caldwell presents each of his workers with a bilingual "employee information card." Just above the signature line, Caldwell has printed in boldface: *I am not*

*A similar case involves "Robert Powers," who hires two hundred and fifty harvesters for a similar period, and owns one labor camp.

willing to supply any information that I have not written on this card. He then submits two more lists to the ALRB, both of which will be judged unsatisfactory.

Accordingly, two charges are filed against Caldwell. The first is *failure to supply complete and accurate information.* This information has been required for almost two decades, but non-agricultural businesses need not provide it until a union election is actually scheduled. In Caldwell's case, the ALRB rules that the transient, illiterate, non-English speaking people who so often perform agricultural labor cannot be contacted as easily as, say, office workers; therefore, Caldwell ought to furnish the required data in a more timely manner. The second charge against him is that he illegally interrogated his workers by means of those information cards as to whether or not they desired to unionize. In effect, said the ALRB, by explicitly allowing them to opt out of providing their addresses, which they had shown no disinclination to do, Caldwell was requiring them to disclose whether they were pro- or anti-union.

For redress, the ALRB orders Caldwell to give the union one hour with workers during work time (which is to say, at his expense); in addition, he must supply a new prepetition list. He complies. The union loses the election.

Why did Caldwell win? Had he successfully intimidated the people who picked his grapes, or were they satisfied with the conditions of their labor? Let's just say that **INDEPENDENT GROWERS KEEP WORKERS HAPPY**.

"LIKE SPIDERS IN THE WEB"

I think there was a lot of political use of that movement on both sides, said Richard Brogan. I don't know that César himself was hands-on director of anything daily. Probably it was like this: César, we have a strike against the large growers in Yuma.—I know that.—César, do you know what they did three hours ago?—Of course not.—There was no cell phone, no fax machine. It was different then. Some things I wouldn't want to talk about, I guess, but there were a few monumental actions on his part. His fasting to support the grape boycott, they knew how to publicize that. You can get five million Hispanics worked up about him missing a meal. When he misses a week's worth they start taking account in all the newspapers in this country. The migrant community was looking for a champion and they got one.

Mr. Brogan sipped his Coke and said: In 1966 or '67, I read an *L.A. Times* series on him and how he had put himself in the migrant homes with those people in Mexicali, saw their conditions, followed them into their daily work efforts in the Imperial Valley. He was about to make a presence at Imperial Valley College, and leading up to this, there was all this news media coverage, especially the grape boycott.

I would caution you that probably a lot of what I'm discussing, I hate to give the impression that I have the last word clarity on some of this stuff.

I honestly think that there are very clever Hispanic activists today who are using César beyond what he dreamed of. You have more young educated Hispanics here in this community who were still in middle school the first year that he died. They probably don't know anything about him. I believe the United Farm Workers movement has probably slowed down to a standstill. But you still get all these demands. Every new street has got to be named César Chávez Boulevard. Well, I'm having second thoughts when I hear a lot of this. I wonder what agendas are being served.

I asked Mr. Brogan if he cared to be more specific, and he replied: I guess I'm saying that there's a lot of hatred toward the UFW on the part of the large landowners, and a lot of that is because they had to account for their actions; they had to create some better environment for the worker; they had to consider the worker and they never *had* considered the worker before; they were just arrogant people. But I can't really say that César himself was the person causing all these changes. There's a lot of litigation; César was never in a courtroom. So tell me.

I asked him how Imperial Valley had been in the 1970s and he replied: It was terrible. There was an awful lot of vandalism at night. There was an awful lot of preparation for security issues, an awful lot of guns being carried.

And when did that stop?

When the large corporate entities signed union contracts. I witnessed some pretty good union activity in those years. In the Yuma Sheriff's Office I stood in picket lines in '73, '74, '75. I was involved in a major shooting. One person just grabbed out of the crowd and grabbed a sheriff and shot him in the head but just grazed him and the sheriff cussed him out. Some said: *He's dead in an orange grove.* But he ran miles and miles into Mexico and then turned himself in.

Jerry Brown was cultivated by the Kennedys, Brogan remarked, and they really, really championed Chávez. Chávez and some of the local Hispanic politicians were involved in migrant advocacy. I think in fact their agenda was beyond the migrant. They all cultivated and supported Jerry Brown. So he initiated the ALRB. And also the California Rural Legal Assistance. They're a legal representative of poor people but I don't think there's English spoken within their doors. One of their first was Judge X.* Elected in—and he named an Imperial town. That first character, the guy with almost a Filipino name, oh, a bad character . . .

One of their early paralegals applied for Westmorland School board. He was

*I have not vetted this information, and removed the name out of libel concerns.

caught smuggling aliens in a California state car. The Hispanic movement advocate just took advantage of that. Unbelievable.

Like spiders in the web was the way Brogan described the union activists.

"A SHAMEFUL PART OF OUR HISTORY"

Up in Coachella, Carolyn Cooke said: We came in 1957, in June, which was a very hot month, and my husband had gotten a job as an accountant at one of the ranches at Thermal, and so he came out. The ranch manager officer offered us one of the employees' apartments, but it had been used by Mexican farmworkers, so it had a cement floor and pea-green walls, and was pretty desperate looking. So I put up drapes and fixed it up. It wasn't a permanent thing. We were there for I guess about three years and then we were able to rent a little house about three miles away.

One of the big grape growers said, you've been recommended to us as an accountant and a bookkeeper, and so I worked for them for about twenty-three years, and once the strikers came it was very tense. The Chavistas were so troublesome and they would come out to the ranches and make so much noise, with drums and horns and they would yell. It was a shameful part of our history. The supervisors would be so exhausted from trying to keep the crews working, and every now and then there would be a fire; someone's plant would burn down. Finally a lot of growers decided to sign with the Teamsters union since it was preferable to the UFW, which was rather an upstart.

César Chávez decided that his people were not being treated fairly, and of course when you have a union, you do get better positions, but the union is also taking part of the money, but of course the people couldn't understand that. The UFW came in.

No, I don't think he was a bad man. I think he was perfectly within his rights to stand up for his people. At that time, conditions were improving in salary and so forth. But he was not far-seeing enough to know that you can't make changes just overnight. You have to go through certain channels. I think that's nature's way of working, really. I mean, some of the people worshipped him. But some of the people who had a little higher caliber remained loyal to their employers.*

*The authorities gave evidence that they, too, were of a higher caliber. The *California Farmer*, proud of its bias, gleefully informs us that in April 1975 United Farm Workers "wanted to hold a major 'rock concert' in the Coachella Valley to feed funds into its ailing coffers," but got refused by the county supervisors, five to zero.

THE FINAL WORD

Well, I don't know that the strikes made that much difference. There was a lot of marching up and down Miles Avenue, said another old-time Coachellan, Mrs. Tyler.

I don't know that there were any conflicts or anything, said her husband. It didn't reflect anything.

A PLAID SHIRT

Who was he? *To be a man is to suffer for others,* he once said. *God help us to be men.*

César Chávez was born to a family who lived on a hundred and sixty acres near Yuma in 1927, the year when Los Angeles's Metropolitan Water District was formed. He died in 1993. Here is *his invariable costume—plaid shirt, work pants, dark suede shoes.* Now do you know him?

He was the first person to tell us that women are equal to men and that we had the same rights. I wish I could hope for such an epitaph.

He was not only visionary, but practical and patient. Here is another of his sayings: *We have nothing else to do with our lives except to continue in this nonviolent fight.*

His "submarines," who cross picket lines and slow down work, may not be nonviolent, but who shot that sheriff in the head? Should Chávez be answerable? Or is he one of those who saved the movement from doing worse? (Affadavit executed at Calexico, 14 March 1979, name of signer withheld: . . . *it is the position of the United Farm Workers and my direction to organizers and picket captains that threats are counterproductive and not to be tolerated in any form. Threats serve only to divide, where the goal of a strike is to unite.*)

He hates Mexican labor contractors. (In these restricted ARLB hearings, the supervisor who threatens his pro-union workers generally himself has a Hispanic name.* Dean Hutchinson, Imperial County, 1934: *Contractors of labor always Mex-*

*A foreman's lot is not always enviable. "Most of the time I'm a worker," said an old man named Celestino Rivas. "I don't like to be a foreman. I have everything; I have the license to be a foreman, but it's very hard, because they want you to push the workers so much, to hurry up, hurry up. And then, they're always stealing time from the workers. They take fifteen minutes, like they'll say you're starting at six-fifteen when it's actually six. It's only fifteen minutes, but with fifty people, that's a lot of time. They don't pay overtime. This area is not like other areas. You have to be here at two or three in the morning even if you start work at eight or nine; they don't give a shit. Right now a lot of people come early, because of the terrorism. I got here at one-o'-clock this morning. There were about ten people. Then some foremen started arriving. Another problem is that I have to carry all the equipment in my car, and the people have to pay to go to Blythe eight to ten dollars a ride for only five hours of work in watermelon, cantaloupe, broccoli. So a lot of people don't want to go, and then that's my problem."

icans. All there now eliminated. These are "chiselers" and pay only 20 C day to worker while he gets 22½. Well, thank Almighty Capital they've all been eliminated!)

In 1959, we find César Chávez organizing in Oxnard: Braceros have taken local workers' jobs! As I write this I can almost see Javier Lupercio before in the park of the Child Heroes in Mexicali, remembering the bracero days. Who will organize for *him*? Who can Lupe Vásquez turn to?

In 1962, Chávez visits Calexico. He quits the Community Service Organization, walks over into Mexicali for a bite, and begins the next phase of his life. The National Farm Workers Union begins operations. Soon it will be called the United Farm Workers.

In the Union offices, there are black-bordered portraits of the murdered Kennedys. Zapata's likeness will later appear in the headquarters of the United Farm Workers, in Delano, of whose pastoral charms an observer writes: *Hard-edged and monotonous as parking lots, the green fields are without life.* Perhaps the ambience resembles that of another place we know: *Imperial Valley is more than a highly-developed farming area—it is a wonderland of factories running 24 hours a day, 365 days a year.* Ironically, a grower in Lamont will soon charge the Chavistas with the following: *The Union is trying to run a farm like a factory and you can't run a farm like a factory.*

Why Delano? Not all grape workers there are migrants; Chávez has a chance of staying in touch with them.

Do you remember how volatile and violent labor relations got in Imperial in the 1930s? The growers won; the unions and the Reds lost. In one of his inimitable handwritten notes, this one on the stationery of the Planters Hotel in Brawley, Dean Hutchinson elucidated the moral for all of us: *Growers & laborers had reached an agreement prior to this. Mexicans ignorant but quiet and peaceful. However inclined to believe anything in print—or told him by well-dressed man.* Dean Hutchinson's condescending diagnosis may actually shed some light on the failure of the Communist-led strikes. Could it be that those agitators told the field workers too much, and listened not enough?

As for César Chávez, he begins by asking people how much they think they should be paid.

He turns down money from the liberal rich. He approaches people who sometimes lack the means to feed their children, and demands that *they* pay, every month. His recollections of those days convey a trifle of pity and guilt; but he insists, to us and to himself, that feeling sorry for poor people is off the mark. Because they sacrifice to render up their dues, they will come to meetings to see how their dollars are being spent. The organization will belong to them. They will not wait for well-dressed men to take care of them.

In 1965, he organizes a grape pickers' strike there in Delano. Here come the picketers with their flags and their shouts: *Compañero!* Growers chase them with pickup trucks, running one man down.

Meanwhile, in Imperial County, striped banners hang from a line across the street. Beneath them, two brunettes in matching miniskirts, one with thick spectacles, one without, march toward us holding the pennant of the Imperial Tigers for the 1965 California Mid-Winter Fair Parade.

In 1967, Lionel Sternberg, landowner and grape grower in Thermal, addresses a marketing order hearing in Coachella with the following request for pity: *We invest some two or three times what the average businessman* in America *invests, and get about half the return.* In the Coachella Valley, *we've seen two out of three grape growers in the last thirty years disappear.*

A certain Mr. Asker interjects that in 1965 there were two hundred and twenty-five growers in Coachella; in 1966 there had been a hundred and fifty. (In an undated photograph I see two aproned girls, the younger of whom is flirting with the camera; the older girl looks away, trying not to smile; they pose behind their slanted crates of grapes: Will S. Fawcett, Heber, Calif.)

Such failures, Mr. Sternberg explains, result from *poor quality and temporary oversupply which destroyed buyer confidence.* But that's done with, boys and girls! Mr. Sternberg is fully prepared to make a patriotic promise: *The trade will know in 1967 that Coachella Valley Growers are awake, and they want to stay in business; they are not going to overburden the markets of the United States . . .*

Then they all sit around and try to figure out what to do.

Max Cook of Heggblade and Marguleas Company, *perhaps the largest table-grape shipper in California,* comes up with a wonderful idea: *Several years ago—prior to the last few years—it was quite in order to pick seven days a week because our deal was only short and fast—it lasted three weeks and everybody picked for seven days and got in and out of the way. But now, with newer and earlier varieties, we find that our deal is extended for eight weeks and this actually forces us to—we can't have over a six-day week. First of all, because you can't talk to the trade on Sundays. Secondly, we've got to give the help a day off . . .*

How bighearted you are, Mr. Cook! And soon César Chávez will be coming to assist you! You'll find that your help will be taking even more days off . . .

And, indeed, in 1968, César Chávez commences the famous California table-grape boycott. He fasts for twenty-five days to assert the cause of nonviolence.

He organizes a harvest strike in the Coachella Valley on 17 June 1968. The United Farm Workers picket from four-thirty in the morning until midnight. (A member tells us: *The Coachella is a very frightened place; it's like Mississippi.*) A car hits one of the picketers, who then gets beaten by devout Ministers of Capital. I wonder what the picketers do in return? Maybe nothing. The glowingly pro-UFW account before me does not say. What is violence? The Agricultural Labor Relations Board will state that throwing tomatoes at scabs, shouting obscenities and abusive threats, *minor scuffles,* and blocking vehicles cannot justify refusing to rehire the perpetrators. I grant that running people down in cars and beating them is much worse.

After ten days, a court order ends the strike. In a sentence that would have drawn a bitter obscenity from Lupe Vásquez, the biographer writes: *The workers who had sacrificed high harvest wages to walk off the job were replaced immediately by scabs trucked in from Mexicali, fifty miles away.*

In May 1969, the United Farm Workers go to Mass in Indio. Then they commence another march: nine days to Calexico. I imagine them pitching their camps on those eight evenings, the sun suddenly egg-yolk yellow, darkness unrolling along the sandy road, twilight on the flats, broken things around them, orange and blue light over the greying sand. In the mornings, when they begin to march again, the heat strikes their throats, foreheads and ears, coming up off the sand in dry shimmers, raking them like the branches of some thorn-tree.

In 1970 they lead an intensive strike against the table grape growers in Coachella and San Joaquin. That same year, their lettuce campaign in Salinas involves forty-five hundred workers; it may be the largest agricultural strike to date in United States history. In 1971 they strike in Imperial County. In 1973 we find them in Coachella, Lamont-Arvin and Delano. (Captain Frank Oswald, California Highway Patrol, Imperial County, 1934: *Lived here 23 years . . . Have never had a strike here. Agitators threatened workers . . . Mexicans want to work—would work if agitators leave them alone . . . If Mexicans make $5 a day for 10 days would then lay off for don't want too much money—Don't know what to do with it.* Sterling Oswald, Chief of Police, El Centro, 1934, who we learn is *also a grower lettuce cantaloupe melons 360 a[cres] in crops this year. Owns some leases some,* but perhaps he is impartial all the same: *Never any labor troubles . . . High type Mexicans very intelligent but apt to go astray. Still others who want to oppress others under him. Exalted idea of himself. Laboring class proud of being a Mexican. Very courteous—go out of way to do you a favor.*)

By the end of 1970 the grape boycott has already accomplished its aim; growers sign union contracts.

They will be undermined in 1973, when the Teamsters cut a deal with the growers and accept lower wages than the United Farm Workers. In that year we find him in Coachella, saying: *We are the people of the fields, the people who have made the trees and the vines the work of our lives.*

THE MOTHER AND THE FATHER

The way a Coachella Valley history describes the events of 1973, *labor organizing efforts by the United Farm Workers disrupted the valley and brought financial distress to workers and farmers.*

The Chavistas saw it differently.

Why shouldn't they? A Nazi Gauleiter once proposed this distinction: The trade union is the nurturing mother; the state is the father who disciplines. Hence there must be opposition between them.

Up in Kern County that year I see a deputy cradling against his potbelly the panicked, agonized and tooth-bared face of the UFW picketer whose throat he is choking with his baton; the picketer's hands are clenched around the baton, trying to work it loose before his adam's apple crunches, and another deputy has his hand on the picketer's arm as if to comfort him. The first deputy, the one who is choking him, gazes at an alert angle (we cannot see the eyes behind the dark sunglasses) at the other deputy; those two remind me of cowboys castrating yearlings.

On 19 January 1974, in the Calexico Armory, César Chávez speaks to two thousand farmworkers following the deaths of nineteen lettuce workers in a bus (he calls it a wheeled coffin) en route to High and Mighty Farms in Blythe. He says: *This tragedy happened because of the greed of the big growers . . .*

"THEY HAVE A SCHOOL NAMED AFTER HIM NOW"

The California Agricultural Labor Relations Act becomes law in 1975. That June, in order to explain and celebrate it, César Chávez leads a march north from Calexico: a thousand miles, fifty-nine days.

Perhaps it is this particular march which is remembered by the La Londes.

Helen La Londe, who came with her husband to settle in the Coachella Valley shortly before midcentury, said to me: Some of my friends were grape growers and didn't like César Chávez. Some of them sold out.

Oh, they used to walk from Mecca to Indio, said her husband. At the Thermal school they had an air-conditioning unit that was cooled by water. And when the air-conditioning unit got too hot, the water would flow. When they came to Thermal, they went to the school. The water would just flow when the compressor runs. We have the same system here, and we waste water at seven and a half gallons a minute. Anyway, they came, and right when they were getting a drink of water, the compressor turned off and they were upset and thought that someone had turned it off, just to deny 'em a drink. It was on Saturday, and I got the phone call and went down to say, It's not us, it's automatic. And then the water went back on.

They have a school named after him now, he remarked in bemusement.

By 1978, strikers are obtaining contracts in the Imperial Valley.

THE STORY OF TASTY FOODS

Here is one case of redress thanks to the California Agricultural Labor Relations Act.

Do you remember the Imperial County company that fired a man for being tired after he had irrigated onions for twenty-eight hours straight while the levee crumbled away?

On another occasion, workers are harvesting for three hours on a Saturday for the same company. They make about nine dollars, which is less than their guaranteed four-hour minimum; and I have begun to understand how much time and money field workers spend going to and from the furrows. So they approach the foreman, get nowhere, threaten to file a charge with the Agricultural Labor Relations Board, and are fired as troublemakers.

This noble outfit, which I will call "Tasty Foods," is, if you like, a self-sufficient family farm, specializing in asparagus harvesting and shipping, not to mention iceberg lettuce, mixed lettuce, cantaloupes, cabbage and onions. It owns some fields and leases others.

In 1977, the United Farm Workers petition for certification at Tasty Foods, hold an election and win. The resulting collective bargaining agreement holds good for two years. But in February 1979, strikes shake the Imperial Valley, and negotiations between the union and management reach their inevitable impasse.

This happens to be a very strategic time for a strike, since the first asparagus cutting of January enjoys high demand, there being no other asparagus on the market—praise Imperial! By March, glut befalls the market, and the canneries begin to order cheap machine-cut asparagus. Thus Tasty Foods finds itself in the middle of its brief season of high income and high need when the United Farm Workers walk out.

(*California Farmer,* Question of the Month: *To be fair to all parties, when should contracts between growers and labor be negotiated?*

(Lee Anderson, Junior, from Indio: *Harvest time is not fair.*

(John Volker from Brawley: *The unions will say at harvest time and farmers will say after harvest.*)

Do you remember the broad and sinister motives of the mid-1930s, when the Communists launched a similarly strategic lettuce strike, and failed? Repression saved the growers then. What about now?

"Carlos Martínez," one of the strikers, now stands on the corner of Imperial and

Ninth in Calexico, waiting for his friend "Manuel Solís" to come from work, because Solís owes him money. Suddenly, Martínez's supervisor drives past in his pickup, backs up, stops, calls Martínez lazy and also *montonero,* meaning a troublemaker, then invites him to drink a beer with him. Martínez prudently refuses. At this point, the supervisor, "Alberto García," threatens to make him disappear, and points a pistol at him twice.

García will later insist that Martínez promised to *hurt* Tasty Foods and *break the buses.* In any event, the two men argue for forty-five minutes (I presume that Solís did not appear to pay his debt). García claims that he carries his .22 only when he is carrying a lot of cash to pay his workers; therefore, he did not have it when he met Martínez.

Martínez's testimony is both detailed and direct, García's, contradictory and vague. No one saw the incident with the pistol, but the ALRB decides to believe Martínez.

Another incident: A striker tries for reinstatement. A Mexican foreman replies: *I do not give work to lazy people because they are strikers.*

In the early 1980s Tasty Foods violates labor laws by declining to rehire two UFW supporters, laying off two others, and threatening a fifth with physical harm. The Agricultural Labor Relations Board hearing will be appealed, sometimes all the way up to the California Supreme Court.

In the end, the defendant's petition for review is denied. The Administrative Law Officer of the ALRB issues an order that Tasty Foods cease and desist from firing and threatening reprisals, that it reinstate and *make whole* unlawfully terminated workers, that it make its internal records available, post copies of the hearing notice, etcetera, and read it in all relevant languages at a convocation of the workers.

LIMITATIONS

What has César Chávez won, really?

The restricted ALRB hearing documents often remark that a four- or five-year interval between the labor violation and the court's remedy for it is not uncommon. (Letter from the ALRB Field Examiner to the El Centro legal firm that represents a certain "Abel Farms": *It has now been almost 5 years since these workers were discriminated against. Most of them have not found steady employment and are currently unemployed.*—In the end, contempt proceedings are filed against Abel in the Court of Appeals, *the first ever,* says the case assignment document.) How are those unemployed workers doing now? What was the cost to their marriages and their health?

But the radicalism of the Agricultural Labor Relations Board must have been shocking to Imperial's growers. For instance: *Respondent is found to have violated the act for an alleged threat that only the discriminatee saw.*

The extremism of some members of the United Farm Workers must have appalled them even more.

A police report from 1979 describes how two hundred strikers from the United Farm Workers have surrounded a labor camp in Monterey. One officer counts over a hundred rocks lying on the ground, arranged by size. Gas cans and soda bottles seem to be in the process of being rigged up as Molotov cocktails. Rocks are already embedded in the wood of the buses; and the labor camp inmates say that they had to run from a rain of rocks. It appears that they have also flooded a field, smashed windows, and sent a worker to the hospital with one of their rocks. Another scab tells the officers that a striker pushed a pistol in his face. The strikers are shaking the cyclone fence around the camp, and they are screaming at the people who were trying to sleep. It will take thirty-nine officers to stop them. The police report sums up the United Farm Workers' motives as follows: *Personal gratification.*

Taking the grower's side, the Agricultural Labor Relations Board imposes an awful punishment: It requires a public apology from the UFW during peak season, or, at the union's option, a simple promise not to do it again. If any restitution for damage was ordered, that appears nowhere in the restricted documents.

This was the starkest example of pro-union violence that I came across in the restricted files; but in Imperial itself, especially in 1979, there were any number of incidents which would have been frightening to experience, and possibly embittered their victims. Eventually, César Chávez himself was forced to concede, at least among friends, that documentary photographs from the Imperial Valley had begun to seriously injure the public image of the UFW.

A certain Imperial grower of lettuce, tomatoes and other commodities (let's call the company "Sylvester & Co."), having unionized and survived, eventually reaches our universal Rubicon: the collective bargaining agreement expires. Negotiations grind on for twenty-four sessions over a period of three months, then fall apart. Sylvester offers a twenty-one-percent wage increase; the United Farm Workers demand a hundred twenty-five to two hundred percent. Later both Sylvester and the UFW will accuse each other of bargaining in bad faith.

Sylvester blames the United Farm Workers for condoning and possibly instigating the following during the strike: They threaten the people who continue to work; they run them off the road, and they even beat them. Property damage is significant. In the face-off, someone shoots a striker dead. This is Rufino Contreras.

Co-petitioning the appeals court with Sylvester & Co. is a grower named "Joffe Brothers." During this same period, the Chavistas rush a crew of Joffe Brothers scabs, shouting obscenities at them and attacking with rocks until they flee to a bus. Back in the thirties, police and Legionnaires might have been doing the same to strikers. Perhaps these actions of the UFW were accordingly excusable and even necessary. I hate to think so.

On another day in those same fields, the picketers metastasize into six or eight hundred rioters. The police command them to disperse; they refuse. *The film shows what happened as the bus began to leave the area. First, the Union picketers broke through police and security lines and intercepted the buses . . . Windows were then shattered by pieces of concrete thrown by the picketers. One bus was forced off of an embankment by the attacking strikers.* They also attack the police.

A memo notes that this case was decided *adversely to the Board . . . Petition for hearing denied . . .* In other words, I presume that the growers won that time.

ELENA PRIETO'S CARD

It is central to the Imperial Idea that when confronted by impediments—for instance, temperatures bordering on the preposterous, or waterlessness, or field workers who not only demand wage increases but intimidate other employees and damage company property—a person clenches his teeth and bulls his way ahead. This was not merely, as Richard Brogan called it, arrogance. I suspect that many growers sincerely believed, as they used to about a minimum wage, that additional expenses might put them out of business. They already had to deal with underproduction, overproduction, leasing and contracting fees. They worried that they might be required to hire someone without qualifications. One foreman fretted: *You're going up against competition, against Bruce Church and Bud Antle. And we can't just fool around with non-experienced people.* Moreover, any human being, and especially an Imperialite, evinces a natural disposition to resist being told what to do. I have never been cheated out of a dollar in my life.

All this being said, the reactions of some Imperial growers to the Chavistas ranged from the ill-advised to the pathetic to the disgusting.

Abel Farms, for instance, the company that won the ALRB's very first contempt-of-court prize, clings very fiercely to its accustomed ways of growing lettuce, cantaloupe, watermelon, alfalfa, cotton, sugar beets, broccoli, carrots, rapini, onions, asparagus and wheat.

The members of this concern (evidently not only field workers but also foremen, perhaps even the big boss) meet before work in a certain shop in Heber to drink coffee, plan out the day and roll dice. Union organizers want to go there before six A.M., so that nobody can be said to be stealing time from management. Nonetheless, Mr. Abel, the man after whom his farms are named, denies access. Not many days after this, an organizer attempts to address the workers on these premises at five in the morning. Mr. Abel expels the man. On the following day he performs a citizen's arrest of five organizers.

(Does he have any right on his side? Mr. Abel will later accuse organizers of crossing his fields and kicking good lettuce into the furrow. His understanding is that they have a right to talk to workers in cars, not in fields. Or they can talk during the lunch break—which lasts an entire ten minutes and does not take place at any set time. He tells the organizers that they can sit at the side of his fields all day but they are not to come *onto* those fields. Defying him, they go from crew to crew, damaging lettuce.)

The election approaches. "Ramón Ortega," supervisor, advises "Elena Prieto" in his weeding and thinning crew to vote for Teamsters; he recommends that she not wear a UFW button. Even though she does not consider it to be such, this will later be charged, rightly I think, as *unlawful interrogation*. At another time, Ortega counsels her to vote for the *caballitos*, the "little horses" on the Teamsters' emblem. She used to ride to work with him; after the election, their friendship cools.

Meanwhile, an irrigator's foreman warns him that *if Chavez's union gets in, everything is going to get fucked up*. The irrigator is holding a bird in his hand, the foreman says. If he lets go of it to reach for many who are flying, he will be left with no bird at all. The irrigator considers this to be a threat that he will get fired if he votes for any union.

Perhaps because of these tactics, the United Farm Workers win the election.

Elena Prieto signs a UFW authorization card given her by a certain woman organizer. Ortega is eating lunch, watching. A quarter of an hour later, when she returns to work, Ortega tells her she should not have signed. And behind Ortega I seem to see, as she perhaps also saw, the Associated Farmers of the 1930s, with their deputies and axe handles. Elena Prieto must have been a brave or desperate woman. Her victory, and the tale of César Chávez, is as miraculous to me as water leaping up and out of the tan desert.

ANOTHER FINAL WORD

César Chávez fasts again at Delano in 1988, at the age of sixty-one. The purpose of this Fast for Love is to warn about the effects of pesticides on field workers' children.

Before this century is done, he says, *there will be an evolution in our values, . . . not because man has become more civilized but because, on a blighted earth, he will have no choice.*

Enemies of César Chávez, take heart! As the twentieth century ends, the

Brawley Chamber of Commerce advises you to **DISCOVER THE RICHES BRAWLEY HAS TO OFFER**, these including *LABOR: Wages 25% lower than the California average. Put our labor force to work for you.* Our convenient twenty-two-percent unemployment rate *(seasonal fluctuations occur due to the predominance of the agricultural industry)* creates *a strong and readily available work force.* Moreover, better than eighty percent of Brawley's private companies remain non-union.

And as Brawley goes, so goes Imperial! Reader, ride north with me out of Duroville, to the Thermal Boxing Club, then into Coachella's tan walls, Avenue 52, a row of palm trees, a 7UP truck, a smog test station. On Sixth and Grapefruit by the Mexican Food Lounge I begin my inventory and discover the following: Riverside Scrap Iron & Metal, Pipe Materials, Seaview Citrus, Medjools, Grapes, a palm grove and gated houses the color of sand . . . Past the two sofas in the sand at Rancho De Lara there is a leafless vineyard; then I find the long lines of cars of migrant workers, two of them kicking a ball around in the dirt shoulder of Avenue 52. Another line of half a dozen cars is silhouetted in an artichoke field. The day is hot and horrible. *They do work Americans wouldn't do.* I approach the power plant of Mecca, which achieves one single twist of smoke . . .

ONE MORE REASON TO BE A WATER FARMER

Richard Brogan had been uttering quite a few remarks about César Chávez—off the record. Later we returned to the subject of water farmers; and he said: You almost might have a backlash against the union farmworker—and I think that Mr. Brogan meant the farmworker of Mexican descent; for, as you may remember, he had expressed bitterness that *in this county there's a significant bias; you can see the anti-white attitude every day*—a sense, he continued, of to hell with them by selling off the water. There's absentee landlords here, too. Somebody opening their check every month, what the hell do they care?

Chapter 140

SUBDELINEATIONS: WATERSCAPES

(1950–1975)

"Get more water to get more people to get more economic growth" is a syndrome to be evaluated, not a principle of necessity. The great Southern California engineer and water developer of earlier days perceived this clearly when he said, "If we don't get the water, we won't need it."

—Paul S. Taylor, 1970*

In 1952, the lawsuit *Arizona v. California* was initiated over Colorado River water. By pure coincidence, it was that very same year when, picking up a pamphlet by the Colorado River Association, which just happened to be located in Los Angeles, we learned that Los Angeles was now buying forty percent of all power produced by Hoover Dam, and that ***OFFICIAL FIGURES SHOW NO COLORADO RIVER WATER AVAILABLE FOR CENTRAL ARIZONA PROJECT***. Poor Arizona! It's not our fault that we'll be taking all that water; ***OFFICIAL FIGURES*** prove that we just have to.†

(By the way, in 1951 Los Angeles had finally annexed Riverside's Eastern Municipal Water District. I'll bet that ***OFFICIAL FIGURES*** demonstrated that it was for the best. All the same, a historian writing in 1971 will conclude that Santa Ana River water rights have been litigated *almost continuously since the 1950s,* the adversaries being Riverside and San Bernardino. If only Los Angeles would swallow up San Bernardino, too! Then the Inland Empire would achieve a state of perfect peace.—Well, my kindred water-drinkers, that day just may come.)

In 1959, California assured the world that *the upper limit of safe annual yield* from the Colorado, excluding the Gila branch, was 5,850,000 acre-feet, although *the safe annual yield may be as little as 5,400,000 acre-feet.* In any case, *we reserve the right to claim more water against the states of the upper division.* Did we have enough water now?

*Needless to say, this point of view was rejected by its intended forum, the Sacramento Bee, because "it is my impression . . ," explained the editor, "that your articles have an emphasis more on criticisms, old and new, of the present system. Goodness knows we have published a great deal of the criticism in recent months."

†Lamentably, in 1963 the Supreme Court ruled in favor of Arizona.

In the 1960s, the water level dropped by three feet per year in Palm Springs, ten feet per year in the southern San Joaquin Valley. Fortunately, those areas lie outside the entity I refer to as Imperial; why worry? As the 1970s neared, California's lowland cities which used to depend largely on pumping were commanded by the state to begin conserving underground water, relying instead on the Colorado and Feather rivers.

In 1965, James J. Doody, the Director of the Southern District of the California Department of Water Resources, gave a speech in San Diego reassuring us all that *the 2,580,200 acre-feet of Northern California water and 4,400,000 acre-feet of Colorado River water would be sufficient to meet the projected net water requirements of Southern California up to about 1990. An additional 1,930,000 acre-feet of supplemental water would be needed to meet projected total net water requirements in 2020.* What to do? Desalinization could be done at three hundred and twenty-five dollars per acre-foot—one dollar per thousand gallons. And praise the Lord, that very year President Johnson had signed a bill *authorizing the Department of the Interior to further investigate the feasibility of saline water conversion. This bill will have its effect on California.*

Forty-one years later, I read in the newspaper that astonishing progress had indeed been made: **LAGUNA BEACH—From where Mike Dunbar stands . . . [in] the South Coast Water District, he sees an agency at the end of the line for water shipped to this arid region from Northern California and the Colorado River . . . That's why Dunbar, like so many coastal water managers before him, dreams that someday his agency's customers will be served in part by desalinated seawater.** I can't help believing in people.*

In short, it was simply needless to question the supply of water, even though California's rivals did. For the questioners, a solution was found in 1965—an eternal solution. The Grand Canyon Workshop of the Colorado Open Space Council reported: *After fighting for twenty years to take Colorado River water from one another, Arizona, California, and other Colorado Basin states have agreed to share the river if they can take enough water from elsewhere to make argument unnecessary . . .*

Well, whom might we take it from? Any guesses, my fellow Northsiders? We've sworn to squirt one point five million acre-feet down to Mexico, *subject to increase or reduction in certain contingencies. No assumption is made here as to the magnitude of such variations in the guaranteed delivery.* However, *there is evidence of underflow of the Colorado River to Mexico which is not measured and hence not credited against the Mexican Treaty obligation.* Well, let's measure and credit it, by God! Someday, we might just line the All-American Canal and save the seepage for *us.* **THE DESERT REAPPEARS.**

*Tijuana built the Rosarito Desalination Plant sometime during the 1960s, but decommissioned it in 1983 on account of its expense.

When I was in the Imperial Valley, said Edith Karpen, nobody started lining ditches. They started only in the seventies. It keeps the water level up in the wells when you don't line them.

But, reader, which wells are we talking about in the present context?—Only Mexican ones.

As a matter of fact, the water in Mexican wells did happen to be dropping.—Between 1958 and 1998, the water table three miles away from Morelos Dam sank by eighteen feet!—So what?—On the Cucapah reservation south of Mexicali, old Carlos remembered when the gringos dammed the Colorado. Well, he shrugged, it's their water. They can do what they like with it.—I asked him what had happened exactly, and he said: The Río Hardy kept dwindling after that. The fishing got worse. Anyway, he finished, they didn't consult me.

The gringos had done that in the 1960s; and it happened to be just then that in Señora Teresa García's words *the land started to lose its strength* in the Mexicali Valley; that was also when the water in her family well stopped being clear.

Has the water table dropped since you were little?

Our water comes from a canal. Our well gets water from the canal.

Can you drink from that well?

No! she laughed. It's very dirty. As a child, the water was really clear but we couldn't drink from it. It stopped being clear many years ago, in the sixties . . .

She *bought* her drinking water nowadays, in big bottles.

What do you suppose happened to her water? I did not sample it on that day in 2004, so I cannot say, but the following prophecy, uttered by one of Northside's hydrological savants in 1958, may not be utterly irrelevant: *Prudent planning for the future requires consideration of the probability that the water available for diversion through the Metropolitan Aqueduct to irrigated areas in Arizona and California, and for deliveries to Mexico, will contain at least 1.5 tons of dissolved solids (dry weight) per acre foot of water when the planned developments in the Upper Basin are carried out.*

That's prudent planning for the future, all right! That's why Mr. Dunbar, like so many coastal water managers before him, dreams that someday his agency's customers will be served in part by desalinated seawater.

HIGH-PRIORITY WATER IMPROVEMENTS

Between 1906 and 1983, the average annual virgin (unregulated) flow of the Colorado River at Colorado River Compact point was fifteen point one million acre-feet. So I would hypothesize that about fifteen point one million yearly acre-feet of Colorado River water (less of course those trifling deductions for Mexico) got withdrawn after 1961.

In 1962, the doomed newsman Ruben Salazar visited Tijuana and wrote: *In what might be described as the "wettest" town in Baja California—alcoholically speaking—most of the residents ration their household water almost by the drop.* A hundred and sixty-six thousand people lived there then; there was enough water for thirty thousand. The solution: Decreto 75, which would enact an aqueduct from the Mexicali Valley at a cost of thirty-two million U.S. dollars.* The journalist Carlos Estrada Sastre wrote against it; he said that poor people would be paying the thirty-two million; and his was no solitary voice, for the Supreme Court of Mexico ruled against the constitutionality of Decreto 75. Perhaps because of Señor Sastre's outspokenness on this subject, perhaps because he accused the Tijuana police of participating in drugs and prostitution, he got his head bashed in with—what could better make their point?—a piece of water pipe. The chief of police and three subordinates were arrested. But all this was the merest Southside peculiarity; who cared about Southside?

In American Imperial, the money for water flowed like water, since **WATER WAS** already and would remain **HERE**. How could we not make beneficial use of *the Colorado River, which makes Imperial County the fifth-ranking United States county in agricultural production?* That encomium was published in 1966, five years after the Colorado's decreasing trickle to the Gulf finally stopped. (José Joaquín Arrillaga, 1796: *As the sun rose, I saw the poplar trees of the Colorado River.* I have stood more or less where he stood on that morning in the Mexicali Valley. There are no poplar trees anymore. There is no water there anymore.)†

Meanwhile, the city of San Diego budgeted almost forty-two million dollars for water utilities in fiscal year 1971. For fiscal year 1972, San Diego required the following municipal capital-improvement expenditures: *PRIORITY IMPROVEMENTS: HIGH PRIORITY WATER improvements made necessary by new system development or unanticipated operational deficiencies:* four hundred thousand dollars, *three-quarters of which was attributable to new housing.* The Mission Gorge Pump Plant near Jackson Drive cost a hundred and forty grand, seventy-five percent of that being attributable to just-arrived residents.

*Specifically, 88% of Baja California's water lies in or under the Mexicali Valley. Why wouldn't Tijuana want to drink that up? Fortunately for us all, in 1977, the end of thirty-one drought years, Baja can expect her 2,634,779 acre-feet to be augmented by rain; for didn't she get a forty-seven-year wet season before the dry time? This reminds me of the pious prayer of the professor in Claremont, California, back in 1904: "We have had ever and anon years that gave a great down pour. We may safely expect another of these very soon, I feel sure. Thus the men that plow in hope and faith, I believe will not reckon without their host."

†The Río Hardy still has some trees, a good number of which are dead. But the Colorado's former mouth is a desert of detritus.

IMPERIAL POOLS

Do you remember how California's nineteenth-century waterscapes eventually washed away the notion of riparian ownership, leaving us instead with the law of appropriation? Here comes a professional restatement of that latter principle: *The one who first appropriated water and put it to beneficial use acquired a vested right to continue to divert and use that quantity of water against all claimants junior to him in time.*

In 1922, the U.S. Supreme Court had ruled in *Wyoming v. Colorado* that this doctrine may apply on the interstate level. Therefore, it certainly applies for water districts. The Imperial Irrigation District was a senior rightholder on the Colorado: Only Thomas Blythe's diversion of 1877 preceded the waterworks of George Chaffey and Charles Rockwood. Hence Imperial County had nothing to fear from, for instance, Los Angeles and San Diego.

Los Angeles waits. San Diego waits.

In the course of a year, Imperial Valley alfalfa used eighty-one inches of water;* Imperial Valley sugar beets, forty-six; Imperial Valley cotton, forty-one; Imperial Valley barley, twenty-two.—Well, that was nothing. Why worry? *The dove abounds in the cut-over alfalfa fields and around the many miles of irrigation ditches and canals. Here they settle so thickly that a single blast from a shotgun often bags the 10-bird daily limit.*

At the beginning of 1975, on the very front page, the *California Farmer* warned: *Irrigation and reclamation must take first national priority. We could be too late now.* But it is simply needless to question the supply of water, as evidenced by a certain stock photo from the Olson Collection: Unlabeled except for the word "desert" scrawled on the back in ballpoint pen and the stamp **PHOTOMAMMOTH MURALS** with an address in North Hollywood, entirely undated, it depicts a palm grove more beautiful than any I have ever seen in my own sojourns in Imperial, because the air is clear so that we can see the snow-covered mountains behind the palms; secondly, the foreground of this image, between two stately palms, is a mirror of grass-speckled water: deepish water, rich in reflections of palms and mountains; soft clouds in the air; there is so much of everything and it is so clean. *Experience in the Coachella Valley indicates that not less than 9 to 12 acre-feet per year should be applied for palms in full production.*

*I assume this is per acre.

Chapter 141

WELLTON-MOHAWK

(1961)

Irrigated agriculture will always be a short-lived enterprise unless the salts accumulated in the root zone are leached out.

—National Research Council, 1989

The drier the climate, the less leaching takes place and hence the more serious the salt buildup. How serious might it now be in Imperial? Turning to her mother, Alice Woodside said: You remember how Dad used to dread the alkali?—But as a sort of reply, the old lady remarked: The city of Imperial was a rice-growing area, because they got so much alkali that they started raising rice there; they'd flooded it to eliminate the alkali. So they would flood the fields and wash the alkali. They fixed the problem and grew melons.—She believed, as I want to, that one really can *fix the problem*. What if one can't?—You'll be happy to know that experiments conducted at Imperial Valley Field Station prove that *plants can flourish when irrigated with water as high as 1,350 parts per million salt content, if the water is applied properly*. Imperial's irrigation water is expected to reach that level by 2000. Well, 2000 remains a long safe quarter-century away.

Fourteen years go by. Salinity at the Colorado River is now up to eight hundred and seventy parts per million. Don't worry.

When did the Mexicans first start complaining? Never mind. Back in 1925, good old Phil Swing had summed up all verities: *God in his infinite wisdom placed Mexico upon the last part of the stream of the Colorado River.*

The 1944 treaty states only: Northside must provide one point five million acre-feet to Mexico. The treaty declines to mention the quality of that water. Mexican protests lead to amendments, the last of which is Minute 242: Average annual salinity of the Colorado upstream of where it enters Mexico at Morelos Dam cannot exceed that of Imperial Dam by more than a hundred and fifty parts per million.

But the salinity of the water we generously give Mexico increases year upon year. The salinity of the Mexicali Valley aquifer increases by twenty point six milligrams per liter* per year. And now Arizona's Wellton-Mohawk district takes up irrigation with a vengeance.

Wellton-Mohawk's sewage carries total dissolved solids of as much as fifteen thousand milligrams per liter, so that at Morelos the Colorado River water sometimes bears a salinity of twenty-five hundred milligrams per liter. *Plants can flourish when irrigated with water as high as 1,350 parts per million.*

A book called *Collapse* informs me: *The major problem affecting California agriculture is salinization as a result of irrigation agriculture, ruining expanses of agricultural land in California's Central Valley, the richest farmland in the United States.* **THE DESERT DISAPPEARS**.

What about Mexican agriculture?—*The bountiful continent is ours, state on state, and territory on territory, to the waves of the Pacific sea.*

It's not okay with the water, said Yolanda Sánchez Ogás in 2003. After fourteen years, Emilio López Samoa, an engineer, made a runoff from Wellton-Mohawk to the Golfo de California. Salt water had destroyed a lot of land here in the Mexicali Valley, and we couldn't get it back. It ruined the cars in the city, the engines. It ruined everything in the valley. So the Mexican government tried to recuperate the land. And they moved the people on the best land to other places: Centinela, Zamora, Progreso. It hurt them a lot, because they didn't have enough water to wash themselves. Now again they have salt! And there's not enough water. And we have to send water to Tijuana.

In 1973, the International Boundary and Water Commission of the United States and Mexico decides that water at Morelos must be no saltier than a hundred and fifteen milligrams per liter.

The Yuma Desalting Plant obligingly appears in 1974. But it's so expensive to run that for a considerable while, just out of the goodness of our hearts, we choose to dilute our effluent with extra water . . .

May I tell you how much water has been bypassed at Morelos from Wellton-Mohawk? These amounts *measure the degree of deprivation of the American water users as a consequence of promulgation of Minute 242.* Poor Americans! "Moisture Means Millions." In 1974, we give Southside over a hundred thirteen thousand needless acre-feet; in 1976, more than two hundred and five thousand acre-feet! A water consultant warns: *The average amount by-passed . . . is about one-fourth of the annual water allotment to the Metropolitan Water District of Southern California. In dry periods . . . these quantities would be damaging to the urban areas of Southern California.*

*Approximately equivalent to parts per million. These figures are all rough. They mask sampling error, incomplete data, and such local variations as the following finding (1954): Two Coachella wells within half a mile of each other, one 565 feet deep, the other only 180, showed the following respective salt concentrations: 400 and 8,500 ppm.

Chapter 142

SUBDELINEATIONS: POISONSCAPES

(1888–2003)

> That is Imperial Valley. It is the "Topsy-Turvy Land" of America . . . Here people look up and not down at sea level . . . The land is fertilized by adding liquid fertilizer to the irrigation water.
>
> —Holtville Chamber of Commerce, 1952

In 1921, certain busybodies dare to raise the idea that maybe the State Board of Health should regulate the proposed Burbank sewer farm. The voice of freedom, the voice of individual right, counter-argues: *The function of the State Board of Health does not appear from any act to "design" sewer systems, but to "guard" against the design and operation of such sewer systems and sewer disposal plants which would create a nuisance and be dangerous to public health.* In other words, the state may be reactive but not proactive. Wasn't this the American Idea once upon a time, and isn't it the Imperial Idea itself?

In 1930, the city of Los Angeles advises in its annual report that *final plans for grease skimming tanks should now be made . . . After such installation the removal of the grease in the sewage flow will . . . greatly improve the physical conditions along the Hyperion Beach. Although all solid matter in the sewage which cannot pass the 1/16th inch slots is intercepted by the screens, the effluent contains considerable oil and grease, which, after being discharged into the ocean, may be carried by winds and currents to beaches some distance from Hyperion. It is therefore recommended that these skimming tanks be built as soon as possible to protect the beaches.*

Next exhibit: a pretty graph which simultaneously depicts the area, population and sewer mileage of Los Angeles between 1900 and 1931. Although all three curves begin near zero, their slopes rise divergently, *area* going up the least, to four hundred and forty-two square miles as of 1930; *population* climbs higher but still linearly, up to one point two million; while *sewer miles* increase exponentially, overtowering its two rival quantities at the princely elevation of twenty-three hundred and thirty-one. Three scales on one axis, doesn't that equate to comparing wormy apples, rotten oranges and tainted Imperial Valley grapefruits? Well, who am I to say that there isn't some profound principle in play all the same? Los Angeles, city of cities, gets denser as it expands, and as it gets denser it requires a maze of sewer pipe! The chief of California's Bureau of Sanitary Engineering has an explanation for this phenomenon: *We take it as a matter of course nowadays that plumbing has passed for a luxury.*

Twenty-three hundred and thirty-one miles of sewer pipe! What does this "mean"? (What does any number "mean"?)

A hundred and fifty-five thousand acre-feet of sewage per year now spews from Los Angeles County into the Pacific Ocean. From Orange County comes only six thousand acre-feet.

In *A SURVEY OF SEWAGE DISPOSAL IN CALIFORNIA AS PRACTICED APRIL 1929: Includes all systems known to us, administered by public authorities*, we're informed that San Diego sends its raw sewage to bays, as does National City with its septic tank effluent; Oceanside eponymously prefers the ocean. Chula Vista's Imhoff tank effluent goes to bays, and Los Angeles's to sloughs; however, Los Angeles's fine screens go to the ocean.

The Department of Public Health, which compiled the survey, concludes: *There are no set standards of sewage disposal.*

A REQUEST

Stop for a moment and consider the implications of that one sentence.

FISH-FEEDING

But a new dawn looms, at least for sewage. *The arrangement is essentially contractual and the result of it is to bring the sewage of many communities to central points for treatment. It is difficult to adequately appraise the importance of these huge centralizing projects in their localities and to the state unless one contemplates what the situation would have been without them. Sanitation and development would have been next to impossible.*

Here is one of the upcoming miracles of bureaucratic centralism: The Los Angeles County Sanitation Districts *embrace thirteen cities entirely, parts of three others, and contemplate the inclusion of ten more within the next few years . . . Before long it will be necessary to . . . convey the effluent into the Pacific Ocean 5000 feet off shore. This is the ultimate plan which will serve upwards of 2,000,000 people.*

"A STREAM IS LIKE A WOMAN"

So much for sewage (almost). What about other feculence? Fortunately, the main industrial wastes of California are still agricultural, deriving from *canneries, milk-plants, sugar factories and olive pickling works.* How safe, how innocent! Because *there are no set standards of sewage disposal,* Lodi, to pick a random example, is one of the towns which *run their cannery wastes, raw, to valuable rivers and channels through special industrial sewers, forming great masses of ugly slime and deposits in the stream.*

But "ugly" is the wrong word here. My attitude is incorrect. For correctness, I refer you to a 1975 column in the *California Farmer*—yes, in 1975 there were still people who missed the good old days in Lodi: *In some respects a stream is like a woman. We instinctively enjoy the beauty of each . . . There are times, however, when the bearer of this beauty must bend her back and dirty her hands at an unbecoming chore. So might it not be necessary for the waters of the purest stream to irrigate a field, drive a turbine, or rinse away the dirt of civilization?*

In this spirit, the cities of El Centro and Imperial in 1916 improve their amenities from *the primitive sewer system of the earliest days* to a grand new *outfall sewer* which *empties into New River.* By century's end, San Diego will be likewise bending her back and dirtying her beautiful hands a trifle: *Chollas Creek is a heavily urbanized watershed tributary to San Diego Bay. The Chollas Creek watershed has been added to the 303(d) list as a result of toxicity measured during wet weather monitoring.*

BURIED TREASURES

There are also instances of trouble caused by paper mill wastes, tanneries and gas plants. How safe and innocent might those instances be?

Consider the Arrowhead manufactured-gas plant in San Bernardino, which operated from approximately 1881 to 1912.* In 1994, investigators found that the soil remained contaminated with unsafe levels of lampblack, lead, arsenic, and petroleum hydrocarbons, including toluene. In the groundwater, trace amounts of cyanide now lay intermingled with dangerous amounts of thallium and the carcinogen benzo(a)anthracene. *The flow model indicates constituents of the soil contaminants first reached groundwater no later than the 1930s.* Fortunately, San Bernardino is out of Imperial; it doesn't affect me.

*Appletons' Annual Cyclopaedia, 1892: "California is the third petroleum-producing State in the Union, ranking only after Pennsylvania and New York . . . the wells of Ventura and Los Angeles Counties turning out a constantly increasing quantity of oil."

IMPERIAL BESIEGED

Now for the Riverside manufactured-gas plant. Dates of operation: 1888–1911. (This is unnerving; this is in the Inland Empire itself, on the border of Imperial.) At the end of the twentieth century, when the document about it entered the State Archives, no groundwater analysis had yet been done, doubtless for lack of committed funds or of desire to know the truth. If I had to guess, why wouldn't I suppose the presence of cyanide, thallium and benzo(a)anthracene? In any event, investigators have already discovered the following treasures in the soil: polycyclic aromatic hydrocarbons in carcinogenic quantities, antimony, arsenic, barium, cadmium, chromium, vanadium. In 1992, two hundred tons of contaminated dirt were hauled away so they could contaminate someplace else.

The data tells similar parables for Long Beach, Colton, Los Angeles, Santa Ana.

W. H. SHEBLEY, DRAGONSLAYER

When would a new dawn come? I can provide an exact date: 6 June 1916, when the Fish and Game Commission advises the public, in circular letter number two thousand and seventy-nine, *In order that the matter of water pollution . . . be handled under one uniform plan for the State, which means that all these various matters must be handled by one person, I recommend that all business of this nature be turned over to W. H. SHEBLEY.*

And Californians lived happily ever after.

A heartwarming fable from 1927, "FOR IMMEDIATE RELEASE."

Trial of the suit against the Shell Oil Company for polluting the waters of Petaluma Creek resulted in a fine of $200 . . . A crew of men were put to work with hoes and shovels and the oil soaked banks of the creek were cleaned up in a highly satisfactory manner . . . Both the commission and the company were well pleased with the outcome of the action.

Meanwhile, the Director, Bureau of Hydraulics (a subdepartment of the Fish and Game Division), writes to the Union Oil Company's Manager of Refineries in Los Angeles: *My dear Mr. Page: . . . The looks of that ditch and the effluent were a distinct disappointment . . . It is the sincere desire of the writer to cooperate and work with the oil companies in the prevention of pollution, but it cannot be indefinitely postponed . . .*

I won't quote many more of these crazily half-friendly, half-adversarial letters involving such perfectly named personalities as Mr. William Groundwater, Manager of Transportation at the Union Oil Building; but the sorrowful Director of the

Bureau of Hydraulics is *taking the liberty of again calling this to your attention. From the reports received, it appears that the oil is again coming down . . .*

In that same year, 1927, almost a hundred oil companies in Huntington Beach receive injunctions for oil pollution. The Orange County Associated Chamber of Commerce worries about the fishing and the beach resorts.

In 1929 the Shell Company of California reassures the Fish and Game Commission that certain allegations about its operations in Los Angeles are unfounded. Oh, yes, the Shell Company denies that *water being discharged from our Wilmington Refinery into Nigger Slough carried considerable traces of oil.* It must be true, then. All's right with the world.

Who on this nobly oil-slicked globe of ours *wouldn't* rather be left alone? Who doesn't subscribe to the Imperial Idea? Why can't Shell piss out from her Wilmington refinery whatever color of urine she likes? In 1954, when the Department of Health, Education and Welfare begins intervening more actively to impose pollution standards on the various states of Northside, a Los Angeles Department of Water and Power typescript *For Intradepartmental Use Only* goes out from the Sanitary Engineering Division to Mr. Burton S. Grant, Chief Engineer of Water Works and Assistant Manager, B U I L D I N G. The Principal Sanitary Engineer grieves: *The matter of Federal interference by the U.S. Public Health Service when unsolicited is of great concern to the State Water Pollution Control Board.* No worries, mates! The Principal Sanitary Engineer will hold the line! In 1963 the United States Department of the Interior continues to admit defeat: *The general objective is maintenance of a minimum dissolved-oxygen content of 4 ppm in the streams receiving the waste. The requirements for waste treatment are generally far in excess of the standards met today . . .*

No doubt that describes the New River. Edith Karpen told me that when she first arrived in the Imperial Valley in 1933, *at that time, the growers would bring workers from the New River gorge.*

How was the smell in the thirties?

When I first got there, it wasn't too bad. It got worse all the time. I had a friend who was very outspoken. And when I was there, he was lobbying, I would say, to build a dam, so that the water couldn't come from Mexico!

(Richard Brogan told me, not without grim pride: You know what the U.S. Department of Health has rated our river? One of the worst in the world! All of mankind's diseases. Polio, tuberculosis.)

In the spring of 1950, *Fortune* magazine asserts: *Chemicals must now be considered the premier industry of the U.S.* And in 1954, Mr. Gifford Price, a corn farmer up in Mecca, informs a marketing order hearing that DDT costs him a hundred and twenty pounds per acre. *You can usually double crop.*

In 1966, the Lockheed Aircraft Company expresses readiness for self-improvement, because *wastes from certain processes, such as degreasing and chemical milling, are being conducted to disposal systems in a manner not considered acceptable engineering practice. The uncontrolled discharge of many of the untreated toxic wastes into the storm sewer produces some extremely hazardous, if not deadly fumes such as cyanide gas . . .* That very year, we are informed that almost seventy percent of southern California's wastes still go home to the Pacific. *About half of the wastes are industrial, many of them being dumped from barges several miles offshore.*

By 1985, California's groundwater contains pesticides from Aldicarb to Zytron—two thousand nine hundred and sixty-three verified incidents; but how serious are they really? Perhaps less than one percent of the aquifer is contaminated; surely our testing has been insufficient; certainly some poison levels will keep rising over the decades. For instance, the nematicide 1,2-dibromo-3-chloropropane (DBCP), employed for twenty years (more than fifty million pounds' worth), then banned in 1977, has now been found in two thousand five hundred and twenty-two wells,* a situation which affects seven hundred thousand Californians; over half these contaminated wells have dangerous concentrations. In 1984, DBCP concentrations in some wells are higher than when first measured in 1979. DBCP boasts a half-life of over a century. In Riverside County, a hundred and ninety-five thousand people, thirteen wells and three towns are contaminated. Imperial County escapes mention, although in a map of DBCP applications from 1972 to 1977 inclusive, I see quite a few thousand tons deployed in Imperial; it's tricky to determine how many, since the map key is so poor; Coachella looks pretty clean, as does the Imperial portion of San Diego; the Central Valley is a black nightmare . . .

How could Imperial be any less poisoned than her neighboring agribusiness Rothkoscapes? As with nematicides, so with pesticides: Data on the map of verified incidents of groundwater contamination from pesticides stains both Riverside and San Diego counties a threatening grey, but Imperial County remains snow white! Why? Is it because almost all the county's water comes from the Colorado River, so that there is no groundwater of relevance? (Never mind the long-gone artesian wells of Holtville.) Could it be that Imperial is simply too poor to warrant detailed study? I won't believe that; I can't help believing in people.

By the way, respiratory disease is three times more prevalent in the Imperial Valley than the national average; the reason, explains Dr. Thomas H. Horiagon, is *probably a combination of factors, culture, genetics and environment.*

You'll be relieved to know that on the other side of the ditch, everything remains as clean as a fifteen-year-old prostitute. A private detective in Tijuana said to me:

*In 1985 California has three-quarters of a million wells, so this works out to less than 0.4% of them.

The Mexican government received a report from these investigators to find out the ecological status of the province. And after they read it, they threw it away. If you use it, you never got it from me.

He let me glimpse the report, but would not let me copy it. In a word, the ecological status of the province was horrible.

Imperial is Mexico; Imperial is California; Imperial is cool clean Southwestern fun! And so in 1985, the State Water Resources Control Board, now coming into its forty-first year of existence, declares: *We are approaching the point where toxic pollution is beginning to affect the overall availability of water in California.* That doesn't count; that's after the happily ever after.

BY THE WAY

So W. H. Shebley saved our rivers forever and ever. What about dirt contaminated with cyanide, thallium and benzo(a)anthracene? I fear that that lay literally beneath, but not under, his jurisdiction.

"NO TRACE REMAINS"

In 1925 the citrus growers of California are advised that they can save themselves from dwarfs and culls with *"Black Leaf 40" the Old Reliable nicotine spray,* made in Kentucky. I wouldn't be surprised if a few tons of that improved the orange-scapes of Imperial. In 1950, potassium cyanate liberates us from weeds on fifteen hundred acres of Imperial Valley onions. At the same period, Coachella Valley dates are being fumigated with menthyl bromide, *a very poisonous gas* which *should be handled with extreme caution and only by responsible persons . . . This warning is given only to handlers, not the consumers of the fruit, as no trace of such gas remains on the date . . .*

Maybe that's true, and if I were going to write a book entitled *Imperial,* and if I were to do it with extreme caution and in a responsible manner, I would need to educate myself, and you, about the half-life and effects of each poison in Imperial. *The flow model indicates constituents of the soil contaminants first reached groundwater no later than the 1930s.* But for all I know, *no trace of such gas remains.* (César Chávez considered methyl bromide sufficiently dangerous to be banned.) Isn't it more relaxing just to throw up my hands and decide that a stream is like a woman?

By 1948, Imperial County was spraying 2,4-D on mesquite, although that *failed to give other than fair control. Check plots using arsenicals in jars with individual plant treatment proved more satisfactory and will be used in this program as well as treatment of Camel Thorn.* Ten years earlier, the California Board of Agriculture had warned:

Cattle like the salt and somewhat sweetish taste of sodium arsenite or sodium chlorate weed killer and will lick it up from the bare ground. Arsenate of lead can find its way onto strawberries . . . By then, lead and arsenic trioxide had put in appearances in produce sampled in Los Angeles; Angelenos were ingesting harmful spray residues in cabbages, cauliflowers, celery, tomatoes and especially cherries . . . I for one prefer to imagine that *no trace of such gas remains.* Don't you? Back to 1948. Imperial County's mission continues: *Chlorate has been used to clean up scattered infestations of Johnson Grass.*

In 1949, nearly three million pounds of insecticides were applied in Imperial County—not quite five pounds per irrigated acre. (Wherever these poisons were actually used, of course, the proportionate poundage would have been higher.) We doubled that in 1950. Chlordane for grasshoppers and crickets, oil emulsion spray for red scale, why not? In Imperial County we trap coyotes in the spring, and then we kill bugs. By 1951, we applied chlordane, oil and flake bran by air at ten pounds per acre. In 1954 the Agricultural Commissioner noted that *cotton, sugar beets and fall vegetable crops required almost continual application of insecticides.*

By now the Imperial Idea was getting discomfited by rumors that growers might need permission from their county agricultural commissions before spraying with parathion, lead arsenate, Paris green, etcetera. A grower in Merced assured the State Bureau of Chemistry that *he'd* never had any problems with his animals! Moreover, insecticides had cut his costs by 60 to 75 percent! *E. F. Kirkpatrick, entomologist of the American Cyanamid Company, stated that the use of parathion dusts containing less than 2 per cent is not particularly dangerous, provided, of course, that . . . the instructions are followed.* But by 1975, Northside had so far decayed that warning notices compulsorily arose for parathion and its kin; moreover, the user could no longer be under eighteen years old.—Do you suppose that some of those chemicals might be bad for us? Boysie Day of the University of California helped us keep our sense of proportion: *Commercial 2,4,5-T is about as toxic as kerosene or aspirin, and neither of these are to be taken in large doses.*

At the century's end, the quantity of insect poisons employed in Imperial County was said to be eight million pounds. Why worry? Very likely *no trace of such gas remains.*

Chapter 143

THE SALTON SEA

(1944–1986)

. . . it seems, in tragedy, that innocence is not enough.

—T. H. White, 1940

As late as 1968, Sand Point Marina and Lido Palms, Inc, both with post office boxes in Salton City, get together to invest in a lovely color photograph, full page, of speedboats and waders crowding the clear and shallow blue-brown waters of the Salton Sea, with mobile homes crowded on a sandy spit and flat desert, then a line of palms, then blue desert mountains in the background. As we moderns love to say: *Bucolic.*

That year a million freshwater gallons per minute flow into the Salton Sea.* It must be pretty pure, then!

Some of that sweet water originates in Mexico. I once asked Mrs. Finnell, the retired Agricultural Commissioner's wife, how the New River had been in the fifties, and she said: It was pretty bad then. It was terrible. Well, you know, they've built some sewage plants down in Mexicali.

Her description was confirmed by Peggy Hudson's 1958 high school yearbook,† which I found in a coffee shop on Main Street in El Centro. *Peggy—When you read this I hope you remember a certain Saturday night and the New River—ummmm! Good luck with Calipatria. Love ya (Paxton), Pam Robertson.*

The barnacles had arrived in 1944, probably from the pontoons of Navy seaplanes; by 1968 one beach is eleven feet thick in barnacles. Don't worry about those. Water-skiers remain almost as thick as barnacles!

During World War II General Patton himself visited a resort at the sea. A Coachella girl met her future husband there, proving that barnacles are no imped-

*Indeed, the sea is rising, thanks to outflow from Imperial County's expanding irrigated acreage. On Imperial County Assessor's Map number 9-12, where the Riverview Cemetery District meets the Niland Fire District, and the Southern Pacific Railroad inscribes a sine wave en route to Yuma, we discover the Salton Sea's recession from 1915 to 1919 and then to 1925, its original vastness beautifully inked in blue, but then posterity's pencil has scrawled in *Est. Water Line 1955*, a line which lives between 1925 and 1919.

†*La Ocotilla.* She was a student at Brawley Union High, where "Milling Cattle, Prancing Horses And Hard Riding Cowboys And Lovely Cowgirls Came Together For The Brawley Cattle Call of 1958."

iment to romance. A booster from 1948 assures us that *the public has been rather slow in adopting the area as a playground, but the day is rapidly approaching, when it will come into its own in a big way . . . Nine known species of edible fish inhabit its blue depths . . . Soon this entire area should become one of the most popular resort sections in the Southland.* In those days the sea was no more saline than ocean water.

Cigar-smoking M. Penn Philips, the W. F. Holt of the 1950s, had thrown all his weight behind *Salton Riviera,* which is to say *the most important development in our history.* He sold out at a fancy price—and he had nineteen thousand six hundred acres to sell. In came the Holly Corporation. In 1968 two hundred residences lord it over twenty-three thousand empty lots. Don't worry about that, either; because in the Salton Sea we now have all the tilapia and corvina you could ever want to catch! The first official health advisory (no fish for children and pregnant women, no more than eight ounces a month for the rest of us) will not be posted until 1986, the very year that a Salton Sea angling map, laden with tips on hooking your corvina right and how to bait tilapia (coincidentally, this helpful document was published in Los Angeles) announces that *"Nature's Magnificent Mistake" is rapidly making another name for itself—"A Fisherman's Paradise."*

The green-winged teal and the ospreys, the cormorants, mallards, sandpipers and herring gulls, I suppose that they've been taking the waters for quite awhile now.

Opening up my special "Inland Empire" edition of the *Imperial Valley Press* in this year of grace 1974, when people have already begun talking about diking off part of the Salton Sea and letting the rest go hang (it approaches the salinity of the Arabian Gulf; by century's end it will comfortably exceed it), I see another map, in fact my favorite old map of

— IMPERIAL VALLEY —

"The West's Favorite Sun and Air"

How full of fun it all is, from the non-existent palm grove between Smugglers' Cave and the Old Border Patrol Station all the way northeast to Palo Verde where an angler in a stylized Stetson hat braces his legs and bows his fishing rod against the giant fish beneath him in Oxbow Lagoon! There's dear old Calipatria, whose flagpole reaches all the way up to sea level! Just above the Ben Hulse Highway, a hunter in full outfit takes aim at a bird in flight toward the East Highline Canal. Above Superstition Mountain it says **SAND SCULPTURES** and **FOSSILS**; here comes an emblem of the Parachute Test Facility. Below, a stagecoach driver whips on his horses. I see Dixieland, although the Mobile of Wilber Clark is long gone. I find Date City, which still sold fresh dates at roadside stands as late as 1939; but

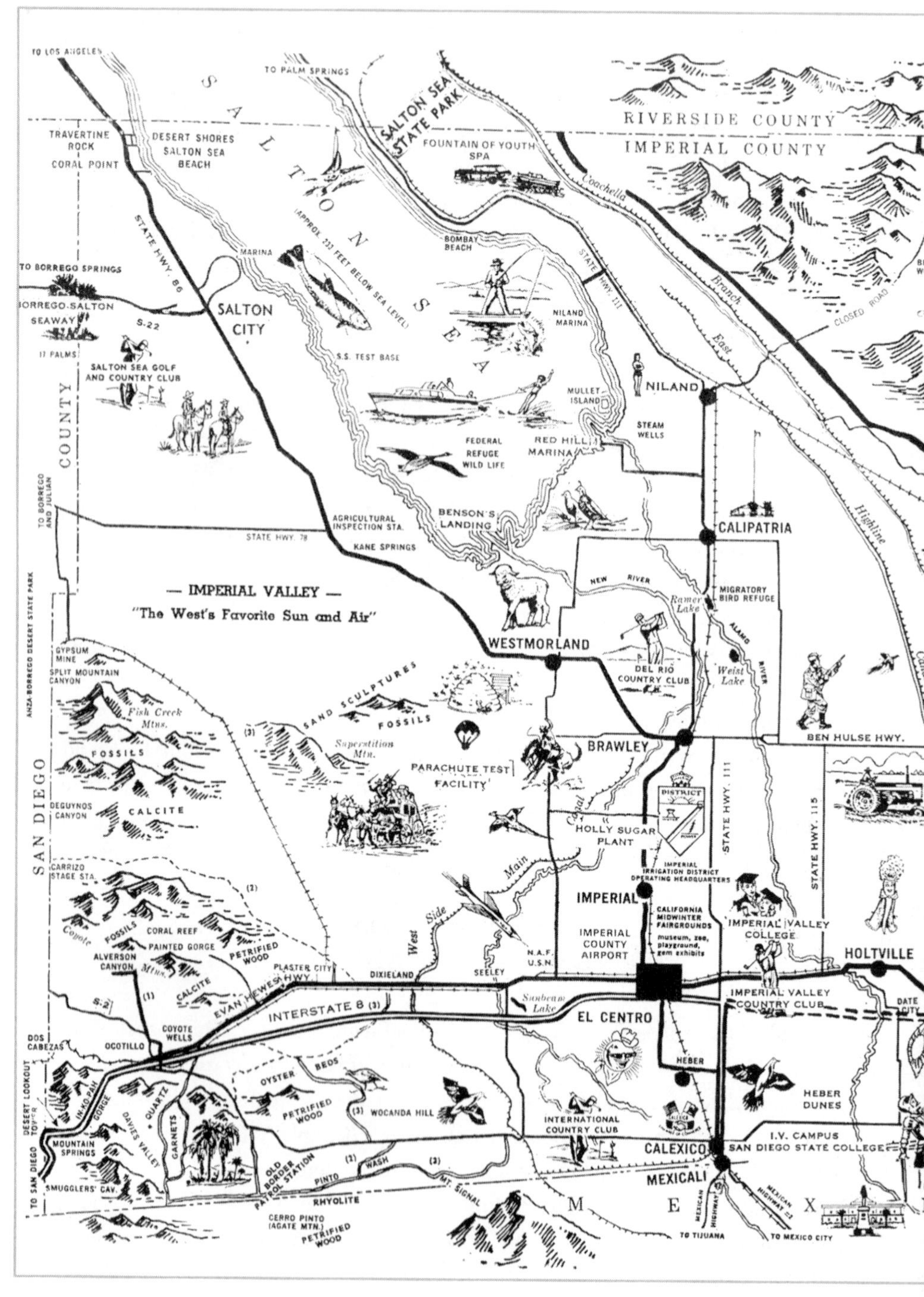
TO LOS ANGELES
TO PALM SPRINGS
SALTON SEA
SALTON SEA STATE PARK
RIVERSIDE COUNTY
IMPERIAL COUNTY
TRAVERTINE ROCK
CORAL POINT
DESERT SHORES
SALTON SEA BEACH
FOUNTAIN OF YOUTH SPA
Coachella
STATE HWY. 86
(APPROX. 232 FEET BELOW SEA LEVEL)
BOMBAY BEACH
MARINA
TO BORREGO SPRINGS
BORREGO-SALTON SEAWAY
S.22
17 PALMS
SALTON CITY
STATE HWY. 111
Branch
East
CLOSED ROAD
NILAND MARINA
S.S. TEST BASE
SALTON SEA GOLF AND COUNTRY CLUB
MULLET ISLAND
NILAND
STEAM WELLS
FEDERAL REFUGE WILD LIFE
RED HILL MARINA
SAN DIEGO COUNTY
TO BORREGO AND JULIAN
BENSON'S LANDING
CALIPATRIA
Highline
AGRICULTURAL INSPECTION STA.
STATE HWY. 78
KANE SPRINGS
ANZA-BORREGO DESERT STATE PARK
NEW RIVER
MIGRATORY BIRD REFUGE
Ramer Lake
— IMPERIAL VALLEY —
"The West's Favorite Sun and Air"
ALAMO RIVER
WESTMORLAND
DEL RIO COUNTRY CLUB
Weist Lake
GYPSUM MINE
SPLIT MOUNTAIN CANYON
SAND SCULPTURES
FOSSILS
Fish Creek Mtns.
Superstition Mtn.
BRAWLEY
BEN HULSE HWY.
FOSSILS
PARACHUTE TEST FACILITY
DISTRICT
DEGUYNOS CANYON
CALCITE
Canal
HOLLY SUGAR PLANT
STATE HWY. 111
STATE HWY. 115
Main
IMPERIAL IRRIGATION DISTRICT OPERATING HEADQUARTERS
CARRIZO STAGE STA.
IMPERIAL
CALIFORNIA MIDWINTER FAIRGROUNDS
museum, zoo, playground, gem exhibits
Side
IMPERIAL VALLEY COLLEGE
Coyote
FOSSILS
CORAL REEF
West
IMPERIAL COUNTY AIRPORT
PAINTED GORGE
PETRIFIED WOOD
ALVERSON CANYON
Mtns.
N.A.F. U.S.N.
HOLTVILLE
PLASTER CITY
DIXIELAND
SEELEY
EVAN HEWES HWY.
S-2
(1)
CALCITE
INTERSTATE 8 (3)
Sunbeam Lake
IMPERIAL VALLEY COUNTRY CLUB
DATE CITY
EL CENTRO
DOS CABEZAS
OCOTILLO
COYOTE WELLS
HEBER
OYSTER BEDS
DESERT LOOKOUT TOWER
IN-KO-PAH GORGE
QUARTZ
PETRIFIED WOOD
(3) WOCANDA HILL
HEBER DUNES
GARNETS
DAVIES VALLEY
INTERNATIONAL COUNTRY CLUB
MOUNTAIN SPRINGS
TO SAN DIEGO
OLD BORDER PATROL STATION
(1) WASH
(3)
PINTO
CALEXICO
I.V. CAMPUS SAN DIEGO STATE COLLEGE
SMUGGLERS' CAV.
RHYOLITE
MT. SIGNAL
MEXICALI
MEXICAN HIGHWAY
M E X
CERRO PINTO (AGATE MTN.)
PETRIFIED WOOD
TO TIJUANA
TO MEXICO CITY

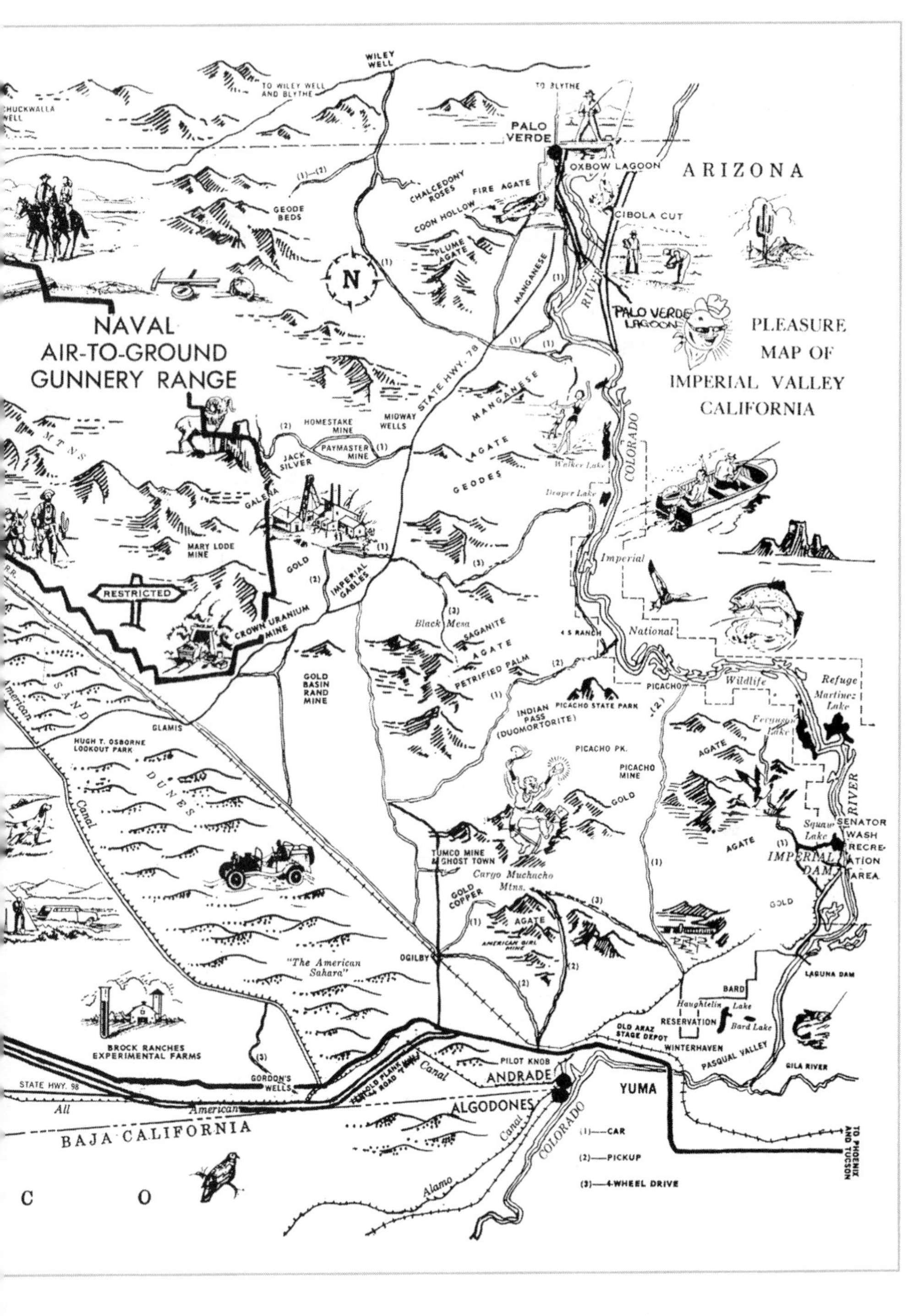
PLEASURE
MAP OF
IMPERIAL VALLEY
CALIFORNIA
ARIZONA
NAVAL
AIR-TO-GROUND
GUNNERY RANGE
WILEY WELL
TO WILEY WELL AND BLYTHE
CHUCKWALLA WELL
TO BLYTHE
PALO VERDE
OXBOW LAGOON
CIBOLA CUT
PALO VERDE LAGOON
CHALCEDONY ROSES
FIRE AGATE
COON HOLLOW
PLUME AGATE
GEODE BEDS
MANGANESE
STATE HWY. 78
HOMESTAKE MINE
MIDWAY WELLS
PAYMASTER MINE
JACK SILVER
GALENA
MARY LODE MINE
GOLD
IMPERIAL GABLES
CROWN URANIUM MINE
RESTRICTED
MTNS
AGATE
GEODES
Walker Lake
Draper Lake
COLORADO
RIVER
Imperial
National
Wildlife
Refuge
Martinez Lake
Ferguson Lake
Black Mesa
SAGANITE
PETRIFIED PALM
4 S RANCH
PICACHO
INDIAN PASS (DUOMORTORITE)
PICACHO STATE PARK
PICACHO PK.
PICACHO MINE
GOLD BASIN RAND MINE
GLAMIS
HUGH T. OSBORNE LOOKOUT PARK
SAND
DUNES
American
Canal
TUMCO MINE & GHOST TOWN
Cargo Muchacho Mtns.
GOLD COPPER
AMERICAN GIRL MINE
Squaw Lake
SENATOR WASH RECREATION AREA
IMPERIAL DAM
LAGUNA DAM
BARD
Haughtelin Lake
Bard Lake
RESERVATION
OLD ARAZ STAGE DEPOT
WINTERHAVEN
PASQUAL VALLEY
GILA RIVER
"The American Sahara"
OGILBY
BROCK RANCHES EXPERIMENTAL FARMS
STATE HWY. 98
GORDON'S WELLS
OLD PLANK ROAD
PILOT KNOB
ANDRADE
YUMA
ALGODONES
All American Canal
Alamo Canal
BAJA CALIFORNIA
C O
TO PHOENIX AND TUCSON
(1)—CAR
(2)—PICKUP
(3)—4-WHEEL DRIVE
N

there is no longer any Meloland. A cartoon carrot epitomizes Holtville. (The Carrot Carnival and Drag Races will run from 26 January to 3 February this year. The Carrot Carnival Parade will be 2 February.) El Centro offers us a smiling sun-face in sunglasses; the International Country Club must have withered by now. Calexico is represented by two flags and a handshake; Mexicali is a large black dot, because whatever that city has to sell, the Northside mapmakers can't cash in on. Now, feeling hot and thirsty, I let my gaze fall back upon the Salton Sea, and am immediately refreshed by a longlegged, bikini'd nymph of a water-skier who raises her left hand at me! I see birds, great fishes, and the carbon copy of the angler from Oxbow Lagoon. (Imperial is the white mummies of fishes and birds; Imperial is people fishing for dinner in what others fear to be a poisoned sea.) In the map, Mullet Island lives on. A stylized girl in a two-piece black bathing suit folds her arms under her bust just west of Niland (the Tomato Festival will take place there in the first three days of February). And there are mountains and Western riders everywhere.

Chapter 144

MARKET PRICES

(1975)

Life is better . . . in Imperial Valley, California

- Where the Action Is!
- Where the People Are!
- Where the Scenery Is!
- Where the Profits Are!

—Imperial Valley Development Agency, 1974

Slaughter steers were going for thirty-nine to forty dollars per cwt.; I found no mention of Imperial, but Stockton and Dixon were ready for you, especially if you wanted hogs and lambs. Cotton was available from the Fresno spot market. Where was Imperial cotton on the fourteenth of March, 1975? You'll have to ask God. As a matter of fact, cotton would end up being number nine on Imperial County's roster of million-dollar crops, which just goes to show that, as my mother says, you never, never know.* Meanwhile, here was something *today* from our favorite Wonderland of Factories: *Asparagus—loose, large crates. Imperial Valley District 15.00.* A year ago this crop had sold for eleven dollars; a month ago it ranged between sixteen and seventeen. Today, fortunately or unfortunately, Stockton Delta District asparagus was two dollars cheaper than the Imperial kind. I wonder which variety the grocery store middlemen went for? (As a wise woman from Imperial laid it out for me: How does a farmer make a million dollars farming? Start out with two million.) Actually, asparagus would be the tenth-place million-dollar crop.

(Does that sound good to you? I regret to inform you that by the beginning of the 1970s, the California Asparagus Association was already worrying about a planetary glut! *We all feel quite strongly that doing further research* on mechanized labor *will only allow other areas, both within the state of California and outside the state of*

*Southsiders had been saying that about cotton ever since the 1950s. In 2003 one rancher in Ejido Morelos told me: "But the trick is that the Americans were screwing over the Mexicans, that the Americans were stealing. They'd say, Cotton is going to be worth a lot this year. Then after we picked it, they'd say, What do you know, the price is low."

California, the United States and foreign countries to start producing asparagus, and thereby really affect our markets to the extent that we may have to go for a production marketing order to hold it down.)

Broccoli was coming in from the Ocean District and Salinas, cabbage from Oxnard. What about Imperial? It wasn't going to show up anywhere in the Agricultural Commissioner's report except for poor Category B: mixed vegetables, whose total combined value was the merest two point seven million. But on the fourteenth of March I saw *carrots—48 1-lb. film bags. Imperial–Coachella Valley District 6.50.* (Carrots would do much better than broccoli, but they had no hopes of qualifying for million-dollar status.) I saw *citrus—f.o.b. plant, shipper's 1st grade cartons:* to be specific, lemons from the Southern California District, oranges from the same; and then *Tangelos—Minneolas, large, Coachella Vly Dist. 2.25–2.50. Grapefruit—Marsh Seedless, 32s, Coach. Vly Dist. 3.00–3.25.* In the Imperial County portion of that valley, grapefruits, lemons, Valencia oranges and tangerines each did far worse than mixed vegetables that year. But let's end with more good news: *Lettuce—2 dozen heads, cartons. Imperial Valley District 2.00–2.25. Palo Verde District 2.50–3.00.* Indeed, lettuce was going to be the number-one million-dollar crop!

Sugar beets were number three; but, unfortunately, our world was just too fertile in 1975; there was too much sugar on the market! Imperial had to live with lower prices for that commodity.

In the end, the Commissioner was forced to sum up 1975 with all too typical agricultural irony:

The 1975 gross income from agricultural production in Imperial County exceeded the half billion mark for the second time in history, but the high prices received in 1974 disappeared in 1975. With a ten percent decrease in gross income and a continued increase in cost of production, the profit posture of our agricultural industry returned to the historic struggle of making ends meet.

Chapter 145

SAN DIEGO

(1975)

> Based on the research and analysis conducted for this report—including that generated during prior studies in San Diego—the key conclusion of Ashley Economic Services, Inc., is that under most circumstances, growth does pay for itself . . .
>
> —A report sponsored by the California Builders Council, 1973

"REVENUES WILL BE RISING DUE TO INCREASED ASSESSED VALUES"

By now, San Diego County has become almost as crowded as a barbershop in San Luis Río Colorado late on a Sunday morning. In 1970 the population was one point two million. In 1980 it will be one point eight million. What will they all drink? How will their excrement get flushed away? How will they all play golf? An academic expert warns: *Today, the county as a whole is about 90 percent dependent on imported water supplies, and that figure will most likely increase in the future.* Fortunately; **WATER IS HERE**. In 1973 we added Pipeline Number Four, *this one again about as large as all previous ones combined;* and *it is hoped,* at least by our academic expert, *that this new line will be sufficient to handle the county's water needs until at least the 1990s;* all the same, in 1982 we'll see fit to add Pipeline Number Five, which, so I'm proudly informed, *brought the Water Authority's total pipeline capacity to about 1 million acre-feet per year, roughly 15 times more than the capacity of the first pipeline alone, which had been built only 35 years earlier.*

Why exactly does San Diego feel compelled to grow so much? Well, you see, all the housing developments examined by Ashley Economic Services, Inc., generate *an overall surplus of cash revenues (including taxes, fees, and other user charges) over expenses for the governing cities or counties.*

At the same time, a detailed study on the rapidly shrinking coastal area between Los Angeles and San Diego concludes: *Urbanization of this strip is now well underway and clearly will result in an incoherent pattern of undifferentiated and environmentally disastrous sprawl unless some logical control is exerted.*

Unquestionably, agrees Ashley Economic Services, Inc., *it is entirely possible that an individual residential development could represent a financial drain to the city if the average assessed valuation per household were extremely low combined with high service cost.* What if, for instance (and this is my instance), there existed a zone of low-salaried service personnel or fluctuating-salaried agricultural workers, who happened to need welfare, schools, health care? *Among all developments surveyed for this report, the only one registering a deficit with the local school district was a rental apartment project with numerous children.* I myself have seen several such places in El Centro and Calexico, not to mention Mexican Imperial. Happily, Ashley Economic Services, Inc., has a solution: Throw in enough high-income housing to pay for the low-income housing.

Ashley Economic Services, Inc., asserts that police and fire services comprise a city's two biggest expenses. (I wonder if they'd like to do away with those?)

Beverly Hills doesn't need to grow much more because *the appreciation of value on existing real estate has more than provided for the increased municipal service cost each year.* In other words, Beverly Hills is a nice, rich place.

But why not build a hundred-and-six-acre commercial center in north San Diego? Ashley Economic Services, Inc., doesn't see any reason why not. *It should be noted that both the city and school district will receive a net surplus of revenues in every year of development. Further, it is not until 1983 that the school district will have any costs resulting from this project, as residential development is not anticipated until this time. In the meantime, revenues will be rising due to increased assessed values.* Besides, who cares about 1983?

MIRACLES

In San Diego, you see, and indeed in all these United States, we believe in miracles. Between 1963 and 1974, San Diego County's agricultural acreage has increased by only one and a half percent, while agricultural income has increased by two hundred and twenty-three percent. If we could only do the same with water . . . !

PARENTHETICALLY

Parenthetically, advises Ashley Economic Services, Inc., *in the absence of new growth, short of a serious cutback in the quality and quantity of municipal services, existing property owners and residents would have been burdened with $11 million in added expenses which they would have to bear alone.* More than two and a half million of that eleven million buys Colorado River water. Why bear that alone? Well, I guess that San Diego is stuck with growing.

Unfortunately, San Diego has junior priority to receive Colorado River water. *Luckily, by the 1970s there was a new source for imported water: water from Northern California.*

Chapter 146

MEXICALI

(1975)

> Water has been the key to Mexicali's growth . . .The result is an agricultural empire in the middle of the desert, served by a proud city with modern commercial and industrial complexes . . . Permeating the Mexicali of the 1970s is a distinct aura of prosperity and vitality.
>
> —Automobile Club of Southern California, 1976

San Diego was growing, to be sure; so was everywhere else, especially Southside. In the middle decade of the twentieth century, the overall population of Mexico rose by thirty-four percent—and in Mexican Imperial, the increase was over eighty-three percent. Well, why not? The winner of the 1970 presidential campaign assured his electorate that they could make their families as large as they wished. He himself had eight children. And between 1910 and 1975, the number of people in Mexicali went up a thousandfold.

Indeed, a Northside historian writes that as the end of the twentieth century approached, Mexico had grown far away from Cárdenas's revolutionary goal, with the microcosm being no longer the *ejido,* but Mexico City itself.

Squatters continued to arrive in Mexicali, building shacks in the obscenely named Colonia Chorizo just south of the line—and what could be more dusty and unclean than the dirt road that ran through that place in 2006, paralleling both the border wall and a stinking greenwater ditch that once used to and perhaps still did receive the excess *aguas negras* of the Río Nuevo?—or going east of the city, or southeast, or south, or southwest—anywhere but north, of course. (There had been squatters even back in Andrade's time; the Colorado River Land Company evicted them as courteously as was practicable.)—In 2004, a lady named Señora Socorro Ramírez said to me: About twenty years ago the invasions started, more or less. When Xicotencatl Leyva Mortera was governor, that is when there were many invasions. But his successor put a stop to it.

Nowadays, I asked her, in places such as Colonia Chorizo, how often do they just invade the land and how often do they buy outright?

About twelve years ago it became illegal to squat, because politicians got involved and they moved people to these places, to get votes and positions.

But I'm sure that people still do it, correct?

No, she insisted. If they do it, they go to prison.

But in 2004 they were still doing it, all right, from Mexicali to Tijuana . . .

Swelling like a ripe orange on a tree at Rancho Roa, Mexicali continued nonetheless to be much the same. I am not saying that history left no marks on the fruit: In 1975 sixteen cases of screwworm were reported in Mexicali livestock, and C. Armando Gallego Moreno was Mayor, and the girls were in their low-cut sundresses, and an old Mexican cowboy limped along all in white, drinking from a white plastic cup; I saw him or his son in 1999; what would he have drunk from in 1975? In 1975 three withered palm trees guarded a vacant lot, and the vendor was nodding over his lemon-boiled corn.

The parking attendant Lupita,* who when I interviewed her in 2003 had lived in Mexicali for exactly thirty years, said that the days of the "white gold" were gone by the time she arrived. I asked what else she remembered from those days, and she said: The airport used to be where the baseball stadium is, and the main road was up here. Where the Kenworth factory is now, on the way to San Felipe, it was all empty.

Was Mexicali better then or is it better now?

Before was the time! she said sadly. Too many robbers now. Too many in my house: Five or six times they've taken my television, my radio.

She had worked then as a security guard in a disco. She smiled and remembered the beauty of the disco prostitutes; and her smile was that same sweet smile I had seen so many times in Imperial when people remembered the past.

And the past was still present, at least to those of us who live now, on this side of it (in other words, the past is past). The *Great Soviet Encyclopedia* (whose information, I grant, might be secondhand and even out of date), describes the Mexicali of this period as follows: *The city is a transportation junction and the center of an irrigated farming region producing cotton, wheat, tomatoes, and oilseed crops.* That entry could have been written about 1950, perhaps even about 1940. Mexicali lay as still and stable as any long alley in the Chinesca, perfectly sunned and shadowed, adorned by her corrugated roofs, from which squares of green-papered light-stripes shone alternately. And if you prefer to hear the same information in Spanish, the same facts offered for sale as neatly as the stuffed sea turtles of San Felipe, I will gladly advise you that in 1978, nearly two hundred and twenty-five *mil hectares* produced more than two and a half *millones de toneladas*. In 1982, fifty *mil hectares*

*The reader has already been introduced to her in "The Chinese Tunnels," p. 422.

more than that produced about half a million *toneladas* less, with various swings and dips in between. By 1975 there might have been a few million people and toneladas more than in 1950, but what of that? Mexicali drowsed and labored on, in the thick of agricultural news.

Señora Olga Márquez, born in 1973, had continued for all her thirty-one years to dwell right there in Colonia Colorado No. 4, which lies a few kilometers east of the Mexicali–San Felipe Highway.

I lived right down the road, she said, and then I got married and moved here. The street went right through here, and this was a parcel of land (she pointed to a yard). They had cows back then. They grew Sudan grass and rye grass. And my grandmother was here. My grandmother made cheese here. They've been fishing in that canal for a long time.

What is the name of that canal?

It has a name, but I can't remember.

How's the life here for you?

I like it. I like the tranquillity and the ranch and the animals. Above all, I like to raise my children here.

What's your opinion of Mexicali?

It's nice. The people there are really nice. The stores are close and everything is close, but I like it even better here because things are more tranquil.

Where else have you been in your life?

Indio, La Quinta, even Bakersfield. I was visiting my uncles. I took my children to Disneyland.

Did you notice any differences between Americans and Mexicans?

The life up there is more enclosed. You go to work and you go home. That's what it seems like to me.

And the life here, will this life stay like this for your children?

It will change, she said, her children smiling beside her.—Who knows? Maybe my children when they grow up will want to live in Mexicali. I want them to have good jobs.

What's the most beautiful thing you've seen or experienced here in your life?

Living right beside my parents. And my brothers and sisters.

Standing outside her little house, with Centinela, known to Northside as Signal Mountain, a translucent blue stegosaurus to the northwest, she intimated that not much had altered here in the course of her entire life; and she liked it that way. Time was a smiling functionary of the municipal park, a man whose hose nourished the grass with the slowest possible water (yes, in Mexicali water travels at a different average speed than in the United States). The Thirteen Negro continued in its glory; I imagine that it was not much different in 1975 than it is tonight in

1998 when the man to my left stares into space and a blonde approaches the table of men to my right, extending her wrist to be kissed by each of them; in the next moment she has withdrawn to the next table to laugh into another woman's ear; they are pointing at the two men and scheming, while the two men are plotting still more seriously with regard to the two women, measuring resources, proclivities and choice, at which point the dance is over, the musicians begin, and it gets so loud that conversation consists of shouting into another human being's ear; at the table behind me, the campesino whom I suspect of being the thief of my baseball cap has now drunk enough to resemble a certain Olmec-style jade mask once offered to the Great Temple of Tenochtitlán: a broad, dark, smooth and shiny face, with downturned black crescent-slits for eyes and fleshy lips downturned in a grimace; that greenish-black mask appears to be stoically experiencing pain or some other unpleasantness, all the while gazing into the land of gods and dreams, as a devout victim might do when the Aztec priests cut his heart out. His eyes dull. His head slumps. He snores in the darkness while the flashing red dances of blood blare on and on. Indeed, the Thirteen Negro continued in its glory, as did the other wide, red-lit bars like happy hells, precursors of the boutique SEXY—SERVICIO PAN AMERICANO DE PERFECCION, SA de CV where orange-faced girls beneath green neon stood yet more steadfast than the pillars of money-changing signs. Mexicali was growing, to be sure; but even in my epoch Imperial mostly appears uninhabited; Imperial is sun and dirt, with accidental concretions of people and wilderness in between.*

In 2000, a middle-aged, sun-honeyed woman with a long lush pigtail wormed through with grey rests her brawny arm upon the back of an old man in a cowboy hat as they watch television together in a restaurant: girls in black swimming suits raising their arms above their heads so that their breasts jut out. The girls smile winningly. It's an exercise program. What might have been on television in 1975? The restaurant was here; it's an old Mexican-Chinese place in the Chinesca. Perhaps there was no television in it then. The middle-aged woman would have been young and her man middle-aged. I ask whether they dined here a quarter-century ago, and she smilingly replies: *Claro!*, which is to say, of course.

*In 1904, the naturalist Hugo De Vries takes a ramble out of Imperial City. "From the inn, located at about the center of the young city, I walked for about one hour along one of the irrigation canals, between luxuriant fields, mainly planted with wheat and barley, some with sorghum and alfalfa and special cultures. After that time, I reached the boundary line of cultivation and hence the desert." Then what? He sees sandhills to the east, the New River to the west. The desert reappears. A century later, that is still the feeling one gets when strolling past the border of one of the *ejidos*, or even Mexicali itself.

Chapter 147

"THE LANGUAGE SEEMS TO BELONG SO TO THIS COUNTRY"

(*ca.* 1960–2003)

> "You seem to be very fond of Spanish, Miss Worth," he said, when the girl came back to the porch . . . Barbara laughed at his evident displeasure. "The language seems to belong so to this country. To me its colors are all soft and warm like the colors of the Desert."
>
> —Harold Bell Wright, 1911

One June morning in 2003, when more-than-hundred-degree days were just starting to feel more likely than less-than-hundred-degree days, I read in the newspaper that five out of eight illegal aliens from Sinaloa had perished in a car crash near Ocotillo. A survivor who identified himself as the driver was, in keeping with the tenderhearted policies of these United States, arrested and charged with five counts of second-degree murder. How had he so identified himself? California Highway Patrolman Richard Bird explained that the man, whose name was Angulo, *indicated he had been driving.* That interview led to Angulo's being arrested. The next day's newspaper continued the story: *In continuing the investigation, Bird said, it was determined Angulo had not been talking about driving the vehicle.* The driver was dead. So it all ended happily for Angulo, whose name was actually Cruz (Angulo being his middle name), and whose fate now would merely be detention and deportation from Imperial. Patrolman Bird's mistake must have been the result of linguistic difficulties.

Someday these difficulties would end; for the language of both American and Mexican Imperial was becoming Spanish, as had once been the case before Imperial got subdivided. American Imperial officially remains English-speaking even now as I write in 2007, but in practice English is sinking into the sand like spilled water. As early as 1934, half of all Calexicans are Mexican or Mexican-American. The Hispanicizing of this region accelerates in the 1950s. By the time the twentieth century had flowed three-quarters away, the Anglos for whose ostensible sake the valley had been irrigated comprise a distinctly less monumental presence than before.

Sixties to seventies, the place was doing some serious changing, said Kay Brockman Bishop. Just becoming more Mexican. You can easily go to Wal-Mart in Calexico and go through ten clerks before you can find one that can speak English. Sometimes I pretend not to speak Spanish just to see how they are. They're nice, but you know. Calexico has worked itself up into a certain mindset, and it's not a mindset that I agree with. I feel that if you're going to come to the United States, then work yourself *into* the United States. Try to fit in. They want to stay Mexican *and* stay on this side. I just don't think that's fair. But they can get away with it in these border towns.

Whatever you might think of her judgment, her analysis remained undeniably valid; and in the random year 1985, the contestants for the Miss Calexico Pageant bore the revealingly non-Anglo-Saxon names of Nora Alicia Bermudez, Nidia G. Castellanos, Siria Eduviguez Calderon, Lucy Trujillo, Martha J. Chong and Fabiola Yuriko Maeda. In the following year, we could still find *Bill Polkinhorn representing De Anza and his Spanish riders;* all the same, the 1986 Miss Calexico was Martha Patricia Castellanos.

(César Chávez, 1984: . . . *twenty and thirty years from now . . . in the Imperial Valley and in many of the great cities of California—these communities will be dominated by farm workers and not by growers . . .*)

A different delineation line has not yet been entirely erased even now. *Contestant must be single, never have been married, nor may she be living with a male partner in lieu of legal marriage . . .* On the other side of the ditch there is a Christmas tree in the lobby of the Nuevo Pacífico and the nearest whore is wearing a festive red miniskirt. On Avenida Tejada all the pretty girls in doorways mouth kisses at me, and I feel warm inside as I wink back at them, not caring that the air stinks like the Río Nuevo. Thus Mexicali. But in Calexico I have almost never seen a whore, no doubt because *a girl's strength of character and personality are reflected in a wholesome appearance.* No matter. In the olden days, Miss Calexico was Barbara Worth, who spoke Spanish for much the same reason that she played the piano. By the 1970s, Miss Calexico was likely to be Mexican-American.

This county was run by the Anglos, said Richard Brogan. The English language was the predominant language, and that's not the case today. In this county there's a significant bias. You can see the anti-white attitude every day.

Brogan named a Mexican-American woman who is mentioned in this book, and he said of her: She has an agenda, that's what I see. Her husband is not as smooth as her; he's not as intelligent. He's a flat-out racist. She's so flat-out smart and savvy that you will never know it from her.

I have already told you what he said about the organization called California

Rural Legal Assistance: *They're a legal representative of poor people but I don't think there's English spoken within their doors . . .*

AND HE IS US

Not only the language is getting Latinized. In his wonderfully evenhanded essay about Northern and Latin American stereotypes of each other, Richard Pike lays out Northside's view of Southside: animalistic, unregulated, hedonistic, servile, ignorant, idolatrous, lascivious, dishonest, corrupt in every sense. Barbara Worth's Caucasian empire never resembled that; the rectitude of W. F. Holt was as reliable and sublimated as the All-American Canal. But now that Barbara has happily married, and Arid America has been syndicated into a wonderland of factories whose operations are almost as efficient as washing machines, we catch our breaths, look about us and perceive that we seem to be living in our own banana republic up here! The Watergate scandal, and Iran-Contra, and the criminality of George W. Bush's administration; televangelists caught with prostitutes, a President and his intern, deficit spending, a politicized judiciary, secret prisons, mercenaries and torture—I do declare, Barbara; I just can't help believing in people! *Latin Americanization,* explains Pike, *implies basically that Americans . . . have themselves assumed the identity of the Latin Other—as traditionally stereotyped.* They *have not become as we are, but* we, *regardless of station of life, have become as they are.*

In Los Angeles a woman watches the infamous beating of the black man Rodney King. The acquittal of the police who did it will set off the riots of 1992. The woman's husband wants to get away from the scene. *And he was just petrified—he grew up in a country where this is prevalent; police abuse is prevalent in Mexico.*

The English language was the predominant language, and that's not the case today. Calexico has worked itself up into a certain mindset, and it's not a mindset that I agree with. *We need have no fear that our lands will not become better and better as the years go by.*

Chapter 148

LOS ANGELES

(1975)

Its water projects today reach out hundreds of miles across the Southwest, while its electrical power is drawn still further from projects scattered throughout six states.

—California Water Atlas, 1979

I don't mean to say we're perfect. We've got a lot to do in the way of extending the paving of motor boulevards.

—Sinclair Lewis, 1922

TÍPICO AMERICANO

The bartender at the Bella Union Hotel in Los Angeles, who *looked as though he had not smiled since his father was hung,* continues to refrain from smiling, having gone off duty sometime since the 1850s. And downtown itself likewise decays.—After the fifties it went away, said Marjorie Sa'adah. By '63, downtown was like *dead.* In the seventies it was like Skid Row.

Today Southern California has lost its booster spirit, concludes the author of a book on water politics. *It has vanished along with the clear skies . . .*

The blue-striped yellow halvah-flesh of the Wilshire Boulevard Temple, whose turreted dome is an anachronism of ornateness, implies by its very singularity that not merely agricultural Imperial-ness has bled almost out of Los Angeles, but also the architectural grandiosity of old times. The cream-colored wedding cake of another old building confronts the wrecking ball, and for what? As early as 1966, a book entitled *Eden in Jeopardy: Man's Prodigal Meddling with His Environment—The Southern California Experience* decries Los Angeles's freeways, which resemble *gigantic watch springs of concrete.* By the end of the century, although the grid of Los Angeles does still give way to green, brown and blue mountainscape decorated by coastal clouds as we go south, the grid then begins again, like immense silicon chips studded with resistors overlaid upon the land; it's all cubes, sometimes set within vegetated squares, sprawling south between the ocean and the first range of mountains to the east. It crawls and crawls, embellished by the ship-wakes like snow-white comet-trails in the blank blue Pacific.

The good news is that Los Angeles had protected her future. The "second barrel" of the Owens Valley Aqueduct was completed in 1969; it is simply needless to question the supply of water.

And let's not accuse Los Angeles of utterly abandoning her past! In 1974 she still grew one-tenth of one percent of California's cantaloupe acres, and slightly under half a percent of California's carrot acres. The market value of her various agricultural productions continued to rise, although naturally she could no longer hope to keep pace with Imperial:

MARKET VALUE OF AGRICULTURAL PRODUCTS SOLD

	1969	*1974*	
Imperial	$293,222,000	$573,938,000	+ 96%
Riverside	223,333,000	374,778,000	+ 68%
San Diego	117,813,000	206,430,000	+ 75%
Los Angeles	106,085,000	146,407,000	+ 38%
CALIFORNIA	3,898,330,000	7,399,623,000	+99%

Note: The 1974 definition of a farm is used.

Source: Census Bureau (1974).

Gross ag receipts of 1974, up two hundred thousand over 1973, were *largely offset by rising costs and decreases in dairy herds and beef cattle held in feedlots.* Los Angeles's accomplishment therefore reminds me of Albert Speer's: As the Allies bombed more and more of the Third Reich's factories and railroads, he actually managed to increase output for a time. In greater Los Angeles, agriculture is on the verge of yielding almost completely to urban sprawl. The county's cantaloupe and carrot productions are heroically doomed holding actions, like similar efforts in the Inland Empire.

In the last decade of the twentieth century, almost eighty-seven thousand jobs will drive away from Los Angeles; close to three hundred and forty-one thousand of them will reappear in the Inland Empire, thereby beating out San Diego and Orange County. The future of Los Angeles's slums, like their nineteenth-century past, is violent crime. We head toward the riots of 1992. In 1993 a renowned observer of Los Angeles remarks that *on the East side we have the worst Latino gang war in history.*

But Los Angeles is not at all in decline. Citywide, countywide, she grows—and grows. She builds, subdivides, booms as much as ever. Moreover, if we consider her from the standpoint of water distribution and consumption, Los Angeles's success is breathtaking. The Metropolitan Water District now reaches deep into the Inland Empire; its tentacles embrace those of the San Diego County Water Authority; **THE DESERT DISAPPEARS**.

Chapter 149

EL CENTRO

(1975)

Good Lord, George, you don't suppose it's any novelty to me to find out that we hustlers, that think we're so all-fired successful, aren't getting much out of it?

—Sinclair Lewis, 1922

By 1980, El Centro, now served by Imperial Airlines, covered five point one square miles of Imperial desert. *The bountiful continent is ours, state on state, and territory on territory, to the waves of the Pacific sea.*

Chapter 150

THE INLAND EMPIRE

(1875–2004)

But, you know, I honestly don't think that we're going to work out psychohistory in time to prevent the Fall of the Empire.

—Isaac Asimov, 1993

As long and clear and verdant as the view used to be looking north on George Chaffey's Euclid Avenue back at the end of the nineteenth century when the San Gabriel Mountains loomed crisply in the air, that was how visible the Inland Empire's history now grew in hindsight, from pedestrians and horses on that three-lane boulevard to cars trapped against each other in the smog, the passengers worrying about getting to the airport on time.

Progress is the delicious Mexicali whore who's just had a happy orgasm with her hand in your hair and your head between her legs; when it's your turn, and the condom breaks, Progress, after asking if she can be your *novia,* volunteers to buy another condom from the lobby man, leaps from the bed, dresses in a flash, expels a few cleansing drops of urine from her hole, promises to return in one minute or less, gravely, almost sternly wags her finger, instructing you: *Confianza! Confianza!* and disappears forever. Where did Ontario go? Where's Upland? I feel sad; all the same, how can I not love Progress? *I have never been cheated out of a dollar in my life.* Where did Progress go? Progress is here; autos are here; **WATER IS HERE**.

Here's Progress for you: *Soon, the Inland Empire . . . had become the land of big-box warehouses.* Progress's instrument: Freeways! Interstate 15 whizzes commodities from Mexico to Vegas; Interstates 10 and 15 move people and things around between the Empire and Los Angeles. At night, headlights resemble those glowing doughnuts of glass beads excavated from Riverside's long dead Chinatown.

Riverside County struggles to hold the line. In 1974 we find her, in defiance of Holtville's world-famous Carrot Festival, doing substantially better than Imperial for carrots (twenty-two farms and more than seventy-nine hundred acres in comparison to Imperial's fifteen farms and less than fifty-four hundred acres).* Even Imperial's signature crop, cantaloupes (this year lumped together with Persian melons), must take Riverside into account in 1974: Her acreage is more than twenty-seven percent of Imperial's, which in turn is seventeen percent of the state's. The Inland Empire's agricultural totals remain nearly as grand as Riverside's palms and towers on Lemon Street.

But Progress does what she has been put on earth to do. Dairy farms become *world-class distribution sites.* Guess what befalls carrot and cantaloupe farms? It all happens by the end of the 1980s, in sight of the Mission Inn's pale umbrellas and citruses.

In 1950 it cost two hundred and fifty dollars an acre to grow oranges. In 1980 it costs fourteen hundred and fifty dollars, in part because smog blights the trees. **Sign of Slow Growth Sends Stocks Lower.** Indeed, in 1975, smog caused five percent of California's milk and beef price increases; you see, *about three times as much alfalfa can be reaped from a field in clean air as from a smoggy field near Riverside.* We now return to 1980's woes: Urban spoilsports frown upon pesticides and smudging; housing developments raise everybody's property values and therefore property taxes go up; finally and mysteriously, water is getting more expensive.

In 1913, the Inland Empire city of Corona, once named South Riverside in homage to the Empire's flagship city, packs out the most oranges in Southern California. In 1982, the citrus plant closes; small houses pop up.

I remember a lovely young queen in a white robe and gold circlet in her hair; she held an orange aloft and a scepter of oranges below; orange groves filled the round world behind her; she gazed at me from the label of Queen Colony Fruit Exchange "Royal," Corona, Riverside, California. Where did she go? She sold out at a fancy price.

*California held 186 carrot farms and 30,760 carrot acres.

Chapter 151

SUBDELINEATIONS: ORANGESCAPES

(or, "It Could Be Called Ambrosia I Suppose")

(1873–2005)

Actually, the orange industry is not faced with overproduction; rather, it's a case of underconsumption.

—J. A. Finley of the Orange Products Company, Ontario, San Bernardino County (1950)

In self-defensive necessity, the late-nineteenth-century citrus dreams of Riverside County *(buds all straight . . . Mediterranean Sweet ORANGES . . . Home Grown, Thrifty Deciduous Fruit Trees of Best Varieties . . .)* were counter-dreamed by San Diego, of course, which insisted in its 1901 city and county directory that Chula Vista was no less than the center of the lemon belt of America! Unimproved citrus land, San Diego informed us, went for fifty to three hundred dollars per acre with water; improved, it started at two hundred dollars and went up, up, up! Rest assured that Los Angeles dreamed, too. Will Wolfskill first planted citrus there back in 1857 (some say 1841); in 1873, by which time Wolfskill was making a thousand dollars an acre, Mrs. H. Shaw's Los Angeles Nursery, two miles below town on San Pedro Street, hawked *my Orange Trees now bearing, . . . raised from seed that I myself brought from Nicaragua, Central America . . . My bearing Lime Trees . . . now a perfect sight to behold.* Thomas A. Garey's Semi-Tropical Nurseries for their part offered THE LARGEST AND MOST COMPLETE STOCK . . .

All the same, California's lemon-orange hopes, let alone Imperial's, remained as speculative as the idea of irrigating desert and turning it into America's Winter Garden. *The club motto is, "The aim if reached or not, makes great the life."* In the penultimate decade of the nineteenth century, Boston, New York and other market cities were already gobbling down barrel-packed oranges grown by our future archrival, Florida; barrels of Florida grapefruit followed before that decade's end. So how could California cash in? The brother of Imperial's Confident Man did his mite. (Of course I mean L. M. Holt.) He was the one who coined the following name for our prospective citrus belt: *Semi-Tropical California*. How much is in a name? For that matter, how much is in a package? Here comes this citrus dispatch from Riverside, just in from the early 1880s: *The Chinamen seemed to be especially expert in this line, as they packed all sizes in the same box and had them come out even at the top, showing the most desirable sizes.* So save the American workingman and run those Chinamen out! Meanwhile, Riverside dreams more dreams, each as grand as her first Citrus Fair in 1879: See the pyramids of cans and fruits stacked like miniature cannonballs on long white-clothed tables while hot white light bursts in between the drapes!

L. M. Holt buys up the newspaper. Now booming and boostering can go full swing!

In 1880, California grows three thousand acres of citrus. In 1893, there's over forty thousand acres! I gaze down through the decades at the dark lushnesses of Riverside orange groves, straight lines of trees fanning out and in according to the whims of topography and perspective, making cleanly inhuman geometries of loveliness upon rolling desert acres, with perfectly empty mountains far below and beyond. This is what *the Inland Empire* means. But in Butte and Ventura and Tulare they have their empires. Why mention Orange County? All California would go orange if she could.

By 1899 our Southern California Agricultural Substation had already proved that oranges did better with deep-furrow irrigation than with wide shallow furrows. But since that only helped a little, let's leave our gladness in the past tense. As late as 1902, with Wilber Clark already in Imperial and water in the ditches, California sent seven thousand one hundred and forty-one carloads of *deciduous fruits* to the Eastern States, among which I don't find citrus listed.

But in the summer of 1904 fancy lemons are going for between fifty cents and a dollar, standard lemons for fifty cents—in 1950 lemons will be two and a half cents per pound; now back to 1904: grapefruits for ninety cents to a dollar, fancy Valencias for two dollars; and at the beginning of that year, the USDA pomologist G. Harold Powell has come west for the first time. He writes his wife: *For two days we travelled across New Mexico, Arizona, and California and saw not a farm comparable to the eastern farms.* He's going to do something about that.

Mr. Powell is now remembered primarily as a citrus man. His experiments will prove that mechanical injury in cutting, packing and sorting cause most of the decay which growers had previously blamed on misfortunes of transit. (Typical California news from 1905: Eighteen carloads of lemons and oranges arrive in Boston, but with a thirty-percent spoilage rate.) Watch this, gentlemen! Two boxes packed with carefully handled oranges, then opened a few days later, exhibit mold damage in only one point one percent of the contents. Two other boxes whose fruit bears "tiny clipper cuts and stem punctures" present an astounding sixty-three-percent damage ratio. The citrus growers praise Powell, banquet him, invite him to dance with their daughters; he's saved them millions. And they have millions to save, millions to spend; disliking the Southern Pacific's freight charges, they even consider financing another transcontinental railroad, assessing themselves ten dollars for each acre they own. Oh, my, what big men! They're almost Imperial men.

One can tell from Powell's letters home that not only does he sincerely care about helping the industry, he also loves the citrus vistas of the Inland Empire. From Whittier, where *the dark green foliage and the flaming yellow fruit of the orange groves made a striking picture,* to "the El Cajon lemon district," to Santa Paula near Fullerton, which he calls *the finest lemon Ranch in California, 300 acres under the most perfect cultivation,* he yields up as much enthusiasm as a ripe navel orange does juice. (His character flaw: silence about the queen of all citrus—grapefruit.) By 1909, on his second trip to California, he's become a bigshot, writing home to Gertrude less about the loveliness of the orange groves than about his expenses, speeches and meetings, as well as (for he was a straightforward husband) a forthcoming rendezvous with his mistress, the sweet-as-citrus-honey Miss Pennington; all the same, new orange vistas do still engage his fancy from time to time. I wonder what he would have made of Imperial? Well, let's read his letter to Gertrude about just that. In April he travels from Yuma to Laguna Dam by mule team, remarking on the dust, which is more impressive even than that of Los Angeles itself, where everyone wears "mixed grey goods" because the dust makes clothes grey anyhow. Now what? In that year Imperial takes particular pride in her butter, poultry, livestock, wool, cotton, miscellaneous fruits and vegetables, and not least in her cantaloupes. More than two hundred and seven thousand acres have been irrigated! On hot light-choked evenings, I've sometimes stood where Powell did, gazing across the Colorado into the pebbly ridges of Imperial's Bard Subdistrict; and sometimes I can smell the freshness of the fields. To Powell, I assume, Imperial looks drier. *I guess we all feel sorry for 'em.* Returning to the barracks in Yuma, he sleeps outdoors in a cot, then rides the very early morning train to Los Angeles. *It was a delightful experience, pretty strenuous but worth while.* That is all he has to say—no mention at all of the Imperial Valley!

But the very next month, an issue of the *Desert Farmer* advises us that *in the future Imperial Valley must be considered one of the orange sections of Southern California.*

In about 1910, California holds six point six million bearing and nonbearing orange trees, nine hundred and forty-one thousand lemon trees and forty-three and a half thousand grapefruit trees. The Inland Empire's orange groves run from Yucaipa and Redlands all the way west to Corona.

Five years later, in December, the Imperial Valley's first shipment of citrus, which happen to be grapefruits, departs L. F. Farnsworth's ranch, which lies not far from the city of Imperial. (Coachella won't start any grapefruit orchards until 1925.) In 1920, the valley's first organization of grapefruit growers charters itself. In 1922 the largest grapefruit orchard is a respectable sixty acres. The following year, forty thousand new grapefuit trees enter the valley. Then Imperial grapefruits start winning prizes.

But this chapter isn't about grapefruits at all; please excuse me for letting them grow in. It's about oranges. Come to think of it, in the era of *The Largest Irrigated District in the World,* who has time to peel oranges anymore? It's more efficient to drink orange juice.

What is orange juice, actually? In 1960, in the Mirror Building in Los Angeles, I overhear a man differentiating between fresh orange juice, frozen fresh orange juice, single-strength frozen orange juice, and reconstituted orange juice, none of which qualify as chilled orange juice. What about orange juice diluted with sugar water? R. J. Smith of Sunnyland Citrus cuts the Gordian Knot: *Well, it could be called ambrosia I suppose and I don't think we have any classification for it here.*

ORANGES AND SNOW

How did we progress from *the flaming yellow fruit of the orange groves* to *it could be called ambrosia I suppose?*

In 1914, the merest year after Mulholland completes the Los Angeles aqueduct, San Fernando grows lush with citrus and other fruits even as the Owens Valley does the opposite. Welcome to San Fernando Rey Brand, whose label sports two vaqueros riding toward an old red-tiled hacienda, with palm trees and flowering prickly pears all around. Indeed, such is San Fernando's success that she almost steals the Citrus Experiment Station away from Riverside—the foiling of which act Riverside celebrates with church bells.

On the frontis of a 1925 number of the *California Cultivator,* we find the legend "Oranges and Snow," and a full-page picture of citrus groves under cloudy mountains. That's the year that the Riverside district ships out twenty-five hundred and forty-one cars of citrus fruit! I can't help believing in people.*

In 1930, the young protagonist of an Upton Sinclair novel (he wants to get into

*Climate does tell: In 1925, southern California ships out nearly twelve thousand traincar lots of oranges—twice the production of central California, and twenty-five times that of northern California. But what does climate tell? Excluding the Colorado River and the westward part of the international line, the entity which I call Imperial is essentially desert. Citrus needs water. But even in Arid America we can do anything, since **WATER IS HERE**.

pictures) gazes out from the freight train he's hopped into Southern California and sees *orange trees—whole groves of them in blosssom, with ripe golden fruit, and an incredibly sweet odor . . . It was the greatest hour of Danny Dane's lifetime . . .*

Southern California keeps on dreaming her citrus dreams right into the Hitler years. We grant that Florida is number one, but the gainful whirling of our Ministry of Capital's prayer wheels may prevent her from being so forever. Regardless, we've created the greatest hour of Danny Dane's lifetime: Oranges used to be so scarce that we employed them to decorate our Christmas trees *(we really looked forward to our holidays, so we could have our one orange at Christmas that came from the far-away and golden state of California);* now oranges are everywhere. Isn't that a victory? The exoticism of yellow- or orange-glowing groves which once enraptured G. Harold Powell—indeed, citrus fruits are more exotic than I ever imagined, for they originated in the Malaysian Archipelago and the jungles of mainland Asia*—has now been subsumed in workaday monoculture, because I have never been cheated out of a dollar in my life and we need have no fear that our lands will not become better and better as the years go by. At the end of the 1935 season, California proudly counts up the *greatest volume of citrus ever exported.* In 1939 I see a white two-horse wagon loaded high with flats of oranges, and many pickers, their majority white-clad, stationed at various heights on heterogeneous ladders, gathering in the golden globes of Riverside, with Mount Rubidoux beyond. Somewhere around the same time I see a young brunette tilting a number-eight-size Sunkist crate toward her with one blurred white-gloved hand, while with the other she reaches into the conveyer belt, picking out number-eight-size oranges, which in the photograph are nearly as white as the part in her hair.

In 1936, when the Paxton Junior lid-nailing machine for orange boxes is in vogue, the Fontana Citrus Association in San Bernardino County shows off its new grapefruit-packing plant, and the San Fernando Lemon Company builds a large new storage building in Van Nuys, although an eighty-acre improved grapefruit ranch in the oasis district of Riverside gets sold. Thank God for the scarcity of Puerto Rican grapefruit! *It is probable that California summer grapefruit will find a ready market in the East this year . . .*

Now, if we could only take those oranges and that snow and can them both! Well, by golly, on 22 April 1950 this newsflash comes in: *Those little six-ounces of frozen concentrated orange juice are shaking the citrus industry to its very foundations . . .*† Concentrate is very popular, all right; as we say in that decade, it's *taking*

*Columbus brought citrus to Haiti in 1493; Ponce de León seems to have established it in Florida in 1513; south of the entity I call Imperial, some of the Mexicans were growing it by the early 1700s.

†What about the orange's sour sister? Among the Imperial County Agricultural Commissioner's papers I came across a time-beiged USDA newsletter from 1915 announcing a NEW SUMMER BEVERAGE.

off to new levels; all the same, we've failed to solve the difficulties of our own success, because there are awfully many oranges in California and Florida; now they're talking about putting in orange groves in Texas and even Mexico.

Just in time, J. A. Finley of the Orange Products Company, Ontario, San Bernardino County, comes to the rescue. He explains that what's required is simply an attitude alteration: *Actually, the orange industry is not faced with overproduction; rather, it's a case of underconsumption.*

"WE HAVE A LEEWAY OF 11.3 BRIX"

Speaking of ambrosia, Michael F. Arlotto of Arlo's Citrus, Incorporated, testifies that *there has been considerable adulteration in the orange juice that has been sold in the State of California.* In other words, if you taste this beverage, you'll realize that **WATER IS HERE**. Well, there's agrarian democracy for you: Each juice processor can set his own standard of purity; moreover (I have never been cheated out of a dollar in my life), he can save up to forty cents per gallon by adding sugar, water and the like, thereby decreasing the orange-juice content to sixty or seventy percent. *The consumer is being cheated,* he affirms, but *it's very hard to tell the difference. It is very palatable, a very acceptable product can be made.*

Did we decide what orange juice might be? Disregard the United States orange-juice standards of 16 June 1959. With the proposed new California standards, Arlotto says, *we have a leeway of 11.3 Brix on the orange juice.*

Brix, by the way, measures fruit-sugar solids. Do you care? In the Mirror Building, several entities care surprisingly—to wit, the Polar Chilled Products Company, Glacier Groves (whose head office is in Cincinnati and whose spokesman objects to more specific standards), Necco Sales, Glenco Citrus Products, Sunnyland Citrus, Golden Citrus, Daisy-Fresh Products (which insists that no orange-juice adulteration whatsoever plagues California), Minute Maid Corporation, and I almost forgot Erb and Company—well, who wouldn't forget Erb and Company? Five "major plants"—we're not told which ones—now make ninety percent of all chilled orange juice in California; we can be pretty sure that they're represented at this hearing. The largest concern excretes four million gallons per year of California orange juice into our mouths. Minute Maid might be my guess. Then there's Erb and Company, from whom we'll hardly hear, but I perceive several other orange-juice jackals snarling over that spilled ten percent which now seems in peril of sinking into the sand of California's moneyscape. I catch whispers of anxiety from

---

Grapefruit Juice Easily Bottled—Simple Method of Making Byproduct. Boil it in an enameled kettle, pour it into a bottle, and hermetically seal. "While as yet, as far as known, there is no commercial market for sterilized grapefruit juice, it is believed that many persons will find it . . . a pleasant variation."

certain retrograde types that small juice companies might get regulated out of the market. *We need have no fear that our lands will not become better and better as the years go by.* Well, there's still a niche for penny-ante freeholders: Dairymen often still "process" the previously bottled orange juice of the Big Five; I guess that means that they pour it into smaller bottles.

Once upon a time, there used to be orange juice price wars, just as California used to suffer from water wars in those unenlightened days before the All-American Canal. Mr. Arlotto remembers how he once got threatened by a competitor *that if I tried to break into the Bakersfield area he would cut the price to where there would be no profit and he said, "If you want to go into there, go ahead."* Thank God that the Big Five are here to save us from that chaos! *He made a success through his own efforts. He sold out at a fancy price.*

Marx and Lenin inform us that capitalism tends to concentrate itself into rival monopolies. When any monopoly wins, we find ourselves that much closer to socialism. In the United States of 1960, we're not quite there yet; but in place of orange juice wars between Stockton and Bakersfield we have orange juice mega-conflicts between California and Florida.

Florida's orange production cost is one-third that of California's, in part due to lower labor costs. (In 2004, a Holtville farmer will tell me that most of the real cost on lemons and grapefruit is labor.) That's not all. Arlotto complains that in Florida you can't legally put sugar in orange juice, while in California you simply have to, in order to *make a good palatable product.* He wants to know how we can protect ourselves from Florida. This question, the most urgent of our time, can be answered only by a citrus man who's never been cheated out of a hundred cents in his life. For my own part, I feel competent merely to address a more basic issue: The reason we simply must add sugar to California orange juice (which, by the way, our new standards will require to be twenty percent fresh juice minimum; the rest may be concentrate) is that Imperial's supposed eternal growing season has failed us! I could pretend that the California orange-juice problem has to do with flavanones, flavones and anthocyanins, but Mr. Arlotto tells it as it is: *In the chilled juice business in California at times we have to use fruit that is low in solids and it by necessity has to be beefed up to a higher fruit solids through the use of concentrate.* Why's that? Well, here's the kicker: *It is not always possible at that time of year to buy fruit on a solids basis.*

In the California of Mr. Powell's day, the citrus industry was getting rationalized and improved, to be sure. But in that epoch, when Wilber Clark's automobile journey from Los Angeles to Imperial was a risky adventure and the first telephone line was little more than a fitfully operational strand of wire (some say barbed wire) strung from fencepost to fencepost, when the drinking water in El Centro was

Huge solar engines imprisoning the heat of the sun may create islands of fertility in icy wastelands, thus vastly increasing the productive food areas of the earth.

100 years from now...

WE MAY GROW ORANGES AT THE POLES!

What will the world be like generations from now? Wonderful new products and methods will make living easier, pleasanter, safer. But in this marvelous new era, one old friend will still serve efficiently. Water and gas will be carried by rugged cast iron pipe laid today. For more than seventy American water and gas utilities, cast iron mains over a century old are still serving dependably. And modern cast iron pipe ...centrifugally cast and quality controlled... is far tougher and more durable.

U.S. Pipe is proud to be one of the leaders in a forward-looking industry whose service to the world is measured in centuries.

U.S.
cast iron
PIPE
FOR WATER, GAS, SEWERAGE
AND INDUSTRIAL SERVICE
CAST IRON

U. S. PIPE AND FOUNDRY COMPANY, General Office: Birmingham 2, Alabama

A WHOLLY INTEGRATED PRODUCER FROM MINES AND BLAST FURNACES TO FINISHED PIPE.

sometimes chocolate colored, and usually had to be strained or filtered, not everybody expected to drink chilled orange juice year round.

I am not for one minute proposing that those times were better. (As Eugene Dahm told me that day in the Pioneers Museum: Well, one of the biggest things is air-conditioning. Before we had electricity, we took a shower and moistened the sheets and tried to sleep before we started to sweat.) On the other hand, could there have been some point between 1899 and 1960 when a fitful supply of fresh orange juice could have resisted replacement by a homogeneously sugared three-hundred-and-sixty-five-day orange juice supply? And would that have preserved democracy in Arid America?

Some years ago, my uncle was trying to start a strange new business. He informed me that it would be quite possible for people to communicate with each other on their computers, and even buy things that way. I inquired why anyone would want to do that, and he replied: *All we have to do is create a demand.*

And now there was a demand for *Home Grown, Thrifty Deciduous Fruit Trees of Best Varieties,* except that they weren't homegrown anymore . . .

What if this dull tale about the sugaring of California orange juice were a parable about Imperial itself? **WATER IS HERE**. Accordingly, people get in the habit of using water. All we have to do is create a demand. The epigraph to this book, written in the year of Powell's train ride through Imperial, is:

> As long as a farmer has an abundance of water, he almost invariably yields to the temptation to use it freely, even though he gets no increased returns as a result.

And so more people use more water, and more, and until—

But that's stupid; we're not running out of orange juice! This chapter isn't about water at all.

"THAT'S JUST THE WAY THE BUSINESS IS"

In the autumn of 2003, in the tiny settlement of Motor, Iowa, a farmer named Heemstra shot a farmer named Lyon in the head with his rifle. They were fighting over the Rodgers Place. As the *New York Times* explained the context: *Increasingly expensive tractors and combines and other mounting overhead costs . . . have led some farmers . . . to farm as much land as possible.* His farm has been highly improved. He made a success through his own efforts. And the murderer told the jury: *You have to spread these costs over more acres. Every farmer feels the need to grow. That's just the way the business is.*

Another farmer remarked: *In twenty years, there's probably going to be twenty farmers in the whole county. It's really depressing.* We need have no fear that our lands will not become better and better as the years go by.

Fortunately, this chapter isn't about farmland at all; it's about oranges and orange juice. Besides, Iowa has nothing to do with California.

FURTHERMORE

This chapter isn't about winter lettuce, either.

NOT TO MENTION POLISHING BRASS

All we have to do is create a demand. Or, in the words of the *California Cultivator,* 1925: *The average housewife little realizes to what a variety of uses an ordinary lemon may be put. A lemon dipped in salt is an excellent brass polisher . . . Lemon juice brightens blond hair in all shades to Titian red.*

But what if blondes want to stay blonde, or families get sick and tired of orange juice? Bank of America, 1941: *In the citrus industry the "on tree" inventory is of record or near record proportions . . . An astute job of marketing will be required.* Goddammit! Moreover, the United States Department of Agriculture has already noted a decline in Southern California citrus profits, thanks to competition with other points in America and the world.* The lovely old lithographed orange box labels give way to photolithographed *standard design elements,* because of *increased competitive pressure.* The Verifine Brand of Riverside obtrudes itself through little more than a glowing white V superimposed over a black pyramid, with colored rays on either side, like the decorative anti-aircraft lights in one of Hitler's Nuremberg rallies. Meanwhile, the label of the Ultimate Brand of the Paramount Citrus Assn., Main Office Los Angeles, has decayed into two simple spoked wheels of red and yellow fire which may have something to do with orange slices. Whatever happened to the peacocks of Sunkist California Dream? That's just the way the business is. Fortunately, Paramount also offers a Star Kiss Brand, whose reddish-blonde heroine, haloed in what

*I have in mind California's navels and Valencias versus Florida's Valencias, Hamlins, pineapples and Parson Browns; we'll panic unless we leave out the Shamouti oranges of Israel, the Peras and Hamlins of Brazil, the blood oranges of Spain. But sometimes, thanks to misfortunes of others, California can sell citrus even in foreign parts. For instance, here come Mussolini and his Fascists! "California has had an unusual opportunity to market lemons in Europe, principally Great Britain, due to the sanctions against Italy . . ."

to me resembles a slice of red onion, gazes long-lashed and red-lipped at two ripe oranges. The College Heights Orange & Lemon Assn. of Claremont, Los Angeles Co., California, introduces all of us to a rakishly fun-loving blonde in a mortarboard; why wouldn't I eat *her* oranges? Siren and Adios, Majorette and Marquita, they're all drop-dead gorgeous, because *attractive women continued to be a favorite subject until the final days of label production.*

Orange groves dwindle.—An old lady who used to live in Riverside told me: The big thing was the smudging, to keep the orange trees warm. It was diesel heat. Our faces would all get black. In the fifties and sixties it started to go away.—Meanwhile, the wooden orange crates become cardboard, and the colored labels likewise go away.

At midcentury the USDA warns us that *eleven large cans of [orange] juice are available annually for each person in the United States.* What to do? (The summer grapefruit market remains good.* For better or worse, grapefruit juice will keep longer in storage than its citrus cousins.) *Use of citrus products must . . . be expanded and new products developed to avoid problems if surpluses of the crop should some time accumulate.* To me, this tale, which Imperial tells in so many ways, seems insane.

But I must be the only one. Bert Cochran, Vice President of McCann-Erickson Advertising Company, appointed to elucidate in 1952 by the Lemon Products Advisory Board, announces that *the basic idea, as we see it, of this . . . cooperative promotion is to finance the expansion of the total market for California lemon juice on a completely equitable basis.* And so everybody cooperatively promotes, equitably or not, growing bigger and more entangled, so that by 1980 an internal Agricultural Labor Relations Board memo finds the relationship between citrus packers, growers and harvesters so potentially tortuous that it may be difficult for case workers to determine who is exploiting whom; but never mind; Bert Cochran's *basic idea* has TRIUMPHED; because at the end of the twentieth century, Italy and the U.S. are the two primary lemon producers; and I'm patriotically proud to report that once again California dominates the American lemonscape.

Hooray for the Sunkist Vitamin C campaign! Whenever we wish to do our health a favor, we eat an orange or drink orange juice; never mind that broccoli and tomatoes contain just as much vitamin C: Oranges are not only sweeter, they're more Californian; they're *fun!* And so our citrusscapes look to be eternal. In the middle of the 1970s a man sets out to cross the border illegally into Northside, and

*The lemon market has continued strong for the moment, but the oncoming fifty-percent reduction on lemon tariff is bad news for California lemons, because we hate it when we have to produce by others' rules. Italian lemons will now muscle their way in to New York: lower labor costs, you see. Currently, lemons go for two and a half cents per pound, which adds up when you realize that California grows fifty percent of the world lemon supply!

consoles his wife: Don't be sad because this time everything's going to be good for me. Raymundo says that San Bernardino is really good with lots of oranges.

Indeed, by 1987, per capita citrus consumption in the United States is twenty-eight point one six pounds—more than fourteen pounds of that oranges, and nearly seven pounds of it grapefruit. In 1988, we manage to swill down seven hundred and ninety-seven million gallons of orange juice!

But in 1992, we drown in citrus nonetheless, and a specialist laments: *Citrus wines have never achieved the high popularity of grape wines due primarily to flavor problems still unsolved.*

By 2004, Brazil can place a pound of frozen orange juice concentrate on the American market for less than seventy-five cents; whereas it costs Florida ninety-nine cents. Thank God for our twenty-nine-cent tariff!

Prudently, Florida puts a million dollars or more a year into research and development. Result: a " canopy shaker" which can harvest a hundred trees in fifteen minutes. Four pickers would have taken all day.

That year Orange County does not have so very much to do with oranges; and as I ride up Highway 91 toward Riverside, enjoying that gentle slope of freeway up to the dusty mountains, my eyes taste another Lemon here, another Euclid there in Fullerton. Fresno, Ventura, Kern and Tulare counties still grow citrus; meanwhile, says a local history, *only tiny lots of old orange or lemon trees remain in production in the Inland Valley.* Across the street from the Riverside courthouse, in front of the parking garage, a clock whose face is an orange slice spills water down a widening V-shaped channel into a fountain. What do oranges mean in Riverside nowadays? Lori A. Yates, President of Victoria Avenue Forever (once upon a time, Victoria Avenue was ten miles long and a hundred and seventy-five feet wide with a thirty-six-foot median garden), finds it necessary to explain *how incredibly important the citrus industry was to the city of Riverside.* Meanwhile, the wall of the Mission Inn Museum informs us that *Frank Augustus Miller (1857–1935) brought to Riverside the vision, dedication and commitment necessary to transform a citrus-based community into an international destination.* In other words, Frank Augustus Miller helped get rid of oranges.

Sprayed with miticides and insecticides, irrigated with the guidance of sunken tensiometers, mechanically pruned, dosed with such growth regulators as 2,4-dichlorophenoxyacetic acid, which *delays and reduces the drop of mature fruit as well as delaying the aging of the fruit,* still picked by human beings on ladders but graded by *an electronic color sorter, at a speed difficult for the eye to discern,* Riverside's oranges continue to grow *in isolated areas which are less visible from our freeways*—for instance, in Coachella.

On Sunset Boulevard in Los Angeles, there is an intersecting street called Orange, and even an El Centro. On Freeway 10, going west from Euclid, evening bestows a reddish-orange glow like neon peaches hanging over us: fiery smog-clouds standing out against the greenish sky; they are extremely beautiful, far more so than the smoke-bruised sunset sky of Mexicali.—I coast by Orange Grove Ave. beneath a fiery-orange sky.—Although grapefruit has been memorialized all the way to Los Angeles's Fourth Street, where the old grimy-white pillar-pairs of the Farmers & Merchants Bank guard the pale fruitlike globes of a chandelier which offers itself to us through the dark-glassed arch of the doorway, the future of Southern California's citriculture, defeated by Florida's, may well be as ghastly white as a trailer park's rooftops under floodlights on Montclair; but never mind; West Covina has a Citrus Street . . .

"THIS WAS *THE* GRAPEFRUIT COUNTRY"

But Imperial, as you may recall, is

NO WINTER -- NO SNOW

NO CROP FAILURES

Therefore, *we need have no fear that our lands will not become better and better as the years go by.*

In 1914, the Southern Pacific Railroad, possibly in alliance with the Chandler Syndicate, puts on the market *several thousand acres of mesa citrus lands* in the northern Imperial Valley *that are expected ultimately to be covered with rich lemon, orange, and grapefruit groves.* This project must have succeeded; because flavonoids, which may in turn be subdivided into flavanones, flavones and anthocyanins, beguiled the young schoolteacher Edith Karpen, when she arrived in Calipatria for the very first time in 1933. (I wish I could have seen what she looked like in that year. In her old age she was a very handsome woman.)

Her future husband showed her the sights.—He took me for a ride on the other side of town, she said, and all I remember about that was the overwhelming smell of grapefruit and orange blossoms.

Where was this? I asked in amazement, for the only thing I had ever smelled in Calipatria was feedlot stench.

We were going west, replied the old lady. Toward San Diego.

Why isn't there citrus in that area now?

The water level later came up and killed them. When I came there, we still had some citrus on the ranch by Mount Signal.

Among the citrus, grapefruit was Emperor of Imperial! Grapefruit, you see, *on account of its earliness has a distinct advantage in California markets over fruit from other sections.*

There might be another reason, if I understand the following numeric tale:

ORANGE TREES IN IMPERIAL COUNTY, 1917–25		
1917	40,295	"Trees brought into the country," 1912–17.
1918	?	No data.
1919	3,938	1,426 nonbearing.
1920	7,000	May include Mexicali Valley.
1921	6,150	4,280 nonbearing.
1922	2,083	"Admitted into Imperial County."
1923	1,600	1,012 nonbearing.
1924	1,600	1,012 nonbearing.
1925	1,600	Number nonbearing not specified.

I conclude from this data that unless the number of *trees brought into the country* was exaggerated by boosters, as perhaps it was, then within a decade, twenty-four out of every twenty-five of them had died.

And yet an eagle snarls, gripping a garland in its claws as it gazes away from an expanding metropolis at the sun-touched Pacific, which nicely curtails itself before the golden border of this award from the California Fruit Exposition of January 21–31, 1926. **This certifies that** Imperial County has been awarded —*First*— **Premium for the Best Twelve Boxes Seedless Grapefruit Sweepstakes.**

Indeed, how could Imperial not win the premium? For that very year, a particularly svelte Barbara Worth cocks her head at me from the ocotillo-studded reddish-mountained desert of an Imperial Valley Grapefruit label (**"No sugar required—The Test is in the Taste"**). In a label of unknown provenance from the Desert Grapefruit Company, Imperial, California, Barbara Worth, pensive and Stetsoned, helps sell Marsh seedless, because **"The Test is** still **in the Taste."**

Unfortunately, **IMPERIAL VALLEY GRAPEFRUIT WILL GET COMPETITON,** warns the *Imperial Valley Press* in that same year. Imperial has planted fifty-five hundred grapefruit acres. *When bearing it will have to compete with about 125,000 acres of grapefruit now planted in other citrus districts of the United States.*

I remember a front-page photo in the *Imperial Valley Press* of two men in suits touching a grapefruit between them, the better to commemorate this occasion *when Senator Shortridge of California converted Senator King of Utah from the latter's belief that Florida had better grapefruits than California.* Oh, yes, Lord be praised; in the end Senator King sees the light and confesses: *The grapefruit of California, as well as all her other products, are known throughout the land. They are not only superior, they are supreme.*

In 1929, Mrs. Adell Lingo buys a ranch called "The Pride of Niland" and plants more than four thousand grapefruit trees. Where are they now?

In 1930, Imperial pronounces itself the seventh most successful grapefruit producer of all counties. Ten years later I see Nana Lee Beck standing in her long white dress in the sandy sunny aisle between her family's grapefruit trees in Calexico; but fifteen years after that, Brawley's Mr. J. E. Harshman, Chairman of the Grapefruit Advisory Board, *which board is composed of the same people who put up the money for the advertising fund,* feels compelled to call for the same measures we have met with for lettuce, cantaloupes, green corn: *The orderly marketing of grapefruit, which will mean consumer satisfaction, is the only safeguard for the grapefruit industry in the desert area.*

Why has acreage declined? Mr. Harshman agrees with Edith Karpen: *In the Imperial Valley grapefruit was planted on a great deal of acreage that was not suitable for the production of grapefruit due to the high salt and high water table . . .The tops of the trees dried, the leaves turned yellow, the quantity of production fell very rapidly, and in those groves it was not economically feasible to continue with grapefruit so they were taken out.*

A certain Mr. Jones slyly interjects: *There is a lot at stake in Coachella Valley today in grapefruit and the future of the Coachella Valley grapefruit is in the hands of a great deal more man-acreage than in Imperial.*

Two years later, a pair of geographers transmit the writing on the wall: *Grapefruit, although the Valley's most important fruit crop, have a total local value of less than five hundred thousand dollars a year.* Mene, mene, tekel, upharsin.

This was *the* grapefruit county in the thirties, said Claude Finnell, whose tenure as Imperial County Agriculture Commissioner lasted for thirty-three years. He was an energetic old gentleman when I interviewed him in 2004.

Right after World War II, he said, there was a big influx of fruit in San Joaquin and Arizona and so forth.* Grapefruit is a good crop but it doesn't make you much money. Used to be, the government used to buy grapefruit juice and give it out to the schools. We have a lot of salt here in the water, and after grapefruits get ten or fifteen years old, they start reacting to the salt. Grapefruit is easily frozen in the wintertime, and that's why it's better in Coachella, since they're a little warmer than we are. So the tree crops just kinda pooped away.

And the date crops?

Same thing, he said with a smile. Soils and salts.

*Even before 1945, Imperial was losing her position. In the state citrus report of 1938, San Joaquin receives the most press; Fresno, Tulare and Kern get nods; there is no mention of Imperial. The Imperial County statistics for that year are very brief, but record forty cars of oranges shipped, eleven hundred and forty-five cars of grapefruit, and no lemons.

In 2003, grapefruits finally become as famous as cherry-lipped Barbara Worth, which is to say that they make the front page of the *New York Times*! It's a three-million-dollar advertising attack, meant to addict twenty-one- to forty-nine-year-old human females to "Sass in a Glass." Desperate times, desperate measures: American grapefruit consumption has declined by one-third between 1998 and 2001. On the other hand, since 2002 we are now selling more grapefruit to Japan than to the U.S. Japanese ladies even buy grapefruit-scented pantyhose.

All this, by the way, has mainly to do with Florida. Here's Imperial's minuscule part: *Texas and California produce grapefruit, too, although far less than Florida.*

WHAT DOES IT ALL MEAN?

In 2005, Imperial County will send to market four hundred and eighty-five thousand, five hundred tons of Valencias, which is to say six hundred and nineteen thousand dollars' worth. (The number of tangerines will be comparable.) In the list of Imperial's top forty crops, lemons are number twenty-three, grapefruits are thirty-three, and miscellaneous citrus (mandarins, tangelos and sour orange) barely makes number forty.

Well, does Imperial produce more oranges in 2005 than in 1925? I wish I could answer that. But over her citrus century, units of measurement change from trees to acres to carloads to tons. I have cynically wondered whether these alterations were intentional obfuscations, orchestrated by boosters with the aim of concealing output declines. When I think of Imperial Valley citrus, only the Bard Subdistrict comes to mind—although there, I must say, it is difficult to resist buying a cardboard box that is fat with blood oranges.

A 2004 number of the *Imperial White Sheet* hawks **FRESH CITRUS,** *Tangelos 5 for $1. Grapefruit 4 for $1. Lemons 6 for $1.* On the Coachella side of the entity I call Imperial, near the northwest shore of the Salton Sea, and then again in Bard, whenever I want to I can take in the *grapefruit light* of Imperial, which, strange as it may seem, I've also experienced in the vicinity of yellow facades on the hottest midmornings of a Russian summer. In the Mexicali Valley, patchy citrusscapes survive in their own way. In another chapter I shall praise the golden treasures of Rancho Roa (a thousand orange and grapefruit trees, all glowing with fruit).—On the road to Algodones, in Ejido Morelos, there was a junkyard whose owner gave me a rusty horseshoe for good luck, and the woman I was with received a rusty iron from him; every third day he ran the water all day to keep his orange, mandarin and lemon trees alive; he was very proud of his water. Claude Finnell had said: *Grapefruit is a good crop but it doesn't make you much money.* But the junkyard's lord did not care about making money from his citrus. He was satisfied to admire his trees, eat some fruit and give the rest away.

Chapter 152

CALICHE

(1975–2005)

O Earth with the mouth of a woman,
release my strength . . .

—María Baranda, 1999

Caliche, said Alice Woodside. That's when they would flood a field, and then the heat would become intense, as it will, and then you would see almost a pavement of dried dirt, and then it would crack. That's bad for the crops. They couldn't break through that.

Once upon a time, in 1910 or 1911, the Holtville high school girls' basketball team gazed into Leo Hetzel's lens. They were seven athletic young ladies all in ankle-length uniform skirts sashed at the waist. Their memory, and the wholesome Anglo Imperial of Barbara Worth, has taken on the wavering roundness of some old piece-of-eight which has been lying in the sands of Mexico since 1609. One side's inscription wanders around a shield subdivided into zones and symbols; the other side sports an artichoke-leaf or acanthus quartered by a cross—are those prancing horses or rampant lions within? How can I say? This coin, already abraded by the centuries, becomes the merest nubbin of gold in my mind because my museum of experiences contains no analogue.

American Imperial was founded by and for the Ministry of Capital. Much of Mexican Imperial was taken over by the same, for which we can thank the Chandler Syndicate. And at first the money-fields sprouted like crazy. Many decades ago, Mr. Leo Hetzel, sleek and paunchy like a successful lizard, raises his finger at me and squeezes the shutter release of his camera, which is as large as a recoilless rifle. Imperial County's photographer portrays himself! It's playfully self-congratulatory; and now as I trudge the vacant lots of Niland and sit in the grass beside the sweaty, exhausted unemployed field workers of Calexico, I wonder where all the self-congratulation went. Leo Hetzel greets me from the time when *The Population Is Increasing at the rate of 40 per cent Every 24 Months.* And now what? Imperial's population continues to increase north and south of the line; but caliche hardens over everything:

San Diego, Los Angeles, Tijuana and Ensenada want Imperial's water. American labor laws and environmental regulations disadvantage Northside Imperial at the expense of Southside, whose campesinos increasingly find themselves working in *maquiladoras* which could move to China at any time. The family farm continues to die. *They couldn't break through that.*

In El Centro one can stroll past Holt and even past Orange. If you wish to dream agricultural dreams, then smell the night hay. For a long time you will be alone as you walk up Imperial Avenue. The swollen moon fuzzes like a dead animal's eyes. The existence of the sad, sad Mexican whore (sadder than I think she would have been in Mexico) in the median strip of Imperial Avenue proves nothing for or against the *ejidos* or the American family farm or silver dimes exploding from the water farmers' sprinklers. She waits for cars and trucks, hoping to be saved by the ministry of capital.

Chapter 153

IMPERIAL REPRISE

(1754–2004)

What have we achieved? We have builded an empire in an unfit place.

—Edgar F. Howe and Wilbur Jay Hall, 1910

1

I *can't help believing in people.* Well, that's started to phase out. But they still use skimpy costumes and you see.

THE DESERT DISAPPEARS. *There's a lot of crying-in-your-beer stuff going on.*

Manufacturing is hitting another level of evolution. A gallon of gasoline or diesel produces more power in an hour than three hundred thousand pounds of horseflesh. *You can't produce things the way you used to.*

Manufacturing is hitting another level of evolution. **THE AZTECS ARE BACK**.

Manufacturing is hitting another level of evolution. The public has been rather slow in adopting the area as a playground, but the day is rapidly approaching, when it will come into its own in a big way . . .

Manufacturing is hitting another level of evolution. I have never been cheated out of a dollar in my life.

I have never been cheated out of a dollar in my life. ***OFFICIAL FIGURES SHOW NO COLORADO RIVER WATER AVAILABLE FOR CENTRAL ARIZONA PROJECT.***

I like the tranquillity and the ranch and the animals. *In the meantime, revenues will be rising due to increased assessed values.*

Before was the time!

The English language was the predominant language, and that's not the case today. Calexico has worked itself up into a certain mindset, and it's not a mindset that I agree with. *And when they can specify that, and the State of California has the authority to do that [and] they can enforce this by legal machinery which can put a man in jail if he doesn't do it, then I say that you are jeopardizing his rights.*

By the time negotiations broke off on February 28, violent and debilitating strikes had been in effect . . . **INDEPENDENT GROWERS KEEP WORKERS HAPPY**.

When we had ten of 'em, a Queen and nine Princesses, we could go to L.A. and get anything on TV we wanted. *No doubt those were the good old days before we had Civil Rights Marches.*

2

In some respects a stream is like a woman. But they still use skimpy costumes and you see.

The looks of that ditch and the effluent were a distinct disappointment . . . It got worse all the time. It's not okay, the water. Again they have salt. And there's not enough water. *Nine known species of edible fish inhabit its blue depths . . . There are no set standards of sewage disposal.*

3

INDEPENDENT GROWERS KEEP WORKERS HAPPY. *No trace of such gas remains.*

PART ELEVEN

POSTSCRIPTS

Chapter 154

THE PROHIBITED BALLADS

(1913–2005)

Those of you who know about these things,
I know you will understand me,
and those who don't get it,
little by little you will.
In this tyrannical world
there are many ways to live.

—*Narcocorrido* "From Nostril to Nostril,"
sung by the band Koely at the Thirteen Negro, 2005

R*elative to Wallace Wilson under arrest for having cocaine in his possession,* Los Angeles advises Calexico in 1913, . . . *you need take no further action in this matter, as you state you have no positive evidence that the goods were smuggled. In this connection I have to advise you that cocaine does not come within the operation of the opium law, as this drug is not a derivative of opium. In future you need take no action against persons having cocaine in their possession, unless further advised by this office.*

But in 2002 in one of my hometown's myriad courtrooms, a baffled, curlyhaired female prisoner, black, gazes over her shoulder at me, her mouth open, looking as if she longs to run. An attorney, drumming fingers on a file, keeps saying something to her. I hear the repeated phrase *two years.*

For cocaine possession, Miss Knox, sixteen months, two years or three years. If you violate probation, you're subject to parole for . . .

Yes, ma'am, she replies to everything.

Do you understand what you are agreeing to? This plea would include all Sacramento County violations. You're required to register as a convicted narcotics offender.

Yes, ma'am.

Do you give up the right to a speedy public trial, the right to confront all witnesses, to testify, to remain silent?

Yes, ma'am.

How do you plead?

Guilty. No contest.

Pick one.

No contest.

If you plead no contest I will find you guilty.

Yes, ma'am, whispers the girl in terrified bewilderment.

Next case. A tall blond boy (possession of meth), awaits punishment, his hands tightly clasped behind his back. The judge warns him he could be subject to sixteen months, two years or three years. If he gets probation he will need to register as a convicted narcotics offender.—*How do you plead?* the voice demands.

Guilty, he says, not only stiffly but monotonously, his fingers writhing behind his back.

He wanders back to his due place in the far rear of the courtroom and slams himself down in his seat with a sad and nervous smirk; his friend claps his shoulder.

And already here's another defendant, gripping a soiled RENO cap behind his back, ruined by getting caught with cocaine! He's a dirty, beaten-down old man whom they are going to beat down a little more. Will their pleasure be sixteen months, thirty-two months or three years? What's the difference? He's a drug criminal; he's human trash.

. . . To all Sacramento County violations, . . . the judge is saying.

He pleads in a blurry mumble: No contest.

A promise of one year in county jail, the judge was saying. Go to probation within two business days and come back to the court on the thirtieth for your sentence.

When he turns around to leave, I see for the first time that he is black. A huge X-shaped bandage mars the lower righthand quadrant of his face.

These are citizens of Northside. Now, what happens when the line gets crossed?

In the village of Coalcomán in Michoacán, a certain Miguel Palominos, illiterate and ignorant of his age (he can't even count), clean of any criminal record and the sole support of his mother and sisters, receives a bus ticket to Nogales, where a coyote brings him across the line and into northern California. Here a man named Jose takes him over. Miguel's salary will be a thousand dollars per month, after the coyote has been paid. His task, shared with four others, is to water thirteen thousand marijuana plants. After two or three months, during which time he receives not a penny, sherriff's deputies appear. Everybody escapes, except for Miguel Palominos, whom prosecutors hope to send away for fifteen years. (This is one of forty or fifty such cases in the past decade in the Sacramento jurisdiction alone. We need have no fear that our lands will not become better and better as the years go by.) His defense attorney tells the jury what seems patently true: This man of about twenty-two years was used as a *throwaway.* The attorney also uses the term *"indentured servitude," which is a polite phrase for slavery.* However, as I see from my newspaper, *federal law allows someone like Palominos to be held responsible for what others have plotted.* How wonderful federal law is. *Sympathy has no place in the courtroom, and the jurors were told that four times . . .*

Thus runs the tale of Miguel Palominos, as complete as I know it: He was arrested in August 2002 and literally *held responsible* until the closing arguments in November 2003. Then what? That didn't make the news.

And in Mexicali, across the street from the Hotel Paris, a woman who is so high that she is literally going through the motions of flying finally apes Icarus and slams face-first on the sidewalk. By the time her escort has accomplished the difficult mission of raising her to her feet, she is weeping with pain, but it is the relaxed, full weeping of a small child, accompanied by easy tears which seem to relieve her. Tomorrow, I suppose, she will more accurately feel and see the damage. Meanwhile at the corner, grey-clad boy soldiers with machine guns send them one disinterested glance. In my country, the soldiers, or rather their police proxies, would come to help that woman, in which process they would arrest her. That's Northside for you! But here we're on the other side of the ditch.

LUPE'S SMILE

Needless to state, it was the great Lupe Vásquez who first informed me of the existence of the *baladas prohibidas.* We were at the Thirteen Negro drinking early in the evening, which is to say that it was not yet midnight and Lupe had not yet blacked out. He had just finished explaining how he determined which of the dancing girls were available, and although I have already quoted this maxim, it deserves to be better remembered,—yea, engraved beneath the first Ten Commandments: *So I just say: Do you want to fuck? If no, that's it. She's fired. They* ***APPRECIATE*** *that, because it saves their time.* Just then the jukebox exploded into another happy song, indistinguishable to my ignorance from the others, and the grim field workers at other tables nearly smiled, while the dancing couples on the metal floor grew livelier, and several men shouted along with the singer. Even Lupe, who trudged bitterly through life and although he called me his friend sometimes walked away from me and at other times, drunken times, shot me glances of the blackest resentment, cheered up when he heard this *corrido,* which was naturally so loud that he had to shout into my ear for me to apprehend that it dealt with the demure ladyfriend of a wanted drug lord who happened to be absent when two Federales visited their residence, promising her that they wouldn't hurt him, so she told them to sit down and wait if so it pleased them; but while fixing refreshments she overheard their plan to liquidate her lover, so she sweetly invited them to rest just a moment longer, then strode out and blew them away! Lupe's hatred of authority exceeded even mine, and for good reason; most days he had to deal with the lordly ways of United States Immigration inspectors, of foremen who might or might not offer him a job and who if they did cared about their production quotas, not about his back; of companies who didn't pay him for the hours he had to sit in buses waiting for the frost to melt off the broccoli; and whenever he got a vacation from these entities, he got to visit the know-it-alls at the employment office in Calexico. Now and then he had also enjoyed the hospitality of Northside's police and judges. His days were not exceptional. No wonder that so many field workers sat drinking or doing heroin in those buses at five in the morning; no wonder that Lupe himself liked to drink—nowadays more often at cantinas such as El Cordobés or intermediate establishments, for instance the Dollar Bar, than the Thirteen Negro, because it practically killed him every time the price of anything went up, and dances were more expensive than when he was young. How bitterly he raged! But wasn't that the way of the world? Throughout Mexicali the *putas* were more expensive, and they charged double to take their tops off so that a man could suck their titties. That was why a few beers at the Thirteen Negro soothed the pain of the Thirteen Negro's prices, and when a certain sort of *corrido* came on the jukebox, Lupe even smiled.

He always had stories about drugs. Once he said: There's an asparagus field near Centinela, and when we're working there we see a lot of burned vehicles from *pollos* and traffickers. Last year the asparagus crew found a lot of weed that somebody left. At first they were scared to get it, in case someone was watching, but they did it; they got it and said fuck it! And they took the marijuana. One guy sold his share for four hundred dollars.

To Lupe this outcome represented not only a significant score (he was always hoping to strike it rich, and one New Year's Day when some of us hiked up the Mexican side of that same Mount Centinela, Lupe vanished for an hour, prowling high in the scree for the legendary gold which Pancho Villa or some ghost had hidden there; I asked what he had found, and he frowningly replied: If I'd found something, I wouldn't tell anybody, not even you!); but also, and I think more fundamentally in his mind, a victory over the official bullies who imprison people for drug possession.

And so that happy ballad about one loving lady's murder of two Federales was ambrosia to Lupe. I asked him how many of those songs there were, and he said: Many. So many that the assholes here have made it illegal to play them on the radio. They're called the *baladas prohibidas*. Some also call them the *narcocorridos*. Of course, the more they try to stamp them out, the more popular they get. Those assholes who try to control us, we just make fun of them.

"A GOOD THING FROM A MARKETING STANDPOINT"

It's been three years that we haven't played any *narcocorridos,* said Alfonso Rodríguez Ibarra, the *programador* at Radiorama Mexicali. Three years ago the people who owned the station and all of their affiliates decided to stop. But a year ago, the government of Baja California made it a policy not to play them.

In your opinion is that a good thing or a bad thing?

A good thing just from the marketing standpoint, he said. If we played *narcocorridos,* there are enough people who would be offended that we would lose the advertising. That's the reason they're not playing them in Sonora, either.

And in Sinaloa?

In Sinaloa I know there is a government decree.

He preferred the traditional *corridos,* the ones about horses and the like. His favorites (and here he started to smile and nod his head as if he could hear them) were "Caballo Blanco," "Katrina y los Rurales," "Lamberto Quintero" and "El Cantador."

You know it's a *corrido* when you listen and it's telling you a story or a legend, not necessarily about love but about a man who fell in love or about a man who had a rooster for his best friend . . .

Here's a story for you, or, if you like, a legend: On Saturday, 22 March 2003, Anna Francis Warner, aged thirty-one, was arrested at Centinela State Prison. *The woman was taken into custody at about 11:45 p.m. and taken to Pioneers Memorial Hospital in Brawley, where an X-ray revealed the contraband hidden in her vagina. Two bindles of methamphetamine weighing 4.5 grams were recovered . . . The woman then implicated a male accomplice who was staying at the Budget Hotel in El Centro.*

What a nasty tale! Who would want to set that to music? I imagine the anxiety she must have felt, then outright dread, and a shock of doom, followed by futile excuses, then the invasive humilation of a policewoman's gloved finger in her womb, followed by arrest, confession, detention, conviction, sentence.—*How do you plead?—Guilty. No contest.* Then what? More punishment, more humiliation. I doubt that it would have brought a smile to Lupe's face. But if what happened to her could be recast as a tragic tale of love and daring—and why not? What if the *male accomplice* were her lover? What if she smuggled with art and grace? What if wretchedness could be magicked into grandeur? Why, then, Anna Francis Warner's fate might become quite *a good thing from a marketing standpoint*—not to Alfonso Rodríguez Ibarra, I grant, nor to María the cleaning lady in Sacramento, who was acquainted with the *narcocorridos* but preferred the ones which were not about drugs; but very possibly *a good thing* to my friends who sleep in abandoned buildings as did José López from Jalisco, who by the way has disappeared and whom I miss; to those who sleep in the park as did the dark street prostitute Érica, who slept only *bit by bit,* as she put it, since otherwise somebody would be sure to cut her purse away from her; I will introduce you to her very soon. For now, let me introduce you to Anna Francis Warner's *narcocorrido* counterpart, "The Queen of the South."

Manola Céspedes said, "Teresa takes risks;
she sells drugs in France, Africa and Italy;
even the Russians buy from the powerful auntie."

She was smart enough to use the Spanish accent;
she showed off her power like a noble lady;
Teresa the Mexican surprised them all!

Sometimes she wore the clothes of her land;
once she wore crocodile boots and an ostrich jacket;
she wore a belt that whistled and drank tequila that jumped.

What happened to Anna Francis Warner? What happened to Miguel Palominos? Why not hope for the best, as the Tigres del Norte did in that *narcocorrido?*

Some say she's in prison, others in Italy,
in California or Miami, somewhere in America.

Anna took risks; she sold drugs in California; Anna surprised them all . . .

The policeman Carlos Pérez said that some of the most famous ballads were about Jesús Malaverde, whom he called *the patron saint of the narcotraffickers.*—They bear his image, he said. For those who use drugs, he's like a saint. Downtown, they show his statues. He lived in Sinaloa. He was Robin Hood. He sold drugs and used the money to help the people. He was killed in a gun battle because he didn't want to give himself up. Some say he was never caught. Some say he died of old age, and others say that he is still alive. Everybody has his own story.*

*Indeed, one folklorist who visited all the Malaverde shrines he could find wondered whether this man had ever existed; no one knew what he looked like, and his life and death (the latter represented by hanging in his prayer cards) might have been a conflation of two other Sinaloan bandits. In any case, prostitutes began to pray at his supposed execution site in the middle of the twentieth century; in time the drug traffickers grew so enthusiastic about him that one Arizona lawman proposed that discovering a Malaverde image in a suspect's wallet, together with the phone number of a house of narcotics, "might be sufficient grounds for indictment." No doubt by the time Malaverde's memory had flown all the way into Imperial, it had grown as immense and distorted as the shadow of a high-flying drug-laden airplane.

I asked him whether he knew any local narco-ballads, and he replied: Most of the bad guys are Sinaloan. Here in Mexicali, there's just middle management. But I've heard a *corrido* about three Colombians in Mexicali. So the three Colombians kill the police commandant . . .

His colleague, Juan Carlos Martínez Caro, explained the genesis of the ballads thus: So the people who were dealing drugs paid singers to write songs about them. It began in the sixties. It's a way to make themselves look good.

I cannot say that I was greatly surprised to learn that Officer Caro preferred those *corridos* praising the police who captured and killed drug traffickers, such as "Comandante Reynosa." What a good thing just from the marketing standpoint! But other individuals, some of whom were to be found at the Thirteen Negro, were fonder of the *corridos pesados,** the heavy ballads, the hardcore ones.

I don't listen to them, said Officer Caro, because they portray the life of drug traffickers as good and it is not. So if you are at a party and they start playing a *narco-corrido,* people get angry at the police. In some places, the government prohibits them since they incite violence . . .

THE CITY OF HAWAII

Just then there came an ex-policeman of eagerly jaunty sadness, bearing roses and dinner for his policewoman wife, who accepted his offerings without enthusiasm. His name was Francisco Cedeño, and he was now Christ's age. He invited me home, so we drove to Colonia Luisa Blanco, where behind a wall of plywood lurked a one-room palace, anonymously male and disarrayed.

He was an ex-policeman who had enlisted in the military in his early teens. A small table was strewn with photographs of his various adventures in uniform. He was immensely proud of these souvenirs, and especially of his police memorabilia, and it caught at my heart when he said straight out: Three years ago I contracted some vices and was fired.

I'm sorry, I said.

He shrugged.—I had to pay the price of life.

Then he said: Not to justify it, but one reason I fell into vices was the lack of love from my parents.

He showed me a photo of a hectare of marijuana in Sinaloa. And here was a photo of an *amapola* drug flower. Here he was in the army at sixteen (it was an important stage of my life, he said wistfully), and here in police uniform at an official reception . . .

*"If you are called *pesado,* you're one of the big guys," said a policeman with a smile.

I got married very young, he said. My wife got pregnant, but because we couldn't have children,* I partied a lot with a lot of women. I was about to lose my marriage when I heard that my biological father wanted to know me before he died of cirrhosis; he sent me a Greyhound bus ticket to Fresno. He bought me some documents and taught me to speak a little English . . .†

He showed me a photo of himself with the father who had actually raised him, the one he loved with all his heart. Here was a photo of the family with a chocolate cake and an eight-year-old boy in a cowboy hat; that was Francisco Cedeño. About the other father, the one in Fresno, he said: He abandoned my mother and didn't think about his kids.

Here's where I got married, he said, showing me a photo of two scared children. You can see she still looks the same.

She didn't, of course. She had become sour and stern, and it wasn't just the uniform. Disappointment has a way of replacing fear with certainty.

My father taught me that you need to give everything to your job, he was explaining. My wife was annoyed most of the time I was involved with the government. So one day I had to choose between my wife and my job. I chose my job. So at that time she told me I had to do everything possible to have a child or she would leave me. So I decided to find out which drug would help me perform sexually. It was crack. It had many vitamins from mares and things like that. I lost my job due to my drug problem.

I nodded in silence.

The story of narcotraffic starts in 1945, he said abruptly. There is no organized crime without protection in government. Here you can find yourself in trouble without wanting to. By the way, this Mafia is run by families. But a person like me, well, I grew up on a ranch; I didn't know anyone. But if I have a brother who's a drug dealer and I'm in the military, I'm not gonna catch my brother. If my brother harvests marijuana, I'm gonna protect him. But to do that I have to share money with my bosses.

First you harvest it, and he showed me another photo. The owner of this field is a politician. It's not easy when you walk with God, but then no one harms you.

The next photograph depicted soldiers destroying a field.—But behind this field, said Francisco Cedeño with what I was already calling the *narcocorrido* smile, there are five more, even bigger! We just took our orders; we were supposed to destroy one and leave five, because if you didn't follow orders you didn't live to tell about it. So they take it, they harvest it, pack it up, hide it in hollow trees, then put it on

*Evidently she had a miscarriage.

†This sentence actually occurs later on in Señor Cedeño's story, but I reproduced it here for narrative purposes. For his capsule border autobiography, see below, "Between the Lines," p. 1045.

boats to San Felipe. Other batches they take by small plane. Doctors who go into the hills to help women and children carry the drugs. Problem is, it grows. And when it takes time to grow, there's risk. So they've developed a new method where you can grow it in any house, little crops in water. They do it in tract houses, motor homes, and especially houses under construction so you can have people outside working, but inside everyone's *really* working.

I heard *narcocorridos* in the military. Everyone enjoyed them. There are people worthy of respect in the military and the police who don't do drugs. But everyone listens.

I composed one for my wife, he said, and here I thought again of that weary, bitter, slender policewoman to whom he brought dinner and roses, and with whom he claimed to read the Bible every day. There was no sign of her in this sweltering concrete cube of a home with one naked mattress halfway sliding off the other—not a slip or a bra, no stray high heel, no lipstick; but I didn't snoop in the closet; maybe all her things were neatly there; but everything I saw was a solitary man's, like a drug runner's, in this one room where rebar stuck out of the wall and dust lay upon his old photos and certificates, not to mention again that bare and grimy mattress with covers merely messing it up and clothes disarraying the covers; his life's metonym might be the open suitcase on the bed, or perhaps the widowed bird (he killed his wife by pecking her, said Francisco). He stayed in shape, however; he cared about his appearance. There lay barbells by the mirror. But this house hidden from the street behind a wall of plywood, this was what I found creepy. Now he began to search everywhere for the *corrido* he had written in honor of his wife, but he couldn't find it, so, changing his clothes and donning a hat to formalize the performance, he sang what snatches he remembered into Terrie's tape recorder, and here is what she transcribed and translated:

In Baja California
there are very valiant women.
Don't take my word for it;
all the people say it!
This *corrido* is for them;
I'm always thinking of them.
There is one I carry in my chest,
or my soul it could be called.
Even for many eggs*
I wouldn't want to trade her.

*Or bigger balls.

The way she carries herself
makes the people respect her.
She's a *norteña,*
this valiant woman.
Some call them *patrona*
because they give us food.
Some love drug dealers;
some love the law!

That was as much as he could remember. The invocations of *valiancy* and *respect* could have been heard in any *narcocorrido,* for instance, in "The Queen of the South"—Teresa the Mexican from the other side of the sea, a valiant woman we'll never forget—and indeed this devout lover of the law had also composed a *narcocorrido,* "The City of Hawaii":

In the year '95,
October thirtieth was the day,
In the city of Hawaii
the story unfolded.
They detained two *narcos*
who sold pure *chiva**
from a pueblo in Nayarit.
They brought the drugs
hidden in a Grand Marquis—
who would even guess?
They dressed like priests
so they wouldn't get searched . . .

That, too, was as much as he could remember. Of course it would end badly, as life does, or else get bad temporarily, then escape from the badness as death does. Did the two false priests, having perhaps employed the power of their Lord to drive across the waves of the Pacific, remain in a Hawaiian jail forever? In its incompleteness, their story mirrored the career of Miguel Palominos, whom I assume to be serving his fifteen years, because *sympathy has no place in the courtroom, and the jurors were told that four times.* When I think of Miguel Palominos, and when I think of Francisco Cedeño, the words of a certain prohibited ballad rush into my mind:

*Heroin.

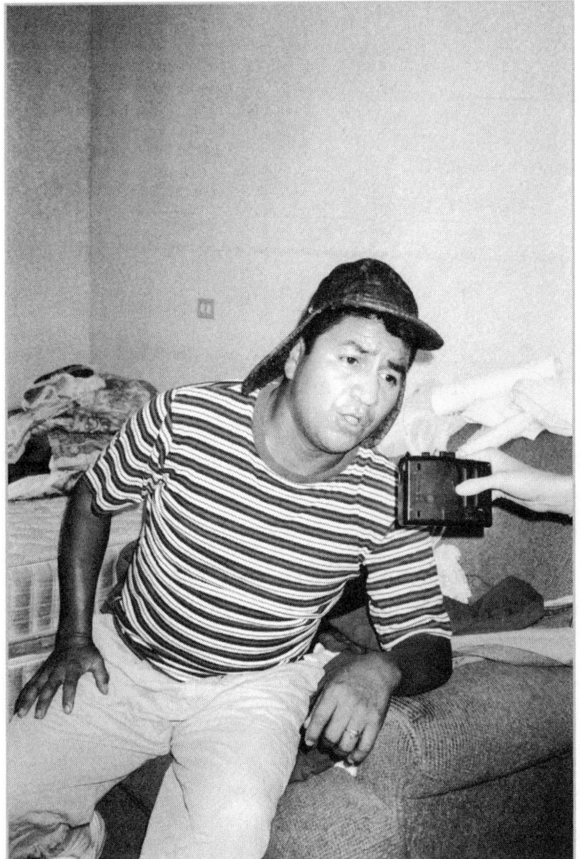

Francisco Cedeño sings "The City of Hawaii."

He dreamed in his delirium
of being free like the wind,
escaping the Presidio.

What happened to the dreamer, who was looking at a long, long stretch of prison years? Why, *his dear wife,* accompanied by a loyal friend, rescued him!

Sinaloa, pretty land,
I sing you goodbye.
I'm off to the Sierra
in the state of Durango,
because the law
looks for me everywhere.

And Francisco Cedeño? Would he win back his valiant policewoman whom he wouldn't trade for ever so many eggs, or testicles? What would the next stanza of his ballad reveal?

Some say she's in prison, others in Italy,
in California or Miami, somewhere in America.

"I SPEND THE NIGHTS FLYING"

As for Emily, oh, as for Emily, she worked at the Thirteen Negro as a *waitress,* not as a *dancer,* she required me to understand; and Mario, the *waiter* who actually brought the drinks, made it clear to me once he was already drunk and I then bought him another beer that although it was over between them he still loved Emily.

I bought Mario a drink, and behind him a fat dancer swerved her fatter bottom from side to side and leaned into a field worker's lap. Streaks of silver and white like phosphorescent fishing line caught everyone's looks from her symphony of hair. Mario was still speaking of Emily. Then the fat dancer's black shoulderstrap slipped diagonally down and she struck her quarry with one giant breast.

I thanked Mario for introducing me to Emily.

She's not a prostitute, said Mario.

Of course not.

She's not a prostitute!

If I don't feel like it, Emily had proudly said, they can ask and ask and I won't do it.

She was talking about dancing.

Last night a man had tried to put his hand up her skirt and she punched him, so he scratched her.

She worked from noon to eight, after which she sometimes went out with friends until three in the morning. I first met her at three in the afternoon, when neither the scathing white light of the streets nor the red side of the beverage truck seen through the open door were as alive as the banks of red bulbs winking in cycles of seduction; but the Thirteen Negro was still asleep enough for the televisions and the white ENTRADA sign to remain almost significant, although already a few men in cowboy hats had swaggered in; and two thin men in moustaches sat side by side in the darkest corner drinking their beers. Before I knew it, a line of straight and bent white-shirted backs conquered the bar stools, and Mario spectacularly twirled my two-hundred-peso note at the bartender to get change. He was still sober then; he was the one who brought me Emily.

Emily gazed up at the ceiling to consider which *narcocorrido* was her favorite and why, smiling, her fingers moving as she recited it, that fine, pale face of hers as fine and pale and silvery-white as her thighs. She had just turned nineteen when she heard her first *narco* on a compact disc in Sonora; she had liked it.

What's necessary to make a *narcocorrido*?

Oh, a good story, said Emily. Her rings were as long and silver as her fingernails.

She was twenty-four. When she was twenty, she had experienced certain problems with her mother. She liked her work except when the men were not respectful. While President Bush looked hunted and evil on the television, Emily waved down Mario for another beer, and then when the black athlete came on, Emily summoned Mario to bear away her beer, which had received the scantest lip service, and to bring her the next beer. I tried to return our paid conversation to the subject of the prohibited ballads, and Emily languidly allowed: Sometimes I'll clean my house and whatever music there is, I'll listen . . .

Would you like to be a drug queen?

She laughed and shook her head.

How about if a drug king fell in love with you and gave you money?

No, because if he had some problems with his friends he would have a problem with me.

Who is worse, the Federales or the Border Patrol?

I've heard the Border Patrol, said Emily, but the Mexican police are just as bad.*

If your boyfriend did drugs and then came off them, would you love him?

No. I don't like drug addicts.

In came a musician with his tuba. He was the lead scout of the Sinaloa band Koely, who in a twinkling had lined up and let loose with the horn and tuba so spectacularly loud that it shocked my heart, and my ears began to sing as if I had just shot off my .50 caliber without using earplugs; and the daylight was safely shut out and the night officially began, Emily now smiling and swaying her head from side to side, showing her white teeth and hopefully as happy as she could be, thanks to those lady-priced beers she kept ordering without asking me—what a predatory little thing! On the other hand, she was nice to Terrie and followed her into the women's restroom to bring her a gift of toilet paper.

*I had expected the prohibited ballads to express more animus against American authority, but once I realized how they were admired in inverse proportion to income it made sense: These poor people went to the United States only illegally, to earn money in discreet snatches of menial work; their encounters with the apparatus of our great nation were apt to be final and brief; whereas back home in Mexico, bereft of gringo toilets to clean, they haunted the streets, so that their unhappy encounters with uniformed officers were quotidian. So it was the Federales more than the Border Patrol, U.S. Immigration or the Drug Enforcement Administration whom the *narcocorridos* delighted to abuse.

It was only 4:41. Now the dance floor held two couples, one with the cowboy's hand on his girl's waist; they looked as if they had grown old together, and it was nice that they had come in together; the other was a more commercial couple with the girl's hand on the man, who smilingly gripped his girl's hips, trying to kiss her while she counter-smilingly shook her head. This was my heaven: a fat blonde waiting on the inner, red-cushioned bench, the band Koely playing *norteño* music; and outside was hot and a dead dog had just begun to stink in the street, but the door had closed and the blonde girl's hair went dim, pulsing in accordance with the curtain of lights within the great wall mirror, and now the bloody red nipples of light begin to wink in the ceiling. An emissary from the band trolled the room for requests at fifty pesos each. Why not a *narcocorrido*? I proposed, but he wanted me to be more specific, because there were an awful lot of those, so I requested "Camelia la Tejana" and he said: *Ohhh,* because everyone knew that one—one of the first, Officer Caro had said; he thought that it dated back to 1972. Accordingly, "Camelia" got enacted. The guitarist in his Hawaiian shirt stood singing very gravely, pleasantly and knowingly this song about a female narcotrafficker who falls in love with a colleague who in turn loves somebody else.—So after they come there from their business in Northside, he says he doesn't want to have anything to do with her again, related Officer Caro, and you will be happy to know that Camelia then showed what she was made of.—He was a real person, said Officer Caro; his name was Emilo Videlo; they only found his body; they never found her.—Camelia's song blared on, while poor Terrie sat at attention, trying to write down and translate a word or two; it was too loud and too distorted there beneath the happy satanic light which flushed and flashed over the drinking men whose stolid expressions did not alter although a few of the dancing girls on the barstools began smiling at Camelia's naughtiness.

Fifty pesos more for Emily's next beer, and fifty more pesos for another *narcocorrido,* which happened to be called "Entre Perico y Perico"—"From Nostril to Nostril."*

> The sun comes up again.
> I don't know what happens to me.
> From nostril to nostril
> I spend the nights flying.

Life grew nearly as grand as the blocky man in the shirt of unearthly whiteness who was blowing out shrieking sounds over the white drum. Field workers in base-

*Or at least this is what they told me it meant. The dictionary definitions are "perìco," parrot, and "Perìco," ladies' man.

ball hats stared at me with gaping eyes, wondering perhaps if I was a DEA agent; and I lost myself amidst the tubas and drums; when they got especially deafening, Emily's somewhat morose face lit up and she swayed her head from side to side, then called for another five-dollar beer. The hilariously blowing tuba player, the long line of men under the red lights and the violinist who sometimes sang slyly or even angrily but usually with nothing more or less than *knowing melodiousness* elaborated the loudness into something crystalline. Most of the drinkers sat in dignified silence, watching the horns and tubas oriented like flowers toward the red lights. Occasionally I did see that *narcocorrido* smile which Lupe Vásquez had first showed me, no doubt on account of the double entendres about airplanes and the feel-good aspects of high altitudes:

There are cantinas here
that I run to constantly
with a beeper in my pocket
that never stops beeping
because all my friends
also want to fly.

But as was the case for so many of the other prohibited ballads, the humor grew bitter and at times left the bitterness entirely naked. Emerson's dictum that *to be great is to be misunderstood* got borne out in the defiant chorus:

Death is looking for me.
I don't want to hide from it.
On the contrary, I want to find it.
I know it will understand me.

Emily heard *narcocorridos* every day. She said: When bad words are sung, the men shout along. A lot of them work in the fields on the other side, harvesting lettuce and onions . . .

She was never tempted to fall in love with them.

Sure, she said, sometimes I'll be dancing with a certain guy, but after awhile he dances with someone else. Sure, there are women who believe they own a man, but that's just a way to get hurt.

Then the song was over, and the two men at the table against the wall sat staring at the bright triangles of light across which a poxed woman in a miniskirt glided.

Once upon a time, one of the ladies who sold tacos outside the Thirteen Negro had told Emily about a place for rent in the Colonia Aguas Calientes to the west of the Río Nuevo and past the man selling Mexican flags for Independence Day; so that was where the silverskinned girl lived, in a place which reminded me of a slave barracks I'd seen in New Orleans: a long shedlike structure with many separate doors—and, by the way, in the Mexican sunlight her skin was actually a lovely reddish-brown. Inside Emily's door there was a stifling concrete-floored kitchen with two chairs, utensils hung neatly on the wall, and bedding piled up against the wall; behind a curtain lay the sanctum, kept by Emily's air conditioner at seventy-eight degrees on that hundred-and-ten-degree day, so Emily definitely wasn't poor; recently her old air conditioner had died and she'd been able to buy this one, not to mention sending money home to Obregón all the time for the betterment of her parents and her four children, whom she visited every three to five months; and it should also be mentioned that Emily owned three cell phones, one of which was used only to chat with her Mama. Why ask what the other two were for? From beneath the mattress of one of the two double beds, she withdrew a heavy-gauge transparent sack of photographs: Here was her favorite uncle, there her seventy-eight-year-old father the rancher, on horseback beside a giant saguaro. Here was her pet goat, whose mother had been killed by a car; her brother had cut the animal's belly open, saved the baby and fed it with bottles of milk. And to complete the entertainment, Emily put on music: pirated compact discs of this band and that, a few of whom, such as Cabrona and Los Tigres del Norte, I now recognized as creators of *narcocorridos.*—What are some of the stories from the *narcocorridos* which stick in your mind? I asked her, and she said without much interest that a lot of them told how drug dealers were killed by the police. It was evident by now that Emily was the sort of person who paid more attention to tunes than to words. But the tunes she never tired of. I will always remember how she began to smile whenever the music at the Thirteen Negro grew so loud that my entire skeleton vibrated; and Emily allowed that last night in this very room she had turned up her music as absolutely loud as it would go even though the landlady didn't really like it (what the landlady *really* didn't like was buying or selling crystal on the premises; the first thing she had asked Emily was whether she had that habit). Probably to please me, Emily now played one of the Tigres del Norte discs, reserving for another occasion the one entitled *Pacto de Sangre,* pact of blood. She was singing along with a *corrido,* her ringed finger dancingly upraised. Oh, yes; her fingers were ornately cylindered with silvery rings which bore the names of her father and her children; she felt naked without them and never took them off, she said, slipping one down an inch to show me the ring of untanned skin beneath like a bikini line; recently she had lost the thumb ring and couldn't rest until she'd bought a replacement. Then she went back to singing. The words of the *corrido* were: *If you're going to leave me, don't come back.*

Happily, she opened and closed the drawer beneath the makeup table, whose most prominent adornment was the image of the Virgin of Guadalupe. It took Emily an hour to put her makeup on whenever she went to work. The hardest part was painting on her eyebrows. Sometimes she didn't like the way they looked; sometimes a friend opined that they weren't quite right; then Emily had to do them all over again. She had the same blood type as her daughter, which was why she chose not to tattoo her eyebrows on, for that would have tainted Emily's blood.

That afternoon, Emily, whose birthday was Valentine's Day, was wearing a white outfit, the gift of some man; so I called her the White Queen and she laughed. She had beautiful young breasts, and did not in the least resemble someone who'd borne children. All her sisters were fat, she said; she was the only slender one. She said that it was a shame that Terrie and I hadn't been at the Thirteen Negro last night because we would have had a laugh to spy the woman who'd come in wearing a see-through dress with a bathing suit beneath it, displaying in the red lights her tattooed boobs and ass. I asked if the men had enjoyed it, and Emily replied that unfortunately the lady had been just a little bit older and also obviously an addict, and sometimes men aren't so attracted to addicts. I asked her how many addicts she saw at work, and she said that there were more here in the *colonia,* in the bar La Baja.

I'm not going to wear that short skirt anymore, she said, because it just causes trouble.—The next night she was wearing a shorter one. I remember Emily on the dancefloor in a pink miniskirt and a black low-cut top of itsy-bitsy straps, swishing her hips, wriggling her bottom, with her fingers spread between a man's shoulderblades; most happily and gloriously and with the same firmness as the gum stuck to the undersides of the Thirteen Negro's tables do I remember Emily on the red bench with her thighs spread so that all the way across the immensity of the scratched and silvery dancefloor and into the darkness where I sat I could see the deep black triangle of her underpants.

DIALOGUE ABOUT ADRENALINE

Are you rich or poor? I asked Javier Armando Gómez Reyes, who stood on a Mexicali street with a collection box, soliciting donations for a drug-free Mexican youth.

Poor, he said promptly.

Why are you poor?

Because my family is poor.

Why are they poor?

My family has always been poor. They've always worked to get ahead and have a house; but I've never had a house.

His collection box boasted him rehabilitated, so I asked him whether he used drugs, and he said yes, ever since he was little, although he had now been walking the sober path for a good two weeks.

Do you listen to *narcocorridos*? I asked, and he commenced to smile so sweetly like all the others; raising his thumb in benediction over good illegal substances, he nodded.

His favorite prohibited ballads were, of course, "Camelia"—he said: I've loved that one since I was a little kid!—and "Golden Pistol Grip," which he summarized as follows: It's about a hired hit man. The Mafia would hire him to kill the competition. It's just a song about him, because he was famous.

Why do most people like the *narcocorridos*?

Adrenaline. It makes people want to be like the people in the songs. It's like when you gringos get drunk and you hear Mexican songs and you go *yee-haw* because it makes you happy!

If you could make money from drugs without risk, would you do it?

Of course, he said. He was one of the most straightforward people I ever met, this Javier Armando Gómez Reyes, from Ciudad Juárez, Chihuaha; he was as clear as a mountain lake.

Which one would you sell?

Coca, heroin, crystal . . . he rattled off with a big smile on his face, and I liked him more and more.

Would you rather sell many drugs or specialize?

It would be a good idea to just sell one, but make sure that it's really strong. If a drug has a lot of chemicals in it, it's cheaper . . .

RESPECTED AT ALL LEVELS

At the beginning of the glorious twenty-first century, the police of my state were running meth scientists out of their labs in the Central Valley. Some of these refugees set up shop in northern California; many reestablished themselves in Southside—for instance, in Mexicali, where my street-friends' favorite drug used to be cocaine of near Colombian purity; then it was crack; and in the year of grace 2005 I asked at a souvenir stand which pipes were best for crystal, and the man immediately opened a discreet box and showed me a glass bowl and stem. Had I been asked to associate a drug with the cheerfully energetic personality of Javier Armando Gómez Reyes, I would have chosen crystal. But for a less hypothetical link with that vitamin, I must refer you to Cookies, whose grandfather was born in Venice, grew up in Spain, married a Yaqui and became a revolutionary.

When did you hear your first *narcocorrido*?

Ooh! A long time ago, said Cookies.

Her colleague María, who'd invited herself to dinner with us at that taco restaurant, put in that she didn't like them because they were *too aggressive*. Cookies quickly said that she had not known what the words meant, but she had wanted to sing them just the same. It was the song called "Camelia." And now María remembered a *narcocorrido* about a piñata which got shot open with bullets to reveal drugs, and she didn't like it:

There once was a piñata
bought by a high-powered man . . .

(And here I beg you to witness María as I did, singing with her sunglasses on the top of her head.)

In America we don't have many of those songs, I said. They are new to me.

Unfortunately, here they are very popular, said María, who bore a mole beneath her heavy left eyebrow, grew long hair down between her breasts like lines of silver, and was built like a sack of potatoes, although she could move fast enough. She went on and on about America and how much she wanted to go there.

They were both from Sonora. They got paid a dollar per dance by their customers at the cantina El Cordobés. The rest was negotiable.

Americans are always very friendly with their big hamburgers, said Cookies. But when I used to go to Tucson even when I had a passport, the American government was very rude to me. I used to dream about living in the United States, but I don't anymore, because I don't like the way I would be treated.

Cookies, what's your favorite drug?

Should I tell you the truth? she wondered absolutely.

Absolutely, said I, with my pen upraised ever so obediently.

Well, then to tell you the truth, I've worked very hard as a prostitute, but I've had to drink a lot and smoke a lot of drugs. I smoke crystal. It helps my work. I've thought about going to a rehab center, a certain Christian rehab center. I really like them. People have offered me crystal to make me thin. I smoke ten dollars' worth of crystal when I'm drunk. There's a white kind, and then when you're drunk there's a green kind that'll end it. You have to know whom to buy it from. You just ask for crystal, but if when you put it on the aluminum foil you start to light it and it's white, it's not gonna do much for you.

I showed them some of the titles of the *narcocorridos* that Terrie had written down at the Thirteen Negro, and María, the one who disliked *narcocorridos,* started smiling and singing, although she had to look down at the lyrics. She remembered one song called "The Mule," about a man who was so successful that police let him cross the border with impunity, so he brought his children along; they got hungry, ate his drugs and died. That tale spoke to María's tragedies, I could see.

Cookies, who was prettier than María but still used up, with floppy old breasts and wrinkled cleavage, sang with relish a song about a man who was also a pirate; they tortured by him by cutting off his testicles, then let him go, and he killed himself by crashing his plane.

In Tijuana, strange things happen
without any reason.
It is said they tortured him
without compassion or regard.

Why had she remembered those lines in particular? What sort of life might she have had?

With skewers they punctured
the noble parts of his body . . .

Was he a hero? I asked her.

No. Just a narcotrafficker.

Maria added: But the thing about him was, he didn't want to deal drugs anymore, and that's why they tortured him.

Both of them were singing it to remember the words, struggling over it.

Why are the prohibited ballads popular?

Mira, said María. Here's how I see it. All the narcotraffickers—no offense, Cookies—all the drug dealers and users listen to them.

Cookies lived with an addict; it scared her.—But those people can't help themselves, she said.

And María said: The brother of the dealer I lived with, they put his head in a plastic bag and shot him. All of his friends are addicts.

What makes the music of a *narcocorrido* good?

Cookies answered: It has to be the music and the beat.

María bitterly said: The music is the costume of the lyrics.

But Cookies was not bitter at all; indeed she sang the following lines with that *narcocorrido* smile:

I am the chief of the chiefs, my friends.
I am respected at all levels.
My name and my photograph
you'll never see in the papers.

Those words came from another Tigres del Norte song, called "Jefe de Jefes," naturally. And the smile they gave to Cookies was the smile of one who can dream for a moment of freedom, power and a good name.

THE SONGS OF ÉRICA

He likes people to sing to him, I had Terrie say, *he pays.* But all the girls in the doorway of the Hotel 16 de Septiembre were asked, and got shy or said they couldn't sing. Fortunately, Érica from Guadalajara was swaying at the intersection across from the Hotel Nuevo Pacífico on that ninety-degree Saturday night which felt so cool after the hundred-and-fifteen-degree day; she was willing to sing prohibited ballads for money in my hotel room. Why not? She used to sing them in the shower, she said. Some of the *corridos* which flew into her head had nothing to do with narcotics, for instance the song about a girl who is in love with a man and he only sees her as a little girl even when she grows up and expresses her love for him and she kisses him and still he only sees her as a little girl:

Put your plans in my hands.
I am the same little girl
but now I am old enough
to say I love you and I can't forget . . .

The *corrido* about the man who drinks and sends his son out to ask for money and his son dies from exposure, and he realizes that he has killed his son, was nearer the mark, especially when sung by Érica in her druggy voice. (I wanted to meet her dealer, and she said that there were some dealers maybe in the Hotel Santa Cruz. Then she said: I know a guy but he's not here in the street. They don't come out. You have to go there and knock and come and get it.) The ballad about the neglected boy seemed not dissimilar to the song about the little boy whose mother is dying at the same time that the father is marrying another woman, and the priest says that anyone knowing anything against this marriage should speak out now, and the child says my mother is dying and the father says I don't know this child. But then Érica remembered the *corrido* (I think by Los Tigres del Norte) about the two inseparable brothers who fall in love with the same girl; they'd fought over drugs and money and would always stay together but once they quarrel over this woman they kill each other:

> Pedro and Pablo were brothers,
> inseparable friends.
> They were abandoned when their parents died.
>
> Pedro it's so good to see you.
> I think we know each other.
> Something erased your smile.
> I cry from happiness . . .
>
> She'd forgotten the words of the climax, but she remembered
>
> Pedro, what has happened to you?
> I cry happy tears . . .

—the dark and slender girl's abscessed arms hunched together like those of a praying mantis, her chin on her fist, the dim silver circlet of her earring hanging limp because she barely moved her weary head, barely opened her gaptoothed mouth.

She remembered the one that María had sung, the one about the piñata shot full of bullets.

She used to go to the Thirteen Negro and the Playboy Club before she had her daughter, she said. She used to drink a lot in those days, she said. I doubt that the Thirteen Negro or the Playboy would have admitted her now. She was twenty-three with two girls. The baby was with her here in Mexicali, just about to turn three.

She said: I think they should get rid of all those *corridos,* since there is so much murder in cold blood. Killing little children, brother against brother. For example, somebody who sells drugs listens to them and they make him feel good.

With many such pieties she sought to please us, scratching her mahogany-red skin, lapsing ino song, swaying. Her arms' many abscesses she explained as being actually the result of Mexicali's airborne viruses; there was something in the dust, she said. The next morning she came to apologize for lying: she had pretended to live in a *colonia* when in fact she slept in the street.

The next scrap of song she sang with the *narcocorrido* smile:

> In a grey truck
> with California plates
> they brought them all fixed up,

but . . .* his girlfriend.
He brought a lot of dollars
to exchange them for drugs.
On the way back to Sinaloa,
Pedro said to Inés:
"I feel like someone's following us.
Maybe we should disappear . . ."

That was all she remembered.

ANGÉLICA AS THE CHIEF OF CHIEFS

Angélica, who was loitering on the street but had an urgent all-night appointment working at a restaurant whose name she couldn't remember, gladly sang a snatch of *narcocorrido* right there on the street and asked which ones I preferred, the ones where they cut people up or *what*? The next morning she staggered upstairs to my hotel room, reeking of urine old and new, bearing a garbage bag of empty cans in each hand, and because she was very tired by then she could sing only snatches of the prohibited ballads, which suited me since I most wanted to hear what she remembered the best.

The first was called "Three Animals," and it began in typical *narco* style by describing the three animals innocuously; then it turned out that the Federales took them away; the hen was marijuana, the goat was *injection* as Angélica put it, which I take to mean heroin; and then the third animal, whose species she momentarily failed to recall,† was cocaine.—In this particular *corrido,* she added, the drug dealers are bragging because they say that, unlike the Federales, *they* are giving the orders.

There are three animals
that I need to live.
This is why I earn money
for my parakeet, my hen and my goat
so the Federales
have me as their target.

So he works as a dealer to earn money, explained Angélica.

Why do you remember this song in particular?

*Here she slurred her words so that the interpreter could not understand.

†It was a parakeet.

You hear it a lot on the border, so it gets stuck in my head. The ones I like the most are the prettier ones, like the traditional ones.

Oh, you don't like the *narcos*?

To tell you the truth, she allowed, I listen to them.

Stinking like a toilet, she used my toilet without flushing it, spraying urine and toilet paper all over the floor. Then she sat back down on the bed, rubbing her reddish-brown skin and apologizing for not having written out the lyrics; she'd been too busy at work. She had five children. Although she was only in her forties she looked as if she were nearing sixty.

She sang the song about three women: I live with three ladies, the blonde is cocaine, the brown hair is shooting up, and the black hair is . . .—she was exhausted; she could hardly stay awake.

Finally she thought she had it. It was called "La Morena y la Rubia"

I'll tell you why I love the brunette
and I love the blonde:
Because these two women
keep me alive!
I love the brunette . . .

It's just that almost all those songs about brunettes and blondes are *narcos*, said Angélica. I like the pretty, traditional songs, but the ones about *narcos* get stuck in my head, little pieces of them . . .

Each recital required her to think for a long time, but then she'd be smiling more and more widely as she sang her snatches of *narcocorridos* whose wicked cleverness animated her glowing, sagging face like a sniff of good meth.

She remembered the lyrics of "Jefe de Jefes" less accurately but more pointedly than Cookies had. She sang:

I am the chief of the chiefs, my friends.
That's why I work against the law.
Even the Federales do what I say . . .

There are many about a drug lord called "Lord of the Skies," she said. There are also some about the Juárez Cartel . . .

Do the *narcocorridos* have different tunes from the other *corridos*?

They are more contemporary. In the time when I really listened to music, there were none. It used to be that the *corridos* sang about famous men who were brave or who were real womanizers. Now they are about men who sell drugs and kill

Federales, and make them larger than life. It's almost always the same story: *I sell them, I do them, I kill them.* There are also some who talk about working your way to the top. You start out helping and then you're the one who's telling the people what to do. I don't really like that. *I kill, I do, I sell, I make fun of.* The Federales tell us what to do and we do it, but the drug dealers are always the big boss and nothing ever happens to them. In all the songs, they never kill the drug dealers.

Why do you think they are so popular?

People like to listen to them when they're drunk in a cantina. In almost all the cantinas you'll find drunks listening to them.

And why do drunks like to listen to them?

For people who sell drugs, it makes them feel valiant.

That was the operating word, I thought. The ex-policeman had used it in the *corrido* that flattered his wife.

And what about those who don't sell drugs?

Because they play them a lot on the radio.

That begged the question, I thought. For me, the answer was this: Mexicans didn't like being told what to do.

If some drug lord fell in love with you and gave you a lot of money, would you be happy?

No.

What would be your ideal?

An opportunity to work very, very hard for myself and for my family.

Then she staggered downstairs stinking, clutching her plastic bags of cans taken from the garbage.

AN ADMIRER OF THE LORD OF THE SKIES

Around the corner from the high-countered office where Francisco Cedeño brought roses and dinner to his policewoman wife, and down a lovely lane of razor-wire, gaped the prison entrance, where all visitors had to pass through metal detectors which happened to be dead; I was hoping to pay drug offenders to sing to me, but that shift's jefe, the chief, a huge thuglike individual whom I would not have wanted to see in authority over me in any capacity, much less to be my jailer, graciously denied me permission to enter, and so did the jefe of the following night; fortunately, I was granted the acquaintance of a young policeman behind a tall desk, a boyish type whom they all teased goodhumoredly because he liked the prohibited ballads. He first heard them when he was three or four, he said.

What kind of melody do they have?

Guitar, he said smilingly. Banjo, tuba . . .

Oh, yes, that was not the first time I'd seen that smile, the *narcocorrido* smile that had crept out on Lupe Vásquez's hard face, and even on Emily's.

The *corrido* that the young policeman remembered best was "Señor de los Cielos," which is to say "Lord of the Skies," about a drug dealer who commanded airplanes and highways in Sinaloa (you may remember that Angélica had made reference to a series of ballads on this topic); and I had the feeling that if this officer and I were in a bar together, or even on the street, instead of conversing with a metal detector between us, no matter that it appeared to be turned off, he would have happily started singing it.

I was twenty years old when I heard my first *narco,* said another policeman. Some are good, some are bad, he opined with a shrug. He liked it *for the music.* It had *pretty tones.* And he shrugged again.

Do you ever hear the prisoners singing them?

The policeman who admired "Señor de los Cielos" said: *We* won't hear them singing *narcocorridos,* but when they are in the cells they will sing them.

They're forbidden on the radio, said a third policeman helpfully.

Then why are they on the jukebox? I wanted to know.

They shrugged together.

A STORY THAT NEVER ENDS

Angélica had said: It's almost always the same lyrics. It's a story that never ends.

She was referring to the *narcocorridos,* but her words applied equally well to the idiotic War on Drugs itself: **NOTICE IS HEREBY GIVEN** that *Nine Thousand Six Hundred ($9,600.00) Dollars, U.S. Currency, was seized on January 13, 2003, from the person of Luz Maria, at 610 Imperial Avenue, Calexico, County of Imperial, CA, by officers of the Imperial County Sheriff Office in violation of Health & Safety Code Section(s) 11359 and 11360 (03-AF-001).* Meanwhile, how many more years does Miguel Palominos have left to serve? Or did the jury, overruling the judge's command against pity, set him free?

There were many good lines in "Jefe de Jefes" which Angélica and Cookies had not sung, such as

Many want to be where I am.
You can see that they're falling.
They wanted to steal my crown
but those who try end up dead.

Who truly wanted to be where they were? That was the sad thing. It was definitely true that those who tried ended up dead. And the *corrido* singers knew this, presenting their knowledge as a kind of fatalistic courage. *They say / that one day they're going to kill me,* runs a stanza of the Tigres del Norte ballad "Pakas de a Kilo," which continues:

They say
that one day they're going to kill me.
The snakes don't scare me!
I know how to lose and how to win.
I carry a goat's horn
for whomever wants to get into it.

"Cruz de Marijuana," by the appropriately named Exterminador, prepares for the future, instructing the hero's survivors:

When I die,
put up a marijuana cross
with ten bottles of wine
and one hundred packs of cards.

This ballad remembers the narrator's life as a luxurious sort of living death:

In my fine coffin,
with grapeshot as my treasure,
I enjoyed every little thing in life:
jewels, women and gold.
I am a drug dealer;
I know the rifle from the dust!

And indeed the blurring of death and life is common in the *narcocorridos.* Valentín Elizalde's "Catarino y los Rurales" is a frankly supernatural tale:

They raised seven men from the dead
who had killed Catarino . . .

Catarino shot bullets;
the *rurales* shot cannons

but Catarino's ghost defies theirs. And the heroes of *narcocorridos* often evince fantastic powers. To quote one last time from "Jefe de Jefes":

I navigate under the water.
I also know how to fly in the sky.
Some say the government watches me;
others say that's a lie.
From up high I entertain myself.
I like them to be confused.

Just as Jesus spoke in parables, likewise the narco-saints—and their listeners. The more desperate they were, the more profoundly the *narcocorridos* sang to them. The hotel clerk Patricia, whom I had known for years, disliked them actively; the barber who always remembered me and said *God bless you* felt the same. The police expressed various tolerations, exasperations and likings from within their collective prison of stolidity. Poor Francisco Cedeño was drawn in equal measures to fantasies of policewomanly valiancy and imaginings of priest-smugglers. Emily liked tunes more than words; *narcocorridos* pleased her on that basis; certainly the so-called drug culture was more normal for her than for many Northsiders; in fact I knew nobody in Mexicali who lived in isolation from it. María knew prohibited ballads in spite of herself; Cookies and Angélica relished them all the more for their prudish affectations; Érica lived the addict's life and half-consciously breathed them; Javier Armando Gómez Reyes, not to mention the great Lupe Vásquez, stood loyally for them; the field workers at the Thirteen Negro who paid Emily's air-conditioning bills shouted the words out.

I've failed to mention the Tucanes de Tijuana, a famous band who composed the first *narcocorridos* Angélica ever heard; I've neglected to relate Alfonso Rodríguez Ibarra's musicological distinctions between *corridos;** I've failed to introduce you to the most famous narcotraffickers, whom even the police speak of with respect: Güero Palma, the brothers Chapo Guzmán and Aureliano Félix from Tijuana; Cárdenas the chief of chiefs, the Valencia brothers . . . But maybe I have showed you that certain individuals of a daringly decorative bent can paint the walls of hell with words as yellow, hot and sulphurous as the Chinesca at three in the morning.

**Corridos,* he said, can be either *banda* or *norteño* style. Very rarely, they can be mariachi style. *Norteño* uses drums, stand-up bass, guitar, and accordion—no horns. *Banda* employs cymbals, tuba, horn, eschewing guitar or stand-up bass. *Tecnobanda* plays keyboard instead of horns. Mariachi involves guitar, trumpet and violin. (Traditionally, harp was also played.) The *narcocorridos* are almost always composed in *norteño* or *banda* style.

Chapter 155

THE *MAQUILADORAS*

(2004)

Q. Are *maquiladoras* good or bad for Mexico, and why?
A. To tell you the truth, I don't know.

—Interview with Señora Candelaria Hernández López, *maquiladora* worker, 2004

In our country, there's reality and there's superficial truth.

—Séñor A., private detective, 2004

Once upon a time in a concrete house on the west bank of the Río Hardy, on one of those hundred-and-ten-degree humid afternoons which in southeast Asia would have imparted an air of Buddhist dreaminess to everything but which in Mexico expressed itself in simple torpidity, a certain Cucapah woman who travelled by slow bus five days out of every seven to the *maquiladora* in Mexicali where she assembled unknown components for the better than average wage of a hundred dollars a week informed me that before she'd given birth to those four children who now sprawled in the dirt, one of them sleeping, two of them playing, the eldest slowly fighting the flies over his can of soda pop, she had worked in a different *maquiladora* managed entirely by men and labor-staffed mostly with single young women like her; in this establishment, the name of which she'd forgotten, every female on the line was required to bring in a bloody tampon each month for inspection. No tampon or no blood, and she got fired. My driver-interpreter Terrie Petree was skeptical. She said that Mexican women usually wore pads, not tampons; and, besides, how difficult would it be to borrow a neighbor's bloody tampon or procure a splash of chicken blood? All the same, I knew a book which seconded the indictment, an angry little book whose certitude glared as inescapably as Imperial sunshine. Its author was none other than Ramón Eduardo Ruiz, whose exaggerations about the feculence of the New River my own laboratory samples had underwhelmingly verified; on the other hand, I credit the man's reassuring consistency for excelling that of the Bible: In brief, Mexicans were mostly right and gringos were always wrong. (His tract ends thus: *A healthy and prosperous American economy will not forever endure if the mass of Mexicans to the south, many of whom labor for greedy American employers, live in Third World dependency.*) What about the Cucapah woman's story? Well, Señor Ruiz was apprised that a certain *maquiladora* in Ciudad Juárez compelled its female employees to bring in bloody tampons each month for the first three months.

What was it about this now-twice-told anecdote of the tampon parade which most offended me? I suppose that it was the violation of dignity. The massive drug testing in American workplaces angers me enough as it is; I see all too well the culture of bullying and cravenness that it leads to. Repeated pregnancy testing as a condition of continued employment is worse; the humiliations of the tampon parade remind me of the anal search to which functionaries of my government once treated me, simply because I was hitchhiking; that was more than twenty years ago now, and I will never forget it. As Emerson wrote, *could not a nation of friends even devise better ways?* To institutionalize such invasiveness with monthly replications would be an easy achievement of the reprehensible.

It really wasn't my concern, because I live over here on Northside, where inexpensive Mexican-assembled products arrive by magic; but I did start wondering how bad it really was in the *maquiladoras. They are very closed,* said everybody, which increased my suspicions. One day Terrie and I breezed into a large feedlot in the Mexicali Valley and the office girl invited me to take any photos I yearned for; all that she asked was that I close whichever gates I opened, so that the stock didn't get loose. A cowboy posed for me; I wandered into another office after closing time, and the man there, who never even asked my name, looked up all the statistics I wanted. On that same day, we had visited a glass factory where our welcome was decidedly different. We would need to apply in advance for authorization, said the man for whom the receptionist had rung. This application must be in writing, delivered by post; and the chances of its being accepted sounded equivalent to those of my being elected President of Mexico. The man was, moreover, inquisitive in that unpleasant fashion of FBI agents. He wanted identification, which for some reason I declined to show him. His clever little eyes never stopped trying to see through me. He was an exemplar of monotonous diligence. He showed no hurry to eject us from the factory; he was perfectly willing to undress our motives for as long as we liked. This must be how one guards trade secrets.

Whenever somebody with a badge tells me not to do something, my inclination is to do it, so I must thank the glass factory's sentinel for encouraging me to peek into a few *maquiladoras,* with or without permission. Of course I'd respect their little trade secrets, excepting a certain ingredient called exploitation.

My high school friend Chuck is a private eye. I asked him how I should proceed. Since his line of work had more to do with trolling databases and standing outside subway stations with the odd suspect's photo hidden in a newspaper, he referred me to his colleagues, Mr. W. and Mr. D.

THE SIXTEEN-HUNDRED-DOLLAR BUTTON

Mr. W.'s profession was to make bug sweeps as mandated for government contractors, to enter the field on surveillance missions, and to assemble covert packages for people such as myself. He was a helpful man who enjoyed his toys, and I ended up liking him. Nothing fancy, I said; accordingly, he recommended a certain "cigarette pack" digital video recorder which could store up to eight hours of video. That would relieve me of five or six hundred dollars. The only question was what to plug into it. There was the cell phone camera, of course, not to mention the pen camera and the button camera. I was receptive, so to speak, to the idea of the cell phone camera since Mexicali stripper-prostitutes had begun to carry those, which meant that some factory girls might, too (Capitalist Axiom Number 807: Call girls set the fashion), but it was bulky; worse yet, it needed to be accidentally-on-purpose laid down on a counter with the antenna pointing at its subject; it did not function in a breast-pocket. So that tool would be in imminent danger of confiscation. As for the pen camera, Mr. W. confessed that it looked flashy. It came in a matched set, in case someone wished to borrow the operative's pen; two pens in one pocket, aside from creating a fifty-percent opportunity for disaster, would further endanger my agent by asserting an inappropriate class statement of abundance. How could it have been otherwise? The items on Mr. W.'s list, being expensive, were for use by the rich against the poor, or by the rich against each other, with the result that flashiness (I mean corporate elegance) was decidedly appropriate. But how could a *maquiladora* worker wear one of his products without attracting attention? Consider the brooch camera, at a price of twelve hundred dollars, and if I were interested in investigating the possible sexual exploitation of Mexican factory women, an issue which had so pervaded common knowledge or at least mythology that Tijuanos used to refer to female *maquiladora* workers as *maquilarañas,* literally factory spiders—"spider" is slang for a prostitute—a woman would be a good choice to film the groping of women, so at first I liked the idea of the brooch-camera, especially because, so Mr. W. now informed me, the process required not only a digital video receiver but also a power supply, which consisted of a four-pack or even an eight-pack of triple-A batteries, so why not find, as Mr. W. recommended, a big-breasted woman to stash all this hardware in her brooch? Sad to say, this item was less appropriate for assembly line workers than for diplomats' wives. When finally I hinted that I might find myself in a blue-collar setting, Mr. W. recommended the jean jacket camera for my consideration, but how inconspicuous would that be on a hundred-and-fifteen-degree day in Mexicali? Besides, what if these *maquiladora* workers wore uniforms? What if factory conveyor belts made longsleeved garments dangerous? Back to the button camera. Incidentally, Mr. W. advised me that *the pen mike works real well,* but I now possessed enough complications without adding sound.

What if I didn't like the button camera? For in this market-driven economy of ours, customer satisfaction is what we agonize over. What if *Playboy,* whose expense check would buy the button camera, regretted that I hadn't bought a vibrator camera instead? Mr. W. and I were both in the same mercantile pickle; we needed to please. But what was not to like?—*It's sweet,* said Mr. W. of this new item; he himself was about to purchase three of them for the office. It came with four matching buttons, which I was supposed to sew onto each garment for which the device was used. On the other hand, the baseball-cap camera required a gizmo-concealing hat clip, which in Mr. W.'s considered opinion looked *weird.* The eyeglasses-case camera was plain and effective; presumably the power supply could go inside it; but what if my spies eschewed glasses or breast-pockets? A similar argument told against the eyeglasses-strap camera. I forgot to tell you that both of these would have required my agent to gracefully wear a wire down the back of her neck. No price too high for beauty, my father used to say, shaking his head.—The cigarette-pack camera tempted me momentarily, but it turned out that it held no cigarettes, which exposed its operative to the same risks as the pen camera. The briefcase camera would definitely drop jaws on the assembly line; the wireless watch camera was out of stock. All right, so I would buy a button camera.

How would I rig it? An athletic bandage and foil would be my friends, instructed Mr. W., and I shouldn't forget the safety pins. He reminded me: If she's well endowed, fix it underneath the breast.

And what if *I* use it? I wanted to know.

The small of the back is okay for a man, but direct line of sight from receiver to transmitter is best for anything wirelesss, due to the water content of the human body. Of course since the button camera is wired, this won't be a problem.

Can I move when the camera is on?

Your video should be stable if the camera is still or slow.

And how much time will the button camera give me?

One hour, said Mr. W.

Enough; I selected the button camera; I bought it; I became another of Mr. W.'s customers. Doubtless it had been assembled in some Chinese *maquiladora.*

By the time everything was all over (and even then it wasn't over), I'd spent sixteen hundred cool green dollars, and it took two more weeks and two hundred dollars more before I got the button camera to work. Ah, the fortunes of war! Now I could understand why the Pentagon sometimes paid six hundred dollars for a toilet seat.

THREE THOUSAND MORE

As for Mr. D., in Chuck's words, *he infiltrates factories for a living.*

I called him up; he was skiing or swimming or something.

Their security is horrible, he explained to me. What you do is you come up with a product you wanna produce. Then you tell their local Chamber of Commerce, and you go in.

He opined that there was worse exploitation in small Mexican industries than in the *maquiladoras,* especially since the latters' facilities are newer.—*Maquiladoras* have created a base of power for Mexican women, he insisted, and I think he was right. He said: The real scandal is the murder of women in Ciudad Juárez.

He did remark that he'd heard a story about a Chinese plant in Tijuana which involved *women from China who were locked in, never let out except to work.* He couldn't say whether this factory was still in operation; and indeed, nobody I met in Tijuana knew anything about this.—Here you have an example of Chinese labor being even cheaper than in Mexicali! he chuckled.

Seven or eight years ago he'd found *maquiladoras* sorting U.S. mail in Mexico. *All these girls out there* were photo-imaging misdelivered mail for corporations despite a federal order not to do it. *US postal workers were upset that their jobs were outsourced down there;* but he thought that *the privacy concerns are overblown.* He was a real card, was Mr. D.

He'd also found Texas motor vehicle records being processed down in Juárez. So I figured that his offer to fly down to Tijuana for two days and three grand might provide me with the knowledge as to where exactly to focus my button camera. He promised me *four or five baddies.* He was a free spirit, too; I liked that about him. He enjoyed playing the guitar.

"YOU WILL NEED A GOOD PRETEXT TO GET IN"

And so at sunset I lay on my bed in a Tijuana hotel room which smelled like pipe smoke and body odor, reading Mr. D.'s report, which began: *We were assigned to conduct an investigation in order to locate maquiladoras in the Tijuana, Mexico region that were abusive to both people and nature.* The sky was paling and the one bare bulb, which illuminated a portion of the ceiling molding quite nicely, could no longer reach my bed, which, after all, was meant to be used for activities pertaining to darkness, so I let my gaze leave the pages of Mr. D.'s report, whose type and whose paper were now nearly the same shade, and I listened to the bells of the cathedral, whose twin towers and whose image of the Virgin of Guadalupe were almost identical with their counterparts on Avenida Reforma in Mexicali; and then I got the white plastic chair which was spattered with brown stains, moved it directly beneath the lightbulb, listened to drumbeats, traffic and barking dogs, then read a little farther into Mr. D.'s report.

Metales y Derivados, read one heading. *This is a shut down battery manufacturing facility that was on four acres and is located in the Ciudad Industrial Nueva Tijuana, above the Ejido Chilpancingo, . . . which was once a fairly clean residential neighborhood . . . [and] is now a fetid, polluted barrio . . . Some estimate that up to 40% of the people in this plant have become ill from the pollution,* which would have cost seven million American dollars to clean up, so it stayed the way it was. *In February of 2004, a Mexican judge issued an arrest warrant for the owner of this plant, Jose Kahn, of the New Frontier Trading Co. He and his [son] both live in San Diego County,* and their addresses and telephone numbers followed.—You'll love this! Mr. D. had instructed me regarding the latter information.

So that sounded promising.

Then a page later, under the heading *Plants With Bad Reputations,* I was first informed of the existence of Óptica Sola, a *maquiladora* which *manufactures all kinds of lenses and is on a pollution watch list (we will check them out further to see if they sell to Lenscrafters or other huge U.S. chains). The production line is predominantly women and the floor and ground below are reportedly contaminated. You will need a good pretext to get in, and as we didn't have anything ready, we were unsuccessful.*

What might it mean to be a *Plant With a Bad Reputation*? Dear reader, would *you* like to have one? I am sure that I would not, even if I had earned it. And Óptica Sola is, let's assume, an adorable company.

Please consider *Plants With Bad Reputations* to be a phrase with entirely less validity than the initial complaint which lures a grand jury into a secret investigation. But since my self-assigned duties demanded that I investigate a few *maquiladoras,* why not report on Óptica Sola?

According to the Secretaría de Medio Ambiente y Recursos Naturales, which is to say the environmental agency of Mexico, Plants I, II and III of a certain Óptica Sola emit contaminants, but this is no evidence of wrongdoing; why, my old high school chemistry textbook insists that a locality's degree of sulphuric acid use is an index of its level of civilization!

A certain "former head" of the Secretaría de Protección al Ambiente Del Estado who now worked in Mexicali and agreed to be interviewed by another private eye on my payroll, a Mr. Adam Raskin (it cost me an extra eight thousand dollars to hire him and his colleagues, but I want you to admire me), *was willing* (runs Mr. Raskin's report) *to make "informal" comments regarding our subject companies, as best as he could recall, from when he was at the state agency . . . Regarding ÓPTICA SOLA,* the "former head" *remembered that there "are files . . . had some problems." Óptica Sola participated in a state program of "autoregulacion [self regulation]," but [he] did not expound on that further.* No, I don't think I would assign Óptica Sola a *Bad Reputation* based on *some problems.*

Mr. Raskin also informs us of two interviews he made with *Jaime Cota, a founder and director at the CENTRO DE INFORMACIÓN PARA TRABAJADORAS Y TRABAJADORES ASOCIACIÓN CIVIL ["CITTAC"] . . . CITTAC is an information gathering, advocacy, and independent association that dealt with individual workers at Maquiladoras,* a word Mr. Raskin capitalizes just for me, *as well as various general political, social, and economic groups in Tijuana and Mexico.*

. . . One of the main activities that CITTAC, and Cota, have undertaken is the presenting of labor "demands [complaints]" against employers at Maquiladoras in the setting of the Junta de Conciliación y Arbitraje. . . . Cota has interviewed hundreds of Maquiladora workers, in some instances formulated their written demands, and appeared at the labor board hearings advocating for those individuals. In the slightly less than 20 years of its existence CITTAC has dealt with above 15,000 workers on different issues.

. . . Cota categorized most labor disputes as related to "unfair termination, low wages," but occasionally for "environmental" reasons. In my follow-up interview with Cota he stated that of our subject group Matsushita, Tompson [sic] *and Óptica Sola had most of the labor complaints he handled.*

. . . Cota corrected that ÓPTICA SOLA was now KARL [sic] *ZEISS VISION, a German firm. He called that Maquiladora one of the "dirtiest in the city." Ten years ago, the El Mexicano newspaper published a list of the most polluting Maquiladoras in Tijuana, and Óptica Sola was on that list.*

In a 2006 issue of the *Boletín Maquilero,* published by and for the workers of Tijuana (the masthead depicts on a blood-red background a blond tophatted Yankee in retreat from a family of brownskinned militants who are shouting at him with doubled fists), under the heading "Chemicals affecting our sexuality and reproduction"—to wit: *KOH, Cellosolve, Metanol, Acetona* and *Ácido Acético*—we read: *There is a great variety of these chemicals utilized in great quantities in maquiladoras such as Óptica Sola . . .* This article comes to you courtesy of Toña, CITTAC, Colectiva Feminista. Might she possibly hold the reputation of Óptica Sola in poor regard? Reader, that's not for me to say. I'm simply a drudge who notes down other people's words.

Back to Mr. D.'s report: *You will need a good pretext to get in, and as we didn't have anything ready, we were unsuccessful.*

Evidently their security was better than Mr. D. had thought. (He later assured me on the phone: I was trying my best bullshit. I kept asking them: Don't you sell *anything* here?)

Well, well. Getting in might have to be my new toy's job.

THE PERFECT SPY

The first time I wore the button camera, my dear friend Shannon helped me duct-tape the button's secret square base to the underside of my shirt, with the real button duct-taped beneath that; we duct-taped the wire to my shirt in a few more places and I then attached the camera input unit to the digital video recorder, plugged in the power pack to both the input unit and the wire, dropped both of these latter modules into my underpants, turned everything on, zipped up my fly, buttoned my shirt, and marched grandly off to Mexicali, with Shannon fussing lovingly over that lone black button like a darling girlfriend. So we came to the border turnstiles, passed through them into Mexico, and I stared sternly at the throngs, confident that I was capturing every face forever. With a *con permiso, señor* to the Mexican officer, I invited myself through the special handicapped entrance to the benches by the border wall where José López from Jalisco awaited me; of course I was so distracted by the button camera that I could hardly understand anything he said. A living skeleton grimaced at me, and I outthrust my chest like a prize turkey, thereby recording him forever with the button camera. Then it was off to the Thirteen Negro Bar and the Hotel Nuevo Pacífico, Shannon smooching me and tenderly mussing up my shirt to make sure that the precious button camera wasn't getting too cockeyed. Outside the Thirteen Negro, she reached passionately into my pants, making a darling little adjustment. That was her role; mine was to move as stiffly as if I were made of glass, choosing to interpret conservatively Mr. W.'s remark that *the video should be stable if the camera is still or slow.* The security guard patted down José, and I got anxious, but that time both Shannon and I, being harmless gringos, were permitted to pass freely through the turnstile into that loud red darkness decades old where men sat glaring balefully at the old cowboys dancing with fat middle-aged women and longhaired young women, some of the women laughing and loving it, or else pretending, the rest grumpily fending off crotch-grabs and butt-pinches, while I sat drinking my *cerveza* like a lord, aiming the center of my chest at the old, old man who nestled his head dreamily between a pockmarked woman's breasts while they slowly trudged out a great circle and she smiled and stroked his hair. How poignant that footage would be! Maybe I should start making art films. There's no feeling quite like discovering that one is far more talented than one thought. In brief, I was so enraptured with my button camera that I stared as crazily as the drunk beside me.

Two hours went by. Mr. W. had advised me that the digital video recorder would last for three. Or was it eight? And hadn't he said that the button camera itself would last for only one? Rushing Shannon back across the border, I found that the poignant art film existed only behind my eyelids. Apparently when Shannon had reached into my pants, she, not knowing that I had turned the power pack on in the United States, turned it *off;* but there wasn't even any footage before that; the living skeleton whom my documentary greed had sought to appropriate would have to remain immortal only to his own circle; I never saw him before or since. It seemed as if the digital video recorder had separated from the input, and I now remembered one moment, ominous in retrospect, when that metal brick, which had been transmitting reassurance of its continued operation by means of a simple yet effective heatwave cipher (translation: it kept scorching my penis), began a slow and searing slide down my left thigh; and I rushed to fortify the elastic in my underwear with a hunk of toilet paper. (See, I'm as good as any *maquiladora* guard at protecting my trade secrets.) Had something gotten disconnected or what? Might I have pushed the record button only once instead of twice? Dazzled but undefeated by these various explanations for my failure, I coolly prepared my second attempt.

This time, in spite of Shannon's objections, I taped the button camera to a long narrow rectangle of cardboard to which I also attached the wire. I duct-taped the recorder, the input module and the power pack into a glorious bomblike affair of sticky silver mummy-wrappings, plopped it into my pants (sizzle, sizzle), zipped myself up and then immediately back down to check on things, discovered that I had just nudged the digital video recorder's power button into the off position, undid the whole apparatus, bought index cards, duct-taped those over the duct tape on either side, wired myself back up, proved once and for all that the power pack's four AAA batteries were now dead, took everything off again while Shannon sighed and set down her purse, replaced the batteries, rewired myself, activated the mess to a setting somewhere between BAKE and TOAST, zipped my fly, gingerly unzipped it again just to admire the glow of the digital video recorder's little square screen through my underpants, rezipped up to zero, took Shannon by the hand, and glided back to Mexico as stiffly as a cardboard cutout, because no untoward bodily kink would disconnect *this* episode! An hour and six minutes later, in the bathroom of the Restaurant Dong Cheng, I verified that the video was still running, then powered off and broke everything down, in order to avoid foreseeable awkwardness with United States Customs and Immigration. Now I was walking on air; I was James Bond! At least, I was Bondish or Bondian.* Pulling the reluctant Shannon back to Calexico (she couldn't see why we couldn't drink one more beer at the Thirteen Negro), I lay down on the bed, played back the video, and watched an hour and six minutes of skies and roofs—did I tell you that the digital video recorder lacked a fast forward? This perfect spy could hardly believe it. Shannon advised me to record the universe from a lower buttonhole next time . . .

Half a week and many batteries later, I had become a reliable videographer of ceiling fans, streetlamps, and the occasional crown of an extremely tall Mexican's head. Every time I was on the American side, I dropped more money and hours at another electronics store, a promising computer repair shop, but I could never transfer even these useless images to my computer, which meant that I had no idea what the actual resolution of my videos might be; moreover, the digital video recorder provided no indication as to how much disk space these videos took up. Was I out of room? I hated to delete everything, especially that first practice video of Shannon dancing for me in the doorway of the Motel Camino Real in Calexico; as for my Mexican movies, I just couldn't believe that there might not somewhere be one good frame, as seemed even more apodictically the case on that stifling July Saturday night when after two long strolls of flirting and communion with Mexicali prostitutes both of the street and of the hotel variety, each walk suitably adorned with romantic button's-eye views of cleavage and streetlit faces (spectacular blue eyeshadow, spiderlike eyelashes and firehouse-red lips which might touch the penis but never the mouth of the client), I came back filled not only with certainty but with pride in a covert job well done, only to find myself the possessor of yet more video clips of awnings, flying birds and the undersides of archways. To be sure, every hotel sign, every *tortillería* advertisement was there as proof that I had truly walked the walk; but first prize at the Cannes Film Festival could not be guaranteed, since my Mexico remained devoid of people, and not incidentally tilted sixty degrees off level. By now the button camera's trial position had descended nearly to my navel; moreover, I had spent half a day in San Diego, pacing the computer specialist's office; the technician failed, sweet-temperedly, to transfer my videos of nothing onto my hard drive. So I was in a fine sulk by midnight, although Sandra at the Hotel 16 de Septiembre had taken the edge off. I erased every last video and took the soldierly resolve to lower the button camera all the way to my bellybutton tomorrow. What else could a perfect spy do?

Sunday was warmer than Saturday, which is to say that it crossed the hundred-and-ten-degree mark, and I could easily have blamed the heat, which has destabilized various of my electronic appliances in Cambodia and the Philippines, for the

*My copy editor suggests: "or Bondage (the French version)."

fact that after a dutiful forty-five-minute trudge first to the doorway of the Hotel Nuevo Pacífico for some closeup flirting with the three prostitutes who held down the fort on that slow afternoon, then to the Thirteen Negro, where the security man *almost* patted me down, I discovered that my digital videographic masterpiece consisted of a pulsing cockeyed image of the inside of my hotel room door, with a shimmering line across it; that was my movie, for forty-five minutes. Honest spy that I was, I confess that on that occasion, four AAA batteries died in vain. But it probably wasn't the heat's fault. I think those rickety connecting pins had come undone again.

Grimly I taped everything up better than ever, threw the old batteries onto the hotel room floor, inserted new ones, recharged the digital video recorder, positioned the button camera one loop above the navel, and this time I actually became the proud possessor of covert footage of my fellow human beings, no matter that my lovely movie remained about forty-seven degrees off from the horizontal. Next time I'd tape the top and bottom of that strip of cardboard to the inside of my shirt; that would keep the button perspective to the straight and narrow. Oh, yes, my fellow private eyes; this is how we learn.

"HERE THERE'S LIFE"

In between these experiments, I interviewed *maquiladora* workers.

We were assigned to conduct an investigation in order to locate maquiladoras in the Tjuana, Mexico region that were abusive to both people and nature. But this project likewise proved more difficult than I had expected. To be human is to complain, so I had anticipated an infinity of criticisms, sob stories and denunciations; but far more emblematic was the old man in the cowboy hat who had once assembled electronic components for a *maquiladora* down on Insurgentes, which lay below us in the smog.

I am sure that you've had many experiences in your life, I began.

Well, naturally. We're old, he said, nodding at his amigo.

The private detective Señor A., whom you will meet in due course, once told me that some factories begin illegally in the basements of large houses, in order to avoid taxes; if they last long enough, the owners build overt factories. And I wondered whether the tale of the *maquiladoras* had begun in this stealthy way, or whether they came heralded by trumpets. That was why I asked the man in the cowboy hat: Do you remember what it was like before the *maquiladoras?*

His reply disappointed me: When we got here, there were already a lot of them in Tijuana.

Where do you come from?

Durango, twenty years ago.

Well, here there's life, he kept saying. There's work! There are lots of *maquiladoras.*

Since he had come twenty years ago, all that he knew about the age of his own neighborhood, which already had concrete sidewalks and shade trees and was called Colonia Azteca, was that it must be at least twenty years old. *Maquiladoras* brought life, he repeated, smiling with his big false teeth.

And I remember the two shy girls I interviewed during their lunch half-hour in front of Óptica Sola, not the main Óptica Sola on Insurgentes which Mr. D. had fingered for me and failed to enter, but a smaller, dirtier plant, more piquant with solvent-perfume, which stood upon the Otay Mesa, in the Nuevo Tijuana Industrial Park. The address was perfect: just off Industrial Avenue.

It's good work, they informed me, and the best thing is the ambience inside. It's very clean and it's air-conditioned.

One girl, the twenty-year-old, had been there for two and a half years; she made ninety-nine pesos a day. Her companion, who had just reached the four-month mark and was a year older, got seventy-four pesos. So both of them were comparatively well off, the daily minimum wage in Tijuana being forty-two pesos, a wage which in a local reporter's words *can't sustain life.*

I might mention that I had begun my engagement with this branch of Óptica Sola on my very best behavior, approaching the windowed booth at the gate whose security guard in his green uniform and sunglasses explained that I would need to get authorization and that unfortunately the sole person or agency who could authorize me (he actually made a phone call) was absent, he couldn't predict for how long; it might be awhile, perhaps as soon as the end of the next Ice Age; he was trying to let me down easy. All the while he kept peering and scrutinizing. Now, as I interviewed the two laughingly reluctant girls (I never could have done it without Terrie, who had to wheedle them until she was nearly exhausted; I also had to pay them), we stood in such a way as to interpose the Óptica Sola shuttlebus between us and the gate, but the girls were getting nervous because the security guard had left his post to come peering and peering around the windshield of the bus; and, by the way, oh, what a smell! It was not an unpleasant smell, really. It took me back to my boyhood when I used to build model rockets in the basement, dabbing airplane glue onto this or that plastic part; I used to get flushed and my heart would race; I loved that smell in those days.

I asked them if there might be any smell inside the factory and they said they didn't know. Then they said no, there wasn't. Then they said that anyhow all factories had that smell.

Is anyone affected by the chemicals?

It depends on which area people work in. But they're very careful with people's security, said the longtime girl piously.

What do you think about that lead plant down the street?

The lead plant was, of course, Metales y Derivados, the one which Mr. D. had flagged for me in his three-thousand-dollar report. It lay in sight.

It has to be bad, they replied, since it smells.

And then the security guard craned his snakelike neck farther around the corner of the bus so that his head became a planetoid with twin sunglasses-lens-craters which I did not want to fall into, and I worried even more about those two girls getting dragged down by the gravitational attraction of that malignantly watchful head, so I ended the interview with my customary question:

Are *maquiladoras* good or bad for Mexicans?

For work they're good, because we need work.

Translation: *Here there's life.*

THE BLACK COUGH

Although that pair almost certainly praised *maquiladoras* because the security guard's presence compelled them to do so, the old man in the cowboy hat who'd sat beneath his shade tree in Colonia Azteca asserted his opinions under no such constraint; and I myself decline to condemn *maquiladoras* as a category. A dapper reporter with a Tijuana paper (he was the one who said that the minimum daily wage couldn't sustain life) was sure that the climate of Baja California rendered *maquiladora* work superior to picking squash or watermelons out in the *campo,* and I'd certainly prefer to work in an air-conditioned office on a hundred-and-eighteen-degree day. Moreover, *maquiladora* wages generally exceeded pay for field work. A legal assessor for a federation of labor unions said to me: Sometimes you can make a little more money working in the *campo* than in the *maquiladoras,* especially with green onions. If the whole family goes and works, they can earn three or four hundred pesos a day. But they only work three or four days a week, and they earn no benefits.

Therefore, exploitation in the *campo* may be worse than exploitation in the *maquiladora.*

I remember a long hot Sunday drive through the eastern farmlands of Mexicali Valley to Ejido Tabasco to inspect a certain barracks for campesinos whose boss, a Mexican like them, had *treated them like slaves.* Those were the words of my guide, the anthropologist-historian Yolanda Sánchez Ogás. Journalists had exposed the conditions here just a day or two ago, Yolanda said; evidently the foreman had fled with his workforce. The barracks, freshly deserted, seemed a ghastly enough place;

I particularly remember a vista down a corridor which was open to the sun through a random series of rectangular holes whose anti-shadows in the hot darkness were unbearable to look at; and on either side (grimy plaster on the right, dirty brick on the left), sweltering windowless cells gaped through doorless doorways, the whole as bereft of any convenience or comfort as some ruined clay-city in the ancient Near East; in one cell there huddled expired votive candles for the Virgin of Guadalupe. The cooking facilities were feculent, as was the toilet. The grimly ugly *hardness* of the site was consonant with some atrocity. And yet who am I to say? I had only Yolanda's word that something evil happened here. Had I come a week ago, I might have seen children playing, or shared a jovial meal with the campesinos, in which case I would have doubtless thought: Here there's life.

Next door to this place stood the house of the newlyweds Elvira Alemán and Marco González. In my view-camera photograph, she stands with her lovely hands resting on him, one cupping his neck, the other on his breast, and she presses herself against him as he sits for me by the metal door, the doorknob level with her hand. They are young and beautiful together; in their faces as they gaze at me is a consciousness of each other, patient and in my uninformed opinion extremely loving. He looks a trifle weary of this last afternoon before he must return to work; and in the young wife's delicate face there is something tenderly protective; although she stands behind him, she is his sentry. What does this portrait say about *maquiladoras*? Only that if life were terrible for them, they'd already look beaten down. Señor González worked in a *maquiladora* in Mexicali making lamps, earning lower wages than the Cucapah woman who'd told the tale of the bloody tampons. His bus ride to work lasted sometimes three hours each way, sometimes four. Yolanda, who was anticapitalist and therefore rather anti-American, thought him very stupid to be exploited in this way, but he seemed quite happy with his situation. The more determinedly he asserted his happiness against her pointed remarks, the more annoyed she became. But in truth he did seem better off than those campesinos must have been in the barracks next door; he had space, a house with windows, a nice wide view of Mexicali sunlight. (What did he think about that barracks? He'd never paid any attention, he said; he knew nothing about the lives of the people who'd lived there.)

Southwest of there and a year later, in the immense Valle de Pedregal development, dirt-colored houses in the dirt formed subdevelopments: Cases Exe, Cuesa Muestra* and God knows what else in the good old Pedregal Esmerelda, which might itself have been a sub- or superdevelopment; the storekeeper I asked neither

*Names spelled for me by residents.

knew nor cared. Almost everybody worked in *maquiladoras.* This cubescape went on as far as I could see, and it brought to life something that the dapper reporter in Tijuana had said: You have many *maquiladora* industries that have a lot of vacancies. They *want* people! Tijuana grows by about a hundred thousand people per year.* It's been that way for at least five years. The *maquiladoras* are good for many people because it's sure work. They come here having nothing at all and the first job they have is a *maquiladora* job. When they enter a *maquiladora,* they have all the social securities that Mexican law permits. First the man comes from a southern state. When he finds a job, he brings with him his family, and the population grows—with one salary. They come to a little wooden house, and they have to rent, without water, without light.

Pedregal was better than those *colonias* in the hills of Tijuana. Here people frequently owned their houses, which were more often than not made of respectable cinderblock; here I saw evidence of electricity, and some of the windows even framed little air conditioners.

Here came a young couple, obviously in a hurry to get to bed for their Sunday afternoon tumble, but they were nice enough to give me a moment; the man, who was older, stood on the wide dirt street with his arm around the shoulders of his dark pretty girl, who made remote controls in the Korema *maquiladora;* I never found any such place but anyhow that was how she spelled it. Her task was to *pack the finished things,* she said. It had been two months now since she'd started there; she wanted to stay.

Would it be good work for all your life?

Yes.

Why do some people work in *maquiladoras* and some become campesinos? Which do you prefer?

She gave me the classic Mexicali answer: The *maquiladora* is more tranquil.

Tranquillity was what they prized in Mexicali. Year after year, that was the word of praise and aspiration I most often heard there. (I rarely heard it in Tijuana.)

And on another dirt street in Pedregal, a man who was lacking teeth conveyed an impression of immense happiness; his own cinderblock house-cube cost a hundred and fifty thousand pesos, which he was now paying off in trifling installments; he worked the night shift in a *maquiladora;* during the day he worked on his house.

His job consisted of placing computer cabinets into a paint-sprayer machine—black paint, obviously, for the man was black around his fingernails, black in his

*He thought that Mexicali was growing by about forty thousand a year.

nose; sometimes he even coughed black, he said. He had worked at the *maquiladora* two months and thought it a very good job; he had no fear that he would ever get sick.

"BECAUSE SONY OWNED EVERYTHING"

For all I knew he really *did* have a good job. If I could only see that he did, I'd gladly give his *maquiladora* a testimonial. If I could only get authorization!

Well, if the *maquiladoras* had had their way, I would never have seen the inside of a single one. Oh, yes; I tried Kimberly-Clark of Mexico, Maquiladora Waste Recovery de Tijuana-Tecate (eternally busy recovering waste, evidently), Kraft Foods of Mexico (no answer), Puntomex Internacional-Maquiladora, whose first and third listed numbers were wrong and whose second number never answered, Ace Industries, which also never answered, Amcor de Mexico, always busy, Automobile Softgoods Manufacturing, an unusual case because someone actually replied; this gentleman, whose name was Rodolfo Gonzales, explained that any visit would be out of the question without press accreditation, so we offered to show him ours the instant we met him, but that wasn't good enough; we had to fax it, which we did, but the number was wrong, so we telephoned him again from the stationery store because he was about to go home for the weekend; he instructed us to fax it to San Diego, which might easily have delayed the resolution by a week; finally he relented and we faxed it to a very special number which I will gladly reveal to you: 622-4290; but now, when the afore-mentioned Rodolfo Gonzales, representative of Automobile Softgoods Manufacturing, discovered that the sponsor of this adventure was *Playboy* magazine, he announced that any meeting, visit or rendezvous with us (no matter that Terrie was an excellent Mormon girl) could hold no conceivable interest for Automobile Softgoods Manufacturing. Fortunately, there was still Foam Fabrication Mexico to call, even though they didn't answer, neither at 627-2376 nor even at 627-2188; as for Fashion Clothing, its functionary referred us to the pleasure of Señor William Chow, who coincidentally proved unavailable.

If I were a racist, I'd shout: Those lazy Mexicans! If I were a bureaucrat, I'd conclude: I need to upgrade my contact information. If I were a leftist troublemaker, I'd say: It's a conspiracy!—Well, who am I? Why do I tend to conflate these blind alleys and refusals with the sharpnosed peering of security guards? If there was a signature experience in this regard, it occurred on the day that Terrie's car, whose underside was at that time nearly virginal with respect to the depredations exacted upon it by Tijuana's so-called speed bumps, was creeping through and adding to traffic on that hot and polluted day; we sought a certain Parque Industrial where Metales y Derivados was supposed to be; and some moments after passing an archway'd wall in the dirt, with dirt inside it, we turned up into Colonia El Lago, continuing upward in the direction of Matamoros, and then at the summit, like fortresses lording it over that smog-greyed valley of grey walls, American fast food restaurants, and here and there, unseen from our eyrie but well remembered, a private security agency upstairs from a stationery store or a restaurant, not to mention the highly visible long wide ugly roofs of manufacturing plants, the heat and dust, the white shinings of walls and dull grey shimmerings of roofs—oh, down there it was grey more than white—stood the *white, white maquiladoras*! Sony in particular was radiantly what it was, in opposition to all that grubby indistinctness below. I remember that my late President Reagan used to speak fondly of America as *a city on a hill;* this must have been exactly what it looked like. How landscaped and grand it was! Never mind the family clinic; there was green grass! I swear to you that I was thinking of the happy, pretty girl who worked at Korema, not of the man with the black cough, when two young women wearing company badges emerged from the company gate and set foot on that beautifully paved street. I murmured to dear Terrie, who, as usual, put them instantly at ease; and with smiles they agreed to be photographed; but just as I raised the camera to my eye, a security guard rushed out to proclaim that taking photographs was prohibited *everywhere,* even across the street in that littered vacant lot, because in his words, *Sony owned everything*. Exasperated, I apologized to the two ladies, who proceeded pensively on their way, but Cerberus wasn't finished with me; he demanded my identification, which I strangely refused to give him. In retrospect, I suppose he was only being kind; he didn't want to expose me to any uneasy doubts about the truth of that verity *here there's life*.

After all, can millions of ecstatic *maquiladora* laborers be wrong? Down in Ejido Chilpancingo, the place which Mr. D.'s report had described as *now a fetid, polluted barrio* thanks to contamination from Metales y Derivados, I interviewed the twenty-four-year-old* Benjamín Prieto, who wore a baseball cap and sat on a park bench. Fifteen years ago, his family had moved here from Mexico City. He had worked in the Hyundai and Honda plants; now he was beginning his second year at Sony and earning a thousand pesos a week.

Which factory is the best?

Sony, because you learn more about electronics. I want to study and get a degree in electromechanical engineering.

Señor Prieto was happily unacquainted with Metales y Derivados; likewise everyone else I interviewed in Chilpancingo. (Summation of the NAFTA report, 11 February 2004: *The level of lead contaminants found on the site is 551 times greater than*

*José López, who was then thirty-eight, said: "I've heard that in the *maquiladoras* they don't like you older than thirty or thirty-five."

that recommended by the EPA . . . for the restoration of contaminated residences. At [a] one mile distance from the plant, the level of lead contamination could still be more than 55 times higher than the highest level based on EPA norms. The Metales y Derivados site is located just 600 meters from Colonia Chilpancingo, home to more than 10,000 residents.)

Did you ever hear any stories about people getting contaminated?

No.

And if someone told you such a story, would you believe it?

No, he said firmly.

Thanking this true believer, I moved on, and sometimes on my travels I even met other exponents of *here there is life.*

THE HOLE

About Metales y Derivados (which on the phone Mr. D. referred to as one of *those old polluting assholes*) I will tell you that it was not quite as easy to find as the aforesaid Mr. D. promised. Fortunately, Terrie and I had all the time and money in the world. Now, where might it be? Well, where might one expect to locate the most distinguished *maquiladoras*?—My hypothesis: in a place where the air tastes metallic on the tongue and the eyes sting a trifle!—Up in the Nuevo Tijuana Industrial Park, which actually didn't appear so new anymore (sparks, heaps of metal, a stink, pallets next to peeling-painted sheds), red buses waited outside a *maquiladora*. A man advised me to go to the delegation where *maquiladoras* are registered. But official channels are rarely one's best connections to bad news, which may sometimes be a synonym for truth. So let's take a spin up and down that central strip of factories along Bellas Artes. Let's ask at Frialsa Frigofor; oh, and here's a satellite Bizco* plant, this one flying the American flag. (Mr. D.'s report: *Babbitcor Bizco Cashcare. In front of Óptica Sola on Insurgentes. Another company with a bad reputation.*)

And then, right on the mesa's edge, the ruin of Metales and Derivados unmistakably stood; and as we got closer there was a salty rancid smell. A sign on the fence warned of danger, but a convenient hole invited us to enter, and in we went. Our eyes began to sting. Mr. D. had said he felt sick the day he strolled about this monument to human selfishness, which in its own way was as eerie as an Indian cliff-dwelling, or even more so, being poisonous, not that I'd ever credit any stories about anyone's getting contaminated. The sharp flapping of black tarps in the wind was the only sound. In other words, here there's life.

*Lacking the financial resources to investigate it, I have changed the company's name.

Rotting metal, said Terrie, who'd not done well in high school chemistry. What rots metal?

We gazed at those corroded drums under the tarps, and after a long time Terrie said: My mouth tastes as if I've been sucking on a penny.

I'm sorry you haven't reproduced, I told her. And I'm glad that I already have.

Under the heaving tarps, squarish skeletons of lead were nightmarish, but nightmares can't hurt you. This comprised, in fact, the corpus delicti: six thousand metric tons of illegally abandoned lead slag. I can't comprehend that; call it a nightmare.

In June 1989, I have read, the place held two lead-smelting furnaces, two crucibles for lead refining and two copper smelting furnaces. In 1993, the final year of operation, three rotary lead-smelting furnaces had existed, but only one remained in use. The cannons I saw must be those furnaces. We need have no fear that our lands will not get better and better as the years go by. I admired the view of the great canyon below, which crawled with houses and shanties. Sunflowers grew near the mountains of old batteries.

Inside the great shed, which felt like the focal point just as the restored gas chamber feels like the focal point of Auschwitz (and isn't this simile overwrought, even unfair? But I have visited Auschwitz, and I remember the *heavy darkness* of the gas chamber, much heavier than here, to be sure; but that memory visited me unbidden as I stood there feeling sickish in several ways, wondering how many children down there in Chilpancingo were enjoying the benefits of lead poisoning; Metales y Derivados felt like a wicked, dangerous place, I can tell you; by comparison, those barracks for the campesinos in Ejido Tabasco began to seem attractive), several huge rusty drumlike apparati were trained like cannons at the barrio below. What were they, those red-crusted hulks? They had wheel-gears on them. I stared at them with my burning eyes; I smelled the sour-metal smell. And those square pits in the concrete floor, those pipes going down, down into the reddish earth, what did they signify?

Across the street, well within smelling-range of that rotten-metal smell, two men sat eating their lunch. I asked if I could photograph them, and they said that I could, but they'd get in trouble if they failed to don their protective gear first; so they laid down their sandwiches, dressed up like astronauts, and stood behind the sign which said **PELIGROSO**, meaning **DANGEROUS**. Meanwhile, a black rat silently rushed past another drum. They were supposed to be cleaning up this place for the company Rimsa, on contract with the Mexican government; and later I met their foreman, who identified himself only as Jaime, and who said: The first thing our government did was try to work with the owners. But it was going to cost so much that the owners left for the U.S.

Metales y Derivados

How will Rimsa clean it up?

We're bringing big dump trucks. They'll take it to the U.S.

How do you feel about this place?

For me it's a criminal act. Mexico opened its door to American people, and the only interest is to make money.

"THEY'VE ALL BEEN PRETTY GOOD"

How many times have I heard this same indictment? The year before we bombed Kosovo, an old Serbian woman shouted at me: You Americans have no souls! You're only about money. But in heaven we'll all be equal.—And now the same accusation rose up against us from smog and grimy white sprawl on grubby grey-green Mexican hills.

The sickness of capitalism, the American sickness, is what gets transmitted at what Marx labels *the cash nexus*. My own theory, which is not particularly Marxian, is that each place possesses its own sickness. Mexicans and Serbs are no healthier than we. If it's the cold American mercantile sickness which seeds the Mexican borderland with such *maquiladoras* as Metales y Derivados, what's the Mexican sickness which allows them to flourish? I'd say it's this: In Mexico, people cut corners and do what's easiest even when it's not what's best. That man in Pedregal ignored the admonition of his own black cough; and I also remember a *maquiladora* worker named Marí (short for María), whom I met in Pancho's bar in Mexicali: Thirty-eight years old, born in Mexicali, the mother of two boys and a girl, she had come to Pancho's with her friend "just to have fun," she said, a little embarrassed. Marí had worked in *maquiladoras* for many years. She was now at the *maquiladora* "Cardinal," which made transparent plastic masks for hospitals. She didn't know who owned it; Mexicans, she thought.*—For me, it's not a good job, she said. I've been working here six years, for eighty-three pesos a day, eight hours a day. I make the masks that go in your nose . . .

How do you make them?

With my hands.

When I asked her how many she made in a day, I saw how the girl sat thinking, struggling with what would have been for anyone with a Northside education an elementary calculation: I don't know how long it takes me to make one. It's really fast. I don't know exactly how many I make in a day, but it's a lot. I make twenty boxes and each box has fifty masks.

She got a half-hour for lunch, and didn't mind that.—It's a really clean factory, she said suddenly. The managers are nice with me. Probably the best thing is that it's air-conditioned and it's very clean . . .

The workers had a kitchen to cook in, and Cardinal also sold food, "everything," very cheaply, just a few pesos.

Marí lived in the *colonia* Seventh of January, which was very far—an hour each way by bus, which cost four pesos fifty. Fortunately, Cardinal provided a free red shuttlebus which took her forty-five minutes, and when I asked her why she had stayed all these years, she said: Maybe because they provide transportation, because my shift ends at eleven-thirty at night, so I can't be wandering around.

It was mainly women who worked at Cardinal—about five hundred people total, she guessed.

*I can find no establishment with this spelling in the Mexicali yellow pages.

Do they ever give pregnancy tests?

There is a pregnancy test only when you begin to work there. But the men get tested for drugs every six months.

Most of the *maquiladoras* where she worked required pregnancy tests at the beginning. Marí had never worked at any facility which required a monthly test.

Do you feel that the pregnancy tests are invasive?

Sometimes the ones who are pregnant can't work, she said in a flat tone. It happened to my friend.

How often has a boss asked you to sleep with him and you feel that your job may be at stake?

It's never happened to me. But there are some people who experience it.

(Terrie believed that something had in fact happened to her which she was too embarrassed or upset to tell; she could see it in her face, Terrie later said.)

Which *maquiladora* job was the best?

They've all been pretty good.

So are the *maquiladoras* good or bad?

I don't have any studies, so they're good for me.

Why not be a campesina?

Because here in Mexicali there's not that opportunity. One must live in the *ejidos.*

Would you prefer to live in an *ejido* and be a campesina?

I used to live in an *ejido* and I worked as a *campo* with my parents, she replied, which I thought was not much of an answer.

So that was Marí, and you've met the man with the black cough, and finally there were those two men who surely understood that Metales y Derivados was an extremely dangerous place, since they had been hired to decontaminate it, yet who sat in the lead-tainted dirt eating lunches seasoned with lead. In short, *here there is life.*

That legal assessor for a federation of labor unions whom I have quoted before (his name was Sergio Rivera Gómez) insisted: The *maquiladoras* are *good* for the population of Baja California, because there is a lot of unemployment in the five Mexico municipalities. And the work that is offered, especially to homeless people, offers benefits.

If there were campesino work for all at the same wage, would people prefer that?

Some would be interested, but the majority would not want to work in the *campo,* thanks to the extreme climate in Mexicali and other regions of Baja California, which makes the work very difficult. In the *maquiladoras,* they have air-conditioning and a lot of advantages.

"WHAT MAKES THE PRODUCT COMFORTABLE"

Above the smog, in the stinging air of the steep hills overlooking Insurgentes Boulevard, in a *colonia* called Villa Cruz, lived a very young-looking young man named Lázaro, small and slender, smoothskinned with a slight moustache. His wet hair was combed back as he stood outside the partly whitewashed, partly greywashed shack where he lived with four others, two of whom worked in *maquiladoras*. In the dirt, an older man, his visiting Pentecostal uncle, stood writing something in the family Bible, using an old refrigerator for a table. We could all see down into the Tijuana Valley, down into its smog and grime; we might as well have been peering down into the poison-clouds of Jupiter. I could make out Óptica Sola below us, wide and white. That was where Lázaro worked nine hours a day, with the usual half-hour break, four-thirty in the afternoon until one in the morning, Monday through Friday, earning eight hundred pesos a week after taxes. (Southside *versus* Northside: They make in a week what we make in a day.*)

He was twenty-two and had already worked at Óptica Sola for four years.

I asked him why he chose that particular place of labor, and he replied: That was my only option.

There are several *maquiladoras* at Los Pinos, I said.

My girlfriend also works here. I met her during her break. She has worked at Óptica Sola for three years.

How much longer do you expect to stay?

Not very long, since the chemicals burn your skin.

I myself could see no traces of skin burns, but Lázaro was dark. At any rate, I asked him: Do you have marks?

Not very often. What happens is that your hands start to burn. The skin gets irritated. You have to wash your hands in really hot water to get the chemicals off. They give you a cream that is very cold, so your hands feel worse.

Do the chemicals cause health problems for any ladies with babies?

When you take the lenses out of the molds, sometimes they stick, and then the chemicals get on the women's clothing. When they go home to hug their kids, the chemicals get on the children's skin.

I found this slow-speaking, girlishly handsome, dark boy believable. He had no reason to say one thing or the other to me.

When you're intoxicated the skin gets red, he continued. It especially affects lightskinned people. It's like a rash. If there's no further contact with the chemicals, it lasts about five days.

*I telephoned the AFL-CIO in hopes of verifying this, but they never returned my phone calls.

Does it happen often?

Just one week ago, a guy who had worked there only three days broke out with a rash, so his boss moved him to another area. When his skin cleared up, his boss moved him back. So he quit. You can't complain since you have your thirty-day contract.

But you're all right?

Fortunately, I'm not so affected. Nor is my girlfriend. She is lightskinned but only in contact with the chemicals ten percent of the time. She opens the molds.

Any union at the plant?

No.

What exactly do you do at Óptica Sola?

I fill the molds with chemicals, I can't tell you which.*

How does it go?

First you fill the mold; then you put it in the oven. It's a big tray. You fill the little trays and put them on the big tray which holds forty-four molds. It takes about

* What might they be? A certain court document entitled "Óptica Sola Labor Demand" records the following complaint: *Regularly, without adequate protection (rubber gloves, safety glasses, protective clothing, eyewash stations, showers, masks, etc), work processes require the use of NOURYSET 200, which causes severe eye, skin and nose irritation; NON-TINTABLE RESIN PG2, which causes eye irritation and can cause blood disorders; RESIN HB 101, which causes eye irritation; HI-GARD RESIN 1080, which causes eye irritation and redness, the skin absorbs it completely and it causes headache, dizziness and other signs of narcosis, its ingestion can cause death; HYDROXIDE OF SODIUM* [sic] *(KOH), which is corrosive to all body tissues it comes into contact with, causing perforations, it can damage respiratory alveoli and pulmonary tissue, it can cause severe burns on the skin and eyes, it can even cause blindness, and chronic exposure provokes dermatitis; ACETONE, which is carcinogenic, can cause headache, dizziness, nausea and loss of consciousness, irritation of the nose and bronchi, severe eye irritation, pain, tearing and inflammation; TINTABLE RESIN, which causes headaches, nausea, weakness, eye and skin irritation, can damage bone marrow, blood, kidneys, liver and testicles; MONÓMERO CR-39, which can cause irritation, burning and pain in the eyes, irritation, cracking and burning in the skin, and if ingested, death; METHANOL, whose fumes can cause dizziness, fatigue, headaches, eye and skin irritation, chronic exposure can cause poisoning, brain disorders, and blindness; ZONIL FLOUROSURFACTANT* [sic], *which can damage the liver, cause dizziness and loss of consciousness, nausea, headaches, severe eye and skin irritation; ZELEC UN LUBRICANT, which can cause dizziness and headaches, skin burns and conjunctivitis; CELLOSOLVE, which can cause cause headaches, nausea, weakness, tearing and eye irritation, chronic exposure can harm the bone marrow, blood, kidneys, liver and testicles; GLACIAL ACETIC ACID, which can damage lungs, irritate the skin and cause dermatitis; EKTASOLVE EP SOLVENT, which can cause blood disorders and eye irritation. Also, we work in poorly ventilated space.* The company responds: *It is denied that the workers have worked without adequate protection. In fact, the company permanently trains workers in the use of work equipment and the handling of dangerous substances, it also provides adequate protective gear; independently, it is denied that the workers have participated in work processes that could have caused any of their symptoms or other consequences they mention. They failed to mention when, in what area, and in what manner they had contact with such substances, or how their health was affected or any work accident caused by the handling of them.* Following this attempt at rebuttal, the court document presents "Safety Data Sheets for Chemicals Used at Óptica Sola." These list all the chemicals mentioned above and the same health risks as mentioned above, plus a few more in some cases. They are signed by Jésus Chávez, Environmental Engineer of Óptica Sola. Since the court documents are dated 1989 through 1996, the *maquiladora*'s facilities and procedures may for all I know be much safer nowadays. However, it does seem likely that the processes of plastic lens manufacture still require at least some of the same chemicals.

one minute. I fill six thousand pieces a day. The chemicals come in a big vat from the lab. I direct the pressurized tube into the molds. There are different lines. Each line is thirty-five people and a manager. There are eight lines.

Sergio Rivera Gómez had said: *In the maquiladoras, they have air-conditioning and lot of advantages.* So I asked Lázaro: Inside, is it air-conditioned, clean, bright?

It's all based on what makes the product comfortable, not on the worker, said Lázaro in his calm slow way. A lot of times when it's hot outside they'll turn on the air conditioners so that you're shivering.

Who owns Óptica Sola?

I think Brazilians.

Are the managers nice with you?

Well, no, they're not actually that nice, since the one thing that concerns them is the quality of the product, not the employee. For example, if you're ten minutes late, they can fill out a report against you. After three reports, you get suspended three days to a week, or they just fire you. I was suspended once for three days because they changed the way I was supposed to fill the molds, but they didn't tell my coworker or me, so I filled three thousand molds wrong.

You don't get trained, he went on. When you show up for your shift, you watch and learn from your coworkers. When you start, you have two days to learn. You get suspended if you don't learn.

I take it that many women work there?

The workforce is mostly female, and most of these women have children.

So the management doesn't mind if the ladies get pregnant and have babies?

No. They get maternity leave.

As I said, I found him calmly credible, and this last remark made him all the more so. He was capable of praising the company as well as blaming it.

Yes, he was still calm then, but he got anxious when I asked whether I could meet any of these chemically affected people he'd mentioned, whose disfigurements I never saw with my own eyes; whatever harm, if any, this factory may be doing its workers is certainly not blatant; for on more than one hot afternoon at shift-change time, Terrie and I approached the vast white facade of Óptica Sola on smoggy Insurgentes, with the steep dirt-hill where Lázaro lived behind us; here came that long white wall with gates and fence-bars set in it, for all the world like the border itself—why not? Isn't it another world? In my button camera video, a nasty guard—I mean an effective guard—neutralizes my attempt to sneak through the gate to the plant itself, which is set far, far back, like an American embassy within its vast perimeter. Farther down the vast wall, other guards lounge in their pillboxes; behind them the parking lot's cars now bustle and twinkle with end-of-shift activity. Workers of all shapes and sizes, mainly women, most often but by no means always young, dark and light, fat and thin, just like Señor A.'s operatives; in the video they look happy but tired; they flip their wrists and smooth their hair. It was at this point that Terrie hunted down for me a lady with interesting blotches on her face and arms, but she turned out to be suffering from postpartum allergic rash. Three women let us photograph them and promised to drink tequila with us, but on the appointed day they must have slipped out another exit gate; I don't think it was because Terrie and I smelled.

Lázaro was going to bring us to one of his chemically injured friends if we gave him time. When we went back to Colonia Villa Cruz, we had to search a good half-hour among other concrete shanties which were variously dust-grey in the ocher hills (we Aztecs prefer to live on hills, not on the ocean, a Tijuana private detective once said); and when we finally found Lázaro's house, he himself was absent and his uncle avoided every question. (Journalistic emendation: The place was very silent; all the same, perhaps Lázaro was inside.—These guys do not go out of the house, the dapper reporter with *La Frontera* had insisted. The ticket for one person for a movie is more than one day of minimum wage! If you want to go with your wife or your children, it's too much.—On the other hand, very likely Lázaro was with his girlfriend.) The uncle wouldn't say when he was back; he didn't know anything; he wouldn't know anything. We left him standing at the doorway, through which I could see a greasy concrete floor with a mattress on it.

"THEY ROB THE PEOPLE OF THEIR BENEFITS"

On Juárez Street in Mexicali, not very far from the Nuevo Pacífico Hotel but closer still to Daniel Ávila's store, there stands a jukebox bar called Pancho's. Here I'd met Marí, the assembler of medical masks; for Pancho's is where women from the *maquiladoras* go on Friday nights in hopes of picking up a dose of happiness.—It's like clockwork, said José López from Jalisco, who introduced me to the place.—Only the faces change. And you know, Bill, there aren't enough men to go around, so some girls always get left out, no matter how quick they hurry here straight from work without even changing out of their sweaty uniforms.

So you try your luck?

Well, I do know the place. The waitress she kind of knows me.

We pushed open the swinging doors and it was very loud with lumbering couples, the feeling somewhat rough but not unfriendly; and beneath the emerald and salmon lights I presently spied the gleam of a particular bottle, the shining of a certain straw which led like the handle of the Big Dipper up through the darkness into a woman's mouth; she was a woman whom the waitress said would talk for money, and she never did give me her name, although I was permitted to photograph her in the end.

She's afraid, José translated. Everybody's afraid.

She was haggard, chunky, blonde and anxious; but she might have been anxious merely to be chosen for a dance. The squat, distorted shapes of cowboys reminded me of dancing bears; prostitutes and *maquiladora* girls swayed heavily in their gleeful clutches.

I've been working here for a year and a half, she said. You can't complain or raise hell or they'll fire you.

How many *maquiladoras* have you worked in?

Oh! It's been a long time. I started when I was eighteen years old. One of 'em, they closed down without paying me after I worked for three years. The company property, the coolers, fans and the rest, we divided them and sold them.

So they didn't pay your wages when they closed?

The wages were paid, but bonuses and vacation pay were not.

Are the *maquiladoras* good or bad?

They're all right. They're the way we survive.

Is it true that they're disappearing?

Yes. A lot of them close down and don't give the people what they deserve.

She gulped her drink, then said in a louder, angrier voice: They just come to a border city, take so much money, rob the people of their benefits, and set up shop in another border city . . .

Who's more unfair to the *maquiladora* workers, Mexicans or foreigners?

The Mexican bosses! When they ask me to stay and work overtime, I do. But when I need anything from them, for instance if there's someone sick in my family and I have to go home, they get mad.

She had reported to her *maquiladora* for two years now at ninety pesos a day, five days a week, six hundred pesos a week (which doesn't add up, but Marí's attempt to multiply twenty times fifty reminds us that many *maquiladora* workers can scarcely read, much less calculate), six-thirty in the morning to three in the afternoon, with one half-hour break, "making parts for a new car."

Four girls sat at a table, giggling over drinks. A battleship-shaped old girl, rejected by one cowboy, stood by the bathroom wiggling her fat buttocks and snuggling up against her next prospect. It did not seem to be such a bad life. How was I to judge? What ought to be acceptable? What minimum standard can we hold a system to? How relative is everything? In Tijuana's Colonia Merida, whose smallish concrete houses, wrought-iron fences and whitewashed brick walls are all seasoned with graffiti and dust, I once went searching for *maquiladora* workers, but failed because, in the politely pointed words of a store proprietor, *this is a profes-*

sional place. By American standards, Colonia Merida did not seem so grand, and my failure to distinguish the grandness offended that storekeeper's class smugness. As for these tired-looking women at Pancho's bar, who brightened up when they were asked to dance, that crude dance floor, those couples loud and happy, wasn't this good enough? In underfed Kinshasa and besieged Sarajevo I had *known;* I had felt the wrongness of existence in those places, where most people I met were sad, angry or fearful. But at Pancho's bar nobody seemed sad; and the sad story which the *maquiladora* blonde was telling me seemed less than real, both to her and to me; I wanted to stay open-minded; I wouldn't condemn the *maquiladoras* without evidence; didn't everybody grouse about work? In one of his discussions of alienated labor, Marx reminds us that how the worker *feels* in the process of creating the product is immaterial to the value of that product; *to go to the slaughter is always the same sacrifice for the ox; this is no reason for beef to have a constant value.* Therefore, why not create productive conditions of *real freedom, whose activity is precisely labor?*

I am skeptical that any such "freedom" can exist when labor is compulsory, but obviously the more the labor experience approaches the sacrificial experience of the ox, the worse.

Standing up all day, the woman remarked, I get blisters on my feet. When you sit down they get on your case . . . Some people faint because their air-conditioning isn't enough.

She had never been compelled to take part in any bloody-tampon parade, but *they check you,* not every month but upon hiring. New workers had to provide urine specimens.—They don't wanna have anyone pregnant, she said.*

I asked whether she thought that was fair, and she said: A pregnant woman wants to work. She wants to get money for her baby. She wants medical insurance. We women with a baby in our body, we have a right to work.

She added: If you miss work for going to the doctor, you get suspended for one or two days or they fire you.

Near the end she dully said: I fell going into work and the company doctor said it's nothing even though my feet are swollen.

THIRTEEN HUNDRED MORE

I sat subtracting numbers. *Playboy* was going to pay me sixteen grand plus four grand in expenses for my research into *maquiladoras,* always assuming that they

*Amelia Simpson of the Environmental Health Coalition in San Diego remarked to me: "Their excuse is always that they want to protect the unborn child. If they really cared about protecting fetuses, they'd have a clean shop floor."

published it. So there was twenty grand. After my agent took her fifteen percent of the sixteen grand, and I paid Mr. D. (whom I liked more and more) for his confidential private-eye report, and I paid Mr. W. for the button camera and its appurtenances, that got me down to nine thousand one hundred. Ten days of my loyal, underpaid driver-translator Terrie made it a round eight thousand. A hundred-dollar plane ticket for me, then hotel rooms for Terrie and me, gas and meals, well, I'd better figure on a hundred twenty a day, especially given hungry new friends and old, so there went two thousand and forty more; and José López from Jalisco would certainly need two hundred, and the button camera had already cost me two hundred more in various miracle devices, absolutely, so now I was down to five thousand five hundred and sixty. (Fortunately, I didn't yet know about the four hundred dollars in hardware and software upgrades which the button camera would necessitate, nor about the eight-hundred-dollar computer doctor's bill to which these upgrades gracefully led.) Meanwhile, getting inside the *maquiladoras,* not to mention Lázaro's house, was less easy than I'd expected. We did try and try, all the way from Insurgentes up to the concrete-cube-clad hills of Matamoros. I think what José López said to me in Pancho's bar in Mexicali was true: They really *were* afraid. Those two young women at Óptica Sola; the haggard blonde who was desperate for money but in the end didn't dare to shoot off a roll for me from a disposable camera; Lázaro, who likewise passed up good money, I really believe not out of indolence but fear; all the people in Tijuana who spoke to us through closed doors, which reminded Terrie of her Mormon mission in Spain . . . In Mexico I have been lied to about subterranean Chinese tunnels; I have been very occasionally cheated and misdirected over the years; but never in Imperial have I felt so walled off by silence as I did when researching the *maquiladoras.* Without the button camera it would have been almost hopeless; thank God I had Terrie to enlist both social grace and feminine charm on my side . . .

It was high time for another private detective. I had looked him up in the Tijuana yellow pages, and Terrie had called him, so I already knew how much he would cost. Once I paid him, I'd have forty-three twenty left—if *Playboy* published the story. If not, easy come, easy go. Probably there would be other expenses, not counting Mexican prostitutes, which it was my American duty to keep employed.

What did I really hope to accomplish?—You should stick to the descriptive stuff you're known for, advised my friend Chuck, first and greatest of all private eyes.—Let's face it, Bill. Investigative reporting is not really your strong suit. There are only two or three decent investigative journalists left. The problem is that to get to the bottom of any story takes months of work and tens of thousands of dollars in expenses. What magazine's going to fund that nowadays?

I told Chuck about the results of my various interviews, and he said kindly: To me that sounds more or less like the sort of material you could uncover about any company in this country, too.

Chuck was right, of course. Chuck was usually right. Every now and then I'd hire him to write me another report on another protagonist in the Imperial Valley, and in the mail another envelope would come with an invoice for a couple of hundred dollars and a report on the subject's properties and convictions, with Chuck's license number and private-eye star at the top. When I'd thank him, he'd always say: Oh, well, it's no more than any news bureau could have done, and then I'd sadly think: Then I must not be as good as a news bureau.

But this time I had Mr. D.'s report, which had led me to several factories "with bad reputations," not that that proved anything at all; I doubt that any manager at Óptica Sola will lose sleep over Mr. D.'s report, which was also noteworthy for its list of contacts all of whose phones were busy or disconnected. What's a bad reputation but bad gossip? And in further extenuation of Óptica Sola, not to mention a hosanna for the perfect Mexican system of *maquiladora* oversight, I insert another anecdote from Mr. Raskin's report: *A certain "Subsecretario de Protección al Ambiente" . . . took me into a small conference room with two younger female office workers. One produced a portable tape recorder, and proceeded to record* the esteemed Subsecretario *explaining to me what Mexican law would allow him to do with my request to view files related to our Maquiladoras. I twice hand copied the list for him. He told me that in order to view files, if such existed, it would be necessary to submit a "formal" written request stating who I was, what information I was looking for, and the reason for my interest in reviewing a file. He then clarified that Mexican law protected all parties, and that he would be required to contact the firms we inquired about, and inform them that we wanted to review the contents of a file . . . A company could contest our request and potentially block review of a file.*

. . . Very informally, the Subsecretario *said he could not "imagine" Óptica Sola caused any water pollution because all they did was "cut glass."*

I had enjoyed Mr. D.'s report, I truly had. But on the principle that the best way to get over an old love affair is to start a new one, I twiddled my thumbs earnestly on my bed in the Scala love hotel, worried about money, sipped from my tequila bottle, and finally knocked at Terrie's door, at which point I committed myself—not to Terrie, who was no worse a Mormon than ever, but to Señor A., whose real name (unless it was something else) was Señor R. and who was now awaiting us in his office over a shoe store in Centro.

This bored, rumpled-looking man was another of those individuals whose sensational stories lose much luster once the deposit has been paid; but the only way to ascertain that is to pay the deposit. Among other things, he assured me of the following: There's a lot of trafficking going on by boat near Ensenada, trafficking in Chinese. One Chinese is worth about ten thousand dollars. It's rumored that some of the Chinese are transported in metal containers. It's very dangerous. People who live on the coast of Ensenada will say: We see line upon line of Chinese on the beach. Needless to say, government officials never find anything.—So far Señor A. was probably telling the literal truth, but the next thing he said was: I know there is a *maquiladora* here that has connections with the sale of Chinese. Someone has already paid the ten thousand. They work it off. Four or five years ago, it took seven or eight years to work it off, maybe through prostitution. But most of them go to the U.S. What I think is that there are *maquiladoras* with a connection; they bring a Chinese over long enough to train Mexican workers; then he moves.

When I heard this, I thought to myself: Señor A. is my man! And I could already see myself lurking outside some *maquiladora*'s gates at midnight, while my button camera flawlessly recorded the unloading of another truckload of Chinese slaves. Well, well. Where would we be without our illusions? Mr. A.'s final report, printed in giant type to enhance its impressive effect, had no more than this to say about the Chinese angle: *We are informed that in the Tijuana Plaza there only exist Taiwanese plants, which are frequently confused with Chinese due to their similar physical characteristics,* blah, blah, blibbedy-dee; and after investigation, *thorough* investigation no doubt, Señor A. discovered that in Ensenada there were also no Chinese plants, only Taiwanese, this information being based in part on confidential reports from the Mexican government; gee whiz.*

I have fat, skinny, tall, short employees, he boasted; and I was in awe; I thought: Wait until Chuck hears how wisely I've chosen!

PERLA'S FIRST RECONNAISSANCE

Actually, Señor A. proved to be worth his weight in pesos, thanks to the pearl he extracted from his treasurehouse of fat, skinny, tall and short operatives, and she literally *was* a pearl, except when she signed a different name on my receipt.

Bubbly, chunky, her hair dyed orange-red, Perla was a woman of a certain age. She cheerfully sacrificed one of her buttons for the sake of that camera. Then we practiced in Señor A.'s office. I was making pretty good button-camera videos by then, so I felt hopeful again; oh, yes, I was certainly confident. And Perla was, as Mr. W. had advised that my operative be, well endowed. All the same, after various experiments we finally chose to place the digital video receiver and power pack against the small of her back. Terrie would lift up Perla's shirt and power her on and off, while I would do my part by averting my eyes and Señor A. would gaze

*Señor A. did locate a factory called Sam Chee in Industrial Park Pacífico. His final report also notes that the *maquiladora* called "Sanchin is owned by Chinese, not by Taiwanese but has no Chinese employees."

boredly into space from behind his desk, which displayed the following items: a huge owl, a Statue of Liberty, a golf ball, a plastic globe and a long lens. I remember that there was another office next to his sanctum; the door was always slightly ajar and on my various visits to Señor A. I would sometimes hear the faint creaking of a swivel chair. Who was this individual? Nobody ever mentioned him in Señor A.'s office, so I confined myself to making postmortem speculations about him with Terrie. How much did he know or see of the wiring-up of Perla? Perhaps I should have hired Señor A. to find out.

For what it is worth, Perla was the first Mexican I ever met who said outright: The *maquiladoras* are bad.

When she was ready, I told Perla that I would make her a *Playboy* centerfold, and she giggled and Señor A. assured me: I've had clients even more disgusting than you.

Now, where should we go first?

By then, Señor A. had shown us a movie which he'd filmed especially for us.

Here is a list of all the *maquiladoras* which use chemicals, he began, handing me a sheaf of photocopies.— We found several that are contaminated. In particular, we found a factory called Thomson.

Then he played his videotape. I think his feelings were hurt whenever Terrie yawned; but the sad truth is that industrial videos, even covert ones, are soporific, especially when shot from outside. It may well be that Terrie's lack of enthusiasm was interpreted by him as a professional challenge, because he kept up a determined flirtation with her by e-mail for weeks afterward. (Speaking as her chaperone, I am proud to tell you that Terrie continued to conduct herself as should a good daughter of the Church of Latter Day Saints.)

The videotape began. White storage tanks stood on a hill.

The wind carries all the contamination away, said Señor A.

Here came more tanks, more factories; Terrie emitted her first yawn.

Here is Baja Imperial.* In Baja Imperial they used to have two hours to eat and now it's been reduced to fifteen or twenty minutes. A person who used to work there I know told me that.

Up on a hill, more chemical tanks stood guard. The private detective said: They pour the chemicals down the hill, with the *colonia* below. The wind always blows the pollution away from the factory.

This is Medimexico.

* I have altered this company's name. The private investigators I hired during the editorial process were not able to discover much about it, except for the following: In 1992 the U.S. EPA initiated a federal civil action against it for illegal export of hazardous waste from California to Mexico. No information about the lunch hour was found.

Another white *maquiladora* stood on a hill. Tons of security, said Señor A. A lot of guards. Only trucks and workers get in. This one is Mexodyne Precision.* They have a lot of contamination.

I saw big tanks, white tanks, pale cylindrical tanks, a sign announcing that Mexodyne Precision sought workers.

How do you know they have contamination? I finally asked.

Because the smoke is very black, explained Señor A.

My opinion of poor Señor A. dropped by two more notches.

This is another burned factory, because it destroys all their problems. Then they also don't have to pay their workers. As you see, a lot of them don't have names, especially the most contaminated. Okay, this is Thomson. Thomson and Óptica Sola probably contribute about the same amount of contamination. The neighbors complain that at night and in the morning, a smoke comes out of the plant that makes the people feel sick. Thomson is gigantic. There are the chemical compounds, he said, pointing to the drums behind the fence. Thomson has bad luck because they're in a little bit of a valley, which means that the air doesn't blow away. All this is Thomson, although it doesn't say Thomson, just N-3, he said, showing how the fence went on and on. You don't see a name. They hide the chemical compounds underneath the floor, he opined. You only know it because of the tubes sticking out. That gravel is just a floor covering. There are gravel and little plants but you can see the holes. They must have very big tanks hidden below.

(Reader, what if Thomson lacked subterranean tanks? What if Thomson employed no chemical compounds whatsoever, or if Thomson's effluvium actually in fact enhanced our entire biosphere? Thomson never did return my phone calls, but like many other insane people I long to be considered "balanced." What if Señor A. were simply, if you'll excuse the expression in this context, blowing smoke? I possess no evidence whatsoever that Thomson might have been imperfect. *In my follow-up interview with Cota* (this is my hired detective Mr. Raskin speaking) *he stated that of our subject group Matsushita, Tompson* [*sic*] *and Óptica Sola had most of the labor complaints he handled.* But labor complaints need not have to do with underground tanks; and besides, I don't know anything about Thomson-related labor complaints, either. Please consider Señor A.'s remarks about Thomson to be the merest local color, devoid of anything but rumors, speculations and Terrie's yawns.)

* Since I was unable to gather much data on this company, I have altered its name. How much contamination, if any, it produces is anyone's guess. It does, however, receive half a dozen mentions in the report of a human rights organization, all related to mandatory pregnancy tests, mistreatment of pregnant women in order to make them quit. One woman claimed to have lost her fetus as a result of being denied permission to go to the hospital; when she went to the bathroom she was told that there was neither aspirin nor even toilet paper.

Now, this is a duct which stops at the street, he continued, showing a white snake running down a hillside into the green grass at the edge of the street. It's to throw out their trash. If they throw it away using their plumbing system they would have explosions, so they let it down on the street.—Okay, here's a very contaminated factory, It's in Cumbre. It's extremely contaminated.

How do you know?

Because employees start to cough as soon as they get close to it.

The video showed workers, and indeed I heard them coughing, coughing. But for all I know, Señor A. had paid them to cough. I have never been cheated out of a dollar in my life.

And what's the name of this *maquiladora*?

Formosa Prosonic México, in Industrial Park Cumbres.

What about Óptica Sola?

The Óptica Sola, we know the schedules of the workers and what chemicals they use inside.

What's your opinion as to how contaminated Óptica Sola is?

I think if you compare Óptica Sola to Formosa, Formosa would win.

Any chance of getting one of your people inside one of these possibly contaminated places and filming it?

They don't have the little camera that you have. Where are the dangerous materials, how many people working? They could do a write-up.

What if I sent someone in with the button camera?

Why not?

And you think you could get somebody inside Formosa?

Yes, especially in the production area. I think my employee can get in all things. She's very smart. It would be very early in the morning, so we have time. Formosa, Matsushita, Óptica Sola, and, if we have time, Thomson or even the battery plant. We can do at least five.

So you think that Formosa is the worst.

Señor A. nodded his weary head; and I remembered something which the dapper reporter had said. I don't know how many of them are breaking the law actually, he had told me. The Mexican law says you have to work forty-eight hours a week in six days and Sunday is sacred. The *maquiladoras* have a lot of side problems. The bigger ones won't dare to risk their investments. The little and medium ones are often doing that. The Chinese and Koreans are the worst.

It's also the circumstances of the ambience, Señor A. continued. Formosa is not on the top of a hill. Neighbors complain about Thomson also because it's in that little valley. The people who notice it the most are those who are not in good locations. By the way, the people that we asked about contamination, especially those who sell food outside the factories, to protect their clientele they would say everything's fine even though they're sick.

That was what he said about those *maquiladoras,* and it was all plausible although he never came close to proving that any of it was true, perhaps because he did not care or was not competent or perhaps because his standards of proof differed from mine, or, most likely, because thanks to the secrecy of the companies and poor record-keeping generally, it simply could not be proved. But let me press on nevertheless in this account of one more deficient attempt to apodictically comprehend the region which this book calls Imperial: I now had Mr. D.'s report and Señor A.'s advice and promises. The plan would be to investigate Formosa and Óptica Sola to see if they were poisoners; and we would investigate Matsushita regarding allegations of sexual exploitation.

I have an ex-employee of Matsushita, Señor A. had said. She can be here on Friday, and she can tell you how they have many modeling contests in Matsushita, frequently. And this is also the factory where they ask women to take the pregnancy test every month.

In the end, the alleged witness of Matsushita's modeling contests (now twenty-one years old, the detective told me; she had supposedly worked in this *maquiladora* from January through June of 2003) did not come, out of anxiety, Señor A. reported. Upon my request, he later forwarded his own transcript of an interview, bearing her full name (which she did not wish to be published) and, among other matter, the following:

Q *What happened between you and the management of Matsushita regarding sexual pressure? Tell us everything that you remember.*

A *Look, it's very embarrassing to talk about the time that I worked there . . . When I first started they assigned me to production. My boss was Díaz, the engineer, and about two weeks after I started working there—it was on a Friday—I was told to call the quality control manager, and he told me that I was going to lose my punctuality bonus because I was getting there late. I told him that my time card said the time that I arrived and that I was not getting there late. When I told him that, he looked at me and said that the time card didn't matter, but if I would agree to go out with him I would continue to receive my punctuality bonus, and I told him no and I left his office.*

Everything seemed fine for about two months until at the beginning of April when they didn't pay me my punctuality bonus. I went to see my production chief and he sent me to a man, a tall white man who was very well-dressed. I explained to him that I had not been paid my punctuality bonus and he said that if I agreed to have a few beers with him, the problem would be taken care of. I told him that I wouldn't put myself in that situation. I left his office and then I only lasted about three more weeks before I changed jobs.

Q *How did this affect you . . . ?*

A *. . . Now I last only a short time on jobs. At first I start out fine but when I hear people laughing, I think they are laughing at me, and then I start to dislike my job. That's why I only last three or four months at the jobs I have had.*

Q *Do you still work in factories?*

A *Not anymore . . . Since then I worked in a bakery and later in a supermarket, and now I don't have a job but I don't want to work in a factory.*

Q *Do you believe that they respect women at Matsushita?*

A *Of course not.*

The evidentiary value of this interview must be considered lower than that of the conversation with Lázaro about Óptica Sola; because I never met the subject, whose existence for all I know may be fabricated, although I don't believe that Señor A. would do this; he did a good mediocre job, entertaining me with occasional colorful exaggerations, to be sure; but I never found him being willfully dishonest.

The young woman's testimony reads credibly to me, although her reaction seems disproportionate. You will have noticed that the modeling contests remained unmentioned. I wish that I could have interviewed her myself, for it is possible that the situation in which she found herself was still more difficult and unpleasant than this brief account states. I especially would have liked to know whether or not she ever got her punctuality bonus.

At any rate, Perla, who was very outspoken and whom I came to admire for her courage and to trust not only for her perfect reliability, her patient caution, her openness about her life, her verifiable knowledge of reality, but most of all for her readiness to admit ignorance and error, assured me that ten or twelve years ago, the employees of Matsushita were *all eighteen- to twenty-five-year-olds in miniskirts.* She used to visit one acquaintance on the job, so she'd seen for herself. She also knew someone who was fired on her twenty-fifth birthday, maybe or maybe not for that reason.

Here in Tijuana, Señor A. had said, they have an event called Miss Maquiladora, and what it becomes is a prostitution ring for high-level executives. There will be a woman who works on the line who gets invited to be an assistant to the President. It normally happens in the springtime. Wives talk about it. Each *maquiladora* sends a woman. They go to a contest in Rosarita. High-level executives attend. It's a meat market. All of a sudden, you'll notice that this poor woman moves to a middle-class neighborhood, and the women who are actually trained to be assistants complain.*

*"There are Mr. Maquiladoras also," he continued. "I once worked for one female client who owned a *maquiladora;* it was a theft case. She had three private secretaries; they were all big muscles. They were too dumb to do anything but one thing."

So Matsushita participates?

Of course.

I am told, but have not verified, that in 1993 or 1994, the head of the federal Procuraduría de los Derechos Humanos investigated sexual harassment at Matsushita. The finding remains unknown to me. The labor activist who relayed this information, Jaime Cota, also *recalled taking complaints from female employees at Matsushita/Panasonic [note: He seemed* to *believe this was the same company] years ago. The women were solderers who fainted because of inhalation of lead . . .* He *categorized most labor disputes as related to "unfair termination, low wages," but occasionally for "environmental" reasons. In my follow-up interview with Cota* (this is my detective Mr. Raskin speaking) *he stated that of our subject group Matsushita, Tompson* [*sic*] *and Optica Sola had most of the labor complaints he handled.*

In addition, Señor Cota furnished Mr. Raskin with a copy of an out-of-court legal settlement between Matsushita and a former employee. From the look of this document, the grievance dates from 1995:

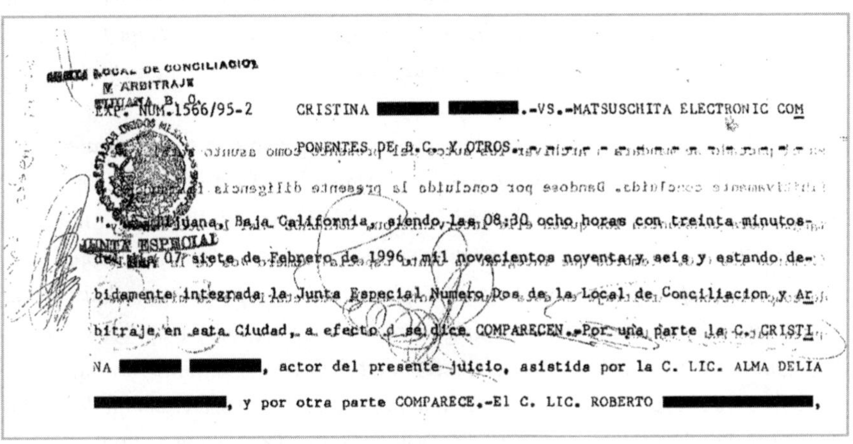

JUNTA LOCAL DE CONCILIACION
Y ARBITRAJE
TIJUANA, B. C.
EXP. NUM.1566/95-2 CRISTINA ████ ████.-VS.-MATSUSCHITA ELECTRONIC COM
PONENTES DE B.C. Y OTROS.

". Tijuana, Baja California, siendo las 08:30 ocho horas con treinta minutos-
JUNTA ESPECIAL
del dia 07 siete de Febrero de 1996, mil novecientos noventa y seis y estando de-
bidamente integrada la Junta Especial Numero Dos de la Local de Conciliacion y Ar
bitraje en esta Ciudad, a efecto d se dice COMPARECEN.-Por una parte la C. CRISTI
NA ████ ████, actor del presente juicio, asistida por la C. LIC. ALMA DELIA
████████, y por otra parte COMPARECE.-El C. LIC. ROBERTO ████████,

From the deposition of Francisco* ———:

3. *When Señora Cristina* ——— ——— *worked at the suede company, you were her supervisor.*
4. *Señora Cristina* ——— ——— *presented several complaints to the Human Resources Dept. of the company against you.*
5. *When Señora Cristina* ——— ——— *worked at the suede company, you knew that she had complained on several occasions that you bothered her by harassing her sexually.*

*Although this document is a semipublic record of sorts, it seemed most ethical to black out the names of the two parties, in order to avoid exposing either one to potential retaliation.

6. *The Dept. of Human Resources ignored her complaints against you.*
7. *On 6/30/95, at approximately 10:00, you forcibly kissed and embraced Señora Cristina ——— ——— when she was at her work station.*

From the settlement:

To the plaintiff, who has been duly confirmed in this judgement, the company agrees to pay 3,000 [handwritten above this: 11,000] *pesos, an amount that will be paid today at 11 am, before this Authority, an amount that covers salary, seniority, vacation time proportionally to the services provided by the plaintiff to the company.*

In this same year 1995, the organization Human Rights Watch investigated forty-three *maquiladoras*. I quote from its report: . . . *Along the U.S.-Mexico border, from Tijuana to Matamoros, we found, with few exceptions, that . . . employers require women applicants to submit to pregnancy exams, most commonly given through urine samples . . . Maquiladora staff also try to determine a woman's pregnancy status by asking intrusive questions about the woman applicant's menses schedule, whether she is sexually active, or what type of birth control she uses . . . Should she become pregnant shortly after starting to work, maquiladora managers sometimes attempt to reassign women to more physically difficult work or demand overtime work in an effort to force the pregnant woman to resign . . .*

Regarding pregnancy tests as compulsory for employment, *the implicated companies* include *Panasonic (Osaka, Japan-based Matsushita Electric Works)*. Dr. Adela Moreno, whom Matsushita employed in 1993, told Human Rights Watch: *It seemed that was all I did. I was appalled, but I did the pregnancy exams. At times I would be so angry . . . and so fed up with how they were exploiting those very young girls that I would tell* the supervisor *that girls were not pregnant when they were . . . An applicant labeled as pregnant was told by the personnel director that she was not qualified, or that all the positions were taken . . . For girls who managed to slip by . . . supervisors made life difficult for them when they realized the girls were pregnant. They would do things like put them on the night shift—which is completely illegal under Mexican labor law.*

In 1998, a *Los Angeles Times* article quoted Dr. Moreno, who claimed that *she watched a manager at Matsushita caress the buttocks of each woman he passed on a welding assembly line. A married mother of six was told to sleep with her boss or lose her job, Moreno said. When she complained, he accused her of stealing. The woman got severance pay only after Moreno made her the cause celebre of a radio campaign . . .*

As you see, even Dr. Moreno made no mention of any "Miss Maquiladora" modeling contest. And from the present millennium I could discover no allegations of any nature against Matsushita, excepting only the following item from the *San Diego Union*, datelined 2002: *In Tijuana, the top producers of highest-risk waste are mainly Asia-based companies, including South Korea's Samsung, Japan's Matsushita, and Taiwan's Merry Tech.*

By then I was sure that Matsushita was a very nice company, really a very sweet company. To prove it, Terrie wired up Perla one last time, and we set out for Matsushita, determined to ascertain the existence or nonexistence of a workforce in white tennis shoes and miniskirts, eighteen to twenty-five, not fat.

Following Perla's directions (over our two working days she seemed to know the whereabouts of every *maquiladora* on earth), we wound up the hill, then back down past Robinson and Robinson, into the valley of dirt and factory-cubes. The first time Perla went into Matsushita (while Terrie and I waited outside another white stucco wall with fenced inserts; she was rereading *A Moveable Feast* and I was worrying about what to do if Perla got in trouble), the dear old button camera didn't record a thing. We went to a fast-food restaurant and I bought giant sodas for the members of my spy team while they retired to the ladies' room to rewire Perla and make more practice videos; in the end they decided to have her carry the digital video receiver in her little purse, prestidigitating the wire into the wire of her cell phone; and this device raised our industrial espionage to an entirely new level. Back to Matsushita she went, returning almost immediately, cheerily swinging her arm, her hair blowing in the breeze, so the next morning early, when *maquiladoras* hired, we wired her up again and sped off to Matsushita, parking not quite in front, since we were discreet individuals, and then for one hour, eleven minutes and forty-six seconds, Terrie reread more of *A Moveable Feast* while I entertained myself with the spymaster's stress of wondering whether Perla's batteries would run out. For variety's sake I sometimes gazed at an installation of barred windows within a courtyard of cheerful green shrubs whose fortifications consisted of barred gate-segments in tracks which slid apart or together by electronic command; the climax came near the end of the hour, when a corrugated cardboard truck entered. This barred gate kept me from learning dreary secrets. Were they secrets only of sickness and death? Or were they secrets which might have made me illicitly rich, *** TRADE SECRETS *** I mean? Answering that was what button cameras were for.

Across the street from that long white regularly windowed factoryscape, a man stood beside a huge white truck which pumped its cargo into a well beneath the street beside the entrance to a *maquiladora* from which four tall and one slightly shorter white cylindrical tanks stood. Some time after I took his photograph, he yawningly knocked the truck with a mallet to see how much of the chemical remained, then put on a mask. It was almost hilarious. The man with the black cough, the two decontamination men who ate their sandwiches in the lead dust of

Metales y Derivados, and now him, what did they all really think? Did they not believe in the danger or did they try not to think because they could see no other choice or did they not care?

Now here came Perla with a big smile on her face; Matsushita had hired her; she'd make eight hundred and seventy pesos a week!

In the covert video we watch the wide street sway with a womanly stride and white storage tanks get closer and closer, then veer away; it is wonderful how briskly Perla walks! Her videos are blurrier than mine because a strand of white thread from her clothing got stuck on the lens beneath the false button and nobody noticed. The long white wall of the *maquiladora* on her left, cars on her right, all swaying back and forth, more gracefully in my male opinion than my own videos do; and presently white wall gives way to black-barred metal fence not unlike the border wall but lower and cleaner; and then after five minutes and seven seconds the security booth swims into sight. Perla obligingly gives a view through the fence from a number of angles; and then the bored belly and upraised hand of the security guard fills part of that magical rectangular world. Halfway through minute six, we see a silhouette running its hands across its head by the fence-bars; then the security guard picks up the phone. Perla paces, providing us with one view after another of the security guard; he gestures to us with kindly paternalism, flipping his head from side to side and moving his lips; he does not seem to be a bad man. What if the only reason my experiences with *maquiladora* guards had been so unpleasant was the simple fact of my own existence? And now, shortly before minute ten, Perla penetrates Matsushita, Kyushu Matsushita-Maquiladora, I mean, whose representative, Antonio Treviño, had previously informed Terrie in no encouraging tone that a visit could scarcely occur until we'd called Fred in San Diego; and a courtyard swims toward us, slightly off level, with a lovely blackish-green fan-shape of a tree to the right; and then that flicks away as we trudge down an arid concrete space with a wall on our left; one of this wall's numbered doors is open; and we abruptly flick inside, with long white incandescent tubes almost horizontal above us and human beings passing with great busyness. The righthand wall contains glossy dark rectangular windows which reflect the incandescent lights; and on the left there are open whitish rooms. Perla turns left. We see a row of what might be pool tables; slowing her step, Perla nears them; they are ordinary long tables with metal chairs along them. The button camera now pauses to afford us an interesting view of a pillar whose notice is almost entirely out of the frame; Perla's errors are frequently the opposite of mine; and here she has positioned her hidden eye too low. Whatever the notice says is blurred to illegibility. She steps back and it is now all there, but still illegible. No one is in the room. Brave Perla ventures into another empty room, and from the quick, choppy quality I can tell that she is not supposed to be here. Then she returns to the hall of windows, one of which she approaches until her silhouetted reflection is pierced by the horizontal spears of many reflected light-tubes. What lies within this window's world? At minute twelve, second fifty-five, we see the holy of holies: the production floor. Perla's silhouette looms over everything like the Virgin of Guadalupe. Far below her shoulders, human outlines move in and out of receding rows of mechanical bays, everything dwindling infinitely like the perspective in two opposed mirrors. A woman nears us and gazes at us, but we cannot see much about her except that she is a woman. Then suddenly a pointing brawny fist intercepts the frame; Perla is being sent about her business! Dutifully, the camera goes down the hall, into another room where no cameras are supposed to be, past a double row of clean metal lockers, then out to the main corridor again. Here's another window; once more the production line fills the world. More figures flash by us. Perla's silhouette raises its phony résumé folder in simulated bewilderment. The button camera swerves back into the room of many tables. We are now making significant inroads on minute fifteen. Perla's spectacles magnify themselves into hugeness as they arc past us; then another young woman, pretty and slender, passes us and offers us her back two tables down; it is time to fill out job applications. Fifteen seconds before the commencement of minute twenty-two, the other woman turns round, rises, and brings her application to Perla's table, evidently requesting help; her face is silhouetted but she is even more evidently well proportioned. Then a man and a woman, both young, each bearing folders, walk toward us and vanish. The woman's lovely brown hands flex upon the foregrounded table for awhile; then the woman who'd passed by with the man returns, and this time we can see that she is also pretty, if not as slender as the first one. So what? They are both merely applicants. Perla's yellow pencil wiggles in the foreground; the slender woman has gone back to her table and bows over the application like a dutiful schoolgirl. More people pass in and out. A plump woman whose badge flaps on her chest comes to fill up our world, extending a hand and a paper. This is the first inside employee whom we have clearly seen, and she does not in the least fit Señor A.'s indictment's profile. At 26:37, Perla offers us a view of her application, which I suppose might be capable of some kind of digital enhancement so that we could actually see what it says; ten minutes later it has been completed (the slender woman is still struggling), and the button camera rears up to lead us back down the hall of glossy black windows. At 36:47 two pretty, slender young women in blue smocks, therefore presumably employees, pass by; to me they do seem to fit the profile. Perla enters another room where more young women, and one man, are all sitting at tables and filling out papers. A busy rainbow doubtless conveys promotion or information on a great video screen. Are they all applicants? At a quarter past thirty-nine minutes,

Perla's application papers magically extend themselves forward at the desk of a pleasant, decidedly plump, middle-aged woman whose face looks friendly and nice. The mummery with pens and documents continues; then she is finished and says goodbye to the slender woman, who continues to pore over her application; at 52:16 three young women in blue smocks rush by us in the hall of windows; a frame-freeze reveals one to be distinctly fat; the middle girl, blurred although she is, would not seem to be conventionally pretty. More peeks through the tinted windows show more blurred figures; then at 53:27 two closed double doors sport red and yellow warning signs, but Perla wisely leaves those alone (an alarm might have sounded) and provides us an interior view of an immaculate, even rather plush, ladies' room; I feel pleased with Matsushita. The camera ascends stairs, passes down an empty corridor to more of the double doors with red and yellow warning signs; gives us a long view of a notice board, swivels furtively to reveal workers in an open doorway (we can't make out their shapes distinctly), swivels past a well-stacked girl in worker-blue, and then brings us back into one more window-framed view of the production line, which looks as clean and modern as any science-fiction spaceship. At 57:47 we see two of these workers more clearly than before; it remains difficult to say whether they are men or women, but from the way in which they stand lounging and chatting, they are probably men (whom we will see more identifiably at 1:35). In the background a pale-clad female figure is definitely not wearing any miniskirt. Then the camera swivels back down the hall, where another applicant approaches us with a folder in her hand; she is beautiful, but the problem is that all Mexican women are beautiful.

At 1:03:05, Perla scores her great coup, breezing her way directly into the production area. A big-breasted, darkfaced female figure approaches us beneath that row of white light-tubes; on our right, the mysterious production bays now resemble nothing so much as the banks of slot machines of Las Vegas. At 1:03:15 we glimpse a line of blue-clad female workers, who are, in the words of two women whom I later asked, *not obese but normal.* None wear miniskirts. A plump-bottomed woman walks away from us; then the camera pans to another line of women, who again seem *not obese but normal.* The closest of the women in 1:03:35 might be stocky; some are wearing miniskirts.

Perla shut down her wire and reported: It's totally changed, even the way they treat the people, the age, the pregnancy test. There are people who are there who are pretty big. They even have music playing in the halls. But also there are several different Matsushitas.

As for me, I was very happy. As far as we could tell from a one-hour video, Matsushita currently offered positions in conditions which were not degrading to women. And the button camera had finally proved itself.

"AND THEN SHE DIDN'T GET THAT OFFICE JOB"

Regarding sexual exploitation in general, I eventually concluded that pressure inflicted by management was probably even more pervasive in Mexico than in the U.S.

Referring to the production line itself, Señor A. had said, and I think he was correct: That's where the people are the most closed, and they won't talk about it. But there's definitely a lot of sexual pressure there. What you have to understand is that the sexual pressure an attractive woman feels comes from her co-workers.

I asked the haggard blonde at Pancho's bar in Mexicali: If a *maquiladora* manager asked you to sleep with him, what would you say?

Thrusting out her chin, she said: It hasn't happened to *me*.

Then she said: Every time they make a pass at me, I stop them cold.

What if the manager said, do it or else?

I would get another job.

But then she said: Once you've reached thirty-five or forty, it's hard to find another job in Mexicali. You've got to have a high school diploma.

What about the other girls in the *maquiladora*? What do they do in that situation?

Some of them do it out of necessity; otherwise they'll lose their jobs. If a girl goes out with the boss, it's just because that way she's going to get more money.

I've heard that on field crews, when a girl sleeps with the foreman in exchange for easier work, the other girls are sometimes jealous. Is it that way in the *maquiladora*?

No, she said wearily. They don't get jealous . . .

Magdalena Ayala Márquez, also of Mexicali, was still more forthright.

How often do the bosses ask to sleep with the female *maquiladora* workers, and do the women have to do it? I asked her.

It does happen lots, Magdalena replied. Where I have work now, I have a daughter, nineteen years old, pretty, *muy bonita,* she laughed, and my daughter is studying computers. At the assembly line one of the supervisors was offering her a job in the office but he was offering her to go out to dinner and like that. Sometimes she would say yes, just to go along, but when the man said, get serious, then she said, no, no, I don't want to go out with you. And then she didn't get that office job. When it's a young pretty woman they get a lot of sexual harassment. One of the supervisors asked me: Do you have a daughter working here? Yes, I said, do you see the prettiest girl here? That's her. He said to me: I've seen that prettiest girl; I've already located her. And then I started feeling anxious.

How about you?

No. I'm old now, said Magdalena. (She was forty-six.) They want the young pretty girl without experience.

"NOW IT'S DONE ALMOST ALWAYS"

What about the bloody tampon? Was that a myth? None of the people I interviewed in 2004 had ever heard of it in their workplaces. The dapper reporter believed that *the maquiladoras used to be harder in the nineties. That's what they told me.* Señor A. was sure that they were no better.

And once again I find Señor A. very plausible. He stated: The *maquiladoras* started the fashion of testing the blood and urine samples of women. Now it's done in Tijuana's industries almost always. But this is when you join, not every month.

As for termination due to pregnancy, most of the workers I interviewed, and certainly almost all of the women, had a story to tell, although it had always happened to someone else. For example, Magdalena Ayala Márquez brought to mind the tale of a friend (evidently not a close friend since Magdalena remembered her as *Maggie something*) about whom the story went: She went to the *maquiladora* doctor and found out she wasn't covered by the insurance anymore so she was basically fired.

Magdalena said that this occurred at a *maquiladora* called Rogers Terminados,* seven or eight years ago. That lapse of time was typical, which I found somewhat comforting. Pregnancy-caused firings were well known, but they hardly happened every day.

The most unpleasant establishment in this regard as in several others was Formosa. After an hour inside (complete with button-camera footage she was so proud of that as soon as she had rushed happily back to the car, she handed the digital video receiver to me, inadvertently unplugging it while it was still on and thereby losing her video forever), Perla told me this:

I got as far as the infirmary where the doctor told me to take off my clothes, so when I was left alone to undress, I left. They all spoke very rudely. The woman who interviewed me told me that they would have to do a pregnancy test and the cost would come out of my paycheck: three hundred pesos! They said I must wear shorts or skirts below the knee. They offered three hundred pesos to work seven in the morning until seven at night. Lunch would cost ten pesos eighty. If I had to do anything during work time, I must take the whole week off. The week I went back, I'd have to work double time. If you get pregnant, you lose your job.

*Listed in the Mexicali yellow pages as "Terminados Roger's," Adolfo L. Mateos, km. 5.

"IT'S GOOD, MORE OR LESS"

Well, so what? By now I'd come to realize that the effect of the *maquiladoras* was, like most effects, ambiguous. Once upon a time, searching for Barrio Chilpancingo, Terrie and I followed a yellow truck which said **CORROSIVE**. (You can find trucks carrying carcinogenic materials easily, insisted Señor A., who might or might not have been exaggerating as usual. Two years ago, the Secretary of Health announced that more than forty percent of Tijuanos over sixty get some kind of cancer. Right now, though, when you're not sixty, you can't detect it.) Mabuchi and Panasonic were soliciting workers. We found our way again: Turn right at Industrial at the big white factory with concertina wire around it and the pipes sticking out of it, then down past Grupo Bafar; down the hill past Tobutsu and Sparkletts. I remember more pipes peeping from Tocabi, and Sano or was it Sanyo on the left.

In the same park where I'd met that true believer in *maquiladoras,* Señor Prieto, I interviewed a mother and daughter from Chiapas. They came a year ago, "to look for work" as the mother put it.

And how did you end up here in Chilpancingo?

Right here is closer to factories.

And how is it for you?

Right now we're looking for work.

But many of these factories have signs: *SE SOLICITAN PERSONAL.*

Because my daughter doesn't know how to read, they don't accept her. She is working at a factory but she got sick, said the mother, and then they refused to give her job back.

What kind of sickness?

She had a growth on her spine.

I said I was sorry, and asked what had caused the growth.

They gave her penicillin to treat it. We don't know the cause.

And what about you, señora?

I work at night.

What sort of work?

A plastic factory.*

Is it good or bad?

It's good, more or less. We're renting, and we need to pay the rent.

It's good, more or less. What did that mean? That dapper reporter had said: The black story of *maquiladoras,* I think there are bad conditions for the workers, but conditions may be better than for workers employed in Mexican industries in the south.

*It sounded as if she said Industrial Ichiwa or Nishiba. She did not say the name very clearly. In a guide to *maquiladoras* I find an Ichia Rubber de México, in Industrial park Valle Sur I.

The daughter took care of a three-month-old at night. The possibility came to mind that she was either retarded, the mother of the baby, or both.

The mother worked a twelve-hour shift, starting at six-thirty at night and finishing at six-forty in the morning. They gave her forty minutes to eat and seven hundred pesos a week. It was a four-day week, which sounded not so bad to me.

How about your health? I asked.

I know that sometimes working with plastics can be hazardous. Well, my eyes are getting worse. It's pretty dim, and because you can't see well and you're tired, it affects your eyes. I examine the little pieces of plastic for telephones and make sure they're clean and not scratched.

They, too, had never heard of Metales y Derivados, whose ruin stood in sight upon the hill.

Are *maquiladoras* good or bad for Mexico, and why?

To tell you the truth, I don't know, the mother said. Her name was Señora Candelaria Hernández López. Her daughter was called Alicia Hernández Hernández.

INDUSTRIAL PARK LOS PIÑOS

It's good, more or less. What if it truly was? I remember the first time I successfully shot covert video inside a production area: Turn right on Campos; that's a dirt road; and on the other side of Canal Libramiento, you'll get to Los Pinos Industrial Park, where by some fluke a few pine trees do remain. They're soliciting female personnel at this *maquiladora* and that. (I quote the dapper reporter: Some are moving to China, but there are forty-eight industrial parks and a hundred thousand people employed in Tijuana! In some places they have five thousand or eight thousand vacancies! Maybe other factories* are offering more.) Passing private security cars in the street, we reach the spot where a security man sits in a doorway with his arm around his girlfriend. Now let's duck into the ornamental thicket, as if to urinate. Switch the power pack to ON. And the button camera aims upward at spare blue skeletonwork of gates and fence, with salmon-colored clouds which on later viewing I won't remember now squiggling across the blank blueness of the entrance gate; did it really look that way or is the button camera employing artistic license? The world wriggles and shifts. Young women's heads rush toward us at the bottom of the frame (especially notable is one copper-faced extremely Indian-looking lady who passes in profile, bearing a majestic knot of black hair); then they all veer rightward, vanishing onto the long sidewalk, which is to say out of the button camera's

*Word interpolated by WTV.

ken. Now, as the security guard gets distracted in his booth, the button camera, accompanied by Terrie for communication and me for locomotion, bears us inside the *maquiladora*'s private world. And presently, at eight minutes thirty-six seconds, we approach the blue-rimmed doorway, number thirteen, with white vertebrae of light running diagonally through its blackness. Closer still, we see a blue-ribbed wall or door on the right, a smoother grey one on the left; now two strings of lights come into view; they are ceiling-tubes, dwindling toward perspective's vertex; and the end of some kind of framelike affair begins to loom out of the darkness, with silhouettes huddled indistinctly around it. Lurching still closer, the button camera abruptly brings us into a warm salmon-colored universe where four people bend over the worktable, two on each side, boy-girl, boy-girl; they could almost be a pair of happy couples playing some board game; they don't seem hurried, weary or grim . . .

GERMÁN'S STORY

It's good, more or less. Here there's life, more or less. And what should a life be?

You and I who both can read are unlikely ever to know what it must have been like to work in Metales y Derivados, but here is a story which approaches that untold tale.

Señor A. said that he found the man named Germán on Saturday, arguing with one of the guards outside Power Sonic. He was a very dark, somber, weary man who was sitting in Señor A.'s waiting room when we arrived. I had thought him another client, and greeted him, but he'd kept silent. In the private detective's office, his face was nearly as dark as his hair.

Two years ago I worked in a battery factory called Power Sony, he said—an error which can be interpreted as suggesting either that he had been coached by Señor A. or that he simply wasn't very literate. I myself believe the latter.

I was supposed to get off at four every day, he said, and I usually didn't get off until seven.

Was this factory affiliated with Metales y Derivados?

I'm not positive, but I know the company had a lot to do with liquids. The batteries were for wheelchairs.

Where was this?

In an industrial area called Pacífico.

Is it near Chilpancingo?

They were going to build one in Chilpancingo but at the time I was working there a factory burned. My boss's name was Jesús López. The first factory burned, so they moved us to another factory although we had thought we would have no job. This was the place called Pacífico. If you go back past the fountain for the Fifth Battalion, there are about thirty factories.

Slamming together the fingers of his big dark hands, he said: I would work extra hours and not get paid. Also, they don't wash all of the equipment. Also, they don't wash the clothes. They were very strict about making us wear goggles because we worked with sulphuric acid but they weren't clean. I'm kind of embarrassed to say it but I got married, and I had to be sure that before I was having sex with my wife I washed so that I didn't get the acid on her.

Did you get sick?

They gave us pills for dizziness, and we often got dizziness.

And did the pills help?

The pills only helped for a little while. Then the schedules changed. I was working from seven until four. But they changed the schedule so I was working from four P.M. to two A.M. And later the acids, there were people, I don't know if it was allergies or what, but you could see their skins . . . After about a year ago, after I had quit, I went to the doctor for an exam and it came out that I was anemic. I had been working for two years. I finally decided to quit because for one thing they paid very little and secondly because I missed work one day and they refused to give me my weekly punctuality bonus of ninety pesos.

Was your wife for or against the decision to quit?

He stretched at his shirt and sniffed at himself. I think she did want me to quit, because it was affecting me, and the smell of *acid, acid,* was so strong that I had to keep my clothes in a separate room. I used to break out on my arms and on my neck. And it affected my sleeping patterns. I only slept three or four hours.

Are you still married now?

Yes.

Are you and your wife both working now?

I'm hoping to find a job in a factory where they recycle cardboard. My wife doesn't work. We have four children.

Congratulations.

I returned to see if I could get my job back, he said then. But they told me no, not anymore. They said, you quit, and a week later we hired people who want to work here, people from Chiapas and the south, people who try to cross but end up staying here.

Why on earth did you try to get your job back?

Because wherever I went, people closed their doors.

I sat looking at him, trying to figure all this out, when he said: And the other thing was—Germán evidently meant the other reason why Señor A. had found him arguing with the *maquiladora* guard—I thought that I would be earning the same, six hundred pesos a week, but now, if I started it would be four hundred and fifty a week.

Why would it be less now?

Because they would have to go back and train me.

Who owns the battery factory?

The manager is Jesús López, but it is American. It's entirely Mexicans who work there, about seven hundred people, counting secretaries. When I was an employee, about four hundred used to work there.

Would you allow your name to be published?

I can't. I worry that I wouldn't be able to get another job if I did.

Have you worked in the *campo*?

Yes, when I was eleven, harvesting lettuce in Ensenada.

Which is better, working in the *campo* or in the *maquiladora*?

Well, in the *campo,* because they pay you by commission. Even if it's lettuce, chilis, if they pay you, say, two pesos a box, you can make out.

Did you ever really consider moving to Mexicali to be a campesino?

I thought about it before, but now that I have a house, I would rather stay here.

Then in a sudden rush he said: I began to work in the factories in 1986. I began in an American factory where they make metals. I was seventeen years old. I worked at the metal factory where they manufactured huge tubes which weighed more than a ton. I was working with a man in the south when one of the tubes fell and broke my leg. But they treated me really well. They paid me for four months. I would have liked to keep working there because I was getting raises and I was about to become the line boss. I knew all about the connectors and I even trained one of the supervisors. But they also used acids there, acetylene. They would place a tube inside and it would come out all covered in chrome. I have some friends who still work there and he is a boss there, a manager. I talked to him and told him that I wanted to work there, but it was very far away and I would have spent fifty pesos on taxis.

I also learned how to install the heating in the car, he said. We used a fabric called *pica-pica,* which means burn-burn. You used gloves and pants but not masks. I worked for five years in Kessler and another two in the battery factory, so I started to worry about my lungs . . .

I gazed into his dark reddish-brown broad and hopeless face, which was heavy with shadows and moustaches, and he said: I've seen a lot of things, especially women shaped like this—he made the motion men make to indicate flaring breasts and hips—who keep getting more raises, and the bosses keep saying to them, we'll go out together. I've been working in factories for nineteen years. I don't really want to work in factories again. Maybe in a vegetable market.

Are the *maquiladoras* good or bad for Mexico?

I live right now thanks to the factories. People say they provide jobs. But they generate a lot of contamination, a lot of trash. Now the factories just throw the trash down the street, even tires. I've had good luck with my jobs, but I've also had friends who after their six-month contract can't keep their work.

Then he said: I used to have a dream that the timer went off saying the battery was done. If you don't take it out on time it will begin to smoke, so I used to have a dream that I needed to disconnect the battery . . .

SALVADOR'S SCAR

And in Colonia Villa Cruz, on the bare hill overlooking Insurgentes, Salvador Santa Cruz (with a naked lady and a United Farm Workers emblem tattooed on him; he revered César Chávez, whom he said was barely known in Mexico) stood outside a relative's grocery store at high noon because he had been suspended from Kimstar Plastics for tardiness; no doubt he, like Germán, might have been somewhat of a troublemaker; all the same, I pitied him when he said, speaking very rapidly:

If I miss work one day, they'll deduct money from me. I started getting five hundred and fifty a week and now I get eight hundred and fifty, but every time you miss work they deduct. And I never miss work, 'cause I got to keep my budget in line. I provide everything to the people who pack. I supply them with foam bags for the computer stuff, and boxes. I don't like to miss work, because I make eight hundred and fifty pesos but every time I miss work I lose two hundred to two hundred and fifty pesos. And sometimes they pay late. That's why we went on strike, because they didn't pay us on payday, but all the same they deduct money from us if we're late.

I've worked there for three years now. The Koreans own it. They're okay. The supervisors are Mexican, of course. My supervisor, ever since he's been there, nobody likes him. They only give us half an hour lunch. As soon as the bell rang I went in, and he said I was eight minutes late and that wasn't right. I told him that's not right. I said, bring your supervisor. They bring the security guard and he was against me, too. I sure didn't wanna sign that paper that said I was eight minutes late, 'cause then I was going to get suspended. Well, I got suspended and here I am.

(In fairness to the *maquiladora* supervisor, I may as well note that Salvador was forty minutes late for our next rendezvous, and he never showed up at all for the last one. And so that sad argument over eight minutes may well have been conducted in perfect self-righteousness on both sides. Foreigners' worship of time clocks, Mexicans' tendency to do things in their own good time, guess which one wins?)

Do many people want your job? I asked him.

Every time they do my job, they quit, 'cause no one can stand my supervisor. I been there three years so maybe I'll make plans to change my job . . .

We've been struggling for two months now, he went on. Sometimes they pay us; sometimes they don't. Last week they were about three days late. So we went on strike. They kept paying the supervisors. Some of us were with the strikers. Some of us were with *them*.

I come out at three-thirty. Sometimes they want me to do a double shift, but I say no, he proudly announced.

His *novia* worked at Sony, where conditions were better, so he thought. But possibly she wasn't his *novia* anymore; it sounded as if he had love problems.

He was born in Michoacán, and came to Tijuana only because the Americans deported him from Fresno, where he'd spent twelve illegal years, the crossing paid for by his mother. He ended up in prison for driving without a license and driving while intoxicated, which was how he caught the attention of our Immigration Department. It had been four years now since his forcible return. They'd put him across at San Ysidro, so the first thing he did was visit his cousin here in TJ. Then he stayed with his aunt, and eventually bought land from her. Now here he was; he'd achieved the Great Mexican Dream; he toiled in a *maquiladora*.

The second time I met him, I noticed his scar.

He'd been making razors for Dorusa in La Presa, his first job, and suddenly razors came shooting out of the machine into his arm; he admitted that he hadn't been carefully watching.—They took me to the hospital, Salvador told me. They said it wasn't that bad. If you get a lawyer, the lawyer charges you money. People don't like to argue with a *maquiladora*. You win this much, and they only pay you half.

No gloves or else the machine will take your fingers off; that had been the rule at Dorusa.—Some guy lost his finger; I saw it, said Salvador. He was using gloves, and the machine got his finger and half his other finger. When we stopped the machines we saw his finger in there . . .

THE PRICE OF A MASK

Like most human records, this account essentially recounts failure; and we never did get button-camera footage of the interior of Óptica Sola; I remember parking yet again in front of Metales y Derivados with the black plastic blowing and us both getting headaches after a moment or two and then Terrie's eyes began to sting. Perla rushed jauntily off, while across the street two men carried an enormous crate on their shoulders into a dark well of barrel-shaped containers. One wore a white mask and a shield. Why not both? The wind blew from Metales y Derivados, and I began to get a sore throat, although only slightly. That sour-salty smell of something poisonous was in my nose and mouth; it was blowing right into the loading dock where those men lifted crates. I remembered that terrifying science-fiction novel *On the Beach,* when the entire world perished bit by bit from silent radioactive contamination; one couldn't feel it right away, one character explained to another, but I've already got it and you've got it and the baby's got it.—The flapping tarps and stinking wind were very disturbing. Needless to say, those two men from Rimsa who were supposed to be cleaning up the place had done nothing; at least they weren't sitting on the ground eating more lead sandwiches today. It was three-twenty; halfway down the block, blue buses pulled up in front of Óptica Sola; this shift must get out at three-thirty; then Perla returned, shaking her head and laughing: *Nada!* The guard had denied her entrance since there was no work to spare. She then bravely tried to walk through the open door into the production line, at which point another guard called her over and reiterated that they weren't hiring women right now.

My self-disappointment at failing to enter that immense fortress has since been mitigated by an article I read in the newspaper *El Sol de Tijuana,* a sweet little story, in fact a charming story:

A large mobilization of emergency crews was provoked by the spill of a non-toxic but extremely flammable chemical inside a factory, where 80 workers were forced outside and a security supervisor detained for preventing entry of firemen.

The event occurred at 10:30 yesterday at Óptica Solare on Insurgentes Blvd. . . .*

The questionable part of the event was that the spill of perchloride happened at 8 am and was not reported by the owners in order to not "alarm the workers," but area residents reported it to the fire chief.

When the firemen arrived at the plant they found the entry locked with a chain and padlock, and the security guard refused to let them enter. They had to wait for the police to arrive, enter by force, and detain the guard.

The firemen then entered and rescued the 89 workers, some of them with vomiting, nausea, and dizziness, in the paramedic's opinion all psychological, since the spilled chemical was not a mortal danger to health.

But since a conflagration could start at any moment since it is highly flammable when exposed to heat, the police proceeded to cordon off the area and prohibit entry.

In the opinion of the assistant fire chief, the executives at Óptica Solare made a grave

*This must be an error for Óptica Sola, since a Web search found no company named Solare, and since Sola is also on Boulevard Insurgentes.

error in blocking entry and in keeping the workers inside working. He estimated it would take several hours to make the air breathable because of the poor handling of the chemical in a space with no ventilation . . .

So if even firemen can't get into Óptica Sola when the place is in imminent danger of bursting into flames, why should this second-rate investigative journalist feel humiliated that he, too, was foiled?

Off we sped to Formosa Prosonic, happily unaware that Perla's videotaping there would prove as useless as it was going to be unpleasant. Out by the Playas the pale ocher earth cut away again; past the new Mormon church (count on Terrie to notice each one of those, and now I know her secret: no cross on the steeple), a few houses huddled in the dirt; by then we were coming up to Plaza de Cumbres on its hill of sand and earth; we were right up on the summit with the Pacific below and on the right a triple-stranded barbed wire fence. The blue-and-white-striped factoryscape of Formosa beguiled us, right next to Fluidmaster Mexico-Maquiladora, whose representative had been either busy or away, I forget which, when Terrie had called to request an appointment.

We parked around the corner from Formosa's main gate, but it was still Formosa. A big pipe ran down the bare hillside. I couldn't see where it started. Señor A.'s theory that many of these *maquiladoras* excreted untreated poisons into the earth through such vessels had come to seem unerringly plausible; it would certainly be an explanation for the smell. Of course the degree, if any, to which Formosa emits dangerous chemicals into its surroundings remains unknown to me. I lacked the budget to take soil and water samples as I had done when researching the Salton Sea and the Río Nuevo; besides, as you remember, the results of those latter tests cannot be called dramatic.

So what can I tell you about these factories? The social responsibility of at least one *maquiladora* may be gauged from the following cassette tape, which I have in my possession, and which is the record of a telephone call made to Thomson, which Señor A. claimed to be the worst or one of the worst polluters. The caller (Perla, I suspect) is pretending to be one of the factory's neighbors:

Every night we have to deal with a really bad smell, says the woman. It smells like something burning. My kids are getting sick.

Well, replies Thomson, if your kids have allergies, it's not our problem.

I don't know what to do; I can't help you, the Thomson woman keeps saying. Finally she comes up with the ideal solution: I'll have you talk to someone else.

A man comes on the line.

There are toxic fumes coming from behind your factory and it's affecting our children, the woman repeats. Their throats and eyes hurt. Can't you do anything to control the smoke?

I'm not really in charge of the smoke but I can call you back, says the man. What's your number?

She gives him one which is no doubt invented.

We don't have any harmful toxic fumes, he reassures her.

What about the smoke?

Oh, is there smoke coming out from behind our factory? asks the man in surprise, and it is all one can do not to laugh or maybe curse; in Señor A.'s video of Thomson one can see the black, black smoke . . .

Meanwhile, behind that graffiti'd fence, before the wall of pipes, Formosa's workers hauled long flexible strips of metal, two workers per strip, and they laid them carefully side by side in the dirt. My eyes began to sting.

Now we waited for the flatvoiced girl with glasses to come; she worked at Fluidmaster now, from six-thirty in the morning to three-twenty in the afternoon; she had only two fifteen-minute breaks.

The fat, flatvoiced girl with glasses was named Lourdes. Before I met the girl, I'd already met her chest X-rays and her case file, **NOTA DE ATENCIÓN MÉDICA**, dated 27 10 2002, for **A———** (PATERNO) **B———** (MATERNO) **Lourdes** (NOMBRES). There was something ugly about her personality, I thought. Terrie didn't think so; Terrie thought her brave and she was, but her bravery came from some bitter, brutalized place; I felt disliked and suspected by her. I sometimes have the same feeling when I interview a rape victim.

We were sitting in the car in La Jolla Industrial Park. Terrie and Perla were wiring Lourdes up for another button camera which was going to fail, and when Lourdes came out of Fluidmaster the security guard seemed to be searching her body, at which point I was almost ready to vomit for anxiety; my rule in these adventures was to take full responsibility for the people working for me, and I was wondering how I was going to get Lourdes out of this and what would happen to me, when she waved cheerfully to the security guard and strolled back to the car; that is what I mean when I say that she was brave.

I asked what had happened to her at Formosa and she said wearily: I got pneumonia and also tuberculosis. I assembled radio speakers.

Why did you get sick?

Because of the glue, which had toxic chemicals in it.

How do you know it was from the glue?

Because it was what everyone was breathing in all the time.

And what did the glue smell like?

I'm not sure how to say it, but it was strong and ugly. It burns the throat.

When you're coming to work at Fluidmaster, can you smell it?

Sometimes but not really.

25/oct/02 HGZ #20

INSTITUTO MEXICANO DEL SEGURO SOCIAL
SEGURIDAD Y SOLIDARIDAD SOCIAL

DIRECCION DE PRESTACIONES MEDICAS

NOTA DE ATENCION MEDICA

NUMERO DE SEGURIDAD SOCIAL 2 1 9 8 3 8 7 5 2 1 F 1 9 8 3 AGREGADO

PACIENTE ████ Lourdes.

PATERNO MATERNO NOMBRE(S)

CURP

UNIDAD DE ADSCRIPCION

No. CONSULTORIO TURNO

DIA	MES	AÑO	HORA	ESTATURA	PESO	TEMPERATURA	PRESION ARTERIAL	FRECUENCIA CARDIACA	FRECUENCIA RESPIRATORIA
27	10	2002							

RESUMEN CLINICO:

NOTA DE ALTA DE MEDICIAN INTERNA.
FECHA DE INGRESO:17-10-02
FECHA DE EGRESO: 27-10-02
DIAGNOSTICO DE INGRESO:HEMOPTISIS EN ESTUDIOS
DIAGNOSTICO DE EGRESO: HEMOPTISIS EN ESTUDIO
RESUMEN: femenino de 19 años de edad que ingreso con diagnostico antes mencionado, se le realizaron Estudios como:Anticuerpos anti-Tb y anticocci;Se realizo broncoscopia tomado muestras para citologico.y microbiologicos. completo esquema de antibiotico con cefalosporinas de tercera generacion y amikacina.
Plan:alta del servicio.
cita abierta a urgencias en caso necesario.
receta por acetaminofe "PRN" fiebre.
Salbutamol 2 inhalaci nes c/8hrs.
ambroxol 10mlc/8hrs
cita C de Mi Dr Glz Control 1 consu tolrio 7 en 4 semanas.
Incapacidad se otorgo a partir del dia
17-10-02 por catorde dias como enfermedadm general, NEUMONIA Vs TBP Vs Coccio.
Al termino de la misma pegresa a trabajar,en caso de no poder realizar su trabajo acudir a CE de MF con este resumen.
-NOTA requiere recabar estudios subrrogados en Lab GAmboa anticuerpos anti TB y cocci.
recabar estudios de lab Citologicos(reporte de patologia)
microbiologicos en lab. cultivos con antibiogramas.
-PRONOSTICO:Reservado hasta tener evidencia de enf. Se explica a paciente y familiar(esposo).
Dr Glz/RIMI Calderon/Mip G. calvo

DIAGNOSTICO (S):

TRATAMIENTO Y MANEJO INTEGRAL:

1- Rifater 2 tabletas c/12
2- Etambutol 1 c/8 horas
3- Complejo B 1 c/12 horas
4-

Anexar BAAR + positivo y copia de Ac Anticocci, Ac anti TB y VIH asi como panel hepatitis.

INCAPACIDAD: SERIE Y FOLIO DIAS

INICIAL SUBSECUENTE RECAIDA

FECHA DE INICIO EG RT

MATERNIDAD FECHA DE EXPEDICION

NOMBRE, MATRICULA Y FIRMA DEL MEDICO

ANVERSO MF -8/2000

Lourdes's medical chart.
She believed that her symptoms resulted from her work in a *maquiladora*.

How many years did you work at Formosa?

Two years eight months.

When you brought in the X-rays, what did they say?

They didn't care. They sent me some insurance.

And how are you feeling now?

Okay. I had a treatment. Pills and a spray.

(When I asked Perla whether Lourdes's health had been ruined permanently, she answered: It has not improved. She still has a cough.—That was what Perla said, although during the hour or so I spent with Lourdes, she never coughed. I suppose it is possible that she coughs at night.—Did Formosa's glue injure her? How can I say?)

Are the *maquiladoras* good or bad for Mexico?

Well, said Lourdes, more or less, the thing is—we have to work.

So they're good?

More or less, she said in what I believe to have been quiet fury.

Can you tell me what happened after the doctor X-rayed you?

I went back to work after getting better and got sick all over again.

I've already told you that in the coarse yellow-brown envelopes of the Instituto Mexicano del Seguro Social lay those two X-rays, dated October 2002, which Perla claimed show pneumonia and which I photographed; I have not yet had a doctor look at my negative, and even if pneumonia can be proven, I see no further proof that the glue at Formosa either caused or exacerbated Lourdes's pneumonia. But here is one thing that somebody at Formosa ought to get barbequed in hell for, if what Perla and Lourdes both told me happened next did happen: When Lourdes recovered and returned, she asked Formosa to give her a mask, and Formosa refused.

That was why she quit, because she didn't wish to continue getting sick. She said that they gave her two hundred and fifty dollars as a settlement to keep her from suing them.*

And how is it now, working at Fluidmaster?

It's really good. I do a lot of work with my hands. I sit at a table. It's comfortable. I sit and pack. What we make is the floating thing inside the toilet . . .

*"So they had her sign something?" I later asked Perla, who replied: "Lourdes told them that she quit because she was sick, so they offered her the two hundred and fifty dollars, and when they saw that she wasn't going to make any trouble, they didn't make her sign anything. Sometimes they do sue and get up to three thousand dollars, when they've complained a lot."

WINDOWS OF DARKNESS, JELLYFISHES OF LIGHT

This concludes the so-called investigative aspect of my story, which is to say the chronicle of hasty interviews, often unwillingly given, and shallow forays into the closed worlds of the *maquiladoras*. Oh, I have a few more button-camera videos weighing down the hard drive of my computer; I've done Óptica Sola more than once from the outside; I've wandered past the gate and into the introductory labyrinth of loading docks at Kimstar, where Salvador worked; and so what? I didn't learn any secrets. In Mexicali I never got inside the Parque Industrial Nelson, the Desierto Industrial Parque, the Parque Industrial Pimas, or any of the other Parques Industriales which marched on and on to the southeast. I tried and tried; I accomplished what I could; someday I'll try again, not only because I want to be of service to people but also because (why not admit it?) any little stroll with the button camera is an adventure. My walk from the Motel Lizvan, a clean and private establishment which sold vaginal lubricant at the office window, to the Philips *maquiladora* facade, was only about two minutes; but in the night time, with the button camera peering from a rolled-up plastic bag because my bluejeans were too sopping wet to encase fragile electronics, and the reason for *that* was that both Terrie and I were burning, itching, headachy and nauseous from our unauthorized exploration of Metales y Derivados, so I'd seen fit to wash my jeans in the shower, the two minutes seemed longer in that cool dark night of palm trees, sand and dust, a night which was almost bereft of humanity although glowing with traffic, including two great trucks without insignia which rolled slowly past me on Insurgentes as if they were heavily laden, then turned down a dirt road. In the button-camera video, the night is corrugated with scan lines, and the lights glowed like pears, jellyfish and almost-frozen white explosions which lurched from side to side. Hugging pale walls and gratings, I presently approached something which shone like a great blue television in the darkness. First came a fence with parked cars behind it, and a white ball of coldly slobbering light atop it; then the fence became translucent corrugated skeleton-bars in the night and the blue and white television swayed in and out of view, with another whitish sun hovering to the left of it. Rounding the corner and coming to the beginning of the narrow sidewalk in front of Philips, I met a darkskinned dirty man who hunched beneath a tree; he was silent. From under the long white overhanging facade of Philips, light spilled down on the sidewalk. Ahead was another white jellyfish of glare. I walked toward it until the button camera became entirely dazzled for a moment; then the blue television filled my eyes, framed by its lurching dark gratings. What it really was was a window, of course, a long barred window of blueness, with yellow-white blobs of light on its surface; and within stretched a vast blue-washed factory world empty of

Covert photo taken with disposable camera inside Kimstar *maquiladora,* Tijuana

everything but pallets and mysteries; then came the chroming plant, Baja Platinadora; and far away the security guard from Kimstar had left his box and sat beneath a tree, watching me. I got as close as I dared, which proved not to be close enough for the button camera to see anything but darkness . . .

What else goes on in the *maquiladoras*? Señor A. insisted that in some establishments it is permissible to use crystal meth because it increases productivity; the police cannot search within a factory's gates. He likened the drugs in these factories to a duty-free shop at the airport. This could easily be another of his speculative exaggerations; on the other hand, he assures me that one of his clients was a mother whose son became a drug addict after working at such a place. I would have liked to investigate this, and discover whether the atmosphere in that *maquiladora* was simply lax or whether it actively encouraged methamphetamine use. Señor A. also claimed that workers frequently stole the crystals used in computer manufacture and sold them to other *maquiladoras;* I would have enjoyed meeting these free marketeers. Amelia Simpson at the Environmental Health Coalition in San Diego told me that she'd documented many cases of *maquiladora* restrooms being so inadequate, and time to use them so restricted, that some women wore diapers rather than waste their one half-hour break standing in line for the toilet, and other women developed kidney infections from holding their urine too long. None of the workers I interviewed ever said any such thing; I frequently asked about the bathrooms and heard no complaints. This does not signify that I've proven or disproven

Restroom in unnamed *maquiladora* in Mexicali;
photo taken covertly by worker with disposable camera

anything, only that my sample remains necessarily small. Amelia Simpson gave me the name of such a factory, and I promised to send Perla there with the button camera later this year. This factory is further alleged to employ lead solder and to withhold masks from its workforce, which is primarily female, so that one can imagine lead being transmitted to the next generation in breast milk. Who knows? If Perla were able to steal an inch of solder for testing, then perhaps this *maquiladora* could be exposed and lives saved.

So send me another ten thousand dollars, quick! Maybe I could do it for seven or for twenty. Now here came Power Sonic up the hill; that was the place where Germán used to get his acid treatments at company expense (shall I throw an "allegedly" in there for legal reasons?); we drove up the highway, with hillside *colonias* left and right; then on a raw-ochered hill which was graffiti'd, a lovely brown girl in white shorts and a white tanktop, her bobbed black hair shining, strode across the naked earth. From around the corner came a smell of solvents; then I saw the *maquiladora* with blue tanks down in the gorge. The immense blue and white cube of AOL Systems Mexico, a gas station, mountains in the distance—don't tell me Tijuana wasn't pretty! My eyes were watering but maybe it was my imagination. We then turned right onto Pacífico, ascending a hill toward an immense gate as we passed the white cube of Kyomex on the left. I remember Ensenada and Pacífico. Up high, another Kyomex and a splendid view of striped hillsides and far *colonias* as we drove along the parking lot of Robinson and Robinson regaled us, Terrie laughing and joking with Perla; then came many tall cylindrical tanks, the smell of solvent more and more sickening. For a second I thought I would vomit. I recollect an endless gate with black glass and white factory cubes behind. Then we parked and waited for Perla to come out. Once I went outside, and the wind was blowing; I couldn't smell solvent anymore. Well, so they offered Perla another job! Which chemicals? I'd told her to ask. The guy replied to her: I don't know. A lot.—As for Perla, she couldn't smell any. What should the perfect spy do? Pay Perla for a week, while she works at Power Sonic and makes videotapes of acid-burned people working without masks, or of well-masked people without acid—why assume the worst? Maybe Germán's a liar; or maybe Power Sonic, like Matsushita, has cleaned up its act. If not, pay Perla to smuggle out chemical samples (good thing *she's* reproduced!).

What *is* the secret? There may be no secret, no horrid one, anyway. I credit myself with being an empathetic and experienced interviewer; therefore, much of what I believe to be true may actually be true. While the stories of Germán and Lourdes can by no means be twisted into glowing encomiums to the *maquiladoras,* the tale of the bloody tampons and Señor A.'s thriller-chiller about Chinese slaves can't be substantiated, either; the plain truth is that most of the workers I met, not least the man with the black cough, expressed satisfaction with the factories in which they were employed. Isn't so much of the interest which other people's lives hold for us based on the divergence between their and our expectations? In Tecate, a lady who lived in a shack on that border-facing dirt road called Avenida México and had labored for the *maquiladoras* until she got old considered herself *pretty normal economically.* She had raised eleven children.—If you're talking about jobs, she went on, my son was working for a factory and it closed. It took him a month to find another job. I've lived here for four years and finally I'm going to build a bathroom . . .—And on Northside we would have thought it intolerable to live bathroomless and overshadowed by that ghastly metal wall thirty paces from the front door, a wall which went on infinitely. But the old woman, who needless to say was not as old as she looked, was kept company in her home by three images large and small of the Virgin of Guadalupe; her water jugs and bare rafters were ordinary to her, and her *maquiladora* work had been the same, until she lost her youth and became the dependent of her children. (From eighteen to thirty you can find work in a factory, she said philosophically.) Although she herself wasn't given a *quinceañera,* since her mother had been a single parent, she had managed to provide that experience for the first four of her six daughters.—And now I have appliances, she said. My new washer is less than a year old.—Her television had been bought with her labor in a *maquiladora.* (By the way, in 2003 fifty percent of all the TVs purchased in Canada, Mexico or the U.S. were made in Tijuana.) No, they were not enthusiastic, those factory hands (who is?); yes, they did often seem strangely unwilling to talk, a phenomenon which I interpreted, based on my prior experience in this region, as being predicated on distrust or fear, depending on the individual.

The *maquiladoras* are ripe for their own César Chávez, of whom many Mexicans have never heard. The haggard blonde in Mexicali said to me: The other day some lawyers and union reps came over and the bosses threw them out.

Of course, if the concessions which the new Chavistas squeezed out of them became too costly, the *maquiladoras* would doubtless up stakes to China, imitating Metales y Derivados if they needed to, leaving behind poisonous holes in the ground.

That is one reason no revolution is imminent. The other is this: I mostly reject the Marxist notion of false consciousness; I believe that a worker can think for himself, and if he doesn't claim to be exploited, why then, he probably isn't. MEXHON Honeywell on Insurgentes: ***SOLICITA PERSONAL***, work to start immediately, and chances are that some new arrival from the south will be thrilled. **SE SOLICITA PERSONAL** at AMAG; ***SE SOLICITA PERSONAL FEMENINA*** in Los Pinos Industrial Park; and the tall white towers of a landscape more than boring and less than ghastly bewildered me. At three in the afternoon, a stream of women poured out of Los Pinos; they assembled medical instruments, they said. Were their lives as sad as the Circus Vásquez Brothers' blue tents and grubby elephants? I don't believe so. They were smiling and giggling; they liked the work, they said.

A man was waiting for his wife to get off work at the Philips Plant Number Two; he stood on a shady part of the concrete sidewalk. When she came, young and pretty in her business clothes, they embraced, then walked hand in hand across Insurgentes and up the steep hillside toward their *colonia*.

I do think that the *maquiladoras* sometimes show a shocking disregard for people's health; the subtle effects of chemical exposure over time and the generally low level of education among *maquiladora* laborers conspire together to be accomplices in the endangerment of human beings for the sake of a few extra pesos.

The *maquiladoras* are a necessary evil, and perhaps not even as evil as I believe. But if their windows were less dark and their gates guarded less unilaterally, if button cameras became unnecessary as a means of verification, they would definitely be better places.

THE CHOICE OF SERGIO RIVERA GÓMEZ

I remember the union legal assessor, Sergio Rivera Gómez, sitting in his office on that extremely hot day in Mexicali when the walls were abloom with a glory of newspaper clippings and girlie pictures, and I remember the waist-high heaps of cans awaiting recycling, not to mention the Pope and the Virgin of Guadalupe.

Does it worry you that foreigners control many of these *maquiladoras*? I asked.

Yes, he replied. A hundred percent of the *maquiladoras* in Baja California are owned by foreigners. And they pay very low salaries to the workers. But they offer social security, pension plans. The workers are happy with their jobs because right now in Mexicali there's a big problem with unemployment—and then he added, I don't believe with any irony whatsoever—a problem with *maquiladoras* moving to China, India, and Central America.

(How serious might this "problem" be? In 1994, when NAFTA went into effect, Mexico possessed five hundred and fifty thousand *maquiladora* jobs, which had risen to one point three million by the year 2000, but over two hundred and thirty thousand positions then disappeared by 2004. How significant is an eighteen-percent decline? Economic graphs are always zigs and zags. Perhaps in another four years, the number of *maquila* jobs would have doubled!)

Señor Gómez, I said, when I go around the Mexicali Valley, I feel that its soul lives in the *ejidos*. Everyone in the *ejidos* always tells me that he's happy, that his children are happy, that he needs nothing. Can the *maquiladoras* harm that?

Of course it will affect the *ejidos,* he replied, because a lot of women and some men come to the city.

I assumed that I understood him, but he went on: If the *maquiladoras* continue to leave, it will diminish the quality of life in the *ejidos.*

And if the *maquiladoras* continue to come?

Maquiladoras bring a lot of toxic contamination, but it won't affect the *campo,* the fields, because people still come from the south to work the fields. So if the *maquiladoras* bring more workers, Mexicali will grow and develop more.

How much would you like Mexicali to develop? To Tijuana's level?

I would like Mexicali to develop more, but not with *maquiladoras,* he said to me. He paused, then said: Livestock businesses, not *maquiladoras.*

THE CHOICE OF JOSÉ LÓPEZ

Well, what I know, Bill, they been around here in Mexicali for awhile, right? I never worked in one, thank God, or maybe my bad luck, who knows? If I'd gone into one I might even have gotten a good position, since I do speak a little English. But for the salaries and all that, Bill, you know, that's what disappoints me. That's the main reason, maybe the only reason. I can think of many reasons why I want to work in one, especially since the majority are girls, know what I mean? And since girls can do it, it's really not backbreaking. I think I can make a more decent living here on the *línea.* But I don't have medical insurance here. But even in the *maquiladora,* if you're insured, you go to the hospital when you're injured and you find your insurance is just paper for the trashcan. And unjustified firings, this has happened to people I've talked to. Then they change managers and just because the supervisor don't like this person, the way he dresses, the way he walks, he gets all the sudden fired.

This guy was telling me, they been hearing also, it's just rumors, but it always starts like that, then rumor becomes reality, that they been thinking they wanna move operations to China. Because in China they get away with paying one dollar a day when here they pay ten if we're lucky.

MOVING THEIR OPERATIONS TO CHINA: ANOTHER ADDENDUM

The *New York Times,* Thursday, September 30, 2004, World Business section:

> **Outsourcing Finds Vietnam**
>
> Very low wages and strong math skills are a combination that has made believers of some experts.

MOVING THEIR OPERATIONS TO CHINA: STILL ANOTHER ADDENDUM

THE COMMONWEALTH OF TOIL

(Air: "Nellie Grey")

By Ralph Chaplin, International Workers of the World (before 1923)

In the gloom of mighty cities
   Mid the roar of whirling wheels
We are toiling on like the chattel slaves of old
   And our masters hope to keep us
Ever thus beneath their heels,
   And to coin our very life blood into gold.

MOVING THEIR OPERATIONS TO CHINA: ONE MORE ADDENDUM

On April 15, 2003, at about nine A.M., said Magdalena Ayala Márquez, all the workers were called into the office. The person from public relations, Margarita, I don't know her last name, called us in, and there was the manager, Alfonso Caballero Camou.* They wanted to know if we had our ID with us, some kind of elector's card we had. And since we were a lot of workers, we were over a hundred workers, some said yes and some said no. The ones that didn't have their ID could get time and go all the way to their houses, but they had to bring their IDs. Some people lived far and had to take two or three hours to come back, and we were all curious about why we needed our IDs. So when we were all back, all of us were led into a cold room, empty, where we usually† kept all the avocados. Once we were in there, we were locked in that cold room. They locked the big doors. They locked us in.‡ They said then they had some bad news and some good news to tell us. The bad thing is, there's no more work. The owners of Flor de Baja, they said they couldn't maintain the *maquiladora* no more; they couldn't keep it running. But that the good thing was, that if we would stay united together, we could keep the machinery. They can sell it and that way they can give the workers some money because of the unjust firing. By this time they had already had some kind of form. They were misleading the people and they just wanted to get all the signatures. The man said there was still more avocado and we could work that before we took off. He said he would give us another job in another *maquiladora* also. He was just buttering us up so that we would not ask too many questions. Each person would get a five-hundred-peso loan and get to keep a share of the *maquiladora*. But the money, Camou said it was gonna be just a little bit of money, so there wouldn't be a lot of red tape. We were kept in that cold room from twelve in the afternoon until six, when everyone put down a signature. And we never knew what we had signed.

Can most of those people read?

Yes, but Margarita showed a sheaf of papers with a little tiny crack of each page,

*Magdalena spelled his name "Kamu." However, a UABC article about this incident gives the above spelling, which seems more plausible to me. I have not verified the spelling or even the man's existence.

†This word interpolated by WTV.

‡ The UABC article merely reports that the workers were locked in. A posting by the Centro de Información para Trabajadoras y Trabajadors repeats the detail that they were locked into the refrigerator. I read that the workers later asked the Governor of Baja California to intervene and demonstrated in front of his office in Mexicali for over a month. When they went to the Labor Department and asked for a copy of their contract, their supposed attorney, Nahum Rodríguez Lara, allegedly said: *What for? Are you going to frame it and hang it in your living room?* As you can imagine, they achieved great success. Magdalena and her daughter were demonstrating and collecting money for this campaign when I met them.

so we were never allowed to know what we had signed. After everybody signed we were sent home.

What would have happened if someone had refused to sign?

Camou asked everybody, do you agree, do you agree? I was the only one who said, Caballero, we are putting our trust in you. And he said, no, I won't let you people down. Then on my way home I started thinking, what did I sign?

When you were being locked in, were you afraid?

No, no, no. Because the guys were there. Caballero and the rest. The day we signed those papers, we were given an appointment for the next Friday so they would give us a loan. I arrived late that Friday, and most of my coworkers were already leaving. I asked them: Where are you girls going?—To Paper Mate, since that's the place where they had gotten them a job. I asked if they had given them the money, and they answered me no. I said, we have to go get our loan, and we went back, and they did give us five hundred pesos each, and we signed. By signing I got a bad feeling and felt that we were basically giving up our rights. I told my coworker that we hadn't received a copy of the documents we had signed. And I told Margarita that I wanted a copy of that, and Margarita said we weren't going to get a copy.

What happened next?

They started placing guards over the *maquiladora* property. Caballero said he'd given the owners a ten-day limit so they'd pay the people what they were entitled to. It was on April twenty-fifth. And the owners didn't come to the appointment they had. Since they weren't present the workers decided to take over the property.

What's the status now?

They never came to pay us.

What's happening to the machinery now?

Some social organization has it. Some mediators. It's in the Industrial Park Las Californias, on the road to San Luis, kilometer ten and a half.

If you go there now, what do you see?

The Americans gave the keys to the owners of the industrial park. So now they start fighting with the workers. Anyhow, there's something else there now. The people from industrial park, they make some paperwork with government to get the machinery out of that building . . .

So whom do you blame?

Caballero.

Are there any workers who want to take the machinery by violence?

The oliveskinned lady with the long, greying hair and the slightly weathered face did not answer this directly, but replied: The owners tell us that our money is no problem because it's so small, but the problem is that Caballero wants so many thousands of pesos. What Caballero did was, he made us sign papers to give us consent to take machinery from the Americans with the pretense to pay the workers. He wants to sell the machinery and keep everything. It's been fourteen months. Every day he adds two hundred and seventy thousand dollars in wages to what he says he is owed. The law says I should get back pay for those fourteen months. But nothing is happening. The law is crooked.

How can we find Caballero?

He lives in Calexico. A brother of his has another *maquiladora* here in Mexicali next to Bimbo. Fluvamex is the name of it. It processes spices and vegetables. Also the conditions are similar to Flor de Baja.

The *maquiladora* where Magdalena Ayala Márquez had worked, Flor de Baja,* made avocados into guacamole, which they shipped worldwide. I am proud to report that in March 2003, this glorious enterprise produced *** **THE BIGGEST TACO IN THE WORLD!** *** A month later the owners shut it down. Who they truly were and where they might be found I cannot tell you. In 1994, when in a rare display of international reach the Environmental Protection Agency over in Northside subpoenaed some companies about the chemicals they discharged into the New River, a certain Brown International Corporation replied in the name of Flor de Baja. (They were very good, it appeared; their factory excreted nothing but avocados.†) In 2004 their head office reportedly existed in Chicago, and for all I know it may have been connected with this same Brown International Corporation. Who knows? And that, reader, is the only official information I can supply. If, however, you would enjoy enhancing your vocabulary of Spanish bird words, then in addition to *pollo* I will teach you *golondrina,* meaning swallow; this is Southside slang for a fly-by-night *maquiladora.*

Magdalena was a Big Knife. She had to cut twenty-seven avocados a minute, ten hours a day, Monday through Friday, from six-thirty in the morning until four-o'-clock. (Compensation: ninety-five pesos a day. Breaks: one per day, at ten-thirty for

*Misioneros y Frailes, Parque Industrial.

†In fact their guacamole might have contained a secret ingredient, for the year before the Brown Corporation made this declaration, the newspaper *El Mexicano* reported the following: *A total of 19 gravely poisoned women was the result . . . at an avocado treatment plant at kilometer 10.5 on the road to San Luis Rio Colorado, Sonora, the plant called Flor de Baja California, also with a location at the back of The Californias Industrial Park . . . Captain César Martínez Salomón and Lieutenant Santos Moreno Cota . . . led a large police operation to protect the female workers at the plant who were suffering from terrible poisoning. According to the Fire Captain, it was all due to an involuntary error . . . The workers, at least 50 in all, wear rubber gloves which must be disinfected at the end of each day in 3 ounces of calcium hypochloride. But on this day, by error, one of the employees used more than 3 ounces, resulting in a spill that led to the 19 young women being poisoned. Ambulances came and took the women to the Social Security Clinic on Avenida Lerdo.*

half an hour. One could go to the bathroom and drink water anytime.) She said that during the three months which her employment lasted, her wrists became injured. She also said that some people got arthritis and frostbite from working with ice in the cold room.*

Magdalena said: Margarita and others were getting invented people on the time sheets so the real ones had to work harder. There were a hundred people working at Flor de Baja and two hundred time sheets.

Did any of the Americans know about this?

She shrugged. I don't know. I don't think so.

So who is responsible for the bad conditions, the Americans or the Mexican middle management?

The local people are to blame, the people in the office. I've heard of thousands of dollars going into people's offices. They steal your wages, all your bonuses. But if you say something you're going to get fired and get blackballed.†

Well, it sounds like a very effective way to get rich.

The people who do that, they get so much money out of the *maquiladora,* they have the money to open up their own business. I think also the American businessmen have to be blamed since they shouldn't leave this kind of business in others' hands knowing what goes on here. They should at least have someone keep an eye on it.

In your opinion, was Flor de Baja among the best, the worst or in the middle?

It was a good *maquiladora.* It received several certificates. It was one of the best for productivity, but for the way they treated the workers, it is one of the worst.

Right now, which one is the worst?

They're all the same. They demand a lot of work, and if they fire you, they don't give you what you're entitled to. When you demand your rights, they blackball you.

Have you been blackballed?

No, because the last time I was working for some other plant I made an agreement; I got a certain amount of money; it was less than what I was entitled to, but with the condition that I wouldn't be blackballed.

She was now working at another *maquiladora,* from ten at night until six in the morning.—The schedule is the only thing I don't like, she said. I make air-conditioning ducts at AMP Industrial Mexicana, which is owned by Americans. The wages are about the same.

* Although I personally believe Magdalena's story, I have not been able to cross-check its details with other former workers or managers.

†The Tijuana private detective Señor A. independently told me that "in Tijuana when an employee sues her *maquiladora* for her rights, then her name is put on a list and circulated so that she can't find work."

Suddenly she said: You can't demand your rights. They demand a lot of work from you. They'll just step on you and fire you. You can't form a union or they'll fire you quick. I know organizers who are blackballed to the point where they have to do construction work just to survive although they have degrees. One man (and she named him) applied for a job just at the assembly line so they wouldn't investigate him, but the second day he came, they found out and they fired him.

You know for a fact that they fired him for being a union organizer, or you just heard that that was the reason?

I just heard . . .

Why not end here, with one more instance of disputed fact? We'll each believe what we wish. This almost perfectly incomplete portrait of the *maquiladoras* ends, as every honest investigation should, in midair. *(Let's face it, Bill. Investigative reporting is not really your strong suit.)* It is ever so difficult to begin to comprehend *maquiladoras* as they are, with their chemicals, fences and secrets; as for the future, well, from Tijuana I remember a tiny square of mostly unbuilt freeway, high in the air, souvenir of a broken bridge; and at the very end of it, lording it over empty space, a huge handmade cross with scraps of white plastic bag fluttering in the brown wind.

Chapter 156

SUBDELINEATIONS: WATERSCAPES

(1975–2005)

Thriving young towns will be born between Holtville and Yuma. That newer region will be dotted with happy farm homes, traversed by gleaming canals, crossed with busy highways.

—Robert Hays, 1930

To all to whom these presents shall come:

WATER IS HERE. WATER IS HERE. At least, they promised me that **WATER IS HERE.** How could I doubt it? Back in 1920, Mr. Leonard Coates from Fresno revealed the secret to make water last forever: Stir the soil frequently; then it will conserve moisture! That's all. Mr. Coates advised us to consider the following analogy: Powdered sugar on top of a sugar cube will hold water better than will a sugar cube on top of a sugar cube . . .

Gee whiz, somebody must not have been kicking enough dirt around, because Imperial's waterscape was beginning to look as patchily arid as ever!

"IMPERIAL ATTITUDE"

How should I put this? For a little longer, American Imperial continued to dream her watermelon dreams, secure in her bed of perpetual entitlements. *His farm has been highly improved. He made a success through his own efforts.* In 1999 Imperial County's average yield was four hundred and thirty-two honeydews and miscellaneous melons per acre; we'll ignore the dip one year later to three hundred eighty, because the year after *that* it was seven hundred and seventy-seven.* Just think what Otis P. Tout and the other dead boosters would have made of her triumph! The rest of southern California might be thirsty and thirstier for Colorado River water, but do you know what? American Imperial (we'll ignore her Mexican sister) had been here first! Other water districts are, in the Imperial Irrigation District's

*In 2002 it was eight hundred and twenty-four, a rise no longer meteoric; all the same, Imperial could continue to cry: *Ever upward!*

considered legal opinion, *junior rightholders*. The pioneers, from Wilber Clark to the Colorado River Land Company, had bought their rectangles of desert in good faith and irrigated them in hope and trust. *We need have no fear that our lands will not become better and better as the years go by.*

I sit in Sacramento alone on a hot August night, with Wilber Clark's land patent before me, and its words are as benevolently steadfast as anything in the Four Gospels.

The United States of America, *To all to whom these presents shall come, Greeting.* That is how the document begins.

If only I could express to you how those words make me feel! Earlier this evening I was reading a message sent from a despairing man in Senegal to an uneasy observer in my own country who in turn posted it on an electronic bulletin board where a friend of mine in Japan discovered it, sadly printed it out, and mailed it to me. The message was about my President, and it informed me, among other things, that *more than fifteen hundred persons have been arrested and put in jail between Thursday and Monday. Hopefully they will be released now that the Big Man is gone . . . All trees in places where Bush would pass have been cut. Some of them are more than a hundred years old.* On Goree Island, *for "security reasons" . . . the local population was chased out of their houses from five to twelve a.m. They were forced by the American security to leave their houses and leave everything open, including their wardrobes, to be searched by special dogs brought from the U.S.* This is the President I have now. This is my country. *There are now thousands of Senegalese who believe that for all Americans the world is their territory.* How much of this is true? Maybe none; I'd rather not know. What I read in the morning newspaper is bad enough. Well, so what? I prefer to imagine that I live in Wilber Clark's America, which is to say, **The United States of America,** ornate and proud—and archaic, to be sure; we need not say obsolete. Maybe I am obsolete, too. **The United States of America,** *To all to whom these presents shall come, Greeting.* And I seem to see America herself, personified by the Statue of Liberty, greeting all to whom these presents shall come.

Whereas, *a Certificate of the Register of the Land Office at Los Angeles, California, has been deposited in the General Land Office, whereby it appears that full payment has been made by the claimant Wilber Clark according to the provisions of the Act of Congress of April 24, 1820 . . .* **NOW KNOW YE,** *That the* UNITED STATES OF AMERICA, *in consideration of the premises, and in conformity with the several Acts of Congress in such case made and provided,* **HAS GIVEN AND GRANTED,** *and by these presents* **DOES GIVE AND GRANT,** *unto the said claimant and to the heirs of the said claimant* *the Tract above described;* **TO HAVE AND TO HOLD** *the same, together with all the rights, privileges, immunities, and appurtenances, of whatsoever nature, thereunto belonging, unto the said claimant and to the heirs and assigns of the said claimant forever.* To have and to hold forever; this I like very much and wish to believe in even though I'm aware that forever is an illusion. Moreover, now come the qualifications: *And to the heirs and assigns of the said claimant forever;* ***subject to any vested or accrued water rights*** *for mining, agricultural, manufacturing, or other purposes, and* ***rights to ditches and reservoirs used in connection with such water rights*** *, as may be recognized and acknowledged by the local customs, laws, and decisions of courts; and there is reserved from the lands hereby granted,* ***a right thereon for ditches or canals*** *constructed by the authority of the United States.*

In short, Northside can do as she pleases; other interests can try to get what *they* want. All the same, the lands have been hereby granted, to have and to hold, forever, and the United States of America greets all to whom these presents shall come. (Taft was President then, in the year of our Lord 1911, and of the independence of the United States the one hundred and thirty-fifth.) And the farms of Imperial had likewise been granted, to have and hold forever, together with all the rights, privileges, immunities, and appurtenances, of whatsoever nature, which is why during the drought of 1987, the Colorado River Project suffered *no reductions in deliveries.*

Not every water agency forgave that. By 1989, one out of every four Californians had fallen subject to mandatory water rationing; by 1991 it was three out of four, but the Colorado River Project suffered *no reductions in deliveries,* no matter that the years 1987-91 were drier than the previous five! Imperial County found that state of affairs convenient, especially in regard to lettuce.—Field crops are cheap to grow, said Richard Brogan. You can miss a day of water. You don't do that in lettuce. You work with laptop computers in the field making decisions, and if you don't apply chemicals in a twelve-hour period, they'll fire you. So they know in the hothouse, the broccoli is going to grow. They order water in advance. It's very time-sensitive. On the other hand, your flat crops, your Bermuda grass or wheat, tomorrow doesn't matter . . .

You want your broccoli year-round, don't you? Imperial asked the world. And you want it at a low price, right? Well, then no reductions in water deliveries for us, please, not ever!

WATER IS HERE. *In fact, earlier this year the Metropolitan Water District of Southern California, which supplies half the water delivered on the coastal plain from Ventura south to the Mexican border, received approval to run its Colorado River*

Aqueduct at full capacity. This will provide Southern California with a much-needed 1.2 million acre-feet of water supplies.

These words appear in a book whose authorship is appropriate: the Association of California Water Agencies. Which agencies, I wonder? The next sentence, written, so I suspect, in sentiments of spite and rage, gives a hint as to one of them: *MWD is entitled to only half that amount.* Who gets the other half, I wonder? They are the people who happened to get there first, and became entitled, so their patents imply, to have and hold forever their local waterscapes.

I sit in Sacramento, and read in my newspaper that these individuals are guilty of an *Imperial attitude.*

Imperial is a long, wide ditch with grass and trees on either side; I see a man and child fishing—no, I don't; this is not Imperial, not anymore.

Or is it? Kay Brockman Bishop said to me in 2006: You can still fish in the cement ditches. I must have seen four hundred little fish in there, from catfish to little bass . . .

"A TOTALLY OBSOLETE AND WASTEFUL ACTIVITY"

What should a waterscape be—a perfect checkerboard of sugarcube-fields in water, or a slurry of sugar-water? Instead, it's a sugary desert straining to suck up a pool of water.

In 1984, the State Water Resource Board decides a lawsuit against the Imperial Irrigation District, determining that it has *wasted* four hundred thousand acre-feet per year.

American Imperial wakes up anxious. All this time, she'd been dreaming that the Mexicans were the enemy! Now she can hear Tamerlane's warriors coming. Who will rescue her? She cannot trust even the empty round blue eye-sockets filled with darkness, the empty blue stone lips and red fangs of the darkness-filled mouth: Tlaloc the Aztec rain god. How many inches of rain did Brawley get last year?

Slowly, slowly, she falls back asleep. And in 1986 a longtime resident of Ocotillo complains about how *our life's blood, our water, was being hemorrhaged away as the noisy diesel trucks from Mexicali ground through the main street of our small hamlet, on their way to pick up water* from the Clifford Well, which had been *selling water to Mexicali businessmen* since sometime after 1958. Why did no Northsiders absent themselves from Ocotillo's nightmares?

By the middle of the 1990s, sixty percent of the Imperial Valley enjoys the wonders of absentee ownership. Two of those absentee owners, the infamous Bass brothers, construct a corporation called Western Farms. Their greed is as bare as the dirt of a Mexican cemetery. Promising that they have all but one of the Imperial Irrigation District's directors in their pocket, they offer *half a million annual acre-feet of water* to San Diego, taken from the water rights of their idled land.

San Diego hesitates, perhaps because Western Farms may not actually be able to sell those water rights. She decides to approach the Imperial Irrigation District directly. Meanwhile, Western Farms accepts suitable compensation to convey its forty-two thousand acres to the company called U.S. Filter, which gloats: *The water we have is 81 billion gallons a year in perpetuity.*

Are the Bass brothers villains or not?—You know, said Richard Brogan, when the Bass brothers came in, that was marginal, field crop ground. Bermuda grass.

And I remember how the same accusation once got leveled against the sellouts of the Owens Valley: *If the city did wrong in buying, they did wrong in selling.*

(Back at the beginning of the twentieth century, George Chaffey and the California Development Company were the first water farmers in the region. A historian writes: *The company was not planning to farm, but to sell water.*)

So which of Imperial's great and powerful was never a water farmer?

Tamerlane's warriors approach. In 2003, Andy Horne, the Director of Imperial Irrigation District One, coins a bitter definition: *Agriculture: Once thought to be an essential means of providing food and fiber for the nation, now a totally obsolete and wasteful activity engaged in by greedy farmers for the sole purpose of selfishly depriving cities and fish of their rightful share of water.*

Across the county line, Eleanor Shimeall, President of the Borrego Water District's Board of Directors, warns the San Diego County Board of Supervisors that her aquifer is becoming "fatally" overdrafted. A decade ago, groundwater was receding by one to two feet per year. Now it falls by two to five feet per year. What will save Borrego Springs? All the editors of the local newspaper can propose is to *give local farmers an equity mechanism for selling their land.* The citrus plantations on the north end are the worst water-wasters. Wouldn't it be nice if we could tear them out and replace them with golf courses and trailer parks?

In the unincorporated little town of Cabazon just west of Palm Springs, Harvey Williamson, the water board President, *watches the district's big wells drop a foot a month. The cause for the decline is a mystery.* The mysterious cause might be the Arrowhead bottling plant, a conjecture which Arrowhead naturally denies. What should Harvey Williamson do? *"We don't expect to run out next year," he says . . . "But if water levels keep dropping, we will run out someday." Imported water flowing through a pipeline could be the answer, he says.* In other words, let's buy or steal it from somebody else.

A seasoned private detective from San Diego tells me: All the incestuous, evil little politics going on, that's gone. Now all the corrections money, that has dramatically changed the towns. Before, there were little Chinese markets everywhere. Now it's all Sears, Wal-Marts, Kmarts. Bottom line is, it's just exploded. I just remain stunned at the way that from Temecula to El Centro the desert is booming like crazy! And the water, where's it going to come from? They're going to be fighting over water really soon . . .

I refuse to believe that. Once a man told me that the United States dollar could not keep weakening against other currencies, and when I asked him how he knew that, he confidently replied: Because any other possibility would be unthinkable!—In his dauntless spirit, I insist that Imperial's future remains as white as the clouds of steam arising from Tecate's brewery!

So does California's. Therefore, California keeps right on growing.

Back in 1967, the National Advisory Commission on Rural Poverty recommended that *no more public money be invested in developing privately owned farmland* until the nation needed more farm products.—Well, then, let's develop other zones of California!—And so the San Fernando Valley, which once comprised a subdivision of Mulholland-watered citrusscapes sold off by the Chandler Syndicate, has now boomed into true greatness on this cool moist October moment, the smog at bay, everything convenient thanks to wide streets with thirteen-stranded power poles, the turn signal resembling a sick child clicking its throat, the driver's consciousness low on the pavement as he speeds through intersections, heading east toward the mountains. A teenaged girl in pink pushes the button for a walk signal, the light going fast now from the orange sky, and that mall clock on a pillar shaped like a double-bladed axe proves that it is 5:07; 71°; the cold yellow orange digital display comprised of glossy spheres like flying fish eggs. Turning south on 405, one finds oneself heading for mountains behind an immense blue truck which screams **SAFE AND COURTEOUS**. A plane, blinking at the navel, slowly labors behind power wires; one then proceeds west past Pigeon World, and enters a very dark tunnel with a mural of fishes, and garages glowing red and blue in the direction of the wool-clot clouds, the beer factory silhouetted like children's toy pyramids, its pink smoke rising into the sky. *Hola* to La Brea Immanuel Mission Church! Then it's on to Koreatown, the crawling lights around the Young Dong Restaurant on Wilshire, and we ride through the night of Koreatown up to the stubby light-pixelated phalli and tombstones of skyscrapers beneath which tiny people scuttle, silhouetted by the cold colored lights of downtown Los Angeles.

Imperial's a miracle, all right; the All-American Canal's another miracle; housing "developments" are miracles, too, and even if we exclude our meditations to agriculture alone, I can think of a certain other place, oh, yes, and almost half a thousand miles it runs, green and tan, red and brown, that wide, flat groove between the Sierra Nevada and the Coast Range—yes, flat above all, dusty in summer, foggy in winter, and at rare snatches so clear that all the agricultural puzzle-pieces of it suddenly become as distinct as the silhouettes of the crows on its road-signs. It runs from Mount Shasta all the way south to Grapevine, split down the middle by the blue doglegging of the California Aqueduct. Black cows at sea in yellow grass, almond orchards laid out in vast grids which resemble military cemeteries, the shadowy hollows of tan-grassed hills, roads and houses infesting this outstretched land in whose midst hunkers the state capital, Sacramento; thus our great Central Valley, from which, they say, half of California's agricultural profit comes, vibrating like the I-5 Freeway itself. In comparison, the Imperial Valley's half a million irrigated acres mean little.

And more houses come to the Central Valley (whose residents never imagined they would compete with distant Imperial), and more cities grow. I wonder where their water will come from?

Here in the capital, the newspaper gives me fifteen "water-wise tips" including:

1. **Incorporate hardscape elements into your yard such as paths, boulders, decks and patios. None requires water.**

That comes from the "Drips and Drops" feature.

Will California's future years truly be pale as mummified fishes on gravel by night at Bombay Beach? Never! An oracle named Angela Anderson gets quoted in "Drips and Drops." She happens to be the water conservation administrator for Sacramento. *"We just ask that water is used efficiently so that we have an ample water supply for new developments and existing homes," says Anderson.*

New developments! Well, then **WATER** must still be **HERE**. What a relief!

Herbert Marcuse, 1955: *The individual comes to the traumatic realization that full and painless gratification of his needs is impossible. And after this experience of disappointment . . . the reality principle supersedes the pleasure principle.*

But here at the San Diego County Water Authority, we now sell almost six hundred thousand acre-feet of water per year to our thirty-two members—everyone from Chula Vista to Ramona to Oceanside, not to mention twenty-nine others, and, to be frank, we don't subscribe to the reality principle. We don't need to, since **WATER IS HERE**. More strictly speaking, water is in Imperial, but we have never been cheated out of a water-drop in our lives. (At the Travelodge in San Diego I asked old Dick: Do you think it will rain today?—He proudly replied: It never rains in southern California.) So let's sit down with Metropolitan and Interior to prepare our ambush. Imperial is weak; so let *her* discover the reality principle! That way, we can enjoy the pleasure principle a few years longer . . .

EIGHTY PERCENT

In the month of May, 1991, when Los Angeles finds itself compelled to live with a water-usage reduction of twenty-six point five percent (the Marin Municipal Water District suffers worst of all, with a fifty-percent cutback), certain selfish nobodies, whose identity the Association of California Water Agencies tactfully reserves for another page, experience no water shortage at all!

Not being tactful, I'll let you in on the secret right away: These sinners inhabit the Imperial and Coachella valleys. Sharing their guilt are the parasites of the Yuma Indian Reservation Project and the Palo Verde Irrigation District. Almost *eighty percent* of California's share of Colorado River water goes to those four, simply because they were there first! To those water-accountants among you who crave hard numbers, read on: The All-American Canal continues to spill as much as three million delicious acre-feet of Colorado River water into the Coachella and Imperial valleys every year—twice the quantity that the Mexicali Valley gets. Never mind Mexico; what about *us*? My fellow San Diegans and Angelenos, oh, my dear thirsty brethren in National City, my cousin victims in Escondido, my angry friends in Long Beach, would you call the distribution of water-wealth in our great state equitable? Just as California lemons run the risk of turning grey and oozing with sour rot fungus, so our patience nears blight or outright spoliation; I'm referring to our long-standing, self-denying, and ultimately preposterous forbearance with the yokels of Imperial! ***TO HAVE AND TO HOLD,*** *forever.* Never fear; we have money and numbers. We're going to get them.

THE EARTHQUAKE WITHOUT CASUALTIES

And so as the millennium turned, Imperial's eponymous county got squeezed by San Diego, Los Angeles, to whose vast water district San Diego had belonged for half a century now, and even the United States Interior Department.

(I asked Richard Brogan: Would you say there's more pressure on Imperial from San Diego, Los Angeles, Coachella or the Inland Empire?

He replied: In my very general and brief experience, I think the Metropolitan Water District is the biggest, the most capable and the least open.)

The urbans, as Imperial County called them, requested her to sign a water-transfer agreement which would begin to dry up the farms in whose name she had come into being. (We need have no fear that our lands will not become better and better as the years go by.) Ask the ghost of Phil Swing what would happen should water be withdrawn from a preexisting huddle of human beings. *It would constitute the economic murder of any community which we stood by and permitted to develop with the use of this water,* he replies. (That's 1925. He's talking about Mexican Imperial. He wants us to get that water first and build the All-American Canal, before Mexicali and Tijuana grow too big.) One academic compared the economic losses which the water transfer would exact upon Imperial County as similar to those of an earthquake with a magnitude of 7.5. San Diego restated his conclusion as follows: *The urban agencies, which used to divert this water from the river at virtually no cost, will now be paying to implement agricultural water conservation programs that make transfer water available without economically harming the agricultural community.* And on Coronado and Wilshire, trees and silver-grey building-windows cool your gaze; then, whirling round the corner in your Los Angeles automobile, you meet a burst of sun, more glorious trees and a fountain's white spurt.

OTHER AUTHORIZED USES

WATER IS HERE. *We just ask that water is used efficiently so that we have an ample water supply for new developments and existing homes.* There is an abundant supply of water. *Surely one of Coachella Valley's defining images into the next millennium is of beautiful green fairways and blue lakes, often ringed with the rugged rocks and desert plants they have replaced.*

And California's smacking her thirst-cracked lips! She's not particular anymore; she longs even to slurp up the *aguas negras* of the New River, then wash it down with selenium-salted gulps of the Salton Sea! In 1983, the year after La Quinta incorporates and two years before the urban population of Baja California reaches one million, three hundred and fifty thousand, the United States informs Mexico that even the seepage waters drooling out of the All-American Canal belong to *us.* We reserve the right to lay down concrete, thereby preserving our water from crossing without permission to Southside. A laudatory biography of William Mulholland concludes: *In spite of rationing, and even with the possibility of a new aqueduct, it is unlikely that the region's critical water problems can be solved. As the twenty-first century approached, the same problems that challenged William Mulholland confronted the city* of Los Angeles *again.* Well, one can't blame Los Angeles for trying to solve it! In 2003, she applies for nearly half a million acre-feet of New River water *(purpose of use: municipal and industrial).* Eagerly seconding her, the federal government, Imperial County's new enemy, decries the fact that so much water fails to return to the Colorado River, as opposed to *the return flows of many other,* I presume saintlier, *water contractors within the Lower Colorado River Basin.* (Why doesn't it return? Because the Imperial Valley is at or below sea level.) Oh, the outrage of that! You see, since they dead-end in the Salton Sea, the stinking fluids of the New River, the Alamo and the Whitewater *are no longer available for other authorized uses or users.*

In response, American Imperial sends out this cry to *My Fellow Farmers Throughout California:* We need *your support to withstand the largest attack on agricultural water rights in California since Owens Valley.* Warning: *This is a precedent for ag communities all across California and the rest of the arid southwest.*

SHOT 107

```
. . . The Emir stares before him, whispering:

"He who controls water--is the victor . . ."
```

"We just ask that water is used efficiently so that we have an ample water supply for new developments and existing homes," says Anderson.

SHOT 108

```
. . . Tamerlane's warriors gallop into the
square . . .
```

"AN ABUNDANT SUPPLY OF WATER"

Fortunately, Southside suffers no such worries. The Mexicali yellow pages for 2002–03 assure me, in prose which could have been written about Imperial County in 1950:

> **Fertile Lands Surrounded by the Desert**
> The Valley of Mexicali is the most important agrarian region in the state. There is an abundant supply of water, and, with a watering capacity for 220,000 hectares, it has proved its fertility for the cultivation of cotton and other grains.

Meanwhile in Tijuana, whose people drink up water from wells, the subterranean source of the La Misión stream, the Tijuana and Las Palmas rivers and of course the Colorado, the television announces **SUSPENSION OF WATER** and rapidly lists many *colonias* in small type. But their water has suffered a suspension mainly because their arteries needed cleaning. Call it the merest *inconvenience,* not a *shortage.* An agronomist in Tijuana informs his visitor: *At this moment, we are not in a water crisis.* He continues: *Agriculture goes well in this state, but not in Tijuana. It's mostly because of the water here.*

In 2005, Mexico files suit against the United States in an attempt to halt the lining of the All-American Canal, which will result in a loss to the Mexicali Valley of between sixty-six and eighty-one thousand acre-feet per year. The practical effects of Northside's frugality will be a fourteen-percent decrease in the water that the valley can draw on, a nine- to twenty-foot drop in the water table near the canal, and significantly increased salinity. One commentator worries about a possible eco-catastrophe. Another predicts a nine-percent decrease in crop productivity. In other words, *there is an abundant supply of water.*

In 2003 Richard Brogan had said to me: Have you ever been down along the Mexican side of the All-American Canal? And now the Americans are talking about lining the canal. Imagine what's going to happen there. That's how they live there, from that water.

Stella Mendoza, the former President of the Imperial Irrigation District, had said: Well, you know that now that they're going to line the All-American Canal, and that water that's been seeping out—it's about sixty, seventy thousand gallons—the Mexicali farmers have been pumping that out. What's going to happen to them? That's something that we as the IID need to talk about. The lining, the engineering has already started, so it's going to happen within the next five years.

The San Diego Water Authority refused comment as usual.

(The private investigator in San Diego comforted me by explaining that Mexicans were worse than Americans: They'll starve out a whole *colonia* of people to sell water to the United States. If you want to exploit a Mexican, put another Mexican in charge! The exploitation will reach heights we can never dream of.)

There was a hairdresser in Luis Río de Colorado named Evalía Pérez de Navarro. She had lived in that place since about 1968. In 2003 she said: My grandfather had a ranch thirty years ago. There was like a canal, a very big canal. When I was seven or eight and on Grandfather's ranch, it was very pretty. There used to be a lot of foliage—small bushes and small pines—and it kept the water from spreading out. My uncle was the President of the organization for cleaning the water.

When did the river start to change?

Thirty or forty years ago. The first thing I noticed was that I could see a lot of salt on the highway and the cotton wasn't growing as much.

No one drinks out of the tap anymore, she said. If you spill on the floor, it leaves white salt. If you drive to Mexicali, you can see where the salt has deposited on the land. It happens when it rains. A week or two after the rain has dried, you can see the white part. And in my garden, some things are more difficult. For gardening we buy soil from other places. We can use it a year or less.

So, how would you describe the water situation?

It's not normal, but it's not something that we can really fix.

And in Mexicali?

The water in Mexicali is bad. It smells bad.*

*"I haven't talked to the folks in the Mexicali Valley," said Stella Mendoza. "All I know is that when the water gets to Mexico from Algodones, it's not so good."

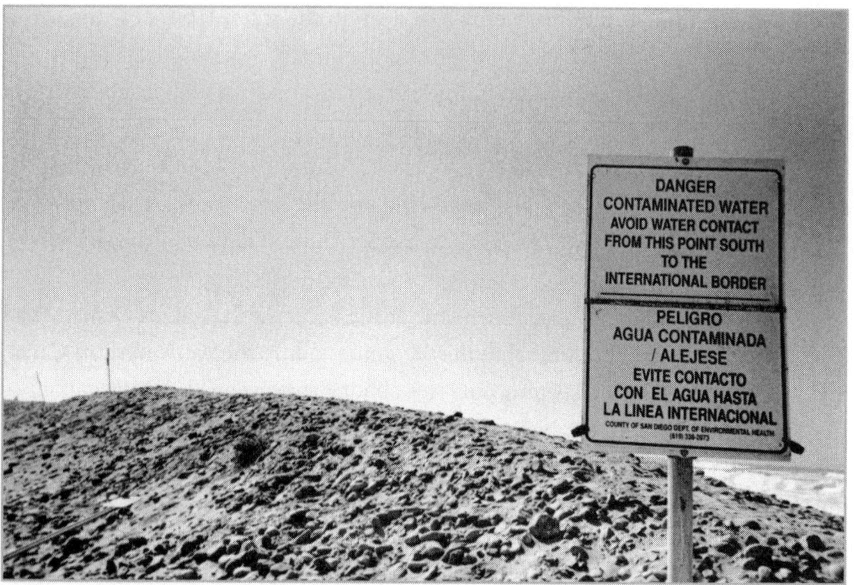

Pacific Ocean, Imperial Beach, 2002

IT'S ALL RELATIVE

Please recall that at the beginning of the twentieth century, when the Imperial and Mexicali valleys first began to drink from the Colorado in earnest, the salinity of that river-water was four hundred parts per million. Now at the century's end five Mexican scientists lament the impending loss of All-American Canal seepage, treasuring this *good-quality groundwater* whose salinity is nine to thirteen hundred parts per million. Northside's act will nearly double the salinity of Mexicali's aquifer over the next twenty years. Cotton, wheat, rye and sorghum production should be unaffected; alfalfa will decline by twenty percent and green onions, a crop which *generates the largest need for labor in the area,* by fifty-eight percent.

But why despair? Mexican Imperial might be able to save some water by irrigating as efficiently as they do in Northside . . .

NEWS FLASH FROM CALEXICO

By the way, how *is* water quality up in Northside?

The water comes in out of the cement ditch there and it comes into our own cistern, Kate Brockman Bishop was saying to me. That blue pump tower down there, that's water we give to the Mexicans that goes to Ensenada. It's been there fifteen, twenty years.

I asked about salinity on her land, and she said: It's worse now than it used to be.

NO TIME TO WORRY

In 1985, a paper was delivered by Eduardo Paredes Arellano, Secretaria de Agricultura y Recursos Hidráulicos, Mexicali. *The greatest danger threatening the future of our civilization is the rapid reduction of water resources, . . .* he advised us. Someday industries might fail and cities disperse due to lack of water! *"We just ask that water is used efficiently so that we have an ample water supply for new developments and existing homes," says Anderson.* Fortunately, Mexican Imperial was enjoying a period of high rain in those years: Between 1979 and 1981, nearly nine thousand million cubic meters of Río Colorado water drained into the Mexicali Valley. **WATER IS HERE**. Moreover, the aqueduct from the Río Colorado to Tijuana was nearly done; ten more waterworks were proposed. Then Baja California would enjoy an abundant supply of water, I'm sure. Here came still another suggestion, made in a spirit of sincere international neighborliness: *It should be pointed out that along the international boundaries between Mexico and the United States the water basin of the Tijuana-Alamar rivers is one of the few that flows toward the United States of America, for which reason its immediate exploitation,* in other words its complete retention by Mexico, *is required and recommended.* More wonderful news: In Irrigation District 014 of the Colorado River, which included Mexicali, the authorities of Mexico were working with the Banco de Crédito Rural to "recuperate" salt-infiltrated soils. We need have no fear that our lands will not become better and better as the years go by. *It is pertinent to point out that all of the privately owned wells for agricultural uses* have outlived their usefulness,* which must mean that they've gone salty or dry. *Therefore it is necessary to implement the financing that would allow their total rehabilitation.*

In Mexican Imperial, people must buy two kinds of water: the kind they drink, and the other kind. At the turn of the century, household water (for washing and the like) cost between a hundred and two hundred pesos a month. Bottled water was the same again or more.†

Northwest of San Luis Río Colorado, in the *ejido* called Ciudad Morelos, Don Carlos Cayetano Sanders Collins told me: It's not hard to get it, but the problem is, it's very expensive. Although I only pay a hundred and fifty pesos a month for what we use in our household, I pay ten pesos per liter for agricultural use. One five-day

*In the district there were 236 of them.

†The interviews through which I obtained this information appear in the references to this chapter.

cycle takes a hundred and ten liters for my thirty hectares. So it costs me four or five thousand pesos per month.

That *is* expensive, I agreed.

It comes from electric sprinklers, he added, a little proudly, I thought.

Is there much salt in the water, or not much?

He nodded. It puts my crops in danger. But ten or fifteen miles up the road, there's Presa Morelos. When it goes through the *presa,* then it's okay.

Which of your crops is the most endangered by salt?

Cotton.*

And which crop needs the most water?

It's all the same.

Are you worried about the future of your water?

There's no time to worry. I have enough to do, paying for it now.

E. J. Swayne, townsite of Imperial, California, 1901: *It is simply needless to question the supply of water.*

IN WHICH THE ARTESIAN WELLS COME BACK TO LIFE

Who are you and I, to disagree with E. J. Swayne? Leonard Coates from Fresno backs him up. And if you want more proof, do you remember all those artesian wells which a work of alarmist fiction entitled *Imperial* insists have dried up? In the Motor Transport Museum in Campo, where the former Julian stagecoach lay in state (a quack in Borrego Springs replaced its transmission with a generator in order to sell his patients therapeutic electric shocks), old Carl Calvert, having shown off this marvel to me, referred in a voice of experience to a carbonated well from the turn of the last century; one could still see it bubbling, he said; moreover, there'd been artesian wells in Rancho Santa Fe just last week!—Do you know what fed them? he laughed. Runoff from lawn irrigation from a development up the hill . . .

*In fact. although cotton does need a lot of water, and this might be the factor that he had in mind, it remains an extremely salt-tolerant crop.

Chapter 157

AS PRECIOUS AS THIS

(2003)

And behold the people, the subjects are perishing! . . .
The breast of our mother and father, Lord of the Earth, is dry . . .

—Aztec hymn to Tláloc the rain god

How will Tamerlane's warriors feint? In which poison will they dip their arrows? American Imperial warns **My Fellow Farmers** that here's what will happen: *MWD will pay higher prices for short-term water transfers to maintain the appearance of reliability, while at the same time attacking agricultural uses, on the basis of inefficiency or whatever, in order to procure a long-term water supply . . .*

. . . for instance, the All-American Canal, which flows blue or brown or grey, depending on the sky, between berms of dirt, with reeds on either side to give the pretense that there is more to it than utility; once the canal gets lined, the reeds will die. Here's Pilot Knob, a rolling purplish dark hunk of something volcanic, sprawling on the horizon with white streaks of salt or mineral wriggling down it. Not far away runs a long white wriggling geoglyph of the four-headed snake which the Quechan creator-spirit Kumat threw into the sea a long time ago, to save people from its rattles. The snake came back, and Kumat had to kill it with a stone knife. Then another snake of reddish-brown water slithered here, when George Chaffey opened his main gate and the Imperial Valley began to turn green.

And the All-American Canal bores on through the desert as far as I can see in both directions, just dirt-lips and a smile of water in between; far away, perhaps in Andrade, a child's voice takes to the wind.

MWD will pay higher prices. MWD is but one of Tamerlane's divisions. Don't forget San Diego, Coachella, Nevada, Arizona, Interior . . .

It is simply needless to question the supply of water.

And so California's entities argue angrily, pettily, and pathetically about who is using water best. Whose proof of reasonable and beneficial use will prevail?

Here is how Imperial argues.—Wait; I admit that there *is* no one Imperial. The water farmers draw the line against the farmers of cantaloupes, lettuce and tomatoes. (Richard Brogan shook his head and said: The sad part of it, a lot of these families are starting to feud. The old men put something together during the Second World War and accumulated thousands of acres. Now they got sons and daughters who are feuding).*—But if there *were* one Imperial, and if there were a "we," this is how we would argue against the world:

Even American Imperial's archfoe, the Bureau of Reclamation, confesses that our "on-farm efficiency" of water use in Imperial has achieved between seventy-two and eighty-three percent over the past sixteen years; while Coachella's was only fifty-seven to seventy percent. As for Los Angeles, *MWD admits that 30–70% of residential use is in outdoor landscaping.*† . . . *MWD's "efficiency" is thus well below 70%, and without careful measuring of the inflow or outflow.* While we in Imperial go innocently about our business of raising *food and fiber for the nation,* MWD spends too much time regulating flush toilets and not enough time slapping down golf courses. After all, Los Angeles is, among other things, the restaurant Crustacean in Beverly Hills, whose slogan is "Cuisine from Another World," because *when you enter, you are drawn to another world: Indochina of the 1930s. An 80-foot-long river filled with exotic koi elegantly leads you to the dining room.* That's what I call reasonable and beneficial use.

From 1936 to 2002 (the latest year for which I have figures), the Imperial Irrigation District has consistently used between two point seven and three million acre-feet per year—about twice what Mexico gets. No doubt it could save water, but certainly it has not drunk more than its allotment for a very long time.

MWD has its own argument. San Diego possesses an argument. Who cares *what* they all argue? I'll tell you *how* they argue: My friend Lupe Vásquez always kept his broccoli knife in his backpack, not on his belt, because he knew his own temper when he got provoked. The last time he'd fought was thirteen years ago

*At the beginning of this book I remarked on the necessary secrecy of life itself in sunstruck Imperial, and that hiddenness extended itself to the water transfer. One of my favorite memories from 2002 was awarded me by the local reporter on whom I dropped in to ask in all innocence for pointers as I wrote my book about his valley; he said that he didn't know anything, and would I please not put him in my book? I asked whether he had any opinions about the water transfer to San Diego and he didn't, although twenty steps away, in the hot brightness just outside that office cube, was a vending machine through whose window the upper front page of the newspaper revealed itself, and precisely there shone an article about the water transfer; the article bore his byline. He explained, and I pitied him for his cowardice, that he strove simply to report the facts, so as not to offend anybody, and maybe that would have impressed me had he not (in that hot slow world where most people dismissed unwanted callers by means of phased withdrawal or wearily shrugging indifference; they rarely scuttle away with outright precipitation; for Imperial is the dirty man in Mexicali who carefully carries both his broom and his filth-encrusted dustpan for an entire block in order to empty the latter in the one receptacle; this operation has been known to take as long as ten minutes) had he not, I said, been so desperate to get rid of me; he might simply have felt overwhelmed by some deadline, but he seemed to me *afraid.*

†In one of the IID's legal briefs from this same period, the figure, and the way that it is stated, varies slightly: ". . . of the total 9.6 MAF [million acre-feet] of water use in Southern California in 1995, *about 1.893 MAF (28%) was used to irrigate urban landscapes*" (italics in original).

when a kid kept throwing lettuce on his table when it was already full because the woman packer was getting behind. Lupe told him to stop, but he didn't, so Lupe called the foreman, who made the kid stop. Then, when it might have been over, Lupe threw some lettuce on the kid's table, *just to show him what it was like.* The kid wanted to fight him right there on the field. Lupe told him to wait. So he followed Lupe down the street after they had finished in the broccoli field. Lupe told him it was over, but the kid wouldn't listen; Lupe accordingly swung at him and kept swinging until a bystander pulled him off; and when he got to this part, Lupe remarked that he had been lucky that nobody called the police. I wonder whether anybody at least dragged the kid into the shade or whether they left him lying in the street. At any rate, here comes the punchline: Next day the kid didn't show up for work.—I'll never forget the vengeful sparkling of Lupe's eyes as he told me this.—Los Angeles, San Diego and Imperial argue about water in that spirit.

Those birds squeaking and chuckling in a plantation of date palms in Coachella, they must be drinking something somewhere; doesn't that imply on-farm inefficiency?

In beleaguered Imperial County, near the border and east of the Highline Canal, on the white soft dirt the grass is as lush as a collie-dog's hair. More inefficiency! The silhouette of a dragonfly occludes one after another in a series of parallel power wires, and then a bird calls. The cool fragrant shadows begin to outstretch from the bushes beneath which they slept. I can smell water—that means water's a-wasting!

On a Mexicali morning, men on the arch-roofed sidewalks are chatting with the vendors with their multicolored juices in huge transparent jug-shaped jars; now it's hot; people sweat and lick their lips; in the jars the juices are beautiful; water is as precious as this.

Chapter 158

ONE ACRE-FOOT

(1903–2003)

Those politicians, they're just promising and promising, very eloquently as my father always used to say, but when they're by themselves, they're thinking, how can I make dough?

—Lupe Vásquez, 2002

In 1975, the *California Water Atlas* defines an acre-foot as the amount needed by a family of five for a year, *including lawn and garden irrigation*. In 2003, the San Diego County Water Authority explains that an acre-foot is *the amount of water used by two typical households in a year*. So we're getting more efficient, aren't we?

We have already noted that in 1950, the average per capita water usage in San Diego County was not quite eighty-one gallons per day. In 2000, that figure is a hundred and twenty-five gallons per day. Well, why not? **WATER IS HERE**.

The Mexicali Valley contains as many irrigated acres as the Imperial, but gets only half as much water, thanks to the All-American Canal. But in 2000, Mexicali uses a San Diego–like hundred and seventeen gallons per day per capita. So there must be poor people who use less, quite a bit less—for instance José López from Jalisco. On a hot March midmorning the sunlight probes inside the doorway of the Hotel Nuevo Pacífico to reveal a whore whose electric-blue miniskirt clashes perfectly with her huge red slabs of crossed thigh-flesh; José, who would certainly be more of a ladies' man had his circumstances permitted, refrains from peeking; he is especially embarrassed about his two black front teeth, which continue to decay because he so often lacks good water to brush them with; moreover, his clothes smell in the heat; we must thank him for saving water for Northside.

Tijuana's "normal requirement"* is between two hundred fifty and three hundred fifty liters per capita per day—call it eighty gallons. Tijuana actually gets a hundred and eighty-nine liters per day, or five-eighths of the desired amount.

* Mid-1980 figures, the most recent available.

In 1920, water availability in Baja California was more than twenty-five cubic meters per capita per year; in 1984, it was four point five cubic meters.

An essay called "U.S.–Mexico Border Environment by the Numbers" estimates that at the beginning of the twenty-first century, average per capita water consumption in Mexico border communities is a hundred gallons per day. In Albuquerque, it is two hundred gallons per day. I can't help believing in people.

In 1998, farmers in Imperial County pay thirteen dollars and fifty cents per acre-foot. San Diego is prepared to pay two hundred and forty-nine dollars.

One acre of alfalfa in the Imperial Valley needs six acre-feet of water. That will cost the farmer eighty-one dollars. On the other hand, if he fallows his field and becomes a water farmer, he could sell those six acre-feet to San Diego for fourteen hundred and ninety-four dollars. How much can he get for an acre of alfalfa? I see that the county's yield per acre in 1998 was seven point six five tons, each ton of which sold for ninety-three dollars and sixty-four cents. Call his income seven hundred and sixteen dollars—half of what San Diego would pay him to fallow. If we factor in his labor and expenses, water farming looks even nicer. And, remember, alfalfa is one of the most cost-effective crops an Imperialite can raise.*

One acre-foot—what is it but a unit of power?—Richard Brogan once said of a certain farming family in the Imperial Valley, and I have changed the name: His wife is extremely involved in Farm Bureau politics. He and she, they are extremely huge.† *I understand that they can order a thousand acre-feet of water every twenty-four hours,* he said, folding his arms.—In Smith Farms, when everything is done, it's all planted right now, they want that first cutting before June. *Smith Farms alone can draw down the level of the All-American Canal.*

One acre-foot: How should it be used—to maintain a family farm that no one quite believes in, or for profit? Judge Farr again, 1918: *As has already been learned by the reader of this volume, the financial end of the great project in this Valley has overshadowed every other feature from its inception.*

*Report ftom Paul Foster, farmboy turned programmer: "Alfalfa is an ag economist's dream of the benefits of comparative advantage. Heat-tolerant, highly responsive to irrigation, and a major beneficiary of a long growing season (this results in more cuttings and higher yields for the later cuttings), alfalfa is the shining exception to the general rule of declining field crops over the decades" in Imperial County. "Despite dramatic swings in market prices, alfalfa has been a reliable performer, especially when measured by the $/acre yardstick . . . I suspect that only cantaloupes and melons would rival it for consistency in its contribution to the Imperial economy. It has also benefited from improvements in harvest technology, dramatically lowering the labor component required."

†"The Smith family haven't been wealthy very long. You hear a lot of stuff. Especially that second wife. She's an heir to"—and Mr. Brogan named a very big company.

Chapter 159

OPERATION GATEKEEPER

(1994)

"Criminals" is what they are even if you try to sugarcoat it by saying they are dreamers. How would you feel if you lost a loved one because an alien slammed into your family's car? I bet you would sue the Border Patrol for negligence. Heck, that is where the money is . . .

To finalize this letter, I ask you, what is enough, 1 million illegals, 10 million or until the other countries are empty. Use your college education to figure it out.

—Juan Arvizu, letter to the editor, 2003

In 1962, the journalist Ruben Salazar assured us that from one end to the other of that eighteen-hundred-mile border, not a single soldier stood on either side. *A chain link fence is all that separates the two nations for about half that distance; the waters of the Rio Grande do the job for the rest of the way.*

A quarter century went by; and in 1986, the year that Leonard Knight buckled down to his true life's work and began painting Salvation Mountain, the U.S. Immigration Reform and Control Act solved a certain problem for eternity by punishing employers of illegal workers and amnestying four-year permanent residents. The very same page of the history book I got this fact out of informs me that in 1989, earnings posted to Mexico by illegal workers were *the country's third largest source of foreign exchange.* Perhaps the prospects for denying illegals access into American Imperial were approximately as flat as the desert on the eastern shore of the Salton Sea.

In 1949, there had been a hundred and seven thousand braceros, but more than two hundred and thirty-three thousand illegals got caught by the Border Patrol.

In 1974, they nabbed almost seven hundred and ten thousand illegals. In the early 1990s, they bagged forty thousand *bodies* per year in Sector El Centro alone.

Once upon a time, Southside was our frontier. We raped away half of Mexico and convinced ourselves that it was for *their* good, too. We extended the Imperial

Irrigation District right into the Mexicali Valley. We passed the Volstead Act, then roared into Southside whenever we wanted to get drunk.

But *they* started coming over here.

This is the biggest drug corridor in California, said the woman from Jacumba. If they're bringing *bodies,* the *bodies* have drugs, because that's their ticket. I'm sick of it. People from China ending up on my doorstep! Chinese! I live one mile from the border and I'm sick of it. They're all convicted felons. No one can do a thing because they can just run twenty feet and they're across the border. Out here, you can't be out here by yourself. You need a dog. Too many weirdos. Close the goddamn borders! They have to build some kind of infrastructure and maintain it. All this traffic coming across, it's gotta stop. But by the time we're dead it'll have already changed because of all the foreigners comin' in. You go from here to Kearny Mesa, it's all in Chinese and Japanese. The whole frigging town! That's bullshit. We gotta limit immigration, really limit it. First thing we gotta do is clean house and get rid of all the illegals.

What would it take to stop them? Why, first a fence, and then a better fence!

It was time for Operation Gatekeeper, to which *pollos* and coyotes responded with the hollowed-out gas tank, the child in the piñata, the plank beneath the car. In 1995, eighty percent of the people apprehended along the California-Mexico border were pedestrians. By 2004, eighty percent of them were in vehicles.

The line kept straining to hold, especially at the Pacific, because in the 1980s, half of all illegal border-crossers along the entire stretch between Northside and Southside went through Tijuana. That was why Operation Gatekeeper would set out to harden that sector. I remember when they caught eight El Sal juveniles at ten-thirty at night when it was time to take off the uniforms and go home. A Border Patrolman told me, not without pride: Our shift isn't over until everybody we caught is processed.

In 1989, Northside officially launched the War on Drugs. Guess which industry would now enjoy a great future down in Southside?

In 1994, Northside began Operation Gatekeeper. Guess which growing business got to raise its prices in Southside?

In the ringing words of Adele Fasano, Southern California Director of Field Operations, United States Customs and Border Patrol, *it all comes down to desperation, and the smugglers—being as depraved as they are—they prey on people's desperation and human misery,** unlike Adele Fasano herself, who gets paid to try to repress that

*Salvation Mountain's Leonard Knight, whom I had never before heard speak ill of anybody, said of certain coyotes: "I think it's disgusting. I heard they hung some people up in a tree last year and leave 'em to die. But I guess we're all doin' the best we can . . ."—I asked what he thought about illegal labor, and he said: "I don't think those rich orchard owners should give 'em a job."

human misery by keeping it in Southside. Meanwhile, American produce remains cheap, and wages to field workers accordingly low. *The constant threat of heavy shipments . . . seemed to be the depressing factor.* We read that sentence years ago; it applied to Imperial Valley lettuce prices. It seems no less apposite in relation to the incomes *pollos* can command.

Read on if you dare; the very next paragraph retails and details the true story of a depraved smuggler!

Once I asked a man named José López—not the Jose Lopez with whom I rafted on the New River but the one you and I now know better, the person from Jalisco who became my long-term friend, the unwashed middle-aged man of thirty-eight who frequently slept on one of the shaded sidewalk benches just a few steps Mexico-ward of the line—which had been the smoothest of his sixteen illicit crossings, and he replied: They cut a hole in the fence about three years ago;* they cut out a bar, actually. There was a parked car right next to the old Immigration office. The guy who owned that car was a friend of mine. Well, I went through; I crossed the line. I was sure that the Border Patrol had seen me but they hadn't. And I hid in the car. My friend came in about five minutes and he took me to San Diego. That was an easy one, real easy! He's from Mexico, but he has a green card. The relationship we had, as friends, it means that we've done favors for each other without expecting money or anything like that. Yeah, that was an easy one. I stayed four months in San Diego. Then I went to Bakersfield to pick lettuce for a month. I was supposed to go to Salinas, but I got caught . . .

He claimed that seventy-five percent of the time he came back voluntarily. He sent his dollars home to Mexico by Western Union.

I requested his opinion of the border. He said: Sometimes when I get to thinking about it, I've had bad feelings toward them, their American system. They play it off to being just and equal, but they're just as corrupt as anybody. I still think that California and all those states that were robbed from Mexico, I don't know, I don't know; I don't have the words. Like when I get caught by Immigration and thrown out of a place that used to be Mexico, I get pissed off.

I am proud to report that in 1996, in Sector El Centro alone, the Border Patrol saved Northside from sixty-six thousand, six hundred and eighty people like him.

In 1997 they caught a hundred and forty-six thousand, two hundred and ten.

In 1998 they caught two hundred thousand.

Well, if a merely upgraded fence failed to stop them, we might require a *militarized* fence! Accordingly, our eager, grateful and well-informed taxpayers rushed to fund the next phase of Operation Gatekeeper.

*Which would have been in 2000.

Over its first decade, more than three thousand illegals would perish *since,* as a Mexican source explains it, *Operation Gatekeeper . . . increased the vulnerability and mortality of undocumented immigrants.* One newspaper calculates that these deaths constituted a five-hundred-percent increase, although whether that is a per capita or absolute figure I cannot tell. We need have no fear that our lands will not become better and better as the years go by.

There were more than two hundred and fifty illegal-alien deaths along the border from October 2002 until October 2003—a record. Seventy of those corpses were found in the Imperial Valley. That was what the newspaper said.* On the same page, I read that a dead illegal alien had been found in Ash Canal; a second body was found an hour later. On the next page, a woman in Los Angeles got sentenced to nine years for imprisoning and beating illegal immigrants who couldn't pay her coyote fee.

In 2003 about twenty-five thousand people were apprehended hidden in vehicles crossing from Mexico to California.

In 2004, it was almost fifty thousand.

But do you remember what Border Patrolwoman Gloria Chavez said to me? *Before Gatekeeper, we were arresting half a million people a year. In 1998 there were only two hundred and forty-eight thousand in detention.* So please help yourself to whichever numbers suit your agenda.

FOLK WISDOM FROM THE HUNGRIEST STATE

Up in Oregon, which of course was never in Old Mexico, a teacher sought to help his students understand what he called *The Line Between Us.* Operation Gatekeeper then was a decade old. (North of Ciudad Juárez, Operation Hold the Line was making splendid progress; Operation Safeguard was improving the world in Nogales.) The teacher asked his pupils what they made of it all.

One student said: If we treat them good, there'll be more of them who want to come.

Oregon is the hungriest state, said another. People here are dying of starvation. Why should we support people who don't belong here?

MORE DEPRAVITY

Lamentably for these supporters of Operation Gatekeeper, the *pollos* were going to keep right on coming no matter how badly they got treated, no matter how hungry Oregonians might be.

*Along the entire border, someone now meets death each day attempting to come into Northside. Fortunately for this book, only a small proportion of the line runs through the entity that I call Imperial.

José López once said to me: This summer I'm gonna try to get as much work as I can, guiding tourists. I'll try to pay a coyote. That's my surest shot. Just to jump, since I cannot save eighteen hundred dollars, so I'm praying to God I can at least pay four hundred, four-fifty, just to jump the fence. Thank God, I know a little bit of English.

Then he said what would have gladdened the patriotic guardians of *the hungriest state:* If by summer's end I don't have any success, I'm gonna have to go back home, Bill. Save money and try again. It's just a constant goal.

Why not bring your family here?

Because, Bill, sometimes I suffer too much, Bill. At least they have a roof over their heads. I mean, there are two young kids, man.

He had no success that summer, which was 2003. All the same, he stayed put in 2004 and 2005. In 2006 I didn't see him. *Why should we support people who don't belong here?*

At the beginning of President Zedillo's term, which approximated the commencement of Gatekeeper, Subcomandante Marcos and the insurgents of Chiapas constituted a continuing embarrassment to a government which had swung far rightwards of the Revolution, weakening its power to coax in foreign capital. The peso lost nearly half its value between December 1994 and January 1995; then it continued dropping. Northside loaned Mexico twenty billion dollars; improvements in the economy resulted; and those solved everything.

Thirteen years into Operation Gatekeeper, it seemed to me that Mexican Imperial was more Americanized, which meant among other things more materially prosperous. Much of rural Mexico, however, had grown poorer. In brief, *it all comes down to desperation, and the smugglers—being as depraved as they are—they prey on people's desperation and human misery,*

I asked a woman in Ejido Netzahualcóyotl whether many people jumped the border near her home, and she said: Right now not really, but four or five years ago, tons of people used to cross here. They used to ask us for water and I would give it to them, with their little kids in the heat . . .

What a depraved smuggler she was!

In a photograph, three young Mexicans, two women and a man, nestle helplessly in a trunk into which a Border Patrolman peers with calm alertness. *If we treat them good, there'll be more of them who want to come.* So raise a toast to Operation Gatekeeper, now serving you at the gas station in Winterhaven whose proprietor had been there since the seventies but was originally from Michigan; he said that we had just caught eight more illegals right *here* this morning (May 2003); he came out, portly and sweating, to stand beside me and watch three more getting frisked up against the side of a white jail-on-wheels, three submissive darkskinned men in dusty clothes.

Chapter 160

THE FARM WATER QUALITY MANAGEMENT PLAN

(2003)

Gatekeeper's surveillance and control exemplified a fashion in Northside, where we need have no fear that our lands will not become better and better as the years go by; and to prove it, the newspaper now informed our loyal citizens that by 1 September 2003, every field in Imperial County *(this includes duck ponds and fields that don't drain on a regular basis)* would require its own written Farm Water Quality Management Plan, including *Best Management Practices (BMPs): existing and planned* and *Sediment Control Goals,* not to mention other required data. And in material advantages they were already well supplied. *If the Regional Water Quality Control Board . . . catches a farmer who has not turned in these forms by the deadline . . . the RWQCB may fine that person $1000 per day per drain.* I can't help believing in people.

Chapter 161

PRIVATIZING THE *EJIDOS*

(1992–2006)

We have to create a new world economy.

—President Bill Clinton, 1993

And when did Mexico stop creating *ejidos*? I asked Yolanda Sánchez Ogás.

You can still do it, she said. But now they'd give you an *ejido* with just rocks . . .

As a matter of fact, in 1992, when the North American Free Trade Agreement partially undid Imperial's original subdelineation of 1848 by creating a common market between the United States and Mexico, Presidente Salinas, ever the ally of easy financial liquidity, gave a speech saying that the revolutionary land redistribution of the Cárdenas era had *brought justice to the countryside,* but *today it is unproductive and impoverishing.* Who am I to judge him incorrect? A book about the Revolution's formation of a campesino identity winds up the twentieth century with this bitter conclusion: *The persistent impoverishment of the countryside in Mexico has in fact homogenized rural people in economic terms, diminishing some of the material differences that once distinguished* the various subcategories of those who lived on and worked the land with varyingly small degrees of fortune and entitlement. Indeed, our historian bluntly says: *Many ejidos today do not possess enough agricultural land to sustain their members.*

Salinas's solution: Let the campesinos sell or mortgage their *ejido* shares as they saw fit. An *ejido* could also vote to disband itself. And why not bring back sharecropping? All these improvements were duly enacted, to the benefit of new Chandler Syndicates.

Imperial is the Rothkoscapes of agribusiness, the sandy acres of water farmers; Imperial is horizon-crowding plains of monoculture-for-export; but once upon a time, Imperial was also the homestead of Wilber Clark, no matter that Wilber Clark failed; and ever since Cárdenas, and almost certainly long before him, Imperial was subsistence hectares in the Mexicali Valley, not to mention the ranchos of Tecate and the former ranchos around the capricious streams of Tijuana. How can I imagine Mexican Imperial without *ejidos*? Never mind; Article Twenty-seven of the Mexican Constitution is no longer in force.

Before 1992, said an official of Mexicali's Tribunal Unitario Agrario Distrito Dos, the law stipulated that you could leave the land to whomever you wanted but it had to be someone whose existence would depend on the land, since otherwise the *ejidos* would fold. But that's no longer true.

I asked him how he felt about this, but he never answered; perhaps he did not wish to say.

It was predicted that two million rural families would become landless once the *ejidos* became alienable; but, after all, you can't produce things the way you used to. Besides, privatization is most appealing precisely for those who intend to sell their land for nonagricultural purposes; and why shouldn't Mexico "develop" just as much as Northside? Jaime Serra Puche, the Mexican Secretary of Commerce, helped us all comprehend that one of NAFTA's intentions was to replace subsistence farming with export crops, so why should we cry in our beer? *Manufacturing is hitting another level of evolution.* Hurrah for Southside's prospective water farmers!

In the *ejidos* of the Mexicali Valley nobody had much to say about privatization.

How about the life for you, Don Carlos? I asked a rancher in Morelos.—Is it getting better or worse?

Worse, said the sleepy *ejidatario.*

Why?

All of the funding and the loans from the government come from Mexico City and sometimes it takes months and months.

Was it better under the PRI?*

No. The political parties back then, they didn't help the people.

I took these replies to mean that his life, like mine, was simply continuing in its customary state of imperfection. When I asked whether NAFTA had affected his family—this was a decade after that agreement had been enacted—he had nothing to say, so his wife replied: The only people who know about those things are the people who make them up, the lawyers.

I don't think the valley will change, a restaurant proprietress in the Mexicali Valley said bravely. Yes, there are many American companies who are coming and renting the land, but I think that's okay since the parcels will stay active as farmland. Many factories around here have something to do with agriculture, for instance something to do with carrots. The countryside will stay the same, since the

*The Partido Revolucionario Institucional, which remained in power for many years.

river is here (she meant the Colorado) and the people are dedicated to agriculture. Another reason that agriculture will remain here is that it's not like before when they used to just kind of guess what to grow; now they use a lot of technology and export our produce all over the world, crops like pumpkins and carrots.

Many American companies are leasing the land from Mexicans and using it to grow crops, said a rancher lady in nearby Colonia Sieto de Cierro Prieto.*—Yes, they harvest asparagus right over here, some American company. I don't see it's a bad thing because this gives the people money. It takes a lot of people to harvest asparagus. Because of that, it gives a lot of jobs, although only for a couple of months. Before, we planted the pumpkins and watermelons only for ourselves.

Why did *you* stop planting for yourselves?

Well, we started getting married, and we started planting a lot of cardamom for the oil, and *cevada,* which is like wheat for the cattle. And right now we don't have the tools for the watermelons. Before, we had the tractors, Caterpillars, all the machinery.

What happened to them?

She laughed.—I got married. My brothers were left in charge of it.

"THEY KEEP THE PEOPLE IN SLAVE CONDITIONS"

What patterns does analysis incline us to? In the spring of 2003 I rode down Highway 2 past Desierto Industrial Park and Parque Industrial Nelson; the signs offered one and a half hectares for sale or sometimes more; were these bits of privatized *ejidos* or previously forgotten scraps of desert that had never belonged to any subsistence farmer? And had Señora García gotten squeezed by cruel market forces until it no longer benefited her to grow her own watermelons, or was it simply that her brothers had manhandled the tractors?

Following her own tendency for dramatization, Yolanda Sánchez Ogás described Colonia Carranza in the center of the valley, and by extension much of the area around the Río Colorado, as follows: Foreign companies rent it. They keep the people in slave conditions. They bring the people to work from Sinaloa and Oaxaca. They bring the people into rooms where there aren't even any beds. They just sleep on the floor. Sometimes the people die. Two weeks ago a little boy died from heat exposure here. The women put their babies in fruit baskets when they work in the fields. This happened in Ejido Tabasco.

As already told, we went to Ejido Tabasco to look at the place where the workers

*Stella Mendoza, the past President of the Imperial Irrigation District, once remarked to me that the farmers in Imperial County were complaining about the global economy, "but meanwhile they do it to themselves; they go to Mexicali."

had been kept *in slave conditions* and where the little boy had died, but the barracks, hot and grim though they certainly were, were empty; and the newlywed *maquila* workers next door, who were very open and friendly, knew nothing about the barracks, nothing that they could say.

Had two million *ejidatario* families become landless yet? Why did I not yet smell in most of Mexican Imperial the overpowering reek of class hatred that makes Colombia so dangerous to rich and poor alike? The answer might simply have been that Mexican Imperial is unlike the rest of Mexico, a nation about which after all these years and pages I remain largely ignorant . . .

Or perhaps the progressing privatization of the *ejidos* was not much of a tragedy at all, because manufacturing was simply hitting another level of evolution.

THOUGHTS ABOUT A COTTONWOOD TREE

A young señora who had lived in Ejido Netzahualcóyotl for twenty years stood beside a younger man* in the dust in front of their house; she did not invite us in. One pleasant aspect of her life was that *you don't have to go all the way into Mexicali for food.*† Her son and her husband both worked in the fields: wheat and cotton.

She said that most land in the vicinity had fallen into the possession of the United States. The *ejidos* were permitted to sell their land bit by bit and the American companies bought it. Her father-in-law still had his parcel, but it comprised less than eighty hectares.

To what patterns was the mind of this Alma Rosa Hernández inclined? I believe that she blamed Northside for the erosion of the *ejidos,* and there she was partially right. Perhaps President Salinas might also have borne a trifle of the responsibility.—Who else? By the time Article Twenty-seven got undone, the Revolution's land reforms had redistributed forty-two percent of the nation's surface, including three-fourths of all farmland. But crops paid less than they used to; the government no longer offered agricultural credit. The *ejidatarios* remained poor. Might some of them truly be "better off" as Northside's field workers?

At the edge of Ejido Netzahualcóyotl, in a ditch, there is a single gracious cottonwood whose yellowing leaves catch the low sun which hangs like a glowing peach at the side of the white-dust road. Dust to the north, green crops to the south, thus this picture of delineation, moneyscape and waterscape. The new Zapatistas,

*Their names were Alma Rosa Hernández and Hugo Heriberto Herrera.

†I asked her what was best and worst about the *ejidos,* and she began by replying, as they always did: "Here, life is more tranquil than in Mexicali." She then continued: "But if you want to buy things, such as clothes, it takes forty minutes by bus to get there, and you have to catch the bus from another *ejido,* so it takes fifty-five minutes total."

who had risen up when NAFTA was signed, asserted in a communiqué of their Clandestine Revolutionary Indigenous Committee that *capitalism makes merchandise of people, of nature, of culture, of history, of conscience.* What about that cottonwood in the ditch? Who had planted it, on whose property? What would de-*ejido*-ization do to that tree, not to mention nature, culture, history and conscience? Suspicious as I am of the sentimentalism underlying the Zapatistas' attack on capitalism's merchandise-ification of those entities, I cannot help dreading the disappearance of the *ejidos*. Most *ejidatarios* plant shade trees around their homes. I wonder how many cottonwoods are in the Mexicali Valley's future?

Chapter 162

ASSETS FORFEITURE

(2003)

Offhand, I know of nothing more deleterious to my liver than being the useful, contributing member of society the Occupation seems bent on making of us all.

—Oliver Lange, 1971

And while Southside was privatizing her *ejidos*, the trustworthy guardians of Northside were deprivatizing personal sovereignty in still other ways, always for the best of reasons, and expressed in phrases as smooth to the touch as the paint on Salvation Mountain.

The Imperial Idea, which was once the American Idea, cannot survive without private property. If my home is not my castle, if I cannot make my own mistakes, then I become merely one of what Imperialites refer to as *the urbans.*

The Farm Water Quality Management Plan was now extended to *the urbans.* They might be called upon to report how much money they had in their wallets; they learned to show identification upon demand.

Northside's authorities declared a War on Drugs. Volstead had failed, and they did not want the War on Drugs to fail, so they voted themselves the power to appropriate the cash and assets of enemy drug warriors. They liked that; it extended their budgets.

Some cities, including the one in which I live, declared a War on Prostitution and helped themselves to the cars of individuals who bought sex. They liked that recompense equally well.

The Border Patrol launched Operation Gatekeeper and awarded themselves the assets of certain people-smugglers, under certain conditions, always for the purpose of protecting you and me. I can't help believing in people.

. . . And so today in Holtville's *Imperial Valley Weekly* I'm informed by Kenneth R. Stitt, Chief Patrol Agent, that *because of the alleged use in commission of a violation of Section 274(a) of the Immigration and Nationality Act,* forty-seven vehicles, each with its own asset identification number, stand *subject to forfeiture except as provided in 8 CFR 274.5(b) and 18 USC 983.* What is likely to happen to this 1997 Jeep Cherokee seized in Westmorland, that 1989 Mercury Sable snatched in Calexico, the 1982 Lincoln Town Car limo gleaned in Niland, the 1977 Dodge van (my God, twenty-six years old and still running!) appropriated near Seeley? I'll tell you what! *Sale or other disposal if declared forfeited.*

Why not? After all, we have to create a new world economy.

Chapter 163

WE SHOULD HAVE HAD A BETTER NEGOTIATING POSITION

(2002–2003)

San Diego County sees such water transfers as part of the solution to potential future water shortages.

—The San Diego County Water Authority, 2003

This puts in place the basic building block of future agreements to meet water needs.

—Gale Norton, Secretary of the Interior, 2003

The taxi driver who used to be a babysitter, and before that, years and years before, when she was thirty-three, a field worker, would never forget how unpleasant tomato-picking had been, because everything she wore got indelibly stained, even her underwear; but she'd hated cantaloupes the most, their harvest being so hot and unprotected. When she told me this, I remembered an ancient Hetzel photo of a truckload of boxed cantaloupes, the driver inside the truck, his skin very dark against his white hat and white shorts; and the wheels, as crude as a wagon's, had sunk deep in white dirt, with tall trees behind them. That must have been around 1920, I would guess. Had picking cantaloupes been better or worse in those days? I finished wondering and paid her, because we'd now arrived at the Imperial Irrigation District meeting in El Centro. It was the autumn of 2002.

The idea, and I scarcely mean Imperial's, was to transfer two hundred thousand acre-feet per year (let's be twenty-first century and call it **200 KAFY**; that way we don't have to get tired counting all the zeroes) from the Imperial Irrigation District to San Diego, and possibly Los Angeles would get some, too. That might require the Imperial Valley to *conserve* here and there, I'm afraid. For instance, why couldn't her water-wasters reduce tailwater on the fields?

One of Imperial's consultants concluded that the *environmental mitigation cost* (I love that phrase) of, for instance, a three-hundred-thousand acre-foot reduction for 2003—after all, why should Imperial's enemies stop with two hundred thousand?—would be a hundred and twelve dollars per acre-foot. In addition, *construction/*

operation would cost a hundred dollars per acre-foot. The farmers of Imperial County were currently paying sixteen dollars per acre-foot, *the highest per–acre foot charge of any irrigators receiving Colorado River [water] in the Lower Basin.* So tailwater reduction would increase their fees by a factor of thirteen. As Border Patrol Officer Gloria Chavez said: I think we all feel sorry for 'em.

Well, but the water transfer might pay fifty million dollars every year (*"Moisture Means Millions"*)! And only thirty thousand acres (seven percent of the county's farmland) would get fallowed. To be sure, fallowing would reduce the incomes of seed merchants, car and tractor dealerships, etcetera, not to mention effects on the businesses they patronized; but don't worry; we need have no fear that our lands will not become better and better for water farmers. One simply fallows low-value crops! (Andy Horne, Director of the Imperial Irrigation District, will now define low-value crops: *Those crops being grown with water someone else wants.*)

Let's not be selfish, boys and girls! Los Angeles and San Diego *need* that water! Besides, they'll use it responsibly. Look! They've even prepared an urban water-management plan! (Andy Horne defines "urban water management plan": *Highly detailed and complex volumes of documents which, among other things, attempt to explain why it is considered perfectly acceptable to devote one-half of all water in cities to ornamental landscaping. In the middle of the desert. In the middle of a drought.*)

Andy Horne and Stella Mendoza will vote against the water transfer. Bruce Kuhn, Rudy Maldonado and Lloyd Allen will vote in favor.

Later that year, when she was no longer President, Stella Mendoza sat in her kitchen in Brawley and said to me: When they talked about conserving water through fallowing, that really hit me through what I understood. That would hurt the agricultural workers and the agricultural businesses. Who's going to help those people? We were up in Sacramento talking to Senator Machada. He's an arrogant little prick. I told him, what are those people going to do? He said, *they can just leave this valley.*

You look at this valley. It's so hot during the summer. What do we have of value? We have the water and we have the land. It's like when you have a jar of pickles, it's really hard to unscrew the lid, and once you do, all the pickles get eaten.

The other Board members said, *If we don't sell the water, they'll take the water.* I said: Hell no! These other Board members, I think they're being extremely short-sighted. Rudy Maldonado said we're spoiled; he's out telling the world that that we have too much water. What an idiot.

An important message from the San Diego County Water Authority

The IID-Water Authority Transfer is the talk of the town in Imperial Valley. While making presentations to various groups, representatives of the Water Authority have received a lot of questions regarding the Agreement. Rightfully so. We understand that not everyone can be at these presentations. So we have compiled the most frequently asked questions we are hearing from you and will be sharing these and our answers in this and upcoming columns.

You've been asking...

Q. What if the water transfer does not go through?

A. The failure of the Transfer Agreement would cause a "house of cards" effect in California, jeopardizing the entire state's current Colorado River water use. Because the IID holds nearly 70 percent of California's entire Colorado River water allotment, the region's water use has come under scrutiny.

The state government, Secretary of the Interior, and other Colorado River basin states, as well as other water agencies within California, are watching closely. If the transfer and other water use efficiency measures committed to under the Quantification Settlement Agreement are not fulfilled, delicately crafted agreements that would bring peace on the Colorado River will crumble and Imperial Valley's water would certainly be at risk. Specifically, a "no water transfer" scenario could result in water being taken involuntarily from the Imperial Valley.

Conversely, the Transfer Agreement provides an opportunity for the Imperial Valley to get paid for saving water and will strengthen IID's long-standing water rights. By demonstrating its voluntary reduction of Colorado River water use, the IID guards itself against future water use challenges, can sell some of its water and can infuse the Imperial Valley with up to or more than $50 million a year.

We hope this information has been helpful,

Maureen Stapleton
General Manager

San Diego County Water Authority

For more information, please call the San Diego County Water Authority Public Affairs Office
(760) 352-4656 from Imperial Valley
or (858) 522-6700 from San Diego
4677 Overland Ave.
San Diego, CA 92123

THE ROOM

The room where these public meetings took place was in part bricked, and on the bricks were blue diamond-shaped tiles which I suppose were meant to remind us of water-drops' preciousness. In the corner, a beautiful Latina in a miniskirt sometimes sat at her computer with her white cowboy hat on the table beside it. She must have been the stenographer. Behind the long high desk at which the Board sat hung a curtain as blue as water, on either side of which was a door bearing the following political caution: **WATCH YOUR STEP**.—This reminds me of a conversation between Hitler and his architect. The new Marble Gallery was so hyper-polished that Speer worried that some foreign Ambassador might fall down and break a leg.—All to the good, replied the Führer, diplomats need to be adept at traversing slippery surfaces.

Not every board member of the Imperial Irrigation District seemed adept at slipperiness. Stella Mendoza in particular seemed out of her depth, which is precisely why I admired her. I will never forget her love for the valley in which she was born. She never had a chance.

Small-town democracy must always have been in part a myth; nonetheless, to the extent that it existed at all, it might have existed in Imperial. Tamerlane's warriors did not plan to let it get in their way. If need be, all their persuasions would become as cruel as the painted water on Salvation Mountain.

Imperial is bare dirt. Imperial is green fields. Imperial is the regular meeting of the Board of Supervisors in this same room, on Tuesday, 14 October 2003, in El Centro, a meeting which begins: At this time, please bow your heads and say a prayer for all those young people in harm's way in Iraq. We lost three of 'em yesterday.

After that prayer, the pastor prayed that this county be considered pleasing in the sight of God, and that God rain down His blessings on it. Then came the Pledge of Allegiance; all rose. And the pastor said: The county is still in step when we say, one nation *under God.*

I myself believe that our war against Iraq was and will always be an unjust war. I believe that public prayer at a civic function is appropriate and pleasing in, say, Iraq, but inappropriate and odious in the United States of America, which is supposed to be founded on freedom of religion, which in turn implies freedom *from* religion to all who wish it. At the same time, I was touched by the pastor's expressions of concern and care. I was sorry about our soldiers who had been killed, and I truly wanted every possible blessing for Imperial. Finally—how can I best say this?—I preferred a community's united expression of feeling, no matter that for some people present that expression might be *pro forma* or even hypocritical, to the absence of any expression of feeling. I preferred love for the home to love for money. I believed that Imperial was what she was because water was here. That was why I didn't think that the cities of California had any right to her water.

Imperial is Joe Maruca, Chairman, who says: At ten-fifteen we will take in closed session the item of the Sierra Club versus the EPA.

He explains: We're expecting a phone call from an attorney who is representing us in this EPA matter.

The Sierra Club wants to shut down the whole valley, and we can all go to San Diego, he says bitterly. With our *water.*

This is Imperial; this is Joe Maruca, Chairman.

I support the Sierra Club, and that's irrelevant. I disagree with Stella Mendoza about the Salton Sea, and that's irrelevant, too. (By the way, Gale Norton, the Interior Secretary, has been quoted as saying that *the Bush administration does not see preserving the inland lake as a funding priority.*)

Imperial is Joe Maruca. Imperial is Stella Mendoza. Imperial is Leonard Knight, who lays another coat of paint on Salvation Mountain and says: *When I get too close to people, they always want me to do it their way. And then it looks like I want to do it my way. And most of the times, their way is right. But I still like to do it my way.*

Imperial has now been surrounded, like an old Victorian in Riverside with gables and round windows which resemble compass dials, an old house ringed round with freeways.

Imperial is what she is, outspokenly. What about Imperial's enemies? The Department of the Interior's e-mails to the Metropolitan Water District *suggest that the federal government may have worked behind the scenes . . . to develop a Colorado River-sharing pact that favors the giant Los Angeles-based wholesaler.* The Imperial Irrigation District bitterly declares for the record that Interior's Regional Director, Mr. Robert Johnson, secretly met with MWD in 2002 to formulate a "gameplan" against them. *Mr. Johnson formed his opinions long ago.* Meanwhile, Ruth Thayer, a subordinate of Mr. Johnson's, e-mails another Interior employee named Jayne Harkins. Poor Ruth wants to know what she should do. Having revised her notes, she feels ready to push the **SEND** button, but she's been cautioned that electronic communications are potentially public documents, in which case *IID will be able to get them.* Wouldn't that be awkward in this aboveboard, impartial public review process? We need have no fear that our lands will not become better and better as the years go by. *Another e-mail suggested that Metropolitan and Interior officials discussed "how to bulletproof" a federal order to take some of Imperial's water.* Tamerlane's warriors come galloping into the square.

IMPERIAL REPRISE

Standing today by the grave of that infant civilization which blossomed, amidst such hardships, upon a desert, we would fain lift the veil and see the unthought-of transformation which fifty years will bring.

Tuesday, December 10, 2002: EL CENTRO—**In a stunning move that could lead to a statewide water crisis, Imperial Valley officials Monday rejected a controversial proposal to reduce their water use and sell the excess to San Diego . . . "We want to transfer water, but we want to do it on our terms," said board President Stella Mendoza, who voted against the sale.**

`Tamerlane's warriors gallop into the square.`

EPITAPHS FOR A DONE DEAL

So on that day in 2002 they began with the Pledge of Allegiance. The auditorium was mostly full. An anxious man asked: Madam Chairman, is this the time to discuss the water transfer?

Not yet, said Stella Mendoza.

Finally a Mr. Carter began to speak. He was one of the Imperial Irrigation

District's lawyers.—We have negotiated an agreement, he began. Inflow into the Salton Sea will not be different than it would have been absent the program.

But after fifteen years, he said, that could be changed. San Diego will only receive half of what she wanted during that fifteen years.—Reassuringly, Mr. Carter said: IID has a right to reset our agreement in Year Six.—The socioeconomic impacts of fallowing, he said, would be *tracked, monitored and mitigated.*

Stella Mendoza said: I think you all know how I stand on the water transfer. I can't support it on a personal level.

Bruce Kuhn said: I on the other hand believe that no action could have put us in a worse situation.

Rusty Jordan from Brawley was saying: I looked up another word called *extortion . . .*

And someone else said: I don't know that it's wise to negotiate with people that threaten, because it colors the result.

In all, five million acre-feet are going away, said a greyhaired man named Larry Porter, his voice almost trembling.

Cliff Hurley from El Centro, a whitehaired man, shakily requested to know whose farms would be fallowed.

A youngish, cleancut man named Steve Olson said: What you're embarking on is a grave mistake. I'm telling you, you need to have some serious legal counsel. Succinctly put, once they have it for five years, they'll have it forever.

In a trembling voice, Stella asked if this was true.

Hitching up his belt, a man named John Pierre said: Lloyd Allen asked all of us farmers to stick together. When Lloyd was there he conducted himself as a gentleman. Mr. Maldonado conducted himself as a gentleman.

A man said: I think you've given us the best deal we can possibly get.

DEFINITION OF A POINT SOURCE

As the Imperial Irrigation District's lawyers later told the tale, *Interior sought to push IID into the QSA* by rejecting IID's estimated water "order" for 2003 and promising IID water to junior right holders* unless *IID signed the QSA by December 31, 2002 . . . IID approved a revised QSA on December 31, 2002, and signed an agreement with SDCWA.† However, Interior rejected the form of the QSA approved by IID.*

On December 27, 2002, Interior notified IID that Interior would not deliver IID's

*Quantification Settlement Agreement. Legalese for the water-transfer plan.

†San Diego County Water Authority.

Stella Mendoza at the fateful IID meeting

2003 water estimate of 3.1 MAFY. Interior informed CWD, which is to say Coachella, *that it would receive its full request of 347 KAFY, even though CWD's rights are junior in priority . . .*

(A year later, Richard Brogan said: Coachella, what I would find here, I believe their ag producing ground is decreasing. However, they've got more golf courses per capita there than anywhere in the country. We're talking monumental. Rancho Mirage, Palm Desert. Are we going to create a lifestyle for certain people who thrive because of growth? You don't have your average everyday laborer going to golf, because of hundred dollar green fees.)

Meanwhile, continued the Imperial Irrigation District's lawyers, *Interior informed MWD that it would receive 713 KAFY of water (assuming no execution of the QSA), rather than the 550 KAFY that is allocated to MWD at priority 4.* Imperial Irrigation District lost three hundred and thirty thousand, four hundred acre-feet to

which it possessed senior vested right. For Interior, it must have been as easy as killing squirrels with Cyan-o-Gas back in 1925. *It costs a dollar to feed a squirrel. It costs 2c to kill him. Let's kill him.*

On 18 March 2003, a federal district court judge ordered the government of the United States to deliver the Imperial Irrigation District's quota of water, uncut. Judge Thomas J. Whelan cited irreparable harm to the Imperial Irrigation District and failure of the government to establish its case or respect its own procedures. But in much the same way that in the Hotel 16 de Septiembre in Mexicali the whores use any available room that's not locked, make love rapidly on top of smelly blankets, throw the condom on the floor, remake the bed if the blankets have moved out of place, remake their iron-stiff hair, then rush back downstairs in search of new business, so the Interior Department altered a few paragraphs of its water reduction order in a flash, without mussing up the blankets, and sent it right back. (Definition: A point source is a specific site of pollutant discharge. In this case, the point source is our incorruptible Interior Department.)

On 15 March the federal district court published its decision, and in that document stated that there was a *very strong likelihood that the defendants,* namely the Interior Department, *breached the Seven Party Agreement* between the Colorado River states.

WATER'S SAVIORS

If you like, Imperial's attitude toward Los Angeles was a mirror of Owens Valley's in 1924: *an American community . . . driven to defense of its rights,* says the Inyo County Register. The Owens Valley was divided, needless to say, and so was the Imperial Valley.

Even as the Imperial Irrigation District struggled in court against Interior, a coalition of water farmers called the Imperial Group filed suit against the Imperial Irrigation District, accusing it, among other things, of *wasting water.*

In the newspapers, the Imperial Group appeared to be most frequently associated with a man named Mike Morgan. A search of property records located twenty-six parcels, many of which were labeled, as we might expect from a water farmer, *waste land, marsh, swamp, submerged-vacant land.*

You may remember that Rudy Maldonado was one of the two Board members who voted straightaway in favor of the water transfer. Mr. Ray Naud of El Centro found it *interesting,* he writes in to the paper, *that Allen and Maldonado both have supported the sale of water and fallowing since they have been on the board.* He informs us that he visited the county recorder's office, discovering that among those who donated between five hundred and a thousand dollars to Maldonado's campaign was a certain Mike Morgan.

Mike Morgan, said Richard Brogan slowly. He's very aloof, very difficult to reach. A very private person. He's someone who grew up with extra houses in Colorado, in Mexico. He probably grew up wondering, where were the folks last night? In Colorado or Mexico? He's different.

Of Mike Morgan, Richard Brogan also said: You know where his background is in money? He's the grandson of—and Mr. Brogan named a name.—They have that ground around the Salton Sea, he said. It's those people with land like that who have the real strong motives. Morgan can write checks quicker than anybody else could. I don't think he's the richest. I don't know for how long his family will back him in bad business deals. Morgan, his hobbies are hunting and fishing in the Gulf of Mexico. I think he owns a nice little recreational place six, seven hundred miles south on the east side . . .

Who was Mike Morgan? I never got to meet him, so I must repeat the words to you of the old pioneer from Heber: *I don't want you to write that down. This is all just background.*

"IF WE HAVE THE RIGHT TO DECIDE"

I asked Mr. Brogan for his feelings about the water transfer, and he said:

I think this water thing is very minute in the overall picture, but I don't understand how people can't be concerned with the lifestyle change that's coming.

You think it is going to be a dustbowl here?

Well, forty to sixty thousand acres is a lot of jobs. The ag money spent here goes in a circle. It goes to land leasing, to taxes, and so on back to land leasing. Now it's going to be one check from the water users to the landowners. If the landowner chooses to live in a beachfront house in Coronado . . . They'll obviously fallow the less productive ground to start with. But then . . .

I waited, and he said: Well, I have a twofold feeling. If that's gonna happen, then I'm still a believer in the rights of property ownership, so I don't have a problem there. But I think we're being *forced* into that. I think the Department of the Interior is forcing us. I believe in free enterprise, *if* we have the right to decide. A lot of these people like to grow two crops, lettuce and asparagus. High-dollar crops. If the price is up they can learn to make a million dollars with eighty acres, but they can't do that without water. I think that the government is trying to start a precedent. Now, a lot of these people are risk takers. They'd rather try lettuce. Is water better than wheat or alfalfa? Potentially, yes. And then are there middlemen here? Is the government involved in the transaction? Is there sales tax on the water?

After awhile he shook his head and said: We have a government in Washington creating a dustbowl regardless of the human sacrifice.

"IF WE GET PAID ENOUGH"

Kay Brockman Bishop was more resigned. Perhaps she even approved of the water transfer, for she said:

I think it's inevitable. I think we'd better learn how to make money and get more innovative. I think we're wasting water now. I think it's idiotic to think you can do it without fallowing something. In a downtime, you do the extra work.

If we get paid enough for that fallowing, we'll do it fine. I don't know anybody, and I know a lot of farmers, that's shortened up his crew because of fallowing. If you've got workers working for you, you'll keep 'em.

I asked her whether she felt sorry for the people of Owens Valley, and she replied: They simply didn't get what they should have gotten. They let Los Angeles buy up all that land without thinking what was happening or how much they could have been paid for it. They didn't see what it was worth.

So are you for the water transfer or against it? I asked.

Oh, jeez, I don't know. I just get tired of all the fighting . . .

DEMOCRACY

In August 2003, the Imperial Irrigation District asks the federal government for work files. The government refuses. I can't help believing in people. The District files a Freedom of Information Act request. The government replies that the cost will be a thousand dollars, which the District immediately pays, at which point the government announces that actually the cost will be five thousand dollars, which the District pays that very same day. Almost three weeks later, the District asks the government where the documents are, and is told they will come in a week. Eight days later, a letter arrives saying the documents will not come for another fifteen days, which is only three business days before the District's deadline for legal response—in other words, as the District's lawyers remark, *too late for meaningful review.*

Gamely, the lawyers try to present Imperial's case all the same: *C[oachella] V[alley] W[ater] D[istrict] has an undisputed lower on-farm efficiency than IID and has undisputed access to multiple sources of supply. The determination must address why, under these facts, CVWD as a junior rightholder, should receive a large share of the water ordered by senior rightholder IID. The Determination is totally silent [as to], but must address, why IID should replace all (for CVWD) and some (for M[etropolitan] W[ater] D[istrict of Los Angeles]) of the surplus water these junior right holders used to receive, rather than the junior right holders having to live within their normal-flow year entitlements or obtaining water from available non–Colorado River sources.*

The Imperial Irrigation District predicts the results of water reduction: The Salton Sea will die sooner, selenium concentrations in tailwater and leach water will increase in the drains; endangered species such as the desert pupfish will suffer increased pressure in their habitat around Parker Dam. Needless to say, Imperial will enjoy little protection against potentially unlimited liability for environmental mitigation. Her lawyers bitterly quote SWRCB Decision 1600, 1984: *A property right once acquired by the beneficial use of water is not burdened by the obligation of adopting methods of irrigation more expensive than those currently considered reasonably efficient in the locality.*

"THEY HATE MY GUTS"

Stella Mendoza was a pretty woman of indeterminate age. She had reddish-blonde hair and dark eyes. We sat around her kitchen table, and she said:

We have this water transfer for seventy-five years. And one of the concerns that I have, is that these farmers like Mike Morgan and the Imperial Group, they want the water allocated to the gate. The way it is now, the IID is a trustee to the landowners, and the landowners have the right to use water as long as they use it reasonably and beneficially. And Mike Morgan wants to dissolve the IID, and have two boards, one for the water, one for the electricity. It's like the same system they have in Palo Verde. Then the landowners can sell.

I can tell you that of the water we're entitled to, ninety-eight percent is used for ag purposes, she said proudly. Only two percent is used for urban purposes.

There has to be a water history to the land. There are some lands up in the northern part of the valley where the land is very hard to farm. So the water history for those is not as big as the water history in the Holtville area where they grow a lot of produce.

Why does Mr. Morgan want so much land?

His intent is to control the water. The bottom line is greed and money. If he can somehow get the Board to agree to allocate water to the gate and then the water is allocated to the land, that's one step in that direction.

Did the split vote reflect a split in the county generally?

The community is kind of fractured. There's maybe four groups. Right now we have maybe three Board members that are not farmers. And I can understand the mentality of some of the farmers that non-farmers are making decisions that are directed at them: How dare this gal tell them how to use the water? I'm the first woman on the Board and I'm of Mexican descent. What they don't understand is that IID Board doesn't only make decisions on the water but also on the power side.

The farmers feel like they're losing control. There's maybe five hundred in the valley. So they're lashing out.

I would think that they'd adore you.

Hell, no. They hate my guts. John Vesey and Mike Morgan, if they could shoot me and put me in a canal and get away with it, they would.

Are more of them on your side or on their side?

It's hard to tell.—She named one of her supporters and said: He's one of the farmers who wants to just be left alone, who wants to just farm. And then you have some who don't feel that way.

Are there farmers who are not water farmers who support the water transfer?

Many. I guess what they're afraid of, is that the water would just get taken away. But what I tell them is that we're supposed to be a nation of laws. Laws do stand for something. The law stands that we're entitled to twenty-three point two million acre-feet of water. If they try to take it away, I'll see you in court. But they feel that they're outnumbered. Also, you can be paid for not farming. And that's very attractive.

I firmly believe in my heart that ag will always pay a major part in Imperial Valley, she continued. As technology improves, I think the farmers will always be more technology-capable, producing higher yields with less fertilizer.

That would mean fewer farms could produce the same amount of crop, I said. And it seems to me that that's going to mean fewer farms, period.

That's true, she said. And look at Calexico. They're going to convert all that farmland into subdivisions. I would prefer Imperial County to remain rural.

What's your personal feeling about the Salton Sea?

The Salton Sea is a body of water that is evolving, and it's going through changes.* If less water flows into the sea because of this water transfer, well, look, in order to prevent less water flowing into the Salton Sea, the water transfer was amended for additional fallowing. Say, if the water transfer did not go forward, the sea would die anyway. But that is not to say there could be some kind of reparation as with the Dead Sea or the Great Salt Lake. In my mind, they have this North Lake concept. It really sounds good on paper. But where are they going to get this four billion dollars? And my concern is that they're going to come on back to the IID, and they're going to tell us that the cheapest, easiest way to save the sea is to fallow more farmland.

Who gets fallowed?

Right now, they're talking about the cost of an acre-foot is two hundred and fifty-

*Kay Brockman Bishop was less diplomatic: "It would tickle me no end if the Salton Sea dried up. All this hullabaloo, it's just exactly that. I don't think we should be spending a gazillion dollars on it. I don't mind it being there; I don't mind it being gone. They'll figure out something."

eight dollars. The farmers pay about seventeen. Two hundred will go to the farmer and the rest will go for mitigation. Farmers are already signing up. Greed comes into play.

So most people are going to want more water transfers, right?

Unfortunately. And this transfer, according to our attorney, was never about selling water; it was about protecting our water rights. And that's bullshit. Because we don't have an ironclad assurance that Interior won't come back and hit us again! We're shouldering all the liability. We're transferring more water for less money. First they capped our liability at fifteen million, then they came back at fifteen million more, and now it's thirty-four million. And MWD, they're good negotiators, they're not paying a penny for it, and they got off scot free. If we hit a hundred and twenty-two million, if the mitigation goes over that, and we have still more, the state promised us that we would backfill with the money. That's bullshit. The state doesn't have the money. I don't trust them. Andy Horne and myself agree on that. The other Board members trust the state.

She said then: What I don't understand is that *we have the water,* so we should have had a better negotiating position. And what I think is that we were sold out,* and I'm not happy with it. You can write that.

Coachella has always attacked us on our reasonable and beneficial use. They're junior partners. So they're always there being jealous. If we lose the right to that water, that means that they get more water. The idea has always been to work as a partner with the rest of the state. But there's always this envy, this mentality that we're entitled to too much water.

In the urban communities, over sixty percent of the water is for landscaping! Here, almost all of it is for food and fiber. What we told Interior was, that if you're going to attack us on reasonable and beneficial use, do it to the urbans, too. But they won't.

Drearily she said: Unless we have technology, good-paying jobs here in the valley, we're going to become an industrial community with low-paying jobs, people on relief, on welfare. It'll probably be a Third World county . . .†

RIPPLES OF BENEFIT

On the tenth of October, 2003, representatives of the Imperial Irrigation District, the Coachella Valley Water District, the Metropolitan Water District of Southern

* For reasons which I am not permitted to go into, I have made this sentence slightly less specific than it actually was.

†Speaking of enabling low-wage industrialism, an IID brochure from this period boasts of "powering Mexican maquiladoras through first international agreement."

California and of course the San Diego County Water Authority sign the water transfer in Los Angeles. Imperial surrenders two hundred thousand acre-feet a year for seventy-five years; while San Diego also gets seventy-seven thousand acre-feet a year for a hundred and ten years, proffered by Los Angeles; this is for lining the All-American Canal.* In short, *the pact will supply San Diego with about a third of its current water needs—as much as 277,000 acre-feet of water each year.*†

That was on Friday. On Sunday an editorial appeared in the *Imperial Valley Press,* decrying an editorial in the *San Diego Union-Tribune* which proposed that the water

*In their losing struggle against the water transfer, Stella Mendoza's faction of Imperial County insists against Los Angeles that they have exercised reasonable and beneficial use with All-American Canal water. Meanwhile, Mexico insists against Imperial County and San Diego that she has exercised reasonable and beneficial use with All-American Canal seepage over the past sixty-five years. But this is the merest footnote; who cares about the losers?

†In 2003, San Diego would receive 15,000 acre-feet, one-third of it to actually go to the Salton Sea. "For 2004, IID is expected to pay back overruns from 2002."

transfer be considered a "template" for more water transfers.* The *Imperial Valley Press* remarked that this statement *reinforced the idea that "urban interests" have established a beachhead in the Imperial Valley—and their next move will be to construct a siphon . . . Far from being a template for ag-to-urban cooperation and equity, this water study has been a case study in the exercise of raw political power.*

What do you think San Diego would have said about that? What would have spewed out of San Diego's mouth? What would have been the outfall? (Definition of outfall: *the point where sewage is expelled from a system.*) Well, I'll tell what San Diego did say: *The water transfer agreement provides ripples of benefit across the west.*

*A week later, the *New York Times* echoed: "The recent announcement of an armistice in that epic battle could provide a template for compromise elsewhere." In case I haven't told you, "the key to this historic deal is an agreement by the Imperial Valley farmers in California to make do with less water . . . Credit is due to Gale Norton," the Interior Secretary, "for insisting that it go forward despite huge political obstacles . . . The agreement has taught a state that always had trouble controlling its appetites some valuable lessons for living with scarcity."

Chapter 164

YOU MIGHT AS WELL GET OUT OF THE WAY

(2006)

They're building houses in where there used to be farmland, said Kay Brockman Bishop.

I don't agree with Stella. It's just like the bollworms coming in. Things change. You learn to roll with the punches and do something else. A lot of the guys, the contract labor, are going to get hurt more than most.

I think it'll be a suburb before very long. Could be fifty years.

They're going to do what they're going to do, and you might as well get out of the way.

But you can walk across the yard and you can hear the wind going whishing past a bird's wings. You sit someone down on the porch and get 'em a beer or a cup of coffee and say it is sure peaceful here.

. . . I sat with her, watching the sunset coming and smelling the cool smell of the ditches and then the flies went away, and it got cooler and cooler.

Chapter 165

WATER IS HERE (A VIEW FROM ARIZONA)

(1985–2007)

Supplemented by the newly finished All-American Canal and its intake, the Imperial Dam and desilting works, Imperial Valley can claim the most secure, cheapest, dependable and abundant water supply in the United States.

—El Centro Chamber of Commerce, 1939

The unsuspecting traveller who has crossed the Colorado river and entered Southern California, naturally looks around him for the orange groves of which he has so often heard and is astonished not to find himself surrounded by them.

—Mrs. W. H. Ellis, 1912

Between Phoenix and Tucson lies a quasi-Imperial zone which in the words of two climatologists *was mostly agriculture in the 1950s, but is now showing the effects of severe groundwater depletion, economic changes and widespread farm abandonment.* The farm abandonment desertification effect, by the way, is acronymically known as FADE. *FADE may cause up to one-third of the warming which would be brought about by outright urbanization.* FADE may also increase the dust content of the local atmosphere.

But just because farmers are leaving doesn't mean that other thirsty entities cannot replace them. Back in 1927, Arizona's bitterest rival had figured that out: *The relinquishment of agricultural land for urban use does not reduce the total water consumption as cities of fairly mature growth use water in amounts about equal to that required for irrigating the same area. The demand for water, therefore, can never grow less in southern California* . . . I wonder if the same might be true in Arizona?

By the century's end, Arizona has "grown" sufficiently to gobble down her entire allotment of Colorado River water under the Colorado River Compact. Poor California!

Once upon a time, not long before the end of the nineteenth century, there was another Irrigation Convention in Los Angeles; and to there the delegate J. Rice of Arizona boasted, perhaps missing the menacing irony of his own words, that *in days that are forgotten in the history of Arizona there existed large canals, and large cities are now buried . . . that were . . . made possible only by extensive canals . . .*

Arizona certainly needs her extensive canals! If only other states didn't need them, too . . .

I went rafting down the Colorado River near Peach Springs, and my Hualapai Indian guide pointed at the white traces of waterline high above us and said in words as flat and wide as Yuma: That's where the river used to be. Before Boulder Dam. Before California took all that for new cities and Nevada took the rest for Las Vegas . . .*

And what might Arizona be doing with her share? Go to Boulder Dam, also known as Hoover Dam, whose curving, eerily white and dry wall, narrowing as it drops to a distant deck adorned with two powerhouses, looks down, so far down, to the dark brown-blue water whose expanding rings of white air rush up. That is how it looked in 2007. The Colorado went on, narrower. I cannot promise that some was not diverted to Arizona. Perhaps Nevada did sip away a trifle: I remember seeing that most beneficial of uses, the artificial waterfall at the MGM Grand Hotel (never mind the artificial river at the hotel New York New York, in which so many of the Strip's shining signs are reflected). It might have been that California also dipped her fingers in and sucked them. And Arizona?

Go a hundred thirty miles south as the crow flies, to Quartzsite. Now you're even with the entity I call Imperial. Yuma lies another sixty-odd miles ahead, but you'll reach Laguna Dam first. On the Arizona side of the river, on the upside of Laguna Dam, beyond the skin of grass and cress, I remember that a sun glowed in the center of the still, still water—spuriously still, for white ripples streamed around it. This sun was the reflection of the sunset-struck nose of a rocky ridge in Imperial County; the greater part, which was shaded, had now nearly lost itself in the river's greyness, so the peak shone almost alone, yellow-orange, made up of fractured rock; and as I watched and wrote, the water swallowed up ever more of the reflection, because evening's shadow was creeping up the ridge; now the sun in the water was merely a crescent of gold; a moment later, it had gone to green shadow; all the orange was out of the sky now; the sky was white; like the sky in an old silver-gelatin photograph.

Below the dam, dark water flashed like time-scratched shale across the concrete

*Las Vegas possesses rights to 300 acre-feet per year of Colorado, and the *Imperial Valley Press* opines: "The only place where the progress of the QSA is followed more closely than in the Imperial Valley is in Las Vegas, probably because the people there have as much to gain from its implementation as those of us here have to lose."

basin and down between the wide-spaced concrete teeth to spew up in cotton-white clots, which then lost themselves in wider, more white-rippled darkness, then seeming to sink into the green plain of verdure.

Then it narrowed again, and narrowed . . . Perhaps Arizona drank a little bit.

One night on the California side, I gazed at the Colorado from under the Yuma bridge, studying the dull brown glint of it in the rushes. An Indian on the Quechan Reservation said that this was actually just a canal; from the map it seems to have been no less than the Reservation Main Drain. I crossed the bridge and entered Arizona. The Indian had been correct; the Colorado was a slightly wider stretch of slow brown water. As their creation song said:

This is my water, my water.
This is my river, my river.
We love its water . . .
It shall flow forever.
It shall flow forever.

Declining to shop at Yuma Citrus Plaza, I watched a six-locomotive train screeching slowly east of the Yuma yard; it was singing and screaming and rasping all at once, the broken bottle-bits on the sand not yet glittering in the winter morning sun. Then I went to the river where the small, paint-faded houses were; one even had a cupola. Soon I was at First and Gila.

Lieutenant-Colonel Emory, writing at the middle of the nineteenth century, describes the plain where the Colorado and the Gila meet as almost vegetationless except for *Larrea mexicana* and wild wormwood. (He was about six miles east of the confluence of the two rivers, both of which have shifted.) Here is my own description: Take Sixteenth Street, then go left toward San Luis, right to Quartzsite. You'll see De Anza Plaza, Platinum Laserworks, the Inca Lanes bowling alley, and they all need just as much water as their counterparts in California.

Cocopah Casino—Stay on 95.

Turn left to pass the various chain supercenters. Trust in Route 95. Then Yuma ends in flat green fields, with mountains off to the north; cross a winding blue canal, pass the Cocopah Casino; and the mountains and fields of Mexico will be ahead. Susy's Plaza and Yuma Farm & Home Supply both use water, I suspect. Roll on, into Somerton, and after enjoying the sign for *Paradise Water*, feel free to observe the grey-green heavily odorous fields of cauliflowers going on and on. Then comes the wide S-turn of the highway between cauliflower and lettuce, and you've come into Gadsden. All across a long brown field, white buses and brown men in white sombreros are striding and bending in the dirt. White sprinkles of

Colorado River water rise out of green and brown fields. And now you are entering Arizona's last town, San Luis. A long flat pipe with frail side-pipes like fish-ribs lies across the dirt, and the horizon ahead is very low. **DO NOT ENTER**. Here's Friendship Park! A Border Patrolman studies your face. Beside him in his vehicle stands a bottle of water. Next comes Mexico:

PUERTO FRONTERIZO

The taco shop in San Luis Río Colorado offers three bowls of salsa: blood-red with a hint of orange, carrot orange and deep green. Their liquid content derives from Colorado River water . . .

Chapter 166

WATER IS HERE (A VIEW FROM IMPERIAL)

(2003)

While singlemindedly attacking IID's alfalfa and "low value" crops, Interior allows Southern California to fill its pools, water lush lawns, and frolic in water amusement parks.

Chapter 167

RAIN

(2005–2006)

And rain was smashing down on the greyness of Los Angeles and San Diego; even the Los Angeles River sometimes has water in it, reddish-brown with white foam, rushing past the graffiti on the gently slanted concrete bank—it could almost be the Seine!—the skyscrapers had become cloud-towers; silver puddles on grey concrete assured us: *It is simply needless to question the supply of water.*

And in the Owens Valley, the smallish coagulations of clouds in the glowing blue sky graced snow-veined arid mountains, cottonwoods, sagebrush, tall greenish-grey grass. The orange-brown Bishop River had white foam in it. There were cloud-shadows on mountains, a huge golf course, a vacant lot which proclaimed itself the Property of the City of Los Angeles, pale leaves of cottonwoods, and then Bishop was gone. In the high desert, clumps of green trees were not ruined-looking. Big Pine was surprisingly green and lush, the Owens River a dark creek like the Colorado at San Luis . . .

South of Big Pine, the yellow-green desert went grey, balls of sagebrush yellowing and greying. Dust rose from what had been Owens Lake until Mulholland drained it. The steep dusty greenness of the Sierras did not change in the west, but the Whites went grey, yellow and blue under a rare rainstorm. Cool raindrops married dust in the hot air, and the temperature dropped in a couple of minutes from a hundred and one to ninety-five to sixty-nine . . .

Chapter 168

PROBATE

(1901–2003)

> Business . . . was his profession, but it was even more than a profession; it was the expression of his genius. Still more it was, through him, the expression of the age in which he lived, the expression of the master passion that in all ages had wrought in the making of the race.
>
> —Harold Bell Wright, 1911

I have never been cheated out of a dollar in my life, but I've lost the odd dime here and there; oh, yes, Imperial turns my silver into quicksilver and it dribbles down, back into the sandy, silty earth. Barrett's Boring Outfit sought oil in the 1890s and didn't find it; we know what the great flood did to those two rival salt companies (their commercial skeletons must surely be festooned with whiteness now, in the foul depths of the Salton Sea). Next come the homesteaders, determined to profit from the transactions of agrarian democracy. Then the storekeepers and G-men commence operations. The Inland Empire creeps closer; **THE DESERT DISAPPEARS**, but where did it go? Where did Wilber Clark's ranch vanish to? We find ourselves in the same position as the baffled subscriber to *California Cultivator* who writes (in 1920): *In the years past my father obtained patents to numerous property interests in this state from the Mexican government. On his death all of his property was willed to his wife. I have received no share in his property. Later there has been a fire in the house which has burned up all of the papers. I understand that my father was drunk when he signed the will. Much of this property was never probated. What is the position in respect to it?*

How much is it worth? In other words, is Imperial rich or poor? That question could be answered in many ways. Should we find a per capita average income, or a median income, an income for field workers and another income for landowners? Must we, as everyone else does, separate Northside from Southside? Hopefully this book has helped you to make a determination, according to your own favorite category.

A question on which we can probably come to more agreement is: To what extent does Imperial continue to create agricultural wealth? Here are data for American Imperial:

CASH HARVESTS OF SELECTED CALIFORNIA COUNTIES, 2002

	Market Value of Agricultural Products Sold	*Percent of California*	*Rank*
CALIFORNIA	$25,737,173,000	100	—
Counties in the entity which I call Imperial,[a] and their rivals			
Imperial	1,043,279,000	4.1	8
Riverside	1,008,273,000	3.9	10
San Diego	950,761,000	3.6	11
Los Angeles	281,303,000	1.1	21
		12.7	
Highest-ranking counties			
Fresno	2,759,421,000	10.7	1
Tulare	2,338,577,000	9.1	2
Monterey	2,190,121,000	8.5	3
Kern	2,058,705,000	8.0	4
Merced	1,409,254,000	5.5	5
		41.8	

[a]As a very rough measure, the entity that I call Imperial might incorporate 20% of Riverside County, agriculturally speaking, much of western Riverside being now thoroughly smoggified. The San Diego County border strip is less than 10%, but given the continued urbanization of much of the rest of the county, this approximation of agricultural contribution may serve. Then the total market value of Imperial agricultural products sold in 2002 would be $1,340,009,700, or slightly over 5% of California's total production.

Source: USDA, National Agricultural Statistics Service: 2002 Census of Agriculture, County Data (accessed online, 4/4/07).

In short, American Imperial's accomplishments are hardly insignificant, but the boomers and boosters of early days, from W. F. Holt to Otis P. Tout, promised us more.

Were comparable data for Mexican Imperial available, we would surely find that the Mexicali Valley and the border strip produce a higher proportion of Baja California Norte's agricultural yield. The Chandler Syndicate was quite aware of this; and did not trouble to buy much of the Marsscape beyond the delta.

So American Imperial is rich enough, and so is Mexican Imperial. But I met a Pentecostal pastor and his family on the road to Algodones. Those people made bricks, a thousand for thirty dollars. To wash, they swam in a canal of *aguas negras.*

They said that they got so hot that many people they knew had gone to Jesus. They claimed to sometimes drink the *aguas negras.* At first I thought that I was not understanding, and kept pointing to the stinking black water in the ditch, and they nodded; perhaps they strained and boiled it . . .

How will their piece of Imperial be probated?

Chapter 169

SUCH A GOOD LIFE

(2006)

You corn kernels, you coral seeds,
you days, you lots:
may you succeed, may you be accurate

—Popul Vuh, before 900?

Teresa Cruz Ochoa and her husband José de Jesús Galleta Lamas were probably in their fifties but looked older. Both of them were grey, with strong reddish-dark hands. In their kitchen there were jars of candy, a poinsettia on the table, packets of American snacks in cardboard boxes. They had lived three kilometers south of the line in Colonia Borges for thirty years.

He was offered a job here because *a long time ago the owner of this land had cows.*—I don't do anything now. I was a cowboy before. I am from Jalisco, the man said, and she is from Michoacán. We own the land where the house is. We bought it from the owner.

How large is Colonia Borges?

It starts here and goes all the way to Algodones. You'll see houses all over the place.

The wife said: Before, we lived in Colonia Santa Isabel, and he was my father's neighbor. My parents told me not to marry him because he was much older than I was.

They laughed and laughed.

We've been married thirty-four years, she said, and they laughed again. They loved each other.

When you first moved here, were you happy that it was peaceful or did you feel lonely?

I didn't like it at all, she said. I cried a lot. I had never lived in a place like this.

As for me, said the man, I grew up on a ranch, so I liked it.

How close were your neighbors?

We were the last people to arrive here, and we had three neighbors, over there and over there.

What did you do for the water?

We were here for a year before we had running water and light in the house, she said. (Now they owned a refrigerator and a small air conditioner.) He would take the milk from the dairy all the way to San Luis and he brought back the empty milk jars full of water for me. An hour there, and an hour back. It was from somebody's faucet. The people who bought it would fill it with tap water for washing the clothes and dishes.

Once there were more than forty-eight milking cows, he said. *Muchos coyotes!* Lots of doves. Don't think we're talking about the coyotes who cross, although there are plenty of those. Neither one will ever go away.

You can eat the doves, and the ducks, said the wife, they're both really good. A lot of people come to hunt.

It's so tranquil, she said, such a good life. You raise your children without worrying about problems like addiction. And now in the pueblos, it's a disaster. For drugs and addiction, and also because of robbery. I don't cry anymore here! she laughed, showing one missing tooth.

The man said: We've got all our kids married and taken care of. Why *would* she cry?

What are the pros and cons of living in a *colonia* and not an *ejido*?

It is more solitary and more peaceful here in the *colonia,* she said. But the bad part is, even if you have money, you have to get into town to buy things.

Are there any subsistence farmers or family farmers in this area?

If you're talking about people who plant just what they're going to eat, she said, well, companies plant vegetables and things they eat.

There's nobody in the valley that lives that way anymore, the husband added. It hasn't been that long that people did, though. Maybe about twenty years. When we were married, there were people who lived that way and planted their own beans, their own tomatoes. But the father died and the family changed a lot. They did not want to follow the family traditions anymore.

Did you ever want to live that way? I asked the man.

Yeah, I wanted to live that way at one time, but why bother?

We could do it now, she said, but he is bad in the legs and also there is a problem with a lack of water. The people who own the parcels are always trying to get more water from the United States. That's why we are already poor and this is going to leave us more poor, once they line the canal. It will leave us in ruins. Now you have to go sixty feet down or more to dig a well. I have a little well with water to wash clothes and dishes. It used to be only thirty feet down. Now even sixty feet down there is not much water. About six years ago the water really became scarce. Somebody started planting another field around here, and then our well water dropped. We used to just have a pump, but now you can't get water that way anymore. We've only had our well for about three months. Six years ago that was how it was, with thirty feet only.

How does it look over there by the All-American Canal?

Well, it's pretty.

Many Border Patrol people?

Oh, *la migra*? Oh, *muchas*! They say it's really hard to cross now. We sometimes see helicopters. The *pollos,* we see them many times. We see men, women and children. They do not molest us. This is a good place to cross if you do it here. There are a lot of wells and you drink from the canal. If you go farther east, that's where the problem is. You might wander far into the desert. Too many cars, cars, cars! And if they don't have cars, they pass by foot! A hundred pass here each night! If it were a hundred people a week, it would be okay. So what they do is, they kind of watch for the police, and when they go, they cross. The only thing they might do is ask us for a little water when they cross.

The *pollos* come from the south; the coyotes are from here, the man said. You don't see 'em around anywhere. If you see them once or twice, maybe they wave to you. These people have their own contact here. They exploit them.

Have you ever been across the line, into the United States?

I've done some contract work over there, the man said. He was merry-eyed and grey, with a squat, sunburned face.—My wife has a passport, so she's been to Yuma, Los Angeles, Calexico. I go about once a year. My permission is for six months. I go mostly to Yuma.

It's been awhile since I went, he said. They ran me out, he laughed.

With her sweet smile, the woman said: We will have some tamales and pozole for Christmas and we invite you . . .

Chapter 170

STILL A GREAT FARMING COUNTY

(2004)

A thinly populated world of the type I describe either grows moribund and impoverished, falling off into an uncultured near-animal level—or it industrializes. It is standing on a narrow point and topples over in either direction and, as it just so happens, almost every other world in the Galaxy has fallen over into industrialization.

—Isaac Asimov, 1993

Well, it really has had several changes, said sprightly Mr. Claude Finnell, referring to Imperial County, of which he was a retired Agriculture Commissioner.*

Before I came, in the thirties, this was a large citrus area, lots of grapefruit and stuff like that. During the war that was the big thing, and then that began to go out since the San Joaquin Valley didn't have the heat we did. So we slipped into cotton at the time; it was controlled by the government of course. And alfalfa has always been a crop. Wheat, oats and barley have always grown here. Wheat's grown more important. When they had dairies they sold oats to the dairies. Cotton has been a crop in and out ever since the valley was farmed. Vegetables started here way before I came but in the early part of World War II they became a big crop. With vegetables it's been sort of the same here over time, but more and more intense cultivation, and less and less labor. Better varieties.

Bermuda came in not too long ago in the last fifteen or twenty years as a major crop. Bermuda has always been a problem before it became a hay. I guess somebody thought, hey, it's easy to grow, so why not? When I came here in '54, we had

*As Richard Brogan reminds us all, that position "is a big deal, in an agricultural county like this. See, all the enforcement, the environmental issues, they're yours. You can literally tell someone you can start a fire or you can't start a fire. They are not going to have a controversial person. They need a chameleon, a political person. Claude Finnell stayed in there for twenty or thirty years, anointed somebody to be his successor. This guy had unbelievable connections. The cement counties up north, they might change the commissioner periodically. Boy, when you get in this county, it's a huge thing being Ag Commissioner. He has the power to enforce quarantine."

some citrus, and doggone Bermuda grass was a pest! Actually you want it in your yard now, since it's easy to take care of and difficult to get rid of.

What was the biggest challenge you faced as Ag Commissioner?

He laughed. Getting through the summer, I think! No, the biggest problem we had at that time was a new pest, a grain pest, and for some reason we've got it all over the place, and our biggest job was to eliminate that capra beetle. It took about four years. We had to cover the building that was infected and put cyanide in it. That was very difficult and very dangerous.

It was mostly family farms when I came, but there's been a big change over the years, going from farmers living on the farms to the other kind. About in the fifties that began to change as the crops got bigger and you had to have more equipment as the cost began to increase. Most of the farms that were here then were farms that had been picked out and increased and made into a farm. Well, around in the fifties, a lot of those people were getting old and began to sell their farms, so the farms began to get bigger, which meant that with those new machines you either had enough money to farm or you didn't.

It's not the same self-contained farm that it used to be. Really, I'm serious about this. The counties around us, the coastal counties, have gone into manufacturing, building other things. San Diego at one time was one of the top farm counties. One of the top!

I lived in Corona before I met my wife, and my goodness! No farming *there* anymore.

As the farmers who came here and owned the farm and tilled it and so forth died, then, especially following World War II, prices for commodities were not very good, so great numbers of families quit farming and got out. I believe that there's probably fifty or sixty percent of the farms owned by the farmers, but it used to be more like a hundred percent.*

What was the average acreage here when you were Ag Commissioner?

Well, it was probably two hundred acres as an average, and now it's probably three or four. We have some large ones, as you know, forty thousand acres.

Do you think anyone could live on a hundred and sixty acres nowadays?

Values were different, he said then. Being a farmer was a good thing in those days. Being a farmer now is the same as a businessman. You'd have a difficult time, I think, living here on a hundred and sixty acres, unless it's beautiful vegetable ground.

Do you feel bad about that?

I think it's a normal kind of thing. We breed cattle to get bigger and bigger—and

*Here the reader may remember that as early as 1930, three-fifths of Imperial County's farms were operated by tenants, not owners.

better. So we do the same thing to farmers. I don't think we can work on the hundred-and-sixty-acre farm anymore. I do think that we have probably come to an equilibrium in farm size. It's not just a way of life anymore. It's a business, and it does quite well. Now, as people come here over time, they're gonna push out, do away with the land. That's gonna happen with a lot of places.

As I think over Mr. Finnell's implication, I remember a book I read, a small book published in a very limited printing; and there is a place in it when an interviewer asks an ancient rancher: *Have you ever thought about what the* Owens *Valley would be like if the City,* meaning of course Los Angeles, *hadn't come in and bought up the land?* It is 1976, sixty-three years after Mulholland completed the aqueduct, and fifty-seven years after pumping of Owens Valley groundwater began. The rancher has seen it all; he is ninety-two. He blames local greed and factionalism if he blames anything at all; he himself sold out to Los Angeles for a fancy price (after which masked men took to driving past his house and other anonymous defenders of ditch democracy set off dynamite on his field), and he insists that the Owens Valley was never as green as it is remembered to be. He replies: *Well, I have thought about it, but it is a dream, and nobody knows.* And I wonder if people in the Imperial Valley will be uttering similar words about the family farm fifty years from now, or even ten.

This seemed like an appropriate time to ask Mr. Finnell about the water transfer, but he preferred not to be quoted on that because (and here he laughed) *they might shoot me.* He cheerfully informed me what Richard Brogan had already revealed; namely, that he was in the pay of the Metropolitan Water District, and indeed, the phone rang a couple of times from MWD as we sat there at the kitchen table in that unpretentious house in El Centro. (He was not registered by the California legislature as a lobbyist, but in 1988, when IID approached agreeing "in principle" to sell a hundred thousand acre-feet of water to MWD, the *Los Angeles Times* referred to him as the fellow who *advised the MWD during the negotiations.*) Since I respected his wish for me not to take notes at this point in the discussion, I cannot go too thoroughly into his views; I do remember telling him that I was against the water transfer and having him breezily reply that every farmer has a corner of his land, maybe ten percent, which he's not getting much from and farms only out of inertia; it would do no harm to take that out of production, and market forces were going to make that happen anyway. He was probably right.

I was grateful to him for the interview and believed that I had already taken the measure of his opinions, so I let the water transfer go, overtly at least, and asked: Is there any factor which makes Imperial County unique?

Twelve months of growing, he said solemnly. Twelve growing months! The second thing is water, of course.

I think our biggest problem is competition from other countries like Mexico, not water. When I came down here, we actually had a compound for 'em. We could only bring 'em up for ninety days.* Mexico was only making a living. During that time, several or many of the U.S. citizens began to farm down on the coast on the Mexican side, from Texas down. And they could grow all kind of things. And that's just increased. And you cannot compete on this side. Just take lettuce for instance. Here you have to pay your employees seven dollars an hour. Down there they pay fifty cents an hour. Very hard to compete with that. There's an awful lot of disappointed farmers right now.

If you were the Ag Commissioner right now, what would you do about that?

I'd retire! he laughed. It's hard to fix. It's hard to change history as we go along. But by the same token, Mexico is gonna increase their lifestyle and they'll want more money and then some other island somewhere will take over.

We used to compete heavily with Cuba, he added. Sugarcane,† vegetables, before the embargo. We've always had barriers on that. It was a very U.S.-type island.

What do you think the valley's going to look like a hundred years from now?

Well, I don't think they'll be making snowmen! But I think it'll be a lot like it is now, with a lot of people in it. The number-one item will still be agriculture.

Mr. Finnell sat there in silence for a moment, and I sat there wondering whether that was the end.

A hundred-and-twenty-degree summer! he said with a smile, almost to himself. It's still a great farming county, one of the best.

*He must have been referring to the bracero program.

†Speaking of this crop, in 2001 Mr. Finnell was mentioned as the co-founder of the Imperial Valley Sugarcane Growers Association. In 2003 he was listed as a partner in a sugar and sorghum cane ethanol project. The company was registered in Baton Rouge, Louisiana.

Chapter 171

IMPERIAL REPRISE

(1975–2005)

The man of the land. He's part commodities expert. Part businessman. Part grower. And this year, he'll be picking six Dow products to grow bigger . . .

—The *California Farmer* advertisement, 1975

1

WATER IS HERE. Well, here there's life. There's work! There are lots of *maquiladoras.* **Sign of Slow Growth Sends Stocks Lower.**

The level of lead contaminants found on the site is 551 times greater than that recommended by the EPA. I make twenty boxes and each box has fifty masks. They want the young pretty girl without experience.

What happens is that your hands start to burn. A smoke comes out of the plant that makes the people feel sick. Some people faint because their air-conditioning isn't enough. They gave us pills for dizziness, and we often got dizziness. They took me to the hospital. They said it wasn't that bad. *If we treat them good, there'll be more of them who want to come.* If you get a lawyer, the lawyer charges you money. You get suspended if you don't learn. You can't complain or raise hell or they'll fire you. It's good, more or less.

It's good, more or less. I wanted to work there, but it was very far away and I would have spent fifty pesos on taxis.

2

I would have spent fifty pesos on taxis. *I have never been cheated out of a dollar in my life.*

3

You can't complain or raise hell or they'll fire you. Those assholes who try to control us, we just make fun of them. Teresa the Mexican surprised them all!

4

WATER IS HERE. *But if water levels keep dropping, we will run out someday.*

5

We breed cattle to get bigger and bigger—and better. So we do the same thing to farmers. There's a white kind, and then when you're drunk there's a green kind that'll end it.

There's nobody in the valley that lives that way anymore. There were people who lived that way and planted their own beans, their own tomatoes. But the father died and the family changed a lot. They did not want to follow the family traditions anymore.

I guess what they're afraid of is that the water would just get taken away. *"Moisture Means Millions."*

What I don't understand is that *we have the water,* so we should have had a better negotiating position. *Sympathy has no place in the courtroom, and the jurors were told that four times . . .*

6

Americans are always very friendly with their big hamburgers. I used to dream about living in the United States, but I don't anymore, because I don't like the way I would be treated. **To finalize this letter, I ask you, what is enough, 1 million illegals, 10 million or until the other countries are empty.** Why should we support people who don't belong here? *The sheriff's department believes the deaths could outpace last year's record of 95. Sympathy has no place in the courtroom, and the jurors were told that four times . . .*

PART TWELVE

DEFINITIONS

Chapter 172

IF MEXICO WERE ITALY

(2004)

If Mexico were Italy . . .

If Mexico were Switzerland . . . Don't even think that. But if Mexico were Italy, well, that could be possible. Every *supermercado* would be a *supermercato.*

An artificial fountain would be spraying over lemon-covered coconut slices, Romulus and Remus uplifting greedy mouths to the teats of the bronze *lupa;* and Mexicans would be trying to keep illegal Albanians out! *If we treat them good, there'll be more of them who want to come.*

A book called *Imperial,* told through the marble reverberations of Rome, might conceivably be as vivid as the walls of the Vatican's Gallery of Maps: **THE DESERT DISAPPEARS** into white-coasted emerald lands in seas of lapis lazuli, filled with golden sun-stars and calligraphic trails, wakes of word-ships!

In the ruins of the Forum, next to the ice cream wagon, I've truly seen Antonietta Imperial Fruit.

Chapter 173

WHERE DOES LOS ANGELES END?

(1834–2005)

The uncertain air that magnified some things and blotted out others hung over the entire Gulf so that all sights were unreal and vision could not be trusted . . .

—John Steinbeck, 1945

The important place in 1834 was San Pedro Harbor, which *furnished more hides than any port on the coast.* As an afterthought, our American observer wrote that *about thirty miles in the interior was a fine plane country, filled with herds of cattle, in the centre of which was the Pueblo de los Angeles—the largest town in California . . .*

In 1873, we could say definitely that Los Angeles, once sixteen square leagues, had been reduced to *four square leagues, or 17,172.37 acres.* It remained quite distinct from Anaheim, Compton and other such irrigated islands.

In 2004 an Angeleno showed me how Echo Park kept its own character: A beautiful mural of a girl with flowing hair rationalized the land and then we coasted past a *quinceañera* store; on Sunset Boulevard we saw a lovely Mexican-looking girl with a parasol over her head; then down the dip we drove to the Flores Recycling Center and around the corner to a vista of blue-green palm trees on a hill looking down on Silversun Liquor. Hello, **MAGIC** Paint and Body!

This was considered *a fairly hip area,* said the Angeleno as we passed Floyd's Industrial Goods at Hyperion. Indeed, Rough Trade (Sex, Leather and Spurs) was located conveniently across from Jiffly Lube. Then we merged smoggily into Silverlake not long before Tang's Donut. I admired the white frosting on the red facade of the Vista theater. Before I knew it, we were riding on Vermont in Little Armenia, Sunset Boulevard in Hollywood—don't let me forget to tell you about that stretched-out yellow church right next to Crossroads, the French Cottage Motel, then the grand high palm trees on the righthand side of Highland, you know, just before you cross Orange right before Days Inn. Once you reach La Brea, you relax and sit and *sit* in traffic.

It would be more accurate to describe our progress not in paragraphs but like this:

- the Saharan Motor Hotel
- Mexican Hamburgers Hot Dogs
- All-American Burger
- the Seventh Veil: ***Live Nude Revue GIRLS GIRLS 18 & Over***

a stone angel on a plinth in an almost Moorish cobalt-blue niche with white squares subdivided into four diamonds each of which glowed behind her, and the address: 7180

then a once-red pillar above the street number, a haunted looking image of a glamour girl half drowned out by reflection of fences and palm trees from across the street

then

(seen through the sea-cool grating)

a tunnel with a blue ceiling of blue plates

a mural on the lefthand wall of a reclining woman with red drapes on the lush bed behind her, and on the right, black stone steps, probably granite, leading upward to another statue, neoclassical, of the eternal feminine clutching one breast and exposing the other, turning her stone gaze to right where it said OPEN although it was not open

which was why we then got back into the Angeleno's automobile (he was an excellent person; his name was Jared); and before we knew it, we had reached the Crossroads of the World! (**UNIQUE OFFICES.**)

High in the air, a grubby globe whose blue seas were going grey but whose white continents remained white, doubtless thanks to solar bleaching, turned clockwise at a rapid clip; its own wide stand was two white legs connected by steel latticework widening as they descended past the American flag on its pole until they achieved rest upon a glass cylinder with a wavy fence around it; and cars grunted by in packs.

Anything beyond that bank, anything that west, is just ugly, Jared said. Bad, bad traffic.

He said that he lived much of his life in the car, talking and watching the cars crawl by so that it did not matter so much where he went or even quite how much time he passed in the car; being in the car was just like living.

And when he had said this, downtown's skyscrapers blue-grey in a white smoggy air, the half-silhouetted masses of greyish-blue buildings and greenish-grey palm trees appearing and disappearing in the smog, grew strangely beautiful to me.

And in 2005 I was with an ex-Angeleno (my own species); she drove me up 405, *the 405* as locals say, past the Getty Center, getting off at Mulholland Drive (left lane), and up the green coastal hills, and Los Angeles looked like a wellscrubbed beachscape, complete with easy width and sweeping turns of pavement . . .

. . . And she spun me along Mulholland Drive, winding down across Stone Canyon and around the moist green hills with the San Fernando Valley below; white houses, the more expensive the more precious, then came dark trees and more white building-squares and mountains until the San Fernando Valley opened up, with the long straight ribbon called Sepulveda shooting through the white-and-grey-green grid toward the mountains.

In the valley, which Mulholland's Owens Valley water had reclaimed, I saw Mexicali Tires on Van Owen.

Lovely white skyscrapers were sliced by the blinds of the hotel window, and embossed with bluish-black window-dominoes; sharp-angled towers met blue sky. Now in the night the same view altered to random small greenish rectangles of light in a black vertical nightscape, topped with the previously sun-hid words ONE WILSHIRE.

Later that year we were motoring through Irvine, and when I asked her what she saw, she replied: *Offices and cookie-cutter houses.* She insisted that here we were outside Los Angeles. *They were discrete places when I was growing up, and just because they're now filled in with sprawl doesn't mean they're not different now. Anyway, L.A. is not Irvine to me.*

What's the difference?

This is Orange County, she insisted.

But to me, because I could not *see,* it was just hedges, freeways, office-cubes, cars, smog, ***EXECUTIVE PARK***s, the sky whiter than Imperial's, my eyes stinging, the Washingtonia palms and eucalyptus; it felt very Los Angeles to me.

She drove me to Long Beach, Huntington beach, the Liquid Lounge beneath a bright blue-grey sky, Garden Grove, then Cypress, next exit; and we had come home by crossing the Los Angeles County Line. And to her it did feel like Los Angeles. I could not understand why. But here were Cherry Avenue North and South! RIGHT LANE MUST EXIT. **VIVA LAS VEGAS**. ORANGE AVE. ¼.

Artesia Highway and the Imperial Highway, what souvenirs were these? We'd better put them in a book of dull old history called *Imperial.*

A white airplane crossed the freeway silently descending; my chest ached with smog, and plane after plane kept passing. Here hid a Los Angeles bungalow, painted white and adorned with many flags on its small lawn; here were more bungalows beneath the large trees.

Our overpass soared up above eucalyptus and pines on the median. On the

Santa Monica Freeway I inhaled a summer breeze, and the world grew so green and cool, Los Angeles being an oasis here yet, decorated with the ball-shaped trees I remembered from my childhood.

I saw some pedestrians at the crosswalk at Ventura Boulevard, and I asked her whether that wasn't as rare as rain in Imperial, pedestrians in suburban Los Angeles? She did not answer me. There was glaring white evening light on the grey tarmac, light on shiny white car-shoulders, office towers in shadow . . .

Back in 2004, I was sitting beside Jared in his car in Santa Monica, on a street called Centinela.

It would probably be easier to take the 10, he said. Let's see, what time is it? Three-seventeen; yeah, better take the freeway.

Later we were going east on Pico with this green park and that green golf course, those white building-cubes whose windows were partially overprinted by rocket-shaped shadows, and now already we had crossed Motor Avenue. This must be Los Angeles, of course, for I spied the Avenue of the Stars!

Then it was a wide and soothing ride all the way up to Fairfax. The Boulevard Vacuum Company was an old white building like an ancient dowager's frilly underpants.

(In Valencia you're in the evening brightness, towers glowing white, orange, grey-blue, dark grey-blue. Suddenly, gold light seethes bitterly in an infinity of searing square jewels. You've reached the office tower on Wilshire and Figueroa.)

On the freeway, swiveling around dusted treescapes and graffiti'd freeway walls, we came successfully to Lakewood-Bellflower, where Jared's father had gotten clean and sober.

It was always so boring, said Jared.

Bellflower was renowned for its churches and car dealerships.

It actually kind of feels like a No Man's Land, he said, because it's definitely not Orange County but it's definitely not L.A., because nobody's concerned with entertainment out here for their livelihood. It's definitely working-class.

Suddenly, we passed a Disneyland-like island spilling with water.

Buena Park peered down over the freeway at a green world of flat roofs and treetops, a few trees quite grand and gracious, and then we began to ride Highway 91, penetrating the Inland Empire, driving deep toward Riverside. Tyco Flow Control welcomed us with a white cube leering over the freeway on the outskirts of Tustin. Even I could tell the difference between this and the lovely shiny black shoes of businessmen on Downtown's pale sidewalks.

I noted Lakeview Avenue, then the Imperial Highway, Highway 90, dryish mountains ahead. Now we had come into Yorba Linda.

Is this still Los Angeles to you?

I always equate Yorba Linda and Fullerton, said Jared.

They're both Orange County, his girlfriend Caroline explained, which meant that we were definitely out of Los Angeles.

I think Imperial Highway would be a good demarcation, Jared said. That way is all Mission Viejo and Newport Beach . . .

The freeway led us into California's dry and hilly interior.

The red-white-and-blue announcement on the Feather River dam advised us that we had already experienced **200 YEARS OF FREEDOM**; then we were in Riverside County.

It looks a lot newer, said Caroline, like a lot of pink stucco.

And a lot more of these commercial plazas, said Jared, with homogenized aesthetics, all adobe style or faux modern. A lot of RV dealers. Looks like it's just more recreational. I mean, you don't have the beach all that close at hand. I mean, you do; it's only about forty-five minutes; but most people here are more into dirt play than they are into water play. Everything seems less landscaped, more desert.

Now for the Tyler Mall and mile-long Ontario Mills!

We desired to visit Magnolia and Golden in the eleven thousands, so we kept driving east toward the mountains, with palms and shrubs keeping us company in the median strip.

They're not making much use of the vertical space, said Jared. They just keep everything spread out and low.

We rode past a giant corporate hospital, followed by the Magnolia Surgery Center and more palm trees and grassy corporate lawns, America's Tire Co., a coffee chain, a submarine sandwich chain, a boarded-up Victorian in the nine thousands, strip malls now retiring in favor of smaller detached older structures such the public library (white, 1908); whereupon Cindy's Cafe yielded to the carwash and video store.

Caroline said: It's hotter here than in Los Angeles. Also, there are no parking meters; here you can park at the side of the street.

Then here we were at the shaded Heritage House, which I have written about in *Imperial* and which went on sleeping its sleep.

Chapter 174

MEXICANS AND AMERICANS

(1901–2007)

Gringo, in its literal signification, means *ignoramus.* For instance: An American who had not learned to eat chili peppers stewed in grease, throw the lasso, contemplate the beauties of nature from the sunny side of an adobe wall, make a first class cigar out of a corn husk, wear open-legged pantaloons, with bell buttons, dance on one leg, and live on one meal a week. Now the reader knows what a terrible thing it was in early days to be a *gringo.*

—Horace Bell, 1881

Chung Lee's store was burned during the Los Angeles riots of 1992. Richard Kim was shot at, and shot back. At a stoplight, Walter Park was shot in the temple, the bullet passing through his left eye and partially lobotomizing him. His stepson tells us that a black man did this. Many in the mobs who attacked Chung Lee and Richard Kim were black. When my Korean-American in-laws told me about that time, they always emphasized the blackness of the people who had threatened them. But hear a bookkeeper-accountant from South Central tell the story: *Now, they talk about the looting in Koreatown . . . Those wasn't blacks, those wasn't blacks, those was Mexicans . . . We wasn't over there lootin' over there, but here, in this right here.* Who were Mexicans to her? I wonder.

One zoot-suiter whose eardrum got fractured by the police back in 1943 (they must have been white, context tells me) *had a hate in me, even now,* now being the 1990s, and he liked it whenever whites looked afraid of people of color. Who was he? Aside from his negatively defined existence in relation to whites, how did he see himself? Was he American, Latino, Mexican, Chicano?

A muralist in San Diego said: *I think I've considered myself Chicano ever since the late sixties . . . I hate the word* American *because it's such a weird statement for me.*

And here I ought to mention what one Northsider biographer of César Chávez describes as the Mexican perception that *Chicanos are traitors: they are the Mexicans who left and never looked back . . .*

I hate the word *Hispanic,* said Stella Mendoza, the former President of the

Imperial Irrigation District. Hispanic to me is a label they put on anyone who is of a Latin background. I've always considered myself to be Mexican-American. I'm proud to be of Mexican descent, but I'm an American citizen. But these terms, *Chicana, Latina, Hispanic,* I hate those.

Who are we to each other—what we do to each other or what we expect from each other? Most so-called knowledge of the other is as empty as the white concrete benches of the Park of the Child Heroes on that cool night (actually chilly for Mexicali) which happened to follow the Day of the Little Angels: All the couples who usually sat there on summer nights, the women on the men's laps, were gone. The white benches made me feel as if I were in the cemetery. Then up from the ground rose handsome young Carlos from Honduras, deported from Arizona just today for trying to get an honest job. Well, actually, to tell you the truth, brother, he had been caught in MacArthur Park in Los Angeles, selling meth. He wanted a place for the night; he explained to me very gently and cordially that he would do anything to get a place, not that he was a bad person, bro, but in this world you gotta do what you gotta do; and no matter how quickly I walked, he remained at my side, with his huge cousin in the red shirt, another graveyard child, now half a block behind. We passed the doorway of the Nuevo Pacífico, and the girls within looked pale enough to be dead. I remarked to my new friend that since I was a gringo, if anything happened to me, no one would help me; and because I said it simply and without bitterness, he liked me then; he laughed, and for half an hour we talked about women, God, money, broken hearts, standing on the darkish sidewalk in front of the Hotel Chinesca; he had no suspicion that I was staying there. He would much rather have wheedled than robbed me. Finally I put a ten-peso piece into his hand, because I truly did feel sorry for him, preferring not to sleep in parks myself. Carlos wanted five dollars. I said I was sorry. He wanted ten dollars and I said I was really sorry; then I shook his hand and he understood that I stayed here, and his cousin, who had been preparing to loom over me like a mountain on the verge of avalanche, dropped despondently back and then Carlos pretended again that he liked me.

To him, I would say, I was neither more nor less than a gringo: rich as he was not, representative and beneficiary of the system of delineation that excluded him; accordingly, fair prey whenever he could catch me. I could have been Canadian or British and his definition of me would have been the same. And what was he to me? What I had said to him about my vulnerability in Southside was so true that perhaps his non-Mexican-ness was irrelevant, in which case why not extend Southside all the way to Patagonia?

A history of such transnational perceptions characterizes Latin Americans' stereotype of the Northsider soul as the *calculating, cold-hearted materialism of the Caucasian Other.*

In perfect counterpoint, an American observer of Mexican California concluded: *The men are thriftless, proud, extravagant, and very much given to gaming; and the women have but little education, and a good deal of beauty, and their morality, of course, is none of the best . . .*

Another foreign adventurer of that period wrote: *In person, the Californian* caballero *is generally tall and graceful, with jet black hair, having a slight tendency to curl, a brown complexion, expressive black eyes, and features decidedly Roman in their cast . . . I cannot conceive a more perfect type of manly beauty and chivalrous bearing.* Like his colleague, he was extremely aware of Mexicans' pride.

My own summation—or stereotype, if you will—of a Mexican would be someone who is suspicious of outsiders, cynical of authority and distrustful of power, because he has been robbed so many times; someone who desires, perhaps more fiercely than I, to keep and enlarge whatever he has. And, yes, he is proud, so much so that liberty may be more valuable to him than wealth. In every sense he can be harder than I; probably he works harder.

What about me? Am I a calculating, cold-hearted materialist? Naturally, I cannot step far enough back out of my own shadow to see myself as I am. I am methodical because I am less robust than many Southsiders, more easily defeated by sickness or accident. My national inclination, which I mistake for personal, is to see Americans as idealistic, accustomed to believing that problems can be solved, that the pie can be made large enough for all, because we have not suffered as much as Mexicans; thus we are naive and complacent, but also in some ways more generous and optimistic.—What about the Mexican War, and Chinese Exclusion, slavery, the Indian genocide, Operation Gatekeeper and the broccoli days and years of Lupe Vásquez? In each case I excuse myself, my friends and almost everybody I know, thinking something like: Well, of course such things have happened, but the ones that happened a long time ago were possible only because at that time people were "different," and the ones that take place today are the work of politicians and corporations; so I excuse myself.

I remember one time when Lupe Vásquez was complaining to me about the unfairness of Americans to Mexicans; finally, he grew so intemperate as to say, of *all* Americans, and, feeling injured, I said: Well, what about me? If I haven't been fair to you, I'd like to know about it.—After a silence, during which he regarded me with his black eyes sparkling with rage, he finally grudgingly said: You been fair, Bill . . .—a statement which satisfied neither of us, because he felt, I could tell, that I had dragged it out of him, whereas I naturally had hoped to hear him say that I was more than fair: *generous,* a true friend, etcetera.

I know Americans who regard illegal immigration, and the so-called border problem, with outright fear. *If we treat them good, there'll be more of them who want to come.* Most of my neighbors, although they would deny it now, expressed support for the Iraq wars, which appeared as easy and advantageous as raping away half of Mexico.—But I believe in the United States of Northside, and I always will; I couldn't bear it if we weren't good—

And how did Lupe perceive the difference between Northside and Southside?

Well, right here in Calexico and Mexicali the people are actually the same: *Mexican,* he once said. The buildings are different and everything is more organized in the States. In Mexicali you still have a lot of *colonias* where you have unpaved streets. There's more poverty in Mexicali. But on the Mexican side you have more freedom. You can do things that a poor person can't do over here. You can buy a cheap plot of land and build your own house. You can build it starting with one little room. You don't have inspectors coming to see your license.

Although I have been spied on and detained in my own country, I have also been extorted by Mexican officials. They have assessed me fees for nonexistent permits, written my various drivers tickets for the misedemeanor of stopping to ask them directions, and openly charged me protection money. I eternally smile and pay, so we get along famously. And how "free" is Mexico for people such as José López from Jalisco, who cannot pay?

For one survivor of "the movement" of 1968, the forces of the state were personified by *the president's perverse monkey features* and the riot police. *All those guys who lied, who kept us down, who kissed ass, who threatened us—they were the real Mexico,* he decided. *But then we, the new we, made from the many that had been, decided that, fuck it, we were also the real Mexico.*

With those words in my mind, I asked Lupe: Which side is more corrupt?

Lupe did not answer directly. He said: *La mordida,* it used to be that they never left you alone. But little by little it's changing. They don't harass you; they don't ask for *la mordida* no more. A lot of people prefer to pay it, and not go to the fuckin' court and lose a day's work. See, *we* built the *mordida.* The people built it. So we're at fault for that.

What is the main difference between life here and in the United States? I asked an old man in Tecate, and he replied: In the United States, life is easier, because people have a lot of help. For example, an old person here in Mexico, after seventy, they don't get any help. Moreover, here if you didn't work, you won't get anything. But on the other hand, it's better to live in Mexico because there's less pressure. Over there you have to work all the time; you have to get up early; if you want to stand in the street and wait for a job, you can't, because the police will investigate you. Over there, everybody works, and whatever you earn, you end up just paying your rent with it.

Again, what about this freedom that Mexicans kept talking about? Just west of

Mexicali's Colonia Chorizo, and in sight of the border wall, I remember a woman of the garbage dump: long-fingernailed, her smile sawtoothed and crescent-shaped like a citrus pruning knife *circa* 1930. A girl of seven or eight years was also playing in those stinking heaps. When my interpreter and I asked to speak with her, the father, good defender, encouraged our departure with a machete. These people all survived; they stank but seemed vigorous; I doubt that they paid taxes. They were free, weren't they?

We live more freely here, said a government worker in Colonia Santo Niño, but on the other side (meaning Northside) there are many Mexicans, and you won't see them taking an empty can and throwing it into the street. The instant they cross *la línea,* they do that. Right over here, it's all garbage.

The border may indeed be unfortified, wrote Ruben Salazar in 1970, *but it separates two people*[s] *who created the Mexican-American—a person many times tormented by the pull of two distinct cultures.*

But, thanks to the Spanish Conquest, might not bifurcation be a part of *all* Mexican-ness? The syncretic Virgin of Guadalupe rushes back into my mind. The pull of that latest Spain, Northside, now sucks *pollos* out of Mexican villages everywhere. One Mexicana said to a biographer of Cortés's native mistress: *Malinche has always been venerated, here in Tlaxcala.* But perhaps we have been punished for this. People say that is why all our young men leave. They go to the capital, to the north, or even worse, to the United States . . . It's a curse, they say, . . . the allure of foreign things.*

Gringos hoard their ill-gotten riches; Southsiders expropriate. The existence of such stereotypes, which contain some truth, explains why it is that in Mexican Imperial we find such folk saints as the rapist Juan Soldado, the bandit-revolutionary Pancho Villa, and the robber Jesús Malaverde, now the patron of narcotraffickers; while American Imperial has proffered such exemplars as W. F. Holt, also known as Jefferson Worth, Minister of Capital; nor should we forget his fictive daughter Barbara Worth.

Mexican-ness partakes for better and worse of localism.—Josefina Cruz Bermúdez said to me: I am from Mexico City and I only know Tecate. It's the same in other places. You only know your own neighborhood.

As for me, I know many neighborhoods, or think I do. Perhaps I know none. Does

*The question of how well we ever truly *see* the other remains better unanswered. I remember an engraving of Malinche and her nineteen companions who were given to the conquistadors. The artist, who appears never to have seen Mexico, makes the naked nubile females resemble Italians as they cluster shyly together beneath an oaklike forest at the ocean's edge. And if I, Cortés, took Malinche to me, would I be as likely to find her out as she in her cunning desperation would be to tell me what I wished to hear? This thought-experiment leads to the following axiom: "When power relations are unequal, the weaker will know the stronger better than vice versa." Hence Mexicans know Americans better than the other way around.

that make me an American?—Where am I from? I was born in California; I think of myself as a Californian; but when I meet an Oregonian or a New Yorker, in my mind our similarities far outweigh our differences. We are Americans first and last. Meanwhile, in the late 1920s, Paul S. Taylor shockingly *found no recognized word or phrase all-inclusive of the various groups of persons of Mexican ancestry in the Southwest.*

They are all Mexicans to us, of course.

I asked the government worker in Colonia Santo Niño: In your opinion, when somebody crosses the border and decides to live over there in the United States, how soon does he become an American?

On the north side, people who live there are North Americans. On this side there are Latins. Before, there were patrons who would sponsor people to come across the border and would get their papers in order. When they live there three years, that's in my opinion when they stop being Mexicans and start becoming Americans. There was an American governor who said that.

Well, I thought, why not?

THE UNKNOWN

Working hypothesis: To be American is to cross the ditch or not, but in either event to remain unchanged by the other side. To be Mexican is to cross the ditch and be changed, or to be prevented from crossing the ditch and therefore to be changed. (I would never characterize them as hostile, objected the old pioneer from Heber, becoming hostile.) Is there anybody in Mexico, even in the remotest mountain village in Chiapas, whom the reddish-rusty shimmer of the border wall fails to reach? Mexico means Mix-aco; everything and everybody is mixed like a produce market's red, white and green: blackish-red chili pods heaped like a mass of curve-clawed crabs, white garlic and red beans splendiferously abundant in their various tubs, emerald nopal lobes in a boy's hand as he whittles away their spines with a dreamy smile. (I give a Mexican a dollar and his face lights up: Ah! A green peso!) At Algodones, just south of the Quechan Reservation, the line of cars bound for the United States waits for blocks and blocks, while a loudspeaker shouts into Mexico: *All right, everybody, mrphh mrphh mumpph.* Algodones possesses taco stands; Algodones offers serapes for sale in U.S. dollars (once, in Niland, almost in sight of Leonard's mountain, the old lady whose child owned the hotel let me pay for my room in pesos, once and only once; that was an exotic experience). Algodones bears many English-language signs for the better assistance of tourists. In front of one of them a man is hacking up a fallen palm tree. And down below him, on the banks of the Río Colorado, a man in a baseball cap which advertises an American fast-food chain sits all day on a rock surrounded by algaed water whose breath makes him feel a trifle cooler; his beard grows longer; he keeps thinking about invading Northside, but he feels discouraged. He treasures a single cigarette in the breast pocket of his shirt. He crosses his wrists in his lap, deciding what he should do. This side or the other side of the ditch? *Now I hear the people smugglers are getting so brazen, now they got the Humvees with the guns mounted on them.*

MORE UNKNOWNS

I "love Mexico." What does that mean? Would I live there? Only if I had money. Would I marry a Mexicana? Undoubtedly. Would I worry about crime there more than I do now? Yes, because more people in Southside are poor, and my white skin asserts me as a Northsider.*

Would I be more free in Mexico? I honestly believe so. Would I be happier? Are *they* happier? Not particularly . . .

Mexico is the street prostitute Liliana, who keeps reminding her clients: I'm a poor woman.—In the hotel she's all enthusiastic: I want to suck your dick! I need to suck your dick! Please let me suck your dick! and then: I want to be your friend! and then: I want to know all of life, so I want to be a serial killer. And she keeps staring at you with her crazy eyes when she repeats this last thing, so that it's legitimate to wonder whether she'll suddenly caress your throat with a razor. Fertile, sincere and occasionally menacing, that's Liliana; that's Mexico.—I'll be back, she says. She adds: But you said you had no money and you're staying at this expensive hotel! You lied to me. I'm going to wait out in the street for you all night. What do you really want? Just tell me the truth. I'm a poor woman; I've got to go now; I've got to work all night.

America is—what? America is me. I come to buy Mexico's time (I can't even remember anymore whether I slept with her). I want to be her friend, and then I want to write down my notes to put her in this book. What do I really want? Of course I lied to her; if I'd told her how much money I had, she would have robbed me . . .

I'm generous, I tell myself. I always tip José López on top of what I pay him; I invite him into my room to take a shower; he washes his stinking clothes in my sink. I buy him a meal. Then what? I put him in my book and stroll over to Northside, where he cannot go except at extreme risk. Who is he to me? I worry about him. So what? He's a poor man; he's got to work all day.

*In respect to this inherited characteristic of mine, it is strange to think that *Aztlán,* the unknown sacred place where the Aztecs originated, means *whiteness*. Aztlán was not entirely unlike the Colorado River Delta before they dammed the river, for there were many water-birds and fishes. A tall hill rose from the water like Pilot Knob. However, Pilot Knob has no caves that I know of, and the hill Colhuacan, Place of Ancestors, was riddled with grottoes where the ancestors lived.

Proud, sad, yet watchful; portrayed with a downward gaze; hooknosed, with fleshy lips; simply stylized, as Orozco's creations usually are, with bright light on his cheekbones, nose and chin, most of the forehead darkened by inky hair, the rest of his profile in shadow—this gouache is called "Study for head of an Aztec migrant." Who is he to me? Who am I and who can I be to Mexicans, who have enriched my life beyond my most greedy and romantic calculations?

PART THIRTEEN

INSCRIPTIONS

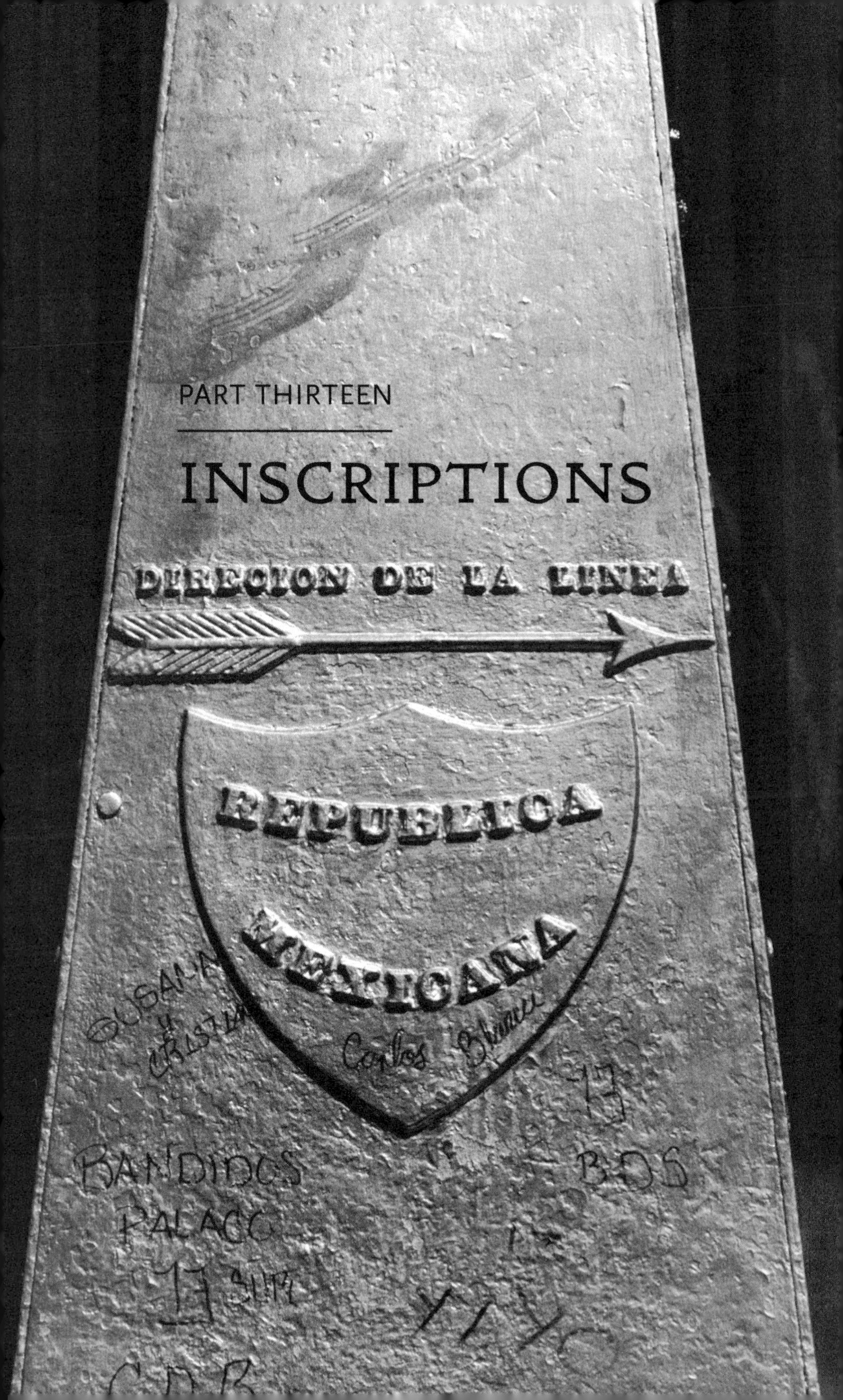

Chapter 175

STILL A MYSTERY

(2003)

Names Appearing in Black Letters IN THIS DIRECTORY are the names of people who ACCOMPLISH THINGS and are entitled to favorable consideration . . . The publishers are honored in thus making them better known to the public.

—Imperial Valley Directory (1930)

I opened the newspaper and read: **JUDGE ORDERS FULL WATER ALLOTMENT** and **TERROR ALERT ORANGE: Calexico: High risk level may cause delays for border-crossers.** That was on page one. On page two I read: **Holtville readies for Schwingfest** and **Man pleads to smuggling ring in S.D.** (a human-smuggling ring, of course) and **County marks end of phase 1** and then, at the bottom of that page, **Identity of dead man found still a mystery.** The identity of a dead man found floating in the All-American Canal west of here Monday was still a mystery due to the advanced state of decomposition . . . According to the deputy coroner, it was not thought the man was trying to enter the country illegally at the time of his death due to the way he was dressed. The man was reportedly wearing a T-shirt and jeans in good condition, black dress shoes and a Mexican military trouser belt.

That was on Wednesday. On Thursday, the front page said: **U.S. INVASION OF IRAQ BEGINS** and page two said: **Filth an ongoing problem, merchants say.** I guess that the identity of the dead man was still a mystery, since the newspaper didn't mention him. Well, after all, how could we be expected to keep track of every death? On Tuesday a lady in the three hundred block of Chisholm Trail in Imperial had discovered a dead bird in her back yard. *An animal control officer was sent to pick up and dispose of the carcass.* That was in the **POLICE BRIEFS** section of another newspaper.

On Friday, the brand-new "Liberation of Iraq" section began with a quotation from the President, and then on page A2 the most dramatic item of local news was **El Centro asparagus thief sought.** The identity of the dead man must have still been a mystery.

I missed Saturday because the newspaper fooled me. Usually it didn't appear in the vending machines until midafternoon of its day of issue, so I foolishly waited until Sunday morning to get Saturday's news, but it turned out that Sunday's paper was already there. Anyhow, on Sunday the front page said: **HALFWAY TO BAGHDAD** and page three said: **Broccoli cartons latest stolen crops.** I can't honestly claim that anybody else had died on the international line; and no doubt I am bigoted; no doubt I tend to think of Imperial as being more correctly represented by the newspaper some months later, which not only reported a **Body found in mountainous area** (a suspected illegal in Mountain Springs Grade) but also bad fishing on the Salton Sea (Ray Garnett, in whose boat I had motored down the lower reaches of the New River, informed me at that time that algal blooms had prevented him from catching a thing for three weeks now), than by **Broccoli cartons latest stolen crops,** which downplayed the gloom and doom, recasting Imperial as nothing more or less tragic than the epitome of provincial dreariness—straight out of Chekhov. Illegals didn't die every day in Imperial,* and the Salton Sea wasn't always terrible. Meanwhile, the identity of that dead man continued to be a mystery.

On Monday the front page said: **U.S.: 'DRAMATIC' PROGRESS SEEN** in Iraq, an extremely helpful bit of news whose accuracy was underlined by **Iraqi resistance slows advance.** Page seven reported: **ASPARAGUS: MARKET SLIGHTLY HIGHER.**

On Tuesday the front page said: **WRITTEN ORDER ON IID SUIT RELEASED** and **SANDSTORMS THWART AIR MISSIONS** and **Border Patrol reports fewer apprehensions.** Page ten noted that five illegals were burned alive in a controlled burn of a sugarcane field near the border; maybe it wasn't so controlled after all, or at least I hope not; anyhow, it happened not in Imperial but in Raymondville, Texas; I must have put it in this book by accident.

On Wednesday nothing at all occurred. I read the newspaper twice, because nothing was taking place in my life, either; all I could make out was that our military continued to make great progress.

On Thursday the front page said: **U.S. VOWS TO INTENSIFY ATTACKS** and **GUARDS POSTED AT IID DAM, NERVE CENTER: TERROR THREAT:**

*Since the entity I define as Imperial is larger than Imperial County, the latter's newspaper frequently excludes from publication such items as the following, since it occurred four miles north of the county line: "Sweeney Pass crash kills woman, injures 7": "A 26-year-old woman from Mexico died and seven people, including a 3-year-old boy, were injured when the Mazda Protege they were riding in flipped over on county road S2 . . . Six people fled the vehicle . . . Claudia Salinas Morales, 26, was declared dead at the scene . . . [Patrolman Ryan] Haley said federal smuggling charges would be filed against 23-year-old Maria Othon of San Diego, who was identified as the driver following an investigation. All seven of her passengers were suspected illegal immigrants."

Beefed-up security aimed at protecting water, power facilities, probably from the broccoli-carton thief. At the bottom of the page, I learned the following: **One dead, 18 hurt in rollover after blowout.** WINTERHAVEN—An unidentified man was killed and 18 others injured when a stolen vehicle suspected of carrying undocumented immigrants overturned near here Wednesday night when one of its tires blew out.

So now it had been a week and a day, and I had to face the likelihood that the name of the dead man in the All-American Canal would continue to be a mystery.

HOLTVILLE

Is this such a terrible thing? Someday, reader, you and I will be forgotten. In this regard I'm reminded of a certain haunting phrase by George Eliot: *unremembered tombs.* How many should we remember? *Leave the dead to bury the dead,* said Christ, in part because there are so many dead! On 12 July 1853, Señor Dolores Martínez of Los Angeles is *found shot by zanja.* A *zanja* is nothing more or less than a water-ditch, the All-American Canal itself being just another *zanja.* Who might Señor Dolores Martínez be to us? His identity will continue to remain an everlasting mystery. Moreover, in 1853 somebody died by violence pretty much every day in Los Angeles. So even if we could somehow come to know this murdered man, what about his three hundred and sixty-four–odd compatriots?

Once upon a time in Imperial—on Friday the eighth of May, 1914, to be exact—the former deputy county clerk, Miss June Bagby, now residing in San Diego, was *reported to be suffering from a slight indisposition, though nothing serious,* and James Hamilton of the Enterprise Grocery approached recovery from having inhaled a fly while being shaved. Aren't these facts history? Don't Miss Bagby and Mr. Hamilton deserve to be remembered just as much as Señor Martinez, even though they failed to accomplish anything as dramatic as dying right then? As the Women's 10,000 Club used to say, *the aim, if reached or not, makes great the life.* And what if there exists no aim whatsoever, or if we'll never discover it?

In the county of Imperial, in the city of Imperial, *1 mi n SP track,* local registered death number twenty-eight occurred on 29 July 1924. Full name: *John Doe unknown Mexican.* He was about thirty-eight, and his occupation was *apparently laborer.* The cause of death was *Heat Stroke found dead on* Southern Pacific *track 1-mi no-Imperial.* His birthplace, parents, etcetera, were all *not known.* They removed him to Mountain View Cemetery in El Centro.*

*His death certificate is reproduced at the beginning of this book, just opposite the dedication.

Local registered death number twenty-nine occurred on 31 July 1924, the place of death being identical with Albert Henry Larson's two years later, namely, *7 miles N West*. Monica Gordins, *female Mexican, single,* three months old, name of father unknown, maiden name of mother, if I can read it, *Yolda Yolda,* died of heat prostration and was buried that same day at Mountain View. Did the baby get no funeral?

So much about those unknown lives will never stop being mysteries. But for mysteries within mysteries, visit the unremembered tombs of Holtville. I suppose that the dead man from the All-American Canal has now taken up residence there. Perhaps they allowed him to keep his black dress shoes.

Go through the green grass beneath which entitled people are buried. Pass beyond the immense hedge and then the shrubby border proper to the furowed naked brown field with the knee-high white crosses imprinted with the pious lie **NO OLVIDADO**, not forgotten; on each there is a paper flower and a cup and saucer. I have not forgotten **ROW 7 24 JOHN DOE**; nor have I forgotten **JANE DOE** beside him; I recollect **ROW 7 10 JOHN DOE** and **ROW 7 11 JOHN DOE**, not to mention **ROW 7 12 JOHN DOE**, **ROW 7 13 JOHN DOE**, **ROW 7 15 JOHN DOE**, **ROW 7 17 JOHN DOE**, all of whose identities remain mysteries, and then, when you are ready for them all to be **OLVIDADO** once more, why, return to the front lawn of Terrace Park Cemetery, where the dead bear names, lying across the highway from a hayfield of whirling sprinklers.

RAG ENIGMAS

In 1531, Juan Diego Cuauhtlatoatzin ("He Who Speaks Like an Eagle") received miraculous winter flowers and wrapped them into his mantle. He carried them to the skeptical Bishop, and their magic left an image of the Virgin of Guadalupe on the very fibers of that garment. Sometimes in Imperial I think of that when I see the abandoned garments of *pollos* beaten down into the hardpacked desert until they've become flat stones. Whom did they belong to? That's a mystery. (Officer Gloria I. Chavez, U.S. Border Patrol: *I think we all feel sorry for 'em.*)

JOSÉ LÓPEZ'S FUTURES

The fact that *the identity of a dead man found floating in the All-American Canal west of here Monday was still a mystery* reminds me that that veteran illegal border-crosser, my friend José López from Jalisco, committed one of his sixteen immigration felonies by means of that same *zanja*.

It's been about six years, he told me; I remember that it was very hot that day in 2002; José was still rich in hopes of crossing the line and emulating the broccoli career of our mutual friend Lupe Vásquez.—It was three of us guys, he said. We had met in that place where, you know, where people wait to get jumped across. We went all the way to where the fence ends, and then there's the canal,* and we tried it there, but Immigration was *hard,* so we went to the other side of Mexicali, the west side, and we saw the Border Patrol, but we saw more probability of making it, so we waited until it was dark and just started. We had heard stories of people drowning there, so we were kinda scared, but our willingness outgrew our fear. Then we waited until that Border Patrol Blazer started to move. It was our first time. We didn't know we were supposed to take our clothes off and put them in plastic bags over our heads, so we came to America with wet clothes. It was winter season, so I got a job harvesting lettuce. Then I went back home. It had been a pretty good season, I remember. I saved about two or three thousand bucks.

How was the current? I asked him.

I don't know if it was the fear, he said, but I didn't find it really hard.

(We pause to insert into the record the testimony of Mr. Rose, who represents *a private corporation down there,* which is to say in Mexican Imperial; despite his professed animosity for Harry Chandler, he must have something to do with the Colorado River Land Company. It is the year 1925. He testifies to the Senate Committee on the Colorado River Basin: *It is nothing uncommon to pull out a dead horse*

*This spot is portrayed from the American side of the canal in my 8" x 10" negative BR-CN-USA-99-05, and from the Mexican side, where José would have tried it, in negatives BR-CN-MEX-99-06 and -04.

or dead cow along the canal, or even a dead man . . . It is an extremely long canal; it is imposible to keep them out. They swim out in the water; you see a whole family out there paddling around in the water; it is a common practice among the Mexican people. But no worries! In answer to the query of Senator Dill, Mr. Rose explains that we filter the water, so that dead Mexicans cannot make us sick.)

José was just then getting ready to make his seventeenth crossing, maybe in a week or two when the harvest started. For now he'd keep sleeping on benches in Mexicali. I asked him where he would try it, and he said: Downtown Calexico, right where the Port of Entry is. It's gonna be on my own, since I don't have no money to pay a coyote . . .

Why not the canal? You did it that other time.

It's too hard, he said, but I saw from the look in his face that if he thought he had to, he would still try it. One day I would come to Mexicali and ask for him, and he would not be here. Perhaps he would have made it into the United States, or perhaps he would drown in the All-American Canal, or it could be that thanks to heatstroke or a panicky driver trying to outrun the Border Patrol, the coroner would already have released him to the potters' field in Holtville, or not improbably he would have given up, temporarily of course, squatting in Colonia Chorizo or returning back home to his two children and their mother in Jalisco. In any case, he'd become a mystery to me.

And in time he'd be as forgotten as a cigarette carton crushed into the dirt of Avenida México.

INFORMAL LIBERTIES

His identity might be forever a mystery, his fate unknown to all who loved him, his purpose unfulfilled, his family perhaps left to fall apart in poverty somewhere in Jalisco, but at least he would be free, a term which I use in the same sense as it was employed in the following Western Union telegram from the Deputy Customs Collector in Los Angeles to the Deputy Customs Collector in Calexico at 1:30 P.M. on a 1913 day: ADMIT CORPSE AND CASKET FREE ON INFORMAL ENTRY.

Chapter 176

THE LINE ITSELF

(2003–2006)

Yet across the gulf of space, minds that are to our minds as ours are to those of the beasts that perish, intellects vast and cool and unsympathetic, regarded this earth with envious eyes, and slowly and surely drew their plans against us.

—H. G. Wells, 1898

Our primary mission is to prevent terrorism and terrorist weapons from entering our country," El Centro Chief Border Patrol Agent Michael McClafferty said, and in my mind's eye I can see these agents of delineation, far less self-questioning or half-ashamed than on that first coolish night in 1999 when I rode along with Border Patrolman Dan Murray, who was now retired; his primary mission had been simply to keep unauthorized Mexicans out. It wasn't that anybody who hated Border Patrol agents liked them better now, and they must have known that; but they themselves and the people whom they ostensibly protected from Southside now shared the fear, I repeat, *shared the fear;* they stood shoulder to shoulder together against their fear of Islamic murderers which seared Northside like sunshine itself; they could uniform themselves in haughty secrets now; they could be brisker and probably more brutal than they had been for many years; we submitted without a whisper. New powers and titles nourished them. There was a measure afoot to triple the wall where Imperial met the sea; leveling canyon and mesa, they'd be granted advance immunity from any legal or environmental questions. They were the sole adults in Northside; the rest of us were children or worse.

Once upon a time in 1915, the Treasury Department admonished the Collector of Customs: *The general belief that opium in powdered form, pearls, aigrettes or other merchandise must be illegally introduced into the United States is not sufficient warrant for subjecting every pedestrian crossing the border to such a search as was made in the case of Mr. Edmonston. You will be governed accordingly.* Oh, that was once upon a time, all right!

Near the beginning of this book I wrote about the first time they detained me, which was comparatively jolly. The second time I got to visit their little room, three years later, I suffered from optimism: We wouldn't remain there long, since we hadn't last time. At my ease, I took note of the love-word MEXICO scratched upon the metal bench on which we waited. I was with somebody else by then, a woman whose lineage and place of birth tied her, at least in the conviction of Northside's new department called Homeland Security, to Arabs. I will never forget the way she went from irritated to furious to unbelieving to frightened in the course of that seven hours.

The shame that they inflicted upon her (among other acts, they browsed publicly and contemptuously through her diary, much of which consisted of descriptions of her erotic feelings for me), caused me to hate them. The calm anger, not shame at all, which I myself felt when they emptied my wallet's papers onto the counter and every officer who happened by could frown over my parking receipts or, worse yet, the following incendiary anti-American document, which will appear in its own proper place in the infamous terrorist manifesto entitled *Imperial:* hard and gleaming tomatoes, coated with food-grade vegetable-mineral-beeswax and/or lac-resin-based wax or resin to maintain freshness . . . was irrelevant in comparison. They humiliated the woman I loved.

Sitting on that hard metal bench, from which I was not allowed to rise even to request a cup of water (they brought that to me), I lost my desire to imagine stories. When a man with a gun took me to the toilet and observed my urination, I hated him personally and wished him the worst. Either he or I should not have been a citizen of this country. *You will be governed accordingly.*

I became familiar with the partition which separated me from her; they did not forbid us from leaning forward and speaking to each other occasionally, but I was not allowed to sit beside her or hold her hand. Above all, the supposition that whether or not we were criminals we had no right to question why we were under suspicion, or to know when if ever this would end, or sit together, or even read, was educational. (Every time the door would open I would see her lean anxiously into my view, hoping that this would be the end.) *It all comes down to desperation, and the smugglers—being as depraved as they are—they prey on people's desperation and human misery.* The waiting and waiting, the not being allowed to comfort her or get my belongings, the bitterness that I couldn't even entertain myself with a pencil and a piece of paper while I awaited their convenience, these wore me down, to be sure, but in the end they accomplished something positive: I stopped being sorry for these officials and began to hate them. I still hate them. My plan is to hate them for the rest of my life, and to incite others to hate these un-Americans.

If I were a Mexican field worker, and they treated me like filth over and over, how would I feel about them then?

They took her away first, through the steel door marked ***BROKEN*** because it slammed. She was gone a quarter-hour. Then it was my turn to be fingerprinted. They did not like it when I looked out the window into Mexico, or when I asked what system they were using. But the woman who held my hand was female and gentle in her official way; I enjoyed surrendering each finger to her to be electronically scanned even though when I later looked back on the four-and-a-half-hour detention I found that being fingerprinted without my consent and having my fingerprints added to an unknown database offended me the most. They did something to my laptop computer, too; I suppose that they downloaded everything. If they infected it with spyware, all the better.

Whom did I *really* hate, though? Not the man with the nearly shaved head, nor Fatso at the desk, and certainly not the courteously hard-bitten FBI agent from El Centro with the twang in her voice, nor most of the various male officers who escorted me to and from the restroom whenever I needed to urinate, nor the kind female officer who got me a prison box lunch at about three-thirty in the afternoon. None of these had crossed *my* line. The man who ran his hands over me, first requiring me to lean forward with my hands above my head and against the wall so that I was off balance, at his mercy, I hate him and sometimes imagine punching him in the mouth. Well, wasn't he just doing his job? If I had a chance to punch him, I would not; I'd never touch him.

Should I have blamed Eleven Negro, which was what Mexicans called September 11? I forgive the authorities their ignorance, but not their disrespect. We need have no fear that our lands will not become better and better as the years go by.

As for Southside, precisely because that utterly alien zone contaminated with multiple criminalities justified their existence, they must have feared it, as did the Pyrrans in Harry Harrison's Deathworld Trilogy, hunkering behind their patchwork redoubt of flamethrowers and steel plates, on the defensive against alien lifeforms which constantly mutated against them. *"The southern border is literally under siege . . . ," Representative Solomon P. Ortiz, Democrat of Texas, said at a Congressional hearing.* Or, as the Deathworld Trilogy explains: *Hundreds of thousands of years of genetic weeding-out have produced things that would give even an electronic brain nightmares.* Do you want to hear more? *"Praise Perimeter!" she breathed. "They found the napalm. One of the new horrors is breaking through to Ward Area 13 . . ."* In that connection, I remember what Dan Murray (who was not such a bad sort) always used to say: *They'll pop their heads up again in a minute.*

The functionaries of Operation Gatekeeper liked to advise me not to get too close to the fence, in case a Southsider threw rocks. That could have been their experience. Nobody ever threw rocks at *me*. They said that it was dangerous on the other side of the ditch; I can well believe that it might have been so for them. Once upon a time in the hot darkness outside the Thirteeen Negro, a threatening drunk attached himself to me, walking at my side for block after block, demanding not just money but big money; informing me that a broccoli knife stood ready in his pocket, he molested me with his bloodshot gaze, which reminded me of an Aztec stone sculpture of a man's head who glares and grimaces with his white strips of shell inlay for teeth, and his red-smeared shell-eyes with obsidian pupils make him hideous to me; it was with precisely such bloody eyes that this drunk assaulted me; he had just teased me with the third glimpse of his broccoli knife when I reached the Hotel Chinesca, passing inside with much the same relief as a child feels pulling the bedclothes over his head, and he remained outside, glaring redly at me through the glass door, waiting for me to come back out into his power. Could it be that to some Northsiders, *all* Southsiders were of his species?

Tunnel between Mexicali, Calexico discovered, the newspaper announced. *One of the new horrors is breaking through to Ward Area 13*. That wasn't the newspaper; that was the Deathworld Trilogy. But Imperial was science-fictioning itself into Deathworld. *We're going to send a robot down,* announced the Immigration and Customs Service spokeswoman, because who knows what lurked in that tunnel twenty feet down? After all, **Tunnel to U.S. starts inside Mexican home**. *The investigation was not in response to statements by a Mexican man who claimed to have used a tunnel in eastern Calexico to help Chinese terrorists into the country to build a nuclear "dirty bomb" to attack Boston*. So they sent their robot down. They discovered electricity, a closed-circuit security system, and other signs of sinister sophistication. **U.S. officials seize house at end of border tunnel**. *Several altars with flowers and pictures of saints were also found inside.*

Oh, it's not easy holding the line, but they were doing it well enough that Kay Brockman Bishop could tell me: Illegals come through our property very seldom. They've put up some new cameras on our property that have really made a difference. I had one coyote on the Donlevy ranch that would wave to me every morning. But here we've had no problem that I can speak of.

Now let me tell you how that line appears nowadays.

THE LINE ITSELF (2003–2006)

It starts with grey ocean, cafés, *terraza de playas*, ***PESCADOS***, **MARISCOS**. Above the grey sea-swells, coconuts hang from a beam. Each year, Tijuana really does increase its likeness to San Diego. It is clean and grey, with families sitting on the grass. Americans sometimes buy or rent houses here. Going inland, the line becomes less built up, for which we must console ourselves with the following leftwing campaign billboard: ***WHERE THERE IS BREAD YOU LIVE BETTER***. The line continues away from the sea and up the cut in the sand-ridge. In these hills, the box-houses are better than shanties, but as the line goes east they begin to resemble the assemblages of Mexicali's Colonia Chorizo: tires hung in rows on doorways, a broken brickwork skeleton which proclaims itself **SE VENDE**, junked cars in steep ravines. Then suddenly there is a rolling vista of white houses with an uprising of green trees.

Going east, it gets grubbier and smoggier. Three beautiful prostitutes and two hotels delight the eye. Often these kind ladies are in white miniskirts, standing with crossed thighs.

From the whores, flies and shoe stores of Centro to the freeway between the two overpasses, from the graffiti'd yellow castle (taste of exhaust in my mouth) to the giant white Jesus on the grimy hill, Tijuana lives with the line. One poet of the illicit secrets of Coahuila Street, of *piss and mortuary candles,* of meth, of *transvestites with enormous bullet tits,* and of above all *las niñas las niñas,* the girls the girls, sings of a certain billard parlor where one must go to obtain *the essential address of the tomb of* that rapist-saint *Juan Soldado,* about whose life and death this book has already written* and *who bestows the miracle of invisibility required to cross the border, without* la migra *seeing, without* la migra *seeing.* That tomb, of course, lies but three blocks south of the border. Someday I will go there, and pray never to become invisible to the girls the girls. What does John the Soldier stand for, but the occasionally crossed divide between evil and sacredness? Yes, in Tijuana the line lies everywhere! Even on Insurgentes, where flocks of young workers pass in and out of that gate in the long stretch of Óptica Solas, while under a blue tarp, two ladies sell tacos and potato chips at a factory's edge, they talk about how the wages are better here than farther south, and how much better still—ten times better—they must be *on the other side.* A woman sells ***EXPRESS FRUIT*** on a metal siding near Metales y Derivados on this drizzly January morning, waiting for customers in the huddles of job-seekers at this or that *maquiladora.* Occasional groups of half a dozen–odd chunky young women in cheap windbreakers pass rapidly, chattering. From Metales y Derivados, the Northsider-conceived nightmare, abandoned to poison the people and other organisms of Southside, there comes a piquant solvent smell in honor of the line.

And the line continues east! In sight of the wall grow a few sunflowers. At the freeway entrance two girls are hitchhiking, one of them holding a baby. Then on a fresh-shaved sandy hillside I see a housing development like some white conglomeration of salt crystals. Ahead, a mountain veils itself in dust. Two wide concrete ditches whose emptinesses echo that of the Los Angeles River mark some kind of delineation best known to engineers; then the highway climbs out of the Tijuana

*In "The Line Itself," p. 563.

Valley, which from above appears more hellish than it really is.* We now say good-bye to the blue restaurant Yi Wa.

In deference to the line, many cars bear California license plates, but Californians can be of any color and these vehicles most often hold brownskinned people.

At the strip malls where the Tecate toll road begins, you can easily find a Pollo Féliz to eat in, along with its American counterpart. Also awaiting you are Industrial Tools de México, Veterinaria Azteca, and a photocopyist. A vendor wheels his cart and rings his bell at the intersection of Industrial and Maquiladora, which is appropriately solvent-smelling; then comes a hill like a double-toothed volcano, a roadside cross in honor of some dead victim, and the Río Tecate, which today is a brownish streamlet. Now begins the ascending desolation; it's similar to what one sees when flying from Los Angeles to Imperial: the same mountains, orangish-tan with wisps of green on top. Rapidly it becomes beautiful. Occasional *rancherías* show off small tan hay bales, as rounded volcanic-looking cones rise over the trees. Whitish round rocks burst out of the reddish grass, just as in California's Sierra foothills. The wall can occasionally be seen.

Next comes Tecate in its rocky, grassy bowl. It is a cool town of generous trees. In many places the wall stands out from far away. It is still possible to slip through the waist-high and shoulder-high gaps; indeed, wall-less segments remain. But Northside keeps building.† Here at sunset there is often a yellow sky over the mountain and behind the Telcel sign and between the Burger King and the Pollo Féliz, from one of whose two silver pipes comes dark smoke.

A man starts to polish the car. I give him ten pesos, enter the taquería, and eat dinner. At the end of the meal he is still earnestly working.

Past a yellow sign for the **TECATE GATEWAY COMPLEJO INDUSTRIAL**, the route arrives at the high country's ranches, many of them for sale, after which we descend into a wide grassy plateau, the grimy air hiding mountains, pine trees, grass, rocks, a Campo Turísto, El Rancho Concordio. Then for a time the wall cannot be seen at all; nor are there any ranches, only the Sierra Juárez, where I am told that there are several old Indian sites where ceremonies of fertility were once conducted: boulders convoluted into massive vulvas. I have not found them here but then I have never asked.

*This reminds me that far down into the Baja Peninsula, once upon a time there was, and perhaps still is for all I know, a hill called "The Grave," and another called "Hell."

†Here is a thought on another wall in another country: "The damage inflicted by the barrier on the idea of a Jewish homeland built by Jews fleeing the walled ghettos of Europe seems enormous. In the Jerusalem area, where the wall is really a wall of concrete, higher than the Berlin wall, the offense to the ideal that was Israel appears incalculable." Could there be any truth to this? If so, might it offer any analogy to the wall now thickening and growing along the southern edge of the Land of the Free?

Then comes Rumorosa, very small and hilly, where the composite rock dolmens begin.

Far below, the Mexicali Valley glows like a sulphurous sun.*

Here at Rumorosa the plateau is especially beautiful just before dusk with the mountains low like purple crystals at the edge of it, and the few cloud-puffs touching it and everything gold or tan or purple-shaded as one goes eastward into that stunning golden light.

The road from Tecate down to Mexicali is called the Cantú Grade. Ahead one sees a maze of rock, and then suddenly the pink and orange cavern of light where Mount Centinela basks and many *pollos* cross, while the violet light gradually turns silver.

From Mexicali the clean, wide, green and brown grids of the Imperial Valley are best seen from between the slats of the border wall while one waits to cross, anticipating constellations of white birds in green fields, mirages on the almost-empty highways (emptier than Mexico), and ever so many longnecked birds.

(Once upon a time, coming into Northside past the long line of Mexicans with papers, I met the stern, tired, bald personification of American paternalism, who questioned me, then curtly, shruggingly gestured me out of his sight. Speechlessly they X-rayed my notebook, and I emerged from the big door crowned by portraits of Bush and Cheney; here was Calexico, whose streets were emptier and more orderly than Mexicali's. There was some English spoken but the people looked mostly the same as in Mexicali. I heard the clink of the turnstile through which people depart the United States. A plump Mexican-American girl with a bun of brownish-blonde hair sat on the sidewalk in front of the burger chain store, smoking a cigarette. A Border Patrol wagon rolled briskly by. Then all fell still. After using the telephone, I went back to Mexico. How easy it was!—But it used to be even easier.)

Reader, shall I tell you what makes Mexicali unique? I know, because I have asked Rosa Pérez in the Park of the Child Heroes this very question, and she replied: For me, there are no boundaries. All is God's. All is the same. The woman is the crown and the man is the creature of the earth.—And here the old lady began to sing: *From cup to cup you ruin your life, drunk for a woman.*

But let us push on through the *ejidos, colonias* and desert of the Mexicali Valley's three thousand square kilometers. (As it happens, the line itself follows squiggly rivers of shadow, DRIFTING SAND NEXT 7 MI at Glamis, then the new world

*José Joaquin Arrillaga, 1796: "From the heights one spies only flat country, of clay, without trees, this being the Laguna Salada, and beyond, the Sierra next to the Colorado." The Mexicali Valley is now dusty, smoggy and hazy with geothermal plumes. It is much harder to see the Sierra de Los Cocopas from far away; as for the Colorado, we know what happened to *that*.

of the dunes, their domes and facets so sharp in the evening, white and blue; they open up, salmon-colored in the dusk, with the mountains of Mexico a series of pink and blue jewels on the horizon.) Halfway between Mexicali and Algodones, cotton bolls and hay bales adorn a green October field; children play in a spilled truckload of cotton while their elders clean it up: three thousand dollars' worth.

San Luis Río Colorado is longer and lower than the heart of Mexicali, the square blocks of bars and restaurants weighing down the pavement, like the smell of disinfectant in the Motel California, which is also the Hotel California. On the old-style wall, which is not see-through strips of landing mat, the top strip angles into Northside palm trees, whose bottoms have been artfully whitewashed. On the Mexican side, the wall has been painted with, for instance, a profile of Nefertiti, a map, hand-painted advertisements.

. . . And they come very very close to me, the tall tattooed boys, staring into my eyes and asking why. When I try to tell them that I am writing a book, they become contemptuous; because to them it is just wall, somewhere between rust-colored and tan against the grey dirt. The sky becomes a lovely yellow-orange over it; and farther away from town the wall is graffiti'd again with a skull and then it goes just blank, blank, a border and then more blankness, then a dairy cow corralled up against the wall.

In this city called San Luis Río Colorado, Francisco Manuel Preciado Martínez weeps on a park bench ten minutes' walking from the line itself. He comes originally from Hermosillo.—I got here in 2004, he says. This is where Immigration brought me from Seattle, Washington.—And he shows me a government document which bears a photo of his wife.—They took her, he says, bursting into tears.

Who took her?

I invited a friend to stay in my house and he took her. It happened on the twenty-third of October of this year.

When was the first time you crossed the border?

In 1963. Into Yuma, Arizona. From here. I walked, he said, weeping, because I did not have money. It took about three days. I saw many things but I was very hungry. I just remember that I was thirsty and I was hungry. It was in June and it was very hot. I wanted to work, he wept, wiping his eyes.

How did you know where to go?

I just went. I walked in the day and in the night. I got to Yuma and jumped a train and went to Los Angeles. That was the first time I had done it but some other people had told me how to do it. The train was stopped and I jumped onto a car. It was a boxcar with three holes up top. Nobody could see you. I was just lifting myself up and looking out of the hole. The train ran alongside the freeway. It took

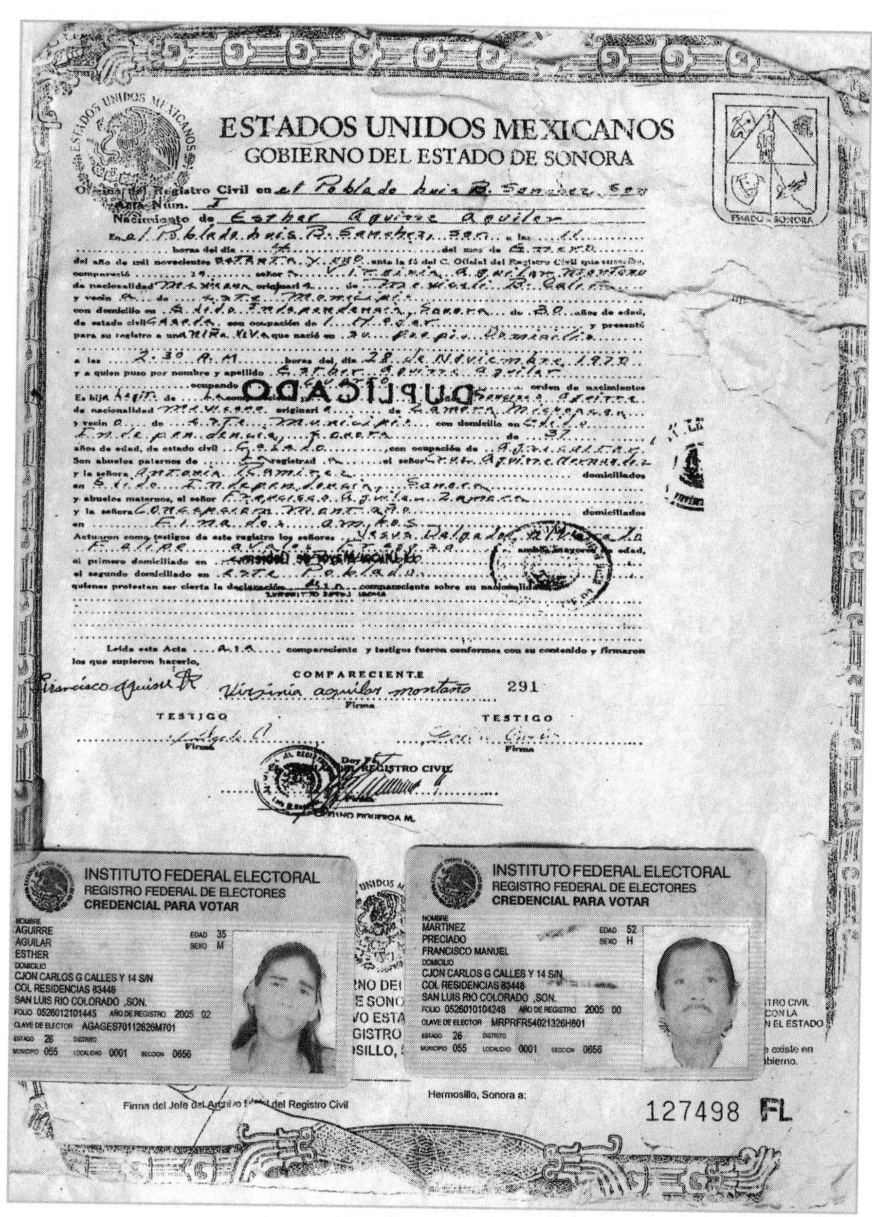

ESTADOS UNIDOS MEXICANOS
GOBIERNO DEL ESTADO DE SONORA

Oficina del Registro Civil en el Poblado Luis B. Sanchez, Son.
Acta Núm. 1
Nacimiento de Esther Aguirre Aguilar

En el Poblado Luis B. Sanchez, Son. a las 11 horas del día 4 del mes de Enero del año de mil novecientos setenta y uno, ante la fé del C. Oficial del Registro Civil que suscribe, compareció la señora Virginia Aguilar Montaño de nacionalidad mexicana originaria de Mexicali, B. Cfa. y vecina de este municipio con domicilio en Ejido Independencia, Sonora de 30 años de edad, de estado civil casada con ocupación de el hogar y presentó para su registro a una niña viva que nació en su propio domicilio a las 2.30 A.M. horas del día 28 de Noviembre 1970 y a quien puso por nombre y apellido Esther Aguirre Aguilar ocupando cuarto orden de nacimientos. Es hija legit. de la compareciente y ... Francisco Aguirre de nacionalidad mexicano originario de Zamora, Michoacan y vecino de este municipio con domicilio en Ejido Independencia, Sonora de 37 años de edad, de estado civil casado, con ocupación de agricultor. Son abuelos paternos de la registrada el señor ... Aguirre Hernandez y la señora Antonia Ramirez domiciliados en Ejido Independencia, Sonora y abuelos maternos, el señor Francisco Aguilar Zamora y la señora Concepcion Montaño domiciliados en Finados ambos. Actuaron como testigos de este registro los señores Jesus Delgado Alvarado, Felipe Avalos Fregoso ambos mayores de edad, el primero domiciliado en ... el segundo domiciliado en este Poblado quienes protestan ser cierta la declaración de la compareciente sobre su nacionalidad.

DUPLICADO

Leída esta Acta a la compareciente y testigos fueron conformes con su contenido y firmaron los que supieron hacerlo,

COMPARECIENTE
Francisco Aguirre R. — Virginia aguilar montaño — 291
Firma

TESTIGO — TESTIGO
Firma — Firma

Doy fé
El Oficial del Registro Civil

INSTITUTO FEDERAL ELECTORAL
REGISTRO FEDERAL DE ELECTORES
CREDENCIAL PARA VOTAR
NOMBRE
AGUIRRE
AGUILAR
ESTHER
EDAD 35
SEXO M
DOMICILIO
CJON CARLOS G CALLES Y 14 S/N
COL RESIDENCIAS 83448
SAN LUIS RIO COLORADO, SON.
FOLIO 0526012101445 AÑO DE REGISTRO 2005 02
CLAVE DE ELECTOR AGAGES70112826M701
ESTADO 26 DISTRITO
MUNICIPIO 055 LOCALIDAD 0001 SECCION 0656

INSTITUTO FEDERAL ELECTORAL
REGISTRO FEDERAL DE ELECTORES
CREDENCIAL PARA VOTAR
NOMBRE
MARTINEZ
PRECIADO
FRANCISCO MANUEL
EDAD 52
SEXO H
DOMICILIO
CJON CARLOS G CALLES Y 14 S/N
COL RESIDENCIAS 83448
SAN LUIS RIO COLORADO, SON.
FOLIO 0526010104248 AÑO DE REGISTRO 2005 00
CLAVE DE ELECTOR MRPRFR54021326H601
ESTADO 26 DISTRITO
MUNICIPIO 055 LOCALIDAD 0001 SECCION 0656

Firma del Jefe del Archivo Estatal del Registro Civil
Hermosillo, Sonora a:
127498 FL

Police report on missing wife,
received by WTV in 2006

eighteen hours. It was right near Los Angeles, Puente Los Angeles, fourteen miles from Los Angeles. I went there because I wanted to work in Washington; I had a good job over there. I knew I would have a job with the Boeing Company, because I could fix airplane parts. So in Los Angeles I went straight to look for work. I went to work in Brooklyn Avenue, East L.A. I slept right there where I worked. They gave me some food and a place to sleep. It was like a tortilla factory and they made chorizo, carnitas, bread. I got paid sixty dollars a week. It was a little room where I slept. Fifteen people were sleeping and working there. Everyone was illegal. I saved my money and went to Washington. They were sad because I worked very hard. A man who was already headed that way, I paid him and he took me in his car. It took thirty-two hours. I paid him a hundred dollars. He dropped me off at the rescue mission on Second Avenue. I went to a placement company and put in an application to work in Alaska. Boeing called me after three months in Seattle, Washington, he says, sniffling, his face bright red, his left hand raised as if he were swearing some oath.—I was in Seattle for three months looking for work and then in Alaska for six months. In Saint Paul, near Russia. It was a contract job in a fishing boat. They paid twenty-five dollars an hour. And then I completed my job and flew back to Seattle on the company plane. When I came back to Seattle, I could afford an apartment. I kept in touch with my boss. And after two months my boss got me the job with Boeing. I had worked with a man from Missoula, Montana, in 1980. Through that friend I met the boss. I started working at Boeing in 1990. Then somebody reported me to Immigration, and here he burst into tears. Boeing paid me a lot of money. *A lot of money!* he shouted. I was working and then the next thing you know I was in an airplane. They grabbed me, just like that. They took me in the plane to Chihuahua. Then I hitchhiked here.

He is fifty-two, and his wife, whose name is Esther Aguilar Aguirre, is thirty-six, according to the color photostat of the police report that he hands me. I buy him a meal and give him money; soon he is in the street getting drunk with his friends.

Pleading for more money, he follows me all the way to the wall, which is painted and rusted, aloof behind its row of whitewashed palm saplings, its fence and yellow curb so very still in the Sunday heat. After a longish time, a fat blonde comes, dragging her steps, with a plastic bag of groceries weighing down her haunch of an arm. This is the first street, where Mexico begins; it's vitiated and poisoned by the wall, or maybe just defined by it.

Coming out of San Luis Río Colorado into Arizona, the twenty miles to Yuma will be wide, perfectly furrowed dirt, with sky-blue reflections in each irrigated furrow—oh, Northside's wide highways are shockingly different—

Chapter 177

SUBDELINEATIONS: MARSSCAPES

(2004)

Could the gray-green areas in an otherwise reddish disk be vast, plant-filled oases sprouting forth from a global desert? And was it possible that those remarkable straight lines some astronomers perceived were canals created by an advanced civilization?

—*Astronomy*, 2003

Possible indeed! May I tell you why? Because **WATER IS HERE**!

To tell the truth, the most Martian place of all isn't Imperial, although I grant that Signal Mountain is somewhat that way, especially mornings and evenings when it glows grey-red; but if you ascend high enough to gaze down into Northside, then you're compelled to believe in aliens, because here's an onion field; there's a haystack; they add up to vast, plant-filled oases sprouting forth from a global desert! *We need have no fear that our lands will not become better and better as the years go by.* That's what the Martians say. But wait a minute! I'm from San Diego; I don't believe in Martians. Better to enjoy the Marsscapes of San Diego County; for instance, near Split Mountain in the Anza-Borrego badlands, not far from Ocotillo, there's a long wide streak of Martian daylight across the shadowed bluff; everything is a shard; red rocks crouch on tanscapes which appear to be made of sand but bear one's weight without even leaving a footprint, like the superfrozen snow of the high Arctic; here on Mars the weird trees are invaders; the bursts of yellowheaded bushes out of fractured rocks shouldn't be here; when from far away a human's grating footsteps sound, that isn't natural. Reddish-yellow shards of daylight lie in fractured marriage with the shadow.—Oh, man, like, see, this would be so cool to hike up to that mountain up there! cries Professor Larry McCaffery on 4 November 2003, smoking his last cigarette ever, the absolutely last before he quits.—And you can imagine the view you'd have!—Larry, also known as Lorenzo, at least when in the alien world of Mexico, takes two steps away while I'm scribbling in a notebook, and then before I know it he's at the top of a ridge! It must be that low Martian gravity. This is the place where Imperial gets crumpled up against the sky.

One reason this must be Mars is that the sky is so dark and cloudless. Leaning strata of sand, fossilized oyster shells, these signifiers of long slow change almost seduce me into imagining an epoch when Martians actually existed, in which case they would have been worthy of my consideration. Oh, give me grooves, wrinkles, yonis and clefts in the rock instead; that way I don't need to recognize anything but the pleasure principle! (What about freckled granite in white sand? I see it but I won't acknowledge it; it's not Martian; it hinders this subdelineation.)

I'm from San Diego. Imperial's more remote than Mars to me. I need the water, so I'll take it. A few million years from now I'll explain to my friends: *Gone are the oases, canals and cities . . . But the abode of Mars as the abode of hostile aliens lives on.*

"WARPED AND CRAWLING THINGS"

Reader, what is Mars to you? To me it's simply Otherwhere, but most science-fictioneers refine that definition at least enough to convey a sense of desiccated deficiency. After all, who dares to claim the desert's superiority to the oasis? A proper Marsscape, then, invites the following clichés: *harsh, dangerous, red, alien.* Never mind cold and thin air, which characterizes no part of Imperial excepting a few mountain-scraps around Tecate, the Sierra Cucapah, the Chocolate range; we know quite well the temperature appropriate to our area of study! Once this latitude has been granted, almost any science-fiction opus set in a dry place will qualify as an Imperial Marsscape—for instance, Walter M. Miller, Jr.'s bitter parable *A Canticle for Leibowitz,* which takes place on Earth. *Gone are the oases, canals and cities,* because nuclear war shattered and poisoned those. *The abode of Mars as the abode of hostile aliens lives on.* Who are they in this case? Mutants: piebald men, two-headed women, freaks and monsters with human souls, which is why the Church prescribes their raising and nurturing, so that they're called *the Pope's children. Their ranks were continually replenished,* we're informed, *by warped and crawling things that sought refuge from the world.* They kill poor Brother Francis with an arrow between the eyes, because they're hungry. Let's call them Martians, unless you want to think of them as illegal aliens. The Martians in H. G. Wells's *War of the Worlds* possess similar habits to the Pope's children; they're even scheming to sneak across the darkness of the interplanetary border and land here! *Now I hear the people smugglers are getting so brazen, now they got the Humvees with the guns mounted on them. They got laws on the books and they're not being enforced.* All head and no digestive system (they live by injecting themselves with human blood), causing the narrator to muse over *the actual accomplishment of . . . a suppression of the animal side of the organism by the intelligence . . . Without the body the brain would, of course, become a mere selfish intelligence, without any of the emotional substratum of the human being.* Miller's Martians are, on the contrary, idiotic bodies bent on their own needs and greeds; while the selfish intelligences he imagines are scientists and politicians who rebuild the world out of its postapocalyptic Dark Age in order to launch another nuclear war. Only the monks and abbots of this Marsscape recognize others' humanity—or their non-Martian-ness, I should say. Wells again: *Those who have never seen a living Martian can scarcely imagine the strange horror of its appearance . . . There was something fungoid in the oily brown skin . . . Even at this first encounter . . . I was overcome with disgust and dread.* In the end, we almost feel sorry for his Martians, who are all carried off by terrestrial pathogens; the last one wails a solitary amplified ululation within its metal spider, then becomes bird-food. But until they perish, their otherness remains coolly malevolent. This is why Miller's vision must be considered superior to Wells's, at least from a standpoint of empathetic accomplishment. Who are we to judge the Pope's children? A dying abbot, half crushed in a nuclear blast, receives the Host from a woman with two heads. The younger head, named Rachel, has taken over the woman's body, and it becomes vigorous, supple and beyond the human exigencies of bleeding and pain. *He did not ask* why *God would choose to raise up a creature of primal innocence from the shoulder of Mrs. Grales . . . One glimpse had been a bounty, and he wept in gratitude.* Then he finishes dying, as does the Earth. Earth becomes Mars—I mean Imperial—so thoroughly that even the Martians are dead! In the words of still another science-fiction writer, J. G. Ballard, *the blighted landscape and its empty violence, its loss of time, would provide its own motives.* In other words: *Though large parts of this may certainly be reclaimed by the waters of the Colorado, we are not at present recommending our desert.*

MORE WARPED AND CRAWLING THINGS

In science fiction, Mars comes and goes. In Frank Herbert's *Dune,* whose world is *the landscape beyond pity, the sand that was form absorbed in itself,* George Chaffey's closest semblance is no careful engineer, but the outcast Paul Atreides, who lives out an exaggeration of Lawrence of Arabia's tale. Indeed, Herbert's Martians are not Mexicans, but robed Arabs who fight a guerrilla war against occupiers as cruel and corrupt as stereotyped Turks. Secret pools of water, much of it distilled from human metabolisms, have been decanted into caves beneath the dunes, building up for the distant time when Mars, here called Arrakis, can become green. *And no man ever again shall want for water.* Then Mars will be called Imperial.

But the desert is always present beneath our crops, waiting. That is why the psychologically deepest Marsscape of all is Ray Bradbury's *Martian Chronicles,* in whose eeriest tale the Third Expedition lands on a Mars which resembles Green Bluff, Illinois. This shows what their home-fantasies were and how cruelly Mars disguised itself. *"Our primary mission is to prevent terrorism and terrorist weapons from entering our country," El Centro Chief Border Patrol Agent Michael McClafferty said.* But Bradbury's spacemen, forgetting to obey the primary mission, rush out to fraternize with the enemy, who take on the semblance of lost girlfriends, dead parents, etcetera, and in the night murder them all. The Other, you see, is most dangerous when he studies Northside's ways and pretends to be one of us. Like the naive spaceman from Earth who cries out at the telepathic Martian woman: "You speak *English!*" we were tricked into believing that Mars was Imperial, but it will never stop being the Valley of Death. *"Our primary mission is to prevent terrorism and terrorist weapons from entering our country," El Centro Chief Border Patrol Agent Michael McClafferty said.* The club motto is, "The aim if reached or not, makes great the life."

Strange to say, the Martians' Northsider facade was not entirely a coldblooded ploy; Bradbury describes the manifold ways in which the Martians helplessly change into us, start looking like us, are drawn to us and trapped by our consciousness while at the same time manipulatively becoming what they wish us to be. Meanwhile they euthanize Earth men as incurable psychotics, or shoot them with guns which fire golden stinging bees.

Who then are the Martians? They are Southsiders, and so we can never understand them.

And what is Mars? What could it ever be, but home? Therefore, even though **THE DESERT DISAPPEARS**, how can it not come back? In J. G. Ballard's already-mentioned masterpiece, *The Drought,* we cannot escape the bitter trip from home to the salty sea, then the return a decade later to sand-rounded desiccations of the past, whose few survivors are more grotesque than ever, the final failing of everything being hastened by self-destructive vanities. *It is simply needless to question the supply of water.* Every setting might as well be Salton City, which is to say a place that Ballard refers to as a terminal zone, an abandoned, ugly, dangerous Detritusville. Once upon a time, Mars was an alien desert, possessed in fits and starts by exotic beauty. We made it into Calexico and Mexicali. *The bountiful continent is ours, state on state, and territory on territory, to the waves of the Pacific sea.* Now the water is going away again. Ruins remain. In Ballard's brilliantly bleak characterization of events, human relationships and even personality itself all gradually dry out. I can't help believing in people.

Chapter 178

RANCHO ROA

(2004–2005)

The caretaker said, This was one of the first ranches in Mexicali. His name was Leobardo Roa. His wife was named Brenda. And she is still the owner.

When did this ranch come into being?

I don't know. But it's more than fifty years old.

So the señora must have been very old.

She's thirty-five. He passed away.

When did the señor pass away?

Now it's been eight years actually since he died, the man said. He wore a gun at his hip and a T-shirt that bore the name of an American company. He was old, dark-brownskinned and wiry, and he could carry a crate of oranges on his shoulder as I can carry a book. Every time I saw him, he was just about to give notice and return to his home district, but for the señora's sake he would remain at Rancho Roa just a month longer. Probably next time I came he would be gone, unfortunately. Each time I came, he was there. He was king of the chirping birds, the palm trees and metal sheds. His name was Natalio Morales Rebolorio.

It was a cattle ranch, he said, all cattle.

How many hectares?

I don't know for sure, but it's a big ranch. It starts over here where you see the trees and it continues over there and it keeps on going back. There are probably a thousand orange trees and grapefruit trees. They come from all over, from Tecate, from Tijuana, from all over, to buy them.* Mostly, people who come by come by to pick a bag.

Once when I visited the old man it was January, and a certain buyer had contracted to box up the produce of the entire orchard.—Today I'm waiting for a man

*Rancho Roa was known even in the capital of the world, Mexicali. Javier Lupercio for instance said: "There's a slaughterhouse next to that place, round about kilometer eight or nine. It started out as a cattle ranch, lots of heads of cattle they had. It was one of the biggest ranches at that time. They also used to plant alfalfa. Up to date, that ranch still has cattle. But it's not as productive as before."

who bought everything, he said. He's bringing his workers to harvest it and take to other places.—Señora Roa still owns it, he reassured me then.—It's all still in her name; basically, people buy it just for the day.

She must be a very rich lady.

Not really, he said proudly, but . . .

I take care of it for her, he said. The trees, the animals. You see, the goats know me really well. I was just about to let them loose for the day. This one here was born only two days ago. The geese over there are just decorative.

Scraping with his plastic-handled machete, he uncovered more goose eggs under the palm trees.

She comes at two and lays the eggs, he said, and then she hides them.

That little white one over there, he said, that goat is only two months old.

A thousand citrus trees total! Valencias on the right, big moonlike grapefuits on the left, trees like islands in the pale golden grass, these were the treasures of Rancho Roa. He said that the custom was to wait for them to fall and pick up only the fallen. The trees went on and on, to the white horse on the horizon.

The season lasted from November through January; in January they harvested. Another time that I visited him, he said: It's ending right now. The Valencias are all gone. So the man is supposed to come today to take all the grapefruits and sell them. If not today, he'll come on Monday.

He said that on a Thursday. I could see that it did not greatly matter when the man would come.

I went with him across a plain of yellow grass, the orchard crowned with its myriad yellow moons. It was cool in the shadows of the grapefruits. The trees grew here and there as they liked.

In Coachella the grapefruit trees stand in straight ranks, I said.

That means they won't develop as much, said the old man. They should have that much space between them, so that the air gets in, so that they can develop.

Which takes more work, the grapefruits or the oranges?

It's the same. These orange trees have been here forty years and will be cut down.

And those palms also, he said, they also give fruit. Dates. Approximately fifty kilos per treee. We have eight trees.

In your opinion, did the Garden of Eden look like this?

Oh, yes, yes. This grove of palm trees, when I came here they were really small. But I've been watering them. It's so pretty to walk beneath them. One of them had so much fruit that the limb broke. Oh, if you could have seen them in November! They were so full!

He broke off a branch for me and another for my interpreter, saying: I give branches to people. After two years it will give fruit . . .

Which fruit do you like the best?

I like the Valencias because you can choose them for juice. Of course you make juice from grapefruits also. On the other side of these grapefuits are the navel oranges. For people who just want to eat an orange, the navels are good because they don't have seeds.

I've always liked the way grapefruits look, I said.

Inside the orchard there are some trees where you can get five or even six bags of grapefruit, he said proudly. Last year a man paid twenty thousand pesos for the whole orchard; he came five or six times.

He showed some of his best-bearing trees, and I felt quite happy between the lovely yellow grass and the brilliant yellow grapefruit. Two or three times he ascended a ladder to see how the ripening was coming along.

So the grapefruits that they've already picked up off the ground, he said, those they use to feed animals. But the ones they sell in the market, for those they use a ladder and cut them off with scissors and cut them and put into a bag. These fruits here, the goats will come and eat them when I let them out.

Later we will flood this with water, he said. There's a canal *there,* and we'll let it in *here* and it will fill up the orchard. It's not very salty because it comes from the Río Colorado. You have to pay for it; it's expensive.

How does it work?

I have to tell the man in charge of the canals to open the gate. And when the orchard is full, I go and tell him, and he turns it off.

How many times a year do you do this?

Every month, he said. Once a month. Look at the earth, how it gets. The hot times are coming. And the roots need the wetness. The hardest part is running the water. And the fertilizing. You have to fertilize when the water has already come through. You only fertilize once a year. You fertilize with ammonia. It's a liquid. You wear gloves and boots. That way the bugs die and the trees live.

Now we were walking once again down the long white shadow-striped avenue of white-limed date trees, and he said: We give the dates away.—Truth to tell, the dates were a trifle hard; Rancho Roa could not compete with the industrial cathedrals of date palms in Coachella.

Citrus trees, as we know from Imperial County, do poorly in saline soils. Unable to believe in a happy future for the Mexicali Valley aquifer, I asked the old man: What is the future of this area?

The life of the trees depends on how well people maintain them, he replied. If a trees is not well maintained it will die.

In his mind, he had answered me accurately and completely. After all, what *was* this area but the pale yellow suns of oranges on the forty-year-old trees? So I asked:

Do you think there will be more roads and houses here in the future? Will there be enough water for everybody? Will the city come here?

Yesterday I was talking about this with the señora, he said. Because some trees are dying. I told her that we need to buy more trees so that the orchard doesn't run out. She agreed. They will send an agricultural engineer who will figure out how many more trees and how much it will cost.

In fifty years, will there still be ranches here or will it all be *maquiladoras*?

I think this ranch will be here in fifty years. The señora has two children, and a couple of days ago a Spaniard came to ask her if she would sell, and she refused because her children will be the owners.

Do you think the Americans are taking control?

I can't really answer that question. I see a lot of Americans who pass on the way to San Felipe in their cars but they never stop, except for that one Spaniard.

I inferred that while a Spaniard was not quite an American, they were approximately the same.

He came from Chiapas, so I asked him what he thought about Subcomandante Marcos and the new Zapatistas whose doings we had heard about even in America, and he said: I don't pay much attention. All I want to do is work. I work, work, work. Because if I don't work, I don't get money. And if I work, I get money. And that is also my honor. The señora trusts me . . .

He reminded me a trifle of Leonard, the visionary of Salvation Mountain. For each of those two very different men, where he was was everything to him. Leonard's backyard was some dreamer's or pensioner's or outlaw's, a part-silhouetted silver trailer with rounded corners and a satellite dish, beads of light upon the glamorous pallor of the Salton Sea, a ragged bar of mountains and then glowing orange sky. For Natalio Morales Rebolorio, there was orange fire-shimmering in the reflections of oranges in the brown water of the furrows. Seventy goats and thirty geese accompanied him, not to mention his black dog. He had hens, *not that many now.* He would always give me a cardboard box filled with fruit, which I sometimes presented to the campesinos who were picking squash or watermelon out in the *ejidos;* they grew joyful then. Once I gave Rancho Roa oranges to my favorite desk clerk at the Hotel Chinesca; she, too, was happy.* It was wonderful for me to become in miniature Natalio Morales Rebolorio, the Santa Claus of citrus! Closing my eyes now to remember him, I see him from the back as I follow him down the pathway through the orange trees.

*Once while detaining me, the guardians of Northside, having inspected my every pill, film canister and dollar, finally discovered my one item of contraband: a single Rancho Roa orange forgotten in the trunk of the car. They seized it triumphantly and paid me a monitory pamphlet in exchange.

Chapter 179

BROCK FARMS

(2004)

Ben Brock was a third-generation asparagus farmer in Holtville. Richard Brogan knew him and said: They used to own a lot of farmland in the central part of the valley. They were really big here in early agriculture. They were the first packing house for asparagus. They were some of the early pioneers going into Mexicali. Lettuce for sure. Not necessarily carrots, I think.

Ben Brock said: In season, Imperial asparagus used to be ninety percent of the crop in the supermarket. That was ten years ago. Now it's down to five percent.*

Yesterday we had to pick, because if we didn't pick, we were going to lose the product. It cost us eight dollars and ninety cents a field box.

He gave the other numbers—for instance, twenty-five cents for cooling, five cents for the rubber band. As numbers will, they added up.

Yesterday was expensive, he said, because we had to pay time and a half.

Our growing cost is about eleven hundred dollars an acre, he said. We're looking at two hundred–plus crates per acre. You can watch the percentage in value in asparagus and it goes down . . .

We're in the state of California, and what happened January first was that the Workers' Comp rate went up by ten to fifteen percentage points. The costs I gave you were based on minimum wage. Anything we get paid below eighty-five cents per pound, we're losing money. Even at a dollar we're not making money. So you add ten percent for Workers' Comp, and that has to come out of the dollars coming out of the field. California is a scary place to do business, because you're waiting for the other shoe to drop. You've got OSHA;† you've got the ALRB,‡ which is a

*I may have misunderstood this. In 2004, asparagus occupied 1,812 Imperial County acres. The yield was 240 thirty-pound cartons per acre, $32.11 per carton. Asparagus was number twenty-four of the top forty crops. In 1994, there had been nearly 6,000 acres of asparagus planted; although the yield was only 147 cartons, the market price had been $35.67 per carton. Asparagus accordingly made number eight on the top forty list.

†Occupational Safety and Health Administration.

‡Agricultural Labor Relations Board. See "Chávez's Grapes," p. 748.

government front for the union. None of us want our workers to go hungry or suffer or work in terrible conditions. However, what is acceptable has changed and keeps changing.

Eighty-five cents a pound for asparagus, he said. Eighty cents of that is labor cost.

The price of water has gone up. It's about ten to fifteen times cheaper here, but you couldn't farm if you had to pay residential rates.

I asked him what he thought about the water transfer, and he smiled sadly and said: As if a couple of farmers have a chance of pulling together against MWD and San Diego!

He gave me a tour, and I saw Mexican-looking ladies sorting the asparagus on a slow belt. It was very cool in there and they did not seem unhappy.

He gave me a box of asparagus to take with me. It was delicious raw.

I asked him about Mexico, and he said: *There's nothing that we can do that Mexicali cannot.*

Chapter 180

SALVATION MOUNTAIN

(1996–2005)

> It's happening more and more. People looking at the mountain, people want me to come to church and listen, and I say no, just come and listen to the mountain!
>
> —Leonard Knight, 2003

Years it's been now since my first visit to Leonard Knight's mountain; back then he told me that his ambition stopped short of extending the accomplishment; he wished simply to overpaint it as many times as he could until death. Up close, it became the world; a few steps away it began to resolve into the puny production of a single human being. Nearly as foolish as my own attempt to express Imperial in a book, it metonymized its near neighbor, Niland, which the 1914 Imperial Valley directory celebrates as *"the Main Line City," and the Wonderland of Activity.* In an undated photograph, the two-storey train depot resembles a Victorian house. The porch-roof says **NILAND**. A small fleet of flatbed wagons awaits in front; men and boys stand wearing Stetson-type hats; two long tall trains adorned with many windows bask upon the two tracks, on the far side of which is a parklike zone of trees fronted by a row of young palms. (Those trees are gone now.) Because of its proximity to various important railroad destinations, the Main Line City's future was assured. *Niland had not an inhabitant on March 14;* had 300 on July 1; will have, it seems certain, thousands within its first eighteen months . . . Niland abolished summer in Imperial Valley.* That was the situation in 1914. Since Harry Chandler happened to be a stockholder in the First National Bank of Niland, I am less than surprised to read that *the opening was attended by trainloads from Los Angeles . . . Many lots were sold.*

In 1930, John D. Reavis promised us all: *Some day Niland's dream of commercial and horticultural greatness will be realized.* We're still waiting.

The building of the All-American Canal will vastly increase the productive area of Niland, prophesied Otis P. Tout. *Because of its reputed frostless climate the entire*

*In fact, Deane Haughtelin's family lived in a caboose in a siding in Niland in about 1902; her father was a Southern Pacific conductor.

district bids fair to become the favored citrus section of the Valley. In 1939 the WPA guide to California reported that Niland possessed *some of the largest ranches in the valley; on one ranch alone are 4,000 grapefruit, 17,000 orange, 6,000 lemon and 2,000 tangerine trees.* I have never seen a single citrus orchard in Niland.

Imperial is failed dreams; Imperial is castles in the air transformed at best into grimy bunkers; Imperial is the Niland Tomato Festival, whose sad carnival rides hang almost empty, and whose tomatoes are nonexistent. *The club motto is, "The aim if reached or not, makes great the life."*

Once upon a time, an old man in Niland said to me: I don't much like it here, but I hate the cold; I hate that cold wind that goes right through you.—These words were spoken on a ninety-five-degree day. His aim had been reached; the same may be said of Salvation Mountain.

INTO MY HEART

Presently Leonard decided to do more than overpaint. He built first a hogan, then a gigantic, walk-in replica of the hot air balloon he'd applied himself to for fourteen years (it failed to leave the ground). The interior of this second structure resembles in its cool reclusiveness the interior of the I. V. Restaurant. I can scarcely describe it except to call it a sort of maze which vaguely resembles a lung's alveoli magnified and garishly colored; the passageways curve, and painted round tree-trunks both rise out of the dirt floor and spread their arms, which resemble strings of mucus, crosswise into the painted walls, where the studs, painted in different hues, bulge out like orifices. Up and in curve the walls, like soft palates; the trees remind me of tonsils. A curving wall of hay bales has not yet been painted. After a moment or two I can smell them; they are better than the best tobacco. Leonard's new hired man is singing around the corner.

Between that wall of hay bales and another just-born hogan, cool goes to hot, moist to dry, painted to tan; for a few steps away, the desert recommences, rising up high in a wall of pale dirt which is actually Salvation Mountain itself; Leonard hasn't painted this section of ridge yet, and maybe he never will.

Imperial is scissors on a closed paint can; Imperial is gobs of paint on a palette, and then another recess whose abstractions of colors and shape approach the complexities of reality itself. I see Leonard's straw hat on a shelf. The tunnel winds around itself; it's an immense negative doughnut, with fibrillations, bas-reliefs and villi.

Above all, Imperial is the navy-blue-striped waterfalls on Leonard's mountain, flowing two-dimensionally over two-dimensional reddish cookie-cutter-like trees and crude flowers of all colors; **WATER IS HERE**. Imperial is the yellow steps ascending, zigzagging in and out of sight on their way to the white cross in the cloudless sky.

Within the balloon-thing, Leonard built those trees ring by ring.

All these trees are made out of tires, he explained. Then this adobe, it's hard, just like cement, isn't it? By the time I got it half built, God knows it got in *Germany* magazine. Now, God showed me this. It started cracking and a couple tractor tires come in, and honest to God I didn't have any idea, but I filled one tire full of adobe and then another, and then I figured if I got eight tires it's gonna look like a tree! I try to learn things that way. And it's *thrilling* me, positively no end. A thousand bales of hay, that's how many there are right now. And I'm makin' a museum over here. Sixteen more tire trees is what I'm aiming for. I shoulda started this thing when I was about nine years old! I wanna make a museum over here. But I'd like to show you this . . .

He always had new things to show me.

What is Imperial to you? Here is what it is to Leonard:

God has given me Scriptures that I really don't dare go against. *You need not that a man teach you.* The Bible tells you not to go to man to learn. God didn't reveal it to the preachers. God revealed it to me.

The sun beats down upon the back of my neck; Leonard's paint is hot to the touch. Everything human must fail. Yet there stands Salvation Mountain, very pure and good, light and bright in the desert.

Isn't that something, he said, how something can be so *simple*? I ran into beautiful people who've given many, many thousands of dollars to the church, and I mention something about letting Jesus into my heart, and they get mad at me.

(Leonard might have been just a bit of a rebel.)

What does Imperial County mean to you? I asked him.

The whole place, and this includes Slab City, too, it's *freedom*. People can come here in Slab City from November until May and it's totally free. They can have picnics, and parties, and it's totally free. I love the people and the whole area. To me, it's freedom. It's the way the United States *should* be.

Does the landscape itself speak to you?

Well, can you see the Salton Sea from here? For me it's beautiful. In 1984 I came in my hot air balloon; I towed it behind my truck. Luckily, it rotted out here; I was stuck here. I realized nineteen or twenty years later, I realized that God put me in the very best place to build a mountain. It's peaceful. It's so darn beautiful.

In 1967 I was running away from God and from my sister, because my sister was talking about God, and all the sudden I said, *Jesus I'm a sinner, come into my life and into my heart,* and I started crying like a baby, and it changed my life, totally, completely. God zapped me in Lemon Grove, 1967, just like He zapped Saul. So I tried to build that hot air balloon that would tell people about Jesus. I built it in Nebraska, but it didn't work. In 1982 I towed it out here, and it came to rest right here in Slab City. We tried to put it up twenty-five or thirty times. And it would kind of go up, then it would sink down.

What was Slab City like back then?

It was almost the way it is now. But in 1990 and 1991 they had a swap meet up here, and both sides of the road were crammed with people. They had maybe about eight thousand people here. The authorities stopped it. There's still about three thousand people who come here in the winter.

And what made you decide to pick this particular mountain?

Well, I was trying to put the balloon up right about here. I just happened to come down here without any thought at all of staying here. That's when I told God, I'll stay down here one week and make an eight-foot replica of my balloon. During that week, which is when I made that heart over there—that was the first part of the mountain—something happened to make me stay longer. A man told me where I could get some broken cement, and I thought, that's friendly. So I stayed another week. Nineteen years later, now I'm here for the duration. At least that's what I hope.

In 1990, after I'd been working on it five years, when it was just cement, because I didn't know about adobe then, the whole mountain fell down. I told God, I got fourteen years making a balloon, and five years making a mountain, and I said: Oh, God, *You* do it! That was the smartest thing I ever did. Why did it take God nineteen years to get me out of the way?

Then those eight bimetallists came in. Before the results came in, I was a toxic nightmare. They wanted to take me down, so they could put in a paid campground. The *Los Angeles Times* said, the laws of God and the laws of man are gonna collide in Niland, California! And once they backed off, they backed off totally.

And nobody's bothered you since?

Not at all. And next two weeks, they're gonna bring in eight hundred gallons of paint!

How much paint can you use in a day?

If I'm painting the ocean floor down there, and it's in five-gallon buckets, I can put in a hundred gallons a day.

What did you do for food in the beginning?

I always got by with food. I can scrounge cans, I got a bicycle, and I can get what I want. I was so happy back then to work all day for Jesus Christ. People think I suffered back then, but I was happy. You know, God can ruffle my feathers; that's a fact. When they told me I was a toxic nightmare, I was upset. Thank You, God, for making me upset, because they made the mountain famous!

At sunset I was sitting at the base of the cross, watching the dark figure of Leonard come scrambling up his moutain. Niland was out of sight, aside from a thin line of lights. *Some day Niland's dream of commercial and horticultural greatness will be realized.* Gaston's Cafe, where I used to get root beer floats, had burned back in about 2001, but Gaston had already sold his café and was still alive; sometimes people still saw him watering his lawn. *He made a success through his own efforts. He sold out at a fancy price.* That was Niland for you. But there was the orange-pinkness of the Salton Sea and the pink stain in the Borrego mountains above it, as I sat there looking straight down on everything.

Who could be a more public figure than Leonard Knight? There was his mountain, which could be seen ten miles away. There was his mission: That is what I want to do, put *God is love* to everybody! My mountain even went on satellite disk to Baghdad! Some soldiers were over there, and when they got back they came to me and said: Leonard, we saw your mountain on television in Baghdad! Can you believe it? I love everybody that goes to church. And I love everybody that don't go to church.

So, Leonard, a hundred years from now, what do you think your mountain is going to look like?

I pray that if I keep painting it thicker and thicker, and if I get it in the Senate, then nobody can fight it.

So if you disappeared from the scene tomorrow, how long would this last?

I think they'll protect it, he replied with a grin.

And who could be a more private figure than Leonard Knight? What Imperial secrets lie sheltered within the cool darkness of any soul? Once he said to me: I was praying in the spirit. All the sudden I got the heavenly language. Since then, thank God, God has showed me many more Scriptures. Twenty years ago I said, God, I want this Holy Ghost fire. And I got it.

He got it, but no one other than Leonard Knight and his God will ever know the heavenly language. No one other than my God and I will ever know mine. What should I do? Should I stop speaking it on that account? Should you and I both lay down our private selves on the altar of a spurious commonality, and leave them to desiccate? I think not. To quote a certain Leonard Knight: If the Bible says something, my attitude is, oh, Lord, You wrote it and I don't understand it but *You wrote it* and I ain't changing one word for nobody!

When darkness came we descended, and now the brightest thing was the line of bluish-white light which was the Salton Sea (so it looks from the base of the mountain), far brighter than the narrowing dome of orange sky in the indigo sky above it. Leonard was getting his brand-new motor scooter; he was getting ready to ride it for the first time; two neighborly men were helping him unload it from the truck.

I have ascended Salvation Mountain by night, the cool wind whickering eventfully out of Slab City, Leonard's cat prowling with magical softness across the inscriptions as a much-loved woman and I climbed that frosted wedding cake. And I have taken Leonard's tour year after year. In 2005 he said: I got about three hundred gallons of paint and I got about four hundred gallons comin' in. Sometimes it's old paint. This mountain has really picked up speed in the last four months. It's almost staggering.

Leonard never became jaded, and so his Imperial Idea never ceased picking up speed. *We need have no fear that our lands will not become better and better as the years go by.*

The mountain itself, pastel at dusk, then a pale analogue of phosphorescence, spread out its pale wings from the great red heart, which was delicious as any Mexicali prostitute's lips, the white legend within as clean and pure as her teeth: JESUS I'M A SINNER PLEASE COME UPON MY BODY AND INTO MY HEART. And Leonard roared off on his scooter, laughing like a boy.

Oh, God, he called out, it's so beautiful! Isn't that beautiful? Jeez! You wanna take a little spin?

And now the mountain was a beautiful ghost of itself, hanging in the dark world which, as the desert and sky took on equal darkness, was all one; **WATER IS HERE**; the Idea moved upon the face of that water, and the mountain was its own cloud and island in Imperial's endless sea.

Chapter 181

SIGNAL MOUNTAIN

(2003)

When America was young to the rest of the world and the Declaration of Independence was announcing there would be a new republic established, Indians made their signal fires at the crest of this crumbling mountain.

—Otis B. Tout, 1931

It's not easy, said José Quintero. They got snakes. But they don't do nothing if you just walk carefully. You just go in the night time when you go up Signal Mountain.

He'd gone to TJ but *just didn't like something about it,* so he'd then proceeded to Mexicali, where he'd passed a month already when I met him, sitting each day five hours on the bench by the border turnstile, then five hours in the park, spending each day ten dollars for a hotel, eighty pesos for food, *and you gotta buy clothes.*

I like water too much. You don't see water right here.—He smiled then, saying: Sometimes I go to the other side to take a shower. Beautiful! I go over there, me and my friends, and we have a swim, have a cold drink of water.—He was pointing to the All-American Canal.—I see the Border Patrol. They don't tell me nothin' 'cause I'm not goin' deep.

The next time I came to Mexicali he was gone. I never saw him again. Perhaps he'd crossed over Signal Mountain.

To Acting Governor Arrillaga it was, rather inelegantly, *the Big Mountain which is lined up from the south to north which I crossed when I passed by the mouth* of the Colorado. He wrote those words in 1796. From the air, at least from American airspace, it is a squat pyramid in the midst of or at least foregrounded by green field-squares; Laguna Salada's hazy whiteness behind it resembles cloud upon field, not sand at all; it looks soft and lush.

Blue Angels Peak at four thousand five hundred forty-eight feet is actually Imperial County's highest. As usual, there are higher places in Mexico.* All the same, the mountain befits the county seal, being the termination of American Imperial,

*Signal Mountain is much less impressive from the Mexicali side, more sprawling, and appears no higher than the surrounding mountains, whereas on the U.S. side it stands alone.

whose concentrated greens, blues and tans might as well be the tones of a black-and-white photograph; suddenly one has reached the verge, the desert.

One of the best views of it I ever had was coming west from Glamis on Highway 78, a smell of feedlot in my face as I rode out into the irrigated acres. In a swarm of young date palms, there was squat Signal Mountain, that translucent turquoise pyramid; now it had centered itself in a field of green, in Bermuda grass, thrusting above road-mirages and golden walls of hay bales. I passed palm-islands in a flat brown field-sea, glimpsed beehives under their tarps, smelled another feedlot whose cattle were darker than the evening shadows. By now I had begun my rushing through a green dream of evening homesteads east of Brawley, with the cool-looking mountains of Anza-Borrego ahead. Sheds and palm trees, flat fallow fields, sunset thunderheads reflected in the Rockwell Canal, flat wet olive-green irrigated acres fading into moist darkness beneath other gilt-edged thunderheads, these were the tissues of Imperial's heart. Imperial's soul was Signal Mountain, which continued to hold its contrast against the earth, by darkening in proportion to the dim sky.

One New Year's Day, Lupe Vásquez and two friends and I decided to walk up Signal Mountain—Centinela, I should say, since we were then in Mexico.

The reddish-grey rocks, probably basalt in my opinion, were middling warmish to the touch. The canyon twisted and climbed fairly gently past the occasional abandoned jug, sock or jacket. I wondered how many of those *pollos* had successfully reached the gardens of Paradise. At the base of the mountain, on the east side, very near to the border, there is a path to a cave, and on another occasion, a woman and I were guided to that cave, where we found many empty water-jugs. The woman was with me today. She was already losing her desire for me. She did not hold my hand even on the wide path, and when it narrowed I let her go ahead to grip those rock-tussocks that were the color of dried blood.

Looking down into the dreamy banded rainbows of Laguna Salada, Lupe said that he'd heard there was once a rainbow above Centinela, a *supernatural rainbow,* he said meaningfully.

He gazed down into Laguna Salada for another moment. Then he said: There used to be shrimp down there, when there was water, twenty years ago.

(Arrillaga describes Laguna Salada simply as *a plain which, on the east and north, reaches the horizon . . . The plain has no pasture whatsoever . . .* This very year, Lupe proudly said, a special stadium would be built there so that the people could hear Pavarotti sing.)

Many squat, multifaceted quartz crystals lay around us. After an hour's easy walk, we stood at the topmost upcurving ridge of the saddle (which of course is not the top of Signal Mountain at all), observing how the trail swung deep down around a lower squat point, after which the bowl widened and deepened infinitely into Northside, where Plaster City resembled frozen snow-clouds on Imperial's reddish-tan ground, beyond which rose the mountains of the Anza-Borrego Badlands. A breeze swept through the gap, strong enough to whirl my cap off my head as I sat writing these very words at the top of a mound of reddish-greyish stones.

This is why the Spaniards in their maps drew California like an island, because it was like *this,* said Lupe almost to himself, pointing north.

I picked up a piece of quartz that was yellowed and veined like very ancient ivory; and here I was; here I was, between the tan peak and the blood-red sprawl; and the trail went on down into my America, which delineated itself by pale green dots; far away, I spied a low range of sand-molars set into the earth's jaw, and one of them was stained yellow like that piece of quartz.

I turned to looked back into the wider endlessness of Mexico.

Lupe said: I wanna look for that treasure, though. It's supposed to be at the top, where they encaved themselves to stop the gringo land grabbers.

He believed that twilight sun-gleams revealed the gold in one of the upper caves. It was not twilight by a long shot, but he went off by himself to search for gold. He was gone for a long time. When he came back I asked if he had found the treasure, and he smiled and said: If I had, do you think I'd tell you?

As for me, I took my pick of treasures from the artifacts bestowed here and there upon the mountain; in particular, the *pollos'* jugs reminded me of the concretions which Eva May Hyde and her friends had discovered at the northern foot of Signal Mountain, back in about 1912. *They were so numerous that we thought little of their scientific value.* A quarter-century later she had not forgotten them, and published a brief essay in *The Mineralogist.* In the photograph, they seem to be spheres, each with its own long tapering beak. Nobody knew how they had been created. People who lived near Signal Mountain proposed this theory: *Each one is formed by a hole being made by a crab or other marine animal and as the water poured in the hole the sand was set in motion. As it went round and round the center solidified and the length of the handle was according to the depth of the hole.* Well, well; that's as good a story as any. By the time I got to Imperial at the end of the twentieth century, the concretions had long since been gleaned away. *We need have no fear that our lands will not become better and better as the years go by.*

In spite of the odd plastic bottle or scrap of cloth, from this spot of vantage, Imperial seemed to have been scarcely stained at all by humanity. I felt as if I'd entered a certain old book which they keep behind the counter at the Calexico Public Library. This volume is entitled *Report of the Boundary Commission Upon the Survey and Re-Marking the Boundary between the United States and Mexico West of the Rio Grande 1891-1896. ALBUM.* Hatted men and horses, numbered boundary steles succeed each other in what begins as empty palm desert; the palms disappear long before we reach Imperial. The numbers increase as we go westward. Sometimes ocotillos seem to grapple with the white obelisks—but not every monument is an obelisk; part of the border's charm back then was the allowable variation; a monument might be thin or squat; moreover, each view in this album was composed from a different distance and perspective. Here's a horse and wagon on the overlook to Las Palomas Valley (station number fifteen); there's a marker built out of bricks; it rises about two-and-a-half times the height of the men who pose around it, one man leaning on his shovel; that's monument number forty. Number seventy-six, in Cañón de Guadalupe, Arizona, is made of iron. By the time we reach one hundred and ninety-three, we're in el Desierto de Yuma, which we now might as well begin calling the Yuma Desert since it's been ours ever since Guadalupe Hidalgo; more ocotillos grope like the desiccated arms of victims of a live burial, straining out of fractured sand. Two markers later, we're still in the Yuma Desert. A man sits on what could be either a barrel or a bedroll; he looks as if the heat is getting to him. Indeed, it's Yuma Desert all the way to monument two hundred and three, which happens to be an iron stele on flat grey sand; then comes number two hundred and four, also iron, old, repaired, claiming for my nation the mesa just east of the Colorado River. So it is that number two hundred and five, which indicates our possession of the river's bottomland, introduces us to Imperial itself, where immense, leafless trees reach high above the stele. (Aren't most of those trees gone now? Closing my eyes, I seem to see only the sprawling mediocrity of Yuma.) On the western side of the Colorado our album depicts more trees; then comes the fateful monument two hundred and seven, built of stone, on the mesa near Pilot Knob, where the irrigation of Imperial will commence. In the album, of course, that's still several years away; who could believe in such a utopian enterprise? A distant figure in a broadbrimmed hat poses with his hands on his hips.

Number two hundred and eight: Flatness west of Pilot Knob. Two hundred and nine: Sandhills west of Pilot Knob. Two hundred ten is an iron syringe which points absurdly erect out of more sandhills west of Pilot Knob . . .

With number two hundred and eleven, whose material is also iron, we find ourselves officially "on the Colorado Desert," whose borders wax and wane most disconcertingly in every new publication about the region. Here we find horses and buggies, not to mention a providential water barrel, and four men, two of whom stand posing at shoveling the flat earth. In fact, it's flat all the way to two hundred and seventeen. Two hundred and eighteen (iron) demarcates a place I'd never before heard of, to wit, the Salton Valley, which is also quite flat, but surprisingly twig-strewn as well as sandy, with low trees or bushes on the horizon. There must be water hereabouts! Two hundred and nineteen (iron) marks title to more of the

Salton Valley; we see a mule team in this photograph—freakish! How could such a miserable spot ever be suitable for agriculture? Number two hundred and twenty (iron again) is squat and tapering with a shield, and the world it possesses flat all around; we are east of the New River. Two hundred and twenty-one brings us west of the New River. Two hundred and twenty-two lies in another place I didn't know existed, the New River Valley—how we love to subdelineate!—and a man with a view camera poses there for us eternally. Two hundred and twenty-three bears the distinction of being the lowest point along the entire boundary. Two hundred and twenty-four stands on a spur of Cerro del Centinela, which is to say Signal Mountain; from where I stand right now, I can't see its successor;* the peak on my right occludes it. Two hundred twenty-six brings us back to the Colorado Desert again. May I skip a few markers? *They were so numerous that we thought little of their scientific value.* By the time we reach two hundred fifty, "on a ridge of Tijuana Valley," everything is quite lush, and we're only still in Imperial because of the pedantic way that I define her; two fifty-seven stands on a high mesa overlooking the Pacific Ocean; then comes the last one, two hundred and fifty-eight, right on the beach, very grand, caged like the altar in a Mexican shrine.

*But you will find it in my negative BR-BS-SIG-01-02.

Chapter 182

BETWEEN THE LINES

(2003–2005)

> The third, or Desert division [of San Diego County], lies east of the second, or San Jacinto range of mountains . . . Along the eastern base of this range extends the great Coahuila Valley, 50 miles in length by 10 in width, connecting southerly with the valley of the New River, which flows from the Colorado in times of freshets and fructifies the fertile lands along its bottoms. The Southern Pacific Railroad crosses this division . . .
>
> —Douglas Gunn, 1887

"I CAN GET ACROSS WHENEVER I WANT"

This book supposes that the damage done to the former coherence of the entity called Imperial is now as sickeningly rich as the stench of the Río Nuevo, which on a summer night remains on one's clothes and even on one's tongue;* on the other hand, as the Río Nuevo crosses the line to become the New River, upon its black sewage and white clots of foam are projected the carnival-like reflections of the border lights—beautiful lights!—and each delineation, every nexus, truly does offer us its own beauty: the rich night-mirror of the Salton Sea, for instance, or the change from Calexico's silent wide streets to Mexicali's crowded wide streets. Meanwhile, considerable coherence remains. I see it in the photographs I've taken: This old man resembles that old man, not just in the face and pose but in the clothes he wears. I see it in the sky: Wherever I go, the solar disk remains as fiery red as the face of a drunken, sleepy Mexican rancher on a Sunday afternoon. Honoring coherence, my Mexican friends go on denying and defying the first line.—When you look at this wall, I asked a man in Tijuana, do you feel sad or angry, or don't you care?—Proudly, he replied: I don't feel blocked in. I can get across whenever I want.—This statement does bear some literal value. Go to Mexicali's tapering silver-painted border stele number two hundred and twenty-one, and you'll see an outright ladder of tires mounted on the wall. To aid the ascender, an image of the Virgin of

*In short, I concur with George Wharton James, who writes *ca.* 1906 in his *Wonders of the Colorado Desert:* "There is a peculiar charm and surprise about the odors of the desert that needs comment."

Guadalupe has been painted nearby. Year by year, a rare sapling further obscures her; to deter him, a massive light, with a camera doubtless attached, stares down from Northside, directly opposite the ladder. Never mind: Read the *New York Times:* **At Mexican Border, Tunnels, Vile River, Rusty Fence.** *Perhaps nowhere is the inexorable nature of the northward migration of Mexicans—and the vulnerability of the United States to infiltration, whether by migrants or terrorists—more apparent than in Mexicali and its sister city, Calexico, Calif.* In other words, *I can get across whenever I want.*

Here let me insert the supernatural trans-border adventures of the ex-policeman Francisco Cedeño, whom you may remember in connection with that immortal *narcocorrido* "The City of Hawaii." He said:

When I went to meet my Dad in Fresno, he bought me some documents and taught me to speak a little English. I was living and working in Irwindale since my father's family did not accept me. I had a birth certificate and a social security card. I made up a story and paid off some American policemen to get a driver's license. So my name is Javier ———, and he showed me the false documents.—My wife didn't say much. She didn't know anything about the documents. I wanted to be an artist. So when I paid all these policemen off, they started threatening me—big brown men—and I said: I'm an artist. So the Department of Motor Vehicles gave me the driver's test and a policeman sold me the guide for the written test. It's the same here and there. I can swear to that. So one day I was here alone and very sad, and I was praying and I heard a voice saying I had to ask for forgiveness from my wife, parents, everyone to whom I had done wrong. So I went to the U.S. Customs and told them I had false papers and was sorry. They took me upstairs to a little room and kept me there for two hours and then they said I was a liar. Who *was* I? they wanted to know. I showed them my Mexican papers, and they said that for all they knew I was a Central American. They told me to get out. So now I can come and go. I have my social security number memorized!

And he laughingly reeled it off.

Did this story contain any embellishments? Who am I to say? Whether or not it's literally true, and it may well be (but if so, its climax must have occurred before the sea-change of September 11), it faithfully expresses a certain theme: *I can get across whenever I want.*

Francisco Cedeño might or might not have crossed the line on his own. Meanwhile, the farmers of oranges, water and lettuce had shown us the way to conceptualize everything—as a commodity which could be artificially *flowed* from origin to market. To the coyotes and other hole-builders, human beings were simply another such commodity. Hurrah for the canny people-farmers! To the guardians of Northside, needless to say, that flow was an endless Salton Sea accident. If *la línea* is a sort of canal, then the Chinese tunnels and other border-piercings may as well be considered weep holes—that is, openings left in retaining walls and the like to allow drainage. But the hydraulic engineers of Northside didn't buy that. Oh, if only they'd employed a double chamber sediment excluder! Ashford shutters, Bengal shutters, Fouracres shutters, automatic and counterweight, over- and under-counterweight, bear trap shutters of the European and non-European types, Whiting's rising sill gate, they might already have tried those, I don't know; for since the Patriot Act was passed, we're not supposed to ask; but there must be *some* way to keep them out! (They'll pop their heads up again in a minute.) All the same, had *I can get across whenever I want* been entirely true, the functionaries of Operation Gatekeeper with their handcuffs and Nightbusters* must have despaired. The wall itself, and the sad deported *pollos* who tell their stories in this book, prove the reverse. **Border deaths hit records**, my newspaper boasted. *A record 460 illegal migrants died crossing the U.S.-Mexico border in the last year, a toll pushed higher by the unusually hot temperatures and a shift of illegal migration routes through the remote desert . . . The dead were mostly Mexicans* . . . And yet the proud man's conception of Imperial, which is Mexican America, asserted itself faithfully, irresistibly. Imperial continued to be herself. Imperial was Elvira, the much-loved and much-raped Mexicali street prostitute whose face had been scarred by car accidents. Delineate her into pieces, and she'd still be Elvira. I'm told that she was stabbed, or maybe strangled. I haven't seen her in years, so chances are that she really has crossed the line, gone beneath the dirt. All the same, she's still Elvira. Cherishing my photographs of her, I refuse to feel blocked in; I can remember Elvira whenever I want . . .

The ancient taxi driver Juan Rodríguez, who spoke *small English,* lived Monday through Friday in the city of Imperial, and weekends in Mexicali. He stayed in the United States solely for the sake of his children's education, he said. I asked him about the wall and he said: It is an insult. But it means nothing.

Stella Mendoza lived in Brawley where she was born, but her orthodontist was in Mexicali, where Lupe Vásquez slept most nights, although his son, who had Down's syndrome, attended "special school" in Heber. Unlike José López, who sat on the south side of the border wall year after year, Lupe could get across whenever he wanted; and in his honor I quote from an end-of-the-century Pancho Villa prayer card: *Beloved brother, you who knew how to conquer your fiercest enemies, cause me to triumph in my most difficult undertakings.* A portrait of that famous revolutionist is captioned GENERAL PANCHO VILLA, THE MAN WHO DARED INVADE THE U.S.A.

On the Day of the Dead, the only live people in Pioneer Cemetery Number One,

*I wish I had permission to show you my snapshot of one of these monsters: white tanklike light-cannons blasting our enlightened radiance at Southside! After I clicked the shutter, a Border Patrolman rolled slowly up, whizzed down his window, and advised me that I was in a closed area.

with the exception of the caretakers, were a couple in late middle age; they dwelled in Northside, up near Fresno, but since three of their fourteen children were buried here in Mexicali, they came each year, she with her broom, he with his wheelbarrow; they'd already bought a crypt for the two of them, and she pointed to the concrete slab and said: All they have to do is slide this out to put our bodies in. It's very well made.—Over there was the grave of the son who'd died in an accident; here was the grave of the daughter who'd died of cancer. The parents had driven down the previous day, stopping in Indio to gamble at Casino Twenty-nine; then, crossing the line, they'd arrived in Mexicali at nine P.M. After their children's tombs were put in order, they'd drive back to Northside to await the Mexican call of death.

In Mexicali, the parking lot attendant Lupita had crossed the line for twenty-nine years now, mainly to go to Las Vegas, which she loved. The year before I interviewed her, the handbag containing her passport got stolen while she was reading a magazine in a fast food restaurant in Calexico. She would have a new passport in two months, she thought; she was certain that she could get across whenever she wanted. *"The aim if reached or not, makes great the life."*

When the sun went down, wide Mónica began to work across the street from Lupita's former spot. She'd come into this world in Fresno, California. Her mother and brothers remained there. She kept her three children with her in Mexicali, where she dwelled because she loved her grandmother so much and because being around her mother made her so sad. She apologized for being so dark; her grandfather had been a nigger, she said. She had to work hard for her children, she said; she worked especially hard on Friday and Saturday nights. She never carried condoms with her nor asked her customers to use any. Her fee was twenty dollars. Her answer to impotence was vitamins and reassurance. She thought that any woman who loved her man enough would always say yes to his desire, because she loved him. It was her *choice* to be here.

In 1916 the Imperial County Development Agent reported that *in Imperial Valley, besides the 39,028 bales ginned on the American side, 24,147 bales were ginned on the Mexican side, making a total valley production of 63,175 bales.* He too saw the valley as all one—at least as far as the Riverside County line. *Up to 1916, the Mexican cotton was ginned on the American side and the production included in the California statistics by the Census bureau.*

Up in Riverside County, in a weird Mexican barrio on Indian land not far from Coachella (the place was called Duroville, and will receive its own chapter), I photographed four young men who leaned against or sat upon a car; and the righthandmost of these, whose name was Benito Ledesma, said to me: I consider myself Mexican. I was born in Riverside. My Mom was born in Mexico. That means I got Mexican blood.

He sometimes went to Mexicali for fun. (He considered the Thirteen Negro Bar too dangerous.) He was Mexican, and yet he said: When I grow up I wanna stay here.

It seemed that to him, too, the line was nearly irrelevant—a hindrance, perhaps, a distortion, certainly, but he was Mexican, emphatically not Mexican-American, it came out; the fact that he had neither been born in Mexico nor lived there, nor intended to do so, made scant difference.

The epigraph to this chapter transacts its narrative in coins of an obsolete currency: San Diego County no longer includes that long valley now dissected by abstraction's knife into sub-valleys, of which neither the New River Valley nor "the great Coahuila Valley" retains its name (for that matter, the immense nation of Kumeyaay Indians out of which so much of San Diego and Imperial counties were violently carved has long since dried up into a very few reservation-puddles); meanwhile, the New River no longer fructifies; it is a horror; the Colorado neither waxes nor wanes, having been *smoothed out* by the Bureau of Reclamation and other agents of control; the Southern Pacific Railroad may still *cross this division,* but highways have robbed it of its prominence. So what? Delineations come and go; Imperial remains Imperial. Thoreau insisted that even when they put him in jail his thoughts could still fly in and out the window. For my part, I don't feel blocked in. I can get across whenever I want, my fantasies adorned with twists of dates from the trees of Rancho Roa.

DIFFERENCES

Meanwhile, Imperial's artificially created subzones, artifcially stimulated into mutual antipathy, insist upon their diffferences.

Desperately arguing against the reduction of its water allotment by the behemoth Interior, Imperial County claims that it has an entirely different soil type from Coachella. The Imperial Valley's fields glisten on their low ends; Coachella's don't. But the Imperial Valley's not wasteful—don't ever think that! *Unlike CWD's service area, where the sandy soil soaks up the water and the runoff to the Salton Sea is underground, the farmers in IID's service area must work with soil that does not allow the water to seep in quickly. Tailwater is the natural result.* (Now to the point: *Interior has not limited IID's tailwater use for over seven decades . . . all parties . . . were well aware of IID's customary irrigation practices.*)

IMPERIAL REPRISE

All the same, I can get across whenever I want.

THE BROAD STREET WELL (1854)

If that's so, what could be less relevant than any official borderline? It's easy to say that Northside is richer than Southside; more graphically, that Northside is to Southside as San Diego is to Tijuana: foggy to smoggy, clean to dirty, spacious to crammed, gridded to mazed, silent to loud, expensive to cheap—all such oppositions being relative, of course, TJ being much more expensive than Mexicali and, in Centro, many of the prices nearly equal San Diego's; but that raises up one more opposition: Southside, many things are negotiable; Northside, they often are not. I've stayed in that San Diego Travelodge half a dozen times now, and in both senses it stinks. The rooms are grubby and damaged; the doors don't lock; flies drift over the courtyard, and now it costs me a hundred dollars. What can I do about it? A tip's not going to make anybody fix my room. In sum, if we zoom in on Northside, we can see such gross variations in moneyscape topography as the following: Within Brawley's zip code 92227, which would seem to be an awfully discrete location, the postal carrier route C003 (West Allen Street, De Anza Place and environs) boasts an average estimated income of $80,595, while carrier route C002 (North First Street, North Imperial Avenue, and so on) in the very same zip code presents an income of $22,692. Where is the money-line? Couldn't it be that Imperial is comprised of as many sub-shapes as that abandoned car's windshield over there, shattered into powder? One prominent information designer would certainly expect this or any book to convey *a sense of* average *and of* variation *about that average—the two fundamental summary measures of statistical data.* I agree with him; I want to know whether the variation about the average is so great that aggregating Imperial into "Northside" and "Southside" is meaningless.

Our information designer, whose name is Edward Tufte, devotes several illustrated pages to the London cholera epidemic of 1854. Although the bacteriological agency of this then extremely lethal disease remained unknown, Dr. John Snow succeeded in isolating what we might call its proximate agency: the well at Broad Street. Ticking off the locations of the deaths on a map which also showed all eleven wells in the affected quarter, Snow was able to literally *see* where the deaths were clustered. Proceeding to the Board of Guardians of Saint James's Parish, he persuaded them to remove the pump handle of the Broad Street well. The cholera deaths ran their course. What Snow did might be supposed to be a crude sort of aggregation. Tufte, however, points out that *aggregations by area can sometimes mask and even distort the true story of the data.* And Tufte draws three specimen maps with the Broad Street well at the center. In the first, one of the six aggregated zones, a trapezoid-like figure with a square notch taken out of the western edge, happens to be centered on the well, and so it is the darkest, most ominous grey. In the second map, five zones comprise the same area, the well touches one boundary of three of them, and they are all, not to mention an adjacent fourth zone, equally grey. In the third map, there are also five zones, but the two smallest ones on either side of the well, and some distance from it, are darkest, while the two larger zones whose joint boundary runs east-west across the well are only mid-grey.

This parable is inspiring, but at the same time cautionary. Should I subdelineate Imperial ignorantly (or, worse yet, misdefine its perimeters), the Broad Street well might remain invisible to me.

"NEARLY EVERYONE YOU MEET HERE IS FROM THE EAST"

Imperial is ghettoization; Imperial is mobility, migration, permanent temporariness. In these border towns, people come from somewhere else. Travelling around San Diego, Los Angeles and the Inland Empire, G. Harold Powell writes home in 1904: *Nearly everyone you meet here is from the east, and a large proportion from New York.* Ninety-nine years later, everybody is still from somewhere else. In Tijuana where *don't* they come from? In Mexicali it's the same. Calexico is growing like crazy, which must mean that people are arriving from somewhere else; it's not just the birthrate.

Since there's no school for his children in Sonora, one paterfamilias moves house to Tecate. Now his daughter has already married here. In fact, all his daughters are married; he has grandchildren; his sons sell furniture. He's been to Northside; he used to work in Los Angeles. Smiling on his park bench, he boasts: I used to have a lot of luck since *la migra* never threw me out.

(In other words, I can get across whenever I want.)

He used to pick oranges, pick lemons, pick all kinds of fruit.—It was really easy back then, he says. I had a passport that let me go and come back. It allowed me to cross; then I could come right back. But I stayed. I worked for fifteen years, in the seventies and eighties. I picked Valencia oranges. I used to climb up into the trees; I had to snip them with little scissors. I used to pick lemons in Santa Paula; that's three hours from Los Angeles to the west (which would have made it another Atlantis, and the interpreter said that he didn't know the word "west"; he'd actually said *where the sun sets*). Oh, he said, there are lots of oranges and lemons and grapefruits in that valley! There was a lot of work, contracted work, ten or twelve hours a day.

And how long have you been in Tecate?

Many years.

The buttery smell of fresh pastries from the bakery at the edge of the park, the other old men on their benches, pensioned—*waiting to die,* as they put it—the palm shadows, the coolness which Tecate enjoys as a result of its elevation, the birds and the statues make me feel that this would not be a bad sector of Imperial in which to end my days, so I ask him if he likes it. He has already told me that he misses his little house in Sonora, and I half expect him to say that he would rather die there, but instead he replies: I live here because I can't live in the U.S. The rent was so high . . .

SURRENDER

And do you recall that indefatiguable *pollo,* hoper and guide, José López from Jalisco? Do you remember his striving and struggling to cross the line? Two and a half years after I first met him just outside the handicapped gate of the entrance into Mexico, with the border wall five paces in front of him and Calexico's taxi stand visible, audible and unattainable beyond, he said this to me:

I mean, at first I didn't wanna do it because I thought I was just passing through. But I seen it was hard. *Hard,* Bill, to pass to the other side! And I would get a pretty good grip of money and spend it on hotels, with the hope of getting to the other side. But this was back in the old days. Thank God, I got about two-three days' work with some white folks. They told me they were gonna pay me good, guiding and translating. The first day, sightseeing and barhopping and checking out the girls. The second day, they said, we want you to go with us to San Felipe, but we only got as far as the Río Hardy. We stopped there. They got new bamboo roofs and four posts and you can put lawn chairs. We stayed there and we started drinking a couple beers and that afternoon we just came to Mexicali. As a matter of fact, we ate around the corner from here, right at that new Chinese restaurant. At the third day, they said, okay, have something planned for us. Earn your money. I thought, man, I ran out of watering spots! Then I said, no problem! At the Caliente, I saw some older guys that I know and they were gambling. They were betting on the pit bull fights. I said, man! Where is that? At Ejido T—— on the way to San Luis! It's not like legal. It's not registered. We might have been raided and shit. So I said, gimme the address. It was at a ranch. So we went there, spent around four or five hours over there, and we saw it all. Each fight went on not till one dropped, just until one cried. Put a pole in to separate them. Then I took 'em to the Miau-Miau. It was four guys. I think I earned my money. Each of 'em have a girl. The girls' drinks are seven bucks. The men's drinks are three-fifty. For me it was like a green light, too. But I wasn't like getting drunk. I had to pay attention. They gave me a hundred-dollar bill, but I really earned my money because it was four guys, four girls. I told them, look, I'm gonna translate for you, but I'm not gonna translate everything the girls say, because my throat was already sore. So they give me another hundred bucks, and another, and then two hundred bonus. And that's when I thought, Bill, since

I haven't been able to come across, and then I always used to go to the Hotel Capri instead of blowing air with a piece of newspaper at the Nuevo Pacífico, why not? When I had that money, Bill, and I sent some home, but still I had two hundred bills and I said I'm not gonna do the same mistake with the Hotel Capri.

I walked for about four or five hours. If you see a lady or a man outside, you ask them, are there any *cuartos*? Anyway, I see a sign. So I stopped there. I liked the place. It's just a little room, but usually you're gonna have to use your shower and restroom with the rest, and this one has it all inside. And I think this is the only one. I asked him how much and he tells me it's about six hundred. I thought it was a little steep. But then I see the shower inside and I think it's worth it. It's six hundred pesos plus the electric bill plus five bucks a month for water. I could have only stayed three or four nights at the Capri, so I think I invested my money good.

And it's just way better. I can do my laundry there. And that's why I got my place, Bill. But I don't wanna get too comfy. I gotta start making my decision. Since this happened with my Mom, I don't even think I wanna go again to the other side. First because it's so damn hard. I dunno. That event changed a lot of things. Changed my mind. I guess I've given more thought to things I didn't think of much before my Mom's death. Man, here I am. It's been so many months I haven't been over there. And maybe I can't do it.

Sometimes I do good, man. I have a little to send home, a little for me. I'm thinking, I'm either going to get to the other side or bring my family over here. If I dedicate myself to what I do, I can live pretty good. Come September, October, it picks up. It picks up. 'Course it's pretty hot now, but . . .

He was silent for an instant, then said in a lower voice: I don't wanna spend too much time like *this,* you know. I don't know if I'm not trying hard enough or what.

Throughout this book I have called him José López from Jalisco, and although he suffered the accident of being born in Mexicali he really *was* from there.—Jalisco, it has beach, he said to me once. That's where Puerto Vallarta is. There's big mountain range. The Sierra Madre runs like through five states! My Dad would drive. There's like cliffs. And I mean, oh, man, it's so nice. We would go at different times of the year. Like, the cliffs, you would see down, and all green! I would always get nervous in that part of the road because the traffic would be like passing in curves. You could see down, and like that way, going towards Guadalajara, you were on the edge of the cliff and you could see houses in the side of the cliff and you could see everything being harvested and you could see banana plantations. My father would go down and he would buy like an arm of bananas. That's what they call it, an arm. We'd be eating bananas all the way to Guadalajara. Well, it's been awhile since then.

Which do like better, Mexicali or Jalisco?

I can survive better here, Bill. Jalisco may be the place where I grew up, sure, but it's not about that; it's about survival. And it's not wild here, like Tijuana. I been to Juárez, too, and Nuevo Laredo. And this is the border where I would like to be doing what I am doing when I have a choice. Tijuana, besides, there's a lot of competition around there, a lot of guys who get deported and stay there in Tijuana. It's been awhile since I been in Tijuana, maybe eight or ten years, and back in that time, you know they deport you right at the border. And I could hear a lot of locals talking English. So this is the place I think I would be. In Jalisco there's hardly any jobs. You would have to own land, and then you would have to work at something.

Why not be a campesino here?

Because of the salary. Even what they pay over there—and he pointed quickly at the wall without looking at it—it's underpaid. Because I knew Bud Antle, and Dole, which took them over; they planted lettuce, and broccoli, cauliflower in the Mexicali Valley, and they were getting more than in the *maquiladora,* but it still wasn't really good.

How much can you make in a day, compared to what you would make in a *maquiladora*?

Well, if it's just like, if I was there all the way to noon and then I seen that I wasn't gonna get nobody to guide, what I do is dedicate myself to helping people with groceries. It depends on how far you take 'em. But on the average, just helping people with groceries, if I stay from eleven until they close the gate at eight P.M., and that don't mean I'll be working all these hours, I can probably make twenty-five or twenty dollars. I'll tell you, Bill, most people will give you ten pesos if you just take 'em to the Hotel del Norte. It's a sure thing.

And how often can you . . . ?

Hook somebody up? Well, then my job is like seasonal, since not a lot of people like this weather. Right now in summertime I would say, to guide, I would say, twice a week. In guiding, it's a cinch. I'm gonna get at least fifty. Then when I escort them just to a cab, I get just a couple dollars. They'll tip me out of their heart.

So how much do you make in a month?

Oh, it varies a lot. It's got to be two hundred, two hundred and fifty a month.

So that was twice what a *maquiladora* worker made. I wanted to ask him how much he sent home to his family in Jalisco, but I didn't.

Like this is one of the times I spent more time here in Mexicali, he remarked. I'm liking it. I don't know if it got so hard to cross the border illegally, but I'm thinking, maybe I don't really have to go to the border side to make a living. They're forcing you to try your luck in the desert and the mountains and I won't try that. Like there, every month there'll be new posters, posters for missing people. Most of the posters, they have a note that says they got a mental illness. If not elderlies, it's real young girls. Oh, man, a lot of things can happen.

A moment later two of the bicycle policemen who had been persecuting him (he especially feared the one in the dark shirt) appeared on the edge of Niños Héroes Park where we sat on that hundred-and-ten-degree morning with sweat slowly sliding down our chests, and they summoned him with a finger-jerk. A moment after he had come up to them and they had patted him down, he was walking away from them and me without looking back. He walked quite rapidly. When I caught up with him, they already had him up against the wall. They assured me that he had been arrested for three robberies. Eventually they let him go, and I thanked them for their attention to security. I wondered whether they would arrest him again when I was gone. But that had not quite happened yet. I took him to the Hotel Chinesca so that he could have a shower. He washed his clothes when he washed himself. Then he said: Like at night time, in that abandoned clinic, I wondered, what am I doing over here? When you're hearing all the rats and cockroaches passing over that uncovered roof, no ceiling. So I got to thinking, man, if I'm gonna be here, might as well make the best of it. That's how I decided to settle down.

He hit me up for a tip, and that was the last time I ever saw him.

Chapter 183

SUBDELINEATIONS: MONEYSCAPES

(1989–2005)

> Attempts at description are stupid: who can all at once describe a human being?. . . We recognise the alphabet; we are not sure of the language.
>
> —George Eliot, 1876

HOLES IN THE MAP

Module F, Social and Economic Data Tables, will depict our moneyscape for today. California in her entirety lies before us, nicely subdivided in money-zones of stepped grey, one county per zone. In this map of median household income in 1989, Imperial County stands out with the whiteness of earnings stripped down to the bone: $20,494 to $24,450. But she has company in her poverty: namely, the great belt from Inyo down to Kern, and up through Kings and Fresno counties—much of the Central Valley, in short. And this whiteness continues even into the Swiss-like counties of Calaveras and Alpine.

San Bernardino and Riverside counties are two full greys darker and richer than this. Their median household income lies between $28,867 and $33,520 inclusive.

Then come Los Angeles and San Diego counties, sharing the next shade of lush darkness at $33,521 to $39,113.

In Module B, we have what first seems to be a negative image of the previous map: white, not black, is now good; for this moneyscape shows **County Unemployment Rates, 1999 Annual Averages**. And so the deep black holes of Imperial, Tulare and Colusa counties stand grimly out from the map: thirteen point five to twenty-two point eight percent unemployment. (Ranked number one of all California counties: Imperial, 1997; Imperial, 1998; Imperial, 1999 . . .) Meanwhile, lying insouciantly alongside Imperial, San Diego County remains pure white, enjoying the lowest unemployment bracket in the state: one point nine to three point nine percent. Fellow club members: Orange County, and that other white coastal zone of Santa Barbara and San Luis Obispo counties. As for Riverside, that county is a pale grey, like San Bernardino and Inyo above it: four to five point nine percent unemployment. The grey zone beginning in Ventura County and sweeping all the way up past Death Valley to the edge of Mono County, should we consider it a sick place or just average? Los Angeles County is grey, too, I see; Imperial County's all alone in her blackness down there.

"SOME OF THE GREATEST INCOME DISPARITIES IN CALIFORNIA"

Palm Springs, Cathedral City and Palm Desert *have some of the greatest income disparities in California . . . In general, resort communities . . . had some of the highest income gaps, as did agricultural areas in the Imperial and Central valleys that rely heavily on immigrant workers.*

Mecca: Median household income is $22,973.

Indio: $34,624.

Indian Wells (six miles from Indio): $93,986. *Retirees have flocked in recent years to dozens of gated communities,* which must be why in the *Desert Sun* one can find such lease bargains as *Sterling Cove: Exclusive Estate/Pool!* for nine thousand dollars a month . . .

RANKINGS

In 1997, a ranking of small-scale American urban clusters for various livability factors assigns the "micropolitan" complex El Centro–Calexico–Brawley a climate rating of zero; an amusement place availability ranking of second to last, just above Hinesville, Georgia; above the bottom ten for personal income (Eagle Pass, Texas, being the loser since it is *a port of entry for immigrants from Mexico*); for *change in per capita income 1990–94, adjusted for inflation,* the El Centro cluster finishes dead last. *In El Centro–Calexico–Brawley, California, the decline partially reflects an influx of immigrants with few initial job skills and low earning potential.* Second to last for percentage of adults with a high school education (once again, Eagle Pass, Texas, is at the bottom), El Centro gets fabulous scores for population growth, percentage of new housing, annual expenditures on health care and other peculiarities. Thus, on the overall report card, Eagle Pass finishes in last place with three hundred seventy-one out of a thousand points; Mount Vernon, Washington, wins at six hundred and five points; and El Centro gets four hundred and thirty-four points, coming in at a national rank of a-hundred-and-eighty-first out of two hundred.

May I tell you more? In 2001, a certain California county called Imperial (leading commodities: cattle, leaf and head lettuce, alfalfa, carrots and livestock) ranks eleventh in the state for total production value. In 2002, it will rank ninth. San Diego (cut flowers, ornamentals, eggs, avocados, tomatoes and the like) ranks just above Imperial at eighth for both years. Fresno and Tulare trade places for first and second; Riverside's at ninth, then eleventh, busily vending its milk, nursery products, table grapes and hay; Los Angeles is halfway down the list at twenty-seventh and twenty-sixth (nursery plants, peaches, etcetera); Alpine is smack at the bottom, poor number fifty-eight, no produce to mention.

Meanwhile, in the year 2000, one out of four Mexicans, some of them doubtless in Imperial, exist *in extreme poverty.*—That year sixteen percent of all Californians were classified as impoverished, while thirty point three percent of Imperial County denizens made the same grade. Every day in every way we are getting better and better: For in 1990, only twenty-three point eight percent of Imperial County's residents had been officially poor. Shall we give praise for the conquest of Arid America?—On a hot June morning in 2003, I walked out of my hotel room to get coffee and found a line of human beings, almost all of them brownskinned or oliveskinned, stretching along the sidewalk and around the corner; I followed them down the sidewalk and around the next corner; they went almost entirely around the four sides of a city block. I asked the girl at the end of the line what she was waiting for, and she said a Ralph's supermarket job. The newspaper said that it was a Food 4 Less; two thousand people had lined up in hopes of getting seventy-five jobs. The first ones had been waiting since three in the morning. Applications were given out beginning at eight.

An essay on Tijuana remarks: *The closer you get to the U.S., the poorer the city becomes.* This is in fact the opposite of what I hear,* but never mind; Tijuana most certainly is poorer than her neighbor, San Diego. A Stanford historian informs us: *The income gap between the United States and Mexico is the largest between any two contiguous countries in the world.*

What does it mean to be ranked? Does one *know one's place*? Does Mecca hate Indian Wells?

Until a large pool of skilled workers willing to work for less began appearing in the Inland Empire, there was no incentive for high-paying firms to migrate to the region. Now, there is. Why, how nice for high-paying firms! Something tells me that in Mexican Imperial a high-paying firm can find any number of people who are willing to work for less. And in material advantages they are well supplied. Imperial's moneyscape may be summed up as *a steep and reliable differential,* whose reliability

*José López said: "Oh, the first thing you notice is the money when you're working. Everything is different, even the houses, the cities. Even in Calexico it's a whole different culture even though we're all Mexicans. Mexicali is better money, and Calexico is even better money, so you get to eat a little better, you dress better, you have a little money to send back, and you can even get a used car. When it gets time to go home I just sell it. Sometimes I sleep in it. Once I got me a used pickup with a camper shell, and a used mattress from a secondhand store, and I slept there. I used to just go to a work camp and pay two dollars for a shower. Just a little bit uncomfortable, but it was worth it."

facilitates the commerce it specializes in. Necessity teaches poor people, as it does *maquila* managers, to map out specialized sub-gradients of particular utility.

In 2003 a man in Tijuana assured me: Most of the tourists are from the U.S., and all the money here is from the U.S. Basically, we live on the U.S.

How did that happen? I asked.

It happened bit by bit. Here basic services, like getting a car fixed, are cheaper that in the U.S., so Americans come to get more for their money.

The man was orginally from Frontera Sur of Chiapas. He said to me: Here in Tijuana there are more people from all over the Republic! A mixture from all the states!

In other words, the international line created a sharp gradient, over which money from Northside accordingly spilled; and Mexicans came from all over Southside to be nourished by that money.*

In a classical economic model of international trade, raw materials, especially agricultural produce, come from the undeveloped country to the developed one. But in Mexicali the Guatemalan who squeezed my fresh orange juice said that his oranges came from across the border, from California, as did his grapefruits, carrots, celery, and even his nopales, whose pulp makes such a lovely bitter green when blended with orange juice; the only exception to this rule of reverse derivation was his bananas, which came from Chiapas. In 2003 he paid two pesos per orange. His profit on each glass of juice he sold was about fifty percent.

And infinitely eastward of there, a good fifty kilometers or more into the steamy furnace of the Mexicali Valley, the renowned fighting-cock breeder Señor Héctor, whose real name I decline to reveal to the law, dwelled in Ejido Monterrey. One of his birds survived seven fights. He'd bought his latest batch of chicks in Indio, where Northside's strictness renders cockfighting more than nominally illegal, and drove them across the line, hiding them beneath the seat of his scarred truck. He gave them vitamins every day, and a shot of anabolic steroids. Up high in rope perches in their cages, the black cock with the flamelike mane and the reddish-brown one were jittering their heads back and forth. When they were young they used to fear being handled. Now they attacked as they were supposed to, which was why when he worked with them, Señor Héctor wore the same heavy canvas shield as lemon-pickers. He'd made a success through his own efforts. He sold them for up to five hundred dollars each; sometimes ten men each pay two hundred dollars to bet on one of his birds, winner take all. In his way Héctor was a great man.

* Another example of knowing one's subgradients: An old man I met in the park in Tecate bought coffee and light sugar in El Cajon when he went to visit his two children; those commodities were cheaper in the United States. Sugar for diabetics was also cheaper, likewise potatoes and canned food. But coffee and meat were more expensive; he tried not to buy them on the other side.

But to know Imperial's moneyscapes, the peaks of richness, the various boundary-lines, the rippling moneycourses which bear wealth away, is to make one inescapably conscious of the resulting inequalities.

Once upon a Mexicali night, my sweetheart and I set out for the Fiesta del Sol. Behind a wall, white tombs crowded each other in the evening dirt. We got into a taxi that rushed us down into the Río Nuevo gorge. Then we paid the woman behind the heavily barred window, who gave us one pasteboard ticket apiece. So we gained entrance to the carnival rides, the even lines of *policía* rigidly enjoying themselves, the darkfaced, proud-breasted girls tapping their feet to the music, with their fingers in the belt-loops of their jeans. There was a basketball hoop contest, a plastic Virgin of Guadalupe for a prize! Teenaged girls screamed in chorus on the twister ride. Meanwhile, accompanied by prerecorded music, all paying children could get their photos taken with Spider-Man!

On the edge of a dirt embankment overlooking the Fiesta, poor children stood in a line, looking down across the street and over a fence into the fun, the Río Nuevo stench coming in from evenly spaced gratings on the lovely cool wind, fountains spouting from a sunburst daisy booth where someone was about to win a Chevrolet.

Chapter 184

SUBDELINEATIONS: MONEYSCAPES

(2003–2006)

MORE HOLES IN THE MAP

Between 2000 and 2003, one out of every six manufacturing jobs in the United States vanishes! *Economists say it's largely the strong increases in productivity that have shrunk demand for workers.*

Where does production go? China, India, Mexico.

But now Mexico's also losing those manufacturing jobs. Where do they go? China, India.

What does Mexico gain? Agricultural revenues. **U.S. opens avocado pipeline: Mexico ramps up exports as trade barriers finally fall.**

Chapter 185

PRESENT AND FUTURE SUCCESSES

(2003)

Hopefully you'll find the data and charts mostly correspond to your impressions of Imperial from your many visits there. I've never been, and I'm not sure I especially want to go. It seems likely to remind me of the Anasazi ruins or some other collapsed civilization, except people still live there, and a version of the collapse is still going on with only a handful of bright spots.

—Paul Foster, 2007

County unemployment rate dips a bit to 22 percent.

OPTIMISTIC OUTLOOK: Local officials point to the housing and retail boom as indicators of present and future successes.

Economic signs have picked up across the country . . . Some of the good news has reached the Imperial Valley.

While the county still has the highest rate of unemployment in the state, there were more workers employed in September than at the same time last year . . .

Chapter 186

MARKET PRICES

(2000)

Now a haze lies upon the land . . . and through it emerges an apparition of monumental cultivation.

—William DeBuys and Joan Myers, 1999

In 1993, when the North American Free Trade Agreement was signed, Northside corn sold for a hundred and ten dollars a ton; Southside corn went for two hundred and forty dollars a ton. At the beginning of the twenty-first century, the price of Mexican corn had fallen by half, bankrupting one point three million small farmers. Well, so Mexicans could buy corn for less. *We need have no fear that our lands will not become better and better as the years go by.*

By the way, in 1989, fifty-four percent of rural Mexicans were classified as poor. In 2001 that figure was eighty-one and a half percent. *There's a lot of crying-in-your-beer stuff going on.*

Up in Imperial, the total agricultural wealth created in 2000 was a bit under nine hundred and twenty million dollars—ten and a half percent less than for the previous year. Only apiaries did better in 2000 than in the previous year. *You can't produce things the way you used to.*

The top five products were, in decreasing order of gross income, those old Imperial standbys cattle, alfalfa, lettuce, carrots and sugar beets. No doubt we will not be able to produce such items the way we used to; and if you wish to know how we used to, I refer you to the taxi driver Angel, who said as he drove me from El Centro to the good city of Imperial, passing a thick cloud of white birds hovering above a brown field over which one sprinkler made many rainbows: You know, lettuce is hard to work, because all day is bend down and cut. Watermelons is start at eleven, so you work only four, five hours. Melons you cut in early morning or late afternoon; watermelons is easier money. The hardest thing with watermelons is to know which is the ripest.

What is the secret? I asked.

They don't tell anyhow, because for their secret they get twenty-five dollars an hour, a hundred bucks for four hours.*

Celery, he continued, is raining, and broccoli is lots of moisture sometimes dropping down; no good. In six hours I make a hundred twenty bucks for celery. For eighty to a hundred pounds they pay eighty-nine cents.

So much for Angel, who undoubtedly has never been cheated out of a dollar in his life. So much for green wealth. Now, what about other reliable Imperial products?

The last time Lupe had been to the Thirteen Negro, the going rate had been five pesos a dance. Now it was ten. He was horrified; he couldn't believe it. *Manufacturing is hitting another level of evolution.*

At the Hotel Nuevo Pacífico, the snooty half-Chinese girl he liked parleyed with him through the glass door; so it came out that she would be two hundred and fifty pesos, naked from the waist down only, probably for ten minutes maximum, so he was despondent; he remembered when that would have been a hundred pesos. *What a great choice!*

A bored and sleepy girl who sat down on the steps of the Hotel Altamirano with her head resting on the wall offered to strip from the waist down and present herself for up to thirty minutes for two hundred and fifty pesos. That's not bad! Lupe remarked. Licking her lips, she milked her giant breasts at him. *And in material advantages they are already well supplied.*

*I have been told that this knowledge is guarded with certain migrant worker families.

Chapter 187

IMPERIAL BEACH

(2005)

Taking the road to the right of the Tia Juana road, we come to the seaside, just beyond the head of the Bay, and find the Initial Monument, which marks the start of the boundary line . . .

—Douglas Gunn, 1887

In fact, Imperial Beach does possess an avenue called Date, but this memorialization of the entity which I call Imperial is silver with fog and weeps with trees. On silver nights one makes the final west turn off Seacoast Drive, onto the long pier where fishermen stand luring dreams as big as swordfish by means of the stinking clams and mussels they won two or three days since at low tide; here lies a clamshell as silver as the fog's ear. Looking over their shoulders I see the white foam-snakes wriggle in upon their sides, parallel to one another in the black water-night. (From my Imperial nights I remember many a train like a darkness-spined beast; I remember occasional trees, the Salton Sea a mirror of purple darkness. The siren songs of trains in Imperial equal the waves of Imperial Beach; both would carry me away if I only had a *pollo*'s courage or need.) Closer to the lights of the city the night is blacker and less alive; that must be beach. House-lights rake sand accidentally; mostly, however, that zone remains as unknown as Imperial itself. But to the south, at the very end of the restless black water, a light pulses in the silver air: that's our Coast Guard, marking the delineation of Northside and Southside which continues indefinitely out to sea.

I love it here. Imperial Beach equals almost perfect blankness, at night, at least; and foggy days are nearly as good as true Imperial nights. I never liked Bombay Beach, whose flat hard streets stink; had I ever made a friend there, I could have entered somebody's boarded-up trailer with a deck on it; from that deck, or even from the levee, which resembles the border wall, I could have dreamed my way into the Salton Sea. Oh, cold bulbs, cold lights! Trailers with no lights, a satellite dish glazed with dust, and the grey mountains of the moon beyond fences! Almost half the houses wore lights on them in Bombay Beach. The winter haze was so rich and cold . . . Give me Imperial Beach! If it's not in Imperial, I'll make it so, going farther and farther away from that accidental and salt-poisoned sea until I've come back to Mother Pacific . . .

But it already is so, and has been ever since the line of 1848 cut away Northside from Southside. Imperial Beach, which resembles El Centro much less than El Centro does, say, Dateland, Arizona, is no less El Centro's sister city for all her ocean fog; the *pollos* make her so.—They do work most Americans wouldn't do, said Border Patrolman Dan Murray. And tonight, in the chilly darkness and in spite of Operation Gatekeeper, somebody must be creeping northward . . .

Chapter 188

SAN DIEGO

(2003–2006)

Subdivisions in various localities have already proven highly successful and flourishing settlements have sprung up on half-barren fields.

—Ludwig Louis Salvator, recollections from the nineteenth century's "Sunny Seventies"

At rainy times San Diego extends all the way to Los Angeles, with water shimmering out of palm trees and white warehouse walls becoming foggy sky. The median strips of freeways turn lush almost instantly; this is how California was supposed to be.

Kindly San Diego, as you know, has offered to pay for the lining of the All-American Canal. All she asks in return is to drink ninety-nine years' worth of the water thus saved from seeping into Mexico.

San Diego may be excluded from the entity which I call Imperial, but she enjoys membership in the Water Drinkers' Club; and on rainy days she grows new houses beneath the same wet skies as in Fullerton or Santa Ana; she excavates sodden meadows as in Irvine; here in San Diego by the ocean where water is trembling on top of ashcans, and in the shadows of recycling barrels on sidewalks, I gaze south to green fields in the fog: "inhumanly" (what does this word mean?) straight fat stripes of green between thin stripes of grey.

Sometimes it does seem at those rainy times that the fog thickens as one goes south from Los Angeles, the foliage ever more flourishing, almost voluptuous; then quite suddenly we have come into a foggy orchard country; white-foamed streams slobber down through the rain; we're in the pages of *Ramona*. The flowers, ferns and fan-palms of San Juan Capistrano can trick me into believing the homestead promotions of the railroad companies. But then the coast grows arid again as one rides into San Diego, whose water-glass is eternally half empty.

And yet, **WATER IS HERE**, nourishing flocks of little white houses and trees, hummocky turf out of Emily Brontë, and then there is the grey-green ocean, with seagulls swooping in and out of the shining pavement-rectangles of another Ocean Parkscape, the fog as thick as ale-foam now over the beach houses, clean black ribbon of wet road, endless rectangle of beach, infinite rectangle of white-scribbled dark sea, trees on parking lots; the sea-horizon has softened; the land-edge is crookeder than usual, thanks to the wind. A pier stands on centipede legs, flying the American flag. The beaches are empty and clean. Sometimes the ocean darkens, particularly over dark stones, but a prominent meteorologist assures me that this phenomenon has more to do with the increasing darkness of the clouds. Now sea and fog comprise one square punctuated by rain-sounds; the square goes upward infinitely but it is underlined by dark greenness.

In San Diego I remember rain on the night-black parking lots of Tijuana, bulky female figures bowing under umbrellas as the green or pink glows from motel lobbies strike them in the shoulders; I remember rain running off roofs, and the taste of solvents coming down from Otay Mesa. San Diego is less smelly, more "natural," richer of course. San Diego's rain is clean.

In San Diego, an Imperial Avenue runs right through the Mexican neighborhoods. Then where does Imperial Avenue go? Follow the old plank road through the Algodones Dunes and then you will know.

San Diego is lovely and perfect. *"Moisture Means Millions."* San Diego is lush white lace on the fat waves, the sea shining simultaneously silver and gold. San Diego is the glints and sparkles of water in tidal estuaries. Poor San Diego! Her water's all salt!

In San Diego it is a cool summer day in December, palm trees whipping in the sea breeze, crisp shadows, blue sky. An American flag flies from atop an old hotel. Banana leaves wave above parking lots of glittering cars. I see a billboard for Mel Gibson's new movie "Apocalypto," and an advertising blimp hovers over so many cars that the farthest ones are washed out by distance. The skyscrapers of San Diego's core huddle compactly amidst the sprawl. The freeways are lush with ivy, ice plants and palm trees. This lovely coast remains verdant between and among the concretions of humanity. But just outside the city we find this verdancy to be actually a human artifact; for the hills, though bushy, are semi-arid, the dirt tan or even white, showing through between grass-clumps like bald patches in a worn carpet.

Chapter 189

TIJUANA

(2003–2005)

> Bring me the sunflower so that I might
> transplant it into burning fields of alkali . . .
>
> —Eugenio Montale, before 1982

At the beach stood the white pyramid to replace the one which had been shrine-caged in wrought iron—oh, that had been a very, very long time ago, when Tijuana was still Aunt Juana's hot springs and there had been no wall. There was wall now, all right. On the stele was incised LIMITE DE LA REPUBLICA MEXICANA and beside those words the graffito FUCK INS.* It was a foggy Sunday afternoon. Every moment, a couple or sometimes just a man would approach, carrying a little child, and pointing at the wall so that the child would understand, its guardian would explain: The gringos stole our land.—These were the words I heard them say, more or less. Occasionally a man would come alone to brood; once a man came with his infant girl clutched against his heart; he gazed at the stele without telling her anything, but his face came alive with anger and hate.

In the course of my journalistic career I have visited quite a number of countries which do not hold the United States of America in great esteem. One of my criteria for categorizing them is how they treated me. I remember Yemen, where they threw stones at me; and Serbia, where one night, fearing the worst, I barricaded the door of my hotel room with furniture; but I also remember Taliban-era Afghanistan, where people's kindness, even if it might frequently be tinctured with reserve, almost never got superseded by their hatred for the nation I came from. What about Southside? Very few Mexicans seemed to hold me personally responsible for what my government had done back in 1848. A weary flick of the hand was my answer when I asked them how they felt about losing half their territory. The inhabitants of Mexican Imperial confessed with engaging graciousness that they benefited from the border economy. They liked American pickup trucks and

*United States Immigration and Naturalization Service.

movies. On the other hand, the existence of the wall, the actions of the Border Patrol and the examinations they endured whenever they crossed the line, all these they considered to be continuing insults. If I associated myself with any of those three things, I could expect to be treated accordingly—not by any means to get a stone in my face as in Yemen, but to be myself insulted or occasionally threatened. When I stood on the Calexico side of the so-called Friendship Wall, gazing through the bars as I waited for José López from Jalisco to give me his latest progress report on the Chinese tunnels, the people on the Mexican side, assuming as I suppose that I was looking at them like animals in a zoo, sometimes sent back toward me unkind words and glances. But as soon as I had gone half a dozen steps into Mexicali, I could almost have been one of them; they were friendly with me; if they wanted something of me, they made their proposition with respect.

In Tijuana that friendliness and that respect were less in evidence than elsewhere in Imperial. I am not saying that people were rude; I have been treated well in Tijuana on any number of occasions; still, it did not feel exactly untoward if when simply going about my business in Tijuana I was made to feel as I felt when I peered through the Friendship Wall.

And so, as I stood by the boundary stele on that hazy white Sunday, I was not made to feel entirely comfortable. For instance, that bearded man with the little girl in his arms, after he glared at the limit of his Republic he also glared at me. Frankly, I felt more defiant than intimidated, for not only had I never fought in the Mexican War, I never supported it; so I looked right back into his face; then we both gazed elsewhere—namely, at the wall itself, which continued westward, painted with figures and rust-continents, descending steeply into the grey sea.

Directly north of the stele itself was a park, closed off perhaps for security reasons; and here a foxlike little dog stared curiously into Southside. (Never mind the white Bronco with the Border Patrolman inside; skip the Nightbuster; of course they were both there, too.) Presently the dog entered a hole and came back into Mexico.

I heard that a hundred years ago there used to be a Tia Juana Hot Spring, I said.

Aguas termales, said a man on the beach. It's still there.

The Fiesta Inn still has water from the hot springs, said a woman.

In the Colonia Twentieth of November there's one, the man said. He was a commercial printer.

What makes Tijuana special?

He grimaced thoughtfully and said: The climate. It always changes, he said proudly.

If you were a millionaire would you stay here or go back to Chiapas?

I'd stay here, because everything is close at hand.

By *everything* I suppose he meant the Otay Mesa on the road toward Tecate, and its inhabitants gazing down through the brown air at a sprawl of grimy little houses, the tomb of Juan the Soldier, the blue-and-pink two-storey hotel in Matamoros whose first storey was a nightclub; the Río Tecate, which comprised approximately as much water as the Río Nuevo; a midget who was not unlike the large-footed young woman sculpted of wood by some long dead Aztec; with inturned hands she offered her conical breasts to the border traffic; her vacant white shell-eyes and the two white shell-teeth in her dark mouth gaped with cunning, holy idiocy; behind her ran the tiny auto-glass shops, seafood restaurants, gas stations, fast food and tire shops; the small lines, mostly of men, seeking jobs at Óptica Sola and Tyco at seven-fifteen on a Monday morning; graffiti'd apartments and mini-malls, taco stands and hubcap stands, a graffiti'd metal fence, then concrete housettes in the dirt mountains; a woman standing on a sidewalk island, holding in her arms her sleeping son who was almost as large as she; clouds swirling behind wires; hissing trucks and buses, layered clouds, solitary men with caps on their heads and hands in their pockets, standing by factory fences; steps made of tires set flat into the steep mud; gasoline haloes in the pothole-puddles; the same smell as at Metales y Derivados, a smell as of pencils—it was the *maquiladora* where they made furniture—white light glaring through the holes in the clouds; and then, beyond a fence, puddles and garbage, swampy ground and green grass and mountains, eroded dirt with many strata.—The worst and best things in the whole country are happening here, said a reporter for *La Frontera*.—Shall I tell you one of the best things? It is that Tijuana's parking lots are so often named after women. Another is that within her blind archway the Virgin of Guadalupe towers over all, contemplating the mysteries across from Dorian's department store.

Chapter 190

TECATE

(2003–2006)

When the heat takes one's breath away in the Imperial Valley, it is windy-warmish at the Desert Viewing Tower and cool in Tecate, over which the great mountain to the west spreads its grey-blue translucent wings. Juan Bandini's old tract has come along considerably: A truck blares canned exultant slogans from the speakers which burden its back; the breeze carries them thankfully away. Bird-songs and snarling cars, men leaning on stick-fences beneath immense trees, a Chinese restaurant, a Mexican flag, these "typical" entities could be found anywhere in Imperial, and in a number of sites and zones outside it.

To be sure, Tecate, cool in July as in October, resembles Imperial Beach in that it would not be Imperial at all without the international line. The Tecate wallscape consists of painted advertisements as long as the road remains paved; then, when it becomes sandy and commences to hump upward to the west, the wall goes bare, wraps around an old tree or two, upstages the official white stele on its mound of bare dirt, and allows itself to express the following extremely original sentiment: ***VIVA MEXICO***.—Coincidentally, the name of the road is Avenida México.—On its south side are little houses. On its north side one can see nothing but the wall, excepting only two crosses.—I have been told that these memorialize not fallen *pollos* but accident victims.

Sometimes the wall is painted white, with blue, red or black advertisements overpainted on it. Then it becomes just army green or black or the usual rust-brown. A white rock has been handpainted to read **GARITA**.

Looking down east along that wall with its tall sunflowers, I imagine infinity, which lies somewhere between my horizon and Mexicali; looking west, my impulsions outward into universal ease are barred not by the wall itself, which runs parallel to my striving, but by a certain mound of graffiti'd rocks, in one hollow of which lie a heap of *pollos'* clothes: I think then of the scraps of cloth ground into the killing fields of Choeung Ek, Cambodia.

For us it used to be very pretty, said an old half-Yaqui woman whose father had emigrated here four decades ago; it was he, the Yaqui, who'd made the shrine to the Virgin of Guadalupe which presided over the dirt behind the fence.

There wasn't any wall and we could see the mountains, she continued; it was really very pretty. People could pass back and forth. We were friends with the people from the United States. There was a path over there, and on that side I remember a few ranches. We were very friendly with them. The Hyde family used to live over there on the hill. Very generous people—Americanos. But once they put up that wall, it got different. They put it up in 1995.

How do you feel when you look at it now?

We don't want it to be there. We wish it wasn't there. We can't see the pretty vistas anymore.

Why is there a city over here and not over there?

Fiercely she replied: Because Americans think that if they put a bunch of stores over there, Mexicans will come to work.

There was no city *over there,* so her answer was senseless, and the anger of its senselessness was itself information.

Tecate used to resemble a very beautiful ranch, she presently went on. People used to sleep indoors, leaving the doors and windows open. But lately many people from other parts of Mexico have been coming here—*pollos* and work seekers. There are many robberies.

How often do you see the *pollos*?

Lately, none have come by. About eight years ago, there were a lot of jumpers, even women and children.

Her little boy tried to say that they saw many every day, but she shushed him.

Two old ladies who were her neighbors told me: We see them every day, walking toward the mountains.

Once they put up that wall, it got different. In the supermarket, a poster against cigarettes depicted the Trojan Horse of Northside leering over the border wall.

THE CENTER OF THE CENTER OF THE UNIVERSE

The Aztec word for city or town is *altepetl,* which contains the words for hill and for water. Tecate is the only Imperial city that truly qualifies, with the exception of some Tijuana shantytowns, and those only in the spring.

So hail Tecate, center of the universe! The center of the center was, of course, the zócalo: benches oriented around the disk of cracked squares of white and greystone shards joined together; sometimes in late afternoon the children swam upon its coolness, while their parents sat in the cool shadows and on the next bench a teenaged boy was bending his teenaged sweetheart backward, kissing and kissing her, his hands up her striped miniskirt, and yes, she parted her knees for him and her snow-white calf-length socks shone like the gypsum of Plaster City and her black buckled shoes were as glossy as the All-American Canal when it carries away the last of the evening light.

AND ITS EDGE

And so the last of the evening light gets carried away to the music of barking dogs, the air cooling, carrying children's voices to the wall, acrosss which four Nightbusters already glow; and above them, over an American mountain, a helicopter blinks.

Steam and hissing issue from the Tecate brewery at Avenida Hidalgo.

Suddenly at nine P.M. the street fills with traffic; the shoe store windows gleam and shine. The Diana Bar grows crowded. On the sidewalk, two little girls stand hip to hip. A man stands beside sweating gratings. A boy on the corner sells roses wrapped in plastic. A boy with his red cap on backward skates down the busy street, followed by four more boys, each with a different colored cap.

In summer there are sharp green evening shadows in contradistinction to the gold zone in La Rumorosa; in winter there are the glowing industrial suburbs.

Ten-o'-clock slides up the steep dirt streets of Tecate, the lateness partially overcome by Christmas tree lights within some rich walled houses and on the walls of shacks. Three boys walk down a hilly *avenida,* all the while lounging and gesturing in that graceful Mexican way. Two girls hold hands as they stride up another street, which is pallid with sand like so many others this close to the line. Turning north at a graffiti'd stop sign, I find myself face to face with that rusty metal reification of delineation which clings grimly to the undulating ridgetop farther in both directions than I will ever be able to comprehend. Nightbusters glow at me from Northside. In the interpreter's car I ride along to the west as I have done so many times before over the years, passing my old graffiti'd acquaintance, Border Stele 245, across the street from which snakes of Christmas lights entwine themselves around the houses, cousins to the pale white graffiti that scrolls and spiders on the dark steel wall.

The street ends in a man-high concrete wall, but on the right, near the border fence, there are two angled concrete baffles not unlike those in the passages down through which rolls the precious sphere in a pinball machine. Cautiously introducing myself to this environment, I discover a plastic bag with a man's T-shirt in it, which shines new and red in the headlights of the interpreter's car; then there is a darkness, and I think the darkness goes deep.

We go south. The concrete wall follows us. Clambering up a bulbous protuberance at its base, I peer down into a deep arroyo and, defeated by the lack of scale, cannot decide whether that pale rectangle I see down below is a shanty or a piece of cardboard.

To our right somebody whistles twice, very close. To our left another whistle comes. I urge the interpreter back into the car, and we drive away, crawling back into the town. After half a dozen turns, where dirt gives way to pavement our headlights catch a lovely plump schoolgirl in a plaid miniskirt, who stares unsmilingly at us from between two low houses. Three young men lounge by a wall. I wave at them and they do not wave back. We roll slowly down a dark dirt alley in the shadow of a black wall, and a hooded man quickly turns his face away from our headlights. Soon we are back on Avenida Juárez, and we go westward into the fog.

My topographic map indicates a fairly short and easy hike northward through or over the border hills just west of Tecate Road on the American side, after which one quickly strikes Highway 94, which squiggles down to San Diego. Not much farther westward, at about the extremity of Tecate as of this writing, two narrow arroyos twist north between Tecate Peak and Little Tecate Peak. One of these must even contain occasional water, for the map shows a blue line called Cottonwood Creek. If I were a *pollo,* I would consider gambling here, for the Border Patrol would need to get out of their vehicles, *in the dark,* to patrol here. Of course they have their Nightbusters now. But given that Tecate remains the most penetrable part of the entire line between American and Mexican Imperial, the *pollos* must cross somewhere around here; and to the east of the official crossing the land smooths out sufficiently to be crisscrossed by jeep trails.

The next morning, crossing legally into Northside after a mere two-hour wait, I will learn that Cottonwood Creek does sport a dirt road along its eastern bank, and here are all-terrain vehicles with Border Patrol officers in them. For now I merely wonder where the *pollos* are.

So we drive as far as Rancho la Puerta, turning back just before committing ourselves to the Tijuana toll road. The foggy glow of that metropolis seethes down on the western horizon.

Tecate possesses a much more desert character in the night: fog, rock, dust and trees.

The eastern side of town seems somewhat affluent. The houses are more stoutly built and fewer of them are graffiti'd. Hugging the wall in the vicinity of stele 244, we roll as far east as we can, until concrete blocks stop us. We park. Strolling through the foggy night along a dirt road, we find ourselves between *la línea* and a long graveyard whose tall pale arches, crosses, blocks and statues are particularly eerie in the foggy night. A square open pit of blackness in a white slab suggests an open tomb. But then we see another of these, and several more. It must be that these crypts, purchased in advance, still await their occupants.

From the cemetery, a figure gazes at us. Is it a man or a statue? If I were a *pollo,* this place would be adequate to wait in, although how I would expect to escape the gaze of the Nightbusters is beyond me. From the cemetery comes the sound of a fountain.

There are as many open graves as gaps in the fence.

Now the pale sand road rises as we begin to ascend the shoulder of the volcanic mountain just outside of town, our footsteps shockingly loud in the sand; and here the Nightbuster glares right over the wall and into the cemetery, bleaching the tombs like a satanically hideous simulacrum of a desert sun.

The dark wall is pitted here and there with holes about the size of a gap that a child could make if he looped his thumb against his forefinger. Placing my eye to one of these, I discover that all I can see at first is blindingly bright fog. Then in time I make out the immense emptiness of the controlled American securityscape. The Nightbusters hurt my eyes.

A few paces farther up the road there is a long gap at the base of the fence, more than a foot wide. I could wriggle under if I had to. Of course, where would I find myself then?

I place my eye to another hole and see something like a giant caltrop over on Northside; actually, what it resembles more than anything is one of the Nazi obstacles that we had to contend with in the Normandie landing on D-day; the GIs called those *Rommel's asparagus.* Beyond that, the vista dips down into the glaring sand of America. Before the wall there must have been a pretty view, as the old half-Yaqui woman had suggested. I think I can see a long meadow of glaring white grass, and then, farther down the hill, just where the light ends, a small shack; but my interpreter, whose eyes are better, points out to me that this is just the base of a Nightbuster.

By day it is all blonde chaparral, olive-hued shrubs and leaden dirt in the rain; and one can easily see over the border fence to the dirt access roads in Northside. By night it is a mirthless alien carnival of surveillance.

Just then somebody whistles from the cemetery, and his whistle gets rapidly answered by someone very close to us, so we return to the car—

Chapter 191

CAMPO

(2005)

They slacked away again when the price of silver went down . . .

—Mary Austin, 1903

Sagebrush crushed in my hands, I rode east toward Jacumba, the tan rocks piled into caches of eggs and topped with green-grey bushes, a rounded pyramid ahead, greenish-brown mounds which got less green the closer I came. Riding west toward Jacumba on Highway 94, I passed the Feed Supply; the old road wound almost empty between boulders, manzanitas, conveying a high oak feeling. It was lush for Imperial, with many green trees. Here came a graceful trestle bridge dark between two ridges by the Golden Acorn Casino (established in 2001), which I hoped was enriching the Campo band of Kumeyaay Indians as well as the entity which had built it. Through the trestle bridge I could see blue mountains to the west, the ground frothy with olive-green shrubs, the road still empty, the land nearly uninhabited. Once upon a time, the people who lived in that valley called it Meelqsh G'tay, Big Open Meadow. *Campo* was not such a bad translation.

After the bend with a white picket fence, there stood a picturebook little red house with a satellite dish, clusters of prickly pear growing right out of the rock, a sign offering fresh eggs, and another sign:

CAMPO MILLING CORPORATION

INDUSTRIAL AND AGRICULTURAL MINERALS

Now here was the Motor Transport Museum, where Carl Calvert wanted to tell me stories. He said:

There was a guy named Haffner who came here in 1913, and he claimed he knew how to seed clouds to make rain. County made a compact to pay him ten thousand dollars. He built a tower. I have some of his formulas at home. I don't know if he knew what he was doing, but it rained. Worst rain in a long time. He didn't get paid; it was just a verbal contract.

He showed me feldspar that had been mined here in Campo and made into powder for glass; they used to add clay.

I like to say the secret of feldspar is in this rod, he said. It works like solder. The steel will not stick by itself. So feldspar is a flux.

He showed me a handcarved wooden mold for a gas pedal. You set it in sand and then poured molten brass into it at eighteen hundred degrees Fahrenheit. Carl Calvert had carved it himself. I could imagine Wilber Clark's gas pedal being made like this.

See that thing? he said. That's the first motor to pump water in Borrego.

Thump, thump, went the motor obligingly.

He caressed a huge flywheel and said: It does not drive.

To start the engine, he said, you need to take this plug out here and smoke a cigarette, then put the cigarette in there and the heat of the cigarette will start it.

And it all seemed very Imperial to me, this sweet turning back to the past.

In his back yard were red-tinted bushes, an omelette of rocks and brush, then Mexico herself . . .

Chapter 192

MEXICALI

(2003)

That's all it is, bad news: crooked politicians, bad pavements, bad treatment from *our neighbor.*

—Lupe Vásquez, summing up the contents of a Mexicali newspaper, 2003

And now Mexicali, founded in 1904, or maybe 1905, perhaps in 1899, becomes officially a hundred years old! They've decided that Mexicali's *centenario* will be 2003, and why not? Within the leather repair shop, the glass case is crammed with rags, boxes, and what seems to be trash; on top are dusty old boots with holes in them; the leather man finds a scrap of leather, scissors out a patch from it, hammers the patch flat upon my ageing rucksack, and while watching the news sharpens his knife on a stele. Now he is already at the thinly humming sewing machine; his gruesome piñata sways in the air (it will soon be the Day of the Dead), and the long-braided, pointy-breasted, naked girl in the sombrero smiles at him over her shoulder on the Depósito Karmen calendar while a very small and canted Virgin of Guadalupe rests on the shelf against his **ABIERTO** sign; the lamp gilds his reddish skin as he rapidly, carefully, eagerly feeds leather and cloth to his sewing machine, and two bimbos on television act prettily stupid; he gazes at them round-eyed while his hands keep working; whenever the bimbos stop wriggling, he darts down a glance at his makings, showing neither resentment nor disinterest; this is not only his living but how he lives. On the wall opposite the Virgin and Señorita Karmen, a newspaper page, already sun-stained to the tan color of Imperial sand, cries:

Felicidades,
Mexicali

What is it, this place on whose very birth no one can agree?

To me, hailing from the other side of the ditch, the "border feeling" of here consists to no inconsiderable extent of Mexican-ness, whereas to José López from Jalisco, Mexicali stands out first of all for the license plates to the cars.—So many

American plates! he cries. Then the dress styles—You can tell right away they're from *the other side*. The language also: lots of Mexicans speaking English. And all the American businesses, like (here he named a bunch of fast food franchises, which scarcely deserve to be advertised by me).—Even though they are all over Mexico now, he confessed, well, they're *more* here.

And isn't he correct? This Mexicali which I'd imagined to be truly herself, namely Centro, grows ever less important in proportion to the swelling sprawling glowings occurring in her name to the south, east and west; thanks to the grimy white walls and reddish-tan dust of her flatlands, and each Parque Industrial's vast secrecies behind a vaster fence, and her graffiti'd walls of junkyards bulging with junk, she has now turned into one of the twenty largest cities in Mexico.* Shouldn't we celebrate that? Mexicali is tawny, blonde, huge-breasted Gloria in the doorway of the Hotel Nuevo Pacífico: If there happens to be more of her, doesn't that make her more perfectly Mexican? So what if her flesh consists to some extent of foreign-controlled industrial parks? And who could deny her plenitude of Mexican-ness? I see more rose vendors in the middle of the street than I ever would in the United States, infinitely more uniformed schoolgirls kissing uniformed schoolboys beneath the huge desert moon! All the same, the new outer Mexicali which keeps growing away from the decaying core I love feels surprisingly like Los Angeles.

In 2003, fifty thousand people worked in the *maquiladoras* of Mexico, and thirty-five thousand more worked in Imperial County. The old Mexican who'd worked from age twenty-seven to age sixty in the Chinese supermarket said to me: In a hundred years we'll grow up against San Diego, since the population is from all over . . .

Zulema Rashid, the fifty-eight-year-old Calexico native, had had most of her important girlhood experiences in Mexicali, and she said: Most of my friends are from Mexicali, and it's not the place that I'm interested in, but the people.

But *physically*, she continued, Mexicali is so dirty, except for the Colonia Nuevo. I think it's ugly, it's dirty, it's just *sad*. I think when I was a girl I just didn't notice. It used to be just dirty. And now it just stinks. A lot of people have moved in from other parts of Mexico. It is filthy like something being abused. That makes me very sad. My brother and sister have a very hard time keeping their business clean, even on this side of the border, because it is so close. The people that are coming there now are just waiting to cross the border, and they are using it as a trampoline.

And in bitter agreement-rebuttal to Zulema's words I quote the lifelong Mexicali resident Yolanda Sánchez Ogás: *We're the garbage can of the United States*. Right now they've put in their new geothermal plants, even though a judge told them

*Between 2000 and 2020, Mexicali's population is expected to double again.

not to. On the American side, they burn their crops only when the wind blows south . . .

One singer's impression of Mexicali rhymes in Spanish, and probably sounds more elegant than a field worker's English translation: *a lot of people, hot like a bitch, and a river full of shit.*

The ancient Aztec divinity Tlazoltéotl, Goddess of Filth, could cleanse Her worshippers of coition's sins, but only by means of such rigorous penances as passing a twig through a hole in the tongue twice a day. I worshipped a Tlazoltéotl Who was filth Herself, a Tlazoltéotl of acceptance, not penance, a living blend, as are all of us, of excrement, sunlight, blood and watermelons. That was one of the reasons that I have loved street prostitutes ever since I was young. And what was the border but another incarnation of Her? Now in the year 2007 as I finish this chapter, my dinghy-ride down the New River with the first Jose Lopez haunts me sweetly. I had expected nothing but filthiness and frightfulness; I'd wanted to "expose," to "investigate," to sound the alarm, in other words, to wallow self-righteously in the excrement of what was supposed to be the most polluted waterway in North America. And I had gotten my fill of that, the bad taste that would not leave my mouth; but I had also, as had this fine Jose Lopez, played at the game of Lewis-and-Clark; and I remember sunlight, tamarisks, spewing pipes, silence, and befouled but undestroyed wildness. And when Zulema said of Mexicali, the city that I cannot stop loving, that *it is filthy like something being abused,* when Yolanda said, *we're the garbage can of the United States,* when Calexicans who smelled the New River complained that they were the toilet of Mexico, I became all the more faithful to Mexicali, third-largest of the border cities, after Ciudad Juárez and Tijuana, to Mexicali, home of *maquiladoras* and *ejidos* alike, Mexicali the hot, slow, sunny, spicy, stinking place, whose most precious jewel is her tranquillity.

Because Mexicali emblematizes the so-called "Black Legend" of Mexican sinfulness, I now reintroduce you to the street prostitute Liliana, who tried to sell me her seventeen-year-old Indian friend Capricorn instead (they weren't lesbians, but they shared the same bed; they weren't friends, but Liliana would rather have had me go with Capricorn than with her). In my room, her eyes got crazy and she kept talking about how she wanted to know serial killers in order to know life. Whatever I said, she kept demanding: *Is it true?* She wanted to be my friend but didn't trust me. She knew for a fact that the Chinese had killed a Mexican woman; she thought Chinese were ugly and ridiculous; she hated them; they owned everything in Mexicali. She was scary, sad, exciting, smelly and beautiful. This book, like the Virgin of Guadalupe Herself, is syncretic; Liliana, like Mexicali, was still more so, for she possessed the supernatural power of spewing diarrhea at the very moment of singing me a beautiful song.

That was on a Saturday night. And on a Sunday afternoon in the cathedral on Reforma, a hot July Sunday afternoon, I should add, a handful of people glided slowly in silence, a young woman helping an older one to rise, gripping her by her bloated arm. Behind the altar Jesus on the cross gazed dreamily upward, as if He, too, had been left languorous by this heat. His dear mother the Virgin of Guadalupe had long since faded into something resembling a tintype, gazing downward at the floral still life.

In the hot breeze, there came a smell of grass.

In the lovely, cool and shady evening in the park at Altamirano and Zuazua (the electronic thermometer said ninety-six degrees Fahrenheit), a man was sweeping the sidewalk around the juice stand; a man in a black sombrero and a red shirt played the accordion; a grimy, weary, middle-aged man who looked to be a *pollo* or was maybe just homeless sat on the curb waiting for darkness, while sparrows snatched up crumbs; an old woman and a young woman passed by, wheeling a little girl in a stroller; a big girl whose black hair fell all the way down her back took her little brother's hand and led him across the street; and then a mariachi band in white sombreros and black dress uniforms began to play beneath the trees. Two ladies chatted with a soldier. A man on a bench was lightly rolling his drumsticks across his drums, getting ready for the night. The accordionist had fallen silent once the mariachi band began, and once it likewise stopped, he stood there under the trees, not quite making music yet, just tuning up or announcing himself or getting ready or something I could not understand; whatever his purpose, he made the most delicate sounds, cool and strange, with the sparrows singing rapidly all around him and the sky getting pinkish-orange behind him at the end of the street. All this life was being lived because the darkness was coming.

Chapter 193

EJIDO NETZAHUALCÓYOTL

(2004)

This is seepage water that Mexicali growers, industrial users and the government have come to depend on over the years, and the prospect of losing it is not a happy one south of the border . . . If the so-called era of limits on the Colorado River applies to the Imperial Valley, and we have frequently questioned whether it applies anywhere else, then it must also apply to Mexico. Our friends and neighbors in Mexicali don't have to like it. But they're undoubtedly going to learn to live with it.

—The *Imperial Valley Press*, 2005

They met at a dance in Ejido Palaco. He was born in Mexicali, and his name was José Castro. She was from Sonora; she never told me her name. She came with two sisters looking for work and found a *maquiladora* job in 1970. Later she didn't even remember which *maquiladora* it had been; she made collars and wristbands for a clothing company, an American company, she didn't recollect which one.

His first job was also in a *maquiladora,* at Kenworth. It was a contract where he would work for a year and have a month off. He was seventeen or eighteen. He assembled entire trucks, he said with pride.

There were a lot of dances but he didn't go very often because he didn't like dancing. They both lived in Palaco at the time. It was her very first year there, 1970. His mother and brothers lived here in Ejido Netzahualcóyotl, so this is where they came. His brother gave them this land. They lived with his mother at first. He had one arm broken from pitching baseball, so he built the adobe house one-armed in a month. It is a good house which they are proud of; they told me that it sways in earthquakes. He confidently believed that it could withstand a big quake, although she was not so sure. In any event, now they had whitewashed it inside, and it possessed a stout concrete floor, a sink, a refrigerator, and a radio, which was playing when they invited me in. Electricity came in 1976 or 1977. By the way, the water in the sink came from a purification plant; one can drink it but they preferred not to.

She no longer worked except in the home. He was now a mechanic, working solo, for himself.

In 1970 there were about thirty families. And now, there are a lot! More than a hundred. It is a good place, they said. Not a lot of crime here. It's quiet. No gangs. Only a few fights. Not any problems and we don't want any. They're putting in many factories nearby, agricultural factories for the onions and grapes, so that will change things. It will get a little better.

In 1970 the water table was thirty or forty meters deep, they said. Now it is sixty or seventy meters deep. The water was starting to get more salty so we moved the well . . .

(They gave me a glass of well water to taste, and it did taste slightly saline but not much.)

When they finish lining the All-American Canal, will you still have water? I asked.

We'll still have water, but it will be lower, maybe a hundred meters.

When you did first hear about this matter?

They've been saying it since last year. On the radio.

Will it be much harder for you?

There's a committee here that's looking at the problem and we think that it will be all right.

That was his answer, which was confident like him. She remarked, and only on the surface did it seem irrelevant, that once there had been a fountain in the park and the water had been white with salt. They used to wash clothes in that water, but the clothes dried with white crystals on them.

What are your aspirations for the future?

That God will bless us and we will keep moving forward, said the woman. What more can you ask?

They didn't believe in the Virgin of Guadalupe, only in God.

She had never been across the border. He had been a couple of times *just to look around.* In fact, he had explored all the way to Los Angeles.

Here there's more freedom, he concluded. In America you work all the time.

Do you have any desire to visit America? I asked her.

Actually, yes, she said smiling. I was praying that God will let me know the other side; I am hungering for it.

Her husband fell silent.

What of America can you see from this side?

Since I've never been there I can't say, but there's a canal.

I asked him: Is there anything you want Americans to understand about Mexicans?

There should be better communication between the two, he replied.

Do you feel badly that the United States took so much of Mexico?

He shrugged and said: Either way there's still a lot of land.

THE DESERT DISAPPEARS

Within the Republic of Northside, lining the All-American Canal would endanger four wetlands totalling six hundred and thirty hectares, three of them along both sides of the canal; the fourth, by far the largest at five hundred and seventy-five hectares and which contained salt cedars, arrowweeds, mesquites and marsh, was between Drops Three and Four. Within Mexico, two thousand two hundred and seventy hectares in the Andrade Mesa would be affected, and two-thirds of that probably lost. These areas were mostly in Ejidos Irapuato and Netz. The second-largest Mexican populations of two bird subspecies, the Yuma clapper rail and the black rail, might disappear. Seventy thousand acre-feet per year would be taken from Mexicali's thirsty maw. I can't help believing in people.

There's a committee here that's looking at the problem and we think that it will be all right.

Anyhow, what was extraordinary about it? It was nothing more than the next reification of subdelineation.

GOLD AND JADE

Mucho calor, muchos mosquitos. It starts in June, and by August . . . the wife said laughing.

Before, it used to get hotter, Señor Castro put in.

She nodded.—Sometimes children and old people would die.

Why is it cooler now?

Because we have water, they explained.

MORE GOLD AND JADE

Oh, yes. **WATER IS HERE**.

The old man from Durango who was sitting in the park in San Luis Río Colorado with his shoes off, in a plaid shirt and a baseball cap with an American logo, said to me:

I've planted and harvested corn and beans. I once owned some land which was expropriated by the *ejido*. I also had some ancestral land until my father died in 1967. My little brother owns it. We plant corn and beans, but it's a very hand to mouth life since there is no irrigation.

What is it like where you come from?

Well, there are just a lot of *ejidos*. In Durango it's all *ejidos*.

And what is different about San Luis?

Here it is all businesses. Down there it is all farmwork, he aphorized, nodding cautiously. He had a thin grey moustache and gold teeth.

If you wanted to farm here you could, he said knowingly, because the land here is *irrigated*.

REPRISE

And in Ejido Morelos, the rancher Gilberto Sanders had reassured me: We have plenty of water here. There's a canal, a concrete canal without a name . . .

YOU, TOO, WILL GO THERE

I supposed that they would all still have water, just less of it.

Down in Colonia Santo Niño I met a man who worked for the State Commission of Public Services in Mexicali. His department concerned itself with issues of potable water. He said that the lining of the All-American Canal would be *a big problem for Mexicali.*

It comes from the valley over near Calexico and it drops over to this side, he said; quite a bit of water comes from there.

Will some of the *ejidos* have to close up and leave?

It will affect them quite a bit, because they're selling the water to San Diego and Los Angeles.

Will they have to leave?

No. But they're going to have to live on a strict quantity.

How about in this *colonia*?

It's measured, but you can use as much as you can pay for. I myself spend about thirty or forty pesos a month for washing water, and for drinking water two hundred and ten pesos in a big jug . . .

So perhaps it would be merely a little worse for the Castros in Ejido Netzahualcóyotl, whose name, by the way, memorializes the Aztec ruler Nezahualcóyotl, Fasting Coyote. Here is one of his poems:

Like a flower,
we will dry up
here on earth. . . .
though you be of jade,
though you be of gold
you will also go there
to the place of the fleshless.

WATER IS HERE.
WATER IS HERE.
WATER IS HERE.

Chapter 194

SAN LUIS RÍO COLORADO

(2006)

His name is Mariano Silvas Contreras, the waitress said. He is a United States citizen. It has been about eight years since I have seen him. I came back here to San Luis to find out about him, because I heard that he was here. I have been here for four months, and I know absolutely nothing about him. I don't know if he died or anything. But if he is alive, I would like to live with him, because he is my father. And since he is a United States citizen, I would like him to help me go there. I know that he was married in the United States but I don't know if they were really married or if they were just living together. It came to the point that my parents did not want to be together anymore. I am not trying to molest him. I think that he would want to see me, because every time we met each other, he would hug me and he would cry. He always drank a lot, and you cannot have a conversation with someone who has been drinking. So the conversations were very short. I am still in touch with my mother but I live here with my sister. I know he worked over *there*—by which the waitress meant Northside—although he lived here. He was a day laborer, a vaquero, so he worked on some ranches. He talked a lot about a place called Casas Blancas. I don't know where that is.

If he helps me with my citizenship, then I can go. But I have never been across even once, to go shopping. To me it sounds a little scary. And besides, I don't have my papers, so I cannot do it. I have been going around asking questions about it and people tell me maybe I could ask Customs if he goes back and forth . . .

She was a beautiful, beautiful girl with a wide golden face and blonde-brown hair, dark brown eyebrows and golden-brownish eyes.

Chapter 195

BLYTHE

(2005)

> Life on Earth never settled down to doing anything very good. Science ran too far ahead of us too quickly . . .
>
> —Ray Bradbury, 1950

In 2005 the columnist George F. Will, whose elegant sentences and rightwing themes had entertained me for years, turned his attention to the following problem (so my hometown paper entitled the editorial): **Old water agreement maroons booming Las Vegas**. Poor Las Vegas! And which boulder blocked that watercourse's way? Thomas Blythe, of course. *Because of the principle "first in time, first in right," California got an abundance.*

One would have supposed that a conservative would favor this principle. *Of course in the classroom my kids didn't talk about it.* ***You can't produce things the way you used to***.

Almost a tenth of all Americans depend on the Colorado River's *water. But agriculture sops up 90 percent of it. The sprawl of Phoenix onto agricultural land actually decreases water use.* So sprawl away, America, sprawl away! Then we'll never be thirsty anymore.

The heroine of Mr. Will's column is *the elegant, no-nonsense Pat Mulroy, 52,* general manager of the Southern Nevada Water Authority. This woman informs the interested Mr. Will that *the Strip accounts for less than 1 percent of the state's water use—while producing 60 percent of the state's economy.* I can't help believing in people.

While Mr. Will does not come out explicitly against *first in time, first in right,* he is clearly on the Southern Nevada Water Authority's side. What would Emerson say? Mr. Will, by the way, is about the only popular commentator of my own epoch who might have actually read Emerson.

What is a conservative? I had thought him to be, among other things, an individual who respects the inviolability of private property—Thomas Blythe's, for instance.

Of course, Thomas Blythe is long dead. His Mexican holdings went back to Andrade, who transferred them to the Colorado River Land Company. As for the property rights invested in his eponymous town, these now hinder the growth of Las Vegas. "*Moisture Means Millions*." *But agriculture sops up 90 percent of it.*

CRIME SCENES

Ride with me along Highway I-10, the boundary of Imperial, on a cloudy ninety-degree July morning, with the green and olive scrub and the sawtoothed mountains on either side. Look with me down into the yellow grass, and then the long gap below mountains ending upon a very distinct flat horizon. It is all bushes and clouds, surprisingly lush for Imperial, and there is a white sign: 150 ACRES.

Look up a splayed ocher canyon lined with pallid rocks; and ahead you will see a low many-toothed shard of blue-grey mountain severed from the earth by a pale horizon-line.

Coming into Blythe, you will find a long fence of citrus trees, hay bales, fields, a row of date palms, a canal, an adobe house bearing an advertisement for bail bonds, and the palm-backdropped Sunlite Bowling Center with a black and peeling billboard. Welcome to the Courtesy Coffee Shop. You need not neglect the Hot Group, nor Erika's Sand Bar. Now it is a hundred and two degrees, and you may as well retreat beneath the old archway'd architecture of Imperial. Yes, old! First in time, first in right—

On a decidedly unincorporated road in the unincoporated realm of Mesa Verde, there is a water tank labeled OASIS. Leaving the petroglyphs and intaglios to their bygoneness, let us drive the dirt road that passes directly between sets of power poles. Now we come into the tall tough greenness of riverbottom vegetation, and then there is a lovely piercing green of fresh-cut alfalfa, with mountains in all directions, a veritable table-land.

What is Imperial to you? To me, today at least, it is small houses, a child swinging beneath stately trees, the trees often nicer than the homes; Imperial is a tall rusty rocketlike tower on spider-legs overlooking the metal sheds; Imperial is the screaming green, the lovely chocolate fields of Palo Verde and Blythe.

Almost a tenth of all Americans depend on the water. But agriculture sops up 90 percent of it.

Imperial is mountains behind and citrus ahead.

Now we have arrived at that awful crime against Las Vegas, the Palo Verde Outfall: green banks on either side of a ditch of slow water; enclosed in labia of green sage, then yellow sage, then sand. That is how it is when one goes away from water: Going south from Palo Verde, one rapidly meets the end of the greenness, fields going to yellow and yellow-green brush; then reddish-grey and bluish-grey desert hills burst forth in the late afternoon, with rare thunderheads over Imperial. It is only a hundred and two degrees as evening comes over the reddish Cargo Muchacho Mountains, shadowing them into varying blue diagonals.

And after a long time one enters the yellow-green fields of Bard, which are jeweled with silver sprinkler-droplets (each another crime against Arizona and Nevada), out of which Signal Mountain rises ahead like a blue whalefin. A yellow-grassed desert swells, scattered with black rocks. Ocotillos reach for the clouds.

I always forget how beautiful this part of Imperial is. Her treasures here are conical mounds of black rock and silver pebbles, more ocotillos, not to mention chollas and Joshua trees.

Then far away I glimpse a lovely horizon-line of dunes, lavender with blue shadows, a thickening horizon-line with a very pale blue line of thicker sky behind it—the sky-blue mountains of Mexico.

Chapter 196

THE INLAND EMPIRE

(2003–2004)

Southern California's housing demand could be reduced by importing Indiana's weather, forcing our children to live in Texas, or telling the world not to want our liberties.

—Rob Leicester Wagner, 2004

During the first two decades of the twenty-first century, the Inland Empire's population is projected to increase more than that of forty-five other states!

I look at an orange box label from the W. R. Strong Company (Riverside, California), and see green groves, people, a horse, Wisconsin-like fields, low snowy mountains and high blue mountains. Although it might never have been like this, I wish that it were. Decades after Riverside's Chinatown had died, archaeologists found red, black and white eyeball-like gambling beads; and a shard or two of an opium pipe whose bowl had been fashioned to resemble a crab. Which of these two survivals is now more exotic?

I look at the label from Old Baldy Brand (California Citrus Union), and find myself returned to the striped gazebo on Euclid Avenue in Upland, with an American flag flying over the orangescaped boulevard, lovely houses on either side and a snowy peak on the horizon.

God bless America, my neighbors say; but, America, where are you? Have you gone west on the street called Mission Inn, past the bell-like streetlamps with their so-called Indian crosses?

Imperial is America. So is the Inland Empire. Once upon a time, the Inland Empire was or pretended to be Old Baldy Brand.

In search of, let's say, Old Baldy, I swim down the highway, following Wilber Clark's hypothetical drive, and presently arrive at the

RIVERSIDE CITY LIMITS
NEXT 12 EXITS

If names can be nut-trees, I'm now in an orchard at Almond and Eleventh; and here comes Chestnut, with the desert's rubbly hills abruptly tamed at the beginning of this street shaded by cool high palms and other trees. Here drowse houses with hammocks and porches, homes where I dream I would have loved to live, and for scenery the occasional American flag. *The bountiful continent is ours, state on state, and territory on territory, to the waves of the Pacific sea.* Riverside begins here. Or, if you like, here it ends, then goes up into grass and dirt which becomes sand and rock.

Once upon a time, in 1906, the stifling, narrow funeral parlor on Main Street offered folding chairs, a piano, two American flags at perfect diagonals, a black cushion or pall embroidered with a white swastika, a chandelier resembling twin trumpets, and on the wallpapered walls, framed pictures that in the badly printed photograph looked faded even then; and I could hardly bear the dreariness, which was to me and my conception of Imperial what the muddy fly-specked provincial towns of Russia must have been to Gogol; and I thanked the omniscient narrator that I had not been condemned to die in Riverside after having lived all my life there.

Never mind; there's space enough to breathe in now!* *What the Inland Empire has that the coastal counties don't . . . is vast amounts of available land for future growth*—twenty-eight thousand square miles!—*and plenty of affordable real estate for your home and business.* My citrus dreams survive weakly here; on the lawns of the old houses with their fences and porches, everything well-painted wood—look, an orange tree!

A house with Japanese fans in the windows, another with a forest of planters, some frat boys chugalugging beer in the lawn, why can't these be metonyms for the Inland Empire? So green and good is Riverside, so nice and humid.

If you drive through Riverside in the correct direction, you'll come first to Lemon, then to Lime Street; and the long humid light of late afternoon will get distilled purer than Imperial's, and cooler and cleaner. There will be a bitter smell, a bitter clean smell of plants, and as a train whistles, the palm fronds will slowly move in the almost cloudless sky.

From Mount Rubidoux, you can now see freeways and mountains in the evening light and hear the cars go by beneath you like wind, the breath of golden California.

Looking down on Riverside, you see an almost jungle-lush zone of trees, almost bluish-green in richness, very sharply demarcated by the square corners of intersecting roads which set them off from the more olive-colored desert scrub and from the railroad tracks and the steep mounds of desert which burst out of the greener lowlands like kinks of eviscerated bowel. Especially in the evening light, the palm

*Speaking of breathing, I read that lettuce salinity experiments "cannot be conclusively done in close proximity to Riverside because the smog negates the scientific validity of the finds."

trees appear more tropical than they really are; and Riverside's streets are narrow ribbons of bluish-greenish-grey which vanish into an almost-imaginary jungle of such delicious potency that it obscures many of the old buildings, only a few new Los Angeles–style skyscrapers breaking through this act of imagination that ends itself both subtly and gently in the beginnings of Imperial which, resolutely defying their own reality, tone their greys, reds, oranges and ochers into a loving orange veil about the jungle which could almost be the sunset sky.

On a smogless evening, Riverside still almost smells of oranges.

Chapter 197

COACHELLA

(2003–2004)

In the Coachella Valley you can roll along the San Andreas Fault on a chuck wagon, lope through a date farm on a camel, soar above 100 golf courses in a motorless sailplane, float over the desert at sunrise in a hot-air balloon . . .

—*Southwest Airlines Spirit* magazine, 2004

They're coming in here so fast that they're shedding a lot of the ranches out, said Carolyn Cooke, who had lived in the Coachella Valley for almost exactly half a century. Before there were houses here where I live, it was a grapefruit ranch.

Does the development worry you?

Well, I think it's inevitable. Of course we can't do a thing to stop it. I think there's been so much development without any planning. A beautiful valley has changed to the point where I'm not sentimental about it.

There was no traffic light in the whole valley when I was first here, she went on after a moment. And coming home from the Chinese restaurant in Palm Desert, you could see every star and every phase of the moonlight, and I was in my seventh heaven. And when we went out of the valley to Los Angeles; and coming back, coming over the pass, there's a pass near Whitewater when you look into the valley, and my eyes would fill with tears and I would get goosebumps and I was so happy that this valley was my home. Now there are acres of houses where there used to be acres of flowers. It's going to be like one of those places where you can't move for traffic.

When and where did the heavy development start?

Well, Indian Wells, the early developers were ranchers now that I think about it. There were citrus ranches and date gardens over there. And then there were hotels, and then there's the tennis garden. In '57 there was hardly anything there. There was an artist there on the south side of Highway 111. I forget his name. And then there was Lucille Ball and Desi Arnaz, who had a hotel that they used to frequent when we were there, and we loved it although we never used to actually *see* Lucille Ball.

The Coachella Valley was green, she said. The areas down around Thermal, Mecca,

Coachella were all ranches and so you saw a variety of greens. Right here in Indio, when we bought this house there was an orange grove on one side of us, and then there was a date garden. Well, now they're both gone. It's all houses. I can't see my mountains anymore. All the animals and the birds are gone.

Was there any specific time when you could say that things had gone far enough?

Miles Avenue when we first came was beautiful to drive on; it was just a double-lane road and you could see these vistas of dunes and wildflowers and mountains. I think the first development was a failure at the corner of Miles at Washington; it was about 1990 maybe when that came in, and then there was another built in next to it and then they jumped a couple of subdivisions in and now Miles Avenue has become a four-way throughway and it's no longer fun to drive.

We need have no fear that our lands will not become better and better as the years go by. I can't see my mountains anymore, but that's what one should expect when **WATER IS HERE**. In the decade since I began this book, Indio and Palm Springs have finally eaten up the space between, thereby perfecting Palm Desert, Rancho Mirage, Desert Hot Springs, La Quinta, Cathedral City . . .

Yes, what about Cathedral City? Cathedral City is actually a great choice with which to end this list, because as *The Coachella Valley's #1 Real Estate Magazine* informs me: *Cathedral City . . . What a Great Choice!*

I had a call girl from Cathedral City once. She came all the way down to my motel in Indio, which was awfully nice of her. It took her awhile because she got stuck in traffic.* *Once a sleepy community, Cathedral City was subdivided in the 1950s and has experienced tremendous growth over the past 10 years . . .* It's all houses. *What a Great Choice!*

The Coachella Valley was green. Well, wasn't it still green? Can't you see the vineyards like living factories on the east side of Mecca, everything squared up? In spite of or because of César Chávez, table grapes continued to be the valley's primary cash crop. On Avenue 52, right at sea level, darkskinned men stooped over green stripes in the tan dirt, and then there was a sign: ***COMING SOON!***

Captioned *North Shore Ranch,* a flat building half-hides itself amidst the shrubs of the flat desert. In the foreground are two sheds which might actually be crates. There is little sense of scale. *Bordered by the All American Canal. See the night lights on Salton Sea on approx. 98 ac., with water and electricity, private but accessible. Some buildings and garages. Only $299,000.* That's an Imperial-style advertisement; that's old style, with its cheapness, dreariness, and gigantic parcel size—why, it's as large as one of those mythical American family farms!

*In 2002 there were almost twelve thousand vehicles on Highway 111. The Department of Transportation expected that number to double in the next twenty years.

Meanwhile, what sort of property would Coachella advertise? Something *subdivided, with tremendous growth*. Southwest Airlines Spirit loves Coachella for *the genuinely casual vibe, the dry desert heat, that effortless quiet, and those intense brown mountains hulking over this little city and its neighboring leisure communities with those names—La Quinta, Indian Wells, Rancho Mirage—that all sounded like even better reasons to retire at 35 and buy some* golf *clubs*. Let's omit agriculture, poverty, migrant workers' suffering, water worries. *What a Great Choice!*

Walking down one of the long cracked-earth avenues between date palm trees in Coachella, I once saw the tracks of a bobcat. The tall furry columns of palm trees are still there; in fact, somebody's planting new palm groves, and we can often spy blue sky and the Chocolate Mountains through them, blue-red on the far side of the Salton Sea.

Chapter 198

INDIO

(2003–2004)

A narrative, in addition to descendancy charts and family group sheets, can be a good way to share stories, letters and documents, or to set the family in the society in which it lived.

—Emily Ann Croom, 2001

A man is stroking a woman's pretty brown foot on Bliss Avenue.

In the real estate guide, a color photo of a little ranch-style homestead with boarded-up windows advises us to cash in on someone's misfortune: *HUD Repo in Indio.* Four bedrooms, two baths, air-conditioning! *Very central location, mature trees, excellent terms. This one won't last!*

Chapter 199

DUROVILLE

(2003–2006)

. . . it's hard to imagine a situation any worse for migrant workers than the dangerous slum growing on an Indian reservation on the northern shore of the Salton Sea.

—*San Diego Union-Tribune*, 2003

When I lay down negative IV-CS-DUR-03-01 upon the light table, what I always notice first is the usual Imperial broad grey emptiness; the lower half of the image consists of pavement alone, stubbled like my chin; the twin passing-lines, yellow or white in "reality," here represent themselves as paler demarcations whose edges bleed into the surrounding asphalt more or less as the pastel bandings of Laguna Salada merge into one another when I gaze down at them from Signal Mountain or Guadalupe Canyon; then the highway continues up past the midpoint of my negative, shadow-hollowed here and there, as if with myriad armpits; I don't remember seeing these at all when I squinted into the ground glass of my view camera; they were probably even shallower than the wind-ridges which form on hardpacked snow in the Arctic. So much for the lower zone of this multiform Rothkoscape. The upper zone is a heavier, more even grey (which is to say that the positive would be pale white), with the white antitheses of power wires spanning it in dips. Then in the middle, below the lighter greynesses of the Chocolate Mountains, which must really be considered a part of the sky-zone, we find Duroville itself, which like sky and pavement runs edge to edge and which makes up no more than twenty percent of the composition. Unlike negative IV-CS-DUR-03-02, negative IV-CS-DUR-03-01 actually records direct evidence of life; for on that hot June Sunday afternoon vehicles sped in and out of Duroville, perhaps one every minute or two, and so I waited to click the shutter until somebody pulled in; accordingly, here's a car, whose motion-blurred license plate I can still read through the loupe; and through the rear window I can see two white anti-silhouettes, the lefthand one being the driver in his sombrero; he turns slightly toward the man in the baseball cap, who, freed by his passenger status from any responsibility for watching the road, faces almost sideways, probably speaking into the driver's ear as they pass the fence topped by the hand-lettered sign for Frank's Auto Sales, which offers the world a telephone number in Thermal. Just left of that entrance road stands a speed limit sign: five miles per hour, please, as explained by the graphic of a child. That's quite official-looking. Then, farther leftward, and higher than Frank's sign, I see, on a rectangular field adorned, like many motel signs in Indio, with palm trees, this welcome:

H. DUROS
TRAILER PARK

and an address, which I omit. (If you want to find it, ask the Torres-Martinez Desert Cahuilla Indians, whose band comprises a hundred and ninety-two members *within the ranchería,* and fifty-seven *adjacent;* their gross acreage is not quite twenty-four thousand, if we ignore the fact that much of it lies under the Salton Sea. Duroville exists proudly *within the ranchería.*)

The trailer park itself? Trailers, fences, roads with absurdly official street signs; here and there the white negative of a tree; it's a flat zone (no two-storey trailers here!); it's dreary and unfriendly. But aren't most new neighborhoods?

The editorial from which this chapter's epigraph was taken goes on to quote a *Los Angeles Times* story which claims that *dioxin-laden smoke and ash from the waste dump waft through the slum of broken-down trailers and plywood shacks. Raw sewage leaks onto the streets, while piles of rotting garbage and other refuse litter the area, which is called Duroville, after its founder, Harvey Duro.*

I never noticed any raw sewage. The garbage pile was on the outskirts of Duroville, and usually it was smoldering.

According to the private investigator I hired, Harvey J. Duro, born in 1947, owned no property appearing in a database of California tax assessors' records. Nor did any corporate or business affiliations appear under his name, although the investigator remarked: *It is probable that records regarding activity on an Indian Reservation would be kept by the tribal government, not by state or county agencies.* As for the man's criminal history, no Imperial County records were available online, but Riverside County case number 062389 (28 August 1996) revealed that Mr. Duro had served thirty days in prison for driving under the influence of alcohol and then resisting arrest. A civil case from 1993 reported a default judgment against Mr. Duro, who failed to appear in court on what seemed to have been a child support matter. In 1991 he was the defendant in a Federal District Court in a real property rental, release and ejectment case, the plaintiff being the All Indian Housing Authority. The case was closed a year later. In 2003 another Federal District Court case of the same nature was filed against him, the plaintiff being the United States of America. This case was still pending. The civil minutes mention that one of the main issues was *whether the court . . . has the authority to order defendant, an Indian allottee, to take certain action to alleviate the human habitation and environmental conditions which prevail on the allotted land pending the eviction of the occupants of the trailers.* The court ruled against the United States's request for a preliminary injunction, arguing that the risk of immediate harm to the occupants of Duroville was less than the hardship which would surely be inflicted upon them should the place be closed down. The case continued.

In 2003, four thousand–odd migrant workers lived in Duroville.

Noe Ponce, born in Duroville, had worn the Virgin of Guadalupe around his neck for two years now. He said: Police come in here every day arresting people for being drunk, fighting, stealing.

Carmen Lopez, aged twelve, wanted to be a cheerleader. She had lived in Duroville for six years. She said: I don't like it here so much, because when they burn things at the dump, my head hurts.

For fun she played. She wanted a cheerleading outfit but did not know where to buy it.

Many men had come from Michoacán, I presume illegally, to work in grapes and bell peppers. They paid two hundred a month to live in those junky trailers. (*$4,500 SE VENDE*, offered one trailer.) I did not ask them whether they had ever proceeded beyond the laundry drying on the fence to visit the **INSTITUTO GNOSTICO DE ANTROPOLOGIA A. C.**

A redhaired man was sitting beside the restaurant trailer. He glared at me.

Aside from trailers, Duroville contained nice cars, dirt streets, stop signs, street signs, fences, some vines, gravel yards, even a lawn or two, a basketball hoop. In spite of the lawn, it reminded me of the ghetto shantytowns of Kingston, Jamaica.

Every now and then I went back there. I never made any friends. Nobody welcomed me; nobody trusted me.

One hot December afternoon I rolled up along the western side of the Salton Sea, the grape leaves on the vineyards quite reddish at this season, and passed that famous landmark the Riverside County Disposal Site. Lincoln Street offered citrus hedges in angled parallels, young palms, some of them mere seedlings; they were ranked like chesspieces in the white dirt. The clump of convenience stores at Highway 195 has grown a trifle wider. Who knew what grandeurs Duroville might have achieved?

Stop Illegal Dumping. Keep Our Reservation Beautiful.

NATIVE SPIRIT DISCOUNT SMOKES

PRIVATE PROPERTY

Then there was an inflatable Santa Claus by a fence, a huge fat shaggy palm, junked cars in the dirt.

POSTED—NO TRESPASSING, KEEP OUT

Imperial was flaky mud, a roadrunner on the pavement. Imperial was **FOR SALE BY OWNER.**

A long silver pipe in a fallow field paralleled the highway, guiding me back into Duroville.

I saw a painted Virgin of Guadalupe on the side of a trailer, crapball fences of various sorts, pickup trucks, additional grimy Santa Claus statues, a dog lying in the street, doubtless doing its best to enforce the sign that said **KEEP OUT—PRIVATE**. A man glared at me through dark sunglasses. Christmas tree lights hung over boarded-up windows and a full garbage can.

A police car blocked the dirt street called Wiley Avenue. Two cops were interrogating a man dressed in his Sunday best on this Tuesday noon, while a crowd of girls and women watched from across the sand.

The redhaired man was sitting in the same spot as before, shooting me a bloodshot glare . . .

Chapter 200

SALTON CITY

(2006)

> Into this long undeveloped land, which nature has so wonderfully fitted for the highest human use, has now come a new race, bringing energy and the most approved modern methods . . .
>
> —Elmer Wallace Holmes, 1912

Fruit for a dollar a bag at the Brawley fruit stand, Palm Avenue, Lalo's Taco Shop on Palm and Main, Brawley Billiards, the Salvation Army, the shut-down Planter's Hotel with scaffolding on it, then Westmorland's tan dormant fields, these are one's early-twenty-first-century landmarks en route to Salton City. Four white geothermal plumes arise in the direction of the Salton Sea. Had I stopped at the Westmorland Dollar Store or Johnny's Liquor, this chapter might have been about Westmorland instead; but the biggest news I ever gathered from my decade of passing through the latter metropolis was that once upon a time, a truckload of lemons spilled on the highway, and children ran out to gather them up by the armload; meanwhile, the traffic squished the fruits, and Westmorland smelled so beautifully like lemon. Now Westmorland is behind; the car curves toward the low grey-blue knife-ridges of mountains, passing a field of chard, and at Bannister Road I first notice the Salton Sea as a sky-blue line of a pencil's thickness. Trifolium Canal is but a wriggly arroyo at present; perhaps it always was; Deep Wash is deep no longer. Here comes the first palm tree. Crossing Alfalfa Ditch I pass a dust-sugared palm grove, then the dry olive-brushed wash of San Felipe Creek. Today the Border Patrol checkpoint is memorialized by an empty white vehicle, and the car speeds through, by which time the Salton Sea has rotated from a bearing two-o'-clock to three-o'-clock, becoming a dusty grey-blue; and at one-o'-clock I soon see the small white shards of Salton City.

SALTON SEA ESTATES—*$10,000 Credit*

WELCOME TO West Shores of the Salton Sea

A mortgage center that was never here before offers

New Custom Homes from the $200,000s

WELCOME TO droopy cacti on Potrero Road, to new homes. The Imperial Idea may linger in this neighborhood! Just now I read about a man on Vista del Mar who boasts that he can dance with his wife on the patio or *talk to your yard bare-ass naked. And nobody can complain.* What of the other grand avenues? Might they be as free-spirited as Vista del Mar? Shore Sand remains empty; then come four new houses, the blue line of sea widening ahead like a lizard's smile; I now catalogue Shore Prince, Shore Maze, and I had better not forget Shore View, where a desert-camouflage-painted Volkswagen Beetle graces a sandy driveway; Yacht Club Drive, a home **FOR SALE BY OWNER** (he sold out at a fancy price); Treasure appears no more or less precious than the other streets, and here's the beach, herring gulls circling and crying over the purple water. On the flats, mummified brown little fat tilapia speckle the world farther than I can see. Why not take a promenade? My driver retches at the ammoniac stench, the fish-corpses flat and crunchy underfoot on the tan sand. As the Department of Parks and Recreation wrote in 1990, *the salty water may cause a slight stinging sensation in your eyes or in open cuts, but old-timers claim that a soak in the Salton Sea can cure almost anything.* Cured, we return to the car. My shoes leave lumps of reeking beach-mortar on the floormat. Off we go. In the blink of a realtor's eye, we have arrived at Seaport Avenue.

The Mexican-American woman, shrugging, fifty-odd years old, fat, has been here for one year. Her five-year-old looks very cute watering sand with the hose. They hail from Coachella.

When I ask what brought her to Salton City, she gives the Imperial answer: I wanted to live in a place more tranquil.

Does the smell bother you?

Yes.

Is it getting better or worse?

Well, it's not improving, and in the summer there are a lot of bugs.

Could it be hazardous for your daughter's health?

It could be, she shrugs.

Are the neighbors nice?

I don't talk to them.

What do you do for fun here?

Go to Coachella. When the smell is bad I don't go outside.

Back at the mortgage center, the pretty young Mexican-American realtor assures us that the Salton Sea possesses a filtration system and that she does not notice the smell more than half the time. I inquire about birth defects, and she claims never to have heard about those, or indeed about any pollution problem with the Salton Sea. I wonder aloud about fun in Salton City. Well, there are a few restaurants, and soon there will be a truck stop.

I ask who has been buying her houses.

We're getting a lot of good people here, she explains. I don't want there to be any bad people.

Departing Salton City, we cross Electra Ditch; at Calyx Ditch the sea suddenly becomes wide, blue and pretty, with the reddish desert hills to our left. Passing Desert Shores, the white shack or shed crowned by the initials of Veterans of Foreign Wars, we find the sea ever so calm, with the brown and red Chocolate Mountains vaguely reflected halfway across it, and already we are coming into date palm groves . . .

Chapter 201

HOLTVILLE

(2003)

But that is the essence of the Valley; so much that is worth noting is silent, unspoken.

—Alice Woodside, 2006

. . . And the golden light on the golden fields brought the land alive as evening always does in Imperial: A lush green zone of chard or radish flashed by, with sky-blue water in between every row of green; a big cloud rested over Signal Mountain; Imperial put on her best perfume (essence of feedlot); and then came the eastward turn toward Holtville.

Imperial was green and the mountains were underlined by a strip of white sand, a line of palm trees, the Planters' Ginning Co.

W. F. Holt would have been glad to see this feedlot of dappled black-and-white cows whose many long bodies kept darkening into silhouettes.

Then the car turned left into Holtville, went left a block and left again on Sixth back out of town to the white crosses in their fresh-graded muck.

Do you remember what they wrote about Mr. Holt? *He works too hard to have time to sit around the corner store stove and whittle with the rest of the fellows, so when they get out to work they find the Holt fields are all plowed . . . Lots of people don't like Holt; lots do.*

That was all these illegal aliens in the cemetery had wanted, to work as hard as Holt did. Bad luck, in an unknown number of cases emblematized as Operation Gatekeeper, had caught them; and so here they were, home forever in Holtville.

Some of the crosses possessed wilted flowers, possibly from the Day of the Dead. A long cross made of carnation heads lay a dead body's length in the muck before one cross with no name, not even **JOHN DOE**, simply **NO OLVIDADO**, and I touched a scattering of white bead-like things in the flowers; they were wax drippings.

When they get out to work they find the Holt fields are all plowed, the sun now glaring right on top of the low trees at the edge of the potters' field, the muck seeming to breathe, giving off a comforting breath of water-freshened earth, and the crosses, small and still and white, beginning almost to shine in the twilight.

And a big truck went by, and Holtville cooled. Birds began to sing. Night arrived; Imperial came alive.

Off the changing wind came a smell of manure.

IMPERIAL

The hatted heads like crops in the 1911 picnic "fiestas" of Holtville, so many ladies in white, the men often in dark suits, those squinting Western faces beneath the trees—where have they all gone? They've ridden away on that plank road of Edith Karpen's memories, the road they used to oil from a cylindrical car pulled by half a dozen horses. They've gone to Yuma and beyond; they're out of Imperial now.

Long trenches with poles across them supporting quarter after quarter of barbequed beef; farmers and neighbors together; that was Christmas in Holtville in 1909. Wilber Clark and his sister might have been present; perhaps Mr. Holt motored down from Redlands with his wife and daughters; the Edgar brothers had already opened a branch of their hardware store there; confident dreamers were growing grapes.

Manufacturing is hitting another level of evolution. You can't produce things the way you used to. So the grapes went away, and the farms dwindled in number and increased in acreage.

JOHN DOE'S PROMOTION

JOHN DOE was born with a Mexican name. *He works too hard to have time to sit around the corner store stove and whittle with the rest of the fellows.* That was why he decided to go to Northside.

NEW TODAY!
Debt Collection Technician

Naturally **JOHN DOE** would never qualify for that exalted position.

NEW TODAY!
Agribusiness Warehouse / Delivery Person

Growing Western agribusiness [the newspaper never says which one] is looking for a Warehouse/Delivery person for our Holtville warehouse.

Once upon a time, in the years before Operation Gatekeeper, **JOHN DOE** could have gotten warehouse employment; even nowadays he might have aspired to such work had he known how to borrow someone's social security number, obediently paying money into a system which would never return it to him in his old age *(they do work most Americans wouldn't do);* a delivery job would have been more problematic, since he surely lacked a driver's license.

NEW TODAY!
Field Labor

Growing Western agribusiness looking for a person who will not complain. No benefits; no job security.

That advertisement never appeared in the newspaper; advertisements were a waste of money in that business; **JOHN DOE** would wait regardless; I suspect he could not read the newspaper.

The sheriff's department believes the deaths could outpace last year's record of 95. **Yet as tragic as these events are, the patrolling policy, known as Operation Gatekeeper, is the correct one.** I can't help believing in people.

Some crosses had fallen; Terrie picked them up and set them right . . .

Chapter 202

CALEXICO

(2003)

Among the outstanding attractions of Calexico are . . . 6.—Six miles of waste-water sewers and new sanitary outfalls.

—Imperial Valley Directory, 1930

At four-thirty in the morning the air smells sulphurous and sweet like Karachi, and a bird sings. A man walks briskly west, toward Donut Avenue, and a block away another man is also walking west. A truck goes down Fourth Avenue. The palm-tree shadows are crisp and still on the parking lots. A police car, a taxicab, a walking man in a work cap, a fingernail moon and a few stars, that's Calexico at four-thirty.

But the deep blue sky is now going pink on the eastern end of Second Street, and men and women are standing at pay phones; people are emerging from the pallid blankness of the border station. Stores are lit but closed. An ancient brown man in a white Panama hat lopes along, carrying a plastic bag. At **FALLAS PAREDES** they're pulling the racks of discount clothes onto the sidewalk because it's already five, and across the street, under the Bank of America sign, half a dozen men sit on the yellow-lit sidewalk. Men stride rapidly toward Donut Avenue.

And in front of Donut Avenue there they are, at least two hundred of them, the lines and crowds of men in the parking lot, each huddle formed like a pearl around each truck or van. A big fat woman stands drinking coffee beside her man. Two men sit behind the dark window of a van, watching and perhaps choosing. In another van a man sits regally in the driver's seat. Another man stands, leaning toward the open passenger door, swinging it idly. Men speak in brisk voices, smiling and even relaxing, with their plastic bags or backpacks slung over their shoulders.

Inside Donut Avenue, they are, of course, eating their doughnuts in paper bags, drinking their coffee, aggregating in threes and fours, most of them men although occasionally a woman will sit with several men. By the bank of video-game machines a man in white-salted boots kneels on the floor, reading a Jehovah's Witness magazine. Most of the men's clothes are clean. They do not speak loudly. Several of those whom I had taken to be chatting I now realize are dully rubbing their noses, gazing away from one another like people in elevators, waiting for the judgment.

A slender man in a cap which says **FOXY** stands in the doorway, one hand in his jacket pocket, the other on his coffee cup, and he strains his eyes, looking. A handsome young couple are flirting; a whitehaired, big-shouldered man in a checked shirt strides in as though he owns the world. A white van, crowded with the chosen, pulls away. Now it is five-thirty, with a few bloody sausage-shaped clouds at the eastern end of the pale blue sky. All the benches at the bus stop are full. A crowd of men listens rapturously to an older man tell a story in a sharp voice. One man whistles at another, who trots obediently toward him, while on a bus bench a third man watches them with narrowed eyes, working away with his toothpick. More of the battered vans head for the fields, honking. Across the street, on the sidewalk in front of Valley Independent Bank, a man begins to drone away with a leaf blower.

The man with the toothpick is very still now beside me. He crosses his legs, uncrosses them, and finally begins walking back to the border.

By seven, all that is over. The foremen have taken all the winners away! In the hotels, the smooth seagull-cries of women in orgasm are just beginning to pass through the walls. The sun is hot on the back of my neck. Lupe Vásquez is surely in the broccoli. *God, so that's my life.*

Then it is eight-o'-clock in Calexico when the wind smells like manure and the cashier inside the Rite Aid, which is still closed, has begun matching and inserting each drawer into each cash register. Rite Aid opens! Half a dozen people, most of them women, rush inside. And then Calexico is silent all day.

Meanwhile, the newspaper reports the coming of *a huge subdivision that could double Calexico's population.*

A young palm gently twitches in the hundred-degree night, and a cavalcade of automobiles—a good three of them—shines its way eastward on Third Avenue. In the windows of LA Selección, light clothes crowd against the glass like refugees peering through the portholes of a sinking ship, and crickets sing. A cockroach emerges from the manhole, scuttles briskly some two feet, takes fright and rushes home. How still it always is in those long hot archways! Is it my imagination or are they more brightly lit than before? There's the old tower, white in the night, and the fence, through which the red brakelights of departing cars shine in Mexico.

Even there it seems quiet, due to the heat. But still, by ones and twos people speak to one another through the heavy mesh. An unshaven man glares piercingly into my eyes.

Chapter 203

EL CENTRO

(2002)

> Some lover of nature, seeking seclusion and health, has erected a cabin home, surrounded it with rustic comfort, and subsists upon the products of the rich responsive soil.
>
> —Wallace W. Elliott, 1885

—And change came; just as the urine of dehydrated people is turbid and dark, failing in transparency, so the evening sunlight, as if heated to exhaustion by and with itself, now lost the glaring whiteness which had characterized it since early morning, and it oozed down upon the pavement to stain it with gold; and suddenly* the lengthening angles of light alongside the railroad tracks and between the faded temples of agricultural success on Commercial Avenue became incredibly beautiful, the goldenness containing within itself an earthern rainbow of tans and browns; the next day I saw that same many-subsuming color in the hair of a woman who called herself Mexican-American and whose boyfriend even though he was thirty-seven could still make a baby if I knew what she meant; she'd had three children by three diferent men and they were all in foster care because the world kept kicking her when she was down; and she bore an ankh, the ancient vulva-based fertility symbol, tattooed on her upper arm; her parents were Christian and her brother was a Satanist, so she knew what was what (and while saying this she made it more than clear that she wanted me to do some business with her); and suddenly she became emblematic to me of Imperial's troubled not to say polluted fertility, with her sun-colored hair and her silt-brown skin, her babies and her happylust to conceive more babies. When is conception a tragedy? When the pioneer generation took root in Imperial, it was "noble," "heroic," "romantic." And now?

And change came. *A cliffhanger decision looms tonight for the most important water deal in California's modern history* . . . That is what the newspaper said. How would the Imperial Irrigation District vote? *All the heavy weight is on the Imperial Valley,* opined a jeweler. *There were all these threats . . . that if we don't do this deal, all these bad things could be done to us.* I think we all feel sorry for 'em.

*" 'Things are moving very rapidly,' said Oscar Rodriguez, the city's director of economic development. 'There is a significant amount of economic development underway,' he said."

YELLOW CAB DISPATCHING PRICES, CITY OF IMPERIAL

(2003)

Posted inside the taxi:

Social Security	\$4
County Jail	\$6
Out of Imperial	\$8, 9, 10 and more

LOS ANGELES

(2002–2005)

The country was completely parched and desolate, but half-way up the hill we could see a green spot where a spring emerged from a mountain. It takes no more than this to create a settlement in Lower California.

—John Steinbeck, 1940

TÍPICO AMERICANO

The aggression of Palm Springs's green lawns, casinos, gated communities, car dealerships and billboards, to say nothing of that literally grey eminence Los Angeles, with its myriads, its neediness and its greediness cushioned within cool smoggy mists, must surely conquer Imperial's tranquil decrepitude, and indeed is already winning mile by mile. *It takes more "nerve" and more coin to invest in a corner lot than it once did, but the promise of returns is still good . . . A new water supply is coming; a mountain river has been annexed at great cost . . .* A booster wrote those words about Los Angeles in 1911. Nearly a century later their veracity has been refreshed, thanks to the water transfer from Imperial County. The promise of returns may indeed be better than ever, at least for the super-rich. Within ten or twenty years, won't Indio be another suburb of Los Angeles? The *Imperial Valley Press* proudly announces the forthcoming appearance of this hotel chain and that fast food franchise in El Centro. When the new border checkpoint opened on the east side of Mexicali, which is to say considerably eastward of Mexicali's puny counterpart Calexico, people told me that another of Northside's industrial parks was going to sprawl and slither there; in some adjoining future year, Calexico will reach at least that far, manifesting what those of us to whom only human concretions are important have named "southern California," meaning lawns and telephone poles, palm trees getting moved in on by baseball fields, the desert turning the color of money: green-green, greeny-green!

It won't be all bad. I love to ride in a car past Citrus Avenue, continuing onward past the immediately following Orange Avenue to the tanning salons, coffeehouses and antique shops around La Brea, whose eponymous tarpits offer up a past whose prehistoric tropicality feels scarcely more alien than the epoch when Citrus Avenue actually grew citrus. (G. Harold Powell: *The dark green foliage and the flaming yellow fruit of the orange groves made a striking picture.* And so did the sabertoothed tigers and dire wolves slowly drowning in tar, upon whose surface the water-mirror of their bygone world trembled and rippled, restoring its choate illusion for the next victim.) In the midst of Miracle Mile, a fountain's jets blossom cotton-white upon a granite altar. Then here come the department stores. Lovely apartments present the prospect of an **IMMEDIATE MOVE-IN** near the Motor Hotel on Hauser. **GROWING PAINS: Residents crowding into L.A. area make it most densely packed in U.S.**

Blotches of Mexicali's south and east already resemble Calexico in a way—a grubbier, more uneven Calexico, to be sure, but here lie ugly signs and industrial peoplelessness nonetheless. (My favorite announcement to the world: *GARY WELLS USA WORLD CHAMPION MOTORCYCLIST*.) A little farther out, Mexicali regains its houses of brilliantly painted brick glazed with dust, its yards of tires and plastic buckets of roses; but in the zone of Gary Wells, one could be in Los Angeles. (An advertisement for a new cemetery: **TÍPICO AMERICANO**.) And San Felipe despite its whale-skull exoticism will in obedience to forces personified by the expatriate entrepreneurs grow from a small to a large American resort enclave, eventually resembling Ensenada or Rosarita Beach, if the hotel owners can only afford the air-conditioning bills. For a more northeasterly preview, cross the California Wasteway and then the reedy weedy Colorado to Yuma Podiatry Associates, Drive Thru, Avenue A, **Palm Plaza**, **AUTHENTIC MEXICAN FOOD**, *Yuma Gardens*, First Church of the Nazarene, an orange tree, a palm tree, the smell of asphalt, *MONTERO CHIROPRACTIC (72°F)*, walls, fences, DISCOUNT LIQUOR, **COLLISION SPECIALIST**, SALT FREE DRINKING WATER and all the rest of Arizona.

Don't think Imperial didn't want to outgrow itself! Maybe Imperial County did continue to be the poorest in the state of California, and in the lowest zone of official plant richness; maybe Mexican Imperial likewise suffered from a high failure rate; still, Imperial (or at least Imperial's developers) never lost sight of the greeny-green dream; Imperial was a sun-abused, abscessed street prostitute in Mexicali who resolutely put herself forward in the best possible light:

> **Imperial**
> This bargain reduced for quick sale.
>
> **Brawley Investment**
> This 17 room with kitchen and office used to me [*sic*] a motel. Priced at $700,000 but seller is anxious.

Imperial Home
Fixer-upper 3 bedroom. Large lot. Zoned for animals, large lot disible [*sic*] location. Owner motivated, priced to sell for only $85,000.

West Indio
Just a few years old! Hurry it won't last.

Acreage in Thousand Palms!
Recently SOLD. Call me if you want to SELL your RANCH or ACRES. I'll get you top dollar for them in 60 days or less GUARANTEED. (Subject to terms and price.)

Repo Property!
In the search for repos, HUD/VA? Call me, I will hook you up with the best deals in town. Don't wait no more! Ask for Ramon Lara . . .

THE DESERT DISAPPEARS, like the lovely oval face of Mary Ellen Tuttle, pioneer teacher. Recently SOLD. *The bountiful continent is ours.* **D r i v e T h r u.** *It is simply needless to question the supply of water.* Hurry it won't last. **WATER IS HERE**. *I can't help believing in people. I have never been cheated out of a dollar in my life.* VISIT ONE OF OUR NEW HOME NEIGHBORHOODS. **Repo Property!** *He sold out at a fancy price.*

He sold out at a fancy price. He sold out at a fancy price. Don't wait no more! *He sold out at a fancy price.*

In the experience of Riverside we may see the commercial romance of irrigation in its striking form. The original sheep pasture, assessed at seventy-five cents an acre, sold readily at twenty-five dollars an acre when irrigation facilities had been supplied . . . The improved orange orchards, which had been evolved from the sheep pasture, were valued, and actually sold, at one thousand to two thousand dollars per acre. Those words were published in 1905. Riverside was a "pioneer orange colony" then. Riverside might as well have been Imperial. And Riverside kept selling out at a fancy price, until finally (don't wait no more!) Riverside was eaten up by Los Angeles.

Actually, that's an exaggeration. It only seems to me, because I'm not from there, that Los Angeles is a monoculture. For example, West Covina's pine trees, grass, smog and fast food seem to me like Los Angeles, but they're really just West Covina.—Well, yes, agreed my friend Jake the Engineer, who's lived in Long Beach for ever so long now, I guess I would have a finer-grained perspective. There's a lot of wilderness here, even at Palos Verdes ten minutes away from my house where I like to bicycle . . .—I asked him when he had last been to Riverside, and he said not for ages. I asked him to describe Riverside as he remembered it, and he said: Hot. Drab. It's probably a checkerboard of new development and orange groves. I'm sure they still have orange groves. It was just twenty-five years ago that they bulldozed some more orange groves to build the campus where I worked in Huntington Beach. And that's Huntington Beach, which is pretty close in. There's so much land out there that I'm sure there's quite a bit left. It isn't wall to wall by any means. They call it the Inland Empire. There are people who will live in the lower-priced houses out there and take the commute from hell. There's a lot more land out there that's already got somebody's hooks in it for preservation or something . . .

You know, Jake said after awhile, they still have unique names as cities around here. Sometimes when you get off the freeway you can find the old main street. You can see these two-storey brick buildings and you can know there must have been a feed store, and sometimes there's still a grain elevator two blocks away. The difference is that there's a big freeway and lots of housing developments . . .

He sounded almost sad, maybe because he was from Kansas originally and had worked on a ranch with me when we were young (he always made the best ice cream) so I asked him if he could board a time machine for southern California *circa* 1900 and live out his days as a homesteader in one of those fresh-born miraculously irrigated farming towns, would he do it, and if so, would he expect to have a better life than the one he was having, and without hesitation he replied: Oh, yes, in spite of the occasional whooping cough. Could be fun . . .

THE DESERT DISAPPEARS.
THE DESERT DISAPPEARS.
THE DESERT DISAPPEARS. TÍPICO AMERICANO.

DELINEATIONS

In Northside, where there are fewer parades and one has to look awfully hard to find the Virgin of Guadalupe painted on any wall, **THE DESERT DISAPPEARS.** So does water. I remember one time when Jake and I explored one straight-edged section of the Los Angeles River; we ran up and down the steepish concrete walls and then stepped over its two inches of flow. `Just a few years old! Hurry it won't last.` Southside, couples sit tightly embracing on the park benches, gazing so seriously into each other's faces. Northside I find Palm Springs' white houses, palms everywhere, quiet money and subdued cubes, poodle-shaped trees, white houses and white walls, white marker-stones, and nobody sitting outside, nobody embracing nobody. *He sold out at a fancy price.* Should I write **IMPERIAL DISAPPEARS**? But what is Imperial? *He sold out at a fancy price.* That's everywhere.

At the turn of the twentieth century, Fullerton was the walnut kingdom; now Fullerton is simply Los Angeles.

At the beginning of this book I wrote that *Imperial is the continuum between Mexico and America.* Well, then what might Los Angeles be? Because I love Imperial and because it comes naturally to me to preach graveside elegies, I began my as yet unwritten novel by hating Los Angeles, which I intended to define in terms of the simpering yellow star of the hamburger franchise on Sunset Boulevard; for hadn't Los Angeles slain Imperial? `Tamerlane's warriors gallop into the square`. One car advertisement on a billboard, another billboard of a human silhouette in the midst of an ecstatic writhe (that was supposed to sell a certain computer product); could I really insist that such images, not to mention the white cube of that Cadillac dealership in sight of the Oasis Christian Center, were really any more vulgar or "un-American" than some turn-of-the-century Imperial boomer complacently announcing that *I have never been cheated out of a dollar in my life*? And the expensive lawn-greened homes of Highland Park, the neoclassical banalities of Youngwood Court, wasn't I bemused and even attracted by them? Even if I chose to be so cruelly unfair as to pretend that Los Angeles had become all present, that nothing significant remained of the orange trees and vineyards, the Los Angeles River, the old pueblo, the Indian land, so that only yellow hamburger-franchise stars and car advertisements could be offset against the shabby past upon which Imperial's half-moribund present was painted; if I closed my eyes to Los Angeles's art deco towers and all the rest, even so, didn't I like the palm trees in the median strip of Wilshire Boulevard? What right had I to fail to include in my definition of Los Angeles lush lawns, hedges, banana trees, palms, purple-blue flower-trees like Fourth of July fireworks, hedges, property-walls cushioned by ivy and poppies?

Never mind. *Imperial is the continuum between Mexico and America.* The fact that on Avenida Reforma in Mexicali the Consultorio Dental, the Piano Bar, the *distribuidor autorizado* of Telcel could easily be found in Los Angeles, where even the streets of Koreatown are rapidly Latinizing, makes me wonder whether Los Angeles is eating Imperial or the other way around. (From *The City Observed: Los Angeles, A Guide to Its Architecture and Landscapes,* published in 1988, I extract the following: *Broadway, downtown's old main artery, now resembles a giant Mexican village in perpetual fiesta.*) At the mega-discount store we can buy dozen-count boxes of hard and gleaming tomatoes, *coated with food-grade vegetable-mineral-beeswax- and/or lac-resin-based wax or resin to maintain freshness,* the official name of this product being item number eighty-three thousand six hundred, grown and protected by Del Campo y Asociados S.A. de CV in Sinaloa, distributed by Tam Produce in Fullerton, which is to say in greater Los Angeles—Fullerton, where almost next to the train station a warehouse offers Orange County Produce. I remember two snobbish girls; they were even Hispanic girls; they kept praising the clothing shops of San Diego, then complaining about the unfortunate Third Worldization, by which they meant Mexicanization, of Los Angeles! **TÍPICO AMERICANO**. *We need have no fear that our lands will not become better and better as the years go by,* in which case the hybrid which I've been calling Imperial may not really be threatened at all; indeed, it may prove to be as voracious and victorious as a pond weed.

SUBDELINEATIONS

I know a place whose lake is a salt-rimmed silver mirror. This place is part of California, but it lies above and northward of Imperial. The gold, ochers and russets of its scrub in springtime fill me with joy. The hard rock of it, the fragile crags, the scree, the high mounds with their geological ambiguities, the dry mountains all around me, comprise the floor and walls of the only house where I have truly felt at home.

En route to Tecate one must enter the purplish-grey mountains which I heard one Mexicali man call "the end of home" because as soon as one journeys up there, it starts to feel cool.—And what we call home, he explained, it has to be *hot.*—The mountains of my home are higher and, in the winter, considerably colder. From an Imperialite's point of view, this place lies beyond the end of the world. Tempted by glibness, I started to call it High Imperial just now, but it's not that at all. (If anything is "like" Imperial it would be the Canadian Arctic with its flatness and its plenitude of sky.) This high valley holds many Indian secrets, and on horseback I used to seek and find arrowheads by their gleam in the winter twilight sun. I know it so much better than I'll ever know Imperial. This is where Jake and I worked on that ranch. **THE DESERT DISAPPEARS**? Never! *He sold out at a fancy price?* Not here, not anyone I know. That dark-lipped vulva in the mountainside over there leads, I know, to the drunken Roman grandeur of Marble Canyon, where I used to camp. (Actually, now that I've been going to Imperial so often, its formations bring to mind the crowded white extravagances of a Mexican cemetery.) And the pale, crumbly ridge to the northeast, I've camped there, too, far past the stone phallus, and I remember the ledge where I used to find perfect rodent skulls; and I know where to gather quartz crystals, and I've gathered pine nuts and boiled Mormon tea. These wafers of rock on the slopes, and the crumbly clack of rock dislodged onto rock as one climbs, and these rocks the color of bloody water, and these steps of rock in the hills which go up and up, they're all mine, and my knowledge of this place and my love for it are braided together like the grey flesh of the ancient little trees. Rusty mounds of stones, dark clouds, they're my riches, which I'll have forever. What does it mean to be attuned to a place? Well, what does anything mean? On this winter night I'm lying on my back in a sloping sandy wash, with the waist-high sagebrush towering over me; since it's ten or twenty degrees below freezing, the tip of my nose feels cold, but for some reason my breath does not obscure the many stars. I know that I'll sleep happily and well. I love the high, cold desert feeling. This place is akin to Imperial, as I said, and to me more beautiful, simply because I know it better, each grain of its sand being a happy memory of my youth and my freedom. I look up into these stars which are far more numerous, precise, brilliant and massive than my human eyes can ever make out, and their greatness exalts me. When I get to Imperial I won't be able to see them except from the summit of Signal Mountain or from one of those other mounds, cones and peaks which in my opinion belong to Imperial only thanks to various trivial accidents of location. Here in this other zone for which I don't have a name, this place where I've always felt literally at home whereas Imperial for its part will never cease to strike and scorch me with the sunbeats of utter alienness, I love to fall into the stars every night, leaving my body, swimming between galaxies into astral entities which I call starways, not constellations, because they are so inhuman, beyond all associations and understanding, that they might lead me to something beyond myself. What will happen to the universe finally? Where will the stars go? Where will I go? Where should I go? We call these questions sophomoric only because we can't answer them. The black mountains all around me, the pallor of sand-humps in the darkness, and above all the spill of stars, I am lying in the middle of all this, so happy and grateful to witness the mystery. This place, or at least this landscape with its rotating starscape, remains almost exactly as it was a quarter-century ago, and it welcomes me, or I welcome myself in it, but it is gone all the same because my youth is gone. Here I feel calm; I begin to know what I already knew but had forgotten that I knew. For how many years now have I neglected to listen to myself? I "never have time," which means that I've lost myself, that I've failed to live my life and to apprehend the lives of others. But tonight I see another chance to ascend the starways. Where will the stars go? Where will I go? Maybe one reason that I chose Imperial to write about was that this secret high desert valley has been too much loved by me, too much roamed over, so that I've fallen into this illusion of recovering myself. Imperial, however, lies beyond the starways, in the great white light beyond the blackness of Pluto. There seems to be something about the dark flatness of Imperial's fields at night, Imperial's horizon studded with meaningless lights or, far more often, with no lights; something about the heavy sky, from which even the rare clouds must sink exhausted—well, what is that something? Can't I delineate it? The *Geological Atlas of California* does so rather beautifully, inscribing the pure sky-blue of the Salton Sea within a lobster-claw of yellow (Quaternary lake deposits: obsidian, rhyolite, pumice, etc.), and then, running parallel to the northeast shore, our atlas presents to us a palish blotch of recent alluvium (the same hue as those white, wide-streeted empty towns), followed by the Chocolate Mountains brown and pink with various Mesozoic granitic rocks. But now comes sunset over the scrub, dim shadows under the awning; Louise sits silhouetted against sky, drinking her beer, delighting in telling me another story about how she gave a cop the finger and told him to shove his attitude up his ass, and her dogs are barking because a strange car's nosing into the Drops; the moon's already high, the sky's red-orange over the trailers; and darkness licks away the low purple mountains over the orange sky. If I had the atlas with me now, I couldn't read it. Like an earthworm, darkness has long since ingested Imperial's vast fields horizoned by low half-silhouetted haystacks which are separated by narrow gaps, so that they resemble gated walls; in the morning all this will emerge from the worm's other end where Louise's cop might as well have placed his attitude, and it will be just a little darker and richer for the experience; right now there are no green-on-green hay bale checkerboards on fields; there is no atlas, and near Plaster City that ruined, semiskeletonized building with the word **APPLES** lettered on a rafter deep inside exists only as solid darkness. The humid mysteries of Imperial's flatness, the blackness of the night's canals, that solitary lamp which glows so yellow between the palm tree and the shed, all this overlies me with a heavy ephemerality, like a woman I love lying on top of me kissing me so long and so sweetly that I can hardly breathe; after awhile she will rise and go away, and I'll go with her or without her, after which this hired bed which was ours will support its next passion or sleep; Imperial's endless, mostly treeless horizontality accepts activity and even fecundation just as it drinks poisons and salts; cruelly hot and indifferent to harvests raped from it or the barrenness of its own slumber, Imperial blesses me with perfection expressed as perfect imperviousness. Imperial is those Mexicali men in jackets who offer me deals in soft, unhurried whispers; they enter restaurants to discuss their propositions, but, respecting the restaurants if not this writer, never go farther than just inside each doorway; if need be, they'll wait an hour for me to finish my meal, then loyally accompany me outside. None of my refusals can touch them. To them as to Imperial itself I can never be any more than one of those silver-grey water-mirages on the road where the double lane of border traffic almost moves, then doesn't move; and, occluding the zebra-stripe curves of the international wall's distorted reflection in a van's curved windows, two men stride down the pavement's center, bearing on their shoulders a huge Christ on His cross which they would sell to someone if they could; their doleful slowness, and the immensity of the bleeding figure they bear, reenacts the crucifixion. I have seen them there many times with their Christ; nobody ever wants to take Him. They continue nonetheless. Now it is twilight at last and they are still there, even though Imperial's greenish-white glare is fading into a celestially white horizon-line beneath blue mountains. Imperial is the father and son who sit high and gently swinging in one car of the otherwise unoccupied ferris wheel which reigns over a sandy night carnival in San Felipe; the lesser counterpart rides, spiderlegged with neon tubes, slowly spin to loud music, but the ferris wheel will not demean itself to turn for nothing; hence the father and son, who hold hands, must wait for somebody else to buy a ride so that it will become worth the man's while to pull the lever; they're not impatient; they're content, and a quarter-hour later, when three girls finally pay to be whirled around and utter happy screams, the father strokes the boy's head, and then I see their tranquil smiles as they're borne high into the cool darkness above everything. Needing nothing, Imperial can nourish itself on a tree-shaped shadow, watching the pigeons and crawling flies. Imperial dresses itself in long lines of palm-tree silhouettes below its mountains; Imperial speaks in the sounds of trains day and night like rushing winds. But silence and nakedness would not diminish it. *Both the Imperial and Mexicali Valleys are gradually being filled in by siltation from the Colorado River and peripheral canals . . . Ultimately this silt will raise the floor of the Gulf sufficiently to cause tidal flooding of the entire adjacent low desert region.* And then what? **WATER IS HERE**. Sometime after that, water will not be here. We can't deny that. In 1849 Colonel Cave Johnson Couts writes in his journal, and in 2849 or maybe 2249 it will be this way again: *Marched from Colorado [River] on morning of 19th,* heading westwards into Imperial, *ult. making about 18 miles to a* sandhill *which we had to pull the wagons over by hand. Up to this hill we passed through a mesquite bottom which bears every sign of once having been* extensively cultivated. *The irrigating ditches are very numerous and as plain as if now in use.* I'm sure that the bed of the All-American Canal will remain visible for a very long time. *Twelve miles from Colorado we passed what is called the* 1st well *or wells . . . We scraped them out but no trace of water was to be found. Nothing in the world was to be found where we encamped but mesquite.* And so they press onward, their mules beginning to die of thirst, and the men not far behind in failing. *The mirage was most beautiful about midday, presenting beautiful lakes and no small number did it sadly disappoint . . .* **WATER IS HERE**. None of this makes any difference. Nothing can touch this marriage of land and sky, of heat and salt, this hammer and anvil, this procreating couple whose only child is a plain which unlike a rainforest, an empire or a work of art can outlast anything the planet itself can, anything, even human beings, even water or waterlessness; and if, God forbid, Imperial does someday get riddled with cities, its character will remain almost unaffected; it will go on and on, true to itself, long after such temporary superficialities as "the U.S.A." and "Mexico" have become as washed out as old neon hotel signs in the searing daylight of Indio.

Chapter 206

HOLTVILLE

(1914)

A little boy in a cowboy hat squints out from the Model T; his sister in boots and a white dress is older, and almost doesn't squint; there's flat dirt all around . . .

In about but not exactly 1858, in a place called *California* and without any recorded subsequent baptism, a child named Miguel came into the world. His father's name and his mother's remain illegible; he had no surname; all we know of him is that he *resided Los Angeles City; Indian in William Wolfskill household.*

And now he's gone, not that he was ever more than half a name with no face; and that little boy from Holtville has been buried with equal finality; of him we have a face with no name; the Holtville of 1914, onetime emblem of the reclamation of Arid America, and therefore of America itself, empire of ingenuity, progress, equality, enrichment and self-sufficiency and now a wavering half-symbol of imperiled decrepitude, has grown as mysterious and wonderful to me as Indian California . . .

Chapter 207

IMPERIAL REPRISE

(1901–2004)

Then they talked of the Seer's new expedition that would start south at daybreak, and it seemed to Barbara that the very air was electric with the coming of a mighty age when the race would direct its strength to the turning of millions of acres of desolate, barren waste into productive farms and beautiful homes for the people.

—Harold Bell Wright, 1911

1

I can't help believing in people . . . I have never been cheated out of a dollar in my life. **WATER IS HERE**. *We need have no fear that our lands will not become better and better as the years go by.* ***Stories of a polluted Salton Sea are greatly exaggerated.*** **Q.** Do you have any problems with the smell? Does it ever make you sick? **A.** We're used to it.

Sign of Slow Growth Sends Stocks Lower. *He sold out at a fancy price.* **THE DESERT DISAPPEARS**. *"Moisture Means Millions."* **WATER IS HERE**. *It is simply needless to question the supply of water. The bountiful continent is ours, state on state, and territory on territory, to the waves of the Pacific sea.* It's good, more or less. *And in material advantages they are already well supplied.* **Q.** How about the fish, Ray? **A.** I've been eatin' 'em since 1955, and I'm still here, so there's nothin' wrong with 'em. *The sheriff's department believes the deaths could outpace last year's record of 95.* It's just another die-off. It's natural. **WATER IS HERE**. **WATER IS HERE**. I think we all feel sorry for 'em.

2

Suddenly, as a beast checked in its spring, they were still and motionless. By the side of the old frontiersman on the platform under the light stood Barbara. **THE AZTECS ARE BACK**. *They live together like cigarettes. They came out like ants.* We need to get these criminals behind bars where they can't harm anyone.

Get out! an officer yelled at them. They turned and slowly, slowly walked back into Mexico across the humming throbbing bridge. *What a Great Choice!*

I think we all feel sorry for 'em.* *The sheriff's department believes the deaths could outpace last year's record of 95.* They'll pop their heads up in a minute.

3

"Our primary mission is to prevent terrorism and terrorist weapons from entering our country," El Centro Chief Border Patrol Agent Michael McClafferty said. `Tamerlane's warriors gallop into the square.` The club motto is, "The aim if reached or not, makes great the life."

4

UNLESS YOU TAKE ACTION TO PROTECT YOUR PROPERTY, IT MAY BE SOLD AT A PUBLIC SALE. It would be so convenient to carry on a farm . . . when all the hard and dirty work is performed by apprentices. *Of course in the classroom my kids didn't talk about it.* You can't produce things the way you used to. *He sold out at a fancy price. Yes, just such a man you will see, a hundred times every day in Imperial Valley—the laborer.* I think we all feel sorry for 'em. **`Imperial.`** `This bargain reduced for quick sale.`

5

The essence of the industrial life which springs from irrigation is its democracy. *The club motto is, "The aim if reached or not, makes great the life."* We are praying for rain this winter, because if we do not get it I do not know where we will be. I think we all feel sorry for 'em.

6

A lot of movie stars came there. *The pictures are the result of an Imperial mirage.* I can't see my mountains anymore. I can get across whenever I want. It's the most productive fishery in the world. So, sign the coupon and send it in *today.*

*Dashiell Hammett, 1924: "You hear now and then of detectives who have not become callous, who have not lost what you might call the human touch. I always feel sorry for them . . ."

7

WATER IS HERE. THE DESERT DISAPPEARS. Tamerlane's warriors gallop into the square.

8

That's nothing new. They find 'em every week. That's just accidents. They're just tryin' to get across illegally. *The club motto is, "The aim if reached or not, makes great the life."*

9

The club motto is, "The aim if reached or not, makes great the life." God, so that's my life.

10

Standing today by the grave of that infant civilization which blossomed, amidst such hardships, upon a desert, we would fain lift the veil and see the unthought-of transformation which fifty years will bring. It's progressing along real nice. I think we all feel sorry for 'em.

Chapter 208

THE CONQUEST OF ARID AMERICA

(1905)

Accordin' to my notion hit's this here same financierin' game that's a-ruinin' the West. The cattle range is about all gone now. If they keeps it up we won't be no better out here than some o' them places I've heard about back East.

—Harold Bell Wright, 1911

In the earlier edition of this work, written in 1899, I spoke of this locality as follows:

It is popularly regarded as an empire of hopeless sterility, the silence of which will never be broken by the voices of men . . . Neither animal life nor human habitation breaks its level monotony. It stretches from mountain-range to mountain-range, a brown waste of dry and barren soil. And yet it only awaits the touch of water . . . It is more like Syria than any other part of the United States, and the daring imagination may readily conceive that here a new Damascus will arise more beautiful than that of old.

Six short years have passed, yet the dream has already come true. The very name of "The Colorado Desert" has vanished from the minds of men, and in its place we have . . . "The Imperial Valley."

. . . There could be no more wonderful example of the miracle of irrigation.

CONCERNING THE MAPS

These five maps comprise an attempt in progress to define the borders of the imaginary entity called Imperial.

THE ENTITY CALLED IMPERIAL

The first map (page xxiv) brings our attention to the southeastern corner of California, a state whose vastness is the bezel in which the jewel called Imperial has been set. By Greyhound bus it takes about fifteen hours to travel from Sacramento to Calexico*—not much longer than it takes to fly from Sacramento to Paris. In this depiction we also see the greater vastnesses of the Colorado River and of Northside's formerly Mexican territories.

CLOSEUP OF IMPERIAL

Once upon a time, the second map (page xxv) overlay a reference grid of the relevant counties as they are currently defined:

First, the pre-Conquest territorial boundaries of those Indian tribes in the general region of Imperial.

Second, the landform called the Colorado Desert, whose boundaries of course vary according to the delineator.† (The *Imperial Press and Farmer* informs us that *in January, 1900, the Colorado Desert was one vast barren waste, more desolate and worthless than any other section of arid America that has ever been reclaimed. It was so barren that no human being had ever snatched an acre of it from the Public Domain.* Perhaps the Indians didn't count.)

Third, the simple biological construct, based on temperature differentials, called

*When the connections are good. It sometimes takes eighteen or longer.

†For example, George Wharton James in his opus of 1911 reins it in by San Gorgonio Pass to the northwest, Mounts San Gorgonio and San Jacinto to the northeast, the line between San Bernardino and Riverside counties as the northern boundary generally, the Colorado River to the east, the Mexican border to the south, and the San Jacinto range to the west. "That it extends beyond the Colorado River into Arizona, and also below the boundary line into Mexico, all are well aware, but I shall practically ignore these extensions in the following pages." A botanist proposes that the Colorado Desert is really a representative subset of the Sonoran Desert.

the Desert Lower Sonoran Life Zone,* which shows us that the forbidding heat of Imperial is not confined to the Colorado Desert.

Fourth, the boundary, based on artifacts recovered from archaeological sites, between the material cultures of the Indian tribes whose territories existed more or less in the Desert Lower Sonoran Life Zone, and those tribes whose territories lay elsewhere. In the area of interest to us there were three: the Southern Culture along the southwest crescent of California, the Colorado River Culture to the east of it, and the Great Basin Culture to the north, in what are now Inyo and San Bernardino counties. The boundaries between these cultures were delineated in this map.

Fifth, the perimeter of the style of Indian rock art, called "Great Basin," which pervaded Imperial and many areas northward of it; and finally

Sixth, the zone in which the Hokan family of Indian languages was spoken; this zone overlaps with all but the northern tip of Imperial. Other Hokan language islands appear on the map of Indian California; for the sake of completeness, those have been indicated here.

My assumption is that the lifeways of the Indian tribes along the western side of the Colorado River and the California-Mexico border were in their material respects sufficiently homogeneous to help define the Imperial area. I believe this because, as the second map shows, parts of those tribal territorial, linguistic and cultural boundaries are identical. Surely people who lived as "close to the land" as Indians did would be nourished and constrained by the characteristics of that land (for an obvious instance, the heat of it, as delineated by the "life zone" concept). Don't the strictures of the Colorado Desert even now mold human life there sternly, inescapably? Therefore, if these native American material and linguistic cultures seemed to be mutually similar, and if their territories corresponded to such physically homogeneous areas as landforms, then why not define their borders as Imperial's wherever I could?

To be sure, their so-called cultural group boundary extended considerably northward, incorporating all of Cahuilla and Serrano territory, where no Hokan language was spoken, then continuing through much or all of the counties of San Bernardino, Los Angeles and Kern. Obviously much of this land extends beyond the Imperial "life zone." A good compromise seemed to be to extend Imperial north of the Hokan language line only where the Colorado Desert bulges into Cahuilla territory. This boundary corresponds more or less to the noticeable change in the landscape as one goes east on Highway 10 through Beaumont and Banning into what "feels like"

*Scientists gave it this awkward name to distinguish it from the Valley Lower Sonoran Life Zone northwestward of it.

Imperial.* This is also more or less the frontier between the Colorado River Culture and the Southern Culture. Accordingly, I expelled the Southern Culture from Imperial except as detailed in a sub-essay on Mexican considerations.

The rock art style called "Great Basin" was again far too inclusive, but the Californian portion of Imperial proved to be contained within it; that is, there is no rock art style other than "Great Basin" in Imperial north of the Mexican border. (To the south, the rock art style is unknown to me.)

In accordance with the "life zone" concept, my next step was to trim off the west coast of California except at the Mexican border itself.† Climatologically as well as culturally, this lush, foggy area hardly belongs to Imperial. Several islets of the Desert Lower Sonoran Life Zone do appear in this area, but I have excluded them for the sake of simplicity.

Now what about Mexican lifeway delineations? Early on in this book I decided that *Imperial is the continuum between Mexico and America.* Where does this continuum attenuate itself into a relatively pure Mexican-ness or American-ness?‡ Since we have been talking about Northside up to now, let's continue to do so for the moment. The dominant culture of southern California is so obviously Hispanic nowadays that any hypothetical perimeter of Latino-ness obviously stretches far beyond the boundaries of Imperial in any direction. I have therefore focused my intuition on illegal immigration. The resulting boundary, which is highly speculative, centers on the international border, namely from *a point on the Colorado river 20 m[iles] below the mouth of the Gila river, thence northward to the mouth of the Gila, and thence, nearly due W., along the old line between Upper and Lower California to a point on the Pacific coast one marine league S. of the southernmost point of San Diego Bay.* Much of what used to be Diegueño territory has since been colonized by very un-Imperial urban entities, but every night illegal immigrants take some of it back. In short, Imperial pulsates between Mexicali and San Diego; it waxes and wanes. Here is one case where overmuch specificity would seem pedantically absurd. Accordingly, let's represent the border ribbon from Arizona to the ocean as a geometer would any other ideal line, namely, as something to

*There are place-scraps of pseudo-Imperial to be found as far north as Sacramento: worn, flat sandy patches at the railroad yards, freckled by low grey grass; and over here's a freeway; the sky's hot and pale; by all means, I say to myself, this could be Imperial; but then when I'm back in Imperial itself, where everything is so much hotter and brighter, I realize how weakly my memory can hold an image, so that even a watered-down (literally, for Sacramento has two rivers), cooler, generally diminished approximation convinces me.

†As it happens, every part of the U.S. sector of Imperial lies within the former San Diego County, which included all of the present Imperial County, almost all of the counties of Riverside and San Bernardino, and some of Inyo County.

‡The word "American" excites considerable exasperation on the part of Mexicans, Canadians and other inhabitants of the American continent. Unfortunately, we have no other term for ourselves which is not either pedantic or rude.

which the thickness of a pencil cannot really do justice. A wave-pattern to the north of the border would seem like a simple way to indicate Imperial's temporal flows.

Next I had to account for the fact that some of Imperial lies south of the international border. How much, exactly? From the bicultural standpoint which we have been considering in the previous paragraph, Imperial might extend indefinitely down the Baja Peninsula, where petroglyphs are matched by Anglo-owned resorts. (One Mexican historian claims that the border region *extends out at least sixty miles in both directions. By this calculation, the border region exceeds in square miles the territory of nations such as Spain and France.*) That may be true for the border as a whole, which continues alongside Arizona, New Mexico and Texas. But one of Imperial's most notable characteristics is *slowness,* in evidence of which I advance the tortoiselike promenades of Mexicali's citizens on cool afternoons, the almost-empty black streets, the angle-parked cars which remain in place for days, the stands of fruit awaiting their once-per-hour buyers. It made intuitive sense, given the un-Imperial, hustling, honkytonk character of Tijuana, and the equally foreign busyness and American-ness of the tourist resorts in Baja California below it—and also given the fact that on a pretty map I have, entitled "Phytogeographic Regions of Baja California," this northwest corner of the peninsula has been colored emerald green, in deference to coastal scrub—to rein back Imperial's frontier here to a few more border pulsations which will appear quite pretty in symmetry with the ones we've now agreed to establish to the Northside, while permitting the eastern portion of Imperial to extend much farther south—say, to the resort town of San Felipe, which was historically an entry point for illegal Chinese immigration into Imperial. You'll be ecstatic to hear that "Phytogeographic Regions of Baja California" endorses my stand, for the tan zone called "San Felipe Desert," driest of all the peninsula's many arid places, runs neatly down the eastern side, outpacing its emerald green opposite, which quits at El Rosario.

And why should we stop at San Felipe? The tan zone keeps going, all the way past Bahía de los Angeles to the jade-colored coniferous zone. Not knowing the answer in advance,* I feel obliged to take you on a trip:

Mexicali, if we ignore the zone consecrated to GARY WELLS USA WORLD CHAMPION MOTORCYCLIST, fades with graceful irregularity into Imperial desert, its house-cubes and *carnicerías,* which are sometimes broken-windowed, colored like the illustrations in children's books, then dusted over again; and gradually there are fewer cubes and there is more dust. Between two lanes of

*Nor does anybody else. José López from Jalisco believed that the Mexicali Valley extended "all the way to San Luis Colorado," but he didn't know how far south it went. José the crackhead from Mexicali claimed the entire Baja Pensinsula. Nor were their delineations the only ones.

traffic, a man is selling plastic bags of strawberries. Smoke transects the concrete cube of VIDEO LUCY'S. At the side of the freeway, a cowboy is posting, gathering in his dark cows. Here Imperial's fences begin to incarnate themselves in posts of saguaro cacti. A feedlot with its wall of bales could have been stolen from Northside. Next comes a palm orchard, the trees smaller and more densely planted than around the Salton Sea. Following Cerro Prieto at Kilometer 22, there comes the tan country, whose rivelled sand could have lain in any of the washes between Bombay Beach and Niland if it hadn't borne such a wealth of grey-green brush. Two roadside crosses with immaculate plastic flowers, a beehive kiln in the dirt, a roadside restaurant built to resemble a six-pack of Corona beer, bottletops and all, any one of these might mark the end of Mexicali's sprawl; certainly by Kilometer 50's mounds of gravel and sand we're in the midst of what the woman I was with called "that vast feeling," that dream of emptiness as wholeness. For awhile the valley floor grows carpeted with olive-hued shrubs (mainly creosote bush). In early spring there are many yellow blossoms here. Farther south, around Kilometer 70, the vegetation begins to thin out again, the soil to blanch and crack. By Kilometer 75 the earth is naked, reddish, nearly vegetationless, a plain marked only by occasional ruined tires or the rarer salt-rimmed pool, around one of which I see men fishing to the accompaniment of a guitar. Right after the military checkpoint (green-clad soldiers jittering their machine guns at each approaching car), creamy sand dunes like better-vegetated cousins to those in Algodones mark another Imperial trick, and before I know it, the vegetation has grown up into rich green trees. This would seem to be the boundary of the Desert Lower Sonoran Life Zone. Cones of reddish lava bedeck the world. According to some sources, the Mexicali Valley, which of course is the Mexican half of the Imperial Valley, ends right here. Why not end Imperial itself here in that case? Well, the main reason is that I *want* to go farther. But here's a rationalization, too: Highway 5 is about to go back down again, back into the Desert Lower Sonoran Life Zone. Kilometer 99 offers Imperial's trademark extreme flatness on the left, jagged volcanoes on the right. From a distance, the salt flats around the cinder cones far ahead resemble shimmering water. And so the highway descends from the reddish lava-hills into this other vast plain striped with salt more or less as Jupiter is striped with gases: softly, colorfully and luminously. Nodding to the Sierra las Pintas at around Kilometer 120, the road passes a broken concrete encomium to a disco which died or never happened; Imperial is loved not only for its corrals of agave sticks but also for its high failure rate. Off to the left, the white-rimmed Colorado follows and borders Imperial, but at some point, it's turned into the widening electric-blue line of the Gulf of California, which John Steinbeck described as *a long, narrow, highly dangerous body of water.** Thus at around

*Here is a mid-nineteenth-century observer's description of that water: "Near the mouth of the Rio Colorado . . . a wild and somewhat interesting scene opens . . . The general aspect, however, is far from

Kilometer 186, we've reached San Felipe, a decent place to eat steamed clams and fish tacos while vendors walk slowly past, selling postcards and fourth-rate jewelry. The sea-fog makes it feel a little like San Diego. A round white sign says: **SAN DIEGO BEACH OK**. Isn't this far enough south? The San Felipe Desert and the Desert Lower Sonoran Life Zone stretch on, and we're only halfway to Puerto Refugio, where in 1940 the *Sea of Cortez* achieved her farthest north and swung round to sail down the east coast of the Gulf; but San Felipe seems pretty deep in Mexico just the same; we've left the Mexicali Valley behind. By fiat, Imperial ends here.*

This version of the second map will remain unpublished. I had orginally envisioned *Imperial* as containing detailed chapters about all the native American groups within this area of study. My failure to do so rendered the old version of the map arcane to the general reader. This recapitulation of what it contained was prompted not only by the spirit of querulous attachment but also by an abiding belief that the boundaries of the entity I call Imperial do "mean something" from a material point of view.

The current version of the second map simply indicates Imperial's territory, eschewing comment.

PERSONS AND PLACES IN IMPERIAL

The third map (page xxvi) locates a few people and places mentioned in the text.

RIVERS AND CANALS IN IMPERIAL

The next map (page xxvii) roughly delineates some of Imperial's major waterways. My two base maps were from 1906 (to show where the New River / Río Nuevo used to flow from) and 1962, when the All-American Canal and Wellton-Mohawk were both in place. Canals on the Mexican side are grossly underrepresented because what depictions I found were inconsistent.

MY NEW RIVER CRUISES

The last map (page 84) is a closeup of the American portion of the New River as I met it in 2001.

pleasing. There is such a vastness of monotonous desolation; so dry, so blistered with volcanic fires; so forbidding to the wants of thirsting and hungering men; that one gladly turns his eye upon the water, the *mar de Cortez* . . ."

*Since writing this, I picked up a book called *Salt Dreams* and found it devoted to exactly the same territory, excluding only the border strip to the Pacific. The entity I call Imperial coheres within more gazes than mine.

A CHRONOLOGY OF IMPERIAL

BEGINNINGS TO 1500

"Millions of years ago"
Gulf of California reaches beyond the site of Indio.
"Perhaps as early as 40,000 B.C."
First migration to Mexico
ca. 700–*ca.* 900
Water in Salton Sink.
ca. 1000–*ca.* 1400
Water in Salton Sink.
ca. 1100 Indians settle in the Coachella Valley.
After 1400–*ca.* 1500
Water in Salton Sink.
1494 Treaty of Partition of the Oceans gives Spain dominion over the American continent.

1500–1600

1502–20 Reign of Moctezuma II (Xocoyótzin).
ca. 1510 Ordoñez de Montalvo publishes his romance *Sergas de Esplandián*, which mentions an island called California, "very near to the Earthly Paradise," and inhabited by Amazon-like black women.
1519 Cortés arrives in Mexico, taking as his concubine a "mistress of vassals" from Jalisco whom he christens Doña Marina. Their son is the first recorded mestizo in Mexico.
1520 (June–Oct.)
Cuitláhuac succeeds Moctezuma as Aztec Emperor.
1520–21 Cuauhtémoc succeeds Cuitláhuac.
1521 Cortés completes his conquest of Mexico City (Tenochtitlán). Mexico is now New Spain.
1521–1821 Spanish rule over New Spain.
1524 Cortés replaced as head of state by functionaries of the Spanish Crown.
1531 The Aztec convert Juan Diego (Cuauhtlatoatzin) sees four separate apparitions of the Virgin of Guadalupe (conflated by some with the Aztec goddess Tonantzin).
ca. 1531 Conquistadors explore Mexico as far north as San Luis Potosí.
1535 Cortés discovers and, some say, names the Californian peninsula, presumably after the never-never land in Esplandián's romance.
1537 Cabeza de Vaca lands on the California coast.
1539 Francisco de Ulloa explores the Sea of Cortés all the way to the mouth of the Colorado River: "The sea there is vermilion in color; the tides rise and fall regularly."
1540–41 Mixtón War between Spaniards and Mexican Indians.
1540 Hernando de Alarcón sails from Acapulco to Yuma.
1540 Melchior Díaz passes close by Yuma.
1541 Conquistadors break native rebellions around Guadalajara, so that they can now push farther northwest.
1542 Juan Rodríguez Cabrillo makes harbor in San Diego or perhaps San Pedro. His expedition continues northward to Cape Mendocino, Cabrillo dying on the way.

1545 The Virgin of Guadalupe's intercession credited for ending a typhus epidemic in Mexico.
1547 Death of Cortés in Seville.
1548 Death of Juan Diego.
1548 Loyola Cavello discovers Upper California.
1549 Supposed end of forced Indian labor in Mexico.
1550s Supposed abolition of Indian slavery (which continues in northern Mexico).
1556 Fray Francisco de Bustamante dismisses the image of the Virgin of Guadalupe as "an Indian painting."
1571 The Jesuits arrive in Mexico.
1571 Establishment of the Inquisition in Mexico.
1571–1746 335 Chinese employed in shipbuilding in Lower California.
1574 First auto-da-fé in Mexico (5 people burned, others flogged).
1579 Sir Francis Drake lands in or near San Francisco Bay.
1584 Francisco Gali reaches Cape Mendocino.
1595 Sebastián Rodríguez de Cermeñon runs aground at Point Reyes.

1600–1700

ca. 1600–*ca.* 1700 Water in Salton Sink (Lake Cahuilla).
1602 Sebastián Vizcaíno lands in San Diego Bay.
1604 Juan de Oñate descends the Colorado, we know not precisely from where to where.
1609 Foundation of Santa Fe, New Mexico.
1633–34 Failed Spanish colony at La Paz.
1687 Foundation of Mission Dolores, the first Spanish foothold in the Pimería Subdistrict, whose northwestern terminus touches Imperial at the Gila River.
1693–94 Fathers Kino and Salvatierra explore the Gila River and the northern Gulf.
1697 Foundation of Loreto, the first Jesuit mission in Lower California.
1697–1721 The Jesuits Ugarte, Salvatierra and Kuhn explore the Sea of Cortés.

1700–1800

1700–1702 Francisco Eusebio Kino (in Lower California 1683–85) explores the Colorado River from the Gila to the Gulf. The junction of the Gila and Colorado rivers will later demarcate the U.S.-Mexico border, and also the frontier of the entity which I call Imperial.
1709 Completion of the basilica for the Virgin of Guadalupe.
1718–21 Ugarte explores the Gulf to the Colorado's mouth.
1730 Spanish population of Pimería reaches 300.
1737 Upon proclamation of the Viceroy-Archbishop, the Virgin of Guadalupe becomes Patroness of New Spain and stops a plague.
1754 The Virgin of Guadalupe's new status ratified by Pope Benedict XIV.
1768 Jesuits expelled from their 15 missions in Lower California. Junípero Serra and his Franciscans appointed to replace them. Spanish colonization of Upper California begins.
1769 Foundation of San Diego by Gaspar de Portolá.
1770 Foundation of the Presidio of Monterey. Monterey made capital of Alta California.
1771 The Jesuit Father Baegert prints his account of the missions in Lower California.
1771 Fray Francisco Gardés explores the Colorado Desert as far as Signal Mountain.
1774 First expedition of Captain Juan Batista de Anza. Dispatched overland from Sonora (Pimería) to Monterey, California, he passes through the Cahuilla (now Coachella) Valley.
1774 First colonists arrive in San Diego.
1775 Second de Anza expedition explores the Yuha Desert.

1775 Fray Luis Jayme martyred by Yuman Indians at Mission San Diego de Alcalá on the San Diego River.
1776 California separated from New Spain and made a semi-autonomous territory.
1777 Yuman chief Palma baptized in Mexico City and confirmed in Durango, with de Anza as his godfather.
1777 De Anza appointed Governor of New Mexico.
1778 First public execution in what will be Upper California: 4 insurgent Indian chiefs shot by firing squad in San Diego.
1779 Foundation of 2 missions at the junction of the Colorado and Gila rivers: Portezuela de la Concepción (the future site of Fort Yuma), and Puerto de San Diablo about 10 miles southward. (Alternate names: Mission Purísima and Mission San Pedro y San Pablo.)
1779 Palma baptized.
1780 Colonists arrive at the 2 Colorado missions. They treat the Indians badly. Beginning of gold mining in Cargo Muchacho area of Imperial.
1781 The Yuma Massacre: Both missions get wiped out by Indians. Men massacred, women and children taken captive, later ransomed. Spanish reprisals accomplish little. No further attempt to raise missions in this area.
1781 Foundation of Los Angeles.
1785 Governor of the Californias Pedro Fages and Ensign José Velázquez explore Laguna Salada, the Colorado Delta and part of Imperial Valley in search of a land route to Alta California to replace the one through the former Yuma missions. The Cucapahs are hostile.
1791 Spanish-speaking population of Los Angeles is 139.
1796 Acting Governor José Joaquín Arrillaga leads a new expedition through northern Baja, Laguna Salada and the Delta up to the Río Hardy. He winds up in San Diego.
1798 Foundation of Mission San Luis Rey de Francia, 13½ leagues from San Diego.

1800–1850

1800–1900 Water in Salton Sink half a dozen times.
1800 More than 17,000 inhabitants of California.
1800 About 6 million people in Mexico.
1803 U.S. makes Louisiana Purchase from France. Southwestern (Mexican) boundary of this remains vague.
1804 Upper California incorporated as a province called Nueva California.
1810 A Mexican priest raises up the Virgin of Guadalupe's image as an icon of independence from Spain.
1819 Adams-Onis Treaty demarcates the Mexican-American border. Within Mexico: the future California, Nevada, Utah, Arizona, New Mexico, Texas and then some.
1820 Abolition of the Inquisition in Mexico.
1821 Francisco Novella becomes last pre-Independence Mexican head of state (Juan O'Donojú succeeds him but does not serve).
1821 Birth of Cave Johnson Couts.
1821–22 Under Augustín de Iturbide, Mexico declares independence from Spain. September 16 becomes a national holiday.
1821–23 Reign of Iturbide.
1822 California also declares independence from Spain, affirms dependence on Mexico.
1824–30 James O. Pattie travels from Kentucky to California and back again, trapping beavers on the Colorado River and trekking across the desert of Imperial.
1824 Mexican constitution abolishes slavery, affirms preeminence of Catholic Church, grants President emergency dictatorial powers.
1824 Nueva California becomes Alta California.
1826 Kumeyaay Indians kill 3 soldiers and injure 3 others at Fort Pacheco, the only Mexican

fort in Alta California. Location: half a mile west of present city of Imperial, on western bank of the New River.

1827 Los Angeles boasts 82 houses.

1827 U.S. offers Mexico $1 million for Texas.

1828 U.S. offers Mexico $5 million for Texas.

1829 Mexico defeats a Spanish attempt to reconquer the country.

1830 Juan Bandini receives a grant to the 1,600 hectares of Cañada de Tecate, site of the future city.

1831 Treaty of Limits recognizes Mexican sovereignty over Texas.

1831–40 California divided into 5 districts.

1832 Act of Secularization confiscates Franciscan estates in Mexico (not put into rigorous effect until 1846; but weakens power of California missions).

1833–55 Antonio López de Santa Anna in and out of office.

1833 Secularization of missions begins in Upper and Lower California.

1834–35 Richard Henry Dana, Jr., visits Mexican California as a common sailor.

1835 Los Angeles becomes the territorial capital of Alta California.

1835–36 Texas Wars of Independence.

1836 Texas declares itself a sovereign republic.

1836 American Californians raise a one-star flag and revolt against Mexico. They are appeased with lower taxes.

1839–40 William Hartnell serves as Visitador General of the Missions of Alta California.

1840 L. M. Holt born in Michigan.

1841 American immigrants reach Los Angeles.

1841 Eugène Duflot de Mofras visits California. When he returns to France the following year, he publishes a memoir estimating the area at 500,000 square miles and the population at 5,000 excluding Indians (4,000 people of Spanish origin, 90 Mexicans, 900-odd Anglos and Americans).

1842 General John C. Frémont scouts out the Coachella Valley.

1844 In his essay "The Young American," Emerson writes, "The bountiful continent is ours."

1844 U.S. and Texas sign the Texas Annexation Treaty.

1844 Wagon route to California established.

1845 Mexico grants 3,000 square leagues of California, including San Francisco Bay, to an Irish priest.

1845 U.S. formally annexes Texas and offers Mexico $5 million for it.

1845 (?) Captain James Hobbs finds the remains of 17 immigrants who died of thirst not far from the New River.

1846 Lieutenant W. H. Emory writes a report whose purview includes the Colorado River and the Imperial Valley.

1846–47 Mexican War.

1846–47 Donner Party resorts to cannibalism.

1846 American flag raised over San Diego.

1847 Battle of San Gabriel near Los Angeles ends Mexican control of Alta California.

1848 Treaty of Guadalupe Hidalgo cedes half of Mexico to U.S., including much of the area which I call Imperial. U.S. pays Mexico $15 million.

1848 James Marshall finds gold near Sutter's Mill. California Gold Rush begins.

1848 (?) First few Chinese arrive in California, possibly via Peru or on the brig *Eagle*.

1849 Texan ferrymen at Yuma crossing massacred in revenge for their continued and repeated rapes of Indian and Mexican women passengers.

1849 First steamboat ascends Colorado River from Sea of Cortés.

1849 Colonel Cave Johnson Couts, following more or less the same route as Hobbs, finds Imperial tolerably dry. He establishes Camp Salvation (present-day location: Rockwood Plaza in Calexico) as a rest stop for goldseekers. Camp Salvation lasts from September through December.

1849 Draft California constitution ratified in Monterey by popular vote.

1849 Dr. Oliver M. Wozencraft, "Father of the Imperial Valley," arrives in California, visits the Imperial Valley, and sees how fertile it could become given irrigation.

1849–50 6,000–10,000 Mexican miners take the de Anza route to and through Imperial. Altogether, 100,000 "Forty-Niners" are estimated to pass through Imperial.

1850–1900

1850 Population of Mexico is 7.6 million.

1850 California admitted to the Union as the 31st state, with 18 counties, which become 27 that same year. Population is 92,597. Total assessed value of California property is $57,670,689.

1850 Creation of Los Angeles County. The city of Los Angeles incorporates (population: 1,610).

1850 Creation of San Diego County, which comprises nearly all of present-day San Diego, Imperial, Riverside and San Bernardino counties—not to mention all the American territory of the entity I call Imperial.

1850 Foreign Miners' Tax penalizes Mexican miners in California.

ca. 1850 Gold rediscovered, probably by Mexican prospectors, in the Imperial Valley at Tumco and Picacho.

ca. 1850 Fort Yuma esablished.

ca. 1850 Cave Johnson Couts estimates the number of Indians in San Diego County (excluding "desert and Colorado River Indians") as 3,500.

1851 2,719 Chinese arrive in California, coming mostly from Kwantung (Guangdong) Province.

1851 Los Angeles County enlarged.

1851 Mormons found an irrigated colony at Rancho del San Bernardino (abandoned in 1857 due to a confrontation with the U.S. government in Utah).

1852–59 Lifespan of California's Pautah County, which just happens to lie in Utah Territory (present-day Nevada).

1852 Population of Mexico is 7,663,000.

1853 New treaty revises and refines Mexican-American frontier. Junction of Colorado and Gila rivers now claimed as a border point.

1853 The Tennessee lawyer William Walker invades La Paz, hoping to be dictator of Sonora. He proclaims the Republic of Lower California. Introduces black slavery. Captured, returned to U.S., acquitted.

1853 The geologist William Blake explores the Salton Sink and names Lake Cahuilla.

1853 San Bernardino County split off from Los Angeles County, much of which was in turn taken from San Diego County in 1853.

1854 In Los Angeles, the gambler Dave Brown complains about getting lynched by "a lot of *Greasers.*" White men oblige him.

1854 Most Mexican miners now gone from California due to race prejudice.

1854 Captain Christopher S. Lovell writes report on Cahuilla Indians at Rancho Jurupa.

1855 Commencement of Reform period in Mexican government.

1855–72 Benito Juárez is Mexican head of state.

1855 California Foreign Miners' Tax seeks to protect whites against Chinese and Mexicans.

1855 Chinese Passenger Tax penalizes Chinese immigration to California.

1855 William Walker attacks Nicaragua.

1858 Expedition against the Mohave Indians.

1858 California Chinese Exclusion Act.

1858–61 The Butterfield Stage Route carries mail from the east to California by way of the future Imperial County. This is the first real trail through the area.

1859 Oliver Wozencraft gets the rights to the Salton Sink, but fails to get backing to irrigate the Imperial Valley.

1860	Walker and his followers captured and executed in Honduras.
1860	California's population is 379,999 (a 310% increase from 1850).
1860	Pony Express begins operation.
1860	Gold discovered by an Indian at Picacho in the future Imperial County.
1860	German immigrants establish the irrigated colony of Anaheim.
1861	California Swamp and Overflow Act results in many Chinese laborers' building levees in the Sacramento Delta.
1862–64	Bad drought in California destroys many large cattle ranches.
1862?	Wilber Clark born in Iowa.
1862	Act for the Protection of White Labor in California.
1862	Mexican prospectors commence operations at Picacho.
1864–67	Emperor Maximilian von Hapsburg rules Mexico.
1864	W. F. Holt born.
1866	Completion of the Central Pacific Railroad, which promptly recruits Chinese laborers for further construction.
1866?	Birth of Albert Henry Larson.
1869	Completion of the U.S. Transcontinental Railroad.
1870s	Economic depression reaches California. Also the time of "orange fever" in southern California.
1870	California's population is 560,247.
1870	First successful American planting of the navel orange, by William Saunders of the USDA.
1870	Foundation of the city of Riverside. Digging of its first canal.
1870–72	Near present Interstate I-8, 2.3 miles east of western Imperial County border, Mountain Springs Station stone tollhouse (built as a storehouse in 1862) in use by San Diego and Fort Yuma Turnpike Co.
1871	First orange tree planted in Riverside.
1871	In Los Angeles, the "Chinese Massacre" wipes out anywhere from 18 to 72 Chinese (depending on which sources you read) after a Chinese kills a Caucasian who tries to stop a tong killing.
1872	L. M. Holt arrives in Riverside.
1872	Southern Pacific survey crew chooses a railroad line near Indian Wells, which soon will be called Indio.
1874	Death of Cave Johnson Couts.
1874	Population of Los Angeles reaches 11,000.
1874	Guillermo Andrade's syndicate, comprised mostly of Mexicans living in San Francisco, begins operation. They establish Colonia Lerdo in the Mexicali Valley. In short order they will sell out to Thomas Blythe.
ca. 1875	Mrs. L. C. Tibbetts plants the first navel orange in Riverside.
1876–1911	The Porfiriato, or era of Porfirio Díaz.
1876–80	First period in which Porfirio Díaz is Mexican head of state.
1876	116,000 Chinese in California; 151,000 in all U.S., including 6,000 women.
1876	The Southern Pacific Railroad reaches Los Angeles. Service to and from Indio begins. Town of Coachella (then called "Woodspur") founded shortly after.
1877	Old Beach railroad stop established. In 1914 it will become Niland. Southern Pacific line crosses the Colorado River, putting the steamboat to Yuma out of business.
1877	Thomas Blythe irrigates Palo Verde using Colorado River water.
1879	First Citrus Fair in Riverside.
1880	California's population is 864,694.
1882	Chinese Exclusion Act forbids further immigration from China for 10 years and prohibits Chinese already resident in the U.S. from becoming American citizens.
1882	George Chaffey founds the irrigated colony of Etiwanda.

1882	Chaffey founds the irrigated colony of Ontario at Rancho Cucamonga.
1883	The city of Riverside incorporates.
1883	Construction of the Sweetwater Dam to bring water to San Diego and National City. (See entry for 1916.)
1883–84	New Liverpool Salt Co. begins operations in Salton Sink.
1884–1911	Second period in which Porfirio Díaz is Mexican head of state.
1884–1914	Duration of operations at the Tumco Mine in the future Imperial County.
1885–87	Beginning of new land boom and speculation in Los Angeles.
1885	Elizabeth Clark, *née* Schultz, born in Germany.
1885	Foundation of Tecate.
1885	First store in Indio.
1885	Burning of first Chinatown in Riverside.
1885	White settlement begins at Agua Caliente, the future Palm Springs.
1885	George Chaffey founds the irrigated colony of Mildura in Australia. In 1893 stockholders charge him with flawed engineering.
1886	Establishment of second Chinatown in Riverside, outside the business district.
1887	Wozencraft dies.
1887	In California, the Wright Act (California Irrigation District Act) overturns riparian water law to allow the creation of local irrigation districts.
1887	By special permission of the Pope, the Virgin of Guadalupe's image is crowned.
1888	Scott Act adds new restrictions to Chinese immigration.
1889	Creation of Orange County.
1890	California's population is 1,208,130. In southern California, 217,000 acres lie under irrigation, all of it small scale.
1890	Modest New River flood.
ca. 1890	Barrett's Boring Outfit begins seeking oil in the Imperial Valley.
1890s	Growing Chinese population in Ensenada.
1891	Formation of the California Irrigation Company, whose goal is to divert a portion of the Colorado River into the Salton Sink.
1892–1905	California Fruit Growers' Exchange comes into being.
1892	Geary Act keeps the Chinese Exclusion Act in force for 10 years more.
1893–94	Worst depression so far in U.S. history.
1893	The California Irrigation Company goes bankrupt. The company engineer, Charles Robinson Rockwood, founds the California Development Company.
1893	First school and church in Indio (same building).
1893	A dozen new California counties authorized, but only 3 created, including Riverside (whose southern portion comprises some of the territory which I call Imperial). Riverside County is made up of 6,044 square miles of San Diego County and 590 square miles of San Bernardino County. The part which will most often be mentioned in this book is the Coachella Valley, which stretches from the Salton Sea northwestwards for 60 miles.
1894	Miners at Gold Rock (future Tumco) build a 12-mile pipeline from the Colorado River to their sluices.
1895	John Wesley Powell explores the Colorado River, which still "rolls, a mad, turbid stream, into the Gulf of California."
bef. 1898	Farming begins at Mecca.
1898	The California Land and Cattle Company, precursor to the Colorado River Land Company, buys 832,337 acres of the Mexicali Valley from the Mexican government.
1898	Settlement on La Laguna del Alamo, the future site of Mexicali.
1898–99	Cantaloupe price boom in Mecca.

1899	California ranks 14th in U.S. for value of farm produces.
1899	Mexico and China sign the Treaty of Amity, Commerce and Navigation.

1900

1900–1920	Los Angeles population will increase by a factor of 5.
1900–1950	California population will increase by a factor of 10.
1900–1947	Period of relatively high rainfall in Baja California.
1900	California's population is 1,489,053, of which 41.5% is rural. Total assessed value of California property is $1,217,648,863.
1900	Population of Los Angeles is 102,479.
1900	Population of Mexico is 13,606,000.
1900	Per capita U.S. water consumption for agricultural, industrial, personal, and all other uses is 600 gallons per year. (Compare with 1975 figure.)
1900	10 registered voters in Blue Lake (the future Silsbee). White population of Imperial Valley: about 20.
1900	George Chaffey becomes President of the California Development Company and coins the name "Imperial Valley." Establishment of the Imperial Land Company.
1901	Name of town and valley of Cahuilla changed to Coachella ("Cahuilla" + "concha" = small seashells). Officially approved by USGS in 1909.
1901	Name of the Coachella Valley town Kokell (foundation date unrecorded) changed to Thermal.
1901	Imperial (town) founded.
1901	Imperial Valley's first school founded beside Main Canal near Calexico.
1901	Wilber Clark arrives in the Imperial Valley with his father John and his sister Margaret, who becomes the first postmistress.
1901	The town of Coachella gets its first postmaster.

1901	With the completion of the Imperial Canal (later called the Alamo Canal), irrigation begins in the Imperial Valley. **WATER IS HERE**. Farmer-stockholders pay 50¢ per acre-foot. Salton Sink still dry.

1901	Standard Salt Co. begins competing with New Liverpool Salt Co. in Salton Sink.
1902	Brawley founded (initial population: 2 men); Silsbee incorporated.
1902	Birth of the U.S. Reclamation Service (later, the Bureau of Reclamation). The Reclamation Act (17 June) sets a 160-acre homestead limit, or 320 acres for husband and wife.
1902	Birth of the Colorado River Land Company.
1902	First school in Mecca.
1902	Farming begins in Marshall Cove, which will later be called La Quinta.
1902	Imperial Canal completed.
1902	Chinese Exclusion Act made perpetual.
1902	42 Chinese workers set out on foot from San Felipe to Mexicali; 35 die.
bef. 1903	Foundation of Arabia in Coachella Valley (died slowly after cotton gin moved to Thermal in 1920).
1903	Population of Imperial Valley increases from 2,000 to 7,000; 50,000 acres now under cultivation.
1903	John C. Van Dyke publishes *The Desert: Further Studies in Natural Appearances*. At the Colorado's mouth "the red river rushes under, the blue tide rushes over."
1903	Flume over New River.
1903	Mexicali founded.
1903	Incorporation of Holtville (originally Holton).
1903	First Japanese arrive in Coachella Valley.
1904–42	Imperial and Mexicali valleys share Colorado River water through the Alamo Canal.

1904 Pope Pius upgrades the Virgin of Guadalupe's shrine to a basilica.

1904 "Mexican officials decided it was time to establish a customs post on the Mexican side of the boundary line."

1904 Incorporation of Imperial on second attempt.

1904 Harry Lyon, a native of Turkey, arrives in the Imperial Valley with his wife Julia.

1904 USDA establishes an experimental date station near Mecca, using cuttings from Egypt and Arabia.

1904 Arrival of the Colorado River Land Company in the Mexicali Valley.

1904 Since their canals are silting up and since Congress won't grant them any American water rights, the Imperial Valley water companies make a cut in the Colorado River in Mexican territory for the new Imperial Canal. A series of floods widens this cut dangerously.

1905 William E. Smythe publishes his triumphalist revision of *The Conquest of Arid America.*

1905 Rural population of California is 32%.

1905 Population of Los Angeles is 200,000.

1905 Population of the Imperial Valley is 10,000.

1905 Founding of El Centro (originally called Cabarker).

1905 Closing of gold mine at Hedges (Tumco).

1905 Birth of Imperial Hazel Deed.

1905 First airplane lands at Imperial.

1905 Widening of the Mexican cut now catastrophic. Colorado River floods the New River channel. Salton Sea formed.

1905 Salinity of Salton Sea 3,350 parts per million (ppm).

1906–83 A average annual virgin flow of Colorado River at Colorado River Compact point = 15.1 million acre-feet.

1906 San Diego and Arizona Railways incorporated.

1906 Old Beach railroad stop becomes Imperial Junction.

1906 Colorado River now drops 14 feet through Mexican cut. Mexicali washed away by the New River flood. Silsbee abandoned.

1907 Southern Pacific Railroad seals off the Mexican cut.

1907 Imperial County breaks away from (or in some versions is sloughed off of) San Diego County on 15 August. Area: 2,741,760 acres (9th-largest county in the state). El Centro becomes the county seat.

1907 Population of Calexico is 500, of Mexicali, 100.

1907 First school in Thermal.

1907 Los Angeles passes a bond initiative to finance the Owens Valley Aqueduct.

1908 El Centro, Brawley, Holtville and Calexico incorporate.

1909 Estimated population of El Centro is 2,000.

1909 Estimated population of Los Angeles is 352,000.

1909 Total assessed value of property in Imperial County is $71,168,146. Acres irrigated: 181,545. Value of produce excluding cantaloupes: $53,000.

1909 Southern Pacific Railroad asks to be reimbursed $1,633,136.40 by U.S. government for closing the Colorado River break.

1909 Flow of Colorado River at Yuma is 26 million acre-feet. (See entry for 1934.)

1909 First gambling house opens in Mexicali.

1910

1910–20 Imperial County is the third-fastest-growing county in the U.S.

1910 Almost 20,000 people in the Imperial Valley. (Later California Board of Equalization estimate: 13,591, or 0.57% of California total.)

1910 California is 95% white.
1910 Incorporation of Westmorland.
1910 Henry Stroven of Holtville taps the first artesian well in the Imperial Valley.
1910 The Virgin of Guadalupe proclaimed Patroness of all Latin America.
1910 Population of Mexico is 15,160,000.
1911–13 Francisco I. Madero is President of Mexico.
1911 Harold Bell Wright, ensconced at Rancho El Tecolote (present site: Country Club Drive between Barbara Worth and Calexico roads), publishes *The Winning of Barbara Worth.*
1911 Formation of the Imperial Irrigation District (IID).
1911 Founding of Seeley on the west side of the New River. Seeley approximates the now-defunct Silsbee.
1911 Mexican Revolution begins.
1911 Border post near Calexico razed by arson.
1911 Mexican and American adventurers try to launch a "revolution" in Mexicali; suppressed by Colonel Esteban Cantú.
1911 Overthrow of Ching Dynasty creates unrest in China and furthers desire of Chinese to immigrate to the U.S.A.
1911 A fire at the Triangle Shirtwaist Factory in New York kills 146 and galvanizes the labor movement.
1912 Maier Brewing Company opens first legal liquor joint in Imperial County.
1912 Cotton introduced in Imperial and Mexicali valleys.
1912 First known discovery of concretions in Imperial, on north side of Signal Mountain.
1913–14 Victoriano Huerta is interim President of Mexico, following a brief stint by Pedro Lascuráin.
1913 Completion of the first Los Angeles Aqueduct, which runs 233 miles from the Owens Valley.
1913 Water enters the East High Line Canal.
1913 Arrival in El Centro of Leo Hetzel, better known as "Hetzel the Photographer." His photographs are probably the best single visual record of Imperial during the first half of the twentieth century.
1913 According to Eduardo Auyón Gerardo, Mexicali now has 1,000 Chinese inhabitants, who grow 13,560 hectares of cotton.
1914 Opening of the Panama Canal.
1914 Francisco S. Carbajal is interim President of Mexico.
1914, 1915–20 Venustiano Carranza is President of Mexico.
1914 Fearing the continued revolution in Mexico, Calexico forms home guard volunteers. District Attorney Phil Swing requests that the Imperial Valley be declared neutral in case of a war between the U.S. and Mexico.
1914 Earthquake in the Imperial and Mexicali valleys.
1914 Imperial Junction becomes Niland (which as of this writing remains unincorporated). Founding of Calipatria.
1914 San Diego County sends Imperial County some lumber to begin the famous Plank Road in the eastern sandhills. The Plank Road remains the main thoroughfare to Yuma until 1927; used sporadically after that.
1915–20 Colonel Esteban Cantú is Governor of the District of Baja California
1915 Barbara Worth Hotel opens in El Centro.
1915 Coachella Valley Stormwater District established.
1915 Commencement of the famous plank road across the sandhills of southern Imperial County.
1915 California outlaws horseracing and prostitution. Guess what moves to Mexico?
1915 Harry Chandler is indicted for allegedly seeking to change the government of Baja California. He gets acquitted.

1915 Mexicali becomes the capital of Baja California Norte.
1916 The Sweetwater Dam collapses.
1916 Whitewater River flood cuts a gorge through Coachella Valley. Mecca, Thermal, Coachella underwater; Indio flooded.
1916 Imperial Irrigation District buys the assets of the bankrupt California Development Company for $3 million.
1917 California outlaws pro boxing and dance halls. Guess what moves to Mexico?
1917 Tecate becomes a municipality.
1918 Coachella Valley County Water District established.
1919 Los Angeles begins pumping groundwater from the Owens Valley.
1919 Riverside County's boundaries get written into the California political code.
1919 Completion of railroad between El Centro and San Diego.
1919 Incorporation of Calipatria ("California" + "fatherland").
1919 United States restricts Chinese immigration.
1919 Confederation of Mexicali's 28-odd Chinese organizations into the Asociación China de Mexicali.
1919 According to Eduardo Auyón Gerardo, Mexicali has 11,000 Chinese, 1,500 Mexicans, 500 Japanese and 200 Indians. The Chinese raise cotton on 29,752 out of the 37,190 available hectares in the Mexicali Valley.
1919 Assassination of Emiliano Zapata.
1919 Volstead Act prohibits liquor in the U.S. Guess what moves to Mexico? Eugene Dahm, Imperial Valley farmer: "They had some real nice nightclubs until, oh, about, 1955."

1920

1920 Adolfo de la Huerta is interim President of Mexico.
1920 Population of Los Angeles is 575,480, of which there are 33,644 Chicanos.
1920 Population of Imperial County is 43,453, or 0.127% of California total. Total assessed property value is $40,350,450; population is 55,000.
1920 Imperial Hazel Deed (named simply Hazel Deed on her death certificate) dies in Fresno County, aged 14, of appendicitis.
1920 C. Luis M. Salazar is Governor of the District of Baja California for 5 weeks; succeeded by Engineer Manuel Valarezo.
1920 According to Eduardo Auyón Gerardo, 50,000 hectares are now under cultivation in the Mexicali Valley.
1921 C. Epigmenio Ibarra becomes Governor of the District of Baja California.
1921 Inauguration of Indio Date Festival
1921 A time bomb fails to destroy the Virgin of Guadalupe's image.
1921 Mexico bans importation of unskilled Chinese labor.
1922 Lic. Jose Inocencio Lugo becomes Governor of the District of Baja California.
1922 Imperial County becomes America's number-one lettuce producer.
1922 Imperial Irrigation District finally takes over the valley's remaining mutual water companies, which had been bankrupted by the Salton Sea accident.
1922 Colorado River Compact divides the river's waters between 4 upper-basin and 3 lower-basin states, with 7.5 million acre-feet to each basin, and provision for lower basin to get 1 million acre-feet more. (Virgin flow of entire river: approximately 15 million acre-feet.)
1922–29 Bert Vaughn, resident of Jacumba, builds the Desert View Tower.
1923–30 General Abelardo I. Rodríguez is Governor of the District of Baja California.
1923 Final delineation of Imperial County's borders, resulting in slightly more territory. Boundaries of Los Angeles, San Diego and Riverside counties also fixed. Riverside County is 7,240 square miles.
1923 Population of Cahuilla Indians is approximately 750.
1923 First major fire destroys most of Mexicali's Chinesca.

1923 William Mulholland and associates raft down the Colorado River seeking sites for the All-American Canal.

1923 Upton Sinclair arrested in San Pedro, California, for reading aloud from the Bill of Rights.

1924 U.S. Border Patrol established.

1924 Johnson-Reed Immigration Act restricts the entry of Mexicans into the U.S.A.

1924 End of the real estate boom in southern California.

1924 Death of "John Doe unknown Mexican," aged about 38, of heatstroke on Southern Pacific Railroad track 1 mile north of Imperial city. Local registered death number 28.

1924 Death of Mónica Gordins, aged 3 months, father unknown, mother Mexican, of heat prostration, in Imperial city. Local registered death number 29.

1924 Owens Valley ranchers dyanamite Los Angeles Aqueduct near Alabama Gate, causing minor damage.

1925 Pueblo in Los Angeles said to contain largest Mexican population outside of Mexico City. All the same, strong anti-Mexican feeling is noted in L.A. for the rest of the decade.

1925 *Puente Blanco* (New Town Bridge) connects Mexicali to Colonia Pueblo Nuevo. Municipal theater and library constructed.

1925 The Ku Klux Klan opens shop in Riverside; in the thirties they threaten George Wong in Chinatown and he chases them off with a shotgun.

Late 1920s Gradual demise of Riverside's Chinatown.

1926 First lots sold in Cathedral City.

1926 Levee breach causes no damage to the Imperial Valley and mild damage to Mexicali.

1926 Death of Albert Henry Larson, farmer, 7 miles northwest of Imperial city. Death certificate reads: "Suicide by shooting and slashing wrist with a razor."

1927 Owens Valley farmers plant more bombs in Los Angeles Aqueduct; Los Angeles instigates a state audit which finds Owens Valley banks guilty of fraud. Los Angeles then wins the "water war."

1927 Formation of Metropolitan Water District (MWD), which in 2003 comprises 27 agencies, including Los Angeles and San Diego.

1927 Birth of César Chávez, near Yuma.

1928 Collapse of the Saint Francis Dam built by William Mulholland for Los Angeles. About 500 deaths result.

1928 A California constitutional amendment finally allows appropriative to dominate over riparian water rights.

1928 Swing-Johnson bill to fund the All-American Canal passes.

1928 Imperial Valley workers form La Unión de Trabajadores del Valle Imperial. When their demand for an increase in cantaloupe pickers' wages is denied, wildcat strikes begin but are crushed.

1929 California Limitation Act grants the state a ceiling of 4.4 million acre-feet of Colorado River Water plus up to half of any remaining unclaimed surplus water.

1929 "The waters of Salton Sea are almost as salty as the ocean."

1929 Great Depression begins.

1930

1930s "Twenty-five percent of California's land was owned by only 2 percent of its farmers . . ."

1930s W. T. Ratcliffe carves stone animals in rock garden around the Desert View Tower.

1930 Population of Imperial County is 60,903, or 1.07% of California total. (Imperial Valley Directory estimate: "About 50,000 . . . Local est. 65,000.") Total assessed value of tangible property peaks at $6,257,231. It will decline until 1939. (Directory assessment of assessed value in 1929: $55,718,654.)

1930	Chicano population of Los Angeles is 97,116.
1930	Los Angeles begins Mono County extension of its 1913 first aqueduct.
1930	Indio incorporates.
1930	Imperial Valley growers reduce wages for fruit and vegetable pickers, resulting in more strikes. The local union acts timidly, driving the laborers into the arms of the Communist-controlled Agricultural Workers Industrial League, which will later be called the Cannery and Agricultural Workers Industrial Union.
1930	Mass meeting of AWIL in El Centro broken up by farmers and law enforcement. Over 100 arrests; 8 Communist leaders given prison sentences, although all will be paroled by 1933.
1931–34	13,332 Mexicans from Los Angeles County and 3,492 from San Bernardino County forcibly repatriated.
1931–52	The District of Baja California becomes the Northern Territory of Baja California.
1931	California passes "County of Origin" law to prevent one place from taking another place's water, *à la* Owens Valley.
1931	The flow of the Colorado River begins to be "smoothed out."
1931	18,142 illegal aliens of various races deported.
1931	Marshall Cove renamed La Quinta.
1931	Leonard Knight born in Vermont.
1932	Death of George Chaffey.
1933	Prohibition repealed.
1933	President Roosevelt instigates the Subsistence Homestead Program, saying that he would like "to put 25,000 families on farms at an average cost of $1,000 per family."
1933	Massive cotton strike in San Joaquin Valley. Mexicans killed near Arvin and Pixley. Nonunion laborers brought up from the Imperial Valley.
1934–40	Lázaro Cárdenas is President of Mexico. He redistributes more land than any of his predecessors.
1934	5,000 lettuce workers in the Imperial Valley participate in a strike led by the Cannery and Agricultural Workers Industrial Union. The strike fails.
1934	The ACLU lawyer A. L. Wirin, visiting the Imperial Valley in connection with the labor unrest, is kidnapped by anti-union men, robbed, left to walk 11 miles barefoot across the desert.
1934	Imperial Valley growers join their colleagues in other parts of California to create the anti-union Associated Farmers of America, led by E. Raymond Cato.
1934	Construction of the All-American Canal begins.
1934	Flow of Colorado River at Yuma is 4 million acre-feet.
1934	Rancho Mirage Community Association established.
1935	Completion of Hoover Dam.
1935	3 government camps for California migrants built. There will be 13 camps in the state by 1941.
1935	Los Angeles forms a Committee on Indigent Alien Transients and sends police to turn back anyone without jobs or money. After 2 months this practice is prohibited by California's Attorney General.
1936–37	Colorado River Land Company forced to sell out to Mexican government.
1936–38	More than 200,000 Okies arrive in California.
1936	Sonora-Baja Railroad enacted by decree number 1276.
1936	Using violent methods, the Associated Farmers of America break a lettuce strike in Salinas.
1937	Using nonviolent but perhaps intimidating methods, campesinos in Mexicali and Nayarit expropriate large ranches.
1937	Formation of the Colorado River Board of California.
1938	Palm Springs incorporates.
1938	Imperial Dam constructed (capacity: 85,000 acre-feet).
1938	Parker Dam constructed (capacity: 648,000 acre-feet).

1939	Flood in Coachella Valley.
1939	Aggregate income for "civilian residents" of Imperial County is $28,624.
1939	Cárdenas visits Mexicali.

1940

1940	Population of Imperial County is 59,740 (0.86% of California figure). 9,335 people (45% of the county's workforce) engage in agriculture. Total civilian income is $30,043,000.
1940	Mexican Revolution enters a consolidation period. Manuel Ávila Camacho becomes President.
1940	Completion of first section of the All-American Canal's Coachella branch.
1941	Pumping for the Los Angeles Aqueduct (see 1913) drains four of Mono Lake's tributary creeks completely dry.
1941	First water enters the MWD's Colorado River Aqueduct.
1942	The All-American Canal commences operation. Retirement of the old Alamo Canal through Mexico.
1942	Mexican Imperial is now irrigating ¼ million acres.
1942	Roosevelt signs Executive Order 9066, which authorizes the detention of Japanese Americans. Imperial and Coachella valleys affected.
1942 (?)	Opening of General George Patton's Desert Training Center in eastern Coachella valley. The concrete slabs laid down near Niland will become Slab City.
1942–47	Bracero Program admits 200,000 Mexican field workers to U.S.
1943	Repeal of Chinese Exclusion Act. (See entries for 1882, 1892, 1902.)
1943	Mexico protests high U.S. consumption of Colorado River water.
1944	Closing of Desert Training Center in Coachella Valley.
1944	Imperial County becomes California's number-one county for carbon dioxide production.
1944	Mexican-American Water Treaty grants Mexico 1.5 million acre-feet per year of Colorado River water.
1944	Formation of the San Diego County Water Authority.
1944	Death of Harry Chandler.
1945	California State Water Resources Board established.
1945	Enactment of the Riverside County Flood Control and Water Conservation District.
1945	The city center of Mexicali now counts 134 Chinese businesses.
1945 or '46	Second major fire destroys much of Mexicali's Chinesca.
1948	Imperial County contains 696 farms, 1,700 businesses, and 50,000–60,000 residents.
1946	Aggregate income for "civilian residents" of Imperial County is $92,172,000 (more than triple the 1939 figure).
1946	City of Coachella incorporates.
1946	The San Diego County Water Authority joins the Metropolitan Water District.
1946	Bones of Cortés discovered in a secret niche of Hospital de Jesús, Mexico City.
1947–52	Lic. Alfonso García González is Governor of Baja California.
1947–78	Low rainfall in Baja California.
1947	First San Diego Aqueduct connects to MWD's Colorado River Aqueduct.
1947	Carrot Festival launched in Holtville.
1947	Date Festival in Indio begins selecting a Date Queen and Date Princess.
1947	Imperial County's total bank deposits at year's end are $25,514,74.
1948	Imperial County's land is assessed at $24 million. 70% of its 2.7 million acres is taxable, but only ½ million acres are "productive."
1948	Population of Brawley is 13,000. Population of El Centro is 13,500.
1948	First water through Coachella Branch of the All-American Canal, which is completed in 1949.

1949	Population of Imperial County is 51,400 (preliminary figure), or 0.50% of California's total.
1949	Death of "Hetzel the Photographer."

1950

1950	Population of Mexicali is 64,660.
1950	Population of Imperial County is 62,513. Total civilian income is $122,555,000. Cultivated, urban or industrial land is 507,000 acres. Desert or barren land is 2,222,000 acres. The Salton Sea, says the *California Blue Book* for that year, is "destined to disappear."
1950	Regarding San Diego, "no part of the country maintains so high a claim for the amiable and sociable qualities of the fairer portion of its inhabitants."
1950	California is now the second most populous state in the U.S. More than 10% of U.S. cash income from agriculture earned by California farmers.
1950	Salinity of Salton Sea 3,800 ppm.
1951–64	Bracero Program reactivated to admit 4.5 million Mexican field workers to U.S.
1951	W. F. Holt dies.
1952	The Northern Territory of Baja California becomes the Estado Libre y Soberano de Baja California.
1952	Initiation of the *Arizona v. California* lawsuit over Colorado River water.
1954	Operation Wetback (General Joseph May Swing in command) deports 1 million illegal aliens.
1950	Population of Mexicali is 80,000.
1954–86	Claude Finnell is Agriculture Commissioner in Imperial County.
1955	Church on Reforma in Mexicali consecrated.
1958–64	Adolfo López Mateos is President of Mexico.
1958	Population of Imperial County has increased by 7,800 since 1950, a 12% increase, but only a quarter the average rate for southern California as a whole.
1958	U.S. Supreme Court unanimously upholds the 1902 160-acre limitation in its famous *Ivanhoe* decision.
1959	César Chávez organizes in Oxnard against the granting of California field work to lower paid braceros in place of Mexican-Americans.

1960

1960	Second San Diego aqueduct.
1960	Salinity of Salton Sea 3,550 ppm.
1960	Population of Mexicali is 174,544. The municipality as a whole also contains 106,793 rural people.
1961	The Colorado River is now so heavily utilized that it peters out in the desert before reaching the Gulf of California.
1961	Arizona's Wellton-Mohawk Irrigation and Drainage District raises the salinity level of the Colorado River to a point where Mexican crops show signs of poisoning; Mexican farmers protest.
1962	Arson destroys the Barbara Worth Hotel in El Centro.
1962	César Chávez resigns from the Community Service Organization and begins to build his own movement.
1963	Population of the Imperial Valley is about 80,000.
1963	Desert Hot Springs incorporates.
1963	Supreme Court decision in *Arizona v. California* reduces California's share of Colorado River water.
1964–70	Los Angeles constructs a second aqueduct in the Owens Valley.
1964–70	Gustavo Díaz Ordaz is President of Mexico.
1965	Population of Calexico is 10,000.

1965 Discriminatory measures against Chinese immigration finally rescinded completely. (See entries for 1882, 1892, 1902, 1943.)
1965 César Chávez organizes a grape pickers' strike in Delano, California.
1966 Pope Paul VI gives the Virgin of Guadalupe's shrine a golden rose.
1966 Death of Colonel Cantú.
1967 In San Diego, Leonard Knight accepts Jesus as his savior.
1967 Indian Wells incorporates to prevent absorption by Palm Desert.
1968 A hundred-day leftwing strike in Mexico City ends in massacre: 400 activists killed by the army at Tlatelolco.
1968 César Chávez calls for a boycott of table grapes.
1968 César Chávez's United Farm Workers strike in the Coachella Valley.
1969 Los Angeles completes a "second barrel" of the Owens Valley Aqueduct.
1969 César Chávez leads a nine-day march from Indio to Calexico.

1970

1970–76 Luis Echeverría Álvarez is President of Mexico.
1970 Salinity of Salton Sea 3,870 ppm.
1971–75 Lic. Milton Castellanos Everardo is Governor of Baja California.
1973 U.S. agrees to desalinize the outflow of Wellton-Mohawk.
1973 Completion of California Aqueduct.
1973 Palm Desert and Rancho Mirage incorporate.
1974 Salinity of Salton Sea reaches 39,000 ppm.
1974 Congress passes the Colorado River Basin Salinity Act, which requires salinity levels in the lower basin not to exceed those of 1972.
1975 Per capita U.S. water consumption for agricultural, industrial, personal and all other uses reaches 1,800 gallons per year. (Compare with 1900 figure.)
1975 Los Angeles uses 600,000 acre-feet of water, mostly from the Owens Valley, for a population of 3 million.
1975 "The Colorado River . . . today supplies water to half the state's population . . ."
1975 Mexican Imperial and the Imperial Irrigation District now irrigating half a million acres each.
1975 Agricultural Labor Relations Act goes into effect (28 August). United Farm Workers launch certification drive across American Imperial; César Chávez leads a 59-day, thousand-mile march north from Calexico. Many strikes in Imperial and Coachella valleys for the next several years.
1976–82 José López Portillo is President of Mexico.
1976 The Virgin of Guadalupe's image transferred to a new circular temple.
1977 "Nearly three-fourths of the 675,000 acres receiving irrigation water from the Colorado in California . . . lay within the Imperial district, where crops and livestock that year were valued at more than half a billion dollars."
1978–85+ Another interval of relatively plentiful rain in Baja California.
1978 United Farm Workers' strikes begin to win union contracts for field labor in the Imperial Valley.

1980

1980–86 In Nebraska, Leonard Knight attempts to build a hot air balloon to lead people to Jesus.
1980 1,024,000 illegal aliens enter California from Mexico (about half the U.S. total for that year).
1980 Per capita income of Mexicali is about 1½ times the national average, and slightly higher than Ensenada's and Tijuana's.
1980 75% of southern California's water comes from the Colorado River.

1981 Philip L. Fradkin publishes *A River No More*. At the Gulf of California, he says, the presence of the Colorado "depends on when the toilet is being flushed."

1981 Cathedral City incorporates.

1982–88 Miguel de la Madrid is President of Mexico.

1982 La Quinta incorporates.

1983 The U.S. informs Mexico that seepage from the All-American Canal is American property.

1985 Baja California urban population reaches 1,350,000.

1985 Disastrous earthquake in Mexico City.

1986 Leonard Knight begins painting Salvation Mountain.

1986 The television show "Sixty Minutes" calls the New River the most polluted river in the world.

1986 The U.S. Immigration Reform and Control Act punishes employers of illegal workers and amnesties some permanent residents.

1988–94 Carlos Salinas de Gortari is President of Mexico.

1989 Salvation Mountain collapses because sand was used in the adobe. Leonard starts over.

1989 Earnings sent from illegal workers to Mexico now at $1.25 billion a year.

1989 ⅓ of California population subject to water rationing, due to the drought of 1987. By 1991, that figure will rise to ¾. Due to senior water rights, Imperial County, the Coachella Valley, the Yuma Indian reservation and Blythe are lagely unaffected.

1990

1990 After heavy rains Salvation Mountain collapses; Leonard promptly begins redoing the work.

1990 Imperial County's gross agricultural income surpasses $1 billion for the first time.

1991 or '92 Third major fire destroys most of Mexicali's Chinesca.

1992 North American Free Trade Agreement (NAFTA) creates a common market consisting of Canada, the U.S. and Mexico.

1992 President Salinas privatizes the *ejidos*.

1992 Mexico replaces Japan as the second-largest importer of U.S. manufactures.

1993 Death of César Chávez.

1994–2000 Ernesto Zedillo is President of Mexico.

1994 Operation Gatekeeper begins.

1994 NAFTA comes into effect.

1994 Imperial County and the state of California attempt to bulldoze Salvation Mountain, calling it a "toxic nightmare." Independent testing finds no poisons; Salvation Mountain is saved.

1994 The Tijuana *maquiladora* Metales y Derivados gets shut down by the Mexican government. An arrest warrant is issued for its owner, José Kahn, who has illegally abandoned six thousand metric tons of lead slag. Kahn escapes to San Diego, where he dies a free man.

1999 7.5 million tilapia in a single day die in the Salton Sea.

2000

2000–2006 Vicente Fox ends PRI stranglehold and becomes President of Mexico.

2000 Rural population of California is 5.5%.

2000 Population of Imperial County is more than 142,000.

2000 "Significant salinization is damaging about 35 percent of the irrigated land in California and nearly 70 percent of that in the lower Colorado River basin."

2000 Deaths of *pollos* along the entire Mexico-U.S. border set a record of 383.

2001	Salinity of Salton Sea 46,000 ppm.
2002	Imperial Irrigation District farmers pay $15.50 per acre-foot of water (31 times the 1901 figure). San Diego wants to buy it at $250 per acre-foot.
2002	Senator Barbara Boxer proclaims Salvation Mountain a national treasure.
2003	The Mexicali *maquiladora* Flor de Baja produces the largest taco in the world. Then it shuts down. At this juncture the workers are allegedly locked together in the cold room until they sign away many of their rights.
2005	Deaths of *pollos* along the entire Mexico-U.S. border set a new record of 460, "mostly Mexicans," and 261 of them "while crossing the Arizona deserts."
2006	Los Angeles agrees to release 9,000 acre-feet of water back into the Owens River.
2008	A prototype of the new "virtual border" fails to guard Northside from Southside.

SOURCES

To save space, citations are given here in abbreviated form. Full references appear in the bibliography. Sources for illustrations appear on pages 1301–2.

General epigraph: "As long as a farmer has an abundance of water . . ."—USDA Yearbook (1909), p. 202 (Carl S. Scofield, Bureau of Plant Industry, "The Problems of an Irrigation Farmer").

Brief Glossary

Literal meaning of the term "campesino"—Boyer, p. 19.
Probable first use by Catholics of same—Ibid., p. 163.

PART ONE
INTRODUCTIONS

1. The Gardens of Paradise (1999)

Imperial County: Lowest median tax income in the state—*Imperial Valley Press*, Thursday, July 6, 1999, p. A4. (Note: At the beginning of the twentieth century this publication was known first as the *Imperial Press and Farmer*, then as the *Imperial Press*.)

"The goal is to create a system that can alert authorities . . ."—*Sacramento Bee Final*, April 23, 1999, p. A4 ("Capitol/State" section, "Canal wired to deter immigrants").

Deaths of illegal aliens [on the California-Mexico border]: 254 in 1998—*Calexico Chronicle*, Wednesday, July 7, 1999, p. 6.

"Our Opinion" section: "As important as agriculture is to the county . . ."—*Imperial Valley Press*, Thursday, July 6, 1999, p. A4.

"NOTICE OF TRUSTEE'S SALE . . ."—*Indio Post*, Thursday, July 1, 1999.

Tom Wacker: "We are trying to identify . . ."—*Calexico Chronicle*, cover, July 8, 1999.

Calexico Chronicle's version of the tale of the burned Dodge van—Thursday, July 1, 1999, p. 7. The incident referred to occurred on June 24.

"Imperial Catechism" of 1903: "What kind of labor can be had for ranch work?"—*Imperial Press and Farmer*, vol. II, no. 44 (Saturday, February 14, 1903), p. 1.

My hometown newspaper: "At least 168 people have died . . ."—*Sacramento Bee Final*, April 20, 1999, p. B6 ("Opinion" section, "Gatekeeper's toll: Illegal immigrants die in risky border crossings").

Calexico Chronicle: "Border Patrol Unveils Public Service Announcements . . ."—Thursday, July 1, 1999, p. 7. The incident referred to occurred on June 24.

2. Delineations (2000)

Epigraph: "Our eyes scan only a small angle . . ."—Ansel Adams, p. 67.

"A step over the ditch, and I was in Mexican territory . . ."—*Imperial Press and Farmer*, vol. II, no. 32 (Saturday, November 22, 1902), p. 4 ("A Chatty Letter," repr. from the *Santa Ana Herald*).

Hay prices and yields not long after 1907—*USDA Yearbook* (1909), pp. 499–500, 1908–9 figures. The national average yield per acre of hay was 1.42 bushes. The California and Arizona figures were 1.70 and 3.30 bushels, respectively. The *Yearbook* notes (p. 11) that hay was America's fourth-most-valuable crop, but "considerably below wheat" and "far below cotton." Corn was the premier crop. Nine decades later, when I was visiting Imperial, hay was easily the most conspicuous of these four moneymakers. An EPA scientist whom I interviewed in 2001 told me that alfalfa was by a wide margin the most water-wasteful of Imperial's crops, and that it would probably be necessary to put many of the old-style inefficient family hay farms out of business.

Footnote: "The presence of a boundary. . ."—*Bol'shaia Sovetskaia Entsiklopediia*, vol. 13, p. 324 (entry on the finite).

Footnote: The prevalence of the name "Imperial" in the entity I call Imperial—Description after an ICHSPM photograph, uncatalogued as of 1999.

Footnote: Extract from the Treaty of Guadalupe Hidalgo—Castillo, p. 187 (Appendix 2, text of treaty, Article V).

"Our Dutchman insisted that the plain over which we passed . . ."—Pattie, p. 207.

Old newspapers: "A section of Arid America."—*Imperial Press and Farmer*, vol. II, no. 38 (Imperial, California, Saturday, January 3, 1903), p. 3 ("To Make the Desert Blossom with the Homes of Men").

"A northwestern extension of the basin in which the Gulf of California lies"—Oakeshott, p. 10.

One-armed Major Powell: "Coahuila Valley, the most desolate region on the continent."—John Wesley Powell, p. 3.

My floral guide to Baja California: "Vast agricultural areas of the Mexicali Valley . . ."—Roberts, p. 33. "Tamarisk" was capitalized in the original.

"There appears to be a widespread impression . . ."—Ibid., 1909, p. 201 (Scofield).

Phrases from *Barbara Worth* dust jacket—Wright.

"Often as Barbara sat looking over that great basin . . ."—Ibid., p. 62; also, caption to frontispiece.

"The pioneers in Barbara's Desert . . ."—Ibid., p. 335.

Statistics of the 1910 census—*Thirteenth Census of the United States, Taken in the Year 1910*, vol. 2, pp. 139, 143, 166. In 1910 the population of California was 2,377,549, and the population of Imperial County was 13,591.

The Kentucky boy who finds "much to my surprize and disappointment, not one white person among them" in New Mexico—Pattie, p. 59.

"Prominent among the wide-awake and progressive businessmen of Brawley . . ."—Farr, p. 436 (biography of Walter P. Casey).

"The wholesome, challenging lure of an unmarred womanhood" and "warmly browned"—Wright, p. 57.

"The sea there is vermilion in color . . ."—Gómara, p. 403.

3. *The Water of Life (2001)*

Death of 7.5 million African perch (tilapia) on one August day in 1999—*Environmental News Service* website: accessed June 2001.

The Salton Sea as "one of the best and liveliest fishing areas on the West Coast"—Laflin, *Salton Sea: California's Overlooked Treasure*, p. 52.

"Stories of a polluted Salton Sea are greatly exaggerated . . ."—Ibid., p. 57.

"Believing the largely negative articles . . ."—Ibid., p. 60.

"A wonderful sense of what is right . . ."—Loc. cit. The 1910 description of Howe and Hall (p. 175) is also quite bucolic.

The Salton Sea as "a stinking reddish-brown sump . . ."—Dawson and Brechin, p. 167.

Length of the Alamo River (52 miles)—Kreissman, p. 46 ("Rivers and Streams").

The New River as "the filthiest stream in the nation . . ."—Dawson and Brechin, loc. cit. According to another writer, "the state of California and county officials in the Imperial Valley label the New River, which arises in the United States" [it doesn't] "and then flows through the sprawling city of Mexicali . . . 'the dirtiest river in America'" (Ruiz, p. 198).

That confederation of counties and water districts called the Salton Sea Authority—The Authority is, according to its own leaflet, "a joint powers agency formed in 1993 by the Coachella Valley Water District, the Imperial Irrigation District, Riverside County and Imperial County."

"Myth #5" and all succeeding quotations in this paragraph are from a leaflet entitled "Myths and Realities," sent to me by the Salton Sea Authority in 2001.

Blue Lake of the New River: "Bordered with mesquit trees, which hang gracefully over its banks . . ."—*Imperial Press and Farmer*, vol. I, no. 1 (Saturday, April 20, 1901), p. 4 ("To Indian Wells via Blue Lake"). Blue Lake was 8 miles from Imperial and 2 miles from Indian Wells.

Length of the New River (60 miles)—Kreissman, p. 46 ("Rivers and Streams").

Mr. L. M. Holt: "Unmistakeable evidences of water having flowed" from the Colorado River "through innumerable channels . . . "—*Imperial Press and Farmer*, vol. II, no. 38 (Imperial, California, Saturday, January 3, 1903), p. 3 ("To Make the Desert Blossom with the Homes of Men").

In fact, we find the name in Bartlett's old narrative of 1850–53.—Excerpted in *Wonders of the Colorado Desert*, p. 62.

Footnote: "From Fort Yuma, we started again . . ."—Hobbs, pp. 217–18.

Chart of disease rates per 100,000: Environmental Protection Agency website: "Status Report on the Water and Wastewater Infrastructure Project for the U.S.-Mexico Borderlands," accessed June 2001. The North American Development Bank, the Border Cooperation Commission, the U.S. Environmental Protection Agency and various other such entities were helping to lead Mexico into a bright new day with a wastewater-treatment facility, a pumping plant, and God knows what else. Nobody I talked to seemed to have much idea about any of it.

Footnote: Dr. F. W. Peterson on typhoid—Farr, p. 218 (F. W. Peterson, "Medical History").

The effluvium of eight hundred thousand people—This was the most common population estimate I heard while in Mexicali, and it was endorsed by *La Opinión*. An American source says: "The present population of Mexicali is reported as 438,377, but some believe it is much greater—approaching 1 million" (California Regional Water Control Board District 7 website, http://www.swrcb.ca.gov.rwqcb7/newriver/nr-intro.html, accessed June 2001).

Footnote: California Environmental Protection Agency report—California Environmental Protection Agency Regional Water Quality Control Board, Colorado River Basin Region, executive officer's report, January 2001, p. 1 (Phil Gruenberg, "Meeting with Mayor Hermosillo"). Outcome: "The Mayor also indicated he would support a monitoring program of the underground storm drains, but that concurrence would have to be obtained again—from federal authorities." This seems reasonable enough.

Cerro Prieto: "Thrown up by the mirage into the form of a battleship showing plainly the masts and turrets," etc.—Tout, *The First Thirty Years*, pp. 60–61 ("Reminiscences of Imperial's Early Days, by Mrs. W. A. Edgar").

Geological description of the area around Cerro Prieto, and the route to it—Based in part on Lindsay and Hample, p. 34.

Map: "Northern Part of the Colorado River Delta in Lower California, Compiled by California Development Company, W.H. Holabird, Receiver."—California State Archives file no. 192 (map case #1, hole #47), cat. 192: C2803-C2127-1, Box 1 (undated, 2'9" x 4'9").

Footnote: "A 1910 American history of the Imperial Valley": Volcano Lake as the source of the Río Nuevo—Howe and Hall, p. 74.

Scientist from the Environmental Protection Agency: "That's domestic sewage foam . . ."—My informant was Eugenia McNaughton, environmental scientist for the U.S. EPA, Water Division, Region 9, San Francisco office. She happened to be, among other things, a member of the New River Task Force. Her day-to-day work frequently involved her with what she referred to as "lower Colorado River Delta issues." She called the New River "a very solvable problem. The water, murky and chocolaty though it might be, is domestic wastewater."

Flow of the New River at the border (200 cubic feet per second)—Regional Water Quality Control Board, Basin Planning Program, New River/Mexicali Project, introduction, p. 1 of 2 (website http://www.swrcb.ca.gov.rwqcb7/archive/programs/basinplanning/newriver/-hsnr_intro.html, accessed June 2001). According to *The California Water Atlas* (p. 3), the New River's average annual inflow at the border was 45,415 acre-feet in 1975.

Regional Water Quality Control Board: "The pollutants of major concern . . ."—California Environmental Protection Agency Regional Water Quality Control Board, Colorado River Basin Region, June 10, 1999, executive officer's report (Jose Angel, "Request for Information by U.S. Senator Dianne Feinstein"); at the web address http://www.swrcb.ca.gov.rwqcb7/documents/eo_reports/eo-99-06.10.html, accessed June 2001 (henceforth CEPA, June 10, 1999).

Ninety-five percent of California's wetlands were already gone—*San Jose Mercury News*, Friday, January 14, 2000, Dara Akiko Williams, AP ("Plan to save Salton Sea: Reducing salinity of the dying lake a priority, official at conference says").

The sea's ecoystem was doomed unless nine million tons of salt could be removed every year.—Ibid.

Précis of "The Problems of an Irrigation Farmer"—*USDA Yearbook* (1909), esp. pp. 203–5 (Scofield).

Sabine Huynen, Salton Sea Database Project, University of Redlands—Phone interview, October 2001.

The "Audubon Society fellow" and his claim of "nine million pounds of pesticides a year on Imperial Valley fields."—Mr. Fred Cagle, telephone interview with author, 2001.

Thoreau: "No face which we can give to a matter . . ."—Henry D. Thoreau, *The Illustrated Walden*, p. 327.

The United States Congressional General Accounting Office "finds that sewage from Mexico poses a health risk to public health"—CEPA, June 10, 1999.

Selenium health advisory (not more than 4 ounces of Salton Sea fish-meat per 2 weeks)—SDSU website, accessed June 2001. Advisory isued by California's Health Advisory Board.

One journalist's magnificent words: "A vast salt and selenium bed of dust . . ."—*Western Outdoors*, February 2001, p. 50 (Bill Karr, "Secrets of the Salton Sea"). Like Fred Cagle, Eugenia McNaughton of the EPA thought that this might be exaggerated. But she allowed: "There is speculation about what will happen as the shoreline is exposed."

California Blue Book for 1950: "The county is drained by the Whitewater River . . ."—P. 935.

Percentage of Salton Sea inflow not from Mexico (90%)—SDSU website, accessed June 2001.

Area of the Salton Sea (352 square miles)—Kreissman, p. 52 ("Lakes and Reservoirs").

"Pursuant to Section 303(d) of the U.S. Clean Water Act . . ."—CRWQCB-CRBR 11-12-99 EO's Report, p. 5 of 9 ("Statutory Requirements"); from the website http://www.swrcb.ca.gov/rwqcb7/documents/eo_reports/eo-99-11-12.html. As of January 2000, California was the proud possessor of 509 bodies of water labeled "impaired," meaning too degraded for recreation (*San Diego Union-Tribune*, Friday, January 14, 2000, Terry Rodgers, "Group plans solution to pollution 509 contaminated water sites prompt statewide suit," which is one of the most incomprehensible headlines I've ever read). In February 2000, the Salton Sea watershed was listed as a Category I (Impaired) Priority.

4. *Subdelineations: Lovescapes (2001)*

Epigraph: ". . . an intelligent species . . ."—Midgley, p. 121.

Descartes: " There is nothing in all that I formerly believed . . ."—*Descartes–Spinoza,* p. 76 (*Meditations of the First Philosophy*, trans. Elizabeth S. Haldane and G. R. T. Ross, Meditation I).

Footnote: "Such simple 'sand maps' . . ."—Heizer and Elsasser, pp. 8–9.

5. *The Widemouthed Pipe (2002)*

Epigraph: "We attribute motives . . ."—Laing, p. 27.

Thoreau: "I should not talk so much about myself . . ."—Thoreau, *A Week on the Concord and Merrimack Rivers,* etc., p. 325 *(Walden).*

6. *Then and Now (1844–2002)*

Epigraph: 'Standing today by the grave of that infant civilization . . ."—Farr, p. iii.

Mr. V. Gant: "My experience this season . . ."—*Imperial Press and Farmer*, vol. II, no. 38 (Imperial, California, Saturday, January 3, 1903), p. 6 ("To Make the Desert Blossom . . .").

A. W. Patten: "The weather is not uncomfortable . . ."—Ibid., vol. II, no. 15 (Saturday, July 26, 1902), p. 1 ("Big Imperial Crops").

The Imperial Valley's per capita electricity consumption—Gottlieb and FitzSimmons, p. 72.

"Some of the finest specimens will be presented to the Chamber of Commerce."—*Imperial Press and Farmer*, vol. II, no. 42 (Saturday, January 31, 1903), p. 8 ("Imperial Iron Wood $500 a Cord").

Footnote: "A man who was there . . . : 'Calexico, which derives its name from a combination of California and Mexico . . .' "—Farr, p. 126 (narrative of C. R. Rockwood, 1909).

J. B. Hoffman "invented the open air jail . . ."—Tout, *The First Thirty Years*, p. 79.

William E. Smythe: "Potash, lime, magnesia . . ." and "On the other hand, these elements have been accumulating . . ."—Op. cit., pp. 37–38.

" . . . it took the Government a half century to wake up . . ."—*Imperial Press and Farmer*, vol. II, no. 38, p. 3 ("To Make the Desert Blossom with the Homes of Men").

"Throughout this history the almost pitiful dependence of the settlers on outside capital will be noted."—Howe and Hall, p. 33 ("Enter Capital").

"WATER IS HERE," etc.—*Imperial Press and Farmer*, vol. I, no. 10 (Saturday, June 22, 1901), front page.

"THE DESERT DISAPPEARS"—Ibid., vol. I, no. 11 (Saturday, June 29, 1901)), front page.

Emerson in "The Young American": "The bountiful continent is ours," and other excerpts—Op. cit., pp. 213–17.

A successful candidate for Senator: "There are so many things to be done . . ."—*The Annals of America*, vol. 12, p. 202 (Albert J. Beveridge, "The Taste of Empire," from his campaign speech of 16 September 1898. Source: *Modern Eloquence*, vol. IX).

The birth of Imperial Hazel Deed—Tout, *The First Thirty Years*, p. 178.

"Niland's Future": "Give Salton Sea a new name . . ."—Ibid., p. 410 (John D. Reavis, "Niland's Future").

Smythe: "Irrigation . . . is a religious rite . . ."—Op. cit., p. 330.

Smythe: "All this lay beyond the reach of the individual . . ."—Ibid., p. 31.

"The natural antagonism of any people living under a large water system"—Farr, p. 129 (narrative of C. R. Rockwood, 1909).

Smythe: "The essence of the industrial life . . ."—Op. cit., p. 43.

Smythe: "TWO YEARS AND FOUR MONTHS PRIOR . . ."—Ibid., p. 31.

Figure on California's rural population in 1860—*The California Water Atlas*, p. 28. This number fell to 41½% in 1900 and 32% a decade later, which is to say five years after Smythe's caption was published.—*The Britannica Year-Book 1913*, p. 774 (entry on California).

Figure on California's rural population in 2000—U.S. Census Bureau, Detailed Tables, p. 5. ("Urban and Rural [7]—Universe—Total Population"), data set: Census 2000 Summary File 3 (SF 3)—Sample Data. In this table, the total population given for California was 33,871,648. The urban population (now subdivided, you'll be happy to know, into the inhabitants of urbanized areas and of urban clusters) was 31,994,895. The rural population (subdivided in turn into farming and nonfarming bipeds) was 1,876,753. I divided the rural population into the urban and multiplied by 100%. (Website accessed 6 September 2002.)

Footnote: Figure on Imperial County's rural population in 2000—same source (henceforth referred to as U.S. Census Bureau, Detailed Tables, p.5), different search parameters. The urban population is given as 121,303, and the rural population as 21,058.

"The great cities of the western valleys . . ."—Smythe, p. 46.

A hundred dollars an acre from Brawley cantaloupes in 1905—Tout, *The First Thirty Years*, p. 178.

"Nearly 3000 carloads of this delicious table dessert . . ."—Farr, p. 17.

The cantaloupe season of 1926 and its accompanying refrigerator cars—*Imperial Valley Press*, Monday, May 3, p. 1.

Two hundred thousand metric tons of cantaloupes from Mexico—*Imperial Valley Press*, Thursday, May 30, 2002, pp. 1, 6 (Laura Mitchell, "U.S. cantaloupe growers want Mexico to clean up act").

My interview with the old pioneer from Heber took place in June 2002.

"This marvelous Valley where the land valuations have increased . . ."—Farr, p. 17.

The death of Rogelio Contreras-Navarette—*Imperial Valley Press*, Thursday, May 30, 2002, p. A2 (Mario Rentería, "Man's body found west of Calexico").

"The city's No. 1 priority is that as growth occurs . . ."—*Imperial Valley Press*, Friday, May 24, 2002, p. A1 (Rudy Yniguez, "El Centro: Meeting growing city's needs is No. 1 priority").

Information on Wilber Clark—Farr, pp. 464–65.

The most lucrative crop as I write this book is winter lettuce.—This is according to Gottlieb and FitzSimmons, p. 72.

Average annual precipitation at Brawley—Hundley, p. 14 (map, "Mean Annual Precipitation"). "The northwest corner of our state" goes south from the Oregon border for 50-odd miles. It is about 20 miles wide, and its western boundary is 10 miles from the Pacific. The average annual precipitation at Gasquet Ranger Station, which lies within this zone, is 94.32 inches.

"In no section of Arid America . . ."—*Imperial Press and Farmer*, vol. II, no. 38 (Saturday, January 3, 1903), p. 3 ("To Make the Desert Blossom with the Homes of Men").

E. J. Swayne: "It is simply needless to question the supply of water."—Ibid., vol. I, no. 2 (Saturday, April 27, 1901), p. 1 ("New River Country: What Is Actually Being Done on the Desert").

Cost of water per inch and acre-foot in Imperial and in Riverside—Ibid., vol. II, no. 38 (Saturday, January 3, 1903), p. 4 ("To Make the Desert Blossom . . .").

Article on "Water Wasting"—Ibid., vol. II, no. 20 (Saturday, August 30, 1902), p. 2.

Footnote: "Feds get involved in state water issues . . ."—Ibid. (now called the *Imperial Valley Press*), vol. 103, no. 29, Thursday, June 12, 2003, p. C1 (by Seth Hettena, Associated Press staff writer).

The promoter who had his display cases and tables filled with oranges . . .—Farr, p. 102 (narrative of C. R. Rockwood, 1909).

Hypothetical Colorado River ferry at Algodones, 1915—N.A.R.A.L. Record Group 36. Records of the U.S. Customs Service. Calexico Customs Office. Incoming Official Correspondence (91-60). October 15, 1902–March 23, 1916. Box 4 of 5: July 1914–June 1915. Bound volume labeled "Letters." Copy of report of W. J. Smith, Deputy Collector and Inspector of Andrade, Cal., in re situation at Algodones, on or bef. February 4, 1915; pp. 1–2.

Judge Farr: "It is therefore apparent that the water supply in this vast area is inexhaustible."—Op. cit., p. 17.

"An Angeleno": "The water problem seems to be solved for all time."—Carr, p. 217.

"Smoothing out" of the Colorado River in 1931—Colorado River Board of California (1962), p. 8. How much did the flow vary before the smoothing? Here are some calculations from *Out West*, vol. XXIV, no. 1, January 1906, pp. 12, 20–21 (Edwin Duryea, Jr., C.E., "The Salton Sea Menace"): Our civil engineer gives the total flow of the Colorado River in February 1905 as 30,000 cubic feet per second (cfps) and, on June 5, as twice that. Generally speaking, he considered the Colorado's minimum flow to be 3,000 cfps, the maxium, 100,000 cfps, and the average, 15,000 cfps.

President Herbert Hoover, on Mexicans' rights to the Colorado: "We do not believe they ever had any rights."—Fradkin, p. 299.

Total area irrigated in 1942 by Mexican farmers—Colorado River Board of California (1962), p. 17. The more exact figure was 260,000 acres.

Area in Mexico and the Imperial Valley irrigated by the Colorado in 1975: about half a million acres each—Fradkin, p. 296.

"With our magnificent water system . . ."—*Imperial Press and Farmer*, vol. II, no. 38 (Saturday, January 3, 1903), p. 7 ("Imperial and Alfalfa").

Jokes—Ibid., vol. II, no. 17 (Saturday, August 9, 1902), p. 6; also vol. II, no. 28 (Saturday, October 27, 1902), p. 8 (which includes the news, which I have footnoted in the text, on Negroes and the baseball craze).

"No desert is a fit place for an idle or dissolute man."—Howe and Hall, p. 108.

Salinity of the Salton Sea in 1905 and 1950—Gottlieb and FitzSimmons, p. 78.

Mr. Otis B. Tout: "It is a surprise to many people today . . ."—*The First Thirty Years*, p. 21 ("Lake Cahuilla—Salton Sea").

Salinity of the Salton Sea in 1974 (39,000 mg/l)—Fradkin, p. 297.

Salinity of the Salton Sea in 2001 (46 g/kg = 46,000 ppm, if I've done the math right; that's almost 14 times more than the 1905 figure of 3,350 ppm)—I am using my own data, gathered when I was writing "The Water of Life."

"The Forum finds no reason to recommend changes in the numeric salinity criteria . . ."—Colorado River Basin Salinity Control Forum, unnumbered.

"The waters of the Colorado river carry a very large amount of commercial fertilizers . . ."—*Imperial Press and*

Farmer, vol. I, no. 1 (Saturday, April 20, 1901), p. 1 ("A Few Facts About a Great Agricultural Enterprise—A Year's Record").

Table: "Salt content of Colorado River water at the California-Mexico border"—Figures for Imperial Dam 1951–60 and for both dams 1961–62 come from the Colorado River Board of California (1962), p. 21. Figure for 1966 comes from Morton, p. 8, who states in his preface (p. vi) that the effective date of his data is 1966. His figure is for the Colorado "at Yuma." Figures for 1974 are taken from Fradkin, p. 297, who doesn't attribute them. Figure for Imperial Dam in 1984 is derived from the Colorado River Basin Salinity Control Forum. It is expressed in milligrams per liter. Figures from Francisco Raúl Venegas Cardoso come from Munguía, p. 7. Figures from Saillé et al. are from the same, p. 77.

"The nights are always cool . . ."—Farr, pp. 23–24.

San Luis Río Colorado: "A colorless town with a growing number of *maquiladoras*."—Ruiz, p. 41.

1910 *Britannica* entry on the Colorado: 11th ed., vol. 6, pp. 725ff.

Table: "Flow of the Colorado River at Yuma"—Figures for 1909 and 1934 are from Mary Montgomery, p. 27. Figure on virgin flow is from *The California Water Atlas* (1979), p. 38.

The de Anza Expedition on the Colorado—Font, pp. 33 (30 November 1775), 123 (12 May 1776).

Footnote: Pattie on the Colorado—Op. cit., p. 120.

Governor Arrillaga on the Colorado—Op. cit., p. 76 (19 October 1796).

Colonel Cave Johnson Couts on the Colorado—Op. cit., p. 74.

A man who'd worked for the Bureau of Reclamation from 1948 to 1950—This was Mr. Herb Cilch, interviewed in San Diego in June 2003.

Frank Waters on the Colorado—Waters, pp. 109–116; p. x.

Footnote: Distances from Mexicali to El Mayor and La Bamba—Gerhard and Gulick, p. 68.

Ever since 1961, "not one drop."—Per Colorado River Board of California (1982): "Since 1961, except for minor amounts of uncontrolled flow near the border, essentially no water has flowed toward the Gulf of California."

James O. Pattie, 1827: "We continued to float slowly downwards . . ."—Op. cit., p. 182.

Van Dyke: "After the river crosses the border-line of Mexico . . ."—Op. cit., pp. 72, 74.

John Wesley Powell, 1895: "A million cascade brooks unite . . ."—Op. cit., p. 8.

Philip L. Fradkin, 1981: "To follow the river from Morelos Dam to the gulf . . ."—Op. cit., p. 321. This author points out (p. 322) that the Colorado currently has four ends: the Salton Sea; Laguna Salada, which has always been dry when I've seen it; the Santa Clara Slough, which receives Wellton-Mohawk's brine; and the place in the desert where the river peters out, about fourteen miles north of the Gulf.

"Where two years ago not a living sprig could be found, ripe Thompson's seedless grapes are now being gathered and shipped to Los Angeles."—*Imperial Press and Farmer*, vol. I, no. 4 (Saturday, May 11, 1901), p. 4 ("Desert Redeemed: The New York Times Commends the Great Enterprise").

Mrs. Leroy Holt: The mailbag at Fifteen Mile Tree, the dust storms, "Why did we stay?"—Howe and Hall, pp. 47–49.

"A half-tone portrait of Miss Reed . . ."—*Imperial Press and Farmer*, vol. II, no. 16 (Saturday, August 2, 1902), p. 1 ("An Imperial Baby").

Population of Imperial Valley in 1905—*Out West*, vol. XXIV, no. 1, January 1906.

Population of Imperial Valley in 1910—Howe and Hall, p. 60. California is still 73.2% native white and 21.8% foreign-born white in this decade, in which the population of California as a whole will increase by 60.1%. In San Diego and Imperial counties, growth will be 114.5%; in Los Angeles County, 196%.—*The Britannica Year-Book 1913*, p. 774 (entry on California).

Figure on Imperial County's total population in 2000 (142,361): U.S. Census Bureau, Detailed Tables, p.5

"And in material advantages they are already well supplied."—*Imperial Press and Farmer*, vol. II, no. 1 (Saturday, April 19, 1902), p. 2 ("Believes in Imperial's Prospects: Development in Every Line of That Wonderful New District").

The engineer who was bringing the water to Imperial: "We started out then, about the first of March 1902 . . ."—Farr, p. 125 (narrative of C. R. Rockwood, 1909).

Population of the Imperial Valley in 1904 (7,000)—Tout, *The First Thirty Years*, p. 172 (files of *Imperial Press*).

Mr. Grunsky: The Salton Sea will be gone in twelve to fifteen years "if there were no resupply."—Southern Pacific Imperial Valley Claim (1909), p. 74.

Description of the lobby paintings at the Barbara Worth Hotel, 1915—Tout, *The First Thirty Years*, p. 199, quoting his own article in the *El Centro Progress* for 1914 (evidently the paintings were done a year before the hotel opened).

R. S. Smith of Silsbee wins first prize for his apricots—Ibid., p. 194.

Mr. John Baker: "Paved, well lighted streets . . ."—Farr, p. 274 (John Baker, "Holtville").

A photograph's caption: "W. F. Holt Looks into the Future . . ."—Howe and Hall, p. 114.

W. F. Holt: "I can't help believing in people . . ."—Ibid., p. 117.

Mr. John Baker: "One of the local men . . ."—Farr., p. 275.
Joseph Estudillo "often entertained crowds by shooting dimes tossed in the air"—Tout, *The First Thirty Years*, p. 78.
"A Ten Dollar Bill on the End of a Greased Pole . . ."—Ibid., p. 275. This same game was observed in Mexican California (San Diego) in 1828. See Street, *Beasts of the Field*, p. 21.

7. *The Other Side of the Ditch (1519–2005)*

Epigraph: "No two people will agree . . ."—*Fodor's Mexico, 1992*, p. xv.
"The informal labor sector . . ."—Ruiz, p. 94.
Tale of the Mexican undercover police assaulted and burned alive—*Los Angeles Times*, Valley Edition, Thursday, November 24, 2004, p. A1 (Richard Boudreaux, "Only TV Caught Mob Brutalizing Mexican Police"). This episode occurred in Mexico City.
Incident with the pimp and the two whores—I saw this in December 2006.
Steinbeck: "It is said so often in such ignorance . . ."—*The Log from the* Sea of Cortez, p. 830.
"The very first place of business. . ."—Tout, *The First Thirty Years*, p. 273.
Appearance of the first gaming-houses in Mexicali, 1909—Information in Auyón Gerardo, pp. 41ff. (Terrie Petree's working translation.)
H. M. House: "The Collector states that a town is to be started at Algodones . . ."—N.A.R.A.L. Record Group 36. Records of the U.S. Customs Service. Calexico Customs Office. Incoming Official Correspondence (91-60). October 15, 1902–March 23, 1916. Box No. 3 of 5: November 1913–July 1914. Box 4 of 5: July 1914–June 1915. Letter from H. M. House, Supt. River Division, to J. C. Allsion, Chief Engineer, Calexico, Calif., dated Andrade, Calif., January 14, 1915. COPY.
"I greatly deplore this effort to start a town . . ."—N.A.R.A.L., loc. cit. Letter from W. H. Holabird, Office of the Receiver, the California Development Company, to the United States Collector of Customs, Los Angeles, Calif., January 21, 1915. COPY.
W. J. Smith: "I understand a Mr. Ingraham of Yuma . . ."—N.A.R.A.L., loc. cit. Copy of report of W. J. Smith, Deputy Collector and Inspector of Andrade, California, in re situation at Algodones, on or before February 4, 1915.
Imperial County Board of Supervisors (1920): "Calexico is one of the liveliest cities of its size . . ."—UC Davis, Special Collections, California Local History Collection. Bitler pamphlet, "The Imperial Valley California 1920," p. 28.
"Mexicali's cabarets and bars catered to farmers . . ."—Ruiz, p. 48. In one of his crime stories, written in 1924, Dashiell Hammett itemizes "the crowd that the first Saturday of the racing season across the border had drawn. Movie folk from Los Angeles, farmers from the Imperial Valley" and others complete the list (Hammett, p. 240; "The Golden Horseshoe").
"Two Mexicans in a tent on the Mexican side . . ."—N.A.R.A.L. Record Group 36. Records of the U.S. Customs Service. Port of Campo. General Correspondence 1919–65. Box 1 of 1. Folder: "Historical Letters 1919–1965 [½]." Letter from the Deputy Collector in Charge, Tecate, California, to Collector of Customs, Los Angeles, California, June 15, 1925.
The tale of Dawn Marie Wilson—*Sacramento Bee*, Saturday, December 11, 2004, pp. A1, A18 (Marjie Lundstrom, "Embracing Freedom: San Diego woman learns about Mexican drug law the hard way").
The elderly Coachella Valley resident: "John used to go down to Yuma to a gun show . . ."—Margaret Tyler, born in 1916; interviewed in Palm Desert, 2004.
"Thousands of automobiles cross the line . . ."—Tout, *The First Thirty Years*, p. 365.
"Desirable tracts of from 100 to 100,000 acres."—Advertisement in *Out West*, vol. XXIV, no. 1, January 1906, unnumbered page.
The accident on Interstate 8 and Border Patrol Agent Raleigh Leonard's reaction—*New York Times*, Wednesday, June 26, 2002, p. A14 (Barbara Whitaker, "Mexican Border Crash Kills 6 As Van Hits Oncoming Traffic").
Northside view of Tonantzin: "A statue of this grim goddess . . ." and ". . . projects a visage of fathomless grief . . ."—Johnston, p. 13.
"She Who Tramples the Serpents"—In 1895, Professor D. Mariano Jacabo Rojas, chairman of the Department of Nahuatl at the National Museum, concluded that "Guadalupe" was probably the Nahuatl word "Coatlaxopeuh," with the meaning I have given, "and which again was the equivalent of the Immaculate Conception" (Johnston, p. 47).
"Another name for the Virgin Tonantzin is Coatlalopeuh . . ."—Rothacker, unnumbered p. 13.
Father Florencia: ". . . how they must correct their dress . . ."—Johnston, p. 52.
A migrant worker's child: "Guadalupe predates Christianity . . ."—Hart, p. 202.
"The Virgin of Guadalupe is a figure through which the indigenous people fought back against their colonizers . . ."—Rothacker, unnumbered p. 7.
Observances of the de Anza Expedition relevant to the Virgin of Guadalupe—Font, p. 11 (29 September 1775).

"We carry LA VIRGEN DE LA GUADALUPE, because she is ours."—César Chávez, p. 13 ("The Plan of Delano," March 17, 1966).

Reliance on the Virgin of Guadalupe to conceive children, cure a fright—Hart, pp. 52, 80–81 (re: mid-twentieth century). I have heard the same in my own interviews.

"As a special pleader for sinners . . ."—Pike, p. 77.

The dancer at the Thirteen Negro—Emily, interviewed in September 2005; interpreted by Terrie Petree.

Imperial Valley White Sheet: "GRACIAS VIRGEN de Guadalupe por escuchar oraciones M.P."—Vol. 46, Week 7, Week of February 12–18, 2004; p. 7.

"A poor ordinary man . . ."—León-Portilla and Shorris, p. 338 ("Nican Mopohua," pub. 1645).

Interview with the old woman in Tecate who used to dream about the Virgin—Interviewed in 2003. Terrie Petree interpreted. This person (Josefina Cruz Bermúdez) was one of the two ladies in the 8" x 10" negative MX-TC-WOM-03-01. Zulema Rashid, a 58-year-old Calexico native of Mexican-Lebanese extraction, insisted: "The Virgin of Guadalupe is not that popular here in the north. Our Lady of Guadalupe, no, they didn't talk too much about the Virgin at my Catholic school. My mother, her patron saint is the Sacred Heart of Jesus. She even has a shrine for Him in the house." But Zulema was sheltered and rich.

"A very grand gentleman"—Quoted in Lanyon, p. 60.

It has been asserted that there was no assassination plot.—Ibid., pp. 100–101.

Capsule biography of Doña Marina—Díaz, pp. 82–86. ("God had been very gracious . . ." is taken from p. 86.)

Definition of a *malinchista*—Lanyon, pp. 6–7 (quoting her Mexican informant).

"Do come here . . . Is Quauhtemoc still such a child?"—León-Portilla and Shorris, p. 281 ("The Fall of Tenochitlán, 1518").

"Mexico's problem with Malinche . . ."—Lanyon, pp. 218–19.

" . . .The Spaniards took things from people by force . . ."—León-Portilla and Shorris, p. 285 ("The Fall of Tenochitlán").

"They placed a canopy of varicolored cloth over the Marqués . . ."—León-Portilla and Shorris, ibid., p. 308.

"But when the Captain and Marina saw it they became angry . . ."—León-Portilla and Shorris, ibid., p. 285.

"The White Woman, the great lady."—Ibid., p. 383 (Doña Luz Jiménez stories).

Syncretic capture of the Los Angeles Rangers—Bell, p. 30.

Footnote: "A migrant child of the 1950s" . . . : " 'the dark-skinned daughter in a Mexican family . . .' "—Hart, p. 64.

Footnote: Cortés's marriages and liaisons—Gómara, pp. 408–9.

"The elementary problem of our times: Frightened human beings . . ."—*USA Today*, Wednesday, November 17, 2004, p. 11A, "The Forum" section (Ralph Peters, "Nothing Islamic about human sacrifice: Terrorists in the Middle East are resurrecting a blood cult").

Torturing of Cuauhtémoc by the lieutenants of Cortés, "who could not prevent their actions"—Díaz, p. 410.

8. *Sign of Slow Growth Sends Stocks Lower (2002)*

Epigraph: "Specialization is passing from the consideration . . ."—Polya, p. 190.

Newspaper: "The deaths are full of suffering . . ."—*New York Times*, Tuesday, August 6, 2002, pp. A1, A12 (Evelyn Nieves, "Illegal Immigrant Death Rate Rises Sharply in Barren Areas").

A guidebook: "Mexicali's sights are few and far between . . ."—*Fodor's Mexico, 1992*, p. 159.

Another guidebook: "Mexicali lies at sea level . . ."—John Noble, Dan Spitzer and Scott Wayne, p. 897.

9. *Water Is Here (1849–2002)*

Epigraph: "Possibly there was more rainfall in those days than now . . ."—Van Dyke, p. 48.

Extract from Captain Hobbs's journal—Op. cit., pp. 217–18.

Number of grapefruit and orange trees in Imperial County in 1945—California State Board of Equalization (1949), p. 20.

10. *Preface (2002–2003)*

Epigraph: "The concept of metadata . . ."—*Salton Sea Atlas*, p. 4.

Victor V. Vesey: "They opted for independence and local control."—Vesey, oral history, p. 46.

11. *Subdelineations: Bookscapes (1850–2003)*

Epigraph: "Perhaps you think I will tell you everything . . ."—Schwartz, p. 7 ("The Spider and the Fly").

"The part of 1850 San Diego County . . . no ranchos and no town," and "There are no 1850 Sites to Visit in Imperial County."—Marschner, p. 33 ("Area Within Present-Day Imperial County").

1909 cabbage and grape yields for the Imperial Valley—Tout, *The First Thirty Years*, p. 191 (from the County Assessor's records).

"To look at Barbara Worth was a pleasure . . ."—Wright, p. 57.

Footnote: Tale of "M. B. Davis, commonly known as Bob"—*Imperial Press*, vol. II, no. 51 (Saturday, April 11, 1903), p. 2 ("The Law Triumphant: Liquor Sellers Have a Day of Reckoning in Court").

An agronomist: "Sugar beets grew admirably . . ."—*Imperial Press and Farmer*, vol. II, no. 38 (Saturday, January 3, 1903), p. 10 (letter from Professor A. J. Cook, "Farmers' Institutes in the Desert").

"The dark-faced old plainsman . . ."—Wright, p. 207.

"As she passed, the people turned to follow her . . ."—Ibid., p. 56.

"So good to look at"—Ibid., p. 57.

"She passed into the hotel . . ."—Ibid., p. 95.

"Over the years . . . the flow of the river gradually lessened . . ."—Colorado River Board of California (1962), p. 8.

Steinbeck: "We have a book to write . . ."—Steinbeck, *The Grapes of Wrath and Other Writings*, p. 751 (*The Log from the* Sea of Cortez, orig. pub. 1941; the expedition took place in 1940).

"Silent and hot and fierce in its desolation . . ."—Wright, p. 72.

"Asked to Lead Evil Life, Girl Kills Sister."—Headline in the *Fresno Morning Republican*, Sunday, March 21, 1920, p. 2A.

Portrait of Mrs. Bradshaw, contestant for lead, Barbara Worth film—ICHSPM photograph, cat. P94.10.1.

Otis B. Tout: "Folks, no matter if the river eats up the entire towns of Alexico and Exical . . ."—*Silt*, p. 17.

"Suddenly, as a beast checked in its spring . . ."—Wright, p. 308.

Flaubert: "For half a century the women of Pont-l'Évêque . . ."—Flaubert, p. 17.

Footnote: "The Mexican prepared the horses as Texas had instructed . . ."—Wright, p. 303.

Flaubert: "And as she breathed her last . . ."—Flaubert, p. 56.

Footnote: "Ramona herself is lifeless . . ."—Jackson, p. xv (introduction by Michael Dorris).

Their take-home pay is only one-fifth of hers—According to Ruiz (p. 89), "Most *maquiladora* workers, theoretically, earn the federally mandated minimum of $2.50 a day; but to illustrate what this means, in the electronic *maquiladoras* of Tijuana, take-home pay is less than one-fifth that in the United States." Take-home pay in Mexicali would be the same or less. María gets paid under the table, which means that she gets no minimum wage but also pays no taxes, so one-fifth seems like a fair ballpark estimate.

"Six hundred and thirty thousand of them, 'primarily young women . . . a 29 percent decline in real wages . . .'"—Ibid., p. 62. The statistic in quotation marks is credited to "David Montgomery, a noted economic historian."

"Few hire pregnant women . . . 'bloody tampons for three consecutive months.'"—Ibid., p. 77.

The doctor whose poor patients "seem different—perhaps more lonely . . ."—Robert Coles, *Still Hungry in America*, with photographs by Al Clayton (New York: New American Library/A Plume Book, 1969), p. 106.

Human beings are "preciously unique and different . . ."—Ibid., p. 55.

Francisco de Ulloa: "The game was not worth the candle."—Gómara, p. 403.

Steinbeck, "The Vigilante": "Nigger fiend," "Somebody said he even confessed," "By God, she was right . . ."—Steinbeck, *The Long Valley*, pp. 134, 139.

Steinbeck: "When we get down to business . . . ," "The worse it is, the more effect it'll have."—Steinbeck, *In Dubious Battle*, pp. 261, 89.

Steinbeck's un-American distrust of authority—We might say that Faulkner and Hemingway were not exactly mainstream either, the former spinning out honeysuckled tales of incest, miscegenation and doom, the latter getting involved with Spanish Loyalists (Communists to you, bub); but in both of those writers, the lonely narcissism which characterizes us Americans ultimately obscures social statement. Steinbeck, on the other hand, had specific political things to say.

Steinbeck: "Let us see the fields . . ."—*The Grapes of Wrath &c*, pp. 994 ("The Harvest Gypsies," ch. 1).

Relative rankings of Imperial County "in regard to various unpleasant things"—California county health status profiles (2001), selected tables as indicated.

"The Harvest Gypsies": "Families who had lived for many years. . ."—*The Grapes of Wrath &c*, p. 1025.

12. The Gardens of Paradise (2007)

Epigraph: "Motivations, even if ideological . . ."—Hassig, p. 263.

PART TWO

OUTLINES

13. When Bread Was Light (1768–1848)

Epigraph: "For years they had wandered alone . . ."—Grey, p. 11.

Here and in subsequent chapters, remarks on the distribution of cacti are based on Benson, pp. 84 et seq.

Mr. Samuel T. Black: Op. cit., vol. 1, p. 1.

Acreage of the Mexicali Valley—This was surprisingly hard to come by. Yolanda Sánchez Ogás told me that "the Mexicali Valley contains almost four hundred thousand hectares" (June 2003), so I converted this approximation to acres and hoped for the best: 1 hectare = 2.47 acres.

Lieutenant W. H. Emory (1846): The Imperial Valley "is chiefly covered with floating sand . . ."—Quoted in Howe and Hall, p. 16.

California: "Somewhere on the way from Mexico to India" and "vaguely fixed by such bounds as Asia . . ."—Bancroft, vol. XVIII, p. iii.

Father Baegert on the Baja: "It was altogether one of the most miserable countries in the world . . ."—Quoted in Samuel T. Black, vol. 1, p. 15.

The Indian metaphors: Baegert, quoted in Black, vol. 1, p. 22.

General Sherman on the Baja: "A miserable, wretched, dried-up peninsula."—Sherman, p. 62.

The 1564 map which depicts "the Colorado, largest river in the world . . ."—California Blue Book (1909), p. 717.

"Their duties were to act as body guards . . ."—Baegert, quoted in Black, vol. 1, p. 22.

Footnote: Cruelties to Indians in Baja—Bull, p. 53.

Anecdote by Acting Governor José Joaquín de Arrillaga—Op. cit., p. 31 (26 July).

"When they gave us the holy gospel . . ."—León-Portilla and Shorris, p. 358 (letter of the Cabildo of Huejozingo to the King [of Spain], 1560).

A visitor to Alta California in 1826: "If any of the captured Indians show a repugnance to conversion . . ."—Elliott, *History of Tulare County*, p. 27. The visitor was Captain Beechey, on whose eponymous island in the Canadian Arctic several men of the Franklin Expedition are buried; he is a minor character in my novel *The Rifles*.

Footnote: Dana's observations on California Indians—Op. cit., p. 215.

A California county history . . . "The dress was, for the males . . ."—Loc. cit. These details of the Indian missions were repeated more or less verbatim in the other Elliott county histories I have seen.

Footnote: Fray Junípero Serra's worries about sending letters to Mexico—de Anza, p. 23 (General Archive of the Nation, Internal Provinces 237, Sonora No. 12, Serra to de Anza, 17 April 1776, f.43v).

"Girls reached puberty at the age of twelve . . ."—Baegert, quoted in Black, vol. 1, p. 28.

Palma as the "Capitán and Chief of the Yuma Nation . . ."—de Anza, p. 181 (Archive of the Metropolitan Cathedral of Mexico City, Book of Baptisms of Castes).

Crops of the Yumas—Heizer and Whipple, p. 248 (Pedro Font, "The Colorado Yumans in 1775").

So an American trapper will report half a century later.—The trapper was Pattie, p. 120.

"After mass a proclamation was made . . ."—Font, p. 17 (entry for 29 October 1775).

De Anza enters Imperial: It would be tempting to imagine him to have believed that he had now passed out of Mexico. De Anza to Bucareli, 9 February 1774: "Now that the Colorado River has been joined by the Gila, it very well manifests itself to be the largest river between Mexico and this place . . ." (Bowman and Heizer, p. 111). Of course "Mexico" was merely Mexico City, and the place we call Mexico was New Spain to him.

The New River's shallow canyon (3 feet deep in 1904), not to mention its peppergrass and desert heliotrope—*Journal of San Diego History*, vol. XXI, no. 1 (winter 1976), pp. 35–36 ("The Imperial Valley in 1904: An Account by Hugo de Vries," ed. Peter W. van der Pas).

"It is a miserable place . . ."—Font, p. 35 (9 December 1775).

Homeward route—Ibid., p. 117 (8 May 1776).

Doings and losses of Sebastián Tarabal—Street, *Beasts of the Field*, pp. 17–19.

De Anza's 61-league march to Arroyo de Santa Catharina—Font, pp. 33–39 (4–20 December 1775). These were Mexican leagues of 5,000 yards or 3,000 "geometric paces," which is to say 25% shorter than Spanish leagues (ibid., p. 9).

Bancroft: de Anza's route "cannot be traced exactly"—Op. cit., vol. XVIII, p. 22.

Fonty's map of 1776—Reproduced in Bancroft, vol. XVIII, p. 263.

"We bade farewell to the Yumas . . ."—Font, p. 125 (15 May 1776).

Palma's turquoise nose-bead—Heizer and Whipple, p. 251 (Pedro Font, "The Colorado Yumans in 1775").

Remarks of El Caballero de Croix—Nunis, p. 119 ("Instructions for the Recruitment of Soldiers and Settlers for the California Expedition of 1781," 27 December 1779, item 7).

The nudity of the Yumas has been "discontinued," "seeing that all are covered with reasonable clothing acquired from the fabric of the Pima Nation."—de Anza, p. 23 (General Archive of the Nation, Internal Provinces 237, Sonora No. 12, de Anza to the Most Excellent Lord Commander of Knights, Frey Don Antonio María Bucareli y Urssua [Ursúa], 22 June 1776, ff. 27–27v).

Zorita: "To give a field or other land to a Spaniard . . ."—Op. cit., p. 109.

Estimate of the Conquest's casualties: 4.5 million—Fagan, p. 226. These "costs" are tabulated more precisely, and set against the "costs" of human sacrifice in Aztec Mexico, in the "Defense of Creed" chapter of my book *Rising Up and Rising Down.*

14. Los Angeles (1780)

Epigraph: "Summer was counted from the time frogs were first heard to croak."—*An Illustrated History of Los Angeles County*, p. 13 (quoting the Scotchman Don Perfecto Hugo Reid's observations on the Gabrielino Indians).

15. Los Angeles (1781)

Epigraph: "It is the destiny of every considerable stream . . ."—Austin, p. 139 ("Other Water Borders").

Sometime in June—Nunis, p. 10 ("A New Look at the Founding Families of Los Angeles").

Footnote: Volunteer status of the settlers; married volunteer status of soldiers—Ibid., pp. 120–21 (Instruccion: "Instructions for the Recruitment of Soldiers and Settlers for the California Expedition of 1781," El Caballero de Croix, 27 December 1779. Henceforth "recruitment instructions.").

Soldiers' uniforms—Ibid., p. 135 ("Outfits for Soldiers, Settlers and Families," Antonio Bonilla, 10 February 1780).

Founding of Los Angeles as Our Lady of the Angels of Porciúncula—Ibid., pp. 18–19.

Governor de Neve on the "Pagans"—Ibid., p. 60 (Report No. 83, "Troops," 26 February 1777).

"Docile and without malice . . ."—Ibid., p. 120 (recruitment instructions).

"Taken the necessary steps to prevent transmission of this news . . ."—Ibid., p. 132 ("Correspondence Pertaining to the Polbadores," 10 September 1781).

Itemization of other settlements and missions then present in Upper California—Ibid., pp. 77–78 (Reglamento: "For the Garrison of the Peninsula of Californias . . . ," "Second Title: Footing, pay and gratuities of the Companies . . . ," Pedro Fages, 18 September 1781).

Newness of Santa Barbara—Ibid., p. 129 (recruitment instructions, no. 2 [enclosure]).

Number of Christian converts in the missions—Ibid., p. 86 (same Reglamento, "Fourteenth Title: Political Government and Instructions for Settlement").

"The Head or Father of each family must be a Man of the Soil . . ."—Ibid., p. 120 (recruitment instructions).

Antonio Clemente Féliz Villavicencio and his family—Ibid., p. 26 ("Soldiers and Settlers of the Expedition of 1781").

Their ethnicities and particular possessions—Ibid., p. 141 ("Supplies Purchased for the Pobladores," no. 72, José de Zuñiga, Mission San Gabriel, 18 September 1781).

Settlers' clothes—Ibid., pp. 135–36 ("Outfits for Soldiers, Settlers and Families," Antonio Bonilla, 10 February 1780).

Ethnicities of all the settlers—Ibid., p. 162 ("Padrón of Los Angeles," Joseph Franco. de Ortega); p. 164 ("Note on Races and Castes of Mexico"). See also 1910 *Britannica*, 11th ed., vol. XVIII, p. 337 (entry on Mexico).

"Corn . . . is generally landed wormy . . ."—Ibid., p. 86 (Reglamento: "For the Garrison of the Peninsula of Californias . . . ," "Sixth Title: Supply of articles of clothing and other necessaries . . .").

Bestowals to settlers—Ibid., p. 101 (same Reglamento, "Fourteenth Title").

Details of land distribution—Loc. cit., pp. 101–3.

Population of Los Angeles in 1791—Robinson, p. 39.

16. Tía Juana (1825)

Epigraph: "The dust rises, making swirls, with flowers of death."—Carrasco and Moctezuma, p. 71 ("Warrior Zeal").

Arguello's grant—After Niemann, p. 63.

17. Tecate (1830)

Epigraph: "Before mapping can begin . . ."—Greeley and Batson, p. 16.

Bandini's grant—After Niemann, p. 68.

18. Los Angeles (1845)

Epigraph: "And in spring . . ."—Oppian, p. 253 ("Halieutica," ll. 473–75).

Expenses of the Los Angeles ball, August 1845—Samuel T. Black, vol. 1, p. 64.

Aguardiente: "a sort of cognac, which was very agreeable to the palate . . ."—Elliott, *History of Tulare County,* p. 33.

Footnote: "When the ball broke up . . ."—Pattie, p. 155.

Bancroft: "pre-pastoral California"—Op. cit., vol. XVIII, p. 205.

Date of the first orange tree in Los Angeles—*An Illustrated History of Los Angeles County,* p. 351.

General Sherman: "Every house had its inclosure of vineyard . . . "—Op. cit., pp. 52–53. The date of his visit to Los Angeles was 1847.

Power of the Los Angeles River—Diehl, p. 23 (vol. ix, no. 39, January 20, 1886, "A Fierce Freshet: Los Angeles River on a Rampage, Tears Away Bridges . . . THREE LIVES SACRIFICED").

The flood of 1886—*An Illustrated History of Los Angeles County,* p. 107.

Los Angeles as the destination of runaway Mission Indians—Hartnell, p. 36 (letter to the Prefecture of the Second District—Los Angeles, June 11, 1839).

Per capita income of Mexico, 1800 and 1845—Wasserman, p. 61.

Los Angeles's fields of wild mustard—Gumprecht, p. 23.

The irrigation canal from near Redlands to San Gabriel—Street, *Beasts of the Field,* p. 32.

Renting of Indian field laborers—Ibid., p. 36.

Los Angeles's agricultural surplus, population, etc.—Gumprecht, pp. 46–48.

Tale of the Franciscan vineyards of San Gabriel—Street, p. 30.

Contraction of the Spanish frontier by 1845—Heizer and Whipple, p. 569 (S. F. Cook, "Conflict Between the California Indian and White Civilization").

"An exceedingly lascivious dance . . ."—Bull, p. 31.

Descriptions of men's and women's fashions—Dana, pp. 95, 91–92.

Pattie's scorecard of bull and grizzly combat deaths—Op. cit., p. 293.

Smashing of eggshell—Ryan, vol. I, p. 76. This took place in Monterey but presumably was the same in Los Angeles.

"The laxness and filth of a free brute . . ."—Thomas Jefferson Fernham, 1844; quoted in Pike, p. 99.

19. *West of the River (1803)*

Epigraph: "God, there never was a bigger game! . . ."—Hammett, p. 300 ("Nightmare Town," 1924).

Hamilton's remarks on the territory west of the Mississippi—Op. cit., p. 999 ("Purchase of Louisiana," *New-York Evening Post,* July 5, 1803).

20. *Drawing the Line (1803–1848)*

Epigraph: "We replied that the laws of our country . . ."—Pattie, p. 219.

Jefferson to Bowdoin: "Never did a nation act . . ."—Henry Adams, p. 904.

My 1976 *Britannica*: "The Texan revolution was not simply a fight . . ."—Vol. 18, p. 164 (entry on Texas).

My 1911 *Britannica*: "Three abortive Anglo-American invasions . . ." and "The weakness of the Mexican Liberals . . ."—Vol. XXVI (Submatine Mines–Tom-Tom), pp. 692, 693 (entry on Texas).

Ulysses S. Grant: "We were sent to provoke a fight . . ."—Grant, p. 50.

General Sherman: "California was yet a Mexican province . . ."—Op. cit., p. 55.

Grant: "My pity was aroused . . ."—Op. cit., p. 81.

21. *Ranch Size (1800–1850)*

Epigraph: "Being of or from the Border . . ."—Polkinhorn et al., p. 180 (James Bradley, "Chorizos Fronterizos").

The value of horses in 1836—Dana, pp. 142–43.

Description of Hacienda Sánchez-Navarro—After Wasserman, p. 27.

Horses for poor men in California—Osio, p. 69.

Conversion of the mission territories into private land grants—Hartnell, pp. 11–12 (prologue by Glenn J. Farris).

An official of the district agrarian tribunal in Mexicali—Lic. Carlos E. Tinoco, official of the Tribunal Unitario Agrario Distrito Dos. Interviewed in the tribunal offices in Mexicali, September 2005. Terrie Petree translated.

Maximum allowed size of land grants; owners of Orange County in 1850—Marschner, pp. 5, 46.

Acreages of Mexican ranchos in the Riverside area—After Lechs, pp. 676–78.

22. *Mexico (1821–1911)*

Epigraph: "They did not recognize themselves as the only real hope for the future . . ."—Strugatski and Strugatski, p. 131.

Description of Benito Juárez, and information about him—Engraving reproduced in Wasserman, p. 92, and capsule biography, pp, 93–97.

Footnote about Maximilian and Carlotta—Lowry, p. 15.
"After the nation's humiliating defeat by the North Americans . . ."—Wasserman, p. 93.
Casualties of the Caste War—Ibid., pp. 101–2.
Casualties of Ayutla—Loc. cit.
The Ley Lerdo—Ibid., p. 103. Dwyer claims (p. 28) that the *ejido* lands were in fact exempted.
Footnote: Classes and balance of power during mid-nineteenth century—Wasserman, pp. 54, 71.
Juárez's aim to increase agricultural production—Dwyer, p. 28.
"In the long run . . ."—Wasserman, p. 110.
Increased water needs of haciendas—Ibid., p. 153.
Description of Porfirio Díaz—After an engraving; ibid., p. 161.
My 1910 *Britannica*: "Then came the long, firm rule of Porfirio Díaz. . ."—11th ed., vol. XVIII, p. 322 (entry on Mexico).
The Law of Colonization—Wasserman, p. 169.
Higher wages of Northside and Southside border areas—Ibid., p. 183.
Population of Baja California Norte, 1900–1910—*Britannica* (11th ed.), vol. XVIII, p. 324 (entry on Mexico).
Census data on Mexico, 1900 and 1810—Ibid., p. 322.
Many government lands were vacant only of clear title—See Boyer, p. 71.
Similarity of Dawes Act with American policy in Dominica, 1915—Pike, p. 213.
Luis Terrazas's ten million acres in Chihuahua, etc.—Described in Wasserman, p. 177.
The two waves of expropriation of communal lands—Ibid., p. 187.
"Like so many other Latin American strongmen . . ."—Ibid., p. 166.
"By 1910, most rural folk in Mexico . . ."—Boyer, p. 47. Dwyer writes (p. 29) that 77% to 88% of the people in Baja were "landless rural laborers" in 1910.

23. *The Line Itself (1844–1911)*

Epigraph: "What are the colors of the map without a dream?"—Torre and Wiegers, p. 81 (Alberto Blanco, "Maps," 1998; trans. Michael Wiegers).
"The Californian boasts of California . . ."—Bull, p. 21.

24. *Los Angeles (1850)*

Epigraph: "But I hope as soon as I set forth . . ."—Bowman and Heizer, pp. 111–12 (letter of 9 February 1774).
Dates of Los Angeles's first brick house and first legal hanging—McGroarty, vol. 1, p. 367.
The murder of Juan Diego Valdez—Gostin, pp. 564–65 (records #1562–63).
"The streets were thronged throughout the entire day . . ."—Bell, p. 10.
"All, however, had slung to their rear the never-failing pair of *Colt's* . . ."—Ibid., p. 7.
Violent deaths of unknowns in Los Angeles County, 1850s—Gostin, pp. 596–97 (records #2249, 2243, 2244, 2247, 2261, 2262, 2270, 2269, 2276, 2277).
Los Angeles, "then the greatest cow county in the state . . ."—Bell, p. 11.
"Nigger Alley, which was the most perfect and full grown pandemonium . . ."—Ibid., pp. 12–13.
Information on the Los Angeles County Recorder's register—Gostin, pp. 355–56.
The adventurer from the British Isles: "The portly Californian, under his ample-brimmed *sombrero* . . ." and "I have frequently seen a quiet and respectable party of natives . . ."—Ryan, vol. 1, pp. 72–73, 104. These words were written about Monterey. But why should Los Angeles have been different? The acclaimed novelist Helen Hunt Jackson (op. cit., p. 12) expressed what Mexican Californians must have felt: "The people of the United States have never in the least realized that the taking possession of California was not only a conquering of Mexico, but of California as well; that the real bitterness of the surrender was not so much to the empire which gave up the country, as to the country itself which was given up."
Los Angeles in 1859—Dana, pp. 478–79.
Listing of two Chinese in L.A. 1850 census—The Great Basin Foundation Center for Anthropological Research, vol. 1, chronology.
Various violent deaths 1852–58—Gostin, pp. 492–93 (records #51, 54, 55, 58, 60, 513–19, 524–25); pp. 494–97 (records #126–33); pp. 498–99 (records #175–86), pp. 510–11 (records #444–47), pp. 528–29 (records #819–20), pp. 536–37 (record #958).

25. *Lost Mines (1849–2005)*

Epigraph: "But a few miles from us on the east . . ."—*The City and County of San Diego*, p. 38.
Number of gold seekers crossing the Imperial Valley in 1849—Griffin and Young, p. 172.
The Colorado Desert, which runs a hundred and fifty miles long by fifty miles wide—Figures from Elliott, *History of San Bernardino and San Diego Counties*, p. 173.

"A mere thoroughfare for the adventurers . . ."—Marschner, p. 33.
"Business of every description is reported as being extremely dull."—*The Country Gentleman*, vol. V, no. 16 (April 19, 1855; whole no. 120), p. 256: "CALIFORNIA NEWS."
News of La Paz mines, 1864—*Illustrated History of Los Angeles County*, p. 100.
Crosses, flowers and saints at Mexican mines—Quaife, pp. 243–44 (from ch. XVII of J. D. Borthwick, *Three Years in California*).
The tale of Peg-Leg Smith—Ainsworth, pp. 126–29.
Tumco in 1870—Harris, pp. 51–52.
Gold mines 70 miles north of San Diego—McPherson, p. 61.
Tumco—In this connection let me quote Penn, song number 9 (Tumco Mine): "Howdy do and welcome to you / This is the Tumco mine / Here's your mining hat here's where everything's at / You're gonna have a real fine time . . . There's a hospital in the middle of town / Whitewashed and 40 foot square / It's easy to see and I guarantee / Heat stroke will send you there."
Transactions of the Alexander couple—California State Archives. Microfilmed Imperial County records, 1851–1919. Roll #1433101. Index to Grantors, 1851–1907. May 6, 1886: Book 15, p. 310. July 13, 1894: Book 15, p. 243.
Gold and water statistics for Imperial mines (actually, "mines in the area")—Tumco pamphlet, last page.
United Mines Company telegram—UC Berkeley. Bancroft Library, farm labor situation 1933–34. Folder: "Mexican border incidents." To Governor Hiram Johnson, from Wilbank Johnson, President, UMC, 10:46 A.M., 24 April 1914. 29SF SO 124—3 EX.

26. *White Eyelashes (1853–1926)*

Epigraph: "The discourse of Cortés . . ."—Gómara, p. 25.
"The cause of humanity . . ."—Bancroft, vol. XXIII, p. 603.
The Mexican War: "It is generally admitted that Mexico was provoked into aggression . . ."—1910 *Britannica*, 11th ed., vol. XVIII, p. 340.
"Those spirited men who had gone forth to uphold the broken altars . . ."—D. Gunn, p. 196.
Bancroft on Walker's "seemingly pupilless, grey eyes . . ."—Vol. XXIII (1888), p. 159.
Walker sees Mexico's race-mixing.—Based on his remarks quoted in Pike, p. 147.
Walker's career: San Francisco to Tijuana—D. Gunn, p. 195.
"An anomaly in the history of mankind . . ."—Ibid., p. 198
Walker's 3 expeditions against Nicaragua—Ibid., pp. 196–97.
"A movement to secure the annexation of enough territory . . ."—Tout, *The First Thirty Years*, p. 200.
Story of General Enrique Estrada—Kerig, p. 251.

27. *Colonel Couts's Homestead (1839–ca. 1915)*

Epigraph: "I want and desire . . ."—León-Portilla and Shorris, p. 251, the Bancroft Dialogues.
Epigraph: "Get an Indian wife . . ."—Gilberto Sanders, interviewed on his rancho in Ejido Morelos, 2003. Terrie Petree interpreted.
Syncretism: Let me give you an inkling of the possibilities. On 17 July 1858, William Abbott, aged 24, weds Merced García in Los Angeles, in a Catholic church. In the meantime, Phineas Banning has already married Rebecca Sanford at the home of William T. B. Sanford; while María Eduige (or Edwigo) Soto, whose parents hail from Sonora, has taken Vicente Carrasco to be her lawfully wedded spouse. Antonio Regan has likewise wedded Mary Fay at the Los Angeles Mission Church. In short, as we see from the surnames, either sex is free to legally mate with either race—true democracy, my friends! To be sure, the choice made by Antonio Regan and Mary Fay—a man of the conquered with a woman of the conquerors—will not be so widely emulated.—The four marriages: William Abbott through Mary Fay—Gostin, pp. 360–61 (records #1–5); pp. 364–65 (records #93–95); pp. 368–69 (records #165–66); pp. 398–99 (record #810).
"Make money and marry a Spanish woman. . ."—Muir, p. 544 (*The Mountains of California*, 1894). Muir continues: "People mine here for water as for gold . . . ," and the suitor tells him: "If I chance to strike a good, strong flow, I'll soon be worth $5000 or $10,0000."
Opinion that the señoritas of San Diego, Santa Barbara and Los Angeles "preferred for husbands, not finely dressed, courtly, serenading cavaliers . . ."—Samuel T. Black, vol. 1, p. 73.
Footnote: "Their chief faults they had brought with them in their blood from Mexico . . ."—Ibid., pp. 66–67.
"I was Married on the 4th of November . . ."—D. Mackenzie Brown, p. 32 (Alpheus B. Thompson, Santa Barbara, to his brother, Wildes T. Thompson, Topsham, Maine, March 18, 1835).
"It is two years to-day since my Wife was buried . . ."—Ibid., pp. 59–60 (Alpheus B. Thompson, Santa Barbara, to his sister, Mary Thompson, Topsham, Maine, February 28, 1853).
Tale of the Spanish conquistadors who "heard that ten suns distant from there was an island of Amazons . . ."—Gómara, p. 303.

The name "California"—Industrious, voluminous Bancroft, unable to find the word in any of Cortés's writings, attributes first mention of the real California to the diary of Ulloa's voyage of 1539. The Amazons eluded Ulloa as they had his predecessors; Bancroft plausibly supposes that the name was applied in derision (vol. XVIII; pp. 7, 64, 67).

Syncretism and sensuality: Even nowadays, Imperial frequently likes to clothe herself in a chaste seriousness, in evidence of which I once again bring to mind that 117-degree June day when Rebeca Hernández insisted: "I've never had sex in my life, although I've made love. My sister is still a virgin at twenty-one, and she was shocked when I finally told her that I wasn't. I'll never have sex, ever. That would make me feel so empty . . ."—No doubt this sentiment was in our nineteeth-century Ramona's heart, when she married her American. But this Indian garbage-girl, she's far more alien to me than one of those bygone Hispanicized señoritas of Los Angeles; to go with her, even to hold her hand for an instant, is to accomplish the impossible adventure of Cihuatlán at last. I kiss her hand. She throws her arms around me and kisses me passionately on the mouth. I'm thrilled by the rattling of ice in the juice vendor's glass jars, the creak of unknown things, the sounds of Mexican cars and power tools, the long, slender shadows of people's legs on the wide yellow crosswalk; in other words, *there is much else that is fascinating in connection with this remarkable tribe, such as their habit of "roasting girls" ceremonially at the period of their adolescence* (Samuel T. Black, vol. 1, p. 432); and it gives me comfort to know that I can copulate with her if I want to; I can also enter one of those bars where they shine a flashlight onto your money to see how much you've paid them; when the security guards first hold the door open for you, they always keep it open on their own behalf for a single extra instant, I suppose either to enjoy the coolness or to get a personal peek at the naked dancer shimmying down the stainless steel pole onstage.

Dress of the señoritas in mid-19th-century California—Based on Samuel T. Black, pp. 70–73.

"Sandoval had no desire to fight . . ."—Gómara, p. 300.

"But who is that at the side of the Captain-General? . . ."—León-Portilla and Shorris, p. 179 ("The Imprisonment of Cuauhtémoc," orig, source not given).

Cortés's bedmates—Lanyon, pp. 137–43, 167–68.

Jensen-Alvarado marriage—In the Riverside Directory she is memorialized as *Miss Merced Alvarado, of Compton*, which proves once again that syncretism does work both ways.

"The belle and beauty of Southern California," etc., including Anglicization of Mercedes's name and home—Bynon and Son, p. 54 (biography of Cornelius Jensen).

Tale of the Jensen-Alvarado House—The Great Basin Foundation Center for Anthropological Research, vol. 1, pp. 167–69.

Marriage of Michael White—Wagner, p. 28.

Marriage of Yorba and Smith—Gostin, pp. 402–3 (records #897–98); pp. 406–7 (record #971).

"I could not but feel a pity for him . . ."—Dana, pp. 297–98.

Bandini's ownership of Tecate—Niemann, p. 68.

Footnote on the marriage of Coxcox's daughter—León-Portilla and Shorris, p. 201 ("The Founding of Tenochitlán," from *Crónica Mexicayotl*). In Meyer et al., p. 56, the King is identified as Coxcox, who in fact seems to have been the previous King who gave the Aztecs land when they arrived (León-Portilla and Shorris, p. 200; the King's name is Coxcoxtli). The same tale is related in Carrasco and Moctezuma, p. 16, but there again Coxcox is called Achitometl.

"Orozco's famous painting"—"Cortés and Malinche," painting by José Clemente Orozco, reproduced in color in Lanyon, after p. 12.

American disapproval of miscegenation—Heizer and Whipple, pp. 564–65 (S. F. Cook, "Conflict Between the California Indian and White Civilization").

Discussion of "squaw men"—Pike, p. 145.

"The marriage of Indian women by white men of course involved degradation of the latter."—Hittell, p. 189.

The Tale of Don Hugo Reid—Hartnell, p. 43 (ed. fn.).

William Hartnell's marriage—Ibid., p. 17 (biographical sketch of W.H.).

"I have come to please my blooming vulva . . ."—León-Portilla and Shorris, p. 108 ("Song of the Women of Chalco," from the *Cantares Mexicanos*, collected fifteenth century).

The twentieth-century researcher who studies rural California divorce records—Griswold, pp. 1, 4, 232. The divorce records hail from Santa Clara and San Mateo counties in 1850–90. He assures us of the basic uniformity of rural California at that time, so why not lazily apply his findings to Imperial?

The Mexicali barber—Interviewed in his shop in July 2005. Not the same barber whom I interviewed formally and at length about the Chinese tunnels. He spoke English. When he got excited, he nicked my cheek with his straight razor and said damn.

The marriage and career of Cave Johnson Couts: "the Guajomne Grant, a wedding gift" and "Having been appointed subagent for the San Luis Rey Indians . . ."—Samuel T. Black, vol. 1, p. 417.

Hittell on marital superiority of Mexicanas to Indian women—Op. cit., p. 90.

"Andres, an Indian . . ."—Elliott, *History of San Bernardino and San Diego*, entry for Couts, p. 196.

Description of Arcadia Stearns, *née* Bandini—After a photograph reproduced in Osio, p. 140.
Death of Juan Bandini (4 November 1849)—Gostin, pp. 496–97 (records #156–62).
Map of the Abel Stearns Ranchos—McPherson, advertising end matter, map between pp. II and III.
"One of the worst abusers of Indian field hands . . ."—Street, *Beasts of the Field*, p. 124.
"The soul of honor . . ."—Elliott, *History of San Bernardino and San Diego*, entry for Couts p. 196.
Señorita Couts at the Club Anahuac—Sitton and Deverell, p. 166 (Douglas Monroy, "Making Mexico in Los Angeles").

28. The Indians Do All the Hard Work (1769–1906)

Epigraph: "And as the concomitant differentiation and specialization . . ."—Veblen, p. 348 (*The Theory of Business Enterprise*, 1904).
"The Indians . . . do all the hard work . . ."—Dana, p. 100.
Ordeal of the 42 Cochimi campesinos, 1769—Street, *Beasts of the Field*, pp. 9–11.
Decline of Cochimi labor—Loc. cit. and ff.
Osio's observation on mission registers—Op. cit., p. 124.
"Rape, murder, execution, whippings . . ."—Street, *Beasts of the Field*, p. 23.
Spanish vs. American treatment of Indians—Heizer and Whipple, pp. 564–65 (S. F. Cook, "Conflict Between the California Indian and White Civilization").
"The Indians worked, . . . as if they had a lifetime for the job."—Wasserman, p. 31 (John Lloyd Stephens, 1840s).
"The innumerable Indians loaded like beasts of burden"—Ibid., p. 36 (Fanny Calderón de la Barca, 1840s).
Comanche and Apache raid, 1849—Ibid., p. 110.
History of Indian labor in California, 1833–62—Street, *Beasts of the Field*, pp. 94, 110–11, 146–47, 151.
"Indians did the labor and the white man spent the money . . ."—Bell, p. 2.
"These Indians of California have large bodies . . ."—Salvator, p. 39.
Indian labor in Imperial, 1906—DeBuys and Myers, pp. 115–16.

29. The Inland Empire (1860–1882)

Epigraph: "We wish to form a colony of intelligent, industrious and enterprising people . . ."—Quoted in Holmes et al., p. 24.
Riverside's original name of Jurupa; fate of the vineyards; "essentially a city of homes" and "morally clean"—Riverside Fire Department, pp. 10–11.
The Rubidoux family, their land and history—Bynon and Son, pp. 14, 18–20, 23, 63.
Planting of the first orange tree in Riverside; Mrs. L. C. Tibbetts's navel oranges, etc.—Holmes, p. 44 et seq.
"Nothing contributes more to set off the appearance of a festive table than the orange."—Brown and Boyd, p. 419.
She kept her seedlings alive on dishwater—After Wagner, p. 46.
Parent Tree Brand orange label—Reproduced in McClelland and Last, p. 10.
As of 1989 the tree was still alive—Information from Riverside Municipal Museum, p, 24.
Experiment with opium poppies—Patterson, p. 50.
"Here may be seen large nurseries of orange . . ."—McPherson, p. 60.
The Riverside Fruit Exchange: "The foundation of the organization is the local association, a strictly neighborhood affair."—Holmes et al., p. 123.
James Bettner's accomplishments—Patterson, pp. 159, 221. The Heritage House was erected in 1891, when Riverside was desert, mountains, and long rows of young orange groves—not to mention an opera house.
Entry for Catherine Bettner—Bynon and Son, p. 156.
Riverside's wealth rating in 1895—Riverside Municipal Museum, p. 61 (Vincent Moses, "Machine in the Garden").
The expert from the USDA: "The magnificent hills and valleys with their seas of orange groves . . ."—G. Harold Powell, pp. 39–40 (letter of 11 February 1904, to Gertrude Powell).
"The largest orange and lemon ranch in California"—Ibid., p. 35 (letter of 8 February 1904, to Gertrude Powell).
"In 1907, the California Fruit Growers' Exchange starts advertising, first in Iowa."—Information from the same book, p. 3 (introduction).
Advertisement for the Inland Empire Gas Company in El Centro—Imperial Valley Directory (1930), p. 30.
Descriptions of Etiwanda—Based on Elliott, *History of San Bernardino and San Diego Counties*, Dumke, pp. 106–7.
"Promises Fulfilled"—Patterson, p. 95.
The USDA man on Ontario: "One of the great orange centres . . ."—G. Harold Powell, p. 33 (letter of 8 February 1904, to Gertrude Powell).
Definitions and extensions of the Inland Empire—Wagner, p. 17.

"On the other side is a low range of sandhills . . ."—Elliott, *History of San Bernardino and San Diego Counties*, p. 102.

30. Subdelineations: Waterscapes (1850–1900)

Epigraph: "Nearly all of California that slopes toward the Colorado . . ."—Hall, p. 34.
Epigraph: "Down here, behind the Coast Mountains . . ."—Richards, p. 94.
Statistic on artesian wells of San Bernardino County—Elliott, *History of San Bernardino and San Diego Counties*, p. 104. The exact figure was 16,153,600 gallons per day.
Judge Willis's well—Ibid., p. 103.
The New River as "formed by the surplus waters of the Colorado"—Ibid., p. 172.
"In the southwest . . ."—UC Berkeley. Bancroft Library. Paul S. Taylor papers. Carton 4. Folder 4:34: "Irrigation Crusade, 1969," p. 2 (quote from Walter Gillette Bates, *Scribner's* magazine, 1890).
Number of irrigation companies east of Los Angeles, 1880–1902—Dumke, p. 228.
Area of present-day San Diego County (4,207 square miles)—San Diego Water County Authority, p. 1.
Names and descriptions of western San Diego County's main rivers—Hall, pp. 39–49.
The fact that these 7 rivers all run dry in the summer—San Diego Water County Authority, p. 2.
The 7-fold-plus variation in San Diego rainfall—Pryde, who states (p. 103) that San Diego's rainfall has varied from a high of 25.97 inches in 1883–84 to a low of 3.46 inches in 1960–61. This citation is also given in the "Dissolutions" section, in the chapter "The Water Farmers."
The thirsty citrus groves in 1904—G. Harold Powell, p. 49 (letter of 25 February 1904, to Gertrude Powell).
Reservoir plans of the Mount Tecarte L & W Co.—Ibid., p. 56.
Works of the Riverside Water Company—Hall, p. 199.
Coroner's jury on Saint Francis Dam—William Leslie Davis, p. 238.
"At first, you see, each farmer tried to get a farm that was beside a stream . . ."—Richards, p. 227.
Tale of the wicked water company at Lake Tahoe—*Fresno Morning Republican*, Thursday, March 25, 1920, "Ask Congress to Intervene to Prevent Lowering of Dam."
Fights over water in San Gabriel Cañón—*An Illustrated History of Los Angeles County*, p. 107.
Effusions of *The City and County of San Diego*—Pp. 54–56.
"Riparian doctrine gets superseded," etc.—*The California Water Atlas*, p. 24: ". . . the story of California water rights is consequently in large part a history of the continued assault upon the riparian doctrine by . . . the competing doctrine of appropriation. Under this doctrine, the right to water is awarded to the first person who puts it to a beneficial use. . ."

[Original footnote:] "*Under that doctrine, the owners of lands adjoining a stream were held to share the right to the waters of the stream for use on these adjoining lands to the exclusion of use on other lands."

Footnote: Percentage of Mexican land that is arable—Wasserman, p. 64.
"Those that produce the *best results* from the most *economical* use"—James, *Reclaiming the Arid West*, p. 28.
Language of H.R. 13846: "The right to the use of water shall be perpetually appurtenant to the land irrigated . . ."—Ibid., p. 16. The rememberer of this language was Dr. Frederick H. Newell of the United States Geological Survey.
Footnote: "An era which depended on individualism . . ."—*The California Water Atlas*, p. 27.
Same footnote: 1950 editorial—*California Farmer*, vol. 193, no. 1 (July 1, 1950), p. 4.
"R. R. Sutherland filed notice at Riverside . . ."—*California Cultivator*, vol. XXIII, no. 6 (August 5, 1904), p. 142. In 1906, some ranchers are *suspected of stealing water from the Santa Ana river above Riverside* (*California Cultivator*, vol. XXVII, no. 19 [November 8, 1906], p. 443 ["News of Country Life in the Golden West"]). One wonders what they did that R. R. Sutherland didn't do? Was it simply that they refrained from filing on the water they'd appropriated?
"They sought economic gain . . ."—DeBuys and Myers, p. 80.
Remarks on the Desert Land Act of 1877—UC Berkeley. Bancroft Library Manuscripts Collection. Paul Schuster Taylor, 1895–. Papers, 1895–1984. BANC MSS 84/38. Carton 5. Folder 5:2: "To Make the Desert Bloom Like the Rose, 1969?" Yellow typescript on "The American West" letterhead, entitled "Issue: Colorado Book," pp. 3–5.
"Another boomer," on the subject of Blythe: "water communication from the center of the tract with all the harbors of the world . . ."—Lech, p. 216 (Herb or Hugh Elias to D. W. McLeod of Riverside).
The California Convention of 1878–79—UC Berkeley. Bancroft Library Manuscripts Collection. Paul Schuster Taylor, 1895–. Papers, 1895–1984. BANC MSS 84/38. Carton 5. Folder 5:2: "To Make the Desert Bloom Like the Rose, 1969?" Yellow typescript on "The American West" letterhead, entitled "Issue: Colorado Book," p. 18.
Warning of Francis G. Newlands—UC Berkeley. Bancroft Library. Paul Schuster Taylor papers. Carton 4. Folder 4:34: "Irrigation Crusade, 1969," pp. 5–6.

Remarks on "waterscape improvements" generally—UC Berkeley. Bancroft Library Manuscripts Collection. Paul Schuster Taylor, 1895–. Papers, 1895–1984. BANC MSS 84/38. Carton 5. Folder 5:2: "To Make the Desert Bloom Like the Rose, 1969?" Yellow typescript on "The American West" letterhead, entitled "Issue: Colorado Book," pp. 3–5.
Song of Nanaya: "Dig no canal; let me be your canal . . ."—Leick, p. 93 (Alster 1975); slightly "retranslated" by me for euphony; meaning unchanged. Nanaya was the Sumerian Venus.

31. *Their Needs Are Easily Satisfied (1871–1906)*

Epigraph: "You look at a man's eyes. . ."—Steinbeck, *East of Eden*, p. 164.
An Angeleno: "In fact, now that they are here . . ."—Salvator, pp. 41, 43.
Chinese in Riverside—The Great Basin Foundation Center for Anthropological Research, vol. 1, pp. 2, 13, 175, 178, Chronology sec.
Engraving of the two pigtailed "Celestials"—Ibid., p. 5 (Harry W. Lawton, University of California, Riverside: "Riverside's First Chinatown and the Boom of the Eighties").
Footnote: Leo Klotz's memories—The Riverside Municipal Museum, p. 53.
Riverside historian: "popular antagonism"—Patterson, p. 342.
"It is difficult to see how the present fruit crop . . ."—The Great Basin Foundation Center for Anthropological Research, vol. 1, p. 2. In 1887 the T. E. Langley Ranch in Lugonia employs mainly Chinese and Indians for drying peaches; naturally the Indians' presence is anachronistic (ibid., p. 41).
Unless otherwise stated, all remaining dates and events in this discussion of Chinese labor in California are from the same source's long "Chronology."
Continuation of Chinese history in Riverside, to 1906—Ibid., vol. 1, pp. 5, 195, 38, 46, 49, Chronology sec.
Artifacts excavated from Riverside's Chinatown—The Great Basin Foundation Center for Anthropological Research, vol. 2 (Archaeology), pp. 326–27, 403, 408, 354.

32. *Los Angeles (1875)*

Epigraph: "The constant ripening of fruits . . ."—*An Illustrated History of Los Angeles County*, p. 353.
Indian place-names relating to Los Angeles—Ibid., p. 11.
Editor of the *Los Angeles Star*: "The most degraded race of aborigines upon the North American Continent . . ."—Quoted in Robinson, p. 15.
Miscellaneous other Los Angeles events—*An Illustrated History of Los Angeles County*, pp. 100–103, 105.
L.A. gets title to L.A. River water rights, 1884—Hall, p. 535.
Artesian wells "at pleasure"—McPherson, p. 55.
L.A.'s water supply: "Ample for a very large city . . ."—Ibid., p. 44.
Events of 1887—*An Illustrated History of Los Angeles County*, p. 108.
Depredations of coyotes—Salvator, p. 27.
"A small town," "bituminous pitch"—Pattie, p. 268.
Number of orange trees in 1856—Dumke, p. 13.
Miss Francisca Wolfskill's oranges; the huge beehive—McPherson, pp. 22–23.

33. *The Second Line (1893)*

Epigraph: "A map of the real world . . ."—Torre and Wiegers, p. 77 (Alberto Blanco, "Maps," 1998; trans. Michael Wiegers). The translation gives "the real world," but I have changed the definite article based on the original Spanish on the facing page.
"Most of present-day Riverside County was within 1850 San Diego County . . ."—Marschner, p. 34.
Areas of the two main pieces of Riverside County (printed in roman within the italics of the Marschner quotation)—After Coy, to whom the reader is advised to refer for detailed delineation of each California county.
Discrepancies in the size of Riverside County in comparison to Massachusetts—Holmes et al., pp. in text.
Footnote: "When I first came to Riverside . . ."—Elliott, *History of San Bernardino and San Diego Counties*, p. 376.
W. E. Elliott's map of California in 1883—Elliott, *History of Tulare County*, frontispiece.
A philosopher: "A space is something that has been made room for . . ."—Heidegger, p. 154 ("Building Dwelling Thinking").
Riverside County Directory's remarks—Bynon and Son, rear endpaper, pp. 85 [81], 115 [111], 19 [335], 3–81 [151–230], 180 [336]. (Page numbers in brackets are the rationalized additions of the modern editor.)
A county history: "Though large parts of this may certainly be reclaimed by the waters of the Colorado . . ." —Elliott, *History of San Bernardino and San Diego Counties*, p. 153.

34. The Direct Gaze of the Confident Man (1900)

Epigraph: "We have only one standard in the West, Mr. Holmes . . ."—Wright, p. 93.
Photograph of W. F. Holt by the railroad track—ICHSPM photograph, cat. P92.59.

35. Advertisement of Sale (2002)

Epigraph—*Imperial Valley Press and Farmer*, vol. II, no. 44 (Imperial, California, Saturday, February 14, 1903), p. 2 ("The Imperial Boom").
Excerpts from the advertisement of sale—*Calexico Chronicle*, Thursday, September 26, 2002, p. 11.

36. Imperial Towns (1877–1910)

Epigraph: "He saw the country already dotted . . ."—Wright, p. 145.
"During our passage across it, we saw not a single bird . . ."—Pattie, p. 207. Fray Font's description of the area (p. 117, 8 May 1776) is not much more appetizing.
Commencement of grazing in southwestern Imperial Valley ("early nineties")—Hunt, p. 454.
Appearance of towns decade by decade on the map of Imperial—Based on the maps in Berlo, "Population History Maps," with other dates given in Tout, Laflin, and Holmes et al.
Ogilvy's 21 residents—San Diego City and County Directory (1901), p. 326.
Westmorland as "one of the state's top cotton-producing areas"—ICHSPM, document cat. #A2002.154.2, Ball Advertising, pamphlet: "Visitors' Recreation Guide Book to Imperial County California: 36 Pages of Information" (*ca.* 1964), p. 16.
An old lady in 1956: "The rattler was the most dreaded thing . . ."—ICHSPM, document cat. #A2000.23.1 Letter from Estelle Dalla, 11/8/56, to "My dear Betty." 1 sheet, verso side.
The sour mid-twentieth-century author: "A halfway Utopia of civilized development" and "Blacksmiths' shops were community centers for men . . ."—Lilliard, pp. 49, 52.
Description of Cameron Lake, 1896—ICHSPM photograph, cat. #P91.571.
Chinese railroad workers in 1887—The Great Basin Foundation Center for Anthropological Research, vol. 1, p. 39.
Workers around Indian Wells—The Great Basin Foundation Center for Anthropological Research, vol. 1, "Chronology" sec., entry for 1877.
Date of first homestead in Indio—Lech, p. 293.
Renting an adobe house from the Indians of Palm Springs—Elliott, *History of San Bernardino and San Diego Counties*, pp. 73–74.
Date of first artesian well in Mecca—Laflin, *Coachella Valley*, p. 38. This first artesian well in the Coachella Valley may actually have been in Indio. Cf. Senate Committee on the Colorado River Basin (1925), p. 53 (statement of Dr. Jennings, member of the Board of Directors of the Coachella Valley Water District).
Footnote: Sales information on Palm Springs—Lech, pp. 280–81.
Various founding dates of Tecate—Niemann, p. 68.
Mexicali once a village of Cocopah Indians—Ruiz, p. 40.
Holdings of Andrade in 1888—DeBuys and Myers, p. 142.
Information on Colonia Lerdo—Kerig, p. 54.
Information on Tijuana *ca.* 1890—*An Illustrated History of Southern California*, p. 40.
Tijuana as "the El Paso of California" whose hot springs are as good as those of Arkansas—Dumke, pp. 154–55.
1901 residential listings for "Tia Juana"—San Diego City and County Directory (1901), p. 333.
The book from 1887: "On the southeast, at Tia Juna . . ."—Gunn, p. 38.
Letter to Collector Wadham: "I advise that you carefully search every person that crosses the line . . ."—N.A.R.A.L. Record Group 36. Records of the U.S. Customs Service. Tijuana Customs Office. Letters Received from San Diego and Los Angeles (l-62). February 6, 1894–July 29, 1922. Box 1 of 1. Folder: "Letters Rec'd from Collector—San Diego 1894–1896."

37. The Boomers (1880–1912)

Epigraph: "They sold hundred-dollar property . . ."—Dumke, p. 221.
Mrs. John Kavanaugh: "He stood staunch as Mount Signal" and "He founded Holtville and El Centro . . ." —Harris, p. 25.
A few of Holt's real estate transactions—California State Archives. Microfilmed Imperial County records, 1851–1919. Roll #1433101. Index to Grantors, 1851–1907; Index to Grantees, 1851–1907. References to transactions in the following order: Book 11, p. 308; Book 3, p. 145; Book 19, p. 119; Book 4, p. 211; Book 18, p. 398; Book 4, p. 301; Book 19, p. 117; Book 19, p. 118; Book 18, p. 252; Book 3, p. 145; Book 5, p. 3; Book 7, p. 179; Book 2,

p. 133; Book 18, p. 326; Book 23, p. 28. (On November 20, 1905, Charles T. Collier is the grantor; the Holton Inter-Urban Railway Co. is the grantee. On May 3, 1906, S. A. and Emma G. Adams are the grantors; W. F. Holt is the grantee.)

Holt's reputed 18,000 acres—DeBuys and Myers, p. 82.

Imperial Valley as "Holt country"—E Clampus Vitus website (narrative by Milford Wayne Donaldson).

"One of Mr. Holt's first moves . . ." and details of Canal No. 7 and the Holton Power Co.—Groff article, p. 527.

Letter from Holt re: water stock—ICHSPM document, cat. #A2003.46.2.

Mr. Holt's "firsts" and his financing of the Barbara Worth Hotel—ICHSPM document, cat. #A85.118.1, "Information on Mr. Holt prepared by Mrs. John Kavanaugh for use of Mr. Howard Rose of Pacific Telephone Company in dedication of plaque in El Centro Building April 20, 1955," pp. I–II.

Holt's accomplishments, 1905–06, and his purchase of the *Imperial Valley Press and Farmer* (1902)—*American Biography and Genealogy*, p. 82.

" 'The Little Giant' is a modern Moses . . ."—Groff article, pp. 527–28.

The Holts' Redlands home, and the Redlands capitalists—Groff article, p. 528.

"The fog of this particular kind of war . . ."—DeBuys and Myers, p. 208.

Holt and Wright, 1907 and after—Wright, p. 369 (Appendix I).

"A look of quiet power . . ."—ICHSPM document, cat. #A85.89.1, *Redlands Federal Standard*, 1-11-11—12-19-17, p. 531 (Frances A. Groff, "Western Personalities: The Emperor of Imperial Valley").

"He works too hard . . ."—Howe and Hall, p. 118

On the subject of Progress—On June 1, 1850, Alpheus B. Thompson, now of Santa Barbara, writes to his mother, Mrs. Lydia Thompson, who dwells back east in Topsham, Maine: "Lands, Buildings and house lots have gone up since the great rush of Emigrants to this territory to enormous prices. I sold a dwelling House for the Cattle alluded to (in Barter) 15,000 [dollars] which cost me eight thousand dollars when built; therefore you can see the difference caused by the discovery of Gold . . ." (D. Mackenzie Brown, pp. 52–53 [Alpheus B. Thompson, Santa Barbara, to his mother, Mrs. Lydia Thompson, Topsham, Maine, June 1, 1850.]) Progress assures me that when one kind of gold runs out, there will be another—land, citrus culture, housing subdivisions, big-box warehouses, you name it! And, as you'll surely see, each change will be for the best.

Why did Holt's enterprise flow down into Southside, and not the reverse? I am not the first to note that "Iberian Catholicism's fatalism and its insistence that life on earth was a time of tribulation" (Pike, p. 79) hardly mobilized Mexico's Ministry of Capital to undertake the conquest of Arid America! In American Imperial, God will reward us for our Protestant works of natural improvement. In Mexican Imperial, He will find nothing to reward them for. Accordingly, Mexican Imperial lacks boomers. Her new settlements come to life as Los Angeles did, not with a land rush but with an official expedition of salaried or subsidized colonists escorted by soldiers. A Mexican historian concludes that Southsiders "confined their settlement to regions that seemed to be naturally destined by Providence for man's benefit" (Edmundo O'Gorman; quoted in Pike, p. 114). As for the other regions, such as the Mexicali Valley, Anglo-American capitalists have already begun to study them. They know that Porfirio Díaz is a good man to do business with. He'll give them something for virtually nothing, in hopes of future revenues. The rival systems may be more akin than they appear; for Northside's most successful boomers find their own friends in officialdom. The heroic American cowboy who "civilizes" the desert surely benefits a trifle from the government's more than generous leases of public rangeland; and Imperial County's All-American Canal will in due course be built by the taxpayers. This proposition is contested by my friends in Imperial County. But between 1935 and 1970 the Bureau of Reclamation advanced $64 million on its projects and collected $11 million (Bureau of Reclamation [1970], part i, p. 27). In 2006 I asked the Imperial County native Kay Brockman Bishop her opinion on the 160-acre limitation, and she replied: "My Dad went over and testified against it. They proved that we didn't fall under it because we were not subsidized by the federal government. The All-American was completely paid for by other sources" (interview of December 2006).—Meanwhile here is Paul S. Taylor's opinion (1979): "In 1928 the good people of Imperial County asked Congress to subsidize and build their projects. Congress complied. Now that the courts are holding that "the 160-acre limitation" must be complied with, they are asking Congress to . . . rescind the conditions on which they received the subsidies." (UC Berkeley. Bancroft Library. Paul S. Taylor papers. Carton 4. Folder 4:29 "Imperial Valley, Notes, Drafts." Unnumbered small white sheet, clipped to yellow sheets, dated 1979.) All the same, Southside's hierarchy presses on in obedience to some more or less misinformed project of central authority; whereas Northside's tax giveaways, however much they might be believed in by her Roosevelts and other decisive captains, appear in considerable proximity to this or that boomer's schemes of personal enrichment.—"Iberian Catholicism's fatalism and its insistence that life on earth was a time of tribulation . . ."—Pike, p. 79.—Southsiders "confined their settlement to regions that seemed to be naturally destined by Providence for man's benefit."—Edmundo O'Gorman; quoted in Pike, p. 114.

"In line with his genius for development and expansion . . ."—*American Biography and Genealogy*, pp. 82–83.

The tale of Widtsoe—*Salt Lake Tribune*, 25 August 2002, p. B2 (Will Bagley, "Utah's Many Ghost Towns a Testimony to Broken Dreams and Faded Glory").

Description of Mr. Morrison in Redlands—G. Harold Powell, p. 46 (letter of 21 February 1904, to Gertrude Powell). Redlands sprang into being in longing emulation of Riverside; so did Corona. By 1883, the population of that valley was 3,000. At the 1885 World's Fair at New Orleans, Riverside won out against Florida for best oranges in the world, best oranges in America, and best lemons in the world! By the 1890s, 6,000 carloads of oranges a year rolled out from Riverside's eponymous city. Now, things like that don't just happen; it takes the direct gaze of a confident man! By the time Imperial County was born, things really boomed in Riverside; there was an increase in assessed valuation of more than 30% in 1911–12 alone . . .—*American Biography and Genealogy*, pp. 63, 69, 72; information in the Imperial Valley Directory (1912), p. iii ("Our County"). Next comes a most inspirational Imperial Valley success story: Seeley, whose "remarkable growth from not even under cultivation to the rank of a third-class post office seems to have been largely due to the foresight of Mr. Ferguson"—Allen R. Ferguson, that is—"a splendid example of the men of courage and enterprising spirit, who divided his holdings into town lots and laid off streets and sold most of the lots in the townsite." Good boy, he started with 160 acres! "Mr. Ferguson has financial interests," the biographer crows, "and maintains a fine summer home in Burbank, California." This tribute was published in 1918, a dozen years after the Salton Sea accident washed much of Seeley away. I suppose that wasn't Mr. Ferguson's problem.—Farr, p. 361.

Biography of L. M. Holt—Call him mover and shaker of the Chicago Citrus Fair in 1886, for there and then he persuaded the Inter-Ocean Cold Storage Co. to make iced freight cars available for Riverside citrus! Born in Ann Arbor in 1840, Superindentendent of Schools in Vinton, Iowa, during the Civil War, he had by 1873 moved to Los Angeles, where all boomers must go, and fell into a convenient secretaryship of the Los Angeles Immigration and Co-operative Association. He helped the Association found Artesia in 1875, Pomona in 1877. In January 1880 he arrived in Riverside and began to exert a more direct effect upon the entity that I call Imperial.—The Great Basin Foundation Center for Anthropological Research, vol. 1, p. 3 (Harry W. Lawton, University of California, Riverside: "Riverside's First Chinatown and the Boom of the Eighties"), fn.; Patterson, p. 98.; 1902 photograph in Patterson, p. 87.

There was also a man named L. M. Holt, who happened to be W. F. Holt's brother, or else was no relation, depending on whom you read (everyone gets Leroy the banker and Luther the editor mixed up). He was not W. F. Holt's brother, as a matter of fact. He labored with the good proto-Imperialites of Pasadena, Santa Ana, etc., to organize a big citrus fair in Chicago for the year 1876. After some reverses, the event took place in 1886 and helped start the next southern California boom.—Oh, yes, the verb "to boom" was already in evidence! This Leroy Holt, "the benevolent banker," arrives in Imperial in November of 1900 and establishes the first bank in November 1901. Its name, of course, is the First National Bank of Imperial! Next come his First National Banks of Holtville and El Centro, then the First State Bank of Calexico. In due course the First National Bank of El Centro will become the Bank of Italy, then Bank of America. "Leroy Holt continued as the head officer at the bank's request, until he retired in 1933."—Harris, p. 25.

George Chaffey's fountain—Wagner, p. 126.

Credit to L. M. Holt for naming of Mexicali and Calexio—Hunt, p. 457.

Credit to Colonel Augustín Sangínez for naming of Mexicali and Calexio—Mexicali yellow pages (2002–2003), p. 6.

Description of Holt—After a 1902 photograph in Patterson, p. 87.

"Mr. Holt was a boomer by temperament and training . . ."—Holmes et al., p. 58.

38. Continued from Page A1 (2003)

Epigraph: "To them, the Romantic Hero was no longer the knight . . ."—Lewis, p. 616 *(Babbitt)*.

All text—From the *San Diego Union-Tribune*, Thursday, May 29, 2003, p. A12 ("From the Front Page" section).

39. Los Angeles (1900)

Epigraph: "As you grow bolder . . ."—Snyder, p. 26 ("The Place, the Region, and the Commons").

Urban percentage of U.S. population in 1900—Mott and Roemer, pp. 6–7.

A visitor from the East: The lawns of L.A. and "I have not seen a city so honeycombed . . ."—G. Harold Powell, pp. 18–19 (letter of 25 January 1904, to Gertrude Powell).

Birth of new towns in Los Angeles County—Based on the maps in Berlo, "Population History Maps."

1900 populations of Los Angeles (102,000) and San Francisco (343,000)—Kerig, p. 63.

Tale of C. H. Newcombe—*California Cultivator*, vol. XXIII, no. 6 (August 5, 1904), p. 124 ("A Profitable Lemon Grove").

"The Los Angeles River was the greatest attraction."—William Leslie Davis, p. 258.

Old Mission Brand orange label—McClelland and Last, p. 12.

"Ten thousand people from the east . . ."—*California Cultivator*, vol. XXIII, no. 14 (August 19, 1904), p. 347 ("News Notes of the Pacific Coast").

Los Angeles "has secured options on the Owens river water"—*California Cultivator*, vol. XXV, no. 5 (August 4, 1905), p. 107 ("News of Country Life in the Golden West").

Growth of Los Angeles, Imperial and San Diego counties 1900–1910—*Britannica Year-Book 1913*, p. 774 (entry on California).

"Los Angeles, Ventura and Santa Barbara Counties are leaders in the honey industry"—*California Cultivator*, vol. XXV, no. 5 (August 4, 1905), p. 107 ("News of Country Life in the Golden West").

Description of the Los Angeles Market—After photos and text in the *California Cultivator*, vol. XXIII, no. 4 (July 22, 1904), p. 75.

Tomatoscapes of West Hollywood—Kurutz, p. 76 (photo by C. C. Pierce, *ca.* 1900).

"Onions are still as good as gold mines . . ."—*California Cultivator*, vol. XXIV, no. 14 (April 7, 1905), p. 334 ("The Produce Markets").

Description of the Los Angeles Chamber of Commerce visit to El Centro—ICHSPM photograph, cat. #P92.31 (H. P. Bailey photo, "Los Angeles Chamber of Commerce excursion in El Centro, Cal., Feb. 29th 1908").

Circular from 1913: "Brawley, more than other towns, is possessed of the 'Los Angeles Idea' . . ."—UC Davis, Special Collections, California Local History coll., California Land and Water Co., brochure, "20,000 in 1920," 1913, unnumbered page.

40. The Imperial Idea (1901–2004)

Epigraph: "I am not against packing holidays . . ."—California State Archives, Department of Food and Agriculture, Bureau of Marketing, marketing-order files, 1941–1971, Box 1 (State of California. California Department of Agriculture. Public Hearings—May 2, 1967. Location: Coachella, California. Joan E. Smith, certified shorthand reporter [Rialto, California], p. 66).

A Hetzel image from 1920—ICHSPM photograph, cat. #P85.721 (credit: Hetzel).

Footnote: The Los Angeles booster on schools and the American idea: McGroarty, vol. 1, pp. 287, 289.

Leonard Knight: "I love people . . ."—Op. cit., page facing Plate 37 (words abridged; the ellipsis would fall right before "But when I get too close . . .").

41. Wilber Clark's Homestead (1901–2005)

Epigraph: "For an hour or more Barbara, at the piano, sang for them the simple songs they loved . . ."—Wright, p. 172.

Mr. Frank B. Moson: "The wonderful advantage of the Imperial Valley as a fattening center."—Samuel T. Black, vol. 1, p. 182.

Otis B. Tout: "Before Imperial was laid out . . ."—Tout, *The First Thirty Years*, p. 163.

Imperial Press and Farmer: "More ducks and other water fowl . . ."—Ibid., p. 164.

Imperial townsite's population in March 1901: "Less than a dozen souls"—Howe and Hall, p. 49.

Arrivals of George W. Donley and L. E. Cooley—Tout, *The First Thirty Years*, p. 61. In the anecdote about Mr. Cooley, the subordinate clause actually comes first.

Wilber Clark's automobile—Farr has him "driving down from Los Angeles" (op. cit., p. 464). As I remark, this could well have been by stagecoach.

Photograph of the headgates of the Imperial Canal on 15 May 1901—ICHSPM photograph, cat. #P92.43.

The marriage of Frank Oscar Clark—California State Archives. Microfilmed Imperial County records, 1851–1919. Roll #1433101. Index to Marriages, Men, v. 1–2; 1903–1923.

Dangerous accident involving the two married couples who "tried to drive to the mountains by way of Calexico . . ." —Tout, *The First Thirty Years*, p. 178.

Interview at Motor Transport Museum—With Carl Calvert, October 2003. Terrie Petree was present.

Secondo Guasti's new young realm of grapevines—Wagner and Blackstock, p. 13.

Although 1901 was not a great year for oranges and lemons in Riverside—Information from Riverside Municipal Museum, p. 31 ("Citrus Chronology, 1900–1922").

Photo of the newlywed Pattersons—ICHSPM photograph, cat. #P93.9.

Victor V. Vesey's neighbor: "Drive around the road until you find a crop that looks good . . ."—Vesey, oral history, p. 49.

Voter-registration information on Wilber Clark for 1890—*The California 1890 Great Register of Voters Index*, vol. 1, p. 16.

Hollywood has grown into a handful of houses in empty grey desert.—After Kurutz, double foldout before p. 56 ("Los Angeles, looking toward Hollywood from roof of Belmont Hotel, c. 1889, William Fletcher").

Census information on John L. Clark—California census index (1870) *California 1870 Census Index*, Volume I, A–K, Tule River Two, roll 92, pp. 263, 286.

Date of John Clark's judgeship—*History of the Counties of Fresno, Tulare and Kern*, p. 195.

The narrow escape and rapid marriage of Mrs. Mary A. Clark, *née* Graves, and "Tell the girls . . ."—Stewart, pp. 144, 280.

Miscellaneous information on Wilber Clark and his relatives—Zollinger-Peterson genealogical reports.

Remarks of "a certain Indian Commissioner": "The divine angel of discontent," etc.—Merrill E. Gates, quoted in Pike, p. 175.
Railroad price war of 1887—Dumke, pp. 24–25.
Los Angeles County subdivisions, etc. 1886–88—Ibid., p. 42.
Official closing of American frontier in 1890—Pike, p. 155.
Percentage of San Diego and Los Angeles counties which are irrigated farmland—Dumke, p. 242.
L. M. Holt on "Tropical California"—Lech, pp. 696–97 (Appendix K).
Price of first Imperial Valley cantaloupe of 1919—Imperial Valley Directory (1920), p. xi.
"There is plenty of good land to be had but all Government land worth taking is about gone."—Elliott, *History of San Bernardino and San Diego Counties*, p. 154.
Location of the town of Imperial within Water District No. 1—*Imperial Press and Farmer*, vol. II, no. 38 (Imperial, California, Saturday, January 3, 1903), p. 5 ("To Make the Desert Blossom . . .").
San Diego County as "larger than the State of Masachusetts . . ."—San Diego City and County Directory, p. 7.
Raymond Chandler: "This is the ultimate end of the fog belt . . ."—*Later Novels and Other Writings*, p. 180 (*The Lady in the Lake*, 1943).
Difficulty of the Palm Springs–to–Indio route in 1909—Laflin, *A Century of Change*, unnumbered page, entry for 1909.
View of Brawley road, remarks on dust clouds and the 1921 Studebaker—State of California Department of Transportation. Transportation Library, Sacramento. Imperial folder. Unattributed photocopy of magazine clipping, "Desert Driving Was Tough."
Mention of the Apostle Palm Oasis—Ibid., p. 20.
Photo of Howard Gard—Laflin, *Coachella Valley*, p. 45.
Photo of mesquite loaders—Ibid., p. 50.
Descriptions of Arabia and Mecca—Ibid., pp. 60–61.
Description of Salton—Lech, pp. 300–304.
News of the wagon road to Old Beach—*Los Angeles Times*, dated 28 November 1901, p. 9. Filed from Imperial on November 25 "From The Times' Resident Correspondent."
Los Angeles Times item mentioning Wilber Clark—Loc. cit.
Description of the residence of Joseph Becker—ICHSPM photograph, cat. #P91.42.8.
Correspondence between Imperial Canal and Alamo River—Kerig, p. 45.
Lunar parallel, with melting oxygen—Wells, *The First Men in the Moon*, pp. 53–77.
Footnote: A Coachella company which "proposes to furnish the people of that valley with liquid air"—*California Cultivator*, vol. XXIII, no. 6 (August 5, 1904), p. 142 ("The Produce Market").
Photo of Miss Clark—ICHSPM photograph, cat. #P93.9.
Description of the Browns' hardware store—ICHSPM photograph, cat. #P92.55
W. W. Master's work, the harness store and drugstore—Same *Los Angeles Times* article of 28 November 1901.
"There were enough tents to house a circus now . . ."—DeBuys and Myers, p. 209.
Erection of 4 brick buildings in 1902, including Clark's hardware store—Tout, *The First Thirty Years*, p. 167.
"Water was in the ditches . . ."—Howe and Hall, p. 57.
Clark's ad—*Imperial Valley Press and Farmer*, vol. II, no. 21, Saturday, September 6, 1902, p. 6.
1902 roster of the Farmers' Institute—Howe and Hall, pp 119–20. 1902 is one of the best years ever for hop-growing in California history; there is a substantial crop of sugar beets, a weak honey crop, an average wool crop; these are the highlights of *Appletons' Annual Cyclopaedia*, 1902, p. 701 (entry for United States of America [California]), so it would seem that despite the claims of the boosters and boomers, Imperial has not yet broken out of its own dreams, for I'm sad to say that these items are associated only peripherally with Imperial.
Clark's hunting trip—*Imperial Valley Press and Farmer*, vol. II, no. 25, October 4, 1902, p. 5.
Tale of the Edgar brothers: "They soon founded a farm implement and heavy hardware business in Imperial . . ." —Harris, p. 23.
1903 mention of hardware store in the newspaper—From information in Tout, *The First Thirty Years*, p. 168.
Wilber Clark's acreage in 1903—*Imperial Valley Press and Farmer*, vol. II, no. 38, Saturday, January 3, 1903, p. 11 ("Land Owners Under Imperial System").
Imperial Valley crop acreage increase in 1903—Nadeau, p. 145.
Clark's ads in 1903—*Imperial Valley Press and Farmer*, vol. II, no. 44, Saturday, February 14, 1903, p. 5; no. 51, Saturday, April 11, 1903, p. 3.
"Our popular businessman, Wilber Clark."—Michael Banta, *Conquest of a Continent: Nine Generations on the American Frontier*, no publication information since forwarded to me by a researcher (his report is a restricted file in my papers at Ohio State University), p. 384. This must have been an article in the *Imperial Valley Press and Farmer*.
Officially registered land transactions of the Clarks as grantors—California State Archives. Microfilmed Imperial County records, 1851–1919. Roll #1433101. Index to Grantors, 1851–1907. On March 10, 1903, and March 20,

1904, Margaret Clark is the grantor and the County of San Diego is the grantee in two transactions recorded in Book 14, pp. 59 and 60. This same Margaret S. Clark, although the County Recorder's index adds to her surname "(or Prest)," so we know that she has married, is the grantor and the Imperial Land Company is the grantee in another transaction recorded in Book 18, p. 210. On September 11, 1903, Wilber Clark is the grantor and the County of San Diego is the grantee in a transaction recorded in Book 14, p. 35. On March 15, 1906, Wilber Clark is the grantor and G. W. McCollum is the grantee in a transaction recorded in Book 18, page 386. (Sale of hardware store to A. L. Hill, September 1904: This is not recorded in the county index; or if it is, the county clerk and I failed to find it. I have already cited Farr for this.)

Depiction of 1904 auction of lots in Imperial—ICHSPM photograph, cat. #P94.16.10.

California Development Company as controller of water rights—Kerig, p. 44.

Constant economic losses caused by the irregular water supply through 1903–4 season—*National Geographic* magazine, 1906 (?), vol. XVIII, no. 1, Arthur P. Davis, Assistant Chief Engineer, "The New Inland Sea (An Account of the Colorado River Break)," p. 38.

Otis B. Tout: "Thirty-seven votes were cast, although the town had 800 inhabitants."—*The First Thirty Years*, p. 174.

Officially registered land transactions of the Clarks as grantees—Loc. cit. Index to Grantees, 1851–1907. On May 19, 1904, Margaret S. Clark is the grantee and the Imperial Town Co. the grantor (Book 10, p. 278). On May 28, 1904, Margaret S. Clark is the grantee and the Imperial Town Co. the grantor (Book 10, p. 139). On September 20, 1902, Wilber Clark is the grantee and the Imperial Town Co. the grantor, in a transaction recorded in Book 10, p. 111. On March 25, 1907, Wilbur (yes, with a *u*) Clark is the grantee and Harry Cross the grantor (Book 8, p. 319). On April 24, 1907, Wilber Clark is the grantee and the Imperial Land (not Town) Co. the grantor in a transaction recorded in Book 10, p. 216.

Hugo de Vries on Imperial: "Like all cities in the west . . ."—*Journal of San Diego History*, vol. XXI, no. 1, p. 38.

"Freight receipts at Imperial . . ."—Tout, *The First Thirty Years*, p. 177.

Description of the Varney brothers' store in Imperial—ICHSPM photograph, cat. #P92.71.

Hog wealth of Mr. McKim, 1906—*California Cultivator*, vol. XXVI, no. 17 (April 27, 1906), p. 403 ("Queries and Replies").

"Sharp's Heading is a cheap wooden structure. . ."—*National Geographic* magazine, 1906 (?), vol. XVIII, no. 1, Arthur P. Davis, Assistant Chief Engineer, "The New Inland Sea (An Account of the Colorado River Break)," p. 41.

De Vries: "I was particularly surprised at the speed with which all kinds of weeds . . ."—*Journal of San Diego History*, same essay, p. 36.

Description of the "submarine"—The old man was Carl Calvert, interviewed in Campo, October 2003. Terrie Petree was present. For a photo of a "submarine" with pipes, see Laflin, *Coachella Valley*, p. 133.

"Cattle and hogs are going forward . . ."—*California Cultivator*, vol. XXVI, no. 14 (April 6, 1906), p. 323 ("News of Country Life in the Golden West").

Raymond Chandler: "There's a peculiar thing about money . . ."—*Later Novels and Other Writings*, p. 612 (*The Long Goodbye*, 1953).

Chandler: "I would have stayed in the town where I was born . . ."—Ibid., p. 625.

First edifices of Calexico—Roemer, p. 16.

The Mexican adobe house and surroundings—Archivos album 1, no. 29.AHM/166.1/2 (Mexicali *ca.* 1904, adobe house).

Barbara Worth as "the 'Imperial Daughter' of the Imperial Valley . . ."—E Clampus Vitus website (narrative by Milford Wayne Donaldson).

Judge Farr on the Imperial Valley's women: "Most of these are country born and bred . . ."—Op. cit., p. 76.

G. W. McCollum: This individual sat on the Calexico Board of Trustees from 1908 through 1912. In 1909 "there was an opportunity to purchase the hardware store of Geo. W. McCollum at Calexico, a larger business than the one [Anderson and Meyers were] already operating at Holtville."—After Tout, *The First Thirty Years*, pp. 282, 393.

Acreage of Clark's property and 1911 title deed—Mr. P., private investigator (see note on restricted names in bibliography). Report of investigation, July 5, 2003. Subject: RESTRICTED, RESTRICTED, Wilber Clark. Page 6, information from 1920 Soundex/Census records.

Edith Karpen's memories of the Clark ranch—Based on an interview in January 2004. Alice Woodside was present.

"*IMPERIAL COUNTY SHOWS RAPID INCREASE . . .*"—Imperial Valley Directory (1912), p. iii ("Our County").

Tale of Chase Creamery—*California Cultivator*, vol. XXIV, no. 26 (June 30, 1905), p. 611 ("News of Country Life in the Golden West").

Tale of Imperial Valley Dairymen's Association and Cardiff Creamery—*California Cultivator*, vol. XXIV, no. 10 (March 10, 1905), p. 227 ("News of Country Life in the Golden West").

Imperial County Development Agent's report on butter production, 1916—Imperial County Agricultural Commission papers. A. M. Nelson, Development Agent, Imperial County, El Centro, California "BUTTER PRODUCTION IN IMPERIAL COUNTY." Page 2 of 2-page typescript (the first page relates to cotton production in the same year and is cited below in the chapter on "Between the Lines").

Hetzel photo of Milk Producers Association—ICHSPM, photo uncoded as of 2002. I have abbreviated the banner.

Number of Imperial County dairies in 1926—Imperial Valley Directory (1926), p. 357.

Number of Imperial County dairies in 1930—Imperial Valley Directory (1930), p. 361.

Number of Imperial County dairies in 2001—Imperial Valley yellow pages (2001), p. 101.

Footnote: ". . . the growth, peak, and total collapse of the Imperial Valley dairy industry . . ."—Paul Foster reports (2007) ("Imperial Color Commentary"). Paul adds: "Today a typical U.S. dairy operation would have several hundred head, would be milking at least 100 cows daily (most likely more), and would have hired hands supporting a centralized operation with automated feeding and milking systems. As a result, dairy has moved from a hobby activity, where a farmer kept a few cows to provide milk and sell the cream for butter production at the local creamery, to a very high capital investment business combined with a high daily labor expenditure, requiring economies of scale that result in the production of thousands of pounds of milk daily."

Lack of reference to Wilber Clark as a dairyman in the 1914 Imperial Valley Directory—Page 321. Ditto for the directories of 1924 (p. 99) and 1926 (p. 98).

Otis P. Tout: "USE THE INDICES"—*The First Thirty Years*, p. 7.

I gather that San Diego men are likewise involved.—I gather this because the Imperial Valley Directory (1912) says so on p. ii.

Footnote: Zane Grey: "A seemingly endless arm of the blue sea . . ."—Op. cit., p. 171.

Completion date of the San Diego and Arizona Railroad—Tout, *The First Thirty Years*, p. 358.

Location of Mormon Battalion's campsite—Farris, p. 13. The place was between Dixieland and Plaster City.

"A siding on the San Diego & Arizona Railway . . ."—Wray, p. 67.

The largest ostrich herd in America—Imperial County Agriculture Commission papers, 1917, p. 2.

"During trading hours the streets are lined . . ."—Farr, p. 281 (Edgar F. Howe).

D. G. Whiting's ranch—Ibid., p. 64.

"The Poole Place"—Ibid., pp. 53–54.

"A profitable express business has been worked up on the same."—Ibid., p. 465.

Description of the Valley Cream Company—Ibid., p. 359.

Hugo de Vries on red purslane—*Journal of San Diego History*, vol. XXI, no. 1, p. 36.

Description of Seeley in 1917—Farr, Seeley chapter.

Footnote: Seeley population, 1910 and 1990—Berlo, "Population History Compilation," p. 437.

"Dixieland was planned . . ."—Tout, *The First Thirty Years*, p. 362.

Customs Service communication: "The latest shipment of opium by this crowd . . ."—N.A.R.A.L. Record Group 36. Records of the U.S. Customs Service. Calexico Customs Office. Incoming Official Correspondence (9L-60). October 15, 1902–March 23, 1916. Box No. 3 of 5: November 1913 to July 1914. Folder "March 1914–July 1914: [4/4]." Letter to the Deputy Collector in Charge, Calexico, Cal., from John B. E. [illegible], Collector, Office of the Collector, Treasury Department, U.S. Customs Service, Port of Los Angeles, Cal., July 14, 1914, p. 1 of 2. See also: Incoming Correspondence Regarding Smuggling (9L-61). July 25, 1914–May 23, 1922. Box 2 of 2: From May 1914 to May 1922. Folder: May 1916–16 December 1916. Letter from unnamed Mounted Inspector (no signature on carbon), Calexico, Cal., to the Deputy Collector in Charge, Calexico, Cal., August 28, 1916.

Footnote: Death of Steffano—Same as latter folder. Letter from unknown Deputy Collector (signature cut off from carbon), Calexico, Calif., to the Collector of Customs, Los Angeles, Calif., August 28, 1916.

Clark's absence from Chambers of Commerce listings—Tout, *The First Thirty Years*, p. 194. Very well. From the western edge of El Centro, which in this map resembles a yellow pistol pointing straight upward, to Seeley, I find the following roads running north-south: Clark, which of course attracts my notice but which is far southeast of wherever Mobile could have been, Ferrell, Austin, Forrester, Gullet, which refuses to actually cross S80, Silsbee, which is almost in Seeley, then Bennett, which terminates in the El Centro U.S. Naval Auxiliary Air Facility; finally comes Drew Road. Silsbee has inscribed itself between Bennett and Drew. If the 1912 Dixieland view was drawn at all to scale, then Mobile would seem to have been somewhere between Forrester and Austin. Hoping to magnify my knowledge of this region, I inspect the inset maps of El Centro and Seeley; unfortunately, the former's westward extremity is Austin, and the latter goes no farther east than Bennett.—What lies between Austin and Bennett on S80? My guess would be: the onetime residence of Clark, Wilber, dairy and vineyard, Mobile, P.O. El Centro.

Listing for the Clarks in 1914—Imperial Valley Directory (1914), p. 76.

Seeley's cotton gins—Farr, Seeley chapter.

Listing for the Clarks in 1920—Imperial Valley Directory (1920), p. 52; Zollinger-Peterson genealogical reports.

Nice lady at County Assessor's office—Here is more data from the interesting object she showed me: Map number 9-9, second standard parallel south, right below the Riverside County boundary. There was the ancient beachline of Lake Cahuilla; there was Salton Sea Beach, not to mention the Desert Shores Community District. While the lady at the desk was chatting on the telephone with her niece, whom she called *chiquita,* I discovered that one square of what seemed to be the Torres-Martinez Indian reservation had been crossed out in favor of the Salton Community Services District. Next came the square labeled Oasis Joint Union 1956 (Dixieland-Westmorland x'd over).

"A home, good friends, a fair day's labor . . ."—Howe and Hall, p. 138.

The Secret of Happy Wives—*California Cultivator,* vol. LXV, no. 10, September 5, 1925, p. 221.

Elizabeth Clark in 1930—Department of Commerce, Bureau of the Census, Fourteenth Census of the United States, 1930, Population Schedule, Enumeration District 19-125A(?), Supervisor's District 15, Sheet 8A, stamped 120, handwritten 6575; image from ancestry.com.

"Oh, Harvest Land . . ."—*I.W.W.T.D. and Book,* p. 62 (T.D. and H, "Harvest Land," before 1923). Needless to say, Wilber Clark would not have had much sympathy for Wobblies. This song, however, seems both apt and apolitical.

42. *Mexicali (1904–1905)*

Epigraph: "Mexican lands are entitled to half the water . . ."—*Los Angeles Times,* December 27, 1925, p. B4 ("Selfish interests").

Baja California's 47-year rainy spell (which began in 1900)—Whitehead et al., p. 307 (Eduardo Paredes Arellano, Secretaría de Agricultura y Recursos Hidráulicos, Mexicali, "Water, the Most Important Natural Resource for the State of Baja California, Mexico").

Image of Mexicali main street—ICHSPM photograph, cat. #P94.16.2.

The layout of Mexicali in 1904—AHMM, photo album 1, map in protective sleeve on back cover, "Proprietarios y construcciones en Mexicali, según el censo de 1904," Dibujo A. Bolio, 1991; CIH UNAM-UABC, p. 177.

Cyanotype of Mrs. Ethel Wellcome's social, 1906—ICHSPM photograph, cat. #P94.16.2

Plans of the Lower California Development Company—*California Cultivator,* vol. XXIII, no. 14 (August 19, 1904), p. 347 ("News Notes of the Pacific Coast").

43. *The Sweet Young Night (2002)*

Epigraph: "But there was always Mexicali . . ."—Waters, pp. 306–7.

"Great wire gates" and "at five minutes to nine began the exodus back to the United States"—Ibid., p. 308.

The nightclub singer's encounter with the "White Slave Law"—*Gringo Gazette,* March 2003, p. 1 ("Editor's Note: March 14th Mexicali turns 100 years old.") "It was all so innocent in those days," she writes.

Imperial Press and Farmer, 1903: "The collection of pictures is unlimited . . ."—Vol. II, no. 38 (Imperial, California, Saturday, January 3, 1903), p. 12 ("The World's Picture Gallery: Sights You Would Travel Miles to See, Are Seen Every Morning in Imperial").

The spy from Northside in 1835—Richard Henry Dana. See Samuel T. Black, vol. 1, p. 61.

"But there was more in Barbara's Desert now than pictures woven magically in the air . . ."—Wright, p. 364.

"Not a vulgar greenback . . ."—Waters, loc. cit.

What happened in 1830s San Diego when ladies danced "El Son"—Samuel T. Black, vol. 1, pp. 63–64.

44. *Imperial's Center (1904–1907)*

Epigraph: "It was with a singular feeling . . ."—Although his book was published in 1911, James *(Wonders of the Colorado Desert)* explicitly dates this observation as having taken place in March 1906.

Photo #P85.13.1—Catalogue number from the ICHSPM.

Photo from Mexicali—Display at Mexicali Casa de Cultura, 2003: "Inundación de Mexicali, 1906."

"Serious and urgent"—Senate Doc. No. 212, Fifty-ninth Congresss, second session. Imperial Valley or Salton Sink Region. Message from the President of the United States relative to the threatened destruction of the overflow of the Colorado River, . . . January 12, 1907. Southern Pacific Imperial Valley Claim (1909).

The immortal words of Otis B. Tout: "Silt—that's the devil we've got to fight!"—Otis B. Tout, *Silt,* p. 3.

The Colorado's silt content exceeded the Nile's tenfold—Information supplied in Montgomery, p. 41.

Once upon an even more prehistoric time (or, as translated by my *Salton Sea Atlas,* millions of years ago), the Gulf of California wetted Indio. But in time the Colorado built a wall of silt across the Imperial Valley, leaving Lake Cahuilla's trapped waters to wax and wane over the centuries in homage to this flood and that; right now the Salton Sink is dry, and had better stay so forever, because we've built saltworks and homesteads there. If anything, we're afraid that it will get too dry, for the Imperial Canal's choking and strangling with—Silt, by Otis B. Tout. **WATER IS HERE**, but only sustained effort can keep it here.

"We hesitated about making this cut . . ."—Farr, p. 127 (narrative of C. R. Rockwood, 1909). The President of Mexico's not precisely averse; the U.S. Congress meanwhile seems disinclined to allow Imperial to suck the Colorado's breast: Better navigation than irrigation! Imperial, being thirsty, disagrees; Imperial must have water;

the Mexicans require a mere 50% of what will flow through our new canal, and maybe not less; we'll put up the capital. Temporarily, I said; we'll figure out something better before high water in 1905.

"Mexican Dwellers Along the Canal"—*Out West*, vol. XXIV, no. 1, January 1906, p. 11 (Edwin Duryea, Jr., C.E., "The Salton Sea Menace").

An engineer: "Sandy soil that eats away like so much sugar."—Southern Pacific Imperial Valley Claim (1909), p. 21.

"J. C. Thompson has rigged a double cable across New River . . ."—Tout, *The First Thirty Years*, p. 178.

"It was he who discovered the source of the water . . ."—*Out West*, vol. XXIV, no. 1, January 1906, p. 11 (Edwin Duryea, Jr., C.E., "The Salton Sea Menace").

"The great cataract, which resembles Niagara Falls . . ."—*National Geographic* magazine, 1906 (?), vol. XVIII, no. 1, Arthur P. Davis, Assistant Chief Engineer, "The New Inland Sea (An Account of the Colorado River Break)," p. 49.

"THE SAFETY OF $100,000,000 IN THE BALANCE."—"The New Inland Sea," p. 41.

"Here was the gay, careless life . . ."—Farr, pp. 211–12 ("Medical History," by Dr. F. Peterson).

Closure of the Colorado break with 11,000 flatcar loads of gravel—Southern Pacific Imperial Valley Claim (1909), p. 22.

A settler: "Characteristically American . . ."—Howe and Hall, p. 104.

45. The Third Line (1907)

Epigraph: "Because no single version of a map can serve all purposes . . ."—Greeley and Batson, p. 16.

San Diego . . . no longer reaches east of the Anza-Borrego badlands—Specifically, Imperial County's western border is a more or less south-north line from Mexico up through the east edge of Anza-Borrego badlands to (and I quote) "the second standard parallel south of San Bernardino Base and Meridian, at the common corner of township nine, range nine east, and township ninety-five, range eight east"—this elaborately labeled point marks the northwest corner of the new Imperial County—dissects off Imperial's west-pointing tail, leaving it to struggle as best it might within the now slightly inimical confines of San Diego County.—Coy, p. 113.

46. Subdelineations: Paintscapes (1903–1970)

Epigraph: "The magnitude, on every level of experience and meaning . . ."—Fondation Beyeler, p. 30 (letter from Rothko to John and Dominique de Menil, 1966).

"Now knowe that all *Paintinge* imitateth nature"—Hilliard, p. 54.

"The goodnes of a picture after the liffe . . ."—Ibid., p. 58.

Photographer's account of the composition of "Clearing Winter Storm"—Ansel Adams, pp. 103–4, 106 (commentary on "Clearing Winter Storm").

Rothko to Stanley Kunitz: "Start new" in "a new land"—Breslin, p. 283.

Breslin on Rothko's multiforms—Ibid., pp. 245, 235.

Painting Number 10: A "humanized sun"—Ibid., p. 277.

"To paint a small picture is to place yourself outside your experience . . ."—Fondation Beyeler, p. 25 (Rothko typescript, 1951 MOMA symposium).

One collector: "What were they made of, after all? . . ."—Fondation Beyeler, p. 180 (essay by Ben Heller).

"Rothko's paintings grow beautiful, reaching out to a viewer with their sensuous color . . ."—Breslin, p. 283.

Breslin: "Rothko's empty canvases are filled with ceaseless movement . . ."—Ibid., p. 278.

Rothko on the Houston Chapel: "Something you don't want to look at."—Breslin, p. 469 (Rothko to Ulfert Wilke, 1967).

One admirer: "All that remains of Rothko's once rich colors . . ."—Fondation Beyeler, p. 31 (essay by Oliver Wick).

47. Imperial Reprise (1781–1920)

Epigraph: "They had all kinds of picturesque names for highways . . ."—Sinclair, p. 79 (*Oil!*, 1927).

PART THREE

REVISIONS

48. Futures (1883–2007)

Epigraph: "In compiling the present report . . ."—Weide and Barker, p. 1.

Wallace W. Elliott: "The future of San Bernardino Valley is fruit culture."—Elliott, *History of San Bernardino and San Diego Counties*, p. 117.

Helen Hunt Jackson: ". . . one of those midsummer days of which Southern California has so many in spring . . ." —Jackson, p. 36.
Wheat and barley in California, 1880–1906—*Britannica*, 11th ed., vol. 5, p. 12 (entry on California).
Wheat rust infection in Imperial County—Farr, p. 188 (Walter E. Packard, "Agriculture").
Wheat as "a classic swing commodity"—Paul Foster reports (2007) ("Imperial Color Commentary," comments on "Wheat: Column G, lines 5–17, Ag Census").
"Two States in the Union produce half of the entire barley crop . . ."—*Appletons' Annual Cyclopaedia*, 1892, p. 73 (entry on California). The greatest production was in the southwest and south, including Ventura, Los Angeles, Orange, and San Bernardino counties, "where this cereal is produced with the aid of irrigation, and without rainfall from seed time to harvest."
Judge Farr: "Barley and wheat were the winter crops . . ."—Op. cit., p. 188 (Walter E. Packard, "Agriculture").
The same, on pears and apricots—Ibid., p. 193 (F. W. Waite, "Horticulture").
Fruit and tree nut gross income in Imperial County, 2005—Imperial County Agriculture Commissioner's papers, 2005, p. 2.
Top five Imperial crops, 2005—Ibid., p. 10.
"During the past years nearly every kind of fruit and nuts grown . . ."—Farr, p. 192 (F. W. Waite, "Horticulture").
"There is in America a nomadic race of beings . . ."—Ibid., p. 150 (Edgar F. Howe, "Irrigation").

49. *Harry Chandler's Homestead (1898–1938)*

Epigraph: "The model ranch of the Valley . . ."—Howe and Hall, p. 169.
Description of the Biltmore—From a visit in 2005.
Description of the CRLC's cotton sampling room—*Los Angeles Times*, April 26, 1925, p. J10 (A. W. Swanson, "A Remarkable Room In Which Cotton Experts Meet").
Image of Chandler and President Obregón, *ca.* 1925—After a photo reproduced in Celso Bernal, p. 268.
Chandler's attendance at Calles's inauguration—Kerig, p. 242.
Tale of the Volcano Lake Compromise—Ibid., pp. 210, 229.
Chandler "took a prominent part in the organization of the company . . ."—*Los Angeles Times*, September 24, 1944, p. 1 ("Harry Chandler Called by Death: Publisher, 80, Succumbs in Hospital Following Two Heart Attacks"), continuation on p. 6.
"Chandler's mistake"—Baja website, p. 2 of 8.
The agrarian mind's "longing for independence . . ."—Kimbrell, p. 9 (Wendell Berry, "The Whole Horse: The Preservation of the Agrarian Mind").
"The fundamental difference between agrarianism and industrialism . . ."—Ibid., pp. 8–9.
Footnote: "One history's" skepticism regarding *I'll Take My Stand*—Watkins, p. 372.
Properties of Earl and Hearst—Magón, p. 69 (essay by editor).
The "undated map of the Mexicali Valley, faded and stained, made probably before 1940"—AHMM, undated map: "Comisión Internacional de Aguas Río Colorado: Plano General de la Region Deltaica . . ."
"The methods of The King's Basin Land and Irrigation Company . . ."—Wright, p. 283.
Holt's special train; his commission from the SP—*Valley Grower*, July/August 2002, pp. 30–31 (Steve Bogdan, "That Man Holt").
The "horrible company that hoarded the land"—Dwyer, p. 59 (statement of 1936).
Chandler's arrival in the Imperial Valley—Frisby, pp. 41–42.
Harry Chandler as 3rd to file in Imperial Valley—Kerig, p. 60.
Composition of the Chandler Syndicate—Ibid., pp. 64–67.
Proposed renaming of Port Isabel to Port Otis—Ibid., p. 260.
Chandler as 85% owner of CRLC stock—Ibid., p. 292.
"There is no doubt that they sought wealth and power . . ."—Ibid., p. 70.
Otis B. Tout: "Henry Auster"—*Silt*, p. 28.
"Purchased outright from the Mexican government"—Tout, *The First Thirty Years*, p. 364.
The tale of Blythe and Andrade (incl. "now held title to virtually the entire Mexican portion of the delta")—Kerig, pp. 40–41; Hendricks, unnumbered pp. 4–8.
Entities, events and acreage of 1898—Tout, *The First Thirty Years*, pp. 363–64.
Footnote: In 1910 W. F. Holt "announced the improvement of 32,000 acres in Mexico"—Ibid., p. 192.
Same footnote, on the Inter-California Land Company—Howe and Hall, p. 119.
Tale of the Sociedad de Irrigación y Terrenos de la Baja California, S.A.—Kerig, pp. 46–48.
"Largest Irrigated Ranch in the World"—*Imperial Valley Press and Farmer*, vol. II, no. 25, October 4, 1902, p. 1.
Ads from the Sociedad de Irrigación y Terrenos—For instance, *Imperial Valley Press and Farmer*, vol. II, no. 38, Saturday, January 3, 1903, p. 2.

Holabird's hunting trip—*Imperial Valley Press and Farmer*, vol. II, no. 11, Saturday, April 11, 1903, p. 1.

Andrade-CRLC transaction, 23 May 1904—California State Archives. Microfilmed Imperial County records, 1851–1919. Roll #1433101. Index to Grantors, 1851–1907. Book 17, p. 190. Nadeau, p. 165, gives the figure of 830,000 acres owned by Chandler's syndicate in the Mexicali Valley. DeBuys and Myers, p. 142, write that the syndicate's holdings were 862,000 acres. Here is Hunt, p. 456: "Securing the interest of General H. G. Otis, owner of the *Los Angeles Times*, the outcome was the purchase of a great ranch of 700,000 acres, lying partly in the United States and partly in Mexico."

SITBC-CRLC transaction, 13 June 1904—California State Archives. Microfilmed Imperial County records, 1851–1919. Roll #1433101. Index to Grantees, 1851–1907.

The California-Mexico Land and Cattle Company accepts delivery of Texas cattle for fattening—*California Cultivator*, vol. XXIII, no. 10 (August 19, 1904), p. 251 ("News Notes of the Pacific Coast").

"Their plan was simple . . ."—DeBuys and Myers, p. 142.

Repetition of charge that CRLC did not pay for water—For instance, "by 1904, land below the Mexican border, much of it American owned, was consuming free of charge seven times as much Colorado River water from the Imperial Canal as was being used in the valley itself."—E Clampus Vitus website (narrative by Milford Wayne Donaldson). The accusation is also leveled at Rockwood.

"It may be said that the Chandler interests are the largest cash customer . . ."—Tout, *The First Thirty Years*, p. 365.

Footnote: "The partners of IID . . ."—Munguía, pp. 142–43. In fact, relations between the Colorado River Land Company and the mostly bankrupt consortium of mutual water companies in Northside that preceded IID soon went bad. The consortium's receiver, Holabird, and the Chandler Syndicate's mouthpiece, the *Los Angeles Times*, found themselves in the peculiar position of promoting land speculation in American and Mexican Imperial while decrying the actions of the new Imperial Irrigation District, not to mention the supposed insults and slanders of various Imperial County journalists.

The sober citizen: "The most valuable portion of the valley . . ."—House of Representatives (1907), p. 20 (testimony of Mr. Newell).

Comparative acreages in 1908—Chamberlin, p. 44.

California-Mexico Land and Cattle Company holdings, 1910—Howe and Hall, p. 169.

". . . this model ranch owned by a Los Angeles stock syndicate . . ."—Farr, p. 65.

Employment figures of CRLC, 1929—Tout, *The First Thirty Years*, p. 366.

Land claims of the Colorado River Land Company in 1904—*Los Angles Times*, July 27, 1904, p. 7 ("ARBITRATE AT IMPERIAL: Truce Arranged Between the Ranchers and Company. President Heber Faces Angry Crowd of Irrigators. Trouble Coming Out of Sale of Water Rights.").

CRLC cotton production value after World War I—Dwyer, p. 41.

History of the Colorado River Land Company through 1920s—Kerig, pp. 58, 80, 82, 83, 275, 255, 269, 257–58, 274, 270, 260.

One of Los Angeles's glorifiers on Chandler: "It was his inspiration . . ."—Carr, p. 324.

"The syndicate's members viewed the entire Colorado River delta . . ."—Kerig, p. 84.

"There is no law nor revolutionary principles . . ."—Quoted in Dwyer, p. 18.

50. *Practically Self-Supporting in Three Years (1865–2004)*

Epigraph: "But this is tremendous!"—Wells, *The First Men in the Moon*, p. 37.

"There is no escaping the stereotype of an ideal agrarian world . . ."—Spencer Museum of Art, p. xi.

John Steuart Curry's "Valley of the Wisconsin"—Ibid., plate 18.

"Many of our old neighbors toiled and sweated . . ."—Muir, pp. 106–7 (*The Story of My Boyhood and Youth*, 1913).

The undated stock photo which strangely resembles Nazi homeland propaganda—California State Archives. Olson Photo Collection. Accession #94-06-27 (238–387). Box 2 of 7. Folder #94-06-27 (331–343): Farms and Farming. Photo #94-06-27-0336. "Flax harvest."

Advertisement for Illinois lands, 1865—*Harper's Weekly* facsimiles, p. 256.

Los Angeles per capita acreage figures for 1880—California census (1880), pp. 2, 8, 1 (note that page numbers repeat in this document according to enumeration district).

The first President Roosevelt: "The object of the Government . . ."—Quoted in Smythe, p. 285.

"The Reclamation Act forbade the delivery of water on any government project . . ."—James, *Reclaiming the Arid West*, p. 30.

1917 advice to "experienced men with small means"—Packard, p. 15.

Judge Farr: "Imperial County was settled in a large part by those who did not have a large amount of capital."—Op. cit., p. 187.

Mention of Wilber Clark's grapes and dates—Ibid., p. 465.

Mr. Reider: "What the hell can I do with ten acres?"—California State Archives, Department of Food and Agriculture, Bureau of Marketing, marketing-order files, 1941–1971, Box 1 (State of California. California Department of Agriculture. Public Hearings—May 2, 1967. Location: Coachella, California. Joan E. Smith, certified shorthand reporter [Rialto, California], p. 95).

Statement of Richard Brogan—Interviewed by WTV, Calexico, April 2004. Terrie Petree was present.

Footnote: Chávez at Riverside Church—César Chávez, p. 113 ("At Riverside Church," spring 1971).

Footnote: Average farm size at the beginning of the twenty-first century—*California Agricultural Directory 2004–2005*, p. 108, figures for 1997–2002.

Paul S. Taylor: "The Reclamation Law provides for tremendous subsidies for water development . . ."—UC Berkeley. Bancroft Library. Paul S. Taylor papers. Carton 4. Folder 4:11: "Fight For Water." Typescript: "HEARINGS BEFORE THE NATIONAL COMMISSION ON URBAN PROJECTS, Volume 2, Testimony of Paul S. Taylor, July 5, 1967, San Francisco." Page number cut off on Bancroft's photocopy.

Señora Teresa García—Interviewed on 19 February 2004. Terrie Petree interpreted.

The proprietress of the small restaurant—Señora Socorro Ramírez, interviewed on the same day. Terrie Petree interpreted.

Footnote: "A community of farmers . . ."—UC Berkeley. Bancroft Library. Paul S. Taylor Papers. Carton 5. Folder 5:17: "National Reclamation in the Imperial Valley: Law vs. Politics, Final Draft, 1981." Page 4.

1918 refinements to acreage limitation—California Board of Agriculture (1918), pp. 8, 10.

Advertisement for Calipatria lots—*Imperial Valley Press*, vol. XIV, no. 8, Thursday evening, May 14, 1914, p. 3.

Harry Chandler as part owner of Calipatria townsite lands—Tout, *The First Thirty Years*, p. 348.

Acreage of IID directors Rose and Aten—Statements of these two individuals, in Senate Committee on the Colorado River Basin (1925), pp. 255, 265.

"These Lyons boys," Dave Williams, Harry Van den Heuvel—Farr, pp. 51, 52, 53.

Farr's acreage—Howe and Hall, p. 159.

Alice Woodside's remarks—Interview of February 2004, Sacramento. On the subject of large holdings she said: "Being a real estate agent, and as somebody who's gone out and bought a lot of property here in Sacramento, you know, residential real estate, and I think, more than any of my contemporaries, I had that drive to do that. I've been willing to go out and gather pieces of property and work with them. If you're willing to go out and work really hard . . . of course it's all right. But I've never had that water issue."—I asked her: "For the sake of argument, if the government subsidized reclamation and one man took control of all the reclaimed acres, how would you feel about it?"—She agreed that that would be wrong.

The fable of Seabrook Farms—*Quick Frozen Foods*, vol. XVII, no. 4, November 1954, p. 129.

Judge Farr: "As has already been learned by the reader of this volume . . ."—Op. cit., p. 60.

"Between 1910 and 1920 there began for the first time . . ."—Mott and Roemer, p. 7.

Advertisement for "Garden Tract Sites"—*Fresno Morning Republican*, Sunday, March 21, 1920, p. 18B.

Roosevelt on Subsistence Homestead Program—Watkins, p. 448, quoting Joseph Lash, *Eleanor and Franklin*.

"No boy should be deprived of the experience of harvesting . . ."—Sloane, p. 159.

Home Brand orange label—McClelland and Last, p. 8.

51. *The* Ejidos *(1903–2005)*

Epigraph: "A calpulli or chinacalli . . ."—Zorita, pp. 105–6.

Description of the view from the cemetery in Islas Agrarias—As seen in April 2004.

Definitions of *ejidos* and *colonias*, and their numbers in Baja and Tijuana in 2004—Augustín Pérez, reporter for *La Frontera* (Tijuana). Interviewed in English in a restaurant in Tijuana Centro, July 2004. Terrie Petree was present. I have interpolated approximate numbers of *ejidos* for Mexicali and Tijuana from Baja California's *VII Censo Ejidal* of 1993 (p. 13), whose figures seem close to Señor Pérez's.

"A colonial-era term that had been used to describe indigenous communities' common lands . . ."—Boyer, p. 75.

Varying interpretations of indigenous land tenure—Zorita, pp. 298–300 (translator's note 19).

Zapata leaves it up to each village to decide the form of property distribution of its *ejido*—Womack, p. 234.

Luis Cabrera: "rights established in the epoch of the Aztecs"—Joseph and Henderson, p. 345 (*The Restoration of the* Ejidos).

The 1912 bill for "the reconstitution of the *ejidos*"—Womack, p. 155.

Extracts from the Plan de Ayala—Womack, pp. 402–3. The entire Plan appears there as an Appendix.

Calles's attitude toward the *ejidos*—Kerig, pp. 245–46.

"Almost from the start, the *ejidos* bore the taste of salty tears."—DeBuys and Myers, p. 143.

José López—Interviewed in English in Mexicali, 2004.

Mexicali's 1915 *ejido* proposal—Kerig, p. 165.

Don Carlos Cayetano Sanders-Collins and his wife—Interviewed in Morelos (southwest of Algodones, in the Mexicali Valley), October 2003, Terrie Petree interpreting.

The restaurant proprietress—Señora Socorro Ramírez, interviewed on 19 February 2004 in her restaurant. Terrie Petree interpreted. Re: creating *fraccionamentos,* I asked her: "If a man does that, is that against the spirit of the reform of Cárdenas?"—"Yes, it goes go against his idea, but I've read that he got that idea from Germany."
Footnote: *Ejidos vs.* ranchos—Kerig, pp. 317, 373, 432.

PART FOUR

FOOTNOTES

53. *What I Wish I Knew About Meloland (1907–1998)*

Epigraph: "Half way between El Centro and Holtville . . ."—Tout, *The First Thirty Years*, p. 362.
Paragraph on Meloland, 1907–1909—*Desert Farmer*, Imperial Valley, May 1909, pp. 180–81 ("Meloland Ranch").
"MELOLAND SOCIAL EVENTS OF THE WEEK"—*Imperial Valley Press*, Friday, May 7, 1926, p. 2.
Califonia state road map—State of California. Department of Transportation. Transportation Library, Sacramento. Single item: State of California, Department of Engineering, California Highway Commission. Road Map of the State of California, Austin B. Fletcher, Highway Engineer, 1916.
Population figures for Meloland—Berlo, "Population History Compilation," pp. 326–27.
The many races of Meloland children—As seen in a 1939 ICHSPM photograph, uncatalogued as of 2002. White faces and brown faces likewise grimace or smile from the 1947 Meloland Elementary School class photo (*Imperial County: The Big Picture*, p. 43).
"Actively developed, highly improved, and is becoming thickly settled."—Same *Desert Farmer* article.
The veteran Imperialite—Kay Brockman Bishop, interviewed December 2006. Terrie Petree was present.
Types of soils in the Imperial and Mexicali valleys——Munguía, p. 11 (Francisco Raúl Venegas Cardoso).

54. *San Diego (1769–1925)*

Epigraph: "San Diego is wedded to her lethergy [*sic*] . . ."—Hendricks, unnumbered p. 10; no date given but must have been in or before 1907, and obviously after 1901.
Acreage of San Diego County, and "the area covered by the Colorado River Desert . . ."—McPherson, pp. 60–61.
Helen Hunt Jackson's description of the Pacific coast north of San Diego—Op. cit., p. 227.
Governor de Neve's report—Nunis, p. 59 (No. 89: Troops, 27 February 1777).
Acting Governor Arrillaga's description of San Diego—Op. cit., p. 98 (27 October 1796).
"Hides are plenty in the Pueblo . . ."—D. Mackenzie Brown, pp. 10–11 (John C. Jones, Bark Volunteer, San Diego, to Alpheus B. Thompson, Santa Barbara, November 7, 1833).
Richard Henry Dana, Jr., on San Diego—Op. cit., p. 143.
William Hartnell's description of San Diego—Op. cit., p. 25 (diary, May 27, 1839).
Most of the Missions' Indians have fled to Los Angeles in search of food and clothing—Information from Ryan, p. 60 (diary, July 14, 1839); p. 36 (letter to the Prefecture of the Second District—Los Angeles, June 11, 1839).
A British adventurer describes San Diego . . .—Ryan, vol. 2, p. 357 (this vol. orig. pub. 1851).
Population 2 decades after the British adventurer (actually 1873), and "it has a large park . . ."—McPherson, p. 63.
Dana on San Diego in 1859—Op. cit., p. 481.
Description of old ranch near Mission San Diego—After an anonymous photo in Kurutz, p. 78.
Date of first transcontinental train and of Sweetwater Dam, and "We may say that San Diego has a population of 150,000 . . ."—Dumke, pp. 137–38.
First reservoir; dams of 1918–24; capacity of county reservoirs, 1925—Pryde, pp. 105, 108.
"Where do the fine fruits come from . . ."—McPherson, p. 64.

55. *In Memoriam, Imperial Hazel Deed (1905–2002)*

Epigraph: ". . . we realize that California at its worst . . ."—*Fresno Morning Republican*, Sunday, March 21, 1920, p. 5, "Blessed California."
Birth preeminence of Ruth Reed—Tout, *The First Thirty Years*, p. 172.
Birth of Imperial Hazel Deed—Ibid., p. 178.
"The birth of a daughter to Mr. and Mrs. A. H. Rehkopf . . ."—Loc. cit.
Oren Deed's name I obtained from his daughter's death certificate. His birthplace is confirmed as Kansas.
Findings of my hired genealogists on the Deed family—Zollinger-Peterson reports. The fact that Imperial's ancestors were likely not native Californians is borne out by the *California 1870 Census Index*, Volume I, A–K (p. 380), which lists only an irrelevant Alexander Deede, aged 40, in San Francisco.

Non-appearance of the Deeds in the county indices—California State Archives. Microfilmed Imperial County records, 1851–1919. Roll #1433101.
The marriage of Samuel Dees and Uloa Harlan—Ibid. Index to Marriages, Men, v. 1–2; 1903–1923.
California Death Index entry for Hazel Deed—Op. cit., 1905–1929, vol. II (C–E), p. 2607.
"Eggplant, Imperial Valley, nominal"—*Fresno Morning Republican*, Sunday, March 21, 1920, p. 16, "Commercial News."
The citrus column—Ibid., Saturday, March 27, 1920, p. 20, "Commercial News."
"PHONE 3700 FOR THESE SPECIALS TODAY . . ."—Ibid., p. 24.

56. *Stolid of Face and Languid (1901–2003)*

Epigraph: "Mexican women turned their tortillas . . ."—Tout, *Silt*, p. 2.
"Potentially . . . the most valuable land in the United States"—House of Representatives (1907), p. 46 (testimony of Mr. Newell).
One study: Migrant farmworkers are "by any reckoning . . . the poorest . . ."—Dunbar and Kravitz, p. 2.
Same study: "Throughout much of the area, Mexican Americans were reduced . . ."—Ibid., p. 10.
Mr. Philip Ricker's letter to the editor—*Imperial Valley Press*, vol. 103, no. 22, Thursday, June 5, 2003, p. A4, "Voice of the People" column ("Farmers losing their grip on I.V.").
"Picture a man in desert garb . . ."—Tout, *The First Thirty Years*, p. 199 (Tout's eyewitness description of the murals written for his *El Centro Progress*).
Re: Waves of laborers of different ethnicities—The Riverside Municipal Museum, pp. 10–11, gives the following chronology for its locality:
1870s, Cahuilla and Yuma are orange workers in Riverside.
1880s–end of century, Chinese from Guangdong replace the Indians.
1893, Geary Act replaces Chinese with Japanese.
1910–onward, mostly Mexican immigrants.
"Suppose, for instance, that every Chinaman is driven out of the Santa Ana Valley . . ."—The Great Basin Foundation Center for Anthropological Research, vol. 1, p. 82 (citing *Rural Californian* 9:4:85).
"You know, maybe when I was a kid . . ."—Alice Woodside, interviewed in Sacramento, February 2004.

57. *The Days of Lupe Vásquez (2003)*

Epigraph: "The Imperial Valley's fertile soil . . ."—Imperial Irrigation District, "Fact Sheet: Imperial Valley Agriculture 2001," unnumbered first page.
Lupe's story—From interviews in Mexicali and Calexico, June 2003.
Footnote: California bans most hand-weeding, "declaring the practice an immediate danger to the health of thousands of workers"—*Los Angeles Times*, Thursday, September 23, 2004; California edition; "California" section, pp. B1, B7 (Miriam Pawel, "Standing Up for Farmworkers: State officials are expected to severely limit hand-weeding in fields, a practice recognized as harmful to laborers").
Footnote on county unemployment rates—Based on data in EDD printout (2001).

58. *"Lupe Is Luckier": The Days of José López from Jalisco (2003)*

Epigraph: "The spectacular incidents connected with the reclamation of the desert . . ."—Farr, p. 184.
José's story—Interview in Mexicali, June 2003.
Footnote: Cost of labor in early-twentieth-century Riverside *vs.* south China—The Great Basin Foundation Center for Anthropological Research, vol. 2 (Archaeology), p. 315.

PART FIVE

ELABORATIONS

60. *The Line Itself (1895–1926)*

Epigraph: "Every now and then a word crosses the border . . ."—Torre and Wiegers, p. 191 (Antonio Deltoro, "Cartography," 1999; trans. Christian Viveros-Fauné).
San Diego's alert to Mr. Wadham: "I have reason to believe that Mexicans . . ."—N.A.R.A.L. Record Group 36. Records of the U.S. Customs Service. Tijuana Customs Office. Letters Received from San Diego and Los Angeles (l–62). February 6, 1894–July 29, 1922. Box 1 of 1. Folder: "Letters Rec'd from Collector—San Diego 1894–1896." Letter from John C. Fisher (?), Collector, Office of the Collector of Customs, Port of San Diego, Cal., to Mr. Fred W. Wadham, Deputy Collector, etc., Tia Juana, Cal., April 27, 1895.

Establishment of English language requirement in naturalization—Crosthwaite, Byrd and Byrd, p. 69 ("Chronology: Changes in Immigration and Naturalization Law").

Arrival of first Immigration inspectors at Calexico—Tout, *The First Thirty Years*, p. 263.

"Of 2,182 Japs arriving at Mazatlan . . ."—Asiatic Exclusion League, p. 12 ("Supplementary Report," 1907).

"It makes sense to use fencing along the border in key locations . . ."—*New York Times*, Friday, May 19, 2006, "National" sec., p. A19 (Elisabeth Bumiller, "Bush Now Favors Some Fencing Along Border").

"I halted two mexicans on 2nd Street . . ."—N.A.R.A.L. Record Group 36. Records of the U.S. Customs Service. Calexico Customs Office. Incoming Official Correspondence (9L-60). October 15, 1902–March 23, 1916. Box No. 3 of 5: November 1913 to July 1914. J. E. Shreve, Deputy Collector of Customs, Report of Seizure, Calexico, Cal., January 4, 1914.

". . . Said W. M. Tiller . . ."—Ibid., Folder: November 15, 1913–Feb. 11, 1914. Report of Seizure #1204 (two five-tael tins of opium), April 9, 1914.

Incident at Cananea—Meyer et al., pp. 468–69.

"The Collector cites our amicable relations . . ."—N.A.R.A.L. Record Group 36, op. cit., Box 4 of 5: July 1914–June 1915. Bound volume labeled "Letters." Letter from W. H. Holabird, Office of the Receiver, The California Development Company, to the United States Collector of Customs, Los Angeles, Cal., January 21, 1915. COPY. Re (enclosed and referred to by Holabird): Letter from H. M. House, Supt. River Division, to J. C. Allison, Chief Engineer, Calexico, Calif., dated Andrade, Calif., Jan. 14, 1915. COPY.

Trans-border acreage of Imperial Irrigation District, 1920—Imperial Valley Directory (1920), front matter.

Footnote: The same, 1918—Imperial County Agricultural Commission papers. Letter of June 29, 1918, to Mr. Phil D. Swing, Chief Counsel, Imperial Irrigation District (1-page typescript).

Easy border crossings of Colorado River Land Company cattle—Kerig, p. 86.

"A New Kind of Pioneering in Imperial."—*Los Angeles Times*, April 11, 1926, p. J3 (Randall Henderson, "A New Kind of Pioneering in Imperial").

Imperial County Assessor's Map 17-15—The ancient bound volume in El Centro, of course.

Customs Collector, 1915: "Would strongly recommend, as a preventive measure . . ."—N.A.R.A.L. Record Group 36, op. cit., Incoming Official Correspondence (9L-60). October 15, 1902–March 23, 1916. Box 4 of 5: July 1914–June 1915. Bound volume labeled "Letters." Copy of report of W. J. Smith, Deputy Collector and Inspector of Andrade, Cal., in re situation at Algodones, on or before Feb. 4, 1915.

Allegations against Harry Chandler—Blaisdell, who concludes (p. 393) that Chandler "was not the grey eminence of Baja California border intrigues in 1914–15 . . ."

Shoot to kill order at beginning of Prohibition—N.A.R.A.L. Record Group 36, op. cit., Letters Received from San Diego and Los Angeles (l–62). February 6, 1894–July 29, 1922. Box 1 of 1. Folder: "Letters Rec'd—Los Angeles 1919–22." Letter from John B. Elliott, Collector of Customs, Los Angeles, to the Deputy Collector in Charge, Calexico, California, December 10, 1919.

Recommendation to place cement blocks at Tecate crossing—N.A.R.A.L. Record Group 36, op. cit., Port of Campo. General Correspondence 1919–1965. Box 1 of 1. Folder: "Historical Letters 1919–1965 [½]." Letter from H. T. Shepherd, Deputy Collector in Charge, Tecate, Calif., to Collector of Customs, Los Angeles, Calif., March 9, 1923.

61. The First Coyote (1895–1926)

Epigraph: "On the 28th of last February . . ."—Bowman and Heizer, p. 115 (10 April 1774).

Re: untracked movement over the border, it would seem that movement has never been accurately tracked. In 1923, for instance, fewer than 62,000 Mexicans came Northside. At least that's what the U.S. government says. The Mexican government says that more than 100,000 came.—Watkins, p. 395.

"PARTIES WILLIAM WALKER AND JAMES CHILLISON"—N.A.R.A.L. Record Group 36, op. cit., Calexico Customs Office. Incoming Official Correspondence (9L-60). October 15, 1902–March 23, 1916. Box 4 of 5: July 1914–June 1915. Bound volume labeled "Letters." Frank B. Ellis, Mounted Inspector, U.S. Department of Labor, Immigration Service, Port of Jacumba, Calif., February 14, 1915.

"Proceed immediately to Thermal . . ."—Ibid. Copy of telegram(?) from Connell, 1:10 a.m., WH Los Angeles, Cal., to Immigration, Calexico, Cal., February 13, 1915.

Foundation of Border Patrol HQ in El Centro; first patrol—Tout, *The First Thirty Years*, p. 263.

62. The First Hobo (1901)

Epigraph: "Two men, declared to be the first hoboes . . ."—Quoted in Tout, *The First Thirty Years*, p. 164.

63. *Twenty Thousand in 1920 (1906–1922)*

Epigraph: "Bigger crops mean bigger money."—*California Cultivator,* vol. LIV, no. 1, January 3, 1920, p. 12 (advertisement for Planet Jr. tools, made by S. L. Allen & Co., Philadelphia).

The brochure from the California Land and Water Company—UC Davis, Special Collections, California Local History coll., California Land and Water Co., brochure, "20,000 in 1920," 1913, front cover.

Date of vote to purchase the Gary Corner—*Imperial Valley Press,* vol. XIV, no. 7, Friday, May 8, 1914; p. 6.

"The club colors are green and white . . ."—Tout, *The First Thirty Years,* p. 339; although Tout calls it "the Woman's 10,000 Club," the sign over the door is definitely in the plural (see my 8" x 10" negative IV-LS-EC-03-03). The absorption of the Woman's Club of Imperial must have occurred after 1912, since the Imperial Valley Directory of that year lists both a Woman's Club of Imperial Valley and a Woman's 10,000 Club (p. x).

Footnote: The old lady who told me: "We used to have bridge parties at the Women's 10,000 Club . . ."—She was Edith Karpen, interviewed in Sacramento in January 2004. Her daughter Alice Woodside was present.

Imperial County as the 3rd-fastest-growing county in the U.S.; 1920 populations of El Centro and Brawley—Tout, *The First Thirty Years,* p. 240.

"YOU MAY FIGURE THAT . . . The Population Is Increasing at the rate of 40 per cent Every 24 Months." —Imperial Valley Directory (1912), p. 11.

Two years later there's even a library at the Colored School!—Imperial Valley Directory (1914), p. viii, list of county libraries.

The two views of the line and Calexico in 1911 and 1920—AHMM, photo album 1, no. 29.AHM/166.1/1 and 29.AHM/166.1/8.

Encomium to Calexico: "Long before the present generation was born . . ."—Farr, p. 269 (F. W. Roach, "Calexico").

Brawley's Sweetwater grapes, grain and melons in 1905—*California Cultivator,* vol. XXIV, no. 26 (June 30, 1905), p. 611 ("News of Country Life in the Golden West").

Land sales of the Brawley Town Company and the Calexico Town Company, and some typical names of grantees—California State Archives. Microfilmed Imperial County records, 1851–1919. Roll #1433101. Index to Grantees, 1851–1907.

". . . so that there will be room for more towns and settlers . . ."—ICHSPM document, cat. #A95.242.5. Southern Pacific Passenger Department, pamphlet: "Wayside Notes Along the Sunset Route East Bound" (San Francisco, 1911), p. 19.

Various personages and occupations in Imperial County, 1912—Imperial Valley Directory (1912), pp. 290–91, 284, 1, 326, 296. Meanwhile, Imperial County boasts 3 ice companies and 17 blacksmiths! Won't both occupations be necessary and useful forever?

Achievement of the aim of the Women's 10,000 Club in 1940, not in 1920—Berlo, "Population History Compilation," p. 205.

Advisory re: Hayward and Hall—N.A.R.A.L. Record Group 36, op. cit., Calexico Customs Office. Incoming Official Correspondence (9L-60). October 15, 1902–March 23, 1916. Box No. 3 of 5: November 1913 to July 1914. Folder: "Nov. 15, 1913–Feb. 11, 1914." Letter to the Deputy Collector of Customs, Calexico, Cal., from John B. [illegible], Collector, Office of the Collector, Treasury Department, U.S. Customs Service, Port of Los Angeles, Cal. December 23, 1913.

Holtville's "Water King"—Imperial Valley Directory (1914), p. xvii.

"Buy Hercules Dynamite . . ."—*California Cultivator,* vol. LIV, no. 1, January 3, 1920, p. 12 (just above Planet Jr. advertisement).

Photograph of the El Centro National Bank—ICHSPM photograph, cat. #P91.35.

"The winning of the desert wastes of Imperial Valley . . ."—Hunt, p. 452.

Imperial County, America's number-one lettuce producer—Tout, *The First Thirty Years,* p. 243.

64. *Coachella Waits (1912–1917)*

Epigraph: "The citrus belt is largely along the foothills from Los Angeles to Redlands . . ."—G. Harold Powell, p. 47 (letter of 21 February 1904, to Gertrude Powell).

"Here, in what was once deemed a hopeless desert . . ."—Holmes et al., p. 134.

Thanks to an army of mules and men—After a photo in *Imperial County: The Big Picture,* p. 3.

Chandler "aided the promotion of the Los Angeles Aqueduct . . ."—*Los Angeles Times,* September 24, 1944, p. 1 ("Harry Chandler Called by Death: Publisher, 80, Succumbs in Hospital Following Two Heart Attacks"), continuation on p. 6.

Soil comparison between the Imperial and Coachella valleys—Griffin and Young, p. 169.

Growth of the cities of Los Angeles, San Diego and Riverside 1900–1910—*Britannica Year-Book 1913,* p. 774 (entry on California). The exact figures were: Los Angeles 102,479 to 319,198; San Diego 17,700 to 39,578; Riverside 7,973 to 15,212.

Riverside's luxurious electric cars and orange-grove character—ICHSPM document, cat. #A95.242.5. Southern Pacific Passenger Department, pamphlet: "Wayside Notes Along the Sunset Route East Bound" (San Francisco, 1911), p. 16.

G. Harold Powell: "I don't expect to have such a time anywhere else in California"—Op. cit., p. 44 (letter of 19 February 1904, to Gertrude Powell).

"There is a grand ball here tonight . . ."—Ibid., p. 43 (letter of 15 February 1904, to Gertrude Powell). The ball took place at the Glenwood Mission Inn in Riverside.

Palm Springs in 1912 and before—Holmes et al., pp. 215–17; James, *Wonders of the Colorado Desert*, pp. 271–98.

"In a moment the warm liquid sand . . ."—James, *Wonders of the Colorado Desert*, p. 287.

Footnote on the fate of Rincon—Ibid., pp. 292–93.

The demise of Palmdale—Ibid., p. 291.

"Ever since 1906 Coachella has overcome the necessity of importing beets . . ."—Information from the *California Cultivator*, vol. XXVI, no. 14 (April 6, 1906), p. 323 ("News of Country Life in the Golden West").

Recollections of Dr. John and Margaret Tyler—Interview conducted in their home in Palm Desert, April 2004. Shannon Mullen was present.

Another old-timer: "In 1911 there was one in Coachella . . ."—Mr. Ray House, interviewed in Coachella, July 2004. Shannon Mullen was present.

"Brawley's cantaloupe-packing sheds . . . remain the largest in the world!"—So claimed by "a local observer and writer" as quoted in *American Biography and Genealogy*, p. 84.

"Where three years ago wells flowed several inches over the casing . . ."—Ibid., p. 366.

"A farmer from near Coachella and Mecca . . ."—*California Cultivator*, vol. XXIII, no. 14 (August 19, 1904), p. 346.

"A plan proposed at an El Centro meeting . . ."—Laflin, *Coachella Valley*, p. 171.

"All the north end of the Salton Sea Valley . . ."—Brown and Boyd, p. 404.

"Waiting only for the application . . ."—Holmes et al., loc. cit.

65. City of Imperial (1925)

Epigraph: "Pavements in time . . ."—Farr, p. 268 (Edgar F. Howe, "Imperial").

Epigraph: "As the Valley's first and oldest settlement . . ."—Tout, *The First Thirty Years*, p. 270.

Epigraph: "Imperial is still an important town in the Valley . . ."—Harris, p. 30.

"Imperial is an up-to-date little city . . ."—*American Biography and Genealogy*, p. 83.

Imperial Hotel no longer listed in 1920 directory—Imperial Valley Directory (1920), p. 399.

"According to the Federal census of 1920 . . ."—Imperial Valley Directory (1926), p. 5r.

"The metropolis of the Imperial Valley"—*Out West*, vol. XXIII, no. 12, January 1905, unnumbered page.

Comparison of business buildings in Imperial and El Centro—Imperial Valley Directory (1926), pp. 50, 47.

Numerical comparisons of the buildings of Brawley, Calexico, El Centro, Holtville, Imperial in 1912—Imperial Valley Directory (1912), pp. vii–xiii.

Description of the Queen City Independent Band—ICHSPM photograph, cat. #P92.70.

Population of Imperial—Tout, *The First Thirty Years*, p. 270, gives the following figures: 1904 pop., 900; 1910 and 1920, 1800, 1920; 1930, 2000. These differ slightly from Berlo, "Population History Compilation," pp. 266–67: 1910, 1,257; 1920, 1,885; 1930, 1,943; 1940, 1,493; 1950, 1,759; 1960, 2,658; 1970, 3,271; 1980, 3,210; 1990, 4,113; 1998, 7,475. It was not until later in the fifties that the city began to grow, nearly doubling by 1970, and more than doubling again by the century's end.

Tale of El Centro, Holt and C. A. Barker—Mount Signal website.

Rockwood's objections to Imperial—Farr, pp. 125–26 (C. R. Rockwood, "Early History of Imperial County").

66. Their Needs Are Even More Easily Satisfied (1893–1927)

Epigraph: "It is an interesting commentary. . ."—Paul S. Taylor, *Mexican Labor in the United States: Migration Statistics. IV*, p. 35.

Chinese and Japanese history in Riverside, 1900–1920—The Great Basin Foundation Center for Anthropological Research, vol. 1, Chronology sec.

Japanese in Imperial Valley, 1904, 1908—Street, *Beasts of the Field*, p. 475.

"Lemons which made the size known as 300s . . ."—*California Cultivator*, vol. XXIII, no. 19 (November 11, 1904), p. 467 ("News Notes of the Pacific Coast").

"The general persistency with which the Japanese are breaking into many industries . . ."—Asiatic Exclusion League, p. 11 (1907).

Japanese as 42% of California farmworkers, 1909—Street, op. cit., pp. 409, 486.

Figures on Japanese ownership and leases, 1912—California Board of Agriculture, 1918. One Chinese and three Japanese business establishments are depicted in the Fire Department's 1906 *Souvenir of the City of Riverside,* which contains mostly photographs of properties owned by people with such names as Anderson or Wardrobe.—Riverside Fire Department, pp. 49, 52, 65.

Masako et al.—ICHSPM, photo #P85.15.9.7.

Japanese collective bargaining—Street, op. cit., pp. 415–23, 432–70.

"The Jap laborers . . ."—*California Cultivator,* vol. XXVII, no. 1 (July 5, 1906), p. 2 ("News of Country Life in the Golden West").

Letter from Edwin A. Meserve—Asiatic Exclusion League, unnumbered page (prob. p. 1), "Views of Men Seeking Public Suffrage, Who Present Correctly Attitude of California," letter of August 5, 1910.

Letter from William Kent—Ibid., p. 5.

"Is the World Going to Starve?"—*California Cultivator and Livestock and Dairy Journal,* vol. LIV, no. 3 (January 17, 1920), p. 1.

The Gentlemen's Agreement: The Great Basin Foundation Center for Anthropological Research reports that by 1920, "Japanese gradually begin leaving the citrus industry, and are replaced by Mexican immigrant agricultural workers."

Airplane-smuggling of 1927—N.A.R.A.L. Record Group 36. Records of the U.S. Customs Service. Communication from William Carr, the Southern California Immigration Director.

"But whereas the Chinese were good losers . . ."—Hunt, p. 422.

67. Negroes and Mexicans for Cotton (1901–1930)

Epigraph: ". . . the Latin-American does not propose that any one shall know him . . ."—*Fresno Morning Republican,* Sunday, March 21, 1920, p. 5B (speech delivered to night school class, reported by Captain A. P. Harris).

"The question of competent labor has become a most serious proposition to the fruit-growers of California . . ."—*Western Fruit-Grower,* vol. 13, no. 4 (April 1903), p. 8.

Footnote: The "Nigger-head" cactus—*California Cultivator,* vol. XXIII, no. 8 (August 19, 1904), p. 171 ("Denizens of the Desert").

Arrival of "basic strata," Swiss, colored people, Muslims and Hindus—Farr, pp. 280–81 (Edgar F. Howe).

"Cotton has been especially valuable . . ."—Farr, p. 190.

"While the history of Chinese immigration . . ."—Hunt, p. 370.

"Some difficulty has been experienced in securing labor . . ."—Farr, p. 190 (Walter E. Packard, "Agriculture").

"Labor was supplied by the Indians . . ."—Laflin, *Coachella Valley.*

Mexican laborers in Inland Empire citrus, 1914–19, 1973—Wagner, p. 55 (exact numbers: 2,317 to 7,004).

"Reliable and efficient men," etc.—Packard, pp. 15–16. In 1909, the *Desert Farmer* advises: "Mexican labor can be secured and is highly satisfactory in this work as in Texas. Planters in Imperial Valley can afford to pay at least a dollar per hundred pounds . . ." (*Desert Farmer,* Imperial Valley, May 1909, p. 89 [Joseph R. Loftus, "The Cotton Culture in Imperial Valley"].)

In the century's second and third decades, acreages of sugar beets and cotton explode. And you'll be thrilled to know that sugar beet samples from the Imperial Valley "resulted in proving 18.3 per cent sugar in the beet and 82.6 purity." (UC Berkeley. Bancroft Library. Paul S. Taylor papers. Carton 5. Folder 5:41: "Perspectives on Mexican-Americans, Final Draft w/Footnotes, 1973." Typescript, "Perspectives on Mexican-Americans," p. 4.) Imperial cotton will be just as fine; soon they'll be calling it "the white gold." Hand labor will be just the ticket for those crops! Whose hands should labor? I wonder. Taylor sees the employment of Mexicans in the sugar beet and cotton industries as setting the stage for them as migrant workers in other large-scale agriculture. "For most Mexican-Americans this meant northward migration to the beet fields in the spring, and southward migration to winter quarters—even return to Mexico—in the fall."

"Camp conditions in 1914 were unspeakably bad . . ."—*Fresno Morning Republican,* Sunday, March 21, 1920, p. 9B, Arthur L. Johnson, Director, Fresno-Bakersfield Offices, State Commission of Immigration and Housing of California, address to San Joaquin Valley Federation of Women's Clubs, Porterville, California, March 11, 1920. By 1920, of course, life is much better. "The community camp is a system whereby a number of farmers, by clubbing together, erect a camp at a spot convenient to all, which serves as a labor center from which workers go out to adjoining farms when needed . . . The problem of part-time work is solved; the owner of a small orchard does not have to worry concerning what he should do with his workers on days when his fruit may not have ripened enough for picking . . . We must assist in the task of taking the raw immigrant and making a good loyal American citizen out of him . . . In Bakersfield, the city employs a home teacher who holds a class for Mexican women three afternoons a week in an empty box car at the Southern Pacific camp, and in addition has a class for immigrant men two evenings a week, where the men can come to learn after their day's work is done." I can't help believing in people.

"The emergency rules will allow farm workers to seek at least five minutes . . ."—*Sacramento Bee,* Friday, August 5, 2005, p. B6 ("Opinion" section, "Some heat relief: Governor alone can't protect farm workers").

So who are the farmers and who will they be? On the old Imperial County Assessor's maps, here are some common names of property owners: Shank, Flint, Waldron, Lewis, Kidd, Allan, Moore, Fristoe, Helsinki, Ledermann, Gee, Lister, Beezler, Bray, not to mention Clark, of course. Here also are Aviles, Singh and Matsumoto; but in Imperial County in 1910, almost 1,100 out of 1,300-odd farmers were native-born whites.

Death records show a different preponderance of names: Contreras, Corrales, Calderon, Castro, Chalaco (for of course I was looking for Clark); Cordova, infant of Tiburcio, deceased Dec. 31, 1945, and properly recorded in certificate number 8, Book 12.

Well, they must not have been farmers, then. They must have been laborers. Paul S. Taylor asserts that even Asian immigrants were able to buy farms in California, but . . . "times had changed greatly when the twentieth century Mexicans arrived. Not only was there no agricultural ladder for them to ascend; the effect of their ready availability to landowners was to check further widespread distribution of ownership, and so to contribute further to the decline of the 'family farm.'"

White and Colored Population in the Entity called Imperial and in Los Angeles County, 1900 and 1910

[*Note: Mexicans were considered white. The 1930 census for the first time introduced category of Mexican-ness.*]

1900

	Race				
County	*White*	*Negro*	*Indian*	*Chinese*	*Japanese*
Riverside	16,421	254	809	316	97
Imperial/San Diego[a]	26,605	216	572	388	148
Total	43,026	470	1,381	704	245
Percent	93.88	1.03	3.01	1.54	0.53
(Total of all races: 45,826)					
L.A.	163,975	2,841	69	3,209	204
Percent	96.28	1.67	0.05	1.88	0.12
(Total of all races: 170,298)					
Grand Total, 1900	207,001	3,311	1,450	3,913	449
(Total of all races: 216,124)					

[a]Because Imperial was part of San Diego County until 1907, there is no convenient way to separate out non-Imperial from Imperial San Diego. But in 1900–1910, the city of San Diego was small enough to distort the county data to a relatively minimal extent.

1910

	Race				
County	*White*	*Negro*	*Indian*	*Chinese*	*Japanese*
Imperial	12,582	65	682	32	217
Riverside	31,613	518	1,590	187	765
San Diego	58,514	684	1,516	430	520
Total	102,709	1,267	3,788	649	1,502

Continued on p. 1188

	Race				
	White	*Negro*	*Indian*	*Chinese*	*Japanese*
Percent	93.44	1.15	3.5	0.59	1.37
(Total of all races: 109,915)					
L.A.	483,478	9,424	97	2,602	8,461
Percent	95.92	1.86	0.02	0.52	1.7
(Total of all races: 504,062)					
Grand Total, 1910	**586,187**	**10,691**	**3,885**	**3,251**	**9,863**
(Total of all races: 613,977)					

Source: California Board of Agriculture, 1918, pp. 36–37 (white and colored population by counties, 1900 and 1910).

T. H. Watkins in his history of the Great Depression asserts that "by the 1930s" Mexican-Americans "dominated California's traditional migrant labor pool," Chinese, Hindus, Japanese, Koreans and Filipinos having come and gone. But a regional geography from 1957 reports that "labor consists of Mexicans, Orientals, Negroes, and migrant Caucasians under the direction of Caucasian foremen." The bountiful continent is ours, state on state, and territory on territory, to the waves of the Pacific sea.

Sources to foregoing inset:

Number of native-born white farmers in Imperial County, 1910 (1,077 out of 1,322)—California Board of Agriculture, 1918, p. 43, Table XIII (other relevant figures: L.A., 5,682 out of 7,919; Riverside, 2,044 out of 2,688; San Diego, 1,591 out of 2,298).

"Times had changed greatly when the twentieth century Mexicans arrived . . ."—UC Berkeley. Bancroft Library. Paul S. Taylor papers. Carton 5. Folder 5:41: "Perspectives on Mexican-Americans, Final Draft w/Footnotes, 1973." Typescript, "Perspectives on Mexican-Americans," p. 5.

T. H. Watkins on Mexican-Americans' place in California migrant agriculture—Op. cit., p. 395.

"Labor consists of Mexicans, Orientals, Negroes . . ."—Griffin and Young, p. 174.

68. Mexicans Getting Ugly (1911–1926)

Epigraph: "Say, old boy, there's something doing in Mexico . . ."—Grey, p. 25.

"First woman JUROR in State of California"—ICHSPM photograph, cat. #P85.51 (credit: N. J. Metz; the court was Judge Cole's).

The flight of the rancher from Nuevo León—Hart, p. 61.

"The Valley was uneasy on account of depredations . . ."—Tout, *The First Thirty Years*, p. 198 (files of *Imperial Valley Press and Farmer*).

"The boss will be leery . . ."—*I.W.W. Songs*, p. 41 (Richard Brazier, "When You Wear That Button").

Extract from "Singing Jailbirds"—Sinclair, pp. 38, 50.

Advance detachments of the Mexican Revolution have already infiltrated the Wobblies . . .—See Pike, p. 223.

Article Twenty-seven; words of the Michoacán woman; casualties as of 1919—Boyer, pp. 75, 62–63, 69.

"When the men of Zapata entered the town, they came to kill . . ."—Wemark, pp. 375–76 ("Life and Death in Milpa Alta").

Carranza's lackluster commitment to expropriating the haciendas—Dwyer, pp. 30–31.

"People grew used to killing . . ."—Orozco autobiography, p. 53. In 1917, Orozco gets expelled from Canada, solely for his nationality, he believes; for by then most Northsiders consider "Mexican" and "bandit" to be synonymous (ibid., p. 67).

"A triumph for capitalism."—Kerig, p. 4.

Confluence of interest and bribery keep CRLC in business—Dwyer, p. 43.

Birth of the word "campesinos"—My brief discussion in this chapter is indebted to Boyer.

Orozco's "Head of a Mexican Peasant," Orozco graphic work, p. 113.

Doings of Cárdenas and the CRMDT—Boyer, pp. 213, 191, 151, 192.

"MEXICO CENTER FOR BOLSHEVISM"—*Fresno Morning Republican*, Monday, March 22, 1920, p. 1.

Weapons of war now permitted to be exported to Mexico—Record Group 36. Records of the U.S. Customs Service. Calexico Customs Office. Incoming Official Correspondence (9L-60). October 15, 1902–March 23, 1916. Box

No. 3 of 5: November 1913 to July 1914. Folder: "Nov. 15, 1913–Feb. 11, 1914." Letter to the Deputy Collector of Customs, Calexico, Cal., from John B. [illegible; probably Cretcher], Collector, Office of the Collector, Treasury Department, U.S. Customs Service, Port of Los Angeles, Cal. February 14, 1914.

"American Troops Save Life . . ." and "Battle of Saltillo . . ."—*Imperial Valley Press*, vol. XIV, no. 16, Tuesday evening, May 18, 1914, p. 1.

"Great Battle" and "Mexicans Puzzled . . ."—Ibid., no. 18, Thursday evening, May 20, p. 1.

"While Mexicans Cut Gringo Pigs' Throats . . ."—Womack, p. 185 (*El Independiente*, April 23, 1914).

Footnote: Number of shells fired into Vera Cruz in Mexican-American War—Bigelow, p. 59.

Footnote: Richard Henry Dana—Op. cit.

Debacle between Andrade and Holabird, 1912—*Los Angeles Times*, August 6, 1912, vol. II, no. 10, "INTERNATIONAL CLAIMS ARE STILL UNSETTLED."

"A marked labor shortage in Imperial . . ."—*California Cultivator*, vol. LXV, no. 21, November 21, 1925, p. 516 ("Agricultural News Notes of the Pacific Coast": "Southern California").

The history of Riverside County: "The miserable half-breed race"—Holmes et al., p. 40.

"The rest being Mexicans, Hindus and other foreigners"—Tout, *The First Thirty Years*, p. 239 (files of *Imperial Valley Press and Farmer*).

The tale of Santiago Gonzales from Las Barrancas—Marilyn P. Davis (testimony of Don Ezekiel Pérez). Señor Santiago crossed in 1914.

Paul S. Taylor on Imperial Valley—UC Berkeley. Bancroft Library. Paul S. Taylor papers. Carton 4. Folder 4:29: "Imperial Valley, Notes, Drafts." Unnumbered small white sheet clipped to yellow sheets dated 1979, p. 4.

"And until 1913 there's not a single labor union in Imperial County."—In 1913 printers formed the first union in the Valley (Tout, *The First Thirty Years*, p. 194).

"The entire equipment of the United States regulars . . ."—*Imperial Valley Press*, vol. XIV, no. 8 (Saturday evening, May 8, 1914), p. 1 ("MEXICAN GUNS AT CALEXICO EQUAL DEPARTED MILITIA").

"Twenty-five Imperial Valley School Teachers . . ."—ICHSPM photograph, uncoded in 2001; found near group #P85.111.1.

1914 page-1 news (embargo, platoon, cotton)—*Imperial Valley Press*, vol. XIV, no. 7, Friday, May 8, 1914. Re: the embargo, the *Press* remarks: "Many Americans are inside the rebel lines and are unwilling to leave."

Doings of Huey Stanley—Roemer, pp. 38–39.

"Horses stolen by insurgents . . ."—ICHSPM, photo, uncoded as of 2002.

"Lieutenant Berthold inspecting insurgent troops . . ."—ICHSPM photo, cat. #P85.115.1 Now here is a photo of "insurgent guards, Mexicali, 1911," one of whom expresses tolerance, one suspicion, one self-satisfaction, one neutrality; one sternly swaggers (he's the only one whose hand rests in his pocket instead of on his rifle); the last appears calmly remote.

Doings of Magón, Pryce, Ferris, Mosby—Niemann, pp. 75–76.

Private army of Americans defend their ranches against Magonistas—Chamberlin, p. 46.

Night letter to Governor Johnson, 1911: "In sympathy with the Mexican Insurrectors"—UC Berkeley. Bancroft Library, farm labor situation 1933–34. Folder: "Mexican border incidents." G. Gordon Whitnall, Secretary of a mass meeting in Los Angeles, to Governor Hiram Johnson, 6 February 1911.

"A certain hardening of the line"—Major Esteban Cantú was Chief of the Line in Mexicali in 1911. He fought revolutionists along the Colorado. In November 1913 he defeats insurgents at Las Islitas and gets promoted to Colonel. Counterrevolutionaries rumored to be affiliated with Harry Chandler try to take over the Mexicali Valley, but Cantú stops that. He becomes famous for summoning pro-American secesssionist soldiers to his presence with these words: "You wish to betray your country. Very well, kill me and betray it if you are bad Mexicans."—Farr, p. 302 (Hector González, "The Northern District of Lower California").

"It is not possible any longer . . ." and Apricot Day—*Imperial Valley Press*, vol. XIV, no. 8 (Saturday evening, May 8, 1914), p. 1 ("MEXICAN OFFICIALS DOUBLE VIGILANCE").

Rumors that Mexicans might cut the canal in 1914—Harris, p. 36.

"Mexicans getting ugly . . ."—UC Berkeley. Bancroft Library, farm labor situation 1933–34. Folder: "Mexican border incidents." Rockwood to Thomas, Adjutant General. COPY. 86SF JO 100 Blue. Heber Cal 1222P, June 25, 1916.

Labor and racial unrest in America in 1919—Pike, p. 221.

Phil Swing: "The uneconomic method of that great irrigation district . . . ," etc.—Senate Committee on the Colorado River Basin (1925), p. 189 (Swing's statement).

Tale of the American weapons smuggler in 1920—*Fresno Morning Republican*, Friday, March 26, 1920, p. 3 ("Attempts Arms Sale to Mexico"). Meanwhile, Cantú has himself considered seceding, but Carranza hears and fires him; he refuses to turn over reins to Baldomero Almada; they send in General Abelardo Rodríguez with troops to depose him.

Report on Mejía or Mejís—*Imperial Valley Press*, Wednesday, August 18, 1926, p. 1 ("INSURRECTORS ARE HELD FOR TRIAL IN SEPTEMBER").

69. *The Next Step* (ca. 1925)

"By the mid-twenties they succeeded in obtaining legislation . . ."—UC Berkeley. Bancroft Library. Paul S. Taylor papers. Carton 4. Folder 4:26: "Future of Mexican Immigration: Draft w/Corrections and Notes, 1976" (published as Chapter 11, Arthur E. Corwin, ed., *Immigrants . . .*), p. 3.

70. *El Centro* (1925)

Epigraph: "The husbandman here . . ."—Pattie, p. 264. He was writing about Mission San Diego.
Description of Roth and Marshall's Feed Store—After an ICHSPM photograph, cat. #P91.45.1. (According to Tout, *The First Thirty Years*, p. 335, in 1920 "W. A. Marshall built a handsome store at Eighth and Main.") The ICHSPM photo is undated.
El Centro Chamber of Commerce: Imperial County is "third richest growing county in the United States . . ." —Imperial County Agriculture Commission papers, "Facts on Imperial County California," comp. by John S. Carmichael, Secretary, El Centro Chamber of Commerce, 1925.
Following crop statistics for 1925—Loc. cit.
"Mr. Cooper richly deserves whatever success has come to him . . ."—Farr, p. 388 (biography of Cooper).
Address of Otis P. Tout—Imperial Valley Directory (1912), p. 262. In 1925 Tout was still living in El Centro, and almost certainly at this address. *The First Thirty Years*, published in 1931, informs us that he dwells in El Centro.
Sinclair Lewis: "He had enormous and poetic admiration . . ." and "a high-colored, banging, exciting region"—Op. cit., p. 548.
"You can't hate them properly . . ."—Ibid., p. 578.
Urban percentage of U.S. population in 1900 and 1925—Mott and Roemer, pp. 6–7.
Description of Main Street in 1918—ICHSPM photograph, cat. #P92.39 ("Main Street, El Centro").
News of the Imperial Valley Motor Agency—Imperial Valley Directory (1926), p. 14.
El Centro's "automobile laundries" and auto dealerships in 1930—Imperial Valley Directory (1930), pp. 347–48.
"El Centro has not acquired a large Japanese population . . ."—Farr, p. 281 (Edgar F. Howe, "El Centro").
View of the Hotel Barbara Worth in 1928—ICHSPM photograph, cat. #P91.201.118.
Miss El Centro 1928—ICHSPM photograph, no cat. number recorded.

71. *Mexicali* (1925)

Epigraph: "Impressed with the success of numerous small commercial farmers in the Imperial Valley . . ."—Kerig, p. 139.
Description of the Puente Blanco in 1925—After a photo reproduced in Celso Bernal, p. 260.
Descriptions of Mexicali *ca.* 1925—AHMM, photo album 3, cat. #29.AHM/166.1/1 and #29.AHM/166.3/17.
Hector González: "Due perhaps to the rosy prospects which the cultivation of cotton offers capital . . ."—Farr, pp. 207–8 ("The Northern District of Lower California").
"The concession policies of the Porfirio Díaz Administration . . ."—Munguía, p. 159 (José Luis Castro Ruiz).
Comparative populations of Mexicali and Tijuana, 1910–30—Ibid., p. 158. In 1921 Mexicali held more than six times as many people as Tijuana.
Remarks of Hermenegildo Pérez Cervantes—Interviewed in the AHMM, December 2006. Terrie Petree interpreted. This man also said: "The major source of employment for us Mexicans at first was business, then construction, and then agriculture. We were building businesses, some apartments, some office buildings. They came from the interior: Guadalajara, Mexico, Mazatlán. They were the people with money. They brought land and built buildings. My father was a worker in that soap factory. There were five children in our family."
Mexicali's land purchase from the CRLC, 1920–21—Kerig, pp. 205–6.
"The entire plant is of steel and concrete . . ."—*Los Angeles Times*, April 11, 1926, p. J3 (Randall Henderson, "A New Kind of Pioneering in Imperial").
Parnership between the ISCP (in Spanish, the Compañía Industrial Jabonera del Pacífico) and the CRLC—Kerig, p. 272.
Description of the premises of the Colorado River Ginning Co.—AHMM, unnumbered photo album. "Es de reciente contrucción, pues en 1923 un incendio destruyó la Planta primitiva."
CLRC's role and motives in building the Mexicali and Gulf Railroad—*Los Angeles Times*, April 26, 1925, p. J10 (A. W. Swanson, "A Remarkable Room in Which Cotton Experts Meet").
Its shipping of cleared trees for firewood—Kerig, p. 84.
Episode of Marcelino Magaña—DeBuys and Myers, p. 142.
CRLC sales of 1927—Tout, *The First Thirty Years*, p. 364.
Mexicans put last among CRKC's parcelees—Munguía, p. 117 (Fernando A. Medina Robles).
Miscellaneous facts and dates about the Chinese in Mexicali—Auyón Gerardo, p. 41ff. (Terrie Petree's working

translation.) Regarding the 50 Chinese ranches in the Mexicali Valley, Duncan for his part (p. 635) prefers to give a figure of "at least 32" out of 105.

Activities of the China Leasing Company, 1926—*Los Angeles Times*, February 7, 1926, p. J6 ("Potatoes to Be Tried Below the Line").

Phil Swing: ". . . There have been 8,000 Chinese imported . . ."—Senate Committee on the Colorado River Basin (1925), p. 191 (Swing's statement).

Cultivated acreage in the Mexicali Valley, 1920—Auyón Gerardo, p. 41ff.

Cotton acreage there, 1920—Duncan, p. 624.

One of the Imperial Irrigation District's five directors: Irrigated acreage on Mexican side, 1925—Senate Committee on the Colorado River Basin (1925), Part 2, p. 259 (statement of C. W. Brockman, Calexico director of IID).

Advertisement for the Climax—Imperial Valley Directory (1930), p. 39. Meanwhile, from Hetzel's files, although not from his shutter (he must have been too busy photographing the expanding perfections of Brawley and El Centro), I find a 1927 photograph of Avenida Obregón, sporting twinned streetlights; the arteries of Mexicali are as empty as ever but the median strip is clearer and more verdant than in my day; I can't believe how clear the horizon's mountains are.

72. Volstead (1919–1933)

Epigraph: "The Mexican side of the border is a place where free-spending Americans go . . ."—Salazar, p. 60 ("No Troops Line Border That Has Become Big Business: Changes Loom," January 7, 1962).

Doings of the WCTU—Farr, pp. 258–59, 261–62. (Mrs. C. Angie Miller, "Woman's Christian Temperance Union").

The WCTU in Riverside—Holmes et al., pp. 84–85. The organization was formed in that city in 1883.

Footnote: Date of first legal liquor establishment in Imperial County (1912)—Tout, *The First Thirty Years*, p. 266.

Same footnote: Poolhalls in Imperial County, 1912—Imperial Valley Directory (1912), pp. 295–96.

Same footnote: The wholesale liquor dealer in Imperial—Imperial Valley Directory (1914), unnumbered page (1 in from back cover).

Same footnote: Imperial's 6 bars—Ibid., p. 352.

Same footnote: Number of bars in 2001—Imperial Valley yellow pages (2001), p. 64.

"Usual to all new countries"—*An Illustrated History of Los Angeles County*, p. 245.

"Average number of violent deaths . . ."—Ibid., p. 98.

Vigilance committee of 1856; first legal hanging—Ibid., pp. 99, 110.

Supposed cause of the Chinese Massacre—Ibid., pp. 249–50.

In 1916 Imperial County voted in favor of Prohibition by the widest margin in California and aftermath ten years later—According to Tout, the ballots went 2 to 1 in favor (*The First Thirty Years*, pp. 201, 248 [poll of *Imperial Valley Press* readers]).

Colonel Esteban Cantú as one of those who "sold their souls to the devil . . ."—Ruiz, p. 43. Volstead didn't create Sin City, as we know. Mexicali was always the other side of the ditch. Five years before Volstead we see something like a feeding trough and chute of a stockyard, overhung by a wooden trapezoid; men are sitting on a pile of lumber. The caption reads: "Gambling place after earthquake, Mexicali" (ICHSPM photograph, cat. #P85.19.1 [1914]).

News of W. F. Holt—Wright, p. 378 (facsimile of article, March 1915).

A Customs Collector in Andrade: "It is very well known that the town of Algodones . . ."—N.A.R.A.L. Record Group 36. Records of the U.S. Customs Service. Calexico Customs Office. Incoming Official Correspondence (9L–60). October 15, 1902–March 23, 1916. Box 4 of 5: July 1914–June 1915. Bound volume labeled "Letters." Copy of report of W. J. Smith, Deputy Collector and Inspector of Andrade, Cal., in re situation at Algodones, on or before February 4, 1915; p. 1.

Description of Aleck Gibson's gambling house—Horace Bell, p. 12.

"'Red light' district was raided by Constable Taggart . . ."—Tout, *The First Thirty Years*, p. 175, *Imperial Press and Farmer* files.

". . . raided thirty gambling joints . . ."—Ibid., p. 239.

Recipe for "Russian punch"—*Imperial Valley Press*, Saturday, May 1, 1926, p. 2.

Remarks of Hermenegildo Pérez Cervantes—Interviewed in the AHMM, December 2006. Terrie Petree interpreted.

Report on Hoy and Coffroth—Record Group 36. Op. cit. Incoming Correspondence Regarding Smuggling (9L-61). July 25, 1914–May 23, 1922. Box 2 of 2: From May 1914 to May 1922. Folder: May 1916–16 December 1916. Letter from F. E. Johnson, Special Agent in Charge, Treasury Department, United States Customs Service, Los Angeles, Cal., to the Collector of Customs, Los Angeles, California, May 1, 1916.

"The evils of gambling, drinking and debauchery in Mexicali"—Tout, op. cit., p. 245.

Ratio of money invested in vice establishments *vs.* in the CRLC—In 1920, in Mexicali, the respective figures were \$3 million and \$40 million (Duncan, p. 629, n. 4; estimate by U.S. Consul).

The take of Mexicali's *jefe político,* 1909—Kerig, p. 120.

". . . Intends running a stage to and from the Gate . . ."—N.A.R.A.L. Record Group 36. Op. cit. Port of Campo. General Correspondence 1919–1965. Box 1 of 1. Folder: "Historical Letters 1919–1965 [1/2]." Deputy Collector, Tecate, Cal., to Collector of Customs, Los Angeles, Cal., June 19, 1925.

Report on Navy men in Tecate—N.A.R.A.L. Record Group 36. Ibid. Letter from James S. McKean, Rear Admiral U.S.N., Commandant, Eleventh Naval District, San Diego, California, to Mr. D. S. Kuykendall, Inspector in Charge, Immigration Service, San Diego, 19 November 1926.

Same matter; lack of Immigration officer at Tecate gate—Ibid., Kuykendall to McKean, November 26, 1926.

"This Tijuana happened to be in Mexico . . ."—Hammett, p. 230 ("The Golden Horseshoe," 1924).

1927 Hetzel photo of WCTU—ICHSPM photo, uncoded as of 2002.

The brandy doll in Boston—*Fresno Morning Republican,* Tuesday, March 23, 1920, p. 3.

"Beautiful Girl Pays Big Fine . . ."—*Imperial Valley Press,* Wednesday, May 5, 1926, p. 2.

The "huge whiskey still"—Ibid., Wednesday, March 24: "Capture Big Whiskey Still."

Volstead gets quoted as saying that 3.75% beer is innocuous—Ibid,. Tuesday, April 1, 1926, p. 1.

Footnote: End of Prohibition decreases Baja population by 35,000—Chamberlin, p. 35. This number, says the author, may be inflated. In any event, vice went on before, during and after Volstead on both sides of the line. A local history of the Imperial Valley (Henderson, p. 44) tells us that "a white woman ran a bar next door, where a phonograph ground out songs at five cents a melody . . . Nearby was a dance hall. Filipinos were preferred customers, and white girls took the dimes." That was El Centro for you. But the WCTU did not entirely fail. Nearly a century later, the telephone directory for all Imperial County, which unlike most California counties continued to be accommodated in one slim volume, listed no strippers, no outcall masseuses, and only one "personal escort agency," whose number I dialled, solely for research purposes, and a lovely-voiced lady explained that they were actually in San Diego and "we don't go out there." I said that in that case I guessed I wouldn't be seeing her, and she replied that she hoped I had a good night. Then I took a stroll outside to Broadway. As it turned out, I needn't have even gone that far, because as soon as it got dark on State Street, here came the fat black girl who panhandled in the afternoons; now she was renting something out. All the taxi drivers knew her. Here came the skinny blonde. Both of them were slowly pacing around the block which began across the street from the Greyhound station.

Case of Casino S. Glenn—N.A.R.A.L. Record Group 36. Op. cit. Incoming Correspondence Regarding Smuggling (9L-61). July 25, 1914–May 23, 1922. Box 2 of 2: From May 1914 to May 1922. Folder: May 21, 1919–October 6, 1921. Letter from S.T.H. Esterbrook [? signature illegible], Special Agent in Charge, Treasury Department, United States Customs Service, Los Angeles, Cal., to Deputy Collector in Charge, Calexico, Calif., September 4, 1917.

Opium in lard cans—N.A.R.A.L. Record Group 36. Ibid. Letter (not in folder) from J. B. Cretcher, Special Deputy Collector, to Deputy Collector in Charge, Calexico, Cal., February 13, 1915. Copy of letter [unsigned] from FBC, Special Deputy Collector, Los Angeles, Cal., to The Deputy Collector of Customs, San Diego, Cal., February 18, 1915.

The opium container disguised as a flashlight battery—N.A.R.A.L. Record Group 36. Ibid. Folder: May 1916–16 December 1916. Letter from J. B. Cretcher, Special Deputy Collector, Los Angeles, to Deputy Collectors in Charge, All Ports and Stations, December 24, 1919.

The letter from Jesús Guaderama—N.A.R.A.L. Record Group 36. Ibid. Folder: June 18, 1917—April 24, 1919. Letter from Jesús Guaderama, San Diego, to David Ochoa, Jerome, Arizona, and forwarded to U.S. Customs by U.S. Marshal Harry Carlson on September 9, 1919.

The case of the druggist and veterinarian in Holtville—N.A.R.A.L. Record Group 36. Ibid. Letter (not in folder) from W. B. Evans, Deputy Collector in Charge, Treasury Department, United States Customs Service, Tia Juana, Calif., to the Collector of Customs, Los Angeles, California, August 16, 1916.

Report on Wolf and Block—N.A.R.A.L. Record Group 36. Ibid. Folder: May 1916–16 December 1916. Letter from F. E. Johnson, Special Agent in Charge, Treasury Department, United States Customs Service, Los Angeles, Cal., to the Collector of Customs, Los Angeles, California, May 1, 1916.

Report on the Alexander Gladstone gang—N.A.R.A.L. Record Group 36. Ibid. Letter (not in folder) from J. B. Cretcher, Special Deputy Collector, Treasury Department, United States Customs Service, Los Angeles, Cal., to the Deputy Collector in Charge, Calexico, Cal., July 6, 1916.

The case of Zurbano and la Fuente—N.A.R.A.L. Record Group 36. Ibid. Letter (not in folder) from J. B. Cretcher, Special Deputy Collector, Treasury Department, United States Customs Service, Los Angeles, Cal., to the Deputy Collector in Charge, Calexico, California, June 7, 1916.

Report on Francisco Gonzales—N.A.R.A.L. Record Group 36. Ibid. Letter (not in folder) from J. B. E. [signature illegible], Collector, Treasury Department, United States Customs Service, Los Angeles, Cal., to the Deputy Collector in Charge, Calexico, California, June 5, 1916.

"Miguel Gonzalez is a Mexican . . ."—N.A.R.A.L. Record Group 36. Ibid. Letter (not in folder) from Deputy Collector in Charge [signature cut off on carbon], Calexico Calif., to Special Agent, Treasury Department, El Paso, Texas, August 19, 1918.

The case of Mark Yeates—N.A.R.A.L. Ibid. Record Group 36. Letter from F. E. Johnson, Special Agent in Charge, Treasury Department, United States Customs Service, Los Angeles, Cal., to the Collector of Customs, Los Angeles, California, June 16, 1916. File 1–157. (2) Letter from F. E. Johnson, Special Agent in Charge, Treasury Department, United States Customs Service, Los Angeles, Cal., to the Collector of Customs, Los Angeles, California, June 13, 1916. COPY. (3) Letter from F. E. Johnson, Special Agent in Charge, Treasury Department, United States Customs Service, Los Angeles, Cal., to the Collector of Customs, Los Angeles, California, June 27, 1916. (4) Letter from E. G. Brown, Deputy Collector in Charge, Port of Calexico, California, to the Collector of Customs, Los Angeles, California, September 16, 1919.

Report on Ben Hodges and Mr. Barrera—N.A.R.A.L. Record Group 36. Ibid. Letter (not in folder) from H.P.L. Beck, Inspector in Charge, Tia Juana, to Inspector in Charge, Immigration Service, San Diego, Calif., August 6, 1919.

Case of A. Leyra and the two unknown Americans—N.A.R.A.L. Record Group 36. Ibid. Folder: October 11, 1921–May 23, 1922 + Index. Letter from C. O. Miller, Deputy Collector in Charge, Tia Juana, to the Collector of Customs, San Diego, Calif., November 11, 1921.

Report on N. Sakiyama—N.A.R.A.L. Record Group 36. Ibid. Folder: October 11, 1921–May 23, 1922 + Index. Memo from Imanaka, U.S. Department of Labor, Immigration Service, Office of Inspector in Charge, Calexico, Calif., March 3, 1922.

Report on Cecil Dennis—N.A.R.A.L. Record Group 36. Ibid. Folder: October 11, 1921–May 23, 1922 + Index. Letter from H. G. Dunlap, Inspector, en route, Train No. 4, S. D. & A., East, to U.S. Customs Service, San Diego, January 29, 1922.

Report on Leon Maddox—N.A.R.A.L. Record Group 36. Ibid. Letter (not in folder) from F. E. Johnson, Special Agent in Charge, Treasury Department, United States Customs Service, Los Angeles, Cal., to the Collector of Customs, Los Angeles, California, April 24, 1916.

Report on Dan Hayes—N.A.R.A.L. Record Group 36. Ibid. Letter from unknown Deputy Collector [signature cut off from carbon], Calexico, Calif., to the Collector of Customs, Los Angeles, Calif., August 16, 1916.

73. *The Chinese Tunnels (1849–2003)*

Epigraph: "Stay home and lose opportunities . . ."—Hom, p. 89 ("Immigration Blues," song no. 16, JSGJ II. IIa), slightly "retranslated" by WTV to cut dead wood out of the English.

My interview with the sisters Hernández took place on Good Friday 2001. They spoke English.

My conversations with Jose Lopez about the tunnels took place in July 2001. He spoke English, and indeed sometimes served as my interpreter that year. He has since disappeared. They say he is in Salinas. José López from Jalisco is a different person.

Information from the owner of the Golden Dragon: History of the tunnels, and Chinese population of Mexicali in 2003: 4,000–5,000—Rosalyn Ng report, 2003 (based on the Ngs' visit in July). The first time I met this man in person was in October 2003.

"In the Chinese district of Mexicali . . ."—Ruiz, p. 48.

Frank Waters: Chinese smuggled "in crates of melons . . ."—Op. cit., p. 314.

My interview with Stella Mendoza took place in October 2003. Most of our conversation had to do with the IID-to-MWD water transfer over whose negotiations she had unwillingly presided at the beginning of the year. The bulk of what she had to say will be found in the chapter "We Should Have Had a Better Negotiating Position," below.

The tale of the Chinese vampire—I heard this independently from a woman at the Reforma church on Good Friday, 2001, from Jose Lopez in 2002, and from a would-be *pollo* named Ramón in April or May of 2003. Jose Lopez was by far the most educated of these three tellers.

My interview with the Mexican journalist on a Sunday took place in front of the cathedral on Reforma, in late May or early June of 2002. He spoke English.

My interview with the Mexican mother in Condominios Montealbán took place in July 2001. She spoke English.

My interview with the Mexican waiter at the "Nuevo Peiping" took place in May or June of 2002. The interpreter was José Quintero, a homeless would-be *pollo* whom I employed for several days with great success (he was also a fine bodyguard) and then never saw again. I miss him.

My interviews with the parking attendant Lupita took place in October and November of 2003. She spoke English and Spanish. When it was the latter, Terrie Petree and José López from Jalisco interpreted.

"Planta Despepitadora de Algodón 'Chino-Mexicana' "—Unnumbered album in the AHMM.

The enrichment of Chung Ming and Cheong Yum—Auyón Gerardo, p. 31ff. (working translation by Terrie Petree).

Statistic on Chinese emigration as of 1852 (20,000 per year)—Bain, p. 205.

One of the white magnates (Charley Crocker): "Wherever we put them we found them good . . ."—Ibid., p. 221.

An Irishman: "Begad if it wasn't for them damned nagurs . . ."—Ibid., p. 222.

Departure of white laborers from L.A. in 1860, "City still rapidly improving" and "The Chinese are a prominent factor"—*An Illustrated History of Los Angeles County*, pp. 99, 105, 255.

Footnote: Account of the Chinese Massacre—Ibid., pp. 249–50. The "other source" which claims that 72 Chinese died is Newmark, whose versions of events tend to be more colorful than others'.

Ma You Yong and the tunnel cave-in—Auyón Gerardo, loc. cit.

"When a striker kills with a brick the man who has taken his place, he has no sense of wrong-doing . . ."—London, *Novels and Social Writings*, pp. 1121–22 ("The Scab," 1904). The reference to Chinese coolies is on p. 1133.

An eyewitness judgment: "They sent up to the mines for their use . . ."—Quaife, p. 237 (from ch. XVII of J. D. Borthwick, *Three Years in California*). The same source reports (p. 240): ". . . with a quick motion of the chopsticks . . . they cause the rice to flow down their throats in a continuous stream."

Clare Ng's interview with the old couple at Condominios Montealbán took place in July 2003. They were the same people whom I have indirectly quoted at the beginning of the "Creation Myths" section. I had to send the Ngs down without me since my pelvis had been fractured in an accident.

The tale of Mariano Ma and Chang Peio—Auyón Gerardo, p. 41ff. (Terrie Petree's working translation, slightly polished by WTV). I have been assured by several older Mexicans that there were Chinese homesteads in the Mexicali Valley before the nineteenth century ended; they were growing cotton on their own, my informants said, but the salt defeated them.

My interviews with the softspoken old shoe-store owner took place in November 2003. This was the uncle of the Dong Chen waitress, Miss Xu. Xu gave me his name but he didn't want me to use it. More of this interview appears at the end, in the "Darkness and Broken Chairs" section. José López from Jalisco interpreted.

My interview with Carmen Jaham took place in November 2003. Terrie Petree was the interpeter.

Chinese arrivals in Mexico beween 1902 and 1921—Auyón Gerardo, p. 34 (Terrie Petree's working translation).

Mexicali's Chinese population in 1913—Ibid., p. 41ff. (Terrie Petree's working translation).

Some Chinese sent for by the Colorado River Land Company—This practice began in 1910, according to Duncan, p. 623.

My interviews with Steve Leung took place in October and November of 2003. He spoke English.

C. B. Williams & Sons storefront—AHMM, photo album 2, cat. #29.AHM/166.2/8.

Chinese as 42% of Mexicali's population in 1915—Kerig, p. 160.

Chinese Masonic lodge—AHMM, photo album 2, cat. #29.AHM/166.2/9. The lodge was on Juárez between Azueta and Altamirano.

Chong Kee general store—AHMM, photo album 2, cat. #29.AHM/166.2/10.

Juan Chong's storefront—AHMM, photo album 2, cat. #29.AHM/166.2/15. Photo dated 1925.

Anti-Chinese rhetoric of the Mexican Labor Party—Quoted in Magón, p. 46 (essay by editor).

The anti-Chinese pogrom in Coahuila—Duncan, p. 626, n. 32.

The tale of the Chinese who were purposefully misdirected from San Felipe was told me several times, always by Mexicans. The footnoted version is quite different. Here is another, told me by Señor Armando in the Café Canton, 2002 (Carlos Guillero Baja Terra interpreted): "In 1906, or maybe 1900, when the Chinese came to Mexicali by ship, San Felipe didn't exist. When the Chinese came by ship from San Francisco, there were usually police watching. Sometimes when the Chinese people come in ship, the ones who live in house say: 'Just walk to north and you can see Mexicali.' But sometimes Chinese come alone and lost in desert and sometimes a hundred and twenty degrees. Too many people died. That's the reason for the name *Chinero*. Hundreds died. The people who lived, they come to Mexicali, lived here with the family. There were more Chinese people than Mexicans. They lived in the Mexicali Valley."

Footnote: Excerpt from *El Dragón en el Desierto*—Auyón Gerardo, p. 31ff. (Terrie Petree's working translation.)

My interview with the fighting-cock breeder whom I met at the match in Islas Agrarias took place in November 2003. He spoke English.

Texan farmhand who'd moved to the Imperial Valley "'cause they told us it was the land of plenty"—Salazar, pp. 79–80 ("Farm Workers' Lot Held Worsening in Southland," November 27, 1962).

"Imperial Catechism" of 1903: "You can get Chinese or Japanese cooks . . ."—*Imperial Press and Farmer*, vol. II, no. 44 (Saturday, February 14, 1903), p. 1 ("Should a rancher board his own men, or can they board themselves?").

Information on Mrs. Julia Lyon—Farr, p. 480.

Bancroft: "These people were truly in every sense aliens . . ."—Op. cit., vol. XXIV (1890), p. 336.

The various remarks and observations of Lupe Vásquez—He was my interpreter and guide for the Chinese tunnels project from the fall of 2002 through June 2003. The *quinceañera* took place in May 2003. Lupe was my friend; he and I continued to work together.

José López from Jalisco began to work for me in early 2003. His presence was sporadic, our friendship and working relationship ongoing. His English was slightly better than Lupe's, which was perfectly adequate; Lupe knew Mexicali better, being a native. José's work on the Chinese tunnels project ended when my fieldwork did, in November 2003.

My interview with Alicia and Luisa in Condominios Montealbán took place in April, May and October 2003. Lupe Vásquez, José López from Jalisco and Terrie Petree interpreted on various occasions.

The very friendly, pretty, educated Chinese waitress who lived in Condominios Montealbán was the Dong Cheng waitress, Miss Xu, whom I interviewed in October and November 2003. The interpreters were Terrie Petree and José López from Jalisco.

Footnote: Mr. Clark of Missouri on "the Chinese problem": *Appletons' Annual Cyclopaedia*, 1902, pp. 187–88 (entry on Congress, section on Chinese Exclusion). To illustrate London's thesis more nakedly I should also quote Mr. Perkins of New York (p. 185): "I shall not, Mr. Chairman, take the time of this committee in discussing the general question of Chinese exclusion, because I imagine that every member of this House is agreed that the admission of Chinese laborers on any large scale would be injurious to the laboring interests of this country . . ."

"*California* has distinctly failed as a land of big things . . ."—Smythe, p. 160.

1910 *Britannica* entry on China—11th ed., vol. 6, p. 17 .

"The older citizens will remember when the back portion of the block . . ."—Holmes et al., p. 56.

The task of Mr. Hutchins, the Chinese inspector—James, p. 408.

Zane Grey character: "Of course, my job is to keep tabs on Chinese . . ."—Grey, p. 58.

Importation into Mexico of 500 Chinese in 1913—Auyón Gerardo, p. 48 (Terrie Petree's working translation).

Footnote: Jack Black on the nonexistence of Chinese tunnels in San Francisco—Op. cit., p. 125.

Dashiell Hammett: "The passageway was solid and alive with stinking bodies . . ."—Op. cit, pp. 422, 440 ("Dead Yellow Women," 1925). There certainly were many Chinese in traditional dress in San Francisco; Hammett didn't make that up. In 1917, José Clemente Orozco was in San Francisco and remarked on the "Chinese girls in their embroidered pantaloons and characteristic tunics" (op. cit., p. 60).

Zulema Rashid's fear of Chinese as torturers—Interviews by WTV, May–June 2003. Zulema is quoted in several other chapters of this book. She spoke English like the American she was.

Chinese and Mexican population of Mexicali in 1919, according to *El Dragón en el Desierto*—Auyón Gerardo, p. 50 (Terrie Petree's working translation).

By 1930, Mexicali's population was one-third Chinese.—Information in Ruiz, p. 40.

Footnote: Census data on Imperial County in 2000—U.S. Census Bureau, Population Division, Table CO-EST2001-07-06, "Time Series of California Population Estimates by County, April 1, 2000, to July 1, 2001." Accessed at the website http://eire.census.gov/popest/data/counties/tables/CO-EST2001-07.php, on 6 September 2002.

Same footnote: Statistics of the 1910 census—Census Bureau (1910), pp. 156, 166.

My interview with Beatriz Limón from *La Crónica* took place in April 2003 and is referenced in other parts of this book. She later accompanied Yolanda Sánchez Ogás, José López from Jalisco and me to some Chinese tunnels in June 2003. José López from Jalisco and Lupe Vásquez interpreted on various occasions.

My relationship with Oscar Sánchez from the Archivo Histórico is ongoing. He has been helping me since 1997. This would have been said sometime in 2002 or 2003.

My conversation with the waiter at the Thirteen Negro took place sometime in 2002.

The tour guide named Carlos worked for me in June 2002. He spoke excellent English.

My interview with Mr. Auyón took place in June 2003. Lupe Vásquez interpreted.

Mr. Auyón as a "world-renowned painter, known especially for his paintings of horses and nude women" —Rosalyn Ng report, 2003.

Terrie's summary of *El Dragón en el Desierto*: "The last twenty to twenty-five years in the book . . ."—Auyón Gerardo, p. 41ff (2nd to last page of Terrie Petree's somewhat selective working translation).

My mother-and-daughter team of Chinese interpreters, on the subject of Mr. Auyón: "*Further cooperation in the future: likely . . .*"—Rosalyn Ng report, 2003.

"ALEXANDER REPORTS ATTEMPT WILL BE MADE TONIGHT . . ."—N.A.R.A.L. Record Group 36. Records of the U.S. Customs Service. Calexico Customs Office. Incoming Official Correspondence (9L–60). October 15, 1902–March 23, 1916. Box No. 3 of 5: November 1913 to July 1914. Bound volume labeled "Letters." Telegram, from Macumber to Collector of Customs in Tijuana, Calexico, February 27, 1915.

My interview with Jasmine Brambilla Auyón and her mother took place in June 2003. Some of it was in English; for the rest, Lupe Vásquez interpreted.

View of the Hotel Cecil in 1948—AHMM, photo album 2, cat. #29.AHM/166.2/13.

My encounters with Leonardo took place in June 2003. Leonardo spoke English.

There'd been gaming-houses in Mexicali since 1909.—Information in Auyón Gerardo, p. 46 (Terrie Petree's working translation).

I first met Yolanda Sánchez Ogás in April 2003. She has done a tremendous amount for me and for this book; interviews with her appear in a number of chapters. Lupe Vásquez, José López from Jalisco and Terrie Petree have translated her words for me on various occasions.

My interview with the barber in Pasajes Prendes took place in June 2003. Yolanda Sánchez Ogás was present; Terrie Petree interpreted. Ditto for my interview with the manager of the Hotel Cecil. Our visit to the first two tunnels followed that same day.

The fire of 1923—The caption to the AHMM's photo album 2, cat. #29.AHM/166.2/17 ("Reconstruction of Avenida Juárez between Altamirano and Azueta" informs us that in May 1923 a terrible fire destroyed "dos manzanas completas, de lo que fuera centro comercial chino."

"Round one-pound tins . . ."—N.A.R.A.L. Record Group 36. Records of the U.S. Customs Service. Calexico Customs Office. Incoming Official Correspondence (91–60). October 15, 1902–March 23, 1916. Box No. 3 of 5: November 1913 to July 1914. Bound volume labeled "Letters." F. E. Johnson, Special Agent, United States Customs Service, Los Angeles, Cal., to the Office of the Special Agent, Collector of Customs, Los Angeles, Cal., January 25, 1915, p. 1.

I visited the tunnel under the Sinai Christian Center in late June 2003.

Footnote: Translator's commentary on receipt—Chinese tunnel letters, Batch 1, I (certificate of receipt/invoice).

"Everything goes well at home, except . . ."—Chinese tunnel letters, Batch 2, VI (a letter from a wife to a husband, undated). "The way I miss you is heavy and long" was actually translated "The missing is dense and long," which I thought could use some help from a native speaker of English.

Rosalyn Ng's description of the tunnel under the Restaurante Victoria, Miguel's reaction, etc.—Rosalyn Ng report, 2003. For narrative reasons I have reversed the order of two self-contained blocks of text.

Footnote: Sex ratios in Imperial County in 1910—Census Bureau (1910), loc. cit.

Same footnote: "Happy phantasm" from the Gold Mountain Songs: "I turn around, and I'm no longer a part of that miserable lot! . . ."—Hom, p. 185 ("Rhapsodies on Gold," song no. 98, JSGJ I.6a).

"The Chinese called the city of Mexicali 'Little Can-Choo' . . ."—Auyón Gerardo, p. 50 (Terrie Petree's working translation).

Mexico bans importation of unskilled Chinese laborers in 1921—Duncan, p. 633.

Footnote: "Every Chinese always believes that every store has a life . . ."—The woman who said this was named Mai. She was my second interpreter in Nan Ning. The year was 2002.

"For a long time, [Mr. Auyón] went on and on . . ."—Rosalyn Ng report, 2003.

Footnote: The three major bases of Chinese tongs—Information from Mr. Auyón in Rosalyn Ng's report, 2003. In my own interview with Mr. Auyón, the same three bases were ranked differently (name, then place, then profession).

"Dear Ging Gei . . ."—Chinese tunnel letters, Batch 1, V (letter on official form from Wong Kong Ja Tong, 8 October 1924).

Assistance for Ting Zen—Chinese tunnel letters, Batch 2, I (Announcement, 1928). I have changed "donators" to "donors."

"I went to the venue where brother Shi-Ping was murdered . . ."—Chinese tunnel letters, Batch 2, II (to Huan-Jiang-Xia General Association, 1911).

Report from 1923: "not capable," etc.—Chinese tunnel letters, Batch 2, III (to Jia-Lan-Jie General Association, 1923).

My interviews with the Victoria's Mexican cook took place in November 2003. Terrie Petree and José López from Jalisco interpreted.

Tong contribution to the Anti-Chinese Discrimination Organization—Chinese tunnel letters, Batch 1, IX (from Wong Kong Ja Tong, on letterhead, 13 January 1925). See also Batch 1, X (20 February 1920).

Tongs' joint subscriptions to periodicals—E.g., Chinese tunnel letters, Batch 1, VI (11 November 1924).

"In response to your letter, I would like to inform you that ten to thirty people were caught here . . ."—Chinese tunnel letters, Batch 1, IV (from Wong Kong Ja Tong, on letterhead, 29 October 1924).

Chinese gambling payoffs to the Mexicali police: 28,000 pesos a month—Ruiz, p. 49.

Governor Rodríguez's measure compelling the hiring of Mexicans at gambling establishments—Ruiz, p. 51.

"Expulsion of pernicious individuals of the Chinese nationality"—Rodríguez, pp. 51–54.

"Once more Tai ran true to racial form . . ."—Dashiell Hammett, p. 143 ("The House in Turk Street," 1924).

"Thanks very much for flattering me and naming me to the position . . ."—Chinese tunnel letters, Batch 2, VI (to: brothers in Huan-Jiang-Xia General Association, 1927). English slightly corrected by WTV.

"5 MEXICAN STATES CLEARED OF CHINESE . . ."—*New York Times*, October 18, 1931, p. 2.

The old shoe-store owner who came to Mexicali in 1957—This was the uncle of the Dong Chen waitress, Miss Xu. My interview with him has already been cited in this chapter, above. I think it unlikely that we will meet again.

"The government has arrested a total of more than two hundred people."—Chinese tunnel letters, Batch 1, XI (letter on official form from Wong Kong Ja Tong, 24 November 1934).

My interviews with the young Chinese man in the alley next to the Victoria took place in June 2003. Terrie Petree interpreted; Yolanda Sánchez Ogás was present.

My interviews with Tim, who lived in that same alley next to the Victoria, took place in my room at the Hotel Chinesca in October 2003. Terrie Petree interpreted. I had not met Tim before; Terrie and the Ngs had found and interviewed him in July.

Interview with Tim: Rosalyn's notes—Rosalyn Ng report, 2003. Some parentheses and other punctuation which I considered extraneous was omitted.

My interview with the Restaurant Nineteen's proprietor took place in June 2003. Beatriz Limón and Yolanda Ogás were present; José López from Jalisco interpreted.

The tunnel described in "The Red Handprints" was explored in June 2003. Terrie Petree and the two Mexican girls from the Boutique Duarte above were present.

1920s vistas of Reforma and the Chinesca—AHMM, photo album 3, cat. #29.AHM/166.3/17, #29.AHM/166.3/24; photo album 2, cat. #29.AHM/166.2/6.

Date of establishment of Chinese consulate in Mexicali—Auyón Gerardo, p. 25 (Terrie Petree's working translation).

Information from the Chinese couple at Condominios Montealbán—Rosalyn Ng report, 2003. In the report, the location is given as Gnu River Apartments, which is a newer name for part of Condominios Montealbán.

Footnote: Information from Clare Ng in direct speech—Interview by WTV.

My interviews with the butcher Daniel Ávila took place in October and November 2003. Terrie Petree and José López from Jalisco interpreted. About the paintings of naked women on velvet, Terrie noted on the margin: "Did I translate that? I don't remember him mentioning anything but paintings on the wall like murals." José López responded: "It's a cantina, right? They're velvet paintings, right? What else can they be but naked women?"

Description of Reforma and Altamirano during the construction of the "Teatro China" in 1920—AHMM, photo album 1, cat. #29.AHM/166.1/45.

My two interviews with the Mexican who took care of his dead Chinese boss's supermarket occurred in October and November 2003. Terrie Petree and José López from Jalisco interpreted.

Footnote: "I recently heard that Huan-Jiang-Xia General Association was burned to ashes . . ."—Chinese tunnel letters, Batch 2, V (no heading, 1923).

Same footnote: "Huan-Jiang-Xia General Association is holding its grand opening in the Third City . . ."—Chinese tunnel letters, Batch 2, VII (invitation card, no date).

Communication about the rebuilt family temple—Chinese tunnel letters, Batch 2, X (no header, no date). English slightly corrected by WTV. "Clan" was actually translated "family/tribe."

74. *Indio (1925)*

The new hotel in Indio and its cost—*California Cultivator,* Vol. LXIV, No. 14, April 4, 1925, p. 416 ("Agricultural News Notes of the Pacific Coast": "Southern California").

75. *The Inland Empire (1925)*

Epigraph: "The citrus industry remained unchallenged . . ."—Patterson, p. 376.

Advertisement for Tetley's Nurseries—*California Cultivator,* vol. LXIV, no. 14, April 4, 1925, p. 438 ("Classified Liners").

View of Upland (1918)—Wagner and Blackstock, pp. 28–29.

View of Pomona (1920)—Ibid., pp. 38–39.

Performances of "Ramona"—Paul, p. 185. The first of the 3 performances was in 1923.

"The World Famous Magnolia Avenue"—*California Cultivator,* vol. XXIV, no. 15 (April 14, 1905), cover.

Electric cars on Magnolia—Patterson, p. 385.

Irrigated area of Riverside, 1906—*California Cultivator,* vol. XXVI, no. 18 (May 4, 1906), p. 419 ("News of Country Life in the Golden West"). Her poor sister, the Coachella Valley, finally achieves 14,500 in 1925; she possesses 6,500 inhabitants. Her major agricultural productions are, in order from greatest to least: dates, grapes, grapefruit, Bermuda onions, cotton. She may give Imperial County a run for her money.—Senate Committee on the Colorado River Basin (1925), p. 53 (statement of Dr. Jennings, physician, rancher and landowner in the Coachella Valley, and member of the Board of Directors of the Coachella Valley Water District).

"A city of American homes . . ."—Riverside City Directory (1921), p. 3.

Inhabitants of Riverside and I.V. Investment Co.—Riverside City Directory (1921), pp. 29, 30, 153, 155.

Opening of first motel—Patterson, p. 385.

Information on Chinese, Chinatown and the Ku Klux Klan—The Great Basin Foundation Center for Anthropological Research, vol. 2, p. 399. The date of appearance of Chinese in Occidental clothing was 1924.

Orange acres in Riverside, 1929—Wagner. p. 51.

Agua Caliente Indians in Palm Springs—*California Cultivator,* vol. LXIV, no. 14, April 4, 1925, p. 438 ("Classified Liners").

Description of Palm Canyon, 1924—Kurutz, p. 54 (photo by Frederick Martin).

76. *Los Angeles (1925)*

Epigraph—"It is a clean city . . ."—McGroarty, vol. 1, p. 366.

Figure on Los Angeles' population in 1900–20—*The California Water Atlas,* p. 33.

Detail on the Crystal Springs wells—California State Archives. Margaret C. Felts papers. Box 1. Loose typescript, *ca.* 20 pp. A. H. Koebig, Consulting Engineer and Special Representative. "Answer to the report of Mr. Hay Goudy, Asst. Engineer, to the State Board of Health of the State of California, No. 269, dated June 14th, 1921. By and for the City of Burbank, California." June 25, 1921. Stamped: "Property of Water Resources Center Archives, University of California, Berkeley, California." Handwritten: MS 80/3 119.24, p. 4.

"The Los Angeles aqueduct will carry ten times as much water as all the famous aqueducts of Rome combined." —*American Biography and Genealogy*, p. 36.

Acknowledgment to William Mulholland in *The Winning of Barbara Worth*—Wright, p. 16.

William Mulholland: "Only water was needed to make this region a rich and productive empire . . ."—William Leslie Davis, p. 93.

Harry Chandler's automotive grid plan, 1924—Sitton and Deverell, pp. 52, 55 (Matthew W. Roth, "Mulholland Highway and the Engineering Culture of Los Angeles in the 1920s").

Subdivision of Los Angeles' acreage in 1923–25—*California Cultivator*, vol. LXV, no. 20, November 14, 1925, p. 504 (C. A. Nidever, "Where Are We Going?").

Upton Sinclair: "subdivisions with no 'restrictions' . . ."—Op. cit., pp. 80–81 (*Oil!*, 1927).

Description of an oilscape—After Bristol, p. 23 ("Signal Hills Field, 1933").

Los Angeles as leading oil exporter—Sitton and Deverell, p. 129 (Nancy Quam-Wickham, " 'Another World': Work, Home and Autonomy in Blue-Collar Suburbs").

The real estate atlas of 1910—Baist, Plate 5, subsection 6.

Chicken-hutches and derricks in suburbs—Sitton and Deverell, p. 85 (Becky M. Nicolaides, "The Quest for Independence: Workers in the Suburbs").

A professional man could still be both an osteopath and a citrus grower.—See, e.g., McGroarty, vol. 2, p. 309 (biography of Charles Milliken).

"Is sometimes referred to as 'earth's biggest city . . .' "—Hunt, p. 496.

Saturday Evening Post: "Countless numbers of American citizens . . ."—Quoted in Watkins, p. 297 (Kenneth Roberts, "And West Is West").

Perception of Mexican women as unreliable, slow, unintelligent employees—UC Berkeley. Bancroft Library. Paul S. Taylor papers. Carton 5. Folder 5:7: "Mexican Women in Los Angeles Industry in 1928, 1980." Offprint: Paul S. Taylor, "Research Note: Mexican Women in Los Angeles Industry in 1928," copyright 1980, in *Azatlan*, vol. 11, no. 1; pp. 128–30.

Mexican employees' relatively lower earnings than those of other women—Paul S. Taylor, op. cit., p. 124. Taylor came to this conclusion from inspecting payroll records in his 12 target industries.

Footnote: Wages of unskilled American and Mexican workers, 1930—Sitton and Deverell, p. 21 (Los Angeles Chamber of Commerce).

Disposition of jobs available to those Mexican women—Sitton and Deverell, p. 112. Paul S. Taylor remarks (loc. cit.) that "two-fifths of them were employed in general labor, one-fifth in skilled machine operation, one-fifth in work such as packing or cutting, one-tenth in work requiring some education and English knowledge."

Description of these working women's homes—Paul S. Taylor, op. cit., pp. 118–19.

"Refrigeration without ice"—*California Cultivator*, vol. LXV, no. 24, December 5, 1925, p. 584.

"Distinguishable on the streets . . ."—Paul S. Taylor, op. cit., p. 116. "The 12.5 percent who lived away from their families was made up of mestizos who . . . stoutly maintained that they were Spanish and not Mexican, which appeared to be an indication of their desire not to be linked with the lower class . . ." (ibid., p. 108).

"These industries, fostered by genial climate and contented population . . ."—McGroarty, vol. 1, pp. 363–64.

Doings of the Lockheed and Vega aircraft companies—California State Archives. Margaret C. Felts papers. Box 1 (B4380), labeled "Environmental Files. Groundwater Contamination. L.A. River Pollution 1919–1938." Daniel, Mann, Johnson, & Mendenhall (Los Angeles, California), *Master Plan for USAF Plant 14, Burbank, California, Prepared for Lockheed-California Co., Division of Lockheed Aircraft Co., Burbank, California* (n.d., probably 1966), p. 12.

Los Angeles is still horses in the streets . . .—After McGroarty, vol. 1, p. 356, illus. "Main and Temple Streets, Opposite Present Postoffice [*sic*] Site," n.d. but must be before or *ca.* 1923.

Advertisement of the Tanaka Citrus Nursery—*California Cultivator*, vol. LXIV, no. 14, April 4, 1925, p. 438 ("Classified Liners").

Henry Kruse's biography—McGroarty, vol. 3, p. 213.

"It is difficult to speak of what the Los Angeles of today is . . ."—Ibid., vol. 1, p. 359.

Description of the Pacific Mutual Life Insurance Company Building—Ibid., vol. 1, p. 362.

The Los Angeles Boosters in El Centro—*Imperial Valley Press*, vol. XIV, no. 18, Monday evening, May 31, 1914, p. 1 ("Los Angeles Boosters Delighted with City").

Descriptions of male and female date flowers—After Dunham, p. 90.

Destination of Olympic Boulevard—Sitton and Deverell, p. 52 (Matthew W. Roth, "Mulholland Highway and the Engineering Culture of Los Angeles in the 1920s").

All remarks by Marjorie Sa'adah in this chapter—From an interview and tour she kindly gave me in September 2004.
Opening date of the Mayan Theater—Miron, p. 88.
News of Lupe Velez and Dolores Del Rio—Sitton and Deverell, pp. 163, 174 (Douglas Monroy, "Making Mexico in Los Angeles").
"Looking north from downtown . . ."—Miron, p. 38.
California Eve Brand orange label—McClelland and Last, p. 43.

77. Tamerlane's Warriors Gallop into the Square (1924–2003)

Epigraph: "The city of Los Angeles is asking for a very modest supply . . ."—Senate Committee on the Colorado River Basin (1925), pp. 108–9 (statement of Mulholland).
"His sole interest was in advancing the public good . . ."—William Leslie Davis, p. 90.
First pumping of Owens Valley groundwater, 1919—Ibid., p. 138.
Description of Owens Lake past and present; interviews with the part-time cowgirl in Independence and the museum lady in Lone Pine—July 2005. Micheline Marcom was present.
Arrest of Upton Sinclair—Sinclair, p. 38 (text of commemorative plaque), p. 39 ("Singing Jailbirds").
Recollections of an Owens Valley resident—Parcher and Parcher, unnumbered p. iii (introduction by R. Coke Wood, 1970).
Bullocks Wilshire: "At a scale that makes window-shopping possible for drivers"—Moore et al., p. 147.
Description of the suction dredge—ICHSPM photograph, cat. #P92.33.8 (Hetzel photo).
Eisenstein script excerpt—Eisenstein, p. 265 (Appendix 7, unpublished script for "Ferghana Canal," 1939).

78. Subdelineations: Waterscapes (1901–1925)

Epigraph: ". . . why, Granddaddy, there couldn't *be* any town without all that water . . ."—Richards, p. 26.
Excerpts from the California Experiment Station's record for 1920—USDA *Experiment Station Record* series (1920), pp. 640–41 ("The effects of alkali on citrus trees," W. P. Kelley and E. E. Thomas, *California Station Bulletin 318 (1920)*, pp. 305–37).
G. Harold Powell on what happened to "the first settled part of Riverside"—Op. cit., p. 38 (letters of "Monday night" and "Wednesday night," February 1904, to Gertrude Powell).
"It is in this regard—the pure democratization of the great irrigation systems . . ."—James, *Reclaiming the Arid West*, p. xii.
Mileage of main and lateral canals, 1909—Hunt, p. 461.
Imperial County Assessor's Map 17–15—The ancient bound volume in El Centro.
Complaints of CRLC and *Times* about IID—*Los Angeles Times*, December 15, 1920, p. II8 ("WATER USERS MAKE PROTEST").
IID as largest irrigation district in the Western Hemisphere—Colorado River Association (1952), p. 18.
. . . by 1922, IID's hegemony will be perfect . . .—In 1920 the Imperial Irrigation District is still only one of 15 water companies in the valley, the others being the almost-bankrupt Imperial Water Companies numbers 1 through 12, the South Alamo Water Company, and the Imperial South Side Water Company (Imperial Valley Directory [1920], p. XVIII). In 1922, IID completes its takeover of the remaining entities. As we will see in another chapter, the Bard Subdistrict remains its own creature.
"By 1919 about a quarter of the irrigated land in Imperial Valley . . ."—Lilliard, p. 153.
"Drainage is the most satisfactory way . . ."—Packard, p. 5.
"The flood had subsided . . ."—James, op. cit., p. 65.
Break of the Volcano Lake levee—Senate Committee on the Colorado River Basin (1925), p. 25 (statement of Earl C. Pound, President, Imperial Irrigation District).
"The area of the present Salton Sea is about 400 square miles . . ."—*National Geographic* magazine, 1906 (?), vol. XVIII, no. 1, Arthur P. Davis, Assistant Chief Engineer, "The New Inland Sea (An Account of the Colorado River Break)," p. 44.
Platting of Salton Sea Beach—Wray, p. 86.
Description of the Salton Sea in 1922—After Brown and Boyd, p. 407.
"California's 'Little Yellowstone'"—State of California. Department of Transportation. Transportation Library, Sacramento. Imperial folder. National [illegible], Robert Johansen, "The Mogul of Mullet Island," November 1932.
Description of Mullet Island—ICHSPM, photo #P91.19.
Mullet Island as a peninsula in 1932—State of California, Department of Transportation, op. cit.
"We have since been accused of gross negligence . . ."—Rockwood, quoted in Farr, p. 138.
The tale of Clarence Dougherty's pump—Stamps, pp. 36–37.
Remarks of the professor in Claremont—*California Cultivator*, vol. XXIII, no. 6 (August 5, 1904), p. 124 ("The Water Supply").

Rockwood's reassurance, etc.—*Los Angeles Times*, June 20, 1915, p. 112 ("The Truth About the Imperial Valley"). In fact, all our plutocrats actually did was graciously give Rockwood the right-of-way. And the *Los Angeles Times* with a sad and forbearing air continues its article "Completely Puncturing a Tissue of Vicious Falsehoods." The *Times* means so well; it has gone to such a great expense to help the world "exploit this inland empire" called Imperial; it has no property interests in the valley whatsoever, "though some individual owners have large individual investments there." So let the water flow! (Waterlessness will not go away all at once. I've seen a photograph from 1921 depicting an Imperial encampment of white tents pentagonal in cross-section, with laundry and children around them in that wide flatness of silt; even in 1921 the desert has not quite disappeared; maybe that will happen in 1922.—ICHSPM photograph, cat. #P94.18.1 [Hetzel image]).

". . . practically twice the present area can be irrigated . . ."—Packard, p. 8.

Depth and yield of Coachella's wells—Ibid., p. 7.

Imperial County's good wells limited to Holtville—Ibid., p. 9.

Other information on Coachella Valley's artesian wells and water table, 1894–1922—Senate Committee on the Colorado River Basin (1925), p. 53 (statement of Dr. Jennings, physician, rancher and landowner in the Coachella Valley and member of the Board of Directors of the Coachella Valley Water District).

Lowering of the groundwater level in Southern California, 1922–25—California State Archives. Margaret C. Felts papers. Box 12: Folder: "1927 POLLUTION." State of California. Department of Public Works. Division of Engineering and Irrigation. Paul Bailey, State Engineer, *Bulletin No. 12: Summary Report on the Water Resources of California and a Coordinated Plan for Their Development: A Report to the Legislature of 1927* (Sacramento: California State Printing Office, 1927), p. 43.

John I. Bacon: ". . . we have, to-day, about four years' supply of water . . ."—Senate Committee on the Colorado River Basin (1925), p. 6 (statement of Bacon).

William Mulholland: ". . . in the last two years we have been close to the edge . . ." and exchange with the Chairman—Senate Committee on the Colorado River Basin (1925), pp. 109–10 (statement of Mulholland).

"We have about 30,000,000 acres in farms . . ."—*California Cultivator*, vol. LXIV, no. 14, April 4, 1925, p. 415 (John Lathrop, "Can We Have a Balanced Farm Program?").

The falling wells in Ventura County, 1925—Ibid., p. 416 ("Agricultural News Notes of the Pacific Coast": "Southern California").

"SOUTHERN CALIFORNIA HAS MUCH WATER."—*Imperial Valley Press*, Monday, May 3, 1926, p. 1.

79. *The Mexican User Is a Customer, Not an Owner (1904–1918)*

Epigraph: "Anything can be removed from water except salt and politics."—California State Archives. Margaret C. Felts papers. Box 1. A. H. Koebig, Charles Kirby Fox, Arthur W. Cory, November 15, 1930, letter to the President and Directors of the Southwest Water League, p. 4 (Leon B. Reynolds, Professor of Sanitary Engineering).

Dimensions of Laguna Dam and "Now that modern irrigation methods . . ."—James, *Reclaiming the Arid West*, pp. 86, 97–98.

"The construction of a series of huge reservoirs . . ."—Farr, pp. 79–80.

Footnote: Catarino Mesina's stage line (from Mexicali to the mouth of the Colorado and another from Mexicali to Ensenada)—N.A.R.A.L. Record Group 36. Records of the U.S. Customs Service. Calexico Customs Office. Incoming Correspondence Regarding Smuggling (9L-61). July 25, 1914–May 23, 1922. Box 2 of 2: From May 1914 to May 1922. Letter (not in folder) from J. P. Conway [?], Deputy Collector and Inspector, Tia Juana, Cal., to Deputy Collector in Charge, Tia Juana, Cal., July 19, 1919.

"I believe that if the river is controlled and conserved . . ."—Senate Committee on the Colorado River Basin (1925), Part 2, p. 253 (C.W. Brockman, Calexico director of IID).

"The Mexican user is a customer . . ."—Ibid., p. 241 (J.C. Allison, civil engineer, representing Colorado River Control Club).

80. *Market Prices (1925)*

Epigraph: "My country is abundant in wheat . . ."—Bowman and Heizer, p. 154 (letter of 26 November 1776).

Produce and cattle prices—*California Cultivator*, vol. LXIV, no. 14, April 4, 1925, p. 410 (Los Angeles market price listings, quoted 31 March 1925).

81. *San Diego (1925)*

Epigraph: ". . . and then I shall return to the solitary church in that enchanted world . . ."—Ballard, *The Crystal World*, p. 154.

County rankings for produce, 1910—California Board of Agriculture (1918).

Escondido's 250 tons of tomatoes—*California Cultivator*, vol. LXIV, no. 14, April 4, 1925, p. 416 ("Agricultural News Notes of the Pacific Coast": "Southern California").

Escondido's new citrus packing house—Ibid., vol. LXV, no. 7, August 15, 1925, p. 140 ("Agricultural News Notes of the Pacific Coast": "Southern California").
The 20-acre apricot orchard for sale in Oceanside—Ibid., vol. LXIV, no. 14, April 4, 1925, p. 438 ("Classified Liners").
"San Diego supports extensive ranches and groves of oranges . . ."—Carolan, p. 48.

82. The Long Death of Albert Henry Larson (1903–1926)

Epigraph: "This is the spirit of the Imperial Valley . . ."—Howe and Hall, p. 132.
Larson's death certificate—County of Imperial. No SI number. LR #10.
Albert Henry Larson's absence from, and Gus/Gustav Larson's transactions in, the Imperial County Recorder's index—California State Archives. Microfilmed Imperial County records, 1851–1919. Roll #1433101. Index to Grantors, 1851–1907. Index to Grantees, 1851–1907. Gustav Larson was the grantee on August 13, 1904, in a transaction involving Charles W. Fernald as grantor (Book 8, p. 122). Gus Larson was the grantee on April 15, 1907, in a transaction involving Nathan D. Nichols (Book 24[?], p. 149).
The Larson of 1917–18—Zollinger-Peterson reports.
Olaf Larson's occupation—Imperial Valley Directory (1912), p. 174.
Howe and Hall on John Larson—Op. cit., 171–72. His name is spelled "Larsen" in the Imperial Valley Directory (1912), p. 174.
Bearded men admiring their own sugar beets—ICHSPM photograph, cat. #P85.241 (credit: Putnam and Valentine). The man in boots and waders and the satisfied pioneer are also Pioneer Museum photographs.
Directory entries on Larson—Imperial Valley Directory (1912), p. 174; I.V. Directory (1920), p. 97; I.V. Directory (1926), p. 198.
Default on mortgage, 1924—County of Imperial, County Recorder's book, pp. 45–47, 11 June 1924.
Larson's 1924 land purchase—Document #936662, serial #CAEC 0005863, SB meridian, township 016S, range 0131, section 31.
Names of the Larsons in the Colorado River Control Club—Senate Committee on the Colorado River Basin (1925), Part 2, p. 217.
Connection between opposition to the All-American Canal and land ownership in Mexico—Nordland, p. 6.
USDA remarks on private land-development agencies—USDA Yearbook (1920), pp. 24–25.
Jack Armstrong's ad—*Imperial Valley Press*, Wednesday, March 31, 1926, p. 7.
Armand Jessup's ad—Loc. cit.
H. L. Boone's ad—*Imperial Valley Press*, Friday, April 30, 1926, p. 7.
Larsons and Larsens in the 1870 California census—*California 1870 Census Index*, Volume II, L–Z, ed. Raeone Christensen Steuart (Bountiful, Utah: Heritage Quest, 2000), California census index (1870), p. 17.
Description of the old plank road—ICHSPM photograph, cat. #P92.54.
A French economist: "The industrial wealth of the United States must not deceive us . . ."—*The Annals of America*, vol. 14 (Henri Hauser, "Observations on American Farming," from *L'Amérique vivante*, 1924).
"MRS. LEROY HOLT HOSTESS AT TWO PRETTY AFFAIRS."—*Imperial Valley Press*, Thursday, May 6, 1926, p. 2. Mr. Than's employment was reported in the Thursday, May 6, issue, p. 1; the first trainload of cantaloupes rolled out on May 6; regarding the biggest cantaloupe season in history, I repeat the following citation for "Then and Now": the cantaloupe season of 1926 and its accompanying refrigerator cars—*Imperial Valley Press*, Monday, May 3, p. 1.
Photo of Jack Brothers and McBurney Co.'s five girls—ICHSPM photograph, cat. #P91.201.160 (credit: Southern Pacific Photo Service, 1927).
Otherwise uncited property transactions of the Larsons until Albert's suicide—County Recorder's Book (vol. unknown), p. 15A, 26 November 1923, Superior Court case no. 9156 (re: lots 21 and 22, block 96, Imperial townsite). County Recorder's Book 2, pp. 409–10, 27 September 1923 (my researcher did not obtain part of the record of this transaction). County Recorder's Book 2, page 409 (ten o'clock in the morning on 14 September 1922; NE qtr of SE qtr and N half of SE qtr of Section 35, Township 15 S, Range 16 E, SBM). County of Imperial, County Recorder's book, pp. 45–47, 11 June 1924 (the chattel mortgage). County Recorder's Book, vol. unknown, pp. 484–87; various July 1925 (conveyance from the Consolidated Title Insurance Company of a Deed of Trust to lots 3 and 5, sec. 4, Township 15 south, Range 13 E, SBM, and part of lot 6 in sec. 4). Recorder's Book 190, pp. 287–88, 16 January 1926; El Centro 06863, 4-1023-R (re: lot 30 sec. 31 Township 16 S of Range 13 E of SBM). County Recorder's Book, vol. unknown, p. 289 (on or after 20 March 1926, Albert Larson's declaration of homestead, lots 3 and 5 and some of lot 6, all in sec. 4; unfortunately I do not have the next page).
Disposition of Albert and Elizabeth Larson's acres after the suicide—although Elizabeth herself sells one piece of the estate to P. C. Johnson for $10, Mr. Veazzie A. Wheelock, the administrator of his will, sells the core of the Larson Ranch to P. C. Johnson for $3,715, retaining only the oil rights. To P. C. Johnson and his wife Hattie, Wheelock sells Elizabeth's holdings in section 35 for $1,840. After 26 March 1928, Elizabeth Larson conveys real estate to William L. Pollard for $50 gold coin. In August 1929, Elizabeth Larson sells Lot 7 of the Larson

Ranch to P. C. Johnson, widower, for what must have been even then the small sum of $10, all tenements and appurtenances of the property included—and also all taxes. For at least some of this time the new owners might also have been struggling; for on 12 May 1927, a certain P. C. Johnson, dairyman, mortgages to the National Trust and Savings Association forty-three cows, heifers and calves, all branded with Albert Larson's mark on the left hip. They are collateral for the $325 at 8% interest. [Sources of foregoing: County Recorder's Book, unknown vol., p. 132, 2 June 1926 (NE qtr of SE qtr and N ½ of NW qtr of SE qtr of Sec. 35, Township 15 S, Range 16E, SBM). County Recorder's Book 149, pp. 151–52 (Deed of Trust, 28 September 1926, re: lots 3 and 5 and part of lot 6, sec. 4, township 15 S, range 13 E, $1840). County Recorder's Book, vol. unknown, 4 October 1926, pp. 3–4 (re: lots 3, 5 and 6, section 4, Township 15 south, range 13 east, SBM). County Recorder's Book, vol. unknown, p. 358. County Recorder's Book, vol. unknown, p. 33, no. 20748, 15 August 1929; lefthand edge of page near staples numbered AAA968. County Recorder's Book 149, pp. 237–28 (12 May 1927).]

84. *Imperial Reprise (1901–1929)*

Epigraph: "The sword created the shape of empire . . ."—Torre and Wiegers, p. 601 (Veronica Volkow, "Arcana IV: The Emperor," trans. Margaret Sayers Peden).

PART SIX

SUBPLOTS

85. *Almost as Efficiently as Washing Machines (1891–1936)*

Epigraph: "So, then, to every man his chance . . ."—Wolfe, p. 484 ("The Promise of America").

Judge J. S. Emory: "Four weeks ago I rode across a farm in Texas . . ."—Bancroft Library. Paul S. Taylor papers. Carton 4. Folder 4:34: "Irrigation Crusade, 1969," p. 7.

The tale of Ed J. Callon—*California Cultivator*, vol. XXIII, no. 1 (July 1, 1904), p. 18 (A. R. Colson, "The Call of the Hen: A Visit to the World's Largest Poultry Farms").

Advertisement on chickens-as-machines—*California Cultivator*, vol. XXVII, no. 1 (July 5, 1906), p. 2.

"The great ranches of South America . . ."—*California Cultivator*, vol. LXV, no. 20, November 14, 1925, p. 485 (C. A. Nidever, "Where Are We Going?").

"The history of agriculture . . ." and "The individual spinners . . ."—Ibid., pp. 504, 505.

Remarks of Mr. Charles Anderson—*California Cultivator*, vol. LXXXIII, no. 15, July 18, 1936, p. 539.

Poultry statistics 1950–73—*California Farmer*, January 4, 1975, p. 25 ("The laying hen—'She's come a long way'").

"Petitioner's operation is more akin to a light industry . . ."—California State Archives. ALRB restricted files. Accession no. 1999-07-08, loc. B7949–7955, Box 2 of 27. Specific location number not indicated on this box. On box: EBR. Since the following is already a public record, I can cite it properly: Bound typescript with orange covers. 4 Civ. 16995. In the Supreme Court of the State of California. Prohoroff Poultry Farms, Petitioner, vs. Agricultural Labor Relations Board, Respondent. Petition for hearing. Following dismissal by the Court of Appeal for the Fourth Appellate District, Division One, of a petition for review of a final order of the Agricultural Labor Relations Board. James K. Smith, Esq., John M. Phelps, Esq., San Diego. Attorneys for petitioner. Dated: May 23, 1979. Stamped: Received, May 29, 1979, p. 3.

Dr. Jennings: "Most of the inability to dispose of farm products . . ." and "We accept in theory and fact the principles of the Colorado River compact . . ."—Senate Committee on the Colorado River Basin (1925), pp. 51, 55 (statement of Jennings).

86. *Subdelineations: Lettucescapes (1922–1975)*

Epigraph: "The main reason we cannot read these early texts . . ."—Aruz, p. 13 ("Uruk and the Formation of the City").

Episodes when San Luis Obispo sugar beets were the nation's earliest—*California Cultivator*, vol. XXIV, no. 26 (June 30, 1905), p. 611 ("News of Country Life in the Golden West").

Cantaloupe chart and remarks—Paul Foster reports (2007) ("Imperial Color Commentary").

Group portrait of the Brawley Cantaloupe Growers' Association, 1910—*Imperial County: The Big Picture*, p. 18.

"This is a lettuce hearing . . ."—California State Archives. Department of Food and Agriculture. Bureau of Marketing. Marketing-order files, Box 3. State of California, Department of Agriculture, Bureau of Markets hearing on proposed marketing order for winter lettuce. Wednesday, December 17, 1958, beginning ten o'clock, a.m., El Centro, California. Page 120 (Reginald Knox).

"There were 12,000 acres planted to lettuce . . ."—Imperial County Agricultural Commission papers. Report from E. F. Waite, Horticultural Commissioner, to the Honorable Board of Supervisors of Imperial County, California; hand-dated 1911–22, perhaps by another hand, in upper lefthand corner; p. 2.

Lettuce news for 1924—Hunt, p. 462.

"Growers in the Imperial Valley are alarmed . . ."—*California Cultivator*, vol. LXV, no. 7, August 15, 1925, p. 140 ("Agricultural News Notes of the Pacific Coast": "Southern California").

News of Ed Miller—*California Cultivator*, vol. LXIV, no. 14, April 4, 1925, p. 416 ("Agricultural News Notes of the Pacific Coast": "Southern California").

The two contestants grapple eternally.—Farm prices are $1.30 per crate in 1934 and $1.35 in 1935 for Imperial Valley growers, $1.60 in 1934 and $1.20 in 1935 for Arizona growers, perhaps because the latter have increased lettuce acreage instead of decreasing it as Imperial did but who can say? Imperial's in deep manure now, boys and girls! In 1936, Arizona decreases acreage, while Imperial increases it, so that the 1,950,000 crates produced in the valley in 1935 become 2,750,000 in 1936. Who will win that gamble? To find out, we must wait for 1937. The beginning of 1936 is marred by low consumption in the eastern United States combined with an overhigh quantity of Imperial Valley lettuce. In consequence, both Imperial and Arizona growers decide to withhold their crop from the market. In 1949 the total cash valuation of Imperial's crops decreases from the previous year, due to a freeze and a general price decline, but in spite of the lukewarm returns, especially from truck crops, "the lettuce deal, due to seasonal conditions, was the exception," the County Agriculture Commissioner consoles us. "Markets were steady and F.O.B. prices were a near high record from January to April when the season closed." Imperial is truly America's winter garden. Lettuce revenues increase 60% from 1951 to 1952.

Lettuce news, Imperial Valley and Arizona 1934–36—University of California, *Time Agricultural Outlooks*, no. 4 (March 1936): John B. Schneider and J. M. Thompson, "Truck Crops," unnumbered p. 2, "Imperial Valley Lettuce." Average yields in both the Imperial Valley and Arizona exceeded those of 1934, so total production, alas, almost equalled that of 1934.

Remarks of Mr. Bunn—California State Archives. Department of Food and Agriculture. Bureau of Marketing. Marketing-order files, Box 3. State of California, Department of Agriculture, Bureau of Markets hearing on proposed marketing order for winter lettuce. Wednesday, December 17, 1958, beginning ten o'clock, a.m., El Centro, California, p. 395.

Crop tales for 1936 (including fn.)—California Board of Agriculture (1936), pp. 540–41.

Crop tales for 1938—California Board of Agriculture (1938), pp. 569, 716, 722 (last 2 refs. are for Imperial Valley lettuce), 723 (carrots), 724 (cantaloupes).

Jean-Jacques Rousseau, 1754: "I have seen men wicked enough to weep for sorrow . . ."—Op. cit., p. 363 (Appendix).

Lettuce news for 1949—Imperial County Agricultural Commission papers. B. A. Harrigan, Agricultural Commissioner, annual report for 1949, p. 7. I asked Richard Brogan (interviewed in Calexico, April 2004) when lettuce became big in Imperial County, and he replied: "I don't think it was a big thing until after the war"—in other words, until about this point in time.

Lettuce news 1951–52—Imperial County Agricultural Commission papers.

"A dollar and a quarter for the best" and marketing-order hearing in 1958—California State Archives. Department of Food and Agriculture. Bureau of Marketing. Marketing-order files, Box 3. State of California, Department of Agriculture, Bureau of Markets hearing on proposed marketing order for winter lettuce. Wednesday, December 17, 1958, beginning ten o'clock, a.m., El Centro, California. Pp. 59, 87, 102, 383–85, 13–14, 185, 203, 70, 229, 56–57, 15, 18, 20, 25, 29–31, 76, 73, 83, 95–96, 99, 105, 107, 10, 110–11, 353, 362–63, 366, 379, 383, 407, 402, 420, 422–23.

87. The Nights of Lupe Vásquez (2003)

Epigraph: ". . . the highest honours within human reach . . ."—Veblen, p. 79 *(The Theory of the Leisure Class)*.

PART SEVEN

CONTRADICTIONS

89. Credit Will Be Restored (1929–1939)

Epigraph: "Credit will be restored and business will hum again . . ."—Tout, *Silt*, p. 313.

Mexican migration to the United States achieves a peak, 1929—Paul S. Taylor, *Mexican Labor in the United States: Migration Statistics. IV*, p. 23.

More than fifty thousand railroad cars of produce went out of the Imperial Valley every year—Figure supplied by Tout, *The First Thirty Years*, p. 252.

Imperial's ranking among agricultural counties, 1919–29—Imperial Valley Directory (1939), p. 11, Chamber of Commerce statement.

1932 figures on unsold Imperial Valley produce—Watkins, p. 97.

Mr. Robert Hays: "The First Thirty Years of Imperial Valley's existence . . ."—Tout, *The First Thirty Years*, p. 410.

Footnote: José Clemente Orozco on the crash—Op. cit., pp. 135, 136.

Imperial County Assessor's statistics and analysis, 1930–39—California State Board of Equalization (1949), p. 16.

57,701 carloads of Imperial Valley products in 1930—Imperial Valley Directory (1930), p. 12.

Otis P. Tout accordingly brings his own *First Thirty Years* to a reassuring close (p. 255): "Despite the stock crashes in New York, Imperial Valley continued to be the white spot on the western map of prosperity, never missing a month for more than two years straight." In other words, it will take a year for the Great Depression to harm Imperial County. After that, tangible property weakens year by year right up to 1939. In 1949, when the county had enjoyed as large a share of the war boom as it was going to get, the Assessor concluded: "Imperial County has lost ground since 1934 in relation to the assessed value of the state as a whole" (California State Board of Equalization [1949], loc. cit. Imperial County's percentage of all locally assessed tangible property values in California: 1929, 0.65%; 1933, 0.72%; 1947, 0.43%).

The photograph captioned "Calipatria 1927"—ICHSPM photograph, uncoded.

A photo from an album: UC Berkeley. Bancroft Library. Powell Studio album. Photo #1945.007:5 ("Sheriff's sale of foreclosed farm").

"Attorneys, Attention!"—Imperial Valley Directory (1930), inside frontispiece.

"Confidence in the continued growth of Imperial Valley's wealth . . ."—Ibid., p. 10.

"Because of market conditions in 1934, the equivalent of 300,000 crates [of lettuce] were unharvested in the Imperial Valley."—University of California, *Time Agricultural Outlooks*, no. 4 (March 1936): John B. Schneider and J. M. Thompson, "Truck Crops," unnumbered p. 2, "Imperial Valley Lettuce."

In 1935 the national unemployment rate remained at almost twenty-two percent.—After Watkins, p. 258.

". . . the Depression . . . altered the political terrain . . ."—UC Berkeley. Bancroft Library. Paul S. Taylor papers. Carton 4. Folder 4:26: "Future of Mexican Immigration: Draft w/Corrections and Notes, 1976" (published as Chapter 11, Corwin, Arthur E. [ed.], *Immigrants . . .*), p. 4. I have used the original, uncorrected version of this sentence. In *Mexican Labor in the United States: Migration Statistics. IV*, p. 25, Table 1 ("Migration of Mexican Citizens . . ."), Taylor shows the following: Between 1930 and 1933 inclusive, 337,000 Mexicans returned to their home country from the United States. About one-tenth of them were tourists. During the same period, 72,000 Mexicans entered the U.S., half of them being tourists.

Excerpts from "How It Feels to Be Broke at Sixty . . ."—Wilsie, pp. 1–3.

"W. E. Wilsie's new home two miles west of El Centro . . ."—Tout, *The First Thirty Years*, p. 195.

Reasons for the loss of Wilsie Ranch—Ibid., p. 4 (Owen Miller's letter to Stacy Vellas).

"Since 1930, the most despised and detested group of men . . ."—Watkins, p. 43, quoting "a British visitor" (source: Allen Nevins, ed., *America Through British Eyes*). How despised might they have been before 1930? In 1922 the state of California had shut down the Farmers & Merchants Bank in Imperial, but, as Otis P. Tout proudly informs us, "local capital came to the rescue, and the bank opened again. It closed for good in 1927" (*The First Thirty Years*, p. 267.) I've found that the way to get your money is to give a man a chance to pay you.

The advertisement of Henry L. Loud—Imperial Valley Directory (1930), p. 38.

Imperial County statistics 1930, from fruit-packing sheds to canals—Imperial County Agriculture Commission Papers. "Imperial County, California. 1930 Statistics."

90. *Market Prices (1919–1931)*

Epigraph: "Sometimes it seems that Fortune deliberately plays with us."—Montaigne, p. 198 ("Fortune is often met in the path of reason").

91. *In a Still More Advantageous Position (1928–1942)*

Epigraph: "Of all the western myths . . ."—Phillips et al., p. 37.

Width of the Imperial Main Canal—Caption to an ICHSPM photograph, cat. #P91.202.2.

Listing of Swing as Imperial County's District Attorney in 1912–13—Imperial Valley Directory (1912), p. v.

"Schemers or impractical dreamers of the Mark Rose type."—*Los Angeles Times*, December 15, 1920, p. II8 ("WATER USERS MAKE PROTEST").

"Swing is energetic, popular and efficient . . ."—Howe and Hall, p. 157.

Face-off between IID and CRLC in 1920—*Los Angeles Times*, December 17, 1920, p. III3 ("RATE PLAN PUT UP TO MEXICO").

Footnote: "Because it had a vested interest in the crucial resource that made its own lands economically useful . . ." —Kerig, p. 48.

Exchange between Swing and CRLC in 1924—*Los Angeles Times*, August 6, 1924, p. 6 ("PROMISE AID IN WATER CRISIS. Letter from Landowners Kills Rumor").

Doings in 1925—Senate Committee on the Colorado River Basin (1925), pp. 1, 3, 66, 108.

Prediction that an All-American Canal will bankrupt 70% of the landowners in the Imperial Valley—*Los Angeles Times*, December 27, 1925, p. B4 ("SELFISH INTERESTS").
Imperial Valley's resolutions of Mayday 1926—*Imperial Valley Press*, Saturday, May 1, pp. 1–2.
A. Giraudo's cantaloupes—Ibid., p. 1.
"The All-American Canal on the eastern shoreline . . ."—Shields Date Gardens, p. 17.
Premier of "The Winning of Barbara Worth"—Wright, p. 382 (Appendix III).
Los Angeles' pro-Boulder-Dam exhibit in Brawley, 1926—Tout, *The First Thirty Years*, p. 249.
Swing-Johnson celebration: "The Western Union telegram has been pinned to the flower-heaped table . . ." —ICHSPM photograph, in cat. #P85.
Eugene Dahm's memories—Interview in Imperial (city), January 2002.
Edith Karpen's memories—Interview in Sacramento, January 2004. Her daughter Alice Woodside was present.
"An inappropriate answer to a misconceived problem . . ."—Munguía, p. xv (Helen Ingram).
"When new lands are added through construction of the All-American Canal . . ."—State of California. Department of Transportation. Transportation Library, Sacramento. Imperial folder. Official map of the city of El Centro, 1931, by Philip W. Knights, City Engineer.
Footnote: fertile county acreage—Imperial Valley Directory (1930), p. 14. The same prediction of a million acres is made here.
Predictions of the El Centro Chamber of Commerce in 1939—Imperial Valley Directory (1939), p. 11.
"Signaling the beginning of work . . ."—Laflin, *A Century of Change*, entry for 1932.
Aqueduct Miners' Day—Laflin, *Coachella Valley*, p. 95.
Photos: All-American Canal dam gates, aqueduct through mountains—Bristol, pp. 48–49 (both from 1941).
Bureau of Reclamation photo from October 1951—California State Archives. Olson Photo Collection. Accession #94–06–27 (395–533). Box 3 of 7. Folder 94–06–27 (395–409): Industry—Dams. Photo #94–06–27–0398. BCP 8648. October 4, 1951, by Mark Swain.
"With the practically limitless Boulder Canyon power now available . . ."—Los Angeles City Directory (1942), p. 13.
"Then he goes happily to bed, his conscience clear . . ."—Lewis, p. 651 *(Babbitt)*.
"Today the trees that bore that crop are again white with blossoms . . ."—Parcher and Parcher, p. 45 ("The Last Apple Crop").
Water use of Los Angeles in 1905—McGroarty, vol. 1, p. 273.
"Bolder than British dreams of Egypt."—Ibid., p. 274.
"Anyone wishing further information concerning Imperial Valley farm lands . . ."—Imperial County Agricultural Commission papers. "Imperial County, California. 1928 Statistics." In the following year, the L.A. address was omitted.
Mulholland: "Well, here's where we get our water."—Nadeau, p. 192.
The respective merits of Boulder Canyon, Bull's Head, etc.—California State Archives. Margaret C. Felts papers. Box 1. A. H. Koebig, Charles Kirby Fox, Arthur W. Cory, Nov. 15, 1930, letter to the President and Directors of the Southwest Water League, p. 3. On p. 2 of the same letter we read: ". . . the conservation of all the water resources in Southern California, both from sewage and from flood control, is an absolute necessity . . . We need that water in addition to the entire water from the Owens River and perhaps Mono Basin, in order to provide the necessary water for domestic and irrigation purposes, to assist the growth of Southern California, and to prevent a check being caused by necessary water not being available until we can obtain additional water from outside sources, mostly mentioned at present from the Colorado River."
Shelly J. Higgins: "With what amounted to secrecy . . ."—San Diego County Water Authority, p. 37.
San Diego gets a hundred and twelve thousand acre-feet per year of Boulder Dam water—Figure from Heilbron et al., p. 328; San Diego County Water Authority, p. 37.

92. *There Is Even Evidence of a Small Fruit Orchard (1931–2005)*

Epigraph: "It is well known that civilization demands water . . ."—Al-Biruni, p. 23.
Still of Gale Robbins—California State Archives, Olson Photo Collection. Accession #94–06–27 (534–713). Box 4 of 7. Folder 94–06–27 (625–645): Night Clubs. Photo #94–06–27–0635 (captioned "Night Clubs, Gale Robbins").
L.A. water consumption, November 1935, November 1936—California State Archives. Margaret C. Felts papers. Box 1. Folder: "December 17, 1936. Department of Water and Power." Department of Water and Power, City of Los Angeles, Bureau of Water Works and Supply, December 17, 1936. Regular monthly report, p. 1. (Exact figures: November 1935, domestic, 201.9 s-f, irrigation, 39.7; November 1936, 220.3 and 64.6, respectively.) (In 1942, the city's daily average domestic water consumption is 119 gallons per capita. The capacity of the aqueduct is 310 million gallons a day.—Los Angeles City Directory [1942], p. 12.)

Information on Mono Lake, 1941—Carle, *Introduction to Water in California*, p. 76.
L.A. principal products—Los Angeles City Directory (1942), p. 12.
The Owens Valley tourist pamphlet—Published by the Independence Chamber of Commerce.

93. *Coachella's Share (1918–1948)*

"The Coachella Valley County Water District board spent years . . ."—Laflin, *Coachella Valley*, p. 173.
Tale of Highline Canal—Canal, pp. 4–5.

94. *Subdelineations: Waterscapes (1925–1950)*

Epigraph: "Only in our own day . . ."—Hunt, p. 440.
Completion date of El Capitan Dam—Pryde, p. 111.
Major Wyman's project report—California State Archives. Margaret C. Felts papers. Box 1. Folder: "1898–1965, 'A History of the L.A. District,'" U.S. Army Corps of Engineers, *A History of the L.A. District*, p. 158.
Next paragraph: previous history of Los Angeles River, channel from San Fernando Valley, Ballona Creek—Ibid., p. 170.
Footnote: ". . . Bureau of Reclamation, 'The river's flow can be manipulated in the same fashion as the garden hose . . .'"—Regional Director Arleigh B. West, 1968; quoted in Fradkin, p. 245.
"Four-fifths of the local supplies on the Pacific slope . . ." etc.—California State Archives. Margaret C. Felts papers. Box 12: Folder: "1927 POLLUTION." State of California, Department of Public Works, Division of Engineering and Irrigation. Paul Bailey, State Engineer, *Bulletin No. 12: Summary Report on the Water Resources of California and a Coordinated Plan for Their Development: A Report to the Legislature of 1927* (Sacramento: California State Printing Office, 1927), pp. 43, 45.
Imperial County, etc., "where rights have been established by long usage," and "These technical priorities, however . . ."—Heilbron et al., p. 330.
1944 Colorado River allotment to Mexico—Munguía, p. 7 (Francisco Raúl Venegas Cardoso).
The Colorado's total discharge at Yuma, April 1926—*Imperial Valley Press*, Tuesday, May 4, 1926, p. 1.
". . . each acre-foot gained by Mexico will lose us five Angelenos."—After Nadeau, p. 239.
"Exterior view of Nevada wing of Hoover Dam power plant . . ."—California State Archives. Olson Photo Collection. Accession #94–06–27 (395–533). Box 3 of 7. Folder 94–06–27 (395–409): Industry—Dams. Photo #94–06–27–0401. [Los Angeles] Department of Water & Power photo #16543.
Decline in aquatic creatures in the Gulf of Mexico—Leigh, p. 315.
"There is something back of the rumors that the Colorado is a changed stream . . ."—Ibid., pp. 292–93.
Prior presence of jaguars in the Colorado Delta—Munguía, p. 13 (Francisco Raúl Venegas Cardoso). Jaguars were seen by Spaniards in the sixteenth century.
"Often we seemed to be going silently down long, lavender aisles . . ."—Ainsworth, p. 16.
Number of wells in Mexicali Valley and annual aquifer draft—Munguía, p. 8 (Francisco Raúl Venegas Cardoso). Two studies from the 1990s are cited. One calculates a draft of 750,640 AFY; the other, 891,771.
Population of Tecate in 1930—Munguía, p. 158 (Ruiz).
Advertisement for "IMPERIAL VALLEY 'TRIPLE A' ARTESIAN WATER"—Imperial Valley Directory (1930), p. 19; see also ICHSPM, document cat. #A2000.31.11, pamphlet: "Hostess Reference Book, Signal Chapter, No. 276, Order of the Eastern Star, El Centro, California," n.d.; *ca.* 1936; p. 4.
Footnote: Discovery of Mexicali aquifer, 1923—Kerig, p. 266.
Riverside water events—Patterson, pp. 311, 314–15, 336.
"The imminent danger of infiltration of immense quantities of sea water . . ."—Leigh, p. 309.

95. *The Line Itself (1927–1950)*

Epigraph: "This drift toward a warlike fatality . . ."—Veblen, p. 566 *(Imperial Germany and the Industrial Revolution)*.
Hermenegildo Pérez Cervantes—Interviewed in the Casa Cultura in Mexicali, December 2006. Terrie Petree interpreted.
"Before they had a border there, his family farmed on the Mexican side without knowing it!"—Kay Brockman Bishop, interviewed on her ranch near Calexico, 2006.
"Down its yellow slopes drops a gangling fence . . ."—Griffing Bancroft, p. n8.
The story of Bing Wong—The Great Basin Foundation Center for Anthropological Research, vol. 1, pp. 311–13. Voyaging to China so as to celebrate his arranged marriage with a lady named Ting, he then resumed his life in Gold Mountain. Ting would come to him—after the customary decade-long wait. It was during this interval that he tried to make it as a restaurateur.
Hetzel's classic photograph of snow on Signal Mountain—*Imperial County: The Big Picture*, p. 96.

The woman who was born near the beginning of the 1940s—Alice Woodside, interviewed in Sacramento, February 2004.
The tale of Juan Soldado—After Griffith, pp. 21–41.

96. *Different from Anything I'd Ever Known (1933–1950)*

Epigraph: ". . . they entered a world where the normal laws of the physical universe . . ."—Ballard, *The Crystal World*, p. 61.
Edith Karpen's memories—Interview in Sacramento, January 2004. Her daughter Alice Woodside was present.
The Depression in Los Angeles—"Everything stopped in L.A. in '31," said Marjorie Sa'adah. "Nothing that wasn't a government building got built" (interviewed September 2004.)—Next up: the Zoot Suit Riots of 1943, when Mexicans and Mexican-Americans will get beaten, some almost to death, by sailors in Chavez Ravine.
Footnote on the Karpen-Donlevy marriage—Karpen obituary.
Footnote on the plank road—Undated newspaper clipping in CA DOT folder "Imperial."

97. *Farm Size (1910–1944)*

"Epigraph: "Our economy is based on the exchange of goods and services through the medium of money . . ." —Mott and Roemer, p. 16.
Increasing proportions of American farms 500 acres and more—Ibid., p. 23.
Minimum gross farm income for viability in 1939, and number achieving this—Ibid., pp. 17–18.
Caveat about potential losses faced by large farms—USDA (1940), *Farm Size in California*, p. 12.
Excerpts from *For Whom the Bell Tolls*—Hemingway, pp. 207–8.
Decrease in California vacant lands 1900–1918—California Board of Agriculture, 1918, p. 4. The exact figures were 42,467,512 to 20,529,034 acres, respectively.
"We have always been able to look beyond the frontier . . ."—USDA Yearbook (1920), p. 5.
Footnote: Need for diversified family farms—USDA (1940), *Farm Size in California*, p. 8.
Social services and their financial burden on farmers—Hutchinson, p. 402.
Figures on harvest, corn crop, prices and "Altogether, in the spring of 1920 . . ." and values of American harvests 1918–20—Ibid., pp. 9, 10, 17.
Footnote: "The farmer buys a tractor . . ."—UC Berkeley. Bancroft Library. Paul S. Taylor papers. Carton 4. Folder 4:20: "Good-by to the Homestead Farm: The Machines Advance in the Corn Belt," n.d., print copy (loose note ascribes it to *Harper's*, May 1941).
"To get his shoestrings . . ."—Thoreau, p. 33.
"If you keep on growing chile peppers, onions, and tomatoes . . ."—Womack, pp. 240–41 (Zapata to Villa de Ayala farmers, 1915).
The advice of D. D. Gage—*California Cultivator*, vol. XXIV, no. 22 (June 2, 1905), p. 515 ("News of Country Life in the Golden West").
Remarks of Norman Ward—California State Archives. Department of Food and Agriculture. Bureau of Marketing. Marketing-order files, Box 3. State of California, Department of Agriculture, Bureau of Markets hearing on proposed marketing order for winter lettuce. Wednesday, December 17, 1958, beginning ten o'clock, a.m., El Centro, California, pp. 143–44.
Paragraph on farm size in California—Information and citation from USDA (1940), *Farm Size in California*, pp. 2, 27, 17.
The *encomienda* and the colonist with 11.6 million acres—Meyer et al., pp. 124, 166.
Figures on farm ownership and tenancy, 1930—Imperial Valley Directory (1930), p. 12. Exact statistics: 4,769 farms, 2,909 of them operated by tenants, 1,860 of them operated by owners.
The tenant farmer on relief in the Imperial Valley, 1936—Dorothea Lange, p. 130 ("Ex-Tenant Farmer on Relief Grant in the Imperial Valley, California, March 1936").
Imperial County farm figures, 1910—California Board of Agriculture (1918), pp. 20–21.
Leasing by Imperial Valley farmers of CRLC acres in Mexicali, 1913—Kerig, p. 197.
Citrus parcels of the Chandler Syndicate, 1914—*Los Angeles Times*, January 18, 1914 ("SOUTHERN PACIFIC SELLS BIG TRACT").
The numbers I possess . . . *seem* to show that between 1928 and 1950, average acreage increased from a hundred and ten to a hundred and eighty-five acres per farm. . .—With the exception of a brief experience as an unskilled ranch hand in California, I have no farming knowledge. Neither am I an economist or a statistician. Tracking farm size over time required several assumptions and approximations. In 1928, Imperial County registered 525,797 irrigated acres and 4,759 farms. In 1950 those numbers were respectively 884,990 and 4,779. I divided the first set by the second. The results are crude because they ignore non-farm irrigated land. For more figures, see the statistical section at the end of this book.

"Between 1928 and 1950, average acreage increased from a hundred and ten to a hundred and eighty-five acres per farm—no more than average California acreage, and probably less."—If we use the Census Bureau's 1974 definition of a farm (Census Bureau [1974], p. 1–1), then in 1940 and 1950 the total number and average acreage of California farms were respectively 132,558 farms (note that by the 1940 definition California had about 150,000 farms) of 230 acres each, and 137,168 farms of 267 acres each. This latter figure is obviously substantially more than the 185-acre 1950 Imperial County figure, but I am forced to say "probably," given the unstable definition of a farm.

Average acreage in Imperial County 1928–50—Calculated from Imperial County Agricultural Commission papers.

Footnote: The tale of Willis F. Beal—Farr, p. 439.

Table: "Average acreages of farms in Imperial County"—Information in California State Board of Equalization (1949), pp. 5, 19; California Blue Book (1950), p. 854; Imperial Valley Directory (1930), p. 12; California Board of Agriculture (1918), pp. 20–21; Imperial County Agricultural Commissioner's papers (1920), p. 2.

Total acreage in the county approximately doubled—My researcher Paul Foster concludes that "with only a couple of exceptions, the overall acreage farmed" in Imperial "is stable, stabilizing in 1925 at 525,000 acres, growing to 613,000 acres over the next 15 years, then growing suddenly with a 1942 addition of 270,000 acres bringing the total to 883,000 acres of 'farmable land.' However, the numbers quoted are misleading due to double-cropping, multiple cuttings of hay (especially alfalfa), and the intensive use of land for nuts, apiary, and feeder cattle" (Paul Foster reports, "Imperial Color Commentary").

"Sharp Reduction in acreage . . ."—UC Berkeley. Bancroft Library. Farm labor situation 1933–34. Carton #C-R 84. Folder: 6. Dean Hutchinson's handwritten notes. Sheets 4, 32.

"About 40 percent of the total number of farm owners do not live in the valley . . ."—UC Berkeley. Bancroft Library. Paul S. Taylor papers. Carton 5. Folder 5:17: "National Reclamation in the Imperial Valley: Law vs. Politics, Final Draft, 1981," p. 5, citing the Bureau of Agricultural Economics.

Percentage of Imperial County workforce in agriculture, 1940 (45%)—California State Board of Equalization (1949), p. 15.

"Populated by a small handful of owners and operators . . ."—Munguía, p. 122 (Fernando A. Medina Robles).

"It did not take long for the Imperial Valley, eventually subsidized by the reclamation-built All American Canal . . ."—E Clampus Vitus website (narrative by Milford Wayne Donaldson).

"From the first years of settlement to the present . . ."—DeBuys and Myers, p. 164.

Edith Karpen's memories—Based on an interview in January 2004.

Losses of Harry Chandler (1938)—Nadeau, p. 234, who gives the peculiar, and to me seemingly vastly understated, figure of 287,000 acres. Dwyer (p. iii) believes that 420,000 acres were expropriated outright.

Petition of the Peasant Union for CRLC lands, 1927—Dwyer, p. 52.

Scheme of the Colorado River Land Company to bring in Germans, etc., 1927—*Los Angeles Times*, December 22, 1927, p. A12 ("COLONISTS TO MEXICO: Holdings of Big Ranch Company at Mexicali to Be Sold to European Farmers").

H. H. Clark as world's largest cotton rancher—Ibid., April 11, 1926, p. J3 (Randall Henderson, "A New Kind of Pioneering in Imperial").

Table of land ownership in the Colorado River Delta, 1930—Tout, *The First Thirty Years*, p. 364, citing a report by Mr. Frank Adams for the American Section of the International Water Commission.

Statistics on CRLC leasing and ethnicity, 1924, and report to stockholders on superior Chinese stick-to-itiveness—Duncan, p. 636.

Chandler's concerns about letting title go to Mexican peasants—Kerig, p. 277.

Chandler's fantasies of selling to Italians and other ethnic groups—Ibid., pp. 278–79.

Pueblo Brant—Ibid., pp. 279–81.

Pressure on CRLC to provide infrastructure, 1924—Ibid., p. 236.

CRLC in 1930—Ibid., pp. 286–87.

Shenanigans of the Chandler-Sherman Corporation—Ibid., p. 296.

CRLC and Mexicali water rights deriving from Imperial Canal—Ibid., p. 330.

Squatters unable to afford parcel rentals—Dwyer, p. 24.

Land invasion of 1930 and aftermath—Kerig, pp. 310–12, 324, 344, 356–58.

Details on Felipa Velázquez—Dwyer, pp. 55–57.

Manifesto of the Bar and Restaurant Employees Union—Ibid., p. 61.

CRLC colonization agreement of 1936—Ibid., pp. 45–46, 49–50.

Expulsion of CRLC tenants: Most were Chinese.—Dwyer (p. 19) simply writes that "the agraristas threw off the Chinese tenant famers . . ."

Yolanda Sánchez Ogás—Interviewed in a car in June 2003, en route to Ejido Tabasco. Terrie Petree interpreted.

Footnote: Average parcel size in Oaxaca—RDI (2004), p. 18.

The restaurant proprietress who told the anecdote about Cárdenas—Socorro Ramírez, interviewed on 19 February 2004 in her restaurant. Terrie Petree interpreted.

Footnote: Cárdenas's reponsibility for the closing of gambling dens—Kerig, p. 343.

Hectares granted by Cárdenas, and number of recipients—Boyer, p. 7. Dwyer (p. 35) claims that "by the end of his term" Cárdenas "had distributed around 44 million acres of land to 800,000 ejidatarios." On p. 68 the same source gives 414,943 acres expropriated from the CRLC. I have converted that figure to hectares.

"Desperate straits" of Zapata's hometown—Womack, p. 381.

Loss of cultivated area in Mexicali *ejidos*, 1943—Kerig, pp. 388–89.

"Cárdenas's agrarian reform paid off . . ."—Dwyer, p. 35.

The rancher's wife in the *ejidos* west of Algodones—She was the señora of Don Carlos Cayetano Sanders-Collins, whom I interviewed with his family in Morelos, October 2003, Terrie Petree interpreting.

Confiscation of CRLC lands, March–August 1937, and aftermath—Kerig, pp. 365, 380, 385, 387, 425, 440.

Number of *ejidos* in Mexicali Valley—Yolanda Sánchez Ogás, same interview.

Hermenegildo Pérez Cervantes—Interviewed in the Casa Cultura in Mexicali, December 2006. Terrie Petree interpreted. "There were no gunfights when it happened," Señor Cervantes had said and yet that probable mouthpiece of the Chandler Syndicate, the *Los Angeles Times*, reported that "five colonists were beaten severely and brought into Mexicali bound with ropes," because in good or bad faith they had made the mistake of buying their ranchos from the Colorado River Land Company. "More than 100,000 acres of American-owned or financed land has been ordered seized for division . . ."—April 18, 1937, p. 1 ("Agrarians Beat Colonists Refusing to Yield Lands").

"Yet was it a country with free speech . . . ?"—Lowry, p. 112.

Interview with Lic. Carlos E. Tinoco, official of the Tribunal Unitario Agrario Distrito Dos—In the tribunal offices in Mexicali, September 2005. Terrie Petree translated.

Footnote: ". . . most women . . . are not full *ejidatarios*."—RDI (2004), p. 14.

Camacho's balancing act; reconciliation of landowners and *ejidatarios*—Boyer, p. 230. On pp. 236–37 he notes that the meaning of the word "campesino" became more diffuse and almost banal.

Even the American Ambassador thought so—He was Josephus Daniels, and his enconium of Cárdenas is quoted in Pike, p. 273.

My opinions here, like those about Northside, are at best based on arbitrary localizations, such as this one: In a certain Informe de las Refacciones of something illegible de 1943–44, I find the names of 26 farmers, from Genaro C. Aguirre right down to Carlos Vélez, who owned property in the Colorado River Land Company's Division Two; specifically in Division Two's *colonias* 1, 2, 3, 4, 5, and 10 all mixed together; no one had more than 27 hectares (Pedro Espinsos [?]); the lowest was Braulio Sánchez at 3.2 hectares; the total was 385.40 hectares, so the average was 14.8 hectares—36.5 acres, or less than a quarter of the 160 acres mandated in Northside by the Homestead Act, a smaller proportion still of the 185 average acres toward which Imperial County was tending by midcentury.—AHMM, Chata Angulo coll., Box no. 3, folder "Informe de los Refacciones [illegible] de 1943–44." Lista de Terrenenos en las colonias en la division numero dos, vendidos por la Colorado River Land Company, S.A., sembrados en el año de 1943, con refacción o habilitación proporcionada por la despepitadora de Mexicali, S.A.

"Although accurate data are lacking . . ."—USDA (1940), *Farm Size in California*, p. 15.

Trade-off between efficiency and family farms—This summary is based on, and elaborated from, the same source, p. 13.

98. *The Line Itself: Japanese Addendum (1941–1945)*

Epigraph: " 'Well, that's the way the world goes . . .' "—Anderson, p. 318 ("The Shadow," 1847).

Edith Karpen's memories—Same interview as previous chapter.

99. *Broad and Sinister Motives (1928–1946)*

Epigraph: "Finally, the Committee recommends . . ."—UC Berkeley. Bancroft Library, farm labor situation 1933–34. Folder "Reports": Hutchinson et al., "The Imperial Valley Farm Labor Situation," pp. 30–31.

The dusty old truck with "DISARM THE RICH FARMER . . ."—UC Berkeley. Bancroft Library. Powell Studio album. Photo #1945.007:1.

Footnote: Pickers in 1933 cotton strike, and proportion of them who were Mexican—UC Berkeley. Bancroft Library. Paul S. Taylor papers. Carton 4. Typescript: "In the fields, by Paul S. Taylor & Anne Loftis," n.d. (another slightly different version in the same folder reads: "Revised Sept. 15, 1981"), p. 15.

Edith Karpen's memories—Based on an interview in January 2004.

Re: Helen Marston, Dean Hutchinson writes in his notes (sheet 12): "Helen Marsten [*sic*] San Diego furnished $1,500 bail for Hoffman & Emma Cutter agitators. Also $500 for Mrs. Johnson wife of an attorney on charge of possession of weapon. Has spoken at meetings also furnished gasoline to parade with. When this meeting failed they turned attention to pea fields at Calipatria. Same group Dorothy Ray Stanley Hancock Chambers etc. who have been in lettuce strike. Three women Marsten, Posey, Stevens, particularly active advised to picket fields & run out the peaceable workers."—UC Berkeley. Bancroft Library. Farm labor situation 1933–34. Carton #C-R 84. Folder: 6.

"A tubby, ageing man in a white shirt . . ."—UC Berkeley. Bancroft Library. Powell Studio album. Photo #1945.007:6 ("Pickets on the highway calling workers from the fields—1933 cotton strike").

EPIC program platform—Sinclair, pp. 179, 186, 189 (*EPIC Answers*, 1934).

Remarks on Soviet collectivization—Abstracted from the "Defense of Class" chapter of my *Rising Up and Rising Down*. For the best study of this tragedy, see Robert Conquest, *The Harvest of Sorrow: Soviet Collectivization and the Terror-Famine* (New York: Oxford University Press, 1986).

"There is no compromise or arbitration . . ."—UC Berkeley. Bancroft Library. Paul S. Taylor papers. Carton 4. Folder 4:33: "Irrepressible Conflict? Draft & Notes, Aug., 1943," probably unpublished. Typescript, p. 2.

Dorothea Lange to her boss (Roy Stryker): ". . . what goes on in the Imperial is beyond belief . . ."—Fleischhauer et al., p. 114 (communication of 16 February 1937).

"THE GOVERNOR SENDS AID TO PIXLEY . . ."—UC Berkeley. Bancroft Library. Powell Studio album. Photo #1945.007:4 ("Cotton strike—1933").

"JOIN THE PICKET LINES. DON'T SCAB"—UC Berkeley. Bancroft Library. Powell Studio album. Photo #1945.007:3 ("Picket caravan—1933 cotton strike").

The brown girl getting water—Street, *Photographing Farmworkers*, p. 115 (Dorothea Lange photograph, 1935).

The three Hispanic murderers—*Fresno Morning Republican*, Thursday, March 25, 1920, p. 24 ("Murderers Are Caught After Long Chase").

The "circulars urging measures to prevent the entry of Mexican workers . . ."—Ibid., Saturday, March 27, p. 11 ("Try to Stop Labor Going Into U.S.").

Imperial Valley wages for cotton, 1909, 1938—Street, *Photographing Farmworkers*, p. 156 (caption to Dorothea Lange photograph, 1938).

"We farmers want to be fair . . ."—Sanders, p. 21.

"Men who wore white pajamas and sandals to work . . ."—Womack, p. 100.

"Forced to that belief against my own prejudices . . ."—UC Berkeley. Bancroft Library. Paul S. Taylor papers. Carton 4. Folder 4:33: "Irrepressible Conflict? Draft & Notes, Aug., 1943," probably unpublished. Typescript, p. 6.

Imperial Valley Press article, 1926—Dateline Sacramento.

"IMPERIAL QUALITY" lard—Hostess Reference Book (1936), p. 18.

"The huge irrigated farms of California's Imperial Valley . . ."—Watkins, pp. 392–93.

Mexicali authorities send home campesinos, 1925—Kerig, p. 252.

37,000 migrant children in 1927—UC Berkeley. Bancroft Library. Paul S. Taylor papers. Carton 3. Folder 3:14: "An American Exodus: A Record of Human Erosion, Galleys with Corrections, 1969." Paul S. Taylor, speech to Commonwealth Club of California in 1935, "The Migrants and California's Future," unnumbered p. 1.

Role of the Mexican consulate as mediator between growers and strikers; surrounding events of 1930–34—González article; Daniel, pp. 224–28; Watkins, pp. 416–17.

Events in Imperial County, 1928–30—Watkins, pp. 403–8. The three Communist organizers were Frank Waldron, Harry Harvey and Tsuji Horiuchi.

"What land have they given us, Melitón? . . ."—Rulfo, p. 15 ("They Gave Us the Land").

". . . the demands . . . came at a time when the farm owners were least able to meet them."—WPA, p. 640 (referring specifically to 1930).

Events of 1931 in Mexicali—*New York Times*, February 22, 1931, p. 9 ("BIG MOB THREATENS TO LOOT MEXICALI"). Meanwhile, considerably south of Imperial, in Michoacán, in fact, where the horn of Mexico begins to curve eastward, agrarian activists mobilize the campesinos of Hacienda Nueva Italia to unionize. The union comes into being in 1931. Instantly the campesinos strike, forcing the hacienda to raise wages from $4.60 a week to $6.00! The aftermath, of course, is violence. "These episodes led the foundation for an enduring atmosphere of hostility that pitted unionized field hands against other hacienda laborers and the state government for years to come." (Boyer, pp. 198–99).

"Working and living conditions, which had long been recognized as the worst in the state . . ."—Daniel, p. 224.

Repatriation of Mexicans and their new work in the Colorado River Delta, 1933—*Los Angeles Times*, March 26, 1933, p. I10 (Jack Starr-Hunt, "The Mexicans Who Went Home").

Sketch of the Oklahoma land rush of 1889, and excerpt about "a model empire" (from Edna Ferber's *Cimarron*, 1929)—Pike, pp. 154–55.

"A typical scene of the 'Dirty Thirties' . . ."—Spencer Museum of Art, pp. 67 (Plate 40: Herschel C. Logan, "Dust Storm," 1938), 66 (Plate 39: same artist, "Victim of the Dust," 1938), 62 (Plate 35: Mervin Jules, "Dust," 1933).

The tale of Wallace Case—Uys, p. 51.

"Yuma and the Imperial Valley where you could usually pick up a few days' work on a ranch or farm . . ."—Fox, p. 138.

Footnote: Origin of "Okie"—Sanders, p. 7.

H. T. Roach's memories—Uys, p. 36.

Committee on Indigent Alien Transients—Watkins, pp. 436–37.

Philip Bonosky—Ibid., pp. 244–45.

Remarks of Mr. E. B. Goodman—UC Berkeley. Bancroft Library. Farm labor situation 1933–34. Carton #C-R 84. Folder: 6. Dean Hutchinson's handwritten notes. Sheet 7: Mr. E. B. (Ben) Goodman. El Centro (writer).

Wage differential between Mexican and American Imperial (3 pesos vs. 9)—Ibid., sheet 11.

"Consul last year made a survey of whole valley . . ."—Dean Hutchinson's notes, sheet 20.

"Consul: Mexicans recognize they & the growers have a common problem . . ."—Ibid., sheet 21.

"The camp site at Corcoran, Calif."—UC Berkeley. Bancroft Library. Powell Studio album. Photo #1945.007:2 ("1933 cotton strike. Camp where evicted striking workers concentrated. Corcoran, Calif.").

First establishment of pro rate system in Imperial County—*Imperial Valley Press*, Wednesday, January 24, 1934, p. 3.

Report on squatters' camps, 1934—Paul S. Taylor, speech to Commonwealth Club, unnumbered p. 4 (United States Special Commission on Agricultural Labor Disturbances in Imperial Valley, report of February 11, 1934).

Water "FOR FAMILY USE ONLY"—*Imperial County: The Big Picture*, p. 128. How many people were on the dole? The only statistic I found was that from July 1937 through December 1938, Imperial County had (if I quote the handwritten tally and do my own arithmetic, since the original doesn't quite add up) 192 aliens on relief at Imperial County Hospital, the cost being $4.00 per head per day; 172 of these people were Mexican. Obviously many more people who were capable of sheltering themselves must have been on the rolls. (Statistics on aliens on relief July 1937–December 1938—California State Archives, legislative papers. Statement on number of aliens, 1939, 2 files. Cat. P14.43.44, D10, Box 1. Yellowed telegrams from Imperial Valley to Sacramento via Western Union. List dated 13 January 1939. W. H. Hodkinson, M.D., was the resident physician.)

Men at California Employment Relief Station Camp, 1934—Street, *Photographing Farmworkers*, p. 112 (Hetzel photo).

Dean Hutchinson's labor notes, written on the stationery of the Hotel Barbara Worth: "Agricultural field workers could be organized here in El Centro!," *ca.* 1934—UC Berkeley. Bancroft Library. Farm labor situation 1933–34. Carton #C-R 84. Folder: 6.

Imperial Valley events, 1934—Daniel, pp. 224–28. It is this source which describes the two organizers and quotes the Party report on them. It is also this source which details the lettuce growers' counter-offer, and informs us that sheriffs are often growers, that the American Legionnaires show up with clubs, etc.

Extracts from the *Imperial Valley Press* re: lettuce strike—Monday, January 8, 1934; Tuesday, January 9; Wednesday, January 10; Thursday, January 11; Friday, January 12; Saturday, January 13 (ad for the Owl, p. 7); Sunday, January 14; Tuesday, January 16; Wednesday, January 17; Friday, January 19 (and continuation on p. 6); Wednesday, January 24 (and pp. 5, 7); Wednesday, January 31. All citations are from the front page unless otherwise stated.

"Jan 9th crowd formed in Brawley . . ."—Dean Hutchinson's notes, sheet 8.

Description of Dorothy Ray's cell and her comrades' reception in the chain gang; fates of Wirin's colleagues—UC Berkeley. Bancroft Library. Farm labor situation 1933–34. Carton #C-R 84. Folder: Miscellany A–Z correspondence, pp. 14–15, 12–13 of "California's Brown Book."

Re: Wirin's abduction, Dean Hutchinson writes in his notes (sheet 2, 17th Jan.): "A. L. Wirin scheduled as main speaker. Failed to appear. 3–4 others from LA made short talks—one Rev. Beverley L. Oatin Secy So. Calif. Congregational conference. Wirin refused permit to hold meeting by Chief of Police. Wirin showed up in Dr. Wallace office at Calipatria. Dr. reported him in very nervous condition few scratches on feet & face. Asked for & given police protection to Barbara Worth hotel where he staid all night. Next morning with Chester Williams put in car & taken to San Diego by County officers."—"*Brawley Meeting* Azteca Hall 12th January . . ."—UC Berkeley. Bancroft Library. Farm labor situation 1933–34. Carton #C-R 84. Folder: 6. Dean Hutchinson's handwritten notes, sheet 1.

Skepticism about Wirin's kidnapping—Ibid., Folder: Miscellany A–Z correspondence, p. 19 of "California's Brown Book."

Remarks of the San Joaquin Valley Agriculture Labor Bureau—Quoted in Watkins, p. 439.

Brawley ordinance found unconstitutional; growers declare lettuce holiday—*Imperial Valley Press* front pages, January 30, January 27.

Babbitt on the Good Citizens' League—Lewis, p. 835.

"We object most strenuously . . ."—UC Berkeley. Bancroft Library, op. cit. Folder: Reports. Supplement to Report Entitled "The Imperial Valley Farm Labor Situation," May 9, 1934, submitted to the Associated Farmers of California, by Hutchinson et al., p. 18 (speech by Mr. Ralph H. Taylor of Sacramento).

Letter from Los Angleles Chamber of Commerce—UC Berkeley. Bancroft Library, op. cit. Folder: Miscellany A–Z correspondence.

Mexican field worker in a white straw hat and a bandanna . . .—Street, *Photographing Farmworkers*, p. 130 (Dorothea Lange photograph, 1935); also Dorothea Lange, p. 136 ("Mexican Workers Leaving for the Melon Fields, Imperial Valley, California, June 1935").

Dustbowl arrivals in California, 1935–38—Watkins, loc. cit.

Melon statistics, July 1936—*California Cultivator*, vol. LXXXIII, no. 15, July 18, 1936, p. 524 ("Agricultural News Notes of the Pacific Coast": "Southern California").

Memo to Harry E. Drobish—UC Berkeley. Bancroft Library. Paul S. Taylor papers. Carton 3. Folder 3:14: "An American Exodus: A Record of Human Erosion, Galleys with Corrections, 1969." Unnumbered galley pages entitled: "Emergency Relief Administration, State of California. Date: March 15, 1935. To: Harry E. Drobish, Director of Rural Rehabilitation. From: Paul S. Taylor, Regional Director. Subject: Establishment of Rural Rehabilitation Camps for Migrants in California." Item VIIIC.

The man from 1935—Dorothea Lange, p. 57 ("Imperial Valley, California, June 1935").

Events in Orange County, 1935—*California Cultivator*, vol. LXXXIII, no. 15, July 18, 1936, pp. 523, 551 (continuation page) (unattributed editorial, "Labor Troubles in Orange County"). The *Cultivator* also says (same issue, p. 524; Los Angeles Market Review): "The strike of the orange pickers has had little effect . . . There has been a slight dropoff in sales attended by a very small price increase."

The man and wife from Coachella, 1936—Ibid., p. 114 ("Family from Texas Looking for Work in the Carrot Harvest, Coachella Valley, California, March 1936").

"Disappointment was in store in the Imperial Valley . . ."—Carolan, p. 48.

Acts of the Associated Farmers in Salinas, September 1936—Watkins, pp. 440–42.

"When a person's able to work, what's the use of beggin'?"—UC Berkeley. Bancroft Library. Paul S. Taylor papers, op. cit. Paul S. Taylor, speech to Commonwealth Club of California in 1935, "The Migrants and California's Future," unnumbered p. 1.

Caption to a Dorothea Lange photograph—Ibid., "An American Exodus: A Record of Human Erosion, Galleys with Corrections, 1969." Unnumbered galley pages: "Photo Captions."

Photo: "Jobless on Edge of a Pea Field . . ."—Dorothea Lange, p. 15.

"And they trek into California . . ."—Paul S. Taylor, speech to Commonwealth Club, unnumbered p. 2.

"A rural proletariat"—Ibid., unnumbered pp. 3–4.

1937 item in the *Brawley Daily News*—ICHSPM. Not yet catalogued; offprint hand-captioned "A. Vallas" *Brawley Daily News*, Saturday, February 6, 1937, "Garst Says Migratory Labor Camp a Certainty." In 1938, we find the Department of Public Health ranking "among the more important pieces of work for this month" plans for sewage at the Farm Security Resettlement Camps at, among other places, Brawley and Coachella. (Plans for sewage at the Farm Security Resettlement Camps, 1938—California State Archives. Margaret C. Felts papers. Box 12: Folder: "1938 POLLUTION." State of California. Department of Public Health. February 15, 1938. To: W. M. Dickie, M.D., Director. From: C. G. Gillespie. Subject: Resume of the Activities of the Bureau for January, 1938.)

"The seasonal farm workers . . . continue to present a major social problem."—Hutchinson, p. 407.

". . . the Imperial Valley authorities enjoyed an unlimited range of power."—González, p. 63.

Imperial County's gross cash income from agriculture, and state ranking—California State Board of Equalization (1949), p. 18.

100. *Butter Cream Bread* (ca. 1936)

Advertisement for Butter Cream Bread; proportions for 50—Hostess Reference Book (1936), pp. 2, 11.

101. *Coachella* (1936–1950)

Tale of the Riverside County woman who trapped two mountain lions in one month—*California Cultivator*, vol. LXXXIII, no. 15, July 18, 1936, p. 524 ("Agricultural News Notes of the Pacific Coast": "Southern California").

Interview with Dr. John and Margaret Tyler—Conducted in their home in Palm Desert, April 2004. Shannon Mullen was present.

Footnote: Photo of the Salton Sea Regatta—Laflin, *Coachella Valley*, p. 140.

102. *Have You Ever Seen a Flax Field in Bloom?* (1940s)

Epigraph: "Here the land is green . . ."—Polkinhorn et al., p. 625.

Alice Woodside's memories—The descriptions of the flax field and her school days were based on an interview in Sacramento in January 2004 (the same one at which her mother, Edith Karpen, was present). All other material derives from an interview in February, when only she and I were present.

Footnote: Edith Karpen's love of Mount Signal—Karpen obituary.
Footnote: Flax and alfalfa statistics, 1948–49—Imperial Valley Directory (1949), p. 12.
Footnote on Alice Woodside's father—Karpen obituary, separate letter to WTV.

103. *The Days of Carmen Carillo and Susana Caudillo (2003)*

Carmen Carillo and Susana Caudillo—Interviewed in a fast food restaurant in Calexico in 2003 one morning when they did not get work. The great Lupe Vásquez was there and occasionally interpreted.
Footnote: Supposed grape-growing season in the Coachella Valley—*Desert Sun*, Saturday, December 20, 2003, Section E (Business), p. E2 (Lou Hirsch, "Growers Watch CAFTA: Proposed Central American Free Trade Agreement still has opposition").

PART EIGHT

RESERVATIONS

105. *A Definitive Interpretation of the Blythe Intaglios (ca. 13,000 B.C.–2006)*

Epigraph: ". . . there is something unsatisfying . . ."—Heizer and Elsasser, p. 180.
Extracts from the treaty of Guadalupe Hidalgo—Castillo, pp. 190–91 (Appendix 2, text of treaty, Article XI).
Colonel Cave Johnson Couts: "They sold Capt. Kane a small girl . . ."—Op. cit., p. 82 (entry prior to Saturday, December 9).
Footnote: Couts on "Jumas" west of Colorado: "They use blood generally for painting . . ."—Op. cit., pp. 85–86 (entry for Friday, December 1).
"There are educated people in Mexico . . ."—Augustín Aragón; quoted in Pike, p. 108.
Footnote: My 1910 *Britannica* on the Indians of Mexico: ". . . neglect of their children . . ."—11th ed., vol. XVIII, p. 322 (entry on Mexico).
Indian marriages recorded without surnames—Gostin, pp. 415–16 (records #1186, 1183, 1182, 1177, 1156).
Entries for Warner, 1901—San Diego City and County Directory (1901), pp. 335–36.
Agua Caliente statistics a century later—Bureau of Indian Affairs (1999), p. 7. Specifically: Agua Caliente Band of Cahuilla Indians, population 338 souls on a gross acreage of not quite 23,000 on an eponymous reservation in Riverside near Palm Springs.
Indians die nameless—Gostin, pp. 576–95.
A settler in 1910: "The Yuma is quiet and docile now . . ."—Howe and Hall, p. 112.
An educator: "Difficult for the Indians . . . ," etc.—Farr, pp. 163–66 (L. L. Odle, "Fort Yuma Indian School").
The Yuman creation myth—Luthin, p. 475 ("An Acccount of Origins: Quechan [Yuma], 1908; Tsuyukweráu, narrator; J. P. Harrington, collector).
". . . a Kern citizen who has recently visited Imperial": "I am confident there is a great future for this place . . ."—*Imperial Press and Farmer*, vol. II, no. 29 (Saturday, November 1, 1902), p. 7 ("A Kernite at Imperial: Frank Stanley Writes of the Possibilities of the Great Desert under Irrigation").
"INDIAN DWELLINGS ON THE PLAINS . . ."—Ibid., vol. II, no. 28 (Saturday, October 27, 1902), p. 1.
Coachella's Dead Indian Rock and the fish-weirs—Dunham, pp. 146–47.
Cahuilla tale of the Topa Chisera or Devil Gopher—Ainsworth, p. 172.
Maria Encarnacion Esperiaza—Gostin, pp. 328–29 (records #5955 [Esperiaza], 5939 [Ysidora]).
"The Cahuillas have not had a head-chief . . ." and "They nearly all live upon the large ranches . . ."—Elliott, *San Bernardino and San Diego Counties*, pp. 77, 88.
Cahuilla Band and Cabazon Band statistics—Bureau of Indian Affairs (1999), pp. 22–23.
Farr on the Cucapah—Op. cit., p. 27.
The hill of Apache tears—Auto Club of Southern California, p. 220 (km. 113, Route 5, hill to east).
Footnote: The undifferentiated shaded Ipai-Tipai zone—Heizer, *Handbook of North American Indians*, vol. 8, p. 593 (Katharine Luomala, "Tipai-Ipai," fig. 1, "Ipai and Tipai tribal territories").
Same footnote: One mid-twentieth-century anthropologist: "The long arm of the Corn God's northerly conquests . . ." etc.—Amsden, p. 3.
Campo Band figures, 1999—Bureau of Indian Affairs (1999), p. 24.
Anthropologist on vulva stones, etc.—McGowan, pp. 15, 19.
The man who'd worked for the Bureau of Reclamation—Herb Cilch, interviewed in San Diego, 2003.
Captives and alliances—Heizer and Whipple, pp. 444, 431 (Kenneth M. Stewart); Heizer, p. 109.
"Cocopah Indians could get all the liquor they wanted . . ."—Tout, *The First Thirty Years*, p. 273.
Description of Territory "Los Cucapás"—AHMM, Chata Angulo collection. Item 162.1/61: "Terrenos Cucapás—Expropriación" and related sheets (4 pages in all, and partial translation by Terrie Petree).

Cucapá interviews—2003; interpreted from Cucapah into Spanish by Yolanda Sánchez Ogás, then from Spanish into English by Terrie Petree; 2000, interpreted by Lupe Vásquez.

Font's opinions of the Yumans—Heizer and Whipple, pp. 250–51, 249, 252 (Pedro Font, "The Colorado Yumans in 1775").

"The Yuma reservation contains an area of 71–3/4 square miles . . ."—California Board of Agriculture (1918), p. 2.

Richard Brogan on Yuma (Quechan)—Interviewed at Calexico, April 2004.

Cameron and Diana Chino—Interviewed on the Quechan reservation, December 2006. Terrie Petree was present.

L. M. Holt on Palm Springs—Lechs, pp. 696–97 (Appendix K).

106. The Island (2003–2006)

James Wilson—Interviewed 2003.

Kate Brockman Bishop—Interviewed December 2006 on her ranch in Calexico.

PART NINE

CLIMAXES

107. The Largest Irrigated District in the World (1950)

Epigraph—"The extent of Alta California in ancient times was altogether indefinite."—Samuel T. Black, vol. 1, p. 1.

Populations of El Centro and Brawley, 1948—California State Board of Equalization (1949), p. 14.

The Raymond Chandler murder victim supposedly from El Centro—Dr. G. W. Hambleton in *The Little Sister* (1949). *Later Novels and Other Writings*, p. 244.

Menace of coyotes to sheep—Imperial County Agricultural Commission papers. B. A. Harrigan, Agricultural Commissioner, annual report for 1949, p. 8.

Although it was the ninth-largest county in the state, only one-half of one percent of Californians lived there —Figures from California State Board of Equalization (1949), pp. 13–14.

A chubby little plane which wears our American flag and the twin legends TRANS WORLD AIRWAYS and LOS ANGELES AIRWAYS . . .—California State Archives. Olson Photo Collection. Accession #94-06-27 (1–237). Location: C 5266. Box 1 of 7. Folder 94-06-27 (48–53): Aviation: Commercial. Photograph #94-06-27-0048.

Description of "the sea-edge of Los Angeles at midcentury"—Loc. cit., photo #94-06-27-0050 N.

The Salton Sea, "235 feet below sea level," etc.—ICHSPM document. Ball Advertising Co., p. 4.

"About the same as the ocean"—Shields Date Gardens, p. 21.

Launching facilities for power boats; number of visitors to Salton Sea *vs.* Yosemite—Ainsworth, p. 256.

"Low barometric pressure and greater water density . . ."—*National Motorist*, January–February 1950 (vol. and no. unavailable), p. 8 (Evelyn Slack Gist, "Paradox of the Colorado Desert").

The booster from 1962: "At our little desert hideaway near Mecca . . ."—Ibid., p. 98.

"They had a house of crystal pillars on the planet Mars . . ."—Bradbury, p. 2.

"Salton City, a bustling young community of modern homes"—ICHSPM document. Ball Advertising Co., p. 14.

Rothko: "A picture is not its color . . ."—Breslin, p. 201 (draft manifesto with Adolph Gottleib, 1943).

A civic booster: "One of the great sagas of the Old West took place in the twentieth century . . ."—Laflin, *Coachella Valley*, p. 35.

Edgar F. Howe, 1910: "We can see today more clearly the possibility of building a new Egypt . . ."—Howe and Hall, p. 5.

"From the air, the Coachella Valley looks much like the Imperial . . ."—Griffin and Young, pp. 166–67.

Brawley, "Where it's Sun-Day every day!"—ICHSPM document. Ball Advertising Co., p. 4.

Description of Calexico and various fiestas—Ibid., p. 5.

The President of the Imperial Valley Pioneers: "Imperial Valley is more than a highly-developed farming area . . ." —Harris, p. 7 (note by Seth Grimes, 1956).

Retail sales and income for civilian residents had both more than tripled . . .—After information in California State Board of Equalization (1949), pp. 15, 21. For exact figures, see chronology for 1939 and 1947. The 1940 and 1948 income figures (see chronology) and 1950 figure on agriculture as percentage of income are from the *California Blue Book* (1950), p. 854.

The 1950 annual Brawley picnic—ICHSPM photograph, cat. #P94.9.1, 1–57. Date and place given on caption.

Water requirements to produce one pound of beef—*State of California Atlas*, p. 1. (Note: This is a 1975 figure. It is possible, but not likely, that the 1950 figure would have been different. If so, it might well have been even higher, given the freedom with which Imperial County spent its water allotment.)

Imperial County's percentage of California's locally assessed tangible property values remained one-third lower than it had been before the Depression.—After California State Board of Equalization (1949), p. 16. The figures were: 0.65% for 1929, 0.72% for 1933, 0.43% for around 1947.

Proportional shares of county inheritance taxes collected in 1950—[California State Controller (1950–51).] Statement no. 10 (Amounts Each County Contributed to Certain Receipts During the Fiscal Year Ended June 30, 1951), p. 198. Inheritance taxes collected by counties were: Los Angeles $9,291,911.89, San Diego $961,383.46, Riverside $164,426.58, Imperial $24,329.44, with California's total being $20,371,028.51.

A man who'd worked for the Bureau of Reclamation from 1948 to 1950 . . .—This was Mr. Herb Cilch, interviewed by WTV in San Diego in June 2003.

Simone de Beauvoir: "It is because of the abstract climate in which they live . . ."—*The Annals of America*, vol. 16, p. 545 ("Goodbye to America," from *America Day by Day*, French ed. 1948, English ed. 1952).

Lettuce was the most lucrative crop at twenty-five million dollars.—Information from *California Blue Book* (1950), pp. 851–52.

Herbert Marcuse, 1955: "The sacrifice of libido for culture has paid off well . . ."—Op. cit., pp. 3–4.

Increase in Imperial Valley carrot-production norm—*California Farmer*, vol. 193, no. 1 (July 1, 1950), p. 6 ("Agricultural News Notes of the Pacific Coast: Southern California").

"Cut this phase of the labor by a third"—*California Farmer*, vol. 193, no. 1 (July 1, 1950), p. 9 ("Saving Labor in the Orchard").

B. A. Harrigan writes: "I wish to emphasize that these values are Gross Values . . ."—Imperial County Agricultural Commission papers, 1950. Cover letter to the Honorable Board of Supervisors and the State Director of Agriculture.

The 1950 high school commencement program at Wilson School—ICHSPM, document cat. #A99.13.12. Brochure: "Commencement: Wilson School, June 7, 1950, El Centro, California."

Alice Woodside—Interviewed in Sacramento, February 2004.

Carrots (whose high commodity status was a postwar phenomenon)—Richard Brogan, interviewed in Calexico, April 2004.

Alfalfa as number-1 Imperial crop, 1951—Imperial Valley Directory (1952), p. 15.

Kay Brockman Bishop—Interviewed December 2006 on her ranch just west of Calexico. Terrie Petree was present.

An oldtimer: "We had citrus here . . ."—Richard Brogan, same interview.

Cotton acreages, 1951–53—Imperial County Agricultural Commission papers. B. A. Harrigan, Agricultural Commissioner, annual reports for those years. No cotton listed for 1950.

Footnote: W. F. Holt's obituary—*San Rafael Independent Journal*, 24 November 1951, p. 3.

The cotton goddess of 1952—*Imperial County: The Big Picture*, p. 32.

"Orange groves, cotton—new houses . . ."—Kerouac (Brinkley), p. 359 ("Boomin to Yuma").

Former County Agricultural Commissioner on international cooperation against capra beetles—Claude Finnell, interviewed in his home in El Centro, April 2004. Shannon Mullen was present.

Imperial County Assessor's office: "The flourishing fields and the mile-long trains . . ."—California State Board of Equalization (1949), p. 52.

California Blue Book: "Imperial's warm, sunny winters . . ." and "immense green-gold garden"—Op. cit. (1950 ed.), p. 851.

Zulema Rashid's recollections—From 3 interviews in the Sweet Temptations Coffee Shop in summer 2003. Larry McCaffery was present for the third interview. I asked Zulema why she had chosen to become an accountant, and she said: "Just a couple of months before graduation my mother had an accident and she lost an arm. When I was in L.A. with her for rehab, I went to business college because I wanted to be Perry Mason's secretary, but then there was another terrible accident and my father lost his life."

The two extracts from *The Real Causes of Our Migrant Problem*: "If there's one thing I'm certain of . . ." and "It's a sad change that has come over our farm owners . . ."—Sanders, pp. 18, 56.

Richard Brogan: "The nature of the American farmer is that it's a forthright, inquisitive mind . . ."—Same interview in Calexico, April 2004.

Kay Brockman Bishop—Interview at her ranch, 2006.

The mid-1960s doings of "Imperial Valley, the big, sunny, windy Algeria of the 'Southland'"—Lilliard, pp. 87–88.

Local woman: "Why did they come here? Why did they stay? . . ."—Harris, p. 6 (dedication, January 1956).

Imperial is bird-hunting in the tules along the south shore of the Salton Sea.—Information from *National Motorist*, January–February 1950 (vol. and no. unavailable), p. 9 (Evelyn Slack Gist, "Paradox of the Colorado Desert").

B. A. Harrigan: "No other area in the U.S. can produce any more crops per acre . . ."—*Imperial Valley Press*, vol. 103, no. 27, Tuesday, June 10, 2003, p. A4 ("Stories of the Past: 50 years ago").

Honey production, 1950—Imperial County Agricultural Commission papers. B. A. Harrigan, Agricultural Commissioner, annual report for 1950, unnumbered p. 2.

"At Calexico it was Christmas shopping time on Main Street . . ."—Kerouac, *The Dharma Bums*, p. 94.

Richard Campbell's lettuce memories—California State Archives. Department of Food and Agriculture. Bureau of Marketing. Marketing order files, Box 3. State of California, Department of Agriculture, Bureau of Markets hearing on proposed marketing order for winter lettuce. Wednesday, December 17, 1958, beginning ten o'clock, a.m., El Centro, California. P. 393.

Imperial at midcentury is number one among California counties for carbon dioxide production.—California State Board of Equalization (1949), p. 13.

Image of the "Cavalcade Parade"—ICHSPM photograph, cat. #P95.30.23.

108. There Was Always Food on the Table (1950s)

Stella Mendoza—Interviewed at her kitchen table in Brawley, October 2003.

109. Coachella (1950)

Epigraph: ". . . the road was anisotropic . . ."—Strugatski and Strugatski, p. 204.

Coachella green corn acreage estimate for 1947—California State Archives. Department of Food and Agriculture. Bureau of Marketing. Marketing order files, Box 4. State of California, Department of Agriculture, Bureau of Markets hearing on proposed marketing order for Coachella Valley green corn. Wednesday, April 9, 1947, 10:15 o'clock, a.m., Coachella Valley Water District Building, Coachella, California. P. 6.

Footnote: Irrigated areas, 563,000—Griffin and Young, p. 166.

Interview with Mr. and Mrs. La Londe—July 2004, in their home in Coachella. Shannon Mullen was present.

Footnote: Distinction between Coachella and Imperial soils—Dunham, p. 108; Griffin and Young, p. 181.

"America's Garden of Allah"—Dunham, unnumbered endpaper map.

Carolyn Cooke's recollections—Telephone interview, Coachella, April 2004.

Photograph of weed-control boat—ICHSPM photograph, cat. #P92.34.3 (Don Chandler photo, August 1952, Caterpillar Diesel D311 Marine Engine).

Photograph of Preston Ranch, 1904—ICHSPM photograph, cat. number illegible.

Coachella *vs.* Palo Verde, 1952–53—Paul, p. 50 (expressing these ratios as absolute numbers in thousands of dollars).

Footnote on R.M.C. Fullenwider—Fitch, p. 273.

"The scientifically clean dates . . ." and accompanying photograph—Dunham pp. 100, 101 (illustration, "METICULOUSLY CLEAN AND EFFICIENT PACKING HOUSES PROCESS THE DATES FOR MARKET").

C. H. Hollis, 1947—California State Archives. Department of Food and Agriculture. Bureau of Marketing. Marketing-order files, Box 4. State of California, Department of Agriculture, Bureau of Markets hearing on proposed marketing order for Coachella Valley green corn. Wednesday, April 9, 1947, 10:15 o'clock, a.m., Coachella Valley Water District Building, Coachella, California. P. 43.

Gifford Price, 1957—California State Archives. Department of Food and Agriculture. Bureau of Marketing. Marketing-order files, Box 4. State of California, Department of Agriculture, Bureau of Markets hearing on proposed marketing order for desert area green corn. Tuesday, March 18, 1954, 10:00 o'clock, a.m., Coachella Valley Water District Building. Pp. 57, 63–64.

Douglass Nance—Ibid., pp. 17, 28.

Paul Sandoval—Ibid., p. 31.

J. L. Mapes in Indio—Ibid., pp. 42, 44, 41.

"Agriculture was long the chief source of income in the Coachella . . ."—Griffin and Young, p. 166.

"How fortunate we are in planting our grove at this late date . . ."—Dunham, pp. 77–78.

Need for tile drains—Griffin and Young, p. 189.

Population, agricultural economic figures on Riverside County 1940–50, including quoted remarks on the Coachella Valley and Corona—*California Blue Book*, pp. 936–37, 940. Summing up, the main crops in Coachella's deserts were dates, grapefruits, grapes, alfalfa, cotton and vegetables. I expect that you'll probably want to know how citrus was doing in Riverside County, so let me inform you that in 1940 it was valued at $8,997,468 and by 1949 it was up to $16,332,980. "Corona is the lemon center of the citrus belt," but Corona, unfortunately, lies outside of Imperial.

110. Riverside (1950)

Epigraph: "Confidence in the continued growth of Riverside's wealth . . ."—Riverside City Directory (1951), p. 8.

"It took exactly the entire twenty-five miles to get out of the smog of Los Angeles . . ."—Kerouac, *The Dharma*

Bums, p. 91. My assumption that the words were written in 1956 (the publication date is 1958) derives from that date's appearance in the text.
Footnote: County directory on distance of Riverside from L.A.—Riverside City Directory (1951), p. 9.
Beginning of Riverside smog—Patterson, p. 473.
Riverside City slogan—Riverside City Directory (1951), p. 9.
Survival of one original navel orange tree and "Riverside is an ideal residential community . . ."—Ibid., p. 10.
Description of the Ramona Freeway from above—After a photo in Wagner and Blackstock, p. 21.
"Opening the door of suburbia . . ."—Ibid., p. 13.
1950 as beginning of new building boom in Riverside—Patterson, p. 411.
Riverside City statistics, 1950—Riverside City Directory (1951), p. 9.
Description of the street called Lemon—Ibid., pp. 587–88.
Information on citrus grove realtors, the J. H. Jeter Co. and Alger J. Fast—Ibid.; in Buyers' Guide sec., pp. 700, 19, 4.
The Riverside Holts—Ibid., p. 226.
"Predominating nationalities in the city are American and Mexican."—Ibid., p. 9.
Data on the Angels, Acosta and Aguilar—pp. 25, 14, 16.
Anglo names and occupations—Ibid., pp. 227, 439.
"Foreign" names and occupations—Ibid., pp. 16, 526 (the very last residential entry).
" . . . today Riverside is the center of the Citrus Empire . . ."—Ibid., p. 9.
"Ontario is ideally situated in the heart of the citrus belt . . ." and following description of Ontario—Ontario City Directory (1945–46), p. 13.
"Citrus fruits provide the largest parts of the agricultural revenue . . ."—Ibid., p. 15.
Description of Etiwanda the Beautiful—Ibid., p. 469.

111. Market Prices (1950)

Epigraph: "But it is presumably all for the best . . ."—Veblen, pp. 396–97 (*Absentee Ownership*, 1923).
1950 market prices in Los Angeles and San Francisco for produce—*California Farmer*, April 8, 1950, vol. 192, no. 7. These price quotations were on the Los Angeles market, dated 29 March 1950.
1925 prices in Los Angeles for cabbage, carrots, celery, squash—*California Cultivator*, April 4, 1925, vol. LXIV, no. 15, p. 410. Only local celery had been available in 1925 (best quality: $3.75 to $4.00 per crate). On the subject of this commodity, Chula Vista comes into my definition of Imperial, so I'd better list "Sturdee & wirebound crts." of it, "Chula Vista $2.00–2.50," much higher than local Los Angeles celery. Strangely enough, there's no Imperial Valley celery on this fine March day.
1950 Imperial County totals for various commodities—Imperial County Agricultural Commissioner's papers, 1950, pp. 3–4.
Richard Johnson, Jr.—*California Farmer*, vol. 210, no. 12, June 6, 1959, p. 598 (Richard Johnson, Jr., "State's Farm Workers Paid Adequate Wage").
Jack T. Pickett—Ibid., p. 597 (Jack T. Pickett, "Organized Labor Sabotaging Mexican National Program?").

112. Crop Reports (1946–1957)

Epigraph: "If a year's crop were good . . ."—Jackson, p. 56.
Crop reports—Imperial County Agricultural Commission papers. Various Agricultural Commissioners, annual reports 1946–57, inclusive. Before 1946 there are no comments on real farm income.

113. Cantaloupe Anxieties (1958)

Mr. Frank R. Coit—California State Archives. Department of Food and Agriculture. Bureau of Marketing. Marketing order files, Box 6. State of California, Department of Agriculture, Bureau of Markets hearing on a marketing order for California cantaloupes. Thursday, July 24, 1958, beginning ten o'clock a.m., Fresno, California. Pp. 15–16.
Dr. Braun—Ibid., p. 19.
Mr. F. J. Harkness, Jr.—Ibid., pp. 26–33.
Mosaic disease; former melon acreage in Imperial—Griffin and Young, p. 180.

114. The Braceros (1942–1965)

Epigraph: ". . . . Imperial would not be the Magic Land it is today . . ."—Harris, p. 31.
Javier Lupercio—Interviewed in Mexicali, April 2004, José López from Jalisco translating.
Don Ezekiel Pérez in Montana, 1947—Marilyn P. Davis, p. 18.
"After five months his contract ended . . ."—Crosthwaite, Byrd and Byrd, p. 61 (Isaías Ignacio Vázquez Pimentel, "Ña' a ta' ani' mai").

Claude Finnell and his wife—Interviewed in their home in El Centro, April 2004. Shannon Mullen was present.

Number of braceros, 1942–62; poster from 2002—Bigelow, p. 39.

Naked bracero being sprayed with DDT—Street, *Photographing Farmworkers*, p. 115 (Leonard Nadel photograph, taken at an unnamed "border processing center").

A Mexican leans out the window of his train . . .—Described after Dorothea Lange, p. 172 ("After Five Days' Travel, Mexican Field Workers ['Braceros'] Arriving in Sacramento, California, October 6, 1942").

Bracero figures, 1943, 1957–onward—Salazar, p. 131.

Señora Socorro Rámírez—Interviewed on 19 February 2004 in her restaurant. Terrie Petree interpreted.

Braceros as a quarter of California farmworkers; accommodations at the former San Bernardino jail (Cone Camp), firefighting duties and compensation—Wagner, pp. 60–61.

Ray Heckman's costs—California State Archives. Department of Food and Agriculture. Bureau of Marketing. Marketing-order files, Box 4. State of California, Department of Agriculture, Bureau of Markets hearing on proposed marketing order for Coachella Valley green corn. Wednesday, April 9, 1947, 10:15 o'clock, a.m., Coachella Valley Water District Building, Coachella, California. Pp. 6, 45. Some costs are calculated by me from data provided on those pages.

Kay Brockman Bishop—Interviewed December 2006 on her ranch just west of Calexico. Terrie Petree was present.

Zulema Rashid's recollections—From 3 interviews in the Sweet Temptations Coffee Shop in summer 2003. Larry McCaffery was present for the third interview.

C. H. Hollis, corn grower in Thermal—Same 1947 Coachella Valley green corn marketing-order hearing, p. 45.

Kerouac in Fresno—*On the Road*, pp. 78, 89, 91.

Pickers needed and harvest sizes in the San Joaquin, 1949 and 1950 San Joaquin cotton crops—*California Farmer*, vol. 193, no. 1 (July 1, 1950), p. 2.

Paul S. Taylor on labor contractors—UC Berkeley. Bancroft Library. Paul S. Taylor papers. Carton 4. Folder 4:33: "Irrepressible Conflict? Draft & Notes, Aug., 1943," probably unpublished. Typescript, page 5.

Work of a contractor: Trolling a Sonora poolhall, etc.—For instance, California State Archives. ALRB restricted files, 1978–1984. Case VC. Civil.

Attempt to bring back "crossing card" system—*California Farmer*, vol. 192, no. 8 (April 22, 1950), p. 371 (Joe Crosby, "Imperial Farmers Battling for Mexican Labor Permits").

Border Patrolman Dan Murray—Interview of 1999.

The jail cell in 1951—Street, *Photographing Farmworkers*, p. 187 (Loomis Dean photograph for *Life* magazine).

Commuter workers; President Kennedy; Quick, Morales and Yeller; bribes from braceros to Mexican officials—Salazar, pp. 72–74, 78–79, 136–37.

Don Maclovio Medina—Marilyn P. Davis, pp. 27, 30.

Picket signs in El Centro (1961)—Street, *Photographing Farmworkers*, p. 212 (Arthur Dubinsky photograph).

115. Operation Wetback (1954–1955)

Epigraph: "Why is it estimated that at certain times of the year . . ."—Salazar, p. 252 ("The 'Wetback' Problem Has More Than Just One Side," April 24, 1970).

Jack T. Pickett—*California Farmer*, vol. 210, no. 12, June 6, 1959, p. 597 (Jack T. Pickett, "Organized Labor Sabotaging Mexican National Program?").

Ruben Salazar—Op. cit., p. 252 ("The 'Wetback' Problem Has More Than Just One Side," April 24, 1970).

Details of Operation Wetback—Marilyn P. Davis, p. 24.

Victor Orozco Ochoa—Ibid., p. 293. This raid took place in 1955.

Undated image of Rotary International float (possibly the same "Cavalcade Parade" as cat. #P95.30.23)—ICHSPM photograph, cat. #P95.30.18.

116. Mexicali (1950)

Epigraph: "During the 1940s and 1950s . . ."—Munguía, p. 161 (José Luis Castro Ruiz).

Description of the corn farmer in 1955 and the pyramids of hay bales: AHMM, photo album 9: "Chata Angulo, Valle de Mexicali," cat #29.CHA/166/29 (Serie de Agricultura. Lote 27 colonia cuatro division II. "Rancho Roa" arréo a corrales y establo. 1955.); and cat. #29.CHA/166/13 (Serie Irigación. Perforación de un pozo profondo en el lote 17 del colono J. Jesús Sánchez María en colonia Elias B.C. 1955).

End of Baja California's 47–year wet spell—Whitehead et al., p. 307 (Eduardo Paredes Arellano, Secretaría de Agricultura y Recursos Hidráulicos, Mexicali, "Water, the Most Important Natural Resource for the State of Baja California, Mexico").

Mexicali population, 1950 and 1955—Gerhard and Gulick, p. 16. This differs slightly from Ruiz's version.

Population in entire municipality of Mexicali (Mexicali Valley), 1950—Munguía, p. 162 (José Luis Castro Ruiz, Table 2).

I see a dairy ranch in Colonia Rodríguez.—Information from AHMM, photo album 9: "Chata Angulo, Valle de Mexicali," cat. #29.CHA/166/1/50 (Serie de Agricultura. Lotes 9 y 10 de la colonia Rodríguez. Colonos: Isidro y Guillermo Canchol. Detailles: Ganado lechero).

The Coasters' 1956 hit song—Unfortunately, I have not been able to hear it. I rely on the description in Pike, p. 309. My copy editor now advises: "Go to http://www.last.fm/music/The+Coasters/_/Down+in+Mexico."

"Many times people come to Mexicali hoping to cross to the other side . . ."—Señora Socorro Ramírez, interviewed on 19 February 2004 in her restaurant. Terrie Petree interpreted.

Señor Francisco Arellano Olvera's purchase—AHMM, Chata Angulo collection, box 9, marked simply "34 expedientes," folder "Francisco Arellano Olvera, Sup. 657.76 metros cuadros. Packard. PAGADO."

Mrs. Claude Finnell's recollections—Interviewed with her husband at their home in El Centro, April 2004. Shannon Mullen was present.

Kay Brockman Bishop—Interviewed December 2006 on her ranch just west of Calexico. Terrie Petree was present.

The Dharma Bums' description of Mexicali—Op. cit., pp. 94–95.

View from Mexicali across the line into Calexico—AHMM, photo album 1, cat. #29.AHMM/166.1/11.

Dashiell Hammett on Tijuana, 1924: "Still the same six or seven hundred feet of dusty and dingy streets . . ."—Op. cit., pp. 228–29 ("The Golden Horseshoe," 1924).

Major Ben C. Truman on Los Angeles, 1867: "Crooked, ungraded, unpaved streets . . ."—*An Illustrated History of Los Angeles County*, p. 101.

Remarks of Lupe Vásquez—Interviewed in Mexicali, 2002.

Description of cotton panoramas, *ca.* 1949—AHMM, photo album 9: "Chata Angulo, Valle de Mexicali," cat. #29.CHA/166/1/50 (Serie agricultura. Siembra de trigo en la colonia "La Mariana." Al fondo la Sierra Cucapah. 1955).

Mexicali cotton-production figures, 1912–56—Kerig, p. 481.

Footnote: Distribution and timing of cotton—Señora Socorro Ramírez, same interview.

Receipt no. 6669 and accompanying information—AHMM, Chata Angulo collection, unnumbered box (Vtas. 93–103, 414.2/53–62, folder 1: Venta No. 93—Eusebio Melandrez . . .).

Paragraph on Colonia Hindu and Chinese—AHMM, Chata Angulo collection, box 9, marked "simply 34 expedientes," folder "Aparacion y Annendamientos, Rentos a 31/47." All the information I cite comes from a 29-page list of *colonias* and their inhabitants drawn up in 1947. It is the only information the archives has about property holdings in the overall Mexicali Valley at this time, so it is as representative as we are going to get.

The 134 Chinese businesses in the center of Mexicali—Auyón Gerardo, p. 41ff. (Terrie Petree's working translation, slightly polished by WTV.) The census date was 1945. Duncan (p. 646) reports that of the Chamber of Commerce listings in 1951, 7% of Tijuana's and 10% of Mexicali's inhabitants were Chinese.

"The yellow octopus" and decline in Chinese population in Baja 1930–40—Dwyer, pp. 80–81.

Señor Armando—Interviewed in the Cafe Canton, 2002. Carlos Guillermo Baja Terra interpreted.

Interview with Xu's uncle—As mentioned in "The Chinese Tunnels," my interviews with the "softspoken old shoe-store owner" took place in November 2003. José López from Jalisco interpreted.

Xu's uncle's unexpressed feelings about Mexicans—Might have been reciprocated. An old man from Guanajuato who hated Tijuana, hated San Luis Río Colorado, hated the Fiesta del Sol and had lived in Mexicali for 42 years insisted that in the fifties the police had paid $20 per dead Chinese. "I have something in my heart," he said, touching his temple, "so if I don't like those kinda people, since I don't steal, I know only my job."—"He doesn't quite make sense," said the interpreter (José López, 2002).

Javier Lupercio—Interviewed in Mexicali, April 2004, José López from Jalisco interpreting.

Footnote: "About the only reminder of Mexicali's unsavory past . . ."—Gerhard and Gulick, p. 63.

Señora Teresa García—Interviewed on 19 February 2004, on her family ranch, Rancho García, in Colonia Sieto de Cierro Prieto, not far past the glass factory a few kilometers south of Mexicali. Terrie Petree interpreted.

Señora Socorro Ramírez—Continuation of same interview mentioned earlier.

Richard Brogan—Interviewed in Calexico, April 2004.

117. Subdelineations: Cottonscapes (1796–2007)

Epigraph: "Cotton would grow very well if it were sown."—Arrillaga, p. 88 (20 October 1796).

"No definite conclusion as to the value of Egyptian cotton culture in that region has been reached."—USDA *Experiment Station Record* series (1903–4), p. 135 (Southern California Substation at Pomona).

Sacramento cotton exhibited at State Fair in 1863—California Board of Agriculture (1918), p. 118.

Statistics on Imperial cotton starting, 1902–17—Farr, p. 189. The ICAC papers report the following for 1916: 39,028 bales ginned on the American side of the Imperial Valley, 24,147 on the Mexican side, 4,636 bales ginned in Riverside County. The California total is thus 67,811 bales.

News of Joe Macdonald—*California Cultivator*, vol. XXIII, no. 18 (November 4, 1904), p. 443 ("News Notes of the Pacific Coast").

Imperial takes first prize at New York fair, "Cotton Is King," Hotel King Cotton and number of cotton gins—Imperial Valley Directory (1912–13), pp. xxxii, 307, 326.

Imperial Valley Press, 1914—Vol. XIV, no. 7, Friday, May 8, 1914, p. 1.

Experience of the CRLC foreman in 1910—Kerig, p. 131. Her figure was 1,500 acres, which becomes 607.29 hectares.

Mexicali Valley hectares of cotton, 1912–27, 1930–31—Duncan, p. 624, who actually expresses each year as part of a 2-year cycle. For example, when I write "1912," Duncan writes "1912–13."

Footnote: Mexicali's Chinese population in 1913, and their cotton acreage—Auyón Gerardo, p. 41ff. (Terrie Petree's working translation).

"Cotton—the key to Baja's economic growth and independence"—Ibid., p. 625.

"The yield per acre in the Imperial Valley is much larger than in any other state in the Union" and 1916 yields—California Board of Agriculture (1918), p. 118.

Description of cotton picking and 1933 crop in Kern County—UC Berkeley. Bancroft Library. Paul S. Taylor papers. Carton 3. Folder 3:41: "Documentary History of the Strike of the Cotton Pickers in California, 1933, with Clark Kerr, 1934." Typescript on letterhead of the University of California, Department of Economics, Berkeley. Pp. 6, 5, 7.

New California grade of cotton—Ibid., p. 2.

California, "... where the pattern of cotton culture approximated industrial rather than family farm production"—UC Berkeley. Bancroft Library. Paul S. Taylor papers. Carton 4. Typescript: "In the fields, by Paul S. Taylor & Anne Loftis," n.d. (another slightly different version in the same folder reads: "Revised Sept. 15, 1981"), p. 15.

Cotton in Imperial and San Joaquin, 1920–32—UC Berkeley. Bancroft Library. Paul S. Taylor papers. Op. cit., p. 1. Taylor gives the following Imperial-and-Mexicali Valley yields: 6,000 bales in 1910, 45,000 bales in 1914, 83,000 in 1918.

Footnote: "America's Champion Cotton Grower"—*California Cultivator*, vol. LIV, no. 2, January 10, 1920, p. 1 (profile by M. E. Bemis).

Words of H. H. Clark, 1919—*Los Angeles Times*, April 6, 1929, p. A1 ("COTTON ASSOCIATION MEETS").

In 1930, Imperial County produced 205 carloads of cotton, and 135 of cotton byproducts, valued respectively at $958,375 and $144,373—Imperial Valley Directory (1930), p. 13.

Imperial Valley cotton production, 1932 (1,286 out of 129,371 500-lb. bales)—UC Berkeley. Bancroft Library. Paul S. Taylor papers. Op. cit., Unnumbered sheet ("Table 1: Regional production of cotton in California, 1919–1933 [500 lb. bales]).

National crop limitation of 1933—UC Berkeley. Bancroft Library. Paul S. Taylor papers. Op. cit., p. 7.

Imperial County cotton acreage, 1953, 1957—Griffin and Young, p. 176 (exact figures: 112,895 acres in 1953 and 43,955 in 1957).

"Many fell into it": *California Cultivator*, vol. LXIV, no. 14, April 4, 1925, p. 435 ("Can We Have a Balanced Farm Program?" cont'd). That same year, "San Diego shipped 11,000 bales of Imperial Valley cotton to Mexican mills, November 13."—*California Cultivator*, vol. LXV, no. 21, November 21, 1925, p. 516 ("Agricultural News Notes of the Pacific Coast": "Southern California").

Imperial Valley average yield, 1917: a bale per acre (b/a)—Packard, p. 24.

Average yield, 1953, 1954 (1.54 b/a and 1.89 b/a)—Imperial County Agricultural Commission papers. B. A. Harrigan, Agricultural Commissioner, annual reports for relevant years.

Lettuce grower's remarks, 1958—California State Archives. Department of Food and Agriculture. Bureau of Marketing. Marketing-order files, Box 3. State of California, Department of Agriculture, Bureau of Markets hearing on proposed marketing order for winter lettuce. Wednesday, December 17, 1958, beginning ten o'clock, a.m., El Centro, California. P. 365 (testimony of Richard Campbell).

The Minnesota farmboy's take—Paul Foster reports (2007) ("Imperial Color Commentary").

California second only to Texas for cotton, 1965—California Department of Agriculture (1965), p. 18.

Profitability of Imperial County cotton, 1965—ICAC papers, p. 6.

"Some of the land between the Colorado River and the Salton Sea is irrigated ..."—*Bol'shaia Sovetskaia Entsiklopedia*, vol. 17, p. 77 (entry on the Imperial Valley).

Footnote: Imperial, Riverside and Los Angeles cotton figures, 1974—Census Bureau, 1974, pp. 11, 31, 32 (cotton, 1974). Exact Imperial numbers: 241 farms, 73,164 acres, 185,189 bales harvested, from which I calculate a yield of 2.53 b/a.

Mexicali Valley cotton figures, 2000—Munguía, p. 84 (Saillé et al.). Exact numbers: 71,320 acres of cotton in irrigation modules five and six.

Richard Brogan—Interviewed in Calexico, April 2004.

Footnote: World cotton figures, 2004—*New York Times*, Tuesday, June 29, 2004, "World Business" sec., p. W1 (Todd Benson, "Brazil's Big Stake in Cotton Likely to Become Bigger," sidebar: "Cotton Kings"). Same article,

p. W7: U.S. cotton production is projected to decline by 29% if the World Court ruling against American cotton subsidies ($19 billion a year) is upheld.
Cotton performance in Imperial County, 2005—ICAC papers, p. 10.

118. San Luis Río Colorado (ca. 1968)

Epigraph: "And when the carpenters had hurried on . . ."—Bradbury, p. 78.
The hairdresser—Evalía Pérez de Navarro, interviewed in her establishment in San Luis while she was cutting my hair, October 2003, Terrie Petree interpreting.

119. Certified Seed (1959)

Epigraph: "Nor can I sing in lyric strains . . .":—*I. W.W. Songs*, p. 39 (Joachim Raucher, "Renunciation").
New categories of agricultural commodities—Imperial County Agricultural Commission papers. Agricultural Commissioner Claude M. Finnell, annual report, 1959, pp. 4 and 5.
Complaint of lettuce grower: chain stores are controlling the buying more; lettuce shippers lose control of processing.—California State Archives. Department of Food and Agriculture. Bureau of Marketing. Marketing order files, Box 3. State of California, Department of Agriculture, Bureau of Markets hearing on proposed marketing order for winter lettuce. Wednesday, December 17, 1958, beginning ten o'clock, a.m., El Centro, California. P. 212 (S. M. Beard).

120. Subdelineations: Ocean Parkscapes (1966–1993)

Epigraph: ". . . the tension of 'something about to happen' . . ."—Diebenkorn, p. 41 (Jane Livingston).
Diebenkorn moves into Ocean Park (1966)—Ibid., p. 57 (Jane Livingston).
"Rarely has an artist been more finely attuned to nuances. . ."—Ibid., p. 75 (Jane Livingston).
He describes the flattening out of his paintings in L.A.—Ibid., p. 58.
"Ocean Park No. 107"—Ibid., p. 76 (Figure 39).
"Each one creates its own, self-contained chromatic universe" and primacy of Diebenkorn over Rothko—Ibid., p. 65 (Jane Livingston).
"Well off the mark"—Ibid., p. 68.
"Finally, when all hands were seated . . ."—Bell, p. 3.
"The hesitant-yet-defining diagonal cutaway" and "the half-erased boundary"—Ibid., p. 73 (Jane Livingston).
Diebenkorn on his enjoyment in altering—Ibid., p. 72.
"A visibly imperfect surface that shows signs of its repair"—Ibid., p. 109 (John Elderfield).
"Ocean Park No. 32"—Diebenkorn, p. 68 (Figure 33).
"Ocean Park No. 14½" and "Ocean Park No. 24"—Ibid., pp. 202–3 (Figures 151–52).
"Ocean Park No. 116"—Ibid., p. 225 (Figure 180).
"An architecture . . . increasingly . . . eroded of complexity"—Ibid., p. 112 (John Elderfield).
"Untitled (Ocean Park)"—Ibid., p. 245 (Figure 201).
"Ocean Park No. 128"—Ibid., p. 252 (Figure 208).
"Ocean Park No. 133"—Ibid., p. 255 (Figure 210).
"Ocean Park No. 27"—Ibid., p. 203 (Figure 153).
"Still, he always seemed to be in the process of leaving . . ."—Ibid., p. 114 (John Elderfield).
Diebenkorn in Salt River Canyon, 1970—Ibid., p. 39 (Jane Livingston).
Descriptions of two Salt River works—Ibid., p. 38 (Figures 12, 13).

121. Los Angeles (1950)

Epigraph: "The Indians sternly beckoned us . . ."—Pattie, p. 201.
Mr. R. J. Smith: "Well, I think that there are a number of people, Harry . . ."—California State Archives. Department of Food and Agriculture. Bureau of Marketing. Marketing-order files, 1941–1971. Box 3. State of California, Department of Agriculture, Bureau of Markets. Hearing upon a proposed marketing order for chilled orange juice. Held in Mirror Building, Los Angeles, California, Tuesday and Wednesday, August 2 and 3, 1960. Alice Book, certified shorthand reporter. Pp. 51–52.
"Imperial County since the war . . ."—Tout, *The First Thirty Years*, p. 236.
"A great, screaming frenzy of cars"—Kerouac, *On the Road*, p. 99. By the way, in *On the Road*, Indio and Blythe are lumped in with "the Arizona desert" (loc. cit).
"In about 1950 they first started complaining about parking downtown. . ."—Marjorie Sa'adah, interviewed September 2004.
"The city's transportation system resulted not from conspiracy . . ."—Sitton and Deverell, p. 68 (Matthew W. Roth, "Mulholland Highway and the Engineering Culture of Los Angeles in the 1920s").
"A regular hell is L.A."—Kerouac, *The Dharma Bums*, p. 89.

Appurtenances of the Los Angeles River in 1955—California State Archives. Margaret C. Felts papers. Box 1. Folder: "1898–1965, 'A History of the L.A. District,' U. S. Army Corps of Engineers," p. 181.

"New residents come to California, and come and come . . ."—Lilliard, pp. 4–5.

My parents' memories—Thomas and Tanis Vollmann recollections (2003), all 3 pages.

"From Swim Suit to Ski Lift . . ."—Orange County Directory (1951), unnumbered preliminary pages.

Opinions of Jake on the above—Jake Dickinson, interviewed by phone, May 2007.

Kerouac on South Main Street and "little gone girls"—*On the Road*, p. 99.

Length and capacity of the Colorado River Aqueduct—Colorado River Association (1952), p. 15.

Lockheed: Water "in abundant supply at fair costs"—California State Archives. Margaret C. Felts papers. Box 1, *Master Plan for USAF Plant 14* (cited in detail in notes to "Los Angeles 1925"), p. 19. Date: 1966.

122. *San Diego (1920–1960)*

Epigraph: "So, you see, we have to add to Barbara's list of the uses of water . . ."—Richards, p. 105.

Population, water capacity and usage statistics for San Diego in 1950—San Diego City Directory (1950), p. 12. Pryde notes (p. 111) that between 1920 and 1930 more people entered the city of San Diego than made up the entire population in 1910.

San Diego's record crop returns for 1950—*California Farmer*, vol. 192, no. 8 (April 22, 1950), p. 358 ("Agricultural News Notes of the Pacific Coast": "Southern California").

"Luckily the rainy years before the war . . ." and doubling of water consumption during 1941–43 and dates of formation of SDCWA, of SDCWA's joining MWD, of first water flow to San Diego through the All-American Canal—San Diego County Water Authority, pp. 38–39.

Per capita use in San Diego (County, I think, not city, but this is not specified and the figure is probably about the same)—San Diego County Water Authority, p. 2.

And so capacity is doubled—The third pipeline from the second aqueduct was finished in 1960 (Pryde, p. 112).

123. *Tijuana (1966–2065)*

Epigraph: "Tijuana multiplies film's capacity for spectacle . . ."—MOCA San Diego, unnumbered 1st page of essay "Tijuana: Between Reality and Fiction."

Philip K. Dick's Tijuana—Op. cit., pp. 172–73, 199–200, 202.

Census data on Mexicali and Tijuana, 1960–2000—Munguía, p. 158 (José Luis Castro Ruiz).

Description of Tijuana in 1932—Griffing Bancroft, pp. 9, 11, 13.

My parents' memories—Thomas and Tanis Vollmann recollections (2003), unnumbered pp. 2–3.

124. *Tecate (1950)*

The old man on the park bench in Tecate—Unnamed, but in 8" x 10" neg MX-TC-LOC-03–01, interviewed and photographed in 2003.

"Nobody cares about Tecate! . . ."—Augustín Pérez Aguilar, reporter for *La Frontera* (Tijuana). Interviewed in English in a restaurant in Tijuana Centro, July 2004. Terrie Petree was present.

During the second half of the century, Tecate will grow by a larger factor than either of her two sisters, but if we follow these cities over the entire century, we find that Mexicali has multiplied more than half a million (that being her population in 2000), Tijuana, by less than 5,000; Tecate, by 613.

Year	*Mexicali*	*Tecate*	*Tijuana*
1900	Near zero	127	242
1910	462	?	733
1921	6,782	493	1,028
1930	14,842	566	8,384
1940	18,775	?	16,486
1950	65,749	3,679	59,952
1960	179,539	7,074	152,473
1970	263,498	14,738	277,306
1980	341,559	30,540	461,257
1990	439,756	51,946	702,228
2000	549,873	77,795	1,148,681
Multiple of 1900 size in 2000 for these cities:	549,873	613	4747
Multiple of 1950 size in 2000	8	21	19

Census data on Mexican cities, 1900–2000—Munguía, p. 158 (José Luis Castro Ruiz). I have done the "multiple of" calculations.

125. *Holtville (1905–1964)*

Epigraph: "The 'Carrot Capital of the World' . . ."—Imperial Valley Directory (1952), p. 320.

Holtville news from 1905—*California Cultivator*, vol. XXIV, no. 26 (June 30, 1905), p. 611 ("News of Country Life in the Golden West").

Holtville advice from 1964—Imperial County Pioneers Museum, item cat. #A2002.154.2, Ball Advertising, pamphlet: "Visitors' Recreation Guide Book to Imperial County California: 36 Pages of Information" (*ca.* 1964), p. 8.

The undated photograph—ICHSPM photograph, cat. #P2204.102.18.

126. *What a Cold Starry Night Used to Be Like (1949–1989)*

Epigraph: "And giants lived in this Sun."—Joseph and Henderson, p. 59 (Anonymous, "The Origin of the Aztecs").

Alice Woodside's memories—Interview of February 2004, Sacramento.

PART TEN
DISSOLUTIONS

128. *Probably the Weather (2002–2003)*

Epigraph: "There is no ill which lasts a hundred years . . ."—Hart, p. 133, slightly "retranslated."

The following data analysis is indicative. From Paul Foster reports (2007) ("Imperial Color Commentary"):

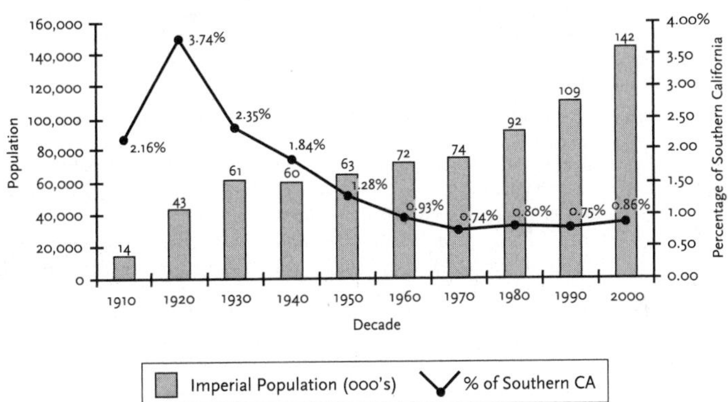

"Population: *(Population worksheet, and Percentage of Southern California chart, reproduced above)* This is probably the most discouraging of the Imperial statistics. After a surge of agricultural migrations in the 1910–20s, population growth was stagnant for 40 years (1930–70, average annual growth was 3%, with no growth from 1930–50). Imperial may be first (well, maybe Inyo) among the California counties for its undesirability as a place to live. Its proportion of the population of Southern California peaked in 1920, declined steadily until it bottomed out at 0.74% in 1970 and recovered modestly to 0.86% in 2000. Meanwhile, Riverside County has shown at least 30% growth every decade and currently has 30% of Southern California's population. Did I mention lately that Imperial is too hot?

"This decline undoubtedly influenced some of its farmers' choices for agricultural production, since Imperial didn't have a growing labor force and relied on migrant workers for picking many of its crops. Population stagnancy is almost certainly also related to the decline of the dairy industry, but which affected the other more strongly is difficult to say. (The *Percent of Southern CA* chart above offers a graphic illustration of Imperial's vertiginous slide. More data is available on the spreadsheet which shows Imperial falling further and further behind Riverside County in population.)"

The slender cowgirl—ICHSPM, document cat. #A2002.154.2, Ball Advertising Co. pamphlet: "Visitors' Recreation Guide Book to Imperial County California: 36 Pages of Information" (*ca.* 1964), cover.

Original meetings of Fraternal Order of Eagles in Holtville—Based on that organization's address listing in the Imperial Valley Directory (1912), p. xii.

"TAKE NOTICE. . . ."—An advertisement which frequently appears in the Imperial Valley Directory (1912).

Advertisement: "SAVE WITH ICE"—Imperial Valley Directory (1930), p. 32.

A book on citrus diseases: "A large list of special fruit rots and spots occurs . . ."—Fawcett, p. 35. In the original the phrase "dry rot," which I have de-italicized to indicate an insertion, occurs just before "the last one has been found only in the Imperial Valley."

129. From Ten Gals Down to Three (1914–2004)

Epigraph: "All Riverside County 'shows off' during this one week period . . ."—Shields Date Gardens, p. 13.

Ray House and his friend Art La Londe—Interviewed at the La Londe residence in Coachella, July 2004. Shannon Mullen was present.

Provenance of Miss Helen Shaw—Tout, *The First Thirty Years*, p. 197.

Mario—Interviewed at his workplace, the Thirteen Negro, in September 2005, Terrie Petree interpreting.

130. You Can't Produce Things the Way You Used To (2003–2004)

Epigraph: "Migratory working man . . ."—*I. W. W. Songs*, p. 59 (T.B.S. [author's initials], "A Worker's Plea," stanza III).

The tale of Prince Industries and Winzeler Gear—*Sacramento Bee*, Monday, December 1, 2003, p. D2 (Dave Carpenter, Associated Press, "For factories, it's change or fold: . . .).

"There's still much cotton in the valley . . ."—Señora Socorro Ramírez, interviewed on 19 February 2004 in her restaurant. Terrie Petree interpreted.

In California, annual crop production has increased . . .—Fact from California Department of Agriculture (1965), p. 5.

"The widespread use of Great Lakes seed . . ."—California State Archives. Department of Food and Agriculture. Bureau of Marketing. Marketing order files, Box 3. State of California, Department of Agriculture, Bureau of Markets hearing on proposed marketing order for winter lettuce. Wednesday, December 17, 1958, beginning ten o'clock, a.m., El Centro, California. P. 211.

Citrus packers in Riverside, 1940s and 1996—Patterson, p. iv.

California farm acreages, averages sizes and total numbers, 1950 and 2000—*California Agricultural Directory 2004–2005*, p. 108.

"It's a great feeling, when winter bears down or a drouth comes along . . ."—Sue Sanders, p. 69.

"Starting in 1975, the new definition of farm[s] . . ."—*California Agricultural Directory 2004–2005*, loc. cit.

"In short, democracy—once created through bloodshed . . ."—Hanson, p. 244.

Paul S. Taylor: "U.S. agriculture is the most productive in the world . . ."—UC Berkeley. Bancroft Library. Paul S. Taylor papers. Carton 4. Typescript: "In the fields, by Paul S. Taylor & Anne Loftis," n.d. (another slightly different version in the same folder reads: "Revised Sept. 15, 1981"). P. 19.

Richard Brogan on the Agricultural Stabilization Board—Interviewed in Calexico, April 2004.

New dehydrating method now allows Imperial County to sell its asparagus to Europe—*California Farmer*, April 5, 1975, p. 12 ("West Coast News Notes: Southern California").

Status of Imperial County agricultural production, 1982—Division of Agricultural Sciences (1982), p. 129.

The private investigator from San Diego: "The really rich ones own or control eighty-five percent of all agribusiness . . ."—George Michael Newman, Tactical Investigative Services. I interviewed him by telephone in 2003.

ICAC reports, 1970, 1980, 1990—Imperial County Agricultural Commission papers; Commissioners' letters for those years.

Eric Sloane: "The extraordinary family spirit . . ."—Op. cit., p. 65.

New York Times extract: "American agriculture is at a dangerous crossroads . . ."—*New York Times*, Thursday, December 9, 2004, "Op-Ed" section, p. A31 (Victor Hanson Davis, "A Secretary for Farmland Security").

Richard Brogan: "I personally feel that this country can't depend on the Mexican industrial sector . . ." —Interviewed in Calexico, April 2004.

131. The Aztecs Are Back (2004)

Epigraph: "He was beginning to yearn for Mexico . . ."—Jackson, p. 359.

Description of Coatlicue—After a photograph in Carrasco and Moctezuma, p. 42.

132. The Line Itself (1950–2006)

Epigraph: ". . . in the new landscape around them . . ."—Ballard, *The Drought*, p. 82.

Javier Lupercio—Interviewed in Mexicali, April 2004, José López from Jalisco translating. And, yes, it was the jobs. One afternoon in San Luis I asked an old man from Durango (he had never been to the United States) what was different about the border, and he said: "The ambiance is very different here, because you get the feeling that all the men are going to the U.S. to work. And here you see the women working in business. Back home, they don't work." He did not want to be named. Interviewed in San Luis, December 2006. Terrie Petree interpreted.

Port of Entry headline—*Imperial Valley Press*, Inland Empire edition, 1974, p. 12 (Don Quinn, "POE opens new door to Mexico in era of friendship").

Leslie Marmon Silko's recollections—Crosthwaite, Byrd and Byrd, p. 72 (Leslie Marmon Silko, "The Border Patrol State").

Ruben Salazar: "The Mexican-American has the lowest education level . . ."—Op. cit., p. 267 ("The Mexican-Americans NEDA Much Better School System").

Salazar again: "Anyone who has seen the fetid shacks in which potential wetbacks live . . ."—Ibid., p. 253 ("The 'Wetback' Problem Has More Than Just One Side," April 24, 1970).

Mexican illegals apprehended in the U.S., 1964 (43,840) and 1974 (709,959)—Dunbar and Kravitz, p. 14 (Table 1–1; based on INS Annual Reports).

César Chávez: "The worst invasion of illegal aliens in our history . . ."—Ibid., p. 21 (statement of 18 July 1974).

133. *Farm Size (1950–2006)*

Epigraph: "As the number of farmers decrease [*sic*] . . ."—*California Farmer*, vol. 210, no. 2 (January 17, 1959), cover.

The field of Mrs. Josephine Runge—*Imperial County: The Big Picture*, p. 68.

Percentages of American *vs.* Mexican farmers at beginning of twenty-first century—Bigelow, p. 79.

Information on Mexicali Valley *colonia* size, 1947, and paragraph on Colonias Villarreal and Zacatecas—AHMM, Chata Angulo collection, box 9, marked "simply 34 expedientes," folder "Aparación y Annendamientos, Rentos a 31/47." (If we make average rather than per capita lot size the basis of our comparison, then Villarreal represents 79 acres, Zacatecas 157½—near about Roosevelt's famous 160.) More examples: In Colonia Alvarado, lot size ranged from 19.8 to 95.8 hectares. Most were in the twenties, a few in the fifties. In Colonia Astorago, one man owned lot number 5 at only 20, but the other 4 settlers all possessed from 60 to 85.6 hectares. The average rounded size for Colonia B. Juárez was 47 hectares; one of the 12 colonists subsisted (or not) on only 5. Colonia Bravo's 10 owners averaged 25.5 hectares apiece. The average for Colonia Terrenos Indios was 29. Colonia Robertson's 8 lots averaged 30 hectares. Colonia Chapultepec had 59 owners or renters; the average was 38.2. Colonia Silva must have been a haven of the rich, for it encompassed 78 landholders at around 50 hectares each.

					Number of Hectares	
Year	Colonia	*Irrigated Area (hectares)*	*Number of Lots*	*Number of Landholders*[a]	*per Lot*	*per Capita*
1947	Villarreal	802.65	25	18	32.10	44.59
1947	Zacatecas	26,617.87	417	352	63.83	75.61

[a]"Landholders" may be buyers or renters, individuals, families or partnerships.

Source: Calculated by me from Archivo Histórico del Municipio de Mexicali, Chata Angulo collection, box 9, marked "simply 34 expedientes," folder "Aparacion y Annendamientos, Rentos a 31/47," 29-page list of *colonias* and their inhabitants drawn up in 1947. As noted elsewhere, this is the only information the archives have about property holdings in the overall Mexicali Valley at this time.

An official of the Tribunal Unitario Agrario—Lic. Carlos E. Tinoco, official of the Tribunal Unitario Agrario Distrito Dos. Interviewed in the tribunal offices in Mexicali, September 2005. Terrie Petree translated.

"Farming is characterized by highly commercialized large scale operations . . ."—Griffin and Young, p. 174.

"Two statements made by Nixon should prove popular . . ."—UC Berkeley. Bancroft Library. Paul S. Taylor papers. Carton 4. Folder 4:11: "Fight For Water." *Brawley News*, 1949, no page ("Nixon Meets With Valley GOP Leaders").

Chairman Clinton P. Anderson of the Subcommittee on Irrigation and Reclamation to the Committee on Interior and Insular Affairs: "It should be made clear to every Member of the Senate . . ."—UC Berkeley. Bancroft Library. Paul S. Taylor papers. Carton 4. Folder 4:11: "Fight For Water." Committee on Interior and Insular Affairs

(1958). [*Committee Print.*] *Ivanhoe (California) Acreage Limitation (Reclamation) Opinion of the Supreme Court of the United States: Memorandum of Chairman Clinton P. Anderson of the Subcommittee on Irrigation and Reclamation to the Committee on Interior and Insular Affairs, United States Senate, Eighty-fifth Congress, Second Session, June 26, 1958* (Washington, D.C.: United States Government Printing Office, 1958). P. 4.

Mr. Barrett: "I say to the Senator from New Mexico . . ."—Loc. cit.

The regional geography just quoted from this period: ". . . Mexicans, Orientals, Negroes, and migrant Caucasians under the direction of Caucasian foremen . . ."—Griffin and Young, pp. 173–74 (partly already quoted in "Stolid of Face and Languid").

The tale of Harold Hunt's ranch—*California Farmer*, vol. 193, no. 1 (July 1, 1950), 29 (Joe Crosby, "Hunt Proves Brahmans Have a Place in Imperial").

Coachella *vs.* Imperial Valley acreage, 1962; acreage of Steven H. Elmore—Ruiz, pp. 280, 286.

"Far from fulfilling William Smythe's breathless promise . . ."—DeBuys and Myers, p. 164.

Number of farms in California in 1974, by 2 definitions—Census Bureau (1974), p. xii.

Total and average California farm acreage, 1969–74; total and average California farm acreage 1940–74; farm profit 1974—Ibid., pp. xiv, xiii, xvi, 1–1, xvii; IV-73.

The California Department of Agriculture (1965) notes (p. 4) that in 1935 California had 150,360 farms; in 1959, only 99,274 farms. In 1959, farms of 1,000 acres and over were 76% of all farmland (p. 5). Average acreage of California farms in 1959 was 372; however, farms of 1,000 acres and more had almost half (46%) the state's cropland harvest in 1959 (p. 10).

Farm shrinkage table, and following paragraph about average acreages in the 4 relevant counties (calculated by me from the following)—Census Bureau (1974), p. II-1.

Debts of farm operators by county, 1974—Ibid., p. II-36 (farm operator debt for farms with sales of $2,500 and over: 1974). Average debt per farm: Imperial, $249,970; Los Angeles, $78,450; Riverside, $177,993; San Diego, $76,546.

Sonoran expropriations of 1976—Meyer et al., p. 649.

"Is it 'unfair' to require residents of Imperial Valley to observe reclamation law?"—UC Berkeley. Bancroft Library. Paul S. Taylor papers. Carton 4. Folder 4:29: "Imperial Valley, Notes, Drafts." Yellow sheet: "Imperial Valley, California. Paul S. Taylor, memo 1978." Pp. 1–2.

Footnote: The summary paragraph relating to the limitation law's vicissitudes is likewise based on Taylor (loc. cit.), who references Interior District Counsel Coffey, February 4, 1933; 1945 71 Interior Dec. 553, 548; the 1957 memorandum in behalf of the United States with respect to relevance of noncompliance with acreage limitations of reclamation law, No. 10 original, *Arizona v. California* 357 U.S. 902 (1957); 71 Interior Dec. 466, 555 (1964); 71 Interior Dec. 517. 1964.

Imperial County farm statistics, 1982—Division of Agricultural Sciences (1982), p. 129.

Doings of the Bass brothers—DeBuys and Myers, p. 165.

Celestino Rivas—Interviewed in Calexico, 2003. Lupe Vasquez was present and introduced me.

Imperial County has ⅓ fewer farms in 2002 than in 1959—Information from same source as table immediately above. Of course this number was always subject to immense fluctuation over the decades, with corresponding affected average acreage—the latter being a much less meaningful figure anyhow than a median would have been, since farm fallowings, failures and abandonments cannot alter the size of other farms, unless those bankrupt acres promptly get amalgamated into somebody else's holdings. Unfortunately, for much of the valley's irrigated life, medians were in short supply.

Addendum to previous note: In 2001 the IID's fact sheet on Valley agriculture listed 6,200 "farm accounts," of which more than 2,000 were owner-operated and the rest tenant-operated.

Kay Brockman Bishop—Interviewed on her ranch near Calexico, December 2006.

The following figures (Census Bureau [1974], p. 1–1) express farm-size trends in California during this period:

	All Farms	*Average Acreage*
1940	132,658	230
1945	138,917	252
1950	137,168	267
1954	123,075	307
1959	99,274	372
1964	80,852	458
1969	77,875	454
1974	67,674	493

Here are slightly different statistics from the *California Agricultural Directory 2004–2005*, p. 108:

Year	*Number of Farms*	*Average Farm Size*
1950	144,000	260
1960	108,000	359
1970	64,000	572
1980	81,000	417
1990	85,000	362
2000	87,500	318
2002	84,000	330

134. *We Now Worry About the Sale of the Fruit Cocktail in Europe (1948–2003)*

Epigraph: "The concept of progress acts as a protective mechanism . . ."—Herbert, p. 330.

"Science in the Agriculture of Tomorrow"—USDA Yearbook series (1950–1951), pp. 1–2.

"The kind of year farmers pray for"—*California Farmer*, January 4, 1975, p. 45 ("Freestone Report").

Editorial on peaches—*Sacramento Bee*, Saturday, July 5, 2003, "Opinion" section, p. B6 ("Just too peachy: Why 14.5 million tons of fruit are rotting").

California pear prices and "It behooves every grower . . ." (emphasis mine)—*California Farmer*, April 5, 1975, pp. 31–32 ("Pear growers must fight for marketing orders").

"We now worry about the sale of the fruit cocktail in Europe."—Ibid., p. 40B ("Growers urged to listen more to urban concerns").

135. *The Water Farmers (1951–2003)*

Epigraph: "In the first place, we might look into the American's greed . . ."—*Annals of America*, vol. 12, p. 592 (Hugo Münsterberg, "The American Passion for Money Explained," from *The Americans*, 1904).

Alice Woodside's remarks—Interview of February 2004, Sacramento.

Proportion of irrigated farms, 1959—California Department of Agriculture (1965), p. 9.

San Diego rainfall, 1883–84 and 1960–61—Pryde, p. 103. The unrounded figures given are: high of 25.97 inches in 1883–84, low of 3.46 inches in 1960–61.

Rousseau: "Easy to see, from the very nature of agriculture. . ."—Op. cit., p. 3365 (Appendix to *On the Origin of Inequality*).

Robert Hays: "As the increasing population of the seacoast cities in California . . ."—Tout, *The First Thirty Years*, p. 410.

Paul S. Taylor: "What is agricultural land today is urban land tomorrow."—UC Berkeley. Bancroft Library. Paul S. Taylor papers. Carton 4. Folder 4:11: "Fight For Water." Typescript: "HEARINGS BEFORE THE NATIONAL COMMISSION ON URBAN PROJECTS, Volume 2, Testimony of Paul S. Taylor, July 5, 1967, San Francisco." Page number cut off on Bancroft's photocopy, possibly p. 235.

El Centro statistics, 1970—Imperial Valley Directory (1970), pp. viii–ix (courtesy El Centro Chamber of Commerce). The same source records IID's gross acreage as over 900,000, "of which 430,398 acres are actually cultivated croplands."

Head-lettuce statistics, 1974—Census Bureau (1974), p. III-12. For the other two types of lettuce, Imperial's 8 farms approximate San Diego's, but the former's acreage is much larger.

The boomers of 1922—See final citation to the chapter "Twenty Thousand in 1920."

Broccoli statistics, 1974—Census Bureau (1974), p. III-11.

Asparagus holdings and difficulties of the Irvine Company, 1971—California State Archives. Department of Food and Agriculture. Bureau of Marketing. Marketing-order files, 1941–1971. Box 1. State of California, Department of Agriculture, Bureau of Marketing. Proposed Marketing Order for California Asparagus Research, as Amended. Tuesday, August 10, 1971, beginning 10 o'clock, a.m. Stockton, California (testimony of James R. Manassero of the Irvine Company, 13042 Myford Road, Santa Ana, California). P. 18.

A resident of Holtville: *"The crops in the Valley are only 1/27 . . ."*—*Imperial Valley Press*, vol. 103, no. 22, Thursday, June 5, 2003, p. A4, "Voice of the People" column (Philip Ricker, "Farmers losing their grip on I.V.").

Footnote: Kay Brockman Bishop—Interviewed December 2006 on her ranch just west of Calexico. Terrie Petree was present.

Ray Heckman: "an even flow of corn into the Los Angeles market"—California State Archives. Department of Food and Agriculture. Op. cit. Box 4. State of California, Department of Agriculture, Bureau of Markets hearing on proposed marketing order for Coachella Valley green corn. Wednesday, April 9, 1947, 10:15 o'clock, a.m., Coachella Valley Water District Building, Coachella, California. P. 7.

Norman Ward: "A more orderly flow of melons to the consuming public." California State Archives. Department of Food and Agriculture. Op. cit. Box 3. State of California, Department of Agriculture, Bureau of Markets hearing on proposed marketing order for winter lettuce. Wednesday, December 17, 1958, beginning ten o'clock, a.m., El Centro, California. P. 142.

King's metaphor: grapes as water—California State Archives. Department of Food and Agriculture. Op. cit. Box 1. State of California. California Department of Agriculture. Public Hearings: May 2, 1967. Location: Coachella, California. P. 50; the two phrases separated by ellipses have actually been reversed.
Photograph of "a parade!"—ICHSPM photograph, cat. #P191.44.8 (IVDA photo).
"Imperial is TOO HOT . . ."—Paul Foster reports (2007) ("Imperial Color Commentary").

136. Coachella (1975)

Epigraph: "Welcome to the Coachella Valley . . ."—Glenn, prefatory note.
"The wildest dreams of men in the first 40 years of this century have been exceeded . . ."—Nordland, p. 2.
Coachella acreage increase, 1940s–60s—Nordland, p. 61.
Agricultural income of Coachella Valley, 1975—*California Farmer*, April 5, 1975, p. 12 ("West Coast News Notes: Southern California").
"This 1973 aerial view . . ."—Laflin, *A Century of Change*, 2nd full-page photo following entry for 1976.

137. The Imperial Idea (1950–2000)

Epigraph: "He was fast becoming that most tragic yet often sublime sight . . ."—Jackson, pp. 35–36.
Alice Woodside's memories—Interview of January 2004, Sacramento. Edith Karpen was present.
The two airlines of Imperial County—*Imperial Valley Press*, Inland Empire edition, 1974, pp. 42–44 (Nancy Meher, "High flying hopes view airport as ever-soaring Valley economic asset").
The gazetteer from 1985: "Principal economic base: market gardens, cotton, sugar beets, alfalfa, gypsum quarries."—*California Gazetteer*, p. 135.
Powers and duties of the Agricultural Commissioner—As described in his annual report, 1954; Imperial County Agricultural Commission papers. This marks the end of B. A. Harrigan's era and the beginning of Claude M. Finnell's.
Richard Campbell's remarks—California State Archives. Department of Food and Agriculture. Bureau of Marketing. Marketing-order files, Box 3. State of California, Department of Agriculture, Bureau of Markets hearing on proposed marketing order for winter lettuce. Wednesday, December 17, 1958, beginning ten o'clock, a.m., El Centro, California. Pp. 353–54, 373, 356, 400.
"Public assistance came to be highly valued . . ."—UC Berkeley. Bancroft Library. Paul S. Taylor papers. Carton 5. Folder 5:17: "National Reclamation in the Imperial Valley: Law vs. Politics, Final Draft, 1981." P. 4.
The two U.S. Supreme Court decisions that weakened property control against collective-bargaining agents—*Republic Aviation Corp v. NLRB*, 324 U.S. 793 [65 S. Ct. 982] and *NLRB v. Babcock & Wilcox Co.*, 351 U.S. 105 [76 S. CDt. 679].
Simon Bale's interrogation in *Nickel Mountain*—Gardner, pp. 153, 181–86.
Excerpts from *Vandenberg*—Oliver Lange, pp. 45, 122–23, 104, 126, 146.
Kay Brockman Bishop—Interviewed in 2006 on her ranch near Calexico.
Description of the family in the pumpkin field—California State Archives. Olson Photo Collection. Accession #94–06–27 (238–387). Box 2 of 7. Folder 94–06–27 (331–343): Farms and Farming. Photo #94–06–27–0334. Caption: "Farms C-3250."
"Nihilism . . . is the recognition of the long *waste* of strength . . ."—Nietzsche, p. 12 (November 1887–March 1888).
Richard Brogan—Interviewed in Calexico, April 2004.
Imperial Valley's agricultural subsidies, 1965—"Imperial Valley, Notes, Drafts." Unnumbered small white sheet. clipped to yellow sheets, dated 1979. Yellow sheet: "Imperial Valley, California. Paul S. Taylor, memo 1978." P. 2.
The document from 1949 concerning Conrad C. Caldwell et al.—AHMM, Chata Angulo collection, box no. 132, labeled "Col. Villarreal, L:1–27," folder, "Lote No. 23, Col. Villarreal, Archivero #7, Gaveta b; 1949.
José López—Interviewed in Mexicali, 2003.
The man in Colonia Santo Niño—Interviewed in 2004. Terrie Petree interpreted.

138. It Seems Like the Money Is Being Taken by Somebody (2003)

Lupe Vásquez—Interviewed in Calexico, 203.

139. Chávez's Grapes (1962–2006)

Epigraph: Proclamation of the Delano grape workers—*Annals of America*, vol. 19, p. 48 (source: *El Malcriado*).
Tale of Jim Holcomb and aside on "Civil Rights Marches"—Reed, pp. 167, 169.
"INDEPENDENT GROWERS KEEP WORKERS HAPPY"—*California Farmer*, January 4, 1975, p. 28.
Tale of the lemon workers' strike—Ibid., p. 17 ("Combatting the boycott").
UFW's falling-out with CML—The UFW accused the Confederation of Mexican Laborers of being scabs, while at a rally at San Luis Río Colorado the CML replied that UFW used violence against them. Same article.

The growers' counter-measures—Ibid., January 4, 1975, p. 12 ("UFW loses Mexican support").

Case of the man who is irrigating onions on Good Friday—California State Archives. ALRB restricted files, 1978–1984. Case GF. Court of Appeal.

"Among the results of delay by Mexican-Americans . . ."—UC Berkeley. Bancroft Library. Paul S. Taylor papers. Carton 5. Folder 5:41: "Perspectives on Mexican-Americans, Final Draft w/Footnotes, 1973." Typescript, "Perspectives on Mexican-Americans," pp. 6–7.

Edith Karpen's memories—Based on an interview in January 2004, Sacramento, California. Alice Woodside was present.

Delmira Treviño: "I will *not* follow in my mother's footsteps . . ."—Hart, p. 45.

Richard Brogan—Interviewed in Calexico, 2004.

Photograph from the folder labeled "Apricots"—ICHSPM photograph, cat. #P91.90.3 (undated Hetzel image; the archivist told me that it looked as if it came from the 1940s; Hetzel died in 1949).

The worker who lost his job the day before the union election—California State Archives. ALRB restricted files, 1978–1984. Case AFB-2. Court of Appeal.

"The birth of serious hope for a farm union"—Matthiessen, p. 15.

Details of the march from Coachella to Calexico, 1969; the murder of Rufino Contreras—Salazar, pp. 210–12; Griffith, p. 10.

"On this day greed and injustice struck down our brother Rufino Contreras . . ."—César Chávez, p. 167 ("Rufino Contreras," February 14, 1979).

Enthusiasm of the nurseryman from Fresno—*California Cultivator*, vol. XXIV, no. 14 (April 7, 1905), p. 323 ("News of Country Life in the Golden West").

"In five years' time, Imperial valley will be recognized . . ."—Ibid., vol. XXVI, no. 18 (May 4, 1906), p. 419 ("News of Country Life in the Golden West").

$600 offer to Coachella grape grower—Ibid., vol. XXVII, no. 1 (July 5, 1906), p. 2 ("News of Country Life in the Golden West").

"One of the most profitable industries in this section . . ."—Packard, p. 40.

Calipatria and Mount Signal districts have greatest grape acreage in Imperial County—Griffin and Young, p. 181.

The tale of "Horace Caldwell"—California State Archives. ALRB restricted files, 1978–1984. Cases HC and RP. California Supreme Court.

Richard Brogan—Interviewed in Calexico, April 2004. Terrie Petree was present.

Interview with Carolyn Cooke—April 2004, in Indio.

Footnote: Tale of the UFW rock concert—*California Farmer*, April 5, 1975, p. 10 ("UFW denied concert site").

Interview with the Tylers—Palm Desert, April 2004. Shannon Mullen was present.

"To be a man is to suffer for others . . ."—McGregor, p. 1 (Marc Grossman).

Details of Chávez's birth—Matthiessen, p. ix.

"His invariable costume . . ."—Ibid., p. 9.

"He was the first person to tell us that women are equal to men . . ."—McGregor, p. 15 (Jessie De La Cruz).

"We have nothing else to do with our lives . . ."—Matthiessen, p. vii.

The "submarines"—Ibid., p. 34.

Affadavit executed at Calexico, 14 March 1979—ALRB restricted files, 1979. Case WG. A sprawling file which has to do with a strike in Salinas and in which we find a UFW affadavit executed at Calexico.

Chávez's hatred for Mexican labor contractors—Matthiessen, p. 18.

"Contractors of labor always Mexicans . . ."—UC Berkeley. Bancroft Library. Farm Labor situation 1933–34. Carton #C-R 84. Folder: 6. Dean Hutchinson's handwritten notes. Sheet 21.

Footnote: Celestino Rivas—Interviewed in Calexico, 2003. Lupe Vásquez was present and introduced me.

Chávez in Oxnard—Matthiessen, p. 51.

Portraits of the Kennedys and Zapata—Ibid., p. 40.

"Hard-edged and monotonous . . ."—Ibid., p. 32.

The Lamont grower's complaint—Ibid., p. 80.

"Growers & laborers had reached an agreement prior to this . . ."—UC Berkeley. Bancroft Library. Farm labor situation 1933–34. Carton #C-R 84. Folder: 6. Dean Hutchinson's handwritten notes. Sheet 2.

Events in Delano—Ibid., pp. 54, 57, 80.

Description of the 1965 California Mid-Winter Fair Parade—After *Imperial County: The Big Picture*, photo on p. 58.

Events of the marketing order hearing in Coachella (1967)—California State Archives. Department of Food and Agriculture. Bureau of Marketing. Marketing order files, 1941–1971. Box 1. State of California. California Department of Agriculture. Public Hearings: May 2, 1967. Location: Coachella, California. Joan E. Smith, certified shorthand reporter (Rialto, California). Pp. 7–10, 32, 30 (Lionel Sternberg, president of David Freedman and Company), pp. 11, 29 (Mr. Asker), pp. 46–47 (Max Cook of Heggblade and Marguleas Company).

Fawcett grape girls—ICHSPM photograph, cat. #P91.166.
Events in Coachella, 1968—Matthiessen, pp. 90–92.
ALRB on tomato-throwing, etc.—California State Archives. ALRB restricted files, 1978–1984. Case GF. Court of Appeal.
The march of May 1969—Griswold del Castillo and Garcia, pp. 89–90.
UFW strikes, 1970–71—California State Archives. ALRB restricted files, 1978–1984. Case MG.
Remarks of Frank Oswald and Sterling Oswald, 1934—UC Berkeley. Bancroft Library. Farm labor situation 1933–34. Carton #C-R 84. Folder: 6. Dean Hutchinson's handwritten notes. Sheets 44–45.
The table grape boycott accomplishes its aim, 1970—McGregor, p. 2.
"We are the people of the fields . . ."—César Chávez, p. 144 ("In Coachella," 1973).
"Labor organizing efforts by the United Farm Workers disrupted the valley . . ."—Laflin, *A Century of Change*, entry for 1973.
The Nazi Gauleiter's distinction between trade union and state—Krebs, p. 17.
The scene from Kern County—Street, *Photographing Farmworkers*, p. 251 (anonymous UFW photograph, possibly by Gayanne Fietinghoff).
"This tragedy happened because of the greed of the big growers . . ."—César Chávez, p. 147 ("After a Bus Accident," February 11, 1974).
March of June 1975—Hammerback and Jensen, p. 104.
Interview with Mr. and Mrs. La Londe—July 2004, in their home in Coachella. Shannon Mullen was present.
Contracts obtained in the Imperial Valley, 1978—Griswold del Castillo and Garcia, p. 131.
The tale of Tasty Foods—California State Archives. ALRB restricted files, 1978–1984. Case GF. Court of Appeal.
Question of the Month—*California Farmer*, November 19, 1977, p. 23.
The tale of Abel Farms—California State Archives. ALRB restricted files, 1978–1984. Case AFB. Court of Appeal.
"Respondent is found to have violated the act for an alleged threat that only the discriminatee saw."—California State Archives. ALRB restricted files, 1978–1984. Case GF. Court of Appeal.
Police report on UFW strike at Monterey—California State Archives. ALRB restricted files, 1978–1984. Case WG.
Chávez admits that UFW violence in Imperial is bad PR.—Street, *Photographing Farmworkers*, p. 259 (text by Street).
The tale of Sylvester & Co. and Joffe Brothers—California State Archives. ALRB restricted files, 1978–1984. Case CJM. Court of Appeal, petition for review.
"You're going up against competition . . ."—California State Archives. ALRB restricted files, 1978–1984. Case VC. Civil. Respondent's brief.
More about Abel Farms—California State Archives. ALRB restricted files, 1978–1984. Case AFB, AFB-2. Court of Appeal.
The Fast for Love—McGregor, p. 11 (Arturo S. Rodriguez).
"Before this century is done . . ."—Matthiessen, p. 29.
Brawley Chamber of Commerce's description of alluring labor qualities—Brawley Business Directory, p. 8.
Richard Brogan—Interviewed in Calexico, April 2004.
Historical note: In October of 2003 I happened to be in Brawley during a strike of the union workers of a certain southern California supermarket chain. They were out there picketing; you'd think they'd want to educate me, but when I asked about the history of labor in the region, their spokesman waved me off, advising me, incredibly enough, to go to City Hall, because "they have a lot of old newspapers there."

140. *Subdelineations: Waterscapes (1950–1975)*

Epigraph: " 'Get more water to get more people to get more economic growth' . . ."—UC Berkeley. Bancroft Library. Paul S. Taylor papers. Carton 4. Folder 4:24: "A Fresh Look at Fresh Water: Drafts 1 & 2, w/Corrections, 1970." Various typescript bundles on yellow paper, corrected. Top bundle, p. 4.
Footnote: "It is my impression . . ."—Paul S. Taylor papers, loc. cit. Folder 4:24. Robert J. Markson, Associate Editor, to Paul S. Taylor, January 16, 1970 (letter on McClatchy Newspapers letterhead).
Fact and factoid from the Colorado River Association (1952)—Op. cit., pp. 10, 21.
Footnote: 1963 United States Supreme Court ruling against California, "favoring, by California standards, development in Arizona"—Rogers and Nichols, p. 20.
Date of annexation of EMWD by MWD—Riverside City Directory (1951), p. 9.
Santa Ana River water "litigated 'almost continuously since the 1950s' "—Patterson, p. 307.
"The upper limit of safe annual yield," etc.—California Department of Justice (1959), pp. 31–32. Between 1928 and 1979, the average annual flow of the Colorado River was 13,900,000 acre-feet, which is to say 4,000,000

acre-feet below the estimate of the Hoover Colorado River Compact Commission. But it was simply needless to question the supply of water. (Average annual flow of the Colorado River, 1928–79—Warne, p. 1.)

Declining aquifers and increased use of the Colorado and Feather rivers, 1960s—Lilliard, pp. 139–40.

James J. Doody: "The 2,580,200 acre-feet of Northern California water . . ."—California State Archives. Margaret C. Felts papers. Box 1. Loose typescript (10 pages). James J. Doody, District Director, Southern District, Department of Water Resources, The Resources Agency of California, State of California, *Meeting Southern California's Water Needs.* Presented before the Southern California Section, Society of American Foresters, San Diego, December 10, 1965. P. 5.

Immediately following remarks on desalinization—Ibid., p. 10.

The tale of Mike Dunbar—*Sacramento Bee,* July 11, 2006, p. B7 (Daniel Weintraub, "Orange County tries new approach to desalinization"). The article lists several objections to desalinization plants, including: deaths of sea creatures pumped up into the system and difficulties of proper filtration, both of which might well be addressed by pumping brackish groundwater instead of seawater.

"After fighting for twenty years to take Colorado River water . . ."—UC Berkeley. Bancroft Library. Paul S. Taylor papers. Carton 5. Folder 5:2: "To Make the Desert Bloom Like the Rose, 1969?" Yellow typescript on "The American West" letterhead, entitled "Issue: Colorado Book." P. 51.

"Subject to increase or reduction in certain contingencies . . ."—California Department of Justice (1959), pp. V-26–27.

Edith Karpen's memories—Based on an interview in January 2004.

Water-table drop near Morelos, 1958–98—Munguía, p. 62 (Barrientos et al.).

Old Carlos—Interviewed very briefly in El Major Indigenes Cucapá, 2003. Terrie Petree interpreted.

Señora Teresa García—Interviewed on 19 February 2004, on her family ranch, Rancho García, in Colonia Sieto de Cierro Prieto, not far past the glass factory a few kilometers south of Mexicali. Terrie Petree interpreted.

"Prudent planning for the future . . ."—California Department of Justice (1959), Appendix F, "Extracts from Testimony on the Future Quality and Composition of Colorado River Water, California Exhibit 5585, A Memorandum Dated August 15, 1958, from Raymond A. Hill to Northcutt Ely Re Future Salt Burden of Colorado River," p. 18.

Average virgin flow of the Colorado 1906–83—Bureau of Reclamation, Sandra J. Owen-Jogre and Lee H. Raymond, in cooperation with the Bureau of Reclamation, U.S.G.S. Water Supply Paper 2407: An Accounting System for Water and Consumptive Use Along the Colorado River, Hoover Dam to Mexico (Washington, D.C.: U.S. Government Printing Office, 1996), p. 2.

Ruben Salazar: "In what might be described as the 'wettest' town in Baja California . . ."—Op. cit., p. 61 ("Murder of a Crusader Underlines Tijuana Choice: Reform or Go Red," January 8, 1962).

Footnote: Mexicali Valley and Baja water statistics, mid-1970s—Whitehead et al., p. 307 (Eduardo Paredes Arellano, Secretaría de Agricultura y Recursos Hidráulicos, Mexicali, "Water, the Most Important Natural Resource for the State of Baja California, Mexico"). Until 1977, which was the last in a long series of drought years, Baja California got 3,250 million cubic meters of water per year, either surface or underground, 2,950 in the Mexicali Valley. (Never mind that this second statistic calculates out to nearly 91%, not 88%). Baja's 3,250 total cubic meters I calculate out to 2,634,779 acre-feet, based on 1 acre-foot = 1,233.5 cubic meters. The high rain in Baja from 1900 to 1947 and again from 1978 to the time of writing (*ca.* 1985) is mentioned on pp. 308–9.

"The Colorado River, which makes Imperial County the fifth-ranking United States county . . ."—Lilliard, p. 153.

"As the sun rose, I saw the poplar trees of the Colorado River."—Arrillaga, p. 75 (19 October).

San Diego's nearly $42 million for water utilities in fiscal 1971—The California Builders Council, p. IV-352 (Table IV-99). The breakdown was as follows: Water Utilities Administration Division $322,877; Water Quality Division $2,983,764; Utilities Systems Division $5,950,891; Utilities Engineering Division $1,233,084; Water—Joint Accounts $23,209,780; Sewerage—Joint Accounts $7,633,502; Utilities Customer Service $832,031; *less:* Bond Funds of (—$347,892). Total: $41,818,037.

San Diego's water costs for fiscal 1972—Ibid., p. IV-357 (Table IV-100).

Professional restatement of the law of appropriation—Rogers and Nichols, p. 125 (sec. 92).

Yearly usage figures for various Imperial Valley crops—*California Farmer,* January 4, 1975, p. 16 ("Irrigation tests with a giant flower pot").

"The dove abounds in the cut-over alfalfa fields . . ."—ICHSPM, document cat. #A2002.154.2, Ball Advertising, pamphlet: "Visitors' Recreation Guide Book to Imperial County California: 36 Pages of Information" (*ca.* 1964), p. 21.

"Irrigation and reclamation must take first national priority . . ."—*California Farmer,* January 4, 1975, p. 1 (Hartt Porteous, "Water—A National Priority").

The stock photo from the Olson Collection: California State Archives. Olson Photo Collection. Accession #94–06–27 (238–387). Box 2 of 7. Folder 94–06–27 (279–310): Desert. Photo #94–06–27–0279.

"Experience in the Coachella Valley indicates . . ."—Dunham, p. 82.

141. *Wellton-Mohawk (1961)*

Epigraph: "Irrigated agriculture will always be a short-lived enterprise . . ."—Committee on Irrigation-Induced Water Quality Problems, p. 39.

Alice Woodside's memory of her father's alkali dread, and Edith Karpen's subsequent remarks on the city of Imperial—Based on an interview in January 2004.

Experiment results at Imperial Valley Field Station; salinity of the Colorado River in 1975—*California Farmer*, January 4, 1975, p. 1 ("Irrigating with salty water").

Phil Swing: "God in his infinite wisdom . . ."—Senate Committee on the Colorado River Basin (1925), p. 190.

The 1944 treaty and Minute 242—104th Congress, 1st Session, Senate Calendar No. 46, report no. 104–24, "Control of Salinity Upsteam [*sic*] of Imperial Dam, April 3 (legislative day, March 27, 1995).

Increasing salinity of Mexican water; TDS of Wellton-Mohawk water and result at Morelos—Munguía, pp. 78, 89 (Gerardo Garcia Saillé, Ángel López López and J. A. Navarro Urbina).

Footnote on same: The 2 Coachella wells—USDA Yearbook (1955), p. 321 (Milton Fireman and H. E. Hayward, "Irrigation Water and Saline and Alkaline Soils").

TDS (total dissolved solids) figures in Upper Colorado and the Colorado at the Mexican line—Committee on Irrigation-Induced Water Quality Problems, p. 40.

"The major problem affecting California agriculture . . ."—Diamond, p. 502. Mares, *Encyclopedia of Deserts* (1999), p. 494, entry on salinization: "About 25 percent of irrigated soils in the western United States are affected by salinization to the point where crop yields are reduced. Globally 25–30 percent of irrigated soils in arid regions are salinized. Human-induced soil salinization is usually the result of applying excessive amounts of water to irrigated lands and raising water tables. Evaporation of groundwater concentrates the salts that are always present in soils . . ."

Yolanda Sánchez Ogás—Interviewed in Mexicali, 2003. Terrie Petree interpreted.

Amounts of water bypassed at Morelos, and the water consultant's opinions of that—ICHSPM, document cat. #A84.48.1, William E. Warne, Water Resources Consultant, Sacramento, California, "The Stormy Past and Clouded Future of Desalting in the Colorado River Basin," repr. from *WSIA Journal*, July 1984. Pp. 1–2, 11.

142. *Subdelineations: Poisonscapes (1888–2003)*

Epigraph: "That is Imperial Valley . . ."—Imperial Valley Directory (1952), p. 320.

"The function of the State Board of Health . . ."—California State Archives. Margaret C. Felts papers. Box 1. Koebig, answer to Goudy (cited in full in the source notes to "Los Angeles [1925]"), p. 8.

City of Los Angeles: "final plans for grease skimming tanks should now be made . . ."—California State Archives. Margaret C. Felts papers. Box 1. Loose typescript. City of Los Angeles, Annual Report, 1929–30, p. 38.

The "pretty graph" of area, population and sewer mileage—Ibid., p. 45.

"We take it as a matter of course nowadays that plumbing has passed for a luxury."—Felts papers. Box 1. State of California. Department of Public Health. Bureau of Sanitary Engineering. C. G. Gillespie, Chief, Bureau of Sanitary Engineering. *The Sewage Situation in California* (prepared April 22, 1929, for the School of Public Administration, University of Southern California, Los Angeles, California), p. 1.

Annual acre-feet of sewage into ocean from Los Angeles and Orange counties—Felts papers. Box 1. A. H. Koebig, Charles Kirby Fox, Arthur W. Cory, November 15, 1930, letter to the President and Directors of the Southwest Water League, p. 2.

"A SURVEY OF SEWAGE DISPOSAL IN CALIFORNIA . . ."—Felts papers. Op. cit., unnumbered p. 29.

"There are no set standards of sewage disposal."—Ibid., p. 18.

"The arrangement is essentially contractual . . ." and "embrace thirteen cities entirely . . ."—Ibid., p. 5.

"Canneries, milk-plants . . ." and "run their cannery wastes, raw . . ."—Ibid., p. 15.

"In some respects a stream is like a woman . . ."—*California Farmer*, January 4, 1975 (vol. info no longer given), page before p. 1, "The reality of natural resource use," quoting "an editorial written in Georgia."

Outfall sewer of El Centro and Imperial, 1916—Farr, p. 280 (Edgar F. Howe, "El Centro").

"Chollas Creek is a heavily urbanized watershed tributary . . ."—At www.dgs.ca.gov\contracts (?). Printout is incomplete. But this website was generated by the San Diego Regional Water Quality Control Board, CWA Section 205(j) Grant Program, January 20, 2000.

"There are also instances of trouble . . ."—Felts papers. Box 1. Gillespie report, loc. cit.

Pollution caused by the Arrowhead manufactured-gas plant—Felts papers. Box 12: "Pollution Files. Manu. Gas Plants; Water Quality. Dept of Water & Power (L.A.) 1881–1943." Loc.: B4384. Folder: "1/1/1881: San Bernardino. manufactured gas plant. Pollution docs, Felts files." Undated 6-page typescript: "San Bernardino (Arrowhead Site Summary)" evidently a legal document. In margin: "Troop Meisinger Steuber & Paisch, LLP," Los Angeles.

Footnote: *Appletons' Annual Cyclopaedia* on petroleum-producing states—1892 ed., p. 72, entry on California. The 1902 *Cyclopaedia* informs us (p. 700, entry for United States of America [California]) that in that year there were 2,152 producing oil wells in California, making 13,692,514 barrels of black gold.

Pollution caused by the Riverside manufactured-gas plant—Felts papers. Same box. Folder: "1/1/1888: Riverside manufactured gas plant. Pollution docs, Felts files." Undated 3-page typescript: "Riverside Site Summary," evidently a legal document. In margin: "Troop Meisinger Steuber & Paisch, LLP," Los Angeles.

Pollution caused by the Long Beach, Colton, Los Angeles and Santa Ana manufactured-gas plants—Same box, counterpart legal site summaries.

"In order that the matter of water pollution . . . be handled under one uniform plan . . ."—Felts papers. Box 12: Folder: "1916 POLLUTION." Circular letter #2079, on letterhead of State of California, Fish and Game Commission, dated at San Francisco, June 7, 1916, to Mr. Scofield, from the Executive Officer, whose name is appropriately illegible.

"FOR IMMEDIATE RELEASE" (1927)—Felts papers. Box 12: Folder: "1927 POLLUTION." "FOR IMMEDIATE RELEASE." 2-page typescript.

"My dear Mr. Page: . . . "—Felts papers. Same folder. Letter from the Director (who in this file copy didn't give his name, but is probably J. Spencer), Bureau of Hydraulics, Natural Resources Division, Fish & Game Division, to Mr. A. G. Page, Manager of Refineries, Union Oil Co., Los Angeles; San Francisco, September 27, 1927.

"Taking the liberty of again calling this to your attention."—Felts papers. Same folder. Letter from the Director (again nameless, and again probably J. Spencer), Bureau of Hydraulics, Natural Resources Division, Fish & Game Division, to Mr. William Groundwater, Manager of Transportation at the Union Oil Building, dated at San Francisco, October 10, 1927.

Almost a hundred oil companies in Huntington Beach receive injunctions for oil pollution—Information from Felts papers. Same folder. "FOR IMMEDIATE RELEASE." Probably a Fish & Game press release, 1927.

Shell's reassurance about Wilmington Refinery—Felts papers. Same folder. Letter on Shell Company of California letterhead, dated at San Francisco, August 2, 1929, to Mr. Spencer at the Fish & Game Commission.

"The matter of Federal interference by the U.S. Public Health Service . . ."—California State Archives. Margaret C. Felts papers. Box 17: "Pollution Files. Misc. Docs 1950s–1980s." Loc: B4386. Loose typescript. Department of Water and Power. For Intradepartmental Use Only. Sanitary Engineering Division. December 9, 1954. To Mr. Burton S. Grant, Chief Engineer of Water Works and Assistant manager, B U I L DI N G. From Ray L. Derby, Principal Sanitary Engineer.

Department of the Interior: "The general objective is maintenance of a minimum dissolved-oxygen content . . ."—Department of the Interior. U.S. Geological Survey (1963), p. 88.

Edith Karpen's memories of the New River—Interview of January 2004.

Richard Brogan—Interviewed in Calexico, April 2004.

Fortune's assertion—March 1950, p. 115 (Lawrence Lessing, "The Chemical Century").

Gifford Price's DDT cost—California State Archives. Department of Food and Agriculture. Bureau of Marketing. Marketing-order files, Box 4. State of California, Department of Agriculture, Bureau of Markets hearing on proposed marketing order for desert-area green corn. Tuesday, March 18, 1954, 10:00 o'clock, a.m., Coachella Valley Water District Building. P. 53.

Lockheed: "Wastes from certain processes, such as degreasing and chemical milling . . ."—California State Archives. Margaret C. Felts papers. Box 1 *Master Plan for USAF Plant 14* (cited in detail in notes to "Los Angeles [1925]"), p. 77.

Characteristics and disposition of southern California wastes, 1966—Lilliard, p. 132.

Information on pesticides and nematicides in California groundwater, 1985—California State Archives. Margaret C. Felts papers. Box 17: "Pollution Files. Misc. Docs 1950s-1980s." Loc: B4386. Folder "1/1/85. Ground Water Contamination . . ." David B. Cohen, Ph.D., Chief, Pollutant Investigations Branch, State Water Resources Control Board, "Ground Water Contamination by Toxic Substances: A California Assessment." Pp. 20, 3, 15 (footnote), 18, 1, 4, 2, 23, 29.

Dr. Thomas H. Horiagon: "Probably a combination of factors, culture, genetics and environment"—*Imperial Valley Weekly*, vol. 98, no. 13 (Thursday, March 27, 2003), p. 1 ("New Doctor at ECRMC to Help Fight Pulmonary Disease in Imperial Valley").

The Mexican private detective—Señor A. See the chapter "The *Maquiladora*." His name is on file at the California State Archives.

"We are approaching the point where toxic pollution . . ."—Felts papers. Box 17, op. cit., p. 5.

Advertisement for "Black Leaf 40"—*California Cultivator*, vol. LXIV, no. 14, April 4, 1925, p. 412: Aphis Insurance for all Citrus Fruits . . .

Good work of potassium cyanate in 1950—*California Farmer*, vol. 192, no. 8 (April 22, 1950), p. 358, "Agricultural News Notes of the Pacific Coast": "Southern California."

Fumigation of dates with menthyl bromide—Dunham, pp. 99–100 (referring presumably to 1948, when the book was published).

Dangers of methyl bromide (in grape production)—César Chávez, p. 195 ("Wrath of Grapes," 1986).

Poisons applied in Imperial County, 1948—Imperial County Agricultural Commission papers. B. A. Harrigan, Agricultural Commissioner, annual report for 1948. Final unnumbered typescript page, headed "WEED CONTROL."

"Cattle like the salt and somewhat sweetish taste . . ." and Los Angeles produce-contamination breakdown, 1938—California Board of Agriculture (1938), pp. 626, 636.

Poisons applied in Imperial County, 1948–49, 1951, 1954, 2000—Imperial County Agricultural Commission papers. B. A. Harrigan, Agricultural Commissioner, annual report for 1949, p. 7. The poundage per acre of insecticide was my computation, based on an "area in irrigated district" given as 612,658 acres (p. 6). There is also a "1942 inclusion" of 272,330 acres. I have not been able to find out what this was, but I assume from the name that it was not irrigated, hence not farmland, so I did not count it. As for the 1950 insecticide figure, that obviously came from the 1950 annual report. Remarks on chlordane, oil emulsion, coyote trapping, 1954 activities: B. A. Harrigan, Agricultural Commissioner, annual report for 1949, p. 7; annual report for 1951, unnumbered p.; annual report for 1954, unnumbered p. The century's end figure comes from DeBuys and Myers, p. 7, sourcing an oral presentation at a workshop in San Luis.

According to the Imperial County Agricultural Commission papers, pesticide applications in Imperial County at midcentury were as follows:

1949	"almost 3 million"
1950	6 million
1951	3,716,850
1952	9,719,725
1953	7,217,775 "insecticide dust" for 285,111 acres. (+ 1,221,020 gal. defoliant, weed & other spray and 91 tons usual grasshopper bait)
1954	6,062,243 dust for 377,079 acres, + 1,853,324 gal. spray

Rumors that permission will be required for some pesticides; the grower in Merced; E. F. Kirkpatrick—*California Farmer*, vol. 193, no. 1 (July 1, 1950), p. 7 ("Proposed Spray Permits Arouse Strong Criticism").

Warning notices for parathion—*California Farmer*, January 4, 1975, p. 22.

Boysie Day's reminder—*California Farmer*, April 5, 1975, p. 16E, "California Weed Conference Report—Taking a look at farm chemicals," quoting Boysie Day from the University of California, Berkeley.

143. The Salton Sea (1944–1986)

Epigraph: ". . . it seems, in tragedy . . ."—White, p. 312.

The lovely color photograph from 1968—Windsor Publications, inside front cover.

Gallons per minute into the Salton Sea in 1968; arrival of barnacles and effects—*Westways*, March 1968, p. 33ff. (some page numbers cut off) (V. Lee Oertie, "Some Salton Sea Tales").

Mrs. Finnell—Interviewed with her husband in their home in El Centro, April 2004. Shannon Mullen was present.

Anecdotes of Patton and of the Coachella girl—Laflin, *Coachella Valley*, p. 109.

"The public has been rather slow in adopting the area . . ."—Dunham, pp. 67–68.

The words of M. Penn Philips, and his proclivity for cigars—DeBuys and Myers, pp. 206–7.

His acreage—Ibid., p. 208.

The Holly Corporation; number of homes and lots in 1968—Ibid., p. 212.

Health advisory of 1986—Ibid., p. 235.

"A Fisherman's Paradise"—Salton Sea map (1986).

Discussion of Salton Sea dike in 1974—Ibid., p. 247.

Relative salinity of Salton Sea, 1950, 1974, century's end—Recapitulated from the sources already given in the "Introductions" chapter entitled "Then and Now." Salinity of Arabian Gulf (43,000 ppm) is taken from Bockris (E. D. Howe, "The Desalinization of Water"), p. 621.

Imperial Valley map—*Imperial Valley Press*, Inland Empire edition, 1974, pp. 36–37.

Activity of Date City in 1939—WPA, p. 639.

Dates of carrot and tomato events—*Imperial Valley Press*, op. cit., p. 18.

144. Market Prices (1975)

Epigraph: "Life is better . . . in Imperial Valley, California . . ."—*Imperial Valley Press*, Inland Empire edition, 1974, p. 18.

Market prices of various commodities, 1975—*California Farmer*, April 5, 1975, p. 45 ("Markets: California Market Prices: Federal-State Market News Service, March 14, 1975").

Footnote: Mexican rancher on cotton prices—Gilberto Sanders, interviewed on his ranch in Ejido Morelos, 2003. Terrie Petree interpreted.

The wise woman from Imperial—Kay Brockman Bishop, interviewed December 2006.

Asparagus: ". . . we all feel quite strongly that doing further research . . ."—California State Archives. Department of Food and Agriculture. Bureau of Marketing. Marketing-order files, 1941–1971. Box 1. State of California, Department of Agriculture, Bureau of Marketing. Proposed Marketing Order for California Asparagus Research, as Amended. Tuesday, August 10, 1971, beginning 10 o'clock, a.m. Stockton, California. P. 34 (testimony of John McCarthy, who works for the Garin Company, an asparagus grower in the Salinas Valley; he is also a member of the advisory board of the CAA). On p. 21 (testimony of Stockton's William P. DePaoli, Manager of the California Asparagus Association, we learn that the CAA represents 156 growers of 74 million pounds of asparagus. The CAA believes hand labor is cheaper than mechanization, so stands against further research.

Status of various Imperial County million-dollar crops—Imperial Valley Agricultural Commission papers, 1975. P. 6 (Recapitulation); p. 4 (Vegetable Crops 1974–1975).

Status of Imperial Valley citrus for that year—Ibid., p. 4.

Commissioner's summary—Ibid. Cover letter by Claude Finnell.

145. San Diego (1975)

Epigraph: "Based on the research and analysis . . ."—The California Builders Council, p. II-1.

San Diego County population, 1970, 1980; total water capacity attained by the construction of Pipeline Number 5—San Diego County Water Authority, p. 41.

"Today, the county as a whole is about 90 percent dependent on imported water supplies . . ."—Pryde, p. 103.

"This one again about as large as all previous ones combined."—Ibid., p. 112. In contradistinction to the SDCWA, Pryde claims that this 4th pipeline (8 feet in diameter), begun in the late 1960s, was finished in 1972, not 1973. I have chosen the latter year, since the SDCWA is more of a primary source on this point.

"It is hoped that this new line will be sufficient . . ."—Loc. cit..

"An overall surplus of cash revenues . . ."—The California Builders Council, loc. cit.

"Urbanization of this strip is now well underway . . ."—Laboratory of Experimental Design, p. 9.

"Unquestionably, it is entirely possible that an individual residential development . . ."—The California Builders Council, p. II-3.

"Among all developments surveyed for this report, the only one registering a deficit . . ."—Ibid., p. II-8.

"The appreciation of value on existing real estate has more than provided for the increased municipal service cost each year."—Ibid., p. II-7.

Specifications and analysis regarding the commercial center in north San Diego—Ibid., pp. IV-222, 230. Phase I: Department stores, retail stores, and a mall. Ladies and gentlemen, can we all get behind that? Phase II: An office tower, a hotel, a conference center, restaurants, an entity called "civic/cultural," which occupies 25,000 square feet, and a skating rink. We need have no fear that our lands will not become better and better as the years go by. Phase III: more "commercial, civic, and cultural," some "office residential," another hotel, and some townhouses.

Increases in San Diego County agricultural acreage and income, 1963–74—Pryde, p. 121.

"Parenthetically, in the absence of new growth . . ."—The California Builders Council, p. IV-345. Pp. IV-347–350 list the $11 million service increases—for instance, a legislative salary increase of $20,895, $1,222 for the Aerospace Museum, $415,223 in retirement-contribution increases "due to actuarial rate changes," and, well, well, "Water Joint Accounts Division: Increase in Colorado River Water purchase due to below average run-off during 1970–71 winter"; that costs San Diego $2,599,000; it all adds up to $11,137,826.

"Luckily, by the 1970s there was a new source for imported water . . ."—San Diego County Water Authority, p. 41.

146. Mexicali (1975)

Epigraph: "Water has been the key to Mexicali's growth . . ."—Automobile Club of Southern California, p. 62.

Growth of "Mexican Imperial" (actually, all Mexican border areas, which of course includes the area I define as Mexican Imperial)—Salazar, p. 57 ("No Troops Line Border That Has Become Big Business: Changes Loom," January 7, 1962). I say "the middle decade of the twentieth century" because Salazar speaks of "the last ten years," which would be from 1952 to 1962; he is probably speaking approximately.

Remarks on family planning in the presidential campaign of 1970—Meyer et al., p. 705.

Increase in Mexicali's population (462 in 1910; 18,775 in 1940, treble that in 1950; 400,000 in 1975)—Fradkin, pp. 295–96.

Mexico's microcosm at twentieth century's end—Pike, p. 347.

Squatters in Andrade's time, and how CRLC dealt with them—Kerig, pp. 106–9. In September 1976, the peso fell from 12½ to 20½ to the dollar. In October, it fell to more than 51 to the dollar (Meyer et al., pp. 648–49). This doubtless encouraged border settlements.

Señora Socorro Ramírez—Interviewed on 19 February 2004 in her restaurant. Terrie Petree interpreted.

Screwworm cases, 1975—*California Farmer*, April 5, 1975, p. 41 ("Screwworms pose threat to Imperial County animals").

Lupita—Interviewed on multiple occasions in her parking lot beside the closed Supermercado, 2003. Terrie Petree interpreted.

Bol'shaia Sovetskaia Entsiklopedia entry on Mexicali—Vol. 16, p. 220. Here the 1970 population of the city is 390,400.

The same information in Spanish—Estado de Baja California (*ca.* 1983), p. 68, *"Superficie y volumen de la producción agrícola en el estado"* of Baja California. The exact figures were: In 1978, 222.46 *miles* de hectares produced 2.61 *millones* de toneladas; in 1982, 275.78 m de h produced 2.15 *millones,* with swings and dips in between.

Olga Liria Márquez—Interviewed on 19 February 2004, outside her little house in Colonia Colorado No. 4, which lies a few kilometers east of Highway 5, the Mexicali–San Felipe road, and not far from Rancho Roa. Terrie Petree interpreted.

Description of the Olmec-style mask—After a photograph in Carrasco and Moctezuma, p. 59.

Footnote: Hugo de Vries on Imperial—*Journal of San Diego History*, vol. XXI, no. 1, p. 38.

147. "The Language Seems to Belong So to This Country" (ca. 1960–2003)

Epigraph: "You seem to be very fond of Spanish, Miss Worth . . ."—Wright, p. 107.

The tale of the five dead illegals from Sinaloa, and the arrest of Angulo—*San Diego Union-Tribune*, Wednesday, June 11, 2003, "Around the Region" section, p. B3 (unattributed item datelined Ocotillo: "Five immigrants die in I-8 crash"). The accident occurred on the 10th.

"Indicated that he had been driving" and "In continuing the investigation . . ."—*Imperial Valley Press*, vol. 103, no. 29, Thursday, June 12, 2003, p. A8 ("FATAL: Driver thought to be dead," cont'd from p. 1).

Angulo, whose name was actually Cruz—He is now named Brigido Angulo Cruz in ibid., vol. 103, no. 30, Friday, June 13, 2003, p. A3 (staff report, "Coroner's Office releases names").

Mexican-ness of Calexico, 1934—Kerig, p. 305 fn.

Remarks of Kay Brockman Bishop—Interview on her ranch just west of Calexico, December 2006. Terrie Petree was present.

Contestants for Miss Calexico Pageant—ICHSPM document, cat. #A.95.232.1. Pamphlet: "Annual Miss Calexico Pageant. Friday, April 12, 1985—7:00 P.M."

Mention of Martha Patricia Castellanos and of contest rules—Same folder, yellow pamphlet: "Miss Calexico Pageant April 18, 1986" [by] "Calexico Chamber of Commerce," pp. 1, 7, 8.

Mention of Bill Polkinhorn—Same folder, "DESERT CAVALCADE PARADE '86 PARADE ENTRY LIST."

". . . Twenty and thirty years from now . . ."—César Chávez, p. 191 ("At the Commonwealth Club of San Francisco," November 9, 1984).

Remarks of Richard Brogan—Interviewed in Calexico, April 2004.

Discussion of Northside's Latin American–ization—Pike, p. 352.

"And he was just petrified—he grew up in a country where this is prevalent . . ."—Smith (Josie Morales, 1992?).

148. Los Angeles (1975)

Epigraph: "Its water projects today . . ."—*The California Water Atlas*, p. 36.

Epigraph: "I don't mean to say we're perfect . . ."—Lewis, p. 650 *(Babbitt)*.

The smile of the Bella Union Hotel's bartender—Bell, p. 6.

"After the fifties it went away . . ."—Marjorie Sa'adah, interviewed September 2004.

"Today Southern California has lost its booster spirit . . ."—Nadeau, p. 5.

"Gigantic watch springs of concrete"—Lilliard, p. 8.

Table: Cantaloupe and carrot statistics for 1969 and 1974—Census Bureau (1974), p. III-11.

Offsets to gross ag receipts of 1974—*California Farmer*, April 5, 1975, p. 12 ("West Coast News Notes: Southern California").

Jobs in last decade of the twentieth century—Wagner, p. 10.

"The worst Latino gang war in history"—Smith, p. 29 (Mike Davis, 1993).

149. El Centro (1975)

Epigraph: "Good Lord, George . . ."—Lewis, p. 542 (*Babbitt*).

Area of El Centro in 1980—Imperial Valley Directory (1980), p. xi, courtesy El Centro Chamber of Commerce.

150. The Inland Empire (1875–2004)

Epigraph: "But, you know, I honestly don't think . . ."—Asimov, p. 9.

"Soon, the Inland Empire . . . had become the land of big-box warehouses."—Wagner, p. 18.

Carrot and cantaloupe statistics for 1974—Census Bureau (1974), p. III-11.

Transformation of dairy farms into "world-class distribution sites"—Wagner, loc. cit.

Orange-growing cost per acre, 1950 and 1980—Wagner and Blackstock, p. 14.
Notes on smog-affected price increases and alfalfa decline, 1975—*California Farmer,* January 4, 1975, p. 14 ("Market Notes").
Premier status of Corona in 1913; closing of plant in 1982—Wagner, p. 51.
The girl on the label of Queen Colony Fruit Exchange oranges—McClelland and Last, p. 97.

151. Subdelineations: Orangescapes (or, "It Could Be Called Ambrosia I Suppose") (1873–2005)

Epigraph: "Actually, the orange industry is not faced with overproduction . . ."—*California Farmer,* vol. 192, no. 8 (April 22, 1950), p. 364 (Joe Crosby, "Frozen Orange Concentrate Has Industry Guessing").
"Buds all straight," etc.—Phrases excerpted from fruit growers' and merchants' advertisements in Bynon and Son, pp. 9 [5], front RH endpaper, 104 [100].
Encomium to Chula Vista; citrus acreage valuations thereabouts—San Diego City and County Directory (1901), p. 7.
Will Wolfskill's citrus planting in Los Angeles—McGroarty, vol. 1, p. 193 ("the first effort to make Los Angeles a citrus fruit center was made"); Riverside Municipal Museum, p. 8.
Wolfskill's profits in the early 1870s—Riverside Municipal Museum, loc. cit.
Advertisements from Mrs. H. Shaw and Thomas A. Garey—McPherson, advertising end matter, pp. x, ix.
First arrivals of Florida citrus in northern American cities—*Encyclopedia of Food Science and Technology,* vol. 1, p. 420ff. (entry on the citrus industry).
L. M. Holt coins "Semi-Tropical California"—The Great Basin Foundation Center for Anthropological Research, vol. 1, p. 3 (Harry W. Lawton, University of California, Riverside: "Riverside's First Chinatown and the Boom of the Eighties").
"The Chinamen seemed to be especially expert in this line . . ."—Ibid., p. 175 ("Paul Wormser, Redlands, California, "Chinese Agricultural Labor in the Citrus Belt of Inland Southern California").
The 1879 citrus fair—Ibid., p. 31 (photograph).
California citrus acreage 1880–93—Wagner, p. 48.
Description of Riverside citrus groves, *ca.* 1885—After a photo in Kurutz, p. 83 (no photographer given).
Deep *vs.* shallow furrows for oranges, 1899—USDA *Experiment Station Record* series (1903–4), p. 195 (entry on irrigation, citing C. H. Shinn, *California Station Bulletin 147,* pp. 65–71, fig. 4).
Catalogue of "deciduous fruit" sent to the Eastern States by California in 1902—*Appletons' Annual Cyclopaedia,* 1902, p. 701 (entry for United States of America [California]).
Citrus prices in 1904—*California Cultivator,* vol. XXIII, no. 6 (August 5, 1904), p. 142 ("The Produce Market").
G. Harold Powell: "For two days we travelled across New Mexico . . ."—Op. cit., p. 18 (letter of 23? January 1904, to Gertrude Powell).
Results of Powell's experiments on boxed fruit—Ibid., p. 7 (introduction).
"Eighteen carloads of lemons and oranges arrive in Boston, but with a thirty-percent spoilage rate."—Information based on *California Cultivator,* vol. XXIV, no. 13 (March 31, 1905), p. 311 ("News of Country Life in the Golden West").
Citrus growers' notion of financing another transcontinental railroad—*California Cultivator,* vol. XXIII, no. 1 (July 1, 1904), p. 7 ("Fruit Growers' League").
G. Harold Powell on Whittier: "The dark green foliage and the flaming yellow fruit of the orange groves made a striking picture."—Op. cit., p. 22 (letter of 27? January 1904, to Gertrude Powell).
"The El Cajon lemon district"—Ibid., p. 48 (letter of 24 February 1904, to Gertrude Powell).
Powell on Santa Paula: "the finest lemon Ranch in California . . ."—Ibid., p. 29 (letter of 4 February 1904, to Gertrude Powell).
Powell on Los Angeles: ". . . everyone wears 'mixed grey goods,' because the dust makes clothes grey anyhow."—Ibid., p. 24 (letter of 28 January 1904, to Gertrude Powell).
Imperial crop accomplishments and irrigated acres, 1909—Imperial County Agriculture Commission papers, 1907–10, pp. 1–3.
Powell's trip to Yuma and through Imperial County by train—Ibid., p. 95 (letter of 13 April 1909, to Gertrude Powell).
". . . in the future Imperial Valley must be considered one of the orange sections of Southern California."—*Desert Farmer,* Imperial Valley, May 1909, p. 101 (Will S. Fawcett, "Orange Culture in Imperial Valley").
California citrus trees, 1910—California Board of Agriculture, 1918, p. 158. I infer the year to be 1910, but this is unclear. The exact figures are: oranges, 6,615.805 bearing trees, 2,093,410 non-bearing; lemons 941,293 bearing and 379,676 non-bearing; and pomelo, 43,424 bearing, 25,589 non-bearing. In 1912 California made $12,951,505 in oranges, $2,976,571 in lemons and $143,180 in pomelos, which you and I call grapefruit. —*Britannica Year-Book 1913,* p. 775 (entry for California).

Early extent of Inland Empire orange groves—Wagner, p. 17.

L. F. Farnsworth's shipment—Tout, *The First Thirty Years*, p. 200.

First grapefruit orchard in Coachella—Nordland, p. 62.

Kinds of orange juice; R. J. Smith's ambrosia—California State Archives. Department of Food and Agriculture. Bureau of Marketing. Marketing-order files, 1941–1971. Box 3. State of California, Department of Agriculture, Bureau of Markets. Hearing upon a proposed marketing order for chilled orange juice. Held in Mirror Building, Los Angeles, California, Tuesday and Wednesday, August 2 and 3, 1960. Alice Book, certified shorthand reporter. Pp. 38–39, 51.

Citrusifying of San Fernando, 1914—William Leslie Davis, p. 120.

Fernando Rey Brand label—McClelland and Last, p. 12.

Near loss of Citrus Experiment Station—Wagner, p. 48.

"Oranges and Snow"—*California Cultivator*, vol. LXIV, no. 15, April 4, 1925, frontispiece.

Riverside's citrus achievement, 1925—Ibid., vol. LXV, no. 21, November 21, 1925, p. 516 ("Agricultural News Notes of the Pacific Coast": "Southern California"). In 1925, California Navels are quoted at 4.50–4.75 per box for 150s and larger and ranging down to 3.00 and 3.25 for 324s. Lemons are reported steady at from 3.75–4.50 per box F.O.B. shipping points. Foreign lemons available during the next 30 days are approximately 250 cars . . .—Same issue, pp. 410–11 ("Citrus Markets").

Footnote: 1925 California orange production figures broken down by region—Ibid., vol. LXIV, no. 14, April 4, 1925, pp. 410–11 ("Citrus Markets"). Lemons show a similar pattern. The exact numbers are: southern California, oranges 11,960 shipments (I assume these must be traincar lots), and lemons 3,215; central California, oranges 5,826 and lemons 115; northern California, oranges 484 and lemons 23.

Danny Dane's greatest hour—Sinclair, p. 113 ("The Golden Scenario," written 1930s, published in 1994).

Rank of California next after Florida in citrus production; change in rarity of oranges between the world wars from Christmas-tree ornaments to everyday objects—USDA Yearbook series (1950–1951), p. 263 (M. K. Veldhuis, "Chemistry and Technology of Citrus").

"We really looked forward to our holidays . . ."—Wagner, p. 47 (memories of Jean Burns, who was a Depression-era child in Iowa).

Origins and early history of citrus—*Encyclopedia of Food Science and Technology*, vol. 1, p. 420ff. (entry on the citrus industry).

Record citrus export from 1935—*California Cultivator*, vol. LXXXIII, no. 15, July 18, 1936, p. 528 ("Orange Freight Revenues Since 1885").

Three citrus news items of 1936—Ibid., vol. LXXXIII, no. 15, July 18, 1936, p. 524 ("Agricultural News Notes of the Pacific Coast": "Southern California").

Orange-picking photo from 1939—Wagner, p. 47.

Undated photo: packing #8 oranges—Wagner and Blackstone, p. 17.

The Paxton Junior lid-nailing machine—Seen at the Mission Inn Museum, Riverside, 2004.

Scarcity of Puerto Rican grapefruit—*California Cultivator*, vol. LXXXIII, no. 15, July 18, 1936, p. 526 ("Better Outlook for Citrus") mentioning early cleanup of Florida grapefruit, limited supplies of Puerto Rican grapefruit. "It is probable that California summer grapefruit will find a ready market in the East this year since there will be practically no competition during July and only the competition of the Isle of Pines during August."

"Those little six-ounces of frozen concentrated orange juice . . ."—*California Farmer*, vol. 192, no. 8 (April 22, 1950), p. 364 (Joe Crosby, "Frozen Orange Concentrate Has Industry Guessing").

Footnote: News about grapefruit juice—United States Department of Agriculture, *Weekly News Letter*, vol. II, no. 40 (May 12, 1915), p. 5.

Michael Arlotto on adulteration and California standards—Chilled orange juice marketing order, pp. 12–13, 17.

Stance of Glacier Groves against specific standards—Ibid., pp. 217–22.

The five major plants that make all chilled orange juice in California, and the output of the largest—Ibid., pp. 18, 56. Dairymen currently accomplish 80% or 90% of distribution of orange juice in California (ibid., p. 119).

The threat of Arlotto's competitor in Bakersfield—Ibid., p. 154.

Florida's orange-production cost is ⅓ those of California's, in part due to lower labor costs—*California Farmer*, vol. 193, no. 1 (July 1, 1950), p. 8 ("Good Valencia Prices Seen; Tariff Cut to Hurt Lemons"). The same source also reports, however, that in 1947 when the canned juice market collapsed, so many Florida canners went bankrupt. Gamely, southern California ships out 33,500 cars of fresh Valencias, 6,000 cars more than in previous year. More than 8,500 cars will be for four million gallons for frozen orange juice concentrate.

The Holtville farmer—Ben Brock, interviewed on the premises of Brock Farms in Holtville, 2004.

Arlotto on Florida *vs.* California orange juice ("a good palatable product")—Chilled orange juice marketing order, p. 159.

California *vs.* Florida: Another wrinkle—Opening my copy of *Fatal Harvest: The Tragedy of Industrial Agriculture*, I find a double-page spread comparing two grapefruit orchards, the one on the right under the purview of "Agrarian Eye: See What You Are Looking At." The 20-acre organic farm of George Cunningham "sits in the heart of California's $60-million-a-year grapefruit industry," and so it might even be in Imperial for all I know, although it looks awfully lush. I see broccoli-colored vegetation on the bouldery ridge in the background, possibly even trees, although the 80%-recycled, 60%-post-consumer-waste paper stock on which this book has been printed does not lend itself to detail; anyhow, the sky is blue above the ridge and there are white cloud-inscriptions on it, so how *could* it be Imperial? The grapefruit trees, pleasantly variable and even unkempt, bear constellations of the rich yellow fruit, and I would enjoy rambling through the tall grass which carpets it all, picking a grapefruit, and eating it on the summit of that ridge. "Instead of the sterile and denuded nature of industrial orchards," I am informed, "Cunningham's farm amounts to a natural nirvana, where spiders, lizards, frogs, and many other species peacefully coexist with his efforts to produce nutritious and mouthwatering grapefruit." On the lefthand page, alas, haunted by the evil "Industrial Eye: See What You Are Looking At," I spy a tall, dark and uniform double row of trees, with many more doubtless hidden behind them; and in the foreground, the lifeless sand is strewn with crowds of fallen grapefruits. This orchard earns its mite of Florida's 70 million annual dollars in grapefruit revenues—not much more than what California takes in, but on 9 times more acreage. "Even though much of Florida's grapefuit gets turned to juice," unlike California's, "that doesn't stop the corporate farmers from dousing their groves unnecessarily with the same toxic arsenal of pesticides thought to be required to maintain a "cosmetic appeal" to consumers."—Kimbrell, pp. 178–79 ("Falling Far from the Tree: The Sterile World of Industrial Orchards").

The new standard of 20%-minimum fresh juice (specifically applying to chilled orange juice)—Chilled orange juice marketing order, p. 34.

Mr. Arlotto: "In the chilled juice business in California . . ."—Ibid., p. 150.

Events in Motor, Iowa, 2003—*New York Times*, p. A14, "National Report" (Monica Davey, "A Farmer Kills Another and Town Asks, How Did It Come to This?: 2 Men Had Known Each Other 30 Years").

"The average housewife little realizes . . ."—*California Cultivator*, vol. LXV, no. 21, November 21, 1925, p. 524 ("The Little Lemon").

"In the citrus industry the 'on tree' inventory . . ."—California Department of Agriculture (1941). J. W. Tapp, Vice President, Bank of America, San Francisco, "Financial Status of California Agriculture," p. 93.

Decreasing profitability of southern California citrus—USDA (1940), *Farm Size in California*, p. 7.

Footnote: "California has had an unusual opportunity to market lemons . . ."—*California Cultivator*, vol. LXXXIII, no. 15, July 18, 1936, p. 530, "Our Export Citrus Market."

Change in orange-box labels—McClelland and Last, p. 55.

Descriptions of orange-box labels in remainder of same paragraph—Ibid., pp. 57, 62–63.

The old lady who used to live in Riverside—Helen La Londe, interviewed in Coachella, July 2004. Shannon Mullen was present.

"Eleven large cans of [orange] juice . . ."—USDA Yearbook series (1950–1951), p. 263 (M. K. Veldhuis, "Chemistry and Technology of Citrus").

Footnote on the lemon market in 1950—*California Farmer*, vol. 193, no. 1 (July 1, 1950), p. 8 ("Good Valencia Prices Seen; Tariff Cut to Hurt Lemons").

Longer storage life of grapefruit juice—Ibid., p. 264.

"Use of citrus products must . . . be expanded . . ."—Ibid., p. 267.

The "basic idea" of Bert Cochran—California State Archives. Department of Food and Agriculture. Bureau of Marketing. Marketing-order files, Box 6. State of California, Department of Agriculture, Bureau of Markets hearing on proposed marketing order for lemon products as amended, pursuant to the provisions of Section 1300.13(b) of the California Marketing Act, Chapter 10, Division 6, of the Agricultural Code. Thursday, June 24, 1952, beginning 9:30 a.m., State Building, 217 West First Street, Los Angeles, California. P. 127.

Complex relationship between citrus packers, growers and harvesters—California State Archives. ALRB restricted files, 1978–1984. Case RRT. Court of Appeal folder, Part I. This case occurred in Ventura County.

Lemon production at the end of the twentieth century—*Encyclopedia of Food Science and Technology*, vol. 1, p. 420ff. (entry on the citrus industry).

The Sunkist Vitamin C campaign; vitamin C in oranges, tomatoes and broccoli—McClelland and Last, p. 40.

The illegal immigrant who expected to enter orange heaven when he got to Northside—Crosthwaite, Byrd and Byrd, p. 66 (Isaías Ignacio Vázquez Pimentel, "Ña' a ta' ani' mai").

Citrus-consumption statistics of 1987–88—*Encyclopedia of Food Science and Technology*, vol. 1, p. 420 (entry on the citrus industry), pp. 424, 434.

"Citrus wines have never achieved the high popularity of grape wines . . ."—Ibid., p. 433.

Brazil, Florida and the "canopy shaker"—*New York Times*, Monday, March 22, 2004 ("National" section), p. A17, cont'd from p. A1 (Eduardo Porter, "For U.S. Fruit Growers, Cheap Labor Is Machines").

"Only tiny lots of old orange or lemon trees . . ."—Wagner and Blackstock, p. 21.

The explanation of Lori A. Yates—*Los Angeles Times*, Thursday, September 23, 2004, California edition, "California" section, p. B2 (Regine Labossiere, "SURROUNDINGS: VICTORIA AVENUE: Riverside's Regal Route Bridges Past and Present: Completed in 1902 and sustained by volunteers, the roadway shows off the city's citrus heritage"). The article continues: "Although most of the citrus groves are gone, fans say the avenue still has a place in Riverside. Its current role is to link downtown Riverside and the remaining orange groves, they say."

Orange and lemon growing, picking and sorting practices as of time of writing—Riverside Municipal Museum, pp. 68–70 (Robert G. Platt, "Current Citrus Industry Practices").

Imperial citrus expectations, 1914—*Los Angeles Times*, January 18, 1914 ("SOUTHERN PACIFIC SELLS BIG TRACT").

Constituents of flavonoids—*Encyclopedia of Food Science and Technology*, vol. 1, p. 423.

Edith Karpen's memories—From an interview by WTV, Sacramento, January 2004. In 2006, Kay Brockman Bishop gave the same explanation for the decline of grapefruit: "The water table went off, and it rotted the roots. Where you're sitting right now, the water table is three feet." (Interviewed December 2006 on her ranch just west of Calexico. Terrie Petree was present.)

"Grapefruit was Emperor of Imperial!"—In 1917, Walter E. Packard offers us his *Agriculture in the Imperial Valley: A Manual for Settlers.* Citron adaptability is poor, he advises, so this fruit cannot be recommended; dates offer excellent adaptability, and in my day they still hold on in the Bard Subdistrict, while in that portion of the Imperial entity known as Coachella, they do much better than hold on; grapes, Packard continues, are a very good Imperial bet, which Wilber Clark is just then putting to the test out in Mobile; lemons are good, especially Eureka and Lisbon; limes are uncertain. Oranges mature earlier and are redder than back East; Packard especially admires the good old Washington navel that is doing so well up in Riverside; he also likes Valencias, and in my era, there will be quite a lot of those (in 2005 all 450 Imperial County acres of oranges will be Valencias); Thompsons are acceptable to him, although I can hardly remember tasting those in Imperial; now he comes to the pomelo (known to you and me as a grapefruit), which "on account of its earliness has a distinct advantage in California markets over fruit from other sections." He votes for the Marsh and seedless varieties. These seem to thrill him the most, more so even than oranges.—Remarks of Packard—Op. cit., pp. 31–32, 38–39.

In 1918, Judge Farr nearly concurs: "The grapefruit trees . . . are short-lived, although their product is superb. This is the only citrus fruit that thrives." F. W. Waite believes grapefruit "the best of the citrus fruits" even if "lemons do very well, growing a very juicy fruit and many varieties of oranges have been tried out; the seedlings produce the best quality of fruit." Accordingly, Sylvanus G. Haskell, "noteworthy among the active, prosperous ranchers of Imperial County," will now build a fancier residence and consecrate 5 of his 80 acres to grapefruit.—"The grapefruit trees . . . are short-lived . . ."—Farr, p. 71.—Opinion of F. W. Waite—Ibid., p. 193 (F. W. Waite, "Horticulture").—Doings of Sylvanus G. Haskell—Ibid., pp. 437–38.

Data in table, "ORANGE TREES IN IMPERIAL COUNTY, 1917–25"—1917: Farr, p. 192 (F. W. Waite). 1920: Imperial Valley Directory (1920). All other dates: Imperial County Agriculture Commission papers. Here follows a more detailed summary:

Citrus Trees in Imperial County

Year	*Grapefruit*	*Orange*
1910	? 0 cr	
1917	70,000 NB[a]	6,048 [lemons 1,491]
1918	?	
1919	?	
1920	44,000[b]	7,000 w/ MX
1921	4,260 + 41,675 NB	1,870 + 4,280 NB
1922	45,040 ad	2,083 ad
1923	? 1950 ac, 53 cr	?
1924	? 4,035 ac, 82 cr	?
1925	? 5,900 ac, 143 cr	?1,600 [lemons 350]
1926	? 5,542 ac	? 25 ac[c] [10 ac lemon, 30 ac tangerine]
1927	? 6,941 ac	? 13,020 ac [4,200 ac tang, 212 ac lem]
1928	? 135 cr	?
1929	? 329 cr	?
1930	? 599 cr	?
1931	? 839 cr	?
1932	? 829cr	?
1933	? 706 cr	?
1934	? 1,010 cr	?
1935	? 1,028 cr	? 26 cr [41 cr tang]
1936	? 1,525 cr	? 26 cr [37 cr tang]

1937	? 1,052 cr	? 132 cr [37 cr tang]
1938	? 1,145 cr	? 40 cr [55 cr tang]
1939	? 1,041 cr	? 74 cr [42 cr tang]
1940	? 1,192 cr	? 135 cr [48 cr tang]
1941	? 1,090 cr	? 135 cr [69 cr tang]
1942	? 1,069 cr	? 135 cr [43 cr tang]
1943	? 1,028 cr	? 105 cr [42 cr tang]
1944	? 3,225 ac;[d] 232 cr + 54 tcr	? 672 ac [252 ac tang + 62 ac lem]; 53 cr + 37 tcr [37 + 37 tang, 0 + 12 lem]
1945	259,487; 863 cr[e]	627,467; 38 cr[f] [38 cr tang, 9 cr lem]
	3,196 ac	667 ac [67 ac lemons]
1946	? 619 cr	? 101 cr [41 cr tang, 13 cr lem]
1947	? 904 cr	? 97 cr [37 cr tang, 6 cr lem]
1948	? 452 cr	? 75 cr [37 cr tang, 11 cr lem]
1949	? 180 cr, 1,154 jt	? 23 jcr [21 cr tang, 17 cr lem]
1950	? 381 cr, 147 jcr	? 140 jcr [44 cr tang, 14 cr lem]
1951	? 366 cr	? 98 cr [40 cr tang, 14 cr lem]
1952	? 210 cr	? 50 cr [26 cr tang, 19 cr lem]
1953	? 264 cr	? 71 cr [27 cr tang, 17 cr lem]
1954	?; 886 ac; 298 cr[g]	?; 341 ac; 42 cr [21 cr tang (190 ac), 4 cr lem (65 ac)]
1955	?; 886 ac; ? cr[h]	?; 341 ac [190 ac tang, 65 ac lem]
1956	?; 872 ac; 154 cr[i]	?; 345 ac; 43 cr [230 ac tang, 26 cr; 263 ac lem, 27 cr; 3 ac lemon seedlings; 1 ac nursery lemons]
1957	?; 1,017 ac; 175 cr[j]	?; 50 cr [226 ac tang, 33 cr; 290 ac lem; 29 cr]
1958	?	?
1959	? 825 ac; 123,777 bx	? 310 ac (Valencia); 34,687 bx [249 ac tang; 35,161 bx]
1960	? 759 ac; yielding 8.25 tons per acre: total = 6,262 tons	? 363 ac (Valencia), yielding 13.3 tons per acre [280 ac or, tang & other, @ 5.4 tons per acre; hence 1,512 tons

Abbreviations: ? = number of trees not reported; ac = acres planted; ad = admitted into Imperial County; bx = boxes; cr = [train]carloads sent out; jcr = juice, in carloads; jt = juice, in tons; NB = non-bearing; tcr = truck-carloads; w/MX = may include part of Mexicali Valley

[a]The figure for grapefruit trees is also given as 46,152.

[b]The Imperial County Agricultural Commission papers list no citrus this year.

[c]In this year the Chamber of Commerce switches from numbers of fruit trees to numbers of acres of fruit trees. I hereby assume that at this point in time, 1,600 orange trees = 25 acres; in other words, 1 acre = 64 orange trees.

[d]Here and in some subsequent years, crops are subdivided into March, August and October acres. For the sake of simplification I list March acres.

[e]By simple division, it would seem that it takes 101 grapefruit trees to fill 1 railroad car of fruit.

[f]By division, it would seem that it takes 16,512 orange trees to produce 1 railroad car of fruit, which would be very sad if true.

[g]We also find the figure of 143 acres mixed citrus, which I omit.

[h]Relevant "Fruit and Nuts" page missing from this copy of the report. Still 143 acres mixed citrus.

[i]108 acres mixed citrus.

[j]113 acres mixed citrus.

Sources: Imperial Valley Directory (1920); California Board of Equalization (1949); all other dates, Imperial County Agricultural Commission papers.

Certificates of merit for grapefruit and mandarin oranges, 1926—ICHSPM, document cat. #A2002.349.1. Another award at the same event, this one merely a certificate of merit, for King Mandarine Orange, to C. C. Conant, or G. G. Ganant.

Barbara Worth on grapefruit label—Wright, back page of commemorative pocket in rear pocket of cover.

"IMPERIAL VALLEY GRAPEFRUIT WILL GET COMPETITION"—*Imperial Valley Press*, Wednesday, April 14, 1926, p. 4.

Photo and text concerning Senators Shortridge and King—Ibid., Friday, May 7, 1926, p. 1.

Mrs. Adell Lingo's ranch—Tout, *The First Thirty Years*, p. 361.
Imperial County citrus statistics, 2005—Imperial County Agriculture Commission papers.
Imperial as the 7th-most-successful grapefruit producer of all counties—Imperial Valley Directory (1939), p. 12. Actually, 7th in production, 5th in value.
Nana Lee Beck—*Imperial County: The Big Picture*, p. 96.
Mr. J. E. Harshman—California State Archives. Department of Food and Agriculture. Bureau of Marketing. Marketing order files, Box 4. State of California, Department of Agriculture, Bureau of Markets hearing on proposed marketing order for California desert grapefruit, as amended. Thursday, May 12, 1955, 10:00 o'clock, a.m., Coachella Valley Water District Building, Coachella, California. Handwritten on upper righthand corner: 50A.9. Pp. 17, 26–27.
Mr. Jones—Ibid., pp. 65–66.
"Grapefruit, although the Valley's most important fruit crop . . ." and list of grapefruit's intolerances—Griffin and Young, p. 181.
Claude Finnell's memories—Based on an interview in his home in El Centro in April 2004. Mrs. Finnell and Shannon Mullen were also present. For corroboration of citrus's salt intolerance (and boron sensitivity), see Lower Colorado Region study, p. X-27, Table 9.
Footnote: State citrus report of 1938—California Board of Agriculture (1938), p. 686.
Grapefruits in the U.S. and Japan, 1998–2001, 2002–2003—*New York Times*, Monday, September 8, 2003, pp. A1, A20 (Abby Goodnough, "Can the Grapefruit Be Hip? Growers Bet on a Makeover").
Imperial Valley White Sheet: "FRESH CITRUS . . ."—Vol. 46, week 7, week of February 12–18, 2004; p. 9.

152. Caliche (1975–2005)

Epigraph: "O Earth with the mouth of a woman . . ."—Torre and Wiegers, p. 25 (María Baranda, "Epistle of the Shipwreck," 1999; trans. Mónica de la Torre).
Alice Woodside on caliche—Interview of January 2004, Sacramento. Edith Karpen was present.
Hetzel photo of Holtville girls' basketball team—ICHSPM, photo uncoded as of 2002.
Description of the old piece-of-eight—After Meyer et al., p. 170.
Hetzel's self-portrait—*Imperial County: The Big Picture*, p. 3.

153. Imperial Reprise (1754–2004)

Epigraph: "What have we achieved? . . ."—Howe and Hall, p. 180.

PART ELEVEN
POSTSCRIPTS

154. The Prohibited Ballads (1913–2005)

Epigraph—*Narcocorrido* "Entre Perico y Perico," sung at my request by the band Koely at the Thirteen Negro in Mexicali, September 2005. This was probably their own creation. They had a sheet of lyrics and lent it to Terrie Petree, who copied and later translated it for me.
"Relative to Wallace Wilson under arrest for having cocaine in his possession . . ."—N.A.R.A.L. Record Group 36. Records of the U.S. Customs Service. Calexico Customs Office. Incoming Official Correspondence (91–60). October 15, 1902–March 23, 1916. Box No. 3 of 5: November 1913 to July 1914. Folder: "Nov. 15, 1913–Feb. 11, 1914." Letter to the Deputy Collector of Customs, Calexico, Cal., from F. B. Cretcher? [illegible], Special Deputy Collector, Office of the Collector, Treasury Department, U.S. Customs Service, Port of Los Angeles, Cal. November 17, 1913.
Sacramento drug defendants and their verdicts—Seen by me in November 2002.
The tale of Miguel Palominos—*Sacramento Bee*, Saturday, November 15, 2003, "Metro" section, pp. B1, B4 (Denny Walsh, "15-year penalty asked in pot trial: The defense asks: Why throw the book at a suspect plucked from Mexico to tend the crop?").
Remarks of Lupe Vásquez—Interviews at the Thirteen Negro in Mexicali and in the Hotel Villa Sur in Calexico, 2003.
Fate of Anna Francis Warner—*Imperial Valley Press*, vol. 102, no. 246, Monday, March 24, 2003, p. A6 (Staff report, "Woman fails in attempt to smuggle drugs into prison").
Excerpts from "The Queen of the South"—A *narcocorrido* by the Tigres del Norte, lyrics translated from the album "Puros Corridos, serie 21," track 1 ("La Reyna del Sur"), by Terrie Petree, 2005. Here and in other *corridos* I have repunctuated Terrie's draft for emphasis.

Footnote about Jesús Malaverde—After Griffith, pp. 66–75.

"He dreamed in his delirium . . ."—Saul Viera ("El Gavilancillo"), "Rodrigo Lopez," translated from the Internet by Terrie Petree.

Interviews with Angélica, Juan Carlos Martínez Caro, Cookies, Emily, Érica, Francisco Cedeño, Alfonso Rodríguez Ibarra, María, Patricia, Carlos Pérez, Javier Armando Gómez Reyes (who makes another appearance in my book *Poor People*)—Late August and early September 2005; all in Mexicali; all as interpreted by Terrie Petree. The *corridos* composed and sung by Francisco Cedeño and the snatches of *corridos* sung by Angélica, Cookies, Érica and María were all recorded, transcribed and translated by Terrie Petree, 31 August to 3 September 2005.

Emigration of meth labs from the Central Valley—*Sacramento Bee*, Friday, October 15, 2004, "Metro" sectio, p. B1 (Christina Jewett, "Meth makers find new places to cook: Once focused in the Valley, labs crop up in the north and south in face of law enforcement pressure").

Excerpts from "Jefe de Jefes"—From the same Tigres del Norte album (track 7), translated by Terrie Petree.

"NOTICE IS HEREBY GIVEN that Nine Thousand Six Hundred ($9,600.00) Dollars . . ."—*Calexico Chronicle*, Friday, June 13, 2003, "Public Notice" section, p. 9.

Excerpts from "Pakas de a Kilo"—From the same Tigres del Norte album (track 13), translated by Terrie Petree.

Excerpts from "Cruz de Marijuana"—Translated from the Internet by Terrie Petree.

Excerpts from "Catarino y los Rurales"—A *narcocorrido* by Valentín Elizalde, lyrics translated from the album "Los Mejores Narco Corridos," track 22, by Terrie Petree, 2005.

155. *The* Maquiladoras *(2004)*

Epigraph: "Are *maquiladoras* good or bad . . ."—Interview with Señora Candelaria Hernández López and her daughter Alicia Hernández Hernández; on a park bench in Ejido Chilpancingo, Tijuana, 14 July 2004. Terrie Petree translated.

Epigraph: "In our country . . ."—First interview with Señor A. (see below). Terrie Petree translated.

Interview with the Cucapah woman—On the Cucapah reservation south of Mexicali, January 2003. Terrie Petree was not present since she only started working for me later that year. My interpreter was the great Lupe Vásquez. The woman did not give her name.

Ruiz: "A healthy and prosperous American economy will not forever endure . . ."—Op. cit., p. 233.

Ruiz's mention of the *maquiladora* in Ciudad Juárez which compelled its female employees to bring in bloody tampons the first three months—Op. cit., p. 77.

Emerson: "Could not a nation of friends . . ."—Op. cit., p. 570 ("Politics").

Interview with Mr. W.—He would not have wanted to be in a book, so I consider his identity to be restricted. It will be placed on file at the California State Archives. See the "NOTE ON RESTRICTED FILES &C" at the beginning of the bibliography. This interview was actually a series of phone conversations which took place on 25, 28 and 29 June 2004.

. . . Female *maquiladora* workers as *maquilarañas*—Information courtesy of the Tijuana private detective Señor A., who will be cited below. This term was current at the beginning of the 1990s, he said.

Interview with Mr. D.—His real name, too, will be on file at the California State Archives. This interview was also a conflation of phone conversations; they occurred on 25 and 28 June and 28 July 2004.

Mr. D.'s report—Private investigator's report, "Re: Tijuana Maquiladoras. Our File No.: 04-7659B." 7 pp. and e-mail cover sheet to Terrie Petree; both cover sheet and report dated 7 July 2004. "ATTORNEY WORK PRODUCT. This is a confidential communication . . . subject to the attorney/client and work product privileges." A copy of this report will be placed on file at the California State Archives, linked to Mr. D.

Companies in the state of Baja California that have been found to produce contaminants—Secretaria de Medio Ambiente website. "Respuesta a solicitud con folio 0001600045304 SECRETARIA DE MEDIO AMBIENTE RECURSOS NATURALES . . . OPERACIONES CLASE MUNDIAL, S.A. de C.V.-**OPTICA SOLA** DE MEXICO S DE R.L DE C.V PL. 1 **OPTICA SOLA** DE MÉXICO, S DE RL D E C.V. PLANTA 2) **OPTICA SOLA** DE MEXICO, S. DE R.L. DE C.V. (PTA. III . . .)."

"Willing to make 'informal' comments regarding our subject companies . . ."—Mr. Raskin's report, p. 4.

Remarks of Jaime Cota—Ibid., pp. 6–7.

"Chemicals affecting our sexuality and reproduction"—*Boletín Maquilero #11*, p. 9 (article by Toña, CITTAC, Colectiva Feminista). In another undated issue of the same publication (e-mail address: cittac@prodigy.net.mx), we read in pp. 18–19 (by Jaime [Cota?], Cittac, June 2003): *Entre los cambios más notorios esgtán que la fabricacíon de moldes metálicos que se hacían en Petaluma se vienen par Óptica Sola III, así miamo se rebucia la fabricación de Gaskets a Sola III . . . Quere obligar a los y trabajadoras de Sola a cambiarse de Otay a Insurgentes es ilegal, pues cuando una entra a trabajar y firma su contrato . . .* And again: *Por cierto esta miasma empresa Sola es conocida por la cantidad de sustancias quinicas de se utilizan sin la protección necesaria.*

Interview with the old man in the cowboy hat in Colonia Azteca, Tijuana—14 July 2004. Terrie Petree translated.

Interview with the Óptica Sola girls—About 14 July; interviewed in front of OS Otay at lunch. Terrie Petree translated.

The "local reporter" who said that the Tijuana minimum daily wage "can't sustain life"—Augustín Pérez Aguilar, reporter for *La Frontera* (Tijuana). Interviewed in English in a restaurant in Tijuana Centro, 9 July 2004. Terrie Petree was present..

A dapper reporter with a Tijuana paper—Again, this was Augustín Pérez Aguilar, and it was the same interview. From here on, the text will refer to him as "the dapper reporter."

Interview with a labor union's legal assessor—He was Sergio Rivera Gómez, Assessor legal de local CROC la Mexicali federación, interviewed 12 July 2004 in his office in the Chinesca. Terrie Petree translated.

The trip to Ejido Tabasco occurred in June 2003. The 8" x 10" portrait of Elvira and Marco has been coded MX-EJ-MAQ-03-01. The photographs of the barracks, taken a few moments earlier, are 35 mm and have not yet been catalogued. Yolanda Sánchez Ogás and Terrie Petree were both present; Terrie translated Elvira and Marco's interview.

Pedregal *colonia* interviews—10 July 2004. Terrie Petree translated. We stopped people in the streets in this new housing development southeast of Mexicali, having good luck since it was Sunday afternoon. The people I had photographed previously in Pedegral did not seem keen on being interviewed or giving their names, so for the interviews cited here I left both camera and notebook in the car. The name of the man with the black cough was Pedro; he did not give his last name.

Interview with Benjamín Prieto—14 July 2004, in park of Barrio Chilpancingo. Terrie Petree interpreted.

Summation of the NAFTA report, 11 February 2004: The level of lead contaminants found on the site . . .—From Terrie Petree's translation of "INFORME JOSÉ KAHN," furnished by the Tijuana private detective Señor A. (see below). This was a supplement to his final report (again, see below), and was e-mailed to Terrie in late July.

Interview with the two Rimsa decontamination workers at Metales y Derivados—14 July 2004, on site. Terrie Petree translated.

The old Serbian woman who shouted at me: "You Americans have no souls!"—Vollmann, vol. 5, pp. 496–97 ("The Avengers of Kosovo").

Interview with Marí (short for María)—10 July 2004, in Pancho's bar, Mexicali; photographed afterwards outside the bar. No last name. Terrie Petree translated.

Footnote: Mexicali yellow pages—Edition of 2002–2003.

Interview with Lázaro (who refused to be photographed or give his last name)—8 July 2004, outside the family shack in Colonia Villa Cruz, TJ. We caught him off guard in the street; otherwise he never would have agreed. Interview conducted in English. Terrie Petree was present, as was Lázaro's uncle. When we went back a week later, only the uncle was present, and he, obviously uneasy, refused to tell us when Lázaro would be back.

Footnote: "Óptica Sola Labor Demand"—35-pp. CITTA labor claim involving Óptica Sola, obtained from Jaime Cota by my hired P.I. Mr. Raskin. Document begins: "Entraron a trabajar OPTICA SOLA DE MEXICO, S. DE R. L. DE C. V. Ubicada en Calle 7 Sur #1 111, Cd. Industrial Nueva Tijuana, con fecha 25 de octubre 1989, la suscrita de nombre ANTONIA ARIAS ESTRADA . . ." and five other individuals. Four out of the six are women. Dates in this first paragraph range from 1989 to 1996. Text translated for WTV by Teresa McFarland. An electronic facsimile of this document will be placed in my archive at Ohio State University.

Interviews with José López—Conducted in various parks, bars and border-gazing sites of Mexicali, on 2, 3 and 12 July 2004, in English. Shannon Mullen was present for the first two, and Terrie Petree for the final interview.

Interview with the "haggard, chunky, blonde and anxious" woman in Pancho's bar, Mexicali—3 July 2004; José López translating. Shannon Mullen was present. The woman refused to give her name.

Marx on alienated labor—Op. cit., pp. 370, 368 (selections from the Grundrisse, 1857–58).

Mr. Raskin's report on the "Subsecretario de Protección al Ambiente"—Op. cit., p. 5.

Interviews with Señor A.—9, 13 and 16 July 2004, in his office in Tijuana. Terrie Petree translated. His operative Perla A. (no relation to Señor A, and anyhow, when I tipped her, she signed the receipt with a different name) was present. His real name, which changed in the course of our acquaintanceship, will also be on file at the California State Archives.

Señor A.'s report—6-p. typescript on yellow paper; first page on letterhead with a postal address; last page signed by the two assigned detectives, Perla A. and a man with a name so anonymous I don't believe that its publication will compromise him: Enrique Hernández. A copy of this report will be placed on file at the California State Archives, linked to Señor A.

Button-camera footage of *maquiladoras* made by WTV and by the Tijuana private detective "Perla"—CD-ROMs and one DVD will be placed on file at the California State Archives, access restricted to protect the *maquiladoras* against any inadvertent privacy infringement or trade-secret exposure. For a detailed catalogue, see the bibliography, category B, item "*maquiladora* videos."

Señor A.'s video—If *Playboy*'s fact-checkers return it to me, I will place it on file with the California State Archives.

"In my follow-up interview with Cota . . ."—Raskin report, p. 7 (already quoted).

Señor A.'s interview with the 21–year-old victim of sexual pressure at Matsushita—From Terrie Petree's translation of "INDICIO DE DATOS DE ENTREVISTA," furnished by Señor A. together with "INFORME JOSÉ KAHN" (see above). As noted, this was a supplement to his final report, and was e-mailed to Terrie in late July. The name of the woman will be placed on file at the California State Archives in my "List of Restricted Names."

I am told, but have not verified, that in 1993 or 1994, the head of the federal Procuraduria de los Derechos Humanos investigated sexual harassment at Matsushita.—Information from Raskin report, p. 7. The informant was Jaime Cota, who said that the head of the Procuraduria was Perez Cansola.

"Recalled taking complaints from female employees . . ."—Loc. cit.

"Categorized most labor disputes as related to 'unfair termination, low wages'. . ."—Loc. cit.

The 1995 legal settlement between Matsushita and a former employee—Attachment #12 to Mr. Raskin's report. Facsimile of document gathered by him, labeled: "Document from sexual harassment claim handled by Cota (CITTA) in 1995 against Matsushita. Cota believed this was the only claim he handled against Matsushita that specifically involved allegations of sexual harassment. The documents are legal size."

Excerpts from Human Rights Watch report—Human Rights Watch Publications, August 1996, vol. 8, no. 6 (B), *Mexico: No Guarantees: Sex Discrimination in Mexico's Maquiladora Sector,* pp. 3–4, 13–15. Related Matsushita material appears on pp. 15 and 55 of this report.

"She watched a manager at Matsushita caress the buttocks . . ."—*Los Angeles Times,* 27 January 1998, home edition, p. A1 (Anne-Marie O'Connor, "Maquiladora Women Finding Freedom [in?] Tijuana . . ."); Factiva Dow Jones, document #latm000020010917dulr006fc.

"In Tijuana, the top producers of highest-risk waste . . ."—*The San Diego Union-Tribune,* May 3, 2002, p. C1 (Diane Lindquist, "Toxic waste risks serious, study finds"); Proquist, document #11781909.

Figures on Metales y Derivados: six thousand metric tons of illegally abandoned lead slag + varying numbers of furnaces and crucibles—Metales y Derivados Final Faculty Record (SEM-98-007) Prepared in Accordance with Article 15 of the North American Agreement on Environmental Cooperation, pp. 13, 22–23. Downloaded from Commission for Environmental Cooperation website.

Interview with Magdalena Ayala Márquez—3 July 2004; in a restaurant in Mexicali. Photographed with her daughter. José López translated; Shannon Mullen was present. For the sense of immediacy, I have sometimes altered "they" to "we" and "she" to "I" when I am certain that José was lapsing into third person instead of translating directly.

Disclaimer of tales of bloody-tampon tests and restricted restroom access—Pretty much every *maquiladora* worker I interviewed denied these. Among the deniers (interviews here cited in their appropriate places): Magdalena Ayala Márquez, Marí and the "haggard, chunky, blonde and anxious" woman, both interviewed at Pancho's bar, Mexicali; Lázaro.

Interview with Señora Candelaria Hernández López and her daughter Alicia Hernández Hernández—14 July 2004, in park of Barrio Chilpancingo. Terrie Petree translated.

Interview with Germán—13 July 2004, in the office of the private detective Señor R. in Tijuana. Señor R. was present, and likewise Terrie Petree, who interpreted. As stated in the interview, Germán preferred not to have his last name be published. He also declined to have his photograph taken. Señor R. later forwarded a digital photo of him, which I will place in the California State Archives along with the file of restricted names.

Interview with Salvador Santa Cruz—8 July 2004, conducted in English, outside a relative's little grocery store in Colonia Villa Cruz, which lies in the hills overlooking the *maquiladoras* on Boulevard Insurgentes. Salvador worked in one of those *maquiladoras* (Kimstar Plastics) and lived in this *colonia.* Terrie Petree was present. A second interview occurred a few days later in front of the Philips *maquiladora,* which stands almost adjacent to Kimstar. I have conflated the two interviews.

Firemen denied entrance at Óptica Solare (probably Óptica Sola)—*El Sol de Tijuana,* sábado 18 de marzo de 2006, p. 1 (Manuel Cordero, "Se derrama químico imflamable: Empleados de la empresada 'Óptica Solare' fureron deslojados y se detuvo al encargado de seguirdad por impedir el eccesso al personal del Cuerpo de Bomberos"). Translated for WTV by Teresa McFarland.

Transcript of cassette of complaint call: Private detective (probably Perla) and Thomson officials—Translated on the fly by Terrie Petree. The cassette will be deposited in the California State Archives.

Interview with Lourdes—In Industrial Park La Jolla, Tijuana inside the car, 16 July 2004. Terrie Petree translated; the PI Perla A. was present. Lourdes bravely went inside her place of work to give us concealed video, but the button camera failed. She did not want her photo or her full name published. The latter, along with a photocopy of her medical record, is on file at the California State Archives.

Statement of Amelia Simpson, Environmental Health Coalition—Phone conversations, early August 2004.

Interview with the old woman on Avenida México in Tecate—Interviewed in 2003. Terrie Petree interpreted. Her name was Josefina Cruz Bermudez, and she was one of the two ladies in the 8" x 10" negative MX-TC-WOM-03–01.

Television-manufacture statistic for 2003—MOCA San Diego, unnumbered p. just before section "This is Tijuana."

Sergio Rivera Gómez—Interviewed in CROC office, Mexicali, on 12 July 2004. Terrie Petree interpreted.

Figures on *maquiladora* jobs, 1994–2004—Bigelow, p. 77.

José López on the *maquiladoras*—Interviewed in Niños Héroes Park, Mexicali, on 12 July 2004. Terrie Petree was present.

Article: "Very low wages and strong math skills . . ."—*New York Times*, Thursday, September 30, 2004, "World Business" section, p. W1 (Keith Bradsher, "Outsourcing Finds Vietnam: Loyalty [and Cheap Labor]").

Song: "In the gloom of mighty cities . . ."—*I. W. W. Songs*, p. 57 (full attribution in text).

Footnote: The UABC article—Ueinternational website, Gemma López Límon, senior researcher at the Instituto de Investigaciones Sociales of the Autonomous University of Baja California, "Mexico's Deplorable Runaway Maquiladoras: Another Example: 'Flor de Baja' " (October? 2004). The alleged words of Nahum Rodriguez Lara also come from this source, which calls Luis Alfonso Caballero Camou "the spokesperson for this fraud . . . also the manager of the firm."

Footnote: "A posting by the Centro de Información para Trabajadoras y Trabajadors"—CITT website. Text begins: "Again, a factory runs away without paying workers their severance benefits! Again, Baja California Labor Board colludes with the company and violate [*sic*] Mexican the Labor Code! . . . The owner ran away to the US[,] abandoning more than 100 workers, without paying salaries and the severance benefits required by Mexican labor law." Information on the protest in front of the Governor's office also comes from this source.

Production of the biggest taco in the world and date of closure—Ueinternational website (Límon).

Brown International Corporation mentioned as responding to an EPA subpoena against Flor de Baja—Factiva, *Pesticide and Toxic Chemical News* (CRC Press), 7 December 1994, vol. 23, no. 6 ("Some Firms Object, Others Claim Error in New River Subpoenas"). Document #penw000020011029dqc70019v.

Footnote: "A total of 19 gravely poisoned women was the result . . ."—*El Mexicano* newspaper, 7 October 1993, David Loyola, "19 Mujeres Intoxicadas en Mexicali: Hipoclorito de Calcio, la Causa," trans. for WTV by Teresa McFarland.

156. Subdelineations: Waterscapes (1975–2005)

Epigraph: "Thriving young towns . . ."—Tout, *The First Thirty Years*, p. 410 (Robert Hays, "The Next Thirty Years").

The secret teaching of Mr. Leonard Coates—*Fresno Morning Republican*, Sunday, March 28, 1920, p. 18B ("Cultivate Now").

Imperial County yields of honeydews and miscellaneous melons, 1999–2002—Imperial County Agricultural Commission papers for those years.

"More than fifteen hundred persons have been arrested . . ."—Social Responsibilities Round Table website.

Richard Brogan: "Field crops are cheap to grow . . ."—Interviewed in Calexico, April 2004.

"In fact, earlier this year the Metropolitan Water District of Southern California . . ."—Association of California Water Agencies, p. 13.

"Imperial attitude"—Already quoted above, in the chapter "Then and Now" ("Imperial attitude: Desert farmers are their own worst enemies," in the *Sacramento Bee*, Sunday, June 2, 2002, "Op-ed" section).

Kay Brockman Bishop—Interviewed December 2006 on her ranch just west of Calexico. Terrie Petree was present.

Decision against IID, 1984—DeBuys and Myers, p. 170.

Description of Tlaloc—After Carrasco and Moctezuma, p. 65 (photo of a polychromed ceramic vessel).

"Our life's blood, our water, was being hemorrhaged away . . ."—Billie Bernal, pp. 120–21.

Absentee ownership in the IV, mid-1990s—DeBuys and Myers, p. 165.

Tale of the Bass brothers—Ibid., pp. 165–67.

Richard Brogan—Interviewed in Calexico, April 2004.

"If the city did wrong in buying, they did wrong in selling."—Nadeau, p. 76.

"The company was not planning to farm, but to sell water."—Hendricks, unnumbered p. 8.

"Agriculture: Once thought to be an essential means . . ."—*Imperial Valley Press*, Wednesday, March 19, 2003, "Voice of the People" column, p. A4: "IID director defines water terminology" (Andy Horne, IID director, El Centro).

Situation of the Borrego Springs aquifer—*Borrego Sun*, vol. 52, no. 12, June 5, 2003, p. 6 (Editorial: "Supervisors need to act on aquifer"). In no. 21 (October 9, 2003), a new headline reported a record rate of decrease in the water levels of northern Borrego, "closest to the agricultural zone." One well declined six feet in one year (p. 4, "Northern well levels decline at record rate").

Dropping water levels in Cabazon—*Press-Enterprise*, Friday, January 14, 2003, pp. A1, A8 (Steve Moore, "Bottler denies blame for drop in well levels").

The seasoned private detective from San Diego: "All the incestuous, evil little politics going on . . ."—George Michael Newman, Tactical Investigative Services. I interviewed him by telephone in 2003.

NACRP: "No more public money be invested . . ."—UC Berkeley, Bancroft Library. Paul S. Taylor papers. Carton 5. Folder 5:2: "To Make the Desert Bloom Like the Rose, 1969?" Yellow typescript on "The American West" letterhead, entitled "Issue: Colorado Book." P. 53.

The newspaper up in the state capital's "water-wise tips" and quote from Angela Anderson—*Sacramento Bee*, Saturday, July 5, 2003, "California Life Home & Garden" section, pp. 13, 15 (Dan Vierra, "Drips and Drops: The smart way to water your lawn and garden").

Marcuse: "The individual comes to the traumatic realization that full and painless gratification of his needs is impossible . . ."—Op. cit., p. 13.

The San Diego County Water Authority's sale of nearly 600,000 acre-feet of water per year to 32 agencies—San Diego County Water Authority, p. 42 (actual figure: 589,062 acre-feet in 2000).

Water cutbacks in Los Angeles and Marin—Ibid., p. 27 (unnumbered table: "Reductions in Water Usage for the Month of May 1991").

No water cutbacks in Imperial and Coachella valleys and Palo Verde Irrigation District—Ibid., p. 17.

80% of California's share of Colorado River water to Imperial and related districts—*The California Water Atlas*, p. 42.

All-American delivery figures to Imperial and Coachella valleys—Munguía, p. 23 (Francisco Zamora Arroyo, Peter Culp and Osvel Hinojosa Huerta). But another essay in the same book [p. 59, Barrientos et al.] gives a figure of only 2.59 MAFY.

Richard Brogan on MWD—Interviewed in Calexico, April 2004.

Phil Swing: "It would constitute the economic murder of any community . . .—Senate Committee on the Colorado River Basin (1925), p. 191 (Swing's statement).

"One academic's" cost comparison between water transfer and an earthquake—*Imperial Valley Press*, Thursday, March 27, 2003, "Farm" section, p. D4 (Juan Guerrero and Karl McArthur, "Economic Theory and Fallowing," part 1 of 4). The academic was Keith Mayberry.

San Diego: "The urban agencies . . ."—San Diego County Water Authority, p. 53.

"Surely one of Coachella Valley's defining images . . ."—Laflin, *A Century of Change*, page after chapter header "1900–1999."

Assertion of American sovereignty over All-American Canal seepage—Munguía, p. vi.

The laudatory biography of Mulholland: "In spite of rationing . . ."—William Leslie Davis, p. 271.

L.A.'s request for New River water, and the federal government's attack on IID about the lack of return flow from the New River et al.—IID objection to Part 417 determination.

American Imperial's cry to "My Fellow Farmers Throughout California"—IID letter to farmers, 9 July 2003, pp. 4, 1.

"Fertile Lands Surrounded by the Desert . . ."—Mexicali yellow pages (2001–2002), p. 10 ("Guía Turística/Tourist Guide").

Television announcement of water suspension to *colonias*—Seen in Tijuana, July 2004. No one seemed bothered or surprised; it was an everyday occurrence.

The agronomist in Tijuana: "At this moment, we are not in a water crisis . . ."—Terrie Petree's translation of Via Oriente, unnumbered p. 13 (interview by Terrie Petree with Javier Melendrez, agronomist, Department of Agriculture, Tijuana, 8/1/2005).

Mexican lawsuit over lining of All-American Canal, and the latter's probable and possible effects—Munguía, pp. viii, 78 (Saillé et al.), xx (intro.), 62–63, 68 (Barrientos et al.), 96 (Saillé et al.). Much of the seepage presently goes to refresh the Mexicali Valley's aquifer.

Interviews: Richard Brogan, by telephone, September 2003; Stella Mendoza, October 2003; George Michael Newman, by telephone, 2003.

The hairdresser Evalía Pérez de Navarro—Interviewed in her establishment in San Luis Río Colorado, October 2003, Terrie Petree translating. She was cutting my hair at the time, and she and I got so interested that she kept right on cutting until I was practically bald.

Salinity of All-American Canal seepage, *ca.* 2000—Munguía, p. 75 (Jaime Herrera Barrientos et al.). This figure was expressed in grams per liter, but the two measurements are nearly equivalent.

Calculated salinity of Mexicali Valley aquifer 20 years after lining of All-American Canal—Ibid., p. 91 (Saillé et al.). The actual figure given is 2,445 mg/L.

Specific crop production declines—Ibid., pp. 94–95 (loc. cit.). According to USDA Handbook no. 60, alfalfa and onions are tolerant when it comes to boron, and cotton semitolerant; barley and cotton are salt-resistant, onions and alfalfa only middlingly so.

Lesser irrigation efficiency of Mexicali Valley—Salinity of All-American Canal seepage, *ca.* 2000—Ibid., p. 46 (Jaime Herrera Barrientos et al.).

Kay Brockman Bishop—Same interview cited earlier in this chapter.

Paper by Eduardo Paredes Arellano: "The greatest danger threatening the future of our civilization . . ."—Whitehead et al., 1988, pp. 305 (Eduardo Paredes Arellano, Secretaría de Agricultura y Recursos Hidráulicos, Mexicali, "Water, the Most Important Natural Resource for the State of Baja California, Mexico").

Water inflow to Mexicali Valley, 1979–81 (8,830 million cubic meters of water)—Ibid., p. 308.

Ten more waterworks proposed—Ibid., p. 309.

"It should be pointed out that along the international boundaries . . ."—Ibid., p. 310.

"Recuperation" of Irrigation District 014—Ibid., p. 311.

"It is pertinent to point out that all of the privately owned wells"—Ibid., p. 312.

"How much do you pay for water?" I asked Josefina Cruz Bermúdez, whose shack sprawled right across the dirt road from the border wall in Tecate.

"It depends. Around a hundred, sometimes a hundred twenty to a hundred fifty pesos per month."

"Where does it come from?"

"I don't know where it comes from," replied the old woman. "I have lived here for fourteen years. For a little while we have plenty of water. But sometimes when they're cleaning the cisterns they warn us on the radio: This neighborhood won't have water for a couple of days. Right now it's Friday and the water went off on Monday."

In the same city, an ancient ex–citrus picker who sat on a green bench in the park every day, *waiting to die* as he put it, told me that he paid about the same: "Normally fourteen or fifteen dollars or two hundred pesos a month. I've lived here thirty-five years, and when Álvarez was President of the Republic he robbed and stole. All the Presidents steal a lot . . ."

"Where does it come from?"

"Now, the water comes from . . ." He thought, then triumphantly cried out: "*Arizona!* I think from the Río Colorado. Yes, that's right. All the Presidents have taken the money and taken it to the other governments . . ."

In Tijuana, a vast lady in Colonia Agrarista in the dry hills overlooking Boulevard Insurgentes got her water bill for the month as I watched; it was a hundred and fifteen pesos for her shack and her mother's shack combined, for washing and everything.—"Not expensive," she said.

That was how much they all paid for household use, between a hundred and two hundred pesos. It took me awhile to realize that of course that wasn't their drinking water; who'd want to drink that water? In Mexicali, the parking lot attendant Lupita said that she paid *poquito* for her water in the house: a hundred pesos. But for drinking water she paid five dollars more (fifty pesos), and a hundred and fifty pesos for when she got thirsty in the street. In the same city, Sergio Rivera Gómez, who was a legal assistant for the Confederación Revolucionaria de Obreros y Campesinos, thought that the average monthly water bill in Mexicali was between five and fifteen dollars *for washing hands and showering,* as he put it. Ninety-nine percent of the people drank bottled water, he thought; the very poor didn't. If he himself drank tap water only once or twice he'd probably be all right; more than that, and he'd get sick.

In San Luis Río Colorado, a juice vendor paid about a hundred and twenty pesos per month for his water. When asked, he proudly informed me that it came from a *presa,* a reservoir. Down the street, a hairdresser paid thirty dollars for her water.

Household and agricultural water prices, Tecate, Mexicali, Ciudad Morelos, San Luis Río Colorado—Interviews by WTV, October 2003, Terrie Petree translating. The hairdresser in the latter town was Evalía Pérez de Navarro.

Household water prices in Tijuana—Interviews by WTV, July 2004, Terrie Petree translating.

E. J. Swayne, 1901—Already quoted and cited in "Then and Now," above.

Carl Calvert on artesian wells, etc.—Interviewed in Campo, October 2003.

The farther west of San Luis they lived (and of course the farther south of the line), the more likely Mexicans were to be sanguine about the water situation. Señora Socorro Ramírez, proprietress of the restaurant Yocojihua, expressed a fairly typical view (interview of 19 February 2004, Terrie Petree interpreting). Señora Ramírez folded her arms and said: "In Mexicali the water comes from the Colorado River and they have a certain quantity from the United States and another quantity which goes to the valley for the farmers. Sometimes we hear that there's a lack, but if it rains a lot up north on the other side then we get extra, too. But they always harvest."—She spread her hands; she wasn't worried.—"The people who have water problems are those who live near the coast. There are always two harvests a year, and sometimes there could be three. It's more salty now," she agreed. But even now it's not as salty now as it once was. Fifty years from now, it will be all right."

157. *As Precious as This (2003)*

Epigraph: "And behold the people . . ."—León-Portilla and Shorris, p. 213 ("Hymn to Tlaloc").
"MWD will pay higher prices for short-term water transfers . . ."—IID letter to farmers, 9 July 2003, p. 4.
Geoglyph of the four-headed snake near Pilot Knob—Von Werlhof, p. 15.
Richard Brogan: "The sad part of it . . ." Interviewed in Calexico, April 2004.
Comparative efficiencies of IID, CVWD and MWD—IID objection to Part 417 determination, p. 19.
Footnote on the amount of water used to irrigate southern California's urban landscapes—IID *de novo* Part 417 brief, p. 74.
MWD spends too much time on flush toilets and not enough time on golf courses.—Based on the argument in the IID *de novo* Part 417 brief, pp. 75–76.
The restaurant Crustacean: "When you enter, you are drawn to another world . . ."—*The Connoisseur's Guide: Los Angeles: The Annual Edition 2002–2003*, p. 88.
IID water use, 1936–2002—Walsh to Platoni e-mail, 2–p. tabular attachment.
Do you want to know how precious water is? In 2002, the California-America Water Company, which I learn from my newspaper (I wouldn't have known otherwise) is the largest private water utility in my state, buys Citizens' Water Resources, which once brought water to the 165,000 people in Sacramento's suburbs. *He sold out at a fancy price.* Coincidentally, California-America Water is a subsidiary of American Water Works Company, Inc., which happens to be the largest private water utility in the United States. "Moisture Means Millions." In 2003, American Water Works gets purchased by Thames Water, an English corporation. *And in material advantages they are already well supplied.* I see that Thames Water is in the process of being acquired by RWE Aktiengesellschaft in Germany; and RWE is the third-largest water company in the entire world. *We need have no fear that our lands will not become better and better as the years go by.* Meanwhile, the ratepayers in Sacramento County get the word that water will now cost them up to 55% more. *I have never been cheated out of a dollar in my life.* Could it be that this is happening everywhere?
The corporate buy-ups of Sacramento's water described in the above paragraph—*Sacramento Bee*, Sunday, October 26, 2003, "Metro" section, p. B1 (Stuart Leavenworth, "Water hike raises queries: Cal-Am says it needs funds for security measures, but some wonder if its purchase by a multinational firm is a factor").

158. *One Acre-Foot (1903–2003)*

Epigraph: "Those politicians . . ."—Lupe Vasquez, private conversation, 2002.
Acre-foot usage defined, 1975—*The California Water Atlas*, glossary, p. vi.
Acre-foot usage defined, 2003—San Diego County Water Authority, p. 2. Here each household consists of 4 people, not 5.
San Diego, 1950: Per capita average water use: 80 gal./day.—San Diego City Directory (1950), p. 12.
San Diego, 2000: "An average person uses 125 gallons per day, or one-eighth of an acre-foot per year." 125 x 365 = 4,5625 gal./yr.—San Diego County Water Authority, p. 2.
Mexicali Valley's acreage and water allotment relative to Imperial Valley—DeBuys and Myers, p. 144.
Mexicali water usage, 2000—Munguía, p. 165 (Ruíz).
Tijuana water usage, mid-1980s—Petree translation of Vía Oriente, pp. 2–3.
Baja California water availability in cubic meters per capita per year—Whitehead et al., 1988 (articles written 1985), p. 306 (Eduardo Paredes Arellano, Secretaría de Agricultura y Recursos Hidráulicos, Mexicali, "Water, the Most Important Natural Resource for the State of Baja California, Mexico"). The figures are:

1920	25.2
1930	21.7
1940	18.3
1950	14.0
1960	10.3
1970	8.7
1980	5.0
1984	4.5

Average per capita water consumption in Mexico border communities and Albuquerque—Crosthwaite, Byrd and Byrd, p. 227 ("U.S.–Mexico Border Environment by the Numbers"). Exact date of statistics not stated, but book was published in 2003.

1998 water prices, Imperial Valley and San Diego—Ibid., pp. 170, 167.

Water requirements of one Imperial Valley acre of alfalfa—DeBuys and Myers, p. 233.

Imperial Valley alfalfa yields and prices, 1998—Imperial County Agricultural Commissioner's report, 1998, p. 5.

Footnote on alfalfa—Paul Foster reports (2007) ("Imperial Color Commentary").

Richard Brogan—Interviewed in Calexico, April 2004.

159. *Operation Gatekeeper (1994)*

Epigraph: "'Criminals' is what they are . . ."—*Imperial Valley Press*, Sunday, October 12, 2003 (on this page, mistakenly dated 2002), "Opinion" section, p. A4 ("Voice of the People" column: "The fact is, illegal immigrants are criminals").

Ruben Salazar: "A chain link fence is all that separates the two nations . . ."—Op. cit., p. 57 ("No Troops Line Border That Has Become Big Business: Changes Loom," January 7, 1962).

Details on the U.S. Immigration Reform and Control Act; 1989 earnings sent to Mexico by illegal workers—Meyer et al., p. 664.

Bracero and arrest figures, 1949 and 1974—Wagner, p. 61. Exact numbers: 1949, 107,000 braceros, but 233,485 illegals caught by Border Patrol; 1974, 709,959 illegals caught by same.

Arrest figures, Sector El Centro, early 1990s, 1996–98—DeBuys and Myers, p. 188.

The 50-year-old woman in Jacumba—A retired real estate broker, about 50 years old. She did not want her name used. I wrote down her remarks verbatim. Interviewed in Jacumba, July 2004. Shannon Mullen was present.—A wise man wrote: "The basic problem is this: Americans remain reluctant to accept the fact that their country has become a frontier for Latin Americans"—and for Chinese, too, evidently (Pike, p. 364).

Pedestrian *vs.* driver-passenger ratios of arrestees, 1995–2004—*Los Angeles Times*, Sunday, April 24, 2005, pp. B1, B6 (Richard Marosi, "Smuggling by Car Accelerates").

Proportion of illegal border-crossers passing through TJ in the 1980s—San Diego MOCA, unnumbered 5th page of essay "This Is Tijuana."

Date of inauguration of War on Drugs—Pike, p. 350.

The words of Adele Fasano, and the photograph of three young Mexicans in a trunk—same *Los Angeles Times* article (Richard Marosi).

José López—Interviewed in Calexico, 2004.

Death of "more than three thousand illegals"—San Diego MOCA, ibid., unnumbered 7th page of essay "The Allure of Tijuana." Bigelow, p. 9, gives the total of 3,200 dead in the first decade. I am skeptical of his precision.

The 500% increase—*Sacramento Bee*, final, Sunday, September 3, 2006, p. A16 (Susan Ferriss: "Border: Thousands have died," cont'd from p. A1, where title is "Breaching the border").—Gatekeeper, not mentioned by name in the article but must be the one referred to given the timeline, has "pushed migration into Arizona's desert and other isolated terrain, resulting in a 500 percent increase in deaths between 1994 and 2004 . . . More than 3,000 fatalities have been recorded since the mid-1990s, and hundreds of bodies and bones remain unidentified."

Illegal-alien deaths October 2002–October 2003, and related Imperial and Los Angeles matters in same paragraph—*Imperial Valley Press*, Thursday, October 16, 2003, p. A2 (Aaron Claverie, "Record number of immigrants die crossing desert"; same author, "Body recovered from Ash Canal"); p. A3 ("Woman sentenced for beating, smuggling immigrants").

Oregon students' remarks on illegal Mexicans—Bigelow, p. 35.

Politico-economic situation of Mexico when Zedillo took office—Meyer et al., pp. 695–96.

The woman in Ejido Netzahualcóyotl—Jose Castro's wife, interviewed February 2004.

160. *The Farm Water Quality Management Plan (2003)*

Information on the Farm Water Quality Management Plan—*Imperial Valley Press*, Thursday, March 27, 2003, p. D4 ("Farm Bureau" column, by Nicole Rothfleisch, program director, Total Maximum Daily Load).

161. *Privatizing the* Ejidos *(1992–2006)*

Epigraph: "We have to create a new world economy."—Bigelow, p. 69 (Clinton's speech "Support the North American Free Trade Agreement").

Yolanda Sánchez Ogás—Interviewed in a car in June 2003, en route to Ejido Tabasco. Terrie Petree interpreted.

"The persistent impoverishment of the countryside in Mexico . . ."—Boyer, pp. 240, 239.

Ability of an *ejido* to privatize either by disbanding itself or by allowing whichever members wish to sell to do so; sharecropping permitted—RDI (2004), pp. 28, 31.

"An official of Mexicali's Tribunal Unitario Agrario Distrito Dos"—Lic. Carlos E. Tinoco, official of the Tribunal Unitario Agrario Distrito Dos. Interviewed in the tribunal offices in Mexicali, September 2005. Terrie Petree translated.

Number of rural families predicted to be displaced by the repeal of Article Twenty-seven, and comments of Jaime Serra Puche—Bigelow, p. 23.

Appeal for privatization for nonagricultural use of land—RDI (2004), p. 9.

The rancher in Morelos—Don Carlos Cayetano Sanders-Collins—Interviewed with his family in Morelos, October 2003, Terrie Petree interpreting.

The restaurant proprietress—Señora Socorro Ramírez, interviewed on 19 February 2004 in her restaurant Yocojihua. Terrie Petree interpreted.

The rancher lady in Colonia Sieto de Cierro Prieto—Señora Teresa García, interviewed on 19 February 2004, on Rancho García. Terrie Petree interpreted.

Alma Rosa Hernández and Hugo Heriberto Herrera—Interviewed in her house or theirs in Ejido Netzahualcóyotl, December 2006, Terrie Petree interpreting.

Statistics on the Revolution's land reform, and remainder of paragraph's remarks on decreasing crop income—Boyer, pp. 223–24.

"Capitalism makes merchandise of people . . ."—Bigelow, p. 24 (Clandestine Revolutionary Indigenous Committee, General Command of the Zapatista Army of National Liberation, 27 June—3 July 2005).

162. Assets Forfeiture (2003)

Epigraph: "Offhand, I know of nothing more deleterious to my liver . . ."—Oliver Lange, p. 45.

Notices of vehicle forfeiture—*Imperial Valley Weekly*, vol. 98. no. 13 (Thursday, March 27, 2003), p. 11 ("Public Notice," dates of publication March 20, March 27, and April 3, 2003).

163. We Should Have Had a Better Negotiating Position (2002–2003)

Epigraph: "San Diego County sees such water transfers . . ."—San Diego County Water Authority, p. 52.

Epigraph: "This puts in place the basic building block . . ."—*Imperial Valley Press*, Thursday, October 16, 2003, p. A1 (Seth Hettena, "Norton to sign water deal: Agreement: Roadmap for future water trades in the West").

Transfer amount (200 KAFY)—IID *de novo* Part 417 brief, p. 15.

Costs of a 300,000 KAFY tailwater reduction—IID *de novo* Part 417 brief, p. 29.

Potential fallowing of 30,000 acres—*San Diego Union-Tribune*, Thursday, May 29, 2003, p. A1 (Michael Gardner, Copley News Service, "Water Pressure: Second in an occasional series: Imperial Valley an Oasis of Opportunity: But many fear that idling of farmland could pull the plug on growth").

Andy Horne's definitions—*Imperial Valley Press*, Wednesday, March 19, p. A4, "Voice of the People" column: "IID director defines water terminology" (Andy Horne, IID director, El Centro). In 2002, Larry Grogan, then Mayor of El Centro, suggests that the city buy farmland and fallow it so that the water rights can be sold to San Diego as part of the increasingly inevitable water-transfer package. He argues that this will keep water transfer dollars within the valley. Andy Horne, the Director of Imperial Irrigation District One, bitterly compares him to the Bass brothers. This strikes me as unfair, for in 2003 we find Grogan, now an El Centro City Councilman, supporting the Imperial Irrigation District's lawsuit against the U.S. government. He opposes the water farmers' "Imperial Group," which proposes that all water-transfer money go directly to landowners. But who can blame Andy Horne for being jittery? (Tale of Larry Grogan: For 2002: Ivpressonline.com, Laura Mitchell, Staff Writer, "Grogan plan to buy, fallow land defeated," http://www.ivpressonline.com/articles/2002/09/05/export16059.prt. For 2003: Ivpressonline.com, Laura Mitchell, Staff Writer, "Grogan asks for anti-Imperial Group action," http://www.ivpressonline.com/articles/2003/03/20/export18999.prt.)

Leonard Knight: "When I get too close to people . . ."—Already cited above, in the chapter "The Imperial Idea (1901–2004)."

Interior Department's conspiratorial e-mails—*San Diego Union-Tribune*, vol. 12, no. 80, Friday, March 21, 2003, p. A3 (Michael Gardner, Copley News Service, "Interior's effect on river sharing raises eyebrows").

"Mr. Johnson formed his opinions long ago."—IID *de novo* Part 417 brief, p. 54.

Ruth Thayer's e-mail to Jayne Harkins—IID *de novo* Part 417 brief, pp. 56–57.

"EL CENTRO—In a stunning move . . ."—*Sacramento Bee* final, Tuesday, December 10, 2002, p. 1 (Stuart Leavenworth and Dale Kasler, "Imperial shuns sale, roils water picture").

"Interior sought to push IID into the QSA . . ."—IID *de novo* Part 417 brief, pp. 15–16.

All remarks by Richard Brogan in this chapter—Interview, Calexico, April 2004.

IID quota cut by 330,400 acre-feet—*Imperial Valley Press,* Wednesday, March 19, 2003.

Advertisement for Cyan-o-Gas—*California Cultivator,* vol. LXIV, no. 14, April 4, 1925, p. 429.

Events of 18 March 2003—*Imperial Valley Press,* Wednesday, March 19, 2003, p. 1 (Rudy Yniguez, staff writer, "Judge orders full water allotment").

"Very strong likelihood that the defendants breached the Seven Party Agreement"—*Imperial Valley Press,* Monday, March 25, 2003, p. A8 ("WATER: Government raised issue"; continued from p. A1).

"An American community . . . driven to defense of its rights"—William Leslie Davis, p. 152.

Imperial Group filing against IID—Ibid., Wednesday, March 19, 2003, p. A4.

Search of property records for Mike Morgan—This information is placed in a restricted file in my papers in Ohio State University.

Assertions of Mr. Ray Naud—IVPressonline.com, from 3/5/03, "Voice: Maldonado's and Allen's contribution lists reveal transfer loyalties."

Richard Brogan's remarks on a potential dustbowl—When I asked Zulema Rashid whether she thought that the water farmers might someday have their way and then her town, Calexico, might become a ghost town, she vehemently replied, pointing to the international line: "It will all be city. You can see city now all the way from San Diego to Jacumba. So it's expanding. But there's still a lot of space here. I don't think this town will ever be a ghost town."

"Too late for meangingful review" and associated narrative—IID objection to Part 417 determination, p. 7, fn. 12.

"CVWD has an undisputed lower on-farm efficiency than IID . . ."—Ibid, p. 16.

Predicted results of water reduction; and SWRCB Decision 1600—Ibid., pp. 53, 69.

Stella Mendoza—Interviewed in her kitchen in Brawley, October 2003. Terrie Petree was present.

The meat of the water transfer (September 25, 2003, QSA between Imperial and San Diego)—Munguía, p. 224 (Vicente Sánchez Munguía).

Footnote: "Powering Mexican maquiladoras . . ."—"Today's IID," verso, center panel.

"The pact will supply San Diego with about a third of its current water needs . . ."—*Imperial Valley Press,* Sunday, October 12, 2003, p. A6 ("Agencies ink landmark water deal").

Footnote: Mexican reasonable and beneficial use—Ibid., pp. 176–77 (Stephen P. Mumme and Donna Lybecker).

Footnoted information on Imperial County's 2003 water obligation to San Diego—*Imperial Valley Press,* Tuesday, October 14, 2003, pp. A1, A6 (Rudy Yniguez, "QSA formally signed, now in effect: WATER: IID must transfer 15,000 acre-feet this year to the San Diego County Water Authority").

Footnote: "The recent announcement of an armistice in that epic battle . . ."—*New York Times,* Wednesday, October 22, 2003, "Editorials/Letters" section, p. A26 ("Living with Scarcity in California").

" . . . reinforced the idea that 'urban interests' have established a beachhead in the Imperial Valley . . ."—*Imperial Valley Press,* Sunday, October 12, 2003, "Our Opinion" section, p. A6 ("How now, San Diego?").

"The water transfer agreement provides ripples of benefit . . ."—San Diego County Water Authority, p. 53.

164. You Might as Well Get Out of the Way (2006)

Kay Brockman Bishop—Interview of 2006.

165. Water Is Here (A View from Arizona) (1985–2007)

Epigraph: "Supplemented by the newly finished All-American Canal . . ."—Imperial Valley Directory (1939), p. 14.

Epigraph: "The unsuspecting traveller who has crossed the Colorado river . . ."—Holmes et al., p. 168 (Mrs. W. H. Ellis, "Moreno Valley").

"Was mostly agriculture in the 1950s . . ."—Whitehead et al., p. 37 (Anthony J. Brazel and Sandra W. Brazel, Laboratory of Climatology, Arizona State University, Tempe, "Desertification, Desert Dust and Climate: Environmental Problems in Arizona").

"FADE may cause up to one-third . . ."—Ibid., p. 39.

"The relinquishment of agricultural land for urban use . . ."—California State Archives. Margaret C. Felts papers. Box 12: Folder: "1927 POLLUTION." State of California. Department of Public Works. Division of Engineering and Irrigation. Paul Bailey, State Engineer, *Bulletin No. 12: Summary Report on the Water Resources of California and a Coordinated Plan for Their Development: A Report to the Legislature of 1927* (Sacramento: California State Printing Office, 1927). P. 43.

Arizona's use of entire Colorado River water allotment—DeBuys and Myers, p. 168.

J. Rice: "In days that are forgotten in the history of Arizona . . ."—UC Berkeley. Bancroft Library Manuscripts Col-

lection. Paul Schuster Taylor, 1895–. Papers, 1895–1984. BANC MSS 84/38. Carton 5. Folder 5:2: "To Make the Desert Bloom Like the Rose, 1969?" Yellow typescript on "The American West" letterhead, entitled "Issue: Colorado Book," p. 21.
Remark of the Hualapai Indian guide—April 2007.
View of Hoover or Boulder Dam in 2007—From that same April visit.
Footnote: "The only place where the progress of the QSA is followed more closely than in the Imperial Valley . . ." —*Imperial Valley Press*, Sunday, July 24, 2005,"Opinion" section, p. A4 ("Learning to Live with Less Water").
"This is my water . . ."—Luthin, p. 482 ("An Account of Origins: Quechan [Yuma], 1908; Tsuyukweráu, narrator; J. P. Harrington, collector; Yuma creation song about the Colorado River).
Emory's observations—Op. cit., p. 92 (entry for 18 November 1846).

166. *Water Is Here (A View from Imperial) (2003)*

"While singlemindedly attacking IID's alfalfa . . ."—IID *de novo* Part 417 brief, p. 15.

168. *Probate (1901–2003)*

Epigraph: "Business . . . was his profession . . ."—Wright, p. 123.
California Cultivator subscriber: "In the years past my father obtained patents to numerous property interests . . ." —Vol. LIV, no. 2, January 10, 1920, p. 68 ("Legal Queries" department).
Interview with Pentecostal family—2003; Larry McCaffery was present.

169. *Such a Good Life (2006)*

Epigraph: "You corn kernels, you coral seeds . . ."—Joseph and Henderson, p. 82 (Anonymous, "Popul Vuh").
Teresa Cruz Ochoa and her husband José de Jesús Galleta Lamas—Interviewed in their home in Colonia Borges in December 2006. Terrie Petree interpreted.

170. *Still a Great Farming County (2004)*

Epigraph: "A thinly populated world of the type I describe . . ."—Asimov, p. 133.
Mr. and Mrs. Claude Finnell—Mrs. Finnell did not give me her name (probably Geraldine). Interviewed in their home in El Centro, 2004. Shannon Mullen was present.
Footnote: Ag Commissioner as "a big deal, in an agricultural county like this"—Richard Brogan, interviewed in Calexico, April 2004. Mr. Brogan also said, and I do not necessarily subscribe to it: "A fellow that would talk to you, one of the cagiest fellows, is Claude Finnell. Well, Claude, after he retired, his job became a lobbbyist for the Metropolitan Water District. Everything that Claude does, he'll do it slowly, and he'll look you in the eye . . . I mean, he is silvertongued. He's paid to meet people such as yourself, people showing interest in the subject. His tentacles are just interwoven in the growth of the farm community here for . . . what? Thirty years."
Q&A with the "ancient rancher" about the Owens Valley—Pearce, pp. 77, 43, 45.
Finnell's status with MWD—*Los Angeles Times*, 14 December 1988, p. 3 (Bill Boyarsky, Metro desk, "MWD Breaks Stalemate in Water Purchase Deal").
Footnote: Finnell's sugarcane group, ethanol project—*Imperial Valley Press*, Friday, December 7, 2001, no page number since from Internet (Laura Mitchell, "Sugar cane can be profitable crop, field day presenters say"), Friday, March 7, 2003, no page number since from Internet (Rudy Yniguez, "Death won't delay plans for sugar cane plant").

In the Paul Foster reports written for this book (2007), the "Imperial Color Commentary" has this to say about the time between Mr. Finnell's administration and the present:

"The end of the Harrigan era in the early 1950s and the rise of Claude Finnell as County Ag Commissioner also coincided with standardization of agricultural reporting throughout California . . . I have inflation-adjusted to 2005 dollars in my chart analysis. This data is reasonably consistent over time and readily available. In addition, the Imperial economy of 2005 would be largely recognizable to the 1955 farmer and vice versa. Also, I have generally used five-year moving averages to smooth out annual bumps in the data and make long-term trends more visible. Some of these trends correlate with trends in the national economy; others are more specific to California and Imperial.

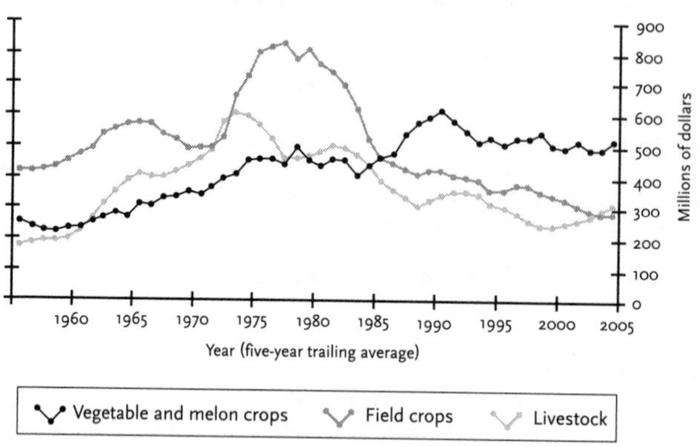

"Ag Trends: The Ag Trends chart is the simplest to follow and mostly tells the tale we'd expect from what we see of Imperial County today. Field crops (feed grains, pasture grasses, some cash crops) grew in importance from 1950–80, peaked in the late 70s, and have diminished in dollar importance ever since. In addition, some specific grains (wheat, barley, milo) have almost disappeared from the radar screen and been lumped into the category "Other field crops" in the annual ag reports. Except for alfalfa, it's generally become less risky to buy feed for livestock than to grow the feed yourself, allowing farmers to make opportunistic forays into livestock.

"Livestock (mainly beef) has been more of a roller coaster, but generally the trend has been downward since 1975. The upticks have mainly followed national trends, but within Imperial, livestock traded swapped [*sic*] in position of importance with vegetables and melons in 1985 and has never really recovered. As mentioned earlier, it seems likely that comparative advantage combined with national trends has given this result. Imperial has no clear advantages in feeder cattle and one big disadvantage in the summer: did I mention lately that Imperial is hot? This almost certainly limits weight gain in the summer months (even today they don't air-condition beef cattle) and hence limits the profitability during that time as well.

"Last, but certainly not least, one can see the rise of vegetable and melon crops through the lens of comparative advantage. Always an important part of the Imperial ag economy, vegetables and melons peaked in the late 1980s, declined through the early 90s, and now seem to occupy a fairly stable place as the leading sector of Imperial's ag economy.

"A look at the Ag Pctg Chart shows that vegetable and melon crops have been a much more volatile component of Imperial's contribution to overall California ag production. This is primarily because Imperial is geographically isolated from the other major California ag counties, giving it different weather patterns, especially for frosts, heavy rains and other unexpected weather that can ruin crops in say, the Central Valley. When the Central Valley catches a cold snap, Imperial doesn't get pneumonia, it usually gets a shot of adrenalin from the higher prices its products bring. On the other hand, when Imperial has its rare crop failure, it may get a double-whammy from the fact that the other lettuce/citrus/whatever-producing counties may have had a bumper crop, driving down prices for its diminished harvest. Over time, though, Imperial has had fewer weather events and so benefits on average from its isolation from the rest of agricultural California.

"Other data on the Ag Pctg Chart show that Fruit and Nut crops have been a small but very steady contributor, while (as expected) Livestock has diminished in importance (compared to the rest of California) after peaking in the 70s. Field Crops have maintained relative importance probably due to the fact that the rest of California has abandoned them more quickly than Imperial, and the opposite would hold true for why Vegetable and Melon crops have declined relative to the rest of California even as they've increased in importance within Imperial. Last but not least, the overall drop in Imperial's total contribution to the California ag economy since the 1970s (it now dwells consistently near the bottom of the top 10 ag counties) is almost certainly due to its continued reliance on field crops and livestock, areas where it doesn't have a comparative advantage, and its lack of greater movement toward citrus, grapes, and other crops for which other California counties have increased their production during the same time period. This is only speculation, though, and I have included enough data from the CA state ag department to allow you to draw this conclusion yourself. The data exists, but it would be a fairly big project in itself to do the analysis that would support this conclusion. Let's just call it a strong hunch that in this case, the slowness of Imperial farmers to move away from crops that they know how to grow (but not especially profitably) to crops they're less familiar with (but that would make them more money) has likely cost Imperial some [of] its share in overall ag production, based on dollar value."

171. *Imperial Reprise (1975–2005)*

Epigraph: "The man of the land . . ."—*California Farmer*, April 5, 1975, advertising insert from Dow Chemical, unnumbered page before p. 29.

PART TWELVE

DEFINITIONS

173. *Where Does Los Angeles End? (1834–2005)*

Epigraph: "The uncertain air that magnified some things and blotted out others . . ."—Steinbeck, *Novels 1942–52*, p. 244 (*The Pearl*, 1945).
L.A. in 1834—Dana, p. 118.
L.A. in 1873—McPherson, p. 33.
The female ex-Angeleno—Micheline Marcom.

174. *Mexicans and Americans (1901–2007)*

Epigraph: "*Gringo*, in its literal signification . . ."—Bell, p. 49.
Chung Lee, Richard Kim, Walter Park, the bookkeeper-accountant—Smith, pp. 84, 87–89, 145–46, 148–49, 129. (The bookkeeper-acccountant was Katie Miller.)
The zoot-suiter with hatred—Smith, pp. 3–4 (Rudy Salas, Sr.).
"I think I've considered myself Chicano . . ."—Marilyn P. Davis, p. 293 (Victor Orozco Ochoa).
"Chicanos are traitors . . ."—Matthiessen, p. xiii.
Stella Mendoza—Interviewed at her home in Brawley, 2003.
"Calculating, cold-hearted materialism of the Caucasian Other"—Pike, p. 45. How would a real estate developer put it? Just as smoke trees prefer sandy washes while palm trees prefer canyons or springs, Northsiders (my clients) want property to invest in while Southsiders want a place to live. That's not to say that Mexicans won't go for the money when they can, but south of the line there is less money to go for.
"The men are thriftless, proud, extravagant . . ."—Dana, pp. 214–15. He continues (p. 96): "From this upper class, they go down by regular shades, growing more and more dark and muddy, until you come to the pure Indian, who runs about with nothing on him but a small piece of cloth . . ."
"In person, the Californian *caballero* is generally tall and graceful . . ."—Ryan, vol. I, pp. 98–99.
Lupe Vásquez—Interviews of 2004, in a bus in Mexicali, and 2003, in Calexico.
"All those guys who lied . . ."—Taibo, p. 36.
The government worker in Colonia Santo Niño—Interviewed in February 2004. Terrie Petree interpreted. This man also said of Northside: "It's cleaner there; the laws are better. I was in Los Angeles, Costa Mesa, Lemon Grove. I have a visa. I was up north somewhere by Salinas, twenty miles from Delano, just there. It's more organized and there's more money."
"The border may indeed be unfortified . . ."—Ruben Salazar, p. 239.
"Malinche has always been venerated . . ."—Lanyon, pp. 98–99.
Footnote: The engraving of Malinche et al.—Meyer et al., p. 99.
Josefina Cruz Bermúdez, Tecate—Interviewed in 2003. Terrie Petree interpreted.
No all-inclusive phrase on Southwest Mexicans—UC Berkeley. Bancroft Library. Paul S. Taylor papers. Carton 5. Folder 5:41: "Perspectives on Mexican-Americans, Final Draft w/Footnotes, 1973." Typescript, "Perspectives on Mexican-Americans," p. 9.
Footnote: Description of *aztlán*—Carrasco and Moctezuma, pp. 179–95.
"Study for head of an Aztec migrant"—Orozco autobiography, gouache, first exhibited 1961–62.

PART THIRTEEN

INSCRIPTIONS

175. *Still a Mystery (2003)*

Epigraph: "Names Appearing in Black Letters . . ."—Imperial Valley Directory (1930), p. 24.
Wednesday's newspaper, p. 1: "Judge orders full water allotment" and "Terror Alert ORANGE"—*Imperial Valley Press*, vol. 102, no. 243, Wednesday, March 19, 2003.
Wednesday's newspaper, p. A2: "Holtville readies for Schwingfest," "Man pleads guilty . . ." and "Identity of dead man . . ."—Same issue. The latter article was by Matthew A. Salorio, staff writer.

Thursday's newspaper, pp. 1–A2: "U.S. invasion of Iraq begins" and "Filth an ongoing problem . . ."—Ibid., vol. 102, no. 244, Thursday, March 20, 2003.

Incident of the dead bird on Tuesday—*Imperial Valley Weekly*, vol. 98, no. 13 (Thursday, March 27, 2003), "Police Briefs" section, p. 7 ("City of Imperial: Tuesday, March 18: It Happens").

Friday's newspaper, "Liberation of Iraq" section, p. 1, quote from the President; p. A2, "Identity of El Centro asparagus thief sought"—*Imperial Valley Press*, vol. 102, no. 245, Friday, March 21, 2003.

Sunday's newspaper, p. A1, "Halfway to Baghdad . . ."; p. A3, "Broccoli cartons . . ."—Ibid., vol. 102, no. 247, Sunday, March 23, 2003.

"Body found in mountainous area"—Ibid., vol. 103, no. 30, Friday, June 13, 2003, p. A2 (staff report). The Salton Sea item appears on "Sports" section, p. B1 (Al Kalin, "Outdoors Report: Poor fishing continues at Salton Sea"). "Fishing success is nonexistent on the Salton Sea as south winds continue to create more algae blooms that rob the water of oxygen and keep the fish from biting."

Footnote: Sweeney Pass accident—*Borrego Sun*, vol. 52, no. 12, June 5, 2003, p. 4.

Monday's newspaper, p. A1, "'Dramatic' progress . . ." and "Iraqi resistance . . ."; p. A7, asparagus news from the "Trading on the Floor" column—*Imperial Valley Press*, vol. 102, no. 246, Monday, March 24, 2003.

Tuesday's newspaper, p. A1, "Written order on IID suit . . . ," "Sandstorms thwart air missions . . ." and "Border Patrol reports fewer apprehensions"; p. A10, deaths of illegal aliens in Texas ("Five immigrants die in field fire")—Ibid., vol. 102, no. 247, Monday, March 25, 2003.

Thursday's newspaper, p. A1, "U.S. vows to intensify attacks" and "Guards posted at IID dam . . ."; same page, Michael A. Salorio, "One dead . . ."—Ibid., vol. 102, no. 249, Thursday, March 27, 2003.

The death of Señor Dolores Martínez—Gostin, pp. 538–39 (records #1011–12).

Figure for 1853 of one violent death a day in Los Angeles—Bell, p. 13.

Great events of 14 May 1914—*Imperial Valley Press*, vol. XIV, no. 7, Friday, May 8, 1914, p. 4.

Testimony of Mr. Rose—Senate Committee on the Colorado River Basin (1924), p. 264.

"ADMIT CORPSE AND CASKET FREE . . ."—N.A.R.A.L. Record Group 36. Records of the U.S. Customs Service. Calexico Customs Office. Incoming Official Correspondence (9L-60). October 15, 1902–March 23, 1916. Box No. 3 of 5: November 1913 to July 1914. Folder: "Nov. 15, 1913–Feb. 11, 1914." Western Union telegram, to Deputy Collector Customs, Calexico Cal. From Cretcher, Deputy Collector. 1:30 PM. Undated but prob. about 2 January 1913.

176. The Line Itself (2003–2006)

Epigraph: "Yet across the gulf of space . . ."—Wells, *The War of the Worlds*, p. 8.

"Our primary mission . . ."—See below, "mission statement of Border Patrol Agent Michael McClafferty."

Treasury Department: "The general belief that opium in powdered form . . ."—N.A.R.A.L. Record Group 36. Records of the U.S. Customs Service. Calexico Customs Office. Incoming Official Correspondence (91–60). October 15, 1902–March 23, 1916. Box 4 of 5: July 1914–June 1915. Bound volume labeled "Letters." Letter from James W. Bevans, Acting Chief, Div. of Customs, Treasury Department, Washington, to the Collector of Customs, Los Angeles, California, March 1, 1915.

"The southern border is literally under siege . . ."—*New York Times*, national ed., Monday, March 14, 2005, p. A16 (Eric Lipton, "Despite New Efforts Along Arizona Border, 'Serious Problems' Remain").

"Hundreds of thousands of years of genetic weeding-out . . ."—Harrison, p. 16.

"'Praise Perimeter!' she breathed . . ."—Ibid., p. 60.

Description of the red-eyed Aztec sculpture—After a photograph in Carrasco and Moctezuma, p. 55.

Mission statement of Border Patrol Agent Michael McClafferty: "We're going to send a robot down" and "The investigation was not in response . . ."—*San Diego Union-Tribune*, February 26, 2005, no page number available (Onell R. Soto, staff writer, "Tunnel between Mexicali, Calexico discovered").

"Tunnel to U.S. starts inside Mexican home"—Ibid., February 28, 2005, no page number available (Sandra Dibble, staff writer, headline as given).

"U.S. officials seize house at end of border tunnel" and "several altars . . ."—Ibid., March 2, 2005, p. B4 (Onell R. Soto and Sandra Dibble, staff writers, headline as given).

Kay Brockman Bishop—Interviewed on her ranch near Calexico, 2006.

Poem about Juan Soldado—Torre and Wiegers, p. 623 (Heriberto Yépez, "On Coahuila Street," 2000; translated by Mark Weiss; "retranslated" here and there by WTV).

Footnote on "The Grave" and "Hell"—Bull, p. 35.

Footnote: Israel's wall—*Berlin Journal: A Magazine from the American Academy in Berlin*, no. 9, fall 2004, p. 19 (Roger Cohen, "Israel's Wall").

Footnote: Arrillaga's view of the Mexicali Valley [from the Sierra Juárez)—Op. cit., p. 65 (21 September 1796).

Rosa Pérez—Interviewed December 2006. Terrie Petree interpreted.

Area of the Mexicali Valley: 3,000 sq. km.—Whitehead et al., p. 307 (Eduardo Paredes Arellano, Secretaría de

Agricultura y Recursos Hidráulicos, Mexicali, "Water, the Most Important Natural Resource for the State of Baja California, Mexico").

Francisco Manuel Preciado Martínez—Interviewed in a restaurant in San Luis Río Colorado, December 2006. Terrie Petree interpreted.

177. Subdelineations: Marsscapes (2004)

Epigraph: "Could the gray-green areas in an otherwise reddish disk . . ."—*Astronomy*, vol. 31, no. 8 (August 2003), p. 20 (Glen Chaple's Observing Basics: "Mars revealed").

"Gone are the oases, canals and cities . . ."—Ibid.

"Their ranks were continually replenished . . ."—Miller, p. 80.

"The actual accomplishment of . . . a suppression . . ."—Wells, *The War of the Worlds*, p. 198.

"Those who have never seen a living Martian . . ."—Ibid., p. 32.

"He did not ask *why* God would choose . . ."—Miller, pp. 276–77.

"The blighted landscape and its empty violence . . ."—Ballard, *The Drought*, p. 49.

Excerpts from *Dune*—Herbert, pp. 398, 326–27, 328.

"You speak *English*!"—Bradbury, p. 16.

A terminal zone—Ballard, op. cit., p. 68.

178. Rancho Roa (2004–2005)

Interviews with Natalio Morales Rebolorio—Conducted on Rancho Roa, February 2004, Terrie Petree interpreting; February 2005, Micheline Marcom interpreting. I visited Rancho Roa briefly on two other occasions in 2004.

Footnote: Javier Lupercio—Interviewed in Mexicali, April 2004, José López from Jalisco translating.

179. Brock Farms (2004)

Richard Brogan—Interviewed in Calexico, April 2004.

Ben Brock—Interviewed on the premises of Brock Farms in Holtville, 2004.

Footnote: Asparagus data, 2004, 1994—ICAC papers, 2004, pp. 6, 11; ICAC papers, 1994, pp. 5, 10.

180. Salvation Mountain (1996–2005)

Epigraph—Leonard Knight, interview with WTV, 2003.

"The Main Line City," etc.—Imperial Valley Directory (1914), p. vi.

Description of the Niland train depot—ICHSPM photograph, cat. #P92.52.

Footnote on Deane Haughtelin's family—ICHSPM document, cat. #A84.20.1: Undated letter to Elizabeth Harris, Holtville, California, from Deane Haughtelin in Winterhaven

Harry Chandler as a stockholder of the First National Bank of Niland—Tout, *The First Thirty Years*, p. 361.

"The opening was attended by trainloads from Los Angeles . . ."—Ibid., p. 195.

John D. Reavis, 1930: "Some day Niland's dream of commercial and horticultural greatness . . ."—Ibid., p. 410.

"The building of the All-American Canal . . ."—Imperial Valley Directory (1914), p. 361.

WPA guide on Niland—WPA, p. 459.

181. Signal Mountain (2003)

Epigraph: "When America was young. . ."—Tout, *The First Thirty Years*, p. 413 ("Scenic Imperial Valley, Land of Desert Oddities").

José Quintero—Interviewed in Mexicali, 2002.

Arrillaga's description of Signal Mountain—Op. cit., p. 92 (23 October 1796).

Arrillaga's description of Laguna Salada—Op. cit., p. 75 (18 October 1796).

Concretions: "They were so numerous that we thought little of their scientific value," etc.—McCollum (Hyde, both of her 2 unnumbered pages).

182. Between the Lines (2003–2005)

Epigraph: "The third, or Desert division . . ."—Douglas Gunn, p. 48.

Footnote: "There is a peculiar charm and surprise about the odors of the desert . . ."—James, *Wonders of the Colorado Desert*, p. 38.

"Perhaps nowhere is the inexorable nature of the northward migration of Mexicans . . ."—*New York Times*, Wednesday, March 23, 2005, p. A8 (James C. McKinley, Jr., "At Mexican Border, Tunnels, Vile River, Rusty Fence").

Francisco Cedeño's story—From an interview at his residence in Mexicali, August 2005. Terrie Petree interpreted.

Definition of weep holes—International Commission on Irrigation and Drainage, after item no. 5198.

"Border deaths hit records" and following text—*Sacramento Bee*, Saturday, October 2, 2005, "National Digest" section, p. A12.

Description of the Pancho Villa prayer card—After Griffith, p. 99. This card was collected sometime between 1994 and 2003.

Imperial County Development Agent's 1916 report—Imperial County Agricultural Commission papers. A. M. Nelson, Development Agent, Imperial County, El Centro, Cal. "CALIFORNIA COTTON PRODUCTION—1916." Page 1 of 2-p. typescript (the second page relates to butter production in the same year and was cited in my chapter on Wilber Clark).

"Unlike CWD's service area, where the sandy soil soaks up the water . . ."—IID *de novo* Part 417 brief, p. 18.

Divergent incomes with Brawley's zip code 92227—Imperial Valley Directory (2000), yellow maps 4 and 5, pink pages (street guide to carrier route), p. 1.

One prominent information designer: ". . . a sense of *average* and of *variation* about that average . . ."—Tufte, *Envisioning Information*, p. 32.

Tufte's remarks on the Broad Street Well—*Visual Explanations*, p. 35.

G. Harold Powell: "Nearly everyone you meet here is from the east . . ."—Op. cit., p. 21 (letter of 25 January 1904, to Gertrude Powell).

José López from Jalisco—Interviewed in Mexicali, July 2004. Shannon Mullen was present during the first interview, and Terrie Petree was there for the second. I have conflated these into one section.

183. Subdelineations: Moneyscapes (1989–2005)

Epigraph: "Attempts at description are stupid . . ."—Eliot, pp. 145–46.

Map of California median household income in 1989—California Employment Development Department (1995), Module F, p. F-1 (Social and Economic Data Tables).

Map: "County Unemployment Rates, 1999 Anual Averages"—Ibid., p. B-vii (dated August 2000).

Number ranking unemployment of Imperial 1997–99—EDD unemployment fact sheet (1997–99).

Median household incomes of Mecca, Indio and Indian Wells; and remark that Palm Springs, Cathedral City and Palm Desert "have some of the greatest income disparities in California . . ."—*Sacramento Bee*, Monday, November 24, 2003, "Capitol & California" section, pp. A3–A4 (Gillian Flaccus, Associated Press, "In posh resort towns of the Palm Springs area, workers can barely afford to live and the income gap is huge").

"Sterling Cove: Exclusive Estate/Pool!"—*Desert Sun*, Saturday, December 20, 2003, "Desert Real Estate" section, p. 75 ("Knowledge Is Power! Luxury Leases, Vacation Rentals"). Another headline in the same issue (Section E [Business], p. E1, Jonathan D. Colburn) informs us: "Valley home prices holding: Median price for a desert home remains $245,000."

Various ratings of El Centro urban complex—Heubusch, pp. 29–31, 69, 107, 113, 112, 146, 131, 434, 438.

California county agricultural commodity rankings and items—*California Agricultural Directory 2004–2005*, p. 109.

1 out of 4 Mexicans "in extreme poverty"—Meyer et al., p. 687.

Californians *vs.* Imperial County Residents in poverty, 2000—Census Bureau, Historical Income Table for Counties: Table C3, Per Capita Income by County, rev. August 22, 2002.

Percentage of Imperial County residents in poverty, 1990—Printout given to me by a clerk in the Employment Development Department in El Centro, *ca.* 2000; no main title; relevant page is headed "1990 CCPH-L-81. table 3. Income and Poverty Status in 1989: 1990. Imperial County, California." This document may come from the U.S. Department of Commerce.

Figures on the number of applicants for the Food 4 Less jobs—*Imperial Valley Press*, vol. 103, no. 27, Tuesday, June 10, 2003, p. A1 (Aaron Claverie, "Thousands bid for jobs at Calexico Food4Less").

"The closer you get to the U.S., the poorer the city becomes."—Crosthwaite, Byrd and Byrd, p. 201 (Juan Villoro, "Nothing to Declare: Welcome to Tijuana").

Footnote: José López—Interviewed in Mexicali, 2003.

A Stanford historian: "The income gap between the United States and Mexico . . ."—*Newsweek*, April 10, 2006, p. 39 (Fareed Zakaria, "To Become an American," quoting David Kennedy).

"Until a large pool of skilled workers willing to work for less . . ."—Wagner, p. 11.

Footnote: The old man who knew what was cheap in Northside—Unnamed, but he appears in 8" x 10" negative MX-TC-LOC-03-01. Interviewed and photographed in Tecate, October 2003. Terrie Petree interpreted.

The juice vendor in Mexicali—Interviewed in 2003.

Señor Héctor—Interviewed in 2003 and 2004. He is portrayed in the 8" x 10" photograph MX-EJ-FCB-03-01.

184. Subdelineations: Moneyscapes (2003–2006)

Decline of U.S. manufacturing jobs 2000–2003 (the 1-in-6 figure is also expressed as 2.8 million lost jobs)—*Sacramento Bee*, Monday, December 1, 2003, p. D2 (Dave Carpenter, Associated Press, "For factories, it's change or fold . . .").

"U.S. opens avocado pipeline . . ."—*Sacramento Bee*, Saturday, October 22, 2005, pp. D1–D2 (story by Chris Kraul, *Los Angeles Times*).

185. Present and Future Successes (2003)

Epigraph: "Hopefully you'll find the data and charts mostly correspond to your impressions of Imperial . . ."—Paul Foster reports (2007) ("Imperial Color Commentary").

All text—*Imperial Valley Press*, Tuesday, October 14, 2003, p. A1 (Marc Schanz, "County unemployment rate dips a bit to 22 percent").

186. Market Prices (2000)

Epigraph: "Now a haze lies upon the land . . ."—DeBuys and Myers, p. 5.

Mexican and American corn prices; Mexican rural poverty statistics—Bigelow, pp. 72, 79.

Imperial County agricultural statistics, 1999 and 2000—Imperial County Agricultural Commissioner's papers, 2000, pp. 3, 11.

The taxi driver Angel—Interviewed between El Centro and Imperial, 2002.

Prices for Thirteen Negro dances, sex, etc.—Investigated with Lupe Vásquez, Mexicali, 2003.

187. Imperial Beach (2005)

Epigraph: "Taking the road to the right of the Tia Juana road . . ."—Douglas Gunn, 1887, p. 38.

188. San Diego (2003–2006)

Epigraph: "Subdivisions in various localities have already proven highly successful . . ."—Salvator, p. 47.

189. Tijuana (2003–2005)

Epigraph: "Bring me the sunflower . . ."—Eugenio Montale, "Portami Il Girasole," translated by Chris Glomski, in *A Public Space*, issue 2 (summer 2006), p. 79.

The Aztec sculpture of a young woman—Carrasco and Moctezuma, p. 60.

"The worst and best things in the whole country are happening here."—Augustín Pérez Aguilar, reporter for *La Frontera* (Tijuana). Interviewed in English in a restaurant in Tijuana Centro, July 2004. Terrie Petree was present.

190. Tecate (2003–2006)

To Terrie Petree, Tecate feels less like a border town than other places. "For some reason in Mexicali it seems like the border tension is palpable."

Definition of *altepetl*—Carrasco and Moctezuma, p. 161.

191. Campo (2005)

Epigraph: "They slacked away again when the price of silver went down . . ."—Austin, p. 165 ("The Little Town of the Grape Vines").

Information on Kumeyaay Indians and their language—Golden Acorn placemat.

Carl Calvert on machines etc.—Interviewed in Campo, October 2003. Terrie Petree was present.

192. Mexicali (2003)

Epigraph: "That's all it is . . ."—Lupe Vásquez, interviewed by WTV, 2003. By "our neighbor" he of course meant the United States.

Size ranking of Mexicali among Mexican cities, number of residents working in the *maquiladoras* and Imperial County—*San Diego Union-Tribune*, Sunday, October 12, 2003, p. E3 ("Mexicali's moment," cont'd from p. E1). For the latter two statistics, Roberto Valero of the Center for Economic Studies is cited.

Footnote: Between 2000 and 2020, the population of Mexicali is expected to double—Munguía, p. 16 (Francisco Raul Venegas Cardoso).

Description of Tlazoltéotl—León-Portilla and Shorris, pp. 222–29 ("prayer to Tlazolteotl," *Florentine Codex*).

Mexicali as third-largest of the border cities—Ruiz, p. 26.

The street prostitute Liliana—I met her in 2004.

193. *Ejido Netzahualcóyotl (2004)*

Epigraph: "This is seepage water that Mexicali growers . . ." and other excerpts from the same editorial—*Imperial Valley Press,* Sunday, July 24, 2005, "Opinion" section, p. A4 ("Learning to Live with Less Water").

José Castro and his wife—Interviewed February 2004. Richard Brogan, by telephone, September 2003; Stella Mendoza, October 2003; George Michael Newman, by telephone, 2003; man in Colonia Santo Niño, interviewed February 2004.

Projected wetlands and bird-species losses caused by lining the All-American Canal—Munguía, pp. 23, 29, 30, 35 (Francisco Zamora Arroyo, Peter Culp and Osvel Hinojosa Huerta).

70,000 acre-feet per year taken from Mexicali by the lining—Same editorial as epigraph.

The old man from Durango—He did not want to be named. Interviewed in San Luis, December 2006. Terrie Petree interpreted.

Gilberto Sanders—Interviewed on his ranch in Ejido Morelos, 2003. Terrie Petree interpreted.

Man in Colonia Santo Niño—Interviewed February 2004.

Netzahualcóyotl's poem—Carrasco and Moctezuma, p. 136.

194. *San Luis Río Colorado (2006)*

The waitress—Anna Silva Reina. She was 25 when I interviewed her at work in December 2006. Terrie Petree interpreted.

195. *Blythe (2005)*

Epigraph: "Life on Earth never settled down to doing anything very good . . ."—Bradbury, pp. 179–80.

George F. Will's column—*Sacramento Bee,* Sunday, February 27, 2005, "Forum" section, p. E5.

196. *The Inland Empire (2003–2004)*

Epigraph: "Southern California's housing demand . . ."—Wagner, p. 9.

Projected population increase—Ibid.

Archaeological discoveries in Riverside's Chinatown—The Great Basin Foundation Center for Anthropological Research, vol. 2 (Archaeology), pp. 387, 383.

Orange-box labels from Strong & Old Baldy—McClelland and Last, pp. 4, 10.

The funeral parlor in 1906—Riverside Fire Department, p. 13 (Chapel of Squire and Flagg's Undertaking Parlors, Main Street).

Footnote on Riverside smog—Imperial Valley Research Center pamphlet, verso, righthand panel of text.

"What the Inland Empire has that the coastal counties don't . . ."—Inland Empire Economic Partnership website, 2003, p. 1 of 2.

197. *Coachella (2003–2004)*

Epigraph: "In the Coachella Valley . . ."—*Southwest Airlines Spirit* magazine, April 2004, p. 94 (Jordan Rane, "A Skeptic's Guide to Palm Springs").

Carolyn Cooke's recollections—Telephone interview, Coachella, April 2004. In another interview the following day, she was blunter: "This valley has been a combination of agricultural and tourism and glamour from the movie industry, and now it is rapidly losing the agriculture aspect and becoming purely a destination and a golf capital and big box stores. It's a beautiful valley, and I just wish somebody had had the foresight to take hold of it and say this will be city and this will be agriculture and this will be desert."

"Cathedral City . . . What a Great Choice! . . ."—*Property Guide 2003,* vol. 17, issue 1, p. 16.

Footnote: Number of vehicles on Highway 111, and 20-year traffic estimate for same—State of California. Department of Transportation. Transportation Library, Sacramento. Imperial folder. Sheet labeled "Maria Contreras-Swet, September 11, 2002, Page 6."

Table grape statistics—*Desert Sun,* Saturday, December 20, 2003, Section E (Business), p. E2 (Lou Hirsch, "Growers watch CAFTA: Proposed Central American Free Trade Agreement still has opposition"). In 2002, table grapes generated one-fourth of the region's $425.6 million.

"North Shore Ranch . . ."—*Property Guide 2003,* op. cit., p. 11.

"The genuinely casual vibe, the dry desert heat . . ."—*Southwest Airlines Spirit,* op. cit., p. 96.

198. *Indio (2003–2004)*

Epigraph: "A narrative, in addition to descendancy charts . . ."—Croom, pp. 227–28.

"HUD Repo in Indio . . ."—*Property Guide 2003,* vol. 17, issue 1, p. 11.

199. *Duroville (2003–2006)*

Epigraph: ". . . it's hard to imagine a situation any worse for migrant workers . . ." and other excerpts from the same editorial—*San Diego Union-Tribune*, Saturday, May 31, 2003, "Editorials" section, p. B6 ("Sovereign slum: Migrants at risk in Salton Sea encampment").

Statistics on the Torres-Martinez Desert Cahuilla Indians—Bureau of Indian Affairs (1999), p. 104.

Private investigator's report on Harvey Duro—Private detective reports, 2003–07. Invoice no. 030728 (July 28, 2003).

Harvey Duro's court cases cited here—(1) U.S. District Court, Central District of California. Civil Minutes—General (2 pp.) Case No. ED CV 03-754 RT (SGLx) July 17, 2003. Title: U.S. v. Harvey Duro, Sr. P. 2. (2) Same case, civil minutes for July 7, 6 pp., pp. 4–6.

Number of migrant workers in Duroville, 2003—*Los Angeles Times*, 25 July 2003, p. B6 (Hannah Cho, "Landfill in Thermal Told to Stop Open Burning of Waste . . .").

Interviews with Noe Ponce and Carmen Lopez—On street, 2004.

Other interviews took place in 2005 and 2006.

200. *Salton City (2006)*

Epigraph: "Into this long undeveloped land . . ."—Holmes et al., p. 6.

The man in Vista del Mar—DeBuys and Myers, p. 218.

The realtor—Araceli Cabadas. I chatted with her in December 2006. Terrie Petree was present. She assumed that Terrie and I were starting a family together and looking for a home. We did nothing to dispel her illusion.

201. *Holtville (2003)*

Epigraph: "But that is the essence of the Valley . . ."—Karpen obituary, Alice Woodside's letter to WTV.

First two advertisements—*Imperial Valley Press*, Sunday, July 23, 2005, pp. E3 and E2. The third advertisement obviously never existed.

202. *Calexico (2003)*

Epigraph: "Among the outstanding attractions of Calexico . . ."—Imperial Valley Directory (1930), p. Y (facing inside back cover).

"A huge subdivision that could double Calexico's population"—*Imperial Valley Press*, Tuesday, October 14, 2003, p. A1 (Aaron Claverie, "Role of CM Ranch consultant unresolved: ENVIRONMENTAL IMPACT REPORT: Parcel owners to pay, but who will do the work?").

203. *El Centro (2002)*

Epigraph: "Some lover of nature. . ."—Elliott, *History of San Bernardino and San Diego Counties*, p. 19.

Footnote: The pronouncement of Oscar Rodriguez—*El Centro Connection*, November 25, 2002, p. 4 (Bill Gay, "$20 million in economic development projects underway").

204. *Yellow Cab Dispatching Prices, City of Imperial (2003)*

Text posted in taxi—I've left out "Brawley $22."

205. *Los Angeles (2002–2005)*

Epigraph: "The country was completely parched . . ."—Steinbeck, *The Log from the* Sea of Cortez, p. 931.

"It takes more 'nerve'" . . .—ICHSPM document, cat. #A95.242.5. Southern Pacific Passenger Department, pamphlet: "Wayside Notes Along the Sunset Route East Bound" (San Francisco, 1911), pp. 12–13.

G. Harold Powell on Whittier: "The dark green foliage and the flaming yellow fruit of the orange groves made a striking picture."—Op. cit., p. 22 (letter of 27? January 1904, to Gertrude Powell). Also quoted in "Subdelineations: Orangescapes [1873–2005]").

"GROWING PAINS: Residents crowding into L.A. area make it most densely packed in U.S."—*Sacramento Bee*, "Capitol & California" section, p. A3 (article by Blaine Harden, *Washington Post*).

Imperial is in the lowest zone of official plant richness—California Department of Fish and Game, p. 25 (Roxanne Bittman, "Plants").

First real estate listings—Century 21 De Oro, *Property Guide Serving the Entire Coachella and Imperial Valleys*, vol. 14, issue 2, pp. 44 (first two items), 39, 28, and 20, respectively.

Real estate listing for "Repo Property!"—*Property Guide 2002: The Coachella and Imperial Valleys* [*sic*] *#1 Real Estate*, vol. 15, issue 1, p. 16.

"In the experience of Riverside we may see the commercial romance of irrigation . . ."—Smythe, p. 100.

"Broadway, downtown's old main artery . . ."—Moore et al., p. 4.

The box of tomatoes with note and item number came from Costco in January 2005.

Geological Atlas of California's colors around the Salton Sea—California Division of Mines and Geology, *Geological Atlas of California* (Olaf P. Jenkins, ed.), 1969, Salton Sea sheet (1967).

"Both the Imperial and Mexicali Valleys are gradually being filled in . . ."—Roberts, p. 33 (remarks on San Felipe Desert subregion).

Journal of Colonel Cave Johnson Couts—Op. cit., pp. 82 (entry for Saturday, December 9), 85 (entry for Friday, December 1).

206. *Holtville (1914)*

Photo from Holtville, 1914—ICHSPM photograph, no cat. number.

The child Miguel—Gostin, pp. 338–39 (record #6315).

207. *Imperial Reprise (1901–2004)*

Epigraph: "Then they talked of the Seer's new expedition . . ."—Wright, p. 69.

Footnote: "You hear now and then of detectives . . ."—Hammett, p. 238 ("The Golden Horseshoe," 1924).

208. *The Conquest of Arid America (1905)*

Epigraph: "Accordin' to my notion hit's this here same financierin' game . . ."—Wright, p. 31.

"In the earlier edition of this work . . ."—Smythe, pp. 151–53.

CONCERNING THE MAPS

Footnote: James's delineation of the Colorado Desert—*Wonders of the Colorado Desert*, p. xxx.

Same footnote—The botanist is Benson; op. cit., p. 60.

"In January, 1900, the Colorado Desert was one vast barren waste . . ."—*Imperial Press and Farmer*, vol. II, no. 38 (Imperial, California, Saturday, January 3, 1903), p. 4 ("To Make the Desert Blossom with the Homes of Men").

California Native American boundaries—Heizer; Heizer maps; Heizer and Elsasser; Heizer and Whipple.

"A point on the Colorado river 20 m[iles] below the mouth of the Gila river . . ."—1910 *Britannica* (11th ed.), vol. XVIII, p. 317 (entry on Mexico). This is the Treaty of Guadalupe Hidalgo boundary, as slightly revised by a later treaty.

One Mexican historian: The border region "extends out at least sixty miles in both directions . . ."—Ruiz, p. 21. The historian was León-Portilla.

The "Phytogeographic Regions of Baja California"—Roberts, second frontispiece map.

Steinbeck on the Gulf of California: "A long, narrow, highly dangerous body of water."—*The Log from the* Sea of Cortez, p. 754.

Footnote: A mid-nineteenth-century observer: "Near the mouth of the Rio Colorado . . ."—Ryan, vol. 1, p. 340 ("from the pen of Mr. Farnham").

Footnote: *Salt Dreams'* version of Imperial—DeBuys and Myers, p. 2.

A CHRONOLOGY OF IMPERIAL

Hydographic history of the Salton Sink—After a graph in the *Salton Sea Atlas*, p. 17.

Many entries for Spanish exploration of California and the Gulf derive from Bancroft, vols. XVIII–XXIV; likewise statistics on population, Chinese immigration, etc., for this period.

Gold mining in east and southeast Imperial County 1775–1905—*Journal of San Diego History*, vol. 42, no. 2 (spring 1996).

Chinese exclusion acts and immigration figures, 1848–1965—After Leung.

1850 and 1900 total assessed value of California property—*California Blue Book* (1909), p. 325.

History of California counties—After Coy.

Population figures for Los Angeles, 1850, 1900, 1920—McGroarty, vol. 1, p. 359.

1850–1900 population statistics for California—*California Blue Book* (1909), p. 323.

Ca. 1850 entry: Cave Johnson Couts's estimate of San Diego County Indian population—Couts, p. 99.

Several dates for Riverside County, 1879–1912—Holmes et al.

1890 irrigation figure for southern California—Howe and Hall, p. 26.

1899 California farm products monetary ranking—*Britannica*, 11th ed., vol. 5, p. 12 (entry on California).

Various population statistcs for Imperial County 1900–31—Tout, ibid.

1900 and 1975 per capita U.S. water-consumption figures—*The California Water Atlas*, p. 1.

1901–73 dates of construction for various California water projects—Taken in part from ibid., p. 25 (map "Historic Water Development").

1901–14 founding/incorporation dates for some Imperial County cities—Henderson; Tout, *The First Thirty Years.*

1904: "Mexican officials decided . . ."—Ibid., p. 174.

1905 population figure for Los Angeles—McGroarty, vol. 1, p. 277.

1909 population statistics for Los Angeles—Ibid., pp. 326, 361.

1909 property values and population statistics for Imperial County—*California Blue Book* (1909), pp. 326, 354.

1910–49 population statistics for Imperial County—California State Board of Equalization (1949), p. 87 (Table 8).

1919 confederation of Mexicali's Chinese organizations—Personal interview with Professor Eduardo Auyón Gerardo, Mexicali, 2003.

1920, 1930 Chicano population of Los Angeles—Watkins, citing Ricardo Romo, *East Los Angeles: History of a Barrio.*

1920 assessed value and population figures for Imperial County—Imperial Valley Directory (1920), p. xi.

1920–77 governors of Baja California—*Agenda de Colonias*, p. 7.

1923 Cahuilla population—Laflin, *Coachella Valley*, p. 28.

1929: "The waters of Salton Sea . . ."—Tout, *The First Thirty Years*, p. 362.

1930s: "Twenty-five percent of California's land . . ."—Watkins, p. 393, citing Kevin Starr, *Endangered Dreams.*

1931–1934 and 1931 deportation/repatriation figures—Ibid., pp. 398, 401.

1936–38 Okie figures—Ibid., p. 436.

1939 and 1946 aggregate civilian income statistics for Imperial County—California State Board of Equalization (1949), p. 15.

1945 Imperial County business and population statistics—Ibid., p. 5.

1947 Imperial County's total bank deposits—Ibid.

1948 Imperial County assessment statistics—Ibid.

1950 population statistics for Imperial County—*California Blue Book* (1950), p. 688.

Respective acreages of cultivated *vs.* desert land in the county—Ibid., p. 854.

1950 opinion that the Salton Sea is "destined to disappear"—Ibid., p. 851.

1950 assessment of San Diego's ladies—Ibid., p. 690.

1950 figure on California cash income for agriculture—Ibid., p. 772.

1950, 1960, 1970 figures on salinity of the Salton Sea—"Visually estimated" from *The California Water Atlas*, p. 43 (Table: "Total Dissolved Solids").

1958 population figure for Imperial County—*California Blue Book* (1958), p. 853.

1960 population figure for Mexicali—Celso Bernal, pp. 389, 393. (On p. 389, the urban figure differs by a count of 4 from the same figure on p. 393.)

1975 water-use and population figures for Los Angeles—*The California Water Atlas*, p. 36.

1975: "The Colorado River . . . today supplies water to half the state's population . . ."—Ibid., p. 38.

1977: "Nearly three-fourths of the 675,000 acres . . ."—Ibid., p. 42.

1980: Figure on illegal aliens—Lowenthal and Burgess, p. 296 (citing U.S. Congress, House Committee on Post Office and Civil Service).

1980: Figure on Mexicali per capita income—Ibid., p. 304 (citing James T. Peach, *Demographic and Economic Change in Mexico's Northern Frontier*).

1985: Baja California urban population—Whitehead et al., p. 307 (Eduardo Paredes Arellano, Secretaría de Agricultura y Recursos Hidráulicos, Mexicali, "Water, the Most Important Natural Resource for the State of Baja California, Mexico").

1989: Earnings sent from illegal workers to Mexico—Meyer et al., p. 664.

1989–91 water-rationing figures—Association of California Water Agencies, pp. 8–9.

2000: "Significant salinization . . ."—Kimbrell, p. 232 ("Water: The Overtapped Resource").

2000 and 2005 illegal-migrant death figures—*Sacramento Bee*, Saturday, October 2, 2005, "National Digest" section, p. A12.

PERSONS INTERVIEWED

Since I interviewed many individuals on more than occasion, or dissected single interviews into widely spaced snippets, this list may help you keep track of who these people are. My great thanks to them, and also to the ones who chose not to be named.

Anglo readers may not be aware, as I was not, that the final word of a Mexican man's last name is his mother's last name. Thus the man in #9 is referred to as Professor Auyón, not as Professor Gerardo.

1. Alicia and Luisa—Mother and daughter in Condominios Montealbán, Mexicali. Luisa's *quinceañera* is described in "The Chinese Tunnels." José López and Terrie Petree interpreted.
2. America—Stripper at the Kaos Gentlemen's Club, Mexicali. Young and beautiful; had been in the life for five years. Interviewed at work, 2005. Terrie Petree interpreted.
3. Angel—Taxi driver and farmworker, in late middle age; interviewed between El Centro and Imperial, 2002.
4. Angélica—Street prostitute in Mexicali. Originally from Zacatecas. In her forties, with 5 children, run-down and unclean. Interviewed in the Hotel Chinesca, 2005. Terrie Petree interpreted.
5. Señor Armando—Mexican habitué of the Cafe Canton in Mexicali, where he was interviewed in September 2002. Carlos Guillermo Baja Terra interpreted.
6. Leonor Cordero Arrceola—Housewife in Ejido Netzahualcóyotl (east of Mexicali). Her husband, whom I didn't meet, worked in construction in Yuma and was about to get her papers. Rancher's daughter. Her father had to sell some land when irrigation became too expensive. I interviewed her in 2004. Terrie Petree interpreted.
7. Daniel Ávila—Elderly butcher in Mexicali who knew quite a bit about Chinese tunnels and had one in his cellar. Interviewed 2003. José López and Terrie Petree interpreted.
8. Jose Angel—Branch Chief of the Regional Water Control Board, Palm Desert. Interviewed by telephone, 2001.
9. Professor Eduardo Auyón Gerardo—A world renowned painter of horses and nude women; also an endlessly helpful discloser of Chinese-tunnel secrets. Interviewed in Mexicali, 2003. Lupe Vásquez, José López and Terrie Petree interpreted.
10. Jasmine Brambilla Auyón—Professor Auyón's niece. Interviewed with her mother in Mexicali, 2003. Lupe Vásquez interpreted.
11. Elderly barber in Pasajes Prendes, Mexicali—Interviewed in 2003 about the tunnels and the old days. Terrie Petree interpreted.
12. Kay Brockman Bishop—Interviewed in 2006 about her life and the Imperial Valley, where she was born in 1947 and where she still lives. Her man Dutch was present and occasionally put in some words.
13. Ben Brock—Third-generation family farmer (Brock Farms: asparagus). In his thirties. Interviewed in Holtville, 2004.
14. Richard Brogan—Private investigator specializing in stolen aircraft recovery. Former deputy sheriff in Imperial County and in Yuma. Some experience of farming. Born in La Jolla in 1944; came to the Imperial Valley in the early fifties. Interviewed in Calexico, 2004.
15. Araceli Cabadas—Thirtyish realtor in Salton City who assured me that the sea had a "filtration system." Interviewed in December 2006. Terrie Petree was present.
16. Fred Cagle—Audubon Society spokesman. Interviewed by telephone, 2001.
17. Carl Calvert—Restorer at the Motor Transport Museum in Campo. Interviewed there, October 2003. Terrie Petree was present.
18. Carmen Carillo—Grape picker who lived in Northside, possibly in Holtville, but she did not say. She looked to be in her mid-thirties. Interviewed in Calexico, 2003. Her friend Susana Caudillo was present, as was Lupe Vásquez.
19. Carlos—Multiply deported *pollo*. Mid-thirties? Interviewed in Mexicali, 1999.
20. Old Carlos—My name for him, to distinguish him from other Carloses. In fact he was ancient. "You just

want to take a photo of me because I'm a relic. I don't like people." Interviewed very briefly in El Mayor Indígenas Cucapá, 2003. Terrie Petree interpreted.

21. Juan Carlos Martínez Caro—Policeman in Mexicali. Late thirties? Interviewed at the station in Mexicali, 2005.
22. Mr. and Mrs. José Castro—Mrs. Castro did not give me her name. Both in late middle age. He was born in Mexicali, and she came from Sonora. Residents of Ejido Netzahualcóyotl (east of Mexicali) since 1970, when they built their house. Interviewed in 2004. Terrie Petree interpreted.
23. Susana Caudillo—Grape picker who lived in Holtville. She looked to be in her mid-thirties. Interviewed in Calexico, 2003. Her friend Carmen Carillo was present, as was Lupe Vásquez.
24. Francisco Cedeño—Ex-policeman, born in 1972. Composer of ballads about narcotraffickers and also about his policewoman wife. Interviewed at home in Colonia Luiso Blanco, 2005. Terrie Petree interpreted.
25. Hermenegildo Pérez Cervantes—Born in 1924. Retired teacher. Fifty years of service. Interviewed in the Casa Cultura in Mexicali, December 2006. Terrie Petree interpreted.
26. Border Patrolwoman Gloria Chavez—Younger. Interviewed in Chula Vista and along the border while on patrol, 1999. Lizzy Kate Gray was present.
27. Cameron and Diana Chino—He was Native American (Quechan), and his wife, who was Caucasian, had spent some of her girlhood on the reservation, where they now lived in a house of their own. Interviewed in December 2006. Terrie Petree was present.
28. Herb Cilch—Worked for the Bureau of Reclamation from 1948 to 1950, surveying the lower Colorado River. Interviewed in San Diego, 2003.
29. Carolyn Cooke—Director of the Coachella Historical Society. Arrived in Coachella in 1957, probably as a newlywed. Worked as a bookkeeper-accountant for a major grape grower in Coachella for twenty-three years. Interviewed in Indio, 2004.
30. Cookies—Heavyset cantina prostitute. Probably younger than she looked. The mother of two. Interviewed in Mexicali over dinner with her colleague María, 2005. Terrie Petree interpreted.
31. José Rigoberto Cruz Córdoba—Workman. He was concreting over the Río Nuevo when I interviewed him in Mexicali in 2001. Rebeca Hernández interpreted.
32. Antonia Torres Cucapá—Fortyish, Cucapah, interviewed in her yard on the reservation in the Mexicali Valley, 2003. Her sisters, Juana Torres Glez Cucapá and Jaziel Soto Torres Cucapá, also put in some words. Terrie Petree interpreted.
33. Eugene Dahm—Elderly Imperial County farmer who remembered Mexicali in the 1940s. Interviewed in 2002 at the Imperial County Historical Society Pioneers Museum along with another "pioneer," the latter being from Heber, who chose not to be named.
34. Mr. D.—Private investigator based in San Rafael. Specialized in infiltrating *maquiladoras*. Interviewed and hired by me in 2004. He went to Tijuana to find the four or five worst *maquiladoras* he could and gave me contact information. His name is on file at the California State Archives.
35. Jacob Dickinson—My college classmate and longtime friend. He married a fellow mechanical engineer and raised a family in Long Beach. Interviewed in various areas of Greater Los Angeles in 1997–2007. He was pushing fifty at the end of this period.
36. Pascuala Saiz Domínguez—Fullbooded Cucupah who claimed to be 115 years old when I interviewed her in the Mexicali Valley in 2003. Lupe Vásquez interperpreted.
37. Employee of the State Commission of Public Services in Mexicali—Elderly man interviewed in his yard in Colonia Santo Niño (southwest of Mexicali Valley), in 2004, Terrie Petree interpreting. Declined to have his name printed in this book.
38. Karina D. Duarte Gonzales—Her family owned a *joyería* in Mexicali's Chinesca. She and her sister provided brave company on an exploration of the Chinese tunnel in their store. She was in her late twenties or early thirties. Interviewed and photographed in June 2003. Terrie Petree interpreted.
39. Old man from Durango—His son was having difficulty with his heart which might become a medical emergency, so the old man had come to visit him. Unfortunately his money was now running out, so he would have to return to Durango. "No, I don't like it here," he said, slowly gesturing up and down (he had shoulders like bull), "because I'm a farmer and I like to be where there's work. From what I hear, there *is* work, especially in the *ejidos* out near Kilometer Fifty-seven, but I have no money to go there." Interviewed in San Luis Río Colorado, December 2006. Terrie Petree interpreted.
40. Emily—Dance hall girl, slender and twenty-four, with four children. She preferred to call herself a "waitress." Interviewed at her place of work, the Thirteen Negro in Mexicali, 2005. Terrie Petree interpreted.
41. Elvira—Addicted street prostitute with a wrecked-up face. Interviewed in Mexicali, 1996–99. After this I never saw her again; the other girls informed me that she had been murdered. I loved her very much.
42. The fifty-year-old woman in Jacumba—A retired real estate broker. She did not want her name used. I wrote down her remarks verbatim. Interviewed in Jacumba, July 2004.
43. Mr. and Mrs. Claude Finnell—Mrs. Finnell did not give me her name (which research indicates to be Ger-

aldine). Mr. Finnell (born probably in 1925) was the Imperial County Agricultural Commissioner from 1954 through 1986. Now retired from that position, he worked as a lobbyist for the Metropolitan Water District. Interviewed in El Centro, 2004.

44. Señor Ramón Flores—Mexicali resident since 1937 who lived in smell's reach of the Río Nuevo. Diabetic; legless. Interviewed in 2001. Rebeca Hernández interpreted.
45. Señora Teresa García—The woman of the house at Rancho Garcia in Colonia Sieto de Cierro Prieto, about twenty kilometers south of Mexicali. Born on this ranch in 1940. Her parents came here in 1936 or 1937. Interviewed in 2004. Terrie Petree interpreted.
46. Ray Garnett—Proprietor of Ray's Salton Sea Guide Service, born *circa* 1923. Had been eating Salton Sea fish since 1955, "and I'm still here, so there's nothin' wrong with 'em." Interviewed on the Salton Sea and on the New River, 2001.
47. Tirso Geraldo—Worked in a juice-squeezing business in San Luis Río Colorado, where he was born. Interviewed in 2003, when he was 21.
48. Juana Torres González—Fortyish Cucapah lady, interviewed in her yard on the reservation in the Mexicali Valley, 2003. Terrie Petree interpreted.
49. Sergio Rivera Gómez—A labor official, or technically *Asesor Legal de la* Federación Local CROC Mexicali. Youngish. Interviewed in his office in 2003, Terrie Petree interpreting.
50. Larry Grogan—Proprietor of Valley Pawn in El Centro. Born in 1942. His term as Mayor of El Centro had just ended when I interviewed him in 2003; he was about to run for Supervisor.
51. Carlos Guillermo Baja Terra—Driver-guide to whom I was referred by the Mexicali Tourist Office, 28 September 2003. He was thirty-three.
52. Guillermo—Originally from the state of Guerrero, he had been in San Luis Río Colorado since 1982. In early middle age. Interviewed there in a park in November 2003, Terrie Petree interpreting.
53. Alma Rosa Hernández and Hugo Heriberto Herrera—Both young adults; he was younger than she. Interviewed in her house or theirs in Ejido Netzahualcóyotl, December 2006, Terrie Petree interpreting.
54. Rebeca and Susana Hernández—Sisters; "border girls" in their early twenties. Rebeca was a choreographer. Interviewed in Mexicali and Calexico, 2001 and 2002.
55. Ray House—Worked in the Indio Date Festival for fifty years starting in 1947. Interviewed in Indio, July 2004.
56. Sabine Huynen—Representative of the Salton Sea Database Project, University of Redlands. Interviewed by telephone, 2001.
57. Alfonso Rodríguez Ibarra—*Programador* (network programmer) at Radiorama Mexicali, an umbrella organization for two AM and three FM stations. Interviewed in his office, 2005. Terrie Petree interpreted.
58. Carmen Jaham—Elderly Chinese-Mexican mestiza who went to school in a tunnel under what is now the Methodist church on Avenida Juarez, Mexicali. Owner of a small chain of shoe stores; widow. Interviewed in Mexicali, 2003. Terrie Petree interpreted.
59. Juan the crackhead—Youngish. Connected to *pollos* and coyotes. Interviewed in Mexicali, 1999.
60. Julio—mid- to late thirties, campesino, panhandler and drunk, interviewed in English in Calexico, July 2005. Information from our conversation also appears in my book *Poor People* (Ecco, 2007). Micheline Marcom was present.
61. Karla—Young street prostitute from one of the *colonias* south of Mexicali. Interviewed in Mexicali, February 2004.
62. Edith Karpen—Retired schoolteacher, born *circa* 1910. Came to Calipatria in 1933; also lived in El Centro, Calexico and on a ranch near Signal Mountain. Mother of Alice Woodside. Interviewed in Sacramento, 2004. She died in 2006.
63. Tom Kirk—Head of the Salton Sea Authority. Interviewed by telephone, 2001.
64. Leonard Knight—Creator of Salvation Mountain, born 1931 in Vermont; arrived in Niland in 1986. Interviewed at the mountain (near Niland), 1997–2005.
65. Art and Helen La Londe—Moved from Riverside to the Coachella Valley in 1945. Interviewed in Indio, July 2004.
66. Leonardo—A pimp specializing in hypothetical young girls and nonexistent Chinese tunnels. A man of his word; a perfect human being. He usually worked in Tijuana. Interviewed in Mexicali, 2003.
67. Steve Leung—AKA Esteban León. Middle-aged photo-store owner; third-generation Chinese immigrant and high-ranking member of the Sam Yap Association. Interviewed in Mexicali, 2003–05.
68. Beatriz Limón—Reporter for *La Crónica* in Mexicali. Interviewed in Mexicali, 2003. Lupe Vásquez and José López interpreted.
69. Carmen Lopez—Aged twelve. Wanted to be a cheerleader. Interviewed in Duroville, Riverside County, 2004.
70. Jose Lopez—Field worker, hotel clerk, ex-Marine, born in Mexicali. In his thirties. Rafted the New River with me. Interviewed in Calexico and Mexicali, 2001.

71. José López from Jalisco—Actually born in Mexicali. Ex–field worker and multiply deported *pollo*. When I knew him, he made his living offering his services to gringos a few steps into Mexico. His wife and children remained in Jalisco. In 2004 he stopped being homeless and began renting a room, but I cannot say for how long. Interviewed in Mexicali, 2002–5.
72. Lourdes—*Maquiladora* worker interviewed in La Jolla Industrial Park, Tijuana, 2004. Terrie Petree interpreted. This nineteen-year-old woman, who gave me a copy of her medical report to insert into this book, had developed TB, she believed as a result of breathing the glue when assembling radio speakers at the Maquiladora Formosa. She bravely employed the button camera to covertly film a *maquiladora*, but the camera failed.
73. Javier Lupercio—Field worker with papers, born in Mexicali in 1945. Interviewed in Mexicali, 2004. Terrie Petree interpreted.
74. Lupita—Middle-aged parking lot attendant in Mexicali; formerly worked at a dance club. Interviewed in 2003. Terrie Petree interpreted.
75. María—Chunky cantina prostitute. Middle-aged, with five children. Interviewed in Mexicali over dinner with her colleague Cookies, 2005. Terrie Petree interpreted.
76. Mario—Longtime waiter at the Thirteen Negro dance hall in Mexicali. He appeared to be in early middle age, but may have been older. Interviewed at work, 2005. Terrie Petree interpreted.
77. Middle-aged Mexican-American woman in Salton City—Declined to give her name. Interviewed in December 2006. Terrie Petree interpreted.
78. Olga Liria Márquez—Resident of Colonia Colorado No. 4, which is about fifteen kilometers southeast of Mexicali. She had lived here thirty-one years and was a housewife and mother. Had visited her uncles in Indio, La Quinta, Bakersfield; had taken her children to Disneyland. Was very happy where she was. Interviewed in 2004. Terrie Petree interpreted.
79. Francisco Manuel Preciado Martínez—Resident of San Luis Río Colorado; fifty-two years old. Disconsolate at having been deported and having also suffered the disappearance of his wife, he lived in the street. Interviewed in December 2006. Terrie Petree interpreted.
80. Professor Larry McCaffery—American literature teacher at San Diego State; literary critic; in his early sixties. Resident of Borrego Springs. Guide and companion in many of my Imperial adventures. Interviewed 1996–2004.
81. Stella Mendoza—Board member of the Imperial Irrigation District. Born 1948. She was President during the crucial juncture at the end of 2002 when the water transfer was voted in (she voted against). Interviewed at her home in Brawley, 2003.
82. Eugenia McNaughton—EPA scientist. Interviewed by telephone in San Francisco, 2001.
83. Border Patrolman Dan Murray—Almost retirement age. Interviewed in Calexico and along the border while on patrol, 1999.
84. Evalía Pérez de Navarro—Hairdresser in late middle age. Interviewed while she cut my hair in San Luis Río Colorado, 2003. Terrie Petree interpreted.
85. George Michael Newman—Chief Executive Officer of Tactical Investigative Services, San Diego. Interviewed by telephone, 2003.
86. Clare Ng—My Chinese interpreter. Went down to Mexicali with her daughter in 2003 to interview Chinese for me about tunnels. Interviewed by me in Sacramento, 2003.
87. Rosalyn Ng—Clare's daughter. Wrote Chinese-tunnels report for me in 2003.
88. Teresa Cruz Ochoa and her husband José de Jesús Galleta Lamas—Married thirty-four years; probably in their fifties but looked older. Had lived in Colonia Borges (three kilometers south of the line) for thirty years. Interviewed at their home in December 2006. Terrie Petree interpreted.
89. Yolanda Sánchez Ogás—Historian of Mexicali (where she was born circa 1940); anthropologist specializing in Cucapah Indians. Interviewed in Mexicali, 2003, 2004. Lupe Vásquez, José López and Terrie Petree variously interpreted.
90. Part-time cowgirl in Independence—How much of a cowgirl she actually was I cannot say, since she was selling sodas and beers in a little store in July 2005. But she claimed to ride horses on Owens Dry Lake, and she seemed honest. She declined to have her name used. Micheline Marcom was present.
91. Augustín Pérez Aguilar—Reporter for *La Frontera* (Tijuana). Interviewed in English at a restaurant in Tijuana Centro, July 2004. Terrie Petree was present.
92. Carlos Pérez—Policeman in Mexicali. Late thirties? Interviewed at the station in Mexicali, 2005. Terrie Petree interpreted.
93. Rosa Pérez—Elderly woman from Sacramento, California. Interviewed December 2006 in the Child Heroes Park in Mexicali, the city of her husband's upbringing. Terrie Petree interpreted.
94. Terrie Petree—A good Mormon girl who all the same somehow liked me. A fearless driver-interpreter, button-camera spy, companion, confidante who in the course of working for me sustained significant damage to her car from burglars and other agents of the Great Road. She turned thirty before the end of this project, but remains unbowed by old age. Many sections of this book benefit from her observations.

95. Noe Ponce—Late teens or early twenties. Interviewed in Duroville, Riverside County, 2004.
96. José Quintero—*Pollo* interviewed in Mexicali, 2002.
97. Señor R.—Private investigator based in Tijuana. Fortyish. Interviewed and hired by me in 2004 for my study of the *maquiladoras*. Perla, who covertly filmed several *maquiladoras* for me with my button camera, was in his employ. His name is on file at the California State Archives. Terrie Petree interpreted.
98. Socorro Ramírez—Proprietress of the roadside restaurant Yocojihua about ten kilometers south of Mexicali. Born in Jalisco; was brought to the Mexicali Valley as a child in 1952; picked cotton with her parents. Interviewed in her restaurant, 19 February 2004. Terrie Petree interpreted.
99. Zulema Rashid—Born in Calexico in 1945; third-generation through Lebanese father (grandfather arrived in Imperial Valley *circa* 1910). Mother Mexican. Interviewed in Calexico, summer 2003.
100. Natalio Morales Rebolorio—Caretaker of Rancho Roa, about ten kilometers south of Mexicali. Interviewed on the ranch in 2004 and 2005. Terrie Petree interpreted.
101. Anna Silva Reina—Waitress in San Luis Río Colorado who wished to find her missing father. Born in San Luis, she had lived there and in Caborca, "to the north." She had never been to Mexicali. She was twenty-five when I interviewed her in December 2006. Terrie Petree interpreted.
102. Rubén—Deported *pollo* working in a taco stand in Mexicali; interviewed in 1999.
103. Celestino Rivas—Sixty-two-year-old field worker, born in Michoacán; came as a bracero and stayed after he got his *mica* (border crossing card). Interviewed in Calexico, 2003. Lupe Vásquez was present and introduced me.
104. Juan Rodríguez—Older taxi driver who lived Monday through Friday in the city of Imperial, and weekends in Mexicali. Spoke very little English. Interviewed in his taxi, 2002.
105. Marjorie Gellhorn Sa'adah—Historian of downtown Los Angeles, and especially of its architecture. Interviewed in her area of specialty, September 2004. She gave a wonderful walking tour.
106. Luz María Salcido—Young housewife, with sixteen-year-old daughter; interviewed in her bare dirt yard in San Luis Río Colorado, where she had lived for years. The conversation took place in October 2003. Terrie Petree interpreted.
107. Don Carlos Cayetano Sanders-Collins—Rancher in middle age; interviewed with his family in his yard in a built-up *ejido* called Ciudad Morelos (southwest of Algodones, in the Mexicali Valley). Born in Ejido Indo. He lived in a house and his two brothers shared the family ranch, which lay some distance away. "Some of the family is here, some in the United States where they work." The interview took place in October 2003, Terrie Petree interpreting.
108. Gilberto Sanders—Rancher in middle age; interviewed with his brother at his ranch in Ejido Morelos. Brother of Don Carlos Cayetano Sanders-Collins. The interview took place in October 2003, Terrie Petree interpreting.
109. Border Patrol Duty Officer Michael Singh—Interviewed at Calexico Station, 1999.
110. Alice Solario—Elderly Filipina married to a Mexican; munitions-factory worker; resident of Mecca since 1986; interviewed there in 2000.
111. Tim—Chinese teenager, probably illegal, interviewed in Mexicali, 2003. Terrie Petree interpreted.
112. Lic. Carlos E. Tinoco—Official of the Tribunal Unitario Agrario Distrito Dos. Interviewed in the tribunal offices in Mexicali, 2005. Terrie Petree interpreted.
113. Dr. John Tyler and his wife Margaret—Retired dentist (born 27 November 1911), who arrived in the Coachella Valley in 1936. She was born on a ranch in Coachella (9 November 1916). Interviewed in Palm Desert, April 2004.
114. David Urbanoski—Manager of the marina at Desert Shores, where I interviewed him in 2001. Long-term resident; older.
115. Lupe Vásquez—Field worker with papers, born in Mexicali; married, with a child. My friend. He must have been about fifty. Interviewed in Mexicali, 2001–2004.
116. Border Patrolman Brian Willett—Youngish. Interviewed at the Chula Vista border checkpoint while on patrol, 1999.
117. Xu—College-age Chinese waitress at the Dong Cheng restaurant in Mexicali; interviewed there and in a nearby tunnel, 2003. Terrie Petree interpreted. In 2004 Xu was no longer at the Dong Cheng.
118. Xu's uncle—The "soft-spoken old shoe-store owner." He was also Chinese, obviously. Xu gave me his name but he didn't want me to use it. Interviewed in his store, November 2003. José López from Jalisco interpreted.
119. Mr. W.—The surveillance-countersurveillance expert who sold me the button camera which I used in my study of the *maquiladoras*. Interviewed by telephone in 2004. His name is on file at the California State Archives.
120. Alice Woodside—Rancher's daughter; real estate broker; born *circa* 1942 in the Imperial Valley near Signal Mountain. Daughter of Edith Karpen. Interviewed in Sacramento, 2004.

BIBLIOGRAPHY

This bibliography is divided into the following sections:

- A **Archival Sources.** Authors are especially proud of these, because inspecting them is inconvenient to most of the people who read our books. That is why these usually get listed first. Allow us our pathetic glory; we need to pretend that we have not wasted our lives.
- B **Ephemeral and Unpublished Sources.** Could probably have been put in the first category, but since they're not all linked with a specific depository I saw fit to indulge an unaccustomed mania for tidiness. (My copies of these will be archived at Ohio State University.) These include dissertations.
- C **Periodical Sources.** It is very important to my image of myself that you know that I sometimes read the *New York Times.* Longish feature articles on specific topics are filed under those topics, an example being "The Chinese and Economic Development of Baja California," which appears in category L.
- D **Websites.** A particularly hated category. Some URLs listed here are now obsolete.
- E **Reference Serials.** A lot of news about mostly nothing.
- F **Government Documents.** Originally classed together with the previous category since congressional records, *California Blue Books,* etc., are in effect an immense, open-ended serial; so in a way are the reports of most government agencies. But I didn't want to annoy you. This category includes vital records such as death certificates and Ted Gostin's privately compiled *Southern California Vital Records* but excludes the *Memoria administrativa* of Abelardo L. Rodriguez (found in category H).
- G **Area Descriptions, Guides and Atlases.** Everything from E. J. Wickson's fossilized *Rural California* (1923) to near-ephemeral tourist books. Nongovernmental economic regional profiles also appear here. Some of this miscellany could easily have gone into the next category, or into the previous one, but what can I do? Archival and ephemeral maps appear under their own respective categories.
- H **Memoirs, Diaries, Correspondence, Histories, Pictorials.** For example, Pat Laflin's unendingly peculiar *Salton Sea: California's Overlooked Treasure.* Some Mexican and many American materials are found here (e.g., Hamilton's writings); Chinese, Native American, Mexican and Los Angeleno materials each get their own category. Memoirs of migrant workers are in category K, as is a monograph on Dorothea Lange.
- I **Agriculture and Ecology.** Professor W. V. Cruess's classic *Commercial Fruit and Vegetable Products* gets the prize. Agricultural atlases remain in category G, as does Gregor's *Agricultural Typology of California.* Being a pictorial, McClelland and Last's *California Orange Box Labels* rests in H. Boyer's book on agrarian struggle in Michoacán is in N.
- J **Irrigation and Water Politics.** Water atlases remain in category G. Histories of the Colorado River and the Salton Sea remain in category H since I tend to cite them in descriptive and historical contexts.
- K **Migrant Workers, Labor Movements and the Border Economy.** Ruben Salazar, César Chávez, Okies, hobos, the Wobblies, etc. Since the Wobblies are here, so are revolutionaries such as Ricardo Flores Magón.
- L **Chinese Sources.** Includes memoirs, fiction, poetry and visual art. The Chinese-tunnel letters are in category B.
- M **Native American Sources.** Includes memoirs, fiction, poetry and visual art.
- N **Miscellaneous Mexican Sources.** Includes memoirs, fiction, poetry and visual art, such as works on and by José Clemente Orozco. Ulysses S. Grant appears here because all I cite from him is his description of Baja California.
- O **Los Angeles.** Excludes water politics (category I). Includes Catalina Island and other holdings of Greater Los Angeles, not to mention Diebenkorn's Ocean Park paintings.
- P **Fiction and Poetry About Imperial.**
- Q **Published Sources Metaphorically Relevant to Imperial.** For instance, works about Mark Rothko.

My arrangement is a compromise between making references easy to browse by category in this bibiography and making citations rational in the notes. For example, one generally cites by author or agency, but why shouldn't the California Death Index be listed under precisely that name instead of under "State of California, Department of Public Health, Bureau of Vital Statistics and Data Processing"? So in the notes I have cited it the easy way. It appears in this bibliography in the "Government Documents" section, under its cumbersomely correct name, but prefixed by and alphabetized under the words "Death Index," with "California Death Index," so that someone who comes across it in the notes can find it.

Citations are filed under title when the author is anonymous. Art monographs are generally cited by the artist's name, not the editor's. If they are primarily biographies, then that is different. In short, I am going to do what I am going to do.

At the end of this bibliography, every work is cited in short form, together with the category in which its full citation appears (for example, "Tout, *The First Thirty Years*, H").

NOTE ON RESTRICTED FILES &C

As will be mentioned below in appropriate spots, the identity of some anonymous informants and details concerning certain restricted files has been noted in a document now at the California State Archives. This document (itself a restricted file) is catalogued under the following heading: "Vollmann, William T. Confidential sources and restricted files cited in *Imperial*." I might have preferred to leave a copy of this document with Ohio State University, which is the repository of most of my papers; however, many of the restricted files I cite come from the California State Archives themselves, so confidentiality would have been breached had I left this information anywhere else. Should the CSA give me permission to do so in future, I will leave an additional copy of this document at OSU.

A. ARCHIVAL SOURCES

1. Archivo Histórico del Municipio de Mexicali.
   a. Albums of mostly uncoded photographs.
   b. Maps as cited.
   c. Chata Angulo collection (about a dozen boxes). Historical documents relating mostly to land and the Colorado River Land Company.
2. California State Archives. Obviously, all departments cited here are state, not federal.
   a. Agricultural Labor Relations Board, restricted files. Hearing and litigation documents, 1978–1984.
   b. Accession #1999–10–13, catalogue #s [which the CSA sometimes also refers to as "locations"] B8096–2 (Box 1), B8096–3 (Box 2), B8097–1 (Box 3), B8097–3 (Box 5), B8098–1 (Box 6), B8099–1 (Box 9).
   c. Accession #1999–10–9, catalogue #s B8101 (Boxes 2, 3). The cataloguing system from (a) to (b) was inconsistent.
   d. Accession #1999–07–08 catalogue #s B7949–7955. Boxes 1–2 of 27. Specific location number not indicated on these boxes. Written on box: "EBR."
      (1) Court cases, being public documents, are referred to by name. Hearing files are private. I have prepared a list of the codes which I have used in this book, and in that list each code matches up with the hearing case numbers. This code list, which is *restricted*, obviously, has been placed on file at the California State Archives under the following heading: Vollmann, William T. Confidential sources and restricted files cited in *Imperial*.
   e. Department of Food and Agriculture. Bureau of Marketing. Marketing order files, 1941–1971, arranged by commodity and chronology. Boxes 1, 3, 4, 6, 7. Accession #88–97, catalogue #B2130–32. [Bound typescripts.]
   f. Margaret C. Felts papers, 1881–2002. Accession #2003–148. Boxes 1, 7, 12 and 17 of 17. Location: B4380–86. Primary and secondary source material on California groundwater contamination.
   g. Legislative papers. Statement on number of aliens, 1939, 2 files. Catalogue #P14.43.44, D10, Box 1. [Part of a survey required of all California counties.]
   h. Maps as cited. [Imperial County and adjacent areas of Mexico 1900–1920.]
   i. Microfilmed Imperial County records, 1851–1919. Location: MF4:4.
   j. Microfilm roll #1433101. Imperial County. Index to Grantors, 1851–1907. Index to Grantees, 1851–1907. Index to Marriages, Men, v. 1–2, 1903–1923. Index to Marriages, Women, v. 1–2, 1903–1923. Marriage Licenses, v. 1–6, 1907–1914.
      (1) Microfilm roll #1433102. Imperial County. Marriage Licenses, 1912–1919.
      (2) Microfilm roll #1433103. Imperial County. Marriage Licenses, 1917–1919.
   k. Olson Photo Collection. Stock photographs, c. 1930–1970. Accession #94–06–27. Catalogue #C 5266. Boxes 1 through 4 of 7.
   l. Victor V. Vesey, oral history; interview by Enid H. Douglas (July & September 1988), for the California State Archives State Government Oral History Program. [Bound typescript volume.]
3. Imperial County Agricultural Commission papers (El Centro), 1915–2002.
   a. Yearly crop yields. Sent by Stephen L. Birdsall, the Agricultural Commissioner, to my researcher Kara

Platoni in 2004. Upon completion of this book I gave these papers to the California State Archives since many were originals. How they will be catalogued is unknown to me, but they should be easy to locate in the archives's finding aids.

4. Imperial County Historical Society Pioneers Museum, city of Imperial. **[Cited: ICHSPM]**
   a. Photograph collection. Includes many Hetzel pictures. These images usually, but not always, bear unique codes; sometimes each member of a series within an envelope or photo is identically labeled. Fortunately, the number of prints within a series is small—usually half a dozen or less—so it will not be much of a chore for any researcher to locate the images cited here.
   b. Document collection. Letters, certificates, pamphlets, advertising circulars, almanacs, yearbooks, etc. Catalogued analogously to the photo collection. Cited sources include:
      (1) Ball Advertising Co., "Visitors' Recreation Guide Book to Imperial County California: 36 Pages of Information,"*ca.* 1964. Pamphlet. ICHSPM document cat. #A2002.154.2
      (2) Colorado River Association (1952). Colorado River Association, pamphlet "California and the Colorado River" (Los Angeles, 1952. Pamphlet. ICHSPM document cat. #A2002.581.1.
      (3) [Hostess Reference Book (1936).] "Hostess Reference Book, Signal Chapter, No. 276, Order of the Eastern Star, El Centro, California," n.d.; *ca.* 1936. Pamphlet. ICHSPM doc. cat. #A2000.31.11.
      (4) William E. Warne, Water Resources Consultant, Sacramento, California, "The Stormy Past and Clouded Future of Desalting in the Colorado River Basin," repr. from WSIA Journal—July 1984. ICHSPM doc. cat. #A84.48.1
      (5) W. E. Wilsie, "How It Feels to Be Broke at Sixty, or, High Finance in Imperial Valley." Five-p. typescript, dated June 1, 2001, but evidently originally written in, or set in, 1916; with a later attachment which could well have been written in 2000. ICHSPM doc. cat. #A2110.17.1.
5. National Archives and Records Administration, Pacific Region (Laguna Niguel, California). **[Cited: N.A.R.A.L.]**
   a. Record Group 36. Records of the U.S. Customs Service. Calexico Customs Office.
      (1) Calexico Customs Office. Incoming Official Correspondence (9L–60). October 15, 1902–March 23, 1916. 5 boxes.
      (2) Calexico Customs Office. Incoming Correspondence Regarding Smuggling (9L-61). July 25, 1914–May 23, 1922. 2 boxes.
      (3) Port of Campo. General Correspondence 1919–1965. 1 box.
      (4) Tiajuana [*sic*] Customs Office. Letters Received from San Diego and Los Angeles (9L-62). February 6, 1894–July 29, 1922. 1 box.
6. State of California. Department of Transportation. Transportation Library, Sacramento. **[Cited: CA DOT.]**
   a. Imperial folder. Miscellaneous maps, highway reports, periodical clippings, one photograph.
   b. Maps. These very large items were brought out to me singly, without any codes on them that I know of.
7. University of California, Berkeley, Bancroft Library.
   a. [Governor] Hiram Warren Johnson correspondence and papers. Subject files (excepting Alien Land Law). Carton #C-B 581, Part II, Box 42. Mexican border incidents. Telegrams to Johnson from G. Gordon Whitnell, Rev. Edwards Burger, H. S. Utley, M. D. Witter, D. K. Adams, Edward Berger, Milbank Johnson. Letter from official of Klauber Wagenheim Co. to Sen. Edgar Luce. Letter from C. R. Rockwood to Adjutant General Thomas.
   b. Farm labor situation 1933–34. [Mostly notes written by, correspondence to, or items gathered by or for Dean Hutchinson.] Carton #C-R 84. Folders:
      (1) Miscellany A–Z correspondence.
      (2) Associated Farmers of California, Inc.
      (3) California Dept. of Agriculture.
      (4) Circulars, handbills.
      (5) Reports: C. B. Hutchinson, W. C. Jacobsen, John Phillips, "The Imperial Valley Farm Labor Situation: Report of the Special Investigating Committee appointed at the request of the California State Board for Agriculture, the California Farm Bureau Federation, and the Agricultural Department of the California State Chamber of Commerce," submitted to the Executive Committee representing the three above groups, Sacramento, California, April 16, 1934 (32 pp.).
      (6) Notes.
      (7) Miscellany.
   c. Powell Studio album. Cotton Strike, Calif. 1933. Transferred from Paul [S.] Taylor papers (C-R-#). Cat. #1945.7 PIC. Miscatalogued online as 1945.002 PIC. Photographs.
   d. [Paul S. Taylor papers.] Bancroft Library Manuscripts Collection. Paul Schuster Taylor, 1895–. Papers, 1895–1984. BANC MSS 84/38. Cartons 3, 4 and 5. Drafts of published and unpublished articles on agriculture, water, migrant labor, the Imperial Valley, Mexicans and Mexican-Americans; correspondents; monographs, reprints.

8. University of California, Davis, General Library, Department of Special Collections.
   a. California Local History and Related Materials Collection. [Formerly and more appropriately entitled "California Promotional Materials Collection."] No accession number; container CAL Box 60; uncatalogued at time of research due to changeover from card to computer. Various pamphlets and brochures as follows:
      (1) Pamphlet, "Artistic Series, Views of Los Angeles and Vicinity," *ca.* 1910.
      (2) Pamphlet, "1901–1915: Imperial Valley," n.d., unnumbered.
      (3) Don C. Bitler, ed., published by Charles E. Miller, issued by the Board of Supervisors of Imperial County, pamphlet, "The Imperial Valley California 1920."
      (4) Imperial Valley Department, California Land and Water Co., brochure, "Imperial Valley: Brawley: 20,000 in 1920", 1913.
      (5) Imperial Valley Farm Lands Owners Association, Schader and Beach, General Sales Agents, California Land and Water Co., Special Agents, brochure, "Nile-Lands Farms, Imperial Valley," 1913.
      (6) California Development Association brochure, "Come to EL CENTRO, CALIFORNIA," *ca.* 1925.
      (7) Imperial Valley Board of Trade brochure, ed. and comp. B. A. Harrigan, County Horticultural Commissioner, "Sunny Imperial Valley, America's Winter Garden," 1927. Unnumbered. Bears the admonition: "Build Boulder Dam!"
      (8) Imperial Valley Board of Trade brochure, "Imperial Valley: America's Winter Garden," *ca.* 1934, with pictorial colored map. Across bottom of front cover: "ALL AMERICAN CANAL GIVES IMPERIAL VALLEY AN ASSURED WATER SUPPLY UNDER CONTROL."
      (9) Imperial County Board of Trade pamphlet, "Imperial County, California: America's Winter Garden," *ca.* 1955 (gives population of 75,000).
   b. Austin C. Chiles papers. Accession #D133; container MC133. "The Coachella Valley Part II: Agriculture and Flood and Earthquake Hazards," Austin C. Chiles, Appraiser, Appraisal Dept., Los Angeles Headquarters [of unnamed bank], August 1953–April 1954. Approx. 300-p. bound typescript. First vol. missing. On lower righthand corner of cover sheet is a number 14, so this may part of a series of assessments of various places.
   c. David Shank papers. Accession #D139. "Theodore Benjamin Shank and his Early Years in the Imperial Valley, California," by David Shank. Three unnumbered typescript pp., 1994.

B. EPHEMERAL AND UNPUBLISHED SOURCES

1. ______, handmade flyer about the disappeared *pollo* Serafín Ramírez Hernández. Given to me in the Park of Child Heroes, Mexicali, 1999.
2. Henry T. Andersen, "The Advertising of California Fruits" (Davis: University of California Ph.D. thesis in agricultural science, 1920).
3. Robert C. Berlo, "Population History Maps of California 1770 to 1998" (Livermore, California, 1998; binder of maps of California regions at ten-year intervals; in case you wondered, Imperial was impressively blank in 1770.)
4. Robert C. Berlo, "Population History of California Places: An edited compilation and analysis of all known population figures for California cities, towns, counties, urban areas, and the state total, including the Spanish and Mexican era" (Livermore, California, November 1998).
5. [Brawley Business Directory.] Brawley Business Directory and Visitors' Guide, "produced with pride" by Mosher-Adams, Inc., "Publishers of Quality Chamber Materials Since 1948," Oklahoma City, 1998.
6. [Chinese-tunnel letters.] Letters found in a tunnel under the Restaurante Victoria in Mexicali, 2003. Discovered by Yolanda Sánchez Ogás, Terrie Petree and WTV in 2003. The restaurant owner, Miguel, might or might not have known of their existence before; he was fairly indifferent, allowed me to borrow them to get them translated, but wanted them back. Some were rat-eaten. They lay in a decrepit old desk, mostly in their original envelopes and mostly addressed to Wong Kong Ja Tong. I hired Clare and Rosalyn Ng to translate as many as I could afford. The letters have been translated in batches. Within each batch, the items are numbered and titled. I have kept photocopies of the Chinese originals in each translated batch, matched up to their English translations. At the conclusion of this project, these materials will be donated to the AHMM. The originals have been returned. Here is a representative citation in *Imperial:* "Chinese-tunnel letters, Batch 2, VI (A letter from a wife to a husband)." In Batch 1, my Roman item number (e.g., IV) corresponds to the translator's Arabic page number (p. 4).
7. [Cruz-Kaegi report, 2008.] Nine text and spreadsheet computer files, including the most important one, ReportMaquilaMexico.doc, organized on a CD-ROM in 2008, for WTV. These items contain the findings of Liz Cruz-Kaegi (CKQuest LLC, Business Intelligence), who electronically searched Mexican government and periodical sources regarding specific *maquiladoras.* At the conclusion of this project, her CD will be sent to Ohio State University.

8. John Joseph Dwyer, "Between the Peasants and the Leviathan: The Expropriation and Spontaneous Seizure of American-Owned Agricultural Property in Mexico, 1934–1941" (University of Illinos at Urbana-Champaign Ph.D. thesis in history, 1998).
9. [Paul Foster reports, 2007.] Statistical data, with analysis, collected and organized on a CD-ROM in 2006–2007, for WTV. The items are: "Crop files" (96 files), "Imperial Stats," "Imperial Stats 2," and "Imperial Color Commentary." At the conclusion of this project, the CD will be sent to Ohio State University.
10. Theodora J. Glenn, Palm Springs Desert Museum, "Birds of the Coachella Valley Checklist" (Palm Springs?: Coachella Valley Audobon Society, dated October 1983 but purchased in new condition in 2004).
11. [Golden Acorn placemat.] As mentioned in the text, the Golden Acorn is the casino on the Kumeyaay reservation at Campo. The information on it is entitled: "History of the Campo Band of Kumeyaay Indians." I collected it in about 2004.
12. "A Guide to Independence, California, 2005–2006" (Independence: Probably published by the Independence Chamber of Commerce.)
13. [IID *de novo* Part 417 brief.] Attorneys for Imperial Irrigation District [Allen Matkins Leck Gamble & Mallory LLP: David L. Osias (Bar #091287), Jeffrey R. Patterson (Bar #126148), Mark J. Hattam (Bar #173667), San Diego; *and* Horton, Knox, Carter & Foote: John Penn Carter (Bar #40716), El Centro, *Imperial Irrigation District* "de novo" *2003 Part 417 brief* [re: United States' *de novo* Part 417 review of Imperial Irrigation District's 2003 water order]. Dated: May 29, 2003.
14. [IID letter to farmers, 9 July 2003.] Imperial Irrigation District Public Information Department, El Centro, open letter of July 9, 2003, to "My Fellow Farmers throughout California," from Lloyd Allen, President, IID Board of Directors. 4 pp.
15. [IID objection to Part 417 determination.] Attorneys for Imperial Irrigation District [same as in previous item], *Imperial Irrigation District objection to the part 417 determinations and recommendations made by Regional Director Robert W. Johnson, and demand for further consultation* [re: United States' *de novo* Part 417 review of Imperial Irrigation District's 2003 water order]. Dated: August 5, 2003.
16. [IID testimony, July 1, 2003.] IID Public Information Department (El Centro), Imperial Irrigation District news release: July 1, 2003: "IID Board president testifies on the QSA." Attached: "Lloyd Allen, President, Board of Directors, Imperial Irrigation District: Testimony Before the Committee on Resources, United States House of Representatives, Hearing on California Water Policy, July 1, 2003." News release cover sheet and 5 numbered pp.
17. [IID water-transportation map.] Imperial Irrigation District map of "Water Transportation: Hoover Dam to User," 1958. Credited to G. A. Reed, May 1958. Dwg [drawing?] no. 8402. In the free stack at the ICHSPM, 2002.
18. Imperial Valley Research Center, 4151 Highway 86; pamphlet, collected *ca.* 2000, written *ca.* 1999. "It began with TRADITION . . . It will continue with your SUPPORT."
19. Jacumba Hot Springs Spa & Cabana Club brochure, collected in 2003.
20. [Karpen obituary.] Alice Woodside, draft obituary for her mother, Edith Karpen (d. 30 November 2006). 1 p. of typescript and letter to WTV.
21. Dorothy Pierson Kerig, "Yankee Enclave: The Colorado River Land Company and Mexican Agrarian Reform in Baja California, 1902–1944" (Irvine: University of California Ph.D. thesis in history, 1988).
22. [*Maquiladora* disposable-camera photos.] Two rolls of film shot for hire in July 2004 by *maquiladora* workers without management authorization, but with some cooperation from coworkers. Prints are on file at Ohio State Univeristy. Access is *restricted* to protect the *maquiladoras* against any inadvertent privacy infringement or trade secret exposure.
    a. Kimstar, Insurgentes, Tijuana. Some coworkers and production-line views. Name of photographer is on file at the California State Archives in my list of restricted names.
    b. Unnamed *maquiladora,* Mexicali. Mainly views of unpleasant bathroom. Shot for me by unnamed man; transaction arranged by José López.
23. [*Maquiladora* videos.] Covert digital videos made with a button camera in Tijuana and Mexicali by WTV and the Tijuana private detective "Perla," July 2004. Originals in AVI format. Copies are on file at Ohio State University. Access is *restricted* to protect the *maquiladoras* against any inadvertent privacy infringement or trade secret exposure. Doubtless their managers will hate me anyhow.
    a. Formosa, Industrial Park La Jolla, Tijuana. Exterior walkthrough and brief entrance into outside gated area, showing payday. Perla.
    b. Industrial Park Los Pinos, Insurgentes, Tijuana. Walkthrough within gated complex and brief entrance into production area. Also some equally forbidden but less revealing doorway views of spray-paint establishments. WTV.
    c. Kimstar and Óptica Sola, Insurgentes, Tijuana. Exterior walkthroughs. WTV.
    d. Matsushita, Otay, Tijuana. Exterior and interior walkthrough, with several revealing glimpses of the production line. 2 videos. Perla.

e. Miscellaneous Mexicali practice videos. No *maquiladoras.* WTV.
f. Miscellaneous Tijuana practice videos. No *maquiladoras.* WTV.
g. Óptica Sola, Otay, Tijuana. Brief exterior and interior walkthrough. Perla.
h. Phillips, Insurgentes, Tijuana. Brief exterior walk-by, night. WTV.

24. Mary Montgomery, "A Plan for Development and Management of Resources of the Colorado River Basin: A Study of Federal Organization" (Berkeley: University of California Ph.D. thesis in political science, 1943).
25. [Rosalyn Ng report, 2003.] "Mexicali-Calexico Trip [by] Rosalyn Ng," 23–24 July 2003. Report to WTV on interviews conducted in Chinese for this project for Rosalyn and her mother Clare, with the location and Spanish-langauge assistance of Terrie Petree. 14-p. unnumbered typescript incl. cover page. At the conclusion of this project, a copy of this document will be donated to the AHMM, and the original will be deposited at Ohio State University.
26. [Petree translation of Vía Oriente.] Unnumbered typescript, 15 pp. Vía Oriente, numero 1, Zona Río, Tjuana, BC, translated by Terrie Petree, Sept. 2005. Includes interview by Terrie with Tijuana agronomist Javier Meléndrez, 8/1/2005.
27. [Private detective reports, 2003–2007.] Prepared by a California private investigator hired by WTV. This person does not wish his name to be published. The originals will be deposited in the California State Archives as described in the "Note on Restricted Files" at the beginning of this bibliography.
28. [Raskin report, 2008.] Seventeen text computer files, some containing holographic legal documents, scanned newspaper articles, etc.; the most important one, "MEMO OF INVESTIGATION re Maquiladoras.doc," contains the draft report of the private investigator Adam Raskin, who compiled these items in Tijuana for WTV, interviewing several "individuals and entities" in the process. This material was organized on a CD-ROM in 2008, for WTV. These items contain the findings of Liz Cruz-Kaegi (CKQuest LLC, Business Intelligence), who electronically searched Mexican government and periodical sources regarding specific *maquiladoras.* At the conclusion of this project, his CD will be sent to Ohio State University.
29. Jordan A. Rothacker, "The Virgin Mary: The Virgin of Guadalupe, Colonialism, and Remaking the Master Narrative." 13-p. unnumbered typescript with references. Written for the Religious Studies Dept. of the University of Georgia at Athens, *ca.* 2003.
30. The Salton Sea Authority, leaflets for public distribution, received 2001.
31. [Salton Sea map (1986).] "Map of Salton Sea No. 1 (with soundings)," Kym's Guide Maps and Charts of Recreation Areas, 1986 by Triumph Press, Inc., L.A., rev. 1986.
32. [Salton Sea map (1990).] "Salton Sea State Recreation Area," California Department of Parks and Recreation #2–91, 1990.
33. Shields Date Gardens, pamphlet, "Coachella Valley Desert Trails and the Romance and Sex Life of the Date" (Indio: 1952).
34. [Thomas and Tanis Vollmann recollections (2003).] Letter to WTV written for this project by my parents, summarizing their memories of his seven and her six years in southern California. 3-p. unnumbered typescript, dated 14 August 2003.
35. ["Today's IID."] Imperial Irrigation District pamphlet, *ca.* 2004, "Today's IID: Our only business is serving you better." Single sheet, folded, with color photos. Jesse Silva is depicted in a hard hat and identified as General Manager.
36. [Tumco pamplet.] "The U.S. Bureau of Land Management and American Girl Joint Mining Venture Welcomes you to Tumco Townsite Historical Walk." Single sheet, folded into 4 pp. N.d.; collected *ca.* 2000.
37. Unnamed Mexican civil engineer, sketch-map attempting to delineate for me the Río Nuevo and its source, Mexicali, 2001.
38. [Walsh to Platoni e-mail.] E-mail from Robert Walsh RWALSH@lc.usbr.gov., re: Imperial County water use research, date: Tue., February 10, 2004, 3:18 pm, to: my researcher Kara Platoni. E-mail exchange is 1 p., followed by 2-p. attachment tabulating IID water use and crop acres from 1914 to 2002 inclusive.
39. Windsor Publications, brochure, "Imperial Valley, California" (Encino, California, 1968).
40. [Zollinger-Peterson genealogical reports.] White binder compiled by Daina Zollinger and Sydney Peterson, both of River Heights, Utah, 2006. Subjects: Hazel Deed, Albert Henry Larson, Wilber/Wilbur Clark, W. F. Holt, Leroy Holt, miscellaneous articles; Luther M. Holt, other Holts. This binder is now in the archives of Ohio State University.

C. PERIODICAL SOURCES

1. *Astronomy.*
2. *Agricultural History* [Urbana, Illinois: The Agricultural History Society.]
3. *The Berlin Journal: A Magazine from the American Academy in Berlin*

4. *Boletín Maquilero.* [Centro de Información para Trabajadoras y Trabajadors, Tijuana. E-mail address : cittac@prodigy.net.mx.] In particular: *Boletín Maquilero #11,* Tijuana, Baja California (June 2006), published by the Red de Trabajadoras y Trabadores de la Maquila).
5. *Borrego Sun* [Borrego Springs, California.]
6. *Calexico Chronicle.*
7. *California Agriculture: Progress Reports of Agricultural Research* [University of California College of Agriculture, Agricultural Experiment Station].
8. *The California Cultivator: An Illustrated Weekly Magazine, Devoted to the Rural Home and Ranch* [Los Angeles and San Francisco]. AKA *The California Cultivator and Livestock and Dairy Journal.* In 1950 this publication became *The California Farmer (Pacific Rural Press* and *California Cultivator).* I have cited it by whichever name appeared on its masthead in a given issue.
9. [Coachella Valley Historical Society, *The Periscope 1995*: See Pat Laflin in Sec. H.]
10. *The Connoisseur's Guide: Los Angeles.* [Beverly Hills: Connoisseur's Guide Publishing, Inc.] Hardbound annual glossy area guide, mainly advertising; placed in expensive hotels.
11. *The Country Gentleman* [Albany, New York]. Nineteenth to twentieth centuries.
12. *Crops and Soils* [Madison, Wisconsin: The American Society of Agronomy].
13. *La Crónica* [Mexicali].
14. *The Desert Farmer* [Imperial Valley]. Cited early twentieth century.
15. *The Desert Sun* [Palm Springs].
16. *The El Centro Connection: A quarterly publication of the City of El Centro, the Central Union High School District, and the El Centro Regional Medical Center.*
17. *El Mexicano* newspaper [Tijuana?].
18. *El Sol de Tijuana.*
19. *Extension Service Review.* Official organ of the Cooperative Extension Service, USDA, Washington, D.C.
20. *Food Technology* [Champaign, Illinois].
21. [*Fortune.*] Duncan Norton-Taylor, ed., *For Some, the Dream Came True: The Best from 50 Years of Fortune Magazine* (Secaucus, New Jersey: Lyle Stuart, Inc., 1981).
22. *The Fresno Morning Republican.*
23. *The Gringo Gazette* [San Felipe].
24. [*Harper's Weekly* facsimiles.] Sidney Rudeau, archivist, *American Civil War Reports as Recorded in Harper's Weekly* (Verplanck, New York: Historical Briefs, Inc. / Monument Printers and Lithographer, Inc., 1994).
25. Human Rights Watch Publications [New York].
26. *The Imperial Valley News* [Brawley].
27. *The Imperial Valley Press* [El Centro]. At the beginning of the twentieth century this publication was known first as the *Imperial Press and Farmer,* then as *The Imperial Press* before settling into its current name.
28. *The Imperial Valley Weekly* [Holtville]. Originally *The Imperial Evening Enterprise* (founded 1906).
29. *The Imperial Valley White Sheet* [Yuma].
30. *The Indio Post.*
31. *The Journal, American Water Works Association* [New York].
32. *The Journal of Farm Economics* [published by the American Farm Economic Association; printed by the George Banta Publishing Co., Menasha, Wisconsin].
33. *The Journal of San Diego History.*
34. *Los Angeles Times.*
35. *El lechugón* [Calexico].
36. *National Geographic.*
37. *National Motorist.*
38. *The New York Times.*
39. *Pesticide and Toxic Chemical News* (CRC Press).
40. *A Public Space* [New York].
41. *The Press-Enterprise: Inland Southern California's Newspaper.* "Since 1878."
42. *Property Guide Serving the entire Coachella and Imperial Valleys,* vol. 14, issue 2 [n.d., gratis at a supermarket in June 2001].
43. *Property Guide 2002: The Coachella and Imperial Valleys.*
44. *Property Guide 2003: Serving the entire Coachella Valley.* [Quarterly; published by Century 21 De Oro; no city of publication given.]
45. *Quick Frozen Foods* [E. W. Williams Publications, Wall Street, New York.]
46. *The Sacramento Bee.*
47. *The San Diego Union-Tribune.*

48. *The San Jose Mercury News.*
49. *Southwest Airlines Spirit.*
50. *The Sun* [Yuma, Arizona].
51. *Time.*
52. [*Time Agricultural Outlooks.*] University of California, College of Agriculture, Berkeley, California, *Time Agricultural Outlooks: Summarizing Supply, Demand, and Price Information on California Crops Supplementing the Annual Agricultural Outlook Reports for California.*
53. [University of California Publications in American Archaeology and Ethnology. See individual authors in Sec. L.]
54. *USA Today.*
55. *The Valley Grower* [El Centro].
56. *The Western Fruit-Grower* [St. Joseph, Missouri].
57. *Western Outdoors.*
58. *Westways.*
59. *WSIA Journal.*

D. WEBSITES

1. Ancestry.com:
   - http://ancestry.com/iexec?htx=prin—u&r=an&dbid=6224&path=California.Los+An . . . Accessed 7/4/2003.
2. Baja:
   - http://www.baja.com/lugares/info_mexicali.htm.
3. California Regional Water Control Board District 7 and California Environmental Protection Agency links. Since, as you see, there are several of these sub-locations, I thought it best to cite each of them in the notes in full.
   - http:/www.swrcb.ca.gov.rwqcb7/newriver/nr-intro.html.
   - http:/www.swrcb.ca.gov.rwqcb7/archive/programs/basinplanning/newriver/~hsnr_intro.html.
   - http:/www.swrcb.ca.gov.rwqcb7/documents/eo_reports/e0-99-06.10.html.
   - http://www.swrcb.ca.gov/rwqcb7/documents/eo_reports/e0-99-11-12.html.
4. CITT website:
   - http://www.clrlabor.org/alerts/2004/aug04-baja.htm. Campaign for Labor Rights: Grassroots Mobilizing Department of the U.S. Anti-Sweatshop Movement, "Support the workers of Flor de Baja, Mexicali California. Information for this alert comes from the Centro de Información para Trabajadoras y Trabajadors, Tijuana and the Red de San Diego en Solidaridad con los y las Trabajadoras de la Maquila. Posted August 4, 2004." 3 pp.
5. Commission for Environmental Cooperation website:
   - http://www.cec.org/home/index.cfm?varlan=english.
6. E Clampus Vitus
   - http://www.hbw.addr.com/eclampusvitus.htm. Accessed 7/17/2006.
7. Environmental Protection Agency
   - http://www.epa.gov/oim/mxsumppt.htm.
8. *Environmental News Service*
   - http://ens.lycos.com/ens/aug99/html.
9. [Hendricks.] San Diego History
   - http://www.sandiegohistory.org/journal/71summer/desert.htm. William O. Hendricks, "Developing San Diego's Desert Empire."
10. Inland Empire Economic Partnership
    - http://www.ieep.com/home.htm, accessed 7/30/2003.
11. Mount Signal:
    - http://home.att.net/ãmcnet3/mountsignal/leohetzel.html. Accessed 17/2006.
12. San Diego State University [SDSU]
    - http://www.sci.sdsu.edu.salton/plSaltonSeaRestorationPlan.html.
13. Secretaria de Medio Ambiente website:
    - Secretaria de Medio Ambiente y Recursos Naturales, at http://www.sisi.org.mx/jspsi/documentos/2005/seguimiento/00016/0001600200705_065.zip. Se incluyó en el buscador el miércoles 07 de marzo de 2007, as accessed in the Cruz-Kaegi report, p. 5.
14. Social Responsibilities Round Table

- gen@awa.or.jp/TUP-ML@egroups.co.jp, posted by Charles Willett on the Social Responsibilities Round Table / Action Council / American Library Association.ysf. Address: srrt-l@ala.org. Date: Saturday, 12 July 2003, 06:19:26-0400.

15. Ueinternational:
    - http://www.ueinternational.org/Mexico—info/mlna—articles.php?id=70.
16. United States Census Bureau. Again, I felt it best to cite each of these sub-locations in the notes in full. For more census sources, see "Department of Commerce, Bureau of the Census" in "Reference Serials" section below.
    - http://factfinder.census.gov/servlet/DTTable?_ts=49391922680.
    - http://eire.census.gov/popest/data/counties/tables/CO-EST2001-07.php.

E. REFERENCE SERIALS

1. *The Annals of America* (Chicago: Encyclopaedia Britannica, 19 vols., 1968). [Cited by titles of original works from which they are excerpted.]
2. [*Antepasados:* See de Anza in section H.]
3. [*Appletons' Annual Cyclopaedia*, 1892.] *Appletons' Annual Cyclopaedia and Register of Important Events of the Year 1892*, new series, vol. XVII; whole series, vol. XXXII (New York: D. Appleton & Co., 1893).
4. [*Appletons' Annual Cyclopaedia*, 1902.] *The Annual Cyclopaedia and Register of Important Events of the Year 1902* (New York: D. Appleton & Co., 1903).
5. *The Britannica Year-Book 1913.*
6. *Diccionario Porrúa: Historia, Biografía y Geografía de México*, tercera edición (Mexico City: Editorial Porrúa, S. A., 1970 corr. repr. of 1964 1st ed.). 2 vols.
7. *Enciclopedia de México* (1987).
8. *Encyclopaedia Britannica* (11th ed. of 1910).
9. *Encyclopaedia Britannica* (15th ed. of 1976).
10. [*Encyclopedia of Food Science and Technology.*] Y. H. Hui, ed.-in-chief, *Encyclopedia of Food Science and Technology* (New York: John Wiley & Sons, Inc. / A Wiley-Interscience Publication, 1992).
11. [*Great Soviet Encyclopedia.*] *Bol'shaia Sovetskaia Entsiklopediia*, ed. A. M. Prokhorov, 3rd. ed. (Moscow: Sovetskaia Entsiklopediia Publishing House, 1973), ed. and trans. Jean Paradise et al., as the *Great Soviet Encyclopedia* (New York: Macmillan, Inc., 1976).
12. *La Ocotilla* [Brawley high school yearbook], (1958).
13. *Machinery's Handbook* (1942).
14. United States Department of Agriculture, *Weekly News Letter* (1915).

F. GOVERNMENT DOCUMENTS (INCLUDING VITAL RECORDS)

1. [California Agricultural Labor Commission (1963).] *Report and Recommendations of the Agricultural Labor Commission*, Julian A. McPhee, Chairman (Sacramento: January 31, 1963).
2. [Boundary Commission, 1891–96.] *Report of the Boundary Commission Upon the Survey and Re-Marking the Boundary between the United States and Mexico West of the Rio Grande 1891–1896. ALBUM.* [Also entitled, with an inexplicable difference in dates, *Views of the Monuments and Characteristic Scenes Along the Boundary between the United States and Mexico West of the Rio Grande 1892–1895.*]
3. [Bureau of Reclamation (1970).] *Summary Report of the Commissioner, Bureau of Reclamation, 1970: Statistical and Financial Appendix, Parts I, II and III.*
4. [Bureau of Reclamation (1988).] U.S. Department of the Interior, Bureau of Reclamation, *1988 Summary Statistics: Water, Land, and Related Data.*
5. [*California 1890 Great Register of Voters Index.*] Janice G. Cloud, ed., California State Genealogical Alliance, *The California 1890 Great Register of Voters Index*, vol. 1 (North Salt Lake, Utah: Heritage Quest, 2001).
6. *California Blue Book, or State Roster* (Sacramento: State Printing Office, 1909, 1950, 1958).
7. [California census index (1870).] *California 1870 Census Index*, 2 vols., Raeone Christensen Steuart, ed. (Bountiful, Utah: Heritage Quest, 2000).
8. [California census (1880).] *California Census 1880* [California State Library microfilm copy], vol. 2, schedule 2: "Productions of Agriculture in Los Angeles, in the County of Los Angeles, State of California, Enumerated by me on the 8th to 14th day of June, 1880" [enumerator's signature, V. A. Heprinco?].
9. [California Board of Agriculture (1918).] Report of the Board of Agriculture, 1918, in the *Appendix to the Journals of the Senate and Assembly of the Forty-Fourth Session of the Legislature of the State of California*, vol. IV (Sacramento: California State Printing Office, 1921).
10. [California Board of Agriculture (1936).] Bulletin of the California Department of Agriculture, Eighteenth

Annual Report, vol. XXVI, no. 4; in the *Appendix to the Journals of the Senate and Assembly of the Fifty-Ninth Session of the Legislature of the State of California* (Sacramento: California State Printing Office, 1936).

11. [California Board of Agriculture (1938).] Bulletin of the California Department of Agriculture, Twentieth Annual Report, vol. XXVIII, no. 6; in the *Appendix to the Journals of the Senate and Assembly of the Sixty-First Session of the Legislature of the State of California* (Sacramento: California State Printing Office, 1938).
12. [California county health-status profiles (2001).] Department of Health Services and California Conference of Local Health Officers, Public Health Week (April 2–8, 2001), *County Health Status Profiles 2001.*
13. [California Death Index.] State of California, Department of Public Health, Bureau of Vital Statistics and Data Processing, *California Death Index 1905–1929.*
14. [California Department of Agriculture (1941).] State of California, Department of Agriculture. Bulletin: *Proceedings: California Agricultural Economic Conference at Stockton, California, December 17 and 18, 1940* (Sacramento: January February March 1941, vol. XXX, no. 1).
15. [California Department of Agriculture (1965).] Ward Henderson, Chief, Bureau of Agricultural Statistics, California Department of Agriculture, *California's Agriculture: A Report Prepared for the Hearings of the National Committee on Food Marketing* (San Francisco: July 8–10, 1965).
16. [California Department of Fish and Game.] State of California. The Resources Agency. Department of Fish and Game, *Atlas of the Biodiversity of California* (2003).
17. California Department of Food and Agriculture, in a joint study with the University of California, Davis, *Energy Requirements for Agriculture in California* (1974).
18. [California Department of Justice (1959).] *Water Supply of the Lower Colorado River Basin: Extracts from Brief and Proposed Findings of Fact and Conclusions of Law Submitted 1 April, 1959, to Hon. Simon H. Rifkind, Special Master, by the California Defendants and Excerpts from the Evidence: Arizona v. California, No. 9 Original, October 1959 Term, Stanley Mosk, Attorney General, State of California, Department of Justice.*
19. [California Department of Water Resources (1978).] State of California. The Resources Agency. Department of Water Resources, Southern District. *District Report: Coachella and Imperial Valleys, Agricultural Land Use Study, 1978* (July 1980).
20. [California Division of Mines and Geology. County geology and mineral reports. See Paul K. Morton, Sec. G.]
21. [California Employment Development Department (1995).] Employment Development Department, Labor Market Information Division, *Projections and Planning Information, Imperial County* (Sacramento, State of California, 1995). 1 vol., loose-leaf pages subject to supersession.
22. [California State Board of Equalization (1949).] California State Board of Equalization, *Property Tax in Imperial County: Report on a Survey Conducted Under the Direction of Section 3693 of the Political Code*, 1949.
23. [California State Controller (1950–51).] Thomas H. Kuchel, State Controller, *California Annual Report of the State Controller for the Fiscal Year Ended June 30, 1951* (Sacramento: Office of the State Controller, 1952).
24. [Census Bureau (1850).] *Seventh Census of the United States. Original Returns of the Assistant Marshals. First Series. White and Free Colored Population* (June 30, 1850).
25. [Census Bureau (1910).] Department of Commerce, Bureau of the Census, *Thirteenth Census of the United States, Taken in the Year 1910* (Washington, D.C.: Government Printing Office, 1913). [Vol. 1: Population: General Report and Analysis.]
26. [Census Bureau (1910, vol. 7).] Ibid., vol. VI: Agriculture, General Report and Analysis.
27. [Census Bureau (1947).] Department of Commerce, Bureau of the Census, *County Data Book: A Supplement to the Statistical Abstract of the United States* (Washington, D.C.: U.S. Government Printing Office, 1947).
28. [Census Bureau (1974).] Department of Commerce, United States of America, Bureau of the Census, *1974 Census of Agriculture*, vol. 1, part 5: California: State and County Data (Washington, D.C.: Issued 1977).
29. [Census Bureau (1975).] U.S. Department of Commerce, Bureau of the Census, *Historical Statistics of the United States, Colonial Times to 1970, Bicentennial Edition, Part 1* (Washington, D.C.: U.S. Government Printing Office, 1975). *For more census sources, see "United States Census Bureau" in "Websites" section above.*
30. Colorado River Basin Salinity Control Forum, "Proposed Report on the 1984 Review Water Quality Standards for Salinity, Colorado River System, Executive Summary," 1984.
31. [Colorado River Board of California (1962).] Colorado River Board of California, *Salinity Problems in the Lower Colorado River Area* (State of California, September 1962).
32. [Colorado River Board of California (1981).] Myron B. Holburt, Chief Engineer, Colorado River Board of California, *The Colorado: Still a Problem River* (Los Angeles: Colorado River Association, n.d., pages unnumbered, *ca.* 1981).
33. Owen C. Coy, Ph.D., Director of the Commission, *California County Boundaries: A Study of the Division of the State into Counties and the Subsequent Changes in Their Boundaries* (Fresno: Valley Publishers, 1973 repr. of 1923 Berkeley ed. published by the California Historical Survey Commission).
34. [Death certificates.] State of California certifications of vital records. [Various bureaucratic incarnations: California State Board of Health, Bureau of Vital Statistics; State of California Department of Heath Services.]

a. County of Fresno.
   (1) Hazel Deed. Died 20 March 1920. State index #20-011526-1036. Local registered #145.
b. County of Imperial.
   (1) John Doe unknown Mexican. Died on or before 29 July 1924. No state index number. Local registered #28.
   (2) Mónica Gordins. Died 31 July 1924. No state index number. Local registered #29.
   (3) Albert Henry Larson. Died 30 March 1926. No state index number. Local registered #10.

35. [Department of the Interior (1933).] United States Department of the Interior, *The Hoover Dam Power and Water Contracts and Related Data, with Introductory Notes by Ray Lyman Wilbur, Secretary of the Interior, and Northcutt Ely, Assistant to the Secretary* (Washington, D.C.: United States Government Printing Office, 1933).
36. [Department of the Interior. U.S. Geological Survey (1963).] C. L. McGuinness, *The Role of Ground Water in the National Water Situation, with State Summaries Based on Reports by District Offices of the Ground Water Branch* (Washington, D.C.: United States Government Printing Office, 1963, Geological Survey Water-Supply Paper 1800).
37. [Department of the Interior, Bureau of Land Management papers on archaeology and related subjects. See Sec. L.]
38. Dirección General de Estadística, *V Censos Agrícola-Ganadero y Ejidal 1970: Baja California* (Mexico, 1975).
39. [EDD printout (2001).] 5-p. printout, "Civilian Labor Force, Employment, and Unemployment—Updated 9/12/2001. Imperial County . . . Source: Employment Development Department, Labor Market Information Division, 916-262-2162."
40. [EDD unemployment fact sheet (1997–99).] 1-p. leaflet: "California Civilian Unemployment Rate Ranked by County 1997–1999," Employment Development Department, Labor Market Information Division, same phone number as previous.
41. [Estado de Baja California (*ca.* 1983).] Impresos y Publicacciones del Gobierno del Estado de Baja California, *Estado de Baja California 1977–1983: Seis Años de Esfuerzo Comunitario* (n.d.; *ca.* 1983).
42. Ted Gostin, comp., *Southern California Vital Records, vol. 1: Los Angeles County 1850–1859* (Los Angeles: Generations Press, 2001).
43. William Ham. Hall, State Engineer, *Irrigation in California (Southern): The Field, Water-Supply, and Works, Organization and Operation in San Diego, San Bernardino, and Los Angeles Counties: The Second Part of the Report of the State Engineer of California on Irrigation and the Irrigation Question* (Sacramento: State Office, J. D. Young, Supt. State Printing, 1888).
44. [House of Representatives (1907).] U.S. Congress (59th), House of Representatives, Committee on the Public Lands, Hearings on Senate Document 227 ("Salton Sea, California, Imperial Valley, and Lower Colorado River"), Friday, January 18, 1907.
45. [Imperial County Assessor's maps.] Assessor's Map Books, County of Imperial, California, n.d., copies obtained from County Assessor's office in 2002. I particularly cite one ancient bound volume, now retired from active use; it was formerly carried into the field if California State Board of Equalization (1949) is to be believed.
46. Instituto Nacional de Estadística Geografía e Informática, *Baja California: Resultados Definitivos, VII Censo Ejidal* (Aguascalientes, Ags., Mexico, 1993).
47. [Lower Colorado Region study (1971).] Lower Colorado Region State-Federal Interagency Group for the Pacific Southwest Interagency Committee, *Lower Colorado Region Comprehensive Framework Study*, Appendix X: Irrigation and Drainage (June 1971).
48. [Senate Committee on the Colorado River Basin (1925).] U.S. Congress, Senate Committee on the Colorado River Basin, *Hearings Before the Committee of Irrigation and Reclamation, United States Senate, Sixty-Ninth Congress, First Session, Pursuant to S. Res. 320; Los Angeles and San Diego, Calif., October 26 and 27, 1925* (Washington, D.C.: Government Printing Office, 1925).
49. [Southern Pacific Imperial Valley Claim (1909).] *Southern Pacific Imperial Valley Claim: Hearing Before Subcommittee of the Committee on Claims of the United States Senate on S. 4170, Thursday, January 21, 1909* (Washington, D.C.: Government Printing Office, 1909).
50. [Smithsonian Institution, Bureau of American Ethnology Bulletins. See Sec. L.]
51. [USDA *Experiment Station Record* series (1903–04, 1920, 1936)]. United States Department of Agriculture, Office of Experimental Stations, *Experiment Station Record:*
   a. Vol. XV, 1903–1904 (Washington, D.C.: Government Printing Office, 1904).
   b. Vol. XLII, January–July, 1920 (Washington, D.C.: Government Printing Office, 1920).
   c. Vol. 75, July–December 1936 (Washington, D.C.: U.S. Government Printing Office, 1937).
52. [USDA *Agricultural Statistics* series (1875).] *Report of the Commissioner of Agriculture for the Year 1875* (Washington, D.C.: Government Printing Office, 1876).
53. [USDA *Agricultural Statistics* series (1900).] United States Department of Agriculture, *Agricultural Statistics 1900* (Washington, D.C.: Government Printing Office, 1901).

54. [USDA *Agricultural Statistics* series (1925).] United States Department of Agriculture, *Agricultural Statistics 1925* (Washington, D.C.: Government Printing Office, 1926).
55. [USDA *Agricultural Statistics* series (1941).] United States Department of Agriculture, *Agricultural Statistics 1941* (Washington, D.C.: U.S. Government Printing Office, 1941).
56. [USDA *Agricultural Statistics* series (1950).] United States Department of Agriculture, *Agricultural Statistics 1950* (Washington, D.C.: U.S. Government Printing Office, 1950).
57. [USDA *Agricultural Statistics* series (1951).] United States Department of Agriculture, *Agricultural Statistics 1951* (Washington, D.C.: U.S. Government Printing Office, 1951).
58. [USDA *Agricultural Statistics* series (2001).] United States Department of Agriculture, National Agricultural Statistics Service, *Agricultural Statistics 2001* (Washington, D.C.: U.S. Government Printing Office, 2001).
59. [USDA *Cotton Literature* series (1940).] Emily L. Day, Library Specialist in Cotton Marketing, Bureau of Agricultural Economics, Washington, D.C., comp., *Cotton Literature: Selected References Prepared in the Library of the United States Department of Agriculture* . . . (vol. 10, nos. 1–12, 1940).
60. [USDA (1940), *Farm Size in California*.] United States Department of Agriculture, Bureau of Agricultural Economics, G. Alvin Carpenter, Associate Agricultural Economist, *Farm Size in California* (Berkeley: October, 1940).
61. [USDA Yearbook series (1900).] *Yearbook of the United States Department of Agriculture*, 1900 (Washington, D.C.: Government Printing Office, 1901).
62. [USDA Yearbook series (1901).] *Yearbook of the United States Department of Agriculture*, 1901 (Washington, D.C.: Government Printing Office, 1902).
63. [USDA Yearbook series (1909).] *Yearbook of the United States Department of Agriculture*, 1909 (Washington, D.C.: Government Printing Office, 1910).
64. [USDA Yearbook series (1910).] *Yearbook of the United States Department of Agriculture*, 1910 (Washington, D.C.: Government Printing Office, 1911).
65. [USDA Yearbook series (1920).] *Yearbook of the United States Department of Agriculture*, 1920 (Washington, D.C.: Government Printing Office, 1921).
66. [USDA Yearbook series (1930).] *Yearbook of the United States Department of Agriculture*, 1930 (Washington, D.C.: Government Printing Office, 1930).
67. [USDA Yearbook series (1931).] *Yearbook of the United States Department of Agriculture*, 1931 (Washington, D.C.: Government Printing Office, 1931).
68. [USDA Yearbook series (1950–1951).] *Crops in Peace and War: The Yearbook of Agriculture 1950–1951* (United States Department of Agriculture, Washington, D.C.: Government Printing Office, 1951).
69. [USDA Yearbook series (1955).] *84th Congress, First Session, House Document no. 32: The Yearbook of Agriculture, 1955: Water* (Washington, D.C.: Government Printing Office, 1956).

G. AREA DESCRIPTIONS, GUIDES AND ATLASES

1. [*Agenda de Colonias*.] Guías y Publicacciones, *Agenda de Colonias Centenario 2003, Mexicali B.C.* (Mexicali, 2002).
2. [*American Biography and Genealogy*.] Robert J. Burdette, D.D., ed., *American Biography and Genealogy, California Edition*, vol. 1 (Chicago: The Lewis Publishing Company, n.d.; *ca.* 1912).
3. [*Atlas of American Agriculture*.] United States Department of Agriculture, *Atlas of American Agriculture* (Washington, D.C.: U.S. Government Printing Office, 1936).
4. [*Atlas of the Biodiversity of California*.] State of California, The Resources Agency, Department of Fish and Game, *Atlas of the Biodiversity of California* (Sacramento? [no place of publication or printer given], 2003).
5. Mary Austin, *The Land of Little Rain* (Albuquerque: University of New Mexico Press, 2003; orig. ed. 1903).
6. Lyman Benson, *The Native Cacti of California* (Palo Alto: Stanford University Press, 1969).
7. A. Bynon and Son, *History and Directory of Riverside County 1893–4*, repr. with foreword by Robert Fitch and intro. by Tom Patterson (Riverside: Historical Commission Press, 1992).
8. [Sponsored by] The California Builders Council, "Fair Share" Committee, *The Fiscal Impact of Urban Growth: California Case Studies* (Newport Beach, California: Ashley Economic Services, Inc., 1973).
9. [*California Agricultural Directory 2004–2005*.] California Farm Bureau Federation, *California Agricultural Directory 2004–2005*, rev. ed. (Sacramento: Omnipress, 2004).
10. [California Division of Mines and Geology. See Paul K. Morton, this section.]
11. [*California Gazetteer*.] American Historical Publications, Inc., *California Gazetteer* (Wilmington, Delaware, 1985).
12. [*The California Water Atlas*.] State of California [Governor's Office of Planning and Research in cooperation with the California Department of Water Resources], *The California Water Atlas* (North Highlands, California: General Services, Publications Section, 1979).
13. Herbert Carolan, *Motor Travels in and out of California* (New York: G. P. Putnam's Sons, 1936).

14. [*The City and County of San Diego.*] [T. S. Van Dyke, who seems to have written the bulk of this book; and T. T. Leberthon and A. Taylor, comps.], *The City and County of San Diego, Illustrated, and Containing Biographical Sketches of Prominent Men and Pioneers* (San Diego: Leberthon and Taylor, 1888).
15. Robert W. Durrenberger with Robert B. Johnson, *California: Patterns on the Land*, 5th ed. (Palo Alto: Mayfield Publishing Co., A California Council for Geographic Education Publication, 1970).
16. Lieut. Col. W. H. Emory, *Notes of a Military Reconnaissance, from Fort Leavenworth in Missouri, to San Diego, in California, including part of the Arkansas, Del Norte, and Gila Rivers* (Washington: Wendell and Van Benthuysen, Printers; for the Thirtieth Congress, First Session, Ex. Doc. No. 41, 1848).
17. Ronald Greeley and Raymond Batson, *The Compact NASA Atlas of the Solar System* (New York: Cambridge University Press, 2001; derived from *The NASA Atlas of the Solar System*, 1997).
18. Howard F. Gregor, *An Agricultural Typology of California* (Budapest: Akadémiai Kiadó, Research Institute of Geography, Hungarian Academy of Sciences, Geography of World Agriculture series, no. 4, 1974).
19. Paul F. Griffin and Robert N. Young, *California: The New Empire State, A Regional Geography* (San Francisco: Fearon Publishers, 1957).
20. Robert Lawrence Griswold, *The Character of the Family in Rural California, 1850–1890*. Stanford University Ph.D. thesis, 1979.
21. [D. Gunn.] (Douglas?) Gunn, *History of California and an Extended History of Its Southern Coast Counties*, 2 vols. (No place of publication given: Historic Record Company, 1907).
22. Douglas Gunn, *Picturesque San Diego, with Historical and Descriptive Notes* (Chicago: Knight and Leonard Co., Printers, 1887).
23. R. J. Halbert, M.D., M.P.H., Associate Director, Preventive Medicine Residency, Center for Health Promotion and Disease Prevention, University of California, Los Angeles, School of Public Health, *The Health Status of Whites in California* (Woodland Hills, California: California Endowment and California HealthCare Foundation [established by Blue Cross of California], April 1997).
24. Kevin Heubusch, *The New Rating Guide to Life in America's Small Cities* (Amherst, New York: Prometheus Books, 1997).
25. Louise L. Hornor, ed., *California Cities, Towns, & Counties: Basic Data Profiles for all Municipalities & Counties* (Palo Alto: Information Publications, 2000).
26. Robert Iacopi, *Earthquake Country* (Menlo Park, California: Lane Book Co. / A Sunset Book, 1964).
27. [Imperial Valley yellow pages (2001).] Pacific Bell SMART Yellow Pages, including White Pages: Imperial County, September 2001 Issue, Area Code 760.
28. [Imperial Valley Directory (1912).] Albert G. Thurston, comp. and pub., *Imperial Valley Business and Resident Directory 1912–1913* (Pasadena and El Centro, 1912).
29. [Imperial Valley Directory (1914).] Albert G. Thurston, comp. and pub., *Imperial Valley Resident Directory 1914–1915* (Pasadena and El Centro, 1914).
30. [Imperial Valley Directory (1920).] Albert G. Thurston, comp. and pub., *Imperial Valley Resident Directory 1920–21* (Los Angeles and El Centro, 1920).
31. [Imperial Valley Directory (1924).] *Imperial Valley Directory* (Los Angeles: Los Angeles Directory Co., 1924).
32. [Imperial Valley Directory (1926).] *Imperial Valley Directory* (Los Angeles: Los Angeles Directory Co., 1926).
33. [Imperial Valley Directory (1930).] *Imperial Valley Directory* (Los Angeles: Los Angeles Directory Co., 1930).
34. [Imperial Valley Directory (1939).] *Imperial Valley Directory* (Los Angeles: Los Angeles Directory Co., 1939).
35. [Imperial Valley Directory (1942).] *Imperial Valley Directory* (Los Angeles: Los Angeles Directory Co., 1942).
36. [Imperial Valley Directory (1949).] *Imperial Valley (California) Directory* (Los Angeles: Los Angeles Directory Co., 1949).
37. [Imperial Valley Directory (1952).] *Imperial Valley (Imperial County, Calif.) Directory* (Los Angeles: R. L. Polk & Co., 1952).
38. [Imperial Valley Directory (1970).] *Imperial Valley (Imperial County, Calif.) Directory* (Monterey Park, California: R. L. Polk & Co., 1970).
39. [Imperial Valley Directory (1980).] *Imperial Valley (Imperial County, Calif.) Directory* (Dallas, Texas: R. L. Polk & Co., 1980).
40. [Imperial Valley Directory (2000).] *2000 Imperial Valley, CA Polk City Directory* (Livonia, Michigan: R. L. Polk & Co., 2000).
41. George Wharton James, *The Wonders of the Colorado Desert (Southern California)*, with drawings by Carl Eytel (Boston: Little, Brown, and Company, 1911; original copyright 1906).
42. Bern Kreissman, assisted by Barbara Lekisch, *California: An Environmental Atlas and Guide* (Davis, California: Bear Klaw Press, 1991).
43. Lowell Lindsay and William G. Hample, eds., *Geological and Geothermal Resources of the Imperial and Mexicali Valleys* (San Diego: San Diego Association of Geologists, 1998).
44. Michael A. Mares, *Encyclopedia of Deserts* (Norman: University of Oklahoma Press, 1999).

45. Allan McCollum, comp., *The Sandspikes from Mount Signal* (Imperial, etc.: Imperial Valley Historical Society Pioneers Museum et al., n.d.; *ca.* 2000). A collection of magazine offprints comprising:
   a. S. C. Edwards, "Sand Concretions from California" (*Rocks and Minerals*, 1934).
   b. Kenneth B. Garner, "Concretions Near Mt. Signal, Lower California" (*American Journal of Science*, 1936).
   c. Eva May Hyde, "Mount Signal Concretions" (*The Mineralogist*, 1937).
   d. Guy E. Hazen, "Sandstone Concretions of the Colorado Delta" (*Earth Science Digest*, 1954).
   e. Frank Dunn, "Treasures of the Badlands" (*Desert*, 1963).
   f. Edmund F. Kiessling, "A Trip to . . . A Concretion Locality" (*Mineral Information Service, State of California Division of Mines and Geology*, 1964).
   g. James R. Mitchell, "Imperial Valley Concretions" (*Rock and Gem*, 1978).
   h. Loran E. Perry, "Mysterious Sandstone Concretions of the Salton Basin" (*Lapidary Journal*, 1981).
46. [Mexicali yellow pages (2002–2003).] Telnor, *Mexicali Diretorio Telefónica*, sección amarilla.
47. Adalberto Walther Meade, *El Valle de Mexicali* (Colonia Nueva, Mexicali: UABC, 1996).
48. Paul K. Morton, geologist; for California Division of Mines and Geology. *County Report 7: Geology and Mineral Resources of Imperial County, California* (Sacramento, 1977; but Morton notes that due to "lack of funding" "the effective date of this report is 1966").
49. Gordon B, Oakeshott, Division of Mines and Geology, State of California, *California's Changing Landscapes: A Guide to the Geology of the State* (New York: McGraw-Hill Book Co., 1971).
50. Yolanda Sánchez Ogás, *Bajo El Sol de Mexicali*, 2nd. ed. (Mexicali, XIV Ayuntamiento: 1998; orig. ed. 1995).
51. [Packard.] University of California, College of Agriculture, Berkeley, Circular No. 159 (January, 1917): Walter E. Packard, "Agriculture in the Imperial Valley: A Manual for Settlers."
52. Arthur G. Paul, President, Riverside Historical Society, *Riverside Community Book* (Riverside: Arthur H. Cawston, 1954).
53. John Malcolm Penn, *California State Landmarks: Imperial County in Story and Song* (Imperial County?: Radio Flier Music, 2003).
54. Philip R. Pryde, ed., *San Diego: An Introduction to the Region* (Dubuque, Iowa: Kendall/Hunt Publishing Co. / prepared by the Department of Geography, San Diego State University, 1976).
55. Irmagarde Richards, *Our California Home*, 3rd. ed. (Sacramento: California State Department of Education, California State Series, 1937 repr. of 1933 ed.).
56. [Riverside City Directory (1921).] *Riverside City Directory 1921, Containing an Alphabetical List of Business Firms and Private Citizens* . . . (Los Angeles: Riverside Directory Co., 1921).
57. [Riverside City Directory (1951).] *Los Angeles Directory Co.'s RIVERSIDE (California) City Directory 1951 . . . Also a BUYERS' GUIDE and a Complete Classified Business Directory* (Los Angeles: Los Angeles Directory Co., 1951).
58. Riverside Fire Department, *Souvenir of the City of Riverside* (Riverside: Riverside Museum Press, 1987; orig. ed. 1906).
59. Norman C. Roberts, *Baja California Plant Field Guide* (La Jolla, California: Natural History Publishing Co., 1989).
60. [*Salton Sea Atlas.*] The Redlands Institute, University of Redlands, *Salton Sea Atlas* (Redlands, California: ESRI Press, 2002).
61. [San Diego City and County Directory (1901).] *San Diego City and County Directory 1901, For the Year March, 1901, to March, 1902* (San Diego: San Diego Directory Co.).
62. [San Diego City Directory (1950).] *San Diego (California) City Directory 1950, Including Chula Vista, Coronado, etc.* (San Diego: San Diego Directory Co., 1950).
63. Ann Foley Scheuring, ed., *A Guidebook to California Agriculture* (Berkeley: University of California Press, 1983).
64. Ellwyn R. Stoddard, Richard L. Nostrand and Jonathan P. West, eds., *Borderlands Sourcebook: A Guide to the Literature on Northern Mexico and the American Southwest* (Norman: University of Oklahoma Press, 1983).
65. E. J. Wickson, *Rural California* (New York: Macmillan Co., Rural State and Province series, 1923).
66. Woods and Poole Economics, Inc., *2003 State Profile California* (Washington, D.C., 2003).
67. [WPA.] *California, A Guide to the Golden State, Compiled and Written by the Federal Writers' Project of the Works Progress Administration for the State of California* (New York: Hastings House, American Guide ser., 1939).
68. Christopher Wray, *The Historic Backcountry: A Geographic Guide to the Historic Places of the San Diego County Mountains and the Colorado Desert* (La Mesa, California: self-published, 2004).
69. John C. Van Dyke, *The Desert: Further Studies in Natural Appearances*, 2nd ed. (New York: Charles Scribner's Sons, 1903).

H. MEMOIRS, DIARIES, CORRESPONDENCE, HISTORIES, PICTORIALS

1. Henry Adams, *History of the United States of America During the Administration of Thomas Jefferson* (1889) (New York: Library of America, 1986).

2. Edward Maddin Ainsworth, *Beckoning Desert*, Bill Bender, ed. (Englewood Cliffs, New Jersey: Prentice-Hall, 1962).
3. David Howard Bain, *Empire Express: Building the First Transcontinental Railroad* (New York: Viking Penguin, 1999).
4. [Griffing Bancroft.] Griffing Bancroft, *Lower California: A Cruise; The Flight of the Least Petrel* (New York: G. P. Putnam's Sons, 1932.)
5. [Bancroft.] *The Works of Hubert H. Bancroft*, vols. XVIII–XXIV (San Francisco: A. L. Bancroft and Co., 1884–90).
6. *Horace Bristol: An American View*, Ken Conner and Debra Heimerdinger, eds. (San Francisco: Chronicle Books, 1996).
7. Billie Bernal, *Ocotillo: A Place in the Sun* (self-published, 1986).
8. Samuel T. Black, *San Diego County, California: A Record of Settlement, Organization, Progress and Achievement*, 2 vols. (Chicago: S. J. Clarke Publishing Co., 1913).
9. D. Mackenzie Brown, *China Trade Days in California: Selected Letters from the [Alpheus B.] Thompson Papers, 1832–1863* (Berkeley: University of California Press, 1947).
10. John Brown, Jr., and James Boyd, *History of San Bernardino and Riverside Counties* (Chicago: Western History Association, Lewis Publishing Co., 1922). Only vol. 1 used.
11. *Journey of James H. Bull, Baja California, October 1843 to January 1844*, Doyce B. Nunis, Jr., ed. (Los Angeles: Dawson's Book Shop, 1965; Baja California Travels ser., no. 1. 1st complete version; abr. version previously pub. by Society of California Pioneers, 1954).
12. *Hepah, California: The Journal of Cave Johnson Couts; From Monterey, Nuevo Leon, Mexico to Los Angeles, California During the Years 1848–1849*, Henry F. Dobyns, ed. (Tucson: Arizona Pioneers' Historical Society, 1961).
13. Harry W. Crosby, *Gateway to Alta California: The Expedition to San Diego, 1769* (San Diego: Sunbelt Publications, 2003).
14. Robert Dawson and Gray Brechin, *Farewell, Promised Land: Waking from the California Dream* (Berkeley: University of California Press, 1999).
15. Álvar Núñez Cabeza de Vaca, *The Narrative of Cabeza de Vaca*, ed., trans. and w. intro. by Rolena Adorno and Patrick Charles Pautz (Lincoln: University of Nebraska Press, 1999 trans. of orig. 1542 Spanish ed.).
16. Richard Henry Dana, Jr., *Two Years Before the Mast: A Personal Narrative* (New York: Houghton Mifflin Company / The Riverside Press, Cambridge, 1911; text dated 1869).
17. Glenn S. Dumke, *The Boom of the Eighties in Southern California* (San Marino, California: Huntington Library, 1944).
18. Wallace W. Elliott, *History of San Bernardino and San Diego Counties, with Illustrations* (San Francisco: Wallace W. Elliott & Co., 1883).
19. [Wallace W. Elliott.] *History of Tulare County, California, with Illustrations* (San Francisco: Wallace W. Elliott & Co., 1883).
20. Ralph Waldo Emerson, *Essays and Lectures* (New York: Library of America, 1983).
21. Brian M. Fagan, *Kingdoms of Gold, Kingdoms of Jade: The Americas Before Columbus* (New York: Thames and Hudson, 1991).
22. [Judge] F. C. Farr, ed., *The History of Imperial County, California* (Berkeley, California: Elms and Franks, 1918).
23. William M. Farris, *The 1847 Crossing of Imperial County, California, and Baja California, Mexico, by the U. S. Mormon Battalion* (El Centro: I. V. C. Museum Society, Occasional Paper No. 2, 1976).
24. Robert J. Fitch, *Profile of a Century: Riverside County, California, 1893–1993* (Riverside: Riverside County Historical Press, 1993).
25. Carl Flesichhauer and Beverly W. Brannan, eds., with essays by Lawrence W. Levine and Alan Trachtenberg, *Documenting America, 1935–1943* (Berkeley: University of California Press in association with the Library of Congress, 1988).
26. Karen J. Frisby, *Imperial Valley: The Greening of a Desert* (Imperial: Imperial Valley College Desert Museum Society, Publisher, Occasional paper No. 9, 1993).
27. Paul W. Gates, ed., *California Ranchos and Farms 1846–1862, Including the Letters of John Quincy Adams Warren of 1861, Being Largely Devoted to Livestock, Wheat Farming, Fruit Raising, and the Wine Industry* (Madison: State Historical Society of Wisconsin, 1967).
28. Alexander Hamilton, *Writings* (New York: Library of America, 2001).
29. [Elizabeth Harris.] Imperial County Historical Society. *The Valley Imperial*, Book I and Book II (Imperial?: Imperial Valley Pioneers/Imperial County Historical Society, 1991 slightly rev. repr. of orig. 1956–58 vols.).
30. *The Diary and Copybook of William E. P. Hartnell, Visitador General of the Missions of Alta California in 1839 and 1840*, Starr Pait Gurcke, trans. and ann., Glenn J. Farris, ed. (Santa Clara, California: California Mission Studies Association, 2004).

31. Carl Heilbron et al., *History of San Diego County* (San Diego: San Diego Press Club, 1936).
32. Tracey Henderson, *Imperial Valley* (San Diego: Neyenesch Printers, Inc., San Diego, 1968).
33. [Leo Hetzel.] Joel Livernois, comp., *Hetzel the Photographer: Impressions of Imperial Valley* (Fresno, California: Pioneer Publishing, 1982).
34. *History of the Counties of Fresno, Tulare and Kern, California, Illustrated* (Chicago: Lewes Publishing Co., n.d., *ca.* 1890).
35. Theodore H. Hittell, *History of California*, vol. III (San Francisco: N. J. Stone & Co., 1897).
36. Captain James Hobbs, of California, *Wild Life in the Far West: Personal Adventures of a Border Mountain Man, Comprising Hunting and Trapping Adventures with Kit Carson and others; Captivity and Life among the Comanches; Services Under Doniphan in the War with Mexico, and in the Mexican War against the French; Desperate Combats with Apaches, Grizzly Bears, etc., etc.* (Glorieta, New Mexico: Rio Grande Press, 1969 repr. of undated 19th-cent. ed.).
37. Elmer Wallace Holmes and other well-known writers, *History of Riverside County, California, with Biographical Sketches* (Los Angeles: Historic Record Company, 1912).
38. Edgar F. Howe and Wilbur Jay Hall, *The Story of the First Decade in Imperial Valley, California* (Imperial, California: Imperial County Historical Society, 1988 repr. of 1910 ed.).
39. Rockwell D. Hunt, A.M., Ph.D., ed., assisted by an advisory board, *California and Californians, Issued in Five Volumes*, vol. II (by Rockwell Hunt) (San Francisco: Lewis Publishing Co., 1926).
40. *An Illustrated History of Southern California* (Chicago: Lewis Publishing Co., 1890). [Front cover is imprinted with *"Pen Pictures from the Garden of the World."*]
41. [*Imperial County: The Big Picture*]. Imperial Valley Press, *Imperial County: The Big Picture*, vol. 1: *Our Towns* (El Centro?: Printed by Quebecor World, 2004).
42. [Kerouac [Brinkley).] Jack Kerouac, *Windblown World: The Journals of Jack Kerouac 1947–1954*, Douglas Brinkey, ed. (New York: Viking, 2004).
43. Leonard Knight, *Salvation Mountain: The Art of Leonard Knight, with Commentary by the Artist* (Los Angeles: New Leaf Press, 1998).
44. Gary F. Kurutz, ed., *California Pastorale: Selected Photographs 1860–1925* (Sausalito: Windgate Press, 1998).
45. Patricia B. Laflin, *Coachella Valley, California: A Pictorial History* (Virginia Beach: Donning Co., 1998).
46. [Pat(ricia) Laflin.] *The Periscope 1995: Salton Sea: California's Overlooked Treasure* (Indio, California: Coachella Valley Historical Society, 1999 repr. of 1995 ed.).
47. [Patricia Baker Laflin.] *The Periscope 2000: A Century of Change in the Coachella Valley* (Indio, California: Coachella Valley Historical Society, 2000).
48. Christopher Landis, *In Search of Eldorado: The Salton Sea* (Palm Springs: Palm Springs Desert Museum, 2000).
49. Steve Lech, *Along the Old Roads: A History of the Portion of Southern California That Became Riverside County 1772–1893* (No place of publication given, but I would hazard Riverside, California: Published by the author, 2004).
50. Randolph Leigh, *Forgotten Waters: Adventure in the Gulf of California* (New York: J. B. Lippincott Company, 1941).
51. Richard G. Lilliard, *Eden in Jeopardy—Man's Prodigal Meddling with His Environment: The Southern California Experience* (New York: Alfred A. Knopf, 1966).
52. Janice Marschner, *California in 1850: A Snapshot in Time* (Sacramento: Coleman Ranch Press, 2000).
53. Gordon T. McClelland and Jay T. Last, *California Orange Box Labels, an Illustrated History* (Santa Ana: Hillcrest Press, 2003 repr. of 1985 ed.).
54. John Muir, *Nature Writings* (New York: Library of America, Literary Classics of the United States, 1997).
55. Ole J. Nordland, *Coachella Valley's Golden Years: The Early History of the Coachella Valley County Water District and Stories About the Discovery and Development of This Section of the Colorado Desert* (Indio: Desert Printing Co., 1978 rev. of 1968 1st ed.).
56. Antonio María Osio, *The History of Alta California: A Memoir of Mexican California*, trans. by Rose Marie Beebe and Robert M. Senkewicz (Madison: University of Wisconsin Press, 1996; orig. Spanish ms. 1851).
57. Tom Patterson, *A Colony for California: Riverside's First Hundred Years*, 2nd. ed. (Riverside: Museum Press of the Riverside Museum Associates, 1996).
58. *The Personal Narrative of James O. Pattie of Kentucky, During an Expedition from St. Louis, through the Vast Regions between that Place and the Pacific Ocean, and then back through the City of Mexico to Vera Cruz . . .*, Timothy Flint, ed. (Santa Barbara: Narrative Press, 2001 repr. of 1831 ed.).
59. John Malcolm Penn, *California State Historical Landmarks: Imperial County in Story and Song* (No place of publication but probably somewhere in San Diego County or Imperial County: Radio Flier Music, 2003). Includes compact disc with recordings of Penn's songs.
60. Sandra S. Phillips, Richard Rodriguez, Aaron Betsky, Eldridge M. Moores, *Crossing the Frontier: Photographs of the Developing West, 1849 to the Present* (San Francisco: San Francisco Museum of Art / Chronicle Books, 1996).

61. G. Harold Powell, *Letters from the Orange Empire*, Richard G. Lillard, ed.; afterword by Lawrence Clark Powell (Los Angeles and Redlands: Historical Society of Southern California and A. K. Smiley Public Library, 1996).
62. John Wesley Powell, *The Exploration of the Colorado River and Its Canyons* (Washington, D.C.: National Geographic Society, 2002 repr. of 1895 ed.).
63. Margaret Romer, M.A., *A History of Calexico*, repr. from the *Annual Publication of the Historical Society of Southern California, 1922.*
64. Milo Milton Quaife, ed., *Pictures from Gold Rush California* (New York: Citadel Press, 1967).
65. Lester Reed, *Old-Timers of Southeastern California* (Redlands, California: Citrograph Printing Co., 1967).
66. W. W. Robinson, *Land in California: The Story of Mission Lands, Ranchos, Squatters, Mining Claims, Railroad Grants, Land Scrip, Homesteads* (Berkeley: University of California Press, 1979 paperback repr. of 1948 ed.).
67. Abelardo L. Rodríguez, *Memoria administrativa del gobierno del Distrito Norte de la Baja California 1924–1927* (Colección Baja California: Nuestra Historia; Secretaría de Educación Pública, 1993 repr. of 1928 ed.).
68. William Redmond Ryan, *Personal Adventures in Upper and Lower California in 1849*, vols. I and II (New York: Arno Press, 1973 repr. of 1850 British ed.).
69. [Upton Sinclair.] *The Land of Orange Groves and Jails: Upton Sinclair's California*, Lauren Coodley, ed. (Santa Clara: Santa Clara University / Berkeley: Heyday Books, 2004; orig. texts 1922–46).
70. Mildred de Stanley, *The Salton Sea Yesterday and Today* (Los Angeles: Triumph Press, A Kym's Book, 1966 listed as pub. date but 1978 is mentioned as "now" in the text).
71. George R. Stewart, *Ordeal by Hunger: The Story of the Donner Party* (New York: Houghton Mifflin Co., 1960 repr. with supplement of 1936 ed.; repr. 1988).
72. John M. Swisher, *Images of America: The Mohave Desert* (Charleston, South Carolina: Arcadia Publishing, 1999).
73. Paco Ignacio Taibo II, *'68*, Donald Nicholson-Smith, trans. (New York: Seven Stories Press, 2004; orig. Spanish-lang. ed. 1991).
74. Alexander S. Taylor, *A Historical Summary of Baja California from Its Discovery in 1532 to 1867*, Walt Wheelock, ed.(Pasadena: Socio-Technical Books, 1971; 1st complete ed. *ca.* 1867).
75. Otis B. Tout, *The First Thirty Years (1901–1931): Being an Account of the Principal Events in the History of Imperial Valley, Southern California, U.S.A.* (Imperial, California: undated Imperial County Historical Society repr. of 1931 ed.).
76. Rob Leicester Wagner, *Sleeping Giant: An Illustrated History of Southern California's Inland Empire* (Las Vegas: Stephens Press, 2004).
77. Rob L. Wagner and Joe Blackstock, eds. *Witness to a Century: The Inland Daily Bulletin* (Upland, California: Dragonflyer Press, 2000).
78. Clifford James Walker, *One Eye Closed, the Other Red: The California Bootlegging Years* (Barstow, California: Back Door Publishing, 1999).
79. T. H. Watkins, *The Hungry Years: A Narrative History of the Great Depression in America* (New York: Henry Holt & Co. / An Owl Book, 2000 repr. of orig. 1999 ed.).

I. AGRICULTURE AND ECOLOGY

1. W. V. Cruess, Professor Emeritus, *Commercial Fruit and Vegetable Products: A Textbook for the Student, Investigator, and Manufacturer*, 4th ed. (New York: McGraw-Hill, 1958).
2. Jared Diamond, *Collapse: How Societies Choose to Fail or Succeed* (New York: Viking, 2005).
3. Division of Agricultural Sciences, University of California, *Agricultural Resources of California Counties (Special Publication 3275)* (Berkeley: March 1982).
4. Wayland A. Dunham, *It's a Date* (Pasadena: Publication Press, 1948).
5. Howard S. Fawcett, Professor of Plant Pathology, *Citrus Diseases and Their Control*, 2nd. ed. [1st. ed. with H. A. Lee] (New York: McGraw-Hill Book Co., 1936).
6. Victor Davis Hanson, *The Land Was Everything: Letters from an American Farmer* (New York: Free Press, 2000).
7. Claude B. Hutchinson, ed., *California Agriculture*, by Members of the Faculty of the College of Agriculture, University of California (Berkeley: University of California Press, 1946).
8. Andrew Kimbrell, ed., *Fatal Harvest: The Tragedy of Industrial Agriculture* (Sausalito, California: Foundation for Deep Ecology, by arrangement with Island Press, 2002).
9. Laboratory for Experimental Design, School of Environmental Design, Department of Landscape Architecture, California State Polytechnic University, Kellogg-Voorhis, Pomona, California, for the Environmental Development Agency of San Diego County as a Component of the Integrated Regional Environmental Management Program, *A Planning System for the Coastal Plain of San Diego County, Phase 1: Northern Sector* (September, 1972).

10. Esther H. Klotz, Harry W. Lawton and Joan H. Hall, eds. Riverside Municipal Museum, *A History of Citrus in the Riverside Area*, rev. ed. (Riverside: Riverside Museum Press, 1989).
11. G. M. Markle, J. J. Baron and B. A. Schneider, *Food and Feed Crops of the United States: A Descriptive List Classified According to Potentials for Pesticide Residues*, 2nd. ed., rev. (Willoughby, Ohio: Meister Publishing Co., Meisterpro Reference Guides, in assoc. with Rutgers University, 1998).
12. Frederick D. Mott, M.D., and Milton I. Roemer, M.D., M.P.H., *Rural Health and Medical Care* (New York: McGraw-Hill Book Co., 1948).
13. Spencer Museum of Art, The University of Kansas, *Remembering the Family Farm: 150 Years of American Prints*, Stephen H. Goddard, ed. (No place of publication: University of Kansas, 2001).

J. IRRIGATION AND WATER POLITICS

1. John A. Adams, Jr., *Damming the Colorado: The Rise of the Lower Colorado River Authority, 1933–1939* (Texas Station: Texas A&M University, The Centennial Series of the Association of Former Students, no. 35, 1990).
2. Association of California Water Agencies, *California's Continuing Water Crisis: Lessons from Recurring Drought, 1991 Update* (Sacramento: ACWA, 1991).
3. J. O'M. Bockris, ed., *Environmental Chemistry* (New York: Plenum Press, 1977).
4. David Carle, *Introduction to Water in California* (Berkeley: University of California Press, California Natural History Guides No. 76, 2004).
5. David Carle, *Water and the California Dream: Choices for the New Millennium* (San Francisco: Sierra Club Books, 2000).
6. Committee on Irrigation-Induced Water Quality Problems, National Research Council, *Irrigation-Induced Water Quality Problems: What Can Be Learned from the San Joaquin Valley Experience* (Washington, D.C.: National Academy Press, 1989).
7. William Leslie Davis, *Rivers in the Desert: William Mulholland and the Inventing of Los Angeles* (Chicago: Olmstead Press, 2001).
8. William deBuys and Joan Myers, *Salt Dreams: Land and Water in Low-Down California* (Albuquerque: University of New Mexico Press, 1999).
9. Philip L. Fradkin, *A River No More: The Colorado River and the West* (Tucson: University of Arizona Press, 1984 repr. of 1981 Knopf ed.).
10. Robert Gottlieb and Margaret FitzSimmons, *Thirst for Growth: Water Agencies as Hidden Government in California* (Tucson: University of Arizona Press, 1991).
11. Blake Gumprecht, *The Los Angeles River: Its Life, Death, and Possible Rebirth* (Baltimore: Johns Hopkins University Press, 1999).
12. Steve Horvitz, Superintendent, Salton Sea Recreation Area, *Salton Sea 101: An Introduction to the Issues of the Salton Sea—California's Greatest Resource* (North Shore, California: Sea and Desert Interpretative Association, 1999).
13. Norris Hundley, Jr., *The Great Thirst: Californians and Water: A History*, rev. ed. (Berkeley: University of California Press, 2001).
14. International Commission on Irrigation and Drainage, *Multilingual Technical Dictionary on Irrigation and Drainage* (New Delhi: printed at the Catholic Press, 1967).
15. George Wharton James, *Reclaiming the Arid West: The Story of the United States Reclamation Service* (New York: Dodd, Mead & Co., 1917).
16. Vicente Sánchez Munguía, ed., *Lining the All-American Canal: Competition or Cooperation for Water in the U.S.-Mexican Border?* (San Diego: San Diego University Press, co-published with the Southwest Consortium for Environmental Research and Policy [SCERP] and El Colegio de la Frontera Norte [COLEF] / SCERP Monograph Series: U.S.-Mexican Border Environment, no. 13, 2006).
17. Remi A. Nadeau, *The Water Seekers*, rev. ed. (Bishop, California: Chalfant Press, 1974; orig. ed. 1950).
18. Marie Louise Parcher and Will C. Parcher, *Dry Ditches* (Bishop, California: Inyo Register Press, 1970 rev. ed.; orig. ed. 1934).
19. Robert A. Pearce, Ph.D., *The Owens Valley Controversy and A. A. Brierly: The Untold Story* (Lincoln, Nebraska: Dageforde Publishing, Inc., 1999).
20. Harold E. Rogers and Alan H. Nichols, *Water for California: Planning, Law & Practice, Finance* (San Francisco: Bancroft-Whitney, 1967), vol. 1.
21. [San Diego County Water Authority.] Written by Kenneth W. Mirvis, Ed.D., and Cathryn M. Delude, both of the Writing Company; for the San Diego County Water Authority, *To Quench a Thirst: A Brief History of Water in the San Diego Region* (San Diego, 2000).
22. William E. Smythe, *The Conquest of Arid America*, with a new introduction by Lawrence R. Lee (Seattle: University of Washington Paperbacks, 1969 repr. of Smythe's rev. ed. of 1905).

23. Frank Waters, *The Colorado* (Athens: Ohio University Press / Swallow Press, 1984 repr. of 1946 ed.).
24. Emily E. Whitehead, Charles F. Hutchinson, Barbara N. Timmermann and Robert G. Varady, eds., *Arid Lands Today and Tomorrow: Proceedings of an International Research and Development Conference, Tucson, Arizona, U.S.A., October 20–25, 1985* (Boulder, Colorado: Westview Press, 1988).

K. MIGRANT WORKERS, LABOR MOVEMENTS, AND THE BORDER ECONOMY

1. Bill Bigelow, *The Line Between Us: Teaching About the Border and Mexican Immigration* (Milwaukee: Rethinking Schools, 2006).
2. Eugene Keith Chamberlin, "Mexican Colonization versus American Interests in Lower California," in *The Pacific Historical Review*, vol. 20, no. 1 (February 1951), pp. 43–55.
3. Cesar Chavez, *An Organizer's Tale: Speeches*, ed. with intro. by Ilan Stavans (New York: Penguin Classics, 2008). [I cite this volume, following *Imperial*'s usage of accent marks, as "César Chávez."]
4. Cletus E. Daniel, *Bitter Harvest: A History of California Farmworkers, 1870–1941* (Ithaca, New York: Cornell University Press, 1981).
5. Marilyn P. Davis, *Mexican Voices / American Dreams: An Oral History of Mexican Immigration to the United States* (New York: Henry Holt & Co., 1990).
6. Tony Dunbar and Linda Kravitz, *Hard Traveling: Migrant Farm Workers in America* (Cambridge, Massachusetts: Ballinger Publishing Co. [a Lippincott subsidiary]), pub. date unavailable, *ca.* 1980).
7. Charles Elmer Fox, *Tales of an American Hobo* (Iowa City: University of Iowa Press / Singular Lives, The Iowa Series in North American Biography, 1989).
8. Gilbert A. González, "Company Unions, the Mexican Consulate, and the Imperial Valley Agricultural Strikes, 1928–1934," in *The Western Historical Quarterly*, vol. 27, no. 1 (spring 1996), pp. 53–73.
9. Richard Griswold del Castillo and Richard A. Garcia, *César Chávez: A Triumph of Spirit* (Norman: University of Oklahoma Press, 1995).
10. John C. Hammerback and Richard J. Jensen, *The Rhetorical Career of César Chávez* (College Station: Texas A&M University Press, 1998).
11. Elva Treviño Hart, *Barefoot Heart: Stories of a Migrant Child* (Tempe, Arizona: Bilingual Press, 1999).
12. [*I.W.W. Song.*] *I.W.W. Songs to Fan the Flames of Discontent: A Facsimile Reprint of the Popular Nineteenth Edition*, 1923 (Chicago: Charles H. Kerr Publishing Co., 1996).
13. [Dorothea Lange.] Pierre Borhan, ed., *Dorothea Lange: The Heart and Mind of a Photographer* (New York: A Bullfinch Press Book / Little, Brown & Co., Marguerite Feitlowitz, trans., 2002; orig. French ed. same year).
14. Abraham F. Lowenthal and Katrina Burgess, eds., *The California-Mexico Connection* (Stanford, California: Stanford University Press, 1993).
15. *Dreams of Freedom: A Ricardo Flores Magón Reader*, Chaz Bufe and Mitchell Cowen Verter, eds. [and trans. by Bufe] (Oakland, California: AK Press, 2005).
16. Peter Matthiessen, *Sal Si Puedes (Escape If You Can): Cesar Chavez and the New American Revolution* (Berkeley: University of California Press, 2000; orig. copyright 1969).
17. Ann McGregor, comp., Cindy Wathen, ed., photos by George Elfie Ballis, *Remembering Cesar: The Legacy of Cesar Chavez* (Clovis, California: Quill Driver Books, 2000).
18. Ramón Eduardo Ruiz, *On the Rim of Mexico: Encounters of the Rich and Poor* (Boulder, Colorado: Westview Press, 1998).
19. Ruben Salazar, *Border Correspondent: Selected Writings, 1955–1970*, Mario T. García, ed. (Berkeley: University of California Press, Latinos in American Society and Culture ser., 1998 paperback repr. of 1995 ed.).
20. Sue Sanders, *The Real Causes of Our Migrant Problem* (privately printed pamphlet, 1940).
21. Richard Steven Street, *Beasts of the Field: A Narrative History of California Farmworkers, 1769–1913* (Stanford, California: Stanford University Press, 2004).
22. Richard Steven Street, *Photographing Farmworkers in California* (Stanford, California: Stanford University Press, 2004).
23. Paul S. Taylor, *Mexican Labor in the United States: Migration Statistics. III* (Berkeley: University of California Press, University of California Publications in Economics, vol. 12, no. 2, 1933). [Note: This and the following monograph are now rare. I found them in the author's papers in the Bancroft Library (see section A of this bibliography), Carton 5, Folder 5:4, "Mexican Labor in the United States, volumes II, III & IV, 1932, 1933, 1934."]
24. Paul S. Taylor, *Mexican Labor in the United States: Migration Statistics. IV* (Berkeley: University of California Press, University of California Publications in Economics, vol. 12, no. 3, 1934).
25. Errol Lincoln Uys, *Riding the Rails: Teenagers on the Move During the Great Depression* (New York: Routedge, 2003).

L. CHINESE SOURCES

1. [Asiatic Exclusion League.] *Proceedings of the Asiatic Exclusion League 1907–1913* (New York: Arno Press, "Anti-Movements in America" series, Gerald N. Grob, advisory ed., 1977).
2. Eduardo Auyón Gerardo, *El Dragón en el Desierto: Los Pioneros Chinos en Mexicali* (Mexicali: Centro de Investigación de la Cultura China, n.d., *ca.* 1991).
3. Jack Black, *You Can't Win* (Edinburgh: AK Press, 2000 repr. of orig. 1926 ed.).
4. Robert H. Duncan, "The Chinese and the Economic Development of Northern Baja California, 1889–1929" in *The Hispanic American Historical Review*, vol. 74, no. 4 (November 1994), pp. 615–47.
5. The Great Basin Foundation Center for Anthropological Research, *Wo Ho Leun: An American Chinatown*, 2 vols. (San Diego: Great Basin Foundation, 1987).
6. Marlon K. Hom, comp., *Songs of Gold Mountain: Cantonese Rhymes from San Francisco Chinatown* (Berkeley: University of California Press, 1987).
7. Peter C. Y. Leung, *One Day, One Dollar: The Chinese Farming Experience in the Sacramento River Delta, California*, 2nd ed. (Taipei: Liberal Arts Press, 1994).
8. Kathleen Kong Wing, with Carolyn Wing Greenlee, *Inside the Oy Quong Laundry*, 3rd ed. (Kelseyville, California: Earthen Vessel Productions, 1998 repr. of 1995 ed.).

M. NATIVE AMERICAN SOURCES

1. Charles Avery Amsden, *Prehistoric Southwesterners from Basketmaker to Pueblo* (Los Angeles: Southwest Museum, 1976 repr. of orig. 1949 ed.).
2. [Bureau of Indian Affairs, 1999.] Bureau of Indian Affairs, Sacramento Area Office, 1999 Tribal Information and Directory.
3. David Carrasco and Eduardo Matos Moctezuma, *Moctezuma's Mexico: Visions of the Aztec World*, rev. ed. (Boulder: University Press of Colorado, 2003).
4. [Delfina Cuero.] *Delfina Cuero: Her Autobiography, an Account of Her Last Years, and Her Ethnobotanic Contributions*, by Florence Connolly Shipek (Menlo Park, California: Ballena Press, 1991).
5. E. W. Gifford, *The Kamia of Imperial Valley* (Washington, D.C.: Smithsonian Institution, Bureau of American Ethnology Bulletin 97, U.S. Government Printing Office, 1931; facsimile repr. by Coyote Press, Salinas, California, n.d.; *ca.* 2004).
6. Ross Hassig, *Aztec Warfare: Imperial Expansion and Political Control* (Norman: University of Oklahoma Press / The Civilization of the American Indian ser., no. 188; 1995 paperback repr. of 1988 ed.).
7. [Heizer maps.] Robert F. Heizer, *Languages, Territories and Names of California Indian Tribes* (Berkeley: University of California Press, 1966).
8. Robert F. Heizer, vol. ed., *Handbook of North American Indians*, vol. 8 (California). (Washington: Smithsonian Institution, 1978).
9. Robert F. Heizer and Albert B. Elsasser, *The Natural World of the California Indians* (Berkeley: University of California Press, California Natural History Guides, 1980).
10. Robert F. Heizer and M. A. Whipple, comp. and ed., *The California Indians: A Source Book*, 2nd ed. (Berkeley: University of California Press, 1971).
11. Miguel León-Portilla and Earl Shorris, et al., eds. and comps., *In the Language of Kings: An Anthology of Mesoamerican Literature—Pre-Columbian to the Present* (New York: Norton, 2001).
12. Herbert W. Luthin, ed., *Surviving Through the Days: Translations of Native California Stories and Songs (A California Indian Reader)* (Berkeley: University of California Press, 2002).
13. Manfred Knaak, *The Forgotten Artist: Indians of Anza-Borrego and Their Rock Art* (Borrego Springs, California: Anza-Borrego Desert Natural History Association, 1988).
14. A. L. Kroeber, *Yuman Tribes of the Lower Colorado* (Berkeley: University of California Press, University of California Publications in American Archaeology and Ethnology, vol. 16, no. 8, pp. 485–575, August 21, 1920; facsimile repr. by Coyote Press, Salinas, California, n.d.; *ca.* 2004).
15. [Esteban Rodríguez Lorenzo.] Miguel León-Portilla, "Indian Place Names of Baja California Sur: A Report attributed to Esteban Rodríguez Lorenzo" (Los Angeles: Southwest Museum Leaflets, no. 38, 1977).
16. Charlotte McGowan, *Ceremonial Fertility Sites in Southern California* (San Diego: San Diego Museum of Man papers, no. 14, 1982).
17. Yolanda Sánchez Ogás, *A La Orilla del Río Colorado: Los Cucapá* (Mexicali, 2000).
18. Elmer M. Savilla, *Along the Trail: A Story of "One Little Indian"* (Quechan reservation near Yuma: Self-published, *ca.* 1996).
19. Leslie Spier, *Southern Diegueño Customs* (Berkeley: University of California Press, University of California Publications in American Archaeology and Ethnology, vol. 20, no. 16, pp. 297–358, December 1923; facsimile repr. by Coyote Press, Salinas, California, n.d.; *ca.* 2004).

20. Edith S. Taylor and William J. Wallace, "Mohave Tattooing and Face-Painting" (Los Angeles: Southwest Museum Leaflets, no. 20, 1947).
21. Robert M. Utley, *The Indian Frontier 1846–1890* (Albuquerque: University of New Mexico Press, 2003 rev. of 1984 ed.).
22. Jay Von Werlhof, *That They May Know and Remember, vol. 2: Spirits of the Earth*, with aerial photographs by Harry Casey (Ocotillo, California: Imperial Valley College Desert Museum Society, 2004).
23. Edwin F. Walker, "Indians of Southern California" (Los Angeles: Southwest Museum Leaflets, no. 10, n.d. but prob. bef. 1947, which is the date of leaflet no. 20).
24. Margaret L. Weide and James P. Barker, with sections by Harry W. Lawton, David L. Weide and Imperial Valley College Museum, Philip L. Wilke, ed., *Background to Prehistory of the Yuha Desert Region* (Riverside, California: Prepared for the United States Dept. of Interior, Bureau of Land Management, California Desert Planning Program, contract no. 52500–CT4–296 (N), June 30, 1974; facsimile repr. by Coyote Press, Salinas, California, n.d.; *ca.* 2004).
25. Anita Alvarez de Williams, *Travelers Among the Cucapá* (Los Angeles: Dawson's Book Shop, 1975; Baja California Travels ser., no. 34; various orig. dates of pub. for source material excerpted).

N. MISCELLANEOUS MEXICAN SOURCES

1. José Joaquín Arrillaga, *Diary of His Surveys of the Frontier, 1796*, trans. by Froy Tiscareno, ed. & annotated by John W. Robinson (Los Angeles: Dawson's Book Shop, 1969; Baja California Travels ser., no. 17).
2. Automobile Club of Southern California, *Baja California* (Los Angeles: Automobile Club of Southern California, 1976).
3. Celso Aguirre Bernal, Miembro de la Asociación de Escritores de Baja California, *Compendio Histórico-Biográfico de Mexicali*, 6th ed. (Mexicali: Escudo de Mexicali,* 1989 repr. of 1966 ed.).
4. Lowell L. Blaisdell, "Harry Chandler and Mexican Border Intrigue 1914–1917," in *Pacific Historical Review*, vol. 35, no. 4 (November 1966), pp. 385–93.
5. J. N. Bowman and R. F. Heizer, *Anza and the Northwest Frontier of New Spain* (Los Angeles: Southwest Museum papers, no. 20, 1967).
6. Christopher R. Boyer, *Becoming Campesinos: Politics, Identity, and Agrarian Struggle in Postrevolutionary Michoacán, 1920–1935* (Stanford, California: Stanford University Press, 2003).
7. Don Hesiquio Treviño Calderón, *Historia y Personajes de Ensenada* (Ensenada: Tipográfica Castañeda, 2003).
8. Luis Humberto Crosthwaite, John William Byrd and Bobby Byrd, *Puro Border: Dispatches, Snapshots & Graffiti from La Frontera* (El Paso, Texas: Cinco Puntos Press, 2003).
9. [Juan Bautista de Anza.] Donald T. Garate, trans. and ed., *Anza's Return from Alta California: Anza Correspondence 1776–1778*, Wade Cox, illus. (San Diego: *Antepasados*, vol. IX, a publication of Los Californianos, 1998).
10. Bernal Díaz, *The Conquest of New Spain*, J. M. Cohen, trans. (New York: Penguin Books, 1963).
11. *Fodor's Mexico, 1992, With the Best of the Beach Resorts and Travel Off the Beaten Path* (New York: Fodor's Travel Publications, 1991).
12. [Fray Pedro Font.] *The Anza Expedition of 1775–76: Diary of Pedro Font*, ed. Frederick J. Teggart, Associate Professor of Pacific Coast History, University of California (Berkeley: University of California Press, Publications of the Academy of Pacific Coast History, vol. 3, no. 1, March 1913).
13. Peter Gerhard and Howard E. Gulick, *Lower California Guidebook: A Descriptive Traveler's Guide* (Glendale, California: Arthur H. Clark Co., 1958).
14. Francisco López de Gómara, *Cortés: The Life of the Conqueror by His Secretary*, Lesley Byrd Simpson, trans. and ed., from 1552 ed. (Berkeley: University of California Press, 1964).
15. Ulysses S. Grant, *Personal Memoirs & Selected Letters* (New York: Library of America, 1990 repr. of 1885–86 ed. and 1967–85 ed., respectively).
16. James S. Griffith, *Folk Saints of the Borderlands: Victims, Bandits and Healers* (Tucson: Rio Nuevo Publishers, 2003).
17. Richard Griswold del Castillo, *The Treaty of Guadalupe Hidalgo: A Legacy of Conflict* (Norman: University of Oklahoma Press, 1990).
18. Francis Johnston, *The Wonder of Guadalupe: The Origin and Cult of the Miraculous Image of the Blessed Virgin of Mexico* (Rockford, Illinois: TAN Books and Publishers, 1981).
19. Gilbert M. Joseph and Timothy J. Henderson, eds., *The Mexico Reader: History, Culture, Politics* (Durham, North Carolina: Duke University Press, 2002).

*Whether or not this is the actual publisher is unclear. It appears on both the front cover and the spine, but in each case as a caption to the coat of arms of Mexicali.

20. Anna Lanyon, *Malinche's Conquest* (Crow's Nest, NSW, Australia: Allen & Unwin, 1999).
21. Michael C. Meyer, William L. Sherman, Susan M. Deeds, *The Course of Mexican History*, 7th ed. (New York; Oxford University Press, 2003; orig. ed. 1979).
22. [MOCA San Diego.] Museum of Contemporary Art San Diego, *Strange New World: Art and Design from Tijuana / Extraño Nuevo Mundo: Arte y diseño desde Tijuana* (La Jolla: MOCA San Diego, distributed by DAP, 2006).
23. Greg Niemann, *Baja Legends: The Historic Characters, Events, and Locations That Put Baja California on the Map* (San Diego: Sunbelt Publications, 2002).
24. John Noble, Dan Spitzer and Scott Wayne, *Mexico, A Travel Survival Kit*, 3rd ed. (Hawthorn, Victoria, Australia: Lonely Planet Publications, 1989).
25. [Orozco autobiography.] José Clemente Orozco, *An Autobiography*, trans. by Robert C. Stephenson, intro. by John Palmer Leeper (Mineola, New York: 2001 repr. of 1962 ed.; orig. Spanish-lang. ed. serially published in Mexico, 1942).
26. [Orozco graphic work.] Jose Clemente Orozco, *José Clemente Orozco: Graphic Work* (Austin: University of Texas Press, Joe R. and Teresa Lozano Series in Latin American and Latino Art and Culture, 2004).
27. Walt Peterson, *The Baja Adventure Book* (Berkeley: Wilderness Press, 1987).
28. Frederick B. Pike, *The United States and Latin America: Myths and Stereotypes of Civilization and Nature* (Austin: University of Texas Press, 1992).
29. Harry Polkinhorn, Gabriel Trujillo Muñoz and Rogelio Reyes, eds., *Border Lives: Personal Essay on the U.S.-Mexico Border* (Calexico / Mexicali: Binational Press, 1995). Bilingual ed.
30. Desmond Rochfort, *Mexican Muralists: Orozco, Rivera, Siquieros* (San Francisco: Chronicle Books, 1998 repr. of 1993 British ed.).
31. Juan Rulfo, *The Burning Plain and Other Stories*, George D. Schade, trans. (trans. of *El llano en llamas*) (Austin: University of Texas Press, Pan American Paperbacks, no. 6, 1971; orig. Mexican ed. 1953).
32. [RDI (2004).] Rural Development Institute Reports on Foreign Aid and Development, no. 120, February 2004 (Jennifer Brown, "Ejidos and Comunidades in Oaxaca, Mexico: Effect of the 1992 Reforms").
33. *The Drawings of Ignacio Tirsch, a Jesuit Missionary in Baja California.* Narrative by Doyce B. Nunis, Jr.; Elsbeth Schulz-Bischof, trans. (Los Angeles: Dawson's Book Shop, 1972; Baja California Travels ser., no. 27; orig, drawings and captions *ca.* 1767).
34. Mark Wasserman, *Everyday Life and Politics in Nineteenth Century Mexico: Men, Women, and War* (Albuquerque: University of New Mexico Press, Diálogos ser., 2000).
35. John Womack, Jr., *Zapata and the Mexican Revolution* (New York: Random House / Vintage, 1970; orig. ed. 1969; copyright 1968).
36. Elizabeth Netto Calil Zarur and Charles Muir Lovell, eds., *Art and Faith in Mexico: The Nineteenth-Century Retablo Tradition* (Albuquerque: University of New Mexico Press, 2001).
37. Alonso de Zorita, *Life and Labor in Ancient Mexico: The Brief and Summary Relation of the Lords of New Spain*, Benjamin Keen, trans. (Norman: University of Oklahoma Press, 1994 repr. of 1963 ed; orig. Spanish ed. 1585).

O. LOS ANGELES

1. C. W. Baist, comp., *Baist's Real Estate Atlas: Surveys of Los Angeles, Cal., Complete in One Volume* (Philadelphia, 1910).
2. Horace Bell, *Reminiscences of a Ranger: Early Times in Southern California* (Norman: University of Oklahoma Press; vol. 65 of the Western Frontier Library, 1999; orig. pub. 1881).
3. Harry Carr, *Los Angeles: City of Dreams* (New York: D. Appleton–Century Co. Inc., 1935).
4. [Diebenkorn.] Jane Livingston, ed., *The Art of Richard Diebenkorn* (New York: Whitney Museum of American Art, in assoc. with University of California Press, 1997).
5. Text by Digby Diehl, *Front Page: A Collection of Historical Headlines from the Los Angeles Times 1881–1987* (New York: Harry Abrams, 1987).
6. C. Milton Hinshilwood and Elena Irish Zimmerman, *Old Los Angeles and Pasadena in Vintage Postcards* (Chicago: Arcadia Publishing, Postcard History ser., 2003 repr. of 2001 ed.).
7. *An Illustrated History of Los Angeles County, California* (Chicago: Lewis Publishing Co., 1889). [Front cover is imprinted with *"Pen Pictures from the Garden of the World."*]
8. Los Angeles City Directory, 1942 (Los Angeles Directory Co., 1941).
9. John Steven McGroarty, ed., *History of Los Angeles County*, 3 vols. (Chicago: American Historical Society, Inc., 1923).
10. W. McPherson, *Homes in Los Angeles City and County, and Description Thereof, with Sketches of the Four Adjacent Counties* (Los Angeles: Mirror Book and Job Printing Establishment, 1873; facsimile repr. by Southern California Chapter, Antiquarian Booksellers Association of America, 1961).

11. George T. Miron, *A Love Affair with the Angels: Vignettes of Old L.A.* and *The Toward-Quiescence and Unity Theory* (Long Beach: University Print, 1979, copy 15).
12. Charles Moore, Peter Becker, and Regula Campbell, *The City Observed: Los Angeles, A Guide to Its Architecture and Landscapes* (Santa Monica: Hennessey and Ingalls, Art + Architecture Books, 1998).
13. Harris Newmark, *Sixty Years in Southern California*, Maurice H. and Marco R. Newmark, eds., 3rd. ed. (Houghton Mifflin, 1930).
14. Doyce B. Nunis, Jr., ed., *The Founding Documents of Los Angeles: A Bilingual Edition* (Los Angeles: Historical Society of Southern California and the Zamorano Club of Los Angeles, 2004).
15. [Ontario City Directory (1945–46).] *Los Angeles Directory Co.'s ONTARIO (California) City Directory 1945–46 Including Upland, Chino, Alta Loma, Cucamonga and Etiwanda. Also a BUYERS' GUIDE and a Complete Classified Business Directory* (Los Angeles: Los Angeles Directory Co., 1946).
16. Ludwig Louis Salvator, *Los Angeles in the Sunny Seventies: A Flower from the Golden Land*, Maguerite Eyer Wilbur, trans. (Los Angeles: Bruce McCallister, printed in a ltd. ed. for Jake Zeitlin, 1929).
17. William Tecumseh Sherman, *Memoirs of General W. T. Sherman* (New York: Library of America, 1990 repr. of 1886 ed.).
18. Tom Sitton and William Deverell, eds., *Metropolis in the Making: Los Angeles in the 1920s* (Berkeley: University of California Press, 2001).
19. Anna Deavere Smith, *Twilight: Los Angeles, 1992* (New York: Random House / Anchor, 1994).
20. [Southern Orange County City Directory (1951).] *Luskey's Official Subscribers' Edition: Southern Orange County (California) City Directory, February 1951 Issue for the cities of Santa Ana, Orange, Tustin, Huntington Beach . . .* (Santa Ana: Directory Service Company, Publishers, 1951).
21. James L. Stamps, honorary editory-in-chief, *The Historical Volume and Reference Works, Covering Artesia*, etc.; vol. 4: Los Angeles County 1965 (Arlington, California: Historical Publishers, 1965).

P. FICTION AND POETRY ABOUT IMPERIAL

1. Raymond Chandler, *Later Novels and Other Writings* (New York: Library of America, 1995).
2. Philip K. Dick, *Now Wait for Last Year* (New York: Daw Books, 1981 repr. of 1966 ed.).
3. Zane Grey, *Desert Gold* (New York: Pocket Books / Simon and Schuster, 1968 repr. of 1913 ed.).
4. Dashiell Hammett, *Crime Stories and Other Writings* (New York: Library of America, 2001).
5. Helen Hunt Jackson, *Ramona* (New York: Signet Classics, a div. of Penguin Putnam, 1988; orig. ed. 1884).
6. Jack Kerouac, *The Dharma Bums* (New York: Penguin Classics Deluxe Edition, 2006; orig. ed. 1958).
7. Jack Kerouac, *On the Road* (New York: Penguin Books, 1981; orig. pub. 1957).
8. Jack London, *Novels and Social Writings* (New York: Library of America, 1982).
9. John Steinbeck, *East of Eden* (New York: Penguin, 1992; orig. ed. 1952).
10. John Steinbeck, *The Grapes of Wrath and Other Writings 1936–1941* (New York: Library of America, 1996).
11. John Steinbeck, *In Dubious Battle* (New York: Penguin; 1986, orig. ed. 1936).
12. John Steinbeck, *The Long Valley* (New York: Penguin; 1986, orig. ed. 1938).
13. John Steinbeck, *Novels 1942–1952* (New York, Library of America, 2001; orig. ed. of *The Pearl* 1945).
14. Mónica de la Torre and Michael Wiegers, eds., *Reversible Monuments: Contemporary Mexican Poetry* (Port Townsend, Washington: Copper Canyon Press, A Kage-An Book, 2002).
15. Otis B. Tout, *Silt: Paula Helps Build Boulder Dam* (San Diego: Hillcrest Publishing Company, 1928).
16. Harold Bell Wright, *The Winning of Barbara Worth*, special numbered and signed limited commemorative edition (Holtville, California: Imperial County Historical Society, in conjunction with the Harold Bell Wright Society; corr. repr. of original 1911 ed.).

Q. PUBLISHED SOURCES METAPHORICALLY RELEVANT TO IMPERIAL

1. Al-Biruni, *Kitab Tahdid al-Amakin: The Determination of the Coordinates of Cities*, Jamil Ali, trans. (Beirut: Centennial Publications, American University of Beirut, 1967; orig. Arabic ed. completed A.D. 1025).
2. James Blish, *Cities in Flight* (New York: Overlook Press, 2005; author's copyright 1970; orig. tetralogy *ca.* 1950–60).
3. Ansel Adams, *Examples: The Making of 40 Photographs* (New York: Little, Brown & Co., 1983).
4. Joan Aruz, *Art of the First Cities: The Third Millennium B.C. from the Mediterranean to the Indus* (New Haven, Connecticut: Yale University Press / Metropolitan Museum of Art, 2003).
5. Isaac Asimov, *Forward the Foundation* (New York: Bantam Books, 1994 Spectra paperback repr. of orig. 1993 ed.).
6. J. G. Ballard, *The Drought* (Harmondsworth, Middlesex, England: Penguin [UK] repr. of orig. 1964 American ed., entitled *The Burning World*).
7. J. G. Ballard, *The Crystal World* (New York: Berkeley Medallion, 1967 repr. of 1966 ed.).

8. James E. B. Breslin, *Mark Rothko, a Biography* (Chicago: University of Chicago Press, 1993).
9. Ray Bradbury, *The Martian Chronicles* (New York: Bantam Books, 1970 21st paperback repr.; orig. Doubleday ed. 1950).
10. Robert Coles, *Still Hungry in America*, with photographs by Al Clayton (New York: New American Library / A Plume Book, 1969).
11. Emily Ann Croom, *Unpuzzling Your Past: The Best-Selling Basic Guide to Genealogy*, 4th ed. (Cincinnati: Betterway Books, 2001).
12. [Descartes.] Robert Maynard Hutchins, editor-in-chief, *Great Books of the Western World*, vol. 31, *Descartes–Spinoza* (Chicago: Encyclopaedia Britannica, 1952).
13. George Eliot, *Daniel Deronda* (New York: Penguin Books, 1982 repr. of 1967 Penguin English Library ed.; orig. ed. 1876).
14. Sergei Eisenstein, *The Film Sense*, Jay Leyda, trans. and ed. (New York: Harcourt Brace Jovanovich / Harvest, 1975 repr. of 1942 ed.; orig. Russian ed. *ca.* 1942, date not given).
15. Gustave Flaubert, *Three Tales*, Robert Baldick, trans. (New York: Penguin, 1961).
16. Fondation Beyeler, ed., *Mark Rothko, "A consummated experience between picture and onlooker"* (Basel: Hatje Cantz Publishers, 2001).
17. John Gardner, *Nickel Mountain: A Pastoral Novel* (New York: Alfred A. Knopf, 1973).
18. Harry Harrison, *The Deathworld Trilogy* (New York: Berkley Medallion, February 1976).
19. Martin Heidegger, *Poetry, Language, Thought*, Albert Hofstadter, trans. (New York: Harper & Row / Colophon, 1975 repr. of 1971 ed.). "Bauen Wohnen Denken," the essay from which I quote, was originally a lecture given in 1951.
20. Ernest Hemingway, *For Whom the Bell Tolls* (New York: P. F. Collier and Son, 1940).
21. Frank Herbert, *Dune* (New York: Ace Books, 1965).
22. Nicholas Hilliard, *A Treatise Concerning the Arte of Limning*, R.K.R. Thornton and T.G.S. Cain, eds. (Manchester, UK: Mid Northumberland Arts Group, Carcanet Press, 1992 repr. of *ca.* 1600 ed.).
23. [Krebs.] *The Infancy of Nazism: The Memoirs of Ex-Gauleiter Albert Krebs 1923–1933*, William Sheridan Allen, ed. and trans. (New York: New Viewpoints, a division of Franklin Watts, 1976).
24. R. D. Laing, *Self and Other*, 2nd. ed. (New York: Penguin Pelican, 1969).
25. Oliver Lange, *Vandenberg* (New York: Bantam 1972 repr. of orig. 1971 ed.).
26. Sinclair Lewis, *Main Street & Babbitt* (New York: Library of America, 1992; orig. text of *Babbitt* 1922).
27. Gwendolyn Leick, *Sex and Eroticism in Mesopotamian Literature* (London: Routledge, 1994).
28. Malcolm Lowry, *Under the Volcano* (New York: HarperCollins Perennial Classics, 2000; orig. pub. 1947).
29. Herbert Marcuse, *Eros and Civilization: A Philosophical Inquiry into Freud*, with a new preface by the author (New York: Vintage Books [Random House], 1961 paperback repr. of 1955 ed.)
30. *Karl Marx: Selected Writings*, David McLellan, ed. (New York: Oxford University Press, 1977).
31. Mary Midgley, *Animals and Why They Matter* (Athens: University of Georgia Press, 1983).
32. Walter M. Miller, Jr., *A Canticle for Leibowitz* (New York: Bantam Books, 15th printing [aft. 1968]; orig. ed. 1959).
33. László Moholy-Nagy, *Painting, Photography, Film*, Janet Seligman, trans. (Cambridge, Massachusetts: MIT Press, 1987 repr. of 1927 2nd German ed.).
34. *The Complete Essays of Montaigne*, Donald M. Frame, trans. (Stanford, California: Stanford University Press, 2002 repr. of 1965 paperback ed.; trans. first pub. 1957; based on final (5th) ed. of 1588).
35. Friedrich Nietzsche, *The Will to Power*, Walter Kaufmann and R. J. Hollingdale, trans.; Walter Kaufmann, ed. (New York: Random House / A Vintage Giant, 1968; orig. German ed. written 1883–88).
36. Oppian, Colluthus, Tryphiodorus, A.W. Mair, D. Litt., trans. (Cambridge, Massachusetts: Harvard University Press / Loeb Classical Library, 1987 repr. of 1928 ed.; original Greek "Halieutica" of Oppian *ca.* A.D. 194).
37. G. Polya, *How to Solve It: A New Aspect of Mathematical Method*, 2nd ed. (Garden City, New York: Doubleday Anchor Books, 1957).
38. Jean-Jacques Rousseau, *A Discourse on the Origin of Inequality, A Discourse on Political Economy, The Social Contract*, G.D.H. Cole, trans. (Chicago: Encyclopaedia Britannica, Great Books ser. [bound with Montesquieu], no. 38, 1952; var. dates for originals. The *Discourse on the Origin of Inequality*, cited in *Imperial*, bears a dedication date of 1754).
39. Howard Schwartz, ed., *Imperial Messages: One Hundred Modern Parables* (New York: Avon Books / Bard, 1976).
40. Eric Sloane, *I Remember America* (New York: Gallery Books, an imprint of W. H. Smith, 1987).
41. Gary Snyder, *The Practice of the Wild* (New York: Farrar, Straus & Giroux / North Point Press, 1990).
42. Arkadi and Boris Strugatski, *Hard to Be a God*, Wendayne Ackerman, trans. (New York: DAW Books, 1973; orig. Russian ed. 1964).
43. Henry D. Thoreau, *The Illustrated Walden*, with photographs from the Gleason Collection, J. Lyndon Shanley, ed. (Princeton: Princeton University Press, 1973).

44. Henry David Thoreau, *A Week on the Concord and Merrimack Rivers*, etc. (New York: Library of America, 1985).
45. Edward R. Tufte, *The Visual Display of Quantitative Information* (Cheshire, Connecticut: Graphics Press, 1983).
46. Edward R. Tufte, *Envisioning Information* (Cheshire, Connecticut: Graphics Press, 1990).
47. Edward R. Tufte, *Visual Explanations: Images and Quantities, Evidence and Narrative* (Cheshire, Connecticut: Graphics Press, 1997).
48. [Thorstein Veblen.] *The Portable Veblen*, Max Lerner, ed. (New York: Viking Press, 1948).
49. William T. Vollmann, *Rising Up and Rising Down: Some Thoughts on Freedom and Urgent Means*, 7 vols. (San Francisco, California: McSweeney's, 2003).
50. H. G. Wells, *The First Men in the Moon* (New York: Dell / Laurel Leaf Library, 1967 repr. of orig. 1901 ed.).
51. H. G. Wells, *The War of the Worlds* (New York: Scholastic Book Services, 1968 repr. of orig. 1898 ed.)
52. T. H. White, *The Once and Future King* (New York: Berkeley Publishing Co. / A Berkeley Medallion Book, 23rd pr., 1966; orig. ed. 1940).
53. *The Complete Short Stories of Thomas Wolfe*, Francis E. Skipp, ed. (New York: Scribner's, 1987; orig. mss. before 1939).

SHORT CITATIONS, AND WHERE THEIR FULL VERSIONS WILL BE FOUND

Websites are omitted, being in category D; so are most periodicals, which will be found in C.

1. Adams, Ansel. Q.
2. Adams, Henry. H.
3. Adams, John A., Jr. J.
4. *Agenda de Colonias*. G.
5. AHMM (= Archivo Histórico del Municipio de Mexicali), photo albums and documents. A.
6. Ainsworth. H.
7. Al-Biruni. Q.
8. *American Biography and Genealogy*. G.
9. Amsden. M.
10. Andersen. B.
11. *The Annals of America*. E.
12. *Appletons' Annual Cyclopaedia*. E.
13. Arrillaga. N.
14. Aruz. Q.
15. Asiatic Exclusion League. L.
16. Asimov. Q.
17. Association of California Water Agencies. J.
18. *Atlas of American Agriculture*. G.
19. *Atlas of the Biodiversity of California*. G.
20. Austin. G.
21. ______, handmade flyer about Serafin Ramírez Hernández. B.
22. Automobile Club of Southern California. *N.*
23. Auyón Gerardo. L.
24. Bain. H.
25. Baist. O.
26. Ball Advertising Co. A. (ICHSPM).
27. Ballard (2 vols.). Q.
28. Bancroft Library, all papers and correspondence. A.
29. Bancroft. H.
30. Bancroft, Griffing. H.
31. Bell. N.
32. Benson. G.
33. Berlo (2 works). B.
34. Bernal, Billie. H.
35. Bernal, Celso Aguirre. N.
36. Bigelow. K.
37. Black, Jack. L.
38. Black, Samuel T. H.
39. Blaisdell. N.
40. Blish. Q.
41. Bockris. J.
42. Boundary Commission, 1891–96. F.
43. Bowman and Heizer. N.
44. Boyer. N.
45. Bradbury. Q.
46. Brawley Business Directory. B.
47. Breslin. Q.
48. Bristol. H.
49. *Britannica Year-Book 1913*. E.
50. Brown, D. Mackenzie. H.
51. Brown and Boyd. H.
52. Bull. H.
53. Bureau of Indian Affairs, 1999. M.
54. Bureau of Reclamation (1970, 1988). F.
55. Bynon and Son. G.
56. Calderón. N.
57. *California 1890 Great Register of Voters Index*. F.
58. *California Agricultural Directory 2004–2005*. G.
59. California Agricultural Labor Commission (1963). F.
60. *California Blue Book*. F.
61. California Board of Agriculture (1918, 1936, 1938). F.
62. The California Builders Council. G.
63. California census (1880). F.
64. California census index (1870). F.
65. California county health-status profiles. F.
66. California Death Index. F.
67. California Department of Agriculture (1941,

1965, 1974). F.
68. California Department of Fish and Game. F.
69. California Department of Food and Agriculture. F.
70. California Department of Justice (1959). F.
71. California Department of Water Resources (1978). F.
72. California Employment Development Department (1995). F.
73. *The California Gazetteer*. G.
74. California State Archives, maps and papers. A.
75. California State Board of Equalization (1949). F.
76. California State Controller (1950–51). F.
77. *The California Water Atlas*. G.
78. Carle (2 vols.). J.
79. Carolan. G.
80. Carr. O.
81. Carrasco and Moctezuma. M.
82. Census Bureau (1850, 1910 [vols. 1, 7], 1947, 1974, 1975). F.
83. Chamberlin. K.
84. Chandler. P.
85. Chávez, César. K.
86. Chinese-tunnel letters. B.
87. *The City and County of San Diego*. G.
88. Coles. Q.
89. Colorado River Association (1952). A. (ICHSPM).
90. Colorado River Basin Salinity Control Forum. F.
91. Colorado River Board (1962, 1981). F.
92. Committee on Irrigation-Induced Water Quality Problems. J.
93. *The Connoisseur's Guide*. C.
94. Couts. H.
95. Coy. F.
96. Croom. Q.
97. Crosby. H.
98. Crosthwaite, Byrd and Byrd. N.
99. Cruess. I.
100. Cruz-Kaegi report. B.
101. Cuero. M.
102. Dana. H.
103. Daniel. K.
104. Davis, Marilyn P. K.
105. Davis, William Leslie. J.
106. Dawson and Brechin. H.
107. De Anza. N.
108. De la Torre and Wiegers. P.
109. De Stanley. H.
110. De Vaca. H.
111. De Williams. M.
112. Death certificates. F.
113. DeBuys and Myers. J.
114. Department of the Interior (1933, 1963). F.
115. Descartes. Q.
116. Diamond. I.
117. Díaz. N.
118. *Diccionario Porrúa*. E.
119. Dick. P.
120. Diebenkorn. O.
121. Diehl. O.
122. Dirección General de Estadística. F.
123. Division of Agricultural Sciences (1982). I.
124. Dumke. H.
125. Dunbar and Kravitz. K.
126. Duncan. L.
127. Dunham. I.
128. Durrenberger with Johnson. G.
129. Dwyer. B.
130. EDD printout (2001). F.
131. EDD unemployment fact sheet (1997–99). F.
132. Eisenstein. Q.
133. Eliot. Q.
134. Elliott, various county histories. H.
135. Emerson. H.
136. Emory. G.
137. *Enciclopedia de México*. E.
138. *Encyclopaedia Britannica* (11th & 15th eds). E.
139. *Encyclopedia of Food Science and Technology*. E.
140. Estado de Baja California (*ca.* 1983). F.
141. Fagan. H.
142. Farr. H.
143. Farris. H.
144. Fawcett. I.
145. Fitch. H.
146. Flaubert. Q.
147. Fleischhauer et al. H.
148. *Fodor's Mexico, 1992*. M.
149. Fondation Beyeler. Q.
150. Font. N.
151. *Food Technology*. C.
152. Paul Foster reports, 2007. B.
153. Fox. K.
154. Fradkin. J.
155. Frisby. H.
156. Gardner. Q.
157. Gates. H.
158. Gerardo. L.
159. Gerhard and Gulick. N.
160. Gifford. M.
161. Glenn. B.
162. Golden Acorn placemat. B.
163. Gómara. N.
164. González. K.
165. Gostin. F.
166. Gottlieb and FitzSimmons. J.
167. Governor Johnson correspondence. A.
168. Grant. N.
169. The Great Basin Foundation [Center for Anthropological Research]. L.
170. *Great Soviet Encyclopedia*. E.
171. Greeley and Batson. G.
172. Gregor. G
173. Grey. P.
174. Griffin and Young. G.
175. Griffith. N.
176. *The Gringo Gazette*. C.
177. Griswold. G.
178. Griswold del Castillo. N..
179. Griswold del Castillo and Garcia. K.

180. "Guide to Independence 2005–2006." B.
181. Gumprecht. I.
182. Gunn. G.
183. D. Gunn. G.
184. Halbert. G.
185. Hall. F.
186. Hamilton. H.
187. Hammerback and Jensen. K.
188. Hammett. P.
189. Hanson. I.
190. *Harper's Weekly* facsimiles. C.
191. Harris. H.
192. Harrison. Q.
193. Hart. K.
194. Hartnell. H.
195. Hassig. M.
196. Heidegger. Q.
197. Heilbron et al. H.
198. Heizer. M.
199. Heizer maps. M.
200. Heizer and Elsasser. M.
201. Heizer and Whipple. M.
202. Hemingway. Q.
203. Henderson. H.
204. Hendricks. D.
205. Herbert. Q.
206. Hetzel. H.
207. Heubusch. G.
208. Hilliard. Q.
209. Hinshilwood and Zimmerman. O.
210. *History of the Counties of Fresno &c.* H.
211. Hittell. H.
212. Hobbs. H.
213. Holmes et al. H.
214. Hom. L.
215. Hornor. G.
216. Horvitz. J.
217. Hostess Reference Book (1936). A. (ICHSPM).
218. House of Representatives (1907). F.
219. Howe and Hall. H.
220. Hundley. J.
221. Hunt. H.
222. Hutchinson. I.
223. Iacopi. G.
224. ICHSPM documents. A.
225. IID letter to farmers, 9 July 2003. B.
226. IID objection to Part 417 determination. B.
227. IID testimony, July 1, 2003. B.
228. IID water-transportation map. B.
229. *An Illustrated History of Los Angeles County*. O.
230. *An Illustrated History of Southern California*. H.
231. Imperial County Agricultural Commission papers. A.
232. Imperial County Assessor's maps. F.
233. *Imperial County: The Big Picture*. H.
234. Imperial County Historical Society Pioneers Museum (ICHSPM), photographs and documents. A.
235. Imperial Valley Directory (1912, 1914, 1920, 1924, 1926, 1930, 1939, 1942, 1949, 1952, 1970, 1980, 2000). G.
236. Imperial Valley Research Center pamphlet. B.
237. Imperial Valley yellow pages (2001). G.
238. Instituto Nacional de Estadística Geografía e Informática. F.
239. International Commission on Irrigation and Drainage. J.
240. *I.W.W. Songs*. J.
241. Jackson. P.
242. James, *Reclaiming the Arid West*. J.
243. James, *Wonders of the Colorado Desert*. G.
244. Johnston. N.
245. Joseph and Henderson. N.
246. *The Journal, American Water Works Association*. C.
247. *The Journal of San Diego History*. C.
248. Karpen obituary. B.
249. Kerig. B.
250. Kerouac (2 vols.). P.
251. Kerouac (Brinkley). H.
252. Kimbrell. I.
253. Klotz, Lawton and Hall. H.
254. Knaak. M.
255. Knight. H.
256. Krebs. Q.
257. Kreissman. G.
258. Kroeber. M.
259. Kurutz. H.
260. *La Ocotilla*. E.
261. Laboratory for Experimental Design. I.
262. Laflin, three histories. H.
263. Laing. Q.
264. Landis. H.
265. Lange, Dorothea. K.
266. Lange, Oliver. Q.
267. Lanyon. N.
268. Lech. H.
269. Leick. Q.
270. Leigh. H.
271. León-Portilla and Shorris. M.
272. Leung. L.
273. Lewis. Q.
274. Lindsay and Hample. G.
275. London. P.
276. Lorenzo. M.
277. Los Angeles City Directory (1942). O.
278. Lotz et al. I.
279. Lowenthal and Burgess. K.
280. Lower Colorado Region study (1971). F.
281. Luthin. M.
282. *Machinery's Handbook*. E.
283. Magón. K.
284. *Maquiladora* disposable camera photos. B.
285. *Maquiladora* videos. B.
286. Marcuse. Q.
287. Mares. G.
288. Markle, Baron and Schneider. I.
289. Marschner. H.
290. Marx. Q.
291. Matthiessen. K.

292. McClelland and Last. H.
293. McCollum [followed by name of author of each cited article]. G.
294. McGowan. M.
295. McGregor. K.
296. McGroarty. O.
297. McPherson. O.
298. Meade. G.
299. Mexicali yellow pages (2002–2003). G.
300. Meyer et al. N.
301. Midgley. Q.
302. Miller. Q.
303. Miron. O.
304. MOCA San Diego. N.
305. Moholy-Nagy. Q.
306. Montaigne. Q.
307. Montgomery. B.
308. Moore et al. O.
309. Mott and Roemer. I.
310. Muir. H.
311. Munguía. J.
312. Nadeau. J.
313. N.A.R.A.L. A.
314. *The New York Times*. C.
315. Newmark. O.
316. Rosalyn Ng report, 2003. B.
317. Niemann. N.
318. Noble, Spitzer and Wayne. N.
319. Nordland. H.
320. Nunis. O.
321. Ogás, *A la Orilla del Río Colorado*. M.
322. Ogás, *Bajo el Sol de Mexicali*. G.
323. Ontario City Directory (1945–46). O.
324. Oppian. Q.
325. Orozco (2 works). N.
326. Osio. H.
327. Packard. G.
328. Parcher and Parcher. J.
329. Patterson. H.
330. Pattie. H.
331. Paul. G.
332. Pearce. J.
333. Penn. G.
334. Peterson. M
335. Petree trans. of Viá Oriente. B.
336. Phillips et al. H.
337. Pike. N.
338. Polkinhorn et al. N.
339. Polya. Q.
340. Powell, G. Harold. H.
341. Powell, John Wesley. H.
342. Private detective reports, 2003–2007. B.
343. *Property Guide*, 2001–2003. C.
344. Pryde. G.
345. Quaife. H.
346. Raskin report. B.
347. RDI (2004). N.
348. Reed. H.
349. Richards. G.
350. Riverside City Directory (1921). G.
351. Riverside City Directory (1951). G.
352. Riverside Fire Department. G.
353. Riverside Municipal Museum. I.
354. Roberts. G.
355. Robinson. H.
356. Rochfort. N.
357. Rodríguez. H.
358. Rogers and Nichols. J.
359. Romer. H.
360. Rothacker. B.
361. Rousseau. Q.
362. Ruiz. K.
363. Rulfo. N.
364. Ryan. H.
365. Salazar. K.
366. *The Salton Sea Atlas*. G.
367. Salton Sea Authority. B.
368. Salton Sea map (1986). B.
369. Salton Sea map (1990). B.
370. Salvator. O.
371. San Diego City and County Directory (1901). G.
372. San Diego City Directory (1950). G.
373. San Diego County Water Authority. J.
374. Sanders. K.
375. Savilla. M.
376. Scheuring. G.
377. Schwartz. Q.
378. Senate Committee on the Colorado River Basin (1925). F.
379. Sherman. O.
380. Shields Date Gardens. B.
381. Sinclair. H.
382. Sitton and Deverell. O.
383. Sloane. Q.
384. Smith. O.
385. Smythe. J.
386. Southern Orange County City Directory (1951). O.
387. Southern Pacific Imperial Valley Claim (1909). F.
388. Spencer Museum of Art. I.
389. Spier. M.
390. Stamps. O.
391. Steinbeck, novels and essays. P.
392. Stewart. H.
393. Stoddard, Nostrand and West. G.
394. Street (both books). K.
395. Strugatski and Strugatski. Q.
396. Swisher. H.
397. Taibo. H.
398. Taylor, Alexander S. H.
399. Taylor, Paul S., *Mexican Labor III* and *IV*. K.
400. Taylor and Wallace. M.
401. Thoreau, several essays. Q.
402. *Time*. C.
403. *Time Agricultural Outlooks*. C.
404. Tirsch. N.
405. "Today's IID." B.
406. Torre and Wiegers. P.
407. Tout, *The First Thirty Years*. H.

408. Tout, *Silt*. P.
409. Tufte, all volumes. Q.
410. Tumco pamphlet. B.
411. University of California, Davis, pamphlets and papers. A.
412. USDA, various yearbooks, reports and statistics. F.
413. Utley. M.
414. Uys. K.
415. Van Dyke. G.
416. Veblen. Q.
417. Vollmann, Thomas and Tanis, recollections (2003). B.
418. Vollmann, William T. Q.
419. Von Werlhof. M.
420. Wagner. H.
421. Wagner and Blackstock. H.
422. Walker. M.
423. Walsh to Platoni e-mail. B.
424. Warne. (ICHSPM) A.
425. Wasserman. N.
426. Waters. J.
427. Watkins. H.
428. Weide and Barker. M.
429. Wells, all novels. Q.
430. White. Q.
431. Whitehead et al. J.
432. Wickson. G.
433. Wilsie. (ICHSPM). A.
434. Windsor Publications. B.
435. Wing. L.
436. Wolfe. Q.
437. Womack. N.
438. Woods and Poole Economics, Inc. G.
439. WPA. G.
440. Wray. G.
441. Wright. P.
442. Zarur and Lovell. N.
443. Zollinger-Peterson genealogical reports. B.
444. Zorita. N.

CREDITS

Previous Publication Information

"The Gardens of Paradise" originally appeared in *Gear* magazine in 1999, in a drastically abridged form.

A truncated version of the "Delineations" chapter appeared in the *Pacific Review* in 2002. I don't recollect getting paid.

"The Water of Life" first appeared in *Outside* magazine in 2002, once again in a much shortened form. This version was reprinted in Houghton Mifflin's *The Best American Travel Writing 2003*. A longer version appeared in 2004 in Larry McCaffery and Michael Hemmingson's *Expelled from Eden: A William T. Vollmann Reader* (New York: Thunder's Mouth Press), in which, by the way, I am incorrectly listed as an editor. The complete version now appears for the first time.

The portion of the "Bookscapes" chapter entitled "Steinbeck, Most American of Us All" was printed (or at least, fourteen hundred words of it was) in *L.A. Weekly* in 2002.

"The Chinese Tunnels" was abridged in *Harper's* magazine in 2004.

"The *Maquiladoras*" was abridged in *Playboy* magazine in 2004 (but the issue was dated January 2005).

"The Prohibited Ballads" was abridged in *Black Book* magazine in 2005.

Black Book, Gear, Harper's, Outside and *Playboy* all paid substantial amounts of money to research the above very-expensive-to-write chapters. I am sincerely grateful to these periodicals.

Illustrations

Pages i–x: Background map, east boundary of the Colorado River Land Company, 1924: courtesy of Archivo Histórico del Municipio de Mexicali

Pages vi–vii, x: Background map, 1904 map of land grants along the Colorado River: courtesy of Archivo Histórico del Municipio de Mexicali

Page xxiv: *The Entity Called Imperial:* courtesy of William T. Vollmann

Page xxv: *Closeup of Imperial:* courtesy of William T. Vollmann

Page xxvi: *Persons and Places in Imperial:* courtesy of William T. Vollmann

Page xxvii: *Rivers and Canals in Imperial:* courtesy of William T. Vollmann

Page 1: Salvation Mountain: courtesy of William T. Vollmann

Page 35: Flyer concerning the disappearance of Serafín Ramírez Hernández: courtesy of William T. Vollmann via its makers, 1999

Page 84: *My New River Cruises:* courtesy of William T. Vollmann

Page 85, *top:* Jose Lopez on the New River, 2001; *bottom:* Ray Garnett on the New River, 2001: courtesy of William T. Vollmann

Page 183: The informative glories of Tumco trailhead: courtesy of William T. Vollmann

Page 275: Wilbur [*sic*] Clark's ad: clipped from facsimile of old *Imperial Valley Press and Farmer,* courtesy of William T. Vollmann

Page 276: W. Clark's ad: clipped from facsimile of old *Imperial Valley Press and Farmer,* courtesy of William T. Vollmann

Page 280: "An Ideal Home Farm," 1927: California Local History Collection, CAL 45:13, Special Collections, University of California Library, Davis

Page 288: Tract 281 in 2005 (Signal Mountain in background): courtesy of William T. Vollmann

Page 311: Amenities of the Salton Sea: courtesy of William T. Vollmann

Page 341: Irrigation ditch, Mexicali Valley, 2004: courtesy of William T. Vollmann

Page 345: Painting on Mexican side of border wall, Colonia Chorizo: courtesy of William T. Vollmann

Page 367: Bar facade, Mexicali: courtesy of William T. Vollmann

Page 400: Rockwood's telegram: The Bancroft Library, University of California, Berkeley

Page 451: Chinese tunnel letters: collected by William T. Vollmann, Terrie Petree, and Yolanda Sánchez Dgás in 2003; now returned to their point of origin

Page 494: Bas-relief of Los Angeles's progress: courtesy of William T. Vollmann

Page 525: Everything a gal could need in El Centro: courtesy of William T. Vollmann
Page 532: Cantaloupe graph: prepared for William T. Vollmann by Mr. Paul Foster, 2007
Page 541: Shuttered floor show one block south of the border: courtesy of William T. Vollmann
Pages 552–53: "Imperial Irrigation District Water Transportation," map, 1958: courtesy of the Imperial Irrigation District
Page 557: Los Angeles enthusiastically obeys legal mandate to environmentally mitigate Owens Lake, 2005: courtesy of William T. Vollmann
Page 564: A limited-use visa for a Mexican national to visit the Northside, 2004: courtesy of William T. Vollmann
Page 580: Circular regarding the sale of Colorado River Land Company plots: Archivo Histórico del Muncipio de Mexicali, Chata Angulo Collection
Page 598: Union flyer: The Bancroft Library, University of California, Berkeley
Page 613: One of the Blythe intaglios: courtesy of William T. Vollmann
Page 629: View of Imperial from commuter plane, *ca.* 2003: courtesy of William T. Vollmann
Page 654: *Riverside City Directory*, 1951: Classified Buyer's Guide section
Page 663: Pay stub of Javier Lupercio: purchased by William T. Vollmann in 2003
Page 701: "Do You Want a Home in Southern California": ad run repeatedly in *Imperial Valley Press and Farmer*, 1901–*ca.* 1905
Page 705: The New River just north of the border; Jose Lopez and William T. Vollmann embarked on their little cruise at this spot: courtesy of William T. Vollmann
Page 724: Page from a list of landholders and renters in Colonia Zacatecas, 1947: courtesy of Archivo Histórico del Municipio de Mexicali, Chata Angulo Collection, box 9, marked "34 Expedientes"; folder, "Aparición y Arrendamientos, Rentas a 31/47"
Pages 784–85: Tourist map of the Imperial Valley: *Imperial Valley Press*
Page 811: Courtesy of U.S. Pipe and Foundry Company
Page 825: Mulholland's aqueduct, San Fernando Valley, *ca.* 2005: courtesy of William T. Vollmann
Page 837: Francisco Cedeño sings "The City of Hawaii": courtesy of William T. Vollmann
Page 874: Metales y Derivados: courtesy of William T. Vollmann
Page 891: Portion of Matsushita settlement document: obtained for William T. Vollmann by Adam Raskin from Jaime Cota, 2008
Page 909: Lourdes's medical chart: furnished directly to William T. Vollmann by Lourdes, 2004
Page 912: Covert photo taken with disposable camera inside Kimstar *maquiladora*, Tijuana: furnished directly to William T. Vollmann by Kimstar worker, 2004
Page 913: Restroom in unnamed *maquiladora* in Mexicali: furnished directly to William T. Vollmann by worker
Page 934: Pacific Ocean, Imperial Beach, 2002: courtesy of William T. Vollmann
Page 957: Message from the San Diego County Water Authority: clipped from *Imperial Valley Press*, courtesy of William T. Vollmann
Page 961: Stella Mendoza at the fateful IID meeting: courtesy of William T. Vollmann
Page 968: "The Devil's in the Details": *Imperial Valley Press*
Page 989: Abandoned clothing, probably of *pollos*, seen on U.S. side of All-American Canal: courtesy of William T. Vollmann
Page 1005: Border stele, Mexicali: west side of Río Nuevo: courtesy of William T. Vollmann
Page 1010: Unknown illegal immigrant's grave at Holtville: courtesy of William T. Vollmann
Page 1021: Police report on missing wife: received by William T. Vollmann in 2005

ACKNOWLEDGMENTS

The ex-farmboy Mr. Paul Foster (to whom I dedicated my very first book) has crunched crop numbers especially for you. You can find his graphs in the notes. Please trust in his honesty and thoroughness. Paul, thank you so much for your friendship, kindness and patience.

Teresa McFarland applied her affectionate care to this manuscript, with particular attention to Spanish and Native American words. She read the entire draft on the computer. She also transcribed Dean Hutchinson's none too legible handwritten notes from 1934. She shared many of my hopes and anxieties during the editing process. Her work was always accurate, her advice intelligent and kind. Teresa, thank you for being in my life. You are my perfect girl.

Terrie Petree was a brave, loyal and practical companion in Imperial for years. Thank you especially for marching boldly up to big tall thugs and asking them if I could take their photographs, for not complaining when a burglar wrecked your front passenger door in Mexicali—and complaining only a trifle when the dirt roads in the steep-hilled *colonias* of Tijuana took their toll on the underside of your car—for remaining unoffended when I requested that you confirm the discreet rectangularity of a digital vido receiver in my underpants, for wiring yourself up with that same DVR and becoming another of this book's PIs, for trusting me with your safety so many times, for listening to my romantic problems and sharing yours, for admiring the grapefruits at Rancho Roa with me, for saving my wallet from policemen on the take, prowling the border wall at night and driving across the border even while suffering Montezuma's Revenge. I love you, Terrie.

The following institutions were especially helpful: the Bancroft Library at UC Berkeley, the Blandford Reading Room at UC Davis, the California Department of Transportation in Sacramento (Deborah Dalton, the history librarian, was as sweet as a bushel of Coachella dates), the California State Archives in Sacramento, the California State Board of Equalization in Sacramento, the California History Room of the California State Library in Sacramento, the Cloud Museum in the Bard Subdistrict of Imperial Couunty (I got to deal with Mr. Cloud himself), the Imperial County Historical Society Pioneers Museum (whose archivist and director of operations, Lynn Housouer, was kind enough to trust me to handle as many of her photographs as I liked), various gracious employees of the Los Angeles Public Library (the unhelpful, overworked photo archivist excepted), the Motor Transport Museum in Campo, California (whose Carl Calvert helped me envision Wilber Clark's very hypothetical automobile journey to Imperial in 1901), the California Department of Transportation.

(The San Diego County Water Authority was rudely unhelpful. I would particularly like to single out the following two unpleasant individuals: John Liarakos, the so-called public affairs officer, who never returned a single phone call, and Dana Friehauf or Fridhof—she never verified the spelling of her name—who required that I put questions to her in writing, then never answered a single one in spite of many requests. In Pasadena, Romaine at the Huntington Library refused to give me a research card, so I was unable to see several photo collections whose images might have benefited my book. The California Department of Motor Vehicles proved indifferent, incompetent and useless regarding research on Wilber Clark.)

Alejandra Lopez at the San Diego County Recorder's office helped me discover that the child who was born Imperial Hazel Deed did not die with the same name.

I would like to thank Señor A., Mr. D., Mr. W., Chuck, Adam Raskin, Liz Cruz Kaegi, and other half-named or unnamed private investigators; Mandy Aftel, whose eleventh edition of the *Britannica* has been a window into another world and whose sympathy and kindness made several of my trips to the Imperial Valley much better; the very patient Jose Angel, Branch Chief of the Regional Water Control Board in Palm Desert; Meagan Atiyeh, for much help and companionship in the Imperial Valley; my designer, Carla Bolte, who as usual took many extra pains on layout, typography, etc., and who remains the *corazon* of my *corazon;* my Viking editor, Paul Slovak, whom I made very tired and who I am sure believes my promise that this will be my last long book (Paul, I'm sorry); his assistant, Dave Martin, who got stuck dealing with permissions because he is a nice man and because by then I was also very tired; my copy editor, Maureen Sugden, whose painstaking work extended to such lengths as verifying the names of streets in Mexicali (not to mention Spanish words I never learned to spell), and who cleaned away a truly shocking number of errors in my manuscript; my production editor, Bruce Giffords, who let me do ever so many things my way; my agent, Susan Golomb, and her assistant, Casey Panell—both of them my friends now; the U.S. Border Patrol, especially Officers Gloria Chavez, Dan Murray, Michael Singh and Brian Willett; Ben Brock of Brock Farms in Holtville; my paid informant, Mr. Richard Brogan, whom I like and respect; Fred Cagle of the Audubon Society for answering many questions about the ecology of the New River and the Salton Sea; Carlos, who I hope has made it over the fence by now; Christofer, to whom I extend the same wish; Mr. Herb Cilch of San Diego; various residents of Condominios Montealbán in Mexicali; Carolyn Cooke, the Director of the Coachella Valley Historical Society, who shared her recollections with me and facilitated other interviews; José Rigoberto Cruz Córdoba; Elvira from Mexicali; Mr. and Mrs. Claude Finnell in El Centro; Ramón Flores, who was used to the Río Nuevo; Ray Garnett, who risked his boat in the New River; Tirso Geraldo of San Luis Río Colorado, who shared his life with me; Lizzy Kate Gray, who helped inspire me to take up this project; the Guanajuato couple in Mecca; Bob Guccione, Jr., for underwriting the Border Patrol chapter; Susana and Rebeca Hernández; Elizabeth Hightower for getting *Outside* magazine to publish and pay for some of my excursions on the Salton Sea and the New River, not to mention the chemical tests; Roger Hodge from *Harper's;* Sabine Huynen of the University of Redlands Salton Sea Database Project; Karla from Mexicali; the late Edith Karpen, who very kindly told me about her life in Calipatria, El Centro and Calexcio; Alex Kasavin, who gave me Charles Elmer Fox's *Tales of an American Hobo;* Tom Kirk of the Salton Sea Authority; Leonard Knight of Salvation Mountain for being so nice year after year; William Linne, whose friendship and photographic capabilities have benefited me; Jose Lopez for being such a fine companion on my first New River excursion; another José López, this one from Jalisco, who was an excellent interpreter and storyteller; Louise and Floyd of Slab City; Bob Love from *Playboy;* Javier Lupercio, whose paid interview made the past a little bit clearer here and there; Juan the cokehead, who might have robbed me but didn't; Micheline Aharonian Marcom, who journeyed with me through Imperial and with whom I experienced much happiness; Larry McCaffery and Sinda Gregory for introducing me to the region and showing me quite a bit of it year after year; Eugenia McNaughton of the Environmental Protection Agency in San Francisco; Shannon Mullen, who presided over my first button camera experiments, kissed me soundly and remained cool when our rental car was crushed to a pancake; Ben Pax, who drove around Imperial with me for a couple of hot days even though he wasn't impressed; Pedro; Ross Peterson, for sharing his recollections of day farming with me; Sydney Peterson, who did genealogical research; my friend Chuck Pfister, for reasons he knows; Mike Pulley, occasional Imperial Valley companion; José Quintero, temporarily of Mexicali; the private detective Adam Raskin, whose work helped me to stand behind my *maquiladoras* chapter with confidence; Natalio Morales Rebolorio of Rancho Roa in the Mexicali Valley; Stephanie Reynolds, without whom I never would have seen the Mixtec shantytown in Tijuana; my good friend Jordan Rothacker at the University of Georgia in Athens, who shared with me some of his insights about the Virgin of Guadalupe; Daniel T. Ryu, who furnished various maps and documents on the Inland Empire; Alice Solario from Mecca; Oscar Sánchez of the Archivo Histórico del Municipio de Mexicali; Amelia Simpson of the Environmental Health Coalition in San Diego; Alejandro José Tamayo of the Archivo Histórico del Municipio de Mexicali (he made perfect copies of maps for free); Maria Thomas, the only nice person I met at the San Diego County Water Authority; Deborah Treisman, whose quiet voice expresses not only mind but heart; Dr. John Tyler and his wife Margaret, who gave a fine interview about the old days in Coachella as we sat in their cool house in Palm Desert; David Urbanoski of Desert Shores; Andrew Wilson at Dawson Books in Los Angeles; Alice Woodside, who was kind enough to share some of her childhood experiences in Calexico; Daina Zollinger, for genealogical research; and I'd better not forget cherry-lipped Barbara Worth. Finally, I want to express my gratitude to all the unnamed illegal aliens who told me their stories.

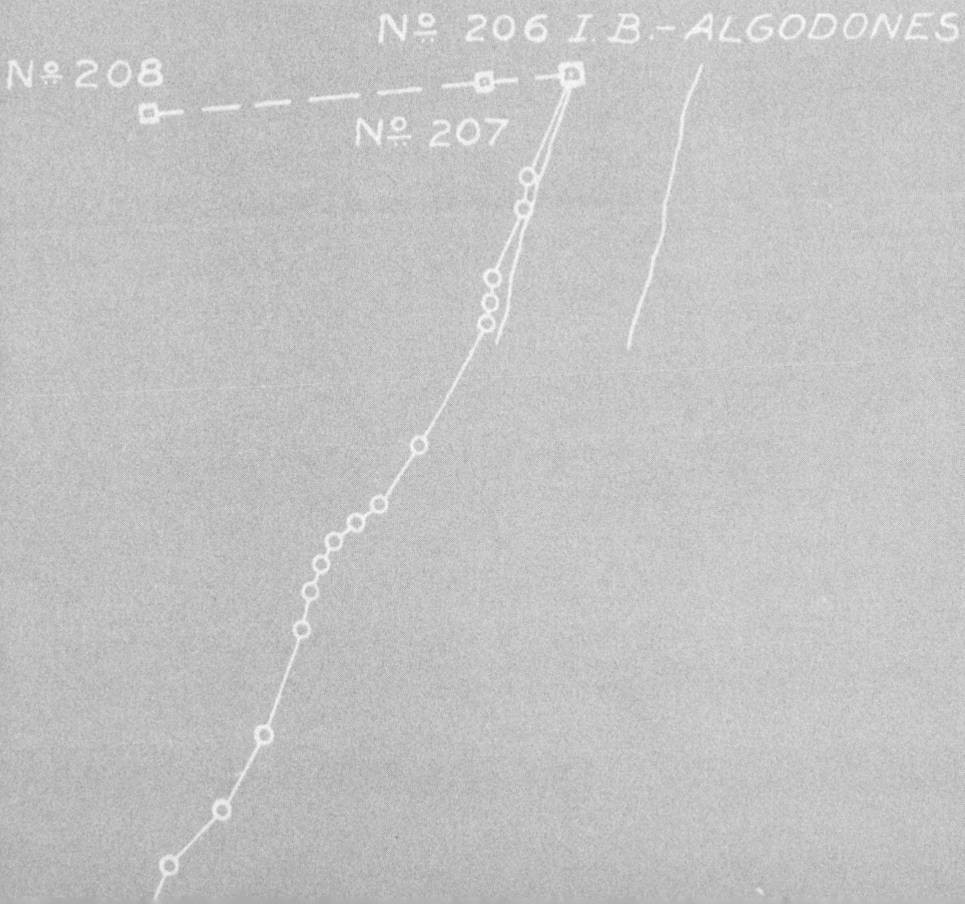

Nº 206 I. B.-ALGODONES

Nº 208

Nº 207

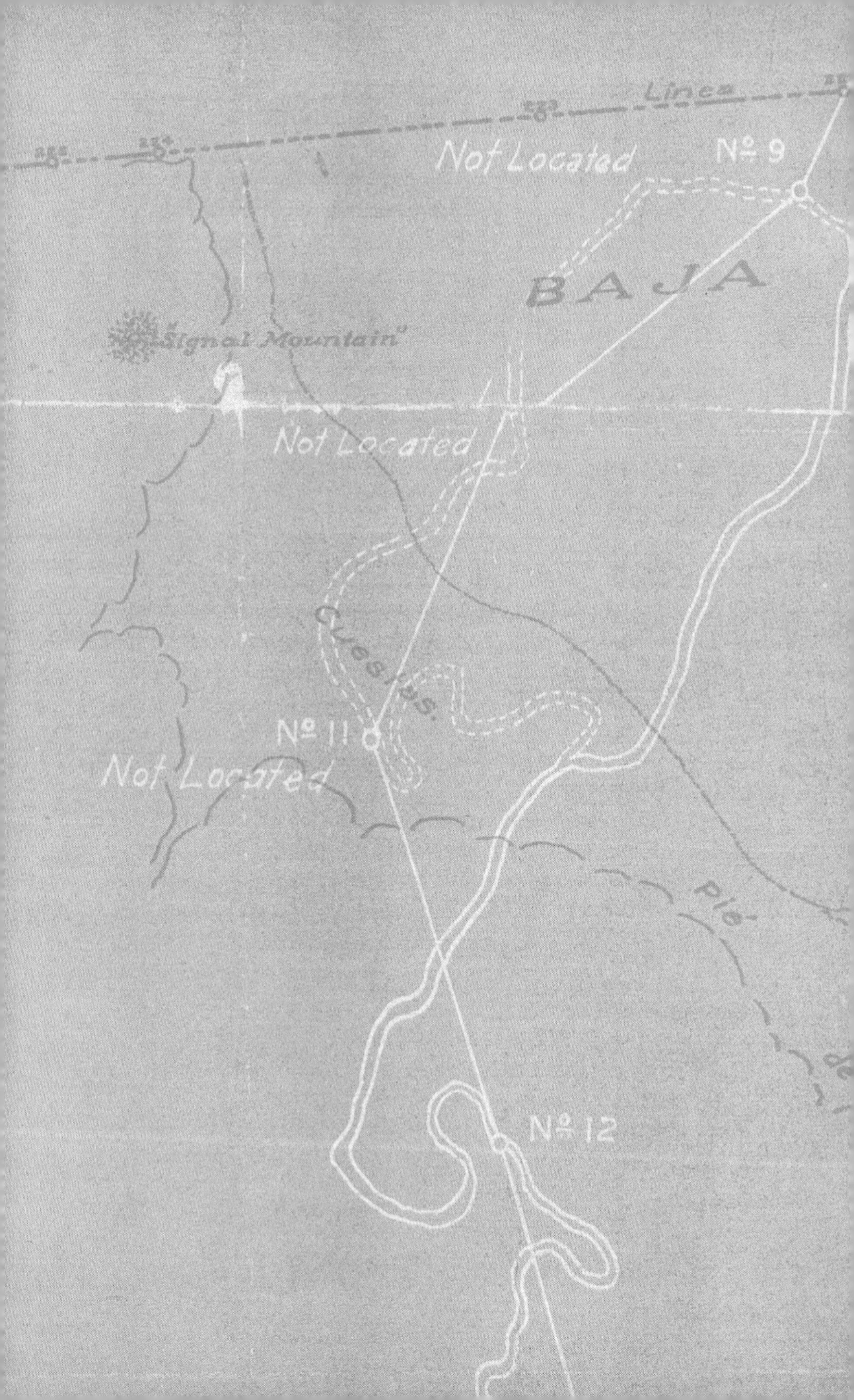

Linea

Not Located

Nº 9

BAJA

"Signal Mountain"

Not Located

Cuesta

Nº 11

Not Located

Pie

de

Nº 12

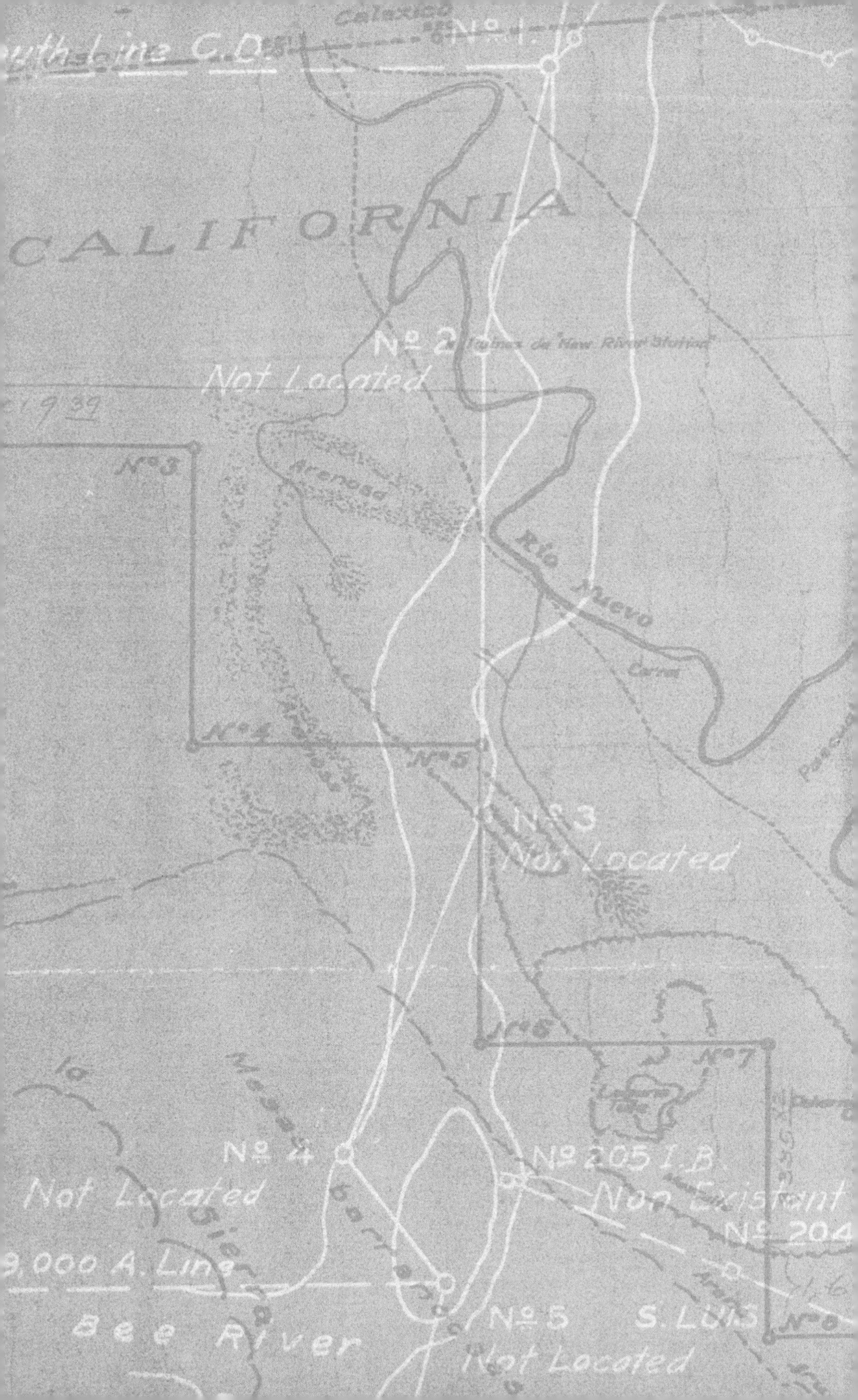

Calexico
No. 1
uth Line C.D.
CALIFORNIA
No. 2 Ruinas de New River Station
Not Located
No 3
Arenosa
Rio Nuevo
No 4
No 5
No. 3
Not Located
No 6
No 7
No. 4
Not Located
No. 205 I.B.
Non Existent
No. 204
9,000 A. Line
Bee River
No. 5
S. Luis
Not Located

№ 9
№ 11

Islita